Beyond Our Borders

Management Perspective

The Legal Environment Today

Business in its Ethical, Regulatory, E-Commerce, and International Setting

5TH EDITION

ROGER LeROY MILLER
Institute for Universiity Studies
Arlington, Texas

FRANK B. CROSS
Herbert D. Kelleher
Centennial Professor in Business Law
University of Texas at Austin

THOMSON
✳
WEST

Australia . Canada . Mexico . Singapore . Spain . United Kingdom . United States

THOMSON

WEST

The Legal Environment Today
Business in Its Ethical, Regulatory, E-Commerce, and International Setting
FIFTH EDITION

Roger LeRoy Miller and Frank B. Cross

Vice President and Editorial Director:
Jack Calhoun

Publisher, Business Law and Accounting:
Rob Dewey

Acquisition Editor:
Steve Silverstein

Senior Developmental Editor:
Jan Lamar

Editorial Assistant:
Todd McKenzie

Executive Marketing Manager:
Lisa L. Lysne

Production Manager:
Bill Stryker

Technology Project Editor:
Christine A. Wittmer

Manufacturing Coordinator:
Charlene Taylor

Marketing Coordinator:
Jenny Stevens

Compositor:
Parkwood Composition Service

Printer:
RR Donnelley, Willard

Art Director:
Linda Helcher

Internal Designer:
Bill Stryker

Cover Designer:
Jennifer Lambert

Web Coordinator:
Scott Cook

For permission to use material from this text or product, submit a request online at

www.thomsonrights.com

For more information, contact:

Thomson Higher Education
5191 Natorp Boulevard
Mason, Ohio 45040
USA

Or, you can visit our Internet site at
www.westbuslaw.com

INTERNATIONAL LOCATIONS

ASIA (including India)
Thomson Learning
5 Shenton Way
#01-01 UIC Building
Singapore 068808

AUSTRALIA/NEW ZEALAND
Thomson Learning Australia
102 Dodds Street
Southbank, Victoria 3006
Australia

LATIN AMERICA
Thomson Learning
Seneca, 53
Colonia Polanco
11560 Mexico
D.F.Mexico

CANADA
Thomson Nelson
1120 Birchmount Road
Toronto, Ontario
Canada M1K 5G4

UK/EUROPE/MIDDLE EAST/AFRICA
Thomson Learning
High Holborn House
50-51 Bedford Road
London WC1R 4LR
United Kingdom

SPAIN (includes Portugal)
Thomson Paraninfo
Calle Magallanes, 25
28015 Madrid, Spain

CONTENTS IN BRIEF

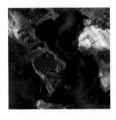

APPENDICES

CONTENTS

CHAPTER 6   Criminal Law and Cyber Crimes   174

UNIT THREE   THE PRIVATE ENVIRONMENT   211

CHAPTER 7   Intellectual Property   212

CHAPTER 8   Contract Formation   241

CHAPTER 12   Creditors' Rights and Bankruptcy   393

UNIT FOUR   THE EMPLOYMENT ENVIRONMENT   437

CHAPTER 13   Employment Relationships   438

UNIT FIVE   THE REGULATORY ENVIRONMENT   531

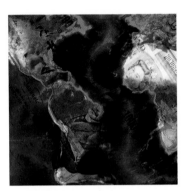

APPENDICES

PREFACE

It is no exaggeration to say that today's legal environment is changing at a pace never before experienced. In many instances, technology is both driving and facilitating this change. The expanded use of the Internet for both business and personal transactions has led to new ways of doing business and, consequently, to a changing legal environment for the twenty-first century. In the midst of this evolving environment, however, one thing remains certain: for those entering the business world, an awareness of the legal and regulatory environment of business is critical.

The Fifth Edition of *The Legal Environment Today: Business in Its Ethical, Regulatory, E-Commerce, and International Setting* is designed to bring this awareness to your students. They will learn not only about the traditional legal environment but also about some of the most significant recent developments in the e-commerce environment. They will also be motivated to learn more through our use of high-interest pedagogical features that explore real-life situations and legal challenges facing businesspersons and consumers. We believe that teaching the legal environment can be enjoyable and so, too, can learning about it.

WHAT'S NEW IN THE FIFTH EDITION

Instructors have come to rely on the coverage, accuracy, and applicability of *The Legal Environment Today*. To make sure that our text engages your students' interest, solidifies their understanding of the legal concepts presented, and provides the best teaching tools available, we now offer the following items either in the text or in conjunction with the text.

ThomsonNOW for *The Legal Environment Today*

For those instructors who want their students to learn how to correctly identify and apply the legal principles they study in this text, we have created an entirely new product for this edition. ThomsonNOW for *The Legal Environment Today* provides interactive, automatically graded assignments for every chapter and unit in this text. We have devised four different categories of multiple-choice homework questions that stress different aspects of learning the chapter materials for each of the twenty-two chapters of the book.

1. **Chapter Review Questions**—The first set of ten to fifteen questions reviews the basic concepts and principles discussed in the chapter.
2. **Brief Hypotheticals**—The next group of seven to ten questions emphasizes spotting the issue and rule of law in the context of a short factual scenario.
3. **Legal Reasoning**—The third category includes five questions that require students to analyze the factual situation provided and apply the rules of law discussed in the chapter to arrive at an answer.
4. **Application and Analysis:** *Reviewing . . .* **Features**—The final set of four questions for each chapter are linked to the new hypothetical scenarios

that have been added at the end of each chapter in the text (the *Reviewing . . .* features, to be discussed shortly). These questions require students to analyze the facts presented, identify the issues in dispute, and apply the rules discussed in the chapter to answer the questions.

5. **Cumulative Questions for Each Unit**—In addition to the questions relating to each chapter, ThomsonNOW for *The Legal Environment Today* provides a set of cumulative questions, entitled "Synthesizing Legal Concepts," for each of the six units in the text.

6. **Additional Advantages of NOW**—Instructors can utilize the NOW system to upload their course syllabi, create and customize the homework assignments, keep track of their students' progress, communicate with their students about assignments and due dates, and create reports summarizing the data for a student or for the whole class.

New Bankruptcy Reform Act of 2005

The chapter on creditors' rights and bankruptcy (Chapter 12) has been significantly revamped due to the passage of the 2005 bankruptcy reform legislation. Bankruptcy reform has been a topic of major debate for many years. Now that the reform act has been enacted, we have overhauled the content of this chapter to reflect the changes.

Reviewing . . . Features in Every Chapter

For the Fifth Edition of *The Legal Environment Today,* we have added a special new feature at the end of every chapter entitled *Reviewing . . . [chapter topic].* Each of these features presents a hypothetical scenario and then asks a series of questions that requires students to identify the issues and apply the legal concepts discussed in the chapter. These features are designed as an assessment tool. Instructors can use these hypotheticals in the classroom to wrap up their discussion of each chapter and assess their students' understanding of the materials covered. Students can also use them for self-assessment, to review the legal principles they have learned and see how they apply in a real-world situation. These features provide a simple and interesting way to review the chapter contents and sharpen legal reasoning skills.

West's Digital Video Library

For this edition of *The Legal Environment Today,* we have provided additional *Video Questions* at the end of selected chapters. Each of these questions directs students to the text's Web site (at **www.thomsonedu.com/westbuslaw/let**) to view a video relevant to a topic covered in the chapter. This instruction is followed by a series of questions based on the video. The questions are again repeated on the Web site, when the student accesses the video. An access code for the videos can be packaged with each new copy of this textbook for no additional charge. If West's Digital Video Library access did not come packaged with the textbook, students can purchase it online at **digitalvideolibrary.westbuslaw.com**.

These videos can be used for homework assignments, discussion starters, or classroom demonstrations and are useful for generating student interest. The new videos are clips from actual movies, such as *The Jerk, Bowfinger,* and *Midnight Run.* By watching a video and answering the questions, students will gain an understanding of how the legal concepts they have studied in the chapter apply to the real-life situation portrayed in the video. **Suggested answers for all of the *Video Questions* are given in both the *Instructor's Manual* and the *Answers Manual* that accompany this text.**

Corporate Governance

Because today's companies are placing a greater emphasis on developing internal rules of corporate governance to prevent corporate misconduct, encourage accountability, and balance potentially conflicting interests, we have added coverage of this topic as appropriate. For example, the chapter on ethics (Chapter 2) includes a subsection discussing corporate governance principles. The chapter covering securities law (Chapter 21) now includes an entire section on corporate governance.

Ethics and Professional Responsibility

For the Fifth Edition of *The Legal Environment Today*, we have included a significantly revised and updated chapter on ethics and professional responsibility (Chapter 2). The chapter now presents a more practical approach to this topic and examines several companies that have been accused of avoiding their ethical obligations (including, for example, the accusations against Merck & Company, which continued to market its popular painkiller Vioxx until late in 2004 despite allegedly knowing that long-term use of the drug was linked to serious health risks). The emphasis on ethics is reiterated in other materials throughout the text—in the numbered *Ethical Issue* sections that appear in the chapters, in "Ethical Considerations" ending many of the cases, and in the case problems entitled *A Question of Ethics* that appear in selected chapters.

Appendix on the Sarbanes-Oxley Act of 2002

In a number of places in this text, we refer to the Sarbanes-Oxley Act of 2002 and the corporate scandals that led to the passage of that legislation. For example, Chapter 2 contains a section examining the requirements of the Sarbanes-Oxley Act relating to confidential reporting systems. We also look at provisions of the Sarbanes-Oxley Act as they relate to public accounting firms and accounting practices. In Chapter 21, we discuss this act in the context of securities law and present an exhibit (Exhibit 21–4) containing some of the key provisions of the act relating to corporate accountability with respect to securities transactions.

Because the act is a topic of significant concern in today's business climate, for the Fifth Edition we have added **excerpts and explanatory comments on the Sarbanes-Oxley Act of 2002 as Appendix N.** Students and instructors alike will find it useful to have the provisions of the act immediately available for reference.

Emphasis on Critical Thinking and Legal Reasoning

Your students' critical-thinking and legal reasoning skills will increase as they work through the numerous pedagogical devices within the book.

- **Case-ending questions**—Many of the cases presented in the text conclude with a section entitled "For Critical Analysis" that raises a question about some aspect of the case for the student to consider. For this edition, we have also added *What If the Facts Were Different?* questions to selected cases throughout the text. These questions require students to analyze how the outcome of the case might be altered if the facts were different.
- **Feature-ending questions**—Concluding each of the boxed-in features entitled *Online Developments* and *Beyond Our Borders* (to be discussed shortly) is a *For Critical Analysis* question that asks the student to explore some of the implications or consequences of the court decision, treaty, or other development discussed in the feature.
- *Reviewing . . .* **hypotheticals**—As already discussed, this new end-of-chapter feature poses a series of questions about a hypothetical scenario that requires the student to apply legal reasoning skills to decide how the principles of law discussed in the chapter should be applied to the situation.
- *Case Briefing Assignment*—In selected chapters of this text, these assignments instruct students to go to the text's Web site to read a case opinion and brief the case. We have included one of these assignments as a case problem in each unit of this text.
- Unit-ending *Cumulative Business Hypotheticals*—At the end of the final chapter in each unit, we present a *Cumulative Business Hypothetical*. The problem introduces a hypothetical business firm and then asks a series of questions about how the law applies to various actions taken by the firm. To answer the questions, the student must consider the laws discussed throughout the unit.

Suggested answers to all critical-thinking questions in the features and all questions following cases can be found in both the *Instructor's Manual* and the *Answers Manual* that accompany this text. Suggested answers to the *Cumulative Business Hypotheticals* are included in the *Answers Manual*.

THE LEGAL ENVIRONMENT TODAY ON THE WEB

For this edition of *The Legal Environment Today*, we have redesigned and streamlined the text's Web site so that users can easily locate the resources they seek. When you visit our Web site at **www.thomsonedu.com/westbuslaw/let**, you will find a broad array of teaching/learning resources, including the following:

- *Relevant Web sites* for all of the *Landmark in the Legal Environment* features and *Landmark and Classic Cases* that are presented in this text.
- *Sample answers for selected case problems*—Included on the Web site is a sample answer to each case problem entitled *Case Problem with Sample Answer*. This case problem, which is set off by a special heading and followed by instructions to the student, appears in the *Questions and Case Problems* at the end of every chapter. This problem/answer set is designed to help your students learn how to analyze and effectively answer case problems by comparing their answers with model answers that are based on the courts' reasoning.
- *Videos* referenced in the new *Video Questions* (discussed previously) that have been added to selected chapters for this edition of *The Legal Environment Today*.

- *Internet exercises* for every chapter in the text (at least two per chapter), many of which are new to this edition. These exercises familiarize students with online legal resources while introducing them to additional information on the topics covered in the chapters.
- *Interactive quizzes* for every chapter in this text.
- *Court case updates* that present summaries of new cases prepared by West Legal Studies in Business from various West legal publications. The case selection is continually updated, and the cases are specifically keyed to chapters in this text.
- *Legal reference materials,* including a "Statutes" page that offers links to the full text of selected statutes referenced in the text, a Spanish glossary, and links to other important legal resources available for free on the Web.
- *Appendix A of the text*—This appendix, which is entitled "How to Brief Cases and Analyze Case Problems," is included both in the text and on the Web site.
- *Cases for Briefing*—Included on the Web site are the cases correlated to each *Case Briefing Assignment* in this text. One of these assignments is included for each of the six units in this text.

ADDITIONAL SPECIAL FEATURES IN THIS TEXT

We have included in the Fifth Edition of *The Legal Environment Today* a number of pedagogical devices and special features, including those discussed here.

Online Developments

Many chapters in the Fifth Edition contain one of these special features. Each feature explores how traditional legal concepts or laws have been applied in cyberspace. As mentioned earlier, a concluding *For Critical Analysis* section asks the student to think critically about some aspect of the issue discussed in the feature. **Suggested answers to these questions are included in both the** *Instructor's Manual* **and the** *Answers Manual* **that accompany this text.**

Management Perspective

Each of these features begins with a section titled "Management Faces a Legal Issue" that describes a practical issue facing management (such as whether employees have a right to privacy in their e-mail communications). A section titled "What the Courts Say" then follows, in which we discuss what the courts have concluded with respect to this issue. The feature concludes with an "Implications for Managers" section that indicates the importance of the courts' decisions for business decision making and offers some practical guidance.

Landmark in the Legal Environment

This feature, which appears in selected chapters, discusses a landmark case, statute, or other law that has had a significant effect on business law. Each of these features includes a section titled *Application to Today's Legal Environment,* which indicates how the law discussed in the feature affects the contemporary legal environment of business. In addition, for the Fifth Edition we have added a *Relevant Web Sites* section that directs students to the book's companion Web site for links to additional information available online.

Beyond Our Borders

These special features give students an awareness of the global legal environment by indicating how international laws or the laws of other nations deal with the specific legal topics being discussed in the text. Because business today is conducted in the global context, it is important for students to understand that what happens beyond our borders can have a significant impact on the legal environment.

Exhibits

When appropriate, we also illustrate important aspects of the law in graphic or summary form in exhibits. For the Fifth Edition of *The Legal Environment Today*, we have added numerous exhibits to facilitate your students' understanding of the materials.

An Effective Case Format

In each chapter, we present cases that illustrate the principles of law discussed in the text. The cases are numbered sequentially for easy referencing in class discussions, homework assignments, and examinations. In selecting the cases to be included in this edition, our goal has been to choose high-interest cases that reflect the most current law or that represent significant precedents in case law.

Each case is presented in a special format, beginning with the case title and citation (including parallel citations). Whenever possible, we also include a URL, just below the case citation, that can be used to access the case online (a footnote to the URL explains how to find the specific case at that Web site). We then briefly outline the background and facts of the dispute, after which the court's reasoning is presented in the words of the court. To enhance student understanding, we paraphrase the court's decision and remedy. Each case normally concludes with a *For Critical Analysis* section. For one case in each chapter, however, we have added a section titled *Why Is This Case Important?* This section clearly sets forth the importance of the court's decision for businesspersons today.

We give special emphasis to *Landmark and Classic Cases* by setting them off with a special heading and logo. These cases also include an *Impact of This Case on Today's Legal Environment* section that stresses the significance of that particular decision for the evolution of the law in that area. For the Fifth Edition, we have added a section titled *Relevant Web Sites* at the conclusion of each landmark and classic case that directs students to additional online resources.

THE MOST COMPLETE SUPPLEMENTS PACKAGE AVAILABLE TODAY

This edition of *The Legal Environment Today* is accompanied by a vast number of teaching and learning supplements, including those listed next. For further information on the items contained in the teaching/learning package, contact your local West sales representative or visit the Web site that accompanies this text at **www.thomsonedu.com/westbuslaw/let**.

Suggestions on how you can adapt the teaching/learning package to fit your particular teaching and learning goals are given in the *Course Planning Guide*, which is available on the Instructor's Resource CD-ROM (IRCD). Furthermore, each chapter of the *Instructor's Manual* contains teaching suggestions, possible discussion questions, and additional information on key statutes or other legal sources that you may wish to use in your classroom. These and numerous other supplementary materials (including printed and multimedia supplements) all contribute to the goal of making *The Legal Environment Today* the most flexible teaching/learning package on the market.

Printed Supplements

- *Online Legal Research Guide*—Packaged with every new copy of the text.
- *Instructor's Manual*—Includes additional cases on point with at least one such case summary per chapter, answers to all *For Critical Analysis* questions in the features and all case-ending questions, and answers for the *Video Questions* at the end of selected chapters (also available on the IRCD).
- *Study Guide.*
- A comprehensive *Test Bank* (also available on the IRCD).
- *Answers Manual*—Includes answers to the *Questions and Case Problems*, answers to the *For Critical Analysis* questions in the features and all case-ending questions, answers for the *Video Questions* that conclude selected chapters, and answers to the unit-ending *Cumulative Business Hypotheticals* (also available on the IRCD).
- *Wall Street Journal*—A subscription is available at a discount to adopters and students.

Software, Video, and Multimedia Supplements

- *Instructor's Resource CD-ROM* (IRCD)—The IRCD includes the following supplements: *Course Planning Guide, Instructor's Manual, Answers Manual, Test Bank,* Case-Problem Cases, Case Printouts, PowerPoint slides, ExamView, *Handbook of Landmark Cases and Statutes in Business Law and the Legal Environment, Guide to Personal Law, Handbook on Critical Thinking and Writing in Business Law and the Legal Environment,* transparencies, and *Instructor's Manual* for the *Drama of the Law* video series.
- *Course Planning Guide*—Identifies and correlates all relevant printed, computerized, multimedia, and video resources for each chapter of the text (available only on the IRCD).
- **ExamView Testing Software** (also available on the IRCD).
- **PowerPoint slides** (also available on the IRCD).
- **WebTutor Toolbox.**
- **Case Printouts**—Provides the full opinion of all cases presented in the text and referred to in selected features (available only on the IRCD).
- **Case-Problem Cases** (available only on the IRCD).
- **Transparencies** (available only on the IRCD).
- **Westlaw®**—Ten free hours on Westlaw are available to qualified adopters.
- **West's Digital Video Library**—Provides access to over sixty-five videos, including the *Drama of the Law* videos and video clips from actual

Hollywood movies. Access to West's Digital Video Library is available in an optional package with each new text at no additional cost. If West's Digital Video Library access did not come packaged with the textbook, your students can purchase it online at **digitalvideolibrary.westbuslaw.com**.

- **VHS Videotapes**—Qualified adopters using this text have access to the entire library of West videos in VHS format, a vast selection covering most business law issues. For more information about these videotapes, visit **www.swlearning.com/blaw/video_library/video_library.html**.
- *LegalTrac*™—Provides indexing for approximately 875 research titles (including major law reviews, legal newspapers, bar association journals, and international legal journals) and law-related articles from more than 1,000 additional business and general-interest titles. *LegalTrac*™ is available as an optional package with a new text.
- **Business & Company Resource Center**—Put a complete business library at your students' fingertips with the Business & Company Resource Center (BCRC). The BCRC is a premier online business research tool that allows you to seamlessly search thousands of periodicals, journals, references, financial information, industry reports, company histories, and much more. The BCRC is a powerful and time-saving research tool for business students—whether they are completing a case study analysis, preparing for a presentation or discussion, creating a business plan, or writing a research paper. Access to the BCRC is available as an optional package with each new text and comes with a user's guide that includes exercises to provide hands-on experience and a real-world context for using the BCRC. For more information, please visit **bcrc.swlearning.com**.
- *Wall Street Journal*—Students and professors have the opportunity to subscribe to the *Wall Street Journal* and to access the *Journal*'s Web site (**wsj.com**) at a discount when bundled with the text. For students, the offer includes a fifteen-week subscription and access to the Web site. Qualifying professors can receive a fifty-two-week subscription, one-year access to the Web site, access to ProfessorJournal.com, and a video instructing students on how to use the *Wall Street Journal*.

ACKNOWLEDGMENTS

Numerous careful and conscientious users of *The Legal Environment Today* were kind enough to help us revise the book. In addition, the staff at West went out of its way to make sure that this edition came out early and in accurate form. In particular, we wish to thank Rob Dewey and Steve Silverstein for their countless new ideas, many of which have been incorporated into the Fifth Edition. Our production manager and designer, Bill Stryker, made sure that we came out with an error-free, visually attractive edition. We will always be in his debt. We also extend special thanks to Jan Lamar, our longtime developmental editor, for her many useful suggestions and for her efforts in coordinating reviews and ensuring the timely and accurate publication of all supplemental materials. We are particularly indebted to Lisa Lysne for her support and excellent marketing advice.

We must especially thank Katherine Marie Silsbee and Lavina Leed Miller, who provided expert research, editing, and proofing services for this project. We also wish to thank William Eric Hollowell, co-author of the *Instructor's Manual, Study Guide, Test Bank,* and *Online Legal Research Guide,* for his excellent research efforts. The copyediting and proofreading services of Suzie

Franklin DeFazio, Mary Berry, and Pat Lewis will not go unnoticed. We also thank Roxanna Lee and Vickie Reierson for their proofreading and other assistance, and Suzanne Jasin for her many special efforts on the project. We are also indebted to the staff at Parkwood Composition, our compositor. Their ability to generate the pages for this text quickly and accurately made it possible for us to meet our ambitious printing schedule.

Finally, numerous thorough and meticulous users of previous editions have been gracious enough to offer us their comments and suggestions on how to improve this text. We are particularly indebted to these reviewers, whom we list below. With their help, we have been able to make this book even more useful for professors and students alike.

Acknowledgments for Previous Editions

Jane Bennett
Orange Coast College

Teri Elkins
University of Houston

Gary Greene
Manatee Community College

Penelope L. Herickhoff
Mankato State University

Susan Key
University of Alabama
at Birmingham

Karrin Klotz
University of Washington

Y. S. Lee
Oakland University

Tom Moore
Georgia College and State University

Michael J. O'Hara
University of Nebraska at Omaha

Mark Phelps
University of Oregon

G. Keith Roberts
University of Redlands

Gary Sambol
Rutgers, the State University of
New Jersey, Camden Campus

Martha Sartoris
North Hennepin Community College

Gwen Seaquist
Ithaca College

Dawn R. Swink
University of St. Thomas

Acknowledgments for the Fifth Edition

Muhammad Abdullah
Pfeiffer University

Brent D. Clark
Davenport University

Richard L. Coffinberger
George Mason University

Teresa Gillespie
Seattle Pacific University

James F. Kelley
Santa Clara University

Martha Wright Sartoris
North Hennepin Community College

Craig Stilwell
Michigan State University

Daphyne Thomas
James Madison University

Wayne Wells
St. Cloud State University

We know that we are not perfect. If you or your students find something you don't like or want us to change, write or e-mail us your thoughts. That is how we can make *The Legal Environment Today,* Fifth Edition, an even better book in the future.

Roger LeRoy Miller
Frank B. Cross

Dedication

To Charley French,
Whose great outlook
on life and continuing
physical exploits serve
as an inspiration
to me and many others.
You have become my
role model. Please stay
that way for at least
another four decades!

R.L.M.

To my parents and sisters.

F.B.C.

UNIT 1

The Foundations

CONTENTS

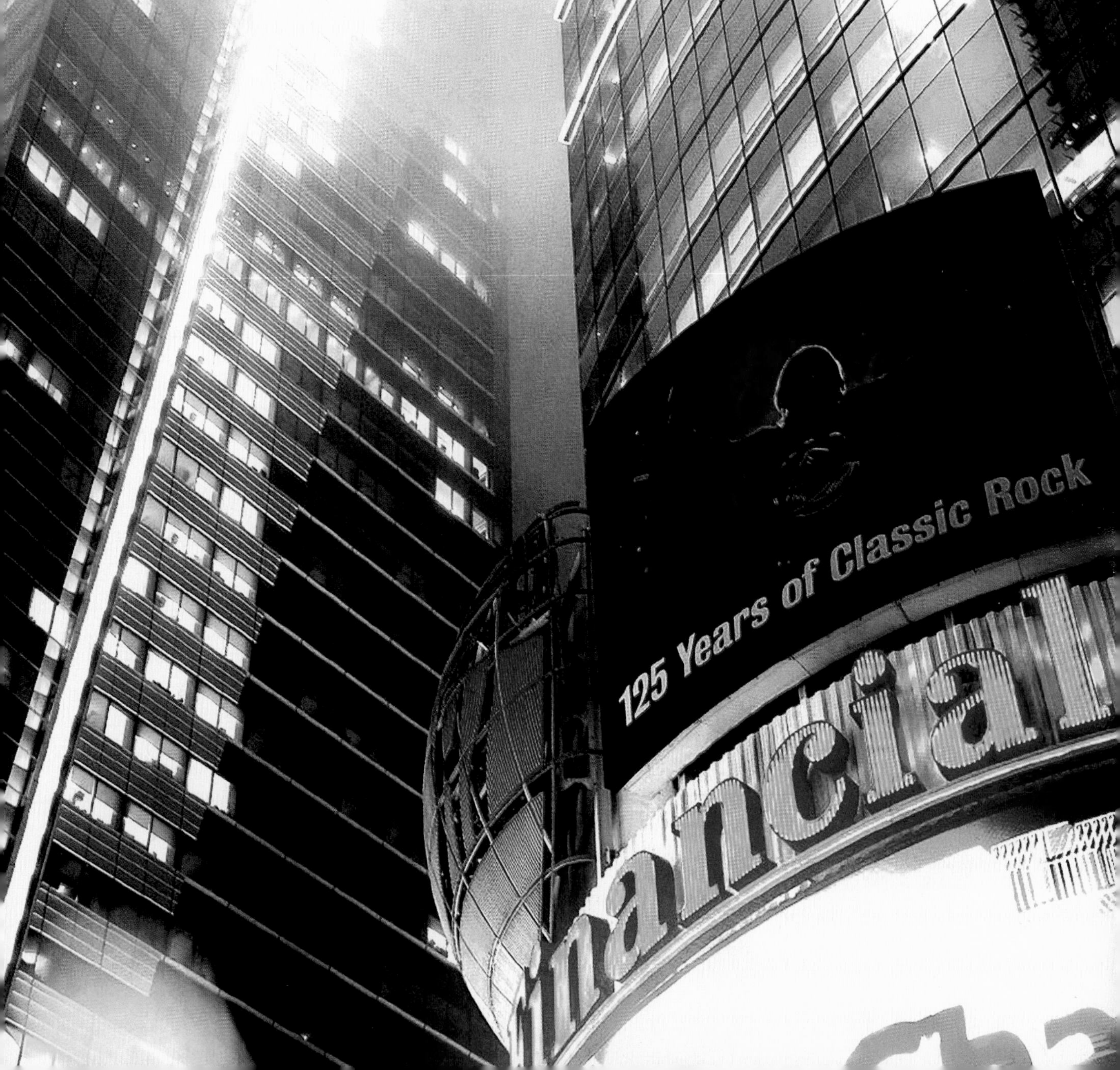

CHAPTER 1

The Legal and International Foundations

CONTENTS

CHAPTER OBJECTIVES

After reading this chapter, you should be able to answer the following questions:

1 What is the Uniform Commercial Code?

2 What is the common law tradition?

3 What is precedent? When might a court depart from precedent?

4 What is the difference between remedies at law and remedies in equity?

5 What are some important differences between civil law and criminal law?

> "The law is of as much interest to the layman as it is to the lawyer."
> —LORD BALFOUR, 1848–1930
> (British prime minister, 1902–1905)

LORD BALFOUR'S ASSERTION in the chapter-opening quotation emphasizes the underlying theme of every page in this book—that law is of interest to all persons, not just to lawyers. Those entering the world of business will find themselves subject to numerous laws and government regulations. A basic knowledge of these laws and regulations is beneficial—if not essential—to anyone contemplating a successful career in today's business environment.

In this introductory chapter, we first look at the nature of law and at some concepts that have significantly influenced how jurists (those skilled in the law, including judges, lawyers, and legal scholars) view the nature and function of law. We then look at an important question for any student reading this text: How does the legal environment affect business decision making? We next describe the basic sources of American law, the common law tradition, and the importance of the common law today. We conclude the chapter with a discussion of some general classifications of law.

THE NATURE OF LAW

LAW
A body of enforceable rules governing relationships among individuals and between individuals and their society.

There have been, and will continue to be, different definitions of law. Although the definitions vary in their particulars, they all are based on the general observation that, at a minimum, **law** consists of *enforceable rules governing relationships among individuals and between individuals and their society*. These "enforceable rules" may consist of unwritten principles of behavior established by a nomadic tribe. They may be set forth in an ancient or a contemporary law code. They may consist of written laws and court decisions created by modern legislative and judicial bodies, as in the United

States. Regardless of how such rules are created, they all have one thing in common: they establish rights, duties, and privileges that are consistent with the values and beliefs of their society or its ruling group.

Those who embark on a study of law will find that these broad statements leave unanswered some important questions concerning the nature of law. Part of the study of law, often referred to as **jurisprudence,** involves learning about different schools of legal thought and discovering how each school's approach to law can affect judicial decision making.

You may think that legal philosophy is far removed from the practical study of business law and the legal environment. In fact, it is not. As you will learn in the chapters of this text, how judges apply the law to specific disputes, including disputes relating to the business world, depends in part on their philosophical approaches to law. We look now at some of the significant schools of legal, or jurisprudential, thought that have evolved over time.

JURISPRUDENCE
The science or philosophy of law.

The Natural Law Tradition

An age-old question about the nature of law has to do with the finality of a nation's laws, such as the laws of the United States at the present time. For example, what if a particular law is deemed to be a "bad" law by a substantial number of that nation's citizens? Must a citizen obey the law if it goes against his or her conscience to do so? Is there a higher or universal law to which individuals can appeal? One who adheres to the natural law tradition would answer this question in the affirmative. **Natural law** denotes a system of moral and ethical principles that are inherent in human nature and that people can discover through the use of their native intelligence.

The natural law tradition is one of the oldest and most significant schools of jurisprudence. It dates back to the days of the Greek philosopher Aristotle (384–322 B.C.E.), who distinguished between natural law and the laws governing a particular nation. According to Aristotle, natural law applies universally to all humankind.

The notion that people have "natural rights" stems from the natural law tradition. Those who claim that a specific foreign government is depriving certain citizens of their human rights are implicitly appealing to a higher law that has universal applicability. The question of the universality of basic human rights also comes into play in the context of international business operations. For example, U.S. companies that have operations abroad often hire foreign workers as employees. Should the same laws that protect U.S. employees apply to these foreign employees? This question is rooted implicitly in a concept of universal rights that has its origins in the natural law tradition.

NATURAL LAW
The belief that government and the legal system should reflect universal moral and ethical principles that are inherent in human nature. The natural law school is the oldest and one of the most significant schools of legal thought.

Legal Positivism

In contrast, **positive law,** or national law (the written law of a given society at a particular point in time), applies only to the citizens of that nation or society. Those who adhere to **legal positivism** believe that there can be no higher law than a nation's positive law. According to the positivist school, there is no such thing as "natural rights." Rather, human rights exist solely because of laws. If the laws are not enforced, anarchy will result. Thus, whether a law is "bad" or "good" is irrelevant. The law is the law and must be obeyed until it is

POSITIVE LAW
The body of conventional, or written, law of a particular society at a particular point in time.

LEGAL POSITIVISM
A school of legal thought centered on the assumption that there is no law higher than the laws created by a national government. Laws must be obeyed, even if they are unjust, to prevent anarchy.

changed—in an orderly manner through a legitimate lawmaking process. A judge with positivist leanings probably would be more inclined to defer to an existing law than would a judge who adheres to the natural law tradition.

The Historical School

The **historical school** of legal thought emphasizes the evolutionary process of law by concentrating on the origin and history of the legal system. Thus, this school looks to the past to discover what the principles of contemporary law should be. The legal doctrines that have withstood the passage of time—those that have worked in the past—are deemed best suited for shaping present laws. Hence, law derives its legitimacy and authority from adhering to the standards that historical development has shown to be workable. Adherents of the historical school are more likely than those of other schools to strictly follow decisions made in past cases.

Legal Realism

In the 1920s and 1930s, a number of jurists and scholars, known as legal realists, rebelled against the historical approach to law. **Legal realism** is based on the idea that law is just one of many institutions in society and that it is shaped by social forces and needs. The law is a human enterprise, and judges should take social and economic realities into account when deciding cases. Legal realists also believe that the law can never be applied with total uniformity. Given that judges are human beings with unique personalities, value systems, and intellects, obviously different judges will bring different reasoning processes to the same case.

Legal realism strongly influenced the growth of what is sometimes called the **sociological school** of jurisprudence. This school views law as a tool for promoting justice in society. In the 1960s, for example, the justices of the United States Supreme Court played a leading role in the civil rights movement by upholding long-neglected laws calling for equal treatment for all Americans, including African Americans and other minorities. Generally, jurists who adhere to the sociological school are more likely to depart from past decisions than are those jurists who adhere to the other schools of legal thought.

BUSINESS ACTIVITIES AND THE LEGAL ENVIRONMENT

As those entering the world of business will learn, laws and government regulations affect virtually all business activities—from hiring and firing decisions to workplace safety, the manufacturing and marketing of products, and business financing, for example. To make good business decisions, a basic knowledge of the laws and regulations governing these activities is beneficial, if not essential. In today's world, though, a knowledge of "black-letter" law is not enough. Businesspersons are also pressured to make ethical decisions. Thus, the study of business law necessarily involves an ethical dimension.

Many Different Laws May Affect a Single Business Transaction

As you will note, each chapter in this text covers a specific area of the law and shows how the legal rules in that area affect business activities. Although compartmentalizing the law in this fashion facilitates learning, it does not indicate the extent to which many different laws may apply to just one transaction. It is important for businesspersons to be aware of this fact and to understand enough about the law to know when to hire an expert for advice.

Example #1 Suppose that you are the president of NetSys, Inc., a company that creates and maintains computer network systems for its clients, including business firms. NetSys also markets software for customers who need an internal computer network but cannot afford an individually designed intranet. One day, Janet, an operations officer for Southwest Distribution Corporation (SDC), contacts you by e-mail about a possible contract involving SDC's computer network. In deciding whether to enter into a contract with SDC, you need to consider, among other things, the legal requirements for an enforceable contract. Are the requirements different for a contract for services and a contract for products? What are your options if SDC **breaches** (breaks, or fails to perform) the contract? The answers to these questions are part of contract law and sales law.

BREACH
The failure to perform a legal obligation.

Other questions might concern payment under the contract. How can you guarantee that NetSys will be paid? For example, if SDC pays with a check that is returned for insufficient funds, what are your options? Answers to these questions can be found in the laws that relate to negotiable instruments (such as checks) and creditors' rights. Also, a dispute may occur over the rights to NetSys's software, or there may be a question of liability if the software is defective. Questions may arise as to whether you and Janet had the authority to make the deal in the first place. Resolutions of these questions may be found in areas of the law that relate to intellectual property, e-commerce, torts, product liability, agency, or business organizations. Finally, if any dispute cannot be resolved amicably, then the laws and the rules concerning courts and court procedures spell out the steps of a lawsuit. Exhibit 1–1 illustrates the various areas of the law that may influence business decision making.

EXHIBIT 1–1 **AREAS OF THE LAW THAT MAY AFFECT BUSINESS DECISION MAKING**

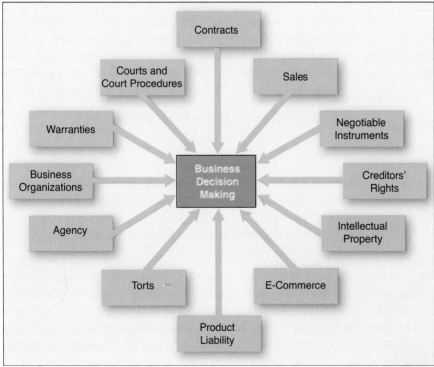

Ethics and Business Decision Making

Merely knowing the areas of law that may affect a business decision is not sufficient in today's business world. Businesspersons must also take ethics into account. As you will learn in Chapter 2, *ethics* is generally defined as the study of what constitutes right or wrong behavior. Today, business decision makers need to consider not just whether a decision is legal, but also whether it is ethical.

Throughout this text, you will learn about the relationship between the law and ethics, as well as about some of the types of ethical questions that often arise in the business context. For example, the *Ethical Issues* in this text are devoted solely to the exploration of ethical dimensions of selected topics treated within the chapter. Additionally, Chapter 2 offers a detailed look at the importance of ethical considerations in business decision making. Finally, various other elements in this text, such as the ethical question that concludes each chapter, are designed to introduce you to ethical aspects of specific cases involving real-life situations.

SOURCES OF AMERICAN LAW

PRIMARY SOURCE OF LAW
Any authority, such as a constitution, a statute, an administrative rule, or a court decision, that establishes the law governing a particular area.

There are numerous sources of American law. **Primary sources of law,** or sources that establish the law, include the following:

- The U.S. Constitution and the constitutions of the various states.
- Statutes, or laws, passed by Congress and by state legislatures.
- Regulations created by administrative agencies, such as the federal Food and Drug Administration.
- Case law (court decisions).

We describe each of these important primary sources of law in the following pages. (See the appendix following this chapter for a discussion of how to find statutes, regulations, and case law.)

SECONDARY SOURCE OF LAW
A publication that summarizes or interprets the law, such as a legal encyclopedia, a legal treatise, or an article in a law review.

Secondary sources of law are books and articles that summarize and clarify the primary sources of law. Legal encyclopedias, compilations (such as *Restatements of the Law,* which summarize court decisions on a particular topic), official comments to statutes, treatises, articles in law reviews published by law schools, and articles in other legal journals are examples of secondary sources of law. Courts often refer to secondary sources of law for guidance in interpreting and applying the primary sources of law discussed here.

Constitutional Law

CONSTITUTIONAL LAW
The body of law derived from the U.S. Constitution and the constitutions of the various states.

The federal government and the states have separate written constitutions that set forth the general organization, powers, and limits of their respective governments. **Constitutional law** is the law as expressed in these constitutions.

The U.S. Constitution is the supreme law of the land. As such, it is the basis of all law in the United States. A law in violation of the Constitution, if challenged, will be declared unconstitutional and will not be enforced no matter what its source. Because of its paramount importance in the American legal system, we discuss the U.S. Constitution at length in Chapter 4 and present the complete text of the Constitution in Appendix B.

The Tenth Amendment to the U.S. Constitution reserves to the states all powers not granted to the federal government. Each state in the union has its own constitution. Unless it conflicts with the U.S. Constitution or a federal law, a state constitution is supreme within the state's borders.

Statutory Law

Statutes enacted by legislative bodies at any level of government make up another source of law, which is generally referred to as **statutory law.**

Federal Statutes   Federal statutes are laws that are enacted by the U.S. Congress. Any federal statute that violates the U.S. Constitution will be held unconstitutional if it is challenged.

Federal statutes that affect business operations include laws regulating the purchase and sale of securities (corporate stocks and bonds—discussed in Chapter 21), consumer protection statutes (discussed in Chapter 17), and statutes prohibiting employment discrimination (discussed in Chapter 14). Whenever a particular statute is mentioned in this text, we usually provide a footnote showing its **citation** (a reference to a publication in which a legal authority—such as a statute or a court decision—or other source can be found). In the appendix following this chapter, we explain how you can use these citations to find statutory law.

State and Local Statutes and Ordinances   State statutes are laws enacted by state legislatures. Any state law that is found to conflict with the U.S. Constitution, with federal laws enacted by Congress, or with the state's constitution will be declared invalid if challenged. Statutory law also includes the **ordinances** passed by cities and counties, none of which can violate the U.S. Constitution, the relevant state constitution, or federal or state laws.

State statutes include state criminal statutes (discussed in Chapter 6), state corporation statutes (discussed in Chapter 11), state deceptive trade practices acts (referred to in Chapter 17), and state versions of the Uniform Commercial Code (to be discussed shortly). Local ordinances include zoning ordinances and local laws regulating housing construction and such matters as the overall appearance of a community.

A federal statute, of course, applies to all states. A state statute, in contrast, applies only within the state's borders. State laws thus vary from state to state.

Uniform Laws   The differences among state laws were particularly notable in the 1800s, when conflicting state statutes frequently created difficulties for the rapidly developing trade and commerce among the states. To deal with these problems, a group of legal scholars and lawyers formed the National Conference of Commissioners on Uniform State Laws (NCCUSL) in 1892 to draft uniform ("model") statutes for adoption by the states. The NCCUSL still exists today and continues to issue uniform statutes.

Each state has the option of adopting or rejecting a uniform law. *Only if a state legislature adopts a uniform law does that law become part of the statutory law of that state.* Note that a state legislature may adopt all or part of a uniform law as it is written, or the legislature may rewrite the law however the legislature wishes. Hence, even when a uniform law is said to have been adopted in many states, those states' laws may not be entirely "uniform."

Young students view the U.S. Constitution on display in Washington, D.C. Can a law be in violation of the Constitution and still be enforced? Why or why not? (Michael Evans/Corbis Sygma)

STATUTORY LAW
The body of law enacted by legislative bodies (as opposed to constitutional law, administrative law, or case law).

CITATION
A reference to a publication in which a legal authority—such as a statute or a court decision—or other source can be found.

ORDINANCE
A regulation enacted by a city or county legislative body that becomes part of that state's statutory law.

The earliest uniform law, the Uniform Negotiable Instruments Law, was completed by 1896 and was adopted in every state by the early 1920s (although not all states used exactly the same wording). Over the following decades, other acts were drawn up in a similar manner. In all, over two hundred uniform acts have been issued by the NCCUSL since its inception. The most ambitious uniform act of all, however, was the Uniform Commercial Code.

The Uniform Commercial Code (UCC)   The Uniform Commercial Code (UCC), which was created through the joint efforts of the NCCUSL and the American Law Institute,[1] was first issued in 1952. The UCC has been adopted in all fifty states,[2] the District of Columbia, and the Virgin Islands. The UCC facilitates commerce among the states by providing a uniform, yet flexible, set of rules governing commercial transactions. The UCC assures businesspersons that their contracts, if validly entered into, normally will be enforced.

Because of its importance in the area of commercial law, we cite the UCC frequently in this text and discuss the provisions of Articles 2 and 2A of the UCC more fully in Chapter 10. We also present Article 2 of the UCC in Appendix D.

Administrative Law

Another important source of American law is **administrative law,** which consists of the rules, orders, and decisions of administrative agencies. An **administrative agency** is a federal, state, or local government agency established to perform a specific function. Administrative law and procedures, which will be discussed in detail in Chapter 16, constitute a dominant element in the regulatory environment of business. Rules issued by various administrative agencies now affect virtually every aspect of a business's operation, including the firm's capital structure and financing, its hiring and firing procedures, its relations with employees and unions, and the way it manufactures and markets its products.

At the national level, numerous **executive agencies** exist within the cabinet departments of the executive branch. For example, the Food and Drug Administration is within the Department of Health and Human Services. Executive agencies are subject to the authority of the president, who has the power to appoint and remove officers of federal agencies. There are also major **independent regulatory agencies** at the federal level, including the Federal Trade Commission, the Securities and Exchange Commission, and the Federal Communications Commission. The president's power is less pronounced in regard to independent agencies, whose officers serve for fixed terms and cannot be removed without just cause.

There are administrative agencies at the state and local levels as well. Commonly, a state agency (such as a state pollution-control agency) is created as a parallel to a federal agency (such as the Environmental Protection Agency). Just as federal statutes take precedence over conflicting state statutes, so do federal agency regulations take precedence over conflicting state regulations.

ADMINISTRATIVE LAW
The body of law created by administrative agencies (in the form of rules, regulations, orders, and decisions) in order to carry out their duties and responsibilities.

ADMINISTRATIVE AGENCY
A federal or state government agency established to perform a specific function. Administrative agencies are authorized by legislative acts to make and enforce rules to administer and enforce the acts.

EXECUTIVE AGENCY
An administrative agency within the executive branch of government. At the federal level, executive agencies are those within the cabinet departments.

INDEPENDENT REGULATORY AGENCY
An administrative agency that is not considered part of the government's executive branch and is not subject to the authority of the president. Independent agency officials cannot be removed without cause.

---

1. This institute was formed in the 1920s and consists of practicing attorneys, legal scholars, and judges.
2. Louisiana has adopted only Articles 1, 3, 4, 5, 7, 8, and 9.

ETHICAL ISSUE 1.1   *Do administrative agencies exercise too much authority?*

Administrative agencies, such as the Federal Trade Commission, combine functions normally divided among the three branches of government in a single governmental entity. The broad range of authority that agencies exercise sometimes poses questions of fairness. After all, agencies create rules that are as legally binding as the laws passed by Congress—the only federal government institution authorized by the Constitution to make laws. To be sure, arbitrary rulemaking by agencies is checked by the procedural requirements set forth in the Administrative Procedure Act (APA), as well as by the courts, to which agency decisions may be appealed. Yet some people claim that these checks are not enough.

Consider that in addition to *legislative rules,* which are subject to the procedural requirements of the APA, agencies also create *interpretive rules*—rules that specify how the agency will interpret and apply its regulations. The APA does not apply to interpretive rulemaking. Additionally, although a firm that challenges an agency's rule may be able to appeal the agency's decision in the matter to a court, the courts generally defer to agency rules, including interpretive rules, and to agency decisions.

Case Law and Common Law Doctrines

The rules of law announced in court decisions constitute another basic source of American law. These rules of law include interpretations of constitutional provisions, of statutes enacted by legislatures, and of regulations created by administrative agencies. Today, this body of judge-made law is referred to as **case law.** Case law—the doctrines and principles of law announced in cases— governs all areas not covered by statutory law or administrative law and is part of our common law tradition. We look at the origins and characteristics of the common law tradition in some detail in the pages that follow.

CASE LAW
Case law includes the aggregate of reported cases that interpret judicial precedents, statutes, regulations, and constitutional provisions.

THE COMMON LAW TRADITION

Because of our colonial heritage, much of American law is based on the English legal system. A knowledge of this tradition is crucial to understanding our legal system today because judges in the United States still apply common law principles when deciding cases.

Early English Courts

After the Normans conquered England in 1066, William the Conqueror and his successors began the process of unifying the country under their rule. One of the means they used to do this was the establishment of the king's courts, or *curiae regis.* Before the Norman Conquest, disputes had been settled according to the local legal customs and traditions in various regions of the country. The king's courts sought to establish a uniform set of rules for the country as a whole. What evolved in these courts was the beginning of the **common law**—a body of general rules that applied throughout the entire English realm. Eventually, the common law tradition became part of the heritage of all nations that were once British colonies, including the United States.

COMMON LAW
That body of law derived from judicial decisions or custom in English and U.S. courts, not attributable to a legislature.

The court of chancery in the reign of King George I. Early English court decisions formed the basis of what type of law? (From a painting by Benjamin Ferrers in the National Portrait Gallery; Photo, Corbis Bettmann)

Courts developed the common law rules from the principles underlying judges' decisions in actual legal controversies. Judges attempted to be consistent, and whenever possible, they based their decisions on the principles suggested by earlier cases. They sought to decide similar cases in a similar way and considered new cases with care, because they knew that their decisions would make new law. Each interpretation became part of the law on the subject and served as a legal **precedent**—that is, a decision that furnished an example or authority for deciding subsequent cases involving similar legal principles or facts.

In the early years of the common law, there was no single place or publication where court opinions, or written decisions, could be found. Beginning in the late thirteenth and early fourteenth centuries, however, each year portions of significant decisions of that year were gathered together and recorded in *Year Books*. The *Year Books* were useful references for lawyers and judges. In the sixteenth century, the *Year Books* were discontinued, and other reports of cases became available. (See the appendix following this chapter for a discussion of how cases are reported, or published, in the United States today.)

Stare Decisis

The practice of deciding new cases with reference to former decisions, or precedents, eventually became a cornerstone of the English and American judicial systems. The practice forms a doctrine called *stare decisis*[3] ("to stand on decided cases").

PRECEDENT
A court decision that furnishes an example or authority for deciding subsequent cases involving identical or similar facts.

STARE DECISIS
A common law doctrine under which judges are obligated to follow the precedents established in prior decisions.

The Importance of Precedents in Judicial Decision Making   The doctrine of *stare decisis* means that once a court has set forth a principle of law as being applicable to a certain set of facts, that court and courts of lower rank must adhere to that principle and apply it in future cases involving similar fact patterns.

| **Example #2**   Suppose that the lower state courts in California have reached conflicting conclusions on whether drivers are liable for accidents they cause while merging into freeway traffic, even though the drivers looked and did not see any oncoming vehicles and even though witnesses (passengers in their cars) testified to that effect. To settle the law on this issue, the California Supreme Court decides to review a case involving this fact pattern. The court rules that in such a situation, the driver who is merging into traffic is liable for any accidents caused by the driver's failure to yield to freeway traffic—even if the driver looked carefully and did not see an approaching vehicle. The California Supreme Court's decision on the matter will influence the outcome of all future cases on this issue brought before the California state courts. | Similarly, a decision on a given issue by the United States Supreme Court (the nation's highest court) is binding on all other courts.

BINDING AUTHORITY
Any source of law that a court must follow when deciding a case. Binding authorities include constitutions, statutes, and regulations that govern the issue being decided, as well as court decisions that are controlling precedents within the jurisdiction.

Controlling precedents in a *jurisdiction* (an area in which a court or courts have the power to apply the law—see Chapter 3) are referred to as binding authorities. A **binding authority** is any source of law that a court must follow when deciding a case. Binding authorities include constitutions, statutes, and

---

3. Pronounced *ster*-ay dih-*si*-ses.

regulations that govern the issue being decided, as well as court decisions that are controlling precedents within the jurisdiction.

Stare Decisis **and Legal Stability** The doctrine of *stare decisis* helps the courts to be more efficient, because if other courts have carefully reasoned through a similar case, their legal reasoning and opinions can serve as guides. *Stare decisis* also makes the law more stable and predictable. If the law on a given subject is well settled, someone bringing a case to court can usually rely on the court to make a decision based on what the law has been.

Departures from Precedent Although courts are obligated to follow precedents, sometimes a court will depart from the rule of precedent if it decides that a given precedent should no longer be followed. If a court decides that a precedent is simply incorrect or that technological or social changes have rendered the precedent inapplicable, the court might rule contrary to the precedent. Cases that overturn precedent often receive a great deal of publicity.

| **Example #3** In *Brown v. Board of Education of Topeka*,[4] the United States Supreme Court expressly overturned precedent when it concluded that separate educational facilities for whites and blacks, which had been upheld as constitutional in numerous previous cases,[5] were inherently unequal. The Supreme Court's departure from precedent in *Brown* received a tremendous amount of publicity as people began to realize the ramifications of this change in the law. |

When There Is No Precedent At times, courts hear cases for which there are no precedents within their jurisdictions on which to base their decisions. When hearing such cases, called "cases of first impression," courts often look to precedents set in other jurisdictions for guidance. Precedents from other jurisdictions, because they are not binding on the court, are referred to as **persuasive authorities**. A court may also consider a number of factors, including legal principles and policies underlying previous court decisions or existing statutes, fairness, social values and customs, public policy, and data and concepts drawn from the social sciences.

PERSUASIVE AUTHORITY
Any legal authority or source of law that a court may look to for guidance but on which it need not rely in making its decision. Persuasive authorities include cases from other jurisdictions and secondary sources of law.

Equitable Remedies and Courts of Equity

A **remedy** is the means given to a party to enforce a right or to compensate for the violation of a right. | **Example #4** Suppose that Shem is injured because of Rowan's wrongdoing. A court may order Rowan to compensate Shem for the harm by paying Shem a certain amount of money. |

In the early king's courts of England, the kinds of remedies that could be granted were severely restricted. If one person wronged another, the king's courts could award as compensation either money or property, including land. These courts became known as *courts of law*, and the remedies were called *remedies at law*. Even though this system introduced uniformity in the settling of disputes, when plaintiffs wanted a remedy other than economic compensation, the courts of law could do nothing, so "no remedy, no right."

REMEDY
The relief given to an innocent party to enforce a right or compensate for the violation of a right.

---

4. 347 U.S. 483, 74 S.Ct. 686, 98 L.Ed. 873 (1954). See the appendix following this chapter for an explanation of how to read legal citations.
5. See *Plessy v. Ferguson*, 163 U.S. 537, 16 S.Ct. 1138, 41 L.Ed. 256 (1896).

Remedies in Equity   *Equity* refers to a branch of the law, founded in justice and fair dealing, that seeks to supply a fair and adequate remedy when no remedy is available at law. In medieval England, when individuals could not obtain an adequate remedy in a court of law, they petitioned the king for relief. Most of these petitions were decided by an adviser to the king called the *chancellor.* The chancellor was said to be the "keeper of the king's conscience." When the chancellor thought that the claim was a fair one, unique remedies were granted. In this way, a new body of rules and remedies came into being, and eventually formal *chancery courts,* or *courts of equity,* were established. The remedies granted by these courts were called *remedies in equity.* Thus, two distinct court systems were created, each having a different set of judges and a different set of remedies.

PLAINTIFF
One who initiates a lawsuit.

DEFENDANT
One against whom a lawsuit is brought; the accused person in a criminal proceeding.

Plaintiffs (those bringing lawsuits) had to specify whether they were bringing an "action at law" or an "action in equity," and they chose their courts accordingly. **| Example #5** A plaintiff might ask a court of equity to order a **defendant** (a person against whom a lawsuit is brought) to perform within the terms of a contract. A court of law could not issue such an order, because its remedies were limited to payment of money or property as compensation for damages. A court of equity, however, could issue a decree for *specific performance*—an order to perform what was promised. A court of equity could also issue an *injunction,* directing a party to do or refrain from doing a particular act. In certain cases, a court of equity could allow for the *rescission* (cancellation) of the contract so that the parties would be returned to the positions that they held prior to the contract's formation.**|** Equitable remedies will be discussed in greater detail in Chapter 9.

REMEMBER ! **Even though, in most states, courts of law and equity have merged, the principles of equity still apply.**

The Merging of Law and Equity   Today, in most states, the courts of law and equity have merged, and thus the distinction between the two courts has largely disappeared. A plaintiff may now request both legal and equitable remedies in the same action, and the trial court judge may grant either form— or both forms—of relief. The merging of law and equity, however, does not diminish the importance of distinguishing legal remedies from equitable remedies. To request the proper remedy, a businessperson (or her or his attorney) must know what remedies are available for the specific kinds of harms suffered. Today, as a rule, courts will grant an equitable remedy only when the remedy at law (money damages) is inadequate. Exhibit 1–2 summarizes the procedural differences (applicable in most states) between an action at law and an action in equity.

EXHIBIT 1–2   PROCEDURAL DIFFERENCES BETWEEN AN ACTION AT LAW AND AN ACTION IN EQUITY

PROCEDURE	ACTION AT LAW	ACTION IN EQUITY
Initiation of lawsuit	By filing a complaint	By filing a petition
Decision	By jury or judge	By judge (no jury)
Result	Judgment	Decree
Remedy	Monetary damages	Injunction, specific performance, or rescission

LANDMARK IN THE LEGAL ENVIRONMENT
Equitable Principles and Maxims

In medieval England, courts of equity had the responsibility of using discretion in supplementing the common law. Even today, when the same court can award both legal and equitable remedies, it must exercise discretion. Courts often invoke equitable principles and maxims when making their decisions. Here are some of the most significant equitable principles and maxims:

1. *Whoever seeks equity must do equity.* (Anyone who wishes to be treated fairly must treat others fairly.)
2. *Where there is equal equity, the law must prevail.* (The law will determine the outcome of a controversy in which the merits of both sides are equal.)
3. *One seeking the aid of an equity court must come to the court with clean hands.* (Plaintiffs must have acted fairly and honestly.)
4. *Equity will not suffer a wrong to be without a remedy.* (Equitable relief will be awarded when there is a right to relief and there is no adequate remedy at law.)
5. *Equity regards substance rather than form.* (Equity is more concerned with fairness and justice than with legal technicalities.)
6. *Equity aids the vigilant, not those who rest on their rights.* (Equity will not help those who neglect their rights for an unreasonable period of time.)

The last maxim has become known as the *equitable doctrine of laches.* The doctrine arose to encourage people to bring lawsuits while the evidence was fresh; if they failed to do so, they would not be allowed to bring a lawsuit. What constitutes a reasonable time, of course, varies according to the circumstances of the case. Time periods for different types of cases are now usually fixed by **statutes of limitations.** After the time allowed under a statute of limitations has expired, no action can be brought, no matter how strong the case was originally.

Application to Today's Legal Environment

The equitable maxims listed on the left underlie many of the legal rules and principles that are commonly applied by the courts today—and that you will read about in this book. For example, in Chapter 8 you will read about the doctrine of promissory estoppel. Under this doctrine, a person who has reasonably and substantially relied on the promise of another may be able to obtain some measure of recovery, even though no enforceable contract, or agreement, exists. The court will estop (bar, or impede) the one making the promise from asserting the lack of a valid contract as a defense. The rationale underlying the doctrine of promissory estoppel is similar to that expressed in the fourth and fifth maxims.

RELEVANT WEB SITES

To locate information on the Web concerning equitable principles, go to this text's Web site at **www.thomsonedu. com/westbuslaw/let,** *select "Chapter 1," and click on "URLs for Landmarks."*

Equitable Principles and Maxims   Over time, a number of **equitable principles and maxims** evolved that have since guided the courts in deciding whether plaintiffs should be granted equitable relief. Because of their importance, both historically and in our judicial system today, these principles and maxims are set forth in this chapter's *Landmark in the Legal Environment* feature.

CLASSIFICATIONS OF LAW

The huge body of the law may be broken down according to several classification systems. For example, one classification system divides law into **substantive law** (all laws that define, describe, regulate, and create legal rights and obligations) and **procedural law** (all laws that establish the methods of enforcing the rights established by substantive law). Other classification systems divide law into federal law and state law or private law (dealing with relationships between persons) and public law (addressing the relationship between persons and their governments).

STATUTE OF LIMITATIONS
A federal or state statute setting the maximum time period during which a certain action can be brought or certain rights enforced.

EQUITABLE PRINCIPLES AND MAXIMS
General propositions or principles of law that have to do with fairness (equity).

SUBSTANTIVE LAW
Law that defines, describes, regulates, and creates legal rights and obligations.

PROCEDURAL LAW
Law that establishes the methods of enforcing the rights established by substantive law.

ONLINE DEVELOPMENTS

International Jurisdiction and the Internet

As you will learn in Chapter 3, *jurisdiction* is an important legal concept that relates to the authority of a court to hear and decide a case. Within the United States, there is a federal court system, which has jurisdiction over specific types of cases. There are also fifty state court systems, each having jurisdiction over certain types of cases. In today's interconnected world, the issue of jurisdiction has become critical. Specifically, businesses using the Internet can reach individuals in any part of the world. Does that mean that every court everywhere has jurisdiction over, say, an Internet-based company in Chicago? Clearly, this question has significant implications for any business that owns or operates a Web site.

The Minimum-Contacts Requirement

Domestically, jurisdiction over individuals and businesses is based on the requirement of minimum contacts as outlined in *International Shoe Co. v. State of Washington.*[a] Essentially, this requirement means that a business must have a minimum level of contacts with residents of a particular state for that state's courts to exercise jurisdiction over the firm. For example, suppose that a Wisconsin driver, while on vacation in California, crashes into a California resident's car. If the crash resulted from the Wisconsin driver's negligence, a *tort,* or civil wrong (see Chapter 5), will have been committed. This contact will be sufficient to allow a California court to exercise jurisdiction over a lawsuit brought by the California resident. In the international arena, other countries' courts are applying the requirement of minimum contacts as developed in the U.S. courts.

Special International Jurisdictional Challenges

Suppose that a firm located in New Jersey posts a statement on its Web site that is defamatory. (As you will read in Chapter 5, *defamation* is a tort that occurs when someone publishes or publicly makes a false statement that harms another's good name, reputation, or character.) Further suppose that the person who has been defamed, or injured by the statement, lives in Australia. Can the Australian citizen sue the New Jersey firm in an Australian court? Perhaps—but at a minimum, jurisdictional authority would depend on whether the tort occurred in Australia. Thus, the question essentially is as follows: Did the tort occur when the defamatory statement was posted on the Web site (in New Jersey) or when it was downloaded and viewed (in Australia)?

To date, only one nation's highest court—that of Australia—has ruled on this issue. The case involved Joseph Gutnick, a resident of Melbourne, Australia, who sued Dow Jones & Company, the U.S. publisher of the *Wall Street Journal,* for defamation. Dow Jones argued that the Australian court could not exercise jurisdiction over its U.S. servers, which were located in New Jersey. The case ultimately reached Australia's highest court, which rejected Dow Jones's argument. The court concluded that the tort had occurred in Australia, where the article had been downloaded and viewed, and thus the Australian court had jurisdiction over the dispute.[b]

For Critical Analysis   *If the opinion of the Australian high court becomes widely accepted, how might this have a "chilling effect" on Internet communications and on the dissemination of ideas?*

a. 326 U.S. 310, 66 S.Ct. 154, 90 L.Ed. 95 (1945).

b. *Dow Jones & Co., Inc. v. Gutnick,* HCA 56 (December 10, 2002).

CYBERLAW
An informal term used to refer to all laws governing electronic communications and transactions, particularly those conducted via the Internet.

Frequently, people use the term **cyberlaw** to refer to the emerging body of law that governs transactions conducted via the Internet. Cyberlaw is not really a classification of law, nor is it a new *type* of law. Rather, it is an informal term used to describe traditional legal principles that have been modified and adapted to fit situations that are unique to the online world. Of course, in some areas new statutes have been enacted, at both the federal and state levels, to cover specific types of problems stemming from online communications. Throughout this book, you will read how the law in a given area is evolving to govern specific legal issues that arise in the online context. We look at one important issue in this chapter's *Online Developments* feature.

Civil Law and Criminal Law

Civil law spells out the rights and duties that exist between persons and between persons and their governments, and the relief available when a person's rights are violated. Typically, in a civil case, a private party sues another private party (although the government can also sue a party for a civil law violation) to make that other party comply with a duty or pay for the damage caused by the failure to comply with a duty. **| Example #6** If a seller fails to perform a contract with a buyer, the buyer may bring a lawsuit against the seller. The purpose of the lawsuit will be either to compel the seller to perform as promised or, more commonly, to obtain money damages for the seller's failure to perform. |

Much of the law that we discuss in this text is civil law. Contract law, for example, which we discuss in Chapters 8 through 10, is civil law. The whole body of tort law (see Chapter 5) is civil law. Note that *civil law* is not the same as a *civil law system*. As you will read shortly, in the context of different nations' laws, a civil law system is a legal system based on a written code of laws.

Criminal law has to do with wrongs committed against society for which society demands redress. Criminal acts are proscribed by local, state, or federal government statutes. Thus, criminal defendants are prosecuted by public officials, such as a district attorney (D.A.), on behalf of the state, not by their victims or other private parties. Whereas in a civil case the object is to obtain remedies (such as money damages) to compensate the injured party, in a criminal case the object is to punish the wrongdoer in an attempt to deter others from similar actions. Penalties for violations of criminal statutes consist of fines and/or imprisonment—and, in some cases, death. We will discuss the differences between civil and criminal law in greater detail in Chapter 6.

CIVIL LAW
The branch of law dealing with the definition and enforcement of all private or public rights, as opposed to criminal matters.

CRIMINAL LAW
Law that defines and governs actions that constitute crimes. Generally, criminal law has to do with wrongful actions committed against society for which society demands redress.

National and International Law

Although the focus of this book is U.S. business law, increasingly businesspersons in this country engage in transactions that extend beyond our national borders. In these situations, the laws of other nations or the laws governing relationships among nations may come into play. For this reason, those who pursue a career in business today should have an understanding of the global legal environment.

The law of a particular nation, such as the United States or Sweden, is **national law**. National law, of course, varies from country to country because each country's law reflects the interests, customs, activities, and values that are unique to that nation's culture. Even though the laws and legal systems of various countries differ substantially, broad similarities do exist, as discussed in this chapter's *Beyond Our Borders* feature on the following page.

In contrast to national law, international law applies to more than one nation. **International law** can be defined as a body of written and unwritten laws observed by independent nations and governing the acts of individuals as well as governments. International law is an intermingling of rules and constraints derived from a variety of sources, including the laws of individual countries, the customs that have evolved among nations in their relations with one another, treaties, and international organizations. In essence, international law is the result of centuries-old attempts to reconcile the traditional need of each country to be the final authority over its own affairs with the desire of

NATIONAL LAW
Laws that pertain to a particular nation (as opposed to international law).

INTERNATIONAL LAW
The law that governs relations among nations. International customs and treaties are important sources of international law.

National Law Systems

Despite their varying cultures and customs, virtually all countries have laws governing torts, contracts, employment, and other areas, just as the United States does. In part, this is because there are two legal systems that predominate around the globe today. One is the common law system of England and the United States, which we have discussed elsewhere. The other system is based on Roman civil law, or "code law." The term *civil law,* as used here, refers not to civil as opposed to criminal law but to codified law—an ordered grouping of legal principles enacted into law by a legislature or governing body. In a *civil law system,* the primary source of law is a statutory code, and case precedents are not judicially binding, as they normally are in a common law system. Although judges in a civil law system commonly refer to previous decisions as sources of legal guidance, they are not bound by precedent; in other words, the doctrine of *stare decisis* does not apply.

A third, less prevalent, legal system is common in Islamic countries, where the law is often influenced by *sharia,* the religious law of Islam. *Sharia* is a comprehensive code of principles that governs both the public and private lives of Islamic persons, directing many aspects of day-to-day life, including politics, economics, banking, business law, contract law, and social issues. Although *sharia* affects the legal code of many Muslim countries, the extent of its impact and the interpretation of *sharia* vary widely. In some Middle Eastern nations, aspects of *sharia* have become codified in modern legal codes and are enforced by national judicial systems.

The accompanying exhibit lists some countries that today follow either the common law system or the civil law system. Generally, those countries that were once colonies of Great Britain retained their English common law heritage after they achieved independence. Similarly, the civil law system, which is followed in most continental European nations, was retained in the Latin American, African, and Asian countries that were once colonies of those nations. Japan and South Africa also have civil law systems. In the United States, the state of Louisiana, because of its historical ties to France, has in part a civil law system. The legal systems of Puerto Rico, Québec, and Scotland are similarly characterized as having elements of the civil law system.

Realize that although national law systems share many commonalities, they also have distinct differences. Even when the basic principles are fundamentally similar (as they are in contract law, for example), significant variations exist in the practical application and effect of these laws across countries. Therefore, those persons who plan to do business in another nation would be wise to become familiar with the laws of that nation.

For Critical Analysis *Does the civil law system offer any advantages over the common law system, or vice versa? Explain.*

THE LEGAL SYSTEMS OF SELECTED NATIONS

CIVIL LAW		COMMON LAW	
Argentina	Indonesia	Australia	Nigeria
Austria	Iran	Bangladesh	Singapore
Brazil	Italy	Canada	United Kingdom
Chile	Japan	Ghana	United States
China	Mexico	India	Zambia
Egypt	Poland	Israel	
Finland	South Korea	Jamaica	
France	Sweden	Kenya	
Germany	Tunisia	Malaysia	
Greece	Venezuela	New Zealand	

nations to benefit economically from trade and harmonious relations with one another.

The key difference between national law and international law is that national law can be enforced by government authorities. If a nation violates an international law, however, the most that other countries or international organizations can do (if persuasive tactics fail) is to resort to coercive actions against the violating nation. Coercive actions range from the severance of diplomatic relations and boycotts to, at the last resort, war. We will examine the laws governing international business transactions in later chapters (including Chapter 10, which covers contracts for the sale of goods, and Chapter 22).

REVIEWING . . . THE LEGAL AND INTERNATIONAL FOUNDATIONS

Suppose the California legislature passes a law that severely restricts carbon dioxide emissions from automobiles in that state. A group of automobile manufacturers file suit against the state of California to prevent the enforcement of the law. The automakers claim that a federal law already sets fuel economy standards nationwide, and that fuel economy standards are essentially the same as carbon dioxide emission standards. According to the automobile manufacturers, it is unfair to allow California to pass more-stringent regulations than those set by the federal law. Using the information presented in the chapter, answer the following questions.

1. Who are the parties (the plaintiffs and the defendant) in this lawsuit?

2. Are the plaintiffs seeking a legal remedy or an equitable remedy? Why?

3. What is the primary source of the law that is at issue here?

4. Read through the appendix that follows this chapter and then answer the following question: Where would you look to find the relevant California and federal statutes?

KEY TERMS

administrative agency 8
administrative law 8
binding authority 10
breach 5
case law 9
citation 7
civil law 15
common law 9
constitutional law 6
criminal law 15
cyberlaw 14
defendant 12
equitable principles and
   maxims 13

executive agency 8
historical school 4
independent regulatory agency 8
international law 15
jurisprudence 3
law 2
legal positivism 3
legal realism 4
national law 15
natural law 3
ordinance 7
persuasive authority 11

plaintiff 12
positive law 3
precedent 10
primary source of law 6
procedural law 13
remedy 11
secondary source of law 6
sociological school 4
stare decisis 10
statute of limitations 13
statutory law 7
substantive law 13

CHAPTER SUMMARY • THE LEGAL AND INTERNATIONAL FOUNDATIONS

The Nature of Law (See pages 2–4.)	Law can be defined as a body of rules of conduct with legal force and effect, prescribed by the controlling authority (the government) of a society. Four important schools of legal thought, or legal philosophies, are the following: 1. *Natural law tradition*—One of the oldest and most significant schools of legal thought. Those who believe in natural law hold that there is a universal law applicable to all human beings and that this law is of a higher order than positive, or conventional, law. 2. *Legal positivism*—A school of legal thought centered on the assumption that there is no law higher than the laws created by the government. Laws must be obeyed, even if they are unjust, to prevent anarchy. 3. *The historical school*—A school of legal thought that stresses the evolutionary nature of law and that looks to doctrines that have withstood the passage of time for guidance in shaping present laws. 4. *Legal realism*—A school of legal thought, popular during the 1920s and 1930s, that left a lasting imprint on American jurisprudence. Legal realists generally advocated a less abstract and more realistic approach to the law, an approach that would take into account customary practices and the circumstances in which transactions take place.
Sources of American Law (See pages 6–9.)	1. *Constitutional law*—The law as expressed in the U.S. Constitution and the various state constitutions. The U.S. Constitution is the supreme law of the land. State constitutions are supreme within state borders to the extent that they do not violate the U.S. Constitution or a federal law. 2. *Statutory law*—Laws or ordinances created by federal, state, and local legislatures and governing bodies. None of these laws can violate the U.S. Constitution or the relevant state constitutions. Uniform laws, when adopted by a state legislature, become statutory law in that state. 3. *Administrative law*—The rules, orders, and decisions of federal or state government administrative agencies. 4. *Case law and common law doctrines*—Judge-made law, including interpretations of constitutional provisions, of statutes enacted by legislatures, and of regulations created by administrative agencies. Case law—the doctrines and principles announced in cases—governs all areas not covered by statutory law (or agency regulations issued to implement various statutes) and is part of our common law tradition.

The Common Law Tradition
(See pages 9–13.)
	1. *Common law*—Law that originated in medieval England with the creation of the king's courts, or *curiae regis,* and the development of a body of rules that were common to (or applied throughout) the land.
	
	2. *Stare decisis*—A doctrine under which judges "stand on decided cases"—or follow the rule of precedent—in deciding cases. *Stare decisis* is the cornerstone of the common law tradition.
	
	3. *Remedies*—
	  a. Remedies at law—Money or something else of value.
	  b. Remedies in equity—Remedies that are granted when the remedies at law are unavailable or inadequate. Equitable remedies include specific performance, an injunction, and contract rescission (cancellation).

Classifications of Law (See pages 13–17.)	The law may be broken down according to several classification systems, such as substantive or procedural law, federal or state law, and private or public law. Two broad classifications are civil and criminal law, and national and international law.

FOR REVIEW

Answers for the even-numbered questions in this For Review *section can be found in Appendix O at the end of this text.*

1. What is the Uniform Commercial Code?

2. What is the common law tradition?

3. What is a precedent? When might a court depart from precedent?

4. What is the difference between remedies at law and remedies in equity?

5. What are some important differences between civil law and criminal law?

QUESTIONS AND CASE PROBLEMS

1–1. Philosophy of Law. After World War II ended in 1945, an international tribunal of judges convened at Nuremberg, Germany. The judges convicted several Nazi war criminals of "crimes against humanity." Assuming that the Nazis who were convicted had not disobeyed any law of their country and had merely been following their government's (Hitler's) orders, what law had they violated? Explain.

Question with Sample Answer

1–2. This chapter discussed a number of sources of American law. Which source of law takes priority in each of the following situations, and why?

1. A federal statute conflicts with the U.S. Constitution.
2. A federal statute conflicts with a state constitution.
3. A state statute conflicts with the common law of that state.
4. A state constitutional amendment conflicts with the U.S. Constitution.
5. A federal administrative regulation conflicts with a state constitution.

For a sample answer to this question, go to Appendix P at the end of this text.

1–3. Legal Systems. What are the key differences between a common law system and a civil law system? Why do some countries have common law systems and others have civil law systems?

1–4. Reading Citations. Assume that you want to read the entire court opinion in the case of *Thompson v. Altheimer & Gray,* 248 F.3d 621 (7th Cir. 2001). The case deals with whether an attorney may dismiss "for cause" a prospective juror in a case involving racial discrimination. Read the section entitled "Finding Case Law" in the appendix that follows this chapter, and then explain specifically where you would find the court's opinion.

1–5. *Stare Decisis.* In the text of this chapter, we stated that the doctrine of *stare decisis* "became a cornerstone of the English and American judicial systems." What does *stare decisis* mean, and why has this doctrine been so fundamental to the development of our legal tradition?

1–6. Court Opinions. Read through the subsection entitled "Case Titles and Terminology" in the appendix following this

chapter. What is the difference between a concurring opinion and a majority opinion? Between a concurring opinion and a dissenting opinion? Why do judges and justices write concurring and dissenting opinions, given that these opinions will not affect the outcome of the case at hand, which has already been decided by majority vote?

1–7. Binding versus Persuasive Authority. A county court in Illinois is deciding a case involving an issue that has never been addressed before in that state's courts. The Iowa Supreme Court, however, recently decided a case involving a very similar fact pattern. Is the Illinois court obligated to follow the Iowa Supreme Court's decision on the issue? If the United States Supreme Court had decided a similar case, would that decision be binding on the Illinois court? Explain.

1–8. Remedies. Arthur Rabe is suing Xavier Sanchez for breaching a contract in which Sanchez promised to sell Rabe a painting by Vincent van Gogh for $150,000.

1. In this lawsuit, who is the plaintiff and who is the defendant?
2. If Rabe wants Sanchez to perform the contract as promised, what remedy should Rabe seek?
3. Suppose that Rabe wants to cancel the contract because Sanchez fraudulently misrepresented the painting as an original van Gogh when in fact it is a copy. In this situation, what remedy should Rabe seek?
4. Will the remedy Rabe seeks in either situation be a remedy at law or a remedy in equity?
5. Suppose that the court finds in Rabe's favor and grants one of these remedies. Sanchez then appeals the decision to a higher court. Read the subsection entitled "Appellants and Appellees" in the appendix following this chapter. On appeal, which party in the Rabe-Sanchez case will be the appellant (or petitioner), and which party will be the appellee (or respondent)?

A Question of Ethics

1–9. On July 5, 1884, Dudley, Stephens, and Brooks—"all able-bodied English seamen"— and a teenaged English boy were cast adrift in a lifeboat following a storm at sea. They had no water with them in the boat, and all they had for sustenance were two one-pound tins of turnips. On July 24, Dudley proposed that one of the four in the lifeboat be sacrificed to save the others. Stephens agreed with Dudley, but Brooks refused to consent—and the boy was never asked for his opinion. On July 25, Dudley killed the boy, and the three men then fed on the boy's body and blood. Four days later, the men were rescued by a passing vessel. They were taken to England and tried for the murder of the boy. If the men had not fed on the boy's body, they would probably have died of starvation within the four-day period. The boy, who was in a much weaker condition, would likely have died before the rest. [*Regina v. Dudley and Stephens*, 14 Q.B.D. (Queen's Bench Division, England) 273 (1884)]

1. The basic question in this case is whether the survivors should be subject to penalties under English criminal law, given the men's unusual circumstances. You be the judge and decide the issue. Give the reasons for your decision.

2. Should judges ever have the power to look beyond the written "letter of the law" in making their decisions? Why or why not?

Critical-Thinking Legal Question

1–10. John's company is involved in a lawsuit with a customer, Beth. John argues that for fifty years, in cases involving circumstances similar to this case, judges have ruled in a way that indicates that the judge in this case should rule in favor of John's company. Is this a valid argument? If so, must the judge in this case rule as those other judges have? What argument could Beth use to counter John's reasoning?

INTERACTING WITH THE INTERNET

Today, business law professors and students can go online to access information on virtually every topic covered in this text. A good point of departure for online legal research is the Web site for *The Legal Environment Today*, Fifth Edition, at

www.thomsonedu.com/westbuslaw/let

There you will find numerous materials relevant to this text and to the legal environment of business generally, including links to various legal resources on the Web. Additionally, every chapter in this text ends with an *Interacting with the Internet* feature that contains selected Web addresses.

You can access many of the sources of law discussed in Chapter 1 at the FindLaw Web site, which is probably the most comprehensive source of free legal information on the Internet. Go to

www.findlaw.com

The Legal Information Institute (LII) at Cornell Law School, which offers extensive information about U.S. law, is also a good starting point for legal research. The URL for this site is

www.law.cornell.edu

The Library of Congress offers numerous links to state and federal government resources at

www.loc.gov

INTERNET EXERCISES

Go to **www.thomsonedu.com/westbuslaw/let**, the Web site that accompanies this text. Select "Chapter 1" and click on "Internet Exercises." There you will find the following Internet research exercises that you can perform to learn more about topics covered in this chapter.

Internet Exercise 1–1: LEGAL PERSPECTIVE—Internet Sources of Law
Internet Exercise 1–2: MANAGEMENT PERSPECTIVE—Online Assistance from Government
                                                Agencies
Internet Exercise 1–3: SOCIAL PERSPECTIVE—The Case of the Speluncean Explorers

BEFORE THE TEST

Go to **www.thomsonedu.com/westbuslaw/let**, the Web site that accompanies this text. Select "Chapter 1" and click on "Interactive Quizzes." You will find a number of interactive questions relating to this chapter.

Finding and Analyzing the Law

THE STATUTES, agency regulations, and case law referred to in this text establish the rights and duties of businesspersons engaged in various types of activities. The cases presented in the following chapters provide you with concise, real-life illustrations of how the courts interpret and apply these laws. Because of the importance of knowing how to find statutory, administrative, and case law, this appendix offers a brief introduction to how these laws are published and to the legal "shorthand" employed in referencing these legal sources.

FINDING STATUTORY AND ADMINISTRATIVE LAW

When Congress passes laws, they are collected in a publication titled *United States Statutes at Large*. When state legislatures pass laws, they are collected in similar state publications. Most frequently, however, laws are referred to in their codified form—that is, the form in which they appear in the federal and state codes. In these codes, laws are compiled by subject.

United States Code

The *United States Code* (U.S.C.) arranges all existing federal laws of a public and permanent nature by subject. Each of the fifty subjects into which the U.S.C. arranges the laws is given a title and a title number. For example, laws relating to commerce and trade are collected in "Title 15, Commerce and Trade." Titles are subdivided by sections. A citation to the U.S.C. includes title and section numbers. Thus, a reference to "15 U.S.C. Section 1" means that the statute can be found in Section 1 of Title 15. ("Section" may also be designated by the symbol §, and "Sections" by §§.)

Sometimes a citation includes the abbreviation *et seq.*—as in "15 U.S.C. Sections 1 *et seq.*" The term is an abbreviated form of *et sequitur,* which in Latin means "and the following." When used in a citation, it refers to sections that concern the same subject as the numbered section and follow it in sequence.

Commercial publications of these laws and regulations are available and are widely used. For example, West Group publishes the *United States Code Annotated* (U.S.C.A.). The U.S.C.A. contains the complete text of laws included in the U.S.C., as well as notes of court decisions that interpret and apply specific sections of the statutes, plus the text of presidential proclamations and executive orders. The U.S.C.A. also includes research aids, such as cross-references to related statutes, historical notes, and library references. A citation to the U.S.C.A. is similar to a citation to the U.S.C.: "15 U.S.C.A. Section 1."

State Codes

State codes follow the U.S.C. pattern of arranging law by subject. The state codes may be called codes, revisions, compilations, consolidations, general statutes, or statutes, depending on the preferences of the states. In some codes, subjects are designated by number. In others, they are designated by name. For example, "13 Pennsylvania Consolidated Statutes Section 1101" means that the statute can be found in Title 13, Section 1101, of the Pennsylvania code.

"California Commercial Code Section 1101" means the statute can be found under the subject heading "Commercial Code" of the California code in Section 1101. Abbreviations may be used. For example, "13 Pennsylvania Consolidated Statutes Section 1101" may be abbreviated "13 Pa. C.S. § 1101," and "California Commercial Code Section 1101" may be abbreviated "Cal. Com. Code § 1101."

Administrative Rules

Rules and regulations adopted by federal administrative agencies are compiled in the *Code of Federal Regulations* (C.F.R.). Like the U.S.C., the C.F.R. is divided into fifty titles. Rules within each title are assigned section numbers. A full citation to the C.F.R. includes title and section numbers. For example, a reference to "17 C.F.R. Section 230.504" means that the rule can be found in Section 230.504 of Title 17.

FINDING CASE LAW

Before discussing the case reporting system, we need to look briefly at the court system (which will be discussed in detail in Chapter 3). There are two types of courts in the United States, federal courts and state courts. Both the federal and state court systems consist of several levels, or tiers, of courts. *Trial courts,* in which evidence is presented and testimony given, are on the bottom tier (which also includes lower courts handling specialized issues). Decisions from a trial court can be appealed to a higher court, which commonly would be an intermediate *court of appeals,* or an *appellate court.* Decisions from these intermediate courts of appeals may be appealed to an even higher court, such as a state supreme court or the United States Supreme Court.

State Court Decisions

Most state trial court decisions are not published. Except in New York and a few other states that publish selected opinions of their trial courts, decisions from state trial courts are merely filed in the office of the clerk of the court, where the decisions are available for public inspection. (Sometimes they can be found online as well.) Written decisions of the appellate, or reviewing, courts, however, are published and distributed. As you will note, most of the state court cases presented in this book are from state appellate courts. Reported appellate decisions are published in volumes called *reports* or *reporters,* which are numbered consecutively. State appellate court decisions are found in the state reporters of that particular state.

Additionally, state court opinions appear in regional units of the National Reporter System, published by West Group. Most lawyers and libraries have the West reporters because they report cases more quickly and are distributed more widely than the state-published reports. In fact, many states have eliminated their own reporters in favor of West's National Reporter System. The National Reporter System divides the states into the following geographic areas: *Atlantic* (A. or A.2d), *North Eastern* (N.E. or N.E.2d), *North Western* (N.W. or N.W.2d), *Pacific* (P., P.2d, or P.3d), *South Eastern* (S.E. or S.E.2d), *South Western* (S.W., S.W.2d, or S.W.3d), and *Southern* (So. or So.2d). (The *2d* and *3d* in the abbreviations refer to *Second Series* and *Third Series,* respectively.) The states included in each of these regional divisions are indicated in Exhibit 1A–1 on the next page, which illustrates West's National Reporter System.

EXHIBIT 1A-1   NATIONAL REPORTER SYSTEM—REGIONAL/FEDERAL

Regional Reporters	Coverage Beginning	Coverage
Atlantic Reporter (A. or A.2d)	1885	Connecticut, Delaware, District of Columbia, Maine, Maryland, New Hampshire, New Jersey, Pennsylvania, Rhode Island, and Vermont.
North Eastern Reporter (N.E. or N.E.2d)	1885	Illinois, Indiana, Massachusetts, New York, and Ohio.
North Western Reporter (N.W. or N.W.2d)	1879	Iowa, Michigan, Minnesota, Nebraska, North Dakota, South Dakota, and Wisconsin.
Pacific Reporter (P., P.2d, or P.3d)	1883	Alaska, Arizona, California, Colorado, Hawaii, Idaho, Kansas, Montana, Nevada, New Mexico, Oklahoma, Oregon, Utah, Washington, and Wyoming.
South Eastern Reporter (S.E. or S.E.2d)	1887	Georgia, North Carolina, South Carolina, Virginia, and West Virginia.
South Western Reporter (S.W., S.W.2d, or S.W.3d)	1886	Arkansas, Kentucky, Missouri, Tennessee, and Texas.
Southern Reporter (So. or So.2d)	1887	Alabama, Florida, Louisiana, and Mississippi.
Federal Reporters		
Federal Reporter (F., F.2d, or F.3d)	1880	U.S. Circuit Courts from 1880 to 1912; U.S. Commerce Court from 1911 to 1913; U.S. District Courts from 1880 to 1932; U.S. Court of Claims (now called U.S. Court of Federal Claims) from 1929 to 1932 and since 1960; U.S. Courts of Appeals since 1891; U.S. Court of Customs and Patent Appeals since 1929; U.S. Emergency Court of Appeals since 1943.
Federal Supplement (F.Supp. or F.Supp.2d)	1932	U.S. Court of Claims from 1932 to 1960; U.S. District Courts since 1932; U.S. Customs Court since 1956.
Federal Rules Decisions (F.R.D.)	1939	U.S. District Courts involving the Federal Rules of Civil Procedure since 1939 and Federal Rules of Criminal Procedure since 1946.
Supreme Court Reporter (S.Ct.)	1882	United States Supreme Court since the October term of 1882.
Bankruptcy Reporter (Bankr.)	1980	Bankruptcy decisions of U.S. Bankruptcy Courts, U.S. District Courts, U.S. Courts of Appeals, and the United States Supreme Court.
Military Justice Reporter (M.J.)	1978	U.S. Court of Military Appeals and Courts of Military Review for the Army, Navy, Air Force, and Coast Guard.

NATIONAL REPORTER SYSTEM MAP

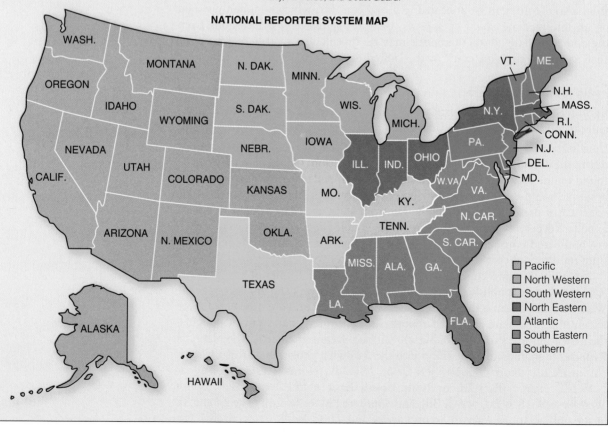

Legend:
- ☐ Pacific
- ☐ North Western
- ☐ South Western
- ■ North Eastern
- ■ Atlantic
- ■ South Eastern
- ■ Southern

After appellate decisions have been published, they are normally referred to (cited) by the name of the case; the volume, name, and page number of the state's official reporter (if different from West's National Reporter System); the volume, name, and page number of the *National Reporter;* and the volume, name, and page number of any other selected reporter. This information is included in the *citation.* (Citing a reporter by volume number, name, and page number, in that order, is common to all citations.) When more than one reporter is cited for the same case, each reference is called a *parallel citation.* For example, consider the following case: *Yale Diagnostic Radiology v. Estate of Harun Fountain,* 267 Conn. 351, 838 A.2d 179 (2004). We see that the opinion in this case may be found in Volume 267 of the official *Connecticut Reports,* on page 351. The parallel citation is to Volume 838 of the *Atlantic Reporter, Second Series,* page 179. In presenting appellate opinions in this text, in addition to the reporter, we give the name of the court hearing the case and the year of the court's decision.

A few states—including those with intermediate appellate courts, such as California, Illinois, and New York—have more than one reporter for opinions issued by their courts. Sample citations from these courts, as well as others, are listed and explained in Exhibit 1A–2 starting on page 26.

Federal Court Decisions

Federal district court decisions are published unofficially in West's *Federal Supplement* (F. Supp. or F.Supp.2d), and opinions from the circuit courts of appeals (federal reviewing courts) are reported unofficially in West's *Federal Reporter* (F., F.2d, or F.3d). Cases concerning federal bankruptcy law are published unofficially in West's *Bankruptcy Reporter* (Bankr.). The official edition of United States Supreme Court decisions is the *United States Reports* (U.S.), which is published by the federal government. Unofficial editions of Supreme Court cases include West's *Supreme Court Reporter* (S.Ct.) and the *Lawyers' Edition of the Supreme Court Reports* (L.Ed. or L.Ed.2d). Sample citations for federal court decisions are also listed and explained in Exhibit 1A–2.

Unpublished Opinions and Old Cases

Many court opinions that are not yet published or that are not intended for publication can be accessed through Westlaw® (abbreviated in citations as "WL"), an online legal database maintained by West Group. When no citation to a published reporter is available for cases cited in this text, we give the WL citation (see Exhibit 1A–2 for an example).

On a few occasions, this text cites opinions from old, classic cases dating to the nineteenth century or earlier; some of these are from the English courts. The citations to these cases may not conform to the descriptions given above because the reporters in which they were published have since been replaced.

READING AND UNDERSTANDING CASE LAW

All of the court opinions in this text consist of excerpts from the full text of the courts' opinions. For those wishing to review court cases for future research projects or to gain additional legal information, the following sections will provide useful insights into how to read and understand case law.

EXHIBIT 1A–2 HOW TO READ CITATIONS

STATE COURTS

271 Neb. 454, 712 N.W.2d 280 (2006)[a]

N.W. is the abbreviation for West's publication of state court decisions rendered in the *North Western Reporter* of the National Reporter System. *2d* indicates that this case was included in the *Second Series* of that reporter. The number 712 refers to the volume number of the reporter; the number 280 refers to the page in that volume on which this case begins.

Neb. is an abbreviation for *Nebraska Reports*, Nebraska's official reports of the decisions of its highest court, the Nebraska Supreme Court.

125 Cal.App.4th 949, 23 Cal.Rptr.3d 233 (2005)

Cal.Rptr. is the abbreviation for West's unofficial reports—titled *California Reporter*—of the decisions of California courts.

1 N.Y.3d 280, 803 N.E.2d 757, 771 N.Y.S.2d 484 (2003)

N.Y.S. is the abbreviation for West's unofficial reports—titled *New York Supplement*—of the decisions of New York courts.

N.Y. is the abbreviation for *New York Reports*, New York's official reports of the decisions of its court of appeals. The New York Court of Appeals is the state's highest court, analogous to other states' supreme courts. In New York, a supreme court is a trial court.

267 Ga.App. 832, 600 S.E.2d 800 (2004)

Ga.App. is the abbreviation for *Georgia Appeals Reports*, Georgia's official reports of the decisions of its court of appeals.

FEDERAL COURTS

___ U.S. ___, 126 S.Ct. 1503, ___ L.Ed.2d ___ (2006)

L.Ed. is an abbreviation for *Lawyers' Edition of the Supreme Court Reports*, an unofficial edition of decisions of the United States Supreme Court.

S.Ct. is the abbreviation for West's unofficial reports—titled *Supreme Court Reporter*—of decisions of the United States Supreme Court.

U.S. is the abbreviation for *United States Reports*, the official edition of the decisions of the United States Supreme Court.

a. The case names have been deleted from these citations to emphasize the publications. It should be kept in mind, however, that the name of a case is as important as the specific page numbers in the volumes in which it is found. If a citation is incorrect, the correct citation may be found in a publication's index of case names. In addition to providing a check on errors in citations, the date of a case is important because the value of a recent case as an authority is likely to be greater than that of older cases.

EXHIBIT 1A–2 HOW TO READ CITATIONS—CONTINUED

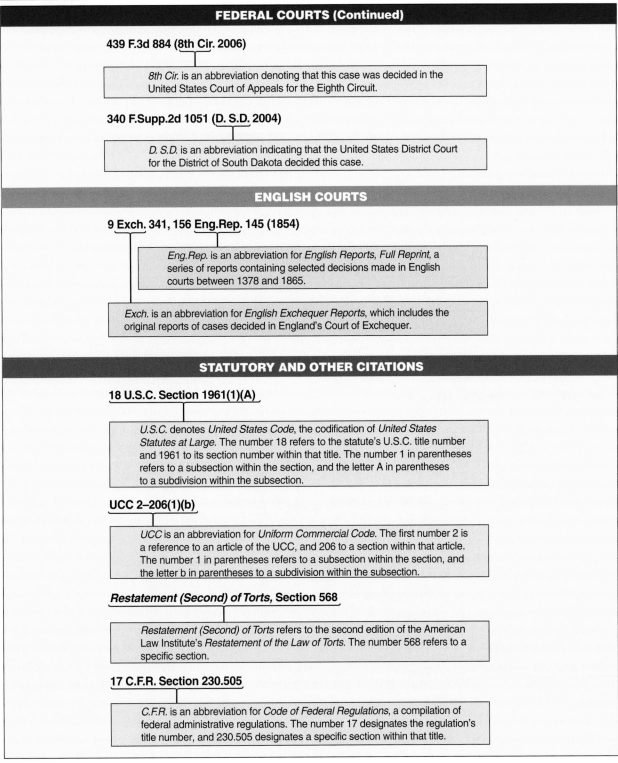

FEDERAL COURTS (Continued)

439 F.3d 884 (8th Cir. 2006)

8th Cir. is an abbreviation denoting that this case was decided in the United States Court of Appeals for the Eighth Circuit.

340 F.Supp.2d 1051 (D. S.D. 2004)

D. S.D. is an abbreviation indicating that the United States District Court for the District of South Dakota decided this case.

ENGLISH COURTS

9 Exch. 341, 156 Eng.Rep. 145 (1854)

Eng.Rep. is an abbreviation for *English Reports, Full Reprint,* a series of reports containing selected decisions made in English courts between 1378 and 1865.

Exch. is an abbreviation for *English Exchequer Reports*, which includes the original reports of cases decided in England's Court of Exchequer.

STATUTORY AND OTHER CITATIONS

18 U.S.C. Section 1961(1)(A)

U.S.C. denotes *United States Code*, the codification of *United States Statutes at Large*. The number 18 refers to the statute's U.S.C. title number and 1961 to its section number within that title. The number 1 in parentheses refers to a subsection within the section, and the letter A in parentheses to a subdivision within the subsection.

UCC 2–206(1)(b)

UCC is an abbreviation for *Uniform Commercial Code*. The first number 2 is a reference to an article of the UCC, and 206 to a section within that article. The number 1 in parentheses refers to a subsection within the section, and the letter b in parentheses to a subdivision within the subsection.

Restatement (Second) of Torts, Section 568

Restatement (Second) of Torts refers to the second edition of the American Law Institute's *Restatement of the Law of Torts*. The number 568 refers to a specific section.

17 C.F.R. Section 230.505

C.F.R. is an abbreviation for *Code of Federal Regulations*, a compilation of federal administrative regulations. The number 17 designates the regulation's title number, and 230.505 designates a specific section within that title.

(Continued)

EXHIBIT 1A-2 HOW TO READ CITATIONS—CONTINUED

Westlaw® Citations[b]

2006 WL 1193212

WL is an abbreviation for Westlaw®. The number 2006 is the year of the document that can be found with this citation in the Westlaw® database. The number 1193212 is a number assigned to a specific document. A higher number indicates that a document was added to the Westlaw® database later in the year.

Uniform Resource Locators (URLs)[c]

http://www.westlaw.com[d]

The suffix *com* is the top-level domain (TLD) for this Web site. The TLD *com* is an abbreviation for "commercial," which usually means that a for-profit entity hosts (maintains or supports) this Web site.

westlaw is the host name—the part of the domain name selected by the organization that registered the name. In this case, West Group registered the name. This Internet site is the Westlaw database on the Web.

www is an abbreviation for "World Wide Web." The Web is a system of Internet servers that support documents formatted in *HTML* (hypertext markup language). HTML supports links to text, graphics, and audio and video files.

http://www.uscourts.gov

This is "The Federal Judiciary Home Page." The host is the Administrative Office of the U.S. Courts. The TLD *gov* is an abbreviation for "government." This Web site includes information and links from, and about, the federal courts.

http://www.law.cornell.edu/index.html

This part of a URL points to a Web page or file at a specific location within the host's domain. This page is a menu with links to documents within the domain and to other Internet resources.

This is the host name for a Web site that contains the Internet publications of the Legal Information Institute (LII), which is a part of Cornell Law School. The LII site includes a variety of legal materials and links to other legal resources on the Internet. The TLD *edu* is an abbreviation for "educational institution" (a school or a university).

http://www.ipl.org/div/news

This part of the Web site points to a static *news* page at this Web site, which provides links to online newspapers from around the world.

div is an abbreviation for division, which is the way that the Internet Public Library tags the content on its Web site as relating to a specific topic.

ipl is an abbreviation for "Internet Public Library," which is an online service that provides reference resources and links to other information services on the Web. The IPL is supported chiefly by the School of Information at the University of Michigan. The TLD *org* is an abbreviation for "organization" (normally nonprofit).

b. Many court decisions that are not yet published or that are not intended for publication can be accessed through Westlaw®, an online legal database.

c. URLs are frequently changed as sites are redesigned and may not be working for other reasons, such as when a Web site has been deleted. If you are unable to find sites in this text with the specified URLs, go to the text's Web site at **www.thomsonedu.com/westbuslaw/ let**, where you may find an updated URL for the site or a URL for a similar site.

d. The basic form for a URL is "service://hostname/path." The Internet service for all of the URLs in this text is *http* (hypertext transfer protocol). Because most Web browsers add this prefix automatically when a user enters a host name or a hostname/path we have omitted the http:// from the URLs listed in this text.

Case Titles and Terminology

The title of a case, such as *Adams v. Jones*, indicates the names of the parties to the lawsuit. The *v.* in the case title stands for *versus*, which means "against." In the trial court, Adams was the plaintiff—the person who filed the suit. Jones was the defendant. If the case is appealed, however, the appellate court will sometimes place the name of the party appealing the decision first, so the case may be called *Jones v. Adams*. Because some reviewing courts retain the trial court order of names, it is often impossible to distinguish the plaintiff from the defendant in the title of a reported appellate court decision. You must carefully read the facts of each case to identify the parties.

The following terms and phrases are frequently encountered in court opinions and legal publications. Because it is important to understand what these terms and phrases mean, we define and discuss them here.

Plaintiffs and Defendants   As mentioned in Chapter 1, the plaintiff in a lawsuit is the party that initiates the action. The defendant is the party against which a lawsuit is brought. Lawsuits frequently involve more than one plaintiff and/or defendant.

Appellants and Appellees   The *appellant* is the party that appeals a case to another court or jurisdiction from the court or jurisdiction in which the case was originally brought. Sometimes, an appellant is referred to as the *petitioner*. The *appellee* is the party against which the appeal is taken. Sometimes, the appellee is referred to as the *respondent*.

Judges and Justices   The terms *judge* and *justice* are usually synonymous and represent two designations given to judges in various courts. All members of the United States Supreme Court, for example, are referred to as justices. And justice is the formal title usually given to judges of appellate courts, although this is not always the case. In New York, a justice is a judge of the trial court (which is called the Supreme Court), and a member of the Court of Appeals (the state's highest court) is called a judge. The term *justice* is commonly abbreviated to J., and *justices* to JJ. A Supreme Court case might refer to Justice Kennedy as Kennedy, J., or to Chief Justice Roberts as Roberts, C.J.

Decisions and Opinions   Most decisions reached by reviewing, or appellate, courts are explained in written *opinions*. The opinion contains the court's reasons for its decision, the rules of law that apply, and the judgment. When all judges or justices unanimously agree on an opinion, the opinion is written for the entire court and can be deemed a *unanimous opinion*. When there is not unanimous agreement, a *majority opinion* is written, outlining the views of the majority of the judges or justices deciding the case.

Often, a judge or justice who feels strongly about making or emphasizing a point that was not made or emphasized in the unanimous or majority opinion will write a *concurring opinion*. That means the judge or justice agrees (concurs) with the judgment given in the unanimous or majority opinion but for different reasons. When there is not a unanimous opinion, a *dissenting opinion* is usually written by a judge or justice who does not agree with the majority. The dissenting opinion is important because it may form the basis of the arguments used years later in overruling the precedential majority opinion. Occasionally, a court issues a *per curiam* (Latin for "of the court") opinion, which does not indicate which judge or justice authored the opinion.

A Sample Court Case

Knowing how to read and analyze a court opinion is an essential step in undertaking accurate legal research. A further step involves "briefing" the case. Legal researchers routinely brief cases by summarizing and reducing the texts of the opinions to their essential elements. (For instructions on how to brief a case, and a brief of the sample court case presented here, go to Appendix A at the end of this text.) The cases contained within the chapters of this text have already been analyzed and partially briefed by the authors, and the essential aspects of each case are presented in a convenient format consisting of three basic sections: *Background and Facts, In the Words of the Court* (excerpts from the court's opinion), and *Decision and Remedy*.

Throughout this text, in addition to this basic format, we sometimes include a special introductory section entitled *Historical and Social [Economic, Technological, Political, or other] Setting*. In some instances, a *Company Profile* is included in place of the introductory setting. These profiles provide a background on one of the parties to the lawsuit. Each case is followed by a brief *For Critical Analysis* section, which presents a question regarding some issue raised by the case; a *Why Is This Case Important?* section, which explains the significance of the case; or a *What If the Facts Were Different?* section, which asks the student to decide whether a specified change in the facts of the case would alter its outcome.

To illustrate the elements in a court opinion, we present an annotated opinion in Exhibit 1A–3. The opinion is from an actual case that the Bankruptcy Appellate Panel of the U.S. Court of Appeals for the Eighth Circuit decided in 2006.[1] Keith Dixon filed a petition in bankruptcy, seeking primarily to prevent his creditors from selling his house to pay his debts. The court ruled that Dixon was not eligible to declare bankruptcy, and he appealed. The question before the Bankruptcy Appellate Panel was whether the lower court erred in dismissing Dixon's petition.

You will note that triple asterisks (* * *) and quadruple asterisks (* * * *) frequently appear in the opinion. The triple asterisks indicate that we have deleted a few words or sentences from the opinion for the sake of readability or brevity. Quadruple asterisks mean that an entire paragraph (or more) has been omitted. Additionally, when the opinion cites another case or legal source, the citation to the case or other source has been omitted to save space and to improve the flow of the text. These editorial practices are continued in the passages from court opinions presented in this text.

The Supreme Court building in Washington, D.C. In what reporters are Supreme Court opinions published? (PhotoDisc)

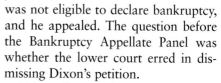

EQUAL JUSTICE UNDER LAW

---

1. A bankruptcy appellate panel is made up of bankruptcy judges from the districts within the circuit for which the panel is established. Its purpose is to hear and to determine appeals from the decisions of the bankruptcy courts in those districts. A panel usually consists of three judges.

EXHIBIT 1A-3 A SAMPLE COURT CASE

Concerning; regarding. This is the usual method of titling a proceeding in which adversary parties do not participate, but there is still something on which a court must rule.	**IN RE DIXON** Bankruptcy Appellate Panel, United States Court of Appeals, Eighth Circuit, 2006. 338 Bankr. 383.
This line gives the name of the judge who authored the opinion of the court.	KRESSEL, Chief Judge. * * * *
The court divided the opinion into parts. The first part of the opinion summarizes the factual background of the case.	**BACKGROUND**

The debtor [Keith Dixon] filed his Chapter 13 case on November 10, 2005. The debtor's case is governed by the Bankruptcy Code as amended by the Bankruptcy Abuse Prevention and Consumer Protection Act [BAPCPA] of 2005. With his petition, the debtor filed a document entitled "Certification Requesting Waiver of Debt Counseling by Individual Debtor." * * * Because the certificate is of the ultimate significance, we set out its [relevant] contents * * * .

One of the sections of the Bankruptcy Code under which a debtor can choose to file a petition with a court, seeking to have his or her debts discharged.

A written assurance that an act has or has not been done, an event has occurred, or a legal formality has been accomplished.

My real estate, residence and homestead was scheduled for foreclosure at 12:00 P.M., November 10, 2005 at the St. Louis County Courthouse, Clayton, MO.

A house in which a family lives, the land on which it sits, and the adjoining land. Under bankruptcy law, a debtor's homestead is exempt to a certain extent from the claims of creditors.

A proceeding in which the sale of a debtor's property is forced so that a debt can be satisfied.

I did not contact an attorney to determine how I could stop said foreclosure until approximately 6:30 P.M., November 9, 2005.

I was advised that I had to file a Chapter 13 Petition prior to 12:00 P.M., on November 10, 2005 to stop the foreclosure * * * .

I was advised that I had to complete credit or debt counseling prior to filing a bankruptcy and given the name of * * * Credit Counseling Centers of America of Dallas, Texas.

* * * I called them and was advised that it would be two weeks before they could provide me with the debt counseling on the phone and that it would be twenty-four hours before they could provide me with the counseling by Internet.

I have no computer and had no access to the Internet.

It was therefore impossible for me to complete credit counseling prior to the time set for foreclosure on my home. * * *

Therefore; a statement providing a reason.

Wherefore, I request waiver of the requirement to obtain budget and credit counseling prior to filing based on exigent circumstances.

Situations that demand unusual or immediate action.

(Continued)

EXHIBIT 1A-3 A SAMPLE COURT CASE—CONTINUED

> A court with the authority to rule on issues arising among debtors and creditors in cases in which the debtors are unable or unwilling to pay their debts.

> In this context, the credit counseling that the debtor must undergo before filing a petition in bankruptcy.

> A party is *eligible to be a debtor* if he or she has met certain requirements to petition a court for a discharge of debts in bankruptcy.

> Ordered that the case be disposed of without a trial of the issues involved.

> The second major section of the opinion analyzes the issue before the court.

> A document giving notice of an intention to appeal filed with the appellate court and the opposing party.

> Required; stipulated; prescribed.

> Essential, with reference to the legal rights and obligations under the statute.

> Opposed; contrary.

> Impending; near at hand.

> Take advantage of; attend.

The bankruptcy court reviewed the certificate and determined that the certificate did not describe exigent circumstances which merited a waiver of the * * * requirement of obtaining a prepetition briefing. As a result, the bankruptcy court held that the debtor was not eligible to be a debtor. In a subsequent order, the bankruptcy court dismissed the debtor's case. * * *

On November 22, 2005, the debtor filed a Notice of Appeal appealing from the two orders of the bankruptcy court * * *.

DISCUSSION

One of the primary amendments enacted by BAPCPA, was a new eligibility requirement for individual debtors. Specifically, [Section] 109(h)(1) states that, as a general rule, all individual debtors must receive an appropriate briefing during the 180 days preceding the date of filing. * * * It is the clear expectation of the statute that all individual debtors receive such a briefing *prior* to filing. * * *

* * * *

The debtor in this case admittedly did not obtain the mandated briefing. Rather, he attempted to establish his eligibility under [Section] 109(h)(3) which provides that the briefing requirement does not apply with respect to a debtor who submits to the court "a certification" * * * which * * * "describes exigent circumstances that merit a waiver of the requirements * * * ."

* * * *

As courts have pointed out, that brief sentence has at least two substantive components: first, there must be exigent circumstances and, second, those circumstances must merit a waiver of the briefing requirements. In this context, it is fair to say that "exigent" indicates that the debtor finds himself in a situation in which adverse events are imminent and will occur before the debtor is able to avail himself of the statutory briefing. Virtually all of the cases in which the exigent circumstances certificate is filed will, in fact, involve exigent circumstances. After all, the reason that such debtors are filing bankruptcy quickly and before they receive the briefing is because they feel that they are unable to wait. The real question for

EXHIBIT 1A-3   A SAMPLE COURT CASE—CONTINUED

the court in such certifications will usually be whether or not those exigent circumstances merit the * * * waiver.

In this case the bankruptcy court found that the certificate filed by the debtor did not merit a waiver. The bankruptcy court observed that [Missouri Revised Statutes Section] 443.310 requires twenty days notice of foreclosure * * * . In the face of that much notice of the impending foreclosure sale, the bankruptcy court determined that his exigent circumstances did not merit the waiver of the prebankruptcy briefing requirement. * * * A review of the reported decisions on facts similar to these discloses that most courts have come to the same conclusion. * * *

* * * *

Once the bankruptcy court denied the debtor's request for a waiver, it concluded correctly that under [Section] 109(h), the debtor was not eligible to be a debtor under the Bankruptcy Code. It determined, as virtually every court that has visited this issue has, that once that determination is made, dismissal of the case is appropriate.

* * * *

The final section of the opinion, in which the court includes its order.

CONCLUSION

We think the bankruptcy court did not abuse its discretion in

Fail to exercise reasonable discretion; commit an error of law; reach a conclusion that is clearly illogical and erroneous.

determining that the debtor had not demonstrated exigent circumstances meriting a waiver of the prepetition briefing requirement. We agree with the bankruptcy court's conclusion that the debtor was therefore not eligible to be a debtor and that, therefore, dismissal of his case was appropriate. We, therefore, affirm.

Uphold; declare that a judgment is valid and stands as rendered.

2 Ethics and Professional Responsibility

CHAPTER OBJECTIVES

After reading this chapter, you should be able to answer the following questions:

1 What is ethics? What is business ethics? Why is business ethics important?

2 How can business leaders encourage their companies to act ethically?

3 What are corporate compliance programs?

4 What duties do professionals owe to those who rely on their services?

5 What types of ethical issues might arise in the context of international business transactions?

> "New occasions teach new duties."
>
> —JAMES RUSSELL LOWELL, 1819–1891
> (American editor, poet, and diplomat)

DURING THE EARLY part of the 2000s, the American public was shocked as one business ethics scandal after another became headline news. Each scandal involved serious consequences. Certainly, those responsible for grossly inflating the reported profits at WorldCom, Inc., ended up not only destroying shareholder value in the company but also facing prison terms. Those officers and directors at Enron Corporation who utilized a system of complicated off-the-books transactions to inflate current earnings saw their company go bankrupt—the largest bankruptcy in U.S. history at that time. They harmed not only their employees and shareholders but also the communities in which they worked—and themselves (some of them were sentenced to prison). The misdeeds of officers and directors at Tyco International landed that company and its shareholders in similar trouble.

In response to the public's outrage over these scandals, Congress passed the Sarbanes-Oxley Act of 2002. This act, which will be discussed in more detail later in this chapter and again in Chapter 21, imposed requirements on corporations that are designed to deter similar unethical and illegal business behavior in the future. As the chapter-opening quotation states, "New occasions teach new duties." Indeed, the ethics scandals of the early 2000s taught businesses throughout the country that corporate governance is not to be taken lightly. Nevertheless, new allegations of unethical business conduct continue to surface.

Business ethics, the focus of this chapter, is not just theory. It is practical, useful, and essential. Although a good understanding of business law and the legal environment is critical, it is not enough. Understanding how one should act in her or his business dealings is equally—if not more—important in today's business arena.

BUSINESS ETHICS

Before we look at business ethics, we need to discuss what is meant by ethics generally. **Ethics** can be defined as the study of what constitutes right or wrong behavior. It is the branch of philosophy that focuses on morality and the way in which moral principles are derived or the way in which a given set of moral principles applies to one's conduct in daily life. Ethics concerns questions relating to the fairness, justness, rightness, or wrongness of an action. What is fair? What is just? What is the right thing to do in this situation? These are essentially ethical questions.

ETHICS
Moral principles and values applied to social behavior.

What Is Business Ethics?

Business ethics focuses on what constitutes right or wrong behavior in the business world and on how moral and ethical principles are applied by businesspersons to situations that arise in their daily activities in the workplace. Note that business ethics is not a separate *kind* of ethics. The ethical standards that guide our behavior as, say, mothers, fathers, or students apply equally well to our activities as businesspersons. Business decision makers, though, must often address more complex ethical issues and conflicts in the workplace than they face in their personal lives.

BUSINESS ETHICS
Ethics in a business context; a consensus of what constitutes right or wrong behavior in the world of business and the application of moral principles to situations that arise in a business setting.

Why Is Business Ethics Important?

Why is business ethics important? The answer to this question is clear from this chapter's introduction. A keen and in-depth understanding of business ethics is important to the long-run viability of a corporation. A thorough knowledge of business ethics is also important to the well-being of the individual officers and directors of the corporation, as well as to the welfare of the firm's employees and various "stakeholders" in the entity's well-being. Certainly, corporate decisions and activities can significantly affect not only those who own, operate, or work for the company but also such groups as suppliers, the community, and society as a whole.

Note that questions concerning ethical and responsible behavior are not confined to the corporate context. Business ethics applies to *all* businesses, regardless of their organizational forms. In a business partnership, for example, partners owe a *fiduciary duty* (a duty of trust and loyalty) to each other and to their firm. This duty can sometimes conflict with what a partner sees as his or her own best interest. Partners who act solely in their own interests may violate their duties to the other partners and the firm, however. By violating this duty, they may end up paying steep penalties—as the following case illustrates.

CASE 2.1   Time Warner Entertainment Co. v. Six Flags Over Georgia, L.L.C.

Georgia Court of Appeals, 2002.
254 Ga.App. 598,
563 S.E.2d 178.
www.ganet.org/appeals/opinions/index.cgi [a]

BACKGROUND AND FACTS The Six Flags Over Georgia
theme park in Atlanta, Georgia, was developed in 1967 as a
limited partnership known as Six Flags Over Georgia, L.L.C.
(Flags). The sole limited partner was Six Flags Fund, Limited
(Fund). The general partner was Six Flags Over Georgia,
Inc. (SFOG). In 1991, Time Warner Entertainment Company
(TWE) became the majority shareholder of SFOG. The next

year, TWE secretly bought 13.7 acres of land next to the park,
limiting the park's expansion opportunities. Over the following
couple of years, using confidential business information from
the park, TWE began plans to develop a competing park.
Meanwhile, TWE installed no major new attractions at the
park, deferred basic maintenance, withheld financial
information from Fund (the limited partner), and began
signing future employment contracts with SFOG officers. TWE
also charged Flags for unrelated expenses, including over
$4 million for lunches in New York City and luxury automobiles
for TWE officers. Flags and Fund filed a suit in a Georgia state
court against TWE and SFOG, alleging, among other things,
breach of fiduciary duty. A jury awarded the plaintiffs
$197,296,000 in compensatory damages and $257,000,000
in punitive damages. TWE appealed to a state intermediate
appellate court, alleging in part that the amount of the punitive
damages was excessive.

a. At the search screen, click on "Search Court of Appeals Opinions." On
the appellate court's screen, set the search year to "all." You can go to a
case most directly if you use as key words the full name of a party—for
example, "Time Warner Entertainment Co." This Web site is sponsored by
the state of Georgia.

IN THE WORDS OF THE COURT . . . *ELLINGTON,* Judge.

* * * *

We begin our analysis by examining the degree of reprehensibility [wrongfulness] of
appellants' conduct in this case. *In examining the degree of reprehensibility of a defendant's conduct, [there are] a number of aggravating factors [to consider], including
whether the harm was more than purely economic in nature, and whether the defendant's behavior evinced [revealed] indifference to or reckless disregard for the health and
safety of others.* Here, although the harm to Flags and Fund was primarily economic, it
was caused by conduct we find especially reprehensible. Appellants' intentional breach
of its fiduciary duty revealed a callous indifference to the financial well-being of its limited partners and their individual investors. [Emphasis added.]

* * * [T]he evidence [presented] supported the jury's conclusion that appellants
acted in concert to breach SFOG's fiduciary duty to its business partners. * * * [T]his
evidence clearly and convincingly supported an award of punitive damages * * *
because the evidence showed that the appellants withheld vital business information
from Fund and Flags, undertook to compete with them, took money belonging to them,
and carried out a plan to depress the value of their investment, the Six Flags Over
Georgia Park. Moreover, the jury found a specific intent to cause harm * * * .

Appellants' conduct toward its partners and those who invested in the limited partnership was part of a premeditated plan surreptitiously [secretly] executed over a period
of years. Appellants' conduct was deceitful, self-serving, and financially damaging. More
importantly, however, appellants' conduct was a breach of fiduciary duty, a violation of
a confidential relationship of trust requiring the utmost in good faith. * * * Appellants'
conduct was, in short, the kind of behavior we find deserving of reproof [disapproval],
rebuke, or censure; blameworthy—the very definition of reprehensible.
* * * *Trickery and deceit are reprehensible wrongs, especially when done intentionally
through affirmative acts of misconduct.* * * * [Emphasis added.]
* * * *

In this case, the ratio of compensatory to punitive damages is 1 to 1.3. We see no
shocking disparity inherent in this figure. Nor does it appear to approach that fuzzy line
suggesting the bounds of constitutional impropriety. More importantly, however, given

CASE 2.1—CONTINUED the amount of intentional economic damage inflicted by the appellants, corporate entities with collective assets measured in billions of dollars, we believe the award of punitive damages was reasonably calculated to punish them and to deter such conduct in the future.

DECISION AND REMEDY The state intermediate appellate court affirmed the judgment of the lower court, finding that the award of punitive damages was not excessive, considering the defendants' financial status and "reprehensible" conduct toward the plaintiffs.

FOR CRITICAL ANALYSIS—Ethical Consideration *If TWE had proceeded with its plans to build a competing park but had not otherwise acted "reprehensibly" toward Flags and Fund, how might the decision in this case have been different?*

SETTING THE RIGHT ETHICAL TONE

Many unethical business decisions are made simply because they *can* be made. In other words, the decision makers not only have the opportunity to make such decisions but also are not too concerned about being seriously sanctioned for their unethical actions. Perhaps one of the most difficult challenges for business leaders today is to create the right "ethical tone" in their workplaces so as to deter unethical conduct.

The Importance of Ethical Leadership

Talking about ethical business decision making means nothing if management does not set standards. Moreover, managers must apply those standards to themselves as well as to the employees in the company.

Attitude of Top Management One of the most important factors in creating and maintaining an ethical workplace is the attitude of top management. Managers who are not totally committed to maintaining an ethical workplace will rarely succeed in creating one. Surveys of business executives indicate that management's behavior, more than anything else, sets a firm's ethical tone. In other words, employees take their cue from management. If a firm's managers adhere to obvious ethical norms in their business dealings, employees will likely follow their example. In contrast, if managers act unethically, employees will see no reason not to do so themselves. **| Example #1** Suppose that Kevin observes his manager cheating on her expense account. Kevin quickly understands that such behavior is acceptable. Later, when Kevin is promoted to a managerial position, he "pads" his expense account as well—knowing that he is unlikely to face sanctions for doing so. **|**

> " What you do speaks so loudly that I cannot hear what you say. "
> —RALPH WALDO EMERSON,
> 1803–1882
> (American poet and essayist)

Looking the Other Way A manager who looks the other way when she or he knows about an employee's unethical behavior also sets an example—one indicating that ethical transgressions will be accepted. Managers must show that they will not tolerate unethical business behavior. Although this may seem harsh, managers have found that discharging even one employee for ethical reasons has a tremendous impact as a deterrent to unethical behavior in the workplace. The following case illustrates what can happen when managers look the other way.

CASE 2.2   In re the Exxon Valdez

United States District Court,
District of Alaska, 2004.
296 F.Supp.2d 1071.

BACKGROUND AND FACTS   Exxon Shipping Company owned the *Exxon Valdez,* an oil supertanker as long as three football fields with the capacity to hold 53 million gallons of crude oil. The captain of the *Valdez* was Joseph Hazelwood, an alcoholic, who had sought treatment in 1985 but had relapsed before the next spring. Exxon knew that Hazelwood had relapsed and that he drank while onboard ship, but nevertheless allowed him to command the *Valdez.* On March 24, 1989, the *Valdez* ran aground on Bligh Reef in Prince William Sound, Alaska. About 11 million gallons of crude oil leaked from the ship and spread around the sound. Commercial fisheries closed for the rest of the year. Subsistence fishing and shore-based businesses dependent on the fishing industry were disrupted. Exxon spent $2.1 billion to clean up the spilled oil and paid $303 million to those whose livelihoods were disrupted. Thousands of claims were consolidated into a single case tried in a federal district court. The jury awarded, in part, $5 billion in punitive damages against Exxon. Exxon appealed to the U.S. Court of Appeals for the Ninth Circuit, which remanded the case for reconsideration of this award, according to the reprehensibility of the defendant's conduct and other factors. The court also instructed the lower court to reduce the amount if the award was upheld.

IN THE WORDS OF THE COURT . . . *HOLLAND,* District Judge.

* * * *

* * * [T]he question before us is whether, under the circumstances of this case, an award of $5 billion in punitive damages is grossly excessive * * * .

* * * *

* * * *[T]he reprehensibility of the defendant's conduct is the most important* indicium *[indication] of the reasonableness of a punitive damages award* * * * . In determining whether a defendant's conduct is reprehensible, the court considers whether:

> the harm caused was physical as opposed to economic; the tortious conduct evinced an indifference to or a reckless disregard of the health or safety of others; the target of the conduct had financial vulnerability; the conduct involved repeated actions or was an isolated incident; and the harm was the result of intentional malice, trickery, or deceit, or mere accident. * * * [Emphasis added.]

* * * *

The reprehensibility of a party's conduct, like truth and beauty, is subjective. One's view of the quality of [a person's] conduct is the result of complex value judgments. The evaluation of a victim will vary considerably from that of a person not affected by an incident. Courts employ disinterested, unaffected lay jurors in the first instance to appraise the reprehensibility of a defendant's conduct. Here, the jury heard about what Exxon knew, and what its officers did and what they failed to do. Knowing what Exxon knew and did through its officers, the jury concluded that Exxon's conduct was highly reprehensible.

* * * *

* * * *Punitive damages should reflect the enormity of the defendant's offense.* * * * Exxon's conduct did not simply cause economic harm to the plaintiffs. Exxon's decision to leave Captain Hazelwood in command of the *Exxon Valdez* demonstrated reckless disregard for a broad range of legitimate Alaska concerns: the livelihood, health, and safety of the residents of Prince William Sound, the crew of the *Exxon Valdez,* and others. Exxon's conduct targeted some financially vulnerable individuals, namely subsistence fishermen. Plaintiffs' harm was not the result of an isolated incident but was the result of Exxon's repeated decisions, over a period of approximately three years, to allow Captain Hazelwood to remain in command despite Exxon's knowledge that he was drinking and driving again. Exxon's bad conduct as to Captain Hazelwood and his operation of the *Exxon Valdez* was intentionally malicious. [Emphasis added.]

CASE 2.2–CONTINUED

* * * Exxon's conduct was many degrees of magnitude more egregious [than defendants' conduct in other cases]. For approximately three years, Exxon management, with knowledge that Captain Hazelwood had fallen off the wagon, willfully permitted him to operate a fully loaded, crude oil tanker in and out of Prince William Sound—a body of water which Exxon knew to be highly valuable for its fisheries resources. Exxon's argument that its conduct in permitting a relapsed alcoholic to operate an oil tanker should be characterized as less reprehensible than [in other cases] suggests that Exxon, even today, has not come to grips with the opprobrium [contempt that] society rightly attaches to drunk driving. * * * Based on the foregoing, the court finds Exxon's conduct highly reprehensible.

* * * *

* * * [T]he court reduces the punitive damages award to $4.5 billion as the means of resolving the conflict between its conclusion and the directions of the court of appeals.

* * * *

* * * [T]here is no just reason to delay entry of a final judgment in this case. The court's judgment as to the $4.5 billion punitive damages award is deemed final * * * .

DECISION AND REMEDY The court determined that Exxon's conduct was "intentionally malicious" and "highly reprehensible." Concluding that "[p]unitive damages should reflect the enormity of the defendant's offense," the court upheld the award, but reduced the amount to $4.5 billion "as the means of resolving the conflict between its conclusion and the directions of the court of appeals."

WHY IS THIS CASE IMPORTANT? *This case is an excellent illustration of the consequences that a business may face when it ignores a serious risk that has been created by its action (or inaction). By allowing Captain Hazelwood, a relapsed alcoholic, to remain in charge of the* Exxon Valdez, *Exxon created serious risks to the environment and the residents of Prince William Sound. These risks led to severe harms. The consequences for Exxon—$4.5 billion in punitive damages—were also severe.*

Setting Realistic Goals Helps Managers can reduce the probability that employees will act unethically by setting realistic production or sales goals. | **Example #2** Suppose that a sales quota can be met only through high-pressure and unethical sales tactics. Employees trying to act "in the best interests of the firm" may think that management is implicitly asking them to behave unethically. |

Periodic Evaluation Some companies require their managers to meet individually with employees and to grade them on their ethical (or unethical) behavior. | **Example #3** One company asks its employees to fill out ethical checklists each month and return them to their supervisors. This practice serves two purposes: First, it demonstrates to employees that ethics matters. Second, employees have an opportunity to reflect on how well they have measured up in terms of ethical performance. |

Creating Ethical Codes of Conduct

One of the most effective ways to set a tone of ethical behavior within an organization is to create an ethical code of conduct. A well-written code of ethics explicitly states a company's ethical priorities.

Costco—An Example   This chapter includes a foldout exhibit showing a code of ethics created by Costco Wholesale Corporation, a large warehouse-club retailer with over 45 million "members." This code of conduct indicates Costco's commitment to legal compliance, as well as to the welfare of its members (those who purchase its goods), its employees, and its suppliers. The code also details some specific ways in which the interests and welfare of these different groups will be protected. If you look closely at this exhibit, you will also see that Costco acknowledges that by protecting these groups' interests, it will realize its "ultimate goal"—rewarding its shareholders with maximum shareholder value.

Another Necessity—Clear Communication to Employees   For an ethical code to be effective, its provisions must be clearly communicated to employees. Most large companies have implemented ethics training programs, in which managers discuss with employees on a face-to-face basis the firm's policies and the importance of ethical conduct. Some firms hold periodic ethics seminars during which employees can openly discuss any ethical problems that they may be experiencing and learn how the firm's ethical policies apply to those specific problems.

Johnson & Johnson—An Example of Web-Based Ethics Training   Creating a code of conduct and implementing it are two different activities. In many companies, codes of conduct are simply documents that have very little relevance to day-to-day operations. When Johnson & Johnson wanted to "do better" than other companies with respect to ethical business decision making, it created a Center for Legal and Credo Awareness. (Its code of ethical conduct is called its *credo*.)

The center created a Web-based set of instructions designed to enhance the corporation's efforts to train employees in the importance of its code of conduct. Given that Johnson & Johnson has over 110,000 employees in fifty-seven countries around the world, reinforcing its code of conduct and its values has not been easy, but Web-based training has helped. The company established a Web-based legal and compliance center, which uses a set of interactive modules to train employees in areas of law and ethics.

Corporate Compliance Programs

In large corporations, ethical codes of conduct are usually just one part of a comprehensive corporate compliance program. Other components of such a program, some of which were already mentioned, include a corporation's ethics committee, ethical training programs, and internal audits to monitor compliance with applicable laws and the company's standards of ethical conduct.

The Sarbanes-Oxley Act and Web-Based Reporting Systems   The Sarbanes-Oxley Act of 2002[1] requires companies to set up confidential systems so that employees and others may "raise red flags" about suspected illegal or unethi-

---

1. 15 U.S.C. Sections 7201 *et seq.*

cal auditing and accounting practices. The act required publicly traded companies to have such systems in place by April 2003.

Some companies have implemented online reporting systems. In one Web-based reporting system, employees can click on an icon on their computers that anonymously links them with Ethicspoint, an organization based in Vancouver, Washington. Through Ethicspoint, employees may report suspicious accounting practices, sexual harassment, and other possibly unethical behavior. Ethicspoint, in turn, alerts management personnel or the audit committee at the designated company to the possible problem. Those who have used the system say that it is less inhibiting than calling a company's toll-free number.

Corporate Governance Principles   Implementation of the Sarbanes-Oxley Act has prompted many companies to create new rules of corporate governance. As you will read in Chapter 21, *corporate governance* refers to the internal principles establishing the rights and responsibilities of a corporation's management, board of directors, shareholders, and *stakeholders* (those affected by corporate decisions, including employees, customers, suppliers, and creditors, for example). Corporate governance principles usually go beyond what is required to comply with existing laws. The goal is to set up a system of fair procedures and accurate disclosures that keeps all parties well informed and accountable to one another and provides a mechanism for the corporation to resolve any problems that arise. Ultimately, good corporate governance should attract investors and stimulate growth while discouraging unethical behavior and fraud.

Compliance Programs Must Be Integrated   To be effective, a compliance program must be integrated throughout the firm. For large corporations, such integration is essential. Ethical policies and programs need to be coordinated and monitored by a committee that is separate from the various corporate departments. Otherwise, unethical behavior in one department can easily escape the attention of those in control of the corporation or the corporate officials responsible for implementing and monitoring the company's compliance program.

ETHICAL ISSUE 2.1   *Should companies hire chief governance officers?*

According to a survey released by the Ethics Resource Center and the Society for Human Resource Management in April 2003, employee ethical conduct may not be rewarded in today's business world. Indeed, 24 percent of the human resources (HR) managers surveyed felt pressure to compromise ethical standards either all of the time, fairly often, or periodically. In 1997, only 13 percent of the same class of respondents felt the same way. This finding is significant because HR personnel are often caught in the middle between employees who come to them with ethical concerns and company officers who may or may not agree with the HR manager's recommendations as to how the company should respond to specific complaints.

What can companies do to ensure ethical compliance? Should they hire specially trained legal executives, known as chief governance officers (CGOs), to oversee corporate compliance? According to some business ethicists, having a CGO can help a company prevent future governance problems that could be costly. In 1992, pharmaceutical manufacturer Pfizer, Inc., became the first company to hire a CGO. Since then, about sixty other companies have done so. In the wake of the business scandals of the early 2000s and the requirements imposed under the Sarbanes-Oxley Act of 2002, the number of companies that have CGOs is expected to grow rapidly.[2]

Conflicts and Trade-Offs

Management constantly faces ethical trade-offs, some of which may lead to legal problems. As mentioned earlier, firms have implied ethical (and legal) duties to a number of groups, including shareholders and employees.

When a company decides to reduce costs by downsizing and restructuring, the decision may benefit shareholders, but it will harm those employees who are laid off or fired. When downsizing occurs, which employees should be laid off first? Cost-cutting considerations might dictate firing the most senior employees, who generally have higher salaries, and retaining less senior employees, whose salaries are much lower. A company does not necessarily act illegally when it does so. Yet the decision to be made by management clearly involves an important ethical question: Which group's interests—those of the shareholders or those of employees who have been loyal to the firm for a long period of time—should take priority in this situation?

| **Example #4**   In one case, an employer facing a dwindling market and decreasing sales decided to reduce its costs by eliminating some of its obligations to its employees. It did this by establishing a subsidiary corporation and then transferring some of its employees, and the administration of their retirement benefits, to that entity. The company expected the subsidiary to fail, and when it did, some employees and retirees who were left with no retirement benefits sued the company. The plaintiffs claimed that the company had breached a fiduciary duty under a federal law governing employer-provided pensions. Ultimately, the United States Supreme Court agreed with the plaintiffs, stating, among other things, that "[l]ying is inconsistent with the duty of loyalty owed by all fiduciaries."[3] |

BUSINESS ETHICS AND THE LAW

MORAL MINIMUM
The minimum degree of ethical behavior expected of a business firm, which is usually defined as compliance with the law.

Today, legal compliance is regarded as a **moral minimum**—the minimum acceptable standard for ethical business behavior. Had Enron Corporation strictly complied with existing laws and generally accepted accounting practices (discussed later in this chapter), very likely the "Enron scandal" (examined in detail later in this chapter), which came to light in the early 2000s, would never have happened. Simply obeying the law does not fulfill all business ethics obligations, however. In the interests of preserving personal freedom, as well as for practical reasons, the law does not—and cannot—codify all ethical requirements. No law says, for example, that it is illegal to lie to one's family, but it may be unethical to do so.

It might seem that determining the legality of a given action should be simple. Either something is legal or it is not. In fact, one of the major challenges

2. Tamara Loomis, "Companies Are Hiring Chief Governance Officers," *The National Law Journal,* May 5, 2003, p. A15.
3. *Varity Corp. v. Howe,* 516 U.S. 489, 116 S.Ct. 1065, 134 L.Ed.2d 130 (1996).

"Sucks Sites"—Can They Be Shut Down?

Management Faces a Legal Issue In today's online environment, a recurring challenge for businesses is how to deal with cybergripers—those who complain in cyberspace about corporate products, services, or activities. For trademark owners, the issue becomes particularly thorny when cybergriping sites add "sucks," "fraud," "scam," "ripoff," or some other disparaging term as a suffix to the domain name of a particular company. These sites, sometimes collectively referred to as "sucks" sites, are established solely for the purpose of criticizing the products or services sold by the companies that own the marks. In some cases, they have been used maliciously to harm the reputation of a competitor. Can businesses do anything to ward off these cyber attacks on their reputations and goodwill?

What the Courts Say A number of companies have sued the owners of "sucks" sites for trademark infringement in the hope that a court or an arbitrating panel will order the owner of that site to cease using the domain name. To date, however, companies have had little success pursuing this alternative. In one case, Bear Stearns Companies, Inc., sued a cybergriper, Nye Lavalle, alleging that Lavalle infringed its trademark by creating Web sites including "Bear Stearns" in the domain names. Two of these sites were called "BearStearnsFrauds.com" and "BearStearnsCriminals.com."

As you will read in Chapter 7, one of the tests for trademark infringement is whether consumers would be confused by the use of a similar or identical trademark. Would consumers mistakenly believe that Lavalle's sites were operated by Bear Stearns? In the court's eyes, no. The court concluded that Lavalle's "Frauds.com" and "Criminals.com" sites were "unmistakenly critical" of the target company and that no Internet user would conclude that Bear Stearns sponsored the sites.[a]

For cybergripers, the message seems to be clear: the more outrageous or obnoxious the suffix added to a target company's trademark, the less likely it is that the use will constitute trademark infringement. This point is underscored in decisions reached by other courts as well. In *Taubman Co. v. Webfeats*,[b] for example, the court stressed that Internet users were unlikely to be confused by "sucks" sites using the Taubman Company name. Because the allegedly infringing domain names all ended with "sucks.com," the court concluded that they were unlikely to mislead Web site visitors into believing that the trademark owner was the source or sponsor of the complaint. The court also noted in its opinion that, generally, the more vicious an attack site's domain name, the less likely that a cybergriper will be found liable for trademark infringement.

Implications for Managers Business owners likely will not be successful in suits against the owners of "sucks" sites for trademark infringement. (Nor will they be able to sue for trade libel individuals who publish negative opinions about them in printed publications.) Many businesses have concluded that the best defense against cybergripers is to make it more difficult for them by buying up insulting Internet domain names before the cybergripers can do so. In fact, this has become standard practice for many large corporations. Another strategy would be to have someone monitor critical opinion on Web sites for ideas on how the business might improve its products and practices.

a. *Bear Stearns Companies, Inc. v. Lavalle*, 2002 WL 31757771 (N.D.Tex. 2002).
b. 319 F.3d 770 (6th Cir. 2003).

businesspersons face is that the legality of a particular action is not always clear. In part, this is because business is regulated by so many laws that it is possible to violate one of them without realizing it. The law also contains numerous "gray areas," making it difficult to predict with certainty how a court will apply a given law to a particular action. This is especially true when technological developments have raised new types of questions. For example, if a business's trademark is used in a domain name followed by "fraud" or "sucks," is this an infringement of the owner's trademark? For a discussion of this question, see this chapter's *Management Perspective* feature.

Laws Regulating Business

Today's business firms are subject to extensive government regulation. As mentioned in Chapter 1, virtually every action a firm undertakes—from the initial act of going into business, to hiring and firing personnel, to selling products in the marketplace—is subject to statutory law and to numerous rules and regulations issued by administrative agencies. Furthermore, these rules and regulations are changed or supplemented frequently.

Determining whether a planned action is legal thus requires that decision makers keep abreast of the law. Normally, large business firms have attorneys on their staffs to assist them in making key decisions. Small firms must also seek legal advice before making important business decisions because the consequences of just one violation of a regulatory rule may be costly.

Ignorance of the law will not excuse a business owner or manager from liability for violating a statute or regulation. **Example #5** In one case, the court imposed criminal fines, as well as imprisonment, on a company's supervisory employee for violating a federal environmental act. This punishment was imposed even though the employee was completely unaware of what was required under the provisions of that act.[4]

"Gray Areas" in the Law

> " Next to doing the right thing, the most important thing is to let people know you are doing the right thing."
>
> —JOHN D. ROCKEFELLER, 1839–1897
> (American industrialist and philanthropist)

In many situations, business firms can predict with a fair amount of certainty whether a given action would be legal. For instance, firing an employee solely because of that person's race or gender would clearly violate federal laws prohibiting employment discrimination. In some situations, though, the legality of a particular action may be less clear.

Example #6 Suppose that a firm decides to launch a new advertising campaign. How far can the firm go in making claims for its products or services? Federal and state laws prohibit firms from engaging in "deceptive advertising." At the federal level, the test for deceptive advertising normally used by the Federal Trade Commission is whether an advertising claim would deceive a "reasonable consumer."[5] At what point, though, would a reasonable consumer be deceived by a particular ad?

In short, business decision makers need to proceed with caution and evaluate an action and its consequences from an ethical perspective. Sometimes it can be difficult to predict how a court will determine what is reasonable in a particular situation, or how a court will apply existing law in a case involving the Internet. Generally, if a company can demonstrate that it acted in good faith and responsibly under the circumstances, it has a better chance of successfully defending its action in court or before an administrative law judge.

The following case demonstrates that businesses and their customers have differing expectations with respect to the standard of care required in handling personal information. The case also illustrates how the legal standards in this context may be inconsistent and vague.

---

4. *United States v. Hanousek,* 176 F.3d 1116 (9th Cir. 1999).
5. See Chapter 17 for a discussion of the Federal Trade Commission's role in regulating deceptive trade practices, including misleading advertising.

CASE 2.3   Guin v. Brazos Higher Education Service Corp.

United States District Court,
District of Minnesota, 2006.
__ F.Supp.2d __.

BACKGROUND AND FACTS   Brazos Higher Education
Service Corporation, which is based in Waco, Texas, makes
and services student loans. Brazos issued a laptop computer
to its employee John Wright, who works from an office in his
home in Silver Spring, Maryland, analyzing loan information.
Wright used the laptop to store borrowers' personal
information. In September 2004, Wright's home was
burglarized and the laptop was stolen. Based on Federal Trade

Commission (FTC) guidelines and California state law (which
requires notice to all resident borrowers), Brazos sent a letter
to all of its 550,000 customers. The letter stated that "some
personal information associated with your student loan,
including your name, address, Social Security number, and
loan balance, may have been inappropriately accessed by [a]
third party." The letter urged borrowers to place "a free 90-day
security alert" on their credit bureau files and review FTC
consumer assistance materials. Brazos set up a call center to
answer further questions and track any reports of identity theft.
Stacy Guin, a Brazos customer, filed a suit in a federal district
court against Brazos, alleging negligence. Brazos filed a motion
for summary judgment.

IN THE WORDS OF THE COURT . . . *KYLE,* J. [Judge]

* * * *

* * * *N]egligence [is] the failure to exercise due or reasonable care. In order to prevail on a claim for negligence, a plaintiff must prove [among other things] the existence
of a duty of care [and] a breach of that duty* * * * [Emphasis added.]

* * * *

Guin argues that the Gramm-Leach-Bliley Act (the "GLB Act") establishes a statutory-
based duty for Brazos to protect the security and confidentiality of customers' nonpublic personal information. * * * Brazos concedes that the GLB Act applies to these
circumstances and establishes a duty of care. The GLB Act was created "to protect
against unauthorized access to or use of such records which could result in substantial
harm or inconvenience to any customer [of a financial institution]." Under the GLB Act,
a financial institution must comply with several objectives, including:

> Develop, implement, and maintain a comprehensive written information security program that
> is written in one or more readily accessible parts and contains administrative, technical, and
> physical safeguards that are appropriate to your size and complexity, the nature and scope of
> your activities, and the sensitivity of any customer information at issue * * * .

Guin argues that Brazos breached the duty imposed by the GLB Act by (1) "providing Wright with [personal information] that he did not need for the task at hand,"
(2) "permitting Wright to continue keeping [personal information] in an unattended,
insecure personal residence," and (3) "allowing Wright to keep [personal information]
on his laptop unencrypted." * * *

The Court concludes that Guin has not presented sufficient evidence from which a
fact finder could determine that Brazos failed to comply with the GLB Act. In September
2004, when Wright's home was burglarized and the laptop was stolen, Brazos had written security policies, current risk assessment reports, and proper safeguards for its customers' personal information as required by the GLB Act. Brazos authorized Wright to
have access to customers' personal information because Wright needed the information
to analyze loan portfolios * * * . Thus, his access to the personal information was
within "the nature and scope of [Brazos's] activities." Furthermore, the GLB Act does
not prohibit someone from working with sensitive data on a laptop computer in a home
office. Despite Guin's persistent argument that any nonpublic personal information
stored on a laptop computer should be encrypted, the GLB Act does not contain any

CASE 2.3–CONTINUED ➡

such requirement. Accordingly, Guin has not presented any evidence showing that Brazos violated the GLB Act requirements.

DECISION AND REMEDY   The court granted the defendant's motion for summary judgment and dismissed the case. Brazos may have owed Guin a duty of care under the GLB Act, but neither Brazos nor Wright breached that duty. Wright had followed Brazos's written security procedures, which was all that the GLB Act required.

WHAT IF THE FACTS WERE DIFFERENT?   *Suppose that Wright had not been a financial analyst and his duties for Brazos had not included reviewing confidential loan data. How might the opinion of the court have been different?*

APPROACHES TO ETHICAL REASONING

ETHICAL REASONING
A reasoning process in which an individual links his or her moral convictions or ethical standards to the particular situation at hand.

Each individual, when faced with a particular ethical dilemma, engages in **ethical reasoning**—that is, a reasoning process in which the individual examines the situation at hand in light of her or his moral convictions or ethical standards. Businesspersons do likewise when making decisions with ethical implications.

How do business decision makers decide whether a given action is the "right" one for their firms? What ethical standards should they apply? Broadly speaking, ethical reasoning relating to business traditionally has been characterized by two fundamental approaches. One approach defines ethical behavior in terms of duty, which also implies certain rights. The other approach determines what is ethical in terms of the consequences, or outcome, of any given action. We examine each of these approaches here.

Duty-Based Ethics

Duty-based ethical standards are often derived from revealed truths, such as religious precepts. They can also be derived through philosophical reasoning.

Religious Ethical Standards   In the Judeo-Christian tradition, which is the dominant religious tradition in the United States, the Ten Commandments of the Old Testament establish fundamental rules for moral action. Other religions have their own sources of revealed truth. Religious rules generally are absolute with respect to the behavior of their adherents. **| Example #7**   The commandment "Thou shalt not steal" is an absolute mandate for a person, such as a Jew or a Christian, who believes that the Ten Commandments reflect revealed truth. Even a benevolent motive for stealing (such as Robin Hood's) cannot justify the act because the act itself is inherently immoral and thus wrong.**|**

Ethical standards based on religious teachings also involve an element of *compassion.* **| Example #8**   Even though it might be profitable for a firm to lay off a less productive employee, if that employee would find it difficult to find employment elsewhere and his or her family would suffer as a result, this potential suffering would be given substantial weight by the decision makers.**|** Compassionate treatment of others is also mandated—to a certain extent, at least—by the Golden Rule of the ancients ("Do unto others as you would have them do unto you"), which has been adopted by most religions.

Kantian Ethics   Duty-based ethical standards may also be derived solely from philosophical reasoning. The German philosopher Immanuel Kant (1724–1804), for example, identified some general guiding principles for moral behavior based on what he believed to be the fundamental nature of human beings. Kant held that it is rational to assume that human beings are qualitatively different from other physical objects occupying space. Persons are endowed with moral integrity and the capacity to reason and conduct their affairs rationally. Therefore, their thoughts and actions should be respected. When human beings are treated merely as a means to an end, they are being viewed as the equivalent of objects and are being denied their basic humanity.

A central postulate in Kantian ethics is that individuals should evaluate their actions in light of the consequences that would follow if *everyone* in society acted in the same way. This **categorical imperative** can be applied to any action. **| Example #9** Suppose that you are deciding whether to cheat on an examination. If you have adopted Kant's categorical imperative, you will decide not to cheat because if everyone cheated, the examination would be meaningless.**|**

CATEGORICAL IMPERATIVE
A concept developed by the philosopher Immanuel Kant as an ethical guideline for behavior. In deciding whether an action is right or wrong, or desirable or undesirable, a person should evaluate the action in terms of what would happen if everybody else in the same situation, or category, acted the same way.

The Principle of Rights   The principle that human beings have certain fundamental rights (to life, freedom, and the pursuit of happiness, for example) is deeply embedded in Western culture. As discussed in Chapter 1, the natural law tradition embraces the concept that certain actions (such as killing another person) are morally wrong because they are contrary to nature (the natural desire to continue living). Those who adhere to this **principle of rights,** or "rights theory," believe that a key factor in determining whether a business decision is ethical is how that decision affects the rights of others. These others include the firm's owners, its employees, the consumers of its products or services, its suppliers, the community in which it does business, and society as a whole.

A potential dilemma for those who support rights theory, however, is that they may disagree on which rights are most important. When considering all those affected by a business decision, for example, how much weight should be given to employees relative to shareholders, customers relative to the community, or employees relative to society as a whole?

In general, rights theorists believe that whichever right is stronger in a particular circumstance takes precedence. **| Example #10** Suppose that a firm can shut down a plant to avoid dumping pollutants into a river that would negatively affect the health of thousands of people. Alternatively, the firm could keep the plant open (and pollute the river) but save the jobs of the twelve workers in the plant. In this situation, a rights theorist can easily choose which group to favor. (Not all choices are so clear-cut, however.)**|**

PRINCIPLE OF RIGHTS
The principle that human beings have certain fundamental rights (to life, freedom, and the pursuit of happiness, for example). Those who adhere to this "rights theory" believe that a key factor in determining whether a business decision is ethical is how that decision affects the rights of various groups. These groups include the firm's owners, its employees, the consumers of its products or services, its suppliers, the community in which it does business, and society as a whole.

Outcome-Based Ethics: Utilitarianism

"Thou shalt act so as to generate the greatest good for the greatest number." This is a paraphrase of the major premise of the utilitarian approach to ethics. **Utilitarianism** is a philosophical theory developed by Jeremy Bentham (1748–1832) and then advanced, with some modifications, by John Stuart Mill (1806–1873)—both British philosophers. In contrast to duty-based ethics, utilitarianism is outcome oriented. It focuses on the consequences of an action, not on the nature of the action itself or on any set of preestablished moral values or religious beliefs.

UTILITARIANISM
An approach to ethical reasoning that evaluates behavior not on the basis of any absolute ethical or moral values but on the consequences of that behavior for those who will be affected by it. In utilitarian reasoning, a "good" decision is one that results in the greatest good for the greatest number of people affected by the decision.

COST-BENEFIT ANALYSIS
A decision-making technique that involves weighing the costs of a given action against the benefits of that action.

Under a utilitarian model of ethics, an action is morally correct, or "right," when, among the people it affects, it produces the greatest amount of good for the greatest number. When an action affects the majority adversely, it is morally wrong. Applying the utilitarian theory thus requires (1) a determination of which individuals will be affected by the action in question; (2) a **cost-benefit analysis**, which involves an assessment of the negative and positive effects of alternative actions on these individuals; and (3) a choice among alternative actions that will produce maximum societal utility (the greatest positive net benefits for the greatest number of individuals).

The utilitarian approach to decision making commonly is employed by businesses, as well as by individuals. Weighing the consequences of a decision in terms of its costs and benefits for everyone affected by it is a useful analytical tool in the decision-making process. At the same time, utilitarianism is often criticized because its objective, calculated approach to problems tends to reduce the welfare of human beings to plus and minus signs on a cost-benefit worksheet and to "justify" human costs that many find totally unacceptable.

PROFESSIONAL RESPONSIBILITY

Business ethics goes hand in hand with professional responsibility. As you will learn in Chapter 5, all individuals, including businesspersons, owe a duty of care to others. Professionals—those who have knowledge or skills in a specific area such as accounting or law—are expected to perform their work in a manner consistent with that status. Generally, professionals are required to deliver competent services and are obligated to adhere to standards of performance commonly accepted within their professions. A professional who fails to abide by professional standards may be sued for malpractice. If the action also constitutes a statutory violation, the professional may face liability (or even criminal penalties) under the relevant statute. Here we examine some of the duties owed by two groups of professionals—accountants and attorneys—whose work can significantly affect business decision making.

Accountants' Duty of Care

Accountants play a major role in a business's financial system. Accountants have the necessary expertise and experience in establishing and maintaining accurate financial records to design, control, and audit record-keeping systems; to prepare reliable statements that reflect an individual's or a business's financial status; and to give tax advice and prepare tax returns.

An *audit* is a systematic inspection, by analyses and tests, of a business's financial records. The purpose of an audit is to provide the auditor with evidence to support an opinion on the reliability of the business's financial statements. A normal audit is not intended to uncover fraud or other misconduct. An accountant may be liable for failing to detect misconduct, however, if a normal audit would have revealed it or if the auditor agreed to examine the records for evidence of fraud or other misconduct that should have been obvious.

Standard of Care Generally, an accountant must possess the skills that an ordinarily prudent accountant would have and must exercise the degree of care that an ordinarily prudent accountant would exercise. The level of skill expected of accountants and the degree of care that they should exercise in performing their services are reflected in what are known as **generally accepted accounting principles (GAAP)** and **generally accepted auditing standards (GAAS)**. The Financial Accounting Standards Board (FASB, usually pronounced "faz-bee") determines what accounting conventions, rules, and procedures constitute GAAP at a given point in time. GAAS are standards concerning an auditor's professional qualities and the judgment that he or she exercises in auditing financial records. GAAS are established by the American Institute of Certified Public Accountants. GAAP and GAAS are also reflected in the rules established by the Securities and Exchange Commission (see Chapter 21).

Violations of GAAP and GAAS   A violation of GAAP and GAAS will be considered *prima facie* (on its face) evidence of negligence on the accountant's part. Compliance with GAAP and GAAS, however, does not necessarily relieve an accountant from potential legal liability. An accountant may be held to a higher standard of conduct established by state or federal statute and by judicial decisions. If an accountant is found to have been negligent in the performance of accounting services for a client, the client may collect damages for any losses that arose from the accountant's negligence. An accountant may also be liable to third parties, such as investors or corporate managers, who rely on accountants' opinions when making decisions.

Attorneys' Duty of Care

The conduct of attorneys is governed by rules established by each state and by the American Bar Association's Model Rules of Professional Conduct. All attorneys owe a duty to provide competent and diligent representation. Attorneys are required to be familiar with well-settled principles of law applicable to a case and to discover law that can be found through a reasonable amount of research. The lawyer must also investigate and discover facts that could materially affect the client's legal rights.

Standard of Care   In judging an attorney's performance, the standard used will normally be that of a reasonably competent general practitioner of ordinary skill, experience, and capacity. If an attorney holds himself or herself out as having expertise in a special area of law (for example, corporate taxation), then the attorney's standard of care in that area is higher than for attorneys without such expertise.

Liability for Malpractice   When an attorney fails to exercise reasonable care and professional judgment, she or he breaches the duty of care (which will be discussed in Chapter 5) and can be held liable for *malpractice* (professional negligence). In malpractice cases—as in all cases involving allegations of negligence—the plaintiff must prove that the attorney's breach of the duty of care actually caused the plaintiff to suffer some injury. **| Example #11** Suppose an attorney allows the statute of limitations (a statute that establishes the time period within which a lawsuit may be brought) to lapse on a client's claim. The attorney can be held liable for malpractice because the client can no longer file a cause of action in this case and has lost a potential award of damages.**|**

Traditionally, to establish causation, the client normally had to show that "but for" the attorney's negligence, the client would not have suffered the injury.

GENERALLY ACCEPTED ACCOUNTING PRINCIPLES (GAAP)
The conventions, rules, and procedures necessary to define accepted accounting practices at a particular time. The source of the principles is the Financial Accounting Standards Board (FASB).

GENERALLY ACCEPTED AUDITING STANDARDS (GAAS)
Standards concerning an auditor's professional qualities and the judgment exercised by him or her in the performance of an examination and report. The source of the standards is the American Institute of Certified Public Accountants.

In recent years, however, several courts have held that plaintiffs in malpractice cases need only show that the defendant's negligence was a "substantial factor" in causing the plaintiff's injury.

Statutory Duties of Accountants

Both civil and criminal liability may be imposed on accountants under securities laws. Accountants are also subject to criminal liability under the Internal Revenue Code.

The Duty of Accountants under Securities Laws   Securities laws are designed to promote disclosure and prevent fraud in the purchase and sale of *securities*—corporate stocks and bonds. As you will read in Chapter 21, the Securities Act of 1933 governs initial sales of stock by businesses. The act requires that all essential information concerning the issuance of securities be made available to the investing public when the securities are registered with the Securities and Exchange Commission (SEC). The SEC is the federal agency that administers and enforces securities laws. The Securities Exchange Act of 1934 regulates the markets in which securities are sold by maintaining a continuous disclosure system for all corporations with securities on the securities exchanges.

Accountants frequently prepare and certify the issuer's financial statements that are included in the registration statement that is filed with the SEC. If a financial statement contains a misstatement or omission of a material fact, the accountant may be liable to any purchasers of the security. To avoid liability under the 1933 act, accountants must show that they used *due diligence*—a standard of care that accountants must meet—in the preparation of the financial statements. Among other things, due diligence requires that the accountant follow GAAP and GAAS. Accountants may also face liability for false or deceptive statements, reports, or other documents under the antifraud provisions of the Securities Exchange Act of 1934.

Potential Criminal Liability of Accountants   Criminal penalties may also be imposed on accountants for violating securities laws. For *willful* violations of the 1933 act, accountants may be imprisoned for up to five years and/or be subject to a fine of up to $10,000. For willful violations of the 1934 act, an accountant may be imprisoned for up to ten years and fined up to $100,000. The Sarbanes-Oxley Act of 2002, which will be discussed later in this chapter, provides that for a securities filing that is accompanied by an accountant's false or misleading certified audit statement, the accountant may be fined up to $5 million, imprisoned for up to twenty years, or both.

Accountants are also subject to criminal liability under the Internal Revenue Code, as well as under both state and federal criminal codes. The Internal Revenue Code makes aiding or assisting in the preparation of a false tax return a felony punishable by a fine of $100,000 ($500,000 for a corporation) and imprisonment for up to three years. This provision does not apply solely to accountants but to anyone who prepares tax returns for others for compensation. A penalty of $250 per tax return is levied on tax preparers for negligent understatement of the client's tax liability, and a penalty of $1,000 is imposed for willful understatement of tax liability or the reckless or intentional disregard of rules or regulations. In addition, those who prepare tax returns for others may be fined $1,000 per document for aiding and abetting another's understatement of tax liability (the penalty is increased to $10,000 in corporate cases).

COMPANIES THAT DEFY THE RULES

One of the best ways to learn the ethical responsibilities inherent in operating a business is to look at the mistakes made by other companies. In the following subsections, we describe some of the ethical failures of companies that have raised public awareness of corporate misconduct and highlighted the need for ethical leadership in business.

Enron's Growth and Demise in a Nutshell

The Enron Corporation was one of the first companies to benefit from the deregulated electricity market. By 1998, Enron was the largest energy trader in the market. When competition in energy trading increased, Enron diversified into water, power plants, and eventually high-speed Internet and fiber optics (the value of which soon became negligible). Because Enron's managers received bonuses based on whether they met earnings goals, they had an incentive to inflate the anticipated earnings on energy contracts, which they did. Enron included these anticipated earnings in its current earnings profits reports, which vastly overstated the company's actual profit. Then, to artificially maintain and even increase its reported earnings, Enron created a complex network of subsidiaries that enabled it to move losses to its subsidiaries and hide its debts.

The overall effect of these actions was to increase Enron's apparent net worth. These "off-the-books" transactions were also frequently carried out in the Cayman Islands to avoid paying federal income taxes. In addition, Enron's

Former Enron CEO, Kenneth Lay, and his wife are shown here being escorted from a Houston courthouse in 2006. During the long-awaited trial, Lay argued in his defense that there was never any "evil" intent on his part. Can such an argument be used to justify past corporate accounting practices that gave a very inaccurate picture of the corporation's true growth in profits? Under what circumstance might intent be an important argument in ascertaining the guilt of a corporate officer? (AP Photo/Pat Sullivan)

Prohibition against the Bribery of Foreign Officials   The first part of the FCPA applies to all U.S. companies and their directors, officers, shareholders, employees, and agents. This part prohibits the bribery of most officials of foreign governments if the purpose of the payment is to get them to act in their official capacity to provide business opportunities.

The FCPA does not prohibit payment of substantial sums to minor officials whose duties are ministerial. These payments are often referred to as "grease," or facilitating payments. They are meant to accelerate the performance of administrative services that might otherwise be carried out at a slow pace. Thus, for example, if a firm makes a payment to a minor official to speed up an import licensing process, the firm has not violated the FCPA.

Generally, the act, as amended, permits payments to foreign officials if such payments are lawful within the foreign country. The act also does not prohibit payments to private foreign companies or other third parties unless the U.S. firm knows that the payments will be passed on to a foreign government in violation of the FCPA.

Accounting Requirements   In the past, bribes were often concealed in corporate financial records. Thus, the second part of the FCPA is directed toward accountants. All companies must keep detailed records that "accurately and fairly" reflect the company's financial activities. In addition, all companies must have an accounting system that provides "reasonable assurance" that all transactions entered into by the company are accounted for and legal. These requirements assist in detecting illegal bribes. The FCPA further prohibits any person from making false statements to accountants or false entries in any record or account.

Penalties for Violations   In 1988, the FCPA was amended to provide that business firms that violate the act may be fined up to $2 million. Individual officers or directors who violate the FCPA may be fined up to $100,000 (the fine cannot be paid by the company) and may be imprisoned for up to five years.

Workers at their sewing machines in a garment plant in Micronesia. How might cultural differences affect what businesspersons consider ethical conduct? If, for example, employees in a particular region typically work fifteen-hour days, is it unethical for an American business operating in that region to require the same number of hours? Why or why not? Would it be any more ethical if the American company subcontracted with another company whose employees were required to work fifteen-hour days? (AP Photo/Charles Hanley)

Other Nations Denounce Bribery

For twenty years after its passage in 1977, the FCPA was the only law of its kind in the world, despite attempts by U.S. political leaders to convince other nations to pass similar legislation. That situation is now changing. In 1997, the Organization for Economic Cooperation and Development created a convention (treaty) that made the bribery of foreign public officials a serious crime. By 2006, thirty countries had adopted the convention, which obligates them to enact legislation within their nations in accordance with the treaty. In addition, other international institutions, including the European Union, the Organization of American States, and the United Nations, have either passed or are in the process of negotiating rules against bribery in business transactions.

REVIEWING . . . ETHICS AND PROFESSIONAL RESPONSIBILITY

Isabel Arnett is the chief executive officer (CEO) of Tamik, Inc., a pharmaceutical company that manufactures a vaccine called Kafluk, which supposedly provides some defense against bird flu. The company began marketing Kafluk throughout Asia. After numerous media reports that bird flu may soon become a worldwide epidemic, the demand for Kafluk increased, sales soared, and Tamik earned record profits. Tamik's CEO, Arnett, then began receiving disturbing reports from Southeast Asia that in some patients, Kafluk had caused psychiatric disturbances, including severe hallucinations, and heart and lung problems. Arnett was informed that six children in Japan had committed suicide by jumping out of windows after receiving the vaccine. To cover up the story and prevent negative publicity, Arnett instructed Tamik's partners in Asia to offer cash to the Japanese families whose children had died in exchange for their silence. Arnett also refused to authorize additional research within the company to study the potential side effects of Kafluk. Using the information presented in the chapter, answer the following questions.

1. In this scenario, it is not clear that the other corporate officers and Tamik's board of directors were aware of the actions of its CEO, Arnett. How might an integrated corporate governance system ensure that these parties were informed of Arnett's conduct?

2. Would a person who adheres to the principle of rights theory consider it ethical for Arnett not to disclose potential safety concerns and to refuse to perform additional research on Kafluk? Why or why not?

3. If Kafluk prevented fifty Asian people who were infected with bird flu from dying, would Arnett's conduct in this situation be ethical under a utilitarian model of ethics? Why or why not?

4. Did Tamik or Arnett violate the Foreign Corrupt Practices Act in this scenario? Why or why not?

KEY TERMS

business ethics   35
categorical imperative   47
cost-benefit analysis   48
ethical reasoning   46
ethics   35

generally accepted accounting
   principles (GAAP)   49
generally accepted auditing
   standards (GAAS)   49

moral minimum   42
principle of rights   47
utilitarianism   47

CHAPTER SUMMARY • ETHICS AND PROFESSIONAL RESPONSIBILITY

Business Ethics (See pages 35–37.)	Ethics can be defined as the study of what constitutes right or wrong behavior. Business ethics focuses on how moral and ethical principles are applied in the business context.

(Continued)

CHAPTER SUMMARY • ETHICS AND PROFESSIONAL RESPONSIBILITY—CONTINUED

Setting the Right Ethical Tone (See pages 37–42.)	1. *Role of management*—Management's commitment and behavior are essential in creating an ethical workplace. Most large firms have ethical codes or policies and corporate compliance programs to help employees determine whether certain actions are ethical. 2. *Ethical trade-offs*—Management constantly faces ethical trade-offs because firms have ethical and legal duties to a number of groups, including shareholders and employees.
Business Ethics and the Law (See pages 42–46.)	1. *The moral minimum*—Lawful behavior is a moral minimum. The law has its limits, though, and some actions may be legal but not ethical. 2. *Legal uncertainties*—It may be difficult to predict with certainty whether particular actions are legal given the numerous and frequent changes in the laws regulating business and the "gray areas" in the law. 3. *Technological developments and legal uncertainties*—Technological developments can also lead to legal uncertainties until it is clear how the law will be applied to the questions raised by these developments.
Approaches to Ethical Reasoning (See pages 46–48.)	1. *Duty-based ethics*—Ethics based on religious beliefs; philosophical reasoning, such as that of Immanuel Kant; and the basic rights of human beings (the principle of rights). 2. *Outcome-based ethics (utilitarianism)*—Ethics based on philosophical reasoning, such as that of John Stuart Mill, and focusing on the consequences of actions rather than the actions themselves.
Professional Responsibility (See pages 48–51.)	1. *Duty of care*—Accountants and attorneys are held to standards of care established by their respective professions. Failure to meet the required standard of care may result in liability for negligence. The standard of care expected of accountants is reflected in generally accepted accounting principles (GAAP) and generally accepted auditing standards (GAAS). The standard of care expected of attorneys is reflected in rules established in each state and by the American Bar Association's Model Rules of Professional Conduct. 2. *Statutory duties of accountants*—Accountants are subject to requirements established by securities laws. Violations of these requirements may result in both civil and criminal penalties. Accountants are also subject to criminal liability under the Internal Revenue Code.
Companies That Defy the Rules (See pages 51–54.)	The Enron debacle—involving one of the largest bankruptcies in U.S. history—serves as an example of a culture that fostered unethical and, in part, illegal business behavior. Another example is Merck & Company, Inc., which became the target of much criticism (and many lawsuits) when it continued to market its painkiller Vioxx until 2004, despite its awareness of studies indicating that the drug significantly increased the risk of heart attacks and strokes.
The Sarbanes-Oxley Act of 2002 (See pages 54–55.)	Imposes strict requirements on domestic and foreign public accounting firms that provide auditing services to companies selling securities to the public. Establishes an oversight board and rules to keep auditors independent and prevent the destruction or falsification of records.
Business Ethics on a Global Level (See pages 56–59.)	Businesses must take account of the many cultural, religious, and legal differences among nations. Notable differences relate to the role of women in society, employment laws governing workplace conditions, and the practice of giving side payments to foreign officials to secure favorable contracts.

FOR REVIEW

Answers for the even-numbered questions in this For Review *section can be found in Appendix O at the end of this text.*

1. What is ethics? What is business ethics? Why is business ethics important?

2. How can business leaders encourage their companies to act ethically?

3. What are corporate compliance programs?

4. What duties do professionals owe to those who rely on their services?

5. What types of ethical issues might arise in the context of international business transactions?

Costco Background

Costco Wholesale Corporation operates a chain of cash-and-carry membership warehouses that sell high-quality, nationally branded, and selected private-label merchandise at low prices. Its target markets include both businesses that buy goods for commercial use or resale and individuals who are employees or members of specific organizations and associations. The company tries to reach high sales volume and fast inventory turnover by offering a limited choice of merchandise in many product groups at competitive prices.

The company takes a strong position on behaving ethically in all transactions and relationships. It expects employees to behave ethically. For example, no one can accept gratuities from vendors. The company also expects employees to behave ethically, according to domestic ethical standards, in any country in which it operates.

COSTCO™

CODE OF ETHICS

By Jim Sinegal

OBEY THE LAW

The law is irrefutable! Absent a moral imperative to challenge a law, we must conduct our business in total compliance with the laws of every community where we do business.

- Comply with all statutes.
- Cooperate with authorities.
- Respect all public officials and their positions.

TAKE CARE OF OUR EMPLOYEES

To claim "people are our most important asset" is true and an understatement. Each employee has been hired for a very important job. Jobs such as stocking the shelves, ringing members' orders, buying products, and paying our bills are jobs we would all choose to perform because of their importance. The employees hired to perform these jobs are performing as management's "alter egos." Every employee, whether they are in a Costco warehouse, or whether they work in the regional or corporate offices, is a Costco ambassador trained to give our members professional, courteous treatment.

Today we have warehouse managers who were once stockers and callers, and vice presidents who were once in clerical positions for Costco. We believe that Costco's future executive officers are cur-

...rently working in our warehouses, depots, buying offices, and accounting departments, as well as in our home offices.

To that end, we are committed to these principles:

- Provide a safe work environment.

- Pay a fair wage.

- Make every job challenging, but make it fun!

- Consider the loss of any employee as a failure on the part of the company and a loss to the organization.

- Teach our people how to do their jobs and how to improve personally and professionally.

- Promote from within the company to achieve the goal of a minimum of 80% of management positions being filled by current employees.

- Create an "open door" attitude at all levels of the company that is dedicated to "fairness and listening."

RESPECT OUR VENDORS

Our vendors are our partners in business and for us to prosper as a company, they must prosper with us. It is important that our vendors understand that we will be tough negotiators, but fair in our treatment of them.

- Treat all vendors and their representatives as you would expect to be treated if visiting their places of business.

- Pay all bills within the allocated time frame.

- Honor all commitments.

- Protect all vendor property assigned to Costco as though it were our own.

- Always be thoughtful and candid in negotiations.

- Provide a careful review process with at least two levels of authorization before terminating business with an existing vendor of more than two years.

- Do not accept gratuities of any kind from a vendor

> These guidelines are exactly that - guidelines, some common sense rules for the conduct of our business. Intended to simplify our jobs, not complicate our lives, these guidelines will not answer every question or solve every problem. At the core of our philosophy as a company must be the implicit understanding that not one of us is required to lie or cheat on behalf of PriceCosto. In fact, dishonest conduct will not be tolerated. To do any less would be unfair to the overwhelming majority of our employees who support and respect Costco's commitment to ethical business conduct.
>
> If you are ever in doubt as to what course of action to take on a business matter that is open to varying ethical interpretations, take the high road and do what is right.

- Avoid all conflict of interest issues with public officials.

- Comply with all disclosure and reporting requirements.

- Comply with safety and security standards for all products sold.

- Exceed ecological standards required in every community where we do business.

- Comply with all applicable wage and hour laws.

- Comply with all applicable anti-trust laws.

- Protect "inside information" that has not been released to the general public.

TAKE CARE OF OUR MEMBERS

The member is our key to success. If we don't keep our members happy, little else that we do will make a difference.

- Provide top-quality products at the best prices in the market.

- Provide a safe shopping environment in our warehouses.

- Provide only products that meet applicable safety and health standards.

- Sell only products from manufacturers who comply with "truth in advertising/packaging" standards.

- Provide our members with a 100% satisfaction guaranteed warranty on every product and service we sell, including their membership fee.

- Assure our members that every product we sell is authentic in make and in representation of performance.

- Make our shopping environment a pleasant experience by making our members feel welcome as our guests.

- Provide products to our members that will be ecologically sensitive.

> Our member is our reason for being. If they fail to show up, we cannot survive. Our members have extended a "trust" to Costco by virtue of paying a fee to shop with us. We can't let them down or they will simply go away. We must always operate in the following manner when dealing with our members:
> Rule #1 – The member is always right.
> Rule #2 – In the event the member is ever wrong, refer to rule #1.
>
> There are plenty of shopping alternatives for our members. We will succeed only if we do not violate the trust they have extended to us. We must be committed at every level of our company, with every ounce of energy and grain of creativity we have, to constantly strive to "bring goods to market at a lower price."

QUESTIONS AND CASE PROBLEMS

2–1. Business Ethics. Some business ethicists maintain that whereas personal ethics has to do with right or wrong behavior, business ethics is concerned with appropriate behavior. In other words, ethical behavior in business has less to do with moral principles than with what society deems to be appropriate behavior in the business context. Do you agree with this distinction? Do personal and business ethics ever overlap? Should personal ethics play any role in business ethical decision making?

Question with Sample Answer

2–2. Human rights groups, environmental activists, and other interest groups concerned with unethical business practices have often conducted publicity campaigns against various corporations that those groups feel have engaged in unethical practices. Do you believe that a small group of well-organized activists should dictate how a major corporation conducts its affairs? Discuss fully.

For a sample answer to this question, go to Appendix P at the end of this text.

2–3. Business Ethics and Public Opinion. Assume that you are a high-level manager for a shoe manufacturer. You know that your firm could increase its profit margin by producing shoes in Indonesia, where you could hire women for $100 a month to assemble them. You also know, however, that a competing shoe manufacturer recently was accused by human rights advocates of engaging in exploitative labor practices because the manufacturer sold shoes made by Indonesian women for similarly low wages. You personally do not believe that paying $100 a month to Indonesian women is unethical because you know that in their country, $100 a month is a better-than-average wage rate. Assuming that the decision is yours to make, should you have the shoes manufactured in Indonesia and make higher profits for your company? Should you instead avoid the risk of negative publicity and the consequences of that publicity for the firm's reputation and subsequent profits? Are there other alternatives? Discuss fully.

2–4. Ethical Decision Making. Shokun Steel Co. owns many steel plants. One of its plants is much older than the others. Equipment at that plant is outdated and inefficient, and the costs of production at that plant are now twice as high as at any of Shokun's other plants. The company cannot raise the price of steel because of competition, both domestic and international. The plant is located in Twin Firs, Pennsylvania, which has a population of about 45,000, and employs over a thousand workers. Shokun is contemplating whether to close the plant. What factors should the firm consider in making its decision? Will the firm violate any ethical duties if it closes the plant? Analyze these questions from the two basic perspectives on ethical reasoning discussed in this chapter.

Case Problem with Sample Answer

2–5. Richard Fraser was an "exclusive career insurance agent" under a contract with Nationwide Mutual Insurance Co. Fraser leased computer hardware and software from Nationwide for his business. During a dispute between Nationwide and the Nationwide Insurance Independent Contractors Association, an organization representing Fraser and other exclusive career agents, Fraser prepared a letter to Nationwide's competitors asking whether they were interested in acquiring the represented agents' policyholders. Nationwide obtained a copy of the letter and searched its electronic file server for e-mail indicating that the letter had been sent. It found a stored e-mail that Fraser had sent to a co-worker indicating that the letter had been sent to at least one competitor. The e-mail was retrieved from the co-worker's file of already received and discarded messages stored on the server. When Nationwide canceled its contract with Fraser, he filed a suit in a federal district court against the firm, alleging, among other things, violations of various federal laws that prohibit the interception of electronic communications during transmission. In whose favor should the court rule, and why? Did Nationwide act ethically in retrieving the e-mail? Explain. [*Fraser v. Nationwide Mutual Insurance Co.,* 352 F.3d 107 (3d Cir. 2004)]

After you have answered this problem, compare your answer with the sample answer given on the Web site that accompanies this text. Go to www.thomsonedu.com/westbuslaw/let, select "Chapter 2," and click on "Case Problem with Sample Answer."

2–6. Ethical Conduct. Unable to pay more than $1.2 billion in debt, Big Rivers Electric Corp. filed a petition to declare bankruptcy in a federal bankruptcy court in September 1996. Big Rivers' creditors included Bank of New York (BONY), Chase Manhattan Bank, Mapco Equities, and others. The court appointed J. Baxter Schilling to work as a "disinterested" (neutral) party with Big Rivers and the creditors to resolve their disputes; the court set an hourly fee as Schilling's compensation. Schilling told Chase, BONY, and Mapco that he wanted them to pay him an additional percentage fee based on the "success" he attained in finding "new value" to pay Big Rivers' debts. He said that without such a deal, he would not perform his mediation duties. Chase agreed; the others disputed the deal, but no one told the court. In October 1998, Schilling asked the court for nearly $4.5 million in compensation, including the hourly fees, which totaled about $531,000, and the percentage fees. Big Rivers and others asked the court to deny Schilling any fees on the basis that he had improperly negotiated "secret side agreements." How did Schilling violate his duties as a "disinterested" party? Should he be denied compensation? Why or why not? [*In re Big Rivers Electric Corp.,* 355 F.3d 415 (6th Cir. 2004)]

2-7. Ethical Conduct. Eden Electrical, Ltd., owned twenty-five appliance stores throughout Israel, at least some of which sold refrigerators made by Amana Co. Eden bought the appliances from Amana's Israeli distributor, Pan El A/Yesh Shem, which approached Eden about taking over the distributorship. Eden representatives met with Amana executives. The executives made assurances about Amana's good faith, its hope of having a long-term business relationship with Eden, and its willingness to have Eden become its exclusive distributor in Israel. Eden signed a distributorship agreement and paid Amana $2.4 million. Amana failed to deliver this amount in inventory to Eden, continued selling refrigerators to other entities for the Israeli market, and represented to others that it was still looking for a long-term distributor. Less than three months after signing the agreement with Eden, Amana terminated it without explanation. Eden filed a suit in a federal district court against Amana, alleging fraud. The court awarded Eden $12.1 million in damages. Is this amount warranted? Why or why not? How does this case illustrate why business ethics is important? [*Eden Electrical, Ltd. v. Amana Co.*, 370 F.3d 824 (8th Cir. 2004)]

2-8. Ethical Conduct. Ernest Price suffered from sickle cell anemia. In 1997, Price asked Dr. Ann Houston, his physician, to prescribe Oxycontin, a strong narcotic, for pain. Over the next several years, Price saw at least ten different physicians at ten different clinics in two cities, and used seven pharmacies in three cities, to obtain and fill simultaneous prescriptions for Oxycontin. In March 2001, when Houston learned of these activities, she refused to write more prescriptions for Price. As other physicians became aware of Price's actions, they also stopped writing his prescriptions. Price filed a suit in a Mississippi state court against Purdue Pharma Co. and other producers and distributors of Oxycontin, as well as his physicians and the pharmacies that had filled the prescriptions. Price alleged negligence, among other things, claiming that Oxycontin's addictive nature caused him injury and that

this was the defendants' fault. The defendants argued that Price's claim should be dismissed because it arose from his own wrongdoing. Who should be held *legally* liable? Should any of the parties be considered *ethically* responsible? Why or why not? [*Price v. Purdue Pharma Co.*, __ So.2d __ (Miss. 2006)]

Critical-Thinking Ethical Question

2-9. If a firm engages in "ethically responsible" behavior solely for the purpose of gaining profits from the goodwill it generates, the "ethical" behavior is essentially a means toward a self-serving end (profits and the accumulation of wealth). In this situation, is the firm acting unethically in any way? Should motive or conduct carry greater weight on the ethical scales in this situation?

Video Question

2-10. Go to this text's Web site at **www.thomsonedu.com/westbuslaw/let** and select "Chapter 2." Click on "Video Questions" and view the video titled *Ethics: Business Ethics an Oxymoron?* Then answer the following questions.

1. According to the instructor in the video, what is the primary reason why businesses act ethically?
2. Which of the two approaches to ethical reasoning that were discussed in the chapter seems to have had more influence on the instructor in the discussion of how business activities are related to societies? Explain your answer.
3. The instructor asserts that "[i]n the end, it is the unethical behavior that becomes costly, and conversely ethical behavior creates its own competitive advantage." Do you agree with this statement? Why or why not?

INTERACTING WITH THE INTERNET

For updated links to resources available on the Web, as well as a variety of other materials, visit this text's Web site at

www.thomsonedu.com/westbuslaw/let

You can find articles on issues relating to shareholders and corporate accountability at the Corporate Governance Web site. Go to

www.corpgov.net

For an example of an online group that focuses on corporate activities from the perspective of corporate social responsibility, go to

www.corpwatch.org

Global Exchange offers information on global business activities, including some of the ethical issues stemming from those activities, at

www.globalexchange.org

INTERNET EXERCISES

Go to **www.thomsonedu.com/westbuslaw/let**, the Web site that accompanies this text. Select "Chapter 2" and click on "Internet Exercises." There you will find the following Internet research exercises that you can perform to learn more about topics covered in this chapter.

Internet Exercise 2–1: LEGAL PERSPECTIVE—Ethics in Business
Internet Exercise 2–2: MANAGEMENT PERSPECTIVE—Environmental Self-Audits

BEFORE THE TEST

Go to **www.thomsonedu.com/westbuslaw/let**, the Web site that accompanies this text. Select "Chapter 2" and click on "Interactive Quizzes." You will find a number of interactive questions relating to this chapter.

Courts and Alternative Dispute Resolution

CHAPTER OBJECTIVES

After reading this chapter, you should be able to answer the following questions:

1 What is judicial review? How and when was the power of judicial review established?

2 Before a court can hear a case, it must have jurisdiction. Over what must it have jurisdiction? How are the courts applying traditional jurisdictional concepts to cases involving Internet transactions?

3 What is the difference between a trial court and an appellate court?

4 In a lawsuit, what are the pleadings? What is discovery, and how does electronic discovery differ? What is electronic filing?

5 How are online forums being used to resolve disputes?

> "The Judicial Department comes home in its effects to every man's fireside: it passes on his property, his reputation, his life, his all."
>
> —JOHN MARSHALL, 1755–1835
> (Chief justice of the United States Supreme Court, 1801–1835)

AS CHIEF JUSTICE John Marshall remarked in the chapter-opening quotation, ultimately, we are all affected by what the courts say and do. This is particularly true in the business world—nearly every businessperson will face either a potential or an actual lawsuit at some time or another. For this reason, anyone contemplating a career in business will benefit from an understanding of American court systems, including the mechanics of lawsuits.

In this chapter, after examining the judiciary's overall role in the American governmental scheme, we discuss some basic requirements that must be met before a party may bring a lawsuit before a particular court. We then look at the court systems of the United States in some detail and, to clarify judicial procedures, follow a hypothetical case through a state court system. Even though there are fifty-two court systems—one for each of the fifty states, one for the District of Columbia, plus a federal system—similarities abound. Keep in mind that the federal courts are not superior to the state courts; they are simply an independent system of courts, which derives its authority from Article III, Sections 1 and 2, of the U.S. Constitution. The chapter concludes with an overview of some alternative methods of settling disputes, including methods for settling disputes in online forums.

Note that technological developments are affecting court procedures just as they are having an impact on all other areas of the law. In this chapter, we also indicate how court doctrines and procedures, as well as alternative methods of dispute settlement, are being adapted to the needs of a cyber age.

THE JUDICIARY'S ROLE IN AMERICAN GOVERNMENT

As you learned in Chapter 1, the body of American law includes the federal and state constitutions, statutes passed by legislative bodies, administrative law, and the case decisions and legal principles that form the common law. These laws would be meaningless, however, without the courts to interpret and apply them. This is the essential role of the judiciary—the courts—in the American governmental system: to interpret and apply the law.

Judicial Review

As the branch of government entrusted with interpreting the laws, the judiciary can decide, among other things, whether the laws or actions of the other two branches are constitutional. The process for making such a determination is known as **judicial review.** The power of judicial review enables the judicial branch to act as a check on the other two branches of government, in line with the checks-and-balances system established by the U.S. Constitution.

JUDICIAL REVIEW
The process by which a court decides on the constitutionality of legislative enactments and actions of the executive branch.

The Origins of Judicial Review in the United States

The power of judicial review was not mentioned in the Constitution, but the concept was not new at the time the nation was founded. Indeed, prior to 1789 state courts had already overturned state legislative acts that conflicted with state constitutions. (For a discussion of judicial review in other nations, see this chapter's *Beyond Our Borders* feature.) Additionally, many of the founders expected the United States Supreme Court to assume a similar role with respect to the federal Constitution. Alexander Hamilton and James Madison both emphasized the importance of judicial review in their essays urging the adoption of the new Constitution. To learn more about the establishment of the doctrine of judicial review, see this chapter's *Landmark in the Legal Environment* feature on the next page.

BEYOND OUR BORDERS
Judicial Review in Other Nations

The concept of judicial review was pioneered by the United States. Some maintain that one of the reasons the doctrine was readily accepted in this country was that it fit well with the checks and balances designed by the founders. Today, all established constitutional democracies have some form of judicial review—the power to rule on the constitutionality of laws—but its form varies from country to country.

For example, Canada's Supreme Court can exercise judicial review but is barred from doing so if a law includes a provision explicitly prohibiting such review. France has a Constitutional Council that rules on the constitutionality of laws *before* the laws take effect. Laws can be referred to the council for prior review by the president, the prime minister, and the heads of the two chambers of the parliament. Prior review is also an option in Germany and Italy, if requested by the national or a regional government. In contrast, the United States Supreme Court does not give advisory opinions; the Supreme Court will render a decision only when there is an actual dispute concerning an issue.

For Critical Analysis *In any country in which a constitution sets forth the basic powers and structure of government, some governmental body must decide whether laws enacted by the government are consistent with that constitution. Why might the courts be best suited to handle this task? What might be a better alternative?*

Marbury v. Madison (1803)

In the edifice of American law, the *Marbury v. Madison*[a] decision in 1803 can be viewed as the keystone of the constitutional arch. The facts of the case were as follows. John Adams, who had lost his bid for reelection to the presidency to Thomas Jefferson in 1800, feared the Jeffersonians' antipathy toward business and toward a strong central government. Adams thus worked feverishly to "pack" the judiciary with loyal Federalists (those who believed in a strong national government) by appointing what came to be called "midnight judges" just before Jefferson took office. All of the fifty-nine judicial appointment letters had to be certified and delivered, but Adams's secretary of state (John Marshall) had succeeded in delivering only forty-two of them by the time Jefferson took over as president. Jefferson, of course, refused to order his secretary of state, James Madison, to deliver the remaining commissions.

Marshall's Dilemma   William Marbury and three others to whom the commissions had not been delivered sought a writ of *mandamus* (an order directing a government official to fulfill a duty) from the United States Supreme Court, as authorized by Section 13 of the Judiciary Act of 1789. As fate would have it, John Marshall had stepped down as Adams's secretary of state only to become chief justice of the Supreme Court. Marshall faced a dilemma: If he ordered the commissions delivered, the new secretary of state (Madison) could simply refuse to deliver them—and the Court had no way to compel action, because it had no police force. At the same time, if Marshall simply allowed the new administration to do as it wished, the Court's power would be severely eroded.

Marshall's Decision   Marshall masterfully fashioned his decision. On the one hand, he enlarged the power of the Supreme Court by affirming the Court's power of judicial review. He stated, "It is emphatically the province

a. 5 U.S. (1 Cranch) 137, 2 L.Ed. 60 (1803).

and duty of the Judicial Department to say what the law is. . . . If two laws conflict with each other, the courts must decide on the operation of each. . . . So if the law be in opposition to the Constitution . . . [t]he Court must determine which of these conflicting rules governs the case. This is the very essence of judicial duty."

On the other hand, his decision did not require anyone to do anything. He stated that the highest court did not have the power to issue a writ of *mandamus* in this particular case. Marshall pointed out that although the Judiciary Act of 1789 specified that the Supreme Court could issue writs of *mandamus* as part of its original jurisdiction, Article III of the Constitution, which spelled out the Court's original jurisdiction, did not mention writs of *mandamus*. Because Congress did not have the right to expand the Supreme Court's jurisdiction, this section of the Judiciary Act of 1789 was unconstitutional—and thus void. The decision still stands today as a judicial and political masterpiece.

Since the Marbury v. Madison *decision, the power of judicial review has remained unchallenged. Today, this power is exercised by both federal and state courts. For example, as you will read in Chapter 4, several of the laws that Congress has passed in an attempt to protect minors from Internet pornography have been held unconstitutional by the courts. If the courts did not have the power of judicial review, the constitutionality of these acts of Congress could not be challenged in court—a congressional statute would remain law until changed by Congress. Because of the importance of* Marbury v. Madison *in our legal system, the courts of other countries that have adopted a constitutional democracy often cite this decision as a justification for judicial review.*

To locate information on the Web concerning the Marbury v. Madison *decision, go to this text's Web site at* **www.thomsonedu.com/westbuslaw/let**, *select "Chapter 3," and click on "URLs for Landmarks."*

BASIC JUDICIAL REQUIREMENTS

Before a court can hear a lawsuit, certain requirements must first be met. These requirements relate to jurisdiction, venue, and standing to sue. We examine each of these important concepts here.

Jurisdiction

In Latin, *juris* means "law," and *diction* means "to speak." Thus, "the power to speak the law" is the literal meaning of the term **jurisdiction.** Before any court can hear a case, it must have jurisdiction over the person against whom the suit is brought or over the property involved in the suit. The court must also have jurisdiction over the subject matter.

JURISDICTION
The authority of a court to hear and decide a specific action.

Jurisdiction over Persons   Generally, a court can exercise personal jurisdiction (*in personam* jurisdiction) over any person or business that resides in a certain geographic area. A state trial court, for example, normally has jurisdictional authority over residents (including businesses) in a particular area of the state, such as a county or district. A state's highest court (often called the state supreme court)[1] has jurisdiction over all residents of that state.

In addition, under the authority of a state **long arm statute,** a court can exercise personal jurisdiction over certain out-of-state defendants based on activities that took place within the state. Before exercising long arm jurisdiction over a nonresident, however, the court must be convinced that the defendant had sufficient contacts, or *minimum contacts,* with the state to justify the jurisdiction.[2] Generally, this means that the defendant must have enough of a connection to the state for the judge to conclude that it is fair for the state to exercise power over the defendant. | **Example #1** If an out-of-state defendant caused an automobile accident or sold defective goods within the state, a court will usually find that minimum contacts exist to exercise jurisdiction over that defendant. Similarly, a state may exercise personal jurisdiction over a nonresident defendant who is sued for breaching a contract that was formed within the state.|

In regard to corporations,[3] the minimum-contacts requirement is usually met if the corporation does business within the state. | **Example #2** Suppose that a Maine corporation has a branch office or a manufacturing plant in Georgia. Does this Maine corporation have sufficient minimum contacts with the state of Georgia to allow a Georgia court to exercise jurisdiction over it? Yes, it does. If the Maine corporation advertises and sells its products in Georgia, those activities will also likely suffice to meet the minimum-contacts requirement, even if the corporate headquarters are located in a different state.|

LONG ARM STATUTE
A state statute that permits a state to exercise personal jurisdiction over nonresident defendants. A defendant must have certain "minimum contacts" with that state for the statute to apply.

Jurisdiction over Property   A court can also exercise jurisdiction over property that is located within its boundaries. This kind of jurisdiction is known as *in rem* jurisdiction, or "jurisdiction over the thing." | **Example #3** Suppose that a dispute arises over the ownership of a boat in dry dock in Fort Lauderdale, Florida. The boat is owned by an Ohio resident, over whom a Florida court normally cannot exercise personal jurisdiction. The other party to the dispute is a resident of Nebraska. In this situation, a lawsuit concerning the boat could be brought in a Florida state court on the basis of the court's *in rem* jurisdiction.|

James Madison. If Madison had delivered the last seventeen of the fifty-nine judicial appointment letters, would the United States Supreme Court today have the power of judicial review? Why did the Court not force Madison to deliver the remaining commissions? (Library of Congress)

---

1. As will be discussed shortly, a state's highest court is frequently referred to as the state supreme court, but there are exceptions. For example, in New York, the supreme court is a trial court.
2. The minimum-contacts standard was established in *International Shoe Co. v. State of Washington,* 326 U.S. 310, 66 S.Ct. 154, 90 L.Ed. 95 (1945).
3. In the eyes of the law, corporations are "legal persons"—entities that can sue and be sued. See Chapter 11.

Jurisdiction over Subject Matter   Jurisdiction over subject matter is a limitation on the types of cases a court can hear. In both the federal and state court systems, there are courts of *general* (unlimited) *jurisdiction* and courts of *limited jurisdiction*. An example of a court of general jurisdiction is a state trial court or a federal district court. An example of a state court of limited jurisdiction is a probate court. **Probate courts** are state courts that handle only matters relating to the transfer of a person's assets and obligations after that person's death, including matters relating to the custody and guardianship of children. An example of a federal court of limited subject-matter jurisdiction is a bankruptcy court. **Bankruptcy courts** handle only bankruptcy proceedings, which are governed by federal bankruptcy law (discussed in Chapter 12). In contrast, a court of general jurisdiction can decide a broad array of cases.

A court's jurisdiction over subject matter is usually defined in the statute or constitution creating the court. In both the federal and state court systems, a court's subject-matter jurisdiction can be limited not only by the subject of the lawsuit but also by the amount in controversy, by whether a case is a felony (a more serious type of crime) or a misdemeanor (a less serious type of crime), or by whether the proceeding is a trial or an appeal.

Original and Appellate Jurisdiction   The distinction between courts of original jurisdiction and courts of appellate jurisdiction normally lies in whether the case is being heard for the first time. Courts having original jurisdiction are courts of the first instance, or trial courts—that is, courts in which lawsuits begin, trials take place, and evidence is presented. In the federal court system, the *district courts* are trial courts. In the various state court systems, the trial courts are known by differing names, as will be discussed shortly.

The key point here is that, normally, any court having original jurisdiction is known as a trial court. Courts having appellate jurisdiction act as reviewing courts, or appellate courts. In general, cases can be brought before appellate courts only on appeal from an order or a judgment of a trial court or other lower court.

Jurisdiction of the Federal Courts   Because the federal government is a government of limited powers, the jurisdiction of the federal courts is limited. Article III of the U.S. Constitution establishes the boundaries of federal judicial power. Section 2 of Article III states that "[t]he judicial Power shall extend to all Cases, in Law and Equity, arising under this Constitution, the Laws of the United States, and Treaties made, or which shall be made, under their Authority."

Whenever a plaintiff's cause of action is based, at least in part, on the U.S. Constitution, a treaty, or a federal law, then a **federal question** arises, and the case comes under the judicial power of the federal courts. Any lawsuit involving a federal question can originate in a federal court. People who claim that their rights under the U.S. Constitution have been violated can begin their suits in a federal court.

Federal district courts can also exercise original jurisdiction over cases involving **diversity of citizenship.** Such cases may arise between (1) citizens of different states, (2) a foreign country and citizens of a state or of different states, or (3) citizens of a state and citizens or subjects of a foreign country. The amount in controversy must be more than $75,000 before a federal court can take jurisdiction in such cases. For purposes of diversity jurisdiction, a

---

PROBATE COURT
A state court of limited jurisdiction that conducts proceedings relating to the settlement of a deceased person's estate.

BANKRUPTCY COURT
A federal court of limited jurisdiction that handles only bankruptcy proceedings. Bankruptcy proceedings are governed by federal bankruptcy law.

FEDERAL QUESTION
A question that pertains to the U.S. Constitution, acts of Congress, or treaties. A federal question provides a basis for federal jurisdiction.

DIVERSITY OF CITIZENSHIP
Under Article III, Section 2, of the Constitution, a basis for federal district court jurisdiction over a lawsuit between (1) citizens of different states, (2) a foreign country and citizens of a state or of different states, or (3) citizens of a state and citizens or subjects of a foreign country. The amount in controversy must be more than $75,000 before a federal district court can take jurisdiction in such cases.

corporation is a citizen of both the state in which it is incorporated and the state in which its principal place of business is located. A case involving diversity of citizenship can be filed in the appropriate federal district court, or, if the case starts in a state court, it can sometimes be transferred to a federal court. A large percentage of the cases filed in federal courts each year are based on diversity of citizenship.

Note that in a case based on a federal question, a federal court will apply federal law. In a case based on diversity of citizenship, however, a federal court will apply the relevant state law (which is often the law of the state in which the court sits).

Exclusive versus Concurrent Jurisdiction   When both federal and state courts have the power to hear a case, as is true in suits involving diversity of citizenship, **concurrent jurisdiction** exists. When cases can be tried only in federal courts or only in state courts, **exclusive jurisdiction** exists. Federal courts have exclusive jurisdiction in cases involving federal crimes, bankruptcy, patents, and copyrights; in suits against the United States; and in some areas of admiralty law (law governing transportation on the seas and ocean waters). States also have exclusive jurisdiction over certain subject matters—for example, divorce and adoption. The concepts of exclusive and concurrent jurisdiction are illustrated in Exhibit 3–1.

When concurrent jurisdiction exists, a party has a choice of whether to bring a suit in, for example, a federal or a state court. The party's lawyer will consider several factors in counseling the party as to which choice is preferable. The lawyer may prefer to litigate the case in a state court because he or she is more familiar with the state court's procedures, or perhaps the attorney believes that the state court's judge or jury would be more sympathetic to the client and the case. Alternatively, the lawyer may advise the client to sue in federal court. Perhaps the state court's **docket** (the court's schedule listing the cases to be heard) is crowded, and the case could be brought to trial sooner in a federal court. Perhaps some feature of federal practice or procedure could offer an advantage in the client's case. Other important considerations include the law

CONCURRENT JURISDICTION
Jurisdiction that exists when two different courts have the power to hear a case. For example, some cases can be heard in either a federal or a state court.

EXCLUSIVE JURISDICTION
Jurisdiction that exists when a case can be heard only in a particular court or type of court.

DOCKET
The list of cases entered on a court's calendar and thus scheduled to be heard by the court.

EXHIBIT 3–1 EXCLUSIVE AND CONCURRENT JURISDICTION

Exclusive State Jurisdiction
Cases involving all matters not subject to federal jurisdiction— for example, divorce and adoption cases

Concurrent Jurisdiction
Cases involving federal questions and diversity-of-citizenship cases

Exclusive Federal Jurisdiction
Cases involving federal crimes, federal antitrust law, bankruptcy, patents, copyrights, trademarks, suits against the United States, some areas of admiralty law, and certain other matters specified in federal statutes

in a particular jurisdiction, how that law has been applied in the jurisdiction's courts, and what the results in similar cases have been in that jurisdiction.

Jurisdiction in Cyberspace

The Internet's capacity to bypass political and geographic boundaries undercuts the traditional basic limitations on a court's authority to exercise jurisdiction. These limits include a party's contacts with a court's geographic jurisdiction. As already discussed, for a court to compel a defendant to come before it, there must be at least minimum contacts—the presence of a salesperson within the state, for example. Are there sufficient minimum contacts if the only connection to a jurisdiction is an ad on the Web originating from a remote location?

The "Sliding-Scale" Standard   Gradually, the courts are developing a standard—called a "sliding-scale" standard—for determining when the exercise of jurisdiction over an out-of-state defendant is proper. In developing this standard, the courts have identified three types of Internet business contacts: (1) substantial business conducted over the Internet (with contracts and sales, for example); (2) some interactivity through a Web site; and (3) passive advertising. Jurisdiction is proper for the first category, improper for the third, and may or may not be appropriate for the second.[4] An Internet communication is typically considered passive if people have to voluntarily access it to read the message, and active if it is sent to specific individuals.

In certain situations, even a single contact can satisfy the minimum-contacts requirement. | **Example #4**   A Texas resident, Davis, sent an unsolicited e-mail message to numerous Mississippi residents advertising a pornographic Web site. Davis falsified the "from" header in the e-mail so that it appeared that Internet Doorway had sent the mail. Internet Doorway filed a lawsuit against Davis in Mississippi claiming that its reputation and goodwill in the community had been harmed. The U.S. district court in Mississippi held that Davis's single e-mail to Mississippi residents satisfied the minimum-contacts requirement for jurisdiction. The court concluded that Davis, by sending the e-mail solicitation, should reasonably have expected that she could be "haled into court in a distant jurisdiction to answer for the ramifications."[5] | In the following case, the court considered whether jurisdiction could be exercised over defendants whose only contacts with the jurisdiction were through their Web site.

---

4. For a leading case on this issue, see *Zippo Manufacturing Co. v. Zippo Dot Com, Inc.*, 952 F.Supp. 1119 (W.D.Pa. 1997).
5. *Internet Doorway, Inc. v. Parks*, 138 F.Supp.2d 773 (S.D.Miss. 2001).

CASE 3.1   **Bird v. Parsons**

United States Court of Appeals,
Sixth Circuit, 2002.
289 F.3d 865.

financia.com. Dotster, Inc., a domain name registrar incorporated in Washington, operates its registry at **www.dotster.com**.[a] Dotster allows registrants who lack an

a. Dotster's registration process is in conjunction with the Domain Registration of Internet Assigned Names and Numbers, which is maintained by Network Solutions, Inc. (owned by VeriSign), and regulated by the Internet Corporation for Assigned Names and Numbers (ICANN). Dotster is an ICANN-accredited registrar.

BACKGROUND AND FACTS   Darrell Bird, a citizen of Ohio, has operated Financia, Inc., a national computer software business, since 1983. Financia, Inc., owns the domain name

Internet server to which a name can be assigned to park their names on Dotster's "Futurehome" page. Marshall Parsons registered the name efinancia.com on Dotster's site in 2000 and "parked" the name on the Futurehome page with the address **www.efinancia.com**. George DeCarlo and Steven Vincent, on behalf of Dotster, activated Parsons's site. The name efinancia.com was soon offered for sale at **www.afternic.com**, an auction site for the sale of domain names. Bird filed a suit against Dotster and others in a federal district court, alleging, in part, trademark infringement, copyright

infringement, and cybersquatting.**b** Dotster, DeCarlo, and Vincent (the "Dotster defendants") asked the court to dismiss the complaint against them for, among other reasons, lack of personal jurisdiction. The court dismissed the suit. Alleging that Dotster sold 4,666 registrations to Ohio residents, Bird appealed to the U.S. Court of Appeals for the Sixth Circuit.

b. *Cybersquatting* is registering another person's trademark as a domain name and offering it for sale. This is a violation of the Anticybersquatting Consumer Protection Act of 1999. Cybersquatting and trademark and copyright infringement will be discussed in more detail in Chapter 7.

IN THE WORDS OF THE COURT . . . *RONALD LEE GILMAN*, Circuit Judge.

* * * *

* * * [J]urisdiction over the Dotster defendants is permissible only if their contacts with Ohio satisfy [a] three-part test * * * :

First, the defendant must purposefully avail himself of the privilege of acting in the forum state [the state in which the lawsuit is initiated] or causing a consequence in the forum state. Second, the cause of action must arise from the defendant's activities there. Finally, the acts of the defendant or consequences caused by the defendant must have a substantial enough connection with the forum state to make the exercise of jurisdiction over the defendant reasonable.

* * * We conclude that by maintaining a website on which Ohio residents can register domain names and by allegedly accepting the business of 4,666 Ohio residents, the Dotster defendants have satisfied the *purposeful-availment requirement.* * * * [Emphasis added.]

The second requirement * * * involves an analysis of whether Bird's claims arise from the Dotster defendants' contacts with Ohio. * * *

The operative facts in the present case include Bird's allegation that the Dotster defendants committed copyright and trademark law violations by registering Parsons's domain name efinancia.com. Both the Dotster defendants' contacts with Ohio and Bird's claim of copyright and trademark violations stem from these defendants' operation of the Dotster website. As a result, the operative facts are at least marginally related to the alleged contacts between the Dotster defendants and Ohio. * * *

The final requirement * * * is that the exercise of jurisdiction be reasonable in light of the connection that allegedly exists between the Dotster defendants and Ohio. * * *

Although the Dotster defendants might face a burden in having to defend a lawsuit in Ohio, they cannot reasonably object to this burden given that Dotster has allegedly transacted business with 4,666 Ohio residents. Ohio has a legitimate interest in protecting the business interests of its citizens, *even though all of Bird's claims involve federal law.* Bird has an obvious interest in obtaining relief, and *Ohio might be the only forum where jurisdiction would exist over all of the defendants.* Although the state of Washington also has an interest in this dispute, because the claim involves its citizens, this interest does not override the other factors suggesting that personal jurisdiction in Ohio is reasonable. [Emphasis added.]

DECISION AND REMEDY The U.S. Court of Appeals for the Sixth Circuit concluded that the lower court erred in granting the Dotster defendants' motion to dismiss for lack of personal jurisdiction. Bird had established that the court's exercise of jurisdiction over the Dotster defendants was proper.

WHY IS THIS CASE IMPORTANT? *This case illustrates how defendants can be sued in states in which they may never have been physically present, provided they have had sufficient contact with that state's residents over the Internet.*

International Jurisdictional Issues   As noted in Chapter 1, because the Internet is international in scope, international jurisdictional issues understandably have come to the fore. What seems to be emerging in the world's courts is a standard that echoes the "minimum-contacts" requirement applied by the U.S. courts. Most courts are indicating that minimum contacts—doing business within the jurisdiction, for example—are enough to compel a defendant to appear and that a physical presence is not necessary. The effect of this standard is that a business firm must comply with the laws in any jurisdiction in which it targets customers for its products.

Venue

VENUE
The geographic district in which an action is tried and from which the jury is selected.

Jurisdiction has to do with whether a court has authority to hear a case involving specific persons, property, or subject matter. **Venue**[6] is concerned with the most appropriate location for a trial. Two state courts (or two federal courts) may have the authority to exercise jurisdiction over a case, but it may be more appropriate or convenient to hear the case in one court than in the other.

Basically, the concept of venue reflects the policy that a court trying a suit should be in the geographic neighborhood (usually the county) where the incident leading to the lawsuit occurred or where the parties involved in the lawsuit reside. Venue in a civil case typically is where the defendant resides, whereas venue in a criminal case is normally where the crime occurred. Pretrial publicity or other factors, though, may require a change of venue to another community, especially in criminal cases when the defendant's right to a fair and impartial jury has been impaired. **│Example #5**   A change of venue from Oklahoma City to Denver, Colorado, was ordered for the trials of Timothy McVeigh and Terry Nichols, who had been indicted in connection with the 1995 bombing of the Alfred P. Murrah Federal Building in Oklahoma City. (At trial, both McVeigh and Nichols were convicted. McVeigh received the death penalty and was put to death by lethal injection in early 2001. Nichols was sentenced to life imprisonment.)│

Standing to Sue

STANDING TO SUE
The requirement that an individual must have a sufficient stake in a controversy before he or she can bring a lawsuit. The plaintiff must demonstrate that he or she has been either injured or threatened with injury.

Before a person can bring a lawsuit before a court, the party must have **standing to sue,** or a sufficient "stake" in a matter to justify seeking relief through the court system. In other words, to have standing, a party must have a legally protected and tangible interest at stake in the litigation. The party bringing the lawsuit must have suffered a harm, or have been threatened by a harm, as a result of the action about which she or he has complained. At times, a person will have standing to sue on behalf of another person. **│Example #6** Suppose that a child suffered serious injuries as a result of a defectively manufactured toy. Because the child is a minor, a lawsuit could be brought on his or her behalf by another person, such as the child's parent or legal guardian.│

JUSTICIABLE CONTROVERSY
A controversy that is not hypothetical or academic but real and substantial; a requirement that must be satisfied before a court will hear a case.

Standing to sue also requires that the controversy at issue be a **justiciable**[7] **controversy**—a controversy that is real and substantial, as opposed to hypothetical or academic. **│Example #7**   In the above example, the child's parent could not sue the toy manufacturer merely on the ground that the toy was

---

6. Pronounced *ven*-yoo.
7. Pronounced jus-*tish*-uh-bul.

defective. The issue would become justiciable only if the child had actually been injured due to the defect in the toy as marketed. In other words, the parent normally could not ask the court to determine, for example, what damages might be obtained if the child had been injured, because this would be merely a hypothetical question.

THE STATE AND FEDERAL COURT SYSTEMS

As mentioned earlier in this chapter, each state has its own court system. Additionally, there is a system of federal courts. Although state court systems differ, Exhibit 3–2 illustrates the basic organizational structure characteristic of the court systems in many states. The exhibit also shows how the federal court system is structured. We turn now to an examination of these court systems, beginning with the state courts.

State Court Systems

Typically, a state court system will include several levels, or tiers, of courts. As indicated in Exhibit 3–2, state courts may include (1) trial courts of limited jurisdiction, (2) trial courts of general jurisdiction, (3) appellate courts, and (4) the state's highest court (often called the state supreme court). Generally, any person who is a party to a lawsuit has the opportunity to plead the case before a trial court and then, if he or she loses, before at least one level of appellate court. Finally, if a federal statute or federal constitutional issue is involved in the decision of the state supreme court, that decision may be further appealed to the United States Supreme Court.

Judges in the state court system are usually elected by the voters for a specified term. State judicial elections or appointments vary significantly, however, from state to state. For example, in Iowa the governor appoints judges, and then the general population decides whether to confirm their appointment in the next general election. The states usually specify the number of years that

EXHIBIT 3–2 FEDERAL COURTS AND STATE COURT SYSTEMS

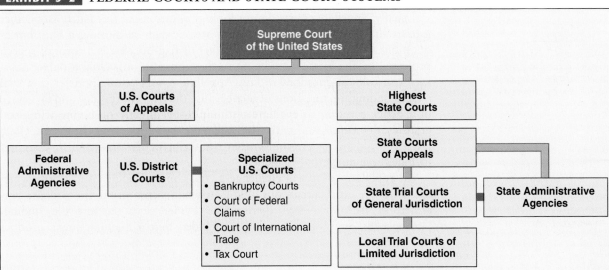

the judge will serve. In contrast, as you will read shortly, judges in the federal court system are appointed by the president of the United States and, if they are confirmed by the Senate, hold office for life—unless they engage in blatantly illegal conduct.

Trial Courts   Trial courts are exactly what their name implies—courts in which trials are held and testimony taken. State trial courts have either general or limited jurisdiction. Trial courts that have general jurisdiction as to subject matter may be called county, district, superior, or circuit courts.[8] The jurisdiction of these courts is often determined by the size of the county in which the court sits. State trial courts of general jurisdiction have jurisdiction over a wide variety of subjects, including both civil disputes and criminal prosecutions.

Some courts of limited jurisdiction are called special inferior trial courts or minor judiciary courts. **Small claims courts** are inferior trial courts that hear only civil cases involving claims of less than a certain amount, such as $5,000 (the amount varies from state to state). Suits brought in small claims courts are generally conducted informally, and lawyers are not required. In a minority of states, lawyers are not even allowed to represent people in small claims courts for most purposes. Another example of an inferior trial court is a local municipal court that hears mainly traffic cases. Decisions of small claims courts and municipal courts may sometimes be appealed to a state trial court of general jurisdiction.

Other courts of limited jurisdiction as to subject matter include domestic relations courts, which handle primarily divorce actions and child-custody disputes, and probate courts, as mentioned earlier.

Appellate, or Reviewing, Courts   Every state has at least one court of appeals (appellate court, or reviewing court), which may be an intermediate appellate court or the state's highest court. About three-fourths of the states have intermediate appellate courts. Generally, courts of appeals do not conduct new trials, in which evidence is submitted to the court and witnesses are examined. Rather, an appellate court panel of three or more judges reviews the record of the case on appeal, which includes a transcript of the trial proceedings, and determines whether the trial court committed an error.

Usually, appellate courts do not look at questions of *fact* (such as whether a party did, in fact, commit a certain action, such as burning a flag) but at questions of *law* (such as whether the act of flag-burning is a form of speech protected by the First Amendment to the Constitution). Only a judge, not a jury, can rule on questions of law. Appellate courts normally defer to a trial court's findings on questions of fact because the trial court judge and jury were in a better position to evaluate testimony—by directly observing witnesses' gestures, demeanor, and nonverbal behavior during the trial. At the appellate level, the judges review the written transcript of the trial, which does not include these nonverbal elements.

An appellate court will challenge a trial court's finding of fact only when the finding is clearly erroneous (that is, when it is contrary to the evidence presented at trial) or when there is no evidence to support the finding. **| Example #8**   Suppose that a jury concluded that a manufacturer's product

SMALL CLAIMS COURT
A special court in which parties may litigate small claims (such as those involving $5,000 or less). Attorneys are not required in small claims courts and, in some states, are not allowed to represent the parties.

---

8. The name in Ohio is court of common pleas; the name in New York is supreme court.

harmed the plaintiff but no evidence was submitted to the court to support that conclusion. In that situation, the appellate court would hold that the trial court's decision was erroneous. (The options exercised by appellate courts will be further discussed later in this chapter.)

Highest State Courts   The highest appellate court in a state is usually called the supreme court but may be called by some other name. For example, in both New York and Maryland, the highest state court is called the court of appeals. The decisions of each state's highest court are final on all questions of state law. Only when issues of federal law are involved can a decision made by a state's highest court be overruled by the United States Supreme Court.

The Federal Court System

The federal court system is basically a three-tiered model consisting of (1) U.S. district courts (trial courts of general jurisdiction) and various courts of limited jurisdiction, (2) U.S. courts of appeals (intermediate courts of appeals), and (3) the United States Supreme Court.

Unlike state court judges, who are usually elected, federal court judges—including the justices of the Supreme Court—are appointed by the president of the United States and confirmed by the U.S. Senate. All federal judges receive lifetime appointments (because under Article III they "hold their offices during Good Behavior").

U.S. District Courts   At the federal level, the equivalent of a state trial court of general jurisdiction is the district court. There is at least one federal district court in every state. The number of judicial districts can vary over time, primarily owing to population changes and corresponding caseloads. Currently, there are ninety-four federal judicial districts.

U.S. district courts have original jurisdiction in federal matters. Federal cases typically originate in district courts. There are other courts with original, but special (or limited) jurisdiction, such as the federal bankruptcy courts and others shown in Exhibit 3–2 on page 73.

U.S. Courts of Appeals   In the federal court system, there are thirteen U.S. courts of appeals—also referred to as U.S. circuit courts of appeals. The federal courts of appeals for twelve of the circuits, including the U.S. Court of Appeals for the District of Columbia Circuit, hear appeals from the federal district courts located within their respective judicial circuits. The Court of Appeals for the Thirteenth Circuit, called the Federal Circuit, has national appellate jurisdiction over certain types of cases, such as cases involving patent law and cases in which the U.S. government is a defendant.

The decisions of the circuit courts of appeals are final in most cases, but appeal to the United States Supreme Court is possible. Exhibit 3–3 on the following page shows the geographic boundaries of the U.S. circuit courts of appeals and the boundaries of the U.S. district courts within each circuit.

The United States Supreme Court   The highest level of the three-tiered model of the federal court system is the United States Supreme Court. According to the language of Article III of the U.S. Constitution, there is only one national Supreme Court. All other courts in the federal system are considered "inferior."

A mother talks with a social worker after a court awarded the mother custody of her child. Are child-custody matters decided by federal or state courts? (*Albuquerque Journal*, Mark Holm/AP Photo)

BE CAREFUL   The decisions of a state's highest court are final on questions of state law.

EXHIBIT 3-3 BOUNDARIES OF THE U.S. COURTS OF APPEALS AND U.S. DISTRICT COURTS

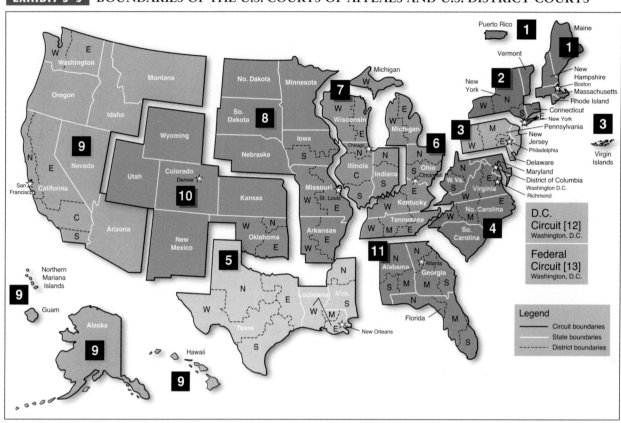

Source: Administrative Office of the United States Courts.

Congress is empowered to create other inferior courts as it deems necessary. The inferior courts that Congress has created include the second tier in our model—the U.S. courts of appeals—as well as the district courts and any other courts of limited, or specialized, jurisdiction.

The United States Supreme Court consists of nine justices. Although the Supreme Court has original, or trial, jurisdiction in rare instances (set forth in Article III, Section 2), most of its work is as an appeals court. The Supreme Court can review any case decided by any of the federal courts of appeals, and it also has appellate authority over some cases decided in the state courts.

Appeals to the Supreme Court. To bring a case before the Supreme Court, a party requests the Court to issue a writ of *certiorari*. A **writ of *certiorari***[9] is an order issued by the Supreme Court to a lower court requiring the latter to send it the record of the case for review. The Court will not issue a writ unless at least four of the nine justices approve of it. This is called the **rule of four.** Whether the Court will issue a writ of *certiorari* is entirely within its discretion. The Court is not required to issue one, and most petitions for writs are denied. (Thousands of cases are filed with the Supreme Court each year; yet it

WRIT OF *CERTIORARI*
A written order from a higher court asking the lower court for the record of a case.

RULE OF FOUR
A rule of the United States Supreme Court under which the Court will not issue a writ of *certiorari* unless at least four justices approve of the decision to issue the writ.

9. Pronounced sur-shee-uh-*rah*-ree.

hears, on average, fewer than one hundred of these cases.)[10] A denial is not a decision on the merits of a case, nor does it indicate agreement with the lower court's opinion. Furthermore, a denial of the writ has no value as a precedent.

Petitions Granted by the Court. Typically, the Court grants petitions when cases raise important constitutional questions or when the lower courts are issuing conflicting decisions on a significant issue. Similarly, if federal appellate courts are rendering inconsistent opinions on an important issue, the Supreme Court may review the case and issue a decision to define the law on the matter. The justices, however, never explain their reasons for hearing certain cases and not others, so it is difficult to predict which type of case the Court might select.

FOLLOWING A STATE COURT CASE

To illustrate the procedures that would be followed in a civil lawsuit brought in a state court, we present a hypothetical case and follow it through the state court system. The case involves an automobile accident in which Kevin Anderson, driving a Mercedes, struck Lisa Marconi, driving a Ford Taurus. The accident occurred at the intersection of Wilshire Boulevard and Rodeo Drive in Beverly Hills, California. Marconi suffered personal injuries, incurring medical and hospital expenses as well as lost wages for four months. Anderson and Marconi are unable to agree on a settlement, and Marconi sues Anderson. Marconi is the plaintiff, and Anderson is the defendant. Both are represented by lawyers.

During each phase of the **litigation** (the process of working a lawsuit through the court system), Marconi and Anderson will be required to observe strict procedural requirements. A large body of law—procedural law—establishes the rules and standards for determining disputes in courts. Procedural rules are very complex, and they vary from court to court and from state to state. There is a set of federal rules of procedure as well as various sets of rules for state courts. Additionally, the applicable procedures will depend on whether the case is a civil or criminal proceeding. Generally, the Marconi-Anderson civil lawsuit will involve the procedures discussed in the following subsections. Keep in mind that attempts to settle the case may be ongoing throughout the trial.

LITIGATION
The process of resolving a dispute through the court system.

The Pleadings

The complaint and answer (and the counterclaim and reply)—all of which are discussed below—taken together are called the **pleadings**. The pleadings inform each party of the other's claims and specify the issues (disputed questions) involved in the case. Because the rules of procedure vary depending on the jurisdiction of the court, the style and form of the pleadings may look quite different in different states.

PLEADINGS
Statements made by the plaintiff and the defendant in a lawsuit that detail the facts, charges, and defenses involved in the litigation. The complaint and answer are part of the pleadings.

The Plaintiff's Complaint Marconi's suit against Anderson commences when her lawyer files a **complaint** with the appropriate court. The complaint

COMPLAINT
The pleading made by a plaintiff alleging wrongdoing on the part of the defendant; the document that, when filed with a court, initiates a lawsuit.

---

10. From the mid-1950s through the early 1990s, the Supreme Court reviewed more cases per year than it has in the last few years. In the Court's 1982–1983 term, for example, the Court issued opinions in 151 cases. In contrast, in its 2005–2006 term, the Court issued opinions in only 87 cases.

contains a statement alleging (asserting to the court, in a pleading) the facts necessary for the court to take jurisdiction, a brief summary of the facts necessary to show that the plaintiff is entitled to a remedy, and a statement of the remedy the plaintiff is seeking. Exhibit 3–4 illustrates how the complaint might read in the Marconi-Anderson case. Complaints may be lengthy or brief, depending on the complexity of the case and the rules of the jurisdiction.

EXHIBIT 3-4   **EXAMPLE OF A TYPICAL COMPLAINT**

IN THE LOS ANGELES SUPERIOR COURT
COUNTY OF LOS ANGELES, STATE OF CALIFORNIA

Lisa Marconi
 	
        Plaintiff,
 	
        v.
 	
Kevin Anderson
 	
        Defendant.
	CIVIL NO. 8–1026
	
	COMPLAINT

Comes now the plaintiff and for her cause of action against the defendant alleges and states as follows:

1. The jurisdiction of this court is based on Section 86 of the California Civil Code.
2. This action is between plaintiff, a California resident living at 1434 Palm Drive, Anaheim, California, and defendant, a California resident living at 6950 Garrison Avenue, Los Angeles, California.
3. On September 10, 2007, plaintiff, Lisa Marconi, was exercising good driving habits and reasonable care in driving her car through the intersection of Rodeo Drive and Wilshire Boulevard when defendant, Kevin Anderson, negligently drove his vehicle through a red light at the intersection and collided with plaintiff's vehicle. Defendant was negligent in the operation of the vehicle as to:

   a. Speed,
   b. Lookout,
   c. Management and control.

4. As a result of the collision, plaintiff suffered severe physical injury that prevented her from working and property damage to her car. The costs she incurred included $10,000 in medical bills, $9,000 in lost wages, and $5,000 for automobile repairs.

WHEREFORE, plaintiff demands judgment against the defendant for the sum of $24,000 plus interest at the maximum legal rate and the costs of this action.

By *Roger Harrington*

Roger Harrington
Attorney for the Plaintiff
800 Orange Avenue
Anaheim, CA 91426

After the complaint has been filed, the sheriff, a deputy of the county, or another *process server* (one who delivers a complaint and summons) serves a **summons** and a copy of the complaint on defendant Anderson. The summons notifies Anderson that he must file an answer to the complaint with both the court and the plaintiff's attorney within a specified time period (usually twenty to thirty days). The summons also informs Anderson that failure to answer may result in a **default judgment** for the plaintiff, meaning the plaintiff will be awarded the damages alleged in her complaint.

The Defendant's Answer   The defendant's **answer** either admits the statements or allegations set forth in the complaint or denies them and outlines any defenses that the defendant may have. If Anderson admits to all of Marconi's allegations in his answer, the court will enter a judgment for Marconi. If Anderson denies any of Marconi's allegations, the litigation will go forward.

Anderson can deny Marconi's allegations and set forth his own claim that Marconi was in fact negligent and therefore owes him for the damage to his Mercedes. This is appropriately called a **counterclaim.** If Anderson files a counterclaim, Marconi will have to answer it with a pleading, normally called a **reply,** which has the same characteristics as an answer.

Anderson can also admit the truth of Marconi's complaint but raise new facts that may result in dismissal of the action. This is called *raising an affirmative defense.* For example, Anderson could assert the expiration of the time period under the relevant statute of limitations (a state or federal statute that sets the maximum time period during which a certain action can be brought or rights enforced) as an affirmative defense.

Motion to Dismiss   A **motion to dismiss** requests the court to dismiss the case for stated reasons. A defendant often makes a motion to dismiss before filing an answer to the plaintiff's complaint. Grounds for dismissal of a case include improper delivery of the complaint and summons, improper venue, and the plaintiff's failure to state a claim for which a court could grant relief (a remedy). For example, if Marconi had suffered no injuries or losses as a result of Anderson's negligence, Anderson could move to have the case dismissed because Marconi had not stated a claim for which relief could be granted.

If the judge grants the motion to dismiss, the plaintiff generally is given time to file an amended complaint. If the judge denies the motion, the suit will go forward, and the defendant must then file an answer. Note that if Marconi wishes to discontinue the suit because, for example, an out-of-court settlement has been reached, she can likewise move for dismissal. The court can also dismiss the case on its own motion.

Pretrial Motions

Either party may attempt to get the case dismissed before trial through the use of various pretrial motions. We have already mentioned the motion to dismiss. Two other important pretrial motions are the *motion for judgment on the pleadings* and the *motion for summary judgment.*

At the close of the pleadings, either party may make a **motion for judgment on the pleadings,** or on the merits of the case. The judge will grant the motion only when there is no dispute over the facts of the case and the sole issue to be resolved is a question of law. In deciding on the motion, the judge may consider only the evidence contained in the pleadings.

SUMMONS
A document informing a defendant that a legal action has been commenced against him or her and that the defendant must appear in court on a certain date to answer the plaintiff's complaint. The document is delivered by a sheriff or any other person so authorized.

DEFAULT JUDGMENT
A judgment entered by a court against a defendant who has failed to appear in court to answer or defend against the plaintiff's claim.

ANSWER
Procedurally, a defendant's response to the plaintiff's complaint.

COUNTERCLAIM
A claim made by a defendant in a civil lawsuit against the plaintiff. In effect, the defendant is suing the plaintiff.

REPLY
Procedurally, a plaintiff's response to a defendant's answer.

MOTION TO DISMISS
A pleading in which a defendant asserts that the plaintiff's claim fails to state a cause of action (that is, has no basis in law) or that there are other grounds on which a suit should be dismissed.

MOTION FOR JUDGMENT ON THE PLEADINGS
A motion by either party to a lawsuit at the close of the pleadings requesting the court to decide the issue solely on the pleadings without proceeding to trial. The motion will be granted only if no facts are in dispute.

In contrast, in a **motion for summary judgment** the court may consider evidence outside the pleadings, such as sworn statements (affidavits) by parties or witnesses or other documents relating to the case. A motion for summary judgment can be made by either party. As with the motion for judgment on the pleadings, a motion for summary judgment will be granted only if there are no genuine questions of fact and the sole question is a question of law.

Discovery

Before a trial begins, each party can use a number of procedural devices to obtain information and gather evidence about the case from the other party or from third parties. The process of obtaining such information is known as **discovery.** Discovery includes gaining access to witnesses, documents, records, and other types of evidence.

The Federal Rules of Civil Procedure and similar rules in the states set forth the guidelines for discovery activity. The rules governing discovery are designed to make sure that a witness or a party is not unduly harassed, that privileged material (communications that need not be presented in court) is safeguarded, and that only matters relevant to the case at hand are discoverable.

Discovery prevents surprises at trial by giving parties access to evidence that might otherwise be hidden. This allows both parties to learn as much as they can about what to expect at a trial before they reach the courtroom. It also serves to narrow the issues so that trial time is spent on the main questions in the case.

Depositions and Interrogatories   Discovery can involve the use of depositions or interrogatories, or both. A **deposition** is the sworn testimony of a party to the lawsuit or any witness that is taken out of court. The person being deposed (the deponent) answers questions asked by the attorneys, and the questions and answers are recorded by an authorized court official and sworn to and signed by the deponent. (Occasionally, written depositions are taken when witnesses are unable to appear in person.) The answers given to depositions will, of course, help the attorneys prepare their cases. They can also be used in court to impeach (challenge the credibility of) a party or a witness who changes testimony at the trial. In addition, the answers given in a deposition can be used as testimony if the witness is not available at trial.

Interrogatories are written questions for which written answers are prepared and then signed under oath. The main difference between interrogatories and written depositions is that interrogatories are directed to a party to the lawsuit (the plaintiff or the defendant), not to a witness, and the party can prepare answers with the aid of an attorney. The scope of interrogatories is broader because parties are obligated to answer questions, even if that means disclosing information from their records and files.

Other Information   A party can serve a written request on the other party for an admission of the truth of matters relating to the trial. Any matter admitted under such a request is conclusively established for the trial. For example, Marconi can ask Anderson to admit that he was driving at a speed of forty-five miles an hour. A request for admission saves time at trial because the parties will not have to spend time proving facts on which they already agree.

A party can also gain access to documents and other items not in her or his possession in order to inspect and examine them. Likewise, a party can gain "entry upon land" to inspect the premises. Anderson's attorney, for example, normally can gain permission to inspect and duplicate Marconi's car repair bills.

When the physical or mental condition of one party is in question, the opposing party can ask the court to order a physical or mental examination. If the court is willing to make the order, which it will do only if the need for the information outweighs the right to privacy of the person to be examined, the opposing party can obtain the results of the examination.

Electronic Discovery Any relevant material, including information stored electronically, can be the object of a discovery request. Electronic evidence, or **e-evidence**, consists of all types of computer-generated or electronically recorded information, including e-mail, voice mail, spreadsheets, word-processing documents, and other data. E-evidence is important because it can reveal significant facts that are not discoverable by other means. For example, whenever a person is working on a computer, information is being recorded on the hard drive disk without ever being saved by the user. This information includes the file's location, path, creator, date created, date last accessed, concealed notes, earlier versions, passwords, and formatting. It reveals information about how, when, and by whom a document was created, accessed, modified, and transmitted. This information can be obtained from the file only in its electronic format—not from printed-out versions.

E-EVIDENCE
A type of evidence that consists of computer-generated or electronically recorded information, including e-mail, voice mail, spreadsheets, word-processing documents, and other data.

The federal rules and most state rules (as well as court decisions) now specifically allow parties to obtain discovery of electronic "data compilations" (or e-evidence). Although traditional means, such as interrogatories and depositions, may still be used to find out about the e-evidence, the parties must usually hire an expert to retrieve the evidence in its electronic format. Using special software, the expert can reconstruct e-mail exchanges to establish who knew what and when they knew it. The expert can even recover from a computer files that the user thought had been deleted. Reviewing back-up copies of documents and e-mail can provide useful—and often quite damaging—information about how a particular matter progressed over several weeks or months.

Although electronic discovery has significant advantages over paper discovery, it is also time consuming and expensive. Who should pay the costs associated with electronic discovery? This chapter's *Online Developments* feature discusses how the law is evolving to address this issue on the next page.

Pretrial Conference

Either party or the court can request a pretrial conference, or hearing. Usually, the hearing consists of an informal discussion between the judge and the opposing attorneys after discovery has taken place. The purpose of the hearing is to explore the possibility of a settlement without trial and, if this is not possible, to identify the matters that are in dispute and to plan the course of the trial.

Jury Selection

A trial can be held with or without a jury. The Seventh Amendment to the U.S. Constitution guarantees the right to a jury trial for cases in federal courts when the amount in controversy exceeds $20. Most states have similar guarantees in their own constitutions (although the threshold dollar amount is

Who Bears the Costs of Electronic Discovery?

Traditionally, the party responding to a discovery request must pay the expenses involved in obtaining the requested materials. If compliance would be too burdensome or too costly, however, the judge can either limit the scope of the request or shift some or all of the costs to the requesting party. How do these traditional rules governing discovery apply to requests for electronic evidence?

Why Courts Might Shift the Costs of Electronic Discovery

Electronic discovery has dramatically increased the costs associated with complying with discovery requests. It is no longer simply a matter of photocopying paper documents. Now the responding party may need to hire computer forensics experts to make "image" copies of desktop, laptop, and server hard drives, as well as removable storage media (including CD-ROMs and DVDs), back-up tapes, voice mail, cell phones, and any other device that digitally stores data.

In cases involving multiple parties or large corporations with many offices and employees, the electronic discovery process can easily run into hundreds of thousands—if not millions—of dollars. For example, in one case concert promoters alleged that thirty separate defendant companies had engaged in discriminatory practices. The federal district court hearing the case found that the complete restoration of the back-up tapes of just one of those defendants would cost $9.75 million. Acquiring 200,000 e-mail messages from another defendant would cost between $43,000 and $84,000, with an additional $247,000 to have an attorney review the retrieved documents. Restoring the 523 back-up tapes of a third defendant would cost $395,000 plus another $120,000 for the attorney to review them. The judge hearing the case decided that both plaintiffs and defendants would share in these discovery costs.[a]

What Factors Do Courts Consider in Deciding Whether to Shift Costs?

Increasingly, the courts are shifting part of the costs of obtaining electronic discovery to the party requesting it (which is usually the plaintiff). At what point, however, should this cost-shifting occur? In *Zubulake v. UBS Warburg LLC,*[b] the court identified a three-step analysis for deciding disputes over discovery costs. First, if the data are kept in an accessible format, the usual rules of discovery apply: the responding party should pay the costs of producing responsive data. A court should consider cost-shifting only when electronic data are in a relatively inaccessible form, such as in back-up tapes or deleted files. Second, the court should determine what data may be found on the comparatively inaccessible media. Requiring the responding party to restore and produce responsive documents from a small sample of the requested medium is a sensible approach in most cases. Third, the court should consider a series of other factors, including, for example, the availability of the information from other sources, the total cost of production compared with the amount in controversy, and each party's ability to pay these costs.

For Critical Analysis   *The court in the* Zubulake *case noted that "as large companies increasingly move to entirely paper-free environments, the frequent use of cost-shifting will have the effect of crippling discovery," especially in cases in which private parties are suing large corporations. Why might cost-shifting thwart discovery? Who would benefit if courts considered cost-shifting in every case involving electronic discovery?*

a. *Rowe Entertainment, Inc. v. William Morris Agency,* 2002 WL 975713 (S.D.N.Y.).

b. 2003 WL 21087884 (S.D.N.Y.).

VOIR DIRE
An old French phrase meaning "to speak the truth." In legal language, the phrase refers to the process in which the attorneys question prospective jurors to learn about their backgrounds, attitudes, biases, and other characteristics that may affect their ability to serve as impartial jurors.

higher than $20). The right to a trial by jury need not be exercised, and many cases are tried without a jury. In most states and in federal courts, one of the parties must request a jury, or the right is presumed to be waived.

Before a jury trial commences, a jury must be selected. The jury selection process is known as **voir dire.**[11] During *voir dire* in most jurisdictions, attorneys for the plaintiff and the defendant ask prospective jurors oral questions

---

11. Pronounced vwahr *deehr.*

to determine whether a potential jury member is biased or has any connection with a party to the action or with a prospective witness. In some jurisdictions, the judge may do all or part of the questioning based on written questions submitted by counsel for the parties.

During *voir dire,* a party may challenge a certain number of prospective jurors peremptorily—that is, ask that an individual not be sworn in as a juror without providing any reason. Alternatively, a party may challenge a prospective juror *for cause*—that is, provide a reason why an individual should not be sworn in as a juror. If the judge grants the challenge, the individual is asked to step down. A prospective juror may not be excluded from the jury by the use of discriminatory challenges, however, such as those based on racial criteria[12] or gender.[13]

> **TAKE NOTE** A prospective juror cannot be excluded solely on the basis of his or her race or gender.

At the Trial

At the beginning of the trial, the attorneys present their opening arguments, setting forth the facts that they expect to provide during the trial. Then the plaintiff's case is presented. In our hypothetical case, Marconi's lawyer would introduce evidence (relevant documents, exhibits, and the testimony of witnesses) to support Marconi's position. The defendant has the opportunity to challenge any evidence introduced and to cross-examine any of the plaintiff's witnesses.

At the end of the plaintiff's case, the defendant's attorney has the opportunity to ask the judge to direct a verdict for the defendant on the ground that the plaintiff has presented no evidence that would justify the granting of the plaintiff's remedy. This is called a **motion for a directed verdict** (known in federal courts as a *motion for judgment as a matter of law*). If the motion is not granted (it seldom is), the defendant's attorney then presents the evidence and witnesses for the defendant's case. At the conclusion of the defendant's case, the defendant's attorney has another opportunity to make a motion for a directed verdict. The plaintiff's attorney can challenge any evidence introduced and cross-examine the defendant's witnesses.

MOTION FOR A DIRECTED VERDICT
In a jury trial, a motion for the judge to take the decision out of the hands of the jury and to direct a verdict for the party who filed the motion on the ground that the other party has not produced sufficient evidence to support her or his claim.

After the defense concludes its presentation, the attorneys present their closing arguments, each urging a verdict in favor of her or his client. The judge instructs the jury in the law that applies to the case (these instructions are often called *charges*), and the jury retires to the jury room to deliberate a verdict. In the Marconi-Anderson case, the jury will not only decide for the plaintiff or for the defendant but, if it finds for the plaintiff, will also decide on the amount of the **award** (the amount to be paid to her).

AWARD
In litigation, the amount awarded to a plaintiff in a civil lawsuit as damages. In the context of alternative dispute resolution, the decision rendered by an arbitrator.

Posttrial Motions

After the jury has rendered its verdict, either party may make a posttrial motion. If Marconi wins, and Anderson's attorney has previously moved for a directed verdict, Anderson's attorney may make a **motion for judgment *n.o.v.*** (from the Latin *non obstante veredicto,* which means "notwithstanding the

MOTION FOR JUDGMENT *N.O.V.*
A motion requesting the court to grant judgment in favor of the party making the motion on the ground that the jury's verdict against him or her was unreasonable and erroneous.

---

12. *Batson v. Kentucky,* 476 U.S. 79, 106 S.Ct. 1712, 90 L.Ed.2d 69 (1986).
13. *J.E.B. v. Alabama ex rel. T.B.,* 511 U.S. 127, 114 S.Ct. 1419, 128 L.Ed.2d 89 (1994). (*Ex rel.* is Latin for *ex relatione.* The phrase refers to an action brought on behalf of the state, by the attorney general, at the instigation of an individual who has a private interest in the matter.)

verdict"—called a *motion for judgment as a matter of law* in the federal courts) in Anderson's favor on the ground that the jury's verdict in favor of Marconi was unreasonable and erroneous. If the judge decides that the jury's verdict was reasonable in light of the evidence presented at trial, the motion will be denied. If the judge agrees with Anderson's attorney, then he or she will set the jury's verdict aside and enter a judgment in favor of Anderson.

Alternatively, Anderson could make a **motion for a new trial,** requesting the judge to set aside the adverse verdict and to hold a new trial. The motion will be granted if the judge is convinced, after looking at all the evidence, that the jury was in error but does not feel it is appropriate to grant judgment for the other side. A new trial may also be granted on the ground of newly discovered evidence, misconduct by the participants or the jury during the trial, or error by the judge.

MOTION FOR A NEW TRIAL
A motion asserting that the trial was so fundamentally flawed (because of error, newly discovered evidence, prejudice, or other reason) that a new trial is necessary to prevent a miscarriage of justice.

The Appeal

Assume here that any posttrial motion is denied and that Anderson appeals the case. (If Marconi wins but receives a smaller monetary award than she sought, she can appeal as well.) A notice of appeal must be filed with the clerk of the trial court within a prescribed time. Anderson now becomes the appellant, or petitioner, and Marconi becomes the appellee, or respondent.

Filing the Appeal   Anderson's attorney files with the appellate court the record on appeal, which includes the pleadings, the trial transcript, the judge's rulings on motions made by the parties, and other trial-related documents. Anderson's attorney will also provide a condensation of the record, known as an *abstract,* which is filed with the reviewing court along with the brief. The **brief** is a formal legal document outlining the facts and issues of the case, the judge's rulings or jury's findings that should be reversed or modified, the applicable law, and arguments on Anderson's behalf (citing applicable statutes and relevant cases as precedents).

BRIEF
A formal legal document submitted by the attorney for the appellant or the appellee (in answer to the appellant's brief) to an appellate court when a case is appealed. The appellant's brief outlines the facts and issues of the case, the judge's rulings or jury's findings that should be reversed or modified, the applicable law, and the arguments on the client's behalf.

Marconi's attorney will file an answering brief. Anderson's attorney can file a reply to Marconi's brief, although it is not required. The reviewing court then considers the case.

Appellate Review   As mentioned earlier, a court of appeals does not hear evidence. Rather, it reviews the record for errors of law. Its decision concerning a case is based on the record on appeal, the abstracts, and the attorneys' briefs. The attorneys can present oral arguments, after which the case is taken under advisement. In general, appellate courts do not reverse findings of fact unless the findings are unsupported or contradicted by the evidence.

If the reviewing court believes that an error was committed during the trial or that the jury was improperly instructed, the judgment will be *reversed.* Sometimes the case will be *remanded* (sent back to the court that originally heard the case) for a new trial. Even when a case is remanded to a trial court for further proceedings, however, the appellate court normally spells out how the relevant law should be interpreted and applied to the case.

| **Example #9**   A case may be remanded for several reasons. For instance, if the appellate court decides that a judge improperly granted summary judgment, the case will be remanded for a trial. If the appellate court decides that the trial judge erroneously applied the law, the case will be remanded for a new

trial, with instructions to the trial court to apply the law as clarified by the appellate court. If the appellate court decides that the trial jury's award of damages was too high, the case will be remanded with instructions to reduce the damages award.| In most cases, the judgment of the lower court is *affirmed,* resulting in the enforcement of the court's judgment or decree.

Appeal to a Higher Appellate Court   If the reviewing court is an intermediate appellate court, the losing party normally may appeal to the state supreme court (the highest state court). Such a petition corresponds to a petition for a writ of *certiorari* from the United States Supreme Court. If the petition is granted (in some states, a petition is automatically granted), new briefs must be filed before the state supreme court, and the attorneys may be allowed or requested to present oral arguments. Like the intermediate appellate court, the supreme court may reverse or affirm the appellate court's decision or remand the case. At this point, unless a federal question is at issue, the case has reached its end.

Enforcing the Judgment

The uncertainties of the litigation process are compounded by the lack of guarantees that any judgment will be enforceable. Even if a plaintiff wins an award of damages in court, the defendant may not have sufficient assets or insurance to cover that amount. Usually, one of the factors considered before a lawsuit is initiated is whether the defendant has sufficient assets to cover the amount of damages sought, should the plaintiff win the case; additional considerations are the time involved and the expenses of litigation.

THE COURTS ADAPT TO THE ONLINE WORLD

We have already mentioned that the courts have attempted to adapt traditional jurisdictional concepts to the online world. Not surprisingly, the Internet has also brought about changes in court procedures and practices, including new methods for filing pleadings and other documents and issuing decisions and opinions. Several courts are experimenting with electronic delivery, such as via the Internet or CD-ROM. Some jurisdictions are exploring the possibility of cyber courts, in which legal proceedings could be conducted totally online.

Electronic Filing

The federal court system first experimented with an electronic filing system in January 1996, in an asbestos case heard by the U.S. District Court for the Northern District of Ohio. Today, most federal courts permit attorneys to file documents electronically in certain types of cases. At last count, more than 200,000 attorneys and others have filed documents electronically in federal courts. The Administrative Office of the U.S. Courts is considering permitting electronic filing in all U.S. district courts nationwide.

State and local courts are also setting up electronic filing systems. Since the late 1990s, the court system in Pima County, Arizona, has been accepting pleadings via e-mail. The supreme court of the state of Washington also now accepts online filings of litigation documents. In addition, electronic filing projects are being developed in other states, including California, Delaware, Georgia, Kansas, Maryland, Michigan, New Hampshire, New Jersey, New Mexico,

New York, North Carolina, Ohio, Pennsylvania, Texas, Utah, and Virginia. The state of Colorado implemented the first statewide court e-filing system and allows e-filing in over sixty courts. Generally, when electronic filing is made available, it is optional, but a trial court judge in the District of Columbia launched a pilot project that *required* attorneys to use electronic filing in certain types of cases.

The expenses associated with an appeal can be considerable, and e-filing can add substantially to the cost. In some cases, appellants who successfully appeal a judgment are entitled to be awarded their costs, including an amount for printing the copies of the record on appeal and the briefs. In the following case, the appellants spent $16,112 for the paper copies and an additional $16,065 to prepare and submit briefs and other documents in an electronic format. Should the appellants be reimbursed for these expenses?

CASE 3.2	Phansalkar v. Andersen, Weinroth & Co.

United States Court of Appeals,
Second Circuit, 2004.
356 F.3d 188.

BACKGROUND AND FACTS Andersen, Weinroth & Company (AW) is a small firm that finds and creates investment opportunities for itself, its partners, and other investors. AW's income includes returns on its investments, fees paid by its investors, and the compensation and other benefits earned by its employees for their service on boards of directors of the companies with which AW does business. Some AW employees receive stock and "investment opportunities" rather than salaries. Rohit Phansalkar worked for AW from February 1998 until June 2000, when he became the chairman and chief executive officer of Osicom Technologies, Inc. After Phansalkar left, AW refused to pay him the returns on certain "investment opportunities" that he had been given while at AW. Phansalkar filed a suit in a federal district court against AW, alleging in part breach of contract. The court awarded Phansalkar more than $4.4 million. AW appealed to the U.S. Court of Appeals for the Second Circuit, which reversed this judgment on the ground that Phansalkar had acted with disloyalty during his employment with AW by failing to disclose compensation and benefits that he received for serving on various boards. AW then asked for an award of the amount that it spent to create copies of the briefs and other documents involved in the appeal in hyperlinked CD-ROM format.

IN THE WORDS OF THE COURT . . . *PER CURIAM:* [By the whole court]

*   *   *   *

On September 16, 2003, this Court reversed a judgment of approximately $4.4 million entered by the U.S. District Court for the Southern District of New York in favor of Phansalkar. On September 29, 2003, the AW parties submitted an itemized bill of costs. As appellants who have won a reversal, they are clearly entitled to costs for the docketing [filing] of the appeal and for printing the "necessary" copies of the regular and special appendices of appellants' main brief and reply brief, an amount totaling $16,112. That entitlement is supported by Rule 39 [of the *Federal Rules of Appellate Procedure* and] by this Court's Local Instructions for Bill of Costs * * * . In addition, the AW parties seek $16,065 in costs associated with preparing and submitting companion appendices and briefs in hyperlinked CD-ROM format.

The AW parties and Phansalkar vigorously dispute whether an agreement was ever reached over how these CD-ROM costs would be allocated between them following this appeal. There is no dispute, however, that if such an agreement was reached, it was never committed to writing * * * . The issue raised by the parties, which this Court has not yet decided, is whether Rule 39 and the rules of this Court contemplate [an award] of the costs of preparing such electronic submissions.

*   *   *

CASE 3.2–CONTINUED

Under Rule 25(a)(2)(D) of the *Federal Rules of Appellate Procedure,*

[a] court of appeals may by local rule permit papers to be filed, signed, or verified by electronic means that are consistent with technical standards, if any, that the Judicial Conference of the United States establishes.

This Court was among the first [federal courts of appeals] to promulgate [publicly establish] such a local rule, by * * * order on October 17, 1997. That order was supplemented on January 30, 1998 with * * * Order 98-2 * * * , which states that the submission of electronic format briefs is "allowed and encouraged" as long as "[a]ll parties have consented * * * or a motion to file has been granted." Several other [federal courts of appeals] have adopted local rules that permit or even require the filing of electronic briefs, usually on companion disks. The submission of an electronic version of a paper brief very likely entails small incremental costs.

CD-ROM submissions that hyperlink briefs to relevant sections of the appellate record are more versatile, more useful, and considerably more expensive. Our January 30, 1998, order allows and encourages the use of such "interactive CD-ROM" formats. The [U.S. Court of Appeals for the] Federal Circuit also allows CD-ROM briefs to be filed with the prior consent of both the court and the opposing party. To date, only the [U.S. Court of Appeals for the] First Circuit appears to have adopted formally a local rule that applies to submission of hyperlinked CD-ROM briefs. Such submissions can assist judicial review and are welcomed, but they are not necessarily [part of an award] as costs.

We have found no local rule or holding from another circuit that allocates CD-ROM costs. No guidance can be found in the relevant text of Rule 39, which authorizes [an award] of costs incurred to produce "necessary" copies of briefs, appendices, and portions of the record relevant to an appeal and a variety of other costs of appeal, such as filing fees. * * * [I]n the absence of a specific textual reference in Rule 39, an expense can be an allowable cost of appeal when it is analogous to one of the costs specifically authorized by Rule 39(e). Citing this test, and our administrative orders encouraging the use of CD-ROMs, the AW parties argue that CD-ROM expenses are allowable costs under Rule 39.

However, * * * several other factors * * * are also important in determining if a cost is authorized by Rule 39: *whether the party seeking disallowance has clearly consented to the expense; whether a court has previously approved the expense; and whether the alternative arrangement costs less than the expense specifically authorized by the Rule.* None of these factors assists the AW parties. In particular, it appears that a substantial portion of the costs were duplicative. Since the AW parties incurred costs both to produce hard copies of their appellate materials *and* to produce hyperlinked CD-ROM copies, Rule 25(a)(2)(D) suggests that the CD-ROM costs in this case were duplicative rather than an analog of hard copy production costs. [Awarding] the CD-ROM costs under such circumstances is inconsistent with our past applications of Rule 39. [Emphasis added.]

Finally, it is decisive that there is no written stipulation or understanding between the parties concerning the allocation of the incremental costs of this useful technology.

DECISION AND REMEDY The U.S. Court of Appeals for the Second Circuit ruled that AW could not recover the costs associated with preparing and submitting electronic copies of the appeal documents. No rule or court decision allocated CD-ROM costs, and in this case, there was no agreement between the parties to allocate the costs and no other relevant factors.

FOR CRITICAL ANALYSIS–Social Consideration *How might the result in this case have been different if the court had required, rather than merely encouraged, the submission of electronic copies of the appeal documents?*

Courts Online

Most courts today have their own Web sites. Of course, each court decides what to make available at its site. Some courts display only the names of court personnel and office phone numbers. Others add court rules and forms. Many include judicial decisions, although generally the sites do not feature archives of old decisions. Instead, decisions are usually available online only for a limited time. For example, California keeps opinions online for only sixty days. In addition, in some states, such as California and Florida, court clerks offer docket information and other searchable databases online.

Appellate court decisions are often posted online immediately after they are rendered. Recent decisions of the U.S. courts of appeals, for example, are available online at their Web sites. The United States Supreme Court also has an official Web site and publishes its opinions there immediately after they are announced to the public. (See the *Interacting with the Internet* section at the end of the chapter for selected court sites.) In fact, even decisions that are designated as unpublished opinions by the appellate courts are often published online.

Cyber Courts and Proceedings

Someday, litigants may be able to use cyber courts, in which judicial proceedings take place only on the Internet. The parties to a case could meet online to make their arguments and present their evidence. This might be done with e-mail submissions, through video cameras, in designated chat rooms, at closed sites, or through the use of other Internet facilities. These courtrooms could be efficient and economical. We might also see the use of virtual lawyers, judges, and juries—and possibly the replacement of court personnel with computer software. Already the state of Michigan has passed legislation creating cyber courts that will hear cases involving technology issues and high-tech businesses. Many lawyers predict that other states will follow suit.

The courts may also use the Internet in other ways. In a groundbreaking decision in early 2001, for example, a Florida county court granted "virtual" visitation rights in a couple's divorce proceeding. Although the court granted custody of the couple's ten-year-old daughter to the father, the court also ordered each parent to buy a computer and a videoconferencing system so that the mother could "visit" with her child via the Internet at any time.[14]

ETHICAL ISSUE 3.1 *How will online access to courts affect privacy?*

From a practical perspective, trial court records, although normally available to the public, remain obscure. Because the decisions of most state trial courts (and some federal courts) are not published, someone must be strongly motivated to go to the trouble of traveling to the relevant courthouse in person to access the documents. As online access to court records increases and electronic filing becomes the norm, this "practical obscurity," as lawyers call it, may soon disappear. Electronic filing on a nationwide basis would open up all court documents to anyone with an

---

14. For a discussion of this case, see Shelley Emling, "After the Divorce, Internet Visits?" *Austin American-Statesman,* January 30, 2001, pp. A1 and A10.

Internet connection and a Web browser. Utilizing special "data-mining" software, anyone could go online and within just a few minutes access information—ranging from personal health records, to financial reports, to criminal violations—from dozens of courts. This means that serious privacy issues are at stake. Should the courts restrict public access to certain types of documents, such as bankruptcy records or documents containing personal information that is not directly related to the legal issue being decided? Many courts are struggling with these questions and have taken a myriad of different approaches. Some courts make civil case information available, but restrict Internet access to criminal case information. Other courts, such as those in Florida, have deemed certain types of documents and court proceedings confidential and no longer post this information online.[15]

ALTERNATIVE DISPUTE RESOLUTION

Litigation is expensive. It is also time consuming. Because of the backlog of cases pending in many courts, several years may pass before a case is actually tried. For these and other reasons, more and more businesspersons are turning to **alternative dispute resolution** (ADR) as a means of settling their disputes.

Methods of ADR range from neighbors sitting down over a cup of coffee in an attempt to work out their differences to huge multinational corporations agreeing to resolve a dispute through a formal hearing before a panel of experts. The great advantage of ADR is its flexibility. Normally, the parties themselves can control how the dispute will be settled, what procedures will be used, and whether the decision reached (either by themselves or by a neutral third party) will be legally binding or nonbinding.

Today, approximately 95 percent of cases are settled before trial through some form of ADR. Indeed, most states either require or encourage parties to undertake ADR prior to trial. Several federal courts have instituted ADR programs as well. In the following pages, we examine various forms of ADR. Keep in mind, though, that new methods of ADR—and new combinations of existing methods—are constantly being devised and employed. In addition, ADR services are now being offered via the Internet. After looking at traditional forms of ADR, we examine some of the ways in which disputes are being resolved in various online forums.

ALTERNATIVE DISPUTE RESOLUTION (ADR)
The resolution of disputes in ways other than those involved in the traditional judicial process. Negotiation, mediation, and arbitration are forms of ADR.

Negotiation

One of the simplest forms of ADR is **negotiation,** a process in which the parties attempt to settle their dispute informally, with or without attorneys to represent them. Attorneys frequently advise their clients to negotiate a settlement voluntarily before they proceed to trial.

Negotiation traditionally involves just the parties themselves and (typically) their attorneys. The attorneys, though, are advocates—they are obligated to put their clients' interests first. Often parties find it helpful to have the opinion and guidance of a neutral (unbiased) third party when deciding whether or how to negotiate a settlement of their dispute. The methods of ADR discussed next all involve neutral third parties.

NEGOTIATION
A process in which parties attempt to settle their dispute informally, with or without attorneys to represent them.

---

15. *In re Report of Supreme Court Workgroup on Public Records*, 825 So.2d 889 (Fla. 2002).

These officers of the Mediation Center of Yavapai County in Arizona review documents for an upcoming dispute-resolution meeting. This organization's president believes that communication breakdowns create many conflicts. How does mediation differ from arbitration? (AP Photo/*The Daily Courier,* Jo. L. Keener)

MEDIATION

A method of settling disputes outside of court by using the services of a neutral third party, who acts as a communicating agent between the parties and assists them in negotiating a settlement.

ARBITRATION

The settling of a dispute by submitting it to a disinterested third party (other than a court), who renders a decision that is (most often) legally binding.

Mediation

In the **mediation** process, the parties themselves attempt to negotiate an agreement, but with the assistance of a neutral third party, a mediator. In mediation, the mediator talks with the parties separately as well as jointly. The mediator emphasizes points of agreement, helps the parties evaluate their positions, and proposes solutions. The mediator, however, does not make a decision on the matter being disputed. The mediator, who need not be a lawyer, usually charges a fee for his or her services (which can be split between the parties). States that require parties to undergo ADR before trial often offer mediation as one of the ADR options or (as in Florida) the only option.

Mediation is not adversarial in nature, as lawsuits are. In litigation, the parties "do battle" with each other in the courtroom, while the judge is the neutral party. Because of its nonadversarial nature, the mediation process tends to reduce the antagonism between the disputants and to allow them to resume their former relationship. For this reason, mediation is often the preferred form of ADR for disputes involving business partners, employers and employees, or other parties involved in long-term relationships. **Example #10** Suppose that two business partners have a dispute over how the profits of their firm should be distributed. If the dispute is litigated, the parties will be adversaries, and their respective attorneys will emphasize how the parties' positions differ, not what they have in common. In contrast, when a dispute is mediated, the mediator emphasizes the common ground shared by the parties and helps them work toward agreement.

Today, characteristics of mediation are being combined with those of arbitration (to be discussed next). In *binding mediation,* for example, the parties agree that if they cannot resolve the dispute, the mediator can make a legally binding decision on the issue. In *mediation-arbitration,* or "med-arb," the parties agree to first attempt to settle their dispute through mediation. If no settlement is reached, the dispute will be arbitrated.

Arbitration

A more formal method of ADR is **arbitration,** in which an arbitrator (a neutral third party or a panel of experts) hears a dispute and renders a decision. The key difference between arbitration and the forms of ADR just discussed is that in arbitration, the third party hearing the dispute makes the decision for the parties. Usually, the parties in arbitration agree that the third party's decision will be legally binding, although the parties can also agree to *nonbinding* arbitration. Additionally, arbitration that is mandated by the courts often is not binding on the parties. If the parties do not agree with the arbitrator's decision, they can go forward with the lawsuit.

In some respects, formal arbitration resembles a trial, although usually the procedural rules are much less restrictive than those governing litigation. In the typical hearing format, the parties present opening arguments to the arbitrator and state what remedies should or should not be granted. Evidence is then presented, and witnesses may be called and examined by both sides. The arbitrator then renders a decision, which is called an *award.*

An arbitrator's award is usually the final word on the matter. Although the parties may appeal an arbitrator's decision, a court's review of the decision will be much more restricted in scope than an appellate court's review of a trial court's decision. The general view is that because the parties were free to frame the issues and set the powers of the arbitrator at the outset, they cannot complain about the results. The award will be set aside only if the arbitrator's conduct or "bad faith" substantially prejudiced the rights of one of the parties, if the award violates an established public policy, or if the arbitrator exceeded her or his powers (arbitrated issues that the parties did not agree to submit to arbitration).

Arbitration Clauses and Statutes   Virtually any commercial matter can be submitted to arbitration. Frequently, parties include an **arbitration clause** in a contract (a written agreement—see Chapter 8); the clause provides that any dispute that arises under the contract will be resolved through arbitration rather than through the court system. Parties can also agree to arbitrate a dispute after a dispute arises.

> **ARBITRATION CLAUSE**
> A clause in a contract that provides that, in the event of a dispute, the parties will submit the dispute to arbitration rather than litigate the dispute in court.

Most states have statutes (often based in part on the Uniform Arbitration Act of 1955) under which arbitration clauses will be enforced, and some state statutes compel arbitration of certain types of disputes, such as those involving public employees. At the federal level, the Federal Arbitration Act (FAA), enacted in 1925, enforces arbitration clauses in contracts involving maritime activity and interstate commerce (though its applicability to employment contracts has been controversial, as discussed later in this chapter). Because of the breadth of the commerce clause (see Chapter 4), arbitration agreements involving transactions only slightly connected to the flow of interstate commerce may fall under the FAA.

The Issue of Arbitrability   When a dispute arises as to whether the parties have agreed in an arbitration clause to submit a particular matter to arbitration, one party may file a suit to compel arbitration. The court before which the suit is brought will decide *not* the basic controversy but rather the issue of arbitrability—that is, whether the matter is one that must be resolved through arbitration. If the court finds that the subject matter in controversy is covered by the agreement to arbitrate, then a party may be compelled to arbitrate the dispute. Even when a claim involves a violation of a statute passed to protect a certain class of people, such as employees, a court may determine that the parties must nonetheless abide by their agreement to arbitrate the dispute. Usually, a court will allow the claim to be arbitrated if the court, in interpreting the statute, can find no legislative intent to the contrary.

> **KEEP IN MIND** Litigation—even of a dispute over whether a particular matter should be submitted to arbitration—can be time consuming and expensive.

No party, however, will be ordered to submit a particular dispute to arbitration unless the court is convinced that the party consented to do so.[16] Additionally, the courts will not compel arbitration if it is clear that the prescribed arbitration rules and procedures are inherently unfair to one of the parties. (See this chapter's *Management Perspective* feature on the following page for a further discussion of this issue.)

The question in the case that starts on the bottom of the next page was whether a court or an arbitrator should consider a claim that an entire contract, including its arbitration clause, is rendered void by the alleged illegality of a separate provision in the contract.

---

16. See, for example, *Wright v. Universal Maritime Service Corp.,* 525 U.S. 70, 119 S.Ct. 391, 142 L.Ed.2d 361 (1998).

MANAGEMENT PERSPECTIVE
Arbitration Clauses in Employment Contracts

Management Faces a Legal Issue Arbitration is normally simpler, speedier, and less costly than litigation. For that reason, business owners and managers today often include arbitration clauses in their contracts, including employment contracts. What happens, though, if a job candidate whom you wish to hire (or an existing employee whose contract is being renewed) objects to one or more of the provisions in an arbitration clause? If you insist that signing the agreement to arbitrate future disputes is a mandatory condition of employment, will such a clause be enforceable?

What the Courts Say As you will read elsewhere in this chapter, the United States Supreme Court has consistently taken the position that because the Federal Arbitration Act (FAA) favors the arbitration of disputes, arbitration clauses in employment contracts should generally be enforced. Nonetheless, some courts have held that arbitration clauses in employment contracts should not be enforced if they are too one sided and unfair to the employee.

In one case, for example, the U.S. Court of Appeals for the Ninth Circuit refused to enforce an arbitration clause on the ground that the agreement was *unconscionable*—so one sided and unfair as to be unenforceable under

"ordinary principles of state contract law." The agreement was a standard-form contract drafted by the employer (the party with superior bargaining power), and the employee had to sign it without any modification as a prerequisite to employment. Moreover, only the employees were required to arbitrate their disputes, while the employer remained free to litigate any claims it had against its employees in court. Among other things, the contract also severely limited the relief that was available to employees. For these reasons, the court held the entire arbitration agreement unenforceable.[a] Other courts have cited similar reasons for deciding not to enforce one-sided arbitration clauses.[b]

Implications for Managers Although the United States Supreme Court has made it clear that arbitration clauses in employment contracts are enforceable under the FAA, business owners and managers would be wise to exercise caution when drafting such clauses. It is especially important to make sure that the terms of the agreement are not so one sided that a court could declare the entire agreement unconscionable.

a. *Circuit City Stores, Inc. v. Adams*, 279 F.3d 889 (9th Cir. 2002).
b. See, for example, *Hooters of America, Inc. v. Phillips*, 173 F.3d 933 (4th Cir. 1999); and *Hardwick v. Sherwin Williams Co.*, 2002 WL 31992364 (Ohio App. 8 Dist. 2003).

CASE 3.3   **Buckeye Check Cashing, Inc. v. Cardegna**

Supreme Court of the United States, 2006.
__ U.S. __,
126 S.Ct. 1204.
163 L.Ed.2d 1038.
straylight.law.cornell.edu/supct/index.html [a]

BACKGROUND AND FACTS Buckeye Check Cashing, Inc., cashes personal checks for consumers in Florida. Buckeye agrees to delay submitting a check for payment in exchange for a consumer's payment of a "finance charge." For each

transaction, the consumer signs a "Deferred Deposit and Disclosure Agreement," which states, "By signing this Agreement, you agree that i[f] a dispute of any kind arises out of this Agreement * * * th[e]n either you or we or third parties involved can choose to have that dispute resolved by binding arbitration." John Cardegna and others filed a suit in a Florida state court against Buckeye, alleging that the "finance charge" represented an illegally high interest rate in violation of Florida state laws, rendering the agreement "criminal on its face." Buckeye filed a motion to compel arbitration. The court denied the motion. On Buckeye's appeal, a state intermediate appellate court reversed this denial, but on the plaintiffs' appeal, the Florida Supreme Court reversed the lower appellate court's decision. Buckeye appealed to the United States Supreme Court.

a. In the "Supreme Court Collection" menu at the top of the page, click on "Search." When that page opens, in the "Search for:" box type "Buckeye Check Cashing," choose "All decisions" in the accompanying list, and click on "Search." In the result, scroll to the name of the case and click on the appropriate link to access the opinion.

CASE 3.3–CONTINUED

IN THE WORDS OF THE COURT . . . Justice *SCALIA* delivered the opinion of the Court.

* * * *

* * * [Section 2 [of the Federal Arbitration Act (FAA)] embodies the national policy favoring arbitration and places arbitration agreements on equal footing with all other contracts:

> A written provision in * * * a contract * * * to settle by arbitration a controversy thereafter arising out of such contract * * * shall be valid, irrevocable, and enforceable, save upon such grounds as exist at law or in equity for the revocation of any contract.

* * * The crux of the [respondents'] complaint is that the contract as a whole (including its arbitration provision) is rendered invalid by the * * * finance charge.

* * * *

* * * [Our holdings in previous cases] answer the question presented here by establishing three propositions. First, as a matter of substantive federal arbitration law, *an arbitration provision is severable from the remainder of the contract.* Second, unless the challenge is to the arbitration clause itself, *the issue of the contract's validity is considered by the arbitrator in the first instance.* Third, *this arbitration law applies in state as well as federal courts.* * * * Applying [those holdings] to this case, we conclude that because respondents challenge the Agreement, but not specifically its arbitration provisions, those provisions are enforceable apart from the remainder of the contract. The challenge should therefore be considered by an arbitrator, not a court. [Emphasis added.]

* * * *

* * * Since, respondents argue, the only arbitration agreements to which [Section] 2 applies are those involving a "contract," and since an agreement void *ab initio* [from the beginning] under state law is not a "contract," there is no "written provision" in or "controversy arising out of" a "contract," to which [Section] 2 can apply. * * * We do not read "contract" so narrowly. The word appears four times in [Section] 2. Its last appearance is in the final clause, which allows a challenge to an arbitration provision "upon such grounds as exist at law or in equity for the revocation of any contract." There can be no doubt that "contract" as used this last time must include contracts that later prove to be void. Otherwise, the grounds for revocation would be limited to those that rendered a contract voidable—which would mean (implausibly) that an arbitration agreement could be challenged as voidable but not as void. Because the sentence's final use of "contract" so obviously includes putative [reputed] contracts, we will not read the same word earlier in the same sentence to have a more narrow meaning.

DECISION AND REMEDY The United States Supreme Court reversed the judgment of the Florida Supreme Court and remanded the case for further proceedings. The United States Supreme Court ruled that a challenge to the validity of a contract as a whole, and not specifically to an arbitration clause contained in the contract, must be resolved by an arbitrator.

WHY IS THIS CASE IMPORTANT? *The result in this case reinvigorated the rule that the Federal Arbitration Act can be the basis for severing from a contract, and separately enforcing, an arbitration clause. The holding in* Buckeye *makes this possible even if the remainder of the contract is later held to be invalid and even if a state law otherwise prohibits the enforcement of an arbitration clause in a contract that is unenforceable under state law.*

Mandatory Arbitration in the Employment Context   A significant question in the last several years has concerned mandatory arbitration clauses in employment contracts. Many claim that employees' rights are not sufficiently protected when they are forced, as a condition of hiring, to agree to arbitrate all disputes and thus waive their rights under statutes specifically designed to protect employees. The United States Supreme Court, however, has generally held that mandatory arbitration clauses in employment contracts are enforceable.

| **Example #11**   In a landmark 1991 decision, *Gilmer v. Interstate/Johnson Lane Corp.*,[17] the Supreme Court held that a claim brought under a federal statute prohibiting age discrimination (see Chapter 14) could be subject to arbitration. The Court concluded that the employee had waived his right to sue when he agreed, as part of a required registration application to be a securities representative with the New York Stock Exchange, to arbitrate "any dispute, claim, or controversy" relating to his employment. | The *Gilmer* decision was controversial and generated much discussion during the 1990s. By the early 2000s, some lower courts began to question whether Congress intended the Federal Arbitration Act (FAA)—which expressly excludes the employment contracts of "seamen, railroad employees, or any other class of workers engaged in foreign or interstate commerce"—to apply to any employment contracts.

In 2001, the United States Supreme Court addressed this issue in *Circuit City Stores, Inc. v. Adams*.[18] In that case, as part of the application process, a sales employee was required to sign an arbitration clause. Two years later, the employee, Adams, filed suit against Circuit City for violating state employment-discrimination laws, and the employer asked the court to compel arbitration. Adams argued that the FAA did not apply to employment contracts, and the U.S. Court of Appeals for the Ninth Circuit agreed. The Supreme Court reversed, however, holding that the act applied to most employment contracts, except those that involve interstate transportation workers.

Other Types of ADR

The three forms of ADR just discussed are the oldest and traditionally the most commonly used. In recent years, a variety of new types of ADR have emerged, some of which were mentioned earlier in the discussion of mediation. Other ADR forms that are used today are sometimes referred to as "assisted negotiation" because they involve a third party in what is essentially a negotiation process. For example, in **early neutral case evaluation,** the parties select a neutral third party (generally an expert in the subject matter of the dispute) to evaluate their respective positions. The parties explain their positions to the case evaluator in any manner they choose. The case evaluator then assesses the strengths and weaknesses of the parties' positions, and this evaluation forms the basis for negotiating a settlement.

Another form of assisted negotiation that is often used by business parties is the **mini-trial,** in which each party's attorney briefly argues the party's case before representatives of each firm who have the authority to settle the dispute. Typically, a neutral third party (usually an expert in the area being

EARLY NEUTRAL CASE EVALUATION
A form of alternative dispute resolution in which a neutral third party evaluates the strengths and weaknesses of the disputing parties' positions. The evaluator's opinion then forms the basis for negotiating a settlement.

MINI-TRIAL
A private proceeding in which each party to a dispute argues its position before the other side and vice versa. A neutral third party may be present as an adviser and may render an opinion if the parties fail to reach an agreement.

---

17. 500 U.S. 20, 111 S.Ct. 1647, 114 L.Ed.2d 26 (1991).
18. 532 U.S. 105, 121 S.Ct. 1302, 149 L.Ed.2d 234 (2001).

disputed) acts as an adviser. If the parties fail to reach an agreement, the adviser renders an opinion as to how a court would likely decide the issue. The proceeding assists the parties in determining whether they should negotiate a settlement or take the dispute to court.

Today's courts are also experimenting with a variety of ADR alternatives to speed up (and reduce the cost of) justice. Numerous federal courts now hold **summary jury trials (SJTs)**, in which the parties present their arguments and evidence and the jury renders a verdict. The jury's verdict is not binding, but it does act as a guide to both sides in reaching an agreement during the mandatory negotiations that immediately follow the trial. Other alternatives being employed by the courts include summary procedures for commercial litigation and the appointment of special masters to assist judges in deciding complex issues.

SUMMARY JURY TRIAL (SJT)
A method of settling disputes, used in many federal courts, in which a trial is held, but the jury's verdict is not binding. The verdict acts only as a guide to both sides in reaching an agreement during the mandatory negotiations that immediately follow the summary jury trial.

Providers of ADR Services

ADR services are provided by both government agencies and private organizations. A major provider of ADR services is the American Arbitration Association (AAA), which was founded in 1926 and now handles over 200,000 claims a year in its numerous offices around the country. Most of the largest U.S. law firms are members of this nonprofit association.

Cases brought before the AAA are heard by an expert or a panel of experts in the area relating to the dispute and are usually settled quickly. Generally, about half of the panel members are lawyers. To cover its costs, the AAA charges a fee, paid by the party filing the claim. In addition, each party to the dispute pays a specified amount for each hearing day, as well as a special additional fee for cases involving personal injuries or property loss.

Hundreds of for-profit firms around the country also provide various forms of dispute-resolution services. Typically, these firms hire retired judges to conduct arbitration hearings or otherwise assist parties in settling their disputes. The judges follow procedures similar to those of the federal courts and use similar rules. Usually, each party to the dispute pays a filing fee and a designated fee for a hearing session or conference.

ONLINE DISPUTE RESOLUTION

An increasing number of companies and organizations offer dispute-resolution services using the Internet. The settlement of disputes in these online forums is known as **online dispute resolution (ODR)**. To date, the disputes resolved in these forums have most commonly involved disagreements over the rights to domain names (Web site addresses—see Chapter 7) and disagreements over the quality of goods sold via the Internet, including goods sold through Internet auction sites.

ONLINE DISPUTE RESOLUTION (ODR)
The resolution of disputes with the assistance of organizations that offer dispute-resolution services via the Internet.

ODR may be best for resolving small- to medium-sized business liability claims, which may not be worth the expense of litigation or traditional ADR methods. Rules being developed in online forums, however, may ultimately become a code of conduct for all of those who do business in cyberspace. Most online forums do not automatically apply the law of any specific jurisdiction. Instead, results are often based on general, universal legal principles. As with offline methods of dispute resolution, any party may appeal to a court at any time.

Negotiation and Mediation Services

The online negotiation of a dispute is generally simpler and more practical than litigation. Typically, one party files a complaint, and the other party is notified by e-mail. Password-protected access is possible twenty-four hours a day, seven days a week. Fees are generally low (often 2 to 4 percent, or less, of the disputed amount).

CyberSettle.com, National Arbitration and Mediation (**namadr.com**), and other Web-based firms offer online forums for negotiating monetary settlements. The parties to a dispute may agree to submit offers; if the offers fall within a previously agreed-on range, they will end the dispute, and the parties will split the difference. Special software keeps secret any offers that are not within the range. If there is no agreed-on range, typically an offer includes a deadline within which the other party must respond before the offer expires. The parties can drop the negotiations at any time.

Mediation providers have also tried resolving disputes online. SquareTrade, for example, has provided mediation services for the online auction site eBay and also resolves disputes among other parties. SquareTrade uses Web-based software that walks participants through a five-step e-resolution process. Negotiation between the parties occurs on a secure page within SquareTrade's Web site. The parties may consult a mediator. The entire process takes as little as ten to fourteen days, and at present no fee is charged unless the parties use a mediator.

Arbitration Programs

A number of organizations, including the American Arbitration Association, offer online arbitration programs. The Internet Corporation for Assigned Names and Numbers (ICANN), a nonprofit corporation that the federal government set up to oversee the distribution of domain names, has issued special rules for the resolution of domain name disputes.[19] ICANN has also authorized several organizations to arbitrate domain name disputes in accordance with ICANN's rules.

Resolution Forum, Inc. (RFI), a nonprofit organization associated with the Center for Legal Responsibility at South Texas College of Law, offers arbitration services through its CAN-WIN conferencing system. Using standard browser software and an RFI password, the parties to a dispute access an online conference room. When multiple parties are involved, private communications and breakout sessions are possible via private messaging facilities. RFI also offers mediation services.

The Virtual Magistrate Project (VMAG) is affiliated with the American Arbitration Association, Chicago-Kent College of Law, Cyberspace Law Institute, National Center for Automated Information Research, and other organizations. VMAG offers arbitration for disputes involving users of online systems; victims of wrongful messages, postings, and files; and system operators subject to complaints or similar demands. VMAG also arbitrates intellectual property, personal property, real property, and tort disputes related to

---

19. ICANN's Rules for Uniform Domain Name Dispute Resolution Policy are online at **www.icann.org/udrp/udrp-rules-24oct99.htm**. Domain names will be discussed in more detail in Chapter 7, in the context of trademark law.

online contracts. VMAG attempts to resolve a dispute within seventy-two hours. The proceedings occur in a password-protected online newsgroup setting, and private e-mail among the participants is possible. A VMAG arbitrator's decision is issued in a written opinion. A party may appeal the outcome to a court.

REVIEWING . . . COURTS AND ALTERNATIVE DISPUTE RESOLUTION

Stan Garner resides in Illinois and promotes boxing matches for SuperSports, Inc., an Illinois corporation. Garner created the concept of "Ages" promotion—a three-fight series of boxing matches pitting an older fighter (George Foreman) against a younger fighter, such as John Ruiz or Riddick Bowe. The concept included titles for each of the three fights ("Challenge of the Ages," "Battle of the Ages," and "Fight of the Ages"), as well as promotional epithets to characterize the two fighters ("the Foreman Factor"). Garner contacted George Foreman and his manager, who both reside in Texas, to sell the idea, and they arranged a meeting at Caesar's Palace in Las Vegas, Nevada. At some point in the negotiations, Foreman's manager signed a nondisclosure agreement prohibiting him from disclosing Garner's promotional concepts unless the parties signed a contract. Nevertheless, after negotiations between Garner and

Foreman fell through, Foreman used Garner's "Battle of the Ages" concept to promote a subsequent fight. Garner filed a suit against Foreman and his manager in a federal district court located in Illinois, alleging breach of contract. Using the information presented in the chapter, answer the following questions.

1. On what basis might the federal district court in Illinois exercise jurisdiction in this case?

2. Does the federal district court have original or appellate jurisdiction?

3. Suppose that Garner had filed his action in an Illinois state court. Could an Illinois state court exercise personal jurisdiction over Foreman or his manager? Why or why not?

4. Assume that Garner had filed his action in a Nevada state court. Would that court have personal jurisdiction over Foreman or his manager? Why or why not?

KEY TERMS

alternative dispute resolution (ADR) 89
answer 79
arbitration 90
arbitration clause 91
award 83
bankruptcy court 68
brief 84
complaint 77
concurrent jurisdiction 69
counterclaim 79
default judgment 79
deposition 80
discovery 80
diversity of citizenship 68
docket 69
early neutral case evaluation 94
e-evidence 81

exclusive jurisdiction 69
federal question 68
interrogatories 80
judicial review 65
jurisdiction 67
justiciable controversy 72
litigation 77
long arm statute 67
mediation 90
mini-trial 94
motion for a directed verdict 83
motion for a new trial 84
motion for judgment *n.o.v.* 83
motion for judgment on the pleadings 79
motion for summary judgment 80
motion to dismiss 79

negotiation 89
online dispute resolution (ODR) 95
pleadings 77
probate court 68
reply 79
rule of four 76
small claims court 74
standing to sue 72
summary jury trial (SJT) 95
summons 79
venue 72
voir dire 82
writ of *certiorari* 76

CHAPTER SUMMARY • COURTS AND ALTERNATIVE DISPUTE RESOLUTION

The Judiciary's Role in American Government (See pages 65–66.)	The role of the judiciary—the courts—in the American governmental system is to interpret and apply the law. Through the process of judicial review—determining the constitutionality of laws—the judicial branch acts as a check on the executive and legislative branches of government.
Basic Judicial Requirements (See pages 66–73.)	1. *Jurisdiction*—Before a court can hear a case, it must have jurisdiction over the person against whom the suit is brought or the property involved in the suit, as well as jurisdiction over the subject matter. a. Limited versus general jurisdiction—Limited jurisdiction exists when a court is limited to a specific subject matter, such as probate or divorce. General jurisdiction exists when a court can hear any kind of case. b. Original versus appellate jurisdiction—Original jurisdiction exists with courts that have authority to hear a case for the first time (trial courts). Appellate jurisdiction exists with courts of appeals, or reviewing courts; generally, appellate courts do not have original jurisdiction. c. Federal jurisdiction—Arises (1) when a federal question is involved (when the plaintiff's cause of action is based, at least in part, on the U.S. Constitution, a treaty, or a federal law) or (2) when a case involves diversity of citizenship (citizens of different states, for example) and the amount in controversy exceeds $75,000. d. Concurrent versus exclusive jurisdiction—Concurrent jurisdiction exists when two different courts have authority to hear the same case. Exclusive jurisdiction exists when only state courts or only federal courts have authority to hear a case. 2. *Jurisdiction in cyberspace*—Because the Internet does not have physical boundaries, traditional jurisdictional concepts have been difficult to apply in cases involving activities conducted via the Web. Gradually, the courts are developing standards to use in determining when jurisdiction over a Web owner or operator in another state is proper. 3. *Venue*—Venue has to do with the most appropriate location for a trial, which is usually the geographic area where the event leading to the dispute took place or where the parties reside. 4. *Standing to sue*—A requirement that a party must have a legally protected and tangible interest at stake sufficient to justify seeking relief through the court system. The controversy at issue must also be a justiciable controversy—one that is real and substantial, as opposed to hypothetical or academic.
The State and Federal Court Systems (See pages 73–77.)	1. *Trial courts*—Courts of original jurisdiction, in which legal actions are initiated. a. State—Courts of general jurisdiction can hear any case; courts of limited jurisdiction include divorce courts, probate courts, traffic courts, small claims courts, and so on. b. Federal—The federal district court is the equivalent of the state trial court. Federal courts of limited jurisdiction include the U.S. Tax Court, the U.S. Bankruptcy Court, and the U.S. Court of Federal Claims. 2. *Intermediate appellate courts*—Courts of appeals, or reviewing courts; generally without original jurisdiction. Many states have an intermediate appellate court; in the federal court system, the U.S. circuit courts of appeals are the intermediate appellate courts. 3. *Supreme (highest) courts*—Each state has a supreme court, although it may be called by some other name; appeal from the state supreme court to the United States Supreme Court is possible only if a federal question is involved. The United States Supreme Court is the highest court in the federal court system and the final arbiter of the Constitution and federal law.
Following a State Court Case (See pages 77–85.)	Rules of procedure prescribe the way in which disputes are handled in the courts. Rules differ from court to court, and separate sets of rules exist for federal and state courts, as well as for criminal and civil cases. A sample civil court case in a state court would involve the following procedures:

CHAPTER SUMMARY • COURTS AND ALTERNATIVE DISPUTE RESOLUTION—CONTINUED

Following a State Court Case—Continued	1. *The pleadings*—

Following a State Court Case—Continued

1. *The pleadings*—

   a. Complaint—Filed by the plaintiff with the court to initiate the lawsuit; served with a summons on the defendant.

   b. Answer—Admits or denies allegations made by the plaintiff; may assert a counterclaim or an affirmative defense.

   c. Motion to dismiss—A request to the court to dismiss the case for stated reasons, such as the plaintiff's failure to state a claim for which relief can be granted.

2. *Pretrial motions (in addition to the motion to dismiss)*—

   a. Motion for judgment on the pleadings—May be made by either party; will be granted if the parties agree on the facts and the only question is how the law applies to the facts. The judge bases the decision solely on the pleadings.

   b. Motion for summary judgment—May be made by either party; will be granted if the parties agree on the facts. The judge applies the law in rendering a judgment. The judge can consider evidence outside the pleadings when evaluating the motion.

3. *Discovery*—The process of gathering evidence concerning the case. Discovery involves depositions (sworn testimony by a party to the lawsuit or any witness), interrogatories (written questions and answers to these questions made by parties to the action with the aid of their attorneys), and various requests (for admissions, documents, and medical examinations, for example). Discovery may also involve electronically recorded information, such as e-mail, voice mail, word-processing documents, and other data compilations. Although electronic discovery has significant advantages over paper discovery, it is also more time consuming and expensive and often requires the parties to hire experts.

4. *Pretrial conference*—Either party or the court can request a pretrial conference to identify the matters in dispute after discovery has taken place and to plan the course of the trial.

5. *Trial*—Following jury selection (*voir dire*), the trial begins with opening statements from both parties' attorneys. The following events then occur:

   a. The plaintiff's introduction of evidence (including the testimony of witnesses) supporting the plaintiff's position. The defendant's attorney can challenge evidence and cross-examine witnesses.

   b. The defendant's introduction of evidence (including the testimony of witnesses) supporting the defendant's position. The plaintiff's attorney can challenge evidence and cross-examine witnesses.

   c. Closing arguments by the attorneys in favor of their respective clients, the judge's instructions to the jury, and the jury's verdict.

6. *Posttrial motions*—

   a. Motion for judgment *n.o.v.* ("notwithstanding the verdict")—Will be granted if the judge is convinced that the jury was in error.

   b. Motion for a new trial—Will be granted if the judge is convinced that the jury was in error; can also be granted on the grounds of newly discovered evidence, misconduct by the participants during the trial, or error by the judge.

7. *Appeal*—Either party can appeal the trial court's judgment to an appropriate court of appeals. After reviewing the record on appeal, the abstracts, and the attorneys' briefs, the appellate court holds a hearing and renders its opinion.

(Continued)

CHAPTER SUMMARY • COURTS AND ALTERNATIVE DISPUTE RESOLUTION—CONTINUED

The Courts Adapt to the Online World (See pages 85–89.)	A number of state and federal courts now allow parties to file litigation-related documents with the courts via the Internet or other electronic means. The federal courts are considering the implementation of electronic filing systems in all federal district courts. Almost every court now has a Web page offering information about the court and its procedures, and increasingly courts are publishing their opinions online. In the future, we may see "cyber courts," in which all trial proceedings are conducted online.
Alternative Dispute Resolution (See pages 89–95.)	1. *Negotiation*—The parties come together, with or without attorneys to represent them, and try to reach a settlement without the involvement of a third party. 2. *Mediation*—The parties themselves reach an agreement with the help of a neutral third party, called a mediator, who proposes solutions. At the parties' request, a mediator may make a legally binding decision. 3. *Arbitration*—A more formal method of ADR in which the parties submit their dispute to a neutral third party, the arbitrator, who renders a decision. The decision may or may not be legally binding, depending on the circumstances. 4. *Other types of ADR*—These include early neutral case evaluation, mini-trials, and summary jury trials (SJTs); generally, these are forms of "assisted negotiation." 5. *Providers of ADR services*—The leading nonprofit provider of ADR services is the American Arbitration Association. Hundreds of for-profit firms also provide ADR services.
Online Dispute Resolution (See pages 95–97.)	A number of organizations and firms are now offering negotiation, mediation, and arbitration services through online forums. To date, these forums have been a practical alternative for the resolution of domain name disputes and e-commerce disputes in which the amount in controversy is relatively small.

FOR REVIEW

Answers for the even-numbered questions in this For Review *section can be found in Appendix O at the end of this text.*

1. What is judicial review? How and when was the power of judicial review established?

2. Before a court can hear a case, it must have jurisdiction. Over what must it have jurisdiction? How are the courts applying traditional jurisdictional concepts to cases involving Internet transactions?

3. What is the difference between a trial court and an appellate court?

4. In a lawsuit, what are the pleadings? What is discovery, and how does electronic discovery differ? What is electronic filing?

5. How are online forums being used to resolve disputes?

QUESTIONS AND CASE PROBLEMS

3–1. Arbitration. In an arbitration proceeding, the arbitrator need not be a judge or even a lawyer. How, then, can the arbitrator's decision have the force of law and be binding on the parties involved?

Question with Sample Answer

3–2. Marya Callais, a citizen of Florida, was walking near a busy street in Tallahassee one day when a large crate fell off a passing truck and hit her, resulting in several injuries. She incurred a great deal of pain and suffering plus numerous medical expenses, and she could not work for six months. She wishes to sue the trucking firm for $300,000 in damages. The firm's headquarters are in Georgia, although the company does business in Florida. In what court may Callais bring suit—a Florida state court, a Georgia state court, or a federal court? What factors might influence her decision?

For a sample answer to this question, go to Appendix P at the end of this text.

3–3. Standing. Blue Cross and Blue Shield insurance companies (the Blues) provide 68 million Americans with health-care financing. The Blues have paid billions of dollars for care attributable to illnesses related to tobacco use. In an attempt to recover some of this amount, the Blues filed a suit in a federal district court against tobacco companies and others, alleging fraud, among other things. The Blues claimed that beginning in 1953, the defendants conspired to addict millions of Americans, including members of Blue Cross plans, to cigarettes and other tobacco products. The conspiracy involved misrepresentation about the safety of nicotine and its addictive properties, marketing efforts targeting children, and agreements not to produce or market safer cigarettes. As a result of the defendants' efforts, many tobacco users developed lung, throat, and other cancers, as well as heart disease, stroke, emphysema, and other illnesses. The defendants asked the court to dismiss the case on the ground that the plaintiffs did not have standing to sue. Do the Blues have standing in this case? Why or why not? [*Blue Cross and Blue Shield of New Jersey, Inc. v. Philip Morris, Inc.,* 36 F.Supp.2d 560 (E.D.N.Y. 1999)]

3–4. Jurisdiction. George Noonan, a Boston police detective and a devoted nonsmoker, has spent most of his career educating Bostonians about the health risks of tobacco use. In 1992, an ad for Winston cigarettes featuring Noonan's image appeared in several French magazines. Some of the magazines were on sale at newsstands in Boston. Noonan filed a suit in a federal district court against The Winston Co., Lintas:Paris (the French ad agency that created the ads), and others. Lintas:Paris and the other French defendants claimed that they did not know the magazines would be sold in Boston and filed a motion to dismiss the suit for lack of personal jurisdiction. Does the court have jurisdiction? Why or why not? [*Noonan v. The Winston Co.,* 135 F.3d 85 (1st Cir. 1998)]

Case Problem with Sample Answer

3–5. Ms. Thompson filed a suit in a federal district court against her employer, Altheimer & Gray, seeking damages for alleged racial discrimination in violation of federal law. During *voir dire,* the judge asked the prospective jurors whether "there is something about this kind of lawsuit for money damages that would start any of you leaning for or against a particular party?" Ms. Leiter, one of the prospective jurors, raised her hand and explained that she had "been an owner of a couple of businesses and am currently an owner of a business, and I feel that as an employer and owner of a business that will definitely sway my judgment in this case." She explained, "I am constantly faced with people that want various benefits or different positions in the company or better contacts or, you know, a myriad of issues that employers face on a regular basis, and I have to decide whether or not that person should get them." Asked by Thompson's lawyer whether "you believe that people file lawsuits just because they don't get something they want," Leiter answered, "I believe there are some people that do." In answer to another question, she said, "I think I bring a lot of background to this case, and I can't say that it's not going to cloud my judgment. I can try to be as fair as I can, as I do every day." Thompson filed a motion to strike Leiter for cause. Should the judge grant the motion? Explain. [*Thompson v. Altheimer & Gray,* 248 F.3d 621 (7th Cir. 2001)]

After you have answered this problem, compare your answer with the sample answer given on the Web site that accompanies this text. Go to www.thomsonedu.com/westbuslaw/let, select "Chapter 3," and click on "Case Problem with Sample Answer."

3–6. Arbitration. Alexander Little worked for Auto Stiegler, Inc., an automobile dealership in Los Angeles County, California, eventually becoming the service manager. While employed, Little signed an arbitration agreement that required all employment-related disputes to be submitted to arbitration. The agreement also provided that any award over $50,000 could be appealed to a second arbitrator. Little was later demoted and terminated. Alleging that these actions were in retaliation for investigating and reporting warranty fraud and thus were in violation of public policy, Little filed a suit in a California state court against Auto Stiegler. The defendant filed a motion with the court to compel arbitration. Little responded that the arbitration agreement should not be enforced in part because the appeal provision was unfairly one sided. Is this provision enforceable? Should the court grant Auto Stiegler's motion? Why or why not? [*Little v. Auto Stiegler, Inc.,* 29 Cal.4th 1064, 63 P.3d 979, 130 Cal.Rptr.2d 892 (2003)]

3–7. Standing to Sue. Lamar Advertising of Penn, LLC, an outdoor advertising business, wanted to erect billboards of varying sizes in a multiphase operation throughout the town of Orchard Park, New York. An Orchard Park ordinance restricted the signs to certain sizes in certain areas, to advertising products and services available for sale only on the premises, and to other limits. Lamar asked Orchard Park for permission to build signs in some areas larger than the ordinance allowed in those locations (but not as large as allowed in other areas). When the town refused, Lamar filed a suit in a federal district court, claiming that the ordinance violated the First Amendment. Did Lamar have standing to challenge the ordinance? If the court could sever the provisions of the ordinance restricting a sign's content from the provisions limiting a sign's size, would your answer be the same? Explain. [*Lamar Advertising of Penn, LLC v. Town of Orchard Park, New York,* 356 F.3d 365 (2d Cir. 2004)]

3–8. Jurisdiction. Xcentric Ventures, LLC, is an Arizona firm that operates the Web sites RipOffReport.com and BadBusinessBureau.com. Visitors to the sites can buy a copy of a book titled *Do-It-Yourself Guide: How to Get Rip-Off Revenge.* The price ($21.95) includes shipping to anywhere in the United States, including Illinois, to which thirteen copies have been shipped. The sites accept donations and feature postings by individuals who claim to have been "ripped off." Some visitors posted comments about George S. May International Co., a management-consulting firm. The postings alleged fraud, larceny, possession of child pornography, and possession of controlled substances (illegal drugs). May filed a suit in a federal district court in Illinois against Xcentric and others, charging in part "false descriptions and representations." The defendants filed a motion to dismiss for lack of jurisdiction. What is the standard for exercising jurisdiction over a party whose only connection to a jurisdiction is through the Internet? How would that standard apply in this case? Explain. [*George S. May International Co. v. Xcentric Ventures, LLC,* 409 F.Supp.2d 1052 (N.D.Ill. 2006)]

A Question of Ethics

3–9. Linda Bender brought an action in a federal court against her supervisor at A. G. Edwards & Sons, Inc., a stockbrokerage firm (the defendants). Bender alleged sexual harassment in violation of Title VII of the Civil Rights Act of 1964, which prohibits, among other things, employment discrimination based on gender. In her application for registration as a stockbroker, Bender had agreed to arbitrate any disputes with her employer. The defendants moved to compel arbitration. The district court judge denied the motion, holding that Bender could not be forced to waive her right to adjudicate Title VII claims in federal court. The appellate court reversed, ruling that Title VII claims are arbitrable. The court held that compelling Bender to submit her claim for arbitration did not deprive her of the right to a judicial forum, because if the arbitration proceedings were somehow legally deficient, she could still take her case to a federal court for review. [*Bender v. A. G. Edwards & Sons, Inc.,* 971 F.2d 698 (11th Cir. 1992)]

1. Does the right to a postarbitration judicial forum equate to the right to initial access to a judicial forum in employment disputes?
2. Should the fact that reviewing courts rarely set aside arbitrators' awards have any bearing on the arbitrability of certain types of claims, such as those brought under Title VII?

Case Briefing Assignment

3–10. Go to **www.thomsonedu.com/ westbuslaw/let**, the Web site that accompanies this text. Select "Chapter 3" and click on "Case Briefing Assignments." Examine Case A.1 [*Rodriquez de Quijas v. Shearson/American Express,*

Inc., 490 U.S. 477, 109 S.Ct. 1917, 104 L.Ed.2d 379 (1989)]. The case has been excerpted there in great detail. Review and then brief the case, making sure that your brief answers the following questions.

1. What is the legislative policy "embodied in the Arbitration Act"?
2. How did the Court reconcile the protections afforded investors under the Securities Act and the legislative policy advanced by the Arbitration Act? Did the Court believe that by submitting to arbitration, investors forgo "substantive rights" given under the Securities Act?

Critical-Thinking Legal Question

3–11. Suppose that a state statute requires that all civil lawsuits involving damages of less than $50,000 be arbitrated and that the case could be tried in court only if a party was dissatisfied with the arbitrator's decision. Suppose further that the statute also provides that if a trial does not result in an improvement of more than 10 percent in the position of the party who demanded the trial, that party must pay the costs of the arbitration proceeding. Would such a statute violate litigants' rights of access to the courts and to trial by jury? Would it matter if the statute was part of a pilot program and affected only a few judicial districts in the state?

Video Question

3–12. Go to this text's Web site at **www. thomsonedu.com/westbuslaw/let** and select "Chapter 3." Click on "Video Questions" and view the video titled *Jurisdiction in Cyberspace.* Then answer the following questions.

1. What standard would a court apply to determine whether it has jurisdiction over the out-of-state computer firm in the video?
2. What factors is a court likely to consider in assessing whether sufficient contacts existed when the only connection to the jurisdiction is through a Web site?
3. How do you think the court would resolve the issue in this case?

INTERACTING WITH THE INTERNET

For updated links to resources available on the Web, as well as a variety of other materials, visit this text's Web site at

www.thomsonedu.com/westbuslaw/let

For the decisions of the United States Supreme Court, as well as information about the Supreme Court, go to

www.supremecourtus.gov

The Web site for the federal courts offers information on the federal court system and links to all federal courts at

www.uscourts.gov

For information on alternative dispute resolution, go to the American Arbitration Association's Web site at

www.adr.org

INTERNET EXERCISES

Go to **www.thomsonedu.com/westbuslaw/let**, the Web site that accompanies this text. Select "Chapter 3" and click on "Internet Exercises." There you will find the following Internet research exercises that you can perform to learn more about topics covered in this chapter.

Internet Exercise 3–1: LEGAL PERSPECTIVE—The Judiciary's Role in American Government

Internet Exercise 3–2: MANAGEMENT PERSPECTIVE—Alternative Dispute Resolution

Internet Exercise 3–3: SOCIAL PERSPECTIVE—Resolve a Dispute Online

BEFORE THE TEST

Go to **www.thomsonedu.com/westbuslaw/let**, the Web site that accompanies this text. Select "Chapter 3" and click on "Interactive Quizzes." You will find a number of interactive questions relating to this chapter.

Joan owns and operates an antique furniture store in Eugene, Oregon. During the five years since she opened the store, the business has thrived. Initially, her customers were from Eugene and other Oregon communities. Today, through her Web site, she sells furniture to buyers around the country.

1. Joan learns that a charming older building that would be an ideal location for her business is being offered for sale. For some time, she has looked for the perfect building for her operations, and now, she realizes, she has finally found it. She forms a contract with the seller of the property to buy the premises. The seller then backs out of the deal and refuses to sell. If Joan sued the seller for breach of contract, would she be entitled to seek the equitable remedy of specific performance (discussed in Chapter 1)? Why or why not?

2. Joan contracts with a furniture manufacturer in Maine to purchase five replicas of an early American dresser from the "federal period." The manufacturer promised her that they would be delivered to Joan's store by March 1. Joan has already formed contracts with three of her customers to sell them the dressers, promising them that the dressers will arrive on March 1. In fact, the dressers are never delivered, despite the manufacturer's continuing promises that they will be completed and shipped "any day now." If Joan decides to sue the manufacturer for breach of contract, can an Oregon state court exercise jurisdiction over the dispute, or will she have to bring her lawsuit in a Maine court? Could she sue the manufacturer in a federal court located in Oregon? Explain.

3. One of Joan's customers, who lives in Kansas, ordered an antique hutch via Joan's Web site. After the customer receives the hutch, he calls Joan and complains that she misrepresented the quality of the hutch in her Web site ads. Joan contends that she did not engage in any deceptive advertising on her Web site and that the customer has no claim against her. Eventually, the customer sues Joan in a Kansas state court. Joan moves to dismiss the case, alleging that the Kansas court lacks jurisdiction. After all, her business is physically located in Oregon, she has no sales representatives in Kansas, and her only contacts with Kansas are through her Web site. Will the court dismiss the suit on the ground that the "minimum-contacts" requirement for jurisdiction over an out-of-state defendant has not been met? Discuss.

4. With respect to the dispute in question 3 above, Joan is certain that the customer does not have a valid claim against her. At the same time, she wants to avoid the expense of litigation. What alternative dispute-resolution methods might Joan suggest to the customer to avoid having to resolve the matter in court? What might Joan have done in the first place to avoid the possibility of having to resolve disputes with customers in court?

5. Rebecca has been Joan's office manager for over five years. For most of those years she was a good worker and a loyal, dependable employee. In fact, Joan has come to rely on Rebecca and her skills extensively. Lately, however, Joan has noticed that Rebecca frequently comes to work late, leaves the office early, and takes time off to tend to matters that, in Joan's mind, do not seem all that important. On several occasions, Joan has talked to Rebecca about her performance, but to no effect. In the meantime, because of Rebecca's negligence, customer orders have been overlooked or mishandled, and Joan is receiving complaints. Joan also notices that some of the employees under Rebecca's supervision have begun to show a similar indifference to work schedules. Joan is thinking about firing Rebecca. Does Joan have an ethical duty to keep Rebecca on the payroll because of Rebecca's past loyalty and good performance record? Or should Joan think about the profits that she could lose if the inefficiency in the office operations continues and fire Rebecca? Would your answer be different if you knew that Rebecca was a single parent who depended on her income from this job and who could never find such a high-paying position elsewhere?

UNIT 2 The Public Environment

4 Constitutional Authority to Regulate Business

CONTENTS

CHAPTER OBJECTIVES

After reading this chapter, you should be able to answer the following questions:

1 What is the basic structure of the U.S. government?

2 What constitutional clause gives the federal government the power to regulate commercial activities among the various states?

3 What constitutional clause allows laws enacted by the federal government to take priority over conflicting state laws?

4 What is the Bill of Rights? What freedoms are guaranteed by the First Amendment?

5 Where in the Constitution can the due process clause be found?

> "The United States Constitution has proved itself the most marvelously elastic compilation of rules of government ever written."
>
> —FRANKLIN D. ROOSEVELT,
> 1882–1945 (Thirty-second president
> of the United States, 1933–1945)

THE U.S. CONSTITUTION is brief.[1] It consists of only about seven thousand words, which is less than one-third of the number of words in the average state constitution. Perhaps its brevity explains why it has proved to be so "marvelously elastic," as Franklin Roosevelt pointed out in the chapter-opening quotation, and why it has survived for over two hundred years—longer than any other written constitution in the world.

Laws that govern business have their origin in the lawmaking authority granted by this document, which is the supreme law in this country. As mentioned in Chapter 1, neither Congress nor any state can enact a law that is in conflict with the Constitution.

In this chapter, we first look at some basic constitutional concepts and clauses and their significance for business. Then we examine how certain fundamental freedoms guaranteed by the Constitution affect businesspersons and the workplace.

THE CONSTITUTIONAL POWERS OF GOVERNMENT

Following the Revolutionary War, the states created a *confederal* form of government. The Articles of Confederation, which went into effect in 1781, established a confederation of independent states and a central (national) government that could exercise only very limited powers. The sovereign power, or supreme authority to govern, rested largely with the states. The limitation on the central government's powers reflected a basic tenet of the

1. See Appendix B for the full text of the U.S. Constitution.

American Revolution—that a national government should not have unlimited power that could be used tyrannically against the states.

The confederation, however, faced serious problems. For one thing, laws passed by the various states hampered national commerce and foreign trade by preventing the free movement of goods and services. By 1784, the nation faced a serious economic depression. Many who could not afford to pay their debts were thrown into "debtors' prisons." By 1786, a series of uprisings by farmer debtors were proving difficult to control because the national government did not have the authority to demand revenues (by levying taxes, for example) to support a militia.

Because of these problems, a national convention was called to amend the Articles of Confederation. Instead of amending the articles, however, the delegates to the convention, now called the Constitutional Convention, wrote the U.S. Constitution. This document, after its ratification by the states in 1789, became the basis for an entirely new form of government. Many of the provisions of the Constitution, including those discussed in the following pages, were shaped by the delegates' experiences during the confederal era (1781–1789).

A Federal Form of Government

The new government created by the Constitution reflected a series of compromises made by the convention delegates on various issues. Some delegates wanted sovereign power to remain with the states; others wanted the national government alone to exercise sovereign power. The end result was a compromise—a **federal form of government** in which the national government and the states *share* sovereign power.

The Constitution sets forth specific powers that can be exercised by the national government and provides that the national government has the implied power to undertake actions necessary to carry out its expressly designated powers. All other powers are "reserved" to the states. The broad language of the Constitution, though, has left much room for debate over the specific nature and scope of these powers. Generally, it has been the task of the courts to determine where the boundary line between state and national powers should lie—and that line changes over time. For most of the twentieth century, for example, the national government met little resistance from the courts when extending its regulatory authority over broad areas of social and economic life. Today, in contrast, the courts, and particularly the United States Supreme Court, are more willing to interpret the Constitution in such a way as to curb the national government's regulatory powers.

FEDERAL FORM OF GOVERNMENT
A system of government in which the states form a union and the sovereign power is divided between the central government and the member states.

The Separation of Powers

To make it difficult for the national government to use its power arbitrarily, the Constitution divided the national government's powers among the three branches of government. The legislative branch makes the laws, the executive branch enforces the laws, and the judicial branch interprets the laws. Each branch performs a separate function, and no branch may exercise the authority of another branch.

Additionally, a system of **checks and balances** allows each branch to limit the actions of the other two branches, thus preventing any one branch from

CHECKS AND BALANCES
The principle under which the powers of the national government are divided among three separate branches—the executive, legislative, and judicial branches—each of which exercises a check on the actions of the others.

exercising too much power. Some examples of these checks and balances are the following:

1. The legislative branch (Congress) can enact a law, but the executive branch (the president) has the constitutional authority to veto that law.
2. The executive branch is responsible for foreign affairs, but treaties with foreign governments require the advice and consent of the Senate.
3. Congress determines the jurisdiction of the federal courts and the president appoints federal judges, with the advice and consent of the Senate, but the judicial branch has the power to hold actions of the other two branches unconstitutional.[2]

The Commerce Clause

To prevent states from establishing laws and regulations that would interfere with trade and commerce among the states, the Constitution expressly delegated to the national government the power to regulate interstate commerce. Article I, Section 8, of the U.S. Constitution expressly permits Congress "[t]o regulate Commerce with foreign Nations, and among the several States, and with the Indian Tribes." This clause, referred to as the **commerce clause,** has had a greater impact on business than any other provision in the Constitution.

COMMERCE CLAUSE
The provision in Article I, Section 8, of the U.S. Constitution that gives Congress the power to regulate interstate commerce.

For some time, the commerce power was interpreted as being limited to *interstate* commerce (commerce among the states) and not applicable to *intrastate* commerce (commerce within a state). In 1824, however, in *Gibbons v. Ogden* (see this chapter's *Landmark in the Legal Environment* feature on page 111), the United States Supreme Court held that commerce within a state could also be regulated by the national government as long as the commerce *substantially affected* commerce involving more than one state.

The Commerce Clause and the Expansion of National Powers In *Gibbons v. Ogden,* the commerce clause was expanded to regulate activities that "substantially affect interstate commerce." As the nation grew and faced new kinds of problems, the commerce clause became a vehicle for the additional expansion of the national government's regulatory powers. Even activities that seemed purely local came under the regulatory reach of the national government if those activities were deemed to substantially affect interstate commerce. **| Example #1** In 1942, in *Wickard v. Filburn,*[3] the Supreme Court held that wheat production by an individual farmer intended wholly for consumption on his own farm was subject to federal regulation. The Court reasoned that the home consumption of wheat reduced the demand for wheat and thus could have a substantial effect on interstate commerce.**|**

The following landmark case involved a challenge to the scope of the national government's constitutional authority to regulate local activities.

---

2. See the *Landmark in the Legal Environment* feature in Chapter 3 on *Marbury v. Madison,* 5 U.S. (1 Cranch) 137, 2 L.Ed. 60 (1803), a case in which the doctrine of judicial review was clearly enunciated by Chief Justice John Marshall.
3. 317 U.S. 111, 63 S.Ct. 82, 87 L.Ed. 122 (1942).

LANDMARK & CLASSIC CASES

CASE 4.1 Heart of Atlanta Motel v. United States

Supreme Court of the United States, 1964.
379 U.S. 241,
85 S.Ct. 348,
13 L.Ed.2d 258.
supct.law.cornell.edu/supct/cases/name.htm[a]

Rights Act of 1964 to prohibit racial discrimination in "establishments affecting interstate commerce." These facilities included "places of public accommodation."

HISTORICAL AND SOCIAL SETTING *In the first half of the twentieth century, state governments sanctioned segregation on the basis of race. In 1954, the United States Supreme Court decided that racially segregated school systems violated the Constitution. In the following decade, the Court ordered an end to racial segregation imposed by the states in other public facilities, such as beaches, golf courses, buses, parks, auditoriums, and courtroom seating. Privately owned facilities that excluded or segregated African Americans and others on the basis of race were not subject to the same constitutional restrictions, however. Congress passed the Civil*

a. This is the "Historic Supreme Court Decisions—by Party Name" page within the "Caselists" collection of the Legal Information Institute available at its site on the Web. Click on the "H" link or scroll down the list of cases to the entry for the *Heart of Atlanta* case. Click on the case name to access the opinion.

BACKGROUND AND FACTS The owner of the Heart of Atlanta Motel, in violation of the Civil Rights Act of 1964, refused to rent rooms to African Americans. The motel owner brought an action in a federal district court to have the Civil Rights Act declared unconstitutional, alleging that Congress had exceeded its constitutional authority to regulate commerce by enacting the act. The owner argued that his motel was not engaged in interstate commerce but was "of a purely local character." The motel, however, was accessible to state and interstate highways. The owner advertised nationally, maintained billboards throughout the state, and accepted convention trade from outside the state (75 percent of the guests were residents of other states). The court ruled that the act did not violate the Constitution and enjoined (prohibited) the owner from discriminating on the basis of race. The owner appealed. The case ultimately went to the United States Supreme Court.

IN THE WORDS OF THE COURT . . . Mr. Justice *CLARK* delivered the opinion of the Court.

* * * *

While the Act as adopted carried no congressional findings, the record of its passage through each house is replete [abounding] with evidence of the burdens that discrimination by race or color places upon interstate commerce * * * . This testimony included the fact that our people have become increasingly mobile with millions of all races traveling from State to State; that Negroes in particular have been the subject of discrimination in transient accommodations, having to travel great distances to secure the same; that often they have been unable to obtain accommodations and have had to call upon friends to put them up overnight. * * * These exclusionary practices were found to be nationwide, the Under Secretary of Commerce testifying that there is "no question that this discrimination in the North still exists to a large degree" and in the West and Midwest as well * * * . This testimony indicated a qualitative as well as quantitative effect on interstate travel by Negroes. The former was the obvious impairment of the Negro traveler's pleasure and convenience that resulted when he continually was uncertain of finding lodging. As for the latter, there was evidence that this uncertainty stemming from racial discrimination had the effect of discouraging travel on the part of a substantial portion of the Negro community * * * . We shall not burden this opinion with further details since the voluminous testimony presents overwhelming evidence that discrimination by hotels and motels impedes interstate travel.

* * * *

It is said that the operation of the motel here is of a purely local character. But, assuming this to be true, "if it is interstate commerce that feels the pinch, it does not

CASE 4.1—CONTINUED ▶

matter how local the operation that applies the squeeze." * * * Thus the power of Congress to promote interstate commerce also includes the power to regulate the local incidents thereof, including local activities in both the States of origin and destination, which might have a substantial and harmful effect upon that commerce.

DECISION AND REMEDY   The United States Supreme Court upheld the constitutionality of the Civil Rights Act of 1964. The power of Congress to regulate interstate commerce permitted the enactment of legislation that could halt local discriminatory practices.

IMPACT OF THIS CASE ON TODAY'S LEGAL ENVIRONMENT
If the Supreme Court had invalidated the Civil Rights Act of 1964, the legal landscape of the United States would be much different today. The act prohibited discrimination based on race, color, national origin, religion, or gender in all "public

accommodations" as well as discrimination in employment based on these criteria. Although state laws now prohibit many of these forms of discrimination as well, the protections available vary from state to state—and it is not certain when (and if) such laws would have been passed had the 1964 federal Civil Rights Act been deemed unconstitutional.

RELEVANT WEB SITES   *To locate information on the Web concerning the* Heart of Atlanta Motel *case, go to this text's Web site at* **www.thomsonedu.com/westbuslaw/let***, select "Chapter 4," and click on "URLs for Landmarks."*

The Commerce Power Today   Today, at least theoretically, the power over commerce authorizes the national government to regulate every commercial enterprise in the United States. Federal (national) legislation governs virtually every major activity conducted by businesses—from hiring and firing decisions to workplace safety, competitive practices, and financing.

In the last decade, however, the Supreme Court has begun to curb somewhat the national government's regulatory authority under the commerce clause. In 1995, the Court held—for the first time in sixty years—that Congress had exceeded its regulatory authority under the commerce clause. The Court struck down an act that banned the possession of guns within one thousand feet of any school because the act attempted to regulate an area that had "nothing to do with commerce."[4] Subsequently, the Court invalidated key portions of two other federal acts on the ground that they exceeded Congress's commerce clause authority.[5]

The current trend of not allowing the federal government to regulate noncommercial activities that take place wholly within a state's borders has led to some controversial decisions in the lower courts. In 2003, for example, the U.S. Court of Appeals for the Ninth Circuit decided a case involving marijuana use on commerce clause grounds. Eleven states, including California, have adopted "medical marijuana" laws that legalize marijuana for medical purposes. Marijuana possession, however, is illegal under the federal Controlled Substances Act (CSA).[6] The case arose after the federal government seized the marijuana that two seriously ill California women were using on the advice of their physicians. The women argued that it is unconstitutional for

---

4. The United States Supreme Court held the Gun-Free School Zones Act of 1990 to be unconstitutional in *United States v. Lopez*, 514 U.S. 549, 115 S.Ct. 1624, 131 L.Ed.2d 626 (1995).
5. See, for example, *Printz v. United States*, 521 U.S. 898, 117 S.Ct. 2365, 138 L.Ed.2d 914 (1997), involving the Brady Handgun Violence Prevention Act of 1993; and *United States v. Morrison*, 529 U.S. 598, 120 S.Ct. 1740, 146 L.Ed.2d 658 (2000), concerning the federal Violence Against Women Act of 1994.
6. 21 U.S.C. Sections 801 *et seq.*

LANDMARK IN THE LEGAL ENVIRONMENT

Gibbons v. Ogden (1824)

The commerce clause, which is found in Article I, Section 8, of the U.S. Constitution, gives Congress the power "[t]o regulate Commerce with foreign Nations, and among the several States, and with the Indian Tribes." What exactly does "to regulate commerce" mean? What does "commerce" entail? These questions came before the United States Supreme Court in 1824 in the case of *Gibbons v. Ogden.*[a]

Background   In 1803, Robert Fulton, the inventor of the steamboat, and Robert Livingston, who was then American minister to France, secured a monopoly on steam navigation on the waters in the state of New York from the New York legislature. Fulton and Livingston licensed Aaron Ogden, a former governor of New Jersey and a U.S. senator, to operate steam-powered ferryboats between New York and New Jersey. Thomas Gibbons, who had obtained a license from the U.S. government to operate boats in interstate waters, competed with Ogden without New York's permission. Ogden sued Gibbons. The New York state courts granted Ogden's request for an injunction—an order prohibiting Gibbons from operating in New York waters. Gibbons appealed the decision to the United States Supreme Court.

Marshall's Decision   Sitting as chief justice on the Supreme Court was John Marshall, an advocate of a strong national government. In his decision, Marshall defined the word *commerce* as used in the commerce clause to mean all commercial intercourse—that is, all

a. 22 U.S. (9 Wheat.) 1, 6 L.Ed. 23 (1824).

business dealings that affect more than one state. The Court ruled against Ogden's monopoly, reversing the injunction against Gibbons. Marshall used this opportunity not only to expand the definition of commerce but also to validate and increase the power of the national legislature to regulate commerce. Said Marshall, "What is this power? It is the power * * * to prescribe the rule by which commerce is to be governed." Marshall held that the power to regulate interstate commerce was an exclusive power of the national government and that this power included the power to regulate any intrastate commerce that substantially affects interstate commerce.

Application to Today's Legal Environment
Marshall's broad definition of the commerce power established the foundation for the expansion of national powers in the years to come. Today, the national government continues to rely on the commerce clause for its constitutional authority to regulate business activities. Marshall's conclusion that the power to regulate interstate commerce was an exclusive power of the national government has also had significant consequences. By implication, this means that a state cannot *regulate activities that extend beyond its borders, such as out-of-state online gambling operations that affect the welfare of in-state citizens. It also means that state regulations over in-state activities normally will be invalidated if the regulations substantially burden interstate commerce.*

RELEVANT WEB SITES
To locate information on the Web concerning the Gibbons v. Ogden *decision, go to this text's Web site at* **www.thomsonedu.com/westbuslaw/let**, *select "Chapter 4," and click on "URLs for Landmarks."*

the federal act to prohibit them from using marijuana for medical purposes that are legal within the state. The federal appellate court agreed. In 2005, however, the United States Supreme Court held that Congress has the authority to prohibit the intrastate possession and noncommercial cultivation of marijuana as part of a larger regulatory scheme (the CSA).[7]

The Regulatory Powers of the States   As part of their inherent sovereignty, state governments have the authority to regulate affairs within their borders. This authority stems in part from the Tenth Amendment to the Constitution, which reserves all powers not delegated to the national government to the

---

7. *Gonzales v. Raich*, 245 U.S. 1, 125 S.Ct. 2195, 162 L.Ed.2d 1 (2005).

This woman was partially paralyzed on the right side of her body until she started smoking medical marijuana. What did the United States Supreme Court decide about states' rights to authorize such uses of marijuana given that federal law still prohibits it? (AP Photo/Ben Margot)

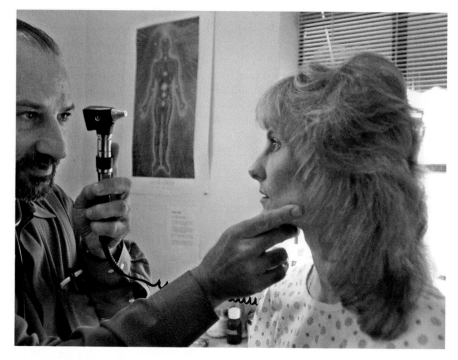

POLICE POWERS
Powers possessed by the states as part of their inherent sovereignty. These powers may be exercised to protect or promote the public order, health, safety, morals, and general welfare.

states. State regulatory powers are often referred to as **police powers.** The term encompasses not only the enforcement of criminal law but also the right of state governments to regulate private activities to protect or promote the public order, health, safety, morals, and general welfare. Fire and building codes, antidiscrimination laws, parking regulations, zoning restrictions, licensing requirements, and thousands of other state statutes covering virtually every aspect of daily life have been enacted pursuant to a state's police powers. Local governments, including cities, also exercise police powers.[8] Generally, state laws enacted pursuant to a state's police powers carry a strong presumption of validity.

The "Dormant" Commerce Clause   The United States Supreme Court has interpreted the commerce clause to mean that the national government has the *exclusive* authority to regulate commerce that substantially affects trade and commerce among the states. This express grant of authority to the national government, which is often referred to as the "positive" aspect of the commerce clause, implies a negative aspect—that the states do *not* have the authority to regulate interstate commerce. This negative aspect of the commerce clause is often referred to as the "dormant" (implied) commerce clause.

   The dormant commerce clause comes into play when state regulations affect interstate commerce. In this situation, the courts normally weigh the state's interest in regulating a certain matter against the burden that the state's regulation places on interstate commerce. Because courts balance the interests involved, it can be extremely difficult to predict the outcome in a particular case.

---

8. Local governments derive their authority to regulate their communities from the state, because they are creatures of the state. In other words, they cannot come into existence unless authorized by the state to do so.

| Example #2 A Michigan statute prohibited out-of-state wineries from shipping wine directly to Michigan residents but allowed in-state wineries to do so. The U.S. Court of Appeals for the Sixth Circuit ruled that the statute violated the dormant commerce clause. The court concluded that the regulations benefited in-state wineries and burdened out-of-state wineries, while failing to promote any legitimate local purpose.[9] Other federal appellate courts, however, had upheld similar statutes on the ground that a state has a legitimate interest in monitoring the flow of alcohol into the state. In 2005, the United States Supreme Court resolved this conflict by affirming the opinion of the Sixth Circuit on the issue.[10] |

What if a state law attempts to regulate the types of materials that may be distributed to state residents via the Internet? Would such a law violate the dormant commerce clause? See this chapter's *Online Developments* feature on page 115 for a discussion of that question.

The court in the following case considered how established law governing the commerce clause applies in cyberspace.

---

9. *Heald v. Engler*, 342 F.3d 517 (6th Cir. 2003).
10. *Granholm v. Heald*, 544 U.S. 460, 125 S.Ct. 1885, 161 L.Ed.2d 796 (2005).

CASE 4.2 **MaryCLE, LLC v. First Choice Internet, Inc.**

Court of Special Appeals of Maryland, 2006.
166 Md.App. 481,
890 A.2d 818.

BACKGROUND AND FACTS The Maryland General Assembly enacted the Maryland Commercial Electronic Mail Act (MCEMA) in 2002 "to curb the dissemination of false or misleading information through unsolicited, commercial e-mail (UCE, or spam—see Chapter 5) as a deceptive business practice." The MCEMA provides that a person may not "initiate," "conspire to," or "assist in" the "transmission of commercial electronic mail" either *from* a computer within Maryland or *to* an e-mail address "that the sender knows or should have known is held by a resident of" Maryland if the mail "[c]ontains false or misleading information." Eric Menhart, a student at George Washington University Law School in Washington, D.C., founded Maryland Consumer Legal Equity, LLC (MaryCLE), to "protect consumers via promotion of responsible marketing practices." MaryCLE's e-mail address is emj@maryland-state-resident.com. In September and October 2003, First Choice Internet, Inc., a marketing firm in New York, sent eighty-three UCE messages to MaryCLE. MaryCLE replied to each with a request to be removed from the mailing list, but each reply was returned as "undeliverable." MaryCLE filed a suit in a Maryland state court against First Choice, claiming violations of the MCEMA. The court dismissed the complaint. The plaintiff appealed to a state intermediate appellate court.

IN THE WORDS OF THE COURT . . . ADKINS, J. [Judge]

* * * *

* * * MCEMA * * * applies to all e-mail advertisers, regardless of their geographic location. It does not discriminate against out-of-state senders. * * * [T]he benefits of MCEMA clearly outweigh the burden on First Choice and other e-mail advertisers. *When the only burden MCEMA imposes is that of sending truthful and nondeceptive e-mail, that First Choice considers MCEMA's requirements inconvenient and even impractical does not mean that statute violates the commerce clause.* [Emphasis added.]

* * * MCEMA does not regulate exclusively extraterritorial [out-of-state] conduct because its focus is not on when or where recipients may open the proscribed * * * messages. Rather, the Act addresses the conduct of spammers in targeting Maryland consumers. The choice to send UCE all over the country, invoking the probability that

CASE 4.2—CONTINUED ▶

CASE 4.2–CONTINUED

it will be received by Maryland residents, is First Choice's business decision. Such a business decision simply does not establish that MCEMA controls conduct occurring wholly outside Maryland.

* * * MCEMA does not have * * * a nationwide reach; nor does it purport to give Maryland any power to determine where an e-mail is sent. It only mandates that all e-mail addressed to Maryland residents be truthful and nondeceptive.

* * * *

MCEMA * * * does not prevent senders of e-mail advertisements from soliciting the residents of other states; it merely regulates those that are sent to Maryland residents or from equipment located in Maryland. The Act does not project Maryland's regulatory scheme into other states because e-mail advertisers remain free to send e-mails to other states.

* * * Although First Choice argues that MCEMA has "an enormous chilling effect on interstate commerce," undoubtedly other states would neither desire the sending of false and misleading e-mails into their borders, nor object to Maryland's exclusion of them.

* * * No state is likely to consider that the welfare of a business that engages in false or misleading advertising is a legitimate interest, worthy of state protection. We therefore conclude that MCEMA does not subject e-mail advertisers to inconsistent obligations.

To be clear, *MCEMA avoids violation of the Commerce Clause because it has built-in safeguards to ensure that it does not regulate conduct occurring wholly outside Maryland.* In order to violate the Act, an e-mail advertiser must either use equipment located in the state of Maryland or send prohibited UCE [spam] to someone he knows or should know is a Maryland resident. * * * Maryland residency is presumed if the sender of UCE can discover that an e-mail address is registered to a Maryland resident. In this case, First Choice could have done so * * * by accessing * * * www.networksolutions.com, and * * * exclud[ing] MaryCLE from its mailing list. [Emphasis added.]

DECISION AND REMEDY The state intermediate appellate court reversed the lower court's judgment and remanded the case for further proceedings, including a possible trial. The appellate court concluded that the MCEMA protects consumers from fraud and the costs associated with spam without unduly burdening interstate commerce and thus "does not offend the Commerce Clause."

WHAT IF THE FACTS WERE DIFFERENT? *If the MCEMA attempted to control conduct that occurred wholly outside Maryland—by, for example, focusing on where spam originates—what might have been the result in this case?*

The Supremacy Clause

Article VI of the Constitution provides that the Constitution, laws, and treaties of the United States are "the supreme Law of the Land." This article, commonly referred to as the **supremacy clause,** is important in the ordering of state and federal relationships. When there is a direct conflict between a federal law and a state law, the state law is rendered invalid. Because some powers are *concurrent* (shared by the federal government and the states), however, it is necessary to determine which law governs in a particular circumstance.

Preemption occurs when Congress chooses to act exclusively in a concurrent area. In this circumstance, a valid federal statute or regulation will take precedence over a conflicting state or local law or regulation on the same general subject. Often, it is not clear whether Congress, in passing a law, intended to preempt an entire subject area against state regulation. In these situations,

ONLINE DEVELOPMENTS
Can States Regulate Internet Commerce?

The Constitution's commerce clause—and most of the United States Supreme Court's decisions interpreting that clause—were created long before the Internet became a reality. Prior to the advent of the Internet, "interstate commerce" typically meant commerce in goods or services that extended beyond a particular state's borders. In the online environment, however, physical boundaries do not exist. Thus, one of the difficulties facing the courts in the last several years has been how to apply this traditional body of law to online transactions.

Traditional Commerce Clause Analysis

The Constitution's commerce clause, as interpreted by the United States Supreme Court, gives the national government the *exclusive* power to regulate interstate commerce. That means, in effect, that states *cannot* regulate interstate commerce. As noted elsewhere in this chapter, this limitation on state powers is referred to as the negative, or "dormant," commerce clause. If a court finds that a state law places too great a burden on interstate commerce, the law will be deemed unconstitutional on the ground that it violates the dormant commerce clause.

By and large, the courts have applied traditional commerce clause analysis in cases challenging the constitutionality of state laws regulating the Internet. As in traditional commerce clause cases, the courts tend to invalidate state laws regulating the Internet if those laws extend to activities beyond their borders and place too great a burden on interstate commerce.

Can Vermont Limit Minors' Access to Web Material?

Consider a case that came before a federal appellate court in *American Booksellers Foundation v. Dean.*[a] The case challenged the constitutionality of a Vermont law that prohibited the Internet distribution to minors of sexually explicit materials that are "harmful to minors."

The effect of this law on out-of-state residents was made clear in the argument put forth by one of the plaintiffs (those who brought the lawsuit), Sexual Health Network, Inc. (SHN). SHN, which was located in Connecticut, operated a Web site on which it posted information concerning a range of sex-related topics. SHN's aim was to provide access to sexuality-related information designed to assist persons with disabilities, illnesses, and changes in their lifestyles. Clearly, SHN could not prevent minors living in Vermont (or any other state—or nation) from accessing its Web site. To avoid possible prosecution for violating Vermont's law, SHN would essentially have to shut down its Web site. SHN and the other plaintiffs, including the American Civil Liberties Union, thus sought a court order barring the enforcement of the Vermont statute on the ground that, among other things, it violated the dormant commerce clause.

The court agreed with the plaintiffs. The court held that the Vermont law violated the dormant commerce clause because it "regulates Internet commerce occurring wholly outside Vermont's borders." The court noted that although Vermont aimed to protect only Vermont minors, in effect the rest of the nation was forced to comply with its regulation or risk prosecution under Vermont's law.

For Critical Analysis *In its opinion, the court pointed out that "at the same time that the Internet's geographic reach increases Vermont's interest in regulating out-of-state conduct, it makes state regulation impracticable." Why does the court here believe that Vermont's regulation is "impracticable"?*

a. 342 F.3d 96 (2d Cir. 2003).

it is left to the courts to determine whether Congress intended to exercise exclusive power over a given area. No single factor is decisive as to whether a court will find preemption. Generally, congressional intent to preempt will be found if a federal law regulating an activity is so pervasive, comprehensive, or detailed that the states have little or no room to regulate in that area. Also, when a federal statute creates an agency—such as the National Labor Relations Board—to enforce the law, matters that may come within the agency's jurisdiction will likely preempt state laws.

The Taxing and Spending Powers

Article I, Section 8, provides that Congress has the "Power to lay and collect Taxes, Duties, Imposts [taxes on imported goods], and Excises [taxes on domestic goods]." Section 8 further provides that "all Duties, Imposts and Excises shall be uniform throughout the United States." The requirement of uniformity refers to uniformity among the states; thus, Congress may not tax some states while exempting others.

Traditionally, if Congress attempted to regulate indirectly, by taxation, an area over which it had no authority, the tax would be invalidated by the courts. Today, however, if a tax measure bears some reasonable relationship to revenue production, it is generally held to be within the national taxing power. Moreover, the expansive interpretation of the commerce clause almost always provides a basis for sustaining a federal tax.

Under Article I, Section 8, Congress has the power "to pay the Debts and provide for the common Defence and general welfare of the United States." Through the spending power, Congress disposes of the revenues accumulated from the taxing power. Congress can spend revenues not only to carry out its enumerated (explicit) powers but also to promote any objective it deems worthwhile, so long as it does not violate the Constitution or its amendments. For example, Congress could not condition welfare payments on the recipients' political views. The spending power necessarily involves policy choices, with which taxpayers may disagree.

BUSINESS AND THE BILL OF RIGHTS

The importance of a written declaration of the rights of individuals eventually caused the first Congress of the United States to submit twelve amendments to the Constitution to the states for approval. The first ten of these amendments, commonly known as the **Bill of Rights,** were adopted in 1791 and embody a series of protections for the individual against various types of interference by the federal government.[11] Some constitutional protections apply to business entities as well. For example, corporations exist as separate legal entities, or legal persons, and enjoy many of the same rights and privileges as natural persons do. Summarized here are the protections guaranteed by these ten amendments (see the Constitution in Appendix B for the complete text of each amendment):

BILL OF RIGHTS
The first ten amendments to the U.S. Constitution.

BE CAREFUL Although most of these rights apply to actions of the states, some of them apply only to actions of the federal government.

1. The First Amendment guarantees the freedoms of religion, speech, and the press and the rights to assemble peaceably and to petition the government.
2. The Second Amendment guarantees the right to keep and bear arms.
3. The Third Amendment prohibits, in peacetime, the lodging of soldiers in any house without the owner's consent.
4. The Fourth Amendment prohibits unreasonable searches and seizures of persons or property.
5. The Fifth Amendment guarantees the rights to *indictment* (formal accusation—see Chapter 6) by grand jury, to due process of law, and to fair payment when private property is taken for public use. In addition, the

---

11. One of these proposed amendments was ratified 203 years later (in 1992) and became the Twenty-seventh Amendment to the Constitution. See Appendix B.

Police search a crack house in Florida. Should the owners and occupants of such houses receive protection from unreasonable searches and seizures under the U.S. Constitution? Why or why not? (Corbis. All rights reserved.)

Fifth Amendment also prohibits compulsory self-incrimination and double jeopardy (trial for the same crime twice).

6. The Sixth Amendment guarantees the accused in a criminal case the right to a speedy and public trial by an impartial jury and with counsel. The accused has the right to cross-examine witnesses against him or her and to solicit testimony from witnesses in his or her favor.

7. The Seventh Amendment guarantees the right to a trial by jury in a civil (noncriminal) case involving at least twenty dollars.[12]

8. The Eighth Amendment prohibits excessive bail and fines, as well as cruel and unusual punishment.

9. The Ninth Amendment establishes that the people have rights in addition to those specified in the Constitution.

10. The Tenth Amendment establishes that those powers neither delegated to the federal government nor denied to the states are reserved for the states.

As originally intended, the Bill of Rights limited only the powers of the national government. Over time, however, the Supreme Court "incorporated" most of these rights into the protections against state actions afforded by the Fourteenth Amendment to the Constitution. That amendment, passed in 1868 after the Civil War, provides in part that "[n]o State shall . . . deprive any person of life, liberty, or property, without due process of law." Starting in 1925, the Supreme Court began to define various rights and liberties guaranteed in the national Constitution as constituting "due process of law," which was required of state governments under the Fourteenth Amendment. Today, most of the rights and liberties set forth in the Bill of Rights apply to state governments as well as the national government.

We will look closely at several of the amendments in the above list in Chapter 6, in the context of criminal law and procedures. Here we examine

---

12. Twenty dollars was forty days' pay for the average person when the Bill of Rights was written.

The Impact of Foreign Law on the United States Supreme Court

As noted in the text, the United States Supreme Court interprets and gives meaning to the rights provided in the U.S. Constitution. It is the Court's role to determine the appropriate balance of rights and protections stemming from the Constitution. Clearly this is a difficult task, especially because society's perceptions and needs change over time. The justices on the Supreme Court are noticeably influenced by the opinions and beliefs of U.S. citizens. This is particularly true when the Court is faced with issues of freedom of speech or religion, obscenity, or privacy. Changing views on controversial topics, such as homosexuality and privacy in an era of terrorist threats, may affect the way the Supreme Court decides a case. The question then becomes, should the Court also consider other nations' laws and world opinion when balancing individual rights in the United States?

Over the last several years, justices on the United States Supreme Court have exhibited an increasing tendency to consider foreign law when deciding issues of national importance. For example, in 2003—for the first time ever—foreign law was cited in a majority opinion of the Supreme Court (references to foreign law have appeared in footnotes and dissents on a few occasions in the past). The case was a controversial one in which the Court struck down laws that prohibit oral and anal sex between consenting adults of the same sex. In the

majority opinion (an opinion that the majority of justices have signed), Justice Anthony Kennedy mentioned that the European Court of Human Rights and other foreign courts have consistently acknowledged that homosexuals have a right "to engage in intimate, consensual conduct."[a] This comment sparked debate in legal circles over whether the Supreme Court, or other U.S. courts, should ever consider world opinion or cite foreign law as persuasive authority.

The practice has many critics, including Justice Scalia, who believes that foreign views are irrelevant to rulings on U.S. law. Other Supreme Court justices, however, including Justices Breyer, Ginsberg, and O'Connor (who is now retired), believe that in our increasingly global community we should not ignore the opinions of courts in the rest of the world.

For Critical Analysis   *Should U.S. courts, and particularly the United States Supreme Court, look to other nations' laws for guidance when deciding important issues—including those involving rights granted by the Constitution? If so, what impact might this have on their decisions? Explain.*

a. *Lawrence v. Texas,* 539 U.S. 558, 123 S.Ct. 2472, 156 L.Ed.2d 508 (2003). Other cases in which the Supreme Court has referenced foreign law include *Grutter v. Bollinger,* 539 U.S. 306, 123 S.Ct. 2325, 156 L.Ed.2d 304 (2003), in the dissent, and *Atkins v. Virginia,* 536 U.S. 304, 122 S.Ct. 2242, 153 L.Ed.2d 335 (2002), in footnote 21 to the majority opinion.

REMEMBER ! **The First Amendment guarantee of freedom of speech applies only to *government* restrictions on speech.**

two important guarantees of the First Amendment—freedom of speech and freedom of religion. These and other First Amendment freedoms (of the press, assembly, and petition) have all been applied to the states through the due process clause of the Fourteenth Amendment. As you read through the following pages, keep in mind that none of these (or other) constitutional freedoms confers an absolute right. Ultimately, it is the United States Supreme Court, as the final interpreter of the Constitution, that gives meaning to these rights and determines their boundaries. (For a discussion of how the Supreme Court may consider other nations' laws when determining the appropriate balance of individual rights, see this chapter's *Beyond Our Borders* feature.)

The First Amendment–Freedom of Speech

Freedom of speech is the most prized freedom that Americans have. Indeed, it forms the basis for our democratic form of government, which could not exist if people were not allowed to express their political opinions freely and criticize government actions or policies. Because of its importance, the courts traditionally have protected this right to the fullest extent possible.

Speech often includes not only what we say, but also what we do to express our political, social, and religious views. The courts generally protect **symbolic speech**—gestures, movements, articles of clothing, and other forms of nonverbal expressive conduct. |**Example #3** In 1989, the Supreme Court held that the burning of the American flag to protest government policies is a constitutionally protected form of expression.[13] Similarly, participating in a hunger strike or wearing a black armband would be protected as symbolic speech.|

Expression—oral, written, or symbolized by conduct—is subject to reasonable restrictions. For example, on the campus of a public high school, certain rights may be circumscribed or denied, in part to protect minors from predatory adults and to protect adults and others from predatory minors. A balance must be struck, however, between a government's obligation to protect its citizens and those citizens' exercise of their rights. These competing interests were at issue in the following case.

SYMBOLIC SPEECH
Nonverbal expressions of beliefs. Symbolic speech, which includes gestures, movements, and articles of clothing, is given substantial protection by the courts.

---

13. See *Texas v. Johnson*, 491 U.S. 397, 109 S.Ct. 2533, 105 L.Ed.2d 342 (1989).

CASE 4.3 Hodgkins v. Peterson

United States Court of Appeals,
Seventh Circuit, 2004.
355 F.3d 1048.

BACKGROUND AND FACTS Shortly after 11 P.M. on August 26, 1999, sixteen-year-old Colin Hodgkins and three friends left a Steak 'n Shake restaurant in Indianapolis, Indiana, where they had stopped to eat after a school soccer game. At the time, an Indiana statute made it illegal for minors between the ages of fifteen and seventeen to be in a public place after 11 P.M. on weeknights unless accompanied by a parent or guardian, with a few exceptions. As Colin and his friends left the restaurant, police arrested and handcuffed them for violating this statute. Colin's mother, Nancy Hodgkins, and others filed a suit in a federal district court against Bart Peterson, the mayor of Indianapolis, and other local government officials, asking the court to order the defendants to stop enforcing the curfew on the ground that it violated the First Amendment. The court ruled in the defendants' favor, and the plaintiffs appealed to the U.S. Court of Appeals for the Seventh Circuit.

IN THE WORDS OF THE COURT . . . *ROVNER*, Circuit Judge.

* * * *

* * * The government claims that plaintiffs cannot mount a * * * challenge to the curfew law * * * because they have not demonstrated either that the curfew law imposes a disproportionate burden on those engaged in First Amendment activities or that it regulates conduct with an expressive element.

We agree that the Indiana curfew ordinance does not disproportionately impact First Amendment rights. As Colin Hodgkins can attest, it burdens minors who want to attend soccer games as much as it burdens those who wish to speak at a political rally. On the other hand, the curfew ordinance regulates minors' abilities to engage in some of the purest and most protected forms of speech and expression. [A] wide range of First Amendment activities occur during curfew hours, including political events, death penalty protests, late night sessions of the Indiana General Assembly, and neighborhood association meetings or nighttime events. A number of religions mark particular days or events with late-night services, prayers, or other activities: many Christians, for example, commemorate the birth of Christ with a midnight service on Christmas Eve and the Last Supper with an all-night vigil on Holy Thursday; Jews observe the first night of

CASE 4.3—CONTINUED ➤

Shavuot by studying Torah all through the night; and throughout the month of Ramadan, Muslims engage in late-evening prayer. Late-night or all-night marches, rallies, and sleep-ins are often held to protest government action or inaction. And it is not unusual for political campaigns, particularly in the whirlwind final hours before an election, to hold rallies in the middle of the night. Thus, during the last weeks of the 1960 presidential campaign, then-Senator John F. Kennedy addressed a group of University of Michigan students at 2:00 A.M. on the steps of the Michigan Union. In unprepared remarks, he asked the students whether they would be willing to devote a few years of their lives working in underdeveloped countries in order to foster better relations between the people of those nations and the United States. The students responded with a petition calling for the creation of the Peace Corps, which came into being the following year. These are but a few examples. *The curfew ordinance regulates access to almost every form of public expression during the late-night hours. The effect on the speech of the plaintiffs is significant.* [Emphasis added.]

    * * * *

    * * * Any juvenile who chooses to participate in a late-night religious or political activity thus runs the risk that he will be arrested if a police officer stops him en route to or from that activity and he cannot prove to the officer's satisfaction that he is out after hours in order to exercise his First Amendment rights.

    * * * *

    * * * The prospect of an arrest is intimidating in and of itself; but one should also have in mind what else might follow from the arrest. * * * We have no doubt that the authorities are well meaning in administering the drug and alcohol testing and in questioning the minor and his parents about his friends and family life. But these are also rather serious intrusions upon one's personal and familial privacy, and they represent a substantial price for a minor to have to pay in order to take part in a late-night political or religious event. *The chill that the prospect of arrest imposes on a minor's exercise of his or her First Amendment rights is patent [evident].* [Emphasis added.]

DECISION AND REMEDY   The U.S. Court of Appeals for the Seventh Circuit reversed the lower court's judgment and ordered a permanent injunction against the enforcement of the curfew. The court held that the curfew law was not narrowly tailored to serve a significant governmental interest and failed to allow for ample alternative channels for expression. The statute restricted a minor's access to any public forum during curfew hours. The concrete possibility of arrest made clear that the statute unduly chilled the exercise of minors' First Amendment rights.

FOR CRITICAL ANALYSIS–Political Consideration   *Can a curfew law be written to protect both the fundamental constitutional rights of minors and the safety of all citizens?*

Corporate Political Speech   Political speech by corporations also falls within the protection of the First Amendment. **|Example #4**   In *First National Bank of Boston v. Bellotti*,[14] national banking associations and business corporations sought United States Supreme Court review of a Massachusetts statute that prohibited corporations from making political contributions or expenditures that individuals were permitted to make. The Court ruled that the Massachusetts law was unconstitutional because it violated the right of corporations to freedom of speech.**|** Similarly, the Court has held that a law prohibiting a corporation from using bill inserts to express its views on controversial issues violates the First Amendment.[15] Although a more conser-

---

14. 435 U.S. 765, 98 S.Ct. 1407, 55 L.Ed.2d 707 (1978).
15. *Consolidated Edison Co. v. Public Service Commission,* 447 U.S. 530, 100 S.Ct. 2326, 65 L.Ed.2d 319 (1980).

vative Supreme Court subsequently reversed this trend somewhat,[16] corporate political speech continues to be given significant protection under the First Amendment.

Commercial Speech   The courts also give substantial protection to "commercial" speech, which consists of communications—primarily advertising and marketing—made by business firms that involve only their commercial interests. The protection given to commercial speech under the First Amendment is not as extensive as that afforded to noncommercial speech, however. A state may restrict certain kinds of advertising, for example, in the interest of protecting consumers from being misled by the advertising practices. States also have a legitimate interest in the beautification of roadsides, and this interest allows states to place restraints on billboard advertising. | **Example #5**   Café Erotica, a nude dancing establishment, sued the state after being denied a permit to erect a billboard along an interstate highway in Florida. The state appellate court decided that because the law directly advanced a substantial government interest in highway beautification and safety, it was not an unconstitutional restraint on commercial speech.[17]|

Generally, a restriction on commercial speech will be considered valid as long as it meets the following three criteria: (1) it must seek to implement a substantial government interest, (2) it must directly advance that interest, and (3) it must go no further than necessary to accomplish its objective. | **Example #6**   The South Carolina Supreme Court held that a state statute banning ads for video gambling violated the First Amendment because the statute did not directly advance a substantial government interest. Although the court acknowledged that the state had a substantial interest in minimizing gambling, there was no evidence that a reduction in video gambling ads would result in a reduction in gambling.[18]|

Unprotected Speech   The United States Supreme Court has made it clear that certain types of speech will not be given any protection under the First Amendment. Speech that harms the good reputation of another, or defamatory speech (see Chapter 5), will not be protected. Speech that violates criminal laws (such as threatening speech) is not constitutionally protected. Other unprotected speech includes "fighting words," or words that are likely to incite others to respond violently.

The Supreme Court has also held that obscene speech is not protected by the First Amendment. The Court has grappled from time to time with the problem of trying to establish an objective definition of obscene speech. In a 1973 case, *Miller v. California*,[19] the Supreme Court created a test for legal obscenity, which involved a set of requirements that must be met for material to be legally obscene. Under this test, material is obscene if (1) the average person finds that it violates contemporary community standards; (2) the work taken as a whole appeals to a prurient (arousing or obsessive) interest in sex;

---

16. See *Austin v. Michigan Chamber of Commerce*, 494 U.S. 652, 110 S.Ct. 1391, 108 L.Ed.2d 652 (1990), in which the Court upheld a state law prohibiting corporations from using general corporate funds for independent expenditures in state political campaigns.
17. *Café Erotica v. Florida Department of Transportation*, 830 So.2d 181 (Fla.App. 1 Dist. 2002); review denied, *Café Erotica/We Dare to Bare v. Florida Department of Transportation*, 845 So.2d 888 (2003).
18. *Evans v. State*, 344 S.C. 60, 543 S.E.2d 547 (2001).
19. 413 U.S. 15, 93 S.Ct. 2607, 37 L.Ed.2d 419 (1973).

(3) the work shows patently offensive sexual conduct; and (4) the work lacks serious redeeming literary, artistic, political, or scientific merit.

Because community standards vary widely, the *Miller* test has had inconsistent applications, and obscenity remains a constitutionally unsettled issue. Numerous state and federal statutes make it a crime to disseminate obscene materials, however, and the Supreme Court has often upheld such laws, including laws prohibiting the sale and possession of child pornography.[20]

Online Obscenity   Congress first attempted to protect minors from pornographic materials on the Internet by passing the Communications Decency Act (CDA) of 1996. The CDA made it a crime to make available to minors online any "obscene or indecent" message that "depicts or describes, in terms patently offensive as measured by contemporary community standards, sexual or excretory activities or organs."[21] The act was challenged as an unconstitutional restraint on speech, and ultimately the United States Supreme Court ruled that portions of the act were unconstitutional. The Court held that the terms *indecent* and *patently offensive* covered large amounts of nonpornographic material with serious educational or other value.[22]

The Child Online Protection Act (COPA) of 1998[23] banned material "harmful to minors" distributed without some kind of age-verification system to separate adult and minor users. Although the COPA was more narrowly tailored than its predecessor, the CDA, it still used "contemporary community standards" to define which material was obscene and harmful to minors. When the act was challenged as violating free speech, the federal court hearing the case granted an injunction suspending the COPA, and the appellate court upheld the injunction.[24] In the same year, however, the Supreme Court reversed that decision and remanded the case, concluding that the reference to contemporary community standards alone was not sufficient to render the entire act unconstitutional.[25] On remand, the appellate court again held that the COPA violated free speech guarantees.[26] In June 2004, the Supreme Court affirmed the appellate court's decision and remanded the case for trial. The Court concluded that the claim that the COPA violated the right to free speech would likely prevail and hence left the injunction in place.[27]

In 2000, Congress enacted the Children's Internet Protection Act (CIPA),[28] which requires public schools and libraries to block adult content from access by children by installing **filtering software.** Such software is designed to prevent persons from viewing certain Web sites by responding to a site's Internet address or its **meta tags,** or key words. The CIPA was also challenged on constitutional grounds, but in 2003 the Supreme Court held that the act did not

FILTERING SOFTWARE
A computer program that includes a pattern through which data are passed. When designed to block access to certain Web sites, the pattern blocks the retrieval of a site whose URL or key words are on a list within the program.

META TAG
A key word in a document that can serve as an index reference to the document. On the Web, search engines return results based, in part, on the tags in Web documents.

20. See, for example, *Osborne v. Ohio,* 495 U.S. 103, 110 S.Ct. 1691, 109 L.Ed.2d 98 (1990).
21. 47 U.S.C. Section 223(a)(1)(B)(ii).
22. *Reno v. American Civil Liberties Union,* 521 U.S. 844, 117 S.Ct. 2329, 138 L.Ed.2d 874 (1997).
23. 47 U.S.C. Section 231.
24. *American Civil Liberties Union v. Reno,* 31 F.Supp.2d 473 (E.D.Pa. 1999); *aff'd,* 217 F.3d 162 (3d Cir. 2002).
25. *Ashcroft v. American Civil Liberties Union,* 535 U.S. 564, 122 S.Ct. 1700, 152 L.Ed.2d 771 (2002).
26. *American Civil Liberties Union v. Ashcroft,* 322 F.3d 240 (3d Cir. 2003).
27. *Ashcroft v. American Civil Liberties Union,* 542 U.S. 656, 124 S.Ct. 2783, 159 L.Ed.2d 690 (2004).
28. 17 U.S.C. Sections 1701–1741.

violate the First Amendment. The Court concluded that because libraries can disable the filters for any patrons who ask, the system was reasonably flexible and did not burden free speech to an unconstitutional extent.[29]

The First Amendment–Freedom of Religion

The First Amendment states that the government may neither establish any religion nor prohibit the free exercise of religious practices. The first part of this constitutional provision is referred to as the **establishment clause,** and the second part is known as the **free exercise clause.** Government action, both federal and state, must be consistent with this constitutional mandate.

The Establishment Clause   The establishment clause prohibits the government from establishing a state-sponsored religion, as well as from passing laws that promote (aid or endorse) religion or that show a preference for one religion over another. The establishment clause does not require a complete separation of church and state, though. On the contrary, it requires the government to accommodate religions.[30]

The establishment clause covers all conflicts about such matters as the legality of state and local government support for a particular religion, government aid to religious organizations and schools, the government's allowing or requiring school prayers, and the teaching of evolution versus fundamentalist theories of creation. The Supreme Court has held that for a government law or policy to be constitutional, it must be secular in aim, must not have the primary effect of advancing or inhibiting religions, and must not create "an excessive government entanglement with religion."[31] Generally, federal or state regulation that does not promote religion or place a significant burden on religion is constitutional even if it has some impact on religion.

| **Example #7**   "Sunday closing laws" make the performance of some commercial activities on Sunday illegal. These statutes, also known as "blue laws" (from the color of the paper on which an early Sunday law was written), have been upheld on the ground that it is a legitimate function of government to provide a day of rest. The United States Supreme Court has held that the closing laws, although originally of a religious character, have taken on the secular purpose of promoting the health and welfare of workers.[32] Even though Sunday closing laws admittedly make it easier for Christians to attend religious services, the Court has viewed this effect as an incidental, not a primary, purpose of Sunday closing laws. |

ESTABLISHMENT CLAUSE
The provision in the First Amendment to the Constitution that prohibits the government from establishing any state-sponsored religion or enacting any law that promotes religion or favors one religion over another.

FREE EXERCISE CLAUSE
The provision in the First Amendment to the Constitution that prohibits the government from interfering with people's religious practices or forms of worship.

ETHICAL ISSUE 4.1   ***Do religious displays on public property violate the establishment clause?***

The thorny issue of whether religious displays on public property violate the establishment clause often arises during the holiday season. Time and again, the courts have wrestled with this issue, but it has never been resolved in a way that satisfies everyone and courts continue to settle

---

29. *United States v. American Library Association*, 539 U.S. 194, 123 S.Ct. 2297, 156 L.Ed.2d 221 (2003).
30. *Zorach v. Clauson*, 343 U.S. 306, 72 S.Ct. 679, 96 L.Ed. 954 (1952).
31. *Lemon v. Kurtzman*, 403 U.S. 602, 91 S.Ct. 2105, 29 L.Ed.2d 745 (1971).
32. *McGowan v. Maryland*, 366 U.S. 420, 81 S.Ct. 1101, 6 L.Ed.2d 393 (1961).

such disputes on a case-by-case basis. In a 1984 case, the United States Supreme Court decided that a city's official Christmas display, which included a crèche (Nativity scene), did not violate the establishment clause because it was just one part of a larger holiday display that featured secular symbols, such as reindeer and candy canes.[33] In a later case, the Court held that the presence of a crèche within a county courthouse violated the establishment clause because it was not in close proximity to nonreligious symbols, including a Christmas tree, which were located outside, on the building's steps.[34] In another instance, in 2005 the Supreme Court ruled that the presence of a six-foot monument depicting the Ten Commandments in a public park in Austin, Texas, did not violate the establishment clause because it was just one of seventeen sculptures. In another ruling issued on the same day, however, the Court held that wall displays of the Ten Commandments in two county courthouses in Kentucky were so overtly religious as to be impermissible.[35] The courts continue to apply this reasoning in cases involving similar issues.

The Free Exercise Clause   The free exercise clause guarantees that a person can hold any religious belief that she or he wants; or a person can have no religious belief. When religious *practices* work against public policy and the public welfare, however, the government can act. For example, regardless of a child's or parent's religious beliefs, the government can require certain types of vaccinations. Similarly, although children of Jehovah's Witnesses are not required to say the Pledge of Allegiance at school, their parents cannot prevent them from accepting medical treatment (such as blood transfusions) if in fact their lives are in danger. Additionally, public school students can be required to study from textbooks chosen by school authorities.

For business firms, an important issue involves the accommodation that businesses must make for the religious beliefs of their employees. For example, if an employee's religion prohibits him or her from working on a certain day of the week or at a certain type of job, the employer must make a reasonable attempt to accommodate these religious requirements. Employers must reasonably accommodate an employee's religious beliefs even if the beliefs are not based on the tenets or dogma of a particular church, sect, or denomination. The only requirement is that the belief be religious in nature and sincerely held by the employee. (We will look further at this issue in Chapter 14, in the context of employment discrimination.)

DUE PROCESS AND EQUAL PROTECTION

Two other constitutional guarantees of great significance to Americans are mandated by the due process clauses of the Fifth and Fourteenth Amendments and the equal protection clause of the Fourteenth Amendment.

33. *Lynch v. Donnelly*, 465 U.S. 668, 104 S.Ct. 1355, 79 L.Ed.2d 604 (1984).
34. See *County of Allegheny v. American Civil Liberties Union*, 492 U.S. 573, 109 S.Ct. 3086, 106 L.Ed.2d 472 (1989).
35. *Van Orden v. Perry*, ___U.S.___, 125 S.Ct. 2854, 162 L.Ed.2d 607 (2005); and *McCreary County, Kentucky v. American Civil Liberties Union of Kentucky*, ___U.S.___, 125 S.Ct. 2722, 162 L.Ed.2d 729 (2005), respectively.

Due Process

Both the Fifth and the Fourteenth Amendments provide that no person shall be deprived "of life, liberty, or property, without due process of law." The **due process clause** of each of these constitutional amendments has two aspects—procedural and substantive.

Procedural Due Process Procedural due process requires that any government decision to take life, liberty, or property must be made fairly. For example, fair procedures must be used in determining whether a person will be subjected to punishment or have some burden imposed on him or her. Fair procedure has been interpreted as requiring that the person have at least an opportunity to object to a proposed action before a fair, neutral decision maker (which need not be a judge). Thus, for example, if a driver's license is construed as a property interest, some sort of opportunity to object to its suspension or termination by the state must be provided.

Substantive Due Process Substantive due process focuses on the content, or substance, of legislation. If a law or other governmental action limits a *fundamental right,* it will be held to violate substantive due process unless it promotes a compelling or overriding state interest. Fundamental rights include interstate travel, privacy, voting, and all First Amendment rights. Compelling state interests could include, for example, the public's safety. **| Example #8** Laws setting speed limits may be upheld even though they affect interstate travel, if they are shown to reduce highway fatalities. The courts uphold these laws because the state has a compelling interest in protecting the lives of its citizens.**|**

In situations not involving fundamental rights, a law or action does not violate substantive due process if it rationally relates to any legitimate governmental end. It is almost impossible for a law or action to fail the "rationality" test. Under this test, virtually any business regulation will be upheld as reasonable—the United States Supreme Court has sustained insurance regulations, price and wage controls, banking limitations, and restrictions of unfair competition and trade practices against substantive due process challenges.

| Example #9 If a state legislature enacted a law imposing a fifteen-year term of imprisonment without a trial on all businesspersons who appeared in their own television commercials, the law would be unconstitutional on both substantive and procedural grounds. Substantive review would invalidate the legislation because it abridges freedom of speech. Procedurally, the law is unfair because it imposes the penalty without giving the accused a chance to defend her or his actions.**|** The lack of procedural due process will cause a court to invalidate any statute or prior court decision. Similarly, the courts will overrule any state or federal law that violates the Constitution by denying substantive due process.

Equal Protection

Under the Fourteenth Amendment, a state may not "deny to any person within its jurisdiction the equal protection of the laws." The United States Supreme Court has used the due process clause of the Fifth Amendment to make the **equal protection clause** applicable to the federal government as well. Equal protection means that the government must treat similarly situated individuals in a similar manner.

DUE PROCESS CLAUSE
The provisions in the Fifth and Fourteenth Amendments to the Constitution that guarantee that no person shall be deprived of life, liberty, or property without due process of law. Similar clauses are found in most state constitutions.

EQUAL PROTECTION CLAUSE
The provision in the Fourteenth Amendment to the Constitution that guarantees that no state will "deny to any person within its jurisdiction the equal protection of the laws." This clause mandates that the state governments treat similarly situated individuals in a similar manner.

Both substantive due process and equal protection require review of the substance of the law or other governmental action rather than review of the procedures used. When a law or action limits the liberty of all persons to do something, it may violate substantive due process; when a law or action limits the liberty of some persons but not others, it may violate the equal protection clause. **| Example #10** If a law prohibits all persons from buying contraceptive devices, it raises a substantive due process question. If a law prohibits only unmarried persons from buying the same devices, it raises an equal protection issue.**|**

Basically, in determining whether a law or action violates the equal protection clause, a court will consider questions similar to those previously noted as applicable in a substantive due process review. Under an equal protection inquiry, when a law or action distinguishes between or among individuals, the basis for the distinction—that is, the classification—is examined. Depending on the classification, the courts apply different levels of scrutiny, or "tests," to determine whether the law or action violates the equal protection clause.

Minimal Scrutiny—The "Rational Basis" Test   Generally, laws regulating economic and social matters are presumed to be valid and are subject to only minimal scrutiny. A classification will be considered valid if there is any conceivable "rational basis" on which the classification might relate to any *legitimate government interest*. It is almost impossible for a law or action to fail the rational basis test. **| Example #11** A city ordinance that in effect prohibits all pushcart vendors except a specific few from operating in a particular area of the city will be upheld if the city proffers a rational basis—such as reducing the traffic in the particular area—for the ordinance. In contrast, a law that provides unemployment benefits only to people over six feet tall would clearly fail the rational basis test because it could not further any legitimate government interest.**|**

Intermediate Scrutiny   A harder standard to meet, that of "intermediate scrutiny," is applied in cases involving discrimination based on gender or legitimacy. Laws using these classifications must be substantially related to *important government objectives*. **| Example #12** An important government objective is preventing illegitimate teenage pregnancies. Because males and females are not similarly situated in this circumstance—only females can become pregnant—a law that punishes men but not women for statutory rape will be upheld. A state law requiring illegitimate children to bring paternity suits within six years of their births, however, will be struck down if legitimate children are allowed to seek support from their biological parents at any time.**|**

Strict Scrutiny   The most difficult standard to meet is that of "strict scrutiny." Very few cases survive strict-scrutiny analysis. Strict scrutiny is applied when a law or action inhibits some persons' exercise of a fundamental right or is based on a suspect trait (such as race, national origin, or citizenship status). Strict scrutiny means that the court will examine the law or action involved very closely, and the law or action will be allowed to stand only if it is necessary to promote a *compelling government interest*. **| Example #13** Suppose that a city gives preference to minority applicants in awarding construction contracts. Because the policy is based on suspect traits (race and national origin), it will violate the equal protection clause *unless* it is necessary to promote a compelling state interest.[36]**|**

---

36. See, for example, *Adarand Constructors, Inc. v. Peña,* 515 U.S. 200, 115 S.Ct. 2097, 132 L.Ed.2d 158 (1995).

PRIVACY RIGHTS

In the past, privacy issues typically related to personal information that government agencies, including the Federal Bureau of Investigation, might obtain and keep about an individual. Later, concerns about what banks and insurance companies might know and transmit to others about individuals became an issue. Since the 1990s, one of the major concerns of individuals has been how to protect privacy rights in cyberspace and to safeguard private information that may be revealed online (including credit-card numbers and financial information). The increasing value of personal information for online marketers—who are willing to pay a high price to those who collect and sell them such information—has exacerbated the situation.

Today, individuals face additional concerns about government intrusions into their privacy. Legislation passed by Congress in the wake of the terrorist attacks of September 11, 2001, has given increased authority to government officials to monitor Internet activities (such as e-mail and Web site visits) and to gain access to personal financial data and student information.[37] Using technology, law enforcement officials can track the telephone and e-mail conversations of one party to find out the identity of the other party or parties. The government must certify that the information likely to be obtained is relevant to an ongoing criminal investigation, but it does not need to provide proof of any wrongdoing to gain access to this information. Privacy advocates argue that this law has adversely affected the constitutional rights of all Americans, and it has been widely criticized in the media, fueling the public debate over how to secure privacy rights in an electronic age.

In this section, we look at the protection of privacy rights under the U.S. Constitution and various federal statutes. Note that state constitutions and statutes also protect individuals' privacy rights, often to a significant degree. Privacy rights are also protected under tort law (see Chapter 5). Additionally, the Federal Trade Commission has played an active role in protecting the privacy rights of online consumers (see Chapter 17). The protection of employees' privacy rights, particularly with respect to electronic monitoring practices, is another area of growing concern (see Chapter 13).

> "There was, of course, no way of knowing whether you were being watched at any given moment."
>
> —GEORGE ORWELL, 1903–1950
> (Author, from his classic novel *1984*)

Constitutional Protection of Privacy Rights

The U.S. Constitution does not explicitly mention a general right to privacy, and only relatively recently have the courts regarded the right to privacy as a constitutional right. In a 1928 Supreme Court case, *Olmstead v. United States*,[38] Justice Louis Brandeis stated in his dissent that the right to privacy is "the most comprehensive of rights and the right most valued by civilized men." At that time, the majority of the justices did not agree, and it was not until the 1960s that a majority on the Supreme Court endorsed the view that the Constitution protects individual privacy rights.

In a landmark 1965 case, *Griswold v. Connecticut*,[39] the Supreme Court invalidated a Connecticut law that effectively prohibited the use of contraceptives. The Court held that the law violated the right to privacy. Justice William

---

37. Uniting and Strengthening America by Providing Appropriate Tools Required to Intercept and Obstruct Terrorism Act of 2001, also known as the USA Patriot Act, was enacted as Pub. L. No. 107-56 (2001) and extended in early 2006 by Pub. L. No. 109-173 (2006).
38. 277 U.S. 438, 48 S.Ct. 564, 72 L.Ed. 944 (1928).
39. 381 U.S. 479, 85 S.Ct. 1678, 14 L.Ed.2d 510 (1965).

O. Douglas formulated a unique way of reading this right into the Bill of Rights. He claimed that "emanations" from the rights guaranteed by the First, Third, Fourth, Fifth, and Ninth Amendments formed and gave "life and substance" to "penumbras" (partial shadows) around these guaranteed rights. These penumbras included an implied constitutional right to privacy.

When we read these amendments, we can see the foundation for Justice Douglas's reasoning. Consider the Fourth Amendment. By prohibiting unreasonable searches and seizures, the amendment effectively protects individuals' privacy. Consider also the words of the Ninth Amendment: "The enumeration in the Constitution of certain rights, shall not be construed to deny or disparage others retained by the people." In other words, just because the Constitution, including its amendments, does not specifically mention the right to privacy does not mean that this right is denied to the people. Indeed, in a recent survey of America Online subscribers, respondents ranked privacy second behind freedom of speech and ahead of freedom of religion as the most important rights guaranteed by the Constitution. A Harris poll showed that almost 80 percent of those questioned believed that if the framers were writing the Constitution today, they would add privacy as an important right.[40]

Federal Statutes Protecting Privacy Rights

In the last several decades, Congress has enacted a number of statutes that protect the privacy of individuals in various areas of concern. In the 1960s, Americans were sufficiently alarmed by the accumulation of personal information in government files that they pressured Congress to pass laws permitting individuals to access their files. Congress responded in 1966 with the Freedom of Information Act, which allows any person to request copies of any information on her or him contained in federal government files. In 1974, Congress passed the Privacy Act, which also gives persons the right to access such information. These and other major federal laws protecting privacy rights are listed and described in Exhibit 4–1.

Responding to the growing need to protect the privacy of individuals' health records—particularly computerized records—Congress passed the Health Insurance Portability and Accountability Act (HIPAA) of 1996.[41] This act, which took effect on April 14, 2003, defines and limits the circumstances in which an individual's "protected health information" may be used or disclosed.

The HIPAA requires health-care providers and health-care plans, including certain employers who sponsor health plans, to inform patients of their privacy rights and of how their personal medical information may be used. The act also generally states that a person's medical records may not be used for purposes unrelated to health care—such as marketing, for example—or disclosed to others without the individual's permission. Covered entities must formulate written privacy policies, designate privacy officials, limit access to computerized health data, physically secure medical records with lock and key, train employees and volunteers on their privacy policies, and sanction those who violate those policies. These protections are intended to assure individuals that their health information, including genetic information, will be properly protected and not used for purposes that the patient did not know about or authorize.

> " There is nothing new in the realization that the Constitution sometimes insulates the criminality of a few in order to protect the privacy of us all. "
>
> —ANTONIN SCALIA, 1936–
> (United States Supreme Court justice, 1986 to present)

---

40. *Public Perspective*, November/December 2000, p. 9.
41. The HIPAA was enacted as Pub. L. No. 104-191 (1996) and is codified in 29 U.S.C.A. Sections 1181 *et seq.*

EXHIBIT 4–1   FEDERAL LEGISLATION RELATING TO PRIVACY

TITLE	PROVISIONS CONCERNING PRIVACY
Freedom of Information Act (1966)	Provides that individuals have a right to obtain access to information about them collected in government files.
Family and Educational Rights and Privacy Act (1974)	Limits access to computer-stored records of education-related evaluations and grades in private and public colleges and universities.
Privacy Act (1974)	Protects the privacy of individuals about whom the federal government has information. Under this act, agencies that use or disclose personal information must make sure that the information is reliable and guard against its misuse. Individuals must be able to find out what data concerning them the agency is compiling and how the data will be used. In addition, the agency must give individuals a means to correct inaccurate data and must obtain their consent before using the data for any other purpose.
Tax Reform Act (1976)	Preserves the privacy of personal financial information.
Right to Financial Privacy Act (1978)	Prohibits financial institutions from providing the federal government with access to customers' records unless a customer authorizes the disclosure.
Electronic Communications Privacy Act (1986)	Prohibits the interception of information communicated by electronic means.
Driver's Privacy Protection Act (1994)	Prevents states from disclosing or selling a driver's personal information without the driver's consent.
Health Insurance Portability and Accountability Act (1996)	Prohibits the use of a consumer's medical information for any purpose other than that for which such information was provided, unless the consumer expressly consents to the use. Final rules became effective on April 14, 2003.
Financial Services Modernization Act (Gramm-Leach-Bliley Act) (1999)	Prohibits the disclosure of nonpublic personal information about a consumer to an unaffiliated third party unless strict disclosure and opt-out requirements are met. Final rules became mandatory on July 1, 2001.

REVIEWING . . . CONSTITUTIONAL AUTHORITY TO REGULATE BUSINESS

A state legislature enacted a statute that required any motorcycle operator or passenger on the state's highways to wear a protective helmet. Jim Alderman, a licensed motorcycle operator, sued the state to block enforcement of the law. Alderman asserted that the statute violated the equal protection clause because it placed requirements on motorcyclists that were not imposed on other motorists. Using the information presented in the chapter, answer the following questions.

1. Why does this statute raise equal protection issues instead of substantive due process concerns?

2. What are the three levels of scrutiny that the courts use in determining whether a law violates the equal protection clause?

3. Which standard, or test, of scrutiny would apply to this situation? Why?

4. Applying this standard, or test, is the helmet statute constitutional? Why or why not?

KEY TERMS

Bill of Rights   116

checks and balances   107

commerce clause   108

due process clause   125

equal protection clause   125

establishment clause   123

federal form of government   107

filtering software   122

free exercise clause   123

meta tag   122

police powers   112

preemption   114

supremacy clause   114

symbolic speech   119

CHAPTER SUMMARY • CONSTITUTIONAL AUTHORITY TO REGULATE BUSINESS

The Constitutional Powers of Government (See pages 106–108.)	The U.S. Constitution established a federal form of government, in which government powers are shared by the national government and the state governments. At the national level, government powers are divided among the legislative, executive, and judicial branches.
The Commerce Clause (See pages 108–114.)	1. *The expansion of national powers*—The commerce clause expressly permits Congress to regulate commerce. Over time, courts expansively interpreted this clause, thereby enabling the national government to wield extensive powers over the economic life of the nation. 2. *The commerce power today*—Today, the commerce power authorizes the national government, at least theoretically, to regulate every commercial enterprise in the United States. In recent years, the Supreme Court has reined in somewhat the national government's regulatory powers under the commerce clause. 3. *The regulatory powers of the states*—The Tenth Amendment reserves to the states all powers not expressly delegated to the national government. Under their police powers, state governments may regulate private activities to protect or promote the public order, health, safety, morals, and general welfare. 4. *The "dormant" commerce clause*—If state regulations substantially interfere with interstate commerce, they will be held to violate the "dormant" commerce clause of the U.S. Constitution. The positive aspect of the commerce clause, which gives the national government the exclusive authority to regulate interstate commerce, implies a "dormant" aspect—that the states do *not* have this power.
The Supremacy Clause (See pages 114–115.)	The U.S. Constitution provides that the Constitution, laws, and treaties of the United States are "the supreme Law of the Land." Whenever a state law directly conflicts with a federal law, the state law is rendered invalid.
The Taxing and Spending Powers (See page 116.)	The U.S. Constitution gives Congress the power to impose uniform taxes throughout the United States and to spend revenues accumulated from the taxing power. Congress can spend revenues to promote any objective it deems worthwhile, so long as it does not violate the Bill of Rights.
Business and the Bill of Rights (See pages 116–124.)	The Bill of Rights, which consists of the first ten amendments to the U.S. Constitution, was adopted in 1791 and embodies a series of protections for individuals—and, in some instances, business entities—against various types of interference by the federal government. Freedoms guaranteed by the First Amendment that affect businesses include freedom of speech and freedom of religion.
Due Process and Equal Protection (See pages 124–126.)	1. *Due process*—Both the Fifth and the Fourteenth Amendments provide that no person shall be deprived of "life, liberty, or property, without due process of law." Procedural due process requires that any government decision to take life, liberty, or property must be made fairly, using fair procedures. Substantive due process focuses on the content of legislation. 2. *Equal protection*—Under the Fourteenth Amendment, a state may not "deny to any person within its jurisdiction the equal protection of the laws." A law or action that limits the liberty of some persons but not others may violate the equal protection clause.
Privacy Rights (See pages 127–129.)	Americans are increasingly becoming concerned over privacy issues raised by Internet-related technology. The Constitution does not contain a specific guarantee of a right to privacy, but such a right has been derived from guarantees found in several constitutional amendments. A number of federal statutes protect privacy rights. Privacy rights are also protected by many state constitutions and statutes, as well as under tort law.

FOR REVIEW

Answers for the even-numbered questions in this For Review *section can be found in Appendix O at the end of this text.*

1. What is the basic structure of the U.S. government?

2. What constitutional clause gives the federal government the power to regulate commercial activities among the various states?

3. What constitutional clause allows laws enacted by the federal government to take priority over conflicting state laws?

4. What is the Bill of Rights? What freedoms are guaranteed by the First Amendment?

5. Where in the Constitution can the due process clause be found?

QUESTIONS AND CASE PROBLEMS

4–1. Commercial Speech. A mayoral election is about to be held in a large U.S. city. One of the candidates is Luis Delgado, and his campaign supporters wish to post campaign signs on lampposts and utility posts throughout the city. A city ordinance, however, prohibits the posting of any signs on public property. Delgado's supporters contend that the city ordinance is unconstitutional because it violates their rights to free speech. What factors might a court consider in determining the constitutionality of this ordinance?

4–2. Commerce Clause. Suppose that Georgia enacts a law requiring the use of contoured rear-fender mudguards on trucks and trailers operating within its state lines. The statute further makes it illegal for trucks and trailers to use straight mudguards. In thirty-five other states, straight mudguards are legal. Moreover, in the neighboring state of Florida, straight mudguards are explicitly required by law. There is some evidence suggesting that contoured mudguards might be a little safer than straight mudguards. Discuss whether this Georgia statute would violate the commerce clause of the U.S. Constitution.

Question with Sample Answer

4–3. Thomas worked in the nonmilitary operations of a large firm that produced both military and nonmilitary goods. When the company discontinued the production of nonmilitary goods, Thomas was transferred to a plant producing military equipment. Thomas left his job, claiming that it violated his religious principles to participate in the manufacture of goods to be used in destroying life. In effect, he argued, the transfer to the war-materials plant forced him to quit his job. He was denied unemployment compensation by the state because he had not been effectively "discharged" by the employer but had voluntarily terminated his employment. Did the state's denial of unemployment benefits to Thomas violate the free exercise clause of the First Amendment? Explain.

For a sample answer to this question, go to Appendix P at the end of this text.

4–4. Equal Protection. With the objectives of preventing crime, maintaining property values, and preserving the quality of urban life, New York City enacted an ordinance to regulate the locations of commercial establishments that featured adult entertainment. The ordinance expressly applied to female, but not male, topless entertainment. Adele Buzzetti owned the Cozy Cabin, a New York City cabaret that featured female topless dancers. Buzzetti and an anonymous dancer filed a suit in a federal district court against the city, asking the court to block the enforcement of the ordinance. The plaintiffs argued in part that the ordinance violated the equal protection clause. Under the equal protection clause, what standard applies to the court's consideration of this ordinance? Under this test, how should the court rule? Why? [*Buzzetti v. City of New York,* 140 F.3d 134 (2d Cir. 1998)]

4–5. Free Speech. The city of Tacoma, Washington, enacted an ordinance that prohibited the playing of car sound systems at a volume that would be "audible" at a distance greater than fifty feet. Dwight Holland was arrested and convicted for violating the ordinance. The conviction was later dismissed, but Holland filed a civil suit in a Washington state court against the city. He claimed in part that the ordinance violated his freedom of speech under the First Amendment. On what basis might the court conclude that this ordinance is constitutional? (Hint: In playing a sound system, was Holland actually expressing himself?) [*Holland v. City of Tacoma,* 90 Wash.App. 533, 954 P.2d 290 (1998)]

Case Problem with Sample Answer

4–6. In February 1999, Carl Adler mailed a driver's license renewal application form and a check for $28 to the New York Department of Motor Vehicles (DMV). The form required Adler's Social Security number, which he intentionally omitted. The DMV returned the application and check and told Adler to supply his Social Security number or send proof that the Social Security Administration could not give him a number. Claiming a right to privacy, Adler refused to comply. The DMV responded that federal law authorizes the states to obtain Social Security numbers from individuals in the context of administering certain state programs, including driver's license programs, and that Adler's application would not be processed until he supplied the number. Adler filed a suit in a New York state court against the DMV, asserting in part that it was in violation of the federal Privacy Act of 1974. Adler asked the court to, among other things, order the DMV to renew his license. Should the court grant Adler's request? Why or why not? [*Adler v. Jackson,* 712 N.Y.S.2d 240 (Sup. 2000)]

After you have answered this problem, compare your answer with the sample answer given on the Web site that accompanies this text. Go to www.thomsonedu.com/westbuslaw/let, select "Chapter 4," and click on "Case Problem with Sample Answer."

4–7. Free Speech. Henry Mishkoff is a Web designer whose firm does business as "Webfeats." When Taubman Co. began building a mall called "The Shops at Willow Bend" near Mishkoff's home, Mishkoff registered the domain name "shopsatwillowbend.com" and created a Web site with that address. The site featured information about the mall, a disclaimer indicating that Mishkoff's site was unofficial, and a link to the mall's official site. Taubman discovered Mishkoff's site and filed a suit in a federal district court against him. Mishkoff then registered other names, including "taubmansucks.com," with links to a site documenting his battle with Taubman. (A Web name with a "sucks.com" moniker attached to it is known as a "complaint name," and the process of registering and using such names is known as "cybergriping.") Taubman asked the court to order Mishkoff to stop using all of these names. Should the court grant Taubman's request? On what basis might the court protect Mishkoff's use of the names? [*Taubman Co. v. Webfeats,* 319 F.3d 770 (6th Cir. 2003)]

4–8. Due Process. In 1994, the Board of County Commissioners of Yellowstone County, Montana, created Zoning District 17 in a rural area of the county and a Planning and Zoning Commission for the district. The commission adopted zoning regulations, which provided, among other things, that "dwelling units" could be built only through "on-site construction." Later, county officials could not identify any health or safety concerns that the on-site construction provision addressed, and there was no indication that homes built off-site would affect property values or any other general welfare interest of the community. In December 1999, Francis and Anita Yurczyk bought two forty-acre tracts in District 17. The Yurczyks also bought a modular home and moved it onto the property the following spring. Within days, the county advised the Yurczyks that the home violated the on-site construction regulation and would have to be removed. The Yurczyks filed a suit in a Montana state court against the county, alleging in part that the regulation violated the Yurczyks' due process rights. Should the court rule in the plaintiffs' favor? Explain. [*Yurczyk v. Yellowstone County,* 2004 MT 3, 319 Mont. 169, 83 P.3d 266 (2004)]

4–9. Supremacy Clause. The Federal Communications Act of 1934 grants the right to govern all *interstate* telecommunications to the Federal Communications Commission (FCC)

and the right to regulate all *intrastate* telecommunications to the states. The federal Telephone Consumer Protection Act of 1991, the Junk Fax Protection Act of 2005, and FCC rules permit a party to send unsolicited fax ads to recipients with whom they have an "established business relationship" if those ads include an "opt-out" alternative. Section 17538.43 of California's Business and Professions Code (known as "SB 833") was enacted in 2005 to give the citizens of California greater protection than that afforded under federal law. SB 833 omits the "established business relationship" exception and requires a sender to obtain a recipient's express consent (for her or him to "opt in") before faxing an ad to that party into or out of California. The Chamber of Commerce of the United States filed a suit against Bill Lockyer, California's state attorney general, seeking to block the enforcement of SB 833. What principles support the plaintiff's position? How should the court resolve the issue? Explain. [*Chamber of Commerce of the United States v. Lockyer,* __ F.Supp.2d __ (E.D.Cal. 2006)]

A Question of Ethics

4–10. In 1999, in an effort to reduce smoking by children, the attorney general of Massachusetts issued comprehensive regulations governing the advertising and sale of tobacco products. Among other things, the regulations banned cigarette advertisements within one thousand feet of any elementary school, secondary school, or public playground and required retailers to post any advertising in their stores at least five feet off the floor, out of the immediate sight of young children. A group of tobacco manufacturers and retailers filed a suit against the state, claiming that the regulations were preempted by the federal Cigarette Labeling and Advertising Act of 1965, as amended. That act sets uniform labeling requirements and bans broadcast advertising for cigarettes. Ultimately, the case reached the United States Supreme Court, which held that the federal law on cigarette ads preempted the cigarette advertising restrictions adopted by Massachusetts. The only portion of the Massachusetts regulatory package to survive was the requirement that retailers had to place tobacco products in an area accessible only by the sales staff. In view of these facts, consider the following questions. [*Lorillard Tobacco Co. v. Reilly,* 533 U.S. 525, 121 S.Ct. 2404, 69 L.Ed.2d 532 (2001)]

1. Some argue that having a national standard for tobacco regulation is more important than allowing states to set their own standards for tobacco regulation. Do you agree? Why or why not?

2. According to the Court in this case, the federal law does not restrict the ability of state and local governments to adopt general zoning restrictions that apply to cigarettes, so long as those restrictions are "on equal terms with other products." How would you argue in support of this reasoning? How would you argue against it?

Critical-Thinking Social Question

4–11. In recent years, many people have criticized the film and entertainment industries for promoting violence by exposing the American public, and particularly American youth, to extremely violent films and song lyrics. Do you think that the right to free speech can (or should) be traded off to reduce violence in in the United States? Generally, in the wake of the September 11, 2001, terrorist attacks on the World Trade Center towers and the Pentagon, should Americans trade off some of their civil liberties for more protection against violence and terrorism?

Case Briefing Assignment

4–12. Go to www.thomsonedu.com/westbuslaw/let, the Web site that accompanies this text. Select "Chapter 4" and click on "Case Briefing Assignments." Examine Case

A.2 [*Austin v. Berryman*, 878 F.2d 786 (4th Cir. 1989)]. This case has been excerpted there in great detail. Review and then brief the case, making sure that your brief answers the following questions.

1. Who were the plaintiff and defendant in this action?
2. Why did Austin claim that she had been forced to leave her job?
3. Why was Austin refused state unemployment benefits?
4. Did the state's refusal to give Austin unemployment compensation violate her rights under the free exercise clause of the First Amendment?
5. What logic or reasoning did the court employ in arriving at its conclusion?

INTERACTING WITH THE INTERNET

For updated links to resources available on the Web, as well as a variety of other materials, visit this text's Web site at

www.thomsonedu.com/westbuslaw/let

For an online version of the Constitution that provides hypertext links to amendments and other changes, as well as the history of the document, go to

www.constitutioncenter.org

For discussions of current issues involving the rights and liberties contained in the Bill of Rights, go to the Web site of the American Civil Liberties Union at

www.aclu.org

INTERNET EXERCISES

Go to **www.thomsonedu.com/westbuslaw/let**, the Web site that accompanies this text. Select "Chapter 4," and click on "Internet Exercises." There you will find the following Internet research exercises that you can perform to learn more about topics covered in this chapter.

Internet Exercise 4–1: LEGAL PERSPECTIVE—Commercial Speech
Internet Exercise 4–2: MANAGEMENT PERSPECTIVE—Privacy Rights in Cyberspace

BEFORE THE TEST

Go to **www.thomsonedu.com/westbuslaw/let**, the Web site that accompanies this text. Select "Chapter 4" and click on "Interactive Quizzes." You will find a number of interactive questions relating to this chapter.

CHAPTER 5

Torts, Cyber Torts, and Product Liability

CHAPTER OBJECTIVES

After reading this chapter, you should be able to answer the following questions:

1. What is the purpose of tort law? What are two basic categories of torts?

2. What are the four elements of negligence?

3. What is meant by strict liability? In what circumstances is strict liability applied?

4. What are the elements of a cause of action in strict product liability?

5. What defenses to liability can be raised in a product liability lawsuit?

> " 'Tort' more or less means 'wrong' . . . . One of my friends [in law school] said that Torts is the course which proves that your mother was right. "
> —SCOTT TUROW, 1949–
> (American lawyer and author)

TORT
A civil wrong not arising from a breach of contract. A breach of a legal duty that proximately causes harm or injury to another.

BUSINESS TORT
Wrongful interference with another's business rights.

AS SCOTT TUROW'S statement in the chapter-opening quotation indicates, torts are wrongful actions.[1] Through tort law, society compensates those who have suffered injuries as a result of the wrongful conduct of others. Although some torts, such as assault and trespass, originated in the English common law, the field of tort law continues to expand. As new ways to commit wrongs are discovered, such as the use of the Internet to commit wrongful acts, the courts are extending tort law to cover these wrongs.

As you will see in later chapters of this book, many of the lawsuits brought by or against business firms are based on the tort theories discussed in this chapter. Some of the torts examined here can occur in any context, including the business environment. Others traditionally have been referred to as **business torts**, which are defined as wrongful interferences with the business rights of others. Included in business torts are such vague concepts as *unfair competition* and *wrongfully interfering with the business relations of others*.

A natural addition to the discussion of tort law is *product liability*. Who is liable to consumers, users, and bystanders for physical harm and property damage caused by a particular good or the use thereof? We examine this topic in the latter part of this chapter.

---

1. The word *tort* is French for "wrong."

THE BASIS OF TORT LAW

Two notions serve as the basis of all torts: wrongs and compensation. Tort law is designed to compensate those who have suffered a loss or injury due to another person's wrongful act. In a tort action, one person or group brings a personal suit against another person or group to obtain compensation (money **damages**) or other relief for the harm suffered.

DAMAGES
Money sought as a remedy for a breach of contract or a tortious action.

The Purpose of Tort Law

Generally, the purpose of tort law is to provide remedies for the invasion of various *protected interests*. Society recognizes an interest in personal physical safety, and tort law provides remedies for acts that cause physical injury or that interfere with physical security and freedom of movement. Society recognizes an interest in protecting real and personal property, and tort law provides remedies for acts that cause destruction or damage to property. Society also recognizes an interest in protecting certain intangible interests, such as personal privacy, family relations, reputation, and dignity, and tort law provides remedies for invasion of these protected interests.

Classifications of Torts

There are two broad classifications of torts: *intentional torts* and *unintentional torts* (torts involving negligence). The classification of a particular tort depends largely on how the tort occurs (intentionally or negligently) and the surrounding circumstances. In the following pages, you will read about these two classifications of torts.

Torts committed via the Internet are sometimes referred to as **cyber torts.** We look at how the courts have applied traditional tort law to wrongful actions in the online environment later in this chapter.

CYBER TORT
A tort committed in cyberspace.

INTENTIONAL TORTS AGAINST PERSONS

An **intentional tort,** as the term implies, requires *intent*. The **tortfeasor** (the one committing the tort) must intend to commit an act, the consequences of which interfere with the personal or business interests of another in a way not permitted by law. An evil or harmful motive is not required—in fact, the person acting may even have a beneficial motive for committing what turns out to be a tortious act. In tort law, intent means only that the person intended the consequences of his or her act or knew with substantial certainty that specific consequences would result from the act. The law generally assumes that individuals intend the *normal* consequences of their actions. Thus, forcefully pushing another—even if done in jest and without any evil motive—is an intentional tort (if injury results), because the object of a strong push can ordinarily be expected to fall down.

This section discusses intentional torts against persons, which include assault and battery, false imprisonment, intentional infliction of emotional distress, defamation, invasion of the right to privacy, appropriation, misrepresentation (fraud), and wrongful interference.

INTENTIONAL TORT
A wrongful act knowingly committed.

TORTFEASOR
One who commits a tort.

Assault and Battery

Any intentional, unexcused act that creates in another person a reasonable apprehension or fear of immediate harmful or offensive contact is an **assault.** Apprehension is not the same as fear. If a contact is such that a reasonable person would want to avoid it, and if there is a reasonable basis for believing that the contact will occur, then the plaintiff suffers apprehension whether or not he or she is afraid. The interest protected by tort law concerning assault is the freedom from having to expect harmful or offensive contact. The occurrence of apprehension is enough to justify compensation.

The *completion* of the act that caused the apprehension, if it results in harm to the plaintiff, is a **battery,** which is defined as an unexcused and harmful or offensive physical contact *intentionally* performed. For example, suppose that Ivan threatens Jean with a gun, then shoots her. The pointing of the gun at Jean is an assault; the firing of the gun (if the bullet hits Jean) is a battery. The interest protected by tort law concerning battery is the right to personal security and safety. The contact can be harmful, or it can be merely offensive (such as an unwelcome kiss). Physical injury need not occur. The contact can involve any part of the body or anything attached to it—for example, a hat or other item of clothing, a purse, or a chair or an automobile in which one is sitting. Whether the contact is offensive or not is determined by the *reasonable person standard.*[2] The contact can be made by the defendant or by some force the defendant sets in motion—for example, a rock thrown, food poisoned, or a stick swung.

A tort may also constitute a crime (see Chapter 6). For instance, in the example of assault and battery given above, Jean could sue under tort law for damages, and the state could bring a criminal action against the perpetrator under criminal law.

Compensation   If the plaintiff shows that there was contact, and the jury agrees that the contact was offensive, the plaintiff has a right to compensation. There is no need to show that the defendant acted out of malice; the person could have just been joking or playing around. The underlying motive does not matter, only the intent to bring about the harmful or offensive contact to the plaintiff. In fact, proving a motive is never necessary (but is sometimes relevant). A plaintiff may be compensated for the emotional harm or loss of reputation resulting from a battery, as well as for physical harm.

Defenses to Assault and Battery   A number of legally recognized **defenses** (reasons why plaintiffs should not obtain what they are seeking) can be raised by a defendant who is sued for assault or battery, or both:

1. *Consent.* When a person consents to the act that damages her or him, there is generally no liability (legal responsibility) for the damage done.
2. *Self-defense.* An individual who is defending his or her life or physical well-being can claim self-defense. In situations of both *real* and *apparent* danger, a person may use whatever force is *reasonably* necessary to prevent harmful contact.

ASSAULT

Any word or action intended to make another person fearful of immediate physical harm; a reasonably believable threat.

BATTERY

The unprivileged, intentional touching of another.

DEFENSE

A reason offered and alleged by a defendant in an action or suit as to why the plaintiff should not recover or establish what she or he seeks.

BE AWARE   Some of these same four defenses can be raised by a defendant who is sued for other torts.

---

2. The *reasonable person standard* is an objective test of how a reasonable person would have acted under the same circumstances. See "The Duty of Care and Its Breach" later in this chapter.

3. *Defense of others.* An individual can act in a reasonable manner to protect others who are in real or apparent danger.
4. *Defense of property.* Reasonable force may be used in attempting to remove intruders from one's home, although force that is likely to cause death or great bodily injury can never be used just to protect property.

False Imprisonment

False imprisonment is the intentional confinement or restraint of another person's activities without justification. False imprisonment interferes with the freedom to move without restraint. The confinement can be accomplished through the use of physical barriers, physical restraint, or threats of physical force. Moral pressure or threats of future harm do not constitute false imprisonment. It is essential that the person being restrained not willingly comply with the restraint.

Businesspersons are often confronted with suits for false imprisonment after they have attempted to confine a suspected shoplifter for questioning. Under the "privilege to detain" granted to merchants in some states, a merchant can use the defense of *probable cause* to justify delaying a suspected shoplifter. Probable cause exists when there is sufficient evidence to support the belief that a person is guilty. Although laws governing false imprisonment vary from state to state, generally they require that any detention be conducted in a *reasonable* manner and for only a *reasonable* length of time.

Intentional Infliction of Emotional Distress

The tort of *intentional infliction of emotional distress* can be defined as an intentional act that amounts to extreme and outrageous conduct resulting in severe emotional distress to another. | **Example #1** A prankster telephones an individual and says that the individual's spouse has just been in a horrible accident. As a result, the individual suffers intense mental pain or anxiety. The caller's behavior is deemed to be extreme and outrageous conduct that exceeds the bounds of decency accepted by society and is therefore **actionable** (capable of serving as the ground for a lawsuit).|

The tort of intentional infliction of emotional distress poses several problems for the courts. One problem is the difficulty of proving the existence of emotional suffering. For this reason, courts in some jurisdictions require that the emotional distress be evidenced by some physical symptom or illness or some emotional disturbance that can be documented by a psychiatric consultant or other medical professional.

Another problem is that emotional distress claims must be subject to some limitation, or they could flood the courts with lawsuits. A society in which individuals are rewarded if they are unable to endure the normal emotional stresses of day-to-day living is obviously undesirable. Therefore, the law usually holds that indignity or annoyance alone is not enough to support a lawsuit based on the intentional infliction of emotional distress. Repeated annoyances (such as those experienced by a person who is being stalked), however, coupled with threats, are enough. In the business context, the repeated use of extreme methods to collect a delinquent account may be actionable.

ACTIONABLE
Capable of serving as the basis of a lawsuit. An actionable claim can be pursued in a lawsuit or other court action.

Defamation

Defamation of character involves wrongfully hurting a person's good reputation. The law has imposed a general duty on all persons to refrain from making false, defamatory statements about others. Breaching this duty orally involves the tort of **slander;** breaching it in writing involves the tort of **libel.** The tort of defamation also arises when a false statement is made about a person's product, business, or title to property. We deal with these torts later in the chapter.

The Publication Requirement   The basis of the tort of defamation is the publication of a statement or statements that hold an individual up to contempt, ridicule, or hatred. *Publication* here means that the defamatory statements are communicated to persons other than the defamed party. **| Example #2**   If Thompson writes Andrews a private letter accusing him of embezzling funds, the action does not constitute libel. If Peters calls Gordon dishonest, two-faced, and incompetent when no one else is around, the action does not constitute slander. In neither case was the message communicated to a third party.**|**

The courts have generally held that even dictating a letter to a secretary constitutes publication, although the publication may be privileged (*privileged* communications will be discussed shortly). Moreover, if a third party overhears defamatory statements by chance, the courts usually hold that this also constitutes publication.[3] Note further that any individual who republishes or repeats defamatory statements is liable even if that person reveals the source of such statements.

Damages for Defamation   Generally, in a case alleging slander, the plaintiff must prove "special damages" to establish the defendant's liability. The plaintiff must show that the slanderous statement caused her or him to suffer actual economic or monetary losses. This requirement is imposed in cases involving slander because slanderous statements have a temporary quality. In contrast, a libelous (written) statement has the quality of permanence, can be circulated widely, and usually results from some degree of deliberation on the part of the author. For that reason, a plaintiff can recover "general damages" for libel and need not prove any special damages.

Exceptions to the burden of proving special damages in cases alleging slander are made for certain types of slanderous statements. If a false statement constitutes "slander *per se,*" no proof of special damages is required for it to be actionable. The following four types of utterances are considered to be slander *per se:*

1. A statement that another has a loathsome communicable disease.
2. A statement that another has committed improprieties while engaging in a profession or trade.
3. A statement that another has committed or has been imprisoned for a serious crime.
4. A statement that a woman is unchaste or has engaged in serious sexual misconduct.

---

3. Defamatory statements made via the Internet are also actionable, as you will read later in this chapter.

Defenses against Defamation Truth is normally an absolute defense against a defamation charge. In other words, if the defendant in a defamation suit can prove that his or her allegedly defamatory statements were true, the defendant will not be liable.

Privileged Communications Another defense that is sometimes raised is that the statements were **privileged** communications, and thus the defendant is immune from liability. Privileged communications are of two types: absolute and qualified. Only in judicial proceedings and certain government proceedings is *absolute* privilege granted. For example, statements made in the courtroom by attorneys and judges during a trial are absolutely privileged. So are statements made by government officials during legislative debate, even if the officials make such statements maliciously—that is, knowing them to be untrue. An absolute privilege is granted in these situations because government personnel deal with matters that are so much in the public interest that the parties involved should be able to speak out fully and freely without restriction.

In other situations, a person will not be liable for defamatory statements because he or she has a *qualified,* or *conditional,* privilege. An employer's statements in written evaluations of employees are an example of a qualified privilege. Generally, if the communicated statements are made in good faith to those parties who have a legitimate interest in the subject, the statements fall within the area of qualified privilege. **| Example #3** Jorge applies for membership at the local country club. After the country club's board rejects his application, Jorge sues the club's office manager for making allegedly defamatory statements to the board concerning a conversation she had with Jorge. Assuming that the office manager had simply relayed what she thought was her duty to convey to the club's board, her statements would likely be protected by a qualified privilege. **|**

Public Figures Public officials who exercise substantial governmental power and any persons who are in the public limelight are considered *public figures.* In general, false and defamatory statements that are made about public figures and published in the press are privileged if they are made without **actual malice.**[4] To be made with actual malice, a statement must be made *with either knowledge of its falsity or a reckless disregard of the truth.* Statements made about public figures, especially when they are made via a public medium, are usually related to matters of general interest; they are made about people who substantially affect all of us. Furthermore, public figures generally have some access to a public medium for answering disparaging (belittling, discrediting) falsehoods about themselves; private individuals do not. For these reasons, public figures have a greater burden of proof in defamation cases (they must prove actual malice) than do private individuals.

Invasion of the Right to Privacy

A person has a right to solitude and freedom from prying public eyes—in other words, to privacy. As discussed in Chapter 4, the Supreme Court has held that a fundamental right to privacy is also implied by various amendments to the U.S. Constitution. Some state constitutions explicitly provide for privacy rights. In addition, a number of federal and state statutes have been enacted to protect individual rights in specific areas. Tort law also safeguards these rights through the tort of *invasion of privacy.* Four acts qualify as an invasion of privacy:

PRIVILEGE
A legal right, exemption, or immunity granted to a person or a class of persons. In the context of defamation, an absolute privilege immunizes the person making the statements from suit, regardless of whether the person's statements were malicious. A qualified privilege immunizes a person from suit only when the statements were made in good faith by a person having an interest in the subject, or a moral or societal duty to speak.

ACTUAL MALICE
Knowledge (by the person who makes a defamatory statement) that a statement is false, or reckless disregard about whether it is true. In a defamation suit, a statement made about a public figure normally must be made with actual malice for liability to be incurred.

---

4. *New York Times Co. v. Sullivan*, 376 U.S. 254, 84 S.Ct. 710, 11 L.Ed.2d 686 (1964).

1. *The use of a person's name, picture, or other likeness for commercial purposes without permission.* This tort, which is usually referred to as the tort of appropriation, will be examined shortly.

2. *Intrusion into an individual's affairs or seclusion.* For example, invading someone's home or illegally searching someone's briefcase is an invasion of privacy. The tort has been held to extend to eavesdropping by wiretap, the unauthorized scanning of a bank account, compulsory blood testing, and window peeping.

3. *Publication of information that places a person in a false light.* This could be a story attributing to the person ideas not held or actions not taken by the person. (Publishing such a story could involve the tort of defamation as well.)

4. *Public disclosure of private facts about an individual that an ordinary person would find objectionable.* A newspaper account of a private citizen's sex life or financial affairs could be an actionable invasion of privacy.

Appropriation

APPROPRIATION
In tort law, the use by one person of another person's name, likeness, or other identifying characteristic without permission and for the benefit of the user.

The use by one person of another person's name, likeness, or other identifying characteristic, without permission and for the benefit of the user, constitutes the tort of **appropriation.** Under the law, an individual's right to privacy normally includes the right to the exclusive use of her or his identity.

| **Example #4** Vanna White, the hostess of the popular television game show *Wheel of Fortune,* brought a case against Samsung Electronics America, Inc. Without White's permission, Samsung included in an advertisement for its videocassette recorders (VCRs) a depiction of a robot dressed in a wig, gown, and jewelry, posed in a scene that resembled the *Wheel of Fortune* set, in a stance for which White is famous. The court held in White's favor, holding that the tort of appropriation does not require the use of a celebrity's name or likeness. The court stated that Samsung's robot ad left "little doubt" as to the identity of the celebrity whom the ad was meant to depict.[5] |

Cases of wrongful appropriation, or misappropriation, may also involve the rights of those who invest time and funds in the creation of a special system, such as a method of broadcasting sports events. Commercial misappropriation may also occur when a person takes and uses the property of another for the sole purpose of capitalizing unfairly on the goodwill or reputation of the property owner.

Misrepresentation (Fraud)

FRAUDULENT MISREPRESENTATION
Any misrepresentation, either by misstatement or omission of a material fact, knowingly made with the intention of deceiving another and on which a reasonable person would and does rely to his or her detriment.

A misrepresentation leads another to believe in a condition that is different from the condition that actually exists. This is often accomplished through a false or incorrect statement. Misrepresentations may be innocently made by someone who is unaware of the existing facts, but the tort of **fraudulent misrepresentation,** or fraud, involves intentional deceit for personal gain. The tort includes several elements:

1. The misrepresentation of facts or conditions with knowledge that they are false or with reckless disregard for the truth.

---

5. *White v. Samsung Electronics America, Inc.,* 971 F.2d 1395 (9th Cir. 1992).

2. An intent to induce another to rely on the misrepresentation.
3. Justifiable reliance by the deceived party.
4. Damages suffered as a result of the reliance.
5. A causal connection between the misrepresentation and the injury suffered.

For fraud to occur, more than mere **puffery**, or *seller's talk*, must be involved. Fraud exists only when a person represents as a fact something he or she knows is untrue. For example, it is fraud to claim that a building does not leak when one knows it does. Facts are objectively ascertainable, whereas seller's talk is not. "I am the best accountant in town" is seller's talk. The speaker is not trying to represent something as fact because the term *best* is a subjective, not an objective, term.[6]

Normally, the tort of misrepresentation or fraud occurs only when there is reliance on a *statement of fact*. Sometimes, however, reliance on a *statement of opinion* may involve the tort of misrepresentation if the individual making the statement of opinion has a superior knowledge of the subject matter. For example, when a lawyer makes a statement of opinion about the law in a state in which the lawyer is licensed to practice, a court would construe reliance on such a statement to be equivalent to reliance on a statement of fact. We examine fraudulent misrepresentation in further detail in Chapter 8, in the context of contract law.

> **PUFFERY**
> A salesperson's often exaggerated claims concerning the quality of property offered for sale. Such claims involve opinions rather than facts and are not considered to be legally binding promises or warranties.

Wrongful Interference

Business torts involving wrongful interference are generally divided into two categories: wrongful interference with a contractual relationship and wrongful interference with a business relationship.

Wrongful Interference with a Contractual Relationship   The body of tort law relating to *intentional interference with a contractual relationship* has expanded greatly in recent years. A landmark case involved an opera singer, Joanna Wagner, who was under contract to sing for a man named Lumley for a specified period of years. A man named Gye, who knew of this contract, nonetheless "enticed" Wagner to refuse to carry out the agreement, and Wagner began to sing for Gye. Gye's action constituted a tort because it wrongfully interfered with the contractual relationship between Wagner and Lumley.[7] (Of course, Wagner's refusal to carry out the agreement also entitled Lumley to sue Wagner for breach of contract.)

Three elements are necessary for wrongful interference with a contractual relationship to occur:

1. A valid, enforceable contract must exist between two parties.
2. A third party must know that this contract exists.
3. The third party must *intentionally* cause either of the two parties to breach the contract.

The contract may be between a firm and its employees or a firm and its customers. Sometimes a competitor of a firm draws away one of the firm's key

> **REMEMBER !** It is the intent to perform an act that is important in tort law, not the motive behind the intent.

---

6. In contracts for the sale of goods, Article 2 of the Uniform Commercial Code distinguishes, for warranty purposes, between statements of opinion *(puffery)* and statements of fact. Warranties will be discussed later in this chapter.
7. *Lumley v. Gye,* 118 Eng.Rep. 749 (1853).

employees. If the original employer can show that the competitor induced the breach—that is, that the former employee would not otherwise have broken the contract—damages can be recovered from the competitor.

The following case illustrates the elements of the tort of wrongful interference with a contractual relationship in the context of a contract between an independent sales representative and his agent (agency relationships will be discussed in Chapter 13). The case was complicated by the existence of a second contract between the sales representative and the third party.

CASE 5.1   Mathis v. Liu

United States Court of Appeals,
Eighth Circuit, 2002.
276 F.3d 1027.

BACKGROUND AND FACTS Ching and Alex Liu own Pacific Cornetta, Inc. In 1997, Pacific Cornetta entered into a contract with Lawrence Mathis, under which Mathis agreed to solicit orders for Pacific Cornetta's products from Kmart Corporation for a commission of 5 percent on net sales. Under the terms, either party could terminate the contract at any time. The next year, Mathis entered into a one-year contract with John Evans, under which Evans agreed to serve as Mathis's agent to solicit orders from Kmart for the product lines that Mathis

represented, including Pacific Cornetta, for a commission of 1 percent on net sales. Under the terms of this contract, either party could terminate it only on written notice of six months. A few months later, Pacific Cornetta persuaded Evans to break his contract with Mathis and enter into a contract with Pacific Cornetta to be its sales representative to Kmart. Evans terminated his contract with Mathis without notice. Two days later, Pacific Cornetta terminated its contract with Mathis. Mathis filed a suit in a federal district court against the Lius and Pacific Cornetta, alleging in part wrongful interference with a contractual relationship. The court issued a judgment that included a ruling in Mathis's favor on this claim, but Mathis appealed the amount of damages to the U.S. Court of Appeals for the Eighth Circuit.

IN THE WORDS OF THE COURT . . . *MORRIS SHEPHARD ARNOLD*, Circuit Judge.

*   *   *   *

* * * *[A] defendant is liable for tortious interference only if the defendant's interference with some relevant advantage was improper. [The] courts [look at several considerations] to determine whether a defendant's interference is improper.* These considerations include the nature of the actor's conduct[,] * * * the actor's motive[,] * * * the interests of the other with which the actor's conduct interferes[,] * * * the interests sought to be advanced by the actor[,] * * * the social interests in protecting the freedom of action of the actor and the contractual interests of the other[,] * * * the proximity or remoteness of the actor's conduct to the interference[,] and * * * the relations between the parties. [Emphasis added.]

We conclude that Mr. Mathis made out a * * * case on this element of his claim. If Mr. Evans's agency arrangement with Mr. Mathis had been purely at will [a legal doctrine under which a contractual relationship can be terminated at any time by either party for any or no reason], we do not believe that Pacific Cornetta's successful effort to hire Mr. Evans * * * would have risen to the level of impropriety necessary to make out a case for tortious interference. That is because a party's interference with an at-will contract is primarily an interference with the future relation between the parties, and *when an at-will contract is terminated there is no breach of it.* In such circumstances, the interfering party is free for its own competitive advantage, to obtain the future benefits for itself by causing the termination, provided it uses suitable means. [Emphasis added.]

Mr. Evans's contract with Mr. Mathis, however, did not create a simple at-will arrangement because Mr. Evans could terminate it only after giving Mr. Mathis six months' notice

CASE 5.1–CONTINUED

of his intention to do so. In these circumstances, we think that the jury was entitled to conclude that Pacific Cornetta's blandishments [flattering statements] were improper, especially since *inducing a breach of contract absent compelling justification is, in and of itself, improper.* [Emphasis added.]

* * * *

Mr. Mathis asked for damages for the loss of anticipatory profits on his tortious interference claim. He argues that the damages that the jury awarded were supported by Mr. Evans's sales of * * * Pacific Cornetta products to Kmart [after Pacific Cornetta terminated the firm's contract with Mathis].

* * * *

We reject this theory * * *. Mr. Mathis's losses on these sales were a result of Pacific Cornetta exercising its right to terminate its contract with him at will, not Pacific Cornetta's tortious interference, and the losses were therefore not recoverable under a theory of tortious interference.

DECISION AND REMEDY The U.S. Court of Appeals for the Eighth Circuit affirmed the judgment of the lower court. The appellate court concluded that the defendants had committed wrongful interference with Mathis's contract with Evans. Evans's sales of Pacific Cornetta products after Pacific Cornetta terminated its contract with Mathis could not furnish

a basis for an award of damages on this claim, however, because the firm's contract with Mathis was terminable at will.

FOR CRITICAL ANALYSIS–Ethical Consideration *Does the ruling in this case mean that Mathis is entirely without recourse? Could he sue Evans for anything?*

Wrongful Interference with a Business Relationship Businesspersons devise countless schemes to attract customers, but they are forbidden by the courts to interfere unreasonably with another's business in their attempts to gain a share of the market. There is a difference between competitive methods and **predatory behavior**—actions undertaken with the intention of unlawfully driving competitors completely out of the market.

The distinction usually depends on whether a business is attempting to attract customers in general or to solicit only those customers who have shown an interest in a similar product or service of a specific competitor. If a shopping center contains two shoe stores, an employee of Store A cannot be positioned at the entrance of Store B for the purpose of diverting customers to Store A. This type of activity constitutes the tort of wrongful interference with a business relationship, which is commonly considered to be an unfair trade practice. If this type of activity were permitted, Store A would reap the benefits of Store B's advertising.

Defenses to Wrongful Interference A person will not be liable for the tort of wrongful interference with a contractual or business relationship if it can be shown that the interference was justified, or permissible. Bona fide competitive behavior is a permissible interference even if it results in the breaking of a contract. |**Example #5** If Antonio's Meats advertises so effectively that it induces Beverly's Restaurant Chain to break its contract with Otis Meat Company, Otis Meat Company will be unable to recover against Antonio's Meats on a wrongful interference theory. After all, the public policy that favors free competition in advertising outweighs any possible instability that such competitive activity might cause in contractual relations.|

PREDATORY BEHAVIOR
Business behavior that is undertaken with the intention of unlawfully driving competitors out of the market.

REMEMBER ! What society and the law consider permissible often depends on the circumstances.

INTENTIONAL TORTS AGAINST PROPERTY

Intentional torts against property include trespass to land, trespass to personal property, conversion, and disparagement of property. These torts are wrongful actions that interfere with individuals' legally recognized rights with regard to their land or personal property. The law distinguishes real property from personal property (see Chapter 19). *Real property* is land and things "permanently" attached to the land. *Personal property* consists of all other items, which are basically movable. Thus, a house and lot are real property, whereas the furniture inside a house is personal property. Money and stocks and bonds are also personal property.

Trespass to Land

TRESPASS TO LAND
The entry onto, above, or below the surface of land owned by another without the owner's permission or legal authorization.

A **trespass to land** occurs whenever a person, without permission, enters onto, above, or below the surface of land that is owned by another; causes anything to enter onto the land; remains on the land; or permits anything to remain on it. Actual harm to the land is not an essential element of this tort because the tort is designed to protect the right of an owner to exclusive possession of his or her property. Common types of trespass to land include walking or driving on someone else's land, shooting a gun over the land, throwing rocks at a building that belongs to someone else, building a dam across a river and thereby causing water to back up on someone else's land, and constructing a building so that part of it is on an adjoining landowner's property.

Trespass Criteria, Rights, and Duties   Before a person can be a trespasser, the owner of the real property (or other person in actual and exclusive possession of the property) must establish that person as a trespasser. For example, "posted" trespass signs expressly establish as a trespasser a person who ignores

This private property has signs indicating that trespassing is not allowed. Why would a private property owner "post" a no trespassing sign? (AP Photo/ Rogelio Solis)

these signs and enters onto the property. A guest in your home is not a tres-passer—unless she or he has been asked to leave but refuses. Any person who enters onto your property to commit an illegal act (such as a thief entering a lumberyard at night to steal lumber) is established impliedly as a trespasser, without posted signs.

At common law, a trespasser is liable for damages caused to the property and generally cannot hold the owner liable for injuries sustained on the prem-ises. This common law rule is being abandoned in many jurisdictions in favor of a "reasonable duty of care" rule that varies depending on the status of the parties; for example, a landowner may have a duty to post a notice that the property is patrolled by guard dogs. Furthermore, under the "attractive nuisance" doctrine, children do not assume the risks of the premises if they are attracted to the property by some object, such as a swimming pool, an aban-doned building, or a sandpile. Trespassers normally can be removed from the premises through the use of reasonable force without the owner's being liable for assault and battery.

Defenses against Trespass to Land   Trespass to land involves wrongful inter-ference with another person's real property rights. One defense against a tres-pass claim is to show that the trespass was warranted, as when a trespasser enters to assist someone in danger. Another defense exists when the trespasser can show that he or she had a license to come onto the land. A *licensee* is one who is invited (or allowed to enter) onto the property of another for the licensee's benefit. A person who enters another's property to read an electric meter, for example, is a licensee. When you purchase a ticket to attend a movie or sporting event, you are licensed to go onto the property of another to view that movie or event. Note that licenses to enter on another's property are *revocable* by the property owner. If a property owner asks a meter reader to leave and the meter reader refuses to do so, the meter reader at that point becomes a trespasser.

Trespass to Personal Property

Whenever an individual unlawfully harms the personal property of another or otherwise interferes with the personal property owner's right to exclusive pos-session and enjoyment of that property, **trespass to personal property**—also called *trespass to personalty*[8]—occurs. If a student takes a classmate's business law book as a practical joke and hides it so that the owner is unable to find it for several days prior to the final examination, the student has engaged in a trespass to personal property.

If it can be shown that the trespass to personal property was warranted, then a complete defense exists. Most states, for example, allow automobile repair shops to hold a customer's car (under what is called an *artisan's lien,* discussed in Chapter 12) when the customer refuses to pay for repairs already completed. Trespass to personal property was one of the allegations in the following case.

TRESPASS TO PERSONAL PROPERTY
The unlawful taking or harming of another's personal property; interference with another's right to the exclusive possession of his or her personal property.

---

8. Pronounced *per*-sun-ul-tee.

CASE 5.2   Register.com, Inc. v. Verio, Inc.

United States Court of Appeals,
Second Circuit, 2004.
356 F.3d 393.

BACKGROUND AND FACTS The Internet Corporation for Assigned Names and Numbers (ICANN) administers the Internet domain name system. (Domain names will be discussed in detail in Chapter 7.) ICANN appoints registrars to issue the names to persons preparing to establish Web sites on the Internet. An applicant for a name must provide certain information, including an e-mail address. An agreement between ICANN and its registrars refers to this information as "WHOIS information" and requires the registrars to provide public access to it through the Internet "for any lawful purposes" except "the transmission of mass unsolicited, commercial advertising or solicitations via email (spam)." A party who wishes to obtain this information must also agree not to use it for this purpose. Register.com, Inc., is an ICANN registrar. Verio, Inc., sells Web site design and other services. Verio devised an automated software program (robot, or bot) to submit daily queries for Register's WHOIS data. Verio would then send ads by e-mail and other methods to the identified parties. Despite Register's request, Verio refused to stop. Register filed a suit in a federal district court against Verio, alleging in part trespass to personal property. The court ordered Verio to, among other things, stop accessing Register's computers by bot. Verio appealed to the U.S. Court of Appeals for the Second Circuit.

IN THE WORDS OF THE COURT . . . *LEVAL,* **Circuit Judge.**

* * * *

* * * Register asserted, among other claims, that Verio was * * * trespassing on Register's chattels [personal property] in a manner likely to harm Register's computer systems by the use of Verio's automated robot software programs. On December 8, 2000, the district court entered a preliminary injunction. The injunction barred Verio from * * * [a]ccessing Register.com's computers and computer networks in any manner, including, but not limited to, * * * software programs performing multiple, automated, successive queries * * * .

* * * *

Verio * * * attacks the grant of the preliminary injunction against its accessing Register's computers by automated software programs performing multiple successive queries. This prong of the injunction was premised on Register's claim of trespass to chattels. Verio contends the ruling was in error because Register failed to establish that Verio's conduct resulted in harm to Register's servers and because Verio's robot access to the WHOIS database through Register was "not unauthorized." We believe the district court's findings were within the range of its permissible discretion.

A trespass to a chattel may be committed by intentionally * * * using or intermeddling [interfering] with a chattel in the possession of another, where the chattel is impaired as to its condition, quality, or value. [Emphasis added.]

The district court found that Verio's use of search robots, consisting of software programs performing multiple automated successive queries, consumed a significant portion of the capacity of Register's computer systems. While Verio's robots alone would not incapacitate Register's systems, the court found that if Verio were permitted to continue to access Register's computers through such robots, it was "highly probable" that other Internet service providers would devise similar programs to access Register's data, and that the system would be overtaxed and would crash. We cannot say these findings were unreasonable.

Nor is there merit to Verio's contention that it cannot be engaged in trespass when Register had never instructed it not to use its robot programs. As the district court noted, Register's complaint sufficiently advised Verio that its use of robots was not authorized and, according to Register's contentions, would cause harm to Register's systems.

CASE 5.2–CONTINUED

DECISION AND REMEDY The U.S. Court of Appeals for the Second Circuit affirmed the lower court's order. Trespass to personal property is "committed by intentionally * * * using or intermeddling with a chattel [personal property] in the possession of another, where the chattel is impaired as to its condition, quality, or value." In this case, Verio's use of search robots "consumed a significant portion of the capacity of Register's computer systems."

FOR CRITICAL ANALYSIS–Technological Consideration
Why should the use of a bot to initiate "multiple automated successive queries" have a different legal effect than typing and submitting queries manually?

- -

Conversion

Whenever personal property is wrongfully taken from its rightful owner or possessor and placed in the service of another, the act of **conversion** occurs. Conversion is defined as any act depriving an owner of personal property without that owner's permission and without just cause. When conversion occurs, the lesser offense of trespass to personal property usually occurs as well. If the initial taking of the property was unlawful, there is trespass; retention of that property is conversion. If the initial taking of the property was permitted by the owner or for some other reason is not a trespass, failure to return it may still be conversion. Conversion is the civil side of crimes related to theft. A store clerk who steals merchandise from the store commits a crime and engages in the tort of conversion at the same time.

Even if a person mistakenly believed that she or he was entitled to the goods, the tort of conversion may occur. In other words, good intentions are not a defense against conversion; in fact, conversion can be an entirely innocent act. Someone who buys stolen goods, for example, is guilty of conversion even if he or she did not know that the goods were stolen. If the true owner brings a tort action against the buyer, the buyer must either return the property to the owner or pay the owner the full value of the property, despite having already paid the thief.

A successful defense against the charge of conversion is that the purported owner does not in fact own the property or does not have a right to possess it that is superior to the right of the holder. Necessity is another possible defense against conversion. **| Example #6** If Abrams takes Mendoza's cat, Abrams is guilty of conversion. If Mendoza sues Abrams, Abrams must return the cat or pay damages. If, however, the cat has rabies and Abrams took the cat to protect the public, Abrams has a valid defense—necessity (and perhaps even self-defense, if he can prove that he was in danger because of the cat).|

Disparagement of Property

Disparagement of property occurs when economically injurious falsehoods are made about another's product or property, not about another's reputation. Disparagement of property is a general term for torts that can be more specifically referred to as *slander of quality* or *slander of title*.

CONVERSION
Wrongfully taking or retaining possession of an individual's personal property and placing it in the service of another.

KEEP IN MIND In tort law, the underlying motive for an act does not matter. What matters is the intent to do the act that results in the tort.

DISPARAGEMENT OF PROPERTY
An economically injurious falsehood made about another's product or property. A general term for torts that are more specifically referred to as *slander of quality* or *slander of title*.

SLANDER OF QUALITY (TRADE LIBEL)
The publication of false information about another's product, alleging that it is not what its seller claims.

Slander of Quality Publication of false information about another's product, alleging that it is not what its seller claims, constitutes the tort of **slander of quality,** or **trade libel.** The plaintiff must prove that actual damages proximately resulted from the slander of quality. In other words, the plaintiff must show not only that a third person refrained from dealing with the plaintiff because of the improper publication but also that there were associated damages. The economic calculation of such damages—they are, after all, conjectural—is often extremely difficult.

An improper publication may be both a slander of quality and a defamation. For example, a statement that disparages the quality of a product may also, by implication, disparage the character of the person who would sell such a product.

SLANDER OF TITLE
The publication of a statement that denies or casts doubt on another's legal ownership of any property, causing financial loss to that property's owner.

Slander of Title When a publication denies or casts doubt on another's legal ownership of any property, and this results in financial loss to that property's owner, the tort of **slander of title** may exist. Usually, this is an intentional tort in which someone knowingly publishes an untrue statement about property with the intent of discouraging a third person from dealing with the person slandered. For example, it would be difficult for a car dealer to attract customers after competitors published a notice that the dealer's stock consisted of stolen autos.

UNINTENTIONAL TORTS (NEGLIGENCE)

NEGLIGENCE
The failure to exercise the standard of care that a reasonable person would exercise in similar circumstances.

criteria   caution

The tort of **negligence** occurs when someone suffers injury because of another's failure to live up to a required *duty of care.* In contrast to intentional torts, in torts involving negligence, the tortfeasor neither wishes to bring about the consequences of the act nor believes that they will occur. The actor's conduct merely creates a *risk* of such consequences. If no risk is created, there is no negligence.

Many of the actions discussed in the section on intentional torts constitute negligence if the element of intent is missing. | **Example #7** If Juarez intentionally shoves Natsuyo, who falls and breaks an arm as a result, Juarez will have committed the intentional tort of assault and battery. If Juarez carelessly bumps into Natsuyo, however, and she falls and breaks an arm as a result, Juarez's action will constitute negligence. In either situation, Juarez has committed a tort.|

In examining a question of negligence, one should ask the following four questions (each of these elements of negligence will be discussed below):

1. Did the defendant owe a duty of care to the plaintiff?
2. Did the defendant breach that duty?
3. Did the plaintiff suffer a legally recognizable injury as a result of the defendant's breach of the duty of care?
4. Did the defendant's breach cause the plaintiff's injury?

The Duty of Care and Its Breach

DUTY OF CARE
The duty of all persons, as established by tort law, to exercise a reasonable amount of care in their dealings with others. Failure to exercise due care, which is normally determined by the "reasonable person standard," constitutes the tort of negligence.

The concept of a **duty of care** arises from the notion that if we are to live in society with other people, some actions can be tolerated and some cannot; some actions are right and some are wrong; and some actions are reasonable and some are not. The basic principle underlying the duty of care is that people are free to act as they please so long as their actions do not infringe on the interests of others.

When someone fails to comply with the duty to exercise reasonable care, a potentially tortious act may have been committed. Failure to live up to a standard of care may be an act (setting fire to a building) or an omission (neglecting to put out a campfire). It may be a careless act or a carefully performed but nevertheless dangerous act that results in injury. Courts consider the nature of the act (whether it is outrageous or commonplace), the manner in which the act is performed (cautiously versus heedlessly), and the nature of the injury (whether it is serious or slight) in determining whether the duty of care has been breached.

The Reasonable Person Standard   Tort law measures duty by the **reasonable person standard.** In determining whether a duty of care has been breached, the courts ask how a reasonable person would have acted in the same circumstances. The reasonable person standard is said to be (though in an absolute sense it cannot be) objective. It is not necessarily how a particular person would act. It is society's judgment on how people *should* act. If the so-called reasonable person existed, he or she would be careful, conscientious, even tempered, and honest. The courts frequently use this hypothetical reasonable person in decisions relating to other areas of law as well.

That individuals are required to exercise a reasonable standard of care in their activities is a pervasive concept in business law, and many of the issues discussed in subsequent chapters of this text have to do with this duty. What constitutes reasonable care varies, of course, with the circumstances.

REASONABLE PERSON STANDARD
The standard of behavior expected of a hypothetical "reasonable person"; the standard against which negligence is measured and that must be observed to avoid liability for negligence.

ETHICAL ISSUE 5.1   ***Does a person's duty of care include a duty to come to the aid of a stranger in peril?***

Suppose that you are walking down a city street and notice that a pedestrian is about to step directly in front of an oncoming bus. Do you have a legal duty to warn that individual? No. Although most people would probably concede that the observer has an *ethical* or moral duty to warn the other in this situation, tort law does not impose a general duty to rescue others in peril. People involved in special relationships, however, have been held to have a duty to rescue other parties within the relationship. A person has a duty to rescue his or her child or spouse if either is in danger, for example. Other special relationships, such as those between teachers and students or hiking and hunting partners, may also give rise to a duty to rescue. In addition, if a person who has no duty to rescue undertakes to rescue another, then the rescuer is charged with a duty to follow through with due care in the rescue attempt.

The Duty of Landowners   Landowners are expected to exercise reasonable care to protect persons coming onto their property from harm. As mentioned earlier, in some jurisdictions, landowners are held to owe a duty to protect even trespassers against certain risks. Landowners who rent or lease premises to tenants (see Chapter 19) are expected to exercise reasonable care to ensure that the tenants and their guests are not harmed in common areas, such as stairways, entryways, laundry rooms, and the like.

BUSINESS INVITEE
A person, such as a customer or a client, who is invited onto business premises by the owner of those premises for business purposes.

Retailers and other firms that explicitly or implicitly invite persons to come onto their premises are usually charged with a duty to exercise reasonable care to protect those persons, who are considered **business invitees.** For example, if you entered a supermarket, slipped on a wet floor, and sustained injuries as a result, the owner of the supermarket would be liable for damages if when you slipped there was no sign warning that the floor was wet. A court would hold that the business owner was negligent because the owner failed to exercise a reasonable degree of care in protecting the store's customers against foreseeable risks about which the owner knew or *should have known*. That a patron might slip on the wet floor and be injured as a result was a foreseeable risk, and the owner should have taken care to avoid this risk or to warn the customer of it. The landowner also has a duty to discover and remove any hidden dangers that might injure a customer or other invitee.

Some risks, of course, are so obvious that the owner need not warn of them. For instance, a business owner does not have to warn customers to open a door before attempting to walk through it. Other risks, however, even though they may seem obvious to a business owner, may not be so in the eyes of another, such as a child. For example, a hardware store owner may not think it is necessary to warn customers not to climb a stepladder leaning against the back wall of the store. It is possible, though, that a child could climb up and tip the ladder over and be hurt as a result and that the store could be held liable.

The Duty of Professionals If an individual has knowledge or skill superior to that of an ordinary person, the individual's conduct must be consistent with that status. Professionals—including physicians, dentists, architects, engineers, accountants, lawyers, and others—are required to have a standard minimum level of special knowledge and ability. Therefore, in determining what constitutes reasonable care in the case of professionals, their training and expertise are taken into account. In other words, an accountant cannot defend against a lawsuit for negligence by stating, "But I was not familiar with that principle of accounting."

If a professional violates her or his duty of care toward a client, the professional may be sued for **malpractice.** For example, a patient might sue a physician for *medical malpractice*. A client might sue an attorney for *legal malpractice*.

MALPRACTICE
Professional misconduct or the lack of the requisite degree of skill as a professional. Negligence—the failure to exercise due care—on the part of a professional, such as a physician, is commonly referred to as malpractice.

The Injury Requirement and Damages

For a tort to have been committed, the plaintiff must have suffered a *legally recognizable* injury. To recover damages (receive compensation), the plaintiff must have suffered some loss, harm, wrong, or invasion of a protected interest. Essentially, the purpose of tort law is to compensate for legally recognized injuries resulting from wrongful acts. If no harm or injury results from a given negligent action, there is nothing to compensate—and no tort exists. **| Example #8** If you carelessly bump into a passerby, who stumbles and falls as a result, you may be liable in tort if the passerby is injured in the fall. If the person is unharmed, however, there normally could be no suit for damages, because no injury was suffered.**|**

As already mentioned, the purpose of tort law is not to punish people for tortious acts but to compensate the injured parties for harm suffered by

Tort Liability and Damages in Other Nations

In contrast to U.S. courts, courts in Europe generally limit damages to compensatory damages; punitive damages are virtually unheard of in European countries. Even when plaintiffs do win compensatory damages, they generally receive much less than would be awarded in a similar case brought in the United States. In part, this is because citizens of European countries usually receive government-provided health care and relatively generous social security benefits. Yet it is also because European courts tend to view the duty of care and the concept of risk differently than U.S. courts do. In the United States, if a swimmer falls off a high diving board and is injured, a court may decide that the pool owner should be held liable, given that such a fall is a

foreseeable risk. If punitive damages are awarded, they could total millions of dollars. In a similar situation in Europe, a court might hold that the plaintiff, not the pool owner, was responsible for the injury.

Tort laws in other nations also differ in the way damages are calculated. For example, under Swiss law and Turkish law, a court is permitted to reduce the amount of damages if an award of full damages would cause undue hardship for a party who was found negligent. In the United States, in contrast, the courts normally do not take this factor into consideration.

For Critical Analysis *Punitive damages are a very important element in American tort litigation. Why is this? What do awards of punitive damages achieve?*

awarding damages. **Compensatory damages** are intended to reimburse a plaintiff for actual losses—to make the plaintiff whole. Occasionally, **punitive damages** are also awarded to punish the wrongdoer and deter others from similar wrongdoing. Punitive damages are rarely awarded in lawsuits for ordinary negligence and usually are given only in cases involving intentional torts. They may be awarded, however, in suits that involve a high degree of negligence, called *gross negligence,* in which a person acts in reckless disregard of the consequences. (Do other nations award punitive damages in tort cases? See this chapter's *Beyond Our Borders* feature for a discussion of tort liability in other countries.)

In *State Farm Mutual Automobile Insurance Co. v. Campbell,*[9] the United States Supreme Court held that to the extent an award of punitive damages is grossly excessive, it furthers no legitimate purpose and violates due process requirements (discussed in Chapter 4). While this case dealt with intentional torts (fraud and intentional infliction of emotional distress), the Court's holding applies equally to punitive damages awards in gross negligence cases.

COMPENSATORY DAMAGES
A money award equivalent to the actual value of injuries or damages sustained by the aggrieved party.

PUNITIVE DAMAGES
Money damages that may be awarded to a plaintiff to punish the defendant and deter future similar conduct.

Causation

Another element necessary to a tort is *causation.* If a person fails in a duty of care and someone suffers injury, the wrongful activity must have caused the harm for a tort to have been committed. In deciding whether there is causation, the court must address two questions:

1. *Is there causation in fact?* Did the injury occur because of the defendant's act, or would it have occurred anyway? If an injury would not have occurred without the defendant's act, then there is causation in fact.

---

9. 538 U.S. 408, 123 S.Ct. 1513, 155 L.Ed.2d 585 (2003).

CAUSATION IN FACT
An act or omission without which an event would not have occurred.

Causation in fact can usually be determined by the use of the *but for* test: "but for" the wrongful act, the injury would not have occurred. Theoretically, causation in fact is limitless. One could claim, for example, that "but for" the creation of the world, a particular injury would not have occurred. Thus, as a practical matter, the law has to establish limits, and it does so through the concept of proximate cause.

PROXIMATE CAUSE
Legal cause; exists when the connection between an act and an injury is strong enough to justify imposing liability.

2. *Was the act the proximate cause of the injury?* **Proximate cause,** or legal cause, exists when the connection between an act and an injury is strong enough to justify imposing liability. **|Example #9** Ackerman carelessly leaves a campfire burning. The fire not only burns down the forest but also sets off an explosion in a nearby chemical plant that spills chemicals into a river, killing all the fish for a hundred miles downstream and ruining the economy of a tourist resort. Should Ackerman be liable to the resort owners? To the tourists whose vacations were ruined? These are questions of proximate cause that a court must decide.|

NOTE Proximate cause can be thought of as a question of social policy. Should the defendant be made to bear the loss instead of the plaintiff?

Probably the most cited case on proximate cause is the *Palsgraf* case, discussed in this chapter's *Landmark in the Legal Environment* feature. In determining the issue of proximate cause, the court addressed the following question: Does a defendant's duty of care extend only to those who may be injured as a result of a foreseeable risk, or does it extend also to a person whose injury could not reasonably be foreseen?

Defenses to Negligence

Defendants often defend against negligence claims by asserting that the plaintiffs failed to prove the existence of one or more of the required elements for negligence. Additionally, there are three basic *affirmative* defenses in negligence cases (defenses that defendants can use to avoid liability even if the facts are as the plaintiffs state): (1) assumption of risk, (2) superseding cause, and (3) contributory and comparative negligence.

ASSUMPTION OF RISK
A doctrine under which a plaintiff may not recover for injuries or damages suffered from risks he or she knows of and has voluntarily assumed.

Assumption of Risk   A plaintiff who voluntarily enters into a risky situation, knowing the risk involved, normally will not be allowed to recover. This is the defense of **assumption of risk.** The requirements of this defense are (1) knowledge of the risk and (2) voluntary assumption of the risk.

The risk can be assumed by express agreement, or the assumption of risk can be implied by the plaintiff's knowledge of the risk and subsequent conduct. For example, a driver entering a race knows that there is a risk of being killed or injured in a crash. Of course, the plaintiff does not assume a risk different from or greater than the risk normally carried by the activity. In our example, the race driver would not assume the risk that the banking in the curves of the racetrack will give way during the race because of a construction defect.

Risks are not deemed to be assumed in situations involving emergencies. Neither are they assumed when a statute protects a class of people from harm and a member of the class is injured by the harm. For example, employees are protected by statute from harmful working conditions and therefore do not assume the risks associated with the workplace. An employee who is injured will generally be compensated regardless of fault under state workers' compensation statutes (discussed in Chapter 13).

Palsgraf v. Long Island Railroad Co. (1928)

In 1928, the New York Court of Appeals (that state's highest court) issued its decision in *Palsgraf v. Long Island Railroad Co.*,[a] a case that has become a landmark in negligence law with respect to proximate cause.

The Facts of the Case The plaintiff, Palsgraf, was waiting for a train on a station platform. A man carrying a small package wrapped in newspaper was rushing to catch a train that had begun to move away from the platform. As the man attempted to jump aboard the moving train, he seemed unsteady and about to fall. A railroad guard on the train car reached forward to grab him, and another guard on the platform pushed him from behind to help him board the train. In the process, the man's package fell on the railroad tracks and exploded, because it contained fireworks. The repercussions of the explosion caused scales at the other end of the train platform to fall on Palsgraf, who was injured as a result. She sued the railroad company for damages in a New York state court.

The Question of Proximate Cause At the trial, the jury found that the railroad guards were negligent in their conduct. On appeal, the question before the New York Court of Appeals was whether the conduct of the railroad guards was the proximate cause of Palsgraf's injuries. In other words, did the guards' duty of care extend to Palsgraf, who was outside the zone of danger and whose injury could not reasonably have been foreseen?

The court stated that the question of whether the guards were negligent *with respect to Palsgraf* depended

on whether her injury was *reasonably foreseeable* to the railroad guards. Although the guards may have acted negligently with respect to the man boarding the train, this had no bearing on the question of their negligence with respect to Palsgraf. This was not a situation in which a person committed an act so potentially harmful (for example, firing a gun at a building) that he or she would be held responsible for any harm that resulted. The court stated that here "there was nothing in the situation to suggest to the most cautious mind that the parcel wrapped in newspaper would spread wreckage through the station." The court thus concluded that the railroad guards were not negligent with respect to Palsgraf because her injury was not reasonably foreseeable.

The *Palsgraf case established* foreseeability *as the test for proximate cause. Today, the courts continue to apply this test in determining proximate cause—and thus tort liability for injuries. Generally, if the victim of a harm or the consequences of a harm done are unforeseeable, there is no proximate cause. Note, though, that in the online environment, distinctions based on physical proximity, such as the "zone of danger" cited by the court in this case, are largely inapplicable.*

To locate information on the Web concerning the Palsgraf *decision, go to this text's Web site at* **www.thomsonedu. com/westbuslaw/let**, *select "Chapter 5," and click on "URLs for Landmarks."*

a. 248 N.Y. 339, 162 N.E. 99 (1928).

Superseding Cause An unforeseeable intervening event may break the connection between a wrongful act and an injury to another. If so, the event acts as a *superseding cause*—that is, it relieves a defendant of liability for injuries caused by the intervening event. **|Example #10** Suppose that Derrick keeps a can of gasoline in the trunk of his car. The presence of the gasoline creates a foreseeable risk and is thus a negligent act. If Derrick's car skids and crashes into a tree, causing the gasoline can to explode, Derrick would be liable for injuries sustained by passing pedestrians because of his negligence. If the explosion had been caused by lightning striking the car, however, the lightning would supersede Derrick's original negligence as a cause of the damage, because the lightning was not foreseeable.**|**

Contributory and Comparative Negligence All individuals are expected to exercise a reasonable degree of care in looking out for themselves. In the past,

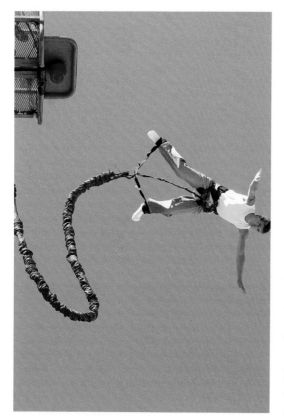

Assume this bungee jumper suffers an eye injury. Why might he not be able to recover any damages? (AP Photo/*Pueblo Chieftain*, Chris McLean)

CONTRIBUTORY NEGLIGENCE
A rule in tort law that completely bars the plaintiff from recovering any damages if the damage suffered is partly the plaintiff's own fault; used in a minority of states.

COMPARATIVE NEGLIGENCE
A rule in tort law that reduces the plaintiff's recovery in proportion to the plaintiff's degree of fault, rather than barring recovery completely; used in the majority of states.

RES IPSA LOQUITUR
A doctrine under which negligence may be inferred simply because an event occurred, if it is the type of event that would never occur in the absence of negligence. Literally, the term means "the facts speak for themselves."

NEGLIGENCE PER SE
An action or failure to act in violation of a statutory requirement.

under the common law doctrine of **contributory negligence,** a plaintiff who was also negligent (failed to exercise a reasonable degree of care) could not recover anything from the defendant. Under this rule, no matter how insignificant the plaintiff's negligence was relative to the defendant's negligence, the plaintiff would be precluded from recovering any damages. Today, only a few jurisdictions still hold to this doctrine. In the majority of states, the doctrine of contributory negligence has been replaced by a **comparative negligence** standard.

Under the comparative negligence standard, both the plaintiff's and the defendant's negligence are computed, and the liability for damages is distributed accordingly. Some jurisdictions have adopted a "pure" form of comparative negligence that allows the plaintiff to recover, even if the extent of his or her fault is greater than that of the defendant. For example, if the plaintiff was 80 percent at fault and the defendant 20 percent at fault, the plaintiff may recover 20 percent of his or her damages. Many states' comparative negligence statutes, however, contain a "50 percent" rule that precludes the plaintiff from any recovery if she or he was more than 50 percent at fault.

Special Negligence Doctrines and Statutes

There are a number of special doctrines and statutes relating to negligence. We examine a few of them here.

Res Ipsa Loquitur   Generally, in lawsuits involving negligence, the plaintiff has the burden of proving that the defendant was negligent. In certain situations, however, when negligence is very difficult or impossible to prove, the courts may infer that negligence has occurred; then the burden of proof rests on the defendant—to prove that he or she was *not* negligent. The inference of the defendant's negligence is known as the doctrine of *res ipsa loquitur,*[10] which translates as "the facts speak for themselves."

This doctrine is applied only when the event creating the damage or injury is one that ordinarily would occur only as a result of negligence. | **Example #11** If a person undergoes surgery to repair a leaking bladder and following the surgery has nerve damage in her spine near the area of the operation, that person can sue the surgeon under a theory of *res ipsa loquitur.* In this instance, the injury would never have occurred in the absence of the surgeon's negligence.[11] | For the doctrine of *res ipsa loquitur* to apply, the event must have been within the defendant's power to control, and it must not have been due to any voluntary action or contribution on the part of the plaintiff.

Negligence *Per Se*   Certain conduct, whether it consists of an action or a failure to act, may be treated as **negligence *per se*** (*per se* means "in or of itself"). Negligence *per se* may occur if an individual violates a statute or an ordinance providing for a criminal penalty and that violation causes another to be

---

10. Pronounced *rehz ihp*-suh *low*-kwuh-tuhr.
11. *Gubbins v. Hurson,* 885 A.2d 269 (D.C. 2005).

injured. The injured person must prove (1) that the statute clearly sets out what standard of conduct is expected, when and where it is expected, and of whom it is expected; (2) that he or she is in the class intended to be protected by the statute; and (3) that the statute was designed to prevent the type of injury that he or she suffered. The standard of conduct required by the statute is the duty that the defendant owes to the plaintiff, and a violation of the statute is the breach of that duty.

| **Example #12** Suppose a statute requires a residential landlord to maintain a building in safe condition and to maintain in good working order all electrical, plumbing, heating, and other facilities supplied by the landlord. The statute is meant to protect tenants and those who are rightfully in the building. Thus, if the landlord violates the statute by failing to keep the lighting in the stairwell in working order and a tenant is thereby injured, a majority of courts will hold that the violation of the statute conclusively establishes a breach of a duty of care—that is, that the landlord's violation is negligence *per se*. |

"Danger Invites Rescue" Doctrine   Sometimes a person who is trying to avoid harm—one who swerves to avoid a collision with an oncoming car, for example—ends up causing harm to another as a result (the driver of another car). In those situations, typically the original wrongdoer is held liable to anyone who was injured, even if the injury actually resulted from an attempt to escape harm. The "danger invites rescue" doctrine extends the same protection to persons who are attempting to rescue another from harm. Under this negligence doctrine, the original wrongdoer is liable not only for the injuries to the person who was placed in danger, but also for injuries to an individual attempting a rescue. The idea is that the rescuer should not be held liable for any damages, because he or she did not cause the danger and because danger invites rescue.

| **Example #13** Lane is a railroad engineer on a train that is traveling through a town at high speed. Lane negligently fails to signal the train's approach by activating a loud, high-pitched whistle and does not notice that a small child is playing on the tracks ahead. A passerby, Frank Yokem, sees the danger to the child and runs to her rescue, throwing her out of the train's path at the last minute to save her life. Yokem, however, is not able to get clear of the tracks and is struck by the train and dies. In a negligence action against the railroad, the "danger invites rescue" doctrine prevents the company from escaping liability for Yokem's injuries by claiming that he was contributorily negligent by placing himself in danger. | Rescuers can injure themselves, or the person rescued, or even a stranger, but the original wrongdoer will still be liable.

Special Negligence Statutes   A number of states have enacted statutes prescribing duties and responsibilities in certain circumstances. For example, most states now have what are called **Good Samaritan statutes.** Under these statutes, someone who is aided voluntarily by others cannot turn around and sue the "Good Samaritans" for negligence. These laws were passed largely to protect physicians and medical personnel who voluntarily render services in emergency situations to those in need, such as individuals hurt in car accidents.

Many states have also passed **dram shop acts,** under which a tavern owner or bartender may be held liable for injuries caused by a person who became intoxicated while drinking at the bar or who was already intoxicated when served by the bartender. In some states, statutes impose liability on *social hosts*

GOOD SAMARITAN STATUTE
A state statute stipulating that persons who provide emergency services to, or rescue, someone in peril cannot be sued for negligence, unless they act recklessly, thereby causing further harm.

DRAM SHOP ACT
A state statute that imposes liability on the owners of bars and taverns, as well as those who serve alcoholic drinks to the public, for injuries resulting from accidents caused by intoxicated persons when the sellers or servers of alcoholic drinks contributed to the intoxication.

(persons hosting parties) for injuries caused by guests who became intoxicated at the hosts' homes. Under these statutes, it is unnecessary to prove that the tavern owner, bartender, or social host was negligent.

CYBER TORTS

It should come as no surprise that torts can also be committed in the online environment. Torts committed via the Internet are often called *cyber torts*. Over the last ten years, the courts have had to decide how to apply traditional tort law to torts committed in cyberspace. Consider, for example, issues of proof. How can it be proved that an online defamatory remark was "published" (which requires that a third party see or hear it)? How can the identity of the person who made the remark be discovered? Can an Internet service provider (ISP), such as America Online, Inc. (AOL), be forced to reveal the source of an anonymous comment made by one of its subscribers? We explore some of these questions in this section, as well as some of the legal issues that have arisen with respect to bulk e-mail advertising.

Defamation Online

Recall from the discussion of defamation earlier in this chapter that one who repeats or otherwise republishes a defamatory statement can be subject to liability as if he or she had originally published it. Thus, publishers generally can be held liable for defamatory contents in the books and periodicals that they publish. Now consider online forums. These forums allow anyone—customers, employees, or crackpots—to complain about a firm's personnel, policies, practices, or products. Whatever the truth of the complaint is, it might have an impact on the business of the firm. One of the early questions in the online legal arena was whether the providers of such forums could be held liable, as publishers, for defamatory statements made in those forums.

Liability of Internet Service Providers   Prior to the passage of the Communications Decency Act (CDA) of 1996, the courts grappled on several occasions with the question of whether ISPs should be regarded as publishers and thus be held liable for defamatory messages made by users of their services. The CDA resolved the issue by stating that "[n]o provider or user of an interactive computer service shall be treated as the publisher or speaker of any information provided by another information content provider."[12] In a number of key cases, the ISP provisions of the CDA have been invoked to shield ISPs from liability for defamatory postings on their bulletin boards.

| **Example #14**   In a leading case on this issue, decided the year after the CDA was enacted, AOL, now part of Time Warner, Inc., was not held liable even though it failed to promptly remove defamatory messages of which it had been made aware. In upholding a U.S. district court's ruling in AOL's favor, a federal appellate court stated that the CDA "plainly immunizes computer service providers like AOL from liability for information that originates with third parties." The court explained that the purpose of the statute is "to maintain the robust nature of Internet communication and, accordingly, to keep government interference in the medium to a minimum."[13] |

---

12. 47 U.S.C. Section 230.
13. *Zeran v. America Online, Inc.,* 129 F.3d 327 (4th Cir. 1997); *cert.* denied, 524 U.S. 934, 118 S.Ct. 2341, 141 L.Ed.2d 712 (1998).

In subsequent cases, the courts have reached similar conclusions.[14] The courts have also extended the immunity to liability provided by the CDA to auction houses, such as eBay.[15]

Piercing the Veil of Anonymity   A threshold barrier to anyone who seeks to bring an action for online defamation is discovering the identity of the person who posted the defamatory message online. ISPs can disclose personal information about their customers only when ordered to do so by a court. Consequently, businesses and individuals are increasingly resorting to lawsuits against "John Does." Then, using the authority of the courts, they can obtain from the ISPs the identities of the persons responsible for the messages.

| **Example #15**   In one case, Eric Hvide, a former chief executive of a company called Hvide Marine, sued a number of "John Does" who had posted allegedly defamatory statements about his company on various online message boards. Hvide, who eventually lost his job, sued the John Does for libel in a Florida court. The court ruled that Yahoo and AOL had to reveal the identities of the defendant Does.[16] |

In other cases, however, the courts have refused to order an ISP to disclose the identity of subscribers.[17] Generally, in these cases the courts must decide which right should take priority: the right to free (anonymous) speech under the First Amendment or the right not to be defamed.

Spam

Bulk, unsolicited e-mail ("junk" e-mail) sent to all of the users on a particular e-mailing list is often called **spam**.[18] Typically, spam consists of a product ad sent to all of the users on an e-mailing list or all of the members of a newsgroup. Because of the problems associated with spam, a majority of the states now have laws regulating spam. In 2003, the U.S. Congress also enacted a law to regulate the use of spam.

SPAM
Bulk, unsolicited ("junk") e-mail.

State Regulation of Spam   In an attempt to combat spam, thirty-six states have enacted laws that prohibit or regulate its use. Many state laws regulating spam require the senders of e-mail ads to instruct the recipients on how they can "opt out" of further e-mail ads from the same sources. For instance, in some states an unsolicited e-mail ad must include a toll-free phone number or return e-mail address through which the recipient can contact the sender to request that no more ads be e-mailed. The most stringent state law is California's antispam law, which went into effect on January 1, 2004. That law follows the "opt-in" model favored by consumer groups and antispam advocates. In other words, the law prohibits any person or business from sending e-mail ads to or from any e-mail address in California unless the recipient has expressly agreed to receive e-mails from the sender. An exemption is made for

---

14. See, for example, *Noah v. AOL Time Warner, Inc.*, 261 F.Supp.2d 532 (E.D.Va. 2003).
15. *Stoner v. eBay, Inc.*, 2000 WL 1705637 (Cal.Super.Ct. 2000).
16. *Does v. Hvide*, 770 So.2d 1237 (Fla.App.3d 2000).
17. See, for example, *Graham v. Oppenheimer*, 2000 WL 33381418 (E.D.Va. 2000).
18. The term *spam* is said to come from a Monty Python song with the lyrics, "Spam spam spam spam, spam spam spam spam, lovely spam, wonderful spam." Like these lyrics, spam online is often considered to be a repetition of worthless text.

e-mail sent to consumers with whom the advertiser has a "preexisting or current business relationship."

The Federal CAN-SPAM Act   In 2003, Congress enacted the Controlling the Assault of Non-Solicited Pornography and Marketing (CAN-SPAM) Act, which took effect on January 1, 2004. The legislation applies to any "commercial electronic mail messages" that are sent to promote a commercial product or service. Significantly, the statute preempts state antispam laws except for those provisions in state laws that prohibit false and deceptive e-mailing practices.

Generally, the act permits the use of unsolicited commercial e-mail but prohibits certain types of spamming activities, including the use of a false return address and the use of false, misleading, or deceptive information when sending e-mail. The statute also prohibits the use of "dictionary attacks"—sending messages to randomly generated e-mail addresses—and the "harvesting" of e-mail addresses from Web sites through the use of specialized software. Additionally, the law requires senders of commercial e-mail to do the following:

1. Include a return address on the e-mail.
2. Include a clear notification that the message is an ad and provide a valid physical postal address.
3. Provide a mechanism that allows recipients to "opt out" of further e-mail ads from the same source.
4. Take action on a recipient's "opt-out" request within ten days.
5. Label any sexually oriented materials as such.

STRICT LIABILITY

Another category of torts is called **strict liability,** or *liability without fault.* Intentional torts and torts of negligence involve acts that depart from a reasonable standard of care and cause injuries. Under the doctrine of strict liability, liability for injury is imposed for reasons other than fault. Strict liability for damages proximately caused by an abnormally dangerous or exceptional activity is one application of this doctrine. Courts apply the doctrine of strict liability in such cases because of the extreme risk of the activity. Even if blasting with dynamite is performed with all reasonable care, there is still a risk of injury. Balancing that risk against the potential for harm, it seems reasonable to ask the person engaged in the activity to pay for injuries caused by that activity. Although there is no fault, there is still responsibility because of the dangerous nature of the undertaking.

There are other applications of the strict liability principle. Persons who keep dangerous animals, for example, are strictly liable for any harm inflicted by the animals. A significant application of strict liability is in the area of *product liability*—liability of manufacturers and sellers for harmful or defective products. We discuss product liability in detail in the following sections.

PRODUCT LIABILITY

Manufacturers, sellers, and lessors of goods can be held liable to consumers, users, and bystanders for physical harm or property damage that is caused by the goods. This is called **product liability.** Product liability may be based on warranty theories, as well as on the theories of negligence, misrepresentation, and strict liability.

Product Liability Based on Warranty Law

Today, warranty law is an important part of the entire spectrum of laws relating to product liability. Most goods are covered by some type of warranty designed to protect consumers. The concept of warranty is based on the seller's assurance to the buyer that the goods will meet certain standards. Because a warranty imposes a duty on the seller, a breach of the warranty is a breach of the seller's promise.

The Uniform Commercial Code (UCC) designates five types of warranties that can arise in a contract for the sale of goods. These include express and implied warranties.

Express Warranties   A seller can create an **express warranty** by making a representation concerning the quality, condition, description, or performance potential of goods at such a time that the buyer could have relied on the representation when he or she agreed to the contract. These representations may be made in advertisements or by a salesperson.

Realize that sellers are allowed to "huff and puff" their wares as they like. Sellers' statements of opinion (such as "this car is a gem") are known as *puffery*, as noted earlier in this chapter in the discussion of the tort of misrepresentation. Normally, a seller's statement of *opinion* does not constitute an express warranty. If a seller makes a statement of *fact*, however, such as "this car has a new engine," this may create an express warranty if the statement goes to the "basis of the bargain"—that is, was essential to the buyer's decision to purchase the car. The line distinguishing puffery from statements that constitute express warranties is often blurred.

Implied Warranties   An **implied warranty of merchantability** that goods are "reasonably fit for the ordinary purposes for which such goods are used" arises automatically in a sale of goods by a merchant who deals in such goods. An **implied warranty of fitness for a particular purpose** arises when any seller—merchant or nonmerchant—knows the particular purpose for which a buyer will use the goods and knows that the buyer is relying on the seller's skill and judgment to select suitable goods.

Liability for Breach of Warranty   Consumers, purchasers, and even users of goods can recover *from any seller* for losses resulting from breach of implied and express warranties. A manufacturer is a *seller*. Therefore, a person who purchases goods from a retailer can recover from the retailer or the manufacturer if the goods are not merchantable. A product purchaser may sue not only the firm from which he or she purchased a product but also a third party—the manufacturer of the product—in product liability.

The UCC does permit warranties to be disclaimed or limited by specific and unambiguous language, provided that this is done in a manner that protects the buyer or lessee from surprise. Therefore, a written disclaimer in language that is clear and conspicuous, and called to a buyer's or lessee's attention, could negate all oral express warranties not included in the written sales contract. Generally speaking, unless circumstances indicate otherwise, the implied warranties of merchantability and fitness are disclaimed by the expressions "as is," "with all faults," and other similar phrases that in common understanding call the buyer's or lessee's attention to the fact that there are no implied warranties.

EXPRESS WARRANTY
A seller's or lessor's oral or written promise, ancillary to an underlying sales agreement, as to the quality, description, or performance of the goods being sold or leased.

IMPLIED WARRANTY OF MERCHANTABILITY
An implicit promise by a merchant seller of goods that the goods are reasonably fit for the general purpose for which they are sold, are correctly packaged and labeled, and are of proper quality.

IMPLIED WARRANTY OF FITNESS FOR A PARTICULAR PURPOSE
An implicit promise made by a seller of goods that the goods are fit for the particular purpose for which the buyer will use the goods. The seller must know the buyer's purpose and be aware that the buyer is relying on the seller's skill and judgment to select suitable goods.

Product Liability Based on Negligence

As defined earlier in this chapter, *negligence* is the failure to exercise the degree of care that a reasonable, prudent person would have exercised under the circumstances. If a manufacturer fails to exercise "due care" to make a product safe, a person who is injured by the product may sue the manufacturer for negligence.

Due Care Must Be Exercised   The manufacturer must exercise due care in designing the product, selecting the materials, using the appropriate production process, assembling the product, and inspecting and testing any purchased products that are used in the final product sold by the manufacturer. The duty of care also extends to the placement of adequate warnings on the label informing the user of dangers of which an ordinary person might not be aware.

RECALL The elements of negligence include a duty of care, a breach of the duty, and an injury to the plaintiff proximately caused by the breach.

Privity of Contract Not Required   A product liability action based on negligence does not require privity of contract between the injured plaintiff and the negligent defendant manufacturer. *Privity of contract* refers to a relationship that exists between the parties to a contract that allows them to sue each other but prevents a third party from doing so (see Chapter 8). In the context of product liability law, privity of contract means a direct relationship between the seller of a product and the person who was injured by it. In the past, because privity was required, only the person who actually bought the product could file a product liability claim. Today, however, an injured party can file a product liability action even if he or she was not the person who purchased the defective product.

As stated in section 395 of the *Restatement (Second) of Torts*, a manufacturer who fails to exercise reasonable care in the manufacture of goods is subject to liability for physical harm caused to those who lawfully use the goods for their intended purpose. In other words, a manufacturer is liable for its failure to exercise due care to any person who sustains an injury proximately caused by a negligently made (defective) product, regardless of whether the injured person is in privity of contract with the negligent defendant manufacturer or lessor. Relative to the long history of the common law, this exception to the privity requirement is a fairly recent development, dating to the early part of the twentieth century.[19]

Suppose that Ford Motor Company installs Firestone tires on all new Ford Explorers. The tires are defective and cause numerous accidents involving people driving new Explorers. Who should bear the costs of the resulting injuries—Ford, Firestone, or the drivers' insurance companies—and why? (AP Photo/Eric Gay)

Product Liability Based on Misrepresentation

When a fraudulent misrepresentation has been made to a user or consumer, and that misrepresentation ultimately results in an injury, the basis of liability may be the tort of fraud. For example, the intentional mislabeling of packaged cosmetics and the intentional concealment of a product's defects would constitute fraudulent misrepresentation.

STRICT PRODUCT LIABILITY

As noted earlier, under the doctrine of strict liability, people may be liable for the results of their acts regardless of their intentions or their exercise of reasonable care. Under this doctrine, liability does not depend on privity of contract. The injured party does not have to be the buyer or a third party beneficiary, as required under contract warranty theory. Indeed, the provisions

19. A leading case in this area is *MacPherson v. Buick Motor Co.*, 217 N.Y. 382, 111 N.E. 1050 (1916).

of the UCC (Uniform Commercial Code—see Chapter 10) do not govern this type of liability in law because it is a tort doctrine, not a principle of the law relating to sales contracts.

Strict Product Liability and Public Policy

Strict product liability is imposed by law as a matter of public policy—the general principle of the law that prohibits actions that tend to be injurious to the public. With respect to strict liability, the policy rests on the threefold assumption that (1) consumers should be protected against unsafe products; (2) manufacturers and distributors should not escape liability for faulty products simply because they are not in privity of contract with the ultimate user of those products; and (3) manufacturers, sellers, and lessors of products are generally in a better position than consumers to bear the costs associated with injuries caused by their products—costs that they can ultimately pass on to all consumers in the form of higher prices.

California was the first state to impose strict product liability in tort on manufacturers. In a landmark 1962 decision, *Greenman v. Yuba Power Products, Inc.*,[20] the California Supreme Court set out the reason for applying tort law rather than contract law in cases involving consumers injured by defective products. According to the court, the "purpose of such liability is to [e]nsure that the costs of injuries resulting from defective products are borne by the manufacturers . . . rather than by the injured persons who are powerless to protect themselves."

Requirements for Strict Liability

Section 402A of the *Restatement (Second) of Torts* indicates how the drafters envisioned that the doctrine of strict liability should be applied. It was issued in 1964, and during the next decade, it became a widely accepted statement of the liabilities of sellers of goods (including manufacturers, processors, assemblers, packagers, bottlers, wholesalers, distributors, retailers, and lessors). Section 402A states as follows:

(1) One who sells any product in a defective condition unreasonably dangerous to the user or consumer or to his [or her] property is subject to liability for physical harm thereby caused to the ultimate user or consumer or to his [or her] property, if
 (a) the seller is engaged in the business of selling such a product, and
 (b) it is expected to and does reach the user or consumer without substantial change in the condition in which it is sold.
(2) The rule stated in Subsection (1) applies although
 (a) the seller has exercised all possible care in the preparation and sale of his [or her] product, and
 (b) the user or consumer has not bought the product from or entered into any contractual relation with the seller.

The Six Requirements for Strict Liability The bases for an action in strict liability as set forth in Section 402A of the *Restatement (Second) of Torts*, and as the doctrine came to be commonly applied, can be summarized as a series of six requirements, which are listed here. Depending on the jurisdiction, if these requirements are met, a manufacturer's liability to an injured party can be virtually unlimited.

---

20. 59 Cal.2d 57, 377 P.2d 897, 27 Cal.Rptr. 697 (1962).

1. The product must be in a defective condition when the defendant sells it.
2. The defendant must normally be engaged in the business of selling (or otherwise distributing) that product.
3. The product must be unreasonably dangerous to the user or consumer because of its defective condition (in most states).
4. The plaintiff must incur physical harm to self or property by use or consumption of the product.
5. The defective condition must be the proximate cause of the injury or damage.
6. The goods must not have been substantially changed from the time the product was sold to the time the injury was sustained.

Unreasonably Dangerous Products   Under the requirements just listed, in any action against a manufacturer, seller, or lessor, the plaintiff does not have to show why or in what manner the product became defective. To recover damages, however, the plaintiff must show (1) that the product was so "defective" as to be "unreasonably dangerous"; (2) that the product caused the plaintiff's injury; and (3) that at the time the injury was sustained, the product was essentially in the same condition as when it left the hands of the defendant manufacturer, seller, or lessor.

A court may consider a product so defective as to be an **unreasonably dangerous product** if either (1) the product is dangerous beyond the expectation of the ordinary consumer or (2) a less dangerous alternative was economically feasible for the manufacturer, but the manufacturer failed to produce it. As will be discussed in the next subsection, a product may be unreasonably dangerous due to a flaw in the manufacturing process, a design defect, or an inadequate warning.

UNREASONABLY DANGEROUS PRODUCT

In product liability, a product that is defective to the point of threatening a consumer's health and safety. A product will be considered unreasonably dangerous if (1) it is dangerous beyond the expectation of the ordinary consumer or if (2) a less dangerous alternative was economically feasible for the manufacturer, but the manufacturer failed to produce it.

Product Defects—*Restatement (Third) of Torts*

Because Section 402A of the *Restatement (Second) of Torts* did not clearly define such terms as "defective" and "unreasonably dangerous," they were interpreted differently by different courts. In 1997, to address these concerns, the American Law Institute issued the *Restatement (Third) of Torts: Products Liability*. The *Restatement* defines the three types of product defects that have traditionally been recognized in product liability law—manufacturing defects, design defects, and inadequate warnings.

Manufacturing Defects   According to Section 2(a) of the *Restatement (Third) of Torts*, a product "contains a manufacturing defect when the product departs from its intended design even though all possible care was exercised in the preparation and marketing of the product." This statement imposes liability on the manufacturer (and on the wholesaler and retailer) whether or not the manufacturer acted "reasonably." This is strict liability, or liability without fault.

Design Defects   A design defect (or an inadequate warning, discussed later in this chapter), by nature, affects all of the units of a particular product. A product "is defective in design when the foreseeable risks of harm posed by the product could have been reduced or avoided by the adoption of a reasonable alternative design by the seller or other distributor, or a predecessor in the commercial chain of distribution, and the omission of the alternative design renders the product not reasonably safe."[21]

***Problems with the* Restatement (Second) of Torts**   In the past, different states applied different tests to determine whether a product had a design defect under Section 402A of the *Restatement (Second) of Torts*. Some of the tests used were controversial, particularly one that focused on "consumer expectations" concerning a product.

***The Test for Design Defect under the* Restatement (Third) of Torts**   The test prescribed by the *Restatement (Third) of Torts* focuses on a product's actual design and the reasonableness of that design. To succeed in a product liability suit alleging a design defect, a plaintiff must show that there is a reasonable alternative design. In other words, a manufacturer or other defendant is liable only when the harm was reasonably preventable. According to the Official Comments accompanying the *Restatement (Third) of Torts*, factors that a court may consider on this point include

> the magnitude and probability of the foreseeable risks of harm, the instructions and warnings accompanying the product, and the nature and strength of consumer expectations regarding the product, including expectations arising from product portrayal and marketing. The relative advantages and disadvantages of the product as designed and as it alternatively could have been designed may also be considered. Thus, the likely effects of the alternative design on production costs; the effects of the alternative design on product longevity, maintenance, repair, and esthetics; and the range of consumer choice among products are factors that may be taken into account.

Inadequate Warnings   Product warnings and instructions alert consumers to the risks of using a product. A "reasonableness" test applies to this material. A product "is defective because of inadequate instructions or warnings when the foreseeable risks of harm posed by the product could have been reduced or avoided by the provision of reasonable instructions or warnings by the seller or other distributor, or a predecessor in the commercial chain of distribution, and the omission of the instructions or warnings renders the product not reasonably safe."[22] Generally, a seller must warn those who purchase its product of the harm that can result from the *foreseeable misuse* of the product as well.

Important factors for a court to consider under the *Restatement (Third) of Torts* include the risks of a product, the "content and comprehensibility" and "intensity of expression" of warnings and instructions, and the "characteristics of expected user groups."[23] For example, children will likely respond more readily to bright, bold, simple warning labels, while educated adults might need more detailed information.

There is no duty to warn about risks that are obvious or commonly known. Warnings about such risks do not add to the safety of a product and could even detract from it by making other warnings seem less significant. The obviousness of a risk and a user's decision to proceed in the face of that risk may be a

The Consumer Product Safety Commission has received complaints about the motor control circuits in this Fisher-Price minibike. If a child was injured by a malfunction of the circuits in the bike, what would the parents have to prove to establish that the bike has a design defect? (AP Photo/Evan Vucci)

21. *Restatement (Third) of Torts: Products Liability*, Section 2(b).
22. *Restatement (Third) of Torts: Products Liability*, Section 2(c).
23. *Restatement (Third) of Torts: Products Liability*, Section 2, Comment h.

defense in a product liability suit based on a warning defect. (This defense and other defenses in product liability suits will be discussed later in this chapter.)

If a warning is provided with a product, can its manufacturer or seller assume that the warning will be read and obeyed? That was one of the questions in the following case.

CASE 5.3   Crosswhite v. Jumpking, Inc.

United States District Court,
District of Oregon, 2006.
411 F.Supp.2d 1228.

BACKGROUND AND FACTS Jumpking, Inc., makes "backyard" trampolines for consumer use. The trampolines are produced with nine warning labels affixed to various components. With each trampoline, Jumpking provides a large, laminated warning placard that is designed for the consumer to attach to the metal frame near the ladder on which jumpers mount the trampoline. Jumpking also includes a *User Manual* and a videotape that explains and illustrates "safe and responsible" trampoline use. In 1999, Jack and Misty Urbach bought a round, fourteen-foot Jumpking trampoline from Costco, Inc., in Oregon. On May 11, 2002, sixteen-year-old Gary Crosswhite, who had six years' experience with trampolines, was jumping on the Urbachs' trampoline with another boy. Crosswhite attempted to perform a back flip. He fell and landed on his head and neck, fracturing his cervical spine, which resulted in paraplegia. Crosswhite filed a suit in a federal district court against Jumpking, grounded in strict liability and other product liability claims, alleging that his injuries were caused by inadequate warnings, among other things. Jumpking filed a motion for summary judgment.

IN THE WORDS OF THE COURT . . . *AIKEN*, J. [Judge]

* * * *

Uniform trampoline safety standards are published by the American Society for Testing and Materials (ASTM). The ASTM standards sets forth specific warning language to accompany trampolines. The record supports defendant's [Jumpking's] allegation that the trampoline at issue, including the warning that accompanied it, complied with all ASTM standards relevant at the time. Moreover, the ASTM standards at that time did not require warnings against users performing somersaults (flips) and/or jumping with multiple people to appear on the trampoline itself[;] however, defendant did affix those warnings to the trampoline as well as on a large warning placard attached to the trampoline at the point of entry or mounting. Specifically, one warning attached to the trampoline frame leg stated:

> **! WARNING**
> **Do not land on head or neck.**
> **Paralysis or death can result, even if you land in the middle of the**
> **trampoline mat (bed).**
> **To reduce the chance of landing on your head or neck, do not do flips.**

Accompanying these warning labels is a "stick-figure" drawing of an individual landing on his head. The drawing is located above the warning language and is enclosed in a circular "x-ed" or "crossed-out" notation, commonly understood to mean that the conduct described should be avoided.

Another pair of warning labels affixed to the trampoline legs read:

> **! WARNING**
> **Only one person at a time on the trampoline. Multiple jumpers**
> **increase the chances of loss of control, collision, and falling off. This can**
> **result in broken head, neck, back, or leg.**

CASE 5.3—CONTINUED

Accompanying these warnings and placed above the warning language is a drawing of two individuals jumping on a single trampoline, which is also enclosed in a "crossed out" or "x-ed" notation. These same warning labels warning users against performing flips or somersaults and against jumping with multiple people were also on the trampoline frame pad, the large 8″ × 11″ warning placard framed by the colors orange and yellow and attached to the trampoline frame at the point of entry, and in various places throughout the *User Manual*. The court notes that these warnings went beyond what was required by the ASTM safety standards.

Further, Jack Urbach testified that the warning placard, which specifically warns against both multiple jumping and performing flips or somersaults and the risk of paralysis, was included in the trampoline he purchased, and that he attached the placard to the trampoline upon its initial assembly. Urbach further testified that he had his entire family watch the safety video provided by defendant prior to assembling and using the trampoline.

* * * [D]efendant is entitled to assume that its many warnings will be read, watched, and heeded.

DECISION AND REMEDY The court issued a summary judgment in Jumpking's favor, holding that its warnings were "adequate as a matter of law." To prevent a product from being unreasonably dangerous, its seller may be required to include a warning about its use. When a warning is provided, the seller may reasonably assume that it will be read and followed, and a product with an adequate warning is not defective or unreasonably dangerous.

WHAT IF THE FACTS WERE DIFFERENT? *If Crosswhite had proved that he had not seen, before his accident, the warnings that Jumpking provided, might the court have considered the trampoline defective or unreasonably dangerous?*

Other Applications of Strict Liability

Although the drafters of Section 402A of the *Restatement (Second) of Torts* did not take a position on bystanders, virtually all courts extend the strict liability of manufacturers and other sellers to injured bystanders. **Example #16** In one case, an automobile manufacturer was held liable for injuries caused by the explosion of a car's motor. A cloud of steam that resulted from the explosion caused multiple collisions because other drivers could not see well.[24]

The rule of strict liability is also applicable to suppliers of component parts. **Example #17** General Motors buys brake pads from a subcontractor and puts them in Chevrolets without changing their composition. If those pads are defective, both the supplier of the brake pads and General Motors will be held strictly liable for the damages caused by the defects.

Statutes of Repose

As discussed in Chapter 1, *statutes of limitations* restrict the time within which an action may be brought. Many states have passed laws, called **statutes of repose**, placing outer time limits on some claims so that the defendant will not

STATUTE OF REPOSE
Basically, a statute of limitations that is not dependent on the happening of a cause of action. Statutes of repose generally begin to run at an earlier date and run for a longer period of time than statutes of limitations.

---

24. For a leading case on this issue, see *Giberson v. Ford Motor Co.*, 504 S.W.2d 8 (Mo. 1974).

be left vulnerable to lawsuits indefinitely. These statutes may limit the time within which a plaintiff can file a product liability suit. Typically, a statute of repose begins to run at an earlier date and runs for a longer time than a statute of limitations. For example, a statute of repose may require that claims be brought within twelve years from the date of sale or manufacture of the defective product. No action can be brought if the injury occurs *after* this statutory period has lapsed. In addition, some of these legislative enactments limit the application of the doctrine of strict liability to new goods only.

DEFENSES TO PRODUCT LIABILITY

Manufacturers, sellers, or lessors can raise several defenses to avoid liability for harms caused by their products. We look at some of these defenses in the following subsections.

Assumption of Risk

Assumption of risk, a defense to negligence, can sometimes be used as a defense in a product liability action. For example, if a buyer fails to heed a product recall by the seller, a court might conclude that the buyer assumed the risk caused by the defect that led to the recall. To establish such a defense, the defendant must show that (1) the plaintiff knew and appreciated the risk created by the product defect and (2) the plaintiff voluntarily assumed the risk, even though it was unreasonable to do so.

These fast-food items often specify the number of calories they contain, as well as other information about the foods' contents. Given the numerous news stories about the correlation between high-caloric foods and weight gain, those who choose to purchase and eat such foods could be deemed to engage in a "commonly known danger." Are there circumstances, nonetheless, which might support a suit against a fast-food outlet if a regular customer becomes overweight? (AP Photo/Tom Gannam)

Product Misuse

Similar to the defense of voluntary assumption of risk is that of misuse of the product. Here, the injured party *does not know that the product is dangerous for a particular use* (contrast this with assumption of risk), but the use is not the one for which the product was designed. The courts have severely limited this defense, however. Even if the injured party does not know about the inherent danger of using the product in a wrong way, if the misuse is *foreseeable*, the seller must take measures to guard against it.

Comparative Negligence

Developments in the area of comparative negligence, or fault (discussed earlier in this chapter), have also affected the doctrine of strict liability—the most extreme theory of product liability. Whereas previously the plaintiff's conduct was not a defense to strict liability, today many jurisdictions, when apportioning liability and damages, consider the negligent or intentional actions of both the plaintiff and the defendant. This means that even if the plaintiff misused the products, she or he may nonetheless be able to recover at least some damages for injuries caused by the defendant's defective product.

Commonly Known Dangers

The dangers associated with certain products (such as sharp knives and guns) are so commonly known that manufacturers need not warn users of those dangers. If a defendant succeeds in convincing the court that a plaintiff's injury resulted from a *commonly known danger,* the defendant normally will not be liable.

| Example #18 A classic case on this issue involved a plaintiff who was injured when an elastic exercise rope that she had purchased slipped off her foot and struck her in the eye, causing a detachment of the retina. The plaintiff claimed that the manufacturer should be liable because it had failed to warn users that the exerciser might slip off a foot in such a manner. The court stated that to hold the manufacturer liable in these circumstances "would go beyond the reasonable dictates of justice in fixing the liabilities of manufacturers." After all, stated the court, "[a]lmost every physical object can be inherently dangerous or potentially dangerous in a sense. . . . A manufacturer cannot manufacture a knife that will not cut or a hammer that will not mash a thumb or a stove that will not burn a finger. The law does not require [manufacturers] to warn of such common dangers."[25] |

---

25. *Jamieson v. Woodward & Lothrop,* 247 F.2d 23, 101 D.C.App. 32 (1957).

REVIEWING . . . TORTS, CYBER TORTS, AND PRODUCT LIABILITY

Two sisters, Darla and Irene, are partners in an import business located in a small town in Rhode Island. Irene is married to a well-known real estate developer and is campaigning to be the mayor of their town. Darla is in her midthirties and has never been married. Both sisters travel to other countries to purchase the goods that they sell at their retail store. Irene buys Indonesian goods, and Darla buys goods from Africa. After a tsunami (tidal wave) destroys many of the cities in Indonesia to which Irene usually travels, she phones one of her contacts there and asks him to procure some items and ship them to her. He informs her that it will be impossible to buy these items now because the townspeople are being evacuated due to a water shortage. Irene is angry and tells the man that if he cannot purchase the goods, he should just take them without paying for them after the town has been evacuated. Darla overhears her sister's instructions and is outraged. They have a falling-out, and Darla decides that she no longer wishes to be in business with her sister. Using the information presented in the chapter, answer the following questions.

1. Suppose that Darla tells several of her friends about Irene's instructing the man to take goods without paying for them after the tsunami disaster. If Irene files a tort action against Darla alleging slander, will her suit be successful? Why or why not?

2. If Irene accepts goods shipped from Indonesia that were wrongfully obtained, has she committed an intentional tort against property? Explain.

3. Darla was in the store one day with an elderly customer, Betty Green, who was looking for a unique gift for her granddaughter's graduation. When the phone rang, Darla left the customer and walked to the counter to answer the phone. Green wandered around the store and eventually went through an open door and into the stockroom area, falling over some boxes on the floor and fracturing her hip. Green files a negligence action against the store. Did Darla breach her duty of care? Why or why not?

4. Suppose that Roland Strum, one of the store's regular customers, purchases a handcrafted knife from Darla that was made in India. The knife looks solid, but the first time Strum uses it at his home, the carved wooden handle breaks in half and the blade slices through his hand and wrist, severing some nerves. If Strum files a product liability lawsuit claiming that the knife was defective due to inadequate warnings, what is the store's best argument to avoid liability?

KEY TERMS

CHAPTER SUMMARY • TORTS, CYBER TORTS, AND PRODUCT LIABILITY

TORTS AND CYBER TORTS

Intentional Torts against Persons (See pages 135–143.)	1. *Assault and battery*—An assault is an unexcused and intentional act that causes another person to be apprehensive of immediate harm. A battery is an assault that results in physical contact.
	2. *False imprisonment*—The intentional confinement or restraint of another person's movement without justification.
	3. *Intentional infliction of emotional distress*—An intentional act that amounts to extreme and outrageous conduct resulting in severe emotional distress to another.
	4. *Defamation (libel or slander)*—A false statement of fact, not made under privilege, that is communicated to a third person and that causes damage to a person's reputation. For public figures, the plaintiff must also prove actual malice.
	5. *Invasion of the right to privacy*—The use of a person's name or likeness for commercial purposes without permission, wrongful intrusion into a person's private activities, publication of information that places a person in a false light, or disclosure of private facts that an ordinary person would find objectionable.
	6. *Appropriation*—The use of another person's name, likeness, or other identifying characteristic, without permission and for the benefit of the user.
	7. *Misrepresentation (fraud)*—A false representation made by one party, through misstatement of facts or through conduct, with the intention of deceiving another and on which the other reasonably relies to his or her detriment.
	8. *Wrongful interference*—The knowing, intentional interference by a third party with an enforceable contractual relationship or an established business relationship between other parties for the purpose of advancing the economic interests of the third party.

CHAPTER SUMMARY • TORTS, CYBER TORTS, AND PRODUCT LIABILITY—CONTINUED

Intentional Torts against Property (See pages 144–148.)	1. *Trespass to land*—The invasion of another's real property without consent or privilege. Specific rights and duties apply once a person is expressly or impliedly established as a trespasser. 2. *Trespass to personal property*—Unlawfully damaging or interfering with the owner's right to use, possess, or enjoy her or his personal property. 3. *Conversion*—Wrongfully taking personal property from its rightful owner or possessor and placing it in the service of another. 4. *Disparagement of property*—Any economically injurious falsehood that is made about another's product or property; an inclusive term for the torts of *slander of quality* and *slander of title*.

Unintentional Torts (Negligence) (See pages 148–156.)	1. *Negligence*—The careless performance of a legally required duty or the failure to perform a legally required act. Elements that must be proved are that a legal duty of care exists, that the defendant breached that duty, and that the breach caused damage or injury to another.
	
	2. *Defenses to negligence*—The basic affirmative defenses in negligence cases are (a) assumption of risk, (b) superseding cause, and (c) contributory or comparative negligence.
	
	3. *Special negligence doctrines and statutes*—
	
	   a. *Res ipsa loquitur*—A doctrine under which a plaintiff need not prove negligence on the part of the defendant because "the facts speak for themselves."
	
	   b. Negligence *per se*—A type of negligence that may occur if a person violates a statute or an ordinance providing for a criminal penalty and the violation causes another to be injured.
	
	   c. Special negligence statutes—State statutes that prescribe duties and responsibilities in certain circumstances. Dram shop acts and Good Samaritan statutes are examples of special negligence statutes.

Cyber Torts (See pages 156–158.)	General tort principles are being extended to cover cyber torts, or torts that occur in cyberspace, such as online defamation and spamming (which may constitute trespass to personal property). Federal and state statutes may also apply to certain forms of cyber torts.
Strict Liability (See page 158.)	Under the doctrine of strict liability, a person may be held liable, regardless of the degree of care exercised, for damages or injuries caused by her or his product or activity. Strict liability includes liability for harms caused by abnormally dangerous activities, by dangerous animals, and by defective products (product liability).
PRODUCT LIABILITY	
Product Liability Based on Warranty Law (See page 159.)	Consumers, purchasers, and users of goods can recover from sellers for losses resulting from the breach of express or implied warranties that were made, or arose automatically, during the sale of goods.
Product Liability Based on Negligence (See page160.)	1. The manufacturer must use due care in designing the product, selecting materials, using the appropriate production process, assembling and testing the product, and placing adequate warnings on the label or product. 2. Privity of contract is not required. A manufacturer is liable for failure to exercise due care to any person who sustains an injury proximately caused by a negligently made (defective) product.
Product Liability Based on Misrepresentation (See page 160.)	Fraudulent misrepresentation of a product may result in product liability based on the tort of fraud.
Strict Liability— Requirements (See pages 161–162.)	1. The defendant must sell the product in a defective condition. 2. The defendant must normally be engaged in the business of selling that product. 3. The product must be unreasonably dangerous to the user or consumer because of its defective condition (in most states).

(Continued)

CHAPTER SUMMARY • TORTS, CYBER TORTS, AND PRODUCT LIABILITY—CONTINUED

Strict Liability— Requirements— Continued	4. The plaintiff must incur physical harm to self or property by use or consumption of the product. (Courts will also extend strict liability to include injured bystanders.)
	5. The defective condition must be the proximate cause of the injury or damage.
	6. The goods must not have been substantially changed from the time the product was sold to the time the injury was sustained.
Product Defects (See pages 162–165.)	A product may be defective in its manufacture, in its design, or in the instructions or warnings that come with it.
Other Applications of Strict Liability (See page 165.)	1. Manufacturers and other sellers are liable for harms suffered by bystanders as a result of defective products.
	2. Suppliers of component parts are strictly liable for defective parts that, when incorporated into a product, cause injuries to users.
Defenses to Product Liability (See pages 166–167.)	1. *Assumption of risk*—The user or consumer knew of the risk of harm and voluntarily assumed it.
	2. *Product misuse*—The user or consumer misused the product in a way unforeseeable by the manufacturer.
	3. *Comparative negligence and liability*—Liability may be distributed between the plaintiff and the defendant under the doctrine of comparative negligence if the plaintiff's misuse of the product contributed to the risk of injury.
	4. *Commonly known dangers*—If a defendant succeeds in convincing the court that a plaintiff's injury resulted from a commonly known danger, such as the danger associated with using a sharp knife, the defendant will not be liable.

FOR REVIEW

Answers for the even-numbered questions in this For Review *section can be found in Appendix O at the end of this text.*

1. What is the purpose of tort law? What are two basic categories of torts?
2. What are the four elements of negligence?
3. What is meant by strict liability? In what circumstances is strict liability applied?
4. What are the elements of a cause of action in strict product liability?
5. What defenses to liability can be raised in a product liability lawsuit?

QUESTIONS AND CASE PROBLEMS

5–1. Defenses to Negligence. Corinna was riding her bike on a city street. While she was riding, she frequently looked back to verify that the books that she had fastened to the rear part of her bike were still attached. On one occasion while she was looking behind her, she failed to notice a car that was entering an intersection just as she was crossing it. The car hit her, causing her to sustain numerous injuries. Three eyewitnesses stated that the driver of the car had failed to stop at the stop sign before entering the intersection. Corinna sued the driver of the car for negligence. What defenses might the defendant driver raise in this lawsuit? Discuss fully.

5–2. Liability to Business Invitees. Kim went to Ling's Market to pick up a few items for dinner. It was a rainy, windy day, and the wind had blown water through the door of Ling's

Market each time the door opened. As Kim entered through the door, she slipped and fell in the approximately one-half inch of rainwater that had accumulated on the floor. The manager knew of the weather conditions but had not posted any sign to warn customers of the water hazard. Kim injured her back as a result of the fall and sued Ling's for damages. Can Ling's be held liable for negligence in this situation? Discuss.

Question with Sample Answer

5–3. In which of the following situations will the acting party be liable for the tort of negligence? Explain fully.

1. Mary goes to the golf course on Sunday morning, eager to try out a new set of golf clubs she has just

purchased. As she tees off on the first hole, the head of her club flies off and injures a nearby golfer.

2. Mary's doctor gives her some pain medication and tells her not to drive after she takes it, as the medication induces drowsiness. In spite of the doctor's warning, Mary decides to drive to the store while on the medication. Owing to her lack of alertness, she fails to stop at a traffic light and crashes into another vehicle, injuring a passenger.

For a sample answer to this question, go to Appendix P at the end of this text.

5–4. Product Liability. Under what contract theory can a seller be held liable to a consumer for physical harm or property damage that is caused by the goods sold? Under what tort theories can the seller be held liable?

5–5. Product Liability. Carmen buys a television set manufactured by AKI Electronics. She is going on vacation, so she takes the set to her mother's house for her mother to use. Because the set is defective, it explodes, causing considerable damage to her mother's house. Carmen's mother sues AKI for the damages to her house. Discuss the theories under which Carmen's mother can recover from AKI.

5–6. Defamation. Lydia Hagberg went to her bank, California Federal Bank, FSB, to cash a check made out to her by Smith Barney (SB), an investment services firm. Nolene Showalter, a bank employee, suspected that the check was counterfeit. Showalter phoned SB and was told that the check was not valid. As she phoned the police, Gary Wood, a bank security officer, contacted SB again and was told that its earlier statement was "erroneous" and that the check was valid. Meanwhile, a police officer arrived, drew Hagberg away from the teller's window, spread her legs, patted her down, and handcuffed her. The officer searched her purse, asked her whether she had any weapons or stolen property and whether she was driving a stolen vehicle, and arrested her. Hagberg filed a suit in a California state court against the bank and others, alleging, among other things, slander. Should the absolute privilege for communications made in judicial or other official proceedings apply to statements made when a citizen contacts the police to report suspected criminal activity? Why or why not? [*Hagberg v. California Federal Bank, FSB*, 32 Cal.4th 350, 81 P.3d 244, 7 Cal.Rptr.3d 803 (2004)]

Case Problem with Sample Answer

5–7. New Hampshire International Speedway, Inc., owned the New Hampshire International Speedway, a racetrack next to Route 106 in Loudon, New Hampshire. In August 1998, on the weekend before the Winston Cup race, Speedway opened part of its parking facility to recreational vehicles (RVs). Speedway voluntarily positioned its employee Frederick Neergaard at the entrance to the parking area as a security guard and to direct traffic. Leslie Wheeler, who was planning to attend the race, drove an RV south on Route 106 toward Speedway. Meanwhile, Dennis Carignan was also driving south on Route 106 on a motorcycle, on which Mary Carignan was a passenger. As Wheeler approached the parking area, he saw Neergaard signaling him to turn left, which he began to do. At the same time, Carignan attempted to pass the RV on its left side, and the two vehicles collided. Mary sustained an injury to her right knee, lacerations on her ankle, and a broken hip. She sued Speedway and others for negligence. Which element of negligence is at the center of this dispute? How is a court likely to rule in this case, and why? [*Carignan v. New Hampshire International Speedway, Inc.*, 858 A.2d 536 (N.H. 2004)]

After you have answered this problem, compare your answer with the sample answer given on the Web site that accompanies this text. Go to www.thomsonedu.com/westbuslaw/let, select "Chapter 5," and click on "Case Problem with Sample Answer."

5–8. Product Liability. In January 1999, John Clark of Clarksdale, Mississippi, bought a paintball gun. Clark practiced with the gun and knew how to screw in the carbon dioxide cartridge, pump the gun, and use its safety and trigger. He hunted and had taken a course in hunter safety education. He was aware that protective eyewear was available for purchase, but he chose not to buy it. Clark also understood that it was "common sense" not to shoot anyone in the face. Chris Rico, another Clarksdale resident, owned a paintball gun made by Brass Eagle, Inc. Rico was similarly familiar with the gun's use and its risks. Clark, Rico, and their friends played a game that involved shooting paintballs at cars whose occupants also had the guns. One night, while Clark and Rico were cruising with their guns, Rico shot at Clark's car, but hit Clark in the eye. Clark filed a suit in a Mississippi state court against Brass Eagle to recover for the injury, alleging in part that its gun was defectively designed. During the trial, Rico testified that his gun "never malfunctioned." In whose favor should the court rule? Why? [*Clark v. Brass Eagle, Inc.*, 866 So.2d 456 (Miss. 2004)]

5–9. Product Liability. Bret D'Auguste was an experienced skier when he rented equipment to ski at Hunter Mountain Ski Bowl, Inc., owned by Shanty Hollow Corp., in New York. The adjustable retention/release value for the bindings on the rented equipment was set at a level that, according to skiing industry standards, was too low—meaning that the skis would be released too easily—given D'Auguste's height, weight, and ability. When D'Auguste entered a "double black diamond" (extremely difficult) trail, he noticed immediately that the surface consisted of ice and virtually no snow. He tried to exit the steeply declining trail by making a sharp right turn, but in the attempt, his left ski snapped off. D'Auguste lost his balance, fell, and slid down the mountain, striking his face and head against a fence along the trail. According to a report by a rental shop employee, one of the bindings on D'Auguste's skis had a "cracked heel housing." D'Auguste filed a suit in a New York state court against Shanty Hollow and others, including the bindings' manufacturer, on a theory of strict product liability. The manufacturer filed a motion for summary judgment. On what basis might the court *grant* the motion? On what basis might the court *deny* the motion? How should the court rule? Explain. [*D'Auguste v. Shanty Hollow Corp.*, 26 A.D.3d 403, 809 N.Y.S.2d 555 (2 Dept. 2006)]

A Question of Ethics

5–10. Intel Corp. has an e-mail system for its employees. Ken Hamidi, a former Intel employee, sent a series of six e-mail messages to 35,000 Intel employees over a twenty-one-month period. In the messages, Hamidi criticized the company's labor practices and urged employees to leave the company. Intel sought a court order to stop the e-mail campaign, arguing that Hamidi's actions constituted a trespass to chattels (personal property) because the e-mail significantly interfered with productivity, thus causing economic damage. The state trial court granted Intel's motion for summary judgment and ordered Hamidi to stop sending messages. When the case reached the California Supreme Court, however, the court held that under California law, the tort of trespass to chattels required some evidence of injury to the plaintiff's personal property. Because Hamidi's e-mail had neither damaged Intel's computer system nor impaired its functioning, the court ruled that Hamidi's actions did not amount to a trespass to chattels. The court did not reject the idea that trespass theory could apply to cyberspace. Rather, the court simply held that to succeed in a lawsuit for trespass to chattels, a plaintiff must demonstrate that some concrete harm resulted from the unwanted e-mail. [*Intel Corp. v. Hamidi*, 30 Cal.4th 1342, 71 P.3d 296, 1 Cal.Rptr.3d 32 (2003)]

1. Should a court require that spam cause actual physical damage or impairment of the computer system (by overburdening it, for example) to establish that a spammer has committed trespass? Why or why not?

2. The content of Hamidi's messages caused much discussion among employees and managers, diverting workers' time and attention and thus interfering with productivity. Why did the court not consider this disruption to be sufficient evidence of harm? Do you agree with the court?

Critical-Thinking Managerial Question

5–11. What general principle underlies the common law doctrine that business owners have a duty of care toward their customers? Does the duty of care unfairly burden business owners? Why or why not?

Video Question

5–12. Go to this text's Web site at **www. thomsonedu.com/westbuslaw/let** and select "Chapter 5." Click on "Video Questions" and view the video titled *Jaws*. Then answer the following questions.

1. In the video, the mayor (Murray Hamilton) and a few other men try to persuade Chief Brody (Roy Scheider) not to close the town's beaches. If Brody keeps the beaches open and a swimmer is injured or killed because he failed to warn swimmers about the potential shark danger, has Brody committed a tort? If so, what kind of tort (intentional tort against persons, intentional tort against property, negligence)? Explain your answer.

2. Can Chief Brody be held liable for any injuries or deaths to swimmers under the doctrine of strict liability? Why or why not?

3. If Chief Brody goes against the mayor's instructions and warns swimmers to stay off the beach, and the town suffers economic damages as a result, has he committed the tort of disparagement of property? Why or why not?

INTERACTING WITH THE INTERNET

For updated links to resources available on the Web, as well as a variety of other materials, visit this text's Web site at

www.thomsonedu.com/westbuslaw/let

You can find cases and articles on torts, including business torts, in the tort law library at the Internet Law Library's Web site. Go to

www.lawguru.com/ilawlib/110.htm

For information on product liability suits against tobacco companies and recent settlements, go to the Web site of the Library & Center for Knowledge Management (maintained by the University of California, San Francisco) at

library.ucsf.edu/tobacco/litigation

You can find articles, cases, and other information on litigation in the area of product liability by going to the following page at the Web site of MegaLaw.com, Inc.:

www.megalaw.com/top/products.php

INTERNET EXERCISES

Go to **www.thomsonedu.com/westbuslaw/let**, the Web site that accompanies this text. Select "Chapter 5" and click on "Internet Exercises." There you will find the following Internet research exercises that you can perform to learn more about topics covered in this chapter.

Internet Exercise 5–1: LEGAL PERSPECTIVE—Negligence and the *Titanic*
Internet Exercise 5–2: MANAGEMENT PERSPECTIVE—Legal and Illegal Uses of Spam

BEFORE THE TEST

Go to **www.thomsonedu.com/westbuslaw/let**, the Web site that accompanies this text. Select "Chapter 5" and click on "Interactive Quizzes." You will find a number of interactive questions relating to this chapter.

CONTENTS

CHAPTER OBJECTIVES

After reading this chapter, you should be able to answer the following questions:

1. What two elements must exist before a person can be held liable for a crime? Can a corporation commit crimes?

2. What are five broad categories of crimes? What is white-collar crime?

3. What defenses might be raised by criminal defendants to avoid liability for criminal acts?

4. What constitutional safeguards exist to protect persons accused of crimes? What are the basic steps in the criminal process?

5. What is cyber crime? What laws apply to crimes committed in cyberspace?

> "No State shall . . . deprive any person of life, liberty, or property without due process of law, nor deny to any person within its jurisdiction the equal protection of the laws."
>
> —FOURTEENTH AMENDMENT TO THE U.S. CONSTITUTION, July 28, 1868

CYBER CRIME
A crime that occurs online, in the virtual community of the Internet, as opposed to the physical world.

VARIOUS SANCTIONS are used to bring about a society in which individuals engaging in business can compete and flourish. These sanctions include damages for violations of tort law (as discussed in Chapter 5), damages for breach of contract (to be discussed in Chapter 9), and the equitable remedies discussed in Chapter 1. Additional sanctions are imposed under criminal law. Many statutes regulating business provide for criminal as well as civil sanctions. Therefore, criminal law joins civil law as an important element in the legal environment of business.

In this chapter, following a brief summary of the major differences between criminal and civil law, we look at how crimes are classified and what elements must be present for criminal liability to exist. We then examine various categories of crime, the defenses that can be raised to avoid liability for criminal actions, and criminal procedural law. Criminal procedural law attempts to ensure that a criminal defendant's right to "due process of law" is enforced. This right is guaranteed by the Fourteenth Amendment to the U.S. Constitution, as stated in the chapter-opening quotation.

Since the advent of computer networks and, more recently, the Internet, new types of crimes or new variations of traditional crimes have been committed in cyberspace. For that reason, they are often referred to as **cyber crime.** Generally, cyber crime refers more to the way particular crimes are committed than to a new category of crimes. We devote the concluding pages of this chapter to a discussion of this increasingly significant area of criminal activity.

CIVIL LAW AND CRIMINAL LAW

Remember from Chapter 1 that *civil law* spells out the duties that exist between persons or between persons and their governments, excluding the duty not to commit crimes. Contract law, for example, is part of civil law. The whole body of tort law, which deals with the infringement by one person on the legally recognized rights of another, is also an area of civil law.

Criminal law, in contrast, has to do with crime. A **crime** can be defined as a wrong against society proclaimed in a statute and punishable by society through fines and/or imprisonment—and, in some cases, death. As mentioned in Chapter 1, because crimes are *offenses against society as a whole,* they are prosecuted by a public official, such as a district attorney (D.A.), not by victims.

CRIME
A wrong against society proclaimed in a statute and punishable by society through fines and/or imprisonment—and, in some cases, death.

Key Differences between Civil Law and Criminal Law

Because the state has extensive resources at its disposal when prosecuting criminal cases, there are numerous procedural safeguards to protect the rights of defendants. One of these safeguards is the higher burden of proof that applies in a criminal case. As you can see in Exhibit 6–1, which summarizes some of the key differences between civil law and criminal law, in a civil case the plaintiff usually must prove his or her case by a *preponderance of the evidence.* Under this standard, the plaintiff must convince the court that, based on the evidence presented by both parties, it is more likely than not that the plaintiff's allegation is true.

In a criminal case, however, the state must prove its case **beyond a reasonable doubt.** In addition, the verdict normally must be unanimous. For the defendant to be convicted, then, *every* juror in a criminal case must be convinced, beyond a reasonable doubt, that the defendant has committed each essential element of the offense with which she or he is charged. In contrast, in civil cases typically only three-fourths of the jurors need to agree that it is more likely than not that the defendant caused the plaintiff's harm. The higher burden of proof in criminal cases reflects a fundamental social value—the belief that it is worse to convict an innocent individual than to let a guilty person go free. We will look at other safeguards later in the chapter, in the context of criminal procedure.

BEYOND A REASONABLE DOUBT
The burden of proof used in criminal cases. If there is any reasonable doubt that a criminal defendant committed the crime with which she or he has been charged, then the verdict must be "not guilty."

Civil Liability for Criminal Acts

Those who commit crimes may be subject to both civil and criminal liability.
| Example #1 Joe is walking down the street, minding his own business, when suddenly a person attacks him. In the ensuing struggle, the attacker stabs Joe

---

EXHIBIT 6–1   KEY DIFFERENCES BETWEEN CIVIL LAW AND CRIMINAL LAW

ISSUE	CIVIL LAW	CRIMINAL LAW
Party who brings suit	Person who suffered harm	The state
Burden of proof	Preponderance of the evidence	Beyond a reasonable doubt
Verdict	Three-fourths majority (typically)	Unanimous
Remedy	Damages to compensate for the harm, or a decree to achieve an equitable result	Punishment (fine, imprisonment, or death)

several times, seriously injuring him. A police officer restrains and arrests the wrongdoer. In this situation, the attacker may be subject both to criminal prosecution by the state and to a tort lawsuit brought by Joe.| Exhibit 6–2 illustrates how the same act can result in both a tort action and a criminal action against the wrongdoer.

CLASSIFICATION OF CRIMES

Depending on their degree of seriousness, crimes are classified as felonies or misdemeanors. **Felonies** are serious crimes punishable by death or by imprisonment in a federal or state penitentiary for more than a year. The Model Penal Code[1] provides for four degrees of felony: (1) capital offenses, for which the maximum penalty is death; (2) first degree felonies, punishable by a maximum penalty of life imprisonment; (3) second degree felonies, punishable by a maximum of ten years' imprisonment; and (4) third degree felonies, punishable by a maximum of five years' imprisonment.

Under federal law and in most states, any crime that is not a felony is considered a **misdemeanor**. Misdemeanors are crimes punishable by a fine or by

FELONY

A crime–such as arson, murder, rape, or robbery–that carries the most severe sanctions, which range from more than one year in a state or federal prison to the death penalty.

MISDEMEANOR

A lesser crime than a felony, punishable by a fine or incarceration in jail for up to one year.

---

1. The American Law Institute issued the Official Draft of the Model Penal Code in 1962. The Model Penal Code is *not* a uniform code. Uniformity of criminal law among the states is not as important as uniformity in other areas of the law. Types of crimes vary with local circumstances, and it is appropriate that punishments vary accordingly. The Model Penal Code contains four parts: (a) general provisions, (b) definitions of special crimes, (c) provisions concerning treatment and corrections, and (d) provisions on the organization of corrections.

EXHIBIT 6–2   **TORT LAWSUIT AND CRIMINAL PROSECUTION FOR THE SAME ACT**

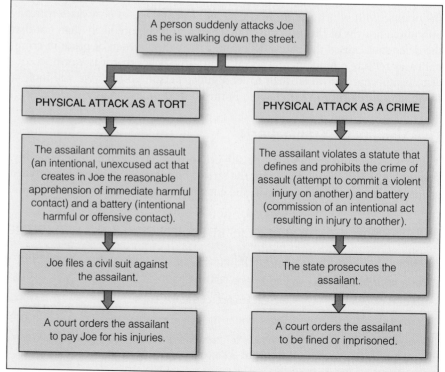

confinement for up to a year. If incarcerated (imprisoned), the guilty party goes to a local jail instead of a prison. Disorderly conduct and trespass are common misdemeanors. Some states have different classes of misdemeanors. For example, in Illinois misdemeanors are either Class A (confinement for up to a year), Class B (not more than six months), or Class C (not more than thirty days). Whether a crime is a felony or a misdemeanor can also determine whether the case is tried in a magistrate's court (for example, by a justice of the peace) or in a general trial court.

In most jurisdictions, **petty offenses** are considered to be a subset of misdemeanors. Petty offenses are minor violations, such as jaywalking or violations of building codes. Even for petty offenses, however, a guilty party can be put in jail for a few days, fined, or both, depending on state or local law.

PETTY OFFENSE
In criminal law, the least serious kind of criminal offense, such as a minor traffic or building-code violation.

CRIMINAL LIABILITY

Two elements must exist simultaneously for a person to be convicted of a crime: (1) the performance of a prohibited act and (2) a specified state of mind or intent on the part of the actor. Every criminal statute prohibits certain behavior. Most crimes require an act of *commission;* that is, a person must *do* something in order to be accused of a crime.[2] In some instances, an act of *omission* can be a crime, but only when a person has a legal duty to perform the omitted act. Failure to file a tax return is an example of an omission that is a crime.

The *guilty act* requirement is based on one of the premises of criminal law—that a person is punished for harm done to society. Thinking about killing someone or about stealing a car may be wrong, but the thoughts do no harm until they are translated into action. Of course, a person can be punished for attempting murder or robbery, but normally only if he or she took substantial steps toward the criminal objective.

A *wrongful mental state*[3] is generally required to establish criminal liability. What constitutes such a mental state varies according to the wrongful action. For murder, the act is the taking of a life, and the mental state is the intent to take life. For theft, the guilty act is the taking of another person's property, and the mental state involves both the knowledge that the property belongs to another and the intent to deprive the owner of it.

Criminal liability typically arises for actions that violate state criminal statutes. Federal criminal jurisdiction is normally limited to crimes that occur outside the jurisdiction of any state, crimes involving interstate commerce or communications, crimes that interfere with the operation of the federal government or its agents, and crimes directed at citizens or property located outside the United States. Federal jurisdiction also exists if a federal law or a federal government agency (such as the U.S. Department of Justice or the federal Environmental Protection Agency) defines a certain type of action as a crime. Today, businesspersons are subject to criminal penalties under numerous federal laws and regulations. We will examine many of these laws in later chapters of this text.

---

2. Called the *actus reus* (pronounced *ak*-tuhs *ray*-uhs), or "guilty act."
3. Called the *mens rea* (pronounced mehns *ray*-uh), or "evil intent."

CORPORATE CRIMINAL LIABILITY

At one time, it was thought that a corporation could not incur criminal liability because, although a corporation is a legal person, it can act only through its agents (corporate directors, officers, and employees). Therefore, the corporate entity itself could not "intend" to commit a crime. Under modern criminal law, however, a corporation may be held liable for crimes. Obviously, corporations cannot be imprisoned, but they can be fined or denied certain legal privileges (such as a license). Today, corporations are normally liable for the crimes committed by their agents and employees within the course and scope of their employment.

Corporate directors and officers are personally liable for the crimes they commit, regardless of whether the crimes were committed for their personal benefit or on the corporation's behalf. Additionally, corporate directors and officers may be held liable for the actions of employees under their supervision. Under what has become known as the "responsible corporate officer" doctrine, a court may impose criminal liability on a corporate officer regardless of whether she or he participated in, directed, or even knew about a given criminal violation.

| **Example #2**   In *United States v. Park*,[4] the chief executive officer of a national supermarket chain was held personally liable for sanitation violations in corporate warehouses in which food was exposed to contamination by rodents. The United States Supreme Court imposed personal liability on the corporate officer not because he intended the crime or even knew about it but because he was in a "responsible relationship" to the corporation and had the power to prevent the violation.| Since the *Park* decision, courts have applied this "responsible corporate officer" doctrine on a number of occasions to hold corporate officers liable for their employees' statutory violations.

TYPES OF CRIMES

The number of acts that are defined as criminal is nearly endless. Federal, state, and local laws provide for the classification and punishment of hundreds of thousands of different criminal acts. Traditionally, though, crimes have been grouped into five broad categories, or types: violent crime (crimes against persons), property crime, public order crime, white-collar crime, and organized crime. Cyber crime—which consists of crimes committed in cyberspace with the use of computers—is, as mentioned earlier in this chapter, less a category of crime than a new way to commit crime. We will examine cyber crime later in this chapter.

Violent Crime

Crimes against persons, because they cause others to suffer harm or death, are referred to as *violent crimes*. Murder is a violent crime. So is sexual assault, or rape. Assault and battery, which were discussed in Chapter 5 in the context of tort law, are also classified as violent crimes. **Robbery**—defined as the taking of cash, personal property, or any other article of value from a person by means

ROBBERY
The act of forcefully and unlawfully taking personal property of any value from another. Force or intimidation is usually necessary for an act of theft to be considered a robbery.

---

4. 421 U.S. 658, 95 S.Ct. 1903, 44 L.Ed.2d 489 (1975).

of force or fear—is also a violent crime. Typically, states have more severe penalties for *aggravated robbery*—robbery with the use of a deadly weapon.

Each of these violent crimes is further classified by degree, depending on the circumstances surrounding the criminal act. These circumstances include the intent of the person committing the crime, whether a weapon was used, and (in cases other than murder) the level of pain and suffering experienced by the victim.

Property Crime

The most common type of criminal activity is property crime—crimes in which the goal of the offender is some form of economic gain or the damaging of property. Robbery is a form of property crime, as well as a violent crime, because the offender seeks to gain the property of another. We look here at a number of other crimes that fall within the general category of property crime.

Burglary   Traditionally, **burglary** was defined under the common law as breaking and entering the dwelling of another at night with the intent to commit a felony. Originally, the definition was aimed at protecting an individual's home and its occupants. Most state statutes have eliminated some of the requirements found in the common law definition. The time at which the breaking and entering occurs, for example, is usually immaterial. State statutes frequently omit the element of breaking, and some states do not require that the building be a dwelling. Aggravated burglary, which is defined as burglary with the use of a deadly weapon, burglary of a dwelling, or both, incurs a greater penalty.

BURGLARY
The unlawful entry or breaking into a building with the intent to commit a felony. (Some state statutes expand this to include the intent to commit any crime.)

Larceny   Any person who wrongfully or fraudulently takes and carries away another person's personal property is guilty of **larceny**. Larceny includes the fraudulent intent to deprive an owner permanently of property. Many business-related larcenies entail fraudulent conduct. Whereas robbery involves force or fear, larceny does not. Therefore, picking pockets is larceny. Similarly, taking company products and supplies home for personal use, if one is not authorized to do so, is larceny.

In most states, the definition of property that is subject to larceny statutes has expanded. Stealing computer programs may constitute larceny even though the "property" consists of magnetic impulses. Stealing computer time can also constitute larceny. So, too, can the theft of natural gas. Trade secrets can be subject to larceny statutes. Obtaining another's phone-card number and then using that number, without authorization, to place long-distance calls is a form of property theft. These types of larceny are covered by "theft of services" statutes in many jurisdictions.

LARCENY
The wrongful taking and carrying away of another person's personal property with the intent to permanently deprive the owner of the property. Some states classify larceny as either grand or petit, depending on the property's value.

The common law distinguishes between grand and petit larceny depending on the value of the property taken. Many states have abolished this distinction, but in those that have not, grand larceny is a felony and petit larceny, a misdemeanor.

Obtaining Goods by False Pretenses   It is a criminal act to obtain goods by means of false pretenses—for example, buying groceries with a check, knowing that one has insufficient funds to cover it. Statutes dealing with such illegal activities vary widely from state to state.

Receiving Stolen Goods   It is a crime to receive stolen goods. The recipient of such goods need not know the true identity of the owner or the thief. All that is necessary is that the recipient knows or should have known that the goods are stolen, which implies an intent to deprive the owner of those goods.

ARSON

The intentional burning of another's dwelling. Some statutes have expanded this to include any real property regardless of ownership and the destruction of property by other means—for example, by explosion.

Arson   The willful and malicious burning of a building (and in some states, personal property) owned by another is the crime of **arson**. At common law, arson traditionally applied only to burning down another person's house. The law was designed to protect human life. Today, arson statutes have been extended to cover the destruction of any building, regardless of ownership, by fire or explosion.

Every state has a special statute that covers a person's burning a building for the purpose of collecting insurance. **| Example #3** If Smith owns an insured apartment building that is falling apart and sets fire to it himself or pays someone else to do so, he is guilty not only of arson but also of defrauding insurers, which is an attempted larceny.| Of course, the insurer need not pay the claim when insurance fraud is proved.

FORGERY

The fraudulent making or altering of any writing in a way that changes the legal rights and liabilities of another.

Forgery   The fraudulent making or altering of any writing in a way that changes the legal rights and liabilities of another is **forgery**. If, without authorization, Severson signs Bennett's name to the back of a check made out to Bennett, Severson is committing forgery. Forgery also includes changing trademarks, falsifying public records, counterfeiting, and altering a legal document.

Public Order Crime

Historically, societies have always outlawed activities that are considered to be contrary to public values and morals. Today, the most common public order crimes include public drunkenness, prostitution, gambling, and illegal drug use. These crimes are sometimes referred to as *victimless crimes* because the offender willingly engages in an act that is illegal but does not directly harm anyone else, so there is no identifiable victim. From a broader perspective, however, they are deemed detrimental to society as a whole because they might create an environment that gives rise to property and violent crimes.

White-Collar Crime

WHITE-COLLAR CRIME

Nonviolent crime committed by individuals or corporations to obtain a personal or business advantage.

Crimes that typically occur only in the business context are commonly referred to as **white-collar crimes**. Although there is no official definition of white-collar crime, the term is popularly used to mean an illegal act or series of acts committed by an individual or business entity using some nonviolent means. Usually, this kind of crime is committed in the course of a legitimate occupation. Corporate crimes fall into this category.

EMBEZZLEMENT

The fraudulent appropriation of funds or other property by a person to whom the funds or property has been entrusted.

Embezzlement   When a person entrusted with another person's funds or property fraudulently appropriates the funds or property, **embezzlement** occurs. Typically, embezzlement involves an employee who steals funds. Banks face this problem, and so do a number of businesses in which corporate officers or accountants "jimmy" the books to cover up the fraudulent conversion of funds for their own benefit. Embezzlement is not larceny, because the wrongdoer does not physically take the property from the possession of another, and it is not robbery, because force or fear is not used.

It does not matter whether the accused takes the funds from the victim or from a third person. If, as the financial officer of a large corporation, Saunders pockets a certain number of checks from third parties that were given to her to deposit into the corporate account, she is embezzling.

Ordinarily, an embezzler who returns what has been taken will not be prosecuted because the owner usually will not take the time to make a complaint, give depositions, and appear in court. That the accused intended eventually to return the embezzled property, however, does not constitute a sufficient defense to the crime of embezzlement.

Mail and Wire Fraud One of the most potent weapons against white-collar criminals is the Mail Fraud Act of 1990.[5] Under this act, it is a federal crime (mail fraud) to use the mails to defraud the public. Illegal use of the mails must involve (1) mailing or causing someone else to mail a writing—something written, printed, or photocopied—for the purpose of executing a scheme to defraud and (2) a contemplated or an organized scheme to defraud by false pretenses. If, for example, Johnson advertises by mail the sale of a cure for cancer that he knows to be fraudulent because it has no medical validity, he can be prosecuted for fraudulent use of the mails.

Federal law also makes it a crime to use wire (for example, the telephone), radio, or television transmissions to defraud.[6] Violators may be fined up to $1,000, imprisoned for up to five years, or both. If the violation affects a financial institution, the violator may be fined up to $1 million, imprisoned for up to thirty years, or both.

Bribery Basically, three types of bribery are considered crimes: bribery of public officials, commercial bribery, and bribery of foreign officials. The attempt to influence a public official to act in a way that serves a private interest is a crime. As an element of this crime, intent must be present and proved. The bribe can be anything the recipient considers to be valuable. Realize that *the crime of bribery occurs when the bribe is offered.* It does not matter whether the person to whom the bribe is offered accepts the bribe or agrees to perform whatever action is desired by the person offering the bribe. *Accepting a bribe* is a separate crime.

Typically, people make commercial bribes to obtain proprietary information, cover up an inferior product, or secure new business. Industrial espionage sometimes involves commercial bribes. For example, a person in one firm may offer an employee in a competing firm some type of payoff in exchange for trade secrets or pricing schedules. So-called kickbacks, or payoffs for special favors or services, are a form of commercial bribery in some situations.

Bribing foreign officials to obtain favorable business contracts is a crime. The Foreign Corrupt Practices Act of 1977, which was discussed in Chapter 2, was passed to curb the use of bribery by American businesspersons in securing foreign contracts.

Bankruptcy Fraud Today, federal bankruptcy law (see Chapter 12) allows individuals and businesses to be relieved of oppressive debt through bankruptcy proceedings. Numerous white-collar crimes may be committed during the

---

5. 18 U.S.C. Sections 1341–1342.
6. 18 U.S.C. Section 1343.

many phases of a bankruptcy proceeding. A creditor, for example, may file a false claim against a debtor, which is a crime. Also, a debtor may fraudulently transfer assets to favored parties before or after the petition for bankruptcy is filed. For example, a company-owned automobile may be "sold" at a bargain price to a trusted friend or relative. Closely related to the crime of fraudulent transfer of property is the crime of fraudulent concealment of property, such as hiding gold coins.

The Theft of Trade Secrets   As will be discussed in Chapter 7, trade secrets (such as customer lists, production methods, and research and development) constitute a form of intellectual property that for many businesses can be extremely valuable. The Economic Espionage Act of 1996[7] made the theft of trade secrets a federal crime. The act also made it a federal crime to buy or possess trade secrets of another person, knowing that the trade secrets were stolen or otherwise acquired without the owner's authorization.

Violations of the act can result in steep penalties. An individual who violates the act can be imprisoned for up to ten years and fined up to $500,000. If a corporation or other organization violates the act, it can be fined up to $5 million. Additionally, the law provides that any property acquired as a result of the violation and any property used in the commission of the violation are subject to criminal *forfeiture*—meaning that the government can take the property. A theft of trade secrets conducted via the Internet, for example, could result in the forfeiture of every computer, printer, or other device used to commit or facilitate the violation.

Insider Trading   An individual who obtains "inside information" about the plans of a publicly listed corporation can often make stock-trading profits by using the information to guide decisions relating to the purchase or sale of corporate securities. **Insider trading** is a violation of securities law and will be considered more fully in Chapter 21. Generally, the rule is that a person who possesses inside information and has a duty not to disclose it to outsiders may not profit from the purchase or sale of securities based on that information until the information is available to the public.

INSIDER TRADING
The purchase or sale of securities on the basis of information that has not been made available to the public.

Organized Crime

As mentioned, white-collar crime takes place within the confines of the legitimate business world. *Organized crime,* in contrast, operates *illegitimately* by, among other things, providing illegal goods and services. For organized crime, the traditional preferred markets are gambling, prostitution, illegal narcotics, and loan sharking (lending funds at higher-than-legal-maximum interest rates), along with more recent ventures into counterfeiting and credit-card scams.

Money Laundering   The profits from illegal activities amount to billions of dollars a year, particularly the profits from illegal drug transactions and, to a lesser extent, from racketeering, prostitution, and gambling. Under federal law, banks, savings and loan associations, and other financial institutions are

---

7. 18 U.S.C. Sections 1831–1839.

required to report currency transactions involving more than $10,000. Consequently, those who engage in illegal activities face difficulties in depositing their cash profits from illegal transactions.

As an alternative to simply storing cash from illegal transactions in a safe-deposit box, wrongdoers and racketeers have invented ways to launder "dirty" money to make it "clean." This **money laundering** is done through legitimate businesses.

| **Example #4** Matt, a successful drug dealer, becomes a partner with a restaurateur. Little by little, the restaurant shows an increasing profit. As a partner in the restaurant, Matt is able to report the "profits" of the restaurant as legitimate income on which he pays federal and state income taxes. He can then spend that after-tax income without worrying that his lifestyle may exceed the level possible with his reported income. |

The Federal Bureau of Investigation estimates that organized crime has invested tens of billions of dollars in as many as a hundred thousand business establishments in the United States for the purpose of money laundering. Globally, it is estimated that more than $700 billion in illegal money moves through the world banking system every year.

The Racketeer Influenced and Corrupt Organizations Act In 1970, in an effort to curb the apparently increasing entry of organized crime into the legitimate business world, Congress passed the Racketeer Influenced and Corrupt Organizations Act (RICO).[8] The act, which was enacted as part of the Organized Crime Control Act, makes it a federal crime to (1) use income obtained from racketeering activity to purchase any interest in an enterprise, (2) acquire or maintain an interest in an enterprise through racketeering activity, (3) conduct or participate in the affairs of an enterprise through racketeering activity, or (4) conspire to do any of the preceding activities.

Racketeering activity is not a new type of substantive crime created by RICO; rather, RICO incorporates by reference twenty-six separate types of federal crimes and nine types of state felonies[9] and declares that if a person commits two of these offenses, he or she is guilty of "racketeering activity." Additionally, RICO is more often used today to attack white-collar crimes than organized crime.

In the event of a violation, the statute permits the government to seek civil penalties, including the divestiture of a defendant's interest in a business (called *forfeiture*) or the dissolution of the business. Perhaps the most controversial aspect of RICO is that, in some cases, private individuals are allowed to recover three times their actual losses (treble damages), plus attorneys' fees, for business injuries caused by a violation of the statute. Under criminal provisions of RICO, any individual found guilty of a violation is subject to a fine of up to $25,000 per violation, imprisonment for up to twenty years, or both. Additionally, the statute provides that those who violate RICO may be required to forfeit (give up) any assets, in the form of property or cash, that were acquired as a result of the illegal activity or that were "involved in" or an "instrumentality of" the activity.

Former Enron president Jeffrey Skilling, on the right, walks to the trial court with his lawyer, Dan Petrocelli. In 2006, Skilling was convicted of many offenses, including one count of insider trading. He faced a maximum sentence of 165 years in prison. (AP Photo/Pat Sullivan)

MONEY LAUNDERING
  Falsely reporting income that has been obtained through criminal activity as income obtained through a legitimate business enterprise–in effect, "laundering" the "dirty money."

8. 18 U.S.C. Sections 1961–1968.
9. See 18 U.S.C. Section 1961(1)(A).

DEFENSES TO CRIMINAL LIABILITY

Among the most important defenses to criminal liability are infancy, intoxication, insanity, mistake, consent, duress, justifiable use of force, entrapment, and the statute of limitations. Many of these defenses involve assertions that the intent requirement for criminal liability is lacking. Also, in some cases, defendants are given immunity and thus relieved, at least in part, of criminal liability for crimes they committed. We look at each of these defenses here.

Note that procedural violations, such as obtaining evidence without a valid search warrant, may operate as defenses as well. As you will read later in this chapter, evidence obtained in violation of a defendant's constitutional rights normally may not be admitted in court. If the evidence is suppressed, then there may be no basis for prosecuting the defendant.

Infancy

The term *infant*, as used in the law, refers to any person who has not yet reached the age of majority (see Chapter 8). In all states, certain courts handle cases involving children who are alleged to have violated the law. In some states, juvenile courts handle children's cases exclusively. In other states, however, courts that handle children's cases may also have jurisdiction over additional matters.

Originally, juvenile court hearings were informal, and lawyers were rarely present. Since 1967, however, when the United States Supreme Court ruled that a child charged with delinquency must be allowed to consult with an attorney before being committed to a state institution,[10] juvenile court hearings have become more formal. In some states, a child may be treated as an adult and tried in a regular court if she or he is above a certain age (usually fourteen) and is charged with a felony, such as rape or murder.

Intoxication

The law recognizes two types of intoxication, whether from drugs or from alcohol: *involuntary* and *voluntary*. Involuntary intoxication occurs when a person either is physically forced to ingest or inject an intoxicating substance or is unaware that a substance contains drugs or alcohol. Involuntary intoxication is a defense to a crime if its effect was to make a person incapable of obeying the law or incapable of understanding that the act committed was wrong. Voluntary intoxication is rarely a defense, but it may be effective in cases in which the defendant was *extremely* intoxicated when committing the wrong.

Insanity

Someone suffering from a mental illness may be judged incapable of having the state of mind required to commit a crime. Thus, insanity may be a defense to a criminal charge. The courts have had difficulty deciding what the test for legal insanity should be, however, and psychiatrists as well as lawyers are critical of the tests used. Almost all federal courts and some states use the relatively liberal standard set forth in the Model Penal Code:

---

10. *In re Gault*, 387 U.S. 1, 87 S.Ct. 1428, 18 L.Ed.2d 527 (1967).

Three suspects were charged with assaulting Matthew Shepard, a gay University of Wyoming student. Shepard was beaten, burned, and tied to a fence like a scarecrow. Should the court allow the defendants to claim that they were temporarily insane because of "homosexual rage"? Why or why not? (AP Photo/Ed Andrieski)

A person is not responsible for criminal conduct if at the time of such conduct as a result of mental disease or defect he [or she] lacks substantial capacity either to appreciate the wrongfulness of his [or her] conduct or to conform his [or her] conduct to the requirements of the law.

Some states use the *M'Naghten* test,[11] under which a criminal defendant is not responsible if, at the time of the offense, he or she did not know the nature and quality of the act or did not know that the act was wrong. Other states use the irresistible-impulse test. A person operating under an irresistible impulse may know an act is wrong but cannot refrain from doing it.

Mistake

Everyone has heard the saying, "Ignorance of the law is no excuse." Ordinarily, ignorance of the law or a mistaken idea about what the law requires is not a valid defense. In some states, however, that rule has been modified. Criminal defendants who claim that they honestly did not know that they were breaking a law may have a valid defense if (1) the law was not published or reasonably made known to the public or (2) the defendant relied on an official statement of the law that was erroneous.

A *mistake of fact*, as opposed to a *mistake of law*, operates as a defense if it negates the mental state necessary to commit a crime. **| Example #5** If Oliver Wheaton mistakenly walks off with Julie Cabrera's briefcase because he thinks it is his, there is no theft. Theft requires knowledge that the property belongs to another. (If Wheaton's act causes Cabrera to incur damages, however, Wheaton may be subject to liability for trespass to personal property or conversion, torts that were discussed in Chapter 5.)**|**

COMPARE "Ignorance" is a lack of information. "Mistake" is a confusion of information.

---

11. A rule derived from *M'Naghten's Case,* 8 Eng.Rep. 718 (1843).

Consent

CONSENT

The voluntary agreement to a proposition or an act of another; a concurrence of wills.

What if a victim consents to a crime or even encourages the person intending a criminal act to commit it? Ordinarily, **consent** does not operate as a bar to criminal liability. In some rare circumstances, however, the law may allow consent to be used as a defense. In each case, the question is whether the law forbids an act that was committed against the victim's will or forbids the act without regard to the victim's wish. The law forbids murder, prostitution, and illegal drug use regardless of whether the victim consents to it. Also, if the act causes harm to a third person who has not consented, there is no escape from criminal liability. Consent or forgiveness given after a crime has been committed is not really a defense, though it can affect the likelihood of prosecution or the severity of the sentence. Consent operates most successfully as a defense in crimes against property.

| **Example #6**   Barry gives Phong permission to hunt for deer on Barry's land while staying in Barry's lakeside cabin. After observing Phong carrying a gun into the cabin at night, a neighbor calls the police, and an officer subsequently arrests Phong. If charged with burglary (or aggravated burglary, because he had a weapon), Phong can assert the defense of consent. He had obtained Barry's consent to enter the premises. |

Duress

DURESS

Unlawful pressure brought to bear on a person, causing the person to perform an act that she or he would not otherwise perform.

Duress exists when the *wrongful threat* of one person induces another person to perform an act that she or he would not otherwise perform. In such a situation, duress is said to negate the mental state necessary to commit a crime. For duress to qualify as a defense, the following requirements must be met:

1. The threat must be of serious bodily harm or death.
2. The harm threatened must be greater than the harm caused by the crime.
3. The threat must be immediate and inescapable.
4. The defendant must have been involved in the situation through no fault of his or her own.

Justifiable Use of Force

SELF-DEFENSE

The legally recognized privilege to protect oneself or one's property against injury by another. The privilege of self-defense protects only acts that are reasonably necessary to protect oneself, one's property, or another person.

Probably the best-known defense to criminal liability is **self-defense.** Other situations, however, also justify the use of force: the defense of one's dwelling, the defense of other property, and the prevention of a crime. In all of these situations, it is important to distinguish between deadly and nondeadly force. *Deadly force* is likely to result in death or serious bodily harm. *Nondeadly force* is force that reasonably appears necessary to prevent the imminent use of criminal force.

Generally speaking, people can use the amount of nondeadly force that seems necessary to protect themselves or their property, or to prevent the commission of a crime. Deadly force can be used in self-defense if there is a *reasonable belief* that imminent death or grievous bodily harm will otherwise result, if the attacker is using unlawful force (an example of lawful force is that exerted by a police officer), and if the defender has not initiated or provoked the attack. Deadly force normally can be used to defend a dwelling only if the unlawful entry is violent and the person believes deadly force is necessary to prevent imminent death or great bodily harm or—in some jurisdictions—if the person believes deadly force is necessary to prevent the commission of a felony (such as arson) in the dwelling.

Entrapment

Entrapment is a defense designed to prevent police officers or other government agents from enticing persons to commit crimes in order to later prosecute them for criminal acts. In the typical entrapment case, an undercover agent *suggests* that a crime be committed and somehow pressures or induces an individual to commit it. The agent then arrests the individual for the crime.

For entrapment to be considered a defense, both the suggestion and the inducement must take place. The defense is intended not to prevent law enforcement agents from setting a trap for an unwary criminal but rather to prevent them from pushing the individual into it. The crucial issue is whether the person who committed a crime was predisposed to do so or acted because the agent induced it.

Statute of Limitations

With some exceptions, such as for the crime of murder, statutes of limitations apply to crimes just as they do to civil wrongs. In other words, criminal cases must be prosecuted within a certain number of years. If a criminal action is brought after the statutory time period has expired, the accused person can raise the statute of limitations as a defense.

Immunity

At times, the state may wish to obtain information from a person accused of a crime. Accused persons are understandably reluctant to give information if it will be used to prosecute them, and they cannot be forced to do so. The privilege against self-incrimination is granted by the Fifth Amendment to the Constitution, which reads, in part, "nor shall [any person] be compelled in any criminal case to be a witness against himself." In cases in which the state wishes to obtain information from a person accused of a crime, the state can grant *immunity* from prosecution or agree to prosecute for a less serious offense in exchange for the information. Once immunity is given, the person can no longer refuse to testify on Fifth Amendment grounds, because he or she now has an absolute privilege against self-incrimination.

Often, a grant of immunity from prosecution for a serious crime is part of the **plea bargaining** between the defendant and the prosecuting attorney. The defendant may be convicted of a lesser offense, while the state uses the defendant's testimony to prosecute accomplices for serious crimes carrying heavy penalties.

CONSTITUTIONAL SAFEGUARDS AND CRIMINAL PROCEDURES

Criminal law brings the power of the state, with all its resources, to bear against the individual. Criminal procedures are designed to protect the constitutional rights of individuals and to prevent the arbitrary use of power on the part of the government.

The U.S. Constitution provides specific safeguards for those accused of crimes. Most of these safeguards protect individuals against state government

ENTRAPMENT
In criminal law, a defense in which the defendant claims that he or she was induced by a public official—usually an undercover agent or police officer—to commit a crime that he or she would otherwise not have committed.

PLEA BARGAINING
The process by which a defendant and the prosecutor in a criminal case work out a mutually satisfactory disposition of the case, subject to court approval; usually involves the defendant's pleading guilty to a lesser offense in return for a lighter sentence.

actions, as well as federal government actions, by virtue of the due process clause of the Fourteenth Amendment. These safeguards are set forth in the Fourth, Fifth, Sixth, and Eighth Amendments.

Fourth Amendment Protections

The Fourth Amendment protects the "right of the people to be secure in their persons, houses, papers, and effects." Before searching or seizing private property, law enforcement officers must obtain a **search warrant**—an order from a judge or other public official authorizing the search or seizure.

SEARCH WARRANT
An order granted by a public authority, such as a judge, that authorizes law enforcement personnel to search particular premises or property.

PROBABLE CAUSE
Reasonable grounds for believing that a person should be arrested or searched.

Search Warrants and Probable Cause   To obtain a search warrant, the officers must convince a judge that they have reasonable grounds, or **probable cause,** to believe a search will reveal a specific illegality. Probable cause requires law enforcement officials to have trustworthy evidence that would convince a reasonable person that the proposed search or seizure is more likely justified than not. Furthermore, the Fourth Amendment prohibits general warrants. It requires a particular description of what is to be searched or seized. General searches through a person's belongings are impermissible. The search cannot extend beyond what is described in the warrant.

There are exceptions to the requirement of a search warrant, as when it is likely that the items sought will be removed before a warrant can be obtained. For example, if a police officer has probable cause to believe an automobile contains evidence of a crime and the vehicle is likely to be unavailable by the time a warrant is obtained, the officer can search the vehicle without a warrant.

Searches and Seizures in the Business Context   Constitutional protection against unreasonable searches and seizures is important to businesses and professionals. As federal and state regulation of commercial activities increased, frequent and unannounced government inspections were conducted to ensure compliance with the regulations. Such inspections were extremely disruptive at times. In *Marshall v. Barlow's, Inc.,*[12] the United States Supreme Court held that government inspectors do not have the right to enter business premises without a warrant, although the standard of probable cause is not the same as that required in nonbusiness contexts. The existence of a general and neutral enforcement plan will justify issuance of the warrant.

Lawyers and accountants frequently possess the business records of their clients, and inspecting these documents while they are out of the hands of their true owners also requires a warrant. No warrant is required, however, for seizures of spoiled or contaminated food. Nor are warrants required for searches of businesses in such highly regulated industries as liquor, guns, and strip mining. General manufacturing is not considered to be one of these highly regulated industries, however.

Of increasing concern to many employers is how to maintain a safe and efficient workplace without jeopardizing the Fourth Amendment rights of employees "to be secure in their persons." Requiring employees to undergo random drug tests, for example, may be held to violate the Fourth Amendment. In Chapter 14, we will discuss Fourth Amendment issues in the employment context, as well as the privacy rights of employees in general, in detail.

---

12. 436 U.S. 307, 98 S.Ct. 1816, 56 L.Ed.2d 305 (1978).

Is a suspicionless checkpoint search conducted in an airport to screen airline passengers permissible under the Fourth Amendment? That was the question in the following case.

CASE 6.1   United States v. Hartwell

United States Court of Appeals,
Third Circuit, 2006.
436 F.3d 174.

BACKGROUND AND FACTS Christian Hartwell arrived at the Philadelphia International Airport on Saturday, May 17, 2003, to catch a flight to Phoenix, Arizona. He reached the security checkpoint, placed his hand luggage on a conveyor belt to be X-rayed, and approached the metal detector. Hartwell's luggage was scanned without incident, but when he walked through, he set off the magnetometer. He was told to remove all items from his pockets and try again. Hartwell removed

several items from his pocket and walked through again. Carlos Padua, a federal Transportation Security Administration (TSA) agent, took Hartwell aside and scanned him with a handheld magnetometer. The wand revealed a solid object in Hartwell's pants pocket. Padua asked what it was, but Hartwell did not respond. Escorted to a private screening room, Hartwell refused several requests to empty his pocket. By Hartwell's account, Padua then reached into the pocket and removed two packages of crack cocaine. Hartwell was arrested and convicted on charges related to the possession of the drugs. He appealed to the U.S. Court of Appeals for the Third Circuit, arguing that the search violated the Fourth Amendment.

IN THE WORDS OF THE COURT . . . *ALITO*, Circuit Judge.

* * * *

Suspicionless checkpoint searches are permissible under the Fourth Amendment when a court finds a favorable balance between the gravity of the public concerns served by the seizure, the degree to which the seizure advances the public interest, and the severity of the interference with individual liberty. [Emphasis added.]

* * * *

In this case, the airport checkpoint passes the * * * test. First, there can be no doubt that preventing terrorist attacks on airplanes is of paramount importance.

Second, airport checkpoints also advance the public interest * * * . [A]bsent a search, there is no effective means of detecting which airline passengers are reasonably likely to hijack an airplane. Additionally, it is apparent that airport checkpoints have been effective.

Third, the procedures involved in Hartwell's search were minimally intrusive. They were well tailored to protect personal privacy, escalating in invasiveness only after a lower level of screening disclosed a reason to conduct a more probing search. The search began when Hartwell simply passed through a magnetometer and had his bag X-rayed, two screenings that involved no physical touching. Only after Hartwell set off the metal detector was he screened with a wand—yet another less intrusive substitute for a physical pat-down. And only after the wand detected something solid on his person, and after repeated requests that he produce the item, did the TSA agents (according to Hartwell) reach into his pocket.

In addition to being tailored to protect personal privacy, other factors make airport screening procedures minimally intrusive in comparison to other kinds of searches. Since every air passenger is subjected to a search, there is virtually no stigma attached to being subjected to search at a known, designated airport search point. Moreover, the possibility for abuse is minimized by the public nature of the search. Unlike searches conducted on dark and lonely streets at night where often the officer and the subject are the only witnesses, these searches are made under supervision and not far from the scrutiny of

CASE 6.1–CONTINUED ▶

the traveling public. And the airlines themselves have a strong interest in protecting passengers from unnecessary annoyance and harassment.

Lastly, the entire procedure is rendered less offensive—if not less intrusive—because air passengers are on notice that they will be searched. Air passengers choose to fly, and screening procedures of this kind have existed in every airport in the country since at least 1974. The events of September 11, 2001, have only increased their prominence in the public's consciousness. It is inconceivable that Hartwell was unaware that he had to be searched before he could board a plane.

DECISION AND REMEDY The U.S. Court of Appeals for the Third Circuit held that Hartwell's search was permissible under the Fourth Amendment, "even though it was initiated without individualized suspicion and was conducted without a warrant. It is permissible * * * because the State has an overwhelming interest in preserving air travel safety, and the procedure is tailored to advance that interest while proving to be only minimally invasive."

WHY IS THIS CASE IMPORTANT? *In this case, the U.S. Court of Appeals for the Third Circuit applied the administrative search doctrine that pertains to highly regulated industries. The United States Supreme Court developed this standard for analyzing suspicionless vehicle checkpoints, such as those used to determine the sobriety of randomly selected drivers. The Supreme Court has not ruled on the legality of airport screenings, however.*

Fifth Amendment Protections

The Fifth Amendment offers significant protections for accused persons. One is the guarantee that no one can be deprived of "life, liberty, or property without due process of law." Two other important Fifth Amendment provisions protect persons against double jeopardy and self-incrimination.

Due Process of Law Remember from Chapter 4 that *due process of law* has both procedural and substantive aspects. Procedural due process requirements underlie criminal procedures. Basically, the law must be carried out in a fair and orderly way. In criminal cases, due process means that defendants should have an opportunity to object to the charges against them before a fair, neutral decision maker, such as a judge. Defendants must also be given the opportunity to confront and cross-examine witnesses and accusers and to present their own witnesses.

DOUBLE JEOPARDY
A situation occurring when a person is tried twice for the same criminal offense; prohibited by the Fifth Amendment to the Constitution.

Double Jeopardy The Fifth Amendment also protects persons from **double jeopardy** (being tried twice for the same criminal offense). The prohibition against double jeopardy means that once a criminal defendant is acquitted (found "not guilty") of a particular crime, the government may not reindict the person and retry him or her for the same crime.

The prohibition against double jeopardy does not preclude the crime victim from bringing a civil suit against the same person to recover damages, however. Additionally, a state's prosecution of a crime will not prevent a separate federal prosecution relating to the same activity, and vice versa. ┃ **Example #7** A person found "not guilty" of assault and battery in a criminal case may be sued by the victim in a civil tort case for damages. A person who is prosecuted for assault and battery in a state court may be prosecuted in a federal court for civil rights violations resulting from the same action. ┃

Self-Incrimination   The Fifth Amendment guarantees that no person "shall be compelled in any criminal case to be a witness against himself." Thus, in any criminal proceeding, an accused person cannot be compelled to give testimony that might subject her or him to any criminal prosecution.

The Fifth Amendment's guarantee against **self-incrimination** extends only to natural persons. Because a corporation is a legal entity and not a natural person, the protection against self-incrimination does not apply to it. Similarly, the business records of a partnership do not receive Fifth Amendment protection.[13] When a partnership is required to produce these records, it must do so even if the information incriminates the persons who constitute the business entity. Sole proprietors and sole practitioners (those who fully own their businesses) who have not incorporated normally cannot be compelled to produce their business records. These individuals have full protection against self-incrimination because they function in only one capacity; there is no separate business entity (see Chapter 11).

Protections under the Sixth and Eighth Amendments

The Sixth Amendment guarantees several important rights for criminal defendants: the right to a speedy trial, the right to a jury trial, the right to a public trial, the right to confront witnesses, and the right to counsel. The Eighth Amendment prohibits excessive bail and fines, as well as cruel and unusual punishment.

The Sixth Amendment right to counsel is one of the rights of which a suspect must be advised when he or she is arrested under the *Miranda* rule (discussed later in this chapter). In many cases, a statement that a criminal suspect makes in the absence of counsel is not admissible at trial unless the suspect has knowingly and voluntarily waived this right. Is the right to counsel triggered when judicial proceedings are initiated through any preliminary step? Or is this right triggered only when a suspect is "interrogated" by the police? In the following case, the Supreme Court considered these questions.

> **BE AWARE** The Fifth Amendment protection against self-incrimination does not cover partnerships or corporations.

SELF-INCRIMINATION
The giving of testimony that may subject the testifier to criminal prosecution. The Fifth Amendment to the Constitution protects against self-incrimination by providing that no person "shall be compelled in any criminal case to be a witness against himself."

---

13. But the protection against self-incrimination has been applied to some small family partnerships. See *United States v. Slutsky*, 352 F.Supp. 1105 (S.D.N.Y. 1972).

CASE 6.2	**Fellers v. United States**

Supreme Court of the United States, 2004.
540 U.S. 519,
124 S.Ct. 1019,
157 L.Ed.2d 1016.
straylight.law.cornell.edu/supct/index.html[a]

BACKGROUND AND FACTS In February 2000, an indictment was issued charging John Fellers, a resident of Lincoln, Nebraska, with conspiracy to distribute methamphetamine. Police officers Michael Garnett and Jeff

a. In the "Search" box, type "Fellers," select "Current decisions only," and click on "submit." In the result, scroll to the name of the case, and click on it to access the opinion. The Legal Information Institute of Cornell Law School in Ithaca, New York, maintains this Web site.

Bliemeister went to Fellers's home to arrest him. They told Fellers that the purpose of their visit was to discuss his use and distribution of methamphetamine. They said that they had a warrant for his arrest and that the charges referred to his involvement with four individuals. Fellers responded that he knew the persons and had used methamphetamine with them. The officers took Fellers to jail and advised him for the first time of his right to counsel. He waived this right and repeated his earlier statements. Before Fellers's trial, the court ruled that his "jailhouse statements" could be admitted at his trial because he had waived his right to counsel before making them. After Fellers's conviction, he appealed to the U.S. Court

CASE 6.2—CONTINUED ▶

CASE 6.2–CONTINUED

of Appeals for the Eighth Circuit, arguing that the officers had elicited his incriminating "home statements" without advising him of his right to counsel and that his "jailhouse statements" should thus have been excluded from his trial as "fruits" of his earlier statements (see the discussion of the exclusionary rule in the next subsection). The appellate court affirmed the lower court's judgment, holding that Fellers had not had a right to counsel at his home because he had not been subject to police "interrogation." Fellers appealed to the United States Supreme Court.

IN THE WORDS OF THE COURT . . . Justice *O'CONNOR* delivered the opinion of the Court.

* * * *

The Sixth Amendment right to counsel is triggered at or after the time that judicial proceedings have been initiated * * * whether by way of formal charge, preliminary hearing, indictment, information, or arraignment. We have held that an accused is denied the basic protections of the Sixth Amendment when there is used against him at his trial evidence of his own incriminating words, which federal agents * * * deliberately elicited from him after he had been indicted and in the absence of his counsel.

We have consistently applied the deliberate-elicitation standard in * * * *Sixth Amendment cases* * * * . [Emphasis added.]

The Court of Appeals erred in holding that the absence of an "interrogation" foreclosed petitioner's claim that the jailhouse statements should have been suppressed as fruits of the statements taken from petitioner [Fellers] at his home. First, there is no question that the officers in this case deliberately elicited information from petitioner. Indeed, the officers, upon arriving at petitioner's house, informed him that their purpose in coming was to discuss his involvement in the distribution of methamphetamine and his association with certain charged co-conspirators. Because the ensuing discussion took place after petitioner had been indicted, outside the presence of counsel, and in the absence of any waiver of petitioner's Sixth Amendment rights, the Court of Appeals erred in holding that the officers' actions did not violate the Sixth Amendment standards * * * .

Second, because of its erroneous determination that petitioner was not questioned in violation of Sixth Amendment standards, the Court of Appeals improperly conducted its "fruits" analysis * * * . Specifically, it * * * [held] that the admissibility of the jailhouse statements turns solely on whether the statements were knowingly and voluntarily made. The Court of Appeals did not reach the question whether the Sixth Amendment requires suppression of petitioner's jailhouse statements on the ground that they were the fruits of previous questioning conducted in violation of the Sixth Amendment deliberate-elicitation standard. We have not had occasion to decide whether [such statements should be excluded from trial] when a suspect makes incriminating statements after a knowing and voluntary waiver of his right to counsel notwithstanding earlier police questioning in violation of Sixth Amendment standards. We therefore remand to the Court of Appeals to address this issue in the first instance.

Accordingly, the judgment of the Court of Appeals is reversed, and the case is remanded for further proceedings consistent with this opinion.

DECISION AND REMEDY The United States Supreme Court reversed the lower court's decision and remanded the case for the determination of a different issue. The Supreme Court held that the Sixth Amendment bars the use at trial of a suspect's incriminating words, deliberately elicited by police after an indictment, in the absence of either counsel or a waiver of the right to counsel, regardless of whether police conduct constitutes an "interrogation."

FOR CRITICAL ANALYSIS–Social Consideration *Should Fellers's "jailhouse statements" also have been excluded from his trial? Why or why not?*

The Exclusionary Rule and the *Miranda* Rule

Two other procedural protections for criminal defendants are the exclusionary rule and the *Miranda* rule.

The Exclusionary Rule   Under what is known as the **exclusionary rule**, all evidence obtained in violation of the constitutional rights spelled out in the Fourth, Fifth, and Sixth Amendments, as well as all evidence derived from illegally obtained evidence, normally must be excluded from the trial. Evidence derived from illegally obtained evidence is known as the "fruit of the poisonous tree." For example, if a confession is obtained after an illegal arrest, the arrest is "the poisonous tree," and the confession, if "tainted" by the arrest, is the "fruit."

The purpose of the exclusionary rule is to deter police from conducting warrantless searches and from engaging in other misconduct. The rule is sometimes criticized because it can lead to injustice. Many a defendant has "gotten off on a technicality" because law enforcement personnel failed to observe procedural requirements. Even though a defendant may be obviously guilty, if the evidence of that guilt was obtained improperly (without a valid search warrant, for example), it normally cannot be used against the defendant in court.

> **EXCLUSIONARY RULE**
> In criminal procedure, a rule under which any evidence that is obtained in violation of the accused's constitutional rights guaranteed by the Fourth, Fifth, and Sixth Amendments, as well as any evidence derived from illegally obtained evidence, will not be admissible in court.

The *Miranda* Rule   In *Miranda v. Arizona,* a case decided in 1966, the United States Supreme Court established the rule that individuals who are arrested must be informed of certain constitutional rights, including their Fifth Amendment right to remain silent and their Sixth Amendment right to counsel. If the arresting officers fail to inform a criminal suspect of these constitutional rights, any statements the suspect makes normally will not be admissible in court. The *Miranda* case is presented as this chapter's *Landmark in the Legal Environment* feature on the next page.

The Supreme Court's *Miranda* decision was controversial, and Congress subsequently attempted to overrule it by enacting Section 3501 of the Omnibus Crime Control Act[14] of 1968. Essentially, Section 3501 reinstated the rule that had been in effect for 180 years before *Miranda*—namely, that statements by defendants can be used against them as long as the statements are made voluntarily. The U.S. Justice Department immediately refused to enforce Section 3501, however. Although the U.S. Court of Appeals for the Fourth Circuit attempted to enforce the provision in 1999, its decision was reversed by the United States Supreme Court in 2000. The Supreme Court held that the *Miranda* rights enunciated by the Court in the 1966 case were constitutionally based and thus could not be overruled by a legislative act.[15]

> **REMEMBER!** Once a suspect has been informed of his or her rights, anything that person says can be used as evidence in a trial.

Exceptions to the *Miranda* Rule   Over time, as part of a continuing attempt to balance the rights of accused persons against the rights of society, the United States Supreme Court has carved out numerous exceptions to the *Miranda* rule. In 1984, for example, the Court recognized a "public safety" exception to the *Miranda* rule. The need to protect the public warranted the admissibility of statements made by the defendant (in this case, indicating where he

---

14. 42 U.S.C. Section 3789d.
15. *Dickerson v. United States,* 530 U.S. 428, 120 S.Ct. 2326, 147 L.Ed.2d 405 (2000).

Miranda v. Arizona (1966)

The United States Supreme Court's decision in *Miranda v. Arizona*[a] has been cited in more court decisions than any other case in the history of American law. Through television shows and other media, the case has also become familiar to most of the adult population in the United States.

The case arose after Ernesto Miranda was arrested in his home, on March 13, 1963, for the kidnapping and rape of an eighteen-year-old woman. Miranda was taken to a Phoenix, Arizona, police station and questioned by two police officers. Two hours later, the officers emerged from the interrogation room with a written confession signed by Miranda.

Rulings by the Lower Courts The confession was admitted into evidence at the trial, and Miranda was convicted and sentenced to prison for twenty to thirty years. Miranda appealed the decision, claiming that he had not been informed of his constitutional rights. He did not claim that he was innocent of the crime or that his confession was false or made under duress. He claimed only that he would not have confessed to the crime if he had been advised of his right to remain silent and to have an attorney. The Supreme Court of Arizona held that Miranda's constitutional rights had not been violated and affirmed his conviction. In forming its decision, the court emphasized that Miranda had not specifically requested an attorney.

The Supreme Court's Decision The *Miranda* case was subsequently consolidated with three other cases involving similar issues and reviewed by the United States

Supreme Court. In its decision, the Supreme Court stated that whenever an individual is taken into custody, "the following measures are required: He must be warned prior to any questioning that he has the right to remain silent, that anything he says can be used against him in a court of law, that he has the right to the presence of an attorney, and that if he cannot afford an attorney one will be appointed for him prior to any questioning if he so desires." If the accused waives his or her rights to remain silent and to have counsel present, the government must be able to demonstrate that the waiver was made knowingly, intelligently, and voluntarily.

Application to Today's Legal Environment

Today, both on television and in the real world, police officers routinely advise suspects of their "Miranda rights" on arrest. When Ernesto Miranda himself was later murdered, the suspected murderer was "read his Miranda rights." Despite Congress's attempt to overrule the Miranda requirements through legislation in 1968, the decision continues to protect the rights of criminal defendants and, as noted in the text, was affirmed by the Supreme Court in 2000 as constitutional.

RELEVANT WEB SITES

*To locate information on the Web concerning the Miranda decision, go to this text's Web site at **www.thomsonedu. com/westbuslaw/let**, select "Chapter 6," and click on "URLs for Landmarks."*

a. 384 U.S. 436, 86 S.Ct. 1602, 16 L.Ed.2d 694 (1966).

placed the gun) as evidence at trial, even though the defendant had not been informed of his *Miranda* rights.[16]

In 1986, the Supreme Court further held that a confession need not be excluded even though the police failed to inform a suspect in custody that his attorney had tried to reach him by telephone.[17] In an important 1991 decision, the Court stated that a suspect's conviction will not be automatically overturned if the suspect was coerced into making a confession. If other, legally obtained evidence admitted at trial is strong enough to justify the conviction

---

16. *New York v. Quarles*, 467 U.S. 649, 104 S.Ct. 2626, 81 L.Ed.2d 550 (1984).
17. *Moran v. Burbine*, 475 U.S. 412, 106 S.Ct. 1135, 89 L.Ed.2d 410 (1986).

Police officers take a suspect into custody. Why must a criminal suspect be informed of his or her legal rights? (Corbis. All rights reserved.)

without the confession, then the fact that the confession was obtained illegally can, in effect, be ignored.[18]

In yet another case, in 1994, the Supreme Court ruled that a suspect must unequivocally and assertively request to exercise his or her right to counsel in order to stop police questioning. Saying, "Maybe I should talk to a lawyer" during an interrogation after being taken into custody is not enough. The Court held that police officers are not required to decipher the suspect's intentions in such situations.[19]

CRIMINAL PROCESS

As mentioned, a criminal prosecution differs significantly from a civil case in several respects. These differences reflect the desire to safeguard the rights of the individual against the state. Exhibit 6–3 on page 196 summarizes the major procedural steps in processing a criminal case. We now discuss three phases of the criminal process—arrest, indictment or information, and trial.

Arrest

Before a warrant for arrest can be issued, there must be probable cause for believing that the individual in question has committed a crime. As discussed earlier, *probable cause* can be defined as a substantial likelihood that the person has committed or is about to commit a crime. Note that probable cause involves a likelihood, not just a possibility (because anything is possible). Arrests may sometimes be made without a warrant if there is no time to get one, as when a police officer observes a crime taking place, but the action of the arresting officer is still judged by the standard of probable cause.

---

18. *Arizona v. Fulminante*, 499 U.S. 279, 111 S.Ct. 1246, 113 L.Ed.2d 302 (1991).
19. *Davis v. United States*, 512 U.S. 452, 114 S.Ct. 2350, 129 L.Ed.2d 362 (1994).

CASE 6.3–CONTINUED

the government's subpoena powers." Yates argued that allowing the testimony would violate her Sixth Amendment right to confront witnesses. The court allowed the witnesses to

testify. A jury found Pusztai and Yates guilty. The defendants appealed to the U.S. Court of Appeals for the Eleventh Circuit.

IN THE WORDS OF THE COURT . . . COX, Circuit Judge:

* * * *

* * * [Pusztai and Yates] contend that their Sixth Amendment rights to confrontation were violated by admission of [the] testimony taken from witnesses who were physically present in Australia while Defendants were in Montgomery, Alabama. * * *

* * * *

The Sixth Amendment provides: "In all criminal prosecutions, the accused shall enjoy the right * * * to be confronted with the witnesses against him." This clause, known as the Confrontation Clause, guarantees the defendant a face-to-face meeting with witnesses appearing before the trier of fact. * * * [Emphasis added.]

* * * [A] defendant's right to confront accusatory witnesses may be satisfied absent a physical, face-to-face confrontation at trial *only where denial of such confrontation is necessary to further an important public policy.* * * * [Emphasis added.]

* * * *

In this case, the district court * * * permit[ted] the Australian witnesses to testify by two-way video conference broadcast on a television monitor at the trial convened in the United States Attorney's Office in Montgomery, Alabama. * * * The district court considered sufficient the Government's stated "important public policy of providing the fact-finder with crucial evidence" and "interest in expeditiously and justly resolving the case." We accept the district court's statement that the witnesses were necessary to the prosecution's case on at least some of the charges, as the record supports the Government's assertion that the testimony was crucial to a successful prosecution of the Defendants and aided expeditious resolution of the case. * * * We hold, however, that, under the circumstances of this case (which include the availability of a [pretrial] deposition), the prosecutor's need for the video conference testimony to make a case and to expeditiously resolve it are not the type of public policies that are important enough to outweigh the Defendants' rights to confront their accusers face to face.

The district court made no case-specific findings of fact that would support a conclusion that this case is different from any other criminal prosecution in which the Government would find it convenient to present testimony by two-way video conference. All criminal prosecutions include at least some evidence crucial to the Government's case, and there is no doubt that many criminal cases could be more expeditiously resolved were it unnecessary for witnesses to appear at trial. If we were to approve introduction of testimony in this manner, on this record, every prosecutor wishing to present testimony from a witness overseas would argue that providing crucial prosecution evidence and resolving the case expeditiously are important public policies that support the admission of testimony by two-way video conference.

DECISION AND REMEDY The U.S Court of Appeals for the Eleventh Circuit vacated the decision of the lower court to allow the overseas witnesses to testify and remanded the case for a new trial. The appellate court reasoned that the admission of the testimony via a live, two-way video teleconference violated the defendants' Sixth Amendment right to confront witnesses.

WHAT IF THE FACTS WERE DIFFERENT? *Suppose that there was only one essential witness in Australia, Paul Christian, who was asked to attend the trial in the United States. Further suppose that Christian was undergoing an intensive course of chemotherapy and was too sick to travel. How might the fact that a witness is unable (as opposed to unwilling) to attend the trial affect the court's opinion on teleconferencing and the Sixth Amendment?*

Sentencing Guidelines

Traditionally, persons who committed the same crime might receive very different sentences, depending on the judge hearing the case, the jurisdiction in which it was heard, and many other factors. Today, however, court judges typically must follow state or federal guidelines when sentencing convicted persons.

At the federal level, the Sentencing Reform Act created the U.S. Sentencing Commission, which was charged with the task of standardizing sentences for federal crimes. The commission fulfilled its task, and since 1987 its sentencing guidelines for all federal crimes have been applied by federal court judges. The guidelines establish a range of possible penalties for each federal crime. Depending on the defendant's criminal record, the seriousness of the offense, and other factors specified in the guidelines, federal judges must select a sentence from within this range.

The commission also created specific guidelines for the punishment of crimes committed by corporate employees (white-collar crimes). These guidelines established stiffer penalties for criminal violations of securities laws (see Chapter 21), antitrust laws (see Chapter 20), employment laws (see Chapters 13 through 15), mail and wire fraud, commercial bribery, and kickbacks and money laundering.[21] The guidelines allow federal judges to take into consideration a number of factors when selecting from the range of possible penalties for a specified crime. These factors include the defendant company's history of past violations, the scope of management's cooperation with federal investigators, and the extent to which the firm has undertaken specific programs and procedures to prevent criminal activities by its employees.

CYBER CRIMES

Some years ago, the American Bar Association defined **computer crime** as any act that is directed against computers and computer parts, that uses computers as instruments of crime, or that involves computers and constitutes abuse. Today, because much of the crime committed with the use of computers occurs in cyberspace, many computer crimes fall under the broad label of cyber crime.

As we mentioned earlier, most cyber crimes are not "new" crimes. Rather, they are existing crimes in which the Internet is the instrument of wrongdoing. The challenge for law enforcement is to apply traditional laws—which were designed to protect persons from physical harm or to safeguard their physical property—to crimes committed in cyberspace. Here we look at several types of activity that constitute cyber crimes against persons or property. Other cyber crimes will be discussed in later chapters of this text as they relate to particular topics, such as banking or consumer law.

COMPUTER CRIME
Any act that is directed against computers and computer parts, that uses computers as instruments of crime, or that involves computers and constitutes abuse.

BE AWARE Technological change is one of the primary factors that lead to new types of crime.

Cyber Theft

In cyberspace, thieves are not subject to the physical limitations of the "real" world. A thief can steal data stored in a networked computer with Internet access from anywhere on the globe. Only the speed of the connection and the thief's computer equipment limit the quantity of data that can be stolen.

---

21. The sentencing guidelines were amended in 2003, as required under the Sarbanes-Oxley Act of 2002, to impose stiffer penalties for corporate securities fraud—see Chapter 21.

Financial Crimes   Computer networks also provide opportunities for employees to commit crimes that can involve serious economic losses. For example, employees of a company's accounting department can transfer funds among accounts with little effort and often with less risk than would be involved in transactions evidenced by paperwork.

Generally, the dependence of businesses on computer operations has left firms vulnerable to sabotage, fraud, embezzlement, and the theft of proprietary data, such as trade secrets or other intellectual property. As will be noted in Chapter 7, the piracy of intellectual property via the Internet is one of the most serious legal challenges facing lawmakers and the courts today.

IDENTITY THEFT
The act of stealing another's identifying information—such as a name, date of birth, or Social Security number—and using that information to access the victim's financial resources.

Identity Theft   A form of cyber theft that has become particularly troublesome in recent years is **identity theft.** Identity theft occurs when the wrongdoer steals a form of identification—such as a name, date of birth, or Social Security number—and uses the information to access the victim's financial resources. This crime existed to a certain extent before the widespread use of the Internet. Thieves would "steal" calling-card numbers by watching people using public telephones, or they would rifle through garbage to find bank account or credit-card numbers. The identity thieves would then use the calling-card or credit-card numbers or would withdraw funds from the victims' accounts.

The Internet, however, has turned identity theft into perhaps the fastest-growing financial crime in the United States. From the identity thief's perspective, the Internet provides those who steal information offline with an easy medium for using items such as stolen credit-card and Social Security numbers while protected by anonymity. An estimated 10 million Americans are victims of identity theft each year, and annual losses are estimated to exceed $50 billion.

Cyberstalking

California enacted the first stalking law in 1990, in response to the murders of six women—including Rebecca Schaeffer, a television star—by men who had harassed them. The law made it a crime to harass or follow a person while making a "credible threat" that puts that person in reasonable fear for his or her safety or the safety of the person's immediate family.[22] Since then, all other states have enacted some form of stalking laws. In about half of the states, these laws require a physical act such as following the victim.

CYBERSTALKER
A person who commits the crime of stalking in cyberspace. Generally, stalking consists of harassing a person and putting that person in reasonable fear for his or her safety or the safety of the person's immediate family.

Cyberstalkers (stalkers who commit their crimes in cyberspace), however, find their victims through Internet chat rooms, Usenet newsgroups or other bulletin boards, or e-mail. To close this "loophole" in existing stalking laws, more than three-fourths of the states now have laws specifically designed to combat cyberstalking and other forms of online harassment.

Note that cyberstalking can be even more threatening than physical stalking in some respects. While it takes a great deal of effort to physically stalk someone, it is relatively easy to harass a victim with electronic messages. Furthermore, the possibility of personal confrontation may discourage a stalker from actually following a victim. This disincentive is removed in cyberspace. Also, there is always the possibility that a cyberstalker will eventually pose a physical threat to her or his target. Finally, the Internet makes it easier to

---

22. See, for example, Cal. Penal Code Section 646.9.

An Arkansas man holds a picture of his thirteen-year-old daughter, who was kidnapped and murdered by a man she met through an Internet chat room. How do cyberstalking laws differ from traditional stalking laws? (AP Photo/Mike Wintroath)

obtain information about the victim, such as where he or she lives or works. (Can Internet sellers of personal information be held responsible for crimes by stalkers who use that information to locate their victims? For a discussion of this issue, see this chapter's *Online Developments* feature on page 202.)

Hacking and Cyberterrorism

Persons who use one computer to break into another are sometimes referred to as **hackers.** Hackers who break into computers without authorization often commit cyber theft. Sometimes, however, their principal aim is to prove how smart they are by gaining access to others' password-protected computers and causing random data errors or making unpaid-for telephone calls.[23] **Cyberterrorists** are hackers who, rather than trying to attract attention, strive to remain undetected so that they can exploit computers for a serious impact. Just as "real" terrorists destroyed the World Trade Center towers and a portion of the Pentagon in September 2001, cyberterrorists might explode "logic bombs" to shut down central computers. Such activities can pose a danger to national security.

Businesses may be targeted by cyberterrorists as well as hackers. The goals of a hacking operation might include a wholesale theft of data, such as a merchant's customer files, or the monitoring of a computer to discover a business firm's plans and transactions. A cyberterrorist might also want to insert false codes or data. For example, the processing control system of a food manufacturer could be changed to alter the levels of ingredients so that consumers of the food would become ill.

A cyberterrorist attack on a major financial institution such as the New York Stock Exchange or a large bank could leave securities or money markets in flux and seriously affect the daily lives of millions of citizens. Similarly, any

HACKER
A person who uses one computer to break into another. Professional computer programmers refer to such persons as "crackers."

CYBERTERRORIST
A hacker whose purpose is to exploit a target computer for a serious impact, such as corrupting a program to sabotage a business.

---

23. The total cost of crime on the Internet is estimated to be many billion dollars annually, but two-thirds of that total is said to consist of unpaid-for toll calls.

ONLINE DEVELOPMENTS
Stalking and Internet Data Brokers

Click here

A cutting-edge issue coming before today's courts has to do with stalking and Internet data brokers—those in the business of selling personal information via the Internet. Suppose that a stalker purchases personal information (such as a home address) from a Web broker and then uses that information to commit a crime (such as murder). The stalker, of course, can be prosecuted under criminal law for the crime of murder. At issue is the broker's responsibility for the crime. Can the broker be sued under tort law (see Chapter 5) for damages?

One Court Weighs In

At least one court has weighed in on this issue. In *Remsburg v. Docusearch, Inc.*,[a] the Supreme Court of New Hampshire concluded that an Internet data broker had a duty to exercise reasonable care when selling personal information online. The case involved Liam Youens, a New Hampshire resident, and Docusearch, Inc., an Internet-based investigation and information service. Youens contacted Docusearch through its Web site and requested information about Amy Boyer. Youens provided his name, address, and phone number and paid Docusearch's fee by credit card. In return, Docusearch provided Boyer's home address, birth date, and Social Security number. Youens also asked for Boyer's workplace address, which Docusearch obtained for him. After Youens had obtained the address of Boyer's place of employment, he drove to the workplace, fatally shot her, and then shot and killed himself.

Helen Remsburg, Boyer's mother, sued Docusearch, claiming that the defendant had acted wrongfully. The

federal district court referred the case to the New Hampshire Supreme Court for a determination of the parties' duties under the state's common law. The state supreme court held that an information broker who sells information about a third person to a client has a duty to exercise reasonable care in disclosing the information.

A Foreseeable Risk?

One of the key issues for the court was whether the crime committed by Youens was a foreseeable risk to Docusearch. Remember from Chapter 5 that under tort law, the test for proximate cause—and the extent of a defendant's duty of care—is the foreseeability of a risk of harm. If certain consequences of an action are not foreseeable, there is no proximate cause.

In determining whether a risk of criminal misconduct was foreseeable to Docusearch, the Supreme Court of New Hampshire found that Docusearch's information disclosure presented two foreseeable risks: stalking and identity theft. Therefore, the company had a duty to exercise reasonable care in disclosing personal information about Boyer to Youens. Because Docusearch had not exercised reasonable care (taken steps to find out if Youens's requests were for a legitimate purpose), Docusearch could be sued for damages for breaching this duty.

For Critical Analysis *What other crimes can you think of, in addition to stalking and identity theft, that might qualify as "foreseeable risks" created by the online sale of personal data by information brokers?*

a. 149 N.H. 148, 816 A.2d 1001 (2003).

prolonged disruption of computer, cable, satellite, or telecommunications systems due to the actions of expert hackers would have serious repercussions on business operations—and national security—on a global level. Computer viruses are another tool that can be used by cyberterrorists to cripple communications networks.

ETHICAL ISSUE 6.1 ***Is it possible to control cyber crime without sacrificing some civil liberties?***

Governments in some countries, such as China, have succeeded in controlling Internet crime to a certain extent by monitoring the e-mail and other electronic transmissions of users of specific Internet service providers. In the United States, however, Americans have been reluctant to allow the government to monitor Internet use to detect criminal conspiracies or terrorist activities. The traditional attitude has been that civil liberties must be safeguarded to the greatest extent feasible.

As noted in Chapter 4, however, after the terrorist attacks on the World Trade Center and the Pentagon in September 2001, Congress enacted legislation, including the USA Patriot Act, to give law enforcement personnel more authority to conduct electronic surveillance, such as monitoring Web sites and e-mail exchanges. For a time, it seemed that the terrorist attacks might have made Americans more willing to trade off some of their civil liberties for greater national security. Today, however, many complain that this legislation has gone too far in curbing traditional civil liberties guaranteed by the U.S. Constitution.

Prosecuting Cyber Crimes

The "location" of cyber crime (cyberspace) has raised new issues in the investigation of crimes and the prosecution of offenders. A threshold issue is, of course, jurisdiction. A person who commits an act against a business in California, where the act is a cyber crime, might never have set foot in California but might instead reside in New York, or even in Canada, where the act may not be a crime. If the crime was committed via e-mail, the question arises as to whether the e-mail would constitute sufficient "minimum contacts" (see Chapter 3) for the victim's state to exercise jurisdiction over the perpetrator.

Identifying the wrongdoers can also be difficult. Cyber criminals do not leave physical traces, such as fingerprints or DNA samples, as evidence of their crimes. Even electronic "footprints" can be hard to find and follow. For example, e-mail may be sent through a remailer, an online service that guarantees that a message cannot be traced to its source.

For these reasons, laws written to protect physical property are difficult to apply in cyberspace. Nonetheless, governments at both the state and federal levels have taken significant steps toward controlling cyber crime, both by applying existing criminal statutes and by enacting new laws that specifically address wrongs committed in cyberspace.

The Computer Fraud and Abuse Act   Perhaps the most significant federal statute specifically addressing cyber crime is the Counterfeit Access Device and Computer Fraud and Abuse Act of 1984 (commonly known as the Computer Fraud and Abuse Act, or CFAA). This act, as amended by the National Information Infrastructure Protection Act of 1996,[24] provides, among other things, that a person who accesses a computer online, without authority, to obtain classified, restricted, or protected data, or attempts to do so, is subject to criminal prosecution. Such data could include financial and credit records, medical records, legal files, military and national security files, and other confidential information in government or private computers. The crime has two elements: accessing a computer without authority and taking the data.

This theft is a felony if it is committed for a commercial purpose or for private financial gain, or if the value of the stolen data (or computer time) exceeds $5,000. Penalties include fines and imprisonment for up to twenty

---

24. 18 U.S.C. Section 1030.

years. A victim of computer theft can also bring a civil suit against the violator to obtain damages, an injunction, and other relief.

Other Federal Statutes   The federal wire fraud statute, the Economic Espionage Act of 1996, and RICO, all of which were discussed earlier in this chapter, extend to crimes committed in cyberspace as well. Other federal statutes that may apply include the Electronic Fund Transfer Act of 1978, which makes unauthorized access to an electronic fund transfer system a crime; the Anticounterfeiting Consumer Protection Act of 1996, which increased penalties for stealing copyrighted or trademarked property; and the National Stolen Property Act of 1988, which concerns the interstate transport of stolen property. Recall from Chapter 4 that the federal government has also enacted laws (many of which have been challenged on constitutional grounds) to protect minors from online pornographic materials. In later chapters of this text, you will read about other federal statutes and regulations that are designed to address wrongs committed in cyberspace in specific areas of the law.

REVIEWING . . . CRIMINAL LAW AND CYBER CRIMES

Edward Hanousek worked for Pacific & Arctic Railway and Navigation Corporation (P&A) as a roadmaster of the White Pass & Yukon Railroad in Alaska. As an officer of the corporation, Hanousek was responsible "for every detail of the safe and efficient maintenance and construction of track, structures, and marine facilities of the entire railroad," including special projects. One project was a rock quarry, known as "6-mile," above the Skagway River. Next to the quarry, and just beneath the surface, ran a high-pressure oil pipeline owned by Pacific & Arctic Pipeline, Inc., P&A's sister company. When the quarry's backhoe operator punctured the pipeline, an estimated 1,000 to 5,000 gallons of oil were discharged into the river. Hanousek was charged with negligently discharging a harmful quantity of oil into a navigable water of the United States in violation of the criminal provisions of the Clean Water Act (CWA). Using the information presented in the chapter, answer the following questions.

1. Did Hanousek have the required mental state *(mens rea)* to be convicted of a crime? Why or why not?

2. Which theory discussed in the chapter would enable a court to hold Hanousek criminally liable for violating the statute regardless of whether he participated in, directed, or even knew about the specific violation?

3. Could the quarry's backhoe operator who punctured the pipeline also be charged with a crime in this situation? Why or why not?

4. Suppose that at trial, Hanousek argued that he could not be convicted because he was not aware of the requirements of the Clean Water Act. Would this defense be successful? Why or why not?

KEY TERMS

arson   180

beyond a reasonable doubt   175

burglary   179

computer crime   199

consent   186

crime   175

cyber crime   174

cyberstalker   200

cyberterrorist   201

double jeopardy   190

duress   186

embezzlement   180

entrapment   187

exclusionary rule   193

felony   176

forgery   180

grand jury   197

hacker   201

identity theft   200

indictment   197

information   197

insider trading   182

larceny   179

misdemeanor   176

CHAPTER SUMMARY • CRIMINAL LAW AND CYBER CRIMES

Civil Law and Criminal Law (See pages 175–176.)	1. *Civil law*—Spells out the duties that exist between persons or between citizens and their governments, excluding the duty not to commit crimes.
	2. *Criminal law*—Has to do with crimes, which are defined as wrongs against society proclaimed in statutes and punishable by society through fines and/or imprisonment—and, in some cases, death. Because crimes are *offenses against society as a whole*, they are prosecuted by a public official, not by victims.
	3. *Key differences*—An important difference between civil and criminal law is that the burden of proof is higher in criminal cases (see Exhibit 6–1 on page 175 for other differences between criminal and civil law).
	4. *Civil liability for criminal acts*—A criminal act may give rise to both criminal liability and tort liability (see Exhibit 6–2 on page 176 for an example of criminal and tort liability for the same act).
Classification of Crimes (See pages 176–177.)	1. *Felonies*—Serious crimes punishable by death or by imprisonment in a penitentiary for more than one year.
	2. *Misdemeanors*—Under federal law and in most states, any crimes that are not felonies.
Criminal Liability (See page 177.)	1. *Guilty act*—In general, some form of harmful act must be committed for a crime to exist.
	2. *Intent*—An intent to commit a crime, or a wrongful mental state, is generally required for a crime to exist.
Corporate Criminal Liability (See page 178.)	1. *Liability of corporations*—Corporations normally are liable for the crimes committed by their agents and employees within the course and scope of their employment. Corporations cannot be imprisoned, but they can be fined or denied certain legal privileges.
	2. *Liability of corporate officers and directors*—Corporate directors and officers are personally liable for the crimes they commit and may be held liable for the actions of employees under their supervision.
Types of Crimes (See pages 178–183.)	1. *Violent crime*—
	a. Definition—Crimes that cause others to suffer harm or death.
	b. Examples—Murder, assault and battery, sexual assault (rape), and robbery.
	2. *Property crime*—
	a. Definition—Crimes in which the goal of the offender is some form of economic gain or the damaging of property; the most common form of crime.
	b. Examples—Burglary, larceny, arson, receiving stolen goods, forgery, and obtaining goods by false pretenses.
	3. *Public order crime*—
	a. Definition—Crimes contrary to public values and morals.
	b. Examples—Public drunkenness, prostitution, gambling, and illegal drug use.
	4. *White-collar crime*—
	a. Definition—An illegal act or series of acts committed by an individual or business entity using some nonviolent means to obtain a personal or business advantage; usually committed in the course of a legitimate occupation.

(Continued)

CHAPTER SUMMARY • CRIMINAL LAW AND CYBER CRIMES—CONTINUED

Types of Crimes—Continued	b. Examples—Embezzlement, mail and wire fraud, bribery, bankruptcy fraud, theft of trade secrets, and insider trading.
	
	5. *Organized crime—*
	
	  a. Definition—A form of crime conducted by groups operating illegitimately to provide the public with illegal goods and services (such as gambling or illegal narcotics).
	
	  b. Money laundering—The establishment of legitimate enterprises through which "dirty" money (obtained through criminal activities, such as organized crime) can be "laundered" (made to appear to be legitimate income).
	
	  c. RICO—The Racketeer Influenced and Corrupt Organizations Act (RICO) of 1970 makes it a federal crime to (1) use income obtained from racketeering activity to purchase any interest in an enterprise, (2) acquire or maintain an interest in an enterprise through racketeering activity, (3) conduct or participate in the affairs of an enterprise through racketeering activity, or (4) conspire to do any of the preceding activities. RICO provides for both civil and criminal liability.

Defenses to Criminal Liability (See pages 184–187.)	Defenses to criminal liability include infancy, intoxication, insanity, mistake, consent, duress, justifiable use of force, entrapment, and the statute of limitations. Also, in some cases defendants may be relieved of criminal liability, at least in part, if they are given immunity.
Constitutional Safeguards and Criminal Procedures (See pages 187–195.)	1. *Fourth Amendment*—Provides protection against unreasonable searches and seizures and requires that probable cause exist before a warrant for a search or an arrest can be issued. 2. *Fifth Amendment*—Requires due process of law, prohibits double jeopardy, and protects against self-incrimination. 3. *Sixth Amendment*—Provides guarantees of a speedy trial, a trial by jury, a public trial, the right to confront witnesses, and the right to counsel. 4. *Eighth Amendment*—Prohibits excessive bail and fines, as well as cruel and unusual punishment. 5. *Exclusionary rule*—A criminal procedural rule that prohibits the introduction at trial of all evidence obtained in violation of constitutional rights, as well as any evidence derived from the illegally obtained evidence. 6. *Miranda rule*—A rule set forth by the Supreme Court in *Miranda v. Arizona* that individuals who are arrested must be informed of certain constitutional rights, including their right to counsel.
Criminal Process (See pages 195–199.)	1. *Arrest, indictment, and trial*—Procedures governing arrest, indictment, and trial for a crime are designed to safeguard the rights of the individual against the state. See Exhibit 6–3 on page 196 for a summary of the procedural steps involved in prosecuting a criminal case. 2. *Sentencing guidelines*—Both the federal government and the states have established sentencing laws or guidelines. The federal sentencing guidelines indicate a range of penalties for each federal crime; federal judges must abide by these guidelines when imposing sentences on those convicted of federal crimes.
Cyber Crimes (See pages 199–204.)	Cyber crime is any crime that occurs in cyberspace. Examples include cyber theft (financial crimes committed with the aid of computers, as well as identity theft), cyberstalking, hacking, and cyberterrorism. Significant federal statutes addressing cyber crimes include the Electronic Fund Transfer Act of 1978 and the Counterfeit Access Device and Computer Fraud and Abuse Act of 1984, as amended by the National Information Infrastructure Protection Act of 1996.

FOR REVIEW

Answers for the even-numbered questions in this **For Review** *section can be found in Appendix O at the end of this text.*

1. What two elements must exist before a person can be held liable for a crime? Can a corporation commit crimes?

2. What are five broad categories of crimes? What is white-collar crime?

3. What defenses might be raised by criminal defendants to avoid liability for criminal acts?

4. What constitutional safeguards exist to protect persons accused of crimes? What are the basic steps in the criminal process?

5. What is cyber crime? What laws apply to crimes committed in cyberspace?

QUESTIONS AND CASE PROBLEMS

6–1. Criminal versus Civil Trials. In criminal trials, the defendant must be proved guilty beyond a reasonable doubt, whereas in civil trials, the defendant need only be proved guilty by a preponderance of the evidence. Discuss why a higher burden of proof is required in criminal trials.

Question with Sample Answer

6–2. The following situations are similar (all involve the theft of Makoto's television set), yet they represent three different crimes. Identify the three crimes, noting the differences among them.

1. While passing Makoto's house one night, Sarah sees a portable television set left unattended on Makoto's lawn. Sarah takes the television set, carries it home, and tells everyone she owns it.

2. While passing Makoto's house one night, Sarah sees Makoto outside with a portable television set. Holding Makoto at gunpoint, Sarah forces him to give up the set. Then Sarah runs away with it.

3. While passing Makoto's house one night, Sarah sees a portable television set in a window. Sarah breaks the front-door lock, enters, and leaves with the set.

For a sample answer to this question, go to Appendix P at the end of this text.

6–3. Types of Crimes. Which, if any, of the following crimes necessarily involve illegal activity on the part of more than one person?

1. Bribery.
2. Forgery.
3. Embezzlement.
4. Larceny.
5. Receiving stolen property.

6–4. Double Jeopardy. Armington, while robbing a drugstore, shot and seriously injured Jennings, a drugstore clerk. Armington was subsequently convicted in a criminal trial of armed robbery and assault and battery. Jennings later brought a civil tort suit against Armington for damages. Armington contended that he could not be tried again for the same crime, as that would constitute double jeopardy, which is prohibited by the Fifth Amendment to the Constitution. Is Armington correct? Explain.

6–5. Fifth Amendment. The federal government was investigating a corporation and its employees. The alleged criminal wrongdoing, which included the falsification of corporate books and records, occurred between 1993 and 1996 in one division of the corporation. In 1999, the corporation pleaded guilty and agreed to cooperate in an investigation of the individuals who might have been involved in the improper corporate activities. "Doe I," "Doe II," and "Doe III" were officers of the corporation during the period when the illegal activities occurred and worked in the division where the wrongdoing took place. They were no longer working for the corporation, however, when, as part of the subsequent investigation, the government asked them to provide specific corporate documents in their possession. All three asserted the Fifth Amendment privilege against self-incrimination. The government asked a federal district court to order the three to produce the records. Corporate employees can be compelled to produce corporate records in a criminal proceeding because they hold the records as representatives of the corporation, to which the Fifth Amendment privilege against self-incrimination does not apply. Should *former* employees also be compelled to produce corporate records in their possession? Why or why not? [*In re Three Grand Jury Subpoenas* Duces Tecum *Dated January 29, 1999,* 191 F.3d 173 (2d Cir. 1999)]

Case Problem with Sample Answer

6–6. The District of Columbia Lottery Board licensed Soo Young Bae, a Washington, D.C., merchant, to operate a terminal that prints and dispenses lottery tickets for sale. Bae used the terminal to generate tickets with a face value of $525,586, for which he did not pay. The winning tickets among these had a total redemption value of $296,153, of which Bae successfully obtained all but $72,000. Bae pleaded guilty to computer fraud, and the court sentenced him to eighteen months in prison. In sentencing a defendant for fraud, a federal court must make a reasonable estimate of the victim's loss. The court determined that the value of the loss due to the fraud was $503,650—the market value of the tickets less the commission Bae would have received from the lottery board had he sold those tickets. Bae appealed, arguing that "[a]t the instant any lottery ticket is printed," it is worth whatever value the lottery drawing later assigns to it; that is, losing tickets have no value. Bae thus calculated the loss at $296,153, the value of his winning tickets. Should the U.S. Court of Appeals for the District of Columbia Circuit affirm or reverse Bae's sentence? Why? [*United States v. Bae,* 250 F.3d 774 (C.A.D.C. 2001)]

After you have answered this problem, compare your answer with the sample answer given on the Web site that accompanies this text. Go to www.thomsonedu.com/westbuslaw/let, select "Chapter 6," and click on "Case Problem with Sample Answer."

6–7. Larceny. In February 2001, a homeowner hired Jimmy Smith, a contractor claiming to employ a crew of thirty workers, to build a garage. The homeowner paid Smith $7,950 and agreed to make additional payments as needed to complete the project, up to $15,900. Smith promised to start the next day and finish within eight weeks. Nearly a month passed with no work, while Smith lied to the homeowner that materials were on "back order." During a second month, footings were created for the foundation, and a subcontractor poured the concrete slab, but Smith did not return the homeowner's phone calls. After eight weeks, the homeowner confronted Smith, who promised to complete the job, worked on the site that day until lunch, and never returned. Three months later, the homeowner again confronted Smith, who promised to "pay [him] off" later that day but did not do so. In March 2002, the state of Georgia filed criminal charges against Smith. While his trial was pending, he promised to pay the homeowner "next week" but again failed to refund any money. The value of the labor performed before Smith abandoned the project was between $800 and $1,000, the value of the materials was $367, and the subcontractor was paid $2,270. Did Smith commit larceny? Explain. [*Smith v. State of Georgia*, 265 Ga.App. 57, 592 S.E.2d 871 (2004)]

6–8. Trial. Robert Michels met Allison Formal through an online dating Web site in 2002. Michels represented himself as the retired chief executive officer of a large company that he had sold for millions of dollars. In January 2003, Michels proposed that he and Formal create a limited liability company (a special form of business organization discussed in Chapter 11)—Formal Properties Trust, LLC—to "channel their investments in real estate." Formal agreed to contribute $100,000 to the company and wrote two $50,000 checks to "Michels and Associates, LLC." Six months later, Michels told Formal that their LLC had been formed in Delaware. Later, Formal asked Michels about her investments. He responded evasively, and she demanded that an independent accountant review the firm's records. Michels refused. Formal contacted the police. Michels was charged in a Virginia state court with obtaining money by false pretenses. The Delaware secretary of state verified, in two certified documents, that "Formal Properties Trust, L.L.C." and "Michels and Associates, L.L.C." did not exist in Delaware. Did the admission of the Delaware secretary of state's certified documents at Michels's trial violate his rights under the Sixth Amendment? Why or why not? [*Michels v. Commonwealth of Virginia*, 47 Va.App. 461, 624 S.E.2d 675 (2006)]

A Question of Ethics

6–9. A troublesome issue concerning the constitutional privilege against self-incrimination has to do with "jail plants"—that is, undercover police officers placed in cells with criminal suspects to gain information from the suspects. For example, in one case the police placed an undercover agent, Parisi, in a jail cell block with Lloyd Perkins, who had been imprisoned on charges unrelated to the murder that Parisi was investigating. When Parisi asked Perkins if he had ever killed anyone, Perkins made statements implicating himself in the murder. Perkins was then charged with the murder. [*Illinois v. Perkins*, 496 U.S. 292, 110 S.Ct. 2394, 110 L.Ed.2d 243 (1990)]

1. Review the discussion of *Miranda v. Arizona* in this chapter's *Landmark in the Legal Environment* feature. Should Perkins's statements be suppressed—that is, not be admissible as evidence at trial—because he was not "read his rights," as required by the *Miranda* decision, prior to making his self-incriminating statements? Does *Miranda* apply to Perkins's situation?
2. Do you think that it is fair for the police to resort to trickery and deception to bring those who have committed crimes to justice? Why or why not? What rights or public policies must be balanced in deciding this issue?

Critical-Thinking Legal Question

6–10. Ray steals a purse from an unattended car at a gas station. Because the purse contains money and a handgun, Ray is convicted of grand theft of property (cash) and grand theft of a firearm. On appeal, Ray claims that he is not guilty of grand theft of a firearm because he did not know that the purse contained a gun. Can Ray be convicted of the crime of grand theft of a firearm even though he did not know that a gun was in the purse?

Video Question

6–11. Go to this text's Web site at www.thomsonedu.com/westbuslaw/let and select "Chapter 6." Click on "Video Questions" and view the video titled *Casino*. Then answer the following questions.

1. In the video, a casino manager, Ace (Robert DeNiro), discusses how politicians "won their 'comp life' when they got elected." "Comps" are the free gifts that casinos give to high-stakes gamblers to keep their business. If an elected official accepts comps, is he or she committing a crime? If so, what type of crime? Explain your answers.

2. Assume that Ace committed a crime by giving politicians comps. Can the casino, Tangiers Corp., be held liable for that crime? Why or why not? How could a court punish the corporation?

3. Suppose that the Federal Bureau of Investigation wants to search the premises of Tangiers for evidence of criminal activity. If casino management refuses to consent to the search, what constitutional safeguards and criminal procedures, if any, protect Tangiers?

INTERACTING WITH THE INTERNET

For updated links to resources available on the Web, as well as a variety of other materials, visit this text's Web site at

www.thomsonedu.com/westbuslaw/let

The Bureau of Justice Statistics in the U.S. Department of Justice offers an impressive collection of statistics on crime at the following Web site:

www.ojp.usdoj.gov/bjs

The following Web site, which is maintained by the U.S. Department of Justice, offers information ranging from the various types of cyber crime to a description of how computers and the Internet are being used to prosecute cyber crime:

www.cybercrime.gov

If you would like to learn more about criminal procedures, the following site offers an "Anatomy of a Murder: A Trip through Our Nation's Legal Justice System":

library.thinkquest.org/2760

INTERNET EXERCISES

Go to **www.thomsonedu.com/westbuslaw/let**, the Web site that accompanies this text. Select "Chapter 6" and click on "Internet Exercises." There you will find the following Internet research exercises that you can perform to learn more about topics covered in this chapter.

Internet Exercise 6–1: LEGAL PERSPECTIVE—Revisiting *Miranda*
Internet Exercise 6–2: MANAGEMENT PERSPECTIVE—Hackers
Internet Exercise 6–3: INTERNATIONAL PERSPECTIVE—Fighting Cyber Crime Worldwide

BEFORE THE TEST

Go to **www.thomsonedu.com/westbuslaw/let**, the Web site that accompanies this text. Select "Chapter 6" and click on "Interactive Quizzes." You will find a number of interactive questions relating to this chapter.

CompTac, Inc., which is headquartered in San Francisco, California, is one of the leading software manufacturers in the United States. The company invests millions of dollars in researching and developing new software applications and computer games that are sold worldwide. It also has a large service department and has taken great pains to offer its customers excellent support services.

1. A customer at one of CompTac's retail stores stumbles over a crate in the parking lot and breaks her leg. The crate had just moments before fallen off a CompTac truck that was delivering goods from a CompTac warehouse to the store. The customer sues CompTac, alleging negligence. Will she succeed in her suit? Why or why not?

2. Roban Electronics, a software manufacturer and one of CompTac's major competitors, has been trying to convince one of CompTac's key employees, Jim Baxter, to come to work for Roban. Roban knows that Baxter has a written employment contract with CompTac, which Baxter would breach if he left CompTac before the contract expired. Baxter goes to work for Roban, and the departure of its key employee causes CompTac to suffer substantial losses due to delays in completing new software. Can CompTac sue Roban to recoup some of these losses? If so, on what ground?

3. Joanna Wexburg enters one of CompTac's retail stores and talks to a salesperson about CompTac's computers. Joanna wants to purchase a computer that will run a complicated new engineering graphics program at a realistic speed. CompTac sells Joanna a computer with a CPU of only 2 gigahertz, even though a speed of at least 3.2 gigahertz would be required to run Joanna's graphics program at a "realistic speed." After discovering that it takes forever to run her program, Joanna returns the computer, asking for a full refund. On what legal theory can Joanna base her claim that she is entitled to a refund? Explain fully.

4. One of CompTac's employees in its accounting division, Alan Green, has a gambling problem. To repay a gambling debt of $10,000, Green decides to "borrow" some money from CompTac to cover the debt. Using his "hacking" skills and his knowledge of CompTac account numbers, Green electronically transfers CompTac funds into his personal checking account. A week later, he is luckier at gambling and uses the same electronic procedures to transfer funds from his personal checking account to the relevant CompTac account. Has Green committed any crimes? If so, what are they?

CONTENTS

CHAPTER 7

Intellectual Property

CONTENTS

CHAPTER OBJECTIVES

After reading this chapter, you should be able to answer the following questions:

1. What is intellectual property?

2. Why are trademarks and patents protected by the law?

3. What laws protect authors' rights in the works they generate?

4. What are trade secrets, and what laws offer protection for this form of intellectual property?

5. What steps have been taken to protect intellectual property rights in today's digital age?

"The Internet, by virtue of its ability to mesh what will be hundreds of millions of people together, ... is ... a profoundly different capability that by and large human beings have not had before."

—TONY RUTKOWSKI, 1943–present
(Executive director of the Internet Society, 1994–1996)

INTELLECTUAL PROPERTY
Property resulting from intellectual, creative processes.

OF SIGNIFICANT CONCERN to businesspersons today is the need to protect their rights in intellectual property. **Intellectual property** is any property resulting from intellectual, creative processes—the products of an individual's mind. Although it is an abstract term for an abstract concept, intellectual property is nonetheless wholly familiar to virtually everyone. The information contained in books and computer files is intellectual property. The software you use, the movies you see, and the music you listen to are all forms of intellectual property. In fact, in today's information age, it should come as no surprise that the value of the world's intellectual property probably now exceeds the value of physical property, such as machines and houses.

The need to protect creative works was voiced by the framers of the U.S. Constitution over two hundred years ago: Article I, Section 8, of the Constitution authorized Congress "[t]o promote the Progress of Science and useful Arts, by securing for limited Times to Authors and Inventors the exclusive Right to their respective Writings and Discoveries." Laws protecting patents, trademarks, and copyrights are explicitly designed to protect and reward inventive and artistic creativity. Exhibit 7–1 offers a comprehensive summary of these forms of intellectual property, as well as intellectual property that consists of *trade secrets*.

An understanding of intellectual property law is important because intellectual property has taken on increasing significance, not only in the United States but globally as well. Today, ownership rights in intangible intellectual property are more important to the prosperity of many U.S. companies than are their tangible assets. As you will read in this chapter, protecting these assets in today's online world has proved particularly challenging. This is because, as indicated in the chapter-opening quotation, the Internet's capability is "profoundly different" from anything we have had in the past.

EXHIBIT 7-1   FORMS OF INTELLECTUAL PROPERTY

	DEFINITION	HOW ACQUIRED	DURATION	REMEDY FOR INFRINGEMENT
Patent	A grant from the government that gives an inventor exclusive rights to an invention.	By filing a patent application with the U.S. Patent and Trademark Office and receiving its approval.	Twenty years from the date of the application; for design patents, fourteen years.	Money damages, including royalties and lost profits, *plus* attorneys' fees. Damages may be tripled for intentional infringements.
Copyright	The right of an author or originator of a literary or artistic work, or other production that falls within a specified category, to have the exclusive use of that work for a given period of time.	Automatic (once the work or creation is put in tangible form). Only the *expression* of an idea (and not the idea itself) can be protected by copyright.	For authors: the life of the author plus 70 years. For publishers: 95 years after the date of publication or 120 years after creation.	Actual damages plus profits received by the party who infringed *or* statutory damages under the Copyright Act, *plus* costs and attorneys' fees in either situation.
Trademark (Service Mark and Trade Dress)	Any distinctive word, name, symbol, or device (image or appearance), or combination thereof, that an entity uses to distinguish its goods or services from those of others. The owner has the exclusive right to use that mark or trade dress.	1. At common law, ownership created by use of the mark. 2. Registration with the appropriate federal or state office gives notice and is permitted if the mark is currently in use or will be within the next six months.	Unlimited, as long as it is in use. To continue notice by registration, the owner must renew by filing between the fifth and sixth years, and thereafter, every ten years.	1. Injunction prohibiting the future use of the mark. 2. Actual damages plus profits received by the party who infringed (can be increased under the Lanham Act). 3. Destruction of articles that infringed. 4. *Plus* costs and attorneys' fees.
Trade Secret	Any information that a business possesses and that gives the business an advantage over competitors (including formulas, lists, patterns, plans, processes, and programs).	Through the originality and development of the information and processes that constitute the business secret and are unknown to others.	Unlimited, so long as not revealed to others. Once revealed to others, they are no longer trade secrets.	Money damages for misappropriation (the Uniform Trade Secrets Act also permits punitive damages if willful), *plus* costs and attorneys' fees.

TRADEMARKS AND RELATED PROPERTY

A **trademark** is a distinctive mark, motto, device, or emblem that a manufacturer stamps, prints, or otherwise affixes to the goods it produces so that they can be identified on the market and their origins made known. At common law, the person who used a symbol or mark to identify a business or product was protected in the use of that trademark. Clearly, by using another's trademark, a business could lead consumers to believe that its goods were made by the other business. The law seeks to avoid this kind of confusion. In the following classic case concerning Coca-Cola, the defendants argued that the Coca-Cola trademark was entitled to no protection under the law because the term did not accurately represent the product.

TRADEMARK
A distinctive mark, motto, device, or emblem that a manufacturer stamps, prints, or otherwise affixes to the goods it produces so that they may be identified on the market and their origins made known. Once a trademark is established (under the common law or through registration), the owner is entitled to its exclusive use.

LANDMARK & CLASSIC CASES

CASE 7.1 **The Coca-Cola Co. v. Koke Co. of America**

Supreme Court of the United States, 1920.
254 U.S. 143,
41 S.Ct. 113,
65 L.Ed. 189.
www.findlaw.com/casecode/supreme.html[a]

BACKGROUND AND FACTS The Coca-Cola Company brought an action in a federal district court to enjoin other

a. This is the "U.S. Supreme Court Opinions" page within the Web site of the "FindLaw Internet Legal Resources" database. This page provides several options for accessing an opinion. Because you know the citation for this case, you can go to the "Citation Search" box, type in the appropriate volume and page numbers for the *United States Reports* ("254" and "143," respectively, for the *Coca-Cola* case), and click on "Get It."

beverage companies from using the words *Koke* and *Dope* for the defendants' products. The defendants contended that the Coca-Cola trademark was a fraudulent representation and that Coca-Cola was therefore not entitled to any help from the courts. By use of the Coca-Cola name, the defendants alleged, the Coca-Cola Company represented that the beverage contained cocaine (from coca leaves). The district court granted the injunction, but the federal appellate court reversed. The Coca-Cola Company appealed to the United States Supreme Court.

IN THE WORDS OF THE COURT . . . Mr. Justice HOLMES delivered the opinion of the court.

* * * *

* * * Before 1900 the beginning of [Coca-Cola's] good will was more or less helped by the presence of cocaine, a drug that, like alcohol or caffein or opium, may be described as a deadly poison or as a valuable item of the pharmacopœa [collection of pharmaceuticals] according to the [purposes of the speaker]. * * * [A]fter the Food and Drug Act of June 30, 1906, if not earlier, long before this suit was brought, it was eliminated from the plaintiff's compound. * * *

* * * Since 1900 the sales have increased at a very great rate corresponding to a like increase in advertising. The name now characterizes a beverage to be had at almost any soda fountain. It means a single thing coming from a single source, and well known to the community. It hardly would be too much to say that the drink characterizes the name as much as the name the drink. In other words Coca-Cola probably means to most persons the plaintiff's familiar product to be had everywhere rather than a compound of particular substances. * * * [B]efore this suit was brought the plaintiff had advertised to the public that it must not expect and would not find cocaine, and had eliminated everything tending to suggest cocaine effects except the name and the picture of the leaves and nuts, which probably conveyed little or nothing to most who saw it. It appears to us that it would be going too far to deny the plaintiff relief against a palpable fraud because possibly here and there an ignorant person might call for the drink with the hope for incipient cocaine intoxication. The plaintiff's position must be judged by the facts as they were when the suit was begun, not by the facts of a different condition and an earlier time.

DECISION AND REMEDY The United States Supreme Court upheld the district court's injunction. The competing beverage companies were enjoined from calling their products "Koke." The Court did not prevent them from calling their products "Dope," however.

IMPACT OF THIS CASE ON TODAY'S LEGAL ENVIRONMENT
In this classic case, the United States Supreme Court made it clear that trademarks and trade names (and nicknames for those marks and names, such as the nickname "Coke" for "Coca-Cola") that are in everyday use receive protection

under the common law. This holding is historically significant because the federal statute later passed to protect trademark rights (the Lanham Act of 1946, to be discussed shortly) in many ways represented a codification of common law principles governing trademarks.

RELEVANT WEB SITES *To locate information on the Web concerning the Coca-Cola Co. decision, go to this text's Web site at **www.thomsonedu.com/westbuslaw/let**, select "Chapter 7," and click on "URLs for Landmarks."*

Statutory Protection of Trademarks

Statutory protection of trademarks and related property is provided at the federal level by the Lanham Act of 1946.[1] The Lanham Act was enacted in part to protect manufacturers from losing business to rival companies that used confusingly similar trademarks. The Lanham Act incorporates the common law of trademarks and provides remedies for owners of trademarks who wish to enforce their claims in federal court. Many states also have trademark statutes.

In 1995, Congress amended the Lanham Act by passing the Federal Trademark Dilution Act,[2] which extended the protection available to trademark owners by creating a federal cause of action for trademark *dilution*. Until the passage of this amendment, federal trademark law prohibited only the unauthorized use of the same mark on competing—or on noncompeting but "related"—goods or services when such use would likely confuse consumers as to the origin of those goods and services. Trademark dilution laws protect "distinctive" or "famous" trademarks (such as Jergens, McDonald's, RCA, and Macintosh) from certain unauthorized uses of the marks *regardless* of a showing of competition or a likelihood of confusion. In 2003, the United States Supreme Court held that to demonstrate dilution under the federal act, some evidence must establish that the allegedly infringing user's mark actually reduces the value of the famous mark or lessens its capacity to identify goods and services.[3] A famous mark may be diluted not only by the use of an *identical* mark but also by the use of a *similar* mark.[4] More than half of the states have also enacted trademark dilution laws.

> "The protection of trademarks is the law's recognition of the psychological function of symbols. If it is true that we live by symbols, it is no less true that we purchase goods by them."
>
> —FELIX FRANKFURTER, 1882–1965
> (Associate justice of the United States Supreme Court, 1939–1962)

Trademark Registration

Trademarks may be registered with the state or with the federal government. To register for protection under federal trademark law, a person must file an application with the U.S. Patent and Trademark Office in Washington, D.C. Under current law, a mark can be registered (1) if it is currently in commerce or (2) if the applicant intends to put the mark into commerce within six months.

In special circumstances, the six-month period can be extended by thirty months, giving the applicant a total of three years from the date of notice of trademark approval to make use of the mark and file the required use statement. Registration is postponed until the mark is actually used. Nonetheless, during this waiting period, any applicant can legally protect his or her trademark against a third party who previously has neither used the mark nor filed an application for it. Registration is renewable between the fifth and sixth years after the initial registration and every ten years thereafter (every twenty years for trademarks registered before 1990).

ETHICAL ISSUE 7.1   ***Should the courts cancel existing trademarks that are disparaging?***

The Lanham Act prohibits the U.S. Patent and Trademark Office from registering trademarks that are immoral, scandalous, or disparaging. Trademark examiners review applications and reject any proposed trademarks that are disparaging (demeaning) by today's standards. But what if

---

1. 15 U.S.C. Sections 1051–1128.
2. 15 U.S.C. Section 1125.
3. *Moseley v. V Secret Catalogue, Inc.,* 537 U.S. 418, 123 S.Ct. 1115, 155 L.Ed.2d 1 (2003).
4. See, for example, *Ringling Bros.–Barnum & Bailey, Combined Shows, Inc. v. Utah Division of Travel Development,* 935 F.Supp. 763 (E.D.Va. 1996).

a trademark that was registered some time ago is perceived as disparaging to a group of people today? Can that registration be canceled? According to a federal district court in 2003, the answer is no. The case involved the Washington Redskins, a professional football team, and six Native Americans (the plaintiffs) who argued that the trademark should be canceled because the term *redskins* is the most derogatory one used for native people.

The federal district court held that the plaintiffs had not presented enough evidence to prove that the mark was disparaging. According to the court, the test is not whether the trademark is disparaging to Native Americans at present but whether it was disparaging at the time it was originally registered. Here, the plaintiffs presented evidence that a number of Native Americans found the term insulting today. The plaintiffs also presented some evidence, including survey results and the testimony of historians and linguists, suggesting that the mark was disparaging when it was first registered in 1967. The court found that evidence insufficient, however, and held that the plaintiffs had waited too long to complain about the trademark. The district court's ruling was affirmed by a federal appellate court in 2005.[5]

Trademark Infringement

Registration of a trademark with the U.S. Patent and Trademark Office gives notice on a nationwide basis that the trademark belongs exclusively to the registrant. The registrant is also allowed to use the symbol ® to indicate that the mark has been registered. Whenever that trademark is copied to a substantial degree or used in its entirety by another, intentionally or unintentionally, the trademark has been *infringed* (used without authorization). When a trade-

---

5. *Pro-Football, Inc. v. Harjo*, 284 F.Supp.2d 96 (D.D.C. 2003); aff'd, at 415 F.3d 44 (C.A.D.C. 2005).

When Google started selling shares to the public, the company's staff was present at the event, as pictured in the large TV monitor on the right. The Google trademark has become well known worldwide. People even refer to doing an Internet search as "googling." If a new company named its search engine Goole or Joogle, how might Google respond? What federal act would help Google defend its trademark? (AP Photo/Kathy Willens)

mark has been infringed, the owner of the mark has a cause of action against the infringer. A person need not have registered a trademark in order to sue for trademark infringement, but registration does furnish proof of the date of inception of the trademark's use.

Only those trademarks that are deemed sufficiently distinctive from all competing trademarks will be protected, however. The trademarks must be sufficiently distinct to enable consumers to identify the manufacturer of the goods easily and to differentiate among competing products.

Strong Marks   Fanciful, arbitrary, or suggestive trademarks are generally considered to be the most distinctive (strongest) trademarks because they are normally taken from outside the context of the particular product and thus provide the best means of distinguishing one product from another.

| **Example #1**   Fanciful trademarks include invented words, such as "Xerox" for one manufacturer's copiers and "Kodak" for another company's photographic products. Arbitrary trademarks include actual words that have no literal connection to the product, such as "English Leather" used as a name for an aftershave lotion (and not for leather processed in England). Suggestive trademarks are those that suggest something about a product without describing the product directly. For instance, "Dairy Queen" suggests an association between its products and milk, but it does not directly describe ice cream. |

Secondary Meaning   Descriptive terms, geographic terms, and personal names are not inherently distinctive and do not receive protection under the law *until* they acquire a secondary meaning. A secondary meaning may arise when customers begin to associate a specific term or phrase, such as "London Fog," with specific trademarked items (coats with "London Fog" labels). Whether a secondary meaning becomes attached to a term or name usually depends on how extensively the product is advertised, the market for the product, the number of sales, and other factors. The United States Supreme Court has held that even a color can qualify for trademark protection.[6] Once a secondary meaning is attached to a term or name, a trademark is considered distinctive and is protected. At issue in the following case was whether a certain mark was suggestive or descriptive.

---

6. *Qualitex Co. v. Jacobson Products Co.*, 514 U.S. 159, 115 S.Ct. 1300, 131 L.Ed.2d 248 (1995).

CASE 7.2   **Menashe v. V Secret Catalogue, Inc.**

United States District Court,
Southern District of New York, 2006.
409 F.Supp.2d 412.

BACKGROUND AND FACTS   In autumn 2002, Victoria's Secret Stores, Inc., and its affiliated companies, including V Secret Catalogue, Inc., began to develop a panty collection to be named "SEXY LITTLE THINGS." In spring 2004, Ronit Menashe, a publicist, and Audrey Quock, a fashion model and actress, began to plan a line of women's underwear also called "SEXY LITTLE THINGS." Menashe and Quock designed their line, negotiated for its manufacture, registered the domain name **www.sexylittlethings.com**, and filed an intent-to-use (ITU) application with the U.S. Patent and Trademark Office (USPTO). In July, Victoria's Secret's collection appeared in its stores in Ohio, Michigan, and California, and, in less than three months, was prominently displayed in all its stores, in its catalogues, and on its Web site. By mid-November, more than 13 million units of the line had been sold, accounting for 4 percent of the company's sales for the year. When the firm applied to register "SEXY LITTLE THINGS"

CASE 7.2–CONTINUED ➡

CASE 7.2–CONTINUED

with the USPTO, it learned of Menashe and Quock's ITU application. The firm warned the pair that their use of the phrase constituted trademark infringement. Menashe and Quock filed a suit in a federal district court against V Secret Catalogue and others, asking the court to, among other things, declare "noninfringement of the trademark."

IN THE WORDS OF THE COURT . . . *BAER,* District Judge.

* * * *

Plaintiffs claim that Victoria's Secret has no right of priority in the Mark because "SEXY LITTLE THINGS" for lingerie is a descriptive term that had not attained secondary meaning by the time Plaintiffs filed their ITU application. Consequently, Plaintiffs assert that they have priority based on * * * their ITU application on September 13, 2004. Victoria's Secret counters that the Mark is suggestive and thus qualifies for trademark protection without proof of secondary meaning. Therefore, Victoria's Secret has priority by virtue of its bona fide use of the Mark in commerce beginning July 28, 2004.

* * * *

To merit trademark protection, a mark must be capable of distinguishing the products it marks from those of others. * * * A descriptive term * * * conveys an immediate idea of the ingredients, qualities, or characteristics of the goods. In contrast, a suggestive term requires imagination, thought, and perception to reach a conclusion as to the nature of the goods. *Suggestive marks are automatically protected because they are inherently distinctive; i.e., their intrinsic nature serves to identify a particular source of a product.* Descriptive marks are not inherently distinctive and may only be protected on a showing of secondary meaning; i.e., that the purchasing public associates the mark with a particular source. [Emphasis added.]

* * * [T]o distinguish suggestive from descriptive marks [a court considers] whether the purchaser must use some imagination to connect the mark to some characteristic of the product * * * and * * * whether the proposed use would deprive competitors of a way to describe their goods.

* * * I find "SEXY LITTLE THINGS" to be suggestive. First, while the term describes the erotically stimulating quality of the trademarked lingerie, it also calls to mind the phrase "sexy little thing" popularly used to refer to attractive lithe [nimble] young women. Hence, the Mark prompts the purchaser to mentally associate the lingerie with its targeted twenty- to thirty-year-old consumers. *Courts have classified marks that both describe the product and evoke other associations as inherently distinctive.* * * * [Also] it is hard to believe that Victoria's Secret's use of the Mark will deprive competitors of ways to describe their lingerie products. Indeed, Victoria's Secret's own descriptions of its lingerie in its catalogues and Web site illustrate that there are numerous ways to describe provocative underwear. [Emphasis added.]

* * * *

* * * Victoria's Secret used "SEXY LITTLE THINGS" as a trademark in commerce beginning on July 28, 2004. Commencing on that date, the prominent use of the Mark in four stores * * * satisfies the "use in commerce" requirement * * * . Similarly, Victoria's Secret's prominent use of the Mark in its catalogues beginning on September 4, 2004, and on its Web site beginning on or about September 9, 2004, together with pictures and descriptions of the goods meets the * * * test * * * . I find that because Victoria's Secret made bona fide trademark use of "SEXY LITTLE THINGS" in commerce before Plaintiffs filed their ITU application, and has continued to use that Mark in commerce, Victoria's Secret has acquired priority in the Mark.

DECISION AND REMEDY The court ruled that Menashe and Quock were not entitled to a judgment of "noninfringement" and dismissed the plaintiffs' complaint. The court concluded that "SEXY LITTLE THINGS" was a suggestive mark that Victoria's Secret used in commerce prior to the time the plaintiffs filed their ITU application. For this reason, Victoria's Secret had "priority in the Mark."

WHY IS THIS CASE IMPORTANT? *This case illustrates how a court distinguishes between trademarks that are "suggestive" (also called strong marks) and trademarks that are merely "descriptive." Only suggestive marks, such as "SEXY LITTLE THINGS," receive automatic protection under trademark law. The case is also notable for the court's characterization of the plaintiffs' suit as "defensive." ITU applicants may defend against other parties' claims of infringement but do not have the right to charge others with infringement. The court, however, "allow[ed] Plaintiffs here to preemptively defend against Victoria's Secret's efforts" to stop the use of the "SEXY LITTLE THINGS" mark.*

Generic Terms Generic terms (general, commonly used terms that refer to an entire class of products, such as *bicycle* or *computer*) receive no protection, even if they acquire secondary meanings. A particularly thorny problem arises when a trademark acquires generic use. For instance, *aspirin* and *thermos* were originally trademarked products, but today the words are used generically. Other examples are *escalator, trampoline, raisin bran, dry ice, lanolin, linoleum, nylon,* and *corn flakes.*

Note that a generic term will not be protected under trademark law even if the term has acquired a secondary meaning. **│Example #2** In one case, America Online, Inc. (AOL), sued AT&T Corporation, claiming that AT&T's use of "You Have Mail" on its WorldNet Service infringed AOL's trademark rights in the same phrase. The court ruled, however, that because each of the three words in the phrase was a generic term, the phrase as a whole was generic. Although the phrase had become widely associated with AOL's e-mail notification service, and thus may have acquired a secondary meaning, this issue was of no significance in this case. The court stated that it would not consider whether the mark had acquired any secondary meaning because "generic marks with secondary meaning are still not entitled to protection."[7]│

Service, Certification, and Collective Marks

A **service mark** is similar to a trademark but is used to distinguish the services of one person or company from those of another. For instance, each airline has a particular mark or symbol associated with its name. Titles and character names used in radio and television are frequently registered as service marks.

SERVICE MARK
A mark used in the sale or advertising of services to distinguish the services of one person from those of others. Titles, character names, and other distinctive features of radio and television programs may be registered as service marks.

Other marks protected by law include certification marks and collective marks. A *certification mark* is used by one or more persons other than the owner to certify the region, materials, mode of manufacture, quality, or accuracy of the owner's goods or services. When used by members of a cooperative, association, or other organization, it is referred to as a *collective mark.* **│Example #3** Certification marks include such marks as "Good Housekeeping Seal of Approval" and "UL Tested." Collective marks appear at the ends of

---

7. *America Online, Inc. v. AT&T Corp.,* 243 F.3d 812 (4th Cir. 2001).

The purple and orange colors displayed on FedEx envelopes, packets, and delivery vehicles (including this airplane) are a distinctive feature of that company. If a start-up company specializing in courier delivery services used those same colors, would the new company be infringing on FedEx's trademark? (Photo Courtesy of FedEx)

the credits of movies to indicate the various associations and organizations that participated in making the movie. The union marks found on the tags of certain products are also collective marks.|

Trade Names

TRADE NAME
A term that is used to indicate part or all of a business's name and that is directly related to the business's reputation and goodwill. Trade names are protected under the common law (and under trademark law, if the name is the same as that of the firm's trademarked property).

Trademarks apply to *products*. The term **trade name** is used to indicate part or all of a business's name, whether the business is a sole proprietorship, a partnership, or a corporation. Generally, a trade name is directly related to a business and its goodwill. Trade names may be protected as trademarks if the trade name is also the name of the company's trademarked product—for example, Coca-Cola. Unless also used as a trademark or service mark, a trade name cannot be registered with the federal government. Trade names are protected under the common law, however. As with trademarks, words must be unusual or fancifully used if they are to be protected as trade names. The word *Safeway*, for instance, was held by the courts to be sufficiently fanciful to obtain protection as a trade name for a grocery chain.[8]

Trade Dress

TRADE DRESS
The image and overall appearance of a product—for example, the distinctive decor, menu, layout, and style of service of a particular restaurant. Basically, trade dress is subject to the same protection as trademarks.

The term **trade dress** refers to the image and overall appearance of a product. Basically, trade dress is subject to the same protection as trademarks. |**Example #4** The distinctive decor, menu, layout, and style of service of a particular restaurant may be regarded as the restaurant's trade dress. Similarly, if a golf course is distinguished from other golf courses by prominent features, such

8. *Safeway Stores v. Suburban Foods*, 130 F.Supp. 249 (E.D.Va. 1955).

as a golf hole designed to look like a lighthouse, those features may be considered the golf course's trade dress. In cases involving trade dress infringement, as in trademark infringement cases, a major consideration is whether consumers are likely to be confused by the allegedly infringing use. Also, features that enhance a product's function will not be protected as trade dress.

CYBER MARKS

In cyberspace, trademarks are sometimes referred to as **cyber marks.** We turn now to a discussion of trademark-related issues in cyberspace and how new laws and the courts are addressing these issues. One concern relates to the rights of a trademark's owner to use the mark as part of a domain name (Internet address). Other issues have to do with cybersquatting, meta tags, and trademark dilution on the Web. The use of licensing as a way to avoid liability for infringing on another's intellectual property rights in cyberspace will also be discussed.

CYBER MARK
A trademark in cyberspace.

> **"**It was not so very long ago that people thought semiconductors were part-time orchestra leaders and microchips were very small snack foods.**"**
> —GERALDINE FERRARO, 1935–present (American politician; Democratic candidate for vice president in 1984)

Domain Names

In the real world, one business can often use the same name as another without causing any conflict, particularly if the businesses are small, their goods or services are different, and the areas where they do business are separate. In the online world, however, there is only one area of business—cyberspace. Thus, disputes between parties over which one has the right to use a particular domain name have become common. A **domain name** is part of an Internet address, such as "westlaw.com." The top level domain (TLD) is the part of the name to the right of the period and indicates the type of entity that operates the site (for example, "com" is an abbreviation for "commercial"). The second level (the part of the name to the left of the period) is chosen by the business entity or individual registering the domain name.

DOMAIN NAME
The last part of an Internet address, such as "westlaw.com." The top level (the part of the name to the right of the period) indicates the type of entity that operates the site ("com" is an abbreviation for "commercial"). The second level (the part of the name to the left of the period) is chosen by the entity.

Conflicts over rights to domain names emerged during the 1990s as e-commerce expanded on a worldwide scale. As e-commerce grew, the *.com* TLD came to be widely used by businesses on the Web. Competition among firms with similar names and products preceding the *.com* TLD led, understandably, to numerous disputes over domain name rights. By using the same, or a similar, domain name, parties have attempted to profit from the goodwill of a competitor, to sell pornography, to offer for sale another party's domain name, and to otherwise infringe on others' trademarks.

As noted in Chapter 3, the federal government set up the Internet Corporation for Assigned Names and Numbers (ICANN), a nonprofit corporation, to oversee the distribution of domain names. ICANN has also played a leading role in facilitating the settlement of domain name disputes worldwide. Since January 2000, ICANN has been operating an online arbitration system to resolve domain name disputes and approve dispute-resolution providers. By 2003, ICANN-approved online arbitration providers were handling over one thousand disputes annually.

Anticybersquatting Legislation

In the late 1990s, Congress passed legislation prohibiting another practice that had given rise to numerous disputes over domain names: cybersquatting. **Cybersquatting** occurs when a person registers a domain name that is the same

CYBERSQUATTING
The act of registering a domain name that is the same as, or confusingly similar to, the trademark of another and then offering to sell that domain name back to the trademark owner.

as, or confusingly similar to, the trademark of another and then offers to sell the domain name back to the trademark owner. During the 1990s, cybersquatting became a contentious issue and led to much litigation. Although it was not always easy for the courts to separate cybersquatting from legitimate business activity, many cases held that cybersquatting violated trademark law.[9]

In 1999, Congress addressed this issue by passing the Anticybersquatting Consumer Protection Act (ACPA), which amended the Lanham Act—the federal law protecting trademarks, discussed earlier in this chapter. The ACPA makes it illegal for a person to "register, traffic in, or use" a domain name (1) if the name is identical or confusingly similar to the trademark of another and (2) if the one registering, trafficking in, or using the domain name has a "bad faith intent" to profit from that trademark. The act does not define what constitutes bad faith. Instead, it lists several factors that courts can consider in deciding whether bad faith exists. Some of these factors are the trademark rights of the other person, whether there is an intent to divert consumers in a way that could harm the goodwill represented by the trademark, whether there is an offer to transfer or sell the domain name to the trademark owner, and whether there is an intent to use the domain name to offer goods and services.

The ACPA applies to all domain name registrations of trademarks, even domain names registered before the passage of the act. Successful plaintiffs in suits brought under the act can collect actual damages and profits, or elect to receive statutory damages of from $1,000 to $100,000.

Meta Tags

Search engines compile their results by looking through a Web site's key-word field. Meta tags, or key words, may be inserted into this field to increase the site's inclusion in search engine results, even though the site may have nothing to do with the inserted words. Using this same technique, one site may appropriate the key words of other sites with more frequent hits, so that the appropriating site appears in the same search engine results as the more popular sites. Using another's trademark in a meta tag without the owner's permission, however, constitutes trademark infringement. One use of meta tags was at issue in the following case.

---

9. See, for example, *Panavision International, L.P. v. Toeppen,* 141 F.3d 1316 (9th Cir. 1998).

CASE 7.3   *Playboy Enterprises, Inc. v. Welles*

United States Court of Appeals,
Ninth Circuit, 2002.
279 F.3d 796.

BACKGROUND AND FACTS   Playboy Enterprises, Inc. (PEI), maintains Web sites to promote *Playboy* magazine and PEI models. PEI's trademarks include the terms *Playboy, Playmate,* and *Playmate of the Year.* Terri Welles is a self-employed model and spokesperson who was featured as the *Playmate* of the Year in June 1981. Welles maintains a Web site titled "Terri Welles—Playmate of the Year 1981." As meta tags, Welles's site uses the terms *Playboy* and *Playmate,* among others. PEI asked Welles to stop using these terms, but she refused. PEI filed a suit in a federal district court against Welles, asking the court to order her to, among other things, stop using those terms as meta tags. On this issue, the court granted a summary judgment in Welles's favor. PEI appealed to the U.S. Court of Appeals for the Ninth Circuit.

CASE 7.3–CONTINUED

IN THE WORDS OF THE COURT . . . *T. G. NELSON*, Circuit Judge.

* * * *

* * * [The] test for nominative use [of a trademark is]:[a]

First, the product or service in question must be one not readily identifiable without use of the trademark; second, only so much of the mark or marks may be used as is reasonably necessary to identify the product or service; and third, the user must do nothing that would, in conjunction with the mark, suggest sponsorship or endorsement by the trademark holder. * * *

* * * *

A large portion of Welles'[s] Web site discusses her association with Playboy over the years. Thus, the trademarked terms accurately describe the contents of Welles'[s] Web site, in addition to describing Welles. Forcing Welles and others to use absurd turns of phrase in their metatags, such as those necessary to identify Welles, would be particularly damaging in the Internet search context. *Searchers would have a much more difficult time locating relevant Web sites if they could do so only by correctly guessing the long phrases necessary to substitute for trademarks.* We can hardly expect someone searching for Welles'[s] site to imagine [a] phrase * * * to describe Welles without referring to Playboy—"the nude model selected by Mr. Hefner's organization * * * ." Yet if someone could not remember her name, that is what they would have to do. Similarly, someone searching for critiques of *Playboy* on the Internet would have a difficult time if Internet sites could not list the object of their critique in their metatags. [Emphasis added.]

There is simply no descriptive substitute for the trademarks used in Welles'[s] metatags. Precluding their use would have the unwanted effect of hindering the free flow of information on the Internet, something which is certainly not a goal of trademark law. Accordingly, the use of trademarked terms in the metatags meets the first part of the test for nominative use.

We conclude that the metatags satisfy the second and third elements of the test as well. The metatags use only so much of the marks as reasonably necessary and nothing is done in conjunction with them to suggest sponsorship or endorsement by the trademark holder. We note that our decision might differ if the metatags listed the trademarked term so repeatedly that Welles'[s] site would regularly appear above PEI's in searches for one of the trademarked terms.

a. A *nominative use* of a trademark is one that does not imply sponsorship or endorsement of a product because the product's mark is used only to describe the thing, rather than to identify its source. See *New Kids on the Block v. News America Publishing, Inc.*, 971 F.2d 302 (9th Cir. 1992).

DECISION AND REMEDY The U.S. Court of Appeals for the Ninth Circuit concluded that Welles's use of PEI's trademarks as meta tags was a permissible, nominative use. The use implied no current sponsorship or endorsement by PEI. Instead, the meta tags identified Welles as a past PEI *Playmate of the Year.*

WHY IS THIS CASE IMPORTANT? *This case illustrates how some uses of another's trademark are permissible and not infringing, provided that the user does not suggest that the trademark owner authorized or sponsored the use.*

Dilution in the Online World

As discussed earlier, trademark *dilution* occurs when a trademark is used, without authorization, in a way that diminishes the distinctive quality of the mark. Unlike trademark infringement, a dilution cause of action does not require proof that consumers are likely to be confused by a connection between the unauthorized use and the mark. For this reason, the products involved do not have to be similar. In the first case alleging dilution on the Web, a court precluded the use of "candyland.com" as the URL for an adult site. The court held that the use of the URL would dilute the value of the "Candyland" mark owned by the maker of the "Candyland" children's game.[10]

In another case, a court issued an injunction on the ground that spamming under another's logo is trademark dilution. In that case, Hotmail, Inc., provided e-mail services and worked to dissociate itself from spam. Van$ Money Pie, Inc., and others spammed thousands of e-mail customers, using the free e-mail provided by Hotmail as a return address. The court ordered the defendants to stop.[11]

Licensing

One of the ways to make use of another's trademark or other form of intellectual property, while avoiding litigation, is to obtain a license to do so. A license in this context is essentially an agreement permitting the use of a trademark, copyright, patent, or trade secret for certain purposes. For instance, a licensee (the party obtaining the license) might be allowed to use the trademark of the licensor (the party issuing the license) as part of the name of its company, or as part of its domain name, without otherwise using the mark on any products or services. Like all contracts, contracts granting licenses must be carefully drafted.

PATENTS

PATENT
A government grant that gives an inventor the exclusive right or privilege to make, use, or sell his or her invention for a limited time period.

A **patent** is a grant from the government that gives an inventor the exclusive right to make, use, and sell an invention for a period of twenty years from the date of filing the application for a patent. Patents for designs, as opposed to inventions, are given for a fourteen-year period. For either a regular patent or a design patent, the applicant must demonstrate to the satisfaction of the U.S. Patent and Trademark Office that the invention, discovery, process, or design is genuine, novel, useful, and not obvious in light of current technology. A patent holder gives notice to all that an article or design is patented by placing on it the word *Patent* or *Pat.* plus the patent number. In contrast to patent law in other countries, in the United States patent protection is given to the first person to invent a product or process, even though someone else may have been the first to file for a patent on that product or process.

At one time, it was difficult for developers and manufacturers of software to obtain patent protection because many software products simply automate procedures that can be performed manually. In other words, the computer programs do not meet the "novel" and "not obvious" requirements previously mentioned. Also, the basis for software is often a mathematical equation or formula, which is not patentable. In 1981, however, the United States Supreme Court held that it is possible to obtain a patent for a process that incorporates a computer program—providing, of course, that the process itself is patentable.[12] Subsequently, many patents have been issued for software-related inventions.

"The patent system . . . added the fuel of interest to the fire of genius."

—ABRAHAM LINCOLN, 1809–1865
(Sixteenth president of the United States, 1861–1865)

---

10. *Hasbro, Inc. v. Internet Entertainment Group, Ltd.,* 1996 WL 84853 (W.D. Wash. 1996).
11. *Hotmail Corp. v. Van$ Money Pie, Inc.,* ___ F.Supp. ___, 47 U.S. Patent Quarterly.2d 1020 (N.D.Cal. 1998).
12. *Diamond v. Diehr,* 450 U.S. 175, 101 S.Ct. 1048, 67 L.Ed.2d 155 (1981).

A significant development relating to patents is the availability online of the world's patent databases. The Web site of the U.S. Patent and Trademark Office provides searchable databases covering U.S. patents granted since 1976. The Web site of the European Patent Office maintains databases covering all patent documents in sixty-five nations and the legal status of patents in twenty-two of those countries.

Patent Infringement

If a firm makes, uses, or sells another's patented design, product, or process without the patent owner's permission, it commits the tort of patent infringement. Patent infringement may exist even though the patent owner has not put the patented product in commerce. Patent infringement may also occur even though not all features or parts of an invention are copied. (With respect to a patented process, however, all steps or their equivalent must be copied for infringement to exist.)

Often, litigation for patent infringement is so costly that the patent holder will instead offer to sell to the infringer a license to use the patented design, product, or process. Indeed, in many cases the costs of detection, prosecution, and monitoring are so high that patents are valueless to their owners; the owners cannot afford to protect them.

Business Process Patents

Traditionally, patents have been granted for inventions that are "new and useful processes, machines, manufactures, or compositions of matter, or any new and useful improvements thereof." The U.S. Patent and Trademark Office routinely rejected computer systems and software applications because they were deemed not to be useful processes, machines, articles of manufacture, or compositions of matter. They were simply considered to be mathematical algorithms, abstract ideas, or "methods of doing business." In a landmark 1998 case, however, *State Street Bank & Trust Co. v. Signature Financial Group, Inc.*,[13] the U.S. Court of Appeals for the Federal Circuit ruled that only three categories of subject matter will always remain unpatentable: (1) the laws of nature, (2) natural phenomena, and (3) abstract ideas. This decision meant, among other things, that business processes were patentable.

Should a software program that allows consumers to make offers for vacation packages via the Internet be considered a "new and useful" process that can be the subject of a business process patent? Why or why not?

After this decision, numerous technology firms applied for business process patents. Walker Digital applied for a business process patent for its "Dutch auction" system, which allowed consumers to make offers for airline tickets on the Internet and led to the creation of Priceline.com. Amazon.com obtained a business process patent for its "one-click" ordering system, a method of processing credit-card orders securely. Indeed, immediately after the *State Street* decision, the number of Internet-related patents issued by the U.S. Patent and Trademark Office increased dramatically.

---

13. 149 F.3d 1368 (Fed. Cir. 1998).

COPYRIGHTS

A **copyright** is an intangible property right granted by federal statute to the author or originator of certain literary or artistic productions. Copyrights are governed by the Copyright Act of 1976,[14] as amended. Works created after January 1, 1978, are automatically given statutory copyright protection for the life of the author plus 70 years. For copyrights owned by publishing houses, the copyright expires 95 years from the date of publication or 120 years from the date of creation, whichever is first. For works by more than one author, the copyright expires 70 years after the death of the last surviving author.

These time periods reflect the extensions of the length of copyright protection enacted by Congress in the Copyright Term Extension Act of 1998.[15] Critics challenged this act as overstepping the bounds of Congress's power and violating the constitutional requirement that copyrights endure for only a limited time. In 2003, however, the United States Supreme Court upheld the act in *Eldred v. Ashcroft*.[16] This ruling obviously favored copyright holders by preventing copyrighted works from the 1920s and 1930s from losing protection and falling into the public domain for an additional two decades.

Copyrights can be registered with the U.S. Copyright Office in Washington, D.C. A copyright owner no longer needs to place a © or *Copr.* or *Copyright* on the work, however, to have the work protected against infringement. Chances are that if somebody created it, somebody owns it.

What Is Protected Expression?

Works that are copyrightable include books, records, films, artworks, architectural plans, menus, music videos, product packaging, and computer software. To obtain protection under the Copyright Act, a work must be original and fall into one of the following categories: (1) literary works; (2) musical works; (3) dramatic works; (4) pantomimes and choreographic works; (5) pictorial, graphic, and sculptural works; (6) films and other audiovisual works; and (7) sound recordings. To be protected, a work must be "fixed in a durable medium" from which it can be perceived, reproduced, or communicated. Protection is automatic. Registration is not required.

Section 102 Exclusions   Section 102 of the Copyright Act specifically excludes copyright protection for any "idea, procedure, process, system, method of operation, concept, principle, or discovery, regardless of the form in which it is described, explained, illustrated, or embodied." Note that it is not possible to copyright an *idea*. The underlying ideas embodied in a work may be freely used by others. What is copyrightable is the particular way in which an idea is *expressed*. Whenever an idea and an expression are inseparable, the expression cannot be copyrighted. Generally, anything that is not an original expression will not qualify for copyright protection. Facts widely known to the public are not copyrightable. Page numbers are not copyrightable because they follow a sequence known to everyone. Mathematical calculations are not copyrightable.

---

14. 17 U.S.C. Sections 101 *et seq.*
15. 17 U.S.C.A. Section 302.
16. 537 U.S. 186, 123 S.Ct. 769, 154 L.Ed.2d 683 (2003).

Compilations of Facts   *Compilations* of facts, however, are copyrightable. Section 103 of the Copyright Act defines a compilation as "a work formed by the collection and assembling of preexisting materials of data that are selected, coordinated, or arranged in such a way that the resulting work as a whole constitutes an original work of authorship." The key requirement for the copyrightability of a compilation is originality. **| Example #5**   The white pages of a telephone directory do not qualify for copyright protection when the information that makes up the directory (names, addresses, and telephone numbers) is not selected, coordinated, or arranged in an original way.[17] In one case, even the Yellow Pages of a telephone directory did not qualify for copyright protection.[18]**|**

Copyright Infringement

Whenever the form or expression of an idea is copied, an infringement of copyright occurs. The reproduction does not have to be exactly the same as the original, nor does it have to reproduce the original in its entirety. If a substantial part of the original is reproduced, there is copyright infringement.

Damages for Copyright Infringement   Those who infringe copyrights may be liable for damages or criminal penalties. These range from actual damages or statutory damages, imposed at the court's discretion, to criminal proceedings for willful violations. Actual damages are based on the harm caused to the copyright holder by the infringement, while statutory damages, not to exceed $150,000, are provided for under the Copyright Act. In addition, criminal proceedings may result in fines and/or imprisonment.

The "Fair Use" Exception   An exception to liability for copyright infringement is made under the "fair use" doctrine. In certain circumstances, a person or organization can reproduce copyrighted material without paying royalties (fees paid to the copyright holder for the privilege of reproducing the copyrighted material). Section 107 of the Copyright Act provides as follows:

> [T]he fair use of a copyrighted work, including such use by reproduction in copies or phonorecords or by any other means specified by [Section 106 of the Copyright Act,] for purposes such as criticism, comment, news reporting, teaching (including multiple copies for classroom use), scholarship, or research, is not an infringement of copyright. In determining whether the use made of a work in any particular case is a fair use the factors to be considered shall include—
>
> (1) the purpose and character of the use, including whether such use is of a commercial nature or is for nonprofit educational purposes;
>
> (2) the nature of the copyrighted work;
>
> (3) the amount and substantiality of the portion used in relation to the copyrighted work as a whole; and
>
> (4) the effect of the use upon the potential market for or value of the copyrighted work.

---

17. *Feist Publications, Inc. v. Rural Telephone Service Co.,* 499 U.S. 340, 111 S.Ct. 1282, 113 L.Ed.2d 358 (1991).

18. *Bellsouth Advertising & Publishing Corp. v. Donnelley Information Publishing, Inc.,* 999 F.2d 1436 (11th Cir. 1993).

Because these guidelines are very broad, the courts determine whether a particular use is fair on a case-by-case basis. Thus, anyone reproducing copyrighted material may be committing a violation. In determining whether a use is fair, courts have often considered the fourth factor to be the most important.

Copyright Protection for Software

In 1980, Congress passed the Computer Software Copyright Act, which amended the Copyright Act of 1976 to include computer programs in the list of creative works protected by federal copyright law. The 1980 statute, which classifies computer programs as "literary works," defines a computer program as a "set of statements or instructions to be used directly or indirectly in a computer in order to bring about a certain result."

Because of the unique nature of computer programs, the courts have had many problems applying and interpreting the 1980 act. Generally, though, the courts have held that copyright protection extends not only to those parts of a computer program that can be read by humans, such as the high-level language of a source code, but also to the binary-language object code of a computer program, which is readable only by the computer.[19] Additionally, such elements as the overall structure, sequence, and organization of a program were deemed copyrightable.[20] The courts have disagreed as to whether the "look and feel"—the general appearance, command structure, video images, menus, windows, and other screen displays—of computer programs should also be protected by copyright. The courts have tended, however, not to extend copyright protection to look-and-feel aspects of computer programs.

Copyrights in Digital Information

Copyright law is probably the most important form of intellectual property protection on the Internet. This is because much of the material on the Internet consists of works of authorship (including multimedia presentations, software, and database information), which are the traditional focus of copyright law. Copyright law is also important because the nature of the Internet requires that data be "copied" to be transferred online. Copies are a significant part of the traditional controversies arising in this area of the law.

The Copyright Act of 1976   When Congress drafted the principal U.S. law governing copyrights, the Copyright Act of 1976, cyberspace did not exist for most of us. The threat to copyright owners was posed not by computer technology but by unauthorized *tangible* copies of works and the sale of rights to movies, television, and other media.

Some issues that were unimagined when the Copyright Act was drafted have posed thorny questions for the courts. For instance, to sell a copy of a work, permission of the copyright holder is necessary. Because of the nature of cyberspace, however, one of the early controversies involved determining at what point an intangible, electronic "copy" of a work has been made. The courts have held that loading a file or program into a computer's random

---

19. See *Stern Electronics, Inc. v. Kaufman,* 669 F.2d 852 (2d Cir. 1982); and *Apple Computer, Inc. v. Franklin Computer Corp.,* 714 F.2d 1240 (3d Cir. 1983).
20. *Whelan Associates, Inc. v. Jaslow Dental Laboratory, Inc.,* 797 F.2d 1222 (3d Cir. 1986).

access memory, or RAM, constitutes the making of a "copy" for purposes of copyright law.[21] RAM is a portion of a computer's memory into which a file, for instance, is loaded so that it can be accessed (read or written over). Thus, a copyright is infringed when a party downloads software into RAM without owning the software or otherwise having a right to download it.[22]

Other rights, including those relating to the revision of "collective works" such as magazines, were acknowledged thirty years ago but were considered to have only limited economic value. Today, technology has made some of those rights vastly more significant.

Further Developments in Copyright Law   In the last several years, Congress has enacted legislation designed specifically to protect copyright holders in a digital age. Prior to 1997, criminal penalties under copyright law could be imposed only if unauthorized copies were exchanged for financial gain. Yet much piracy of copyrighted materials was "altruistic" in nature; that is, unauthorized copies were made and distributed not for financial gain but simply for reasons of generosity—to share the copies with others.

To combat altruistic piracy and for other reasons, Congress passed the No Electronic Theft (NET) Act of 1997. This act extends criminal liability for the piracy of copyrighted materials to persons who exchange unauthorized copies of copyrighted works, such as software, even though they realize no profit from the exchange. The act also imposes penalties on those who make unauthorized electronic copies of books, magazines, movies, or music for *personal* use, thus altering the traditional "fair use" doctrine. The criminal penalties for

21. *MAI Systems Corp. v. Peak Computer, Inc.*, 991 F.2d 511 (9th Cir. 1993).
22. *DSC Communications Corp. v. Pulse Communications, Inc.*, 170 F.3d 1354 (Fed. Cir. 1999).

The Digital Millennium Copyright Act of 1998

The United States leads the world in the production of creative products, including books, films, videos, recordings, and software. In fact, as indicated earlier in this chapter, the creative industries are more important to the U.S. economy than the traditional product industries are. Exports of U.S. creative products, for example, surpass those of every other U.S. industry in value. Creative industries are growing at nearly three times the rate of the economy as a whole.

Steps have been taken, both nationally and internationally, to protect ownership rights in intellectual property, including copyrights. To curb unauthorized copying of copyrighted materials, the World Intellectual Property Organization (WIPO) treaty of 1996, a special agreement under the Berne Convention (discussed later in this chapter), upgraded global standards of copyright protection, particularly for the Internet.

Implementing the WIPO Treaty   In 1998, Congress implemented the provisions of the WIPO treaty by updating U.S. copyright law. The new law—the Digital Millennium Copyright Act of 1998—is a landmark step in the protection of copyright owners and, because of the leading position of the United States in the creative industries, serves as a model for other nations. Among other things, the act established civil and criminal penalties for anyone who circumvents (bypasses, or gets around—through clever maneuvering, for example) encryption software or other technological antipiracy protection. Also prohibited are the manufacture, import, sale, and distribution of devices or services for circumvention.

The act provides for exceptions to fit the needs of libraries, scientists, universities, and others. In general, the law does not restrict the "fair use" of circumvention methods for educational and other noncommercial purposes. For example, circumvention is allowed to test

computer security, conduct encryption research, protect personal privacy, and enable parents to monitor their children's use of the Internet. The exceptions are to be reconsidered every three years.

Limiting the Liability of Internet Service Providers   The 1998 act also limited the liability of Internet service providers (ISPs). Under the act, an ISP is not liable for any copyright infringement by its customer *unless* the ISP is aware of the subscriber's violation. An ISP may be held liable only if it fails to take action to shut the subscriber down after learning of the violation. A copyright holder has to act promptly, however, by pursuing a claim in court, or the subscriber has the right to be restored to online access.

Application to Today's Legal Environment

The application of the Digital Millennium Copyright Act of 1998 to today's world is fairly self-evident. If Congress had not enacted this legislation, copyright owners would have a far more difficult time obtaining legal redress against those who, without authorization, decrypt and/or copy copyrighted materials. Of course, problems remain, particularly because of the global nature of the Internet. From a practical standpoint, the degree of protection afforded to copyright holders depends on the extent to which other nations that have signed the WIPO treaty actually implement its provisions and agree on the interpretation of terms, such as what constitutes an electronic copy.

RELEVANT WEB SITES

To locate information on the Web concerning the Digital Millennium Copyright Act of 1998, go to this text's Web site at **www.thomsonedu.com/westbuslaw/let***, select "Chapter 7," and click on "URLs for Landmarks."*

violating the act are steep; they include fines as high as $250,000 and incarceration for up to five years.

In 1998, Congress passed further legislation to protect copyright holders—the Digital Millennium Copyright Act. Because of its significance in protecting against the piracy of copyrighted materials in the online environment, this act is presented as this chapter's *Landmark in the Legal Environment* feature.

MP3 and File-Sharing Technology

At one time, music fans swapped compact discs (CDs) and recorded the songs that they liked from others' CDs onto their own cassettes. This type of "file-sharing" was awkward at best. Soon after the Internet became popular, a few enterprising programmers created software to compress large data files, particularly those associated with music. The reduced file sizes make transmitting music over the Internet feasible. The most widely known compression and decompression system is MP3, which enables music fans to download songs or entire CDs onto their computers or onto a portable listening device, such as a Rio or an iPod. The MP3 system also made it possible for music fans to access other music fans' files by engaging in file-sharing via the Internet.

Peer-to-Peer (P2P) Networking File-sharing via the Internet is accomplished through what is called **peer-to-peer (P2P) networking.** The concept is simple. Rather than going through a central Web server, P2P involves numerous personal computers (PCs) that are connected to the Internet. Files stored on one PC can be accessed by others who are members of the same network. Sometimes this is called a **distributed network.** In other words, parts of the network are distributed all over the country or the world. File-sharing offers an unlimited number of uses for distributed networks. For instance, thousands of researchers simultaneously allow their home computers' computing power to be accessed through file-sharing software so that very large mathematical problems can be solved quickly. Additionally, persons scattered throughout the country or the world can work together on the same project by using file-sharing programs.

PEER-TO-PEER (P2P) NETWORKING
The sharing of resources (such as files, hard drives, and processing styles) among multiple computers without necessarily requiring a central network server.

DISTRIBUTED NETWORK
A network that can be used by persons located (distributed) around the country or the globe to share computer files.

Sharing Stored Music Files When file-sharing is used to download others' stored music files, copyright issues arise. Recording artists and their labels stand to lose large amounts of royalties and revenues if relatively few CDs are purchased and then made available on distributed networks, from which everyone can get them for free. The issue of file-sharing infringement has been the subject of an ongoing debate over the last few years.

| **Example #6** In the highly publicized case of *A&M Records, Inc. v. Napster, Inc.*,[23] several firms in the recording industry sued Napster, Inc., the owner of the then-popular Napster Web site. The Napster site provided registered users with free software that enabled them to transfer exact copies of the contents of MP3 files from one computer to another via the Internet. Napster also maintained centralized search indices so that users could locate specific titles or artists' recordings on the computers of other members. The firms argued that Napster should be liable for contributory and vicarious[24] copyright infringement because it assisted others in obtaining copies of copyrighted music without the copyright owners' permission. Both the federal district court and the U.S. Court of Appeals for the Ninth Circuit agreed and held Napster liable for violating copyright laws. |

Since the 2001 *Napster* decision, the recording industry has filed and won numerous lawsuits against companies that distribute online file-sharing software. The courts have held these Napster-like companies liable based on two theories: contributory infringement, which applies if the company had reason to know about a user's infringement and failed to stop it; and vicarious

Cary Sherman, president of the Recording Industry Association of America (RIAA), is seen here talking with reporters after announcing that the RIAA is filing hundreds of lawsuits against individuals who shared copyrighted music files via the Internet. Under what theories can a company that distributes file-sharing software also be held liable if individuals use the software to exchange copyrighted music? (AP Photo/George Nikitin)

---

23. 239 F.3d 1004 (9th Cir. 2001).
24. *Vicarious* (indirect) liability exists when one person is subject to liability for another's actions. A common example occurs in the employment context, when an employer is held vicariously liable by third parties for torts committed by employees in the course of their employment.

liability, which exists if the company was able to control the users' activities and stood to benefit financially from their infringement. In the *Napster* case, the court held the company liable under both doctrines, largely because the technology that Napster had used was centralized and gave it "the ability to locate infringing material listed on its search indices, and the right to terminate users' access to the system."

New File-Sharing Technologies   In the wake of the *Napster* decision, other companies developed new technologies that allow P2P network users to share stored music files, without paying a fee, more quickly and efficiently than ever. Today's file-sharing software is decentralized and does not use search indices. Thus, the companies have no ability to supervise or control which music (or other media files) their users are exchanging. Unlike the Napster system, in which the company played a role in connecting people who were downloading and uploading songs, the new systems are designed to work without the company's input.

Software such as Morpheus and KaZaA, for example, provides users with an interface that is similar to a Web browser. This technology is different from that used by Napster. Instead of the company locating songs for users on other members' computers, the software automatically annotates files with descriptive information so that the music can easily be categorized and cross-referenced (by artist and title, for instance). When a user performs a search, the software is able to locate a list of peers that have the file available for downloading. Also, to expedite the P2P transfer and ensure that the complete file is received, the software distributes the download task over the entire list of peers simultaneously. By downloading even one file, the user becomes a point of distribution for that file, which is then automatically shared with others on the network. How the courts have decided the legality of these new digital technologies is discussed in this chapter's *Management Perspective* feature.

TRADE SECRETS

TRADE SECRETS
Business information that is kept confidential to maintain an advantage over competitors.

Some business processes and information that are not or cannot be patented, copyrighted, or trademarked are nevertheless protected against appropriation by a competitor as trade secrets. **Trade secrets** consist of customer lists, plans, research and development, pricing information, marketing techniques, production methods, and generally anything that makes an individual company unique and that would have value to a competitor.

Unlike copyright and trademark protection, protection of trade secrets extends both to ideas and to their expression. (For this reason, and because a trade secret involves no registration or filing requirements, trade secret protection may be well suited for software.) Of course, the secret formula, method, or other information must be disclosed to some persons, particularly to key employees. Businesses generally attempt to protect their trade secrets by having all employees who use the process or information agree in their contracts, or in confidentiality agreements, never to divulge it.

State and Federal Law on Trade Secrets

Under Section 757 of the *Restatement of Torts,* those who disclose or use another's trade secret, without authorization, are liable to that other party if (1) they discovered the secret by improper means, or (2) their disclosure or use

MANAGEMENT PERSPECTIVE

File-Sharing Technology and Copyright Law

Management Faces a Legal Issue Clearly, any person who downloads copyrighted music without permission from the copyright holder is liable for copyright infringement. But what about the companies that provide the software that enables users to swap copyrighted music? In what circumstances will the companies be held liable? For some time, it was difficult for the courts to apply traditional doctrines of contributory and vicarious copyright liability to new file-sharing technologies.

What the Courts Say In 2005, however, the United States Supreme Court addressed this issue in *Metro-Goldwyn-Mayer Studios, Inc. v. Grokster, Ltd.*[a] In that case, organizations in the music and film industry (the plaintiffs) sued several companies that distribute file-sharing software used in P2P networks, including Grokster, Ltd., and StreamCast Networks, Inc. (the defendants). The plaintiffs claimed that the companies were contributorily and vicariously liable for the infringement of their end users.

The federal district court that initially heard the case examined the technology involved and concluded that the defendants were not liable for contributory infringement because they lacked the requisite level of knowledge. It was not enough that the defendants *generally* knew that the software they provided might be used to infringe on copyrights; they also had to have *specific knowledge* of the infringement "at a time when they can use that knowledge to stop the particular infringement." Here, the companies had merely distributed free software. They had

no knowledge of whether users were swapping copyrighted files and no ability to stop users from infringing activities. Further, the two defendants could not be held vicariously liable for the infringement because it was not possible for the companies to supervise or control their users' conduct. The district court's decision was affirmed on appeal.

The United States Supreme Court reversed the lower court's decision and remanded the case for further proceedings. The Court held that "one who distributes a device [software] with the object of promoting its use to infringe the copyright, as shown by clear expression or other affirmative steps taken to foster infringement, is liable for the resulting acts of infringement by third parties." The Court did not, however, specify what kind of "affirmative steps" are necessary to establish liability and left it to the lower court on remand to determine whether the defendants had actually induced their users to commit infringement. In the Court's view, however, there was ample evidence in the record that the defendants had acted with the intent to cause copyright violations by use of their software.

Implications for Managers The Supreme Court's decision in this case shifts the focus in secondary copyright infringement cases away from specific knowledge of acts of infringement to acts that induce or promote infringement. Essentially, this means that file-sharing companies that have taken affirmative steps to promote copyright infringement can be held secondarily liable for millions of infringing acts that their users commit daily. Because the Court did not define exactly what is necessary to impose liability, however, a great deal of legal uncertainty remains concerning this issue.

a. ___ U.S. ___, 125 S.Ct. 2764, 162 L.Ed.2d 781 (2005).

---

constitutes a breach of a duty owed to the other party. The theft of confidential business data by industrial espionage, as when a business taps into a competitor's computer, is a theft of trade secrets without any contractual violation and is actionable in itself.

Until twenty years ago, virtually all law with respect to trade secrets was common law. In an effort to reduce the unpredictability of the common law in this area, a model act, the Uniform Trade Secrets Act, was presented to the states for adoption in 1979. Parts of this act have been adopted in more than thirty states. Typically, a state that has adopted parts of the act has adopted only those parts that encompass its own existing common law. Additionally, in 1996 Congress passed the Economic Espionage Act, which made the theft of trade secrets a federal crime. We examined the provisions and significance of this act in Chapter 6, in the context of crimes related to business.

Trade Secrets in Cyberspace

The nature of new computer technology undercuts a business firm's ability to protect its confidential information, including trade secrets.[25] For instance, a dishonest employee could e-mail trade secrets in a company's computer to a competitor or a future employer. If e-mail is not an option, the employee might walk out with the information on a flash pen drive.

ETHICAL ISSUE 7.2 | ***Does preventing a Web site from posting computer codes that reveal trade secrets violate free speech rights?***

An ongoing issue with ethical dimensions is the point at which free speech rights come into conflict with the right of copyright holders to protect their property by using encryption technology. This issue came before the California Supreme Court in 2003 in the case of *DVD Copy Control Association v. Bunner.*[26] Trade associations in the movie industry (the plaintiffs) sued an Internet Web site operator (the defendant) who had posted the code of a computer program that cracked technology used to encrypt DVDs. This posed a significant threat to the plaintiffs because, by using the code-cracking software, users would be able to duplicate the copyrighted movies stored on the DVDs. In their suit, the plaintiffs claimed that the defendant had misappropriated trade secrets. The defendant argued that software programs designed to break encryption programs were a form of constitutionally protected speech. When the case reached the California Supreme Court, the court held that although the First Amendment applies to computer code, computer code is not a form of "pure speech," and the courts can therefore protect it to a lesser extent. The court reinstated the trial court's order that enjoined (prevented) the defendant from continuing to post the code.

INTERNATIONAL PROTECTION FOR INTELLECTUAL PROPERTY

For many years, the United States has been a party to various international agreements relating to intellectual property rights. For example, the Paris Convention of 1883, to which about ninety countries are signatory, allows parties in one country to file for patent and trademark protection in any of the other member countries. Other international agreements include the Berne Convention and the TRIPS agreement. For a discussion of a treaty that allows a company to register its trademark in foreign nations with a single application, see this chapter's *Beyond Our Borders* feature.

The Berne Convention

Under the Berne Convention of 1886, as amended, an international copyright agreement, if a U.S. author writes a book, every country that has signed the convention must recognize that author's copyright in the book. Also, if a citizen of a country that has not signed the convention first publishes a book in a

---

25. Note that the courts have even found that customers' e-mail addresses may constitute trade secrets. See *T-N-T Motorsports, Inc. v. Hennessey Motorsports, Inc.*, 965 S.W.2d 18 (Tex.App.—Houston [1 Dist.] 1998); rehearing overruled (1998); petition dismissed (1998).
26. 31 Cal.4th 864, 75 P.3d 1, 4 Cal.Rptr.3d 69 (2003).

The Madrid Protocol

In the past, one of the difficulties in protecting U.S. trademarks internationally was that it was time consuming and expensive to apply for trademark registration in foreign countries. The filing fees and procedures for trademark registration vary significantly among individual countries. The Madrid Protocol, however, which President George W. Bush signed into law in the fall of 2003, may help to resolve these problems. The Madrid Protocol is an international treaty that has been signed by sixty-one countries. Under its provisions, a U.S. company wishing to register its trademark abroad can submit a single application and designate other member countries in which it would like

to register the mark. The treaty is designed to reduce the costs of obtaining international trademark protection by more than 60 percent, according to proponents.

Although the Madrid Protocol may simplify and reduce the cost of trademark registration in foreign nations, it remains to be seen whether it will provide significant benefits to trademark owners. Even with an easier registration process, the issue of whether member countries will enforce the law and protect the mark still remains.

For Critical Analysis *What are some of the pros and cons of having an international standard for trademark protection?*

---

country that has signed, all other countries that have signed the convention must recognize that author's copyright. Copyright notice is not needed to gain protection under the Berne Convention for works published after March 1, 1989.

This convention and other international agreements have given some protection to intellectual property on a worldwide level. None of them, however, has been as significant and far reaching in scope as the agreement on Trade-Related Aspects of Intellectual Property Rights, or, more simply, TRIPS.

The TRIPS Agreement

Representatives from more than one hundred nations signed the TRIPS agreement in 1994. The agreement established, for the first time, standards for the international protection of intellectual property rights, including patents, trademarks, and copyrights for movies, computer programs, books, and music. Prior to the agreement, U.S. sellers of intellectual property in the international market faced difficulties because many other countries had no laws protecting intellectual property rights or failed to enforce existing laws. To address this problem, the TRIPS agreement provides that each member country must include in its domestic laws broad intellectual property rights and effective remedies (including civil and criminal penalties) for violations of those rights.

Generally, the TRIPS agreement provides that each member nation must not discriminate (in the administration, regulation, or adjudication of intellectual property rights) against foreign owners of such rights. In other words, a member nation cannot give its own nationals (citizens) favorable treatment without offering the same treatment to nationals of all member countries. For instance, if a U.S. software manufacturer brings a suit for the infringement of intellectual property rights under a member country's national laws, the U.S. manufacturer is entitled to receive the same treatment as a domestic manufacturer. Each member nation must also ensure that legal procedures are available for parties who wish to bring actions for infringement of intellectual property rights. Additionally, a related document established a mechanism for settling disputes among member nations.

Particular provisions of the TRIPS agreement relate to patent, trademark, and copyright protection for intellectual property. The agreement specifically provides copyright protection for computer programs by stating that compilations of data, databases, and other materials are "intellectual creations" and that they are to be protected as copyrightable works. Other provisions relate to trade secrets and the rental of computer programs and cinematographic works.

REVIEWING . . . INTELLECTUAL PROPERTY

Two computer science majors, Trent and Xavier, have an idea for a new video game, which they propose to call "Hallowed." They form a business and begin developing their idea. Several months later, Trent and Xavier run into a problem with their design and consult with a friend, Brad, who is an expert in creating computer source codes. After the software is completed but before Hallowed is marketed, a video game called Halo 2 is released for both the Xbox and Game Cube systems. Halo 2 uses source codes similar to those of Hallowed and imitates Hallowed's overall look and feel, although not all the features are alike. Using the information presented in the chapter, answer the following questions.

1. Would the name "Hallowed" receive protection as a trademark or as trade dress?

2. If Trent and Xavier had obtained a business process patent on Hallowed, would the release of Halo 2 infringe on their patent? Why or why not?

3. Based only on the facts described above, could Trent and Xavier sue the makers of Halo 2 for copyright infringement? Why or why not?

4. Suppose that Trent and Xavier discover that Brad took the idea of Hallowed and sold it to the company that produced Halo 2. Which type of intellectual property issue does this raise?

KEY TERMS

CHAPTER SUMMARY • INTELLECTUAL PROPERTY

Trademarks and Related Property (See pages 213–221.)	1. A *trademark* is a distinctive mark, motto, device, or emblem that a manufacturer stamps, prints, or otherwise affixes to the goods it produces so that they may be identified on the market and their origins made known.
	2. The major federal statutes protecting trademarks and related property are the Lanham Act of 1946 and the Federal Trademark Dilution Act of 1995. Generally, to be protected, a trademark must be sufficiently distinctive from all competing trademarks.
	3. *Trademark infringement* occurs when one uses a mark that is the same as, or confusingly similar to, the protected trademark, service mark, trade name, or trade dress of another without permission when marketing goods or services.

CHAPTER SUMMARY • INTELLECTUAL PROPERTY—CONTINUED

Cyber Marks (See pages 221–224.)	A *cyber mark* is a trademark in cyberspace. Trademark infringement in cyberspace occurs when one person uses, in a domain name or in meta tags, a name that is the same as, or confusingly similar to, the protected mark of another.
Patents (See pages 224–225.)	1. A *patent* is a grant from the government that gives an inventor the exclusive right to make, use, and sell an invention for a period of twenty years from the date of filing the application for a patent. To be patentable, an invention (or a discovery, process, or design) must be genuine, novel, useful, and not obvious in light of current technology. Computer software may be patented. 2. *Patent infringement* occurs when one uses or sells another's patented design, product, or process without the patent owner's permission.
Copyrights (See pages 226–232.)	1. A *copyright* is an intangible property right granted by federal statute to the author or originator of certain literary or artistic productions. Computer software may be copyrighted. 2. *Copyright infringement* occurs whenever the form or expression of an idea is copied without the permission of the copyright holder. An exception applies if the copying is deemed a "fair use." 3. Copyrights are governed by the Copyright Act of 1976, as amended. To protect copyrights in digital information, Congress passed the No Electronic Theft Act of 1997 and the Digital Millennium Copyright Act of 1998. 4. Technology that allows users to share files via the Internet on distributed networks often raises copyright infringement issues. In 2005, the United States Supreme Court made it clear that software companies that have taken affirmative steps to induce or promote infringement may be held liable for their end users' infringement.
Trade Secrets (See pages 232–234.)	*Trade secrets* include customer lists, plans, research and development, and pricing information, for example. Trade secrets are protected under the common law and, in some states, under statutory law against misappropriation by competitors. The Economic Espionage Act of 1996 made the theft of trade secrets a federal crime (see Chapter 6).
International Protection for Intellectual Property (See pages 234–236.)	Various international agreements provide international protection for intellectual property. A landmark agreement is the 1994 agreement on Trade-Related Aspects of Intellectual Property Rights (TRIPS), which provides for enforcement procedures in all countries signatory to the agreement.

FOR REVIEW

Answers for the even-numbered questions in this For Review *section can be found in Appendix O at the end of this text.*

1. What is intellectual property?
2. Why are trademarks and patents protected by the law?
3. What laws protect authors' rights in the works they generate?

4. What are trade secrets, and what laws offer protection for this form of intellectual property?
5. What steps have been taken to protect intellectual property rights in today's digital age?

QUESTIONS AND CASE PROBLEMS

7–1. Patent Infringement. John and Andrew Doney invented a hard-bearing device for balancing rotors. Although they registered their invention with the U.S. Patent and Trademark Office, it was never used as an automobile wheel balancer. Some time later, Exetron Corp. produced an automobile wheel balancer that used a hard-bearing device with a support plate similar to that of the Doneys. Given that the Doneys had not used their device for automobile wheel balancing, does Exetron's use of a similar hard-bearing device infringe on the Doneys' patent?

Question with Sample Answer

7–2. In which of the following situations would a court likely hold Maruta liable for copyright infringement?

1. At the library, Maruta photocopies ten pages from a scholarly journal relating to a topic on which she is writing a term paper.
2. Maruta makes leather handbags and sells them in her small leather shop. She advertises her handbags as "Vutton handbags," hoping that customers might mistakenly assume that they were made by Vuitton, the well-known maker of high-quality luggage and handbags.
3. Maruta owns a small country store. She purchases one copy of several popular movie DVDs from various DVD distributors. Then, using blank DVDs, she makes copies to rent or sell to her customers.
4. Maruta teaches Latin American history at a small university. She has a videocassette recorder and frequently tapes television programs relating to Latin America. She then takes the videos to her classroom so that her students can watch them.

For a sample answer to this question, go to Appendix P at the end of this text.

7–3. Trademark Infringement. Elvis Presley Enterprises, Inc. (EPE), owns all of the trademarks of the Elvis Presley estate. None of these marks is registered for use in the restaurant business. Barry Capece registered "The Velvet Elvis" as a service mark for a restaurant and tavern with the U.S. Patent and Trademark Office. Capece opened a nightclub called "The Velvet Elvis" with a menu, decor, advertising, and promotional events that evoked Elvis Presley and his music. EPE filed a suit in a federal district court against Capece and others, claiming, among other things, that "The Velvet Elvis" service mark infringed on EPE's trademarks. During the trial, witnesses testified that they thought the nightclub was associated with Elvis Presley. Should Capece be ordered to stop using "The Velvet Elvis" mark? Why or why not? *[Elvis Presley Enterprises, Inc. v. Capece, 141 F.3d 188 (5th Cir. 1998)]*

7–4. Trademark Infringement. A&H Sportswear, Inc., a swimsuit maker, obtained a trademark for its MIRACLESUIT in 1992. The MIRACLESUIT design makes the wearer appear slimmer. The MIRACLESUIT was widely advertised and discussed in the media. The MIRACLESUIT was also sold for a brief time in the Victoria's Secret (VS) catalogue, which is published by Victoria's Secret Catalogue, Inc. In 1993, Victoria's Secret Stores, Inc., began selling a cleavage-enhancing bra, which was named THE MIRACLE BRA and for which a trademark was obtained. The next year, THE MIRACLE BRA swimwear debuted in the VS catalogue and stores. A&H filed a suit in a federal district court against VS Stores and VS Catalogue, alleging in part that THE MIRACLE BRA mark, when applied to swimwear, infringed on the MIRACLESUIT mark. A&H argued that there was a "possibility of confusion" between the marks. The VS entities contended that the appropriate standard was "likelihood of confusion" and that, in this case, there was no likelihood of confusion. In whose favor will the court rule, and why? *[A&H Sportswear, Inc. v. Victoria's Secret Stores, Inc., 166 F.3d 197 (3d Cir. 1999)]*

Case Problem with Sample Answer

7–5. In 1999, Steve and Pierce Thumann and their father, Fred, created Spider Webs, Ltd., a partnership, to, according to Steve, "develop Internet address names." Spider Webs registered nearly two thousand Internet domain names for an average of $70 each, including the names of cities, the names of buildings, names related to a business or trade (such as air conditioning or plumbing), and the names of famous companies. It offered many of the names for sale on its Web site and through eBay.com. Spider Webs registered the domain name "ERNESTANDJULIOGALLO.COM" in Spider Webs' name. E. & J. Gallo Winery filed a suit against Spider Webs, alleging, in part, violations of the Anticybersquatting Consumer Protection Act. Gallo asked the court for, among other things, statutory damages. Gallo also sought to have the domain name at issue transferred to Gallo. During the suit, Spider Webs published anticorporate articles and opinions, and discussions of the suit, at the URL "ERNESTANDJULIOGALLO.COM." Should the court rule in Gallo's favor? Why or why not? *[E. & J. Gallo Winery v. Spider Webs, Ltd., 129 F.Supp.2d 1033 (S.D.Tex. 2001)]*

After you have answered this problem, compare your answer with the sample answer given on the Web site that accompanies this text. Go to www.thomsonedu.com/westbuslaw/let, select "Chapter 7," and click on "Case Problem with Sample Answer."

7–6. Trade Secrets. Four Pillars Enterprise Co. is a Taiwanese company owned by Pin Yen Yang. Avery Dennison, Inc., a U.S. corporation, is one of Four Pillars' chief competitors in the manufacture of adhesives. In 1989, Victor Lee, an Avery employee, met Yang and Yang's daughter Hwei Chen. They agreed to pay Lee $25,000 a year to serve as a consultant to Four Pillars. Over the next eight years, Lee supplied the Yangs with confidential Avery reports, including information that Four Pillars used to make a new adhesive that had been developed by Avery. The Federal Bureau of Investigation (FBI) confronted Lee, and he agreed to cooperate in an operation to catch the Yangs. When Lee next met the Yangs, he showed them documents provided by the FBI. The documents bore "confidential" stamps, and Lee said that they were Avery's confidential property. The FBI arrested the Yangs with the documents in their possession. The Yangs and Four Pillars were charged with, among other crimes, the attempted theft of trade secrets. The defendants argued in part that it was impossible for them to have committed this crime because the documents were not actually trade secrets. Should the court acquit them? Why or why not? *[United States v. Yang, 281 F.3d 534 (6th Cir. 2002)]*

7–7. Patent Infringement. As a cattle rancher in Nebraska, Gerald Gohl used handheld searchlights to find and help calving animals (cows giving birth) in harsh blizzard conditions. Gohl thought that it would be more helpful to have a portable searchlight mounted on the outside of a vehicle and remotely controlled. He and Al Gebhardt developed and patented practical applications of this idea—the Golight and the wireless, remote-controlled Radio Ray, which could rotate 360 degrees—and formed Golight, Inc., to make and market these products. In 1997, Wal-Mart Stores, Inc., began selling a portable, wireless, remote-controlled searchlight that was identical to the Radio Ray except for a stop piece that prevented the light from rotating more than 351 degrees. Golight sent Wal-Mart a letter, claiming that its device infringed Golight's patent. Wal-Mart sold its remaining inventory of the devices and stopped carrying the product. Golight filed a suit in a federal district court against Wal-Mart, alleging patent infringement. How should the court rule? Explain. [*Golight, Inc. v. Wal-Mart Stores, Inc.,* 355 F.3d 1327 (Fed. Cir. 2004)]

7–8. Trade Secrets. Briefing.com offers Internet-based analyses of investment opportunities to investors. Richard Green is the company's president. One of Briefing.com's competitors is StreetAccount, LLC (limited liability company), whose owners include Gregory Jones and Cynthia Dietzmann. Jones worked for Briefing.com for six years until he quit in March 2003, and was a member of its board of directors until April 2003. Dietzmann worked for Briefing.com for seven years until she quit in March 2003. As Briefing.com employees, Jones and Dietzmann had access to confidential business data; for instance, Dietzmann developed a list of contacts through which Briefing.com obtained market information to display online. When Dietzmann quit, however, she did not return all of the contact information to the company. Briefing.com and Green filed a suit in a federal district court against Jones, Dietzmann, and StreetAccount, alleging that they appropriated this data and other "trade secrets" to form a competing business. What are trade secrets? Why are they protected? Under what circumstances is a party liable at common law for their appropriation? How should these principles apply in this case? [*Briefing.com v. Jones,* 2006 WY 16, 126 P.3d 928 (2006)]

A Question of Ethics

7–9. Texaco, Inc., conducts research to develop new products and technology in the petroleum industry. As part of the research, Texaco employees routinely photocopy articles from scientific and medical journals without the permission of the copyright holders. The publishers of the journals brought a copyright infringement action against Texaco in a federal district court. The court ruled that the copying was not a fair use. The U.S. Court of Appeals for the Second Circuit affirmed this ruling primarily because the dominant purpose of the use is "archival"—to assemble a set of papers for future reference. The court reasoned that this type of use was not fair because it served the same purpose for which additional subscriptions are normally sold, or for which photocopying licenses may be obtained. [*American Geophysical Union v. Texaco, Inc.,* 60 F.3d 913 (2d Cir. 1994)]

1. Do you agree with the court's decision that the copying was not a fair use? Why or why not?
2. Do you think that the law should impose a duty on every person to obtain permission to photocopy or reproduce any article under any circumstance? What would be some of the implications of such a duty for society? Discuss fully.

Critical-Thinking Managerial Question

7–10. Delta Computers, Inc., makes computer-related products under the brand name "Delta," which the company registers as a trademark. Without Delta's permission, E-Product Corp. embeds the Delta mark in E-Product's Web site, in black type on a blue background. This tag causes the E-Product site to be returned at the top of the list of results on a search engine query for "Delta." Does E-Product's use of the Delta mark as a meta tag without Delta's permission constitute trademark infringement? Explain.

Video Question

7–11. Go to this text's Web site at www. thomsonedu.com/westbuslaw/let and select "Chapter 7." Click on "Video Questions" and view the video titled *The Jerk.* Then answer the following questions.

1. In the video, Navin (Steve Martin) creates a special handle for Mr. Fox's (Bill Macy's) glasses. Can Navin obtain a patent or a copyright protecting his invention? Explain your answer.
2. Suppose that after Navin legally protects his idea, Fox steals it and decides to develop it for himself, without Navin's permission. Has Fox committed infringement? If so, what kind: trademark, patent, or copyright infringement?
3. Suppose that after Navin legally protects his idea, he realizes he doesn't have the funds to mass-produce the special glasses handle. Navin therefore agrees to allow Fox to manufacture the product. Has Navin granted Fox a license? Explain.
4. Assume that Navin is able to manufacture his invention. What might Navin do to ensure that his product is identifiable and can be distinguished from other products on the market?

INTERACTING WITH THE INTERNET

For updated links to resources available on the Web, as well as a variety of other materials, visit this text's Web site at

www.thomsonedu.com/westbuslaw/let

An excellent overview of the laws governing various forms of intellectual property is available at FindLaw's Web site. Go to

profs.lp.findlaw.com

You can find much information about trademark and patent law—and links to registration forms, statutes, international patent and trademark offices, and numerous other related materials—at the Web site of the U.S. Patent and Trademark Office. Go to

www.uspto.gov

For information on copyrights, go to the U.S. Copyright Office at

www.copyright.gov

You can find extensive information on copyright law—including United States Supreme Court decisions in this area and the texts of the Berne Convention and other international treaties on copyright issues—at the Web site of the Legal Information Institute at Cornell University's School of Law. Go to

www.law.cornell.edu/wex/index.php/Copyright

The University of Michigan provides information on copyrights generally and copyrights in digital information at

www.copyright.umich.edu/law.html

INTERNET EXERCISES

Go to **www.thomsonedu.com/westbuslaw/let**, the Web site that accompanies this text. Select "Chapter 7" and click on "Internet Exercises." There you will find the following Internet research exercises that you can perform to learn more about topics covered in this chapter.

Internet Exercise 7–1: LEGAL PERSPECTIVE—Unwarranted Legal Threats
Internet Exercise 7–2: MANAGEMENT PERSPECTIVE—Protecting Intellectual Property across Borders

BEFORE THE TEST

Go to **www.thomsonedu.com/westbuslaw/let**, the Web site that accompanies this text. Select "Chapter 7" and click on "Interactive Quizzes." You will find a number of interactive questions relating to this chapter.

Contract Formation

CHAPTER OBJECTIVES

After reading this chapter, you should be able to answer the following questions:

1. What are the four basic elements necessary to the formation of a valid contract?

2. What elements are necessary for an effective offer?

3. What is consideration?

4. Does an intoxicated person have the capacity to enter into an enforceable contract?

5. What contracts must be in writing to be enforceable?

> "The social order rests upon the stability and predictability of conduct, of which keeping promises is a large item."
> —ROSCOE POUND, 1870–1964
> (American jurist)

PROMISE
A person's assurance that the person will or will not do something.

AS ROSCOE POUND—an eminent jurist—observed in the chapter-opening quotation, "keeping promises" is important to a stable social order. Contract law deals with, among other things, the formation and keeping of promises. A **promise** is an assertion that something either will or will not happen in the future.

Like other types of law, contract law reflects our social values, interests, and expectations at a given point in time. It shows, for example, to what extent our society allows people to make promises or commitments that are legally binding. It distinguishes between promises that create only *moral* obligations (such as a promise to take a friend to lunch) and promises that are legally binding (such as a promise to pay for merchandise purchased). Contract law also demonstrates what excuses our society accepts for breaking certain types of promises. In addition, it indicates what promises are considered to be contrary to public policy—against the interests of society as a whole—and therefore legally invalid. When the person making a promise is a child or is mentally incompetent, for example, a question will arise as to whether the promise should be enforced. Resolving such questions is the essence of contract law. The common law governs all contracts except when it has been modified or replaced by statutory law, such as the Uniform Commercial Code (UCC),[1] or by administrative agency regulations. Contracts relating to services, real estate, employment, and insurance, for example, generally are governed by the common law of contracts.

---

1. See Chapters 1 and 10 for further discussions of the significance and coverage of the UCC. Excerpts from the UCC are presented in Appendix D at the end of this book.

Contracts for the sale and lease of goods, however, are governed by the UCC—to the extent that the UCC has modified general contract law. The relationship between general contract law and the law governing sales and leases of goods will be explored in detail in Chapter 10. In the discussion of general contract law that follows, we indicate in footnotes the areas in which the UCC has significantly altered common law contract principles.

THE FUNCTION AND DEFINITION OF CONTRACTS

The law encourages competent parties to form contracts for lawful objectives. Indeed, no aspect of modern life is entirely free of contractual relationships. Even the ordinary consumer in his or her daily activities acquires rights and obligations based on contract law. You acquire rights and obligations, for example, when you purchase goods or services, when you borrow funds, and when you buy or lease a house. Contract law is designed to provide stability and predictability, as well as certainty, for both buyers and sellers in the marketplace.

CONTRACT
An agreement that can be enforced in court; formed by two or more competent parties who agree, for consideration, to perform or to refrain from performing some legal act now or in the future.

A **contract** is "a promise or a set of promises for the breach of which the law gives a remedy, or the performance of which the law in some way recognizes as a duty."[2] Put simply, a contract is an agreement that can be enforced in court. It is formed between two or more parties who agree to perform or to refrain from performing some act now or in the future. Generally, contract disputes arise when there is a promise of future performance. If the contractual promise is not fulfilled, the party who made it is subject to the sanctions of a court (see Chapter 9). That party may be required to pay damages for failing to perform the contractual promise; in limited instances, the party may be required to perform the promised act.

In determining whether a contract has been formed, the element of intent is of prime importance. In contract law, intent is determined by what is called the *objective theory of contracts,* not by the personal or subjective intent, or belief, of a party. The theory is that a party's intention to enter into a legally binding agreement, or contract, is judged by outward, objective facts as interpreted by a *reasonable* person, rather than by the party's own secret, subjective intentions. Objective facts include (1) what the party said when entering into the contract, (2) how the party acted or appeared (intent may be manifested by conduct as well as by oral or written words), and (3) the circumstances surrounding the transaction.

ELEMENTS OF A CONTRACT

The many topics that will be discussed in these chapters on contract law require an understanding of the basic elements of a valid contract and the way in which a contract is created. These topics also require an understanding of the types of circumstances in which even legally valid contracts will not be enforced.

---

2. *Restatement (Second) of Contracts.* The *Restatement of the Law of Contracts* is a nonstatutory, authoritative exposition of the common law of contracts compiled by the American Law Institute in 1932. The *Restatement,* which is now in its second edition (a third edition is being drafted), will be referred to throughout this chapter on contract law.

Requirements of a Valid Contract

The following list briefly describes the four requirements that must be met before a valid contract exists. If any of these elements is lacking, no contract will have been formed. (Each requirement will be explained more fully later in this chapter.)

1. *Agreement.* An agreement to form a contract includes an *offer* and an *acceptance.* One party must offer to enter into a legal agreement, and another party must accept the terms of the offer.
2. *Consideration.* Any promises made by the parties to the contract must be supported by legally sufficient and bargained-for *consideration* (something of value received or promised, such as money, to convince a person to make a deal).
3. *Contractual capacity.* Both parties entering into the contract must have the contractual *capacity* to do so; the law must recognize them as possessing characteristics that qualify them as competent parties.
4. *Legality.* The contract's purpose must be to accomplish some goal that is legal and not against public policy.

Defenses to the Enforceability of a Contract

Even if all of the above-listed requirements are satisfied, a contract may be unenforceable if the following requirements are not met. These requirements typically are raised as *defenses* to the enforceability of an otherwise valid contract.

1. *Genuineness of assent.* The apparent consent of both parties must be genuine. For example, if a contract was formed as a result of fraud, undue influence, mistake, or duress, the contract may not be enforceable.
2. *Form.* The contract must be in whatever form the law requires; for example, some contracts must be in writing to be enforceable.

TYPES OF CONTRACTS

There are many types of contracts. In this section, you will learn that contracts can be categorized based on legal distinctions as to formation, performance, and enforceability.

Contract Formation

As you can see in Exhibit 8–1 on the next page, three classifications, or categories, of contracts are based on how and when a contract is formed. We explain each of these types of contracts in the following subsections.

Bilateral versus Unilateral Contracts   Every contract involves at least two parties. The *offeror* is the party making the offer. The *offeree* is the party to whom the offer is made. Whether the contract is classified as *unilateral* or *bilateral* depends on what the offeree must do to accept the offer and to bind the offeror to a contract.

If to accept the offer the offeree must only *promise* to perform, the contract is a *bilateral contract.* Hence, a bilateral contract is a "promise for a promise." No performance, such as payment of money or delivery of goods, need take

EXHIBIT 8–1   CLASSIFICATIONS BASED ON CONTRACT FORMATION

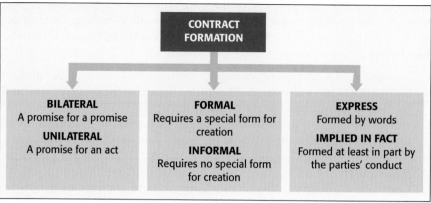

CONTRACT FORMATION		
BILATERAL A promise for a promise **UNILATERAL** A promise for an act	**FORMAL** Requires a special form for creation **INFORMAL** Requires no special form for creation	**EXPRESS** Formed by words **IMPLIED IN FACT** Formed at least in part by the parties' conduct

place for a bilateral contract to be formed. The contract comes into existence at the moment the promises are exchanged. **| Example #1**   Jeff offers to buy Ann's digital camera for $200. Jeff tells Ann that he will give her the money for the camera next Friday, when he gets paid. Ann accepts Jeff's offer and promises to give him the camera when he pays her on Friday. Jeff and Ann have formed a bilateral contract. **|**

If the offer is phrased so that the offeree can accept the offer only by completing the contract performance, the contract is a *unilateral contract.* Hence, a unilateral contract is a "promise for an act."[3] In other words, the time of contract formation in a unilateral contract is not at the moment when promises are exchanged but when the contract is *performed.* **| Example #2**   O'Malley says to Parker, "If you carry this package across the Brooklyn Bridge, I'll give you $20." Only on Parker's complete crossing with the package does she fully accept O'Malley's offer to pay $20. If she chooses not to undertake the walk, there are no legal consequences. **|**

Can a school's or an employer's letter of tentative acceptance to a prospective student or employee qualify as a unilateral contract? That was the question in the following case.

---

3. Clearly, a contract cannot be "one sided," because by definition, an agreement implies the existence of two or more parties. Therefore, the phrase *unilateral contract,* if read literally, is a contradiction in terms. As traditionally used in contract law, however, the phrase refers to the kind of contract that results when only one promise is being made (the promise made by the offeror in return for the offeree's performance).

CASE 8.1   **Ardito v. City of Providence**

United States District Court, District of Rhode Island, 2003. 263 F.Supp.2d 358.

BACKGROUND AND FACTS   In 2001, the city of Providence, Rhode Island, decided to begin hiring police officers to fill vacancies in its police department. Because only individuals who had graduated from the Providence Police Academy were eligible, the city also decided to conduct two training sessions, the "60th and 61st Police Academies." To be admitted, an applicant had to pass a series of tests and be deemed qualified by members of the department after an interview. The applicants judged most qualified were sent a letter informing them that they had been selected to attend the academy if they successfully completed a medical checkup and a psychological examination. The letter for the applicants to the 61st Academy, dated October 15, stated that it was "a conditional offer of employment." Meanwhile, a new chief of police, Dean Esserman, decided to revise the selection process, which caused some of those who had received the letter to be rejected. Derek Ardito and thirteen other newly rejected applicants—who had all completed the examinations—filed a suit in a federal district court against the city, seeking a halt to the 61st Academy unless they were allowed to attend. They alleged in part that the city was in breach of contract.

IN THE WORDS OF THE COURT . . . *ERNEST C. TORRES*, Chief District Judge.

* * * *

* * * [T]he October 15 letter * * * *is a classic example of an offer to enter into a unilateral contract.* The October 15 letter expressly stated that it was a "conditional offer of employment" and the message that it conveyed was that the recipient would be admitted into the 61st Academy if he or she successfully completed the medical and psychological examinations, requirements that the city could not lawfully impose unless it was making a conditional offer of employment. [Emphasis added.]

Moreover, the terms of that offer were perfectly consistent with what applicants had been told when they appeared [for their interviews]. At that time, [Police Major Dennis] Simoneau informed them that, if they "passed" the [interviews], they would be offered a place in the academy provided that they also passed medical and psychological examinations.

The October 15 letter also was in marked contrast to notices sent to applicants by the city at earlier stages of the selection process. Those notices merely informed applicants that they had completed a step in the process and remained eligible to be considered for admission into the academy. Unlike the October 15 letter, the prior notices did not purport to extend a "conditional offer" of admission.

The plaintiffs accepted the city's offer of admission into the academy by satisfying the specified conditions. Each of the plaintiffs submitted to and passed lengthy and intrusive medical and psychological examinations. In addition, many of the plaintiffs, in reliance on the City's offer, jeopardized their standing with their existing employers by notifying the employers of their anticipated departure, and some plaintiffs passed up opportunities for other employment.

* * * *

The city argues that there is no contract between the parties because the plaintiffs have no legally enforceable right to employment. The city correctly points out that, even if the plaintiffs graduate from the Academy and there are existing vacancies in the department, they would be required to serve a one-year probationary period during which they could be terminated without cause * * * . That argument misses the point. The contract that the plaintiffs seek to enforce is not a contract that they will be appointed as permanent Providence police officers; rather, it is a contract that they would be admitted to the Academy if they passed the medical and psychological examinations.

DECISION AND REMEDY The court issued an injunction to prohibit the city from conducting the 61st Police Academy unless the plaintiffs were included. The October 15 letter was a unilateral offer that the plaintiffs had accepted by passing the required medical and psychological examinations.

WHAT IF THE FACTS WERE DIFFERENT? *Suppose that the October 15 letter had used the phrase* potential offer of employment *instead of using the word* conditional. *Would the court in this case still have considered the letter to be a unilateral contract? Why or why not?*

Formal versus Informal Contracts Another classification system divides contracts into formal contracts and informal contracts. *Formal contracts* are contracts that require a special form or method of creation (formation) to be enforceable. One type of formal contract is the *contract under seal*, a formalized writing with a special seal attached. The seal may be actual (made of wax or some other durable substance), impressed on the paper, or indicated simply by the word *seal* or the letters *L.S.* at the end of the document. *L.S.* stands for *locus sigilli* and means "the place for the seal."[4]

A written contract may be considered sealed if the promisor *adopts* a seal already on it. A standard-form contract purchased at the local office supply store, for example, may have the word *seal* (or something else that qualifies as a seal) printed next to the blanks intended for the signatures. Unless the parties who sign the form indicate a contrary intention, when they sign the form, they adopt the seal.

Informal contracts include all other contracts. Such contracts are also called *simple contracts.* No special form is required (except for certain types of contracts that must be in writing), as the contracts are usually based on their substance rather than their form. Typically, businesspersons put their contracts in writing to ensure that there is some proof of a contract's existence should problems arise.

Express versus Implied-in-Fact Contracts   Contracts may also be categorized as *express* or *implied* by the conduct of the parties. In an *express contract,* the terms of the agreement are fully and explicitly stated in words, oral or written. A signed lease for an apartment or a house is an express written contract. If a classmate calls you on the phone and agrees to buy your textbook from last semester for $45, an express oral contract has been made.

A contract that is implied from the conduct of the parties is called an *implied-in-fact contract* or an implied contract. This type of contract differs from an express contract in that the *conduct* of the parties, rather than their words, creates and defines the terms of the contract. For an implied-in-fact contract to arise, the following conditions normally must exist:

1. The plaintiff furnished some service or property.
2. The plaintiff expected to be paid for that service or property, and the defendant knew or should have known that payment was expected.
3. The defendant had a chance to reject the services or property and did not.

| Example #3   Suppose that you need an accountant to complete your tax return this year. You find an accountant at an office in your neighborhood, so you drop by to see her. You go into the accountant's office and explain your problem, and she tells you what her fees are. The next day you return and give her assistant all the necessary information and documents—canceled checks, W-2 forms, and so on. You then walk out the door without saying anything expressly to the assistant. In this situation, you have entered into an implied-in-fact contract to pay the accountant the usual and reasonable fees for her services. The contract is implied by your conduct and by hers. She expects to be paid for completing your tax return, and by bringing in the records she will need to do the work, you have implied an intent to pay her for the services.| (For another example of how an implied-in-fact contract can arise, see this chapter's *Management Perspective* feature.)

---

4. The contract under seal has been almost entirely abolished under such provisions as UCC 2–203 (Section 2–203 of the UCC). In sales of real estate, however, it is still common to use a seal (or an acceptable substitute).

Employment Manuals and Implied Contracts

Management Faces a Legal Issue It is a common practice today for large companies or other organizations to create and distribute to their employees an employment manual or handbook setting forth the conditions of employment. Yet when drafting and distributing such manuals to employees, business owners and managers must consider the following question: Will statements made in an employee handbook constitute "promises" in an implied-in-fact employment contract?

What the Courts Say Increasingly, courts are holding that promises made in an employment manual may create an implied-in-fact employment contract. For example, if an employment handbook states that employees will only be fired for "good cause," the employer may be held to that promise.

This is possible even if, under state law, employment is "at will." Under the employment-at-will doctrine, employers may hire and terminate employees at will, with or without cause. The at-will doctrine will not apply, however, if the terms of employment are subject to a contract between the employer and the employee. If a court holds that an implied employment contract exists,

on the basis of promises made in an employment manual, the employer will be bound by the contract and liable for damages for breaching the contract.[a]

Implications for Managers To avoid being contractually bound by terms in an employment manual, you should avoid making definite statements (such as "employees will only be terminated for good cause") that would cause employees to reasonably believe that those statements are contractual promises. You should also inform employees, when initially giving them the handbook or discussing its contents with them, that it is not intended as a contract. A conspicuous written disclaimer to this effect should also be included in the employment manual.[b] The disclaimer might read as follows: "This policy manual describes the basic personnel policies and practices of our Company. You should understand that the manual does not modify our Company's 'at will' employment doctrine or provide employees with any kind of contractual rights."

---

a. See, for example, *Cisco v. King*, ___ S.W.3d ___ (Ark.App. 2005); and *Parts Depot, Inc. v. Beiswenger*, 170 S.W.3d 354 (Ky. 2005).
b. See, for example, *Ivory v. Specialized Assistance Services, Inc.*, ___ N.E.2d ___ (Ill.App. 1 Dist. 2006).

Contract Performance

Contracts are also classified according to the degree to which they have been performed. A contract that has been fully performed on both sides is called an *executed contract*. A contract that has not been fully performed by the parties is called an *executory contract*. If one party has fully performed but the other has not, the contract is said to be executed on the one side and executory on the other, but the contract is still classified as executory.

Example #4 Assume that you agree to buy ten tons of coal from the Northern Coal Company. Further assume that Northern has delivered the coal to your steel mill, where it is now being burned. At this point, the contract is executed on the part of Northern and executory on your part. After you pay Northern for the coal, the contract will be executed on both sides.

Contract Enforceability

A *valid contract* has the elements necessary to entitle at least one of the parties to enforce it in court. Those elements, as mentioned earlier, consist of (1) an agreement consisting of an offer and an acceptance of that offer, (2) supported by legally sufficient consideration, (3) made by parties who have the legal capacity to enter into the contract, and (4) made for a legal purpose. As you can

EXHIBIT 8-2 ENFORCEABLE, VOIDABLE, UNENFORCEABLE, AND VOID CONTRACTS

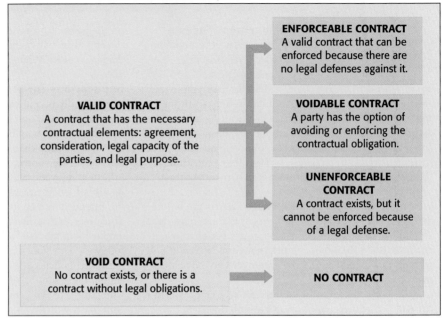

see in Exhibit 8–2, valid contracts may be enforceable, voidable, or unenforceable. Additionally, a contract may be referred to as a *void contract*. We look next at the meaning of the terms *voidable, unenforceable,* and *void* in relation to contract enforceability.

Voidable Contracts   A *voidable contract* is a valid contract but one that can be avoided at the option of one or both of the parties. The party having the option can elect either to avoid any duty to perform or to *ratify* (make valid) the contract. If the contract is avoided, both parties are released from it. If it is ratified, both parties must fully perform their respective legal obligations.

As a general rule, but subject to exceptions, contracts made by minors are voidable at the option of the minor. Contracts entered into under fraudulent conditions are voidable at the option of the defrauded party. In addition, contracts entered into under duress or undue influence are voidable.

Unenforceable Contracts   An *unenforceable contract* is one that cannot be enforced because of certain legal defenses against it. It is not unenforceable because a party failed to satisfy a legal requirement of the contract; rather, it is a valid contract rendered unenforceable by some statute or law. For example, certain contracts must be in writing, and if they are not, they will not be enforceable except in certain exceptional circumstances.

Void Contracts   A *void contract* is no contract at all. The terms *void* and *contract* are contradictory. A void contract produces no legal obligations on any of the parties. For example, a contract can be void because one of the parties was adjudged by a court to be legally insane (and thus lacked the legal capacity to enter into a contract) or because the purpose of the contract was illegal.

AGREEMENT

An essential element for contract formation is **agreement**—that is, the parties must agree on the terms of the contract and manifest their **mutual assent** (agreement) to the same bargain. Ordinarily, agreement is evidenced by two events: an *offer* and an *acceptance*. One party offers a certain bargain to another party, who then accepts that bargain. The agreement does not necessarily have to be in writing. Both parties, however, must manifest their assent to the same bargain. Once an agreement is reached, if the other elements of a contract are present (consideration, capacity, and legality, which will be discussed later in this chapter), a valid contract is formed, generally creating enforceable rights and duties between the parties.

Note that not all agreements are contracts. John and Kevin may agree to play golf on a certain day, but a court would not hold that their agreement is an enforceable contract. A *contractual* agreement arises only when the terms of the agreement impose legally enforceable obligations on the parties.

In today's world, contracts are frequently formed via the Internet. Online offers and acceptances will be discussed in Chapter 10, in the context of electronic contracts, or e-contracts.

Requirements of the Offer

The parties to a contract are the *offeror*, the one who makes an offer or proposal to another party, and the *offeree*, the one to whom the offer or proposal is made. An **offer** is a promise or commitment to do or refrain from doing some specified thing in the future. Under the common law, three elements are necessary for an offer to be effective:

1. The offeror must have a serious intention to become bound by the offer.
2. The terms of the offer must be reasonably certain, or definite, so that the parties and the court can ascertain the terms of the contract.
3. The offer must be communicated by the offeror to the offeree, resulting in the offeree's knowledge of the offer.

Once an effective offer has been made, the offeree has the power to accept the offer. If the offeree accepts, an agreement is formed (and thus a contract arises, if other essential elements are present).

Intention The first requirement for an effective offer to exist is a serious objective intention on the part of the offeror. Intent is not determined by the *subjective* intentions, beliefs, or assumptions of the offeror. Rather, it is determined by what a reasonable person in the offeree's position would conclude the offeror's words and actions meant. Offers made in obvious anger, jest, or undue excitement do not meet the serious-and-objective-intent test. Because these offers are not effective, an offeree's acceptance does not create an agreement.

An expression of opinion is not an offer or a promise. It does not evidence an intention to enter into a binding agreement. **| Example #5** In *Hawkins v. McGee,*[5] Hawkins took his son to McGee, a physician, and asked McGee to operate on the son's hand. McGee said that the boy would be in the hospital three or four days and that the hand would *probably* heal a few days later. The

AGREEMENT
A meeting of two or more minds in regard to the terms of a contract, usually broken down into two events—an offer and an acceptance.

MUTUAL ASSENT
The element of agreement in the formation of a contract. The manifestation of contract parties' mutual assent to the same bargain is required to establish a contract.

OFFER
A promise or commitment to perform or refrain from performing some specified act in the future.

---

5. *Hawkins v. McGee*, 84 N.H. 114, 146 A. 641 (1929).

son's hand did not heal for a month, but nonetheless the father did not win a suit for breach of contract. The court held that McGee did not make an offer to heal the son's hand in three or four days. He merely expressed an opinion as to when the hand would heal.| Similarly, a *statement of intention* is not an offer. |**Example #6** If Ari says "I *plan* to sell my stock in Novation, Inc., for $150 per share," a contract is not created if John "accepts" and tenders the $150 per share for the stock. Ari has merely expressed his intention to enter into a future contract.|

Preliminary negotiations must also be distinguished from an offer. A request or invitation to negotiate is not an offer; it only expresses a willingness to discuss the possibility of entering into a contract. Examples are statements such as "Will you sell Forest Acres?" and "I wouldn't sell my car for less than $5,000." A reasonable person in the offeree's position would not conclude that such a statement evidenced an intention to enter into a binding obligation. Likewise, when the government and private firms need to have construction work done, contractors are invited to submit bids. The *invitation* to submit bids is not an offer, and a contractor does not bind the government or private firm by submitting a bid. (The bids that the contractors submit are offers, however, and the government or private firm can bind the contractor by accepting the bid.) In general, advertisements, mail-order catalogues, price lists, and circular letters (meant for the general public) are treated not as offers to contract but as invitations to negotiate. In the classic case of *Lucy v. Zehmer*, presented next, the court considered whether an offer made "after a few drinks" met the serious-intent requirement.

BE CAREFUL An opinion is not an offer and not a contract term. Goods or services can be "perfect" in one party's opinion and "poor" in another's.

LANDMARK & CLASSIC CASES

CASE 8.2   Lucy v. Zehmer

Supreme Court of Appeals of Virginia, 1954.
196 Va. 493,
84 S.E.2d 516.

BACKGROUND AND FACTS W. O. Lucy and J. C. Lucy, the plaintiffs, filed a suit against A. H. Zehmer and Ida Zehmer, the defendants, to compel the Zehmers to transfer title of their property, known as the Ferguson Farm, to the Lucys for $50,000, as the Zehmers had allegedly agreed to do. Lucy had known Zehmer for fifteen or twenty years and for the last eight years or so had been anxious to buy the Ferguson Farm from Zehmer. One night, Lucy stopped in to visit the Zehmers in the combination restaurant, filling station, and motor court they operated. While there, Lucy tried to buy the Ferguson

Farm once again. This time he tried a new approach. According to the trial court transcript, Lucy said to Zehmer, "I bet you wouldn't take $50,000 for that place." Zehmer replied, "Yes, I would too; you wouldn't give fifty." Throughout the evening, the conversation returned to the sale of the Ferguson Farm for $50,000. At the same time, the parties continued to drink whiskey and engage in light conversation. Eventually, Lucy enticed Zehmer to write up an agreement to the effect that Zehmer would sell to Lucy the Ferguson Farm for $50,000. Later, Lucy sued Zehmer to compel him to go through with the sale. Zehmer argued that he had been drunk and that the offer had been made in jest and hence was unenforceable. The trial court agreed with Zehmer, and Lucy appealed.

IN THE WORDS OF THE COURT . . . BUCHANAN, J. [Justice] delivered the opinion of the court.

* * * *

In his testimony, Zehmer claimed that he "was high as a Georgia pine," and that the transaction "was just a bunch of two doggoned drunks bluffing to see who could talk the biggest and say the most." That claim is inconsistent with his attempt to testify in great detail as to what was said and what was done. * * *

CASE 8.2–CONTINUED

* * * *

The appearance of the contract, the fact that it was under discussion for forty minutes or more before it was signed; Lucy's objection to the first draft because it was written in the singular, and he wanted Mrs. Zehmer to sign it also; the rewriting to meet that objection and the signing by Mrs. Zehmer; the discussion of what was to be included in the sale, the provision for the examination of the title, the completeness of the instrument that was executed, the taking possession of it by Lucy with no request or suggestion by either of the defendants that he give it back, are facts which furnish persuasive evidence that the execution of the contract was a serious business transaction rather than a casual, jesting matter as defendants now contend.

* * * *

In the field of contracts, as generally elsewhere, *[w]e must look to the outward expression of a person as manifesting his intention rather than to his secret and unexpressed intention.* The law imputes to a person an intention corresponding to the reasonable meaning of his words and acts. [Emphasis added.]

* * * *

Whether the writing signed by the defendants and now sought to be enforced by the complainants was the result of a serious offer by Lucy and a serious acceptance by the defendants, or was a serious offer by Lucy and an acceptance in secret jest by the defendants, in either event it constituted a binding contract of sale between the parties.

DECISION AND REMEDY The Supreme Court of Virginia determined that the writing was an enforceable contract and reversed the ruling of the lower court. The Zehmers were required by court order to follow through with the sale of the Ferguson Farm to the Lucys.

WHAT IF THE FACTS WERE DIFFERENT? *Suppose that the day after Lucy signed the real estate sales agreement, he decided that he didn't want the farm after all, and Zehmer sued Lucy to perform the contract. Would this change in the facts alter the court's decision that Lucy and Zehmer had created an enforceable contract?*

IMPACT OF THIS CASE ON TODAY'S LEGAL ENVIRONMENT *This is a classic case in contract law because it illustrates so clearly the objective theory of contracts with respect to determining whether a serious offer was intended. Today, the objective theory of contracts continues to be applied by the courts, and* Lucy v. Zehmer *is routinely cited as a significant precedent in this area.*

RELEVANT WEB SITES *To locate information on the Web concerning* Lucy v. Zehmer, *go to this text's Web site at* **www.thomsonedu.com/westbuslaw/let**, *select "Chapter 8," and click on "URLs for Landmarks."*

Definiteness of Terms The second requirement for an effective offer involves the definiteness of its terms. An offer must have terms that are reasonably definite so that, if it is accepted and a contract formed, a court can determine if a breach has occurred and can provide an appropriate remedy. The specific terms required depend, of course, on the type of contract. Generally, a contract must include the following terms, either expressed in the contract or capable of being reasonably inferred from it:

1. The identification of the parties.
2. The identification of the object or subject matter of the contract (also the quantity, when appropriate), including the work to be performed, with specific identification of such items as goods, services, and land.
3. The consideration to be paid.
4. The time of payment, delivery, or performance.

An offer may invite an acceptance to be worded in such specific terms that the contract is made definite. **| Example #7** Marcus Business Machines contacts

Stein Corporation and offers to sell "from one to ten MacCool copying machines for $1,600 each; state number desired in acceptance." Stein Corporation agrees to buy two copiers. Because the quantity is specified in the acceptance, the terms are definite, and the contract is enforceable.|

Courts sometimes are willing to supply a missing term in a contract when the parties have clearly manifested an intent to form a contract. If, in contrast, the parties have attempted to deal with a particular term of the contract but their expression of intent is too vague or uncertain to be given any precise meaning, the court will not supply a "reasonable" term because to do so might conflict with the intent of the parties. In other words, the court will not rewrite the contract.[6]

Communication   A third requirement for an effective offer is communication of the offer to the offeree, resulting in the offeree's knowledge of the offer. Ordinarily, one cannot agree to a bargain without knowing that it exists. | **Example #8**   Estrich advertises a reward for the return of his lost dog. Hoban, not knowing of the reward, finds the dog and returns it to Estrich. Hoban cannot recover the reward, because she did not know it had been offered.[7]|

Termination of the Offer

The communication of an effective offer to an offeree gives the offeree the power to transform the offer into a binding, legal obligation (a contract) by an acceptance. This power of acceptance, however, does not continue forever. It can be terminated either by the *action of the parties* or by *operation of law.*

Termination by Action of the Offeror   An offer can be terminated by the action of the parties in any of three ways: by revocation, by rejection, or by counteroffer. The offeror's act of withdrawing (revoking) an offer is known as **revocation.** Unless an offer is irrevocable (irrevocable offers will be discussed shortly), the offeror usually can revoke the offer (even if he or she has promised to keep it open) as long as the revocation is communicated to the offeree before the offeree accepts. Revocation may be accomplished by express repudiation of the offer (for example, with a statement such as "I withdraw my previous offer of October 17") or by performance of acts that are inconsistent with the existence of the offer and are made known to the offeree. | **Example #9** Chakir offers to sell some land to Seda. A month passes and Seda, who has not accepted the offer, learns that Chakir has sold the land to Gomez. Because Chakir's sale of the land to Gomez is inconsistent with the continued existence of the offer to sell the land to Seda, the offer to Seda is revoked.|

Termination by Action of the Offeree   The offer may be rejected by the offeree, in which case the offer is terminated. A rejection is ordinarily accomplished by words or conduct evidencing an intent not to accept the offer. As with revoca-

REVOCATION
In contract law, the withdrawal of an offer by an offeror; unless the offer is irrevocable, it can be revoked at any time prior to acceptance without liability.

---

6. See Chapter 10 and UCC 2–204. Article 2 of the UCC specifies different rules relating to the definiteness of terms used in a contract for the sale of goods. In essence, Article 2 modifies general contract law by requiring less specificity.

7. A few states allow recovery of the reward, but not on contract principles. Because Estrich wanted his dog to be returned and Hoban returned it, these few states would allow Hoban to recover on the basis that it would be unfair to deny her the reward just because she did not know it had been offered.

tion, rejection of an offer is effective only when it is actually received by the offeror or the offeror's agent. A **counteroffer** occurs when the offeree rejects the original offer and simultaneously makes a new offer. **|Example #10|** Duffy offers to sell her Picasso lithograph to Wong for $4,500. Wong responds, "Your price is too high. I'll offer to purchase your lithograph for $4,000." Wong's response is a counteroffer, because it terminates Duffy's offer to sell at $4,500 and creates a new offer by Wong to purchase at $4,000.**|**

At common law, the **mirror image rule** requires the offeree's acceptance to match the offeror's offer exactly—to mirror the offer. Any material change in, or addition to, the terms of the original offer automatically terminates that offer and substitutes the counteroffer. The counteroffer, of course, need not be accepted; but if the original offeror does accept the terms of the counteroffer, a valid contract is created.[8]

Termination by Operation of Law   The power of the offeree to transform the offer into a binding, legal obligation can be terminated by operation of law through the occurrence of any of the following events:

1. Lapse of time.
2. Destruction of the specific subject matter of the offer.
3. Death or incompetence of the offeror or the offeree.
4. Supervening illegality of the proposed contract.

An offer terminates automatically by law when the period of time specified in the offer has passed. **|Example #11|** Alejandro offers to sell his camper to Kelly if she accepts within twenty days. Kelly must accept within the twenty-day period, or the offer will lapse (terminate).**|** The time period specified in an offer normally begins to run when the offer is actually received by the offeree, not when it is sent or drawn up. If the offer does not specify a time for acceptance, the offer terminates at the end of a *reasonable* period of time. What constitutes a reasonable period of time depends on the subject matter of the contract, business and market conditions, and other relevant circumstances. An offer to sell farm produce, for example, will terminate sooner than an offer to sell farm equipment because farm produce is perishable and subject to greater fluctuations in market value.

Acceptance

Acceptance is a voluntary act (either words or conduct) by the offeree that shows assent (agreement) to the terms of an offer. The acceptance must be unequivocal (clear) and must be communicated to the offeror.

Unequivocal Acceptance   To exercise the power of acceptance effectively, the offeree must accept unequivocally. This is the *mirror image rule* previously discussed. If the acceptance is subject to new conditions or if the terms of the acceptance *materially* change the original offer, the acceptance may be deemed a counteroffer that implicitly rejects the original offer. An acceptance may be

COUNTEROFFER
An offeree's response to an offer in which the offeree rejects the original offer and at the same time makes a new offer.

MIRROR IMAGE RULE
A common law rule that requires that the terms of the offeree's acceptance adhere exactly to the terms of the offeror's offer for a valid contract to be formed.

ACCEPTANCE
A voluntary act by the offeree that shows assent, or agreement, to the terms of an offer; may consist of words or conduct.

---

8. The mirror image rule has been greatly modified in regard to sales contracts. Section 2–207 of the UCC provides that a contract is formed if the offeree makes a definite expression of acceptance (such as signing the form in the appropriate location), even though the terms of the acceptance modify or add to the terms of the original offer.

unequivocal even though the offeree expresses dissatisfaction with the contract. For example, "I accept the offer, but I wish I could have gotten a better price" is an effective acceptance. So, too, is "I accept, but can you shave the price?" In contrast, the statement "I accept the offer but only if I can pay on ninety days' credit" is not an unequivocal acceptance and operates as a counteroffer, rejecting the original offer.

Certain terms, when added to an acceptance, will not qualify the acceptance sufficiently to constitute rejection of the offer. **| Example #12** Suppose that in response to an offer to sell a piano, the offeree replies, "I accept; please send a written contract." The offeree is requesting a written contract but is not making it a condition for acceptance. Therefore, the acceptance is effective without the written contract. If the offeree replies, "I accept if you send a written contract," however, the acceptance is expressly conditioned on the request for a writing, and the statement is not an acceptance but a counteroffer. (Notice how important each word is!)[9] **|**

Communication of Acceptance   Whether the offeror must be notified of the acceptance depends on the nature of the contract. In a bilateral contract, communication of acceptance is necessary because acceptance is in the form of a promise (not performance) and the contract is formed when the promise is made (rather than when the act is performed). The offeree must communicate the acceptance to the offeror. Communication of acceptance is not necessary, however, if the offer dispenses with the requirement. Additionally, if the offer can be accepted by silence, no communication is necessary.

Because a unilateral contract calls for the full performance of some act, acceptance is usually evident, and notification is therefore unnecessary. Exceptions do exist, however. When the offeror requests notice of acceptance or has no adequate means of determining whether the requested act has been performed, or when the law requires notice of acceptance, then notice is necessary.

Mode and Timeliness of Acceptance   In bilateral contracts, acceptance must be timely. The general rule is that acceptance in a bilateral contract is timely if it is made before the offer is terminated. Problems arise, however, when the parties involved are not dealing face to face. In such cases, acceptance takes effect, thus completing formation of the contract, at the time the acceptance is communicated via the mode expressly or impliedly authorized by the offeror.

This rule traditionally has been referred to as the **mailbox rule,** also called the "deposited acceptance rule," because once an acceptance has been deposited in a mailbox, it is "out of the offeree's possession." Under this rule, if the authorized mode of communication is the mail, then an acceptance becomes valid when it is dispatched by mail (even if it is never received by the offeror). When an offeror specifies how acceptance should be made (for example, by overnight delivery), a contract is created as soon as the offeree delivers the message to the express delivery company.

Technology and Acceptance Rules   Clearly, some of the traditional rules governing acceptance do not seem to apply to an age in which acceptances are commonly delivered via e-mail, fax, or other delivery system, such as FedEx or DHL. For example, the mailbox rule does not apply to online acceptances, which typi-

If an offer expressly authorizes acceptance of the offer by first class mail or express delivery, can the offeree accept by a faster means, such as by fax or e-mail? Why or why not? (Michael Newman/PhotoEdit)

MAILBOX RULE
A rule providing that an acceptance of an offer becomes effective on dispatch (on being placed in an official mailbox), if mail is expressly or impliedly an authorized means of communication of acceptance to the offeror.

---

9. In regard to sales contracts, the UCC provides that an acceptance may still be valid even if some terms are added. The new terms are simply treated as proposed additions to the contract.

cally are communicated instantaneously to the offeror. Nonetheless, the traditional rules—and the principles that underlie those rules—provide a basis for
understanding what constitutes a valid acceptance in today's online environment.
This is because, as in other areas of the law, much of the law governing online
offers and acceptances has been adapted from traditional law to a new context.

While online offers are not significantly different from traditional offers
contained in paper documents, online acceptances have posed some unusual
problems for the court (see Chapter 10).

CONSIDERATION

The fact that a promise has been made does not mean the promise can or will be
enforced. Under Roman law, a promise was not enforceable without some sort of
causa—that is, a reason for making the promise that was also deemed to be a sufficient reason for enforcing it. Under the common law, a primary basis for the
enforcement of promises is consideration. **Consideration** is usually defined as the
value (such as cash) given in return for a promise (such as the promise to sell a
stamp collection on receipt of payment) or in return for a performance.

Often, consideration is broken down into two parts: (1) something of *legally
sufficient value* must be given in exchange for the promise and (2) usually,
there must be a *bargained-for* exchange.

CONSIDERATION
Generally, the value given in return for a
promise. The consideration must be
something of legally sufficient value, and
there must be a bargained-for exchange.

Legal Value

The "something of legally sufficient value" may consist of (1) a promise to do
something that one has no prior legal duty to do, (2) the performance of an
action that one is otherwise not obligated to undertake, or (3) the refraining
from an action that one has a legal right to undertake (called a *forbearance*).
Consideration in bilateral contracts normally consists of a promise in return
for a promise, as explained earlier. For example, suppose that in a contract for
the sale of goods, the seller promises to ship specific goods to the buyer, and
the buyer promises to pay for those goods when they are received. Each of
these promises constitutes consideration for the contract.

In contrast, unilateral contracts involve a promise in return for a perfor-
mance. **| Example #13** Anita says to her neighbor, "When you finish painting
the garage, I will pay you $100." Anita's neighbor paints the garage. The act
of painting the garage is the consideration that creates Anita's contractual obli-
gation to pay her neighbor $100.**|**

What if, in return for a promise to pay, a person refrains from pursuing
harmful habits (a forbearance), such as the use of tobacco and alcohol? Does
such forbearance constitute legally sufficient consideration? That was the issue
before the court in *Hamer v. Sidway,* a classic case concerning consideration
that we present as this chapter's *Landmark in the Legal Environment* feature
on the next page.

Bargained-For Exchange

The second element of consideration is that it must provide the basis for
the bargain struck between the contracting parties. The promise given by the
promisor (offeror) must induce the promisee (offeree) to offer a return promise,
a performance, or a forbearance, and the promisee's promise, performance, or
forbearance must induce the promisor to make the promise.

Hamer v. Sidway (1891)

In *Hamer v. Sidway,*[a] the issue before the court arose from a contract created in 1869 between William Story, Sr., and his nephew, William Story II. The uncle promised his nephew that if the nephew refrained from drinking alcohol, using tobacco, and playing billiards and cards for money until he reached the age of twenty-one, the uncle would pay him $5,000 (about $75,000 in today's dollars). The nephew, who indulged occasionally in all of these "vices," agreed to refrain from them and did so for the next six years. (In 1869, it was legal for a teenager to gamble and to use alcohol and tobacco.) Following his twenty-first birthday in 1875, the nephew wrote to his uncle that he had performed his part of the bargain and was thus entitled to the promised $5,000. A few days later, the uncle wrote the nephew a letter stating, "[Y]ou shall have the five thousand dollars, as I promised you." The uncle said that the money was in the bank and that the nephew could "consider this money on interest."

The Issue of Consideration   The nephew left the money in the care of his uncle, who held it for the next twelve years. When the uncle died in 1887, however, the executor of the uncle's estate refused to pay the $5,000 claim brought by Hamer, a third party to whom the promise had been *assigned*. (The law allows parties to assign, or transfer, rights in contracts to third parties; assignments will be discussed further later in this chapter.) The executor, Sidway, contended that the contract was

a. 124 N.Y. 538, 27 N.E. 256 (1891).

invalid because there was insufficient consideration to support it. The uncle had received nothing, and the nephew had actually benefited by fulfilling the uncle's wishes. Therefore, no contract existed.

The Court's Conclusion   Although a lower court upheld Sidway's position, the New York Court of Appeals reversed and ruled in favor of the plaintiff, Hamer. "The promisee used tobacco, occasionally drank liquor, and he had a legal right to do so," the court stated. "That right he abandoned for a period of years upon the strength of the promise of the testator [one who makes a will] that for such forbearance he would give him $5,000. We need not speculate on the effort which may have been required to give up the use of those stimulants. It is sufficient that he restricted his lawful freedom of action within certain prescribed limits upon the faith of his uncle's agreement."

Application to Today's Legal Environment
Although this case was decided over a century ago, the principles enunciated by the court remain applicable to contracts formed today, including online contracts. For a contract to be valid and binding, consideration must be given, and that consideration must be something of legally sufficient value.

RELEVANT WEB SITES
To locate information on the Web concerning the Hamer v. Sidway *decision, go to this text's Web site at* **www.thomsonedu.com/westbuslaw/let**, *select* "Chapter 8," *and click on* "URLs for Landmarks."

This element of bargained-for exchange distinguishes contracts from gifts. **|Example #14** Suppose that Arlene says to her son, "In consideration of the fact that you are not as wealthy as your brothers, I will pay you $500." The fact that the word *consideration* is used does not, by itself, mean that consideration has been given. Indeed, this is not an enforceable promise because the son need not do anything in order to receive the promised $500.[10] The son need not give Arlene something of legal value in return for her promise, and the promised $500 does not involve a bargained-for exchange. Rather, Arlene has simply stated her motive for giving her son a gift.**|**

Adequacy of Consideration

Legal sufficiency of consideration involves the requirement that consideration be something of legally sufficient value in the eyes of the law. Adequacy of consideration involves "how much" consideration is given. Essentially, adequacy

10. See *Fink v. Cox*, 18 Johns. 145, 9 Am.Dec. 191 (N.Y. 1820).

of consideration concerns the fairness of the bargain. On the surface, fairness would appear to be an issue when the items exchanged are of unequal value. In general, however, a court will not question the adequacy of consideration if the consideration is legally sufficient. Under the doctrine of freedom of contract, parties are normally free to bargain as they wish. If people could sue merely because they had entered into an unwise contract, the courts would be overloaded with frivolous suits.

In extreme cases, however, a court of law may look to the amount or value (the adequacy) of the consideration because apparently inadequate consideration can indicate that fraud, duress, or undue influence was involved or that a gift was made (if a father "sells" a $100,000 house to his daughter for only $1, for example). Additionally, when the consideration is grossly inadequate, the courts may declare the contract unenforceable on the ground that it is unconscionable,[11] meaning that, generally speaking, it is so one sided under the circumstances as to be clearly unfair. (Unconscionability will be discussed further later in this chapter.)

In the following case, the issue was whether consideration existed in a contract to accept lower payments for medical services than the maximum fees allowed under state regulations.

BE AWARE A consumer's signature on a contract does not always guarantee that the contract will be enforced. Ultimately, the terms must be fair.

---

11. Pronounced un-*kon*-shun-uh-bul.

CASE 8.3 **Seaview Orthopaedics v. National Healthcare Resources, Inc.**

Superior Court of New Jersey,
Appellate Division, 2004.
366 N.J.Super. 501,
841 A.2d 917.
lawlibrary.rutgers.edu/search.shtml [a]

BACKGROUND AND FACTS Consumer Health Network (CHN) is a large health-insurance preferred-provider organization (PPO) in New Jersey. CHN provides medical services providers (its clients) with a PPO network in three distinct areas: workers' compensation, group health benefits, and auto insurance. The network includes over 11,000

physicians and nearly 14,000 medical services providers (which include physicians, laboratories, and hospitals). By entering into a contract with CHN, a medical services provider gains potential access to 950,000 enrollees in exchange for accepting reimbursement at rates lower than the maximum rates permitted by New Jersey state regulations. Seaview Orthopaedics is a CHN client that renders services to auto accident victims insured by Allstate Indemnity Company. Allstate pays the CHN rates for Seaview's services through Allstate's claims administrator, National Healthcare Resources (NHR). Seaview and others filed a suit in a New Jersey state court against NHR and others to recover the difference between the CHN rates and the state's maximum rates. The court issued a summary judgment in favor of the defendants. The plaintiffs appealed to a state intermediate appellate court, claiming that the CHN contract was not enforceable, in part because it lacked consideration.

a. Click on "Search by Party Name." On that page, select "Appellate Division" as the court, and type "Seaview Orthopaedics" in the "First Name" box. Click on "Submit Form" to view a synopsis of the case, and then on "click here to get this case" to read the opinion. Rutgers University School of Law in Camden, New Jersey, maintains this Web site.

IN THE WORDS OF THE COURT . . . FISHER, J.A.D. [Judge, Appellate Division]

* * * *

　　　　Plaintiffs * * * argue that their agreement to be bound to the CHN rates for auto accident victims is not supported by consideration. It is well-settled that contracts are not enforceable in the absence of consideration, [that is,] both sides must get something out of the exchange. Consideration may take many forms and may be based upon either a detriment incurred by the promisee or a benefit received by the promisor. Courts, however, do not inquire into the adequacy of consideration in determining whether to

CASE 8.3—CONTINUED ▶

enforce a contract. Any inquiry into the presence of consideration does not depend upon the comparative value of the things exchanged. Instead, when we speak of the need for an exchange of valuable consideration what is meant is that the consideration must merely be valuable in the sense that it is something that is bargained for in fact.

Here, the contract provided benefits to plaintiffs in a variety of ways which either collectively or separately constituted valuable consideration for plaintiffs' promise to accept the CHN rates for reimbursement from auto accident victims (and other types of patients) and not the maximum rate permitted by the [state's] fee schedule. Plaintiffs, for example, obtained the benefit of marketing their businesses in a directory of providers utilized by numerous payors in the workers' compensation and health benefits markets and many thousands of potential patients. Payors make the list available to the largest PPO membership network in New Jersey and, in the health and workers' compensation settings, are generally offered substantial financial incentives when those patients use the providers on the list.

Plaintiffs argue that the likelihood of a provider receiving a referral from the CHN network of an auto accident victim "is practically nil." Defendants dispute this, contending that an auto accident victim, who is in a health benefits or workers' compensation plan that utilized the CHN network, may likely use the same provider that was engaged for these other purposes. This point is, perhaps, debatable. But even if plaintiffs' argument is accurate and the actual benefits received by them in the auto insurance area are illusory, plaintiffs received valuable consideration by being in the network and by obtaining or at least gaining access to patients in the workers' compensation and health benefits areas. That the predominant (or even exclusive) benefits for providers may come from workers' compensation or health benefit sources does not render the contract unenforceable for lack of consideration when services provided for auto accident victims are reimbursed at a lesser rate. We need not, as plaintiffs argue, find some specific monetary benefit for plaintiffs when called upon to provide services for auto accident victims so long as the other aspects of the contract provide, or have the potential to provide, a benefit to plaintiffs. It is the totality of the exchange of promises and benefits that is considered and, in this case, this exchange was sufficient to create an enforceable contract.

* * * *

* * * [W]e reject plaintiffs' contentions in their entirety and affirm the entry of summary judgment dismissing the complaints in these * * * actions. We * * * also affirm the order imposing costs in favor of defendants and against plaintiffs in each action.

DECISION AND REMEDY The state intermediate appellate court affirmed the lower court's summary judgment. The CHN contract did not lack consideration. "Here, the contract provided benefits to plaintiffs in a variety of ways which either collectively or separately constituted valuable consideration for plaintiffs' promise to accept the CHN rates for reimbursement from auto accident victims (and other types of patients) and not the maximum rate permitted by the [state's] fee schedule."

WHY IS THIS CASE IMPORTANT? *As this case illustrates, something need not be of direct economic or financial value to be considered legally sufficient consideration. In many situations, as here, the exchange of promises and potential benefits is deemed sufficient as consideration.*

Agreements That Lack Consideration

Sometimes, one of the parties (or both parties) to an agreement may think that consideration has been exchanged when in fact it has not. Here, we look at some situations in which the parties' promises or actions do not qualify as contractual consideration.

Preexisting Duty   Under most circumstances, a promise to do what one already has a legal duty to do does not constitute legally sufficient consideration. The preexisting legal duty may be imposed by law or may arise out of a previous contract. A sheriff, for example, cannot collect a reward for providing information leading to the capture of a criminal if the sheriff already has a legal duty to capture the criminal.

Likewise, if a party is already bound by contract to perform a certain duty, that duty cannot serve as consideration for a second contract. **| Example #15** Suppose that Bauman-Bache, Inc., begins construction on a seven-story office building and after three months demands an extra $75,000 on its contract. If the extra $75,000 is not paid, Bauman-Bache will stop working. The owner of the land, having no one else to complete the construction, agrees to pay the extra $75,000. The agreement is unenforceable because it is not supported by legally sufficient consideration; Bauman-Bache was under a preexisting contract to complete the building.**|**

Unforeseen Difficulties   The rule regarding preexisting duty is meant to prevent extortion and the so-called holdup game. What happens, though, when an honest contractor who has contracted with a landowner to construct a building runs into extraordinary difficulties that were totally unforeseen at the time the contract was formed? In the interests of fairness and equity, the courts sometimes allow exceptions to the preexisting duty rule. In the example just mentioned, if the landowner agrees to pay extra compensation to the contractor for overcoming unforeseen difficulties, the court may refrain from applying the preexisting duty rule and enforce the agreement. When the "unforeseen difficulties" that give rise to a contract modification involve the types of risks ordinarily assumed in business, however, the courts will usually assert the preexisting duty rule.

Past Consideration   Promises made in return for actions or events that have already taken place are unenforceable. These promises lack consideration in that the element of bargained-for exchange is missing. In short, you can bargain for something to take place now or in the future but not for something that has already taken place. Therefore, **past consideration** is no consideration.

| Example #16   Suppose that Elsie, a real estate agent, does her friend Judy a favor by selling Judy's house and not charging any commission. Later, Judy says to Elsie, "In return for your generous act, I will pay you $3,000." This promise is made in return for past consideration and is thus unenforceable; in effect, Judy is stating her intention to give Elsie a gift.**|**

PAST CONSIDERATION
An act done before the contract is made, which ordinarily, by itself, cannot be consideration for a later promise to pay for the act.

Promissory Estoppel

Sometimes individuals rely on promises, and that reliance may form a basis for contract rights and duties. Under the doctrine of **promissory estoppel** (also called *detrimental reliance*), a person who has reasonably and substantially relied on the promise of another may be able to obtain some measure of recovery. This doctrine is applied in a wide variety of contexts in which a promise is otherwise unenforceable, such as when a promise is not supported by consideration. Under this doctrine, a court may enforce an otherwise unenforceable promise to avoid the injustice that would otherwise result. For the doctrine to be applied, the following elements are required:

PROMISSORY ESTOPPEL
A doctrine that applies when a promisor makes a clear and definite promise on which the promisee justifiably relies; such a promise is binding if justice will be better served by the enforcement of the promise.

1. There must be a clear and definite promise.
2. The promisee must justifiably rely on the promise.
3. The reliance normally must be of a substantial and definite character.
4. Justice will be better served by enforcement of the promise.

If these requirements are met, a promise may be enforced even though it is not supported by consideration. In essence, the promisor will be *estopped* (prevented) from asserting the lack of consideration as a defense. | **Example #17** Suppose that your uncle tells you, "I'll pay you $250 a week so you won't have to work anymore." In reliance on your uncle's promise, you quit your job, but your uncle refuses to pay you. Under the doctrine of promissory estoppel, you may be able to enforce such a promise.[12]|

CAPACITY

In addition to agreement and consideration, for a contract to be deemed valid the parties to the contract must have *contractual capacity*—the legal ability to enter into a contractual relationship. Courts generally presume the existence of contractual capacity, but there are some situations in which capacity is lacking or may be questionable. For example, in many situations, a minor has the capacity to enter into a contract but also has the right to avoid liability under it.

Historically, the law has given special protection to those who bargain with the inexperience of youth or those who lack the degree of mental competence required by law. A person *adjudged by a court* to be mentally incompetent, for example, cannot form a legally binding contract with another party. In other situations, a party may have the capacity to enter into a valid contract but also have the right to avoid liability under it. For example, minors—or *infants*, as they are commonly referred to in legal terminology—usually are not legally bound by contracts. In this section, we look at the effect of youth, intoxication, and mental incompetence on contractual capacity.

Minors

Today, in virtually all states, the *age of majority* (when a person is no longer a minor) for contractual purposes is eighteen years.[13] In addition, some states provide for the termination of minority on marriage. Minority status may also be terminated by a minor's *emancipation,* which occurs when a child's parent or legal guardian relinquishes the legal right to exercise control over the child. Normally, a minor who leaves home to support himself or herself is considered emancipated.

The general rule is that a minor can enter into any contract that an adult can, provided that the contract is not one prohibited by law for minors (for example, the sale of tobacco or alcoholic beverages). A contract entered into by a minor, however, is voidable at the option of that minor, subject to certain exceptions. To exercise the option to avoid a contract, a minor need only manifest an intention not to be bound by it. The minor "avoids" the contract by disaffirming it.

---

12. *Ricketts v. Scothorn,* 57 Neb. 51, 77 N.W. 365 (1898).
13. The age of majority may still be twenty-one for other purposes, such as the purchase and consumption of alcohol.

The technical definition of **disaffirmance** is the legal avoidance, or setting aside, of a contractual obligation. To disaffirm, a minor must express his or her intent, through words or conduct, not to be bound to the contract. The minor must disaffirm the entire contract, not merely a portion of it. For example, the minor cannot decide to keep part of the goods purchased under a contract and return the remaining goods.

DISAFFIRMANCE
The legal avoidance, or setting aside, of a contractual obligation.

Intoxication

Intoxication is a condition in which a person's normal capacity to act or think is inhibited by alcohol or some other drug. A contract entered into by an intoxicated person can be either voidable or valid (and thus enforceable). If the person was sufficiently intoxicated to lack mental capacity, then the transaction may be voidable at the option of the intoxicated person even if the intoxication was purely voluntary. For the contract to be voidable, the person must prove that the intoxication impaired her or his reason and judgment so severely that she or he did not comprehend the legal consequences of entering into the contract.

Mental Incompetence

If a court has previously determined that a person is mentally incompetent and has appointed a guardian to represent the individual, any contract made by the mentally incompetent person is *void*—no contract exists. Only the guardian can enter into binding legal obligations on the incompetent person's behalf.

LEGALITY

For a contract to be valid and enforceable, it must be formed for a legal purpose. A contract to do something that is prohibited by federal or state statutory law is illegal and, as such, void from the outset and thus unenforceable. Also, a contract that calls for a tortious act or an action contrary to public policy is illegal and unenforceable. **| Example #18** Forest offers a young man $10,000 if he refrains from marrying Forest's daughter. If the young man accepts, no contract is formed (the contract is void) because it is contrary to public policy. Thus, if the man marries Forest's daughter, Forest cannot sue him for breach of contract.| It is important to note that a contract or a clause in a contract may be illegal even in the absence of a specific statute prohibiting the action promised by the contract.

Although contracts involve private parties, some are not enforceable because of the negative impact they would have on society. Contracts in restraint of trade (anticompetitive agreements) usually adversely affect the public (which favors competition in the economy) and typically violate one or more federal or state statutes.[14] An exception is recognized when the restraint is reasonable and it is a subsidiary (secondary or subordinate) part of a contract, such as a contract for the sale of a business or an employment contract. Many such contracts involve a type of restraint called a *covenant not to compete,* or a restrictive covenant. Basically, a restriction on competition must be reasonable—that is, not any greater than necessary to protect a legitimate business interest.

---

14. The federal statutes include the Sherman Act, the Clayton Act, and the Federal Trade Commission Act (see Chapter 20).

GENUINENESS OF ASSENT

A contract has been entered into by two parties, each with full legal capacity and for a legal purpose. The contract is also supported by consideration. The contract thus meets the four requirements for a valid contract that were specified previously. Nonetheless, the contract may be unenforceable if the parties have not genuinely assented to its terms. As stated earlier, lack of **genuineness of assent** (voluntary consent) can be used as a defense to the contract's enforceability. Genuineness of assent may be lacking because of a mistake, misrepresentation, undue influence, or duress—in other words, because there is no true "meeting of the minds." In this section, we examine problems relating to genuineness of assent.

Mistakes

We all make mistakes, and it is therefore not surprising that mistakes are made when contracts are formed. It is important to distinguish between *mistakes of fact* and *mistakes of value or quality*. Only a mistake of fact may allow a contract to be avoided.

If a mistake concerns the future market value or quality of the object of the contract, the mistake is one of *value*, and either party can normally enforce the contract. ⎮**Example #19** Suppose that Chi buys a violin from Bev for $250. Although the violin is very old, neither party believes that it is extremely valuable. An antiques dealer later informs the parties, however, that the violin is rare and worth thousands of dollars. Although both parties were mistaken, the mistake is not a mistake of *fact* that warrants contract rescission.⎮

Mistakes of fact occur in two forms—*bilateral* and *unilateral*. A bilateral, or mutual, mistake is made by both of the contracting parties. A unilateral mistake is made by only one of the parties. We look next at these two types of mistakes and illustrate them graphically in Exhibit 8–3.

Bilateral (Mutual) Mistakes of Fact   A bilateral, or mutual, mistake occurs when both parties are mistaken as to some *material fact*—that is, a fact important to the subject matter of the contract. When a bilateral mistake occurs, the contract can be rescinded, or canceled, by either party. ⎮**Example #20** Keeley buys a landscape painting from Umberto's art gallery. Both Umberto and Keeley believe that the painting is by the artist Vincent van Gogh. Later, Keeley discovers that the painting is a very clever fake. Because neither Umberto nor Keeley was aware of this material fact when they made their deal, Keeley can rescind the contract and recover the purchase price of the painting.⎮

A word or term in a contract may be subject to more than one reasonable interpretation. In that situation, if the parties to the contract attach materially different meanings to the term, their mutual mistake of fact may allow the contract to be rescinded because there has been no "meeting of the minds," or true assent, which is required for a contract to arise.

The classic case on bilateral mistake is *Raffles v. Wichelhaus*,[15] which was decided by an English court in 1864. The defendant, Wichelhaus, paid for a shipment of Surat cotton from the plaintiff, Raffles, "to arrive 'Peerless' from Bombay." Wichelhaus expected the goods to be shipped on the *Peerless*, a ship sailing from Bombay, India, in October. Raffles expected to ship the goods on

---

GENUINENESS OF ASSENT
Knowledge of, and voluntary assent to, the terms of a contract. If a contract is formed as a result of a mistake, misrepresentation, undue influence, or duress, genuineness of assent is lacking, and the contract will be voidable.

⎮ "Mistakes are the inevitable lot of mankind."
—Sir George Jessel, 1824–1883
(English jurist)

---

15. 159 Eng.Rep. 375 (1864).

EXHIBIT 8-3   MISTAKES OF FACT

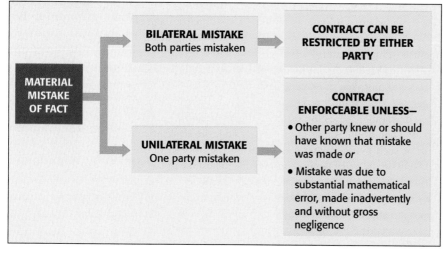

a different *Peerless*, which sailed from Bombay in December. When the goods arrived and Raffles tried to deliver them, Wichelhaus refused to accept them. The court held for Wichelhaus, concluding that no mutual assent existed because the parties had attached materially different meanings to an essential term of the written contract (the ship that was to transport the goods).

In the following case, an injured worker sought to set aside a settlement agreement entered into with his employer, arguing that a physician's mistaken diagnosis of the worker's injury was a mutual mistake of fact on which the agreement was based.

CASE 8.4   **Roberts v. Century Contractors, Inc.**

Court of Appeals of North Carolina, 2004.
162 N.C.App. 688,
592 S.E.2d 215.
www.nccourts.org[a]

BACKGROUND AND FACTS   Bobby Roberts was an employee of Century Contractors, Inc., when a pipe struck him in a work-related accident in July 1993, causing trauma to his neck and back. Dr. James Markworth of Southeastern Orthopaedic Clinic diagnosed Roberts's injuries. After surgery

a. Under the "Favorites" heading, click on "Court Opinions." In the result, click on "2004" under the "Court of Appeals Opinions." Scroll down to "17 February 2004" and select the case name to access the opinion. The North Carolina Appellate Division Reporter maintains this Web site.

and treatment, Markworth concluded that Roberts was at maximum medical improvement (MMI) and stopped treating him. Roberts agreed with Century to accept $125,000 and payment of related medical expenses, and to waive any right to make further claims in regard to his injury. In June 1998, still experiencing pain, Roberts saw Dr. Allen Friedman, who determined that Roberts was not at MMI. Markworth then admitted that his diagnosis was a mistake. Roberts filed a claim for workers' compensation (see Chapter 13), seeking compensation and medical benefits for his injury. He alleged that his agreement with Century should be set aside due to a mutual mistake of fact. The North Carolina state administrative agency authorized to rule on workers' compensation claims awarded Roberts what he sought. Century appealed to a state intermediate appellate court.

IN THE WORDS OF THE COURT . . . LEVINSON, Judge.

*   *   *   *

*   *   * Compromise settlement agreements, including mediated settlement agreements in Workers' Compensation cases, are governed by general principles of contract law.

CASE 8.4—CONTINUED ▶

It is a well-settled principle of contract law that a valid contract exists only where there has been a meeting of the minds as to all essential terms of the agreement. Therefore, where a mistake is common to both parties and concerns a material past or presently existing fact, such that there is no meeting of the minds, a contract may be avoided. [Emphasis added.]

To afford relief, the mistake must be of a certain nature. The fact about which the parties are mistaken must be an existing or past fact. The mistaken fact must also be material * * *. It must be as to a fact which enters into and forms the basis of the contract, or in other words it must be of the essence of the agreement, the *sine qua non* [an essential condition], or, as is sometimes said, the efficient cause of the agreement, and must be such that it animates and controls the conduct of the parties.

Additionally, relief from a contract due to mistake of fact will be had only where *both* parties to an agreement are mistaken. Thus, as a general rule relief will be denied where the party against whom it is sought was ignorant that the other party was acting under a mistake and the former's conduct in no way contributed thereto. Likewise, a party who assumed the risk of a mistaken fact cannot avoid a contract.

A party bears the risk of a mistake when

(a) the risk is allocated to him by agreement of the parties, or
(b) he is aware, at the time the contract is made that he has only limited knowledge with respect to the facts to which the mistake relates but treats his limited knowledge as sufficient, or
(c) the risk is allocated to him by the court on the ground that it is reasonable in the circumstances to do so.

* * * *

* * * The x-rays [examined by Dr. Friedman] after Dr. Markworth or Southern Orthopaedic Clinic had last treated plaintiff [Roberts], indicated Dr. Markworth's diagnosis of maximum medical improvement * * * was a mistake. Dr. Markworth testified * * * that advising plaintiff that he was at maximum medical improvement at that time was a mistake.

* * * *

* * * [T]he finding of maximum medical improvement and the impairment rating given by Dr. Markworth were material to the settlement of this claim and * * * both parties relied on this information in entering into settlement negotiations.

* * * *

* * * [T]he parties believed that plaintiff had reached maximum medical improvement and, further, * * * they materially relied upon this fact in reaching a settlement. Defendants' essential argument on appeal is that because plaintiff either knew that there was a possibility that [he had not reached MMI] or was negligent in not declining to sign the settlement agreement, mutual mistake is a legal impossibility in this case. As the facts * * * support a contrary conclusion, we do not agree.

* * * The plaintiff testified that he based his decision to sign the settlement agreement on Dr. Markworth's diagnosis and that he would not have settled his case if Dr. Friedman had told him that [he had not reached MMI]. Thus, there is competent record evidence to support the * * * findings that the parties were mistaken as to whether plaintiff had reached maximum medical improvement and that this mistaken fact was material. * * *

DECISION AND REMEDY The state intermediate appellate court affirmed the award of compensation and medical benefits to Roberts. The agreement between Roberts and Century was set aside on the basis of a mutual mistake of fact. Markworth's MMI diagnosis was "material to the settlement of this claim and * * * both parties relied on this information." In fact, however, "plaintiff was not at maximum medical improvement."

Unilateral Mistakes of Fact   A unilateral mistake occurs when only one of the contracting parties makes a mistake as to some material fact. The general rule is that a unilateral mistake does not afford the mistaken party any right to relief from the contract. **| Example #21** DeVinck intends to sell his motor home for $17,500. When he learns that Benson is interested in buying a used motor home, DeVinck faxes Benson an offer to sell the vehicle to him. When typing the fax, however, DeVinck mistakenly keys in the price of $15,700. Benson immediately sends DeVinck a fax accepting DeVinck's offer. Even though DeVinck intended to sell his motor home for $17,500, his unilateral mistake falls on him. He is bound in contract to sell the motor home to Benson for $15,700.|

There are at least two exceptions to this general rule.[16] First, if the *other* party to the contract knows or should have known that a mistake of fact was made, the contract may not be enforceable. **| Example #22** In the previous example, if Benson knew that DeVinck intended to sell his motor home for $17,500, then DeVinck's unilateral mistake (stating $15,700 in his offer) may render the resulting contract unenforceable.| The second exception arises when a unilateral mistake of fact was due to a mathematical mistake in addition, subtraction, division, or multiplication and was made inadvertently and without gross (extreme) negligence. If a contractor's bid was significantly low because he or she made a mistake in addition when totaling the estimated costs, any contract resulting from the bid may be rescinded, or canceled. Of course, in both situations, the mistake must still involve some material fact.

Fraudulent Misrepresentation

In the context of contract law, fraud affects the genuineness of the innocent party's consent to the contract. Thus, the transaction is not voluntary in the sense of involving "mutual assent." When an innocent party is fraudulently induced to enter into a contract, the contract usually can be avoided because that party has not *voluntarily* consented to its terms. Normally, the innocent party can either rescind (cancel) the contract and be restored to his or her original position or enforce the contract and seek damages for any injuries resulting from the fraud.

The word *fraudulent* means many things in the law. Generally, fraudulent misrepresentation refers only to misrepresentation that is consciously false and is intended to mislead another. The perpetrator of the fraudulent misrepresentation knows or believes that the assertion is false or knows that she or he does not have a basis (stated or implied) for the assertion. Typically, fraudulent misrepresentation consists of the following elements:

1. A misrepresentation of a material fact must occur.
2. There must be an intent to deceive.
3. The innocent party must justifiably rely on the misrepresentation.

Reliance on the Misrepresentation   To constitute fraud, the deceived party must have a justifiable reason for relying on the misrepresentation, and the misrepresentation must be an important factor in inducing the party to enter into the contract. Reliance is not justified if the innocent party knows the true facts

> "It was beautiful and simple as all truly great swindles are."
> —O. HENRY, 1862–1910
> (American author)

---

16. The *Restatement (Second) of Contracts*, Section 153, liberalizes the general rule to take into account the modern trend of allowing avoidance even though only one party has been mistaken.

or relies on obviously extravagant statements. **| Example #23** If a used-car dealer tells you, "This old Cadillac will get over sixty miles to the gallon," you normally would not be justified in relying on this statement. Suppose, however, that Merkel, a bank director, induces O'Connell, a co-director, to sign a statement that the bank's assets will satisfy its liabilities by telling O'Connell, "We have plenty of assets to satisfy our creditors." This statement is false. If O'Connell knows the true facts or, as a bank director, should know the true facts, he is not justified in relying on Merkel's statement. If O'Connell does not know the true facts, however, *and has no way of finding them out,* he may be justified in relying on the statement.**|**

ETHICAL ISSUE 8.1   *How much information must employers disclose to prospective employees?*

One of the problems employers face is that it is not always clear what information they should disclose to prospective employees. To lure qualified workers, employers are often tempted to "promise the moon" to prospective employees and paint their companies' prospects as bright. Employers must be careful, though, to avoid any conduct that could be interpreted by a court as intentionally deceptive. In particular, they must avoid making any statements about their companies' future prospects or financial health that they know to be false. If they do make a false statement on which a prospective employee relies to her or his detriment, they may be sued for fraudulent misrepresentation.

In one case, for example, an employee accepted a job with a brokerage firm, relying on assurances that the firm was not about to be sold. In fact, as the employee was able to prove in his later lawsuit against the firm for fraud, negotiations to sell the firm were under way at the time he was hired. The trial court awarded the employee over $6 million in damages, a decision that was affirmed on appeal.[17] Generally, employers must be truthful during their hiring procedures to avoid possible lawsuits for fraudulent misrepresentation.

Injury to the Innocent Party   Most courts do not require a showing of injury when the action is to *rescind* (cancel) the contract—these courts hold that because rescission returns the parties to the positions they held before the contract was made, a showing of injury to the innocent party is unnecessary.

For a person to recover damages caused by fraud, however, proof of an injury is universally required. The measure of damages is ordinarily equal to the property's value had it been delivered as represented, less the actual price paid for the property. In actions based on fraud, courts often award *punitive damages,* or *exemplary damages,* which are designed to punish the defendant and to deter similar wrongdoing by others.

Innocent Misrepresentation   Misrepresentations can also be innocently made. If a person makes a statement that he or she believes to be true but that actually misrepresents material facts, an *innocent misrepresentation,* not fraud, has occurred. In this situation, the aggrieved party can rescind the contract but usually cannot seek damages. **| Example #24** Parris tells Roberta that a tract con-

---

17. *McConkey v. AON Corp.,* 354 N.J.Super. 25, 804 A.2d 572 (2002).

tains 250 acres. Parris is mistaken—the tract of land contains only 215 acres—but Parris does not know that. Roberta is induced by the statement to make a contract to buy the land. Even though the misrepresentation is innocent, Roberta can avoid the contract if the misrepresentation is material.|

Undue Influence

Undue influence arises from special kinds of relationships in which one party can greatly influence another party, thus overcoming that party's free will. A contract entered into under excessive or undue influence lacks genuine assent and is therefore voidable.

As mentioned, undue influence arises from relationships in which one party may dominate another party, thus unfairly influencing him or her. Minors and elderly people, for example, are often under the influence of guardians (persons who are legally responsible for another). If a guardian induces a young or elderly ward (the person whom the guardian looks after) to enter into a contract that benefits the guardian, undue influence may have been exerted. Undue influence can arise from a number of confidential or fiduciary relationships: attorney-client, physician-patient, guardian-ward, parent-child, husband-wife, or trustee-beneficiary. The essential feature of undue influence is that the party being taken advantage of does not, in reality, exercise free will in entering into a contract.

Duress

Assent to the terms of a contract is not genuine if one of the parties is *forced* into the agreement. Forcing a party to do something, including entering into a contract, through fear created by threats is legally defined as *duress*. In addition, blackmail or extortion to induce consent to a contract constitutes duress. Duress is both a defense to the enforcement of a contract and a ground for the rescission of a contract.

Generally, for duress to occur the threatened act must be wrongful or illegal. Threatening to exercise a legal right, such as the right to sue someone, ordinarily is not illegal and usually does not constitute duress. **| Example #25** Joan injures Olin in an auto accident. The police are not called. Joan has no automobile insurance, but she has substantial assets. Olin wants to settle the potential claim out of court for $3,000, but Joan refuses. After much arguing, Olin loses his patience and says, "If you don't pay me $3,000 right now, I'm going to sue you for $35,000." Joan is frightened and gives Olin a check for $3,000. Later in the day, Joan stops payment on the check, and Olin later sues her for the $3,000. Although Joan argues that she was the victim of duress, the threat of a civil suit normally is not considered duress. Therefore, a court would not allow Joan to use duress as a defense to the enforcement of her settlement agreement with Olin.|

Adhesion Contracts and Unconscionability

Questions concerning genuineness of assent may arise when the terms of a contract are dictated by a party with overwhelming bargaining power and the signer must agree to those terms or go without the commodity or service in question. Such contracts are often referred to as *adhesion contracts*. An adhesion contract is written *exclusively* by one party (the dominant party, usually the seller or the creditor) and presented to the other party (the adhering party, usually the buyer or the borrower) on a take-it-or-leave-it basis. In other words, the adhering party has no opportunity to negotiate the terms of the contract.

Standard-Form Contracts   Standard-form contracts often contain fine-print provisions that shift a risk naturally borne by one party to the other. A variety of businesses use such contracts. Life insurance policies, residential leases, loan agreements, and employment agency contracts are often standard-form contracts. To avoid enforcement of the contract or of a particular clause, the aggrieved party must show that the parties had substantially unequal bargaining positions and that enforcement would be manifestly unfair or oppressive. If the required showing is made, the contract or particular term is deemed *unconscionable* and is not enforced.

In the following case, the question was whether a standard-form contract clause that mandated individual arbitration of any dispute and precluded class action[18] was unconscionable.

---

18. A *class action* is a lawsuit in which a single person or a small group of people represents the interests of a larger group without every member of the group needing to appear in court.

CASE 8.5   Thibodeau v. Comcast Corp.

Court of Common Pleas of Pennsylvania,
Philadelphia County, 2006.
__ Pa. D. & C.4th __,
__ A.2d __.

BACKGROUND AND FACTS   Philip Thibodeau was a subscriber of Comcast Corporation cable television in Pennsylvania. As part of his subscription agreement, Thibodeau rented two converter boxes and two remote controls, which he thought were necessary to receive broadcasts. At the time, Comcast did not tell its customers that nonpremium programming could be viewed without the boxes and that the remotes were wholly unnecessary. In 2002, Comcast mailed Thibodeau and others a "customer agreement" that mandated the individual arbitration of all disputes and precluded class action. Meanwhile, also in Pennsylvania, Lorena Afroilan bought a cell phone manufactured by Panasonic Corporation and contracted with the AT&T Wireless network for service. With the purchase, Afroilan was given a "Welcome Guide," which required the individual arbitration of all disputes and precluded class action. When Afroilan tried to switch providers, she discovered that her phone had a lock preventing its use on any network other than AT&T's. Thibodeau, Afroilan, and others filed class-action suits in a Pennsylvania state court against Comcast, AT&T, and Panasonic, alleging violations of state law. The court combined the suits. The defendants sought to dismiss the complaints and compel individual arbitration.

IN THE WORDS OF THE COURT . . . *BERNSTEIN, J.* [Judge]

* * * *

Contracts of adhesion are standardized form contracts presented to consumers without negotiation or any option for modification. * * * [A] contract of adhesion is one prepared by one party, to be signed by the party in a weaker position, usually a consumer, who has little choice about the terms. The Comcast and AT&T customer agreements received by the plaintiffs and all other class members are clearly contracts of adhesion. They were sent without any opportunity for customers to negotiate and even without any requirement of assent * * * .

There is nothing *per se* wrong with a contract of adhesion. Not every contract of adhesion contains unconscionable provisions. *A contract of adhesion is only unconscionable if it unreasonably favors the drafter.* * * * In determining whether a clause is unconscionable, the court should consider whether, in light of the general commercial background and the commercial needs of a particular trade, the clause is so one sided that it is unconscionable under the circumstances. [Emphasis added.]

* * * *

Class actions are * * * of great public importance. Class-action lawsuits are an * * * essential vehicle by which consumers may vindicate [assert] their lawful rights. The average consumer, having limited financial resources and time, cannot individually present minor claims in court * * * .

* * * *

It is only the class-action vehicle which makes small consumer litigation possible. Consumers joining together as a class pool their resources, share the costs and efforts of litigation, and make redress possible. Should the law require consumers to litigate or arbitrate individually, defendant corporations are effectively immunized from redress of grievances.

Both the Comcast and AT&T customer agreements attempt to preclude all class action * * * , and attempt to mandate that all customers arbitrate all claims as individuals. The Comcast and AT&T customer agreements are contracts of adhesion unilaterally imposed on all consumers. Consumers including Ms. Afroilan and Mr. Thibodeau are subject to every term without choice. Ms. Afroilan was forced to accept every word of all twenty-five pages of the mass-delivered AT&T customer agreement, or her cellular phone was useless. Mr. Thibodeau was forced to accept every word of all ten pages of the mass-delivered Comcast customer agreement or have no cable television service * * * .

Ms. Afroilan, Mr. Thibodeau, and their class members are claiming minimal damages. Ms. Afroilan and each of the class members allege the cellular phones they purchased for $50 are unusable. Mr. Thibodeau and each of his class members allege they were unlawfully overcharged $9.60 per month. * * * No individual will expend the time, fees, costs, and other expenses necessary for individual litigation or individual arbitration for this small potential recovery. If the mandatory individual arbitration and preclusion of class-action provisions are valid, Comcast and AT&T are immunized from * * * any minor consumer claims. It is clearly contrary to public policy to immunize large corporations from liability by allowing them to preclude all class action.

DECISION AND REMEDY The court denied the defendants' requests to compel individual arbitration of these disputes. The court held that the preclusion of all class action in the defendants' "customer agreement" and "Welcome Guide" was "unconscionable and unenforceable." The court reasoned that the relatively high cost for an individual to obtain a minor recovery would otherwise effectively "immunize [the] corporations from liability."

WHAT IF THE FACTS WERE DIFFERENT? *If the "customer agreement" and "Welcome Guide" had precluded only class litigation and mandated class arbitration, would the court have considered the provisions unconscionable? Why or why not?*

Unconscionability and the Courts Technically, unconscionability under Section 2–302 of the Uniform Commercial Code (UCC) applies only to contracts for the sale of goods. Many courts, however, have broadened the concept and applied it in other situations. For a discussion of whether a contract to prescribe medications via the Internet is unconscionable, see this chapter's *Online Developments* feature on the following page.

It is important to note here that the UCC gives courts a great degree of discretion to invalidate or strike down a contract or clause as being unconscionable. As a result, some states have not adopted Section 2–302 of the

ONLINE DEVELOPMENTS

Is It Unconscionable for Physicians to Prescribe Medication Online?

Anyone with an e-mail address has undoubtedly received scores of messages offering to sell prescription medications, such as Viagra, online. In the past, someone who wanted a prescription for a certain medication—whether it was for allergies, weight loss, or sexual enhancement—had to see a physician and, normally, undergo a physical examination to see if that medication was appropriate. Today, however, it is possible to enter into a contract to obtain a prescription for, and order, many medications via the Internet without ever setting foot in a physician's office. Contracting with a physician online to receive prescription drugs may be ill advised, but are such contracts unconscionable?

A Virtual Diagnosis

The hallmark of an unconscionable contract is that its terms are so oppressive, one sided, or unfair as to "shock the conscience" of the court. Thus, the issue is whether Internet prescription contracts are so unfair that they "shock the conscience" of the court. After all, physicians are trained to examine patients, diagnose medical conditions, and evaluate possible treatments. A physician who is prescribing medication for a person online, however, has no objective way to determine the person's health status or whether the person understands the risks involved. For example, in the online context, a physician cannot tell if a person is truthfully reporting his or her age and weight, which can significantly affect whether a medication is recommended. In addition, physicians who prescribe drugs online cannot monitor the use of these drugs and evaluate their effectiveness.

An Emerging Issue

To date, only a few courts have addressed this issue, and no court as yet has held that prescribing drugs online is unconscionable. For example, in 2003, in a case before

the Kansas Supreme Court, the state attorney general claimed that it was unconscionable for an out-of-state physician to contract with residents to prescribe drugs via the Internet. The case involved three Kansas residents, including a minor, who entered into contracts on the Web to obtain prescription weight-loss drugs (Meridia and phentermine).[a]

The court held that the physician's conduct and the resulting contracts were not unconscionable because there was no evidence that the physician had deceived, oppressed, or misused superior bargaining power. The Web site used by the physician had included a great deal of general information about the specific drugs and their side effects, online questionnaires to obtain medical histories, and waivers of the physician's liability for the prescriptions. The Web site had also provided an online calculator for body weight so that a person could determine if she or he was twenty-five pounds overweight, as required to obtain a prescription for Meridia. Because the court found that the individuals had gotten exactly what they bargained for—the prescription medications they sought—the court refused to step in and declare the contracts unconscionable.

For Critical Analysis *If the physicians are not deceptive, should the courts allow all types of medications to be prescribed over the Internet? Why or why not? Explain whether the practice of prescribing medications via the Internet might reach the point at which it "shocks the conscience" of the court.*

a. *State ex rel. Stovall v. DVM Enterprises, Inc.,* 275 Kan. 243, 62 P.3d 653 (2003); see also *State ex rel. Stovall v. Confimed.com, L.L.C.,* 272 Kan. 1313, 38 P.3d 707 (2002). (The Latin phrase *ex rel.* means "by or on the relation of" and is used in case names when the suit is brought by the government at the request of a private party who is interested in the matter.)

UCC. In those states, the legislature and the courts prefer to rely on traditional notions of fraud, undue influence, and duress.

THE STATUTE OF FRAUDS

A commonly used defense to the enforceability of an oral contract is that it is required to be in writing. Today, almost every state has a statute that stipulates what types of contracts must be in writing. Although the statutes vary slightly from state to state, all states require certain types of contracts to be in writing or evidenced by a written memorandum signed by the party against whom enforcement is sought, unless certain exceptions apply. In this text, we refer to these statutes collectively as the **Statute of Frauds.** The actual name of the Statute of Frauds is misleading because it neither applies to fraud nor invalidates any type of contract. Rather, it denies *enforceability* to certain contracts that do not comply with its requirements. (See this chapter's *Beyond Our Borders* feature on page 272 for a discussion of whether international contracts are required to be in writing.)

STATUTE OF FRAUDS
A state statute under which certain types of contracts must be in writing to be enforceable.

Contracts That Must Be in Writing

The following types of contracts are said to fall "within" or "under" the Statute of Frauds and therefore require a writing:

1. Contracts involving interests in land.
2. Contracts that cannot by their terms be performed within one year from the day after the date of formation.
3. Collateral, or secondary, contracts, such as promises to answer for the debt or duty of another and promises by the administrator or executor of an estate to pay a debt of the estate personally—that is, out of his or her own pocket.
4. Promises made in consideration of marriage (including prenuptial agreements, which are made before marriage).
5. Contracts for the sale of goods priced at $500 or more ($5,000 or more under the 2003 amendments to the Uniform Commercial Code, or UCC, which will be discussed in Chapter 10).

Exceptions to the Statute of Frauds

Exceptions to the applicability of the Statute of Frauds are made in certain situations. In some states, an oral contract that would otherwise be unenforceable under the Statute of Frauds may be enforced under the doctrine of promissory estoppel, based on detrimental reliance. Section 139 of the *Restatement (Second) of Contracts* provides that in these circumstances, an oral promise can be enforceable notwithstanding the Statute of Frauds if the reliance was foreseeable to the person making the promise and if injustice can be avoided only by enforcing the promise. A court might also enforce an oral contract if the party against whom enforcement is sought "admits" in pleadings, testimony, or other court proceedings that a contract for sale was made.

THIRD PARTY RIGHTS

Once it has been determined that a valid and legally enforceable contract exists, attention can turn to the rights and duties of the parties to the contract. A contract is a private agreement between the parties who have entered into it, and traditionally these parties alone have rights and liabilities under the contract. This principle is referred to as *privity of contract.* A *third party*—one who is not a direct party to a particular contract—normally does not have rights under that contract.

There are exceptions to the rule of privity of contract. One exception allows a party to a contract to transfer the rights or duties arising from the contract to another person through an *assignment* (of rights) or a *delegation* (of duties). Another exception involves a *third party beneficiary contract*—a contract in which the parties to the contract intend that the contract benefit a third party.

BEYOND OUR BORDERS

The Statute of Frauds and International Sales Contracts

As you will read in Chapter 10, the Convention on Contracts for the International Sale of Goods (CISG) provides rules that govern international sales contracts between citizens of countries that have ratified the convention (agreement). Article 11 of the CISG does not incorporate any Statute of Frauds provisions. Rather, it states that a "contract for sale need not be concluded in or evidenced by writing and is not subject to any other requirements as to form."

Article 11 accords with the legal customs of most nations, which no longer require contracts to meet certain formal or writing requirements to be enforceable. Ironically, even England, the nation that enacted the original Statute of Frauds in 1677, has repealed all of it except the provisions relating to collateral promises and to transfers of interests in land. Many other countries that once had such statutes have also repealed all or parts of them. Civil law countries, such as France, have never required certain types of contracts to be in writing.

For Critical Analysis *If there were no Statute of Frauds and a dispute arose concerning an oral agreement, how would the parties substantiate their respective positions?*

Assignments

ASSIGNMENT
The act of transferring to another all or part of one's rights arising under a contract.

In a bilateral contract, the two parties have corresponding rights and duties. One party has a *right* to require the other to perform some task, and the other has a *duty* to perform it. The transfer of contractual *rights* to a third party is known as an **assignment.** When rights under a contract are assigned unconditionally, the rights of the *assignor* (the party making the assignment) are extinguished. The third party (the *assignee,* or party receiving the assignment) has a right to demand performance from the other original party to the contract. The assignee takes only those rights that the assignor originally had.

As a general rule, all rights can be assigned. Exceptions are made, however, in some circumstances. If a statute expressly prohibits assignment of a particular right, that right cannot be assigned. When a contract is *personal* in nature, the rights under the contract cannot be assigned unless all that remains is a money payment. A right cannot be assigned if assignment will materially increase or alter the risk or duties of the obligor (the other original party owing performance under the contract).[19] If a contract stipulates that a right cannot be assigned, then *ordinarily* the right cannot be assigned.

There are several exceptions to the rule that a contract can, by its terms, prohibit any assignment of the contract. These exceptions are as follows:

1. A contract cannot prevent an assignment of the right to receive money. This exception exists to encourage the free flow of money and credit in modern business settings.

2. The assignment of rights in real estate often cannot be prohibited, because such a prohibition is contrary to public policy. Prohibitions of this kind are called restraints against *alienation* (transfer of land ownership).

3. The assignment of *negotiable instruments* (which include checks and promissory notes) cannot be prohibited.

4. In a contract for the sale of goods, the right to receive damages for breach of contract or for payment of an account owed may be assigned even though the sales contract prohibits such assignment.

---

19. UCC 2–210(2).

Delegations

Just as a party can transfer rights through an assignment, a party can also transfer duties. The transfer of contractual *duties* to a third party is known as a **delegation.** Normally, a delegation of duties does not relieve the party making the delegation (the *delegator*) of the obligation to perform in the event that the party to whom the duty has been delegated (the *delegatee*) fails to perform. No special form is required to create a valid delegation of duties. As long as the delegator expresses an intention to make the delegation, it is effective; the delegator need not even use the word *delegate*.

As a general rule, any duty can be delegated. Delegation is prohibited, however, in the following circumstances:

1. When special trust has been placed in the obligor.
2. When performance depends on the personal skill or talents of the *obligor* (the person contractually obligated to perform).
3. When performance by a third party will vary materially from that expected by the obligee (the one to whom performance is owed) under the contract.
4. When the contract expressly prohibits delegation.

If a delegation of duties is enforceable, the *obligee* (the one to whom performance is owed) must accept performance from the *delegatee* (the one to whom the duties have been delegated). The obligee can legally refuse performance from the delegatee only if the duty is one that cannot be delegated.

A valid delegation of duties does not relieve the delegator of obligations under the contract. Thus, if the delegatee fails to perform, the delegator is still liable to the obligee.

DELEGATION
The transfer of a contractual duty to a third party. The party delegating the duty (the delegator) to the third party (the delegatee) is still obliged to perform on the contract should the delegatee fail to perform.

Third Party Beneficiaries

Another exception to the doctrine of privity of contract exists when the original parties to the contract intend at the time of contracting that the contract performance directly benefit a third person. In this situation, the third person becomes a **third party beneficiary** of the contract. As an **intended beneficiary** of the contract, the third party has legal rights and can sue the promisor directly for breach of the contract.

The benefit that an **incidental beneficiary** receives from a contract between two parties is unintentional. Because the benefit is *unintentional*, an incidental beneficiary cannot sue to enforce the contract. | **Example #26** Suppose that Bollow contracts with Coolidge to build a recreational facility on Coolidge's land. Once the facility is constructed, it will greatly enhance the property values in the neighborhood. If Bollow subsequently refuses to build the facility, Tran, Coolidge's neighbor, cannot enforce the contract against Bollow, because Tran is an incidental beneficiary. |

THIRD PARTY BENEFICIARY
One for whose benefit a promise is made in a contract but who is not a party to the contract.

INTENDED BENEFICIARY
A third party for whose benefit a contract is formed; an intended beneficiary can sue the promisor if such a contract is breached.

INCIDENTAL BENEFICIARY
A third party who incidentally benefits from a contract but whose benefit was not the reason the contract was formed; an incidental beneficiary has no rights in a contract and cannot sue to have the contract enforced.

REVIEWING . . . CONTRACT FORMATION

Grant Borman, who was engaged in a construction project, leased a crane from Allied Equipment and hired Crosstown Trucking Co. to deliver the crane to the construction site. Crosstown, while the crane was in its possession and without permission from either Borman or Allied Equipment, used the crane to install a transformer for a utility company, which paid Crosstown for the job. Crosstown then delivered the crane to Borman's construction site at the appointed time of delivery. When Allied Equipment learned of the unauthorized use of the crane by Crosstown, it sued Crosstown for damages, seeking to recover the rental value of Crosstown's use of the crane. Using the information presented in the chapter, answer the following questions.

1. What are the four requirements of a valid contract?

2. Did Crosstown have a valid contract with Borman concerning the use of the crane? If so, was it a bilateral or a unilateral contract? Explain.

3. Can Allied Equipment obtain damages from Crosstown based on an implied-in-fact contract? Why or why not?

4. Does the Statute of Frauds apply to this contractual situation? Why or why not?

KEY TERMS

CHAPTER SUMMARY • CONTRACT FORMATION

The Function and Definition of Contracts (See page 242.)	Contract law establishes what kinds of promises will be legally binding and supplies procedures for enforcing legally binding promises, or agreements. A contract is a legally binding agreement between two or more parties who agree to perform or to refrain from performing some act now or in the future.
Elements of a Contract (See pages 242–243.)	1. *Requirements of a valid contract*—Agreement, consideration, contractual capacity, and legality. 2. *Defenses to the enforceability of a contract*—Genuineness of assent and form.
Types of Contracts (See pages 243–248.)	1. *Bilateral*—A promise for a promise. 2. *Unilateral*—A promise for an act (acceptance is the completed—or substantial—performance of the contract by the offeree). 3. *Formal*—Requires a special form for contract formation. 4. *Informal*—Requires no special form for contract formation. 5. *Express*—Formed by words (oral, written, or a combination). 6. *Implied in fact*—Formed at least in part by the conduct of the parties. 7. *Executed*—A fully performed contract. 8. *Executory*—A contract not yet fully performed. 9. *Valid*—A contract that results when the elements necessary for contract formation exist, including an agreement (an offer and an acceptance), consideration, parties with contractual capacity, and a legal purpose. 10. *Voidable*—A contract that may be legally avoided (canceled) at the option of one or both of the parties. 11. *Unenforceable*—A valid contract rendered unenforceable by some statute or legal defense. 12. *Void*—A contract that has no legal force or binding effect and that is treated as if the contract never existed.

CHAPTER SUMMARY • CONTRACT FORMATION—CONTINUED

Requirements of the Offer (See pages 249–252.)	1. *Intent*—The offeror must have a serious, objective intention to become bound by the offer. Offers made in anger, jest, or undue excitement do not qualify. Other situations that may lack the required intent include (a) expressions of opinion; (b) statements of future intent; (c) preliminary negotiations; (d) traditionally, agreements to agree in the future; and (e) generally, advertisements, catalogues, price lists, and circulars.
	2. *Definiteness*—The terms of the offer must be sufficiently definite to be ascertainable by the parties or by a court.
	3. *Communication*—The offer must be communicated to the offeree.
Termination of the Offer (See pages 252–253.)	1. *By action of the parties*—An offer can be revoked or withdrawn at any time before acceptance without liability. A counteroffer is a rejection of the original offer and the making of a new offer.
	2. *By operation of law*—An offer can terminate by (a) lapse of time, (b) destruction of the subject matter, (c) death or incompetence of the parties, or (d) supervening illegality.
Acceptance (See pages 253–255.)	1. Can be made only by the offeree or the offeree's agent.
	2. Must be unequivocal. Under the common law (mirror image rule), if new terms or conditions are added to the acceptance, it will be considered a counteroffer.

Consideration (See pages 255–260.)	1. *Elements of consideration*—Consideration is the value given in exchange for a promise. A contract cannot be formed without sufficient consideration. Consideration is often broken down into two parts:
	  a. Something of *legally sufficient value* must be given in exchange for the promise. This may consist of a promise, an act, or a forbearance.
	  b. There must be a *bargained-for exchange.*

	2. *Adequacy of consideration*—Adequacy of consideration relates to "how much" consideration is given and whether a fair bargain was reached. Courts will inquire into the adequacy of consideration (whether the consideration is legally sufficient) only when fraud, undue influence, duress, or unconscionability may be involved.

	3. *Agreements that lack consideration*—Consideration is lacking in the following situations:
	  a. Preexisting duty—Consideration is not legally sufficient if one is either by law or by contract under a *preexisting duty to* perform the action being offered as consideration for a new contract.
	  b. Past consideration—Actions or events that have already taken place do not constitute legally sufficient consideration.

	4. *Promissory estoppel*—In some situations, when injustice can be avoided only by enforcing a promise that would otherwise be unenforceable, the doctrine of promissory estopppel might allow a contract to be enforced.
Capacity (See pages 260–261.)	1. *Minors*—A minor is a person who has not yet reached the age of majority. In virtually all states, the age of majority is eighteen for contract purposes. Contracts with minors are voidable at the option of the minor.
	2. *Intoxication*—A contract with an intoxicated person is enforceable if, despite being intoxicated, the person understood the legal consequences of entering into the contract. A contract entered into by an intoxicated person is voidable at the option of the intoxicated person if the person was sufficiently intoxicated to lack mental capacity, even if the intoxication was voluntary.
	3. *Mental incompetence*—A contract made by a person whom a court has previously determined to be mentally incompetent is void. Only a guardian can enter into a contract on behalf of an incompetent person.

(Continued)

CHAPTER SUMMARY • CONTRACT FORMATION—CONTINUED

Genuineness of Assent (See pages 262–270.)	1. *Mistakes*—
	    a. Bilateral (mutual) mistakes—When both parties are mistaken about the same material fact, such as identity, either party can avoid the contract. If the mistake concerns value or quality, either party can enforce the contract.
	    b. Unilateral mistakes—Generally, the mistaken party is bound by the contract *unless* (a) the other party knows or should have known of the mistake or (b) the mistake is an inadvertent mathematical error—such as an error in addition or subtraction—committed without gross negligence.
	
	 2. *Fraudulent misrepresentation*—When fraud occurs, usually the innocent party can enforce or avoid the contract. For damages, the innocent party must suffer an injury. When innocent misrepresentation occurs, the contract may be rescinded (canceled), but damages are not available.
	
	 3. *Undue influence*—Undue influence arises from special relationships in which one party can greatly influence another party, thus overcoming that party's free will. Usually, the contract is voidable.
	
	 4. *Duress*—Duress is the tactic of forcing a party to enter a contract under the fear of a threat—for example, the threat of violence or serious economic loss. The party forced to enter the contract can rescind the contract.
	
	 5. *Adhesion contracts and unconscionability*—Questions of genuineness of assent also arise when one party exerts control over the other party and dictates the terms of the contract or when the contract terms are manifestly oppressive and unfair to one party. Courts use their discretion and may not enforce contracts that are deemed to be adhesion contracts or unconscionable.

The Statute of Frauds (See pages 270–271.)	The following types of contracts fall under the Statute of Frauds and must be in writing to be enforceable: 1. Contracts involving interests in land. 2. Contracts that cannot by their terms be performed within one year from the day after the date of formation. 3. Collateral, or secondary, contracts, such as promises to answer for the debt or duty of another. 4. Promises made in consideration of marriage. 5. Under the UCC, contracts for the sale of goods priced at $500 or more ($5,000 or more under the 2003 amendments to the UCC).
Third Party Rights (See pages 271–273.)	1. *Assignments*—An assignment is the transfer of rights under a contract to a third party. The third party to whom the rights are assigned has a right to demand performance from the other original party to the contract. Generally, all rights can be assigned, but there are a few exceptions, such as when a statute prohibits assignment or when the contract calls for personal services. 2. *Delegations*—A delegation is the transfer of duties under a contract to a third party, who then assumes the obligation of performing the contractual duties previously held by the one making the delegation. As a general rule, any duty can be delegated, except in a few situations, such as when the contract expressly prohibits delegation or when performance depends on the personal skills of the original party. 3. *Third party beneficiaries*—A third party beneficiary contract is one made for the purpose of benefiting a third party. If the party was an intended beneficiary, then the third party has legal rights and can sue the promisor directly to enforce the contract. If the contract benefits the third party unintentionally, then the third party cannot sue to enforce the contract.

FOR REVIEW

Answers for the even-numbered questions in this **For Review** *section can be found in Appendix O at the end of this text.*

1. What are the four basic elements necessary to the formation of a valid contract?

2. What elements are necessary for an effective offer?

3. What is consideration?

4. Does an intoxicated person have the capacity to enter into an enforceable contract?

5. What contracts must be in writing to be enforceable?

QUESTIONS AND CASE PROBLEMS

8-1. Contracts. Suppose that Everett McCleskey, a local businessperson, is a good friend of Al Miller, the owner of a local candy store. Every day on his lunch hour, McCleskey goes into Miller's candy store and spends about five minutes looking at the candy. After examining Miller's candy and talking with Miller, McCleskey usually buys one or two candy bars. One afternoon, McCleskey goes into Miller's candy shop, looks at the candy, and picks up a $1 candy bar. Seeing that Miller is very busy, he catches Miller's eye, waves the candy bar at Miller without saying a word, and walks out. Is there a contract? If so, classify it within the categories presented in this chapter.

Question with Sample Answer

8-2. Janine was hospitalized with severe abdominal pain and placed in an intensive care unit. Her doctor told the hospital personnel to order around-the-clock nursing care for Janine. At the hospital's request, a nursing services firm, Nursing Services Unlimited, provided two weeks of in-hospital care and, after Janine was sent home, an additional two weeks of at-home care. During the at-home period of care, Janine was fully aware that she was receiving the benefit of the nursing services. Nursing Services later billed Janine $4,000 for the nursing care, but Janine refused to pay on the ground that she had never contracted for the services, either orally or in writing. In view of the fact that no express contract was ever formed, can Nursing Services recover the $4,000 from Janine? If so, under what legal theory? Discuss.

For a sample answer to this question, go to Appendix P at the end of this text.

8-3. Agreement. Ball writes Sullivan and inquires how much Sullivan is asking for a specific forty-acre tract of land Sullivan owns. In a letter received by Ball, Sullivan states, "I will not take less than $60,000 for the forty-acre tract as specified." Ball immediately sends Sullivan a telegram stating, "I accept your offer for $60,000 for the forty-acre tract as specified." Discuss whether Ball can hold Sullivan to a contract for the sale of the land.

8-4. Requirements of the Offer. The Pittsburgh Board of Public Education in Pittsburgh, Pennsylvania, as required by state law, keeps lists of eligible teachers in order of their rank or standing. According to an "Eligibility List" form made available to applicants, no one may be hired to teach whose name is not within the top 10 percent of the names on the list. In 1996, Anna Reed was in the top 10 percent. She was not hired that year, although four other applicants who placed lower on the list—and not within the top 10 percent—were hired. In 1997 and 1998, Reed was again in the top 10 percent, but she was not hired until 1999. Reed filed a suit in a federal district court against the board and

others. She argued in part that the state's requirement that the board keep a list constituted an offer, which she accepted by participating in the process to be placed on that list. She claimed that the board breached this contract by hiring applicants who ranked lower than she did. The case was transferred to a Pennsylvania state court. What are the requirements of an offer? Do the circumstances in this case meet those requirements? Why or why not? [*Reed v. Pittsburgh Board of Public Education,* 862 A.2d 131 (Pa.Cmwlth. 2004)]

8-5. Intention. Music that is distributed on compact discs and similar media generates income in the form of "mechanical" royalties. Music that is publicly performed, such as when a song is played on a radio, used in a movie or commercial, or sampled in another song, produces "performance" royalties. Each of these types of royalties is divided between the songwriter and the song's publisher. Vincent Cusano is a musician and songwriter who performed under the name "Vinnie Vincent" as a guitarist with the group KISS in the early 1980s. Cusano co-wrote three songs—entitled "Killer," "I Love It Loud," and "I Still Love You"—that KISS recorded and released in 1982 on an album titled *Creatures of the Night.* Cusano left KISS in 1984. Eight years later, Cusano sold to Horipro Entertainment Group "one hundred (100%) percent undivided interest" of his rights in the songs "other than Songwriter's share of performance income." Later, Cusano filed a suit in a federal district court against Horipro, claiming in part that he never intended to sell the writer's share of the mechanical royalties. Horipro filed a motion for summary judgment. Should the court grant the motion? Explain. [*Cusano v. Horipro Entertainment Group,* 301 F.Supp.2d 272 (S.D.N.Y. 2004)]

8-6. Duress. The law firm of Traystman, Coric and Keramidas represented Andrew Daigle in a divorce in Norwich, Connecticut. Scott McGowan, an attorney with the firm, handled the two-day trial. After the first day of the trial, McGowan told Daigle to sign a promissory note in the amount of $26,973, which represented the amount that Daigle then owed to the firm, or McGowan would withdraw from the case, and Daigle would be forced to get another attorney or to continue the trial by himself. Daigle said that he wanted another attorney, Martin Rutchik, to see the note. McGowan urged Daigle to sign it and assured him that a copy would be sent to Rutchik. Feeling that he had no other choice, Daigle signed the note. When he did not pay, the law firm filed a suit in a Connecticut state court against him. Daigle asserted that the note was unenforceable because he had signed it under duress. What are the requirements for the use of duress as a defense to a contract? Are the requirements met here? What might the law firm argue in response to Daigle's assertion? Explain. [*Traystman, Coric and Keramidas v. Daigle,* 84 Conn.App. 843, 855 A.2d 996 (2004)]

Case Problem with Sample Answer

8–7. As a child, Martha Carr once visited her mother's 108-acre tract of unimproved land in Richland County, South Carolina. In 1968, Betty and Raymond Campbell leased the land. Carr, a resident of New York, was diagnosed as having schizophrenia and depression in 1986, was hospitalized five or six times, and subsequently took prescription drugs for the illnesses. In 1996, Carr inherited the Richland property and, two years later, contacted the Campbells about selling the land to them. Carr asked Betty about the value of the land, and Betty said that the county tax assessor had determined that the land's *agricultural value* was $54,000. The Campbells knew at the time that the county had assessed the total property value at $103,700 for tax purposes. A real estate appraiser found that the *real market value* of the property was $162,000. On August 6, Carr signed a contract to sell the land to the Campbells for $54,000. Believing the price to be unfair, however, Carr did not deliver the deed. The Campbells filed a suit in a South Carolina state court against Carr, seeking specific performance of the contract. At trial, an expert real estate appraiser testified that the real market value of the property was $162,000 at the time of the contract. Under what circumstances will a court examine the adequacy of consideration? Are those circumstances present in this case? Should the court enforce the contract between Carr and the Campbells? Explain. [*Campbell v. Carr,* 361 S.C. 258, 603 S.E.2d 625 (App. 2004)]

After you have answered this problem, compare your answer with the sample answer given on the Web site that accompanies this text. Go to www.thomsonedu.com/westbuslaw/let, select "Chapter 8," and click on "Case Problem with Sample Answer."

8–8. Agreement. In 2000, David and Sandra Harless leased 2.3 acres of real property at 2801 River Road S.E. in Winnabow, North Carolina, to Jeanie and Tony Connor (the Harlesses' daughter and son-in-law). The Connors planned to operate a "general store/variety store" on the premises. They agreed to lease the property for sixty months with an option to renew for an additional sixty months. The lease included an option to buy the property for "fair market value at the time of such purchase (based on at least two appraisals)." In March 2003, Tony told David that the Connors wanted to buy the property. In May, Tony gave David an appraisal that estimated the property's value at $140,000. In July, the Connors presented a second appraisal that determined the value to be $160,000. The Connors offered $150,000. The Harlesses replied that "under no circumstances would they ever agree to sell their old store building and approximately 2.5 acres to their daughter . . . and their son-in-law." The Connors filed a suit in a North Carolina state court against the Harlesses, alleging breach of contract. Did these parties have a contract to sell the property? If so, what were its terms? If not, why not? [*Connor v. Harless,* __ N.C.App. __, 626 S.E.2d 755 (2006)]

A Question of Ethics

8–9. When LeRoy McIlravy began working for Kerr-McGee Corp., he was given an employee handbook that listed examples of misconduct that could result in discipline or discharge and spelled out specific procedures that would be used in those instances. When McIlravy was later laid off, he and other former employees filed a suit against Kerr-McGee, contending, among other things, that the handbook constituted an implied contract that Kerr-McGee had breached, because the handbook implied that employees would not be dismissed without "cause." In view of these facts, consider the following questions. [*McIlravy v. Kerr-McGee Corp.,* 119 F.3d 876 (10th Cir. 1997)]

1. Would it be fair to the employer for the court to hold that an implied contract had been created in this case, given that the employer did not *intend* to create a contract? Would it be fair to the employees to hold that no contract was created? If the decision were up to you, how would you decide this issue?

2. Suppose that the handbook contained a disclaimer stating that the handbook was not to be construed as a contract. How would this affect your answers to the above questions? From an ethical perspective, would it ever be fair to hold that an implied contract exists *notwithstanding* such a disclaimer?

Critical-Thinking Legal Question

8–10. Review the list of basic requirements for contract formation given at the beginning of this chapter. In view of those requirements, analyze the relationship entered into when a student enrolls in a college or university. Has a contract been formed? If so, is it a bilateral contract or a unilateral contract? Discuss.

Video Question

8–11. Go to this text's Web site at www.thomsonedu.com/westbuslaw/let and select "Chapter 8." Click on "Video Questions" and view the video titled *Bowfinger.* Then answer the following questions.

1. In the video, Renfro (Robert Downey, Jr.) says to Bowfinger (Steve Martin), "You bring me this script and Kit Ramsey and you've got yourself a 'go' picture." Assume for the purposes of this question that their agreement is a contract. Is the contract bilateral or unilateral? Is it express or implied? Is it formal or informal? Explain your answers.

2. Explain whether Renfro's statement that is quoted in the first part of this question meets the three requirements of an effective offer.

3. Recall from the video that the contract between Bowfinger and the producer was oral. Suppose that a statute requires contracts of this type to be in writing. In that situation, would the contract be void, voidable, or unenforceable? Explain.

INTERACTING WITH THE INTERNET

For updated links to resources available on the Web, as well as a variety of other materials, visit this text's Web site at

www.thomsonedu.com/westbuslaw/let

The 'Lectric Law Library provides information on contract law, including a definition of a contract, the elements required for a contract, and so on. Go to

www.lectlaw.com/lay.html

A good way to learn more about how the courts decide such issues as whether consideration was lacking for a particular contract is to look at relevant case law. To find recent cases on contract law decided by the United States Supreme Court and the federal appellate courts, access Cornell University's School of Law site at

www.law.cornell.edu/wex/index.php/Contracts

The *New Hampshire Consumer's Sourcebook* provides information on contract law, including consideration, from a consumer's perspective. You can access this site at

www.doj.nh.gov/consumer/index.html

To learn what kinds of clauses are included in typical contracts for certain goods and services, you can explore the collection of contract forms made available by FindLaw at

contracts.corporate.findlaw.com/index.html

INTERNET EXERCISES

Go to **www.thomsonedu.com/westbuslaw/let**, the Web site that accompanies this text. Select "Chapter 8" and click on "Internet Exercises." There you will find the following Internet research exercises that you can perform to learn more about topics covered in this chapter.

Internet Exercise 8–1: HISTORICAL PERSPECTIVE—Contracts in Ancient Mesopotamia
Internet Exercise 8–2: ETHICAL PERSPECTIVE—Offers and Advertisements
Internet Exercise 8–3: SOCIAL PERSPECTIVE—Online Gambling

BEFORE THE TEST

Go to **www.thomsonedu.com/westbuslaw/let**, the Web site that accompanies this text. Select "Chapter 8" and click on "Interactive Quizzes." You will find a number of interactive questions relating to this chapter.

Contract Performance, Breach, and Remedies

CHAPTER OBJECTIVES

After reading this chapter, you should be able to answer the following questions:

1 What is a condition precedent, and how does it affect a party's duty to perform a contract?

2 How are most contracts discharged?

3 What is substantial performance?

4 What is the standard measure of compensatory damages when a contract is breached?

5 What equitable remedies can a court grant, and in what circumstances will a court consider granting them?

> "Men keep their engagements when it is to the advantage of both not to break them."
>
> —SOLON, sixth century B.C.E.
> (Athenian legal reformer)

DISCHARGE
The termination of an obligation. In contract law, discharge occurs when the parties have fully performed their contractual obligations or when events, conduct of the parties, or operation of law releases the parties from performance.

PERFORMANCE
In contract law, the fulfillment of one's duties arising under a contract with another; the normal way of discharging one's contractual obligations.

AS THE ATHENIAN POLITICAL LEADER Solon indicated centuries ago, a contract will not be broken so long as "it is to the advantage of both" parties not to break it. In a perfect world, every party who signed a contract would perform his or her duties completely and in a timely fashion, thereby discharging (terminating) the contract. In the real world, however, things frequently become complicated. Certainly, events often occur that may affect our performance or our ability to perform contractual duties. Just as rules are necessary to determine when a legally enforceable contract exists, so also are they required to determine when one of the parties can justifiably say, "I have fully performed, so I am now discharged from my obligations under this contract."

Additionally, the parties to a contract need to know what remedies are available to them if one party decides that he or she does not want to, or cannot, perform as promised. A *remedy* is the relief provided for an innocent party when the other party has breached the contract. It is the means employed to enforce a right or to redress an injury. The most common remedies available to a nonbreaching party include damages, rescission and restitution, specific performance, and reformation. As discussed in Chapter 1, a distinction is made between *remedies at law* and *remedies in equity*. Today, the remedy at law is normally money damages. Equitable remedies include rescission and restitution, specific performance, and reformation, all of which will be examined later in this chapter.

PERFORMANCE AND DISCHARGE

The most common way to **discharge,** or terminate, one's contractual duties is by the **performance** of those duties. For example, a buyer and seller have a contract for the sale of a 2006 BMW for $34,000. This contract will be discharged on the performance by the parties of their obligations under the contract—the buyer's payment of $34,000 to the seller and the seller's transfer of possession of the BMW to the buyer.

The duty to perform under a contract may be *conditioned* on the occurrence or nonoccurrence of a certain event, or the duty may be *absolute*. In the first part of this section, we look at conditions of performance and the degree of performance required. We then examine some other ways in which a contract can be discharged, including discharge by agreement of the parties and discharge by operation of law.

Conditions of Performance

In most contracts, promises of performance are not expressly conditioned or qualified. Instead, they are *absolute promises*. They must be performed, or the parties promising the acts will be in breach of contract. **| Example #1** JoAnne contracts to sell Alfonso a painting for $10,000. The parties' promises are unconditional: JoAnne's transfer of the painting to Alfonso and Alfonso's payment of $10,000 to JoAnne. The payment does not have to be made if the painting is not transferred.**|**

In some situations, however, contractual promises are conditioned. A **condition** is a possible future event, the occurrence or nonoccurrence of which will trigger the performance of a legal obligation or terminate an existing obligation under a contract. If the condition is not satisfied, the obligations of the parties are discharged. **| Example #2** Suppose that Alfonso, in the previous example, offers to purchase JoAnne's painting only if an independent appraisal indicates that it is worth at least $10,000. JoAnne accepts Alfonso's offer. Their obligations (promises) are conditioned on the outcome of the appraisal. Should this condition not be satisfied (for example, if the appraiser deems the value of the painting to be only $5,000), their obligations to each other are discharged and cannot be enforced.**|**

We look here at three types of conditions that can be present in any given contract: conditions precedent, conditions subsequent, and concurrent conditions.

Conditions Precedent A condition that must be fulfilled before a party's promise becomes absolute is called a **condition precedent.** The condition precedes the absolute duty to perform. **| Example #3** In the JoAnne-Alfonso example just given, Alfonso's promise is subject to the condition precedent that the appraised value of the painting must be at least $10,000. Until the condition is fulfilled, Alfonso's promise is not absolute.**|** Insurance contracts frequently specify that certain conditions, such as passing a physical examination, must be met before the insurance company will be obligated to perform under the contract.

Conditions Subsequent When a condition operates to terminate a party's absolute promise to perform, it is called a **condition subsequent.** The condition follows, or is subsequent to, the absolute duty to perform. If the condition occurs, the party need not perform any further. **| Example #4** A law firm hires Julia Darby, a recent law school graduate and a newly licensed attorney. Their contract provides that the firm's obligation to continue employing Darby is discharged if she fails to maintain her license to practice law. This is

CONDITION
A qualification, provision, or clause in a contractual agreement, the occurrence or nonoccurrence of which creates, suspends, or terminates the obligations of the contracting parties.

CONDITION PRECEDENT
In a contractual agreement, a condition that must be met before a party's promise becomes absolute.

CONDITION SUBSEQUENT
A condition in a contract that, if not fulfilled, operates to terminate a party's absolute promise to perform.

a condition subsequent because a failure to maintain the license will discharge a duty that has already arisen.[1]

Generally, conditions precedent are common, and conditions subsequent are rare. Section 224 of the *Restatement (Second) of Contracts* deletes the terms *condition subsequent* and *condition precedent* and refers to both simply as "conditions."

CONCURRENT CONDITIONS

Conditions that must occur or be performed at the same time; they are mutually dependent. No obligations arise until these conditions are simultaneously performed.

Concurrent Conditions   When each party's absolute duty to perform is conditioned on the other party's absolute duty to perform, **concurrent conditions** are present. These conditions exist only when the parties expressly or impliedly are to perform their respective duties *simultaneously.* **| Example #5** If a buyer promises to pay for goods when they are delivered by the seller, each party's absolute duty to perform is conditioned on the other party's absolute duty to perform. The buyer's duty to pay for the goods does not become absolute until the seller either delivers or attempts to deliver the goods. Likewise, the seller's duty to deliver the goods does not become absolute until the buyer pays or attempts to pay for the goods. Therefore, neither can recover from the other for breach without first tendering performance.|

Discharge by Performance

TENDER

An unconditional offer to perform an obligation by a person who is ready, willing, and able to do so.

The great majority of contracts are discharged by performance. The contract comes to an end when both parties fulfill their respective duties by performing the acts they have promised. Performance can also be accomplished by **tender.**

---

1. The difference between *conditions precedent* and *conditions subsequent* is relatively unimportant from a substantive point of view but very important procedurally. Usually, the plaintiff must prove conditions precedent because typically it is the plaintiff who claims that there is a duty to be performed. Similarly, the defendant must normally prove conditions subsequent because typically it is the defendant who claims that a duty no longer exists.

A couple negotiates with a salesperson to purchase a car. Suppose that the parties reach an agreement on the sale, which is conditioned on the dealer's servicing the car's air conditioner. When the couple returns to the lot the following day, they discover that the air conditioner has not been serviced. Are they still obligated to buy the car? Why or why not? What type of condition is this? (Getty Images)

Therefore, a seller who places goods at the disposal of a buyer has tendered delivery and can demand payment. A buyer who offers to pay for goods has tendered payment and can demand delivery of the goods. Once performance has been tendered, the party making the tender has done everything possible to carry out the terms of the contract. If the other party then refuses to perform, the party making the tender can sue for breach of contract.

There are two basic types of performance—*complete performance* and *substantial performance.* A contract may stipulate that performance must meet the personal satisfaction of either the contracting party or a third party. Such a provision must be considered in determining whether the performance rendered satisfies the contract.

Complete Performance   When a party performs exactly as agreed, there is no question as to whether the contract has been performed. When a party's performance is perfect, it is said to be complete.

Normally, conditions expressly stated in a contract must be fully satisfied for complete performance to take place. For example, most construction contracts require the builder to meet certain specifications. If the specifications are conditions, complete performance is required to avoid material breach (material breach will be discussed shortly). If the conditions are met, the other party to the contract must then fulfill her or his obligation to pay the builder. If the specifications are not conditions and if the builder, without the other party's permission, fails to comply with the specifications, performance is not complete. What effect does such a failure have on the other party's obligation to pay? The answer is part of the doctrine of *substantial performance.*

Substantial Performance   A party who in good faith performs substantially all of the terms of a contract can enforce the contract against the other party under the doctrine of substantial performance. Note that good faith is required. Intentionally failing to comply with the terms is a breach of the contract.

Confers Most Benefits Promised in the Contract   Generally, to qualify as substantial, the performance must not vary greatly from the performance promised in the contract, and it must create substantially the same benefits as those promised in the contract. If the omission, variance, or defect in performance is unimportant and can easily be compensated for by awarding damages, a court is likely to hold that the contract has been substantially performed.

| **Example #6**   A couple contracts with a construction company to build a house. The contract specifies that Brand X plasterboard be used for the walls. The builder cannot obtain Brand X plasterboard, and the buyers are on vacation in the mountains of Peru and virtually unreachable. The builder decides to install Brand Y instead, which he knows is identical in quality and durability to Brand X plasterboard. All other aspects of construction conform to the contract. Does this deviation constitute a breach of contract? Can the buyers avoid their contractual obligation to pay the builder because Brand Y plasterboard was used instead of Brand X? Very likely, a court would hold that the builder had substantially performed his end of the bargain, and therefore the couple will be obligated to pay the builder.|

Courts decide whether the performance was substantial on a case-by-case basis, examining all of the facts of the particular situation. For example, in a construction contract, a court would look at the intended purpose of the

> **"**There are occasions and causes and why and wherefore in all things.**"**
> —WILLIAM SHAKESPEARE, 1564–1616
> (English dramatist and poet)

Different brands of construction supplies displayed at a site. If a contract for the construction of a building or house specifies a particular brand, can a product of a different brand of comparable quality be substituted? Why or why not? (Tony Freeman/PhotoEdit)

structure and the expense required to bring the structure into complete compliance with the contract. Thus, the exact point at which performance is considered substantial varies.

Entitles Other Party to Damages   Because substantial performance is not perfect, the other party is entitled to damages to compensate for the failure to comply with the contract. The measure of the damages is the cost to bring the object of the contract into compliance with its terms, if that cost is reasonable under the circumstances. If the cost is unreasonable, the measure of damages is the difference in value between the performance that was rendered and the performance that would have been rendered if the contract had been performed completely.

Performance to the Satisfaction of One of the Parties Contracts often state that completed work must personally satisfy one of the parties. The question then arises whether this satisfaction becomes a condition precedent, requiring actual personal satisfaction or approval for discharge, or whether the test of satisfaction is an absolute promise requiring such performance as would satisfy a *reasonable person* (substantial performance).

Personal-Service Contracts   When the subject matter of the contract is personal, a contract to be performed to the satisfaction of one of the parties is conditioned, and performance must actually satisfy that party. For example, contracts for portraits, works of art, medical or dental work, and tailoring are considered personal. Therefore, only the personal satisfaction of the party will be sufficient to fulfill the condition.

| **Example #7**   Suppose that Williams agrees to paint a portrait of Hirshon's daughter for $750. The contract provides that Hirshon must be satisfied with the portrait. If Hirshon is not, she will not be required to pay for it. The only requirement imposed on Hirshon is that she behave honestly and in good faith. If Hirshon expresses dissatisfaction only to avoid paying for the portrait, the condition of satisfaction is excused, and her duty to pay becomes absolute. (Of course, the jury, or the judge acting as a jury, will have to decide whether she is acting honestly.)[2] |

All Other Contracts   Contracts that involve mechanical fitness, utility, or marketability need only be performed to the satisfaction of a *reasonable* person unless they *expressly state otherwise*. For example, construction contracts and manufacturing contracts are usually *not* considered to be personal, so the party's personal satisfaction is normally irrelevant. As long as the performance will satisfy a reasonable person, the contract is fulfilled.

2. For a classic case illustrating this principle, see *Gibson v. Cranage*, 39 Mich. 49 (1878).

Performance to the Satisfaction of a Third Party At times, contracts expressly require performance to the satisfaction of a third party (not a party to the contract). **Example #8** Assume that you contract to pave several city streets. The contract provides that the work will be done "to the satisfaction of Phil Hopper, the supervising engineer." In this situation, the courts are divided.

A few courts require the personal satisfaction of the third party—in this example, Phil Hopper. If Hopper is not satisfied, you will not be paid, even if a reasonable person would be satisfied. Again, the personal judgment must be made honestly, or the condition will be excused.

A majority of courts, however, require the work to be satisfactory to a reasonable person. Thus, even if Hopper is dissatisfied with the paving work, you will be paid, as long as a qualified supervising engineer would have been satisfied. All of the above examples demonstrate the necessity for *clear, specific wording in contracts.*

Material Breach of Contract A **breach of contract** is the nonperformance of a contractual duty. The breach is *material* when performance is not at least substantial. If there is a material breach, then the nonbreaching party is excused from the performance of contractual duties and has a cause of action to sue for damages resulting from the breach. If the breach is *minor* (not material), the nonbreaching party's duty to perform can sometimes be suspended until the breach has been remedied, but the duty to perform is not entirely excused. Once the minor breach has been cured, the nonbreaching party must resume performance of the contractual obligations undertaken.

> **BREACH OF CONTRACT**
> The failure, without legal excuse, of a promisor to perform the obligations of a contract.

Any breach entitles the nonbreaching party to sue for damages, but only a material breach discharges the nonbreaching party from the contract. The policy underlying these rules allows contracts to go forward when only minor problems occur but allows them to be terminated if major difficulties arise.

Under what circumstances is an employer excused from further performance under a contract with an employee? That was the question in the following case.

CASE 9.1 Shah v. Cover-It, Inc.

Appellate Court of Connecticut, 2004.
86 Conn.App. 71,
859 A.2d 959.

BACKGROUND AND FACTS In November 1997, Cover-It, Inc., hired Khalid Shah to work as its structural engineering manager. Shah agreed to work a flexible schedule of thirty-five hours per week. In exchange, he would receive an annual salary of $70,000 for five years, a 2 percent commission on the sales of products that he designed, three weeks of paid vacation after one year, a company car, time off to attend to prior professional obligations, and certain other benefits. Either party could terminate the contract with ninety days' written notice, but if Cover-It terminated it, Shah would receive monthly payments for the rest of the five-year term.[a] In June 1998, Shah went on vacation and did not return until September. In mid-October, Brian Goldwitz, Cover-It's owner and president, terminated Shah's contract. Shah filed a suit in a Connecticut state court against Cover-It and others. The court determined that Shah had breached the contract and rendered a judgment in the defendants' favor. Shah appealed to a state intermediate appellate court.

a. The contract provided that for up to two years of service, Shah would be paid $20,000 per year; for three years of service, $30,000 per year; and for four years of service, $40,000 per year.

IN THE WORDS OF THE COURT . . . SCHALLER, J. [Judge]

* * * *

On appeal, the plaintiff claims that the court improperly found that he had breached the contract or, in the alternative, that any breach was not material. Specifically, the

CASE 9.1—CONTINUED ▶

plaintiff argues that the court failed to identify an express term or condition that was breached and instead merely found that certain acts, considered together, demonstrated a material breach prior to the termination of his employment. Therefore, according to the plaintiff, the defendants were not relieved of their obligations, under the terms of the contract, to pay his full salary for ninety days and to pay his post-termination salary pursuant to the schedule set forth in the contract. * * *

* * * *

It is a general rule of contract law that a total breach of the contract by one party relieves the injured party of any further duty to perform further obligations under the contract. [Emphasis added.]

* * * Section 241 of the *Restatement (Second) of Contracts* provides:

In determining whether a failure to render or to offer performance is material, the following circumstances are significant: (a) the extent to which the injured party will be deprived of the benefit which he reasonably expected; (b) the extent to which the injured party can be adequately compensated for the part of that benefit of which he will be deprived; (c) the extent to which the party failing to perform or to offer to perform will suffer forfeiture; (d) the likelihood that the party failing to perform or to offer to perform will cure his failure, taking account of all the circumstances including any reasonable assurances; [and] (e) the extent to which the behavior of the party failing to perform or to offer to perform comports with standards of good faith and fair dealing.

The standards of materiality are to be applied in the light of the facts of each case in such a way as to further the purpose of securing for each party his expectation of an exchange of performances. Section 241 therefore states circumstances, not rules, which are to be considered in determining whether a particular failure is material. [Emphasis added.]

In the present case, the court found that the plaintiff took a ten-week vacation, which exceeded the time authorized. After the plaintiff returned, he reported for work only two or three days per week and spent long periods of time visiting Internet Web sites that were unrelated to his professional duties. Additionally, after being instructed by [Cover-It's] human resources manager to document his attendance by use of a time clock, the plaintiff refused and simply marked his time sheets with a "P" for present. Last, the court found that when Goldwitz asked when certain designs would be completed, the plaintiff responded that he was not sure and that he would take his time in completing them. When reviewing those findings in light of the factors set forth in [Section] 241 of the *Restatement (Second) of Contracts,* we conclude that the court's finding of a material breach was not clearly erroneous.

It is clear from the court's findings that the plaintiff failed to perform under the obligations of the employment contract. * * * One cannot recover upon a contract unless he has fully performed his own obligation under it, has tendered performance or has some legal excuse for not performing. As a result of the material breach by the plaintiff, the defendants were excused from further performance under the contract, and were relieved of the obligation to pay the plaintiff his full salary for ninety days and to pay his post-termination salary pursuant to the schedule set forth in the contract.

DECISION AND REMEDY The state intermediate appellate court affirmed the judgment of the lower court. The appellate court held that Shah had materially breached his contract with Cover-It and that this breach excused Cover-It from further performance of its contractual duties, relieving the defendant of any obligation to continue paying Shah's salary.

WHAT IF THE FACTS WERE DIFFERENT? *Suppose that during his ten-week absence Shah was fulfilling prior professional obligations and that on his return he met Cover-It's hours and timekeeping requirements. Further suppose that Shah responded to Goldwitz's questions about his projects with reasonable estimates. Would the outcome of the case have been different? Why or why not?*

Anticipatory Repudiation of a Contract   Before either party to a contract has a duty to perform, one of the parties may refuse to perform her or his contractual obligations. This is called **anticipatory repudiation.**[3] When anticipatory repudiation occurs, it is treated as a material breach of contract, and the nonbreaching party is permitted to bring an action for damages immediately, even though the scheduled time for performance under the contract may still be in the future. Until the nonbreaching party treats this early repudiation as a breach, however, the breaching party can retract the anticipatory repudiation by proper notice and restore the parties to their original obligations.[4]

An anticipatory repudiation is treated as a present, material breach for two reasons. First, the nonbreaching party should not be required to remain ready and willing to perform when the other party has already repudiated the contract. Second, the nonbreaching party should have the opportunity to seek a similar contract elsewhere and may have the duty to do so to minimize his or her loss.

Quite often, an anticipatory repudiation occurs when a sharp fluctuation in market prices creates a situation in which performance of the contract would be extremely unfavorable to one of the parties. **▎Example #9**   Shasta Manufacturing Company contracts to manufacture and sell 100,000 personal computers to New Age, Inc., a computer retailer with 100 outlet stores. Delivery is to be made two months from the date of the contract. One month later, three suppliers of computer parts raise their prices to Shasta. Because of these higher prices, Shasta stands to lose $500,000 if it sells the computers to New Age at the contract price. Shasta writes to New Age, stating that it cannot deliver the 100,000 computers at the agreed-on contract price. Even though you might sympathize with Shasta, its letter is an anticipatory repudiation of the contract, allowing New Age the option of treating the repudiation as a material breach and proceeding immediately to pursue remedies, even though the contract delivery date is still a month away.▎

Discharge by Agreement

Any contract can be discharged by agreement of the parties. The agreement can be contained in the original contract, or the parties can form a new contract for the express purpose of discharging the original contract.

Discharge by Rescission   As mentioned in previous chapters, *rescission* is the process by which a contract is canceled or terminated and the parties are returned to the positions they occupied prior to forming it. For **mutual rescission** to take place, the parties must make another agreement that also satisfies the legal requirements for a contract. There must be an *offer*, an *acceptance*, and *consideration*. Ordinarily, if the parties agree to rescind the original contract, their promises not to perform the acts stipulated in the original contract will be legal consideration for the second contract (the rescission).

Agreements to rescind executory contracts (in which neither party has performed) are generally enforceable, even if the agreement is made orally and even if the original agreement was in writing. An exception applies under the Uniform Commercial Code (UCC) to agreements rescinding a contract for the

ANTICIPATORY REPUDIATION
An assertion or action by a party indicating that he or she will not perform an obligation that the party is contractually obligated to perform at a future time.

REMEMBER !   The risks that prices will fluctuate and values will change are ordinary business risks for which the law does not provide relief.

MUTUAL RESCISSION
An agreement between the parties to cancel their contract, releasing the parties from further obligations under the contract. The object of the agreement is to restore the parties to the positions they would have occupied had no contract ever been formed.

---

3. *Restatement (Second) of Contracts*, Section 253; and UCC 2–610.
4. See UCC 2–611.

sale of goods, regardless of price, when the contract requires a written rescission. Also, agreements to rescind contracts involving transfers of realty must be evidenced by a writing.

When one party has fully performed, an agreement to cancel the original contract normally will not be enforceable. Because the performing party has received no consideration for the promise to call off the original bargain, additional consideration is necessary.

Discharge by Novation   A contractual obligation may also be discharged through novation. A **novation** occurs when both of the parties to a contract agree to substitute a third party for one of the original parties. The requirements of a novation are as follows:

1. A previous valid obligation.
2. An agreement by all the parties to a new contract.
3. The extinguishing of the old obligation (discharge of the prior party).
4. A new contract that is valid.

> **Example #10**   Union Corporation contracts to sell its pharmaceutical division to British Pharmaceuticals, Ltd. Before the transfer is completed, Union, British Pharmaceuticals, and a third company, Otis Chemicals, execute a new agreement to transfer all of British Pharmaceutical's rights and duties in the transaction to Otis Chemicals. As long as the new contract is supported by consideration, the novation will discharge the original contract (between Union and British Pharmaceuticals) and replace it with the new contract (between Union and Otis Chemicals).

A novation expressly or impliedly revokes and discharges a prior contract. The parties involved may expressly state in the new contract that the old contract is now discharged. If the parties do not expressly discharge the old contract, it will be impliedly discharged if the new contract's terms are inconsistent with the old contract's terms.

Discharge by Substituted Agreement   A *compromise*, or settlement agreement, that arises out of a genuine dispute over the obligations under an existing contract will be recognized at law. Such an agreement will be substituted as a new contract, and it will either expressly or impliedly revoke and discharge the obligations under any prior contract. In contrast to a novation, a substituted agreement does not involve a third party. Rather, the two original parties to the contract form a different agreement to substitute for the original one.

Discharge by Accord and Satisfaction   For a contract to be discharged by accord and satisfaction, the parties must agree to accept performance that is different from the performance originally promised. An *accord* is a contract to perform some act to satisfy an existing contractual duty. The duty has not yet been discharged. A *satisfaction* is the performance of the accord agreement. An accord and its satisfaction discharge the original contractual obligation.

Once the accord has been made, the original obligation is merely suspended. The obligor (the one owing the obligation) can discharge the obligation by performing either the obligation agreed to in the accord or the original obligation. If the obligor refuses to perform the accord, the obligee (the one to whom performance is owed) can bring action on the original obligation or seek a decree compelling specific performance on the accord.

| **Example #11** Frazer obtains a judgment against Ling for $8,000. Later, both parties agree that the judgment can be satisfied by Ling's transfer of his automobile to Frazer. This agreement to accept the auto in lieu of $8,000 in cash is the accord. If Ling transfers the car to Frazer, the accord is fully performed, and the debt is discharged. If Ling refuses to transfer the car, the accord is breached. Because the original obligation is merely suspended, Frazer can sue Ling to enforce the original judgment for $8,000 in cash or bring an action for breach of the accord. |

Discharge by Operation of Law

Under certain circumstances, contractual duties may be discharged by operation of law. These circumstances include material alteration of the contract, the running of the statute of limitations, bankruptcy, and the impossibility or impracticability of performance.

Alteration of the Contract   To discourage parties from altering written contracts, the law operates to allow an innocent party to be discharged when the other party has materially altered a written contract without consent. For example, contract terms such as quantity or price might be changed without the knowledge or consent of all parties. If so, the party who was not involved in the alteration can treat the contract as discharged or terminated.

Statutes of Limitations   As mentioned earlier in this text, statutes of limitations restrict the period during which a party can sue on a particular cause of action. After the applicable limitations period has passed, a suit can no longer be brought. For example, the limitations period for bringing suits for breach of oral contracts is usually two to three years; for written contracts, four to five years; and for recovery of amounts awarded in judgments, ten to twenty years, depending on state law. Suits for breach of a contract for the sale of goods generally must be brought within four years after the cause of action has accrued. By their original agreement, the parties can reduce this four-year period to not less than one year, but they cannot agree to extend it.

Bankruptcy   A proceeding in bankruptcy attempts to allocate the assets the debtor owns to the creditors in a fair and equitable fashion. Once the assets have been allocated, the debtor receives a *discharge in bankruptcy*. A discharge in bankruptcy will ordinarily bar enforcement of most of the debtor's contracts by the creditors. Partial payment of a debt *after* discharge in bankruptcy will not revive the debt. (Bankruptcy will be discussed in detail in Chapter 12.)

Impossibility or Impracticability of Performance   After a contract has been made, performance may become impossible in an objective sense. This is known as **impossibility of performance** and may discharge a contract.

Objective Impossibility of Performance   *Objective impossibility* ("It can't be done") must be distinguished from *subjective impossibility* ("I'm sorry, I simply can't do it"). Examples of subjective impossibility include the situation in which goods cannot be delivered on time because of freight car shortages and the situation in which payment cannot be made on time because the bank is closed. In effect, the party in each of these situations is saying, "It is impossible

| "Law is a practical matter."
—ROSCOE POUND, 1870–1964
(American jurist)

IMPOSSIBILITY OF PERFORMANCE
A doctrine under which a party to a contract is relieved of his or her duty to perform when performance becomes objectively impossible or totally impracticable (through no fault of either party).

for me to perform," not "It is impossible for anyone to perform." Accordingly, such excuses do not discharge a contract, and the nonperforming party is normally held in breach of contract. Three basic types of situations, however, generally qualify as grounds for the discharge of contractual obligations based on impossibility of performance:[5]

1. *When one of the parties to a personal contract dies or becomes incapacitated prior to performance.* | **Example #12** | Fred, a famous dancer, contracts with Ethereal Dancing Guild to play a leading role in its new ballet. Before the ballet can be performed, Fred becomes ill and dies. His personal performance was essential to the completion of the contract. Thus, his death discharges the contract and his estate's liability for his nonperformance.|

2. *When the specific subject matter of the contract is destroyed.* | **Example #13** | A-1 Farm Equipment agrees to sell Gudgel the green tractor on its lot and promises to have it ready for Gudgel to pick up on Saturday. On Friday night, however, a truck veers off the nearby highway and smashes into the tractor, destroying it beyond repair. Because the contract was for this specific tractor, A-1's performance is rendered impossible owing to the accident.|

3. *When a change in law renders performance illegal.* For example, a contract to build an apartment building becomes impossible to perform when the zoning laws are changed to prohibit the construction of residential rental property at the planned location.

Commercial Impracticability   Courts may excuse parties from their performance obligations when the performance becomes much more difficult or expensive than originally contemplated at the time the contract was formed. For someone to invoke the doctrine of **commercial impracticability** successfully, however, the anticipated performance must become *extremely* difficult or costly.[6] The added burden of performing not only must be extreme but also *must not have been known by the parties when the contract was made.*

Frustration of Purpose   A theory closely allied with the doctrine of commercial impracticability is the doctrine of **frustration of purpose.** In principle, a contract will be discharged if supervening circumstances make it impossible to attain the purpose both parties had in mind when making the contract.

The origins of the doctrine lie in the old English "coronation cases." A coronation procession was planned for Edward VII when he became king of England following the death of his mother, Queen Victoria. Hotel rooms along the coronation route were rented at exorbitant prices for that day. When the king became ill and the procession was canceled, a flurry of lawsuits resulted. Hotel and building owners sought to enforce the room-rent bills against would-be parade observers, and would-be parade observers sought to be reimbursed for rental monies paid in advance on the rooms. Would-be parade observers were excused from their duty of payment because the purpose of the room contracts had been "frustrated."

Temporary Impossibility   An occurrence or event that makes performance temporarily impossible operates to suspend performance until the impossibility ceases. Then, ordinarily, the parties must perform the contract as originally

COMMERCIAL IMPRACTICABILITY
A doctrine under which a court might excuse the parties from performing a contract when the performance becomes much more difficult or costly due to an event that the parties did not foresee or anticipate at the time the contract was made.

FRUSTRATION OF PURPOSE
A court-created doctrine under which a party to a contract will be relieved of his or her duty to perform when the objective purpose for performance no longer exists (due to reasons beyond that party's control).

---

5. *Restatement (Second) of Contracts,* Sections 262–266; and UCC 2–615.
6. *Restatement (Second) of Contracts,* Section 264.

planned. If, however, the lapse of time and the change in circumstances surrounding the contract make it substantially more burdensome for the parties
to perform the promised acts, the contract is discharged.

|**Example #14** The leading case on the subject, *Autry v. Republic Productions*,[7]
involved an actor who was drafted into the army in 1942. Being drafted rendered
the actor's contract temporarily impossible to perform, and it was suspended until
the end of the war. When the actor got out of the army, the value of the dollar
had decreased so much that performance of the contract would have been sub-
stantially burdensome to the actor. Therefore, the contract was discharged.|

Exhibit 9–1 graphically illustrates the ways in which a contract can be
discharged.

DAMAGES FOR BREACH OF CONTRACT

A breach of contract entitles the nonbreaching party to sue for money (damages). Damages are designed to compensate a party for harm suffered as a
result of another's wrongful act. In the context of contract law, damages compensate the nonbreaching party for the loss of the bargain. Often, courts say
that innocent parties are to be placed in the position they would have occupied had the contract been fully performed.[8]

Realize at the outset, though, that to collect damages through a court judgment means litigation, which can be expensive and time consuming. Also keep
in mind that court judgments are often difficult to enforce, particularly if the
breaching party does not have sufficient assets to pay the damages awarded (as

---

7. 30 Cal.2d 144, 180 P.2d 888 (1947).
8. *Restatement (Second) of Contracts*, Section 347; and UCC 1–106(1).

EXHIBIT 9–1 CONTRACT DISCHARGE

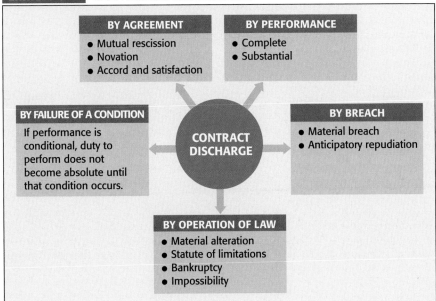

discussed in Chapter 3). For these reasons, the majority of actions for damages (or other remedies) are settled by the parties before trial.

Types of Damages

There are basically four broad categories of damages:

1. Compensatory (to cover direct losses and costs).
2. Consequential (to cover indirect and foreseeable losses).
3. Punitive (to punish and deter wrongdoing).
4. Nominal (to recognize wrongdoing when no monetary loss is shown).

Compensatory and punitive damages were discussed in Chapter 5 in the context of tort law. Here, we look at compensatory and consequential damages in the context of contract law.

> "The duty to keep a contract at common law means a prediction that you must pay damages if you do not keep it—and nothing else."
>
> —OLIVER WENDELL HOLMES, JR.,
> 1841–1935
> (Associate justice of the United States
> Supreme Court, 1902–1932)

Compensatory Damages   Damages compensating the nonbreaching party for the *loss of the bargain* are known as *compensatory damages*. These damages compensate the injured party only for damages actually sustained and proved to have arisen directly from the loss of the bargain caused by the breach of contract. They simply replace what was lost because of the wrong or damage. The standard measure of compensatory damages is the difference between the value of the breaching party's promised performance under the contract and the value of her or his actual performance. This amount is reduced by any loss that the injured party has avoided, however.

| **Example #15**   Wilcox contracts to perform certain services exclusively for Hernandez during the month of March for $4,000. Hernandez cancels the contract and is in breach. Wilcox is able to find another job during the month of March but can earn only $3,000. He can sue Hernandez for breach and recover $1,000 as compensatory damages. Wilcox can also recover from Hernandez the amount that he spent to find the other job.| Expenses that are caused directly by a breach of contract—such as those incurred to obtain performance from another source—are known as *incidental damages*.

The measurement of compensatory damages varies by type of contract. Certain types of contracts deserve special mention. They are contracts for the sale of goods, land contracts, and construction contracts.

Sale of Goods   In a contract for the sale of goods, the usual measure of compensatory damages is an amount equal to the difference between the contract price and the market price. In other words, the amount is the difference between the contract price and the market price at the time and place at which the goods were to be delivered or tendered.[9]

| **Example #16**   Suppose that Chrylon Corporation contracts to buy ten model UTS 400 network servers from an XEXO Corporation dealer for $8,000 each. The dealer, however, fails to deliver the ten servers to Chrylon. The market price of the servers at the time the buyer learns of the breach is $8,150. Chrylon's measure of damages is therefore $1,500 (10 × $150) plus any incidental damages (expenses) caused by the breach.| In a situation in which the buyer breaches and the seller has not yet produced the goods, com-

---

9. See UCC 2–708 and 2–713.

pensatory damages normally equal lost profits on the sale, not the difference between the contract price and the market price.

Sale of Land   Ordinarily, because each parcel of land is unique, the remedy for a seller's breach of a contract for a sale of real estate is specific performance—that is, the buyer is awarded the parcel of property for which she or he bargained (specific performance will be discussed more fully later in this chapter). When this remedy is unavailable (for example, when the seller has sold the property to someone else), or when the breach is on the part of the buyer, the measure of damages is ordinarily the same as in contracts for the sale of goods—that is, the difference between the contract price and the market price of the land. The majority of states follow this rule.

Construction Contracts   The measure of damages in a building or construction contract varies depending on which party breaches and when the breach occurs. The owner can breach at three different stages of the construction:

1. Before performance has begun.
2. During performance.
3. After performance has been completed.

If the owner breaches *before performance has begun,* the contractor can recover only the profits that would have been made on the contract (that is, the total contract price less the cost of materials and labor). If the owner breaches *during performance,* the contractor can recover the profits plus the costs incurred in partially constructing the building. If the owner breaches *after the construction has been completed,* the contractor can recover the entire contract price plus interest.

When the contractor breaches the construction contract—either by failing to begin construction or by stopping work partway through the project—the measure of damages is the cost of completion, which includes reasonable compensation for any delay in performance. If the contractor finishes late, the measure of damages is the loss of use. Exhibit 9–2 illustrates the rules concerning the measurement of damages in breached construction contracts.

Consequential Damages   Foreseeable damages that result from a party's breach of contract are referred to as **consequential damages,** or *special damages.* Consequential damages differ from compensatory damages in that they are caused by special circumstances beyond the contract itself. They flow from the

CONSEQUENTIAL DAMAGES
Special damages that compensate for a loss that does not directly or immediately result from the breach (for example, lost profits). For the plaintiff to collect consequential damages, they must have been reasonably foreseeable at the time the breach or injury occurred.

EXHIBIT 9–2   MEASUREMENT OF DAMAGES—BREACH OF CONSTRUCTION CONTRACTS

PARTY IN BREACH	TIME OF BREACH	MEASUREMENT OF DAMAGES
Owner	Before construction has begun	Profits (contract price less cost of materials and labor)
Owner	During construction	Profits plus costs incurred up to time of breach
Owner	After construction is completed	Contract price plus interest
Contractor	Before construction has begun	Cost above contract price to complete work
Contractor	Before construction is completed	Generally, all costs incurred by owner to complete work

consequences, or results, of a breach. When a seller fails to deliver goods, knowing that the buyer is planning to use or resell those goods immediately, consequential damages are awarded for the loss of profits from the planned resale.

| **Example #17** Gilmore contracts to have a specific item shipped to her—one that she desperately needs to repair her printing press. In her contract with the shipper, Gilmore states that she must receive the item by Monday or she will not be able to print her paper and will lose $950. If the shipper is late, Gilmore normally can recover the consequential damages caused by the delay (that is, the $950 in losses).|

To recover consequential damages, the breaching party must know (or have reason to know) that special circumstances will cause the nonbreaching party to suffer an additional loss. When was this rule first enunciated? See this chapter's *Landmark in the Legal Environment* feature for a discussion of *Hadley v. Baxendale,* a case decided in England in 1854.

Mitigation of Damages

NOTE   A seller who does not wish to take on the risk of consequential damages can limit the buyer's remedies via contract.

In most situations, when a breach of contract occurs, the innocent injured party is held to a duty to mitigate, or reduce, the damages that he or she suffers. Under this doctrine of **mitigation of damages,** the duty owed depends on the nature of the contract.

MITIGATION OF DAMAGES
A rule requiring a plaintiff to do whatever is reasonable to minimize the damages caused by the defendant.

| **Example #18** Some states require a landlord to use reasonable means to find a new tenant if a tenant abandons the premises and fails to pay rent. If an acceptable tenant becomes available, the landlord is required to lease the premises to this tenant to mitigate the damages recoverable from the former tenant. The former tenant is still liable for the difference between the amount of the rent under the original lease and the rent received from the new tenant. If the landlord has not used the reasonable means necessary to find a new tenant, presumably a court can reduce the award made by the amount of rent the landlord could have received had such reasonable means been used.|

In the majority of states, persons whose employment has been wrongfully terminated owe a duty to mitigate damages suffered because of their employers' breach of the employment contract. In other words, wrongfully terminated employees have a duty to take similar jobs if they are available. If the employees fail to do this, the damages they are awarded will be equivalent to their salaries less the incomes they would have received in similar jobs obtained by reasonable means. The employer has the burden of proving that such a job existed and that the employee could have been hired. Normally, the employee is under no duty to take a job of a different type and rank, however.

Liquidated Damages Provisions

LIQUIDATED DAMAGES
An amount, stipulated in the contract, to be paid in the event of a default or breach of contract. The amount must be a reasonable estimate of the damages that would result from a breach in order for the court to enforce it.

A **liquidated damages** provision in a contract specifies that a certain dollar amount is to be paid in the event of a *future* default or breach of contract. (*Liquidated* means determined, settled, or fixed.) For example, a provision requiring a construction contractor to pay $300 for every day he or she is late in completing the construction is a liquidated damages provision. Liquidated damages provisions are frequently used in construction contracts because it is difficult to estimate the amount of damages that would be caused by a delay in completing construction. These clauses are also common in contracts for the

LANDMARK IN THE LEGAL ENVIRONMENT
Hadley v. Baxendale (1854)

The rule that notice of special ("consequential") circumstances must be given if consequential damages are to be recovered was first enunciated in *Hadley v. Baxendale*,[a] a landmark case decided in 1854.

Case Background   This case involved a broken crankshaft used in a flour mill run by the Hadley family in Gloucester, England. The crankshaft attached to the steam engine in the mill broke, and the shaft had to be sent to a foundry located in Greenwich so that a new shaft could be made to fit the other parts of the engine.

The Hadleys hired Baxendale, a common carrier, to transport the shaft from Gloucester to Greenwich. Baxendale received payment in advance and promised to deliver the shaft the following day. It was not delivered for several days, however. As a consequence, the mill was closed during those days because the Hadleys had no extra crankshaft on hand to use. The Hadleys sued Baxendale to recover the profits they lost during that time. Baxendale contended that the loss of profits was "too remote."

In the mid-1800s, it was common knowledge that large mills, such as that run by the Hadleys, normally had more than one crankshaft in case the main one broke and had to be repaired, as happened in this case. It is against this background that the parties argued their respective positions on whether the damages resulting from loss of profits while the crankshaft was out for repair were "too remote" to be recoverable.

The Issue before the Court and the Court's Ruling   The crucial issue before the court was whether the Hadleys had informed the carrier, Baxendale, of the special circumstances surrounding the crankshaft's repair,

a. 9 Exch. 341, 156 Eng.Rep. 145 (1854).

particularly that the mill would have to shut down while the crankshaft was being repaired. If Baxendale had been notified of this circumstance at the time the contract was formed, then the remedy for breaching the contract would have been the amount of damages that would reasonably follow from the breach—including the Hadleys' lost profits.

In the court's opinion, however, the only circumstances communicated by the Hadleys to Baxendale at the time the contract was made were that the item to be transported was a broken crankshaft of a mill and that the Hadleys were the owners and operators of that mill. The court concluded that these circumstances did not reasonably indicate that the mill would have to stop operations if the delivery of the crankshaft was delayed.

Application to Today's Legal Environment

Today, the rule enunciated by the court in this case still applies. When damages are awarded, compensation is given only for those injuries that the defendant could reasonably have foreseen as a probable result of the usual course of events following a breach. If the injury complained of is outside the usual and foreseeable course of events, the plaintiff must show specifically that the defendant had reason to know the facts and foresee the injury. This rule applies to contracts in the online environment as well. For example, suppose that a Web merchant loses business (and profits) due to a computer system's failure. If the failure was caused by malfunctioning software, the merchant normally may recover the lost profits from the software maker if these consequential damages were foreseeable.

RELEVANT WEB SITES

To locate information on the Web concerning Hadley v. Baxendale, *go to this text's Web site at* **www.thomsonedu. com/westbuslaw/let**, *select "Chapter 9," and click on "URLs for Landmarks."*

sale of goods, and Section 2–718(1) of the Uniform Commercial Code (UCC) specifically authorizes the use of liquidated damages clauses.[10]

Liquidated Damages versus Penalties   When a contract specifies a sum to be paid for nonperformance, the issue becomes whether the amount should be treated as liquidated damages or as a penalty. Liquidated damages provisions

10. Note that in 2003, this section was amended. Under the revised version of the statute, only in consumer contracts must the amount of damages be difficult to estimate and be a reasonable prediction. In contracts between merchants, it is no longer required that the damages be difficult to estimate. See Official Comment 2.

PENALTY
An amount, stipulated in the contract, to be paid in the event of a default or breach of contract. When the amount is not a reasonable measure of damages, the court will not enforce it but will limit recovery to actual damages.

are enforceable; penalty provisions are not. Generally, if the amount stated is excessive and the clause is designed to *penalize* the breaching party, a court will consider it a **penalty.** If the amount specified is a reasonable estimation of actual damages, a court may enforce it as a liquidated damages provision.

Factors Courts Consider   To determine if a particular provision is for liquidated damages or for a penalty, two questions must be answered:

1. When the contract was entered into, was it apparent that damages would be difficult to estimate in the event of a breach?
2. Was the amount set as damages a reasonable estimate and not excessive?[11]

If the answers to both questions are yes, the provision normally will be enforced. If either answer is no, the provision normally will not be enforced. For example, in a case involving a sophisticated business contract to lease computer equipment, the court held that a liquidated damages provision that valued computer equipment at more than four times its market value was a reasonable estimate. According to the court, the amount of actual damages was difficult to ascertain at the time the contract was formed because of the "speculative nature of the value of computers at termination of lease schedules."[12]

In the following case, the court considered a liquidated damages provision in the context of an agreement for the lease of a hotel.

---

11. *Restatement (Second) of Contracts*, Section 356(1).
12. *Winthrop Resources Corp. v. Eaton Hydraulics, Inc.*, 361 F.3d 465 (8th Cir. 2004).

CASE 9.2   **Green Park Inn, Inc. v. Moore**

North Carolina Court of Appeals, 2002.
149 N.C.App. 531,
562 S.E.2d 53.
www.nccourts.org [a]

COMPANY PROFILE   *Green Park Inn (**www. greenparkinn.com**) is one of the oldest hotels in the United States. Established in 1882 and listed on the National Register of Historic Places, it is located in the Blue Ridge Mountains near Blowing Rock, North Carolina. Eminent guests have included Annie Oakley, Herbert Hoover, Eleanor Roosevelt, Margaret Mitchell, Calvin Coolidge, and John D. Rockefeller. Green Park Inn is a full-service, first class hotel and restaurant.*

a. Select the link to "Court Opinions," enter "Green Park" in the box labeled "Keywords," and click on "Search." Select the name of the case from the resulting list to access the opinion. The North Carolina Appellate Division Reporter maintains this Web site.

BACKGROUND AND FACTS   Allen and Pat McCain own Green Park Inn, Inc., which operates the Green Park Inn. In 1996, they leased the Inn to GMAFCO, LLC, which is owned by Gary and Gail Moore. The lease agreement provided that, in case of a default by GMAFCO, Green Park, Inc., would be entitled to $500,000 as "liquidated damages." GMAFCO defaulted on the February 2000 rent. Green Park Inn, Inc., gave GMAFCO an opportunity to cure the default, but GMAFCO made no further payments and returned possession of the property to the lessor. When Green Park Inn, Inc., sought the "liquidated damages," the Moores refused to pay. Green Park Inn, Inc., filed a suit in a North Carolina state court against the Moores, GMAFCO, and the Moores' bank to obtain the $500,000. The defendants contended in part that the lease clause requiring payment of "liquidated damages" was an unenforceable penalty provision. The court ordered the defendants to pay Green Park Inn, Inc. The defendants appealed to a state intermediate appellate court.

IN THE WORDS OF THE COURT . . . HUDSON, Judge.

* * * *

The parties agreed to the following in the liquidated damages clause of the Lease Agreement:

CASE 9.2–CONTINUED

Allen and Pat McCain, the only two shareholders of lessor, have actively worked in the day to day operation of the hotel for the past fourteen years, and have steadily built up the clientele, reputation and physical plant of the hotel, and, correspondingly, the revenues/profits of the hotel. In addition, Allen and Pat McCain are 64 and 55 years old respectively, and both retired from the business after this lease was agreed to. The McCains have retired to Florida, and would have to relocate back to Blowing Rock for extended periods of time if they are forced out of retirement to take over operation of the hotel. The parties agree to the following items which will be included in lessor's damages:

(a) restoration of the physical plant;

(b) lost lease payments owed to lessor which will not be paid because of lessee's breach with due consideration having been given to lessor's obligation to mitigate damages;

(c) harm to the reputation of the hotel, which will have to be remedied by lessor;

(d) interruption of business damages caused by the necessity of lessor having to hire new employees to recommence operations.

While some of the items listed in the liquidated damages provision are not indefinite or uncertain, others, such as the harm to the hotel's reputation or the cost to the McCains of being forced out of retirement, clearly would have been difficult to ascertain at the time the Lease Agreement was signed. * * *

Whether a liquidated damages amount is a reasonable estimate of the damages that would likely result from a default is a question of fact. * * * [McCain] stated that, after he and his wife were forced out of retirement and back to Blowing Rock to operate the hotel, "[t]he estimate of $500,000.00 as the fair and reasonable estimate to measure the damages suffered by us in the event of default has proven to be just that fair and reasonable." Additionally, the Lease Agreement states that "[t]he parties have agreed that the sum of Five Hundred Thousand Dollars ($500,000.00) represents a fair and reasonable estimate and measure of the damages to be suffered by lessor in the event of default by lessee." Defendants have proffered [offered] no evidence to show the liquidated damages amount was unreasonable. [Emphasis added.]

DECISION AND REMEDY The state intermediate appellate court affirmed the decision of the lower court. The lease provision satisfied the two-part test for liquidated damages. The amount of the damages would have been difficult to determine at the time that the lease was signed, and the estimate of the damages was reasonable.

WHAT IF THE FACTS WERE DIFFERENT? *If the lease had specified $3 million in damages, would the result in this case have been different? If so, in what way?*

. . . .

ETHICAL ISSUE 9.1

Should liquidated damages clauses be enforced when no actual damages are incurred?

An issue involving liquidated damages clauses that occasionally comes before the courts has to do with deposits on the purchase price of a home or other real estate. For example, in one case a couple signed a contract to buy a home and paid a nonrefundable deposit of $18,000 toward the purchase price. The full agreement was contingent on the buyers' sale of their current home. Because the couple was unable to sell their existing home, they had to back out of the agreement. Shortly thereafter, another buyer agreed to purchase the home for a higher price than the initial buyers had agreed to pay. Thus, the seller incurred no actual damages and, in fact, reaped higher profits as a result of the buyers' inability to perform. In such situations, does a clause requiring the buyers to forgo their deposit constitute a penalty clause rather than a liquidated damages clause?

Not in most cases. The courts routinely hold that such clauses are enforceable liquidated damages clauses. Although this may seem unfair to home buyers who cannot perform due to events beyond their control, consider the alternative: if the courts refused to enforce liquidated damages clauses in these circumstances, it would, in the words of one court, undermine "the peace of mind and certainty of result the parties sought when they contracted for liquidated damages."[13]

EQUITABLE REMEDIES

In some situations, damages are an inadequate remedy for a breach of contract. In these cases, the nonbreaching party may ask the court for an equitable remedy. Equitable remedies include rescission and restitution, specific performance, and reformation. Additionally, a court acting in the interests of equity may sometimes step in and impose contractual obligations in an effort to prevent the unjust enrichment of one party at the expense of another.

Rescission and Restitution

As discussed earlier in this chapter, *rescission* is essentially an action to undo, or cancel, a contract—to return nonbreaching parties to the positions that they occupied prior to the transaction. When fraud, mistake, duress, or failure of consideration is present, rescission is available. The failure of one party to perform under a contract entitles the other party to rescind the contract.[14] The rescinding party must give prompt notice to the breaching party.

RESTITUTION
An equitable remedy under which a person is restored to his or her original position prior to loss or injury, or placed in the position he or she would have been in had the breach not occurred.

CONTRAST Restitution offers several advantages over traditional damages. First, restitution may be available in situations when damages cannot be proved or are difficult to prove. Second, restitution can be used to recover specific property. Third, restitution sometimes results in a greater overall award.

Restitution   To rescind a contract, both parties generally must make **restitution** to each other by returning goods, property, or funds previously conveyed.[15] If the physical property or goods can be returned, they must be. If the property or goods have been consumed, restitution must be made in an equivalent dollar amount.

Essentially, restitution involves the recapture of a benefit conferred on the defendant that has unjustly enriched her or him. **|Example #19** Andrea pays $12,000 to Myles in return for his promise to design a house for her. The next day, Myles calls Andrea and tells her that he has taken a position with a large architectural firm in another state and cannot design the house. Andrea decides to hire another architect that afternoon. Andrea can require restitution of $12,000 because Myles has received an unjust benefit of $12,000.|

Restitution Is Not Limited to Rescission Cases   Restitution may be required when a contract is rescinded, but the right to restitution is not limited to rescission cases. Restitution may be sought in actions for breach of contract, tort actions, and other actions at law or in equity. Usually, restitution can be obtained when funds or property has been transferred by mistake or because of fraud. An award in a case may include restitution of cash or property

---

13. *Kelly v. Marx*, 705 N.E.2d 1114 (Mass. 1999).
14. The rescission discussed here refers to *unilateral* rescission, in which only one party wants to undo the contract. In *mutual* rescission, both parties agree to undo the contract. Mutual rescission discharges the contract; unilateral rescission is generally available as a remedy for breach of contract.
15. *Restatement (Second) of Contracts*, Section 370.

BEYOND OUR BORDERS
Remedies for Breach of Contract

The types of remedies available for breach of contract vary widely throughout the world. In many countries, as in the United States, the normal remedy is damages—money given to the nonbreaching party to compensate that party for the losses incurred owing to the breach. The calculation of damages resulting from a breach of contract, however, may differ from one country to another.

National contract laws also differ as to whether and when equitable remedies, such as specific performance, will be granted. Germany's typical remedy for a breach of contract is specific performance, which means that the party must go forward and perform the contract.

Damages are available only after certain procedures have been employed to seek performance. In contrast, in the United States, the equitable remedy of specific performance usually will not be granted unless the remedy at law (money damages) is inadequate and the subject matter of the contract is unique.

For Critical Analysis *If specific performance were the typical remedy for breaching a contract in the United States, as it is in Germany, would the parties be more likely to perform their obligations and not breach the contract? Discuss.*

obtained through embezzlement, conversion, theft, copyright infringement, or misconduct by a party in a confidential or other special relationship.

Specific Performance

The equitable remedy of **specific performance** calls for the performance of the act promised in the contract. (Interestingly, specific performance is the primary remedy for contract breach in some other nations, as discussed in this chapter's *Beyond Our Borders* feature.) This remedy is quite attractive to the nonbreaching party for three reasons:

1. The nonbreaching party need not worry about collecting the money damages awarded by a court (see the discussion in Chapter 3 of some of the difficulties that may arise when trying to enforce court judgments).
2. The nonbreaching party need not spend time seeking an alternative contract.
3. The performance is more valuable than the money damages.

SPECIFIC PERFORMANCE
An equitable remedy requiring exactly the performance that was specified in a contract; usually granted only when money damages would be an inadequate remedy and the subject matter of the contract is unique (for example, real property).

Suppose that a seller contracts to sell some valuable coins to a buyer. If the seller breaches the contract, would specific performance be an appropriate remedy for the buyer to seek? Why or why not? (Elizabeth Simpson/Getty Images)

Normally, however, specific performance will not be granted unless the party's legal remedy (money damages) is inadequate.[16] For this reason, contracts for the sale of goods rarely qualify for specific performance. The legal remedy—money damages—is ordinarily adequate in such situations because substantially identical goods can be bought or sold in the market. Only if the goods are unique will a court grant specific performance. For example, paintings, sculptures, or rare books or coins are unique, so money damages will not enable a buyer to obtain substantially identical substitutes in the market.

Sale of Land Specific performance is granted to a buyer in a contract for the sale of land. The legal remedy for breach of a land sales contract is inadequate because every parcel of land is considered to be unique. Money damages will not compensate a buyer adequately because the same land in the same location obviously cannot be obtained elsewhere. Only when specific performance is unavailable (for example, when the seller has sold the property to someone else) will money damages be awarded instead.

Is specific performance warranted when one of the parties has substantially—but not *fully*—performed under the contract? That was the question in the following case.

---

16. *Restatement (Second) of Contracts*, Section 359.

CASE 9.3 Stainbrook v. Low

Court of Appeals of Indiana, 2006.
842 N.E.2d 386.

BACKGROUND AND FACTS In April 2004, Howard Stainbrook agreed to sell to Trent Low forty acres of land in Jennings County, Indiana, for $45,000. Thirty-two of the acres were wooded and eight were tillable. Under the agreement, Low was to pay for a survey of the property and other costs, including a tax payment due in November. Low gave Stainbrook a check for $1,000 to show his intent to fulfill the contract. They agreed to close the deal on May 11, and Low made financial arrangements to meet his obligations. On May 8, a tractor rolled over on Stainbrook, and he died. Howard's son David became the executor of Stainbrook's estate. David asked Low to withdraw his offer to buy the forty acres. Low refused and filed a suit in an Indiana state court against David, seeking to enforce the contract. The court ordered specific performance. David appealed to a state intermediate appellate court, arguing in part that his father's contract with Low was "ambiguous and inequitable."

IN THE WORDS OF THE COURT . . . *VAIDIK*, Judge.

* * * *

The Estate [David] * * * contends that Low failed to preserve the remedy of specific performance here because he failed to perform sufficiently under the Agreement. * * * [T]he Estate argues that "[i]n order to be entitled to specific performance, the claimant has the burden to prove *full and complete performance* on their part of the contract." Low * * * argues that specific performance was appropriate because he either *substantially performed* his obligations under the Agreement or offered to do so, and this, rather than full and complete performance, is all that is required to preserve a claim for specific performance.

We agree with Low. Because Low offered to perform his obligations under the Agreement, specific performance was a proper remedy. * * * [T]he Estate argues that Low is not entitled to the remedy of specific performance because he did not pay the November 2004 property taxes. Low, however, * * * offered to make the tax payment and the Estate refused his offer. * * *

CASE 9.3—CONTINUED

The Estate also contends * * * that specific performance was inappropriate because Low failed to tender the purchase price listed in the Agreement and arrange for a survey of the land before the closing date. * * * [T]he Estate's argument assumes that a party may not be granted specific performance unless that party has fully and completely performed under the terms of the contract. On the contrary, * * * specific performance is an appropriate remedy to a party who has *substantially* performed under the terms of the contract. Regarding Low's payment of the purchase price, we note that Low * * * had obtained financing before the closing date, and there is nothing * * * to indicate that he was not prepared to meet his financial obligations at that time. Further, * * * shortly after Stainbrook's death, the Executor of the Estate requested that Low withdraw his offer, and Low declined to do so, indicating that he was prepared to go forward. Regarding Low's failure to order a land survey, the Estate presents no evidence to suggest that this matter, particularly in isolation, reaches the level of failure to perform under the Agreement, and we decline to sanction such a rule. * * *

* * * *

The Estate finally argues that the trial court should not have awarded specific performance here because the Agreement between Low and Stainbrook was unfair. * * * [S]ince Low was twenty-two years old and Stainbrook was eighty-nine at the time of contract, and because the combined estimates of property and timber values was as high as $121,000.00 and Low and Stainbrook had agreed to a $45,000.00 purchase price, the Estate argues that the trial court should have found the contract to be unfair or unconscionable and to have found that Low would be unjustly enriched by its execution. * * *

* * * [T]he Estate stipulated at trial that Stainbrook was competent at the time of contract, and evidence was presented that Stainbrook consulted a lawyer regarding the Agreement and that he insisted upon several handwritten changes to the contract that benefited his own interests. We find no support for the Estate's contention that Stainbrook was anything less than a party entirely capable of entering into this Agreement, nor for its contention that the Agreement was unfair.

DECISION AND REMEDY The state intermediate appellate court held that specific performance was an appropriate remedy in this case and affirmed the lower court's order. The appellate court explained that a contracting party's substantial performance is sufficient to support a court's order for specific performance. Here, "Low both offered to perform and substantially performed his contractual obligations."

WHY IS THIS CASE IMPORTANT? *The court reaffirmed the principle that "[s]pecific performance is a matter of course when it involves contracts to purchase real estate." The circumstances emphasized that "[a] party seeking specific performance of a real estate contract must prove that he has substantially performed his contract obligations or offered to do so." The court's reasoning underscored the importance of focusing on the elements of a principle to resolve a case fairly.*

Contracts for Personal Services Personal-service contracts require one party to work personally for another party. Courts normally refuse to grant specific performance of contracts for personal services. This is because to order a party to perform personal services against his or her will amounts to a type of involuntary servitude, which is contrary to the public policy expressed in the Thirteenth Amendment to the Constitution. Moreover, the courts do not want to monitor contracts for personal services.

| Example #20 If you contract with a brain surgeon to perform brain surgery on you and the surgeon refuses to perform, the court will not compel (and you certainly would not want) the surgeon to perform under these circumstances. There is no way the court can ensure meaningful performance in such a situation.[17]

Reformation

Reformation is an equitable remedy used when the parties have *imperfectly* expressed their agreement in writing. Reformation enables a court to modify, or rewrite, the contract to reflect the parties' true intentions.

When Fraud or Mutual Mistake Is Present   Reformation occurs most often when fraud or mutual mistake (for example, a clerical error) is present. It is almost always sought so that some other remedy may then be pursued. **Example #21** If Keshan contracts to buy a certain parcel of land from Malboa but their contract mistakenly refers to a parcel of land different from the one being sold, the contract does not reflect the parties' intentions. Accordingly, a court can reform the contract so that it conforms to the parties' intentions and accurately refers to the parcel of land being sold. Keshan can then, if necessary, show that Malboa has breached the contract as reformed. She can at that time request an order for specific performance.

Oral Contracts and Covenants Not to Compete   There are two other situations in which the courts frequently reform contracts. The first involves two parties who have made a binding oral contract. They further agree to put the oral contract in writing, but in doing so, they make an error in stating the terms. Normally, the courts will allow into evidence the correct terms of the oral contract, thereby reforming the written contract.

The second situation is when the parties have executed a written covenant not to compete (discussed in Chapter 8). If the covenant is for a valid and legitimate purpose (such as the sale of a business) but the area or time restraints of the covenant are unreasonable, some courts will reform the restraints by making them reasonable and will enforce the entire contract as reformed. Other courts, however, will throw out the entire restrictive covenant as illegal.

Exhibit 9–3 graphically summarizes the remedies, including reformation, that are available to the nonbreaching party.

---

17. Similarly, courts often refuse to order specific performance of construction contracts because courts are not set up to operate as construction supervisors or engineers.

EXHIBIT 9–3   REMEDIES FOR BREACH OF CONTRACT

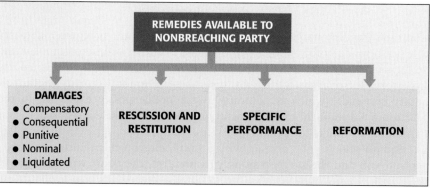

Recovery Based on Quasi Contract

In some situations, when no actual contract exists, a court may step in to prevent one party from being unjustly enriched at the expense of another party. **Quasi contract** is a legal theory under which an obligation is imposed in the absence of an agreement. It allows the courts to act as if a contract exists when there is no actual contract or agreement between the parties. The courts can also use this theory when the parties entered a contract that is unenforceable for some reason.

Quasi-contractual recovery is often granted when one party has partially performed under a contract that is unenforceable. It provides an alternative to suing for damages and allows the party to recover the reasonable value of the partial performance. **Example #22** Ericson contracts to build two oil derricks for Petro Industries. The derricks are to be built over a period of three years, but the parties do not create a written contract. Therefore, the Statute of Frauds will bar the enforcement of the contract (see Chapter 8). After Ericson completes one derrick, Petro Industries informs him that it will not pay for the derrick. Ericson can sue Petro Industries under the theory of quasi contract.

To recover on quasi contract, the party seeking recovery must show the following:

1. The party conferred a benefit on the other party.
2. The party conferred the benefit with the reasonable expectation of being paid.
3. The party did not act as a volunteer in conferring the benefit.
4. The party receiving the benefit would be unjustly enriched by retaining the benefit without paying for it.

QUASI CONTRACT
A fictional contract imposed on parties by a court in the interests of fairness and justice; usually imposed to avoid the unjust enrichment of one party at the expense of another.

ELECTION OF REMEDIES ✓

When one party breaches a contract, the other party—the nonbreaching party—can choose one or more of several remedies. When the remedies are inconsistent with one another, the common law of contracts requires the party to choose which remedy to pursue. This is called *election of remedies.*

The Purpose of the Doctrine

The purpose of the doctrine of election of remedies is to prevent double recovery. **Example #23** Suppose that McCarthy agrees in writing to sell his land to Tally. Then McCarthy changes his mind and repudiates the contract. Tally can sue for compensatory damages *or* for specific performance. If Tally could seek compensatory damages in addition to specific performance, she would recover twice for the same breach of contract. The doctrine of election of remedies requires Tally to choose the remedy she wants, and it eliminates any possibility of double recovery. In other words, the election doctrine represents the legal embodiment of the adage "You can't have your cake and eat it, too."

The doctrine has often been applied in a rigid and technical manner, leading to some harsh results. **Example #24** Beacham is fraudulently induced to buy a parcel of land for $150,000. He spends an additional $10,000 moving onto the land and then discovers the fraud. Instead of suing for damages, Beacham sues to rescind the contract. The court allows Beacham to recover only the purchase price of $150,000 in restitution, but not the additional

BE AWARE Which remedy a plaintiff elects depends on the subject of the contract, the defenses of the breaching party, the advantages that might be gained in terms of tactics against the defendant, and what the plaintiff can prove with respect to the remedy sought.

$10,000 in moving expenses (because the seller did not receive this money, he or she will not be required to return it). So Beacham suffers a net loss of $10,000 on the transaction. If Beacham had elected to sue for damages instead of seeking the remedy of rescission and restitution, he normally could have recovered the $10,000 as well as the $150,000.

The UCC's Rejection of the Doctrine

Because of the many problems associated with the doctrine of election of remedies, the UCC expressly rejects it.[18] As will be discussed in Chapter 10, remedies under the UCC are not exclusive but cumulative in nature and include all the available remedies for breach of contract.

Pleading in the Alternative

Although the parties must ultimately elect which remedy to pursue, modern court procedures do allow plaintiffs to plead their cases "in the alternative" (pleadings were discussed in Chapter 3). In other words, when the plaintiff originally files a lawsuit, he or she can ask the court to order either rescission (and restitution) or damages, for example. Then, as the case progresses to trial, the parties can elect which remedy is most beneficial or appropriate, or the judge can order one remedy and not another. This process still prevents double recovery because the party can only be awarded one of the remedies that was requested.

WAIVER OF BREACH

Under certain circumstances, a nonbreaching party may be willing to accept a defective performance of the contract. This knowing relinquishment of a legal right (that is, the right to require satisfactory and full performance) is called a **waiver.**

WAIVER
An intentional, knowing relinquishment of a legal right.

Consequences of a Waiver of Breach

When a waiver of a breach of contract occurs, the party waiving the breach cannot take any later action on it. In effect, the waiver erases the past breach; the contract continues as if the breach had never occurred. Of course, the waiver of breach of contract extends only to the matter waived and not to the whole contract.

Reasons for Waiving a Breach

Businesspersons often waive breaches of contract to get whatever benefit is still possible out of the contract. | **Example #25** A seller contracts with a buyer to deliver to the buyer ten thousand tons of coal on or before November 1. The contract calls for the buyer to pay by November 10 for coal delivered. Because of a coal miners' strike, coal is hard to find. The seller breaches the contract by not tendering delivery until November 5. The buyer may be well advised to waive the seller's breach, accept delivery of the coal, and pay as contracted.

---

18. See UCC 2–703 and 2–711.

Waiver of Breach and Subsequent Breaches

Ordinarily, the waiver by a contracting party will not operate to waive subsequent, additional, or future breaches of contract. This is always true when the subsequent breaches are unrelated to the first breach. For example, an owner who waives the right to sue for late completion of a stage of construction does not waive the right to sue for failure to comply with engineering specifications on the same job. A waiver will be extended to subsequent defective performance, however, if a reasonable person would conclude that similar defective performance in the future will be acceptable. Therefore, a *pattern of conduct* that waives a number of successive breaches will operate as a continued waiver. To change this result, the nonbreaching party should give notice to the breaching party that full performance will be required in the future.

The party who has rendered defective or less-than-full performance remains liable for the damages caused by the breach of contract. In effect, the waiver operates to keep the contract going. The waiver prevents the nonbreaching party from calling the contract to an end or rescinding the contract. The contract continues, but the nonbreaching party can recover damages caused by defective or less-than-full performance.

CONTRACT PROVISIONS LIMITING REMEDIES

A contract may include provisions stating that no damages can be recovered for certain types of breaches or that damages must be limited to a maximum amount. The contract may also provide that the only remedy for breach is replacement, repair, or refund of the purchase price. Provisions stating that no damages can be recovered are called *exculpatory clauses*. Provisions that affect the availability of certain remedies are called *limitation-of-liability clauses*.

Whether these contract provisions and clauses will be enforced depends on the type of breach that is excused by the provision. For example, a provision excluding liability for fraudulent or intentional injury will not be enforced. Likewise, a clause excluding liability for illegal acts or violations of law will not be enforced. A clause excluding liability for negligence may be enforced in certain cases, however. When an exculpatory clause for negligence is contained in a contract made between parties who have roughly equal bargaining positions, the clause usually will be enforced.

At issue in the following case was the enforceability of a limitation-of-liability clause in a home-inspection contract.

CASE 9.4 **Lucier v. Williams**

Superior Court of New Jersey,
Appellate Division, 2004.
366 N.J.Super. 485,
841 A.2d 907.
lawlibrary.rutgers.edu/search.shtml[a]

BACKGROUND AND FACTS Eric Lucier and Karen Haley, first-time home buyers, contracted to buy a single-family home

a. In the "Search the N.J. Courts Decisions" section, type "Lucier" in the box. In the result, click on the first link to access the opinion. Rutgers Law School in Camden, New Jersey, maintains this Web site.

for $128,500 from James and Angela Williams in Berlin Township, New Jersey. The buyers asked Cambridge Associates, Ltd. (CAL), to perform a home inspection. CAL presented the buyers with a contract that limited CAL's liability to "$500, or 50% of fees actually paid to CAL by Client, whichever sum is smaller. Such causes include, but are not limited to, CAL's negligence, errors, omissions, . . . [or] breach of contract." Lucier reluctantly signed the contract. On CAL's behalf, Al Vasys performed the inspection and issued a report. The buyers paid CAL $385. Shortly after Lucier and Haley

CASE 9.4–CONTINUED ▶

CASE 9.4–CONTINUED

moved into the house, they noticed leaks, which required roof repairs estimated to cost $8,000 to $10,000. They filed a suit in a New Jersey state court against CAL and others, seeking damages for the loss. CAL filed a motion for summary judgment, claiming that under the limitation-of-liability clause, its liability, if any, was one-half the contract price, or $192.50. The court granted the motion. The plaintiffs appealed to a state intermediate appellate court.

IN THE WORDS OF THE COURT . . . *LISA*, J.A.D. [Judge, Appellate Division]

*   *   *   *

We begin our analysis of the enforceability of the limitation of liability clause with the fundamental proposition that contracts will be enforced as written. Ordinarily, courts will not rewrite contracts to favor a party, for the purpose of giving that party a better bargain. However, courts have not hesitated to strike limited liability clauses that are unconscionable or in violation of public policy.

There is no hard and fast definition of unconscionability. * * * *[U]nconscionability is an amorphous [vague] concept obviously designed to establish a broad business ethic. The standard of conduct that the term implies is a lack of good faith, honesty in fact and observance of fair dealing.* [Emphasis added.]

In determining whether to enforce the terms of a contract, we look not only to its adhesive nature [not negotiated by both parties], but also to the subject matter of the contract, the parties' relative bargaining positions, the degree of economic compulsion motivating the adhering party, and the public interests affected by the contract. Where the provision limits a party's liability, we pay particular attention to any inequality in the bargaining power and status of the parties, as well as the substance of the contract.

*   *   *   *

We also focus our inquiry on whether the limitation is a reasonable allocation of risk between the parties or whether it runs afoul of the public policy disfavoring clauses which effectively immunize parties from liability for their own negligent actions. To be enforceable, the amount of the cap on a party's liability must be sufficient to provide a realistic incentive to act diligently.

Applying these principles to the home inspection contract before us, we find the limitation of liability provision unconscionable. We do not hesitate to hold it unenforceable for the following reasons: (1) the contract, prepared by the home inspector, is one of adhesion; (2) the parties, one a consumer and the other a professional expert, have grossly unequal bargaining status; and (3) the substance of the provision eviscerates [removes the essential part of] the contract and its fundamental purpose because the potential damage level is so nominal that it has the practical effect of avoiding almost all responsibility for the professional's negligence. Additionally, the provision is contrary to our state's public policy of effectuating the purpose of a home inspection contract to render reliable evaluation of a home's fitness for purchase and holding professionals to certain industry standards.

*   *   *   *

The foisting of a contract of this type in this setting on an inexperienced consumer clearly demonstrates a lack of fair dealing by the professional. * * *

* * * If, upon the occasional dereliction [neglect of duty], the home inspector's only consequence is the obligation to refund a few hundred dollars (the smaller of fifty percent of the inspection contract price or $500), there is no meaningful incentive to act diligently in the performance of home inspection contracts. To compound the problem, such excessively restricted damage allowance is grossly disproportionate to the potential loss to the homebuyer if a substantial defect is negligently overlooked. The impact upon the homebuyer can be indeed monumental, considering issues such as habitability, health and safety, and financing obligations.

CASE 9.4–CONTINUED

* * * *

Of course, we express no comment on whether or not Vasys or CAL breached any duty to Lucier and Haley under their agreement. Our holding here is only that if they are liable, the extent of any damages for which they should be liable is not limited by the terms of the contract.

DECISION AND REMEDY The state intermediate appellate court held that the provision was unenforceable. The limitation-of-liability clause in the CAL contract did not limit the plaintiffs' recovery. The court reversed the ruling of the lower court and remanded the case for further proceedings.

REVIEWING . . . CONTRACT PERFORMANCE, BREACH, AND REMEDIES

Val's Foods signs a contract to buy 1,500 pounds of basil from Sun Farms, a small organic herb grower, as long as an independent organization inspects and certifies that the crop contains no pesticide or herbicide residue. Val's has a number of contracts with different restaurant chains to supply pesto and intends to use Sun Farms' basil in its pesto to fulfill these contracts. While Sun Farms is preparing to harvest the basil, an unexpected hailstorm destroys half the crop. Sun Farms attempts to purchase additional basil from other farms, but it is late in the season and the price is twice the normal market price. Sun Farms is too small to absorb this cost and immediately notifies Val's that it will not fulfill the contract. Using the information presented in the chapter, answer the following questions.

1. Suppose that the basil does not pass the chemical-residue inspection. Which concept discussed in the chapter might allow Val's to refuse to perform the contract in this situation?

2. Under which legal theory or theories might Sun Farms claim that its obligation under the contract has been discharged by operation of law? Discuss fully.

3. Suppose that Sun Farms contacts every basil grower in the country and buys the last remaining chemical-free basil anywhere. Nevertheless, Sun Farms is only able to ship 1,475 pounds to Val's. Would this fulfill Sun Farms' obligations to Val's? Why or why not?

4. Now suppose that Sun Farms sells its operations to Happy Valley Farms. As a part of the sale, all three parties agree that Happy Valley will provide the basil as stated under the original contract. What is this type of agreement called? Does it discharge the obligations of any of the parties? Explain.

KEY TERMS

CHAPTER SUMMARY • CONTRACT PERFORMANCE, BREACH, AND REMEDIES

Performance and Discharge (See pages 280–291.)	1. *Conditions of performance*—Contract obligations may be subject to the following types of conditions: a. Condition precedent—A condition that must be fulfilled before a party's promise becomes absolute. b. Condition subsequent—A condition that operates to terminate a party's absolute promise to perform. c. Concurrent conditions—Conditions that must be performed simultaneously. Each party's absolute duty to perform is conditioned on the other party's absolute duty to perform. 2. *Discharge by performance*—A contract may be discharged by complete (strict) performance or by substantial performance. In some cases, performance must be to the satisfaction of another. Totally inadequate performance constitutes a material breach of contract. An anticipatory repudiation of a contract allows the other party to sue immediately for breach of contract. 3. *Discharge by agreement*—Parties may agree to discharge their contractual obligations in several ways: a. By rescission—The parties mutually agree to rescind (cancel) the contract. b. By novation—A new party is substituted for one of the primary parties to a contract. c. By substituted agreement—The parties agree to a new contract that replaces the old contract as a means of settling a dispute. d. By accord and satisfaction—The parties agree to render and accept performance different from that on which they originally agreed. 4. *Discharge by operation of law*—Parties' obligations under contracts may be discharged by operation of law owing to one of the following: a. Contract alteration. b. Statutes of limitations. c. Bankruptcy. d. Impossibility or impracticability of performance.
Damages for Breach of Contract (See pages 291–298.)	The legal remedy designed to compensate the nonbreaching party for the loss of the bargain. By awarding money damages, the court tries to place the parties in the positions that they would have occupied had the contract been fully performed. 1. *Compensatory damages*—Damages that compensate the nonbreaching party for injuries actually sustained and proved to have arisen directly from the loss of the bargain resulting from the breach of contract. a. In breached contracts for the sale of goods, the usual measure of compensatory damages is the difference between the contract price and the market price. b. In breached contracts for the sale of land, the measure of damages is ordinarily the same as in contracts for the sale of goods. c. In breached construction contracts, the measure of damages depends on which party breaches and at what stage of construction the breach occurs. 2. *Consequential damages*—Damages resulting from special circumstances beyond the contract itself; the damages flow only from the consequences of a breach. For a party to recover consequential damages, the damages must be the foreseeable result of a breach of contract, and the breaching party must have known at the time the contract was formed that special circumstances existed that would cause the nonbreaching party to incur additional loss on breach of the contract. Also called *special damages*.

CHAPTER SUMMARY • CONTRACT PERFORMANCE, BREACH, AND REMEDIES—CONTINUED

Damages for Breach of Contract—Continued	3. *Mitigation of damages*—The nonbreaching party frequently has a duty to *mitigate* (lessen or reduce) the damages incurred as a result of the contract's breach.
	4. *Liquidated damages*—Damages that may be specified in a contract as the amount to be paid to the nonbreaching party in the event the contract is breached in the future. Clauses providing for liquidated damages are enforced if the damages were difficult to estimate at the time the contract was formed and if the amount stipulated is reasonable. If the amount is construed to be a penalty, the clause will not be enforced.
Equitable Remedies (See pages 298–303.)	1. *Rescission*—A remedy whereby a contract is canceled and the parties are restored to the original positions that they occupied prior to the transaction. Available when fraud, a mistake, duress, or failure of consideration is present. The rescinding party must give prompt notice of the rescission to the breaching party.
	2. *Restitution*—When a contract is rescinded, both parties must make restitution to each other by returning the goods, property, or funds previously conveyed. Restitution prevents the unjust enrichment of the parties.
	3. *Specific performance*—An equitable remedy calling for the performance of the act promised in the contract. This remedy is available only in special situations—such as those involving contracts for the sale of unique goods or land—and when monetary damages would be an inadequate remedy. Specific performance is not available as a remedy in breached contracts for personal services.
	4. *Reformation*—An equitable remedy allowing a contract to be "reformed," or rewritten, to reflect the parties' true intentions. Available when an agreement is imperfectly expressed in writing.
Election of Remedies (See pages 303–304.)	A common law doctrine under which a nonbreaching party must choose one remedy from those available. This doctrine prevents double recovery. Under the UCC, remedies are cumulative for the breach of a contract for the sale of goods.
Waiver of Breach (See pages 304–305.)	A nonbreaching party may choose to accept a defective performance of the contract and thereby waive, or give up, the right to sue for a particular breach. Ordinarily, such a waiver will not operate to waive subsequent, additional, or future breaches, unless it establishes a pattern of conduct between the parties.
Contract Provisions Limiting Remedies (See pages 305–307.)	A contract may provide that no damages (or only a limited amount of damages) can be recovered in the event the contract is breached. Clauses excluding liability for fraudulent or intentional injury or for illegal acts cannot be enforced. Clauses excluding liability for negligence may be enforced if both parties hold roughly equal bargaining power.

FOR REVIEW

Answers for the even-numbered questions in this For Review *section can be found in Appendix O at the end of this text.*

1. What is a condition precedent, and how does it affect a party's duty to perform a contract?
2. How are most contracts discharged?
3. What is substantial performance?
4. What is the standard measure of compensatory damages when a contract is breached?
5. What equitable remedies can a court grant, and in what circumstances will a court consider granting them?

QUESTIONS AND CASE PROBLEMS

9–1. Liquidated Damages. Carnack contracts to sell his house and lot to Willard for $100,000. The terms of the contract call for Willard to pay 10 percent of the purchase price as a deposit toward the purchase price, or as a down payment. The terms further stipulate that should the buyer breach the contract, Carnack will retain the deposit as liquidated damages. Willard pays the deposit, but because her expected financing of the $90,000 balance falls through, she breaches the contract. Two weeks later, Carnack sells the house and lot to Balkova for $105,000. Willard demands her $10,000 back, but Carnack refuses, claiming that Willard's breach and the contract terms entitle him to keep the deposit. Discuss who is correct.

9–2. Junior owes creditor Iba $1,000, which is due and payable on June 1. Junior has been in a car accident, has missed a great deal of work, and consequently will not have the funds on June 1. Junior's father, Fred, offers to pay Iba $1,100 in four equal installments if Iba will discharge Junior from any further liability on the debt. Iba accepts. Is this transaction a novation or an accord and satisfaction? Explain.

For a sample answer to this question, go to Appendix P at the end of this text.

9–3. Impossibility of Performance. In the following situations, certain events take place after the formation of contracts. Discuss which of these contracts are discharged because the events render the contracts impossible to perform.

1. Jimenez, a famous singer, contracts to perform in your nightclub. He dies prior to performance.
2. Raglione contracts to sell you her land. Just before title is to be transferred, she dies.
3. Oppenheim contracts to sell you one thousand bushels of apples from her orchard in the state of Washington. Because of a severe frost, she is unable to deliver the apples.
4. Maxwell contracts to lease a service station for ten years. His principal income is from the sale of gasoline. Because of an oil embargo by foreign oil-producing nations, gasoline is rationed, cutting sharply into Maxwell's gasoline sales. He cannot make his lease payments.

9–4. Specific Performance. In which of the following situations might a court grant specific performance as a remedy for the breach of the contract?

1. Tarrington contracts to sell her house and lot to Rainier. Then, on finding another buyer willing to pay a higher purchase price, she refuses to deed the property to Rainier.
2. Marita contracts to sing and dance in Horace's nightclub for one month, beginning June 1. She then refuses to perform.
3. Juan contracts to purchase a rare coin from Edmund, who is breaking up his coin collection. At the last minute, Edmund decides to keep his coin collection intact and refuses to deliver the coin to Juan.
4. Astro Computer Corp. has three shareholders: Coase, who owns 48 percent of the stock; De Valle, who owns 48 percent; and Cary, who owns 4 percent. Cary contracts to sell his 4 percent to De Valle but later refuses to transfer the shares to him.

9–5. Substantial Performance. Adolf and Ida Krueger contracted with Pisani Construction, Inc., to erect a metal building as an addition to an existing structure. The two structures were to share a common wall, and the frames and panel heights of the new building were to match those of the exist-

ing structure. Shortly before completion of the project, however, it was apparent that the roofline of the new building was approximately three inches higher than that of the existing structure. Pisani modified the ridge caps of the buildings to blend the rooflines. The discrepancy had other consequences, however, including misalignment of the gutters and windows of the two buildings, which resulted in an icing problem in the winter. The Kruegers occupied the new structure, but refused to make the last payment under the contract. Pisani filed a suit in a Connecticut state court to collect. Did Pisani substantially perform its obligations? Should the Kruegers be ordered to pay? Why or why not? [*Pisani Construction, Inc. v. Krueger,* 68 Conn.App. 361, 791 A.2d 634 (2002)]

9–6. Liquidated Damages versus Penalties. Every homeowner in the Putnam County, Indiana, subdivision of Stardust Hills must be a member of the Stardust Hills Owners Association, Inc., and must pay annual dues of $200 for the maintenance of common areas and other community services. Under the association's rules, dues paid more than ten days late "shall bear a delinquent fee at a rate of $2.00 per day." Phyllis Gaddis owned a Stardust Hills lot on which she failed to pay the dues. Late fees began to accrue. Nearly two months later, the association filed a suit in an Indiana state court to collect the unpaid dues and the late fees. Gaddis argued in response that the delinquent fee was an unenforceable penalty. What questions should be considered in determining the status of this fee? Should the association's rule regarding assessment of the fee be enforced? Explain. [*Gaddis v. Stardust Hills Owners Association, Inc.,* 804 N.E.2d 231 (Ind.App. 2004)]

9–7. Train operators and other railroad personnel use signaling systems to ensure safe train travel. Reading Blue Mountain & Northern Railroad Co. (RBMN) and Norfolk Southern Railway Co. entered into a contract for the maintenance of a signaling system that serviced a stretch of track near Jim Thorpe, Pennsylvania. The system included a series of poles, similar to telephone poles, suspending wires above the tracks. The contract provided that "the intent of the parties is to maintain the existing . . . facilities" and split the cost equally. In December 2002, a severe storm severed the wires and destroyed most of the poles. RBMN and Norfolk discussed replacing the old system, which they agreed was antiquated, inefficient, dangerous to rebuild, and expensive, but they could not agree on an alternative. Norfolk installed an entirely new system and filed a suit in a federal district court against RBMN to recover half of the cost. RBMN filed a motion for summary judgment, asserting in part the doctrine of frustration of purpose. What is this doctrine? Does it apply in this case? How should the court rule on RBMN's motion? Explain. [*Norfolk Southern Railway Co. v. Reading Blue Mountain & Northern Railroad Co.,* 346 F.Supp.2d 720 (M.D.Pa. 2004)]

After you have answered this problem, compare your answer with the sample answer given on the Web site that accompanies this text. Go to www.thomsonedu.com/westbuslaw/let, select "Chapter 9," and click on "Case Problem with Sample Answer."

9–8. Waiver of Breach. In May 1998, RDP Royal Palm Hotel, L.P., contracted with Clark Construction Group, Inc., to build the Royal Palms Crowne Plaza Resort in Miami Beach, Florida. The deadline for "substantial completion" was February 28, 2000, but RDP was permitted to ask for changes, and the date would be adjusted accordingly. During construction, Clark faced many setbacks, including a buried sea wall, contaminated soil, the unforeseen deterioration of the existing hotel, and RDP's issue of hundreds of change orders. Clark requested extensions of the deadline, and RDP agreed, but the parties never specified a date. After the original deadline passed, RDP continued to issue change orders, Clark continued to perform, and RDP accepted the work. In March 2002, when the resort was substantially complete, RDP stopped paying Clark. Clark stopped working. RDP hired another contractor to finish the resort, which opened in May. RDP filed a suit in a federal district court against Clark, alleging, among other things, breach of contract for the two-year delay in the resort's completion. In whose favor should the court rule, and why? Discuss. [*RDP Royal Palm Hotel, L.P. v. Clark Construction Group, Inc.*, __ F.3d __ (11th Cir. 2006)]

A Question of Ethics

9–9. Julio Garza was employed by the Texas Animal Health Commission (TAHC) as a health inspector in 1981. His responsibilities included tagging cattle, vaccinating and tattooing calves, and working livestock markets. Garza was injured on the job in 1988 and underwent surgery in January 1989. When his paid leave was exhausted, he asked TAHC for light-duty work, specifically the job of tick inspector, but his supervisor refused the request. In September, TAHC notified Garza that he was fired. Garza sued TAHC and others, alleging, in part, wrongful termination, and an important issue before the court was whether Garza had mitigated his damages. The court found that in the seven years between his termination and his trial date, Garza had held only one job—an unpaid job on his parents' ranch. When asked how often he had looked for work during that time, Garza responded that he did not know, but he had looked in "several" places. The last time he had looked for work was three or four months before the trial. That effort was merely an informal inquiry to his neighbors about working on their ranch. In view of these facts, consider the following questions. [*Texas Animal Health Commission v. Garza*, 27 S.W.3d 54 (Tex.App.—San Antonio 2000)]

1. The court in this case stated that the "general rule as to mitigation of damages in breach of employment suits is that the discharged employee must use reason-able diligence to mitigate damages by seeking other employment." In your opinion, did Garza fulfill this requirement? If you were the judge, how would you rule in this case?

2. Assume for the moment that Garza had indeed been wrongfully terminated. In this situation, would it be fair to Garza to require him to mitigate his damages? Why or why not?

3. Generally, what are the ethical underpinnings of the rule that employees seeking damages for breach of employment contracts must mitigate their damages?

Case Briefing Assignment

9–10. Go to www.thomsonedu.com/westbuslaw/let, the Web site that accompanies this text. Select "Chapter 9" and click on "Case Briefing Assignments." Examine Case A.3 [*AmeriPro Search, Inc. v. Fleming Steel Co.*, 787 A.2d 988 (Sup.Ct.Pa. 2001)]. This case has been excerpted there in great detail. Review and then brief the case, making sure that your brief answers the following questions.

1. What events led to this lawsuit? Did Brauninger (the employment agent) and Kohn (the president of Fleming) agree on how much money AmeriPro would be paid if Fleming hired an engineer recommended by the agency?

2. How did Barracchini (the employee) originally find out about the job opportunity with Fleming Steel in 1993?

3. Who arranged the interview in April 1994, and why did Fleming not hire Barracchini at that time? What about the interview in 1995?

4. What was the trial court's ruling on the question of whether a quasi contract existed?

5. Did the appellate court uphold the lower court's ruling? Why or why not?

Critical-Thinking Social Question

9–11. The concept of substantial performance permits a party to be discharged from a contract even though the party has not fully performed his or her obligations according to the contract's terms. Is this fair? What policy interests are at issue here?

Video Question

9–12. Go to this text's Web site at www.thomsonedu.com/westbuslaw/let and select "Chapter 9." Click on "Video Questions" and view the video titled *Midnight Run*. Then answer the following questions.

1. In the video, Eddie (Joe Pantoliano) and Jack (Robert DeNiro) negotiate a contract for Jack to find the Duke, a mob accountant who embezzled funds, and

bring him back for trial. Assume that the contract is valid. If Jack breaches the contract by failing to bring in the Duke, what kinds of remedies, if any, can Eddie seek? Explain your answer.

2. Would the equitable remedy of specific performance be available to either Jack or Eddie in the event of a breach? Why or why not?

3. Now assume that the contract between Eddie and Jack is unenforceable. Nevertheless, Jack performs his side of the bargain (brings in the Duke). Does Jack have any legal recourse in this situation? Why or why not?

INTERACTING WITH THE INTERNET

For updated links to resources available on the Web, as well as a variety of other materials, visit this text's Web site at

www.thomsonedu.com/westbuslaw/let

For a collection of leading cases involving topics covered in this chapter, go to

www.lectlaw.com/files/lws49.htm

For a summary of how contracts may be breached and other information on contract law, go to Lawyers.com's "General Business" Web page at

www.lawyers.com/lawyers/P~B~General+Business~LDC.html

Then click on "Contracts" and review your options under the "Get Info" section.

The Contracting and Organizations Research Institute (CORI) at the University of Missouri posts a variety of information and articles pertaining to contract law on its Web site at

cori.missouri.edu

INTERNET EXERCISES

Go to **www.thomsonedu.com/westbuslaw/let**, the Web site that accompanies this text. Select "Chapter 9" and click on "Internet Exercises." There you will find the following Internet research exercises that you can perform to learn more about topics covered in this chapter.

Internet Exercise 9–1: LEGAL PERSPECTIVE—Contract Damages and
Contract Theory
Internet Exercise 9–2: ECONOMIC PERSPECTIVE—Anticipatory Repudiation
Internet Exercise 9–3: MANAGEMENT PERSPECTIVE—Commercial Impracticability

BEFORE THE TEST

Go to **www.thomsonedu.com/westbuslaw/let**, the Web site that accompanies this text. Select "Chapter 9" and click on "Interactive Quizzes." You will find a number of interactive questions relating to this chapter.

10 Sales, Leases, and E-Contracts

CHAPTER OBJECTIVES

After reading this chapter, you should be able to answer the following questions:

1 How do Article 2 and Article 2A of the UCC differ? What types of transactions does each article cover?

2 In a sales contract, if an offeree includes additional or different terms in an acceptance, will a contract result? If so, what happens to these terms?

3 What remedies are available to a seller or lessor when the buyer or lessee breaches the contract? What remedies are available to a buyer or lessee if the seller or lessor breaches the contract?

4 What implied warranties arise under the UCC?

5 What are some important clauses to include when making offers to form electronic contracts, or e-contracts?

CONTENTS

THE CHAPTER-OPENING quotation states that the object of the law is to encourage commerce. This is particularly true with respect to the Uniform Commercial Code (UCC). The UCC facilitates commercial transactions by making the laws governing sales and lease contracts uniform, clearer, simpler, and more readily applicable to the numerous difficulties that can arise during such transactions. Recall from Chapter 1 that the UCC is one of many uniform (model) acts drafted by the National Conference of Commissioners on Uniform State Laws and submitted to the states for adoption.[1] Once a state legislature has adopted a uniform act, the act becomes statutory law in that state. Thus, when we turn to sales and lease contracts, we move away from common law principles and into the area of statutory law.

As you will read shortly, the UCC's Article 2 (on sales) and Article 2A (on leases) were amended in 2003 to update their provisions in order to accommodate electronic commerce. Appendix D at the end of this book includes both the existing version of the Article 2 that is now in effect in most states and selected excerpts from the 2003 amendments.

We open this chapter with a look at the scope of Article 2 and Article 2A. Article 2 of the UCC sets out the requirements of sales contracts and how they are formed. Article 2 regulates performance and obligations required under sales

> " The great object of the law is to encourage commerce. "
>
> —J. CHAMBRE, 1739–1823
> (British jurist)

---

1. The UCC has been adopted in whole or in part by all of the states. Louisiana, however, has not adopted Articles 2 and 2A.

contracts. It also delineates when a breach by either the buyer or the seller occurs and what remedies normally may be sought. A sale of goods usually carries with it at least one type of warranty; sales warranties, express and implied, likewise are governed by the UCC. Article 2A covers similar issues for lease contracts.

In the final section of this chapter, we look at how traditional laws are being applied to contracts formed online. We also examine some new laws that have been created to apply in situations in which traditional laws governing contracts have sometimes been thought inadequate. For example, traditional laws governing signature and writing requirements are not easily adapted to contracts formed in the online environment. Thus, new laws have been created to address these issues.

THE SCOPE OF ARTICLE 2–THE SALE OF GOODS

SALES CONTRACT
A contract for the sale of goods under which the ownership of goods is transferred from a seller to a buyer for a price.

Article 2 of the UCC governs **sales contracts,** or contracts for the sale of goods. To facilitate commercial transactions, Article 2 modifies some of the common law contract requirements that were discussed in the previous chapters. To the extent that it has not been modified by the UCC, however, the common law of contracts also applies to sales contracts. For example, the common law requirements for a valid contract—agreement (offer and acceptance), consideration, capacity, and legality—that were discussed in Chapter 9 are also applicable to sales contracts. Thus, you should reexamine these common law principles when studying the law of sales.

In general, the rule is that whenever there is a conflict between a common law contract rule and the UCC, the UCC controls. In other words, when a UCC provision addresses a certain issue, the UCC governs; when the UCC is silent, the common law governs.

In regard to Article 2, you should keep in mind two things. First, Article 2 deals with the sale of *goods;* it does not deal with real property (real estate), services, or intangible property such as stocks and bonds. Thus, if the subject matter of a dispute is goods, the UCC governs. If it is real estate or services, the common law applies. The relationship between general contract law and the law governing sales of goods is illustrated in Exhibit 10–1. Second, in some cases, the rules may vary quite a bit, depending on whether the buyer or the seller is a *merchant.* We look now at how the UCC defines a *sale, goods,* and *merchant status.*

What Is a Sale?

SALE
The passing of title to property from the seller to the buyer for a price.

Section 2–102 of the UCC states that Article 2 "applies to transactions in goods." This implies a broad scope—covering gifts, bailments (temporary deliveries of personal property), and purchases of goods. In this chapter, however, we treat Article 2 as being applicable only to an actual sale (as would most authorities and courts). The UCC defines a **sale** as "the passing of title from the seller to the buyer for a price," where *title* refers to the formal right of ownership of property [UCC 2–106(1)]. The price may be payable in money or in other goods or services.

What Are Goods?

TANGIBLE PROPERTY
Property that has physical existence and can be distinguished by the senses of touch, sight, and so on. A car is tangible property; a patent right is intangible property.

To be characterized as a *good,* an item of property must be *tangible,* and it must be *movable.* **Tangible property** has physical existence—it can be touched or seen. Intangible property—such as corporate stocks and bonds, patents and

EXHIBIT 10-1 LAW GOVERNING CONTRACTS

This exhibit graphically illustrates the relationship between general contract law and the law governing contracts for the sale of goods. Contracts for the sale of goods are not governed exclusively by Article 2 of the Uniform Commercial Code but are also governed by general contract law whenever it is relevant and has not been modified by the UCC.

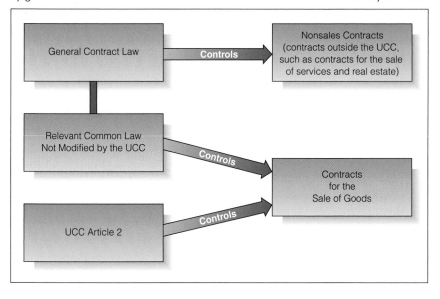

copyrights, and ordinary contract rights—has only conceptual existence and thus does not come under Article 2.[2] A *movable* item can be carried from place to place. Hence, real estate is excluded from Article 2.

Who Is a Merchant?

Article 2 governs the sale of goods in general. It applies to sales transactions between all buyers and sellers. In a limited number of instances, however, the UCC presumes that in certain phases of sales transactions involving merchants, special business standards ought to be imposed because of the merchants' relatively high degree of commercial expertise.[3] Such standards do not apply to the casual or inexperienced seller or buyer ("consumer").

In general, a person is a **merchant** when he or she, acting in a mercantile capacity, possesses or uses an expertise specifically related to the goods being sold. This basic distinction is not always clear-cut. For example, courts in some states have determined that farmers may be merchants, while courts

MERCHANT
A person engaged in the purchase and sale of goods. Under the UCC, a person who deals in goods of the kind involved in the sales contract, or who holds himself or herself out as having skill and knowledge peculiar to the practices or goods involved in the transaction, or who employs a merchant as an intermediary. For definitions, see UCC 2-104.

---

2. The 2003 amendments specifically exclude "information" that is not associated with goods [Amended UCC 2–103(1)(k)]. Nevertheless, Article 2 *may* apply to transactions involving both goods and information when a sale involves "smart goods" (for example, a toy of an automobile that contains embedded computer programs). It is up to the courts to determine whether and to what extent Article 2 should be applied to such transactions.

3. The provisions that apply only to merchants deal principally with the Statute of Frauds, firm offers, confirmatory memoranda, warranties, and contract modification. These special rules reflect expedient business practices commonly known to merchants in the commercial setting. They will be discussed later in this chapter.

in other states have determined that the drafters of the UCC did not intend to include farmers as merchants.

In the following case, the court was asked to determine whether a cattle "order buyer" was a merchant when there was a lapse of time between his transactions.

CASE 10.1　Hammer v. Thompson

Court of Appeals of Kansas, 2006.
35 Kan.App.2d 165,
129 P.3d 609.
www.kscourts.org/kscases[a]

BACKGROUND AND FACTS　In spring 2002, near Richmond, Kansas, Steve Hammer and Ron Howe placed 150 breeding heifers (cows) with Kevin Thompson for grazing. Thompson sold the cattle to Roger Morris, who was doing business as Morris Cattle Company and Auction Service, for $131,750. Morris sold the cattle through Farm Bureau Management Corporation (doing business as BIC Cattle) to

Nick Hunt. Hunt, in business as Clan Farms, Inc., sold the cattle to IBP Foods, Inc. (now known as Tyson Fresh Meats). Hammer and Howe filed a suit in a Kansas state court against Morris and the others, alleging conversion (see Chapter 5). Morris admitted that he bought the cattle, but argued that the claim against him was barred because he was a "buyer in the ordinary course of business" from Thompson, who was a merchant under Article 2.[b] Morris filed a motion for summary judgment in his favor, which the court granted. Hammer and Howe appealed to a state intermediate appellate court.

a. In the body of the text, in the third line, click on the "Court of Appeals" link. On the page that opens, scroll to the name of the case, and click on it to access the opinion. The Kansas courts, the Washburn University School of Law library, and the University of Kansas School of Law library maintain this Web site.

b. Under UCC 2–403, entrusting goods to a merchant *who deals in goods of the kind* gives the merchant the power to transfer all rights to a *buyer in the ordinary course of business* (a person who, in good faith and without knowledge that the sale violates the rights of a third party, buys in ordinary course from the merchant).

IN THE WORDS OF THE COURT . . . *BRAZIL*, J. [Judge]

* * * *

The parties indicate that Thompson was involved in order buying cattle. Thompson described order buying as acting as the middleman between the purchaser and the seller. "I buy the cattle for the man that's purchasing them and try to help the man that's selling them get rid of them or sell them."

* * * *

To support their argument that Thompson was not a merchant, Hammer and Howe argue that Thompson had no intention of being an order buyer of cattle * * * . Hammer and Howe contend there is no evidence that Thompson was running an order buying business in May 2002 when he sold the Hammer/Howe cattle * * * . Hammer and Howe assert that Thompson's documented sales were in the months of October and November 2002, after the May 2002 sale of Hammer and Howe's cattle to Morris.

Morris argues that Thompson was a merchant, pointing to the following facts: Thompson began an order buying business while working at Greeley Farms [in Kansas] and Hammer sold Thompson 300 head of cattle earlier in the summer. Thompson held himself out as a person with specialized knowledge of pasturing cattle, Thompson had documented purchases and sales of cattle as early as March 2001 and had bought or sold cattle as an order buyer in at least 60 different transactions.

* * * *

* * * Between March 15, 2001, and December 20, 2001, there were 25 transactions where Thompson was the buyer and 6 where Thompson was the seller. Additionally, Thompson confirmed * * * his cattle sales and purchases for calendar year 2002. Between October 9, 2002, and November 21, 2002, Thompson was involved in at least one sale and at least 15 purchases as shown by his name listed on the invoices. There

CASE 10.1–CONTINUED were additional invoices * * * where Thompson purchased cattle from Morris in 19 transactions between May 15, 2002, and August 18, 2002.

In the sale at issue, Thompson sold the cattle to Morris on May 18, 2002. There is a lapse in time between December 2001 and May 2002 where there are no records to support that Thompson was involved in order buying cattle. This is consistent with Thompson's testimony that his initial intention was to [engage in a different business] when he moved to Richmond but that he began order buying because he did not have any income. * * * [T]he undisputed facts in the record support a finding that as a matter of law, Thompson was a merchant * * * .

* * * *

The court did not err in finding that Thompson was a merchant.

DECISION AND REMEDY The state intermediate appellate court upheld the finding of the lower court that Thompson was a merchant. The appellate court ruled, however, that Morris had not shown he was a "buyer in the ordinary course of business," which was an essential element of his defense. The court reversed the summary judgment in Morris's favor and remanded the case to the lower court for a determination on this issue.

WHAT IF THE FACTS WERE DIFFERENT? *If neither Thompson nor Morris had any experience in the cattle-trading business, would the result in this case have been different?*

THE SCOPE OF ARTICLE 2A–LEASES

In the past few decades, leases of personal property (goods) have become increasingly common. Consumers and business firms lease automobiles, industrial equipment, items for use in the home (such as floor polishers), and many other types of goods. Until Article 2A was added to the UCC, no specific body of law addressed the legal problems that arose when goods were leased, rather than sold. In cases involving leased goods, the courts generally applied a combination of common law rules, real estate law, and principles expressed in Article 2 of the UCC.

Article 2A of the UCC was created to fill the need for uniform guidelines in this area. Article 2A covers any transaction that creates a **lease** of goods, as well as subleases of goods [UCC 2A–102, 2A–103(k)]. Article 2A is essentially a repetition of Article 2, except that it applies to leases of goods, rather than sales of goods, and thus varies to reflect differences between sales and lease transactions.

Article 2A defines a *lease agreement* as the bargain of the lessor and lessee, as found in their language and as implied by other circumstances [UCC 2A–103(k)]. A **lessor** is one who sells the right to the possession and use of goods under a lease [UCC 2A–103(p)]. A **lessee** is one who acquires the right to the possession and use of goods under a lease [UCC 2A–103(o)]. Article 2A applies to all types of leases of goods, including commercial leases and consumer leases.

LEASE
Under the UCC, a transfer of the right to possess and use goods for a period in exchange for payment.

LESSOR
In a lease of personal property, a person who transfers his or her right to possess and use certain goods for a period to another in exchange for payment (rent).

LESSEE
In a lease of personal property, a person who acquires the right to possess and use another's goods for a period in exchange for paying rent.

THE AMENDMENTS TO ARTICLES 2 AND 2A

For the most part, the 2003 amendments to Articles 2 and 2A mark an attempt by the National Conference of Commissioners on Uniform State Laws to update the UCC to accommodate electronic commerce. Among other things, the amendments revise the definitions of various terms to be consistent with the definitions given in the Uniform Electronic Transactions Act (UETA) and the federal Electronic Signatures in Global and National Commerce

Act (E-SIGN Act) of 2000—discussed later in this chapter. Throughout the amendments, for example, the word *writing* has been replaced by *record*. The term *sign* has been amended to include electronic signatures. Provisions governing electronic contracts, including contracts formed by electronic agents, have also been added.

In addition, the amendments include a number of new protections for buyers, some of which apply only to buyers who are consumers. Other new or revised provisions relate to contract formation (offer and acceptance), the Statute of Frauds, warranties, and other topics. In this chapter, we refer to the amendments, often in footnotes, whenever the amendments significantly change the existing law under Articles 2 and 2A. Note, though, that even when the changes are not substantive, some of the section and subsection numbers may be slightly different under the amended Article 2 due to the addition of new provisions. As mentioned earlier, we include excerpts from the 2003 amendments to Article 2 in Appendix D for further reference.

THE FORMATION OF SALES AND LEASE CONTRACTS

In regard to the formation of sales and lease contracts, the UCC modifies the common law of contracts in several ways. We look here at how Article 2 and Article 2A of the UCC modify common law contract rules. Remember that parties to sales contracts are free to establish whatever terms they wish. The UCC comes into play when the parties have not, in their contract, provided for a contingency that later gives rise to a dispute. The UCC makes this very clear time and again by its use of such phrases as "unless the parties otherwise agree" and "absent a contrary agreement by the parties."

The foldout exhibit that follows this chapter shows an actual sales contract used by Starbucks Coffee Company. The contract illustrates many of the terms and clauses that are typically contained in contracts for the sale of goods.

Offer

In general contract law, the moment a definite offer is met by an unqualified acceptance, a binding contract is formed. In commercial sales transactions, the verbal exchanges, the correspondence, and the actions of the parties may not reveal exactly when a binding contractual obligation arises. The UCC states that an agreement sufficient to constitute a contract can exist even if the moment of its making is undetermined [UCC 2–204(2), 2A–204(2)].

Open Terms   According to contract law, an offer must be definite enough for the parties (and the courts) to ascertain its essential terms when it is accepted. Section 2–204 of the UCC provides that a sales or lease contract will not fail for indefiniteness even if one or more terms are left open as long as (1) the parties intended to make a contract and (2) there is a reasonably certain basis for the court to grant an appropriate remedy. A seller and buyer of goods can thus create an enforceable contract even if several terms, including terms relating to price, payment, and delivery, are left unspecified. For example, if the price term is left open, Article 2 provides that the price will be "a reasonable price at the time of delivery" [UCC 2–305(1)]. If the payment term is left open, Article 2 states that "payment is due at the time and place at which the buyer is to receive the goods" [UCC 2–310(a)]. Under Article 2, the only term that

NOTE   Under the UCC, it is the actions of the parties that determine whether they intended to form a contract.

normally must be specified is the quantity term; otherwise, the court will have no basis for determining a remedy.

ETHICAL ISSUE 10.1 | ***Is it fair for the UCC to impose payment terms when the parties did not agree to those terms?***

Many people buy and sell goods all the time in their daily lives without knowing what the UCC is or how it may apply to their transactions. Is it fair for the UCC to impose terms that the parties never discussed when forming their contract?

Consider, for example, a simple transaction that took place on a farm. Max Alexander agreed to purchase hay from Wagner's farm. Alexander left his truck and trailer at the farm so the seller could load the hay. Nothing was said about when payment was due, and the parties were unaware of the UCC's rules. When Alexander came back to get the hay, a dispute broke out. Alexander claimed that he was not given the quantity of hay that he had ordered and argued that he did not have to pay at that time. Wagner refused to release the hay (or the vehicles on which the hay was loaded) until Alexander paid for it.

Eventually, Alexander jumped into his truck and drove off without paying for the hay. When Alexander was later prosecuted for the crime of theft (see Chapter 6), he claimed that he could not be guilty of taking the property of another because he had bought the hay and was its rightful owner. The court, however, disagreed. Because the parties had failed to specify when payment was due, the court held that UCC 2–310(a) controlled: payment was due at the time Alexander picked up the hay. Thus, Alexander's theft conviction was affirmed.[4]

Merchant's Firm Offer Under regular contract principles, an offer can be revoked at any time before acceptance. The UCC has an exception that applies only to **firm offers** for the sale or lease of goods made by a merchant (regardless of whether or not the offeree is a merchant). A firm offer arises when a merchant gives assurances *in a signed writing* that the offer will remain open. A firm offer is irrevocable without the necessity of consideration for the stated period or, if no definite period is stated, a reasonable period (neither to exceed three months) [UCC 2–205, 2A–205]. **| Example #1** Osaka, a used-car dealer, writes a letter to Saucedo on January 1 stating, "I have a 2005 Suzuki on the lot that I'll sell you for $8,500 any time between now and January 31." This writing creates a firm offer, and Osaka will be liable for breach if he sells the Suzuki to someone other than Saucedo before January 31.**|**

FIRM OFFER
An offer (by a merchant) that is irrevocable without consideration for a stated period of time or, if no definite period is stated, for a reasonable time (neither period to exceed three months). A firm offer by a merchant must be in writing and must be signed by the offeror.

Acceptance

Acceptance of an offer to buy, sell, or lease goods generally may be made in any reasonable manner and by any reasonable means. The UCC permits acceptance of an offer to buy goods "either by a prompt promise to ship or by the prompt or current shipment of conforming or nonconforming goods" [UCC 2–206(1)(b)]. *Conforming* goods accord with the contract's terms; *nonconforming* goods do not. The prompt shipment of *nonconforming goods*

---

4. *State v. Alexander*, 186 Or.App. 600, 64 P.3d 1148 (2003).

constitutes both an *acceptance*, which creates a contract, and a *breach* of that contract. This rule does not apply if the seller seasonably (within a reasonable amount of time) notifies the buyer that the nonconforming shipment is offered only as an *accommodation*, or as a favor. The notice of accommodation must clearly indicate to the buyer that the shipment does not constitute an acceptance and that, therefore, no contract has been formed.

| **Example #2**   McFarrell Pharmacy orders five cases of Johnson & Johnson 3-by-5-inch gauze pads from Halderson Medical Supply, Inc. If Halderson ships five cases of Xeroform 3-by-5-inch gauze pads instead, the shipment acts as both an acceptance of McFarrell's offer and a *breach* of the resulting contract. McFarrell may sue Halderson for any appropriate damages. If, however, Halderson notifies McFarrell that the Xeroform gauze pads are being shipped *as an accommodation*—because Halderson has only Xeroform pads in stock— the shipment will constitute a counteroffer, not an acceptance. A contract will be formed only if McFarrell accepts the Xeroform gauze pads. |

Communication of Acceptance   Under the common law, because a unilateral offer invites acceptance by a performance, the offeree need not notify the offeror of performance unless the offeror would not otherwise know about it. The UCC is more stringent than the common law in this regard. Under the UCC, if an offeror is not notified within a reasonable time that the offeree has impliedly accepted the contract by beginning performance, then the offeror can treat the offer as having lapsed before acceptance [UCC 2–206(2), 2A–206(2)].

Additional Terms   The UCC generally takes the position that if the offeree's response indicates a *definite* acceptance of the offer, a contract is formed even if the acceptance includes additional or different terms from those stated in the offer [UCC 2–207(1)]. If one (or both) of the parties is a *nonmerchant,* the contract is formed according to the terms of the original offer submitted by the original offeror and not according to the additional terms of the acceptance [UCC 2–207(2)]. Any additional terms in that situation are considered merely suggestions or proposals. In contracts *between merchants,* the additional terms automatically become part of the contract unless (1) the original offer expressly limited acceptance to its terms, (2) the new or changed terms materially alter the contract, or (3) the offeror objects to the new or changed terms within a reasonable period of time [UCC 2–207(2)].[5]

Consideration

The common law rule that a contract requires consideration also applies to sales and lease contracts. Unlike the common law, however, the UCC does not require a contract modification to be supported by new consideration. The UCC states that an agreement modifying a contract for the sale or lease of goods "needs no consideration to be binding" [UCC 2–209(1), 2A–208(1)].

---

5. The 2003 amendments to UCC Article 2 do not distinguish between merchants and others in setting out rules for the effect of additional terms in sales contracts. Instead, a court is directed to determine whether (1) the terms appear in the records of both parties, (2) both parties agree to the terms even if they are not in a record, or (3) the terms are supplied or incorporated under another provision of Article 2 [Amended UCC 2–207]. Basically, once adopted, the amendments will give the courts more discretion to include or exclude certain additional terms.

Of course, any contract modification must be made in good faith [UCC 1–203]. | **Example #3** Jim agrees to lease certain goods to Louise for a stated price. Subsequently, a sudden shift in the market makes it difficult for Jim to lease the items to Louise at the given price without suffering a loss. Jim tells Louise of the situation, and Louise agrees to pay an additional sum for leasing the goods. Later, Louise reconsiders and refuses to pay more than the original lease price. Under the UCC, Louise's promise to modify the contract needs no consideration to be binding. Hence, Louise is bound by the modified contract.

In this example, a shift in the market is a *good faith* reason for contract modification. What if there really was no shift in the market, however, and Jim knew that Louise needed the goods immediately but refused to deliver them unless Louise agreed to pay an additional sum of money? This sort of extortion of a modification without a legitimate commercial reason would be ineffective, because it would violate the duty of good faith. Jim would not be permitted to enforce the higher price.|

THE STATUTE OF FRAUDS

[handwritten: for every contract to be forceable must be in written form]

As discussed in Chapter 8, the Statute of Frauds requires that certain types of contracts, to be enforceable, must be in writing or evidenced by a writing. The UCC contains Statute of Frauds provisions covering sales and lease contracts. Under these provisions, sales contracts for goods priced at $500 or more ($5,000 or more under a 2003 amendment) and lease contracts requiring total payments of $1,000 or more must be in writing to be enforceable [UCC 2–201(1), 2A–201(1)].[6]

[handwritten: add promis]

Sufficiency of the Writing

A writing or a memorandum will be sufficient as long as it indicates that the parties intended to form a contract and as long as it is signed by the party (or agent of the party) against whom enforcement is sought. A sales contract normally will not be enforceable beyond the quantity of goods shown in the writing, however. All other terms can be proved in court by oral testimony. For leases, the writing must reasonably identify and describe the goods leased and the lease term.

Special Rules for Contracts between Merchants

Once again, the UCC provides a special rule for merchants engaged in sales transactions (there is no corresponding rule that applies to leases under Article 2A). Merchants can satisfy the requirements of a writing for the Statute of Frauds if, after the parties have agreed orally, one of the merchants sends a signed written confirmation to the other merchant. The communication must indicate the terms of the agreement, and the merchant receiving the confirmation must have reason to know of its contents. Unless the merchant who receives the confirmation gives written notice of objection to its contents within ten days after receipt, the writing is sufficient against the receiving merchant, even though he or she has not

---

6. Note that a 2003 amendment significantly increased the price of goods that will fall under the Statute of Frauds. Under the amended UCC 2–201(1), goods must be priced at $5,000 or more to be subject to the record (writing) requirement.

Can an Employee's E-Mail Constitute a Waiver of Contract Terms?

Under UCC 2–209, an agreement that excludes modification except by a signed writing cannot be otherwise modified. If the written-modification requirement is contained in a form supplied by one merchant to another, the other party must separately sign the form for it to be binding. This rule has an exception, though, which can be significant in the online environment. Under the UCC, *an attempt at modification that does not meet the writing requirement may operate as a waiver* [UCC 2–209(4)]. In other words, the parties can waive, or give up, the right to require that contract modifications be in a signed writing. Can an employee's e-mail communications form a waiver of a contract's written-modification requirement? This issue arose in *Cloud Corp. v. Hasbro, Inc.*[a]

The Contract Terms and the Parties' Relationship

Cloud Corporation contracted to supply packets of a special powder to Hasbro, Inc., for use in Hasbro's new "Wonder World Aquarium." At the time of their initial agreement, Hasbro sent a letter to Cloud containing a "terms and conditions" form, which stated that Cloud, the supplier, could not deviate from a purchase order without Hasbro's written consent. Cloud signed and returned that form to Hasbro as requested, and Hasbro began placing orders. Each time Hasbro ordered packets, Cloud sent back an "order acknowledgment" form confirming the quantity ordered.

After placing several orders, Hasbro told Cloud to change the formula in the packets. As a result, Cloud was able to produce three times as many packets using the same amount of material that it already had on hand to

fill Hasbro's previous orders. Although Hasbro had not ordered any additional packets, Cloud sent Hasbro an order acknowledgment for extra packets at a lower price. Hasbro did not explicitly respond to Cloud's acknowledgment form. One of Hasbro's employees, however, referred to the additional quantities of packets at some point in her e-mail exchanges with Cloud. Several months later, after Cloud had produced the additional packets, Hasbro quit making the Wonder World Aquarium and refused to pay for the packets that it did not order. Cloud then sued Hasbro for breach of contract.

Was the Employee's E-Mail a Waiver?

Ultimately, a federal appellate court held that because Hasbro's employee had referred to the additional packets in at least one e-mail, Hasbro must pay for them. According to the court, the employee's e-mail alone could be sufficient to satisfy the requirement of written consent to modify the contract. Even if it was not, however, the court held that it operated as a waiver. The court stated that for the e-mail to operate as a waiver, Cloud "must show either that it reasonably relied on the other party's having waived the requirement of a writing, or that the waiver was clear and unequivocal." Here, the employee's e-mail had not clearly waived the writing requirement, but there was *reasonable reliance.* According to the court, Hasbro should have advised Cloud if it did not want to be committed to buying the additional quantity rather than "leading Cloud down the primrose path."

For Critical Analysis   *How might the parties to a sales contract prevent their subsequent e-mail communications from waiving the contract's explicit modification requirements? (Hint: How can the parties prevent contract disputes generally?)*

a. 314 F.3d 289 (7th Cir. 2002).

---

signed anything [UCC 2–201(2)]. What happens if a merchant sends a written confirmation of an order that was never placed? For a discussion of this issue, see this chapter's *Online Developments* feature.

Exceptions

The UCC defines three exceptions to the writing requirements of the Statute of Frauds. An oral contract for the sale of goods priced at $500 or more ($5,000 or more under the 2003 amendments) or the lease of goods involving total payments of $1,000 or more will be enforceable despite the absence of a writing in the circumstances described in the following subsections [UCC

2–201(3), 2A–201(4)]. These exceptions and other ways in which sales law differs from general contract law are summarized in Exhibit 10–2.

Specially Manufactured Goods   An oral contract is enforceable if (1) it is for goods that are specially manufactured for a particular buyer or specially manufactured or obtained for a particular lessee, (2) these goods are not suitable for resale or lease to others in the ordinary course of the seller's or lessor's business, and (3) the seller or lessor has substantially started to manufacture the goods or has made commitments for the manufacture or procurement of the goods. In this situation, once the seller or lessor has taken action, the buyer or lessee cannot repudiate the agreement claiming the Statute of Frauds as a defense. **| Example #4** Womach orders custom-made draperies for her new boutique. The price is $1,000, and the contract is oral. When the merchant-seller manufactures the draperies and tenders delivery to Womach, she refuses to pay for them, claiming that she is not liable because the contract was oral. If the unique style and color of the draperies make it improbable that the seller can find another buyer, Womach is liable to the seller.**|** Note that the seller must have made a substantial beginning in manufacturing the specialized item prior to the buyer's repudiation.

Admissions   An oral contract for the sale or lease of goods is enforceable if the party against whom enforcement is sought admits in pleadings, testimony, or other court proceedings that a sales or lease contract was made.[7] In this

REMEMBER ! An admission can be made in documents, including internal memos and employee reports, that may be obtained during discovery prior to trial.

7. Any admission under oath, including one not made in a court, satisfies UCC 2–201(3)(b) and 2A–201(4)(b) under the 2003 amendments to Articles 2 and 2A.

EXHIBIT 10–2   MAJOR DIFFERENCES BETWEEN CONTRACT LAW AND SALES LAW

	CONTRACT LAW	**SALES LAW**
Contract Terms	Contract must contain all material terms.	Open terms are acceptable if parties intended to form a contract, but contract is not enforceable beyond quantity term.
Acceptance	Mirror image rule applies. If additional terms are added in acceptance, counteroffer is created.	Additional terms will not negate acceptance unless acceptance is expressly conditioned on assent to the additional terms.
Contract Modification	Modification requires consideration.	Modification does not require consideration.
Statute of Frauds Requirements	All material terms must be included in the writing.	Writing is required only for sale of goods of $500[a] or more, but contract is not enforceable beyond quantity specified. Merchants can satisfy the writing requirement by a confirmatory memorandum, evidencing their agreement. *Exceptions:* 1. Specially manufactured goods. 2. Admissions by party against whom enforcement is sought. 3. Partial performance.

a. Under a 2003 amendment to the UCC, a writing (record) is required only for the sale of goods priced at $5,000 or more.

An artisan creates a specially designed "bowl within a bowl" out of one piece of clay. If a restaurant orally contracted with the artisan to create twenty of the specially designed bowls for use in its business, at a price of $800, would the contract have to be in writing to be enforceable? Why or why not? (AP/Wide World Photos)

situation, the contract will be enforceable even though it was oral, but enforceability will be limited to the quantity of goods admitted.

| **Example #5** Lane and Byron negotiate an agreement over the telephone. During the negotiations, Lane requests a delivery price for five hundred gallons of gasoline and a separate price for seven hundred gallons of gasoline. Byron replies that the price would be the same, $2.50 per gallon. Lane orally orders five hundred gallons. Byron honestly believes that Lane ordered seven hundred gallons and tenders that amount. Lane refuses the shipment of seven hundred gallons, and Byron sues for breach. In his pleadings and testimony, Lane admits that an oral contract was made, but only for five hundred gallons. Because Lane admits the existence of the oral contract, Lane cannot plead the Statute of Frauds as a defense. The contract is enforceable, however, only to the extent of the quantity admitted (five hundred gallons).|

Partial Performance   An oral contract for the sale or lease of goods is enforceable if payment has been made and accepted or goods have been received and accepted. This is the "partial performance" exception. The oral contract will be enforced at least to the extent that performance *actually* took place.

PERFORMANCE OF SALES AND LEASE CONTRACTS

To understand the obligations of the parties under a sales or lease contract, it is necessary to know the duties and obligations each party has assumed under the terms of the contract. Keep in mind that "duties and obligations" under the contract terms include those specified by the agreement, by custom, and by the UCC.

In the performance of a sales or lease contract, the basic obligation of the seller or lessor is to *transfer and deliver conforming goods*. The basic obligation of the buyer or lessee is to *accept and pay for conforming goods* in accordance with the contract [UCC 2–301, 2A–516(1)]. Overall performance of a sales or lease contract is controlled by the agreement between the parties. When the contract is unclear and disputes arise, the courts look to the UCC.

The Good Faith Requirement

The obligations of good faith and commercial reasonableness underlie every sales and lease contract within the UCC. These obligations can form the basis for a suit for breach of contract later on. The UCC's good faith provision, which can never be disclaimed, reads as follows: "Every contract or duty within this Act imposes an obligation of good faith in its performance or enforcement" [UCC 1–203]. Good faith means honesty in fact. In the case of a merchant, it means honesty in fact and the observance of reasonable commercial standards of fair dealing in the trade [UCC 2–103(1)(b)]. In other words, merchants are held to a higher standard of performance or duty than nonmerchants.[8]

---

8. The 2003 amendments to UCC Articles 2 and 2A apply this definition of *good faith* to all parties, merchants and nonmerchants alike [Amended UCC 2–103(1)(j), 2A–103(1)(m)].

Obligations of the Seller or Lessor

The major obligation of the seller or lessor under a sales or lease contract is to tender conforming goods to the buyer or lessee. **Tender of delivery** requires that the seller or lessor have and hold *conforming goods* at the disposal of the buyer or lessee and give the buyer or lessee whatever notification is reasonably necessary to enable the buyer or lessee to take delivery [UCC 2–503(1), 2A–508(1)]. **Conforming goods** are goods that conform exactly to the description of the goods in the contract.

Tender must occur at a *reasonable hour* and in a *reasonable manner.* For example, a seller cannot call the buyer at 2:00 A.M. and say, "The goods are ready. I'll give you twenty minutes to get them." Unless the parties have agreed otherwise, the goods must be tendered for delivery at a reasonable hour and kept available for a reasonable period of time to enable the buyer to take possession of them [UCC 2–503(1)(a)].

All goods called for by a contract must be tendered in a single delivery unless the parties agree otherwise [UCC 2–612, 2A–510] or the circumstances are such that either party can rightfully request delivery in lots [UCC 2–307].

Place of Delivery   If the contract does not designate the place of delivery for the goods, and the buyer is expected to pick them up, the place of delivery is the *seller's place of business* or, if the seller has none, the *seller's residence* [UCC 2–308]. If the contract involves the sale of *identified goods*—that is, the specific goods provided for in the contract—and the parties know when they enter into the contract that these goods are located somewhere other than at the seller's place of business (such as at a warehouse), then the *location of the goods* is the place for their delivery [UCC 2–308].

The Perfect Tender Rule   Under the **perfect tender rule,** the seller or lessor is required to deliver goods that conform to the terms of the contract in every detail. If the goods or tender of delivery fail *in any respect* to conform to the contract, the buyer or lessee has the right to accept the goods, reject the entire shipment, or accept part and reject part [UCC 2–601, 2A–509].

Exceptions to the Perfect Tender Rule   Because of the rigidity of the perfect tender rule, several exceptions to the rule have been created, some of which we discuss here.

Agreement of the Parties   Exceptions to the perfect tender rule may be established by agreement. If the parties have agreed, for example, that defective goods or parts will not be rejected if the seller or lessor is able to repair or replace them within a reasonable period of time, the perfect tender rule does not apply.

Cure   The UCC does not specifically define the term **cure,** but it refers to the right of the seller or lessor to repair, adjust, or replace defective or nonconforming goods [UCC 2–508, 2A–513]. When any tender of delivery is rejected because of nonconforming goods and the time for performance has not yet expired, the seller or lessor can promptly notify the buyer or lessee of the intention to cure and can then do so *within the contract time for performance* [UCC 2–508(1), 2A–513(1)]. Once the time for performance under the contract has expired, the seller or lessor can still exercise the right to cure if he or

TENDER OF DELIVERY
Under the Uniform Commercial Code, a seller's or lessor's act of placing conforming goods at the disposal of the buyer or lessee and giving the buyer or lessee whatever notification is reasonably necessary to enable the buyer or lessee to take delivery.

CONFORMING GOODS
Goods that conform to contract specifications.

PERFECT TENDER RULE
A rule under which a seller or lessor is required to deliver goods that conform perfectly to the requirements of the contract. A tender of nonconforming goods automatically constitutes a breach of contract.

CURE
The right of a party who tenders nonconforming performance to correct that performance within the contract period [UCC 2–508(1)].

she has *reasonable grounds to believe that the nonconforming tender will be acceptable to the buyer or lessee* [UCC 2–508(2), 2A–513(2)].[9]

The right to cure substantially restricts the right of the buyer or lessee to reject goods. For example, if a lessee refuses a tender of goods as nonconforming but does not disclose the nature of the defect to the lessor, the lessee cannot later assert the defect as a defense if the defect is one that the lessor could have cured. Generally, buyers and lessees must act in good faith and state specific reasons for refusing to accept goods [UCC 2–605, 2A–514].

Substitution of Carriers   When an agreed-on manner of delivery (such as the use of a particular carrier to transport the goods) becomes impracticable or unavailable through no fault of either party, but a commercially reasonable substitute is available, the seller must perform using this substitute [UCC 2–614(1)].

Commercial Impracticability   Occurrences unforeseen by either party when a contract was made may make performance commercially impracticable. When this occurs, the rule of perfect tender no longer holds. According to UCC 2–615(a) and 2A–405(a), delay in delivery or nondelivery in whole or in part is not a breach when performance has been made impracticable "by the occurrence of a contingency the nonoccurrence of which was a basic assumption on which the contract was made." The seller or lessor must, however, notify the buyer or lessee as soon as practicable that there will be a delay or nondelivery.

Can unanticipated increases in a seller's costs that make performance "impracticable" constitute a valid defense to performance on the basis of commercial impracticability? The court dealt with this question in the following case.

---

9. The 2003 amendments to UCC Articles 2 and 2A expressly exempt consumer contracts and consumer leases from these provisions [Amended UCC 2–508, 2A–508]. In other words, cure is not available as a matter of right after a justifiable revocation of acceptance under a consumer contract or lease.

LANDMARK & CLASSIC CASES

CASE 10.2   Maple Farms, Inc. v. City School District of Elmira

Supreme Court of New York, 1974.
76 Misc.2d 1080,
352 N.Y.S.2d 784.

BACKGROUND AND FACTS   On June 15, 1973, Maple Farms, Inc., formed an agreement with the city school district of Elmira, New York, to supply the school district with milk for the 1973–1974 school year. The agreement was in the form of a requirements contract, under which Maple Farms would sell to the school district all the milk the district required at a fixed price—which was the June market price of milk. By December 1973, the price of raw milk had increased by 23 percent over the price specified in the contract. This meant that if the terms of the contract were fulfilled, Maple Farms would lose $7,350. Because it had similar contracts with other school districts, Maple Farms stood to lose a great deal if it was held to the price stated in the contracts. When the school district would not agree to release Maple Farms from its contract, Maple Farms brought an action in a New York state court for a declaratory judgment (a determination of the parties' rights under a contract). Maple Farms contended that the substantial increase in the price of raw milk was an event not contemplated by the parties when the contract was formed and that, given the increased price, performance of the contract was commercially impracticable.

IN THE WORDS OF THE COURT . . . _CHARLES B. SWARTWOOD_, Justice.

* * * *

* * * [The doctrine of commercial impracticability requires that] a contingency—something unexpected—must have occurred. Second, the risk of the unexpected occurrence must not have been allocated either by agreement or by custom. * * *

* * * [H]ere we find that the contingency causing the increase of the price of raw milk was not totally unexpected. The price from the low point in the year 1972 to the price on the date of the award of the contract in June 1973 had risen nearly 10%. And _any businessman should have been aware of the general inflation in this country during the previous years_ * * * . [Emphasis added.]

* * * Here the very purpose of the contract was to guard against fluctuation of price of half pints of milk as a basis for the school budget. Surely had the price of raw milk fallen substantially, the defendant could not be excused from performance. We can reasonably assume that the plaintiff had to be aware of escalating inflation. It is chargeable with knowledge of the substantial increase of the price of raw milk from the previous year's low. * * * It nevertheless entered into this agreement with that knowledge. It did not provide in the contract any exculpatory clause to excuse it from performance in the event of a substantial rise in the price of raw milk. On these facts the risk of a substantial or abnormal increase in the price of raw milk can be allocated to the plaintiff.

DECISION AND REMEDY   The New York trial court ruled that inflation and fluctuating prices did not render performance impracticable in this case and granted summary judgment in favor of the school district.

WHAT IF THE FACTS WERE DIFFERENT?   _Suppose that the court had ruled in the plaintiff's favor. How might that ruling have affected the plaintiff's contracts with other parties?_

IMPACT OF THIS CASE ON TODAY'S LAW   _This case is a classic illustration of the UCC's commercial impracticability_ _doctrine as courts still apply it today. Under this doctrine, increased cost alone does not excuse performance unless the rise in cost is due to some unforeseen contingency that alters the essential nature of the performance._

RELEVANT WEB SITES   _To locate information on the Web concerning_ Maple Farms, Inc. v. City School District of Elmira, _go to this text's Web site at_ **www.thomsonedu.com/ westbuslaw/let**, _select "Chapter 10," and click on "URLs for Landmarks."_

Destruction of Identified Goods   Sometimes, an unexpected event, such as a fire, totally destroys goods through no fault of either party and before risk passes to the buyer or lessee. In such a situation, if the _goods were identified at the time the contract was formed_, the parties are excused from performance [UCC 2–613, 2A–221]. If the goods are only partially destroyed, however, the buyer or lessee can inspect them and either treat the contract as void or accept the damaged goods with a reduction of the contract price.

Cooperation and Assurance   Sometimes the performance of one party depends on the cooperation of the other. The UCC provides that when such cooperation is not forthcoming, the other party can either suspend his or her own performance without liability and hold the uncooperative party in breach or proceed to perform the contract in any reasonable manner [see UCC 2–311(3)(b)].

In addition, if one of the parties to a contract has "reasonable grounds" to believe that the other party will not perform as contracted, he or she may _in_ *writing* "demand adequate assurance of due performance" from the other party. Until such assurance is received, he or she may "suspend" further performance without liability. What constitutes "reasonable grounds" is determined by commercial standards. If such assurances are not forthcoming within a reasonable time (not to exceed thirty days), the failure to respond may be treated as a *repudiation* of the contract [UCC 2–609, 2A–401].

Obligations of the Buyer or Lessee

Once the seller or lessor has adequately tendered delivery, the buyer or lessee is obligated to accept the goods and pay for them according to the terms of the contract.

Payment   In the absence of any specific agreements, the buyer or lessee must make payment at the time and place the buyer or lessee *receives* the goods [UCC 2–310(a), 2A–516(1)]. When a sale is made on credit, the buyer is obliged to pay according to the specified credit terms (for example, 60, 90, or 120 days), not when the goods are received. The credit period usually begins on the *date of shipment* [UCC 2–310(d)]. Under a lease contract, a lessee must make the lease payment specified in the contract [UCC 2A–516(1)].

Payment can be made by any means agreed on between the parties—cash or any other method generally acceptable in the commercial world. If the seller demands cash when the buyer offers a check, credit card, or the like, the seller must permit the buyer reasonable time to obtain legal tender [UCC 2–511].

Acceptance   A buyer or lessee can manifest assent to the delivered goods in the following ways, each of which constitutes acceptance:

1. There is an acceptance if the buyer or lessee, after having had a reasonable opportunity to inspect the goods, signifies agreement to the seller or lessor that the goods are either conforming or are acceptable in spite of their nonconformity [UCC 2–606(1)(a), 2A–515(1)(a)].
2. Acceptance is presumed if the buyer or lessee has had a reasonable opportunity to inspect the goods and has failed to reject them within a reasonable period of time [UCC 2–602(1), 2–606(1)(b), 2A–515(1)(b)].
3. In sales contracts, the buyer will be deemed to have accepted the goods if he or she performs any act inconsistent with the seller's ownership. For example, any use or resale of the goods generally constitutes an acceptance. Limited use for the sole purpose of testing or inspecting the goods is not an acceptance, however [UCC 2–606(1)(c)].

If some of the goods delivered do not conform to the contract and the seller or lessor has failed to cure, the buyer or lessee can make a *partial* acceptance [UCC 2–601(c), 2A–509(1)]. The same is true if the nonconformity was not reasonably discoverable before acceptance. A buyer or lessee cannot accept less than a single commercial unit, however. A *commercial unit* is defined by the UCC as a unit of goods that, by commercial usage, is viewed as a "single whole" for purposes of sale, division of which would materially impair the character of the unit, its market value, or its use [UCC 2–105(6), 2A–103(c)]. A commercial unit can be a single article (such as a machine), a set of articles (such as a suite of furniture or an assortment of sizes), a quantity (such as a bale, a gross, or a carload), or any other unit treated in the trade as a single whole.

Anticipatory Repudiation

What if, before the time for contract performance, one party clearly communicates to the other the intention not to perform? Such an action is a breach of the contract by *anticipatory repudiation*. When anticipatory repudiation occurs, the nonbreaching party has a choice of two responses. One option is to treat the repudiation as a final breach by pursuing a remedy; the other is to wait and hope that the repudiating party will decide to honor the obligations required by the contract despite the avowed intention to renege [UCC 2–610, 2A–402]. (In either situation, the nonbreaching party may suspend performance.)

Should the second option be pursued, the UCC permits the breaching party (subject to some limitations) to "retract" his or her repudiation. This can be done by any method that clearly indicates an intent to perform. Once retraction is made, the rights of the repudiating party under the contract are reinstated [UCC 2–611, 2A–403].

REMEDIES FOR BREACH OF SALES AND LEASE CONTRACTS

Sometimes, circumstances make it difficult for a person to carry out the performance promised in a contract, in which case the contract may be breached. When breach occurs, the aggrieved party looks for remedies. These remedies range from retaining the goods to requiring the breaching party's performance under the contract. The general purpose of these remedies is to put the aggrieved party "in as good a position as if the other party had fully performed." Remedies under the UCC are *cumulative* in nature. In other words, an innocent party to a breached sales or lease contract is not limited to one, exclusive remedy. (Of course, a party still may not recover twice for the same harm.)

Remedies of the Seller or Lessor

A buyer or lessee breaches a sales or lease contract by any of the following actions: (1) wrongfully rejecting tender of the goods, (2) wrongfully revoking acceptance of the goods, (3) failing to make payment on or before delivery of the goods, or (4) repudiating the contract. On the buyer's or lessee's breach, the seller or lessor is afforded several distinct remedies under the UCC, including those discussed here.

The Right to Withhold Delivery   In general, sellers and lessors can withhold or discontinue performance of their obligations under sales or lease contracts when the buyers or lessees are in breach. If a buyer or lessee has wrongfully rejected or revoked acceptance of contract goods (rejection and revocation of acceptance will be discussed shortly), failed to make proper and timely payment, or repudiated a part of the contract, the seller or lessor can withhold delivery of the goods in question [UCC 2–703(a), 2A–523(1)(c)]. If the breach results from the buyer's or lessee's insolvency (inability to pay debts as they become due), the seller or lessor can refuse to deliver the goods unless the buyer or lessee pays in cash [UCC 2–702(1), 2A–525(1)].

The Right to Resell or Dispose of the Goods   When a buyer or lessee breaches or repudiates the contract while the seller or lessor is still in possession of the goods, the seller or lessor can resell or dispose of the goods, holding the buyer or lessee liable for any loss [UCC 2–703(d), 2–706(1), 2A–523(1)(e), 2A–527(1)].[10]

The Right to Recover the Purchase Price or the Lease Payments Due   Under the UCC, an unpaid seller or lessor can bring an action to recover the purchase price or payments due under the lease contract, plus incidental damages, if the seller or lessor is unable to resell or dispose of the goods [UCC 2–709(1), 2A–529(1)].

| **Example #6** Suppose that Southern Realty contracts with Gem Point, Inc., to purchase one thousand pens with Southern Realty's name inscribed on them. Gem Point delivers the pens, but Southern Realty wrongfully refuses to accept them. Gem Point tendered delivery of conforming goods, and Southern Realty, by failing to accept the goods, is in breach. Because Gem Point obviously cannot sell to anyone else the pens inscribed with the buyer's business name, this situation falls under UCC 2–709, and Gem Point can bring an action for the purchase price. |

If a seller or lessor is unable to resell or dispose of goods and sues for the contract price or lease payments due, the goods must be held for the buyer or lessee. The seller or lessor can resell or dispose of the goods at any time prior to collection (of the judgment) from the buyer or lessee but must credit the net proceeds from the sale to the buyer or lessee. This is an example of the duty to mitigate damages.

The Right to Recover Damages   If a buyer or lessee repudiates a contract or wrongfully refuses to accept the goods, a seller or lessor can maintain an action to recover the damages that were sustained. Ordinarily, the amount of damages equals the difference between the contract price or lease payments and the market price or lease payments (at the time and place of tender of the goods), plus incidental damages [UCC 2–708(1), 2A–528(1)].

In the following case, the court had to determine the proper measure of damages after a buyer breached a sales contract.

---

10. Under the 2003 amendments to UCC Articles 2 and 2A, this loss includes consequential damages, except that a seller or lessor cannot recover consequential damages from a consumer under a consumer contract or lease [Amended UCC 2–706(1), 2–710, 2A–527(2), 2A–530]. Consequential damages may also be recovered, except from a consumer under a consumer contract or lease, when a seller or lessor has a right to recover the purchase price or lease payments due or to recover other damages [Amended UCC 2–708(1), 2–709(1), 2–710, 2A–528(1), 2A–529(1), 2A–530]. Subtracted from these amounts, of course, would be any expenses saved as a consequence of the buyer's or lessee's breach.

CASE 10.3   Utica Alloys, Inc. v. Alcoa, Inc.

United States District Court,
Northern District of New York, 2004.
303 F.Supp.2d 247.

BACKGROUND AND FACTS   Alcoa, Inc., through its business, generates scrap metal. Utica Alloys, Inc., buys and processes this type of scrap and sells it to its only user,

General Electric Company (GE), which employs it in land-based power turbines. In July 2001, Utica agreed to buy all of Alcoa's scrap through August 2003. Their contract indexed the monthly price of the scrap to the monthly market price of nickel, but contemplated that the parties would review this price semiannually. In November 2001, GE reduced its production of turbines, which lowered the market value of the scrap. This change was not reflected in Alcoa's arrangement with Utica, however, because the price in their contract was based on the market value of nickel. In January 2002, the opportunity arose to review the price of the scrap, and the parties began to negotiate while they continued to ship and process the scrap. In May, when the parties were unable to agree on a price, Alcoa stated that the contract was over, retrieved the scrap processed after January, and sold it to another party. Utica filed a suit in a federal district court against Alcoa, alleging in part unjust enrichment. Alcoa counterclaimed for breach of contract. The court entered a judgment in Alcoa's favor, holding that Utica breached the agreement by failing to pay for the scrap received after January. Alcoa asked for damages based on the difference between the contract price for the *unprocessed* scrap and the price at which the *processed* scrap sold after it was retrieved.

IN THE WORDS OF THE COURT . . . *HURD,* District Judge.

* * * *

* * * Defendant claims its measure of damages is the difference between the purchase agreement price of the scrap and the price for which it sold the processed scrap it retrieved from plaintiff.

This, however, would serve as a double penalty to Utica Alloys, Inc., for processing the scrap. Absent the purchase agreement, Alcoa, Inc., would have sold the scrap at the unprocessed market price. Because of the purchase agreement, it is entitled to the higher purchase agreement price. The processed feature of the scrap, as Alcoa, Inc., points out numerous times, was not part of the agreement between the parties and actually decreased its value because of the demand reduction in the market for such scrap. However, Alcoa, Inc., accepted return of the processed scrap from Utica Alloys, Inc., when it elected to terminate the purchase agreement in May 2002. It has also refused to pay plaintiff for processing the scrap. Defendant cannot be permitted in one breath to denounce processing as irrelevant to the contractual relationship, while in another embrace the market change of processed scrap as the yardstick for measuring its damages under the contract.

Therefore, *the proper measure of damages is the difference between the purchase price of the unprocessed scrap, as such is calculated under the purchase agreement, and the market value of unprocessed scrap.* The market value of unprocessed scrap is not to be determined solely from the amount for which Alcoa, Inc., was able to sell the scrap in May of 2002. *Rather, because the purchase agreement called for monthly shipments and prices, damages will have to be ascertained for three different time periods.* The following determinations will therefore need to be made, for each of the months from February to April of 2002, before the proper amount of total damages can be calculated: (1) the amount, *in pounds,* of scrap shipped during each of the relevant months; (2) the per pound purchase agreement price, calculated *using the formula in the agreement,* for each of the relevant months; and (3) the per pound *fair market value of unprocessed scrap* for each of the three months. The damages will be calculated for each of the three months, and will then be added together to determine defendant's total damages for plaintiff's failure to pay for the scrap it was shipped. The parties will be permitted to submit * * * only the *three figures,* as well as any facts/figures supporting the same, required *for each month.* [Emphasis added.]

* * * *

* * * Defendant is * * * entitled to judgment on its counterclaim, and may receive as damages for plaintiff's failure to pay for scrap shipped and received under the purchase agreement the difference between the monthly purchase agreement price for such scrap and the monthly fair market value of unprocessed scrap. * * *

CASE 10.3–CONTINUED ➡

CASE 10.3—CONTINUED

DECISION AND REMEDY   The federal district court entered a judgment for the defendant and awarded damages based on the difference between the contract's monthly price for the unprocessed scrap and the monthly fair market value of unprocessed scrap.

FOR CRITICAL ANALYSIS—Economic Consideration   *How, specifically, should the amount of damages in this case be determined, considering that the contract called for monthly shipments and prices?*

Remedies of the Buyer or Lessee

A seller or lessor breaches a sales or lease contract by failing to deliver conforming goods or repudiating the contract prior to delivery. On the breach, the buyer or lessee has a choice of several remedies under the UCC, including those discussed here.

The Right of Cover   In certain situations, buyers and lessees can protect themselves by obtaining **cover**—that is, by buying or leasing substitute goods for those that were due under the contract. This option is available when the seller or lessor repudiates the contract or fails to deliver the goods. It is also available to a buyer or lessee who has rightfully rejected goods or revoked acceptance. Rejection and revocation of acceptance will be discussed shortly.

In obtaining cover, the buyer or lessee must act in good faith and without unreasonable delay [UCC 2–712, 2A–518]. After purchasing or leasing substitute goods, the buyer or lessee can recover from the seller or lessor the difference between the cost of cover and the contract price (or lease payments), plus incidental and consequential damages, less the expenses (such as delivery costs) that were saved as a result of the breach [UCC 2–712, 2–715, 2A–518]. Consequential damages include any loss suffered by the buyer or lessee that the seller or lessor could have foreseen (had reason to know about) at the time of contract formation.

COVER
A buyer or lessee's purchase on the open market of goods to substitute for those promised but never delivered by the seller. Under the UCC, if the cost of cover exceeds the cost of the contract goods, the buyer or lessee can recover the difference, plus incidental and consequential damages.

The Right to Obtain Specific Performance   A buyer or lessee can obtain specific performance when the goods are unique or when the remedy at law is inadequate [UCC 2–716(1), 2A–521(1)]. Ordinarily, an award of money damages is sufficient to place a buyer or lessee in the position he or she would have occupied if the seller or lessor had fully performed. When the contract is for the purchase of a particular work of art or a similarly unique item, however, money damages may not be sufficient. Under these circumstances, equity will require that the seller or lessor perform by delivering exactly the particular goods identified to the contract (a remedy of specific performance).

The Right to Recover Damages   If a seller or lessor repudiates the sales contract or fails to deliver the goods, or the buyer or lessee has rightfully rejected or revoked acceptance of the goods, the buyer or lessee can sue for damages. The measure of recovery is the difference between the contract price (or lease payments) and the market price of (or lease payments that could be obtained for) the goods at the time the buyer (or lessee) *learned* of the breach.[11] The market price or market lease payments are determined at the place where the seller or lessor was supposed to deliver the goods. The buyer or lessee can also

RECALL   Consequential damages compensate for a loss (such as lost profits) that is not direct but was reasonably foreseeable at the time of the breach.

---

11. The 2003 amendments to UCC Article 2 change the rule that the time for measuring damages is the time the buyer learned of the breach. Unless repudiation is involved, the buyer's damages will be based on the market price at the time for tender [Amended UCC 2–713(1)(a)].

recover incidental and consequential damages, less the expenses that were saved as a result of the breach [UCC 2–713, 2A–519].

| Example #7 Schilling orders ten thousand bushels of wheat from Valdone for $5 a bushel, with delivery due on June 14 and payment due on June 20. Valdone does not deliver on June 14. On June 14, the market price of wheat is $5.50 per bushel. Schilling chooses to do without the wheat. He sues Valdone for damages for nondelivery. Schilling can recover $0.50 × 10,000, or $5,000, plus any expenses the breach may have caused him. The measure of damages is the market price less the contract price on the day Schilling was to have received delivery. Any expenses Schilling saved by the breach would be deducted from the damages.**|**

The Right to Reject the Goods   If either the goods or the tender of the goods by the seller or lessor fails to conform to the contract *in any respect,* the buyer or lessee can reject the goods. If some of the goods conform to the contract, the buyer or lessee can keep the conforming goods and reject the rest [UCC 2–601, 2A–509]. The buyer or lessee must reject the goods within a reasonable amount of time after delivery or tender of delivery, and the seller or lessor must be notified *seasonably*—that is, in a timely fashion or at the proper time [UCC 2–602(1), 2A–509(2)].

If a *merchant buyer* or *lessee* rightfully rejects goods, he or she is required to follow any reasonable instructions received from the seller or lessor with respect to the goods controlled by the buyer or lessee. For instance, the seller might ask the buyer to store the goods in the buyer's warehouse until the next day when the seller can retrieve them. The buyer or lessee is entitled to reimbursement for the care and cost entailed in following the instructions [UCC 2–603, 2A–511]. If no instructions are forthcoming, the buyer or lessee may store the goods or reship them to the seller or lessor [UCC 2–604, 2A–512].

The Right to Recover Damages for Accepted Goods   A buyer or lessee who has accepted nonconforming goods may also keep the goods and recover for any loss "resulting in the ordinary course of events . . . as determined in any manner which is reasonable" [UCC 2–714(1), 2A–519(3)]. The buyer or lessee, however, must notify the seller or lessor of the breach within a reasonable time after the defect was or should have been discovered.

When the goods delivered and accepted are not as warranted, the measure of damages equals the difference between the value of the goods as accepted and their value if they had been delivered as warranted, plus incidental and consequential damages if appropriate [UCC 2–714, 2A–519].

Revocation of Acceptance   Acceptance of the goods precludes the buyer or lessee from exercising the right of rejection, but it does not necessarily prevent the buyer or lessee from pursuing other remedies. Additionally, in certain circumstances, a buyer or lessee is permitted to *revoke* his or her acceptance of the goods. Acceptance of a lot or a commercial unit can be revoked if the nonconformity *substantially* impairs the value of the lot or unit and if one of the following factors is present:

1. Acceptance was predicated on the reasonable assumption that the nonconformity would be cured, and it has not been cured within a reasonable period of time [UCC 2–608(1)(a), 2A–517(1)(a)].[12]

---

12. Under the 2003 amendments to UCC 2–508 and 2A–513, after a justifiable revocation of acceptance, cure is *not* available as a matter of right in a consumer contract or lease.

The CISG's Approach to Revocation of Acceptance

Under the UCC, a buyer or lessee who has accepted goods may be able to revoke acceptance under the circumstances mentioned in the text. Provisions of the United Nations Convention on Contracts for the International Sale of Goods (CISG) similarly allow buyers to rescind their contracts after they have accepted the goods.

The CISG, however, takes a somewhat different—and more direct—approach to the problem than the UCC does. In the same circumstances that permit a buyer to revoke acceptance under the UCC, under the CISG the buyer can simply declare that the seller has *fundamentally* breached the contract and proceed to sue the seller for the breach. Article 25 of the CISG states that a "breach of contract committed by one of the parties is fundamental if it results in such detriment to the other party as substantially to deprive him [or her] of what he [or she] is entitled to expect under the contract."

For Critical Analysis *What is the essential difference between revoking acceptance and bringing a suit for breach of contract?*

2. The buyer or lessee did not discover the nonconformity before acceptance, either because it was difficult to discover before acceptance or because the seller's or lessor's assurance that the goods were conforming kept the buyer or lessee from inspecting the goods [UCC 2–608(1)(b), 2A–517(1)(b)].

Revocation of acceptance is not effective until notice is given to the seller or lessor. Notice must occur within a reasonable time after the buyer or lessee either discovers or *should have discovered* the grounds for revocation. Once acceptance is revoked, the buyer or lessee can pursue remedies, just as if the goods had been rejected. (For a discussion of how this issue is handled in international sales contracts, see this chapter's *Beyond Our Borders* feature.)

Is two years after a sale of goods a reasonable time period in which to discover a defect in those goods and notify the seller or lessor of a breach? That was the question in the following case.

CASE 10.4   Fitl v. Strek

Supreme Court of Nebraska, 2005.
269 Neb. 51,
690 N.W.2d 605.
www.findlaw.com/11stategov/ne/neca.html [a]

BACKGROUND AND FACTS   Over the Labor Day weekend in 1995, James Fitl attended a sports-card show in San Francisco, California, where he met Mark Strek (doing business as Star Cards of San Francisco), an exhibitor at the show. Later, on Strek's representation that a certain 1952 Mickey Mantle Topps baseball card was in near-mint condition, Fitl bought the

a. In the "Supreme Court Opinions" section, in the "2005" row, click on "January." In the result, click on the appropriate link next to the name of the case to access the opinion.

card from Strek for $17,750. Strek delivered it to Fitl in Omaha, Nebraska, where Fitl placed it in a safe-deposit box. In May 1997, Fitl sent the card to Professional Sports Authenticators (PSA), a sports-card grading service. PSA told Fitl that the card was ungradable because it had been discolored and doctored. Fitl complained to Strek, who replied that Fitl should have initiated a return of the card within "a typical grace period for the unconditional return of a card, . . . 7 days to 1 month" of its receipt. In August, Fitl sent the card to ASA Accugrade, Inc. (ASA), another grading service, for a second opinion on its value. ASA also concluded that the card had been refinished and trimmed. Fitl filed a suit in a Nebraska state court against Strek, seeking damages. The court awarded Fitl $17,750, plus his court costs. Strek appealed to the Nebraska Supreme Court.

IN THE WORDS OF THE COURT . . . WRIGHT, J. [Justice]

* * * *

Strek claims that the [trial] court erred in determining that notification of the defective condition of the baseball card 2 years after the date of purchase was timely pursuant to [UCC] 2–607(3)(a).

CASE 10.4—CONTINUED * * * The [trial] court found that Fitl had notified Strek within a reasonable time after discovery of the breach. Therefore, our review is whether the [trial] court's finding as to the reasonableness of the notice was clearly erroneous.

Section 2–607(3)(a) states: "Where a tender has been accepted * * * the buyer must within a reasonable time after he discovers or should have discovered any breach notify the seller of breach or be barred from any remedy." [Under UCC 1–204(2)] *"[w]hat is a reasonable time for taking any action depends on the nature, purpose, and circumstances of such action."* [Emphasis added.]

The notice requirement set forth in Section 2–607(3)(a) serves three purposes. * * *

* * * The most important one is to enable the seller to make efforts to cure the breach by making adjustments or replacements in order to minimize the buyer's damages and the seller's liability. A second policy is to provide the seller a reasonable opportunity to learn the facts so that he may adequately prepare for negotiation and defend himself in a suit. A third policy * * * is the same as the policy behind statutes of limitation: to provide a seller with a terminal point in time for liability.

* * * *[A] party is justified in relying upon a representation made to the party as a positive statement of fact when an investigation would be required to ascertain its falsity.* In order for Fitl to have determined that the baseball card had been altered, he would have been required to conduct an investigation. We find that he was not required to do so. Once Fitl learned that the baseball card had been altered, he gave notice to Strek. [Emphasis added.]

* * * [O]ne of the most important policies behind the notice requirement * * * is to allow the seller to cure the breach by making adjustments or replacements to minimize the buyer's damages and the seller's liability. However, even if Fitl had learned immediately upon taking possession of the baseball card that it was not authentic and had notified Strek at that time, there is no evidence that Strek could have made any adjustment or taken any action that would have minimized his liability. In its altered condition, the baseball card was worthless.

* * * Earlier notification would not have helped Strek prepare for negotiation or defend himself in a suit because the damage to Fitl could not be repaired. Thus, the policies behind the notice requirement, to allow the seller to correct a defect, to prepare for negotiation and litigation, and to protect against stale claims at a time beyond which an investigation can be completed, were not unfairly prejudiced by the lack of an earlier notice to Strek. Any problem Strek may have had with the party from whom he obtained the baseball card was a separate matter from his transaction with Fitl, and an investigation into the source of the altered card would not have minimized Fitl's damages.

DECISION AND REMEDY The state supreme court affirmed the decision of the lower court. In the circumstances of this case, notice of a defect in the goods two years after their purchase was reasonable. The buyer had reasonably relied on the seller's representation that the goods were "authentic" (which they were not), and when their defects were discovered, the buyer had given a timely notice.

WHAT IF THE FACTS WERE DIFFERENT? *Suppose that Fitl and Strek had included in their agreement a clause requiring Fitl to give notice of any defect in the card within "7 days to 1 month" of its receipt. Would the result have been different? Why or why not?*

Contractual Provisions Affecting Remedies

The parties to a sales or lease contract can vary their respective rights and obligations by contractual agreement. For example, a seller and buyer can expressly provide for remedies in addition to those provided in the UCC. They can also specifiy remedies in lieu of those provided in the UCC, or they can

Containers sit on ships as they wait to be unloaded at a port in the United States. If the buyer discovers that some of the goods are defective, what remedies under the UCC are available to the buyer? (Susan Goldman/ *Bloomberg News*/Landov)

change the measure of damages. The seller can stipulate that the buyer's only remedy on the seller's breach be repair or replacement of the item, or the seller can limit the buyer's remedy to return of the goods and refund of the purchase price. In sales and lease contracts, an agreed-on remedy is in addition to those provided in the UCC unless the parties expressly agree that the remedy is exclusive of all others [UCC 2–719(1), 2A–503(1)].

If the parties state that a remedy is exclusive, then it is the sole remedy. When circumstances cause an exclusive remedy to fail in its essential purpose, however, it is no longer exclusive [UCC 2–719(2), 2A–503(2)]. **| Example #8** Suppose that a sales contract limits the buyer's remedy to repair or replacement. If the goods cannot be repaired and no replacements are available, the remedy fails in its essential purpose. In this situation, the buyer normally will be entitled to seek other remedies available under the UCC.**|**

SALES AND LEASE WARRANTIES

Warranty is an age-old concept. In sales and lease law, a warranty is an assurance by one party of the existence of a fact on which the other party can rely. Article 2 and Article 2A of the UCC designate several types of warranties that can arise in a sales or lease contract. These warranties include warranties of title, express warranties, and implied warranties.

Because a warranty imposes a duty on the seller or lessor, a breach of warranty is a breach of the seller's or lessor's promise. If the parties have not agreed to limit or modify the remedies available to the buyer or lessee and if the seller or lessor breaches a warranty, the buyer or lessee can sue to recover damages from the seller or lessor. Under some circumstances, a breach can allow the buyer or lessee to rescind (cancel) the agreement.[13]

Warranty of Title

Title warranty arises automatically in most sales contracts under Section 2–312 of the UCC. In most situations, sellers warrant that they have good and valid title to the goods sold and that transfer of the title is rightful [UCC 2–312(1)(a)]. A second warranty of title provided by the UCC protects buyers who are *unaware* of any encumbrances (claims, charges, or liabilities—usually called *liens*[14]) against goods at the time the contract is made [UCC 2–312(1)(b)]. This warranty protects buyers who unknowingly purchase goods that are subject to a creditor's security interest (see Chapter 12). If a creditor legally repossesses the goods from a buyer *who had no actual knowledge of the security interest*, the buyer can recover from the seller for breach of warranty. (The buyer who has *actual knowledge of a security interest* has no recourse against a seller.) Article 2A affords similar protection for lessees [UCC 2A–211(1)]. A merchant seller is also deemed to warrant that the goods delivered are free from any copyright, trademark, or patent claims of a third person [UCC 2–312(3), 2A–211(2)].

In an ordinary sales transaction, the title warranty can be disclaimed or modified only by *specific language* in a contract. For example, sellers may assert that they are transferring only such rights, title, and interest as they have

---

13. *Rescission* restores the parties to the positions they were in before the contract was made.
14. Pronounced *leens*. Liens will be discussed in detail in Chapter 12.

in the goods. In a lease transaction, the disclaimer must "be specific, be by a writing, and be conspicuous" [UCC 2A–214(4)].

Express Warranties

A seller or lessor can create an **express warranty** by making representations concerning the quality, condition, description, or performance potential of the goods. Under UCC 2–313 and 2A–210, express warranties arise when a seller or lessor indicates any of the following:

1. That the goods conform to any affirmation (declaration that something is true) or promise of fact that the seller or lessor makes to the buyer or lessee about the goods. Such affirmations or promises are usually made during the bargaining process. Statements such as "these drill bits will penetrate stainless steel—and without dulling" are express warranties.[15]
2. That the goods conform to any description of them. For example, a label that reads "Crate contains one 150-horsepower diesel engine" or a contract that calls for the delivery of a "wool coat" creates an express warranty.
3. That the goods conform to any sample or model of the goods shown to the buyer or lessee.

Express warranties can be found in a seller's or lessor's advertisement, brochure, or promotional materials, in addition to being made orally or in an express warranty provision in a sales or lease contract. To create an express warranty, a seller or lessor does not have to use formal words such as *warrant* or *guarantee*. It is only necessary that a reasonable buyer or lessee would regard the representation as part of the basis of the bargain [UCC 2–313(2), 2A–210(2)].[16]

Basis of the Bargain   The UCC requires that for an express warranty to be created, the affirmation, promise, description, or sample must become part of the "basis of the bargain" [UCC 2–313(1), 2A–210(1)]. Just what constitutes the basis of the bargain is difficult to say. The UCC does not define the concept, and it is a question of fact in each case whether a representation was made at such a time and in such a way that it induced the buyer or lessee to enter into the contract. Therefore, if an express warranty is not intended, the marketing agent or salesperson should not promise too much.

Statements of Opinion and Value   If the seller or lessor merely makes a statement that relates to the value or worth of the goods, or makes a statement of opinion or recommendation about the goods, the seller or lessor is not creating an express warranty [UCC 2–313(2), 2A–210(2)].

EXPRESS WARRANTY
A seller's or lessor's oral or written promise or affirmation of fact, ancillary to an underlying sales or lease agreement, as to the quality, description, or performance of the goods being sold or leased.

---

15. The 2003 amendments to UCC Article 2 introduce the term *remedial promise*, which is "a promise by the seller to repair or replace the goods or to refund all or part of the price on the happening of a specified event" [Amended UCC 2–103(1)(n), 2–313(4)]. A remedial promise is not an express warranty, so a right of action for its breach accrues not at the time of tender, as with warranties, but if the promise is not performed when due [Amended UCC 2–725(2)(c)].
16. The 2003 amendments to the UCC distinguish between immediate buyers (those who enter into contracts with sellers) and remote purchasers (those who buy or lease goods from immediate buyers) and extend sellers' obligations regarding new goods to remote purchasers. For example, a manufacturer sells packaged goods to a retailer, who resells the goods to a consumer. If a reasonable person in the position of the consumer would believe that a description on the package creates an obligation, the manufacturer is liable for its breach. [See Amended UCC 2–313, 2–313A, and 2–313B.]

| **Example #9**   A seller claims that "this is the best used car to come along in years; it has four new tires and a 150-horsepower engine just rebuilt this year." The seller has made several *affirmations of fact* that can create a warranty: the automobile has an engine; it has a 150-horsepower engine; the engine was rebuilt this year; there are four tires on the automobile; and the tires are new. The seller's *opinion* that the vehicle is "the best used car to come along in years," however, is known as *puffery* and creates no warranty. (**Puffery** is an expression of opinion by a seller or lessor that is not made as a representation of fact.)| A statement relating to the value of the goods, such as "it's worth a fortune" or "anywhere else you'd pay $10,000 for it," usually does not create a warranty.

It is not always easy to determine what constitutes an express warranty and what constitutes puffery. The reasonableness of the buyer's or lessee's reliance appears to be the controlling criterion in many cases. For example, a salesperson's statements that a ladder will "never break" and will "last a lifetime" are so clearly improbable that no reasonable buyer should rely on them.

Implied Warranties

An **implied warranty** is one that *the law derives* by inference from the nature of the transaction or the relative situations or circumstances of the parties. Under the UCC, merchants impliedly warrant that the goods they sell or lease are merchantable and, in certain circumstances, fit for a particular purpose. In addition, an implied warranty may arise from a course of dealing or usage of trade. We examine these three types of implied warranties in the following subsections.

Implied Warranty of Merchantability   An **implied warranty of merchantability** automatically arises in every sale or lease of goods made *by a merchant* who deals in goods of the kind sold or leased [UCC 2–314, 2A–212]. Thus, a merchant who is in the business of selling ski equipment makes an implied warranty of merchantability every time the merchant sells a pair of skis, but a neighbor selling his or her skis at a garage sale does not.

This warranty imposes on the merchant liability for the safe performance of the product. It makes no difference whether the merchant knew of, or could have discovered, that a product was defective (not merchantable).

Goods that are *merchantable* are "reasonably fit for the ordinary purposes for which such goods are used." They must be of at least average, fair, or medium-grade quality. The quality must be comparable to quality that will pass without objection in the trade or market for goods of the same description. The goods must also be adequately packaged and labeled, and they must conform to the promises or affirmations of fact made on the container or label, if any.

Implied Warranty of Fitness for a Particular Purpose   The **implied warranty of fitness for a particular purpose** arises when any *seller or lessor* (merchant or nonmerchant) knows the particular purpose for which a buyer or lessee will use the goods *and* knows that the buyer or lessee is relying on the skill and judgment of the seller or lessor to select suitable goods [UCC 2–315, 2A–213]. A "particular purpose" of the buyer or lessee differs from the "ordinary purpose for which goods are used" (merchantability). Goods can be merchantable but unfit for a particular purpose.

A seller or lessor does not need to have actual knowledge of the buyer's or lessee's particular purpose. It is sufficient if a seller or lessor "has reason to know" the purpose. The buyer or lessee, however, must have *relied* on the skill or judgment of the seller or lessor in selecting or furnishing suitable goods for an implied warranty to be created.

Example #10 Bloomberg leases a computer from Future Tech, a lessor of technical business equipment. Bloomberg tells the clerk that she wants a computer that will run a complicated new engineering graphics program at a realistic speed. Future Tech leases Bloomberg an Architex One computer with a CPU speed of only 2.4 gigahertz, even though a speed of at least 3.8 gigahertz would be required to run Bloomberg's graphics program at a "realistic speed." Bloomberg, after realizing that it takes her forever to run her program, wants her money back. Here, because Future Tech has breached the implied warranty of fitness for a particular purpose, Bloomberg normally will be able to recover. The clerk knew specifically that Bloomberg wanted a computer with enough speed to run certain software. Furthermore, Bloomberg relied on the clerk to furnish a computer that would fulfill this purpose. Because Future Tech did not do so, the warranty was breached.

Implied Warranty Arising from Course of Dealing or Trade Usage Implied warranties can also arise (or be excluded or modified) as a result of a *course of dealing* or *usage of trade* [UCC 2–314(3), 2A–212(3)]. In the absence of evidence to the contrary, when both parties to a sales or lease contract have knowledge of a well-recognized trade custom, the courts will infer that both parties intended for that custom to apply to their contract. For example, if it is an industry-wide custom to lubricate a new car before it is delivered and a dealer fails to do so, the dealer can be held liable to a buyer for damages resulting from the breach of an implied warranty. (This, of course, would also be negligence on the part of the dealer.)

Warranty Disclaimers

Because each type of warranty is created in a special way, the manner in which warranties can be disclaimed or qualified by a seller or lessor varies with the type of warranty.

Express Warranties Express warranties can be excluded or limited by specific and unambiguous language, provided that this is done in a manner that protects the buyer or lessee from surprise. Therefore, a written disclaimer in language that is clear and conspicuous, and called to a buyer's or lessee's attention, could negate all oral express warranties not included in the written sales or lease contract [UCC 2–316(1), 2A–214(1)].

Implied Warranties Generally speaking, unless circumstances indicate otherwise, the implied warranties of merchantability and fitness are disclaimed by the expressions "as is," "with all faults," and other similar expressions that in common understanding for *both* parties call the buyer's or lessee's attention to the fact that there are no implied warranties [UCC 2–316(3)(a), 2A–214(3)(a)].

The UCC also permits a seller or lessor to specifically disclaim an implied warranty either of fitness or of merchantability [UCC 2–316(2), 2A–214(2)]. To disclaim an implied warranty of fitness for a particular purpose, the disclaimer must be in writing and be conspicuous. The word *fitness* does not have to be mentioned in the writing; it is sufficient if, for example, the disclaimer states, "THERE ARE NO WARRANTIES THAT EXTEND BEYOND THE DESCRIPTION ON THE FACE HEREOF." A merchantability disclaimer must be more specific; it must mention *merchantability*. It need not be written; but if it is, the writing must be conspicuous [UCC 2–316(2), 2A–214(4)].[17]

E-CONTRACTS

E-CONTRACT
A contract that is formed electronically.

The basic principles of contract law evolved over a long period of time. Certainly, they were formed long before cyberspace and electronic contracting became realities. Therefore, new legal theories, new adaptations of existing laws, and new laws are needed to govern e-contracts, or contracts entered into electronically. To date, however, most courts have adapted traditional contract law principles and, when applicable, provisions of the UCC to cases involving e-contract disputes.

Online Contract Formation

Today, numerous contracts are being formed online. Although the medium through which these contracts are generated has changed, the age-old problems attending contract formation have not. Disputes concerning contracts formed online continue to center around contract terms and whether the parties voluntarily assented to those terms.

Note that online contracts may be formed not only for the sale of goods and services but also for the purpose of *licensing*. The "sale" of software, for instance, generally involves a license, or a right to use the software, rather than the passage of title (ownership rights) from the seller to the buyer. **| Example #11** Galynn wants to purchase software that allows her to copy DVDs. She goes online and purchases DVD SuperCloner. During the transaction, she has to click on several on-screen "I agree" boxes to indicate that she understands that she is purchasing only the right to use the software and will not obtain any ownership rights. She is also asked to agree to specific terms of use. Once she agrees to these terms, she can download the software to her computer.| As you read through the following pages, keep in mind that although we typically refer to the offeror and offeree as a *seller* and a *buyer,* in many transactions these parties would be more accurately described as a *licensor* and a *licensee.*

Online Offers   Sellers doing business via the Internet can protect themselves against contract disputes and legal liability by creating offers that clearly spell out the terms that will govern their transactions if the offers are accepted. All important terms should be conspicuous and easily viewed by potential buyers.

An important rule for a seller to keep in mind is that the offeror controls the offer, and thus the resulting contract. Important terms may include the following:

1. A provision specifying the remedies available to the buyer if the goods turn out to be defective or if the contract is otherwise breached. Any limitation of remedies should be clearly spelled out.

---

17. Under the 2003 amendments to UCC Articles 2 and 2A, if a consumer contract or lease is set forth in a record (writing), the implied warranty of merchantability can be disclaimed only by language also set forth conspicuously in the record [Amended UCC 2–316(3) and 2A–214(3)].

2. A clause that clearly indicates what will constitute the buyer's agreement to the terms of the offer, such as a box containing the words "I accept" that the buyer can click on to indicate acceptance.
3. A statement specifying the method of payment.
4. A statement of the seller's refund and return policies.
5. Disclaimers of liability for certain uses of the goods. For example, an online seller of business forms may add a disclaimer that the seller does not accept responsibility for the buyer's reliance on the forms rather than on an attorney's advice.
6. A statement explaining how the seller will use the information gathered about the buyer.
7. Provisions relating to dispute settlement, such as an arbitration clause or a **forum-selection clause**—a clause that indicates the forum, or location, for the resolution of any dispute arising under the contract. For a discussion of forum-selection clauses in online contracts, see this chapter's *Management Perspective* feature on the following page.

> **FORUM-SELECTION CLAUSE**
> A provision in a contract designating the court, jurisdiction, or tribunal that will decide any disputes arising under the contract.

The seller's Web site should include a hypertext link to a page containing the full contract so that potential buyers are made aware of the terms to which they are assenting. The contract generally must be displayed online in a readable format such as a twelve-point typeface. All provisions should be reasonably clear. | **Example #12** Suppose that Netquip sells a variety of heavy equipment, such as trucks and trailers, online at its Web site. Because Netquip's pricing schedule is very complex, the schedule must be fully provided and explained on the Web site.|

Online Acceptances Section 2–204 of the UCC, the law governing sales contracts, provides that any contract for the sale of goods "may be made in any manner sufficient to show agreement, including conduct by both parties which recognizes the existence of such a contract." The *Restatement (Second) of Contracts,* a compilation of common law contract principles, has a similar provision. It states that parties may agree to a contract "by written or spoken words or by other action or by failure to act." [18]

Click-On Agreements The courts have used the provisions just discussed to conclude that a binding contract can be created by conduct, including conduct accepting an online offer by clicking on a box indicating "I agree" or "I accept." The agreement resulting from such an acceptance is often called a **click-on agreement.** Generally, the law does not require that all of the terms in a contract must actually have been read by all of the parties to be effective. Therefore, clicking on a button or box that states "I agree" to certain terms can be enough. [19]

> **CLICK-ON AGREEMENT**
> An agreement that arises when a buyer, engaging in a transaction on a computer, indicates his or her assent to be bound by the terms of an offer by clicking on a button that says, for example, "I agree"; sometimes referred to as a *click-on license* or a *click-wrap agreement.*

Browse-Wrap Terms Like the terms of a click-on agreement, **browse-wrap terms** can occur in a transaction conducted over the Internet. Unlike a click-on agreement, however, browse-wrap terms do not require an Internet user to assent to the terms before, say, downloading or using certain software. In

> **BROWSE-WRAP TERMS**
> Terms and conditions of use that are presented to an Internet user at the time certain products, such as software, are being downloaded but to which the user need not agree (by clicking "I agree," for example) before being able to install or use the product.

---

18. *Restatement (Second) of Contracts,* Section 19.
19. See, for example, *i.LANSystems, Inc. v. NetScout Service Level Corp.,* 183 F.Supp.2d 838 (D.Mass. 2002).

The Enforceability of Forum-Selection Clauses

Management Faces a Legal Issue   Because parties to contracts formed online may be located in geographically distant locations, online sellers of goods and services normally include forum-selection clauses in their contracts. These clauses can help online sellers avoid having to appear in court in many distant jurisdictions when customers are dissatisfied with their purchases. Clearly, owners and managers of Internet-based businesses benefit from such clauses, yet purchasers of online goods and services may challenge such clauses as being unfair to them. How have the courts responded to such challenges?

What the Courts Say   Normally, the courts will enforce clauses or contracts to which the parties have voluntarily agreed, and this principle extends to forum-selection clauses in online contracts as well. As one court stated (in a case challenging the enforceability of a forum-selection clause in Microsoft Network's online agreement), "If a forum-selection clause is clear in its purport [meaning] and has been presented to the party to be bound in a fair and forthright fashion, no . . . policies or principles have been violated."[a]

Depending on the jurisdiction, however, a court may make an exception to this rule. Consider a case brought against America Online, Inc. (AOL), by Al Mendoza and other former AOL subscribers living in California. The plaintiffs brought their case in a California state court. They sought compensatory and punitive damages, claiming that AOL had continued to debit their credit cards for monthly service fees, without authorization, for some time after they had terminated their subscriptions. AOL moved to dismiss the action on the basis of the forum-selection clause in its "Terms of Service" agreement with subscribers. That clause required all lawsuits under the agreement to be brought in Virginia, AOL's home state. A California appellate court ultimately held that the clause was unfair and unreasonable, and that public policy was best served by denying enforceability to the clause. The court also noted that Virginia law provides "significantly less" consumer protection than California law, and therefore enforcing the forum-selection clause would violate the "strong California public policy" expressed in the state's consumer protection statutes.[b]

Implications for Managers   Generally, owners and managers of Web-based businesses can assume that forum-selection clauses in their online contracts will likely be enforced. Businesspersons should be aware, though, that different courts have reached varying conclusions on this issue. A court may conclude, as the California court did in the AOL case, that a particular forum-selection clause imposes an unfair burden on those who purchase goods and services from online vendors.

a. *Caspi v. MSN, Inc.,* 323 N.J.Super. 118, 732 A.2d 528 (1999). For another example, see *DeJohn v. The TV Corp. International,* 245 F.Supp.2d 913 (2003).

b. *America Online, Inc. v. Superior Court,* 90 Cal.App.4th 1, 108 Cal.Rptr.2d 699 (2001).

---

other words, a person can install the software without clicking "I agree" to the terms of a license. Offerors of browse-wrap terms generally assert that the terms are binding without the user's active consent.

Critics contend that browse-wrap terms are not enforceable because they do not satisfy the basic elements of contract formation. It has been suggested that to form a valid contract online, a user must at least be presented with the terms before indicating assent.[20] With a browse-wrap term, this would require that a user navigate past it and agree to it before being able to obtain whatever is being granted.

---

20. American Bar Association Committee on the Law of Cyberspace, "Click-Through Agreements: Strategies for Avoiding Disputes on the Validity of Assent" (document presented at the annual American Bar Association meeting in August 2001).

E-Signatures

In many instances, a contract cannot be enforced unless it is signed by the party against whom enforcement is sought. A significant issue in the context of e-commerce has to do with how electronic signatures, or **e-signatures,** can be created and verified on e-contracts.

E-Signature Technologies   Today, numerous technologies allow electronic documents to be signed. These technologies generally fall into one of two categories, *digitized handwritten signatures* and *public-key infrastructure–based digital signatures*. A digitized signature is a graphical image of a handwritten signature that is often created using a digital pen and pad, such as an ePad, and special software. For security reasons, the strokes of a person's signature can be measured by software to authenticate the person signing (this is referred to as *signature dynamics*). In a public-key infrastructure (such as an *asymmetric cryptosystem*), two mathematically linked but different keys are generated—a private signing key and a public validation key. A digital signature is created when the signer uses the private key to create a unique mark on an electronic document. The appropriate software enables the recipient of the document to use the public key to verify the identity of the signer. A *cybernotary,* or legally recognized certification authority, issues the key pair, identifies the owner of the keys, and certifies the validity of the public key. The cybernotary also serves as a repository for public keys.

State Laws Governing E-Signatures   Most states have laws governing e-signatures. The problem is that state e-signature laws are not uniform. Some states— California is a notable example—prohibit many types of documents from being signed with e-signatures, whereas other states are more permissive.

   In an attempt to create more uniformity among the states, in 1999 the National Conference of Commissioners on Uniform State Laws and the American Law Institute promulgated the Uniform Electronic Transactions Act (UETA). To date, the UETA has been adopted, at least in part, by forty-eight states. Among other things, the UETA states that a signature may not be denied legal effect or enforceability solely because it is in electronic form.[21] (We will look more closely at the UETA shortly.)

Federal Law Governing E-Signatures and E-Documents   In 2000, Congress enacted the Electronic Signatures in Global and National Commerce Act (E-SIGN Act),[22] which provides that no contract, record, or signature may be "denied legal effect" solely because it is in an electronic form. In other words, under this law, an e-signature is as valid as a signature on paper, and an e-document can be as enforceable as a paper one.

   For an e-signature to be enforceable, the contracting parties must have agreed to use electronic signatures. For an electronic document to be valid, it must be in a form that can be retained and accurately reproduced.

   The E-SIGN Act does not apply to all types of documents, however. Contracts and documents that are exempt include court papers, divorce decrees, evictions, foreclosures, health-insurance terminations, prenuptial agreements, and wills.

E-SIGNATURE

Under the Uniform Electronic Transactions Act, a signature can be any electronic sound, symbol, or process attached to electronically stored information. This definition is intentionally broad in order to give legal effect to acts that people intend to be the equivalent of their written signatures.

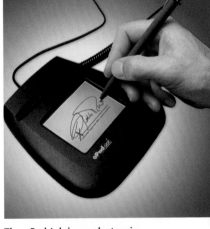

The ePad-Ink is an electronic signature pad that can be used to insert handwritten signatures into electronic documents. What type of e-signature technology does this device utilize? What procedure is used to verify the authenticity of a signature created using this ePad? (Photo Courtesy of Interlink Electronics)

---

21. The 2003 amendments to UCC Article 2 include a similar provision in UCC 2–211.
22. 15 U.S.C. Sections 7001 *et seq.*

Also, the only agreements governed by the UCC that fall under this law are those covered by Articles 2 and 2A and UCC 1–107 and 1–206.

The E-SIGN Act refers explicitly to the UETA and provides that if a state has enacted the uniform version of the UETA, that law is not preempted by the E-SIGN Act. In other words, if the state has enacted the UETA without modification, state law will govern. The problem is that many states have enacted nonuniform (modified) versions of the UETA, largely for the purpose of excluding other areas of state law from the UETA's terms. The E-SIGN Act specifies that those exclusions will be preempted to the extent that they are inconsistent with the E-SIGN Act's provisions.

The Uniform Electronic Transactions Act

As noted earlier, the UETA, promulgated in 1999, represents one of the first comprehensive efforts to create uniformity and introduce certainty in state laws pertaining to e-commerce. The primary purpose of the UETA is to remove barriers to e-commerce by giving the same legal effect to electronic records and signatures as is currently given to paper documents and signatures. The UETA broadly defines an *e-signature* as "an electronic sound, symbol, or process attached to or logically associated with a record and executed or adopted by a person with the intent to sign the record."[23] A *record* is defined as "information that is inscribed on a tangible medium or that is stored in an electronic or other medium and is retrievable in perceivable [visual] form."[24]

The UETA does not apply to all writings and signatures but only to electronic records and electronic signatures *relating to a transaction*. A *transaction* is defined as an interaction between two or more people relating to business, commercial, or governmental activities.[25] The act specifically does not apply to laws governing wills or testamentary trusts or the UCC (other than Articles 2 and 2A).[26] In addition, the provisions of the UETA allow the states to exclude its application to other areas of law.

---

23. UETA 102(8).
24. UETA 102(15).
25. UETA 2(12) and 3.
26. UETA 3(b).

REVIEWING . . . SALES, LEASES, AND E-CONTRACTS

GFI, Inc., a Hong Kong company, makes audio decoder chips, one of the essential components used in the manufacture of MP3 players. Egan Electronics contracts with GFI to buy a total of 10,000 chips, with 2,500 chips to be shipped every three months via Air Express. At the time for the first delivery, GFI delivers only 2,400 chips but explains to Egan that while the shipment is less than 5 percent short, the chips are of a higher quality than those specified in the contract and are worth 5 percent more than the contract price. Egan accepts the shipment and pays GFI the contract price. At the time for the second shipment, GFI makes a shipment identical to the first. Egan again accepts and pays for the chips. At the time for the third shipment, GFI ships 2,400 of the same chips, but this time GFI sends them via Hong Kong Air instead of Air Express. While in transit, the chips are destroyed. Shortly after the third shipment is made, GFI's manufacturing plant burns down and its entire inventory of chips is destroyed. GFI is financially ruined by the fire and unable to continue making decoder chips or to purchase them elsewhere.

Using the information presented in the chapter, answer the following questions.

1. Suppose that Egan had accepted but refused to pay for the first shipment, and instead sued GFI for breach of contract. If a court found that GFI had breached the contract, what would be the measure of damages?

2. Does the substitution of carriers for the third shipment constitute a breach of the contract by GFI? Why or why not?

3. Suppose that the silicon used for the chips becomes unavailable for a period of time and that GFI cannot manufacture enough chips to fulfill the contract, but does ship as many as it can to Egan. Under what doctrine might a court release GFI from further performance of the contract?

4. Suppose that three years after the fire, GFI notifies Egan that it is back in business, has rebuilt its plant, and is now accepting orders via its Web site. The owner of Egan goes to the Web site and places an order for 3,000 chips from GFI, clicking on the "I agree" button without reading the specific terms. What is this type of online contract called? Will a court be likely to enforce the agreement even if one party did not read it?

KEY TERMS

browse-wrap terms 341
click-on agreement 341
conforming goods 325
cover 332
cure 325
e-contract 340
e-signature 343
express warranty 337
firm offer 319

forum-selection clause 341
implied warranty 338
implied warranty of fitness
   for a particular purpose 338
implied warranty of
   merchantability 338
lease 317
lessee 317
lessor 317

merchant 315
perfect tender rule 325
puffery 338
sale 314
sales contract 314
tangible property 314
tender of delivery 325

CHAPTER SUMMARY • SALES, LEASES, AND E-CONTRACTS

The Scope of Article 2—Sales (See pages 314–317.)	Article 2 governs contracts for the sale of goods (tangible, movable personal property). The common law of contracts also applies to sales contracts to the extent that the common law has not been modified by the UCC. If there is a conflict between a common law rule and the UCC, the UCC controls.
The Scope of Article 2A—Leases (See page 317.)	Article 2A governs contracts for the lease of goods. Except that it applies to leases, instead of sales, of goods, Article 2A is essentially a repetition of Article 2 and varies only to reflect differences between sales and lease transactions.

Offer and Acceptance (See pages 318–321.)	1. *Offer—*
	  a. Not all terms have to be included for a contract to be formed (only the subject matter and quantity term must be specified). The price does not have to be included for a contract to be formed.
	  b. A written and signed offer by a *merchant,* covering a period of three months or less, is irrevocable without payment of consideration.
	2. *Acceptance—*
	  a. Acceptance may be made by any reasonable means of communication; it is effective when dispatched.

(Continued)

CHAPTER SUMMARY • SALES, LEASES, AND E-CONTRACTS—CONTINUED

Offer and Acceptance—Continued	b. The acceptance of a unilateral offer can be made by a promise to ship or by prompt shipment of conforming goods, or by prompt shipment of nonconforming goods if not accompanied by a notice of accommodation.
	c. Acceptance by performance requires notice within a reasonable time; otherwise, the offer can be treated as lapsed.
	d. A definite expression of acceptance creates a contract even if the terms of the acceptance vary from those of the offer unless the varied terms in the acceptance are expressly conditioned on the offeror's assent to the varied terms.
	3. *Consideration*—A modification of a contract for the sale of goods does not require consideration.
The Statute of Frauds (See pages 321–324.)	1. All contracts for the sale of goods priced at $500 or more must be in writing. A writing is sufficient as long as it indicates a contract between the parties and is signed by the party against whom enforcement is sought. A contract is not enforceable beyond the quantity shown in the writing.
	2. When written confirmation of an oral contract *between merchants* is not objected to in writing by the receiver within ten days, the contract is enforceable.
	3. Exceptions to the requirement of a writing exist in the following situations:
	a. When the oral contract is for specially manufactured goods not suitable for resale to others, and the seller has substantially started to manufacture the goods.
	b. When the defendant admits in pleadings, testimony, or other court proceedings that an oral contract for the sale of goods was made. In this case, the contract will be enforceable to the extent of the quantity of goods admitted.
	c. The oral agreement will be enforceable to the extent that payment has been received and accepted by the seller or to the extent that the goods have been received and accepted by the buyer.
Performance of Sales and Lease Contracts (See pages 324–329.)	1. The seller or lessor must tender *conforming goods* to the buyer. Tender must take place at a *reasonable hour* and in a *reasonable manner.* Under the perfect tender doctrine, the seller or lessor must tender goods that conform exactly to the terms of the contract [UCC 2–503(1), 2A–508(1)].
	2. If the seller or lessor tenders nonconforming goods prior to the performance date and the buyer or lessee rejects them, the seller or lessor may *cure* (repair or replace the goods) within the contract time for performance [UCC 2–508(1), 2A–513(1)]. If the seller or lessor has reasonable grounds to believe the buyer or lessee would accept the tendered goods, on the buyer's or lessee's rejection the seller or lessor has a reasonable time to substitute conforming goods without liability [UCC 2–508(2), 2A–513(2)].
	3. If the agreed-on means of delivery becomes impracticable or unavailable, the seller must substitute an alternative means (such as a different carrier) if one is available [UCC 2–614(1)].
	4. When performance becomes commercially impracticable owing to circumstances that were not foreseeable when the contract was formed, the perfect tender rule no longer holds [UCC 2–615, 2A–405].
	5. On tender of delivery by the seller or lessor, the buyer or lessee must pay for the goods at the time and place the buyer or lessee receives the goods, even if the place of shipment is the place of delivery, unless the sale is made on credit.
	6. The buyer or lessee can manifest acceptance of delivered goods expressly in words or by conduct or by failing to reject the goods after a reasonable period of time following inspection or after having had a reasonable opportunity to inspect them [UCC 2–606(1), 2A–515(1)]. A buyer will be deemed to have accepted goods if he or she performs any act inconsistent with the seller's ownership [UCC 2–606(1)(c)].

CHAPTER SUMMARY • SALES, LEASES, AND E-CONTRACTS—CONTINUED

Performance of Sales and Lease Contracts—Continued	7. If, before the time for performance, either party clearly indicates to the other an intention not to perform, this is called anticipatory repudiation. Under UCC 2–610 and 2A–402, the nonbreaching party may choose whether to treat the breach as final by pursuing a remedy or wait and hope that the other party will perform. In either situation, the nonbreaching party may suspend performance.
Remedies for Breach of Sales and Lease Contracts (See pages 329–336.)	1. *Remedies of the seller or lessor*—When a buyer or lessee breaches the contract, a seller or lessor can withhold or discontinue performance. If the seller or lessor is still in possession of the goods, the seller or lessor can resell or dispose of the goods and hold the buyer or lessee liable for any loss [UCC 2–703(d), 2–706(1), 2A–523(1)(e), 2A–527(1)]. If the goods cannot be resold or disposed of, an unpaid seller or lessor can bring an action to recover the purchase price or payments due under the contract, plus incidental damages [UCC 2–709(1), 2A–529(1)]. If the buyer or lessee repudiates the contract or wrongfully refuses to accept goods, the seller or lessor can recover the damages that were sustained.
	2. *Remedies of the buyer or lessee*—When the seller or lessor breaches, the buyer or lessee can choose from a number of remedies, including the following:
	a. Obtain cover (in certain situations) [UCC 2–712, 2A–518].
	b. Obtain specific performance (when the goods are unique and when the remedy at law is inadequate) [UCC 2–716(1), 2A–521(1)].
	c. Sue to recover damages [UCC 2–713, 2A–519].
	d. Reject the goods [UCC 2–601, 2A–509].
	e. Accept the goods and recover damages [UCC 2–607, 2–714, 2–717, 2A–519].
	f. Revoke acceptance (in certain circumstances) [UCC 2–608, 2A–517].
	3. The parties can agree to vary their respective rights and remedies in their agreement. If the contract states that a remedy is exclusive, then that is the sole remedy—unless the remedy fails in its essential purpose.
Sales and Lease Warranties (See pages 336–340.)	1. *Title warranties*—Under the UCC, the seller or lessor automatically warrants that he or she has good title, and that there are no liens or infringements on the property being sold or leased.
	2. *Express warranties*—An express warranty arises under the UCC when a seller or lessor indicates, as part of the basis of the bargain, any of the following:
	a. An affirmation or promise of fact.
	b. A description of the goods.
	c. A sample shown as conforming to the contract goods [UCC 2–313, 2A–210].
	3. *Implied warranties*—
	a. The implied warranty of merchantability automatically arises when the seller or lessor is a merchant who deals in the kind of goods sold or leased. The seller or lessor warrants that the goods sold or leased are of proper quality, are properly labeled, and are reasonably fit for the ordinary purposes for which such goods are used [UCC 2–314, 2A–212].
	b. The implied warranty of fitness for a particular purpose arises when the buyer's or lessee's purpose or use is expressly or impliedly known by the seller or lessor, and the buyer or lessee purchases or leases the goods in reliance on the seller's or lessor's selection [UCC 2–315, 2A–213].
	c. Other implied warranties can arise as a result of course of dealing or usage of trade [UCC 2–314(3), 2A–212(3)].

(Continued)

CHAPTER SUMMARY • SALES, LEASES, AND E-CONTRACTS–CONTINUED

Sales and Lease Warranties—Continued	4. Warranties, both express and implied, can be disclaimed or qualified by a seller or lessor, but disclaimers generally must be specific and unambiguous, and often in writing.
E-Contracts (See pages 340–344.)	1. The terms of an online offer should be just as inclusive as the terms in an offer made in a written (paper) document. All possible contingencies should be anticipated and provided for in the offer, including dispute-settlement provisions as well as a forum-selection clause. The offer should be displayed in an easily readable and clear format.
	2. An online offer should also include some mechanism, such as an "I agree" or "I accept" box, by which the customer may accept the offer.
	3. A click-on agreement is created when a buyer, completing a transaction on a computer, is required to indicate her or his assent to be bound by the terms of an offer by clicking on a button that says, for example, "I agree." The courts generally enforce click-on agreements because the offeree has indicated acceptance by conduct.
	4. Browse-wrap terms, which are terms in a license that an Internet user does not have to read or agree to prior to downloading the product (such as software), may not be enforced on the ground that the user is not made aware that he or she is entering into a contract.
	5. The Uniform Electronic Transactions Act (UETA) defines the term *e-signature* as "an electronic sound, symbol, or process attached to or logically associated with a record and executed or adopted by a person with the intent to sign the record."
	6. Although most states have laws governing e-signatures, these laws are not uniform. The UETA provides for the validity of e-signatures and may ultimately create more uniformity among the states in this respect.
	7. Federal law on e-signatures and e-documents, such as the Electronic Signatures in Global and National Commerce Act (E-SIGN Act) of 2000, gave validity to e-signatures by providing that no contract, record, or signature may be "denied legal effect" solely because it is in an electronic form.
	8. Under the Uniform Electronic Transactions Act (UETA), contracts entered into online, as well as other electronic records relating to a transaction, are presumed to be valid. The UETA does not apply to transactions governed by the UCC or to wills or testamentary trusts.

FOR REVIEW

Answers for the even-numbered questions in this For Review *section can be found in Appendix O at the end of this text.*

1. How do Article 2 and Article 2A of the UCC differ? What types of transactions does each article cover?
2. In a sales contract, if an offeree includes additional or different terms in an acceptance, will a contract result? If so, what happens to these terms?
3. What remedies are available to a seller or lessor when the buyer or lessee breaches the contract?

What remedies are available to a buyer or lessee if the seller or lessor breaches the contract?
4. What implied warranties arise under the UCC?
5. What are some important clauses to include when making offers to form electronic contracts, or e-contracts?

QUESTIONS AND CASE PROBLEMS

10–1. Merchant's Firm Offer. On September 1, Jennings, a used-car dealer, wrote a letter to Wheeler in which he stated, "I have a 1955 Thunderbird convertible in mint condition that I will sell you for $13,500 at any time before October 9. [Signed] Peter Jennings." By September 15, having heard nothing from Wheeler, Jennings sold the Thunderbird to another party. On September 29, Wheeler accepted Jennings's offer and tendered the $13,500. When Jennings told Wheeler he had sold the car to another party, Wheeler claimed Jennings had breached their contract. Is Jennings in breach? Explain.

Sample Sales Contract for Purchase of Green Coffee

Starbucks Coffee Company was founded in 1971, when it opened its first store in Seattle's Pike Place Market. Today, Starbucks is the leading roaster and retailer of specialty coffee in the world. The company has more than 5,500 stores in thirty-seven countries. Starbucks's chairman and chief global strategist, Howard Schultz, who has been instrumental in the company's expansion, hopes to have 10,000 stores in fifty countries by the end of 2007.

Schultz joined the company in 1982, when Starbucks was still only a small, but highly respected, roaster and retailer of whole-bean and ground coffee. A business trip to Italy opened Schultz's eyes to the rich tradition and popularity of the espresso bar. Espresso drinks became the foundation of his vision for the company, and when Schultz purchased Starbucks in 1987, Starbucks started brewing. In a few years, the company had expanded to numerous locations in the United States and was available in restaurants, hotels, and airports, as well as by mail-order catalogue. In 1992, Starbucks began to sell shares of the company's stock to the public. The price of Starbucks stock initially was $17 per share. The same share of stock today would be worth about $400—a gain of 2,200 percent.

"In the early days, there were only a few members of the financial community who believed in our viability and staying power," says Schultz. No one dreamed that Starbucks would grow from a company that was worth approximately $270 million in 1992 into a company that is worth nearly $10 billion today. With the forward-thinking Schultz at the helm, however, Starbucks blossomed into one of the world's most admired brands. Since opening its first international location in 1996, Starbucks has expanded to 1,200 international locations throughout North America and Europe, as well as in the Middle East and Pacific Rim. Starbucks coffee is now available in supermarkets and online.

In addition to its uncompromising commitment to buying, roasting, and serving only the finest coffees in the world, Starbucks also produces and sells bottled Frappuccino®, a line of premium ice creams, Tazo® Tea, and a line of compact discs.

The company has also given back to the communities in which it operates—sponsoring cultural events, such as jazz and film festivals, and donating money to charities, especially those that benefit children. Starbucks provides funding for education and literacy programs, college scholarship programs, and international relief organizations. Starbucks is also strongly committed to promoting environmentally sound methods of growing coffee and gave $1 million in support to coffee farmers in 2001.

Photo Credit: Jill Doran for Starbucks Coffee

---

❶ This is a c[...]
their princi[...]
subject to [...]
Goods (CI[...]
places of b[...]
Uniform C[...]

❷ Quantity is[...]
court may [...]

❸ Weight per [...]
stated, usa[...]

❹ Packaging [...]
shipments [...]

❺ A descripti[...]
Warranties[...]
10. Interna[...]

❻ Under the [...]
not set. Se[...]
determina[...]

❼ The terms [...]
be complic[...]
simple, an[...]
ness (for e[...]
cash, the b[...]

❽ *Tender* me[...]
disposition[...]
it be ready[...]
warehouse[...]
goods are [...]

❾ The delive[...]
in breach [...]
within whi[...]
present pr[...]
pass inspe[...]

❿ As part of [...]
when the g[...]
set out in C[...]

⓫ In some co[...]
some loss [...]
example) [...]
to which e[...]

⓬ Document[...]
them word[...]
revised, th[...]
incorporat[...]
provisions[...]

⓭ In internat[...]
brokers are[...]
commissio[...]

ntract for a sale of coffee to be *imported* internationally. If the parties have
al places of business located in different countries, the contract may be
e United Nations Convention on Contracts for the International Sale of
G)—discussed in Chapter 10 and Chapter 22. If the parties' principal
siness are located in the United States, the contract may be subject to the
mmercial Code (UCC).

one of the most important terms to include in a contract. Without it, a
ot be able to enforce the contract. See Chapter 8.

unit (bag) can be exactly stated or approximately stated. If it is not so
e of trade in international contracts determines standards of weight.

equirements can be conditions for acceptance and payment. Bulk
re not permitted without the consent of the buyer.

on of the coffee and the "Markings" constitute express warranties.
in contracts for domestic sales of goods are discussed generally in Chapter
tional contracts rely more heavily on descriptions and models or samples.

UCC, parties may enter into a valid contract even though the price is
Chapter 10. Under the CISG, a contract must provide for an exact
on of the price.

f payment may take one of two forms: credit or cash. Credit terms can
ated and may involve letters of credit. See Chapter 22. A cash term can be
payment may be by any means acceptable in the ordinary course of busi-
ample, a personal check or a letter of credit). If the seller insists on actual
yer must be given a reasonable time to get it.

ns the seller has placed goods that conform to the contract at the buyer's
This contract requires that the coffee meet all import regulations and that
for pickup by the buyer at a "Bonded Public Warehouse." (A *bonded*
s a place in which goods can be stored without payment of taxes until the
emoved.)

y date is significant because, if it is not met, the buyer may hold the seller
the contract. Under this contract, the seller can be given a "period"
h to deliver the goods, instead of a specific day, which could otherwise
plems. The seller is also given some time to rectify goods that do not
tion (see the "Guarantee" clause on page 2).

proper tender, the seller (or its agent) must inform the buyer (or its agent)
ods have arrived at their destination. The responsibilities of agents are
hapter 13.

tracts, delivered and shipped weights can be important. During shipping,
an be attributed to the type of goods (spoilage of fresh produce, for
to the transportation itself. A seller and buyer can agree on the extent
her of them will bear such losses.

are often incorporated in a contract by reference, because including
or word can make a contract difficult to read. If the document is later
whole contract might have to be reworked. Documents that are typically
d by reference include detailed payment and delivery terms; special
and sets of rules, codes, and standards.

onal sales transactions, and for domestic deals involving certain products,
used to form the contracts. When so used, the brokers are entitled to a
.

OVERLAND COFFEE IMPORT CONTRACT
OF THE
GREEN COFFEE ASSOCIATION
OF
NEW YORK CITY, INC.*

SOLD BY: **XYZ Co.**
TO: **Starbucks**

QUANTITY: **Five Hundred** (**500** (Bags) Tons of _____
weighing about **152.117 lbs.** _____ per bag.

PACKAGING: Coffee must be packed in clean sound bags of uniform s
similar woven material, without inner lining or outer cov
and/or machine.
Bulk shipments are allowed if agreed by mutual consent

DESCRIPTION: **High grown Mexican Altura**

PRICE: At **Ten/$10.00 dollars** U. S. C
Upon delivery in Bonded Public Warehouse at ____ **La**

PAYMENT: **Cash against warehouse receipts**

Bill and tender to DATE when all import requirements a
and coffee delivered or discharged (as per contract term
calendar days free time in Bonded Public Warehouse fol

ARRIVAL: During **December** via **truck**
(Period) (N
from **Mexico** for arri
(Country of Exportation)
Partial shipments permitted.

ADVICE OF
ARRIVAL: Advice of arrival with warehouse name and location, to
place of entry, must be transmitted directly, or through S
Broker. Advice will be given as soon as known but not
at the named warehouse. Such advice may be given ver
same day.

WEIGHTS: (1) DELIVERED WEIGHTS: Coffee covered by this co
tender. Actual tare to be allowed.
(2) SHIPPING WEIGHTS: Coffee covered by this contr
weight exceeding **1/2** percent at location named i
(3) Coffee is to be weighed within fifteen (15) calendar
account of **seller**

MARKINGS: Bags to be branded in English with the name of Country
regulations of the Country of Importation, in effect at th
merchandise. Any expense incurred by failure to compl
Exporter/Seller.

RULINGS: The "Rulings on Coffee Contracts" of the Green Coffee
the date this contract is made, is incorporated for all pur
herewith, constitute the entire contract. No variation or
parties to the contract.
Seller guarantees that the terms printed on the reverse he
are identical with the terms as printed in By-Laws and R
York City, Inc., heretofore adopted.
Exceptions to this guarantee are:
ACCEPTED: CON
XYZ Co. s

Seller
BY_____
Agent
Starbucks

Buyer
BY_____
Agent
When this contract is executed by a person acting for an
fully authorized to commit his principal.

Question with Sample Answer

10-2. Flint, a retail seller of television sets, orders one hundred Color-X sets from manufacturer Martin. The order specifies the price and that the television sets are to be shipped by Hummingbird Express on or before October 30. The order is received by Martin on October 5. On October 8, Martin writes Flint a letter indicating that the order was received and that the sets will be shipped as directed, at the specified price. This letter is received by Flint on October 10. On October 28, Martin, in preparing the shipment, discovers it has only ninety Color-X sets in stock. Martin ships the ninety Color-X sets and ten television sets of a different model, stating clearly on the invoice that the ten are being shipped only as an accommodation. Flint claims Martin is in breach of contract. Martin claims the shipment was not an acceptance, and therefore no contract was formed. Explain who is correct and why.

For a sample answer to this question, go to Appendix P at the end of this text.

10-3. Anticipatory Repudiation. Moore contracted in writing to sell her 1996 Ford Taurus to Hammer for $8,500. Moore agreed to deliver the car on Wednesday, and Hammer promised to pay the $8,500 on the following Friday. On Tuesday, Hammer informed Moore that he would not be buying the car after all. By Friday, Hammer had changed his mind again and tendered $8,500 to Moore. Moore, although she had not sold the car to another party, refused the tender and refused to deliver. Hammer claimed that Moore had breached their contract. Moore contended that Hammer's repudiation released her from her duty to perform under the contract. Who is correct, and why?

10-4. Remedies. McDonald has contracted to purchase five hundred pairs of shoes from Vetter. Vetter manufactures the shoes and tenders delivery to McDonald. McDonald accepts the shipment. Later, on inspection, McDonald discovers that ten pairs of the shoes are poorly made and will have to be sold to customers as seconds. If McDonald decides to keep all five hundred pairs of shoes, what remedies are available to her? Discuss.

10-5. Statute of Frauds. Quality Pork International is a Nebraska firm that makes and sells custom pork products. Rupari Food Services, Inc., buys and sells food products from and to retail operations and food brokers. In November 1999, Midwest Brokerage arranged an oral contract between Quality and Rupari, under which Quality would ship three orders to Star Food Processing, Inc., and Rupari would pay for the products. Quality shipped the goods to Star and sent invoices to Rupari. In turn, Rupari billed Star for all three orders but paid Quality only for the first two (for $43,736.84 and $47,467.80, respectively), not for the third. Quality filed a suit in a Nebraska state court against Rupari, alleging breach of contract, to recover $44,051.98, the cost of the third order. Rupari argued that there was nothing in writing, as required by the Uniform Commercial Code (UCC) Section 2–201, and thus there was no enforceable contract. What are the exceptions to the UCC's writing requirement? Do any of those exceptions apply here? Explain. [*Quality Pork International v. Rupari Food Services, Inc.,* 267 Neb. 474, 675 N.W.2d 642 (2004)]

10-6. Perfect Tender. Advanced Polymer Sciences, Inc. (APS), based in Ohio, makes polymers and resins for use as protective coatings in industrial applications. APS also owns the technology for equipment used to make certain composite fibers. *SAVA gumarska in kemijska industria d.d.* (SAVA), based in Slovenia, makes rubber goods. In 1999, SAVA and APS contracted to form *SAVA Advanced Polymers proizvodno podjetje d.o.o.* (SAVA AP) to make and distribute APS products in Eastern Europe. Their contract provided for, among other things, the alteration of a facility to make the products using specially made equipment to be sold by APS to SAVA. Disputes arose between the parties, and in August 2000, SAVA stopped work on the new facility. APS then notified SAVA that it was halting the manufacture of the equipment and "insist[ed] on knowing what is SAVA's intention towards this venture." In October, SAVA told APS that it was canceling their contract. In subsequent litigation, SAVA claimed that APS had repudiated the contract when it stopped making the equipment. What might APS assert in its defense? How should the court rule? Explain. [*SAVA gumarska in kemijska industria d.d. v. Advanced Polymer Sciences, Inc.,* 128 S.W.3d 304 (Tex.App.—Dallas 2004)]

Case Problem with Sample Answer

10-7. Propulsion Technologies, Inc., a Louisiana firm doing business as PowerTech Marine Propellers, markets small steel boat propellers that are made by a unique tooling method. Attwood Corp., a Michigan firm, operated a foundry (a place where metal is cast) in Mexico. In 1996, Attwood offered to produce castings of the propellers. Attwood promised to maintain quality, warrant the castings against defects, and obtain insurance to cover liability. In January 1997, the parties signed a letter that expressed these and other terms—Attwood was to be paid per casting, and twelve months' notice was required to terminate the deal—but the letter did not state a quantity. PowerTech provided the tooling. Attwood produced rough castings, which PowerTech refined by checking each propeller's pitch; machining its interior; grinding, balancing, and polishing the propeller; and adding serial numbers and a rubber clutch. In October, Attwood told PowerTech that the foundry was closing. PowerTech filed a suit in a federal district court against Attwood, alleging in part breach of contract. One of the issues was whether their deal was subject to Article 2 of the Uniform Commercial Code (UCC). What type of transactions does Article 2 cover? Does the arrangement between PowerTech and Attwood qualify? Explain. [*Propulsion Technologies, Inc. v. Attwood Corp.,* 369 F.3d 896 (5th Cir. 2004)]

After you have answered this problem, compare your answer with the sample answer given on the Web site that accompanies this text. Go to www.thomsonedu.com/westbuslaw/let, select "Chapter 10," and click on "Case Problem with Sample Answer."

10–8. Shrink-Wrap Agreements and Browse-Wrap Terms. Mary DeFontes bought a computer and a service contract from Dell Computers Corp. DeFontes was charged $950.51, of which $13.51 was identified on the invoice as "tax." This amount was paid to the state of Rhode Island. DeFontes and other Dell customers filed a suit in a Rhode Island state court against Dell, claiming that Dell was overcharging its customers by collecting a tax on service contracts and transportation costs. Dell asked the court to order DeFontes to submit the dispute to arbitration. Dell cited its "Terms and Conditions Agreement," which provides in part that by accepting delivery of Dell's products or services, a customer agrees to submit any dispute to arbitration. Customers can view this agreement through an *inconspicuous* link at the bottom of Dell's Web site, and Dell encloses a copy with each order when it is shipped. Dell argued that DeFontes accepted these terms by failing to return her purchase within thirty days, although the agreement did not state this. Is DeFontes bound to the "Terms and Conditions Agreement"? Should the court grant Dell's request? Why or why not? [*DeFontes v. Dell Computers Corp.,* __ A.2d __ (R.I. 2004)]

10–9. Warranty Disclaimers. Roger's Fence, Inc., bought a wheel loader made by Hyundai Construction Equipment, U.S.A., Inc., from Abele Tractor and Equipment Co. in Syracuse, New York. Abele faxed the purchase agreement to the vice president of Roger's. The agreement stated, in capital letters directly above the signature line, that the warranty terms were on the reverse side. On the reverse side, Abele disclaimed all implied warranties and limited damages to the repair or replacement of defective parts for two years or 3,000 hours of operation, whichever came first. The reverse side, however, was not faxed to Roger's, whose vice president nevertheless signed a delivery report indicating that he had reviewed and understood the warranty coverage. Certain repairs were made during the warranty period, and after 3,000 hours, the wheel loader was still operating properly. Later, when it broke down, Roger's filed a suit in a New York state court against Abele and Hyundai, alleging, in part, that the warranty disclaimers were invalid. What are the arguments for and against the position of Roger's? In whose favor should the court rule? Why? [*Roger's Fence, Inc. v. Abele Tractor and Equipment Co.,* 26 A.D.3d 788, 809 N.Y.S.2d 712 (4 Dept. 2006)]

A Question of Ethics

10–10. Bobby Murray Chevrolet, Inc., contracted to supply 1,200 school bus chassis to local school boards. The contract stated that "products of any manufacturer may be offered," but Bobby Murray submitted its orders exclusively to General Motors Corp. (GMC). When a shortage in automatic transmissions occurred, GMC informed the dealer that it could not fill the orders. Bobby Murray told the school boards, which then bought the chassis from another dealer. The boards sued Bobby Murray for breach of contract. The dealer responded that its obligation to perform was excused under the doctrine of commercial impracticability, in part because of GMC's failure to fill its orders. Given these facts, answer the following questions. [*Alamance County Board of Education v. Bobby Murray Chevrolet, Inc.,* 121 N.C.App. 222, 465 S.E.2d 306 (1996)]

1. How will the court likely decide this issue? What factors will the court consider in making its decision? Discuss fully.
2. If the decision were yours to make, would you excuse Bobby Murray from its performance obligations in these circumstances? Would your decision be any different if Bobby Murray had specified in its contract that GMC would be the exclusive source of supply instead of stating that "products of any manufacturer may be offered"?
3. Generally, how does the doctrine of commercial impracticability attempt to balance the rights of both parties to a contract?

Video Question

10–11. Go to this text's Web site at www.thomsonedu.com/westbuslaw/let and select "Chapter 10." Click on "Video Questions" and view the video titled *E-Contracts: Agreeing Online.* Then answer the following questions.

1. According to the instructor in the video, what is the key factor in determining whether a particular term in an online agreement is enforceable?
2. Suppose that you click on "I accept" in order to download software from the Internet. You do not read the terms of the agreement before accepting it, even though you know that such agreements often contain forum-selection and arbitration clauses. The software later causes irreparable harm to your computer system, and you want to sue. When you go to the Web site and view the agreement, however, you discover that a choice-of-law clause in the contract specifies that the law of Nigeria controls. Is this term enforceable? Is it a term that should be reasonably expected in an online contract?
3. Does it matter what the term actually says if it is a type of term that one could reasonably expect to be in the contract? What arguments can be made for and against enforcing a choice-of-law clause in an online contract?

Critical-Thinking Technological Question

10–12. Delta Co. buys accounting software from Omega Corp. On the outside of the software box, on the inside cover of the instruction manual, and on the first screen that appears each time the program is accessed is a license that claims to cover the use of the product. The license also includes a limitation on Omega's liability arising from the use of the software. One year later, Delta discovers that the software has a bug that has imposed on Delta a financial loss. Delta files a suit against Omega. Is the limitation-of-liability clause on the software box enforceable?

INTERACTING WITH THE INTERNET

For updated links to resources available on the Web, as well as a variety of other materials, visit this text's Web site at

www.thomsonedu.com/westbuslaw/let

For information about the National Conference of Commissioners on Uniform State Laws (NCCUSL) and links to online uniform acts, go to

www.nccusl.org

The NCCUSL, in association with the University of Pennsylvania Law School, now offers an official site for in-process and final drafts of uniform and model acts. For an index of in-process drafts, go to

www.law.upenn.edu/bll/ulc/ulc.htm

Cornell University's Legal Information Institute offers online access to the UCC, as well as to UCC articles as enacted by particular states and proposed revisions to articles, at

www.law.cornell.edu/ucc/ucc.table.html

INTERNET EXERCISES

Go to **www.thomsonedu.com/westbuslaw/let**, the Web site that accompanies this text. Select "Chapter 10" and click on "Internet Exercises." There you will find the following Internet research exercises that you can perform to learn more about topics covered in this chapter.

Internet Exercise 10–1: LEGAL PERSPECTIVE—E-Contract Formation
Internet Exercise 10–2: MANAGEMENT PERSPECTIVE—A Checklist for Sales Contracts

BEFORE THE TEST

Go to **www.thomsonedu.com/westbuslaw/let**, the Web site that accompanies this text. Select "Chapter 10" and click on "Interactive Quizzes." You will find a number of interactive questions relating to this chapter.

CONTENTS

"[E]veryone thirsteth after gaine."

—SIR EDWARD COKE, 1552–1634
(English jurist and politician)

CHAPTER OBJECTIVES

After reading this chapter, you should be able to answer the following questions:

1. Which form of business organization is the simplest?

2. What are some advantages and disadvantages of doing business as a partnership or a corporation, respectively?

3. How do limited liability companies and limited liability partnerships differ from traditional corporations and partnerships?

4. What is a franchise? What are the most common types of franchises?

5. What are the rights and duties of the directors and officers of a corporation? What are the rights of shareholders in a corporate enterprise?

MANY AMERICANS would agree with Sir Edward Coke's comment in the chapter-opening quotation on the left that most people, at least, "thirsteth after gaine." Certainly, an entrepreneur's primary motive for undertaking a business enterprise is to make profits. An *entrepreneur* is by definition one who initiates and *assumes the financial risks* of a new enterprise and undertakes to provide or control its management.

One of the questions faced by any entrepreneur who wishes to start up a business is what form of business organization he or she should choose for the business endeavor. In this chapter, we first examine the basic features of the three major traditional business forms—sole proprietorships, partnerships, and corporations. We then look at two relatively new, but increasingly significant, business forms: the limited liability company, or LLC, and limited liability partnership, or LLP. The LLC is rapidly becoming an attractive alternative to the traditional corporate form. The LLP is a variation of the LLC. We also discuss private franchises. In the final pages of the chapter, we look at the roles, rights, and duties of corporate directors, officers, and shareholders, and at some of the ways in which conflicts among these corporate participants are resolved.

MAJOR TRADITIONAL BUSINESS FORMS

Traditionally, entrepreneurs have used three major forms to structure their business enterprises: the sole proprietorship, the partnership, and the corporation.

Sole Proprietorships

The simplest form of business is a **sole proprietorship.** In this form, the owner is the business; thus, anyone who does business without creating a separate business organization has a sole proprietorship. Sole proprietorships constitute over two-thirds of all American businesses. They are also usually small enterprises—about 99 percent of the sole proprietorships in the United States have revenues of less than $1 million per year. Sole proprietors can own and manage any type of business from an informal, home-office undertaking to a large restaurant or construction firm.

A major advantage of the sole proprietorship is that the proprietor receives all of the profits (because he or she assumes all of the risk). In addition, it is often easier and less costly to start a sole proprietorship than to start any other kind of business, as few legal forms are involved. This type of business organization also entails more flexibility than does a partnership or a corporation. The sole proprietor is free to make any decision he or she wishes to concerning the business—such as whom to hire, when to take a vacation, and what kind of business to pursue. A sole proprietor pays only personal income taxes on profits, which are reported as personal income on the proprietor's personal income tax form. Sole proprietors are also allowed to establish certain tax-exempt retirement accounts.[1]

The major disadvantage of the sole proprietorship is that, as sole owner, the proprietor alone bears the burden of any losses or liabilities incurred by the business enterprise. In other words, the sole proprietor has unlimited liability, or legal responsibility, for all obligations incurred in doing business. This unlimited liability is a major factor to be considered in choosing a business form. Another disadvantage is that the proprietor's opportunity to raise capital is limited to personal funds and the funds of those who are willing to make loans. The sole proprietorship also has the disadvantage of lacking continuity on the death of the proprietor. When the owner dies, so does the business—it is automatically dissolved. If the business is transferred to family members or other heirs, a new proprietorship is created.

Partnerships

Traditionally, partnerships have been classified as either general partnerships or limited partnerships. The two forms of partnership differ considerably in regard to legal requirements and the rights and liabilities of partners. We look here at the basic characteristics of each of these forms.

General Partnerships A general partnership, or **partnership,** arises from an agreement, express or implied, between two or more persons to carry on a business for profit. Partners are co-owners of a business and have joint control over its operation and the right to share in its profits. No particular form of partnership agreement is necessary for the creation of a partnership, but for practical reasons, the agreement should be in writing. Basically, the partners

---

1. A *Keogh plan* is a retirement program designed for self-employed persons, as is a simplified employee pension (SEP) plan. A person can contribute a certain percentage of income to the plan, and interest earnings will not be taxed until funds are withdrawn from the plan.

SOLE PROPRIETORSHIP
The simplest form of business, in which the owner is the business; the owner reports business income on his or her personal income tax return and is legally responsible for all debts and obligations incurred by the business.

PARTNERSHIP
An agreement by two or more persons to carry on, as co-owners, a business for profit.

What are the advantages of doing business as a sole proprietorship? (James Schnepf/Getty Images)

may agree to almost any terms when establishing the partnership so long as they are not illegal or contrary to public policy.

A partnership is a legal entity only for limited purposes, such as the partnership name and title of ownership and property. A key advantage of the partnership is that the firm itself does not pay federal income taxes, although the firm must file an information return with the Internal Revenue Service (IRS). A partner's profit from the partnership (whether distributed or not) is taxed as individual income to the individual partner. The main disadvantage of the partnership is that the partners are subject to personal liability for partnership obligations. In other words, if the partnership cannot pay its debts, the personal assets of the partners are subject to creditors' claims.

Limited Partnerships   A special and quite popular form of partnership is the **limited partnership,** which consists of at least one general partner and one or more limited partners. A limited partnership is a creature of statute, because it does not come into existence until a *certificate of limited partnership* is filed with the appropriate state office. A **general partner** assumes responsibility for the management of the partnership and liability for all partnership debts. A **limited partner** has no right to participate in the general management or operation of the partnership and assumes no liability for partnership debts beyond the amount of capital he or she has contributed. Thus, one of the major benefits of becoming a limited partner is this limitation on liability, both with respect to lawsuits brought against the partnership and the amount of funds placed at risk.

Corporations

A third and very widely used type of business organizational form is the **corporation.** Corporations are owned by *shareholders*—those who have purchased ownership shares in the business. A *board of directors,* elected by the shareholders, manages the business. The board of directors normally employs *officers* to oversee day-to-day operations.

The corporation, like the limited partnership, is a creature of statute. The corporation's existence as a legal entity, which can be perpetual, depends generally on state law.

One of the key advantages of the corporate form of business is that the liability of its owners (shareholders) is limited to their investments. The shareholders usually are not personally liable for the obligations of the corporation. Another advantage is that a corporation can raise capital by selling shares of corporate stock to investors. A key disadvantage of the corporate form is that any distributed corporate income is taxed twice. The corporate entity pays taxes on the firm's income, and when income is distributed to shareholders, the shareholders again pay taxes on that income.

S Corporations   Some small corporations are able to avoid this double-taxation feature of the corporation by electing to be treated, for tax purposes, as an **S corporation.** Subchapter S of the Internal Revenue Code allows qualifying corporations to be taxed in a way similar to the way a partnership is taxed. In other words, an S corporation is not taxed at the corporate level. As in a partnership, the income is taxed only once—when it is distributed to the shareholder-owners, who pay personal income taxes on their respective shares of the profits.

LIMITED PARTNERSHIP
A partnership consisting of one or more general partners (who manage the business and are liable to the full extent of their personal assets for debts of the partnership) and one or more limited partners (who contribute only assets and are liable only up to the amount contributed by them).

GENERAL PARTNER
In a limited partnership, a partner who assumes responsibility for the management of the partnership and liability for all partnership debts.

LIMITED PARTNER
In a limited partnership, a partner who contributes capital to the partnership but has no right to participate in the management and operation of the business. The limited partner assumes no liability for partnership debts beyond the capital contributed.

CORPORATION
A legal entity formed in compliance with statutory requirements. The entity is distinct from its shareholder-owners.

S CORPORATION
A close business corporation that has met certain requirements as set out by the Internal Revenue Code and thus qualifies for special income tax treatment. Essentially, an S corporation is taxed the same as a partnership, but its owners enjoy the privilege of limited liability.

Qualification Requirements for S Corporations   Among the numerous requirements for S corporation status, the following are the most important:

1. The corporation must be a domestic corporation.
2. The corporation must not be a member of an affiliated group of corporations.
3. The shareholders of the corporation must be individuals, estates, or certain trusts. Partnerships and nonqualifying trusts cannot be shareholders. Under specific circumstances, corporations can be shareholders.
4. The corporation must have one hundred or fewer shareholders.
5. The corporation must have only one class of stock, although not all shareholders need have the same voting rights.
6. No shareholder of the corporation may be a nonresident alien.

LIMITED LIABILITY COMPANIES

The two most common forms of business organization traditionally selected by two or more persons entering into business together are the partnership and the corporation. As already explained, each form has distinct advantages and disadvantages. For partnerships, the advantage is that partnership income is taxed only once (all income is "passed through" the partnership entity to the partners themselves, who are taxed only as individuals); the disadvantage is the personal liability of the partners. For corporations, the advantage is the limited liability of shareholders; the disadvantage is the double taxation of corporate income. For many entrepreneurs and investors, the ideal business form would combine the tax advantages of the partnership form of business with the limited liability of the corporate enterprise.

The limited partnership and the S corporation partially address these needs. The limited liability of limited partners, however, is conditional: limited liability exists only so long as the limited partner does *not* participate in management. The problem with S corporations is that only small corporations (those with one hundred or fewer shareholders) may acquire S corporation status. Furthermore, with few exceptions, only *individuals* may be shareholders in an S corporation; partnerships and corporations normally cannot be shareholders. Finally, no nonresident alien can be a shareholder in an S corporation. This means that if, say, a European investor wanted to purchase shares in an S corporation, it would not be permissible.

Since 1977, every state has adopted legislation authorizing a new form of business organization called the **limited liability company (LLC).** The LLC is a hybrid form of business enterprise that offers the limited liability of the corporation but the tax advantages of a partnership. The origins and characteristics of this increasingly significant form of business organization are discussed in this chapter's *Landmark in the Legal Environment* feature on page 356.

Formation of an LLC

Like the corporation, an LLC must be formed and operated in compliance with state law. About one-fourth of the states specifically require LLCs to have at least two owners, called **members.** In the rest of the states, although some LLC statutes are silent on this issue, one-member LLCs are usually permitted.

To form an LLC, **articles of organization** must be filed with a central state agency—usually the secretary of state's office. Typically, the articles are

> " The art of taxation consists in so plucking the goose as to obtain the largest amount of feathers with the smallest possible amount of hissing. "
>
> —JEAN BAPTISTE COLBERT, 1619–1683
> (French politician and financial reformer)

LIMITED LIABILITY COMPANY (LLC)
A hybrid form of business enterprise that offers the limited liability of the corporation but the tax advantages of a partnership.

MEMBER
The term used to designate a person who has an ownership interest in a limited liability company.

ARTICLES OF ORGANIZATION
The document filed with a designated state official by which a limited liability company is formed.

Limited Liability Company (LLC) Statutes

In 1977, Wyoming became the first state to pass legislation authorizing the creation of a limited liability company (LLC). Although LLCs emerged in the United States only in 1977, they have been in existence for over a century in other areas, including several European and South American nations. The South American *limitada*, for example, is a form of business organization that operates more or less as a partnership but provides limited liability for the owners.

Taxation of LLCs   In the United States, after Wyoming's adoption of an LLC statute, it still was not known how the Internal Revenue Service (IRS) would treat the LLC for tax purposes. In 1988, however, the IRS ruled that Wyoming LLCs would be taxed as partnerships instead of as corporations, providing that certain requirements were met. Prior to this ruling, only one other state—Florida, in 1982—had authorized LLCs. The 1988 ruling encouraged other states to enact LLC statutes, and in less than a decade, all states had done so.

IRS rules that went into effect on January 1, 1997, also encouraged widespread use of LLCs in the business world. These rules provide that any unincorporated business will automatically be taxed as a partnership unless it indicates otherwise on the tax form. The exceptions involve publicly traded companies, companies formed under a state incorporation statute, and certain foreign-owned companies. If a business chooses to be taxed as a corporation, it can indicate this choice by checking a box on the IRS form.

Foreign Entities May Be LLC Members   Part of the impetus behind the creation of LLCs in this country is that foreign investors are allowed to become LLC members. Generally, in an era increasingly characterized by global business efforts and investments, the LLC offers U.S. firms and potential investors from other countries flexibility and opportunities greater than those available through partnerships or corporations.

Application to Today's Legal Environment

Once it became clear that LLCs could be taxed as partnerships, the LLC form of business organization was widely adopted. Members could avoid the personal liability associated with the partnership form of business as well as the double taxation of the corporate form of business. Today, LLCs, which not long ago were largely unknown in this country, are a widely used form of business organization.

RELEVANT WEB SITES

To locate information on the Web concerning limited liability company statutes, go to this text's Web site at **www.thomsonedu.com/westbuslaw/let**, *select "Chapter 11," and click on "URLs for Landmarks."*

required to set forth such information as the name of the business, its principal address, the name and address of a registered agent, the names of the owners, and information on how the LLC will be managed. The business's name must include the words "Limited Liability Company" or the initials "LLC." In addition to filing the articles of organization, a few states require that a notice of the intention to form an LLC be published in a local newspaper.

Jurisdictional Requirements

One of the significant differences between LLCs and corporations has to do with federal jurisdictional requirements. The federal jurisdiction statute provides that a corporation is deemed to be a citizen of the state where it is incorporated and maintains its principal place of business. The statute does not mention the state citizenship of partnerships, LLCs, and other unincorporated associations, but the courts have tended to regard these entities as citizens of every state in which their members are citizens.

The state citizenship of LLCs may come into play when a party sues an LLC based on diversity of citizenship. Remember from Chapter 3 that in some circumstances, such as when parties to a lawsuit are from different states, a federal court can exercise diversity jurisdiction in cases in which the amount in controversy exceeds $75,000. *Total* diversity of citizenship must exist, however. For example, Fong is a citizen of New York who wishes to bring suit against Skycel, an LLC formed under the laws of Connecticut. One of Skycel's members also lives in New York. Fong will not be able to bring a suit against Skycel in federal court on the basis of diversity jurisdiction because the defendant LLC is also a citizen of New York. The same would be true if Fong was bringing suit against multiple defendants and one of the defendants lived in New York.

Advantages of LLCs

A key advantage of the LLC is that the liability of members is limited to the amount of their investments. Another significant advantage is that an LLC with two or more members can choose whether to be taxed as a partnership or a corporation. Unless the LLC indicates that it wishes to be taxed as a corporation, it is automatically taxed as a partnership by the Internal Revenue Service (IRS). This means that the LLC as an entity pays no taxes; rather, as in a partnership, profits are "passed through" the LLC and paid personally by the members. If LLC members want to reinvest profits in the business, however, rather than distribute the profits to members, they may prefer to be taxed as a corporation if corporate income tax rates are lower than personal tax rates. Part of the attractiveness of the LLC for businesspersons is this flexibility with respect to taxation options. For federal income tax purposes, one-member LLCs are automatically taxed as sole proprietorships unless they indicate that they wish to be taxed as corporations. Still another advantage of the LLC for businesspersons is the flexibility it offers in terms of business operations and management (as will be discussed shortly).

CONTRAST A partnership must have at least two partners. In many states, an LLC can be created with only one shareholder-member.

The LLC Operating Agreement

The LLC is also a flexible business entity in another important way. In an LLC, the members themselves can decide how to operate the various aspects of the business by forming an **operating agreement.** Operating agreements typically contain provisions relating to management, decision-making procedures, how profits will be divided, the transfer of membership interests, whether the LLC will be dissolved on the death or departure of a member, and other important issues.

Operating agreements need not be in writing, and indeed they need not even be formed for an LLC to exist. Generally, though, LLC members should protect their interests by forming a written operating agreement. As with any business arrangement, disputes may arise over any number of issues. If there is no agreement covering the topic being disputed, such as how profits will be divided, the state LLC statute will govern the outcome. For example, most LLC statutes provide that if the members have not specified how profits will be divided among the members, they will be divided equally. Generally, with respect to issues not covered by an operating agreement or by an LLC statute, the principles of partnership law are applied. (For a discussion of a case illustrating the importance of having an operating agreement in place, see this chapter's *Management Perspective* feature on the next page.)

OPERATING AGREEMENT
In a limited liability company, an agreement in which the members set forth the details of how the business will be managed and operated. State statutes typically give the members wide latitude in deciding for themselves the rules that will govern their organization.

The Importance of Operating Agreements

Management Faces a Legal Issue   As mentioned elsewhere in this chapter, an operating agreement is not required to form a limited liability company (LLC). As the LLC becomes more commonly utilized as a business form, however, the value of having an operating agreement in place is becoming increasingly evident to LLC members. Suppose, for example, that you and another individual establish a two-member LLC. The other member cashes checks payable to the LLC and pockets the funds for personal use. The LLC, of course, can sue the embezzling member to recover the funds, but if that member does not have funds available to repay the embezzled amount, does the LLC have any other recourse? Can it recover from the entity that cashed the checks? Can it recover from any of the banks involved?

What the Courts Say   A case involving these exact questions came before a New Jersey court in 2004. The case involved a member-managed LLC owned by two members, Clifford Kuhn, Jr., and Joseph Tumminelli. They did not form a written LLC operating agreement. Tumminelli embezzled $283,000 from the company after cashing customers' checks at Quick Cash, Inc., a local check-cashing service. Quick Cash deposited the checks in its checking account, and its bank collected on the checks from the LLC's (drawee's) bank. Kuhn sued Tumminelli and the banks in a New Jersey state court to recover the embezzled funds.

Although the court ordered Tumminelli to pay Kuhn and to transfer his interest in the LLC to Kuhn, the court issued a summary judgment in favor of the banks. The court noted that under the New Jersey Limited Liability Company Act, when an LLC is managed by its members, each member has the authority to bind the company—unless otherwise provided in the operating agreement. In the absence of such an agreement, held the court, Tumminelli, as a 50 percent owner of the LLC, had broad authority to bind the LLC and specific authority to indorse and cash checks payable to the LLC. In the court's eyes, this meant that Tumminelli had the actual authority to receive the checks, indorse them, and cash them at Quick Cash. Thus, neither Quick Cash nor the banks involved could be held liable for cashing and paying the checks, respectively. These institutions had no way of knowing that Tumminelli had "bad intent," and it would defy reason to hold Quick Cash and the banks liable for the wrongdoing. The court emphasized that if Kuhn had wanted to limit Tumminelli's authority, he could have easily done so in an operating agreement. Kuhn appealed the decision, but the state appellate court affirmed the trial court's ruling.[a]

Implications for Managers   The implications of this case for LLC members, particularly in LLCs managed by the members, are clear. Members should spell out in an operating agreement who has authority to indorse and cash or deposit checks. By the time a dispute over this issue or other issues that arise gets to court, it is often too late to prevent losses.

a. *Kuhn v. Tumminelli,* 366 N.J.Super. 431, 841 A.2d 496 (2004).

Management of an LLC

Basically, there are two options for managing an LLC. The members may decide in their operating agreement to be either a "member-managed" LLC or a "manager-managed" LLC. Most LLC statutes provide that unless the articles of organization specify otherwise, an LLC is assumed to be member managed.

In a *member-managed* LLC, all of the members participate in management, and decisions are made by majority vote. In a *manager-managed* LLC, the members designate a group of persons to manage the firm. The management group may consist of only members, both members and nonmembers, or only nonmembers. Managers in a manager-managed LLC owe fiduciary duties to the LLC and its members, including the duty of loyalty and the duty of care, just as corporate directors and officers owe fiduciary duties to the corporation and its shareholders.

ETHICAL ISSUE 11.1

Should members who own a majority of the interests in a member-managed LLC owe a fiduciary duty to the minority members?

If the managers of a manager-managed LLC owe fiduciary duties to the members, what happens in a member-managed LLC? Do the members owe one another fiduciary duties? That question came before a Tennessee court in a dispute among the members of FuturePoint Administrative Services, LLC. FuturePoint's operating agreement allowed members to be expelled from the LLC—with or without cause—provided that the members holding a majority of interests in the company (majority members) agreed to the expulsion by vote or by written consent. Under the agreement, expelled members were to be paid the same price per share on expulsion as they paid to purchase the interest ($150) when the company was started in 2000.

By September 2001, FuturePoint had generated $63,000 in excess cash. The majority members, wanting to keep the $63,000 among themselves, expelled the minority members from the LLC. They paid the minority members the purchase price of their interests and then resold the interests for more than twice that price to another party. Subsequently, the minority members filed suit, claiming that the majority members had breached their fiduciary duties. The majority members argued that Tennessee's LLC statute did not impose any fiduciary obligations on majority shareholders and that the LLC's operating agreement authorized their actions. Ultimately, the appellate court rejected that argument and determined that the majority members in a member-managed LLC do owe fiduciary duties to minority members simply because "[t]hey should."[2]

LIMITED LIABILITY PARTNERSHIP (LLP)

A business organizational form that is similar to the LLC but that is designed more for professionals who normally do business as partners in a partnership. The LLP is a pass-through entity for tax purposes, like the general partnership, but it limits the personal liability of the partners.

LIMITED LIABILITY PARTNERSHIPS

The **limited liability partnership** (LLP) is similar to the LLC. The difference between an LLP and an LLC is that the LLP is designed more for professionals who normally do business as partners in a partnership. The major advantage of the LLP is that it allows a partnership to continue as a pass-through entity for tax purposes but limits the personal liability of the partners.

The first state to enact an LLP statute was Texas, in 1991. Other states quickly followed suit, and by 1997, virtually all of the states had enacted LLP statutes.

LLP Formation and Operation

Like LLCs, LLPs must be formed and operated in compliance with state statutes. The appropriate form has to be filed with a central state agency, usually the secretary of state's office, and the business's name must include either "Limited Liability Partnership" or "LLP."

In most states, it is relatively easy to convert a traditional partnership into an LLP because the firm's basic organizational structure remains the same. Additionally, all of the statutory and common law rules governing partnerships still apply (apart from those modified by the LLP statute). Normally, LLP statutes are simply amendments to a state's already existing partnership law.

Businesspersons routinely make decisions. How are decision-making procedures established in an LLC? (Steve Cole/Getty Images)

---

2. *Anderson v. Wilder,* 2003 WL 22768666 (Tenn.Ct.App. 2003).

Advantages of the LLP

The LLP is especially attractive for two categories of businesses: professional services and family businesses. Professional service companies include law firms and accounting firms. Family limited liability partnerships are basically business organizations in which all of the partners are related. Generally, the LLP allows professionals to avoid personal liability for the malpractice of other partners. Although LLP statutes vary from state to state, generally each state statute limits in some way the liability of partners. For example, Delaware law protects each innocent partner from the "debts and obligations of the partnership arising from negligence, wrongful acts, or misconduct." In North Carolina, Texas, and Washington, D.C., the statutes protect innocent partners from obligations arising from "errors, omissions, negligence, incompetence, or malfeasance." Partners in an LLP are liable for their own wrongful acts, however, as well as the wrongful acts of those whom they supervise.

MAJOR BUSINESS FORMS COMPARED

When deciding which form of business organization would be most appropriate, businesspersons take several factors into consideration. These factors include ease of creation, the liability of the owners, tax considerations, and the need for capital. Each major form of business organization offers distinct advantages and disadvantages with respect to these and other factors. Exhibit 11–1 on pages 362 and 363 summarizes the main advantages and disadvantages of each of the forms of business organization discussed in this chapter.

PRIVATE FRANCHISES

FRANCHISE
Any arrangement in which the owner of a trademark, trade name, or copyright licenses another to use that trademark, trade name, or copyright, under specified conditions or limitations, in the selling of goods and services.

FRANCHISEE
One receiving a license to use another's (the franchisor's) trademark, trade name, or copyright in the sale of goods and services.

FRANCHISOR
One licensing another (the franchisee) to use his or her trademark, trade name, or copyright in the sale of goods or services.

A **franchise** is defined as any arrangement in which the owner of a trademark, a trade name, or a copyright licenses others to use the trademark, trade name, or copyright in the selling of goods or services. A **franchisee** (a purchaser of a franchise) is generally legally independent of the **franchisor** (the seller of the franchise). At the same time, the franchise is economically dependent on the franchisor's integrated business system. In other words, a franchisee can operate as an independent businessperson but still obtain the advantages of a regional or national organization. Well-known franchises include McDonald's, KFC, and Burger King.

Types of Franchises

Because the franchising industry is so extensive (at least sixty-five types of distinct businesses sell franchises), it is difficult to summarize the many types of franchises that now exist. Generally, though, the majority of franchises fall into one of the following three classifications: distributorships, chain-style business operations, or manufacturing or processing-plant arrangements. We briefly describe these types of franchises here.

Distributorship   A *distributorship* arises when a manufacturing concern (franchisor) licenses a dealer (franchisee) to sell its product. Often, a distributorship covers an exclusive territory. An example of this type of franchise is an automobile dealership.

Chain-Style Business Operation   A *chain-style business operation* exists when a franchise operates under a franchisor's trade name and is identified as a member of a select group of dealers that engages in the franchisor's business. Often, the franchisor requires that the franchisee maintain certain standards of operation. In addition, sometimes the franchisee is obligated to deal exclusively with the franchisor to obtain materials and supplies. Examples of this type of franchise are McDonald's and most other fast-food chains.

Manufacturing or Processing-Plant Arrangement   A *manufacturing or processing-plant arrangement* exists when the franchisor transmits to the franchisee the essential ingredients or formula to make a particular product. The franchisee then markets the product either at wholesale or at retail in accordance with the franchisor's standards. Examples of this type of franchise are Coca-Cola and other soft-drink bottling companies.

Laws Governing Franchising

Because a franchise relationship is primarily a contractual relationship, it is governed by contract law. If the franchise exists primarily for the sale of products manufactured by the franchisor, the law governing sales contracts as expressed in Article 2 of the Uniform Commercial Code applies (see Chapter 10). Additionally, the federal government and most states have enacted laws governing certain aspects of franchising. Generally, these laws are designed to protect prospective franchisees from dishonest franchisors and to prohibit franchisors from terminating franchises without good cause.

> **KEEP IN MIND** Because a franchise involves the licensing of a trademark, a trade name, or a copyright, the law governing intellectual property may apply in some cases.

Federal Regulation of Franchising   Automobile dealership franchisees are protected from automobile manufacturers' bad faith termination of their franchises by the Automobile Dealers' Franchise Act[3]—also known as the Automobile Dealers' Day in Court Act—of 1965. If a manufacturer-franchisor terminates a franchise because of a dealer-franchisee's failure to comply with unreasonable demands (for example, failure to attain an unrealistically high sales quota), the manufacturer may be liable for damages.

Another federal statute is the Petroleum Marketing Practices Act (PMPA)[4] of 1979, which prescribes the grounds and conditions under which a franchisor may terminate or decline to renew a gasoline station franchise. Federal antitrust laws (discussed in Chapter 20), which prohibit certain types of anti-competitive agreements, may also apply in particular circumstances.

In 1979, the Federal Trade Commission (FTC) issued regulations that require franchisors to disclose material facts necessary to a prospective franchisee's making an informed decision concerning the purchase of a franchise.

State Regulation of Franchising   State legislation tends to be similar to federal statutes and the FTC regulations. For example, to protect franchisees, a state law might require the disclosure of information that is material to making an informed decision regarding the purchase of a franchise. This could include such information as the actual costs of operation, recurring expenses,

---

3. 15 U.S.C. Sections 1221 *et seq.*
4. 15 U.S.C. Sections 2801 *et seq.*

EXHIBIT 11-1   MAJOR BUSINESS FORMS COMPARED

CHARACTERISTIC	SOLE PROPRIETORSHIP	PARTNERSHIP	CORPORATION
Method of Creation	Created at will by owner.	Created by agreement of the parties.	Charter issued by state—created by statutory authorization.
Legal Position	Not a separate legal entity; owner is the business.	Not a separate legal entity in many states.	Always a legal entity separate and distinct from its owners—a legal fiction for the purposes of owning property and being a party to litigation.
Liability	Unlimited liability.	Unlimited liability.	Limited liability of shareholders—shareholders are not liable for the debts of the corporation.
Duration	Determined by owner; automatically dissolved on owner's death.	Terminated by agreement of the partners, but can continue to do business in most states even when a partner dissociates (withdraws) from the partnership.	Can have perpetual existence.
Transferability of Interest	Interest can be transferred, but individual's proprietorship then ends.	Although partnership interest can be assigned, assignee does not have full rights of a partner.	Shares of stock can be transferred.
Management	Completely at owner's discretion.	Each general partner has a direct and equal voice in management unless expressly agreed otherwise in the partnership agreement.	Shareholders elect directors, who set policy and appoint officers.
Taxation	Owner pays personal taxes on business income.	Each partner pays pro rata share of income taxes on net profits, whether or not they are distributed.	Double taxation—corporation pays income tax on net profits, with no deduction for dividends, and shareholders pay income tax on disbursed dividends they receive.
Organizational Fees, Annual License Fees, and Annual Reports	None or minimal.	None or minimal.	All required.
Transaction of Business in Other States	Generally no limitation.	Generally no limitation.[a]	Normally must qualify to do business and obtain certificate of authority.

a. A few states have enacted statutes requiring that foreign partnerships qualify to do business there.

EXHIBIT 11-1 MAJOR BUSINESS FORMS COMPARED—CONTINUED

CHARACTERISTIC	LIMITED PARTNERSHIP	LIMITED LIABILITY COMPANY	LIMITED LIABILITY PARTNERSHIP
Method of Creation	Created by agreement to carry on a business for a profit. At least one party must be a general partner and the other(s) limited partner(s). Certificate of limited partnership is filed. Charter must be issued by the state.	Created by an agreement of the member-owners of the company. Articles of organization are filed. Charter must be issued by the state.	Created by agreement of the partners. A statement of qualification for the limited liability partnership is filed.
Legal Position	Treated as a legal entity.	Treated as a legal entity.	Generally, treated same as a general partnership.
Liability	Unlimited liability of all general partners; limited partners are liable only to the extent of capital contributions.	Member-owners' liability is limited to the amount of capital contributions or investments.	Varies from state to state, but usually liability of a partner for certain acts committed by other partners is limited.
Duration	By agreement in certificate, or by termination of the last general partner (withdrawal, death, and so on) or last limited partner.	Unless a single-member LLC, can have perpetual existence (same as a corporation).	Remains in existence until cancellation or revocation.
Transferability of Interest	Interest can be assigned (same as general partnership), but if assignee becomes a member with consent of other partners, certificate must be amended.	Member interests are freely transferable.	Interest can be assigned (same as in a general partnership).
Management	General partner or partners only. Limited partners may not retain limited liability if they actively participate in management.	Member-owners can fully participate in management, or management is selected by member-owners who manage on behalf of the members.	Same as a general partnership.
Taxation	Generally taxed as a partnership.	LLC is not taxed, and members are taxed personally on profits "passed through" the LLC.	Same as a general partnership.
Organizational Fees, Annual License Fees, and Annual Reports	Organizational fee required; usually not others.	Organizational fee required; others vary with states.	Fees are set by each state for filing statements of qualification, foreign qualification, and annual reports.
Transaction of Business in Other States	Generally, no limitation.	Generally, no limitation, but may vary depending on state.	Must file a statement of foreign qualification before doing business in another state.

and profits earned, along with facts substantiating these figures. State deceptive trade practices acts may also prohibit certain types of actions on the part of franchisors.

The Franchise Contract

The franchise relationship is defined by a contract between the franchisor and the franchisee. The franchise contract specifies the terms and conditions of the franchise and spells out the rights and duties of the franchisor and the franchisee. If either party fails to perform the contractual duties, that party may be subject to a lawsuit for breach of contract. Generally, the statutory law and case law governing franchising tend to emphasize the importance of good faith and fair dealing in franchise relationships.

Because each type of franchise relationship has its own characteristics, it is difficult to describe the broad range of details a franchising contract may include. We now look at some of the major issues that typically are addressed in a franchise contract.

Payment for the Franchise   The franchisee ordinarily pays an initial fee or lump-sum price for the franchise license (the privilege of being granted a franchise). This fee is separate from the various products that the franchisee purchases from or through the franchisor. In most situations, the franchisor will receive a stated percentage of the annual sales or annual volume of business done by the franchisee.

Business Premises   The franchise agreement may specify whether the premises for the business must be leased or purchased outright. In some cases, construction of a building is necessary to meet the terms of the agreement. The agreement usually will specify whether the franchisor supplies equipment and furnishings for the premises or whether this is the responsibility of the franchisee.

Location of the Franchise   Typically, the franchisor will determine the territory to be served. Some franchise contracts will give the franchisee exclusive rights, or "territorial rights," to a certain geographical area. Other franchise contracts are silent on the issue of territorial rights. Many franchise cases involve disputes over territorial rights, and this is one area of franchising in which the implied covenant of good faith and fair dealing can come into play.

Business Organization of the Franchisee   The business organization of the franchisee is of great concern to the franchisor. Depending on the terms of the franchise agreement, the franchisor may specify particular requirements for the form and capital structure of the business. The franchise agreement may also provide that standards of operation—relating to such aspects of the business as sales quotas, quality, and record keeping—be met by the franchisee. Furthermore, a franchisor may wish to retain stringent control over the training of personnel involved in the operation and over administrative aspects of the business.

Quality Control by the Franchisor   Although the day-to-day operation of the franchise business is normally left up to the franchisee, the franchise agreement may provide for the amount of supervision and control agreed on by the parties. When the franchise is a service operation, such as a motel, the contract often provides that the franchisor will establish certain standards for running the facility. Typically, the contract will provide that the franchisor is permitted to make periodic inspections to ensure that the standards are being maintained in order to protect the franchise's name and reputation.

|**Example #1** Otmar has secured a particular high-quality ice cream franchise. The franchise agreement calls for Otmar to buy all the ice cream from the franchisor; to order and sell all the flavors produced by the franchisor; and to refrain from selling any ice cream stored for more than two weeks after delivery by the franchisor, as the quality of the ice cream declines after that period. After two months of operation, Otmar refuses to order even a limited quantity of the "fruit delight" flavor because of its higher cost. Otmar has also sold ice cream that has been stored longer than two weeks. In this situation, the franchisor could insist that Otmar buy all the flavors and not sell ice cream that has been stored more than two weeks.|

As a general rule, the validity of a provision permitting the franchisor to establish and enforce certain quality standards is unquestioned. Because the franchisor has a legitimate interest in maintaining the quality of the product or service to protect its name and reputation, it can exercise greater control in this area than would otherwise be tolerated. Increasingly, however, franchisors are finding that if they exercise too much control over the operations of their franchisees, they may incur liability under agency theory (see Chapter 13) for the acts of their franchisees' employees. The actual exercise of control, or at least the right to control, is a key consideration. If the franchisee controls the day-to-day operations of the business to a significant degree, the franchisor may be able to avoid liability, as the following case illustrates.

BE AWARE Under agency law (see Chapter 13), an employer may be liable for the torts of his or her employees if they occur within the scope of employment, without regard to the personal fault of the employer.

CASE 11.1 **Kerl v. Dennis Rasmussen, Inc.**

Wisconsin Supreme Court, 2004.
273 Wis.App. 106,
682 N.W.2d 328.

BACKGROUND AND FACTS Arby's, Inc., is a national franchisor of fast-food restaurants. Dennis Rasmussen, Inc. (DRI), is an Arby's franchisee. Under the terms of their franchise contract, DRI agreed to follow Arby's specifications for several aspects of operating the business. DRI hired Cathy Propp as the manager for its Arby's restaurant in 1994. In early 1999, Propp hired Harvey Pierce, a local county jail inmate with work-release privileges after a conviction for sexual assault. On June 11, Pierce left his shift at the restaurant without permission, walked half a mile to a discount store parking lot, and shot his former girlfriend, Robin Kerl; her fiancé, David Jones; and himself. Pierce and Jones died. Kerl survived, but is permanently disabled. Kerl and others filed a suit in a Wisconsin state court against DRI and Arby's, claiming in part that Arby's was vicariously liable for DRI's allegedly negligent hiring and supervision of Pierce. Arby's filed a motion for summary judgment, which the court granted. A state intermediate appellate court affirmed this judgment. The plaintiffs appealed to the Wisconsin Supreme Court.

IN THE WORDS OF THE COURT . . . *DIANE S. SYKES*, J. [Justice]

* * * *

Vicarious liability under the doctrine of respondeat superior *depends upon the existence of a master/servant agency relationship.* Vicarious liability under *respondeat superior* is a form of liability without fault—the imposition of liability on an innocent party for the tortious conduct of another based upon the existence of a particularized agency relationship. As such, *it is an exception to our fault-based liability system, and is imposed only where the principal has control or the right to control the physical conduct of the agent such that a master/servant relationship can be said to exist.* [Emphasis added.]

CASE 11.1–CONTINUED ▶

* * * *

The rationale for vicarious liability becomes somewhat attenuated when applied to the franchise relationship, and vicarious liability premised upon the existence of a master/servant relationship is conceptually difficult to adapt to the franchising context. If the operational standards included in the typical franchise agreement for the protection of the franchisor's trademark were broadly construed as capable of meeting the "control or right to control" test that is generally used to determine *respondeat superior* liability, then franchisors would almost always be exposed to vicarious liability for the torts of their franchisees. We see no justification for such a broad rule of franchisor vicarious liability. If vicarious liability is to be imposed against franchisors, a more precisely focused test is required.

* * * *

Applying these principles here, we conclude that Arby's did not have control or the right to control the day-to-day operation of the specific aspect of DRI's business that is alleged to have caused the plaintiffs' harm, that is, DRI's supervision of its employees.

* * * *

We conclude that the quality, marketing, and operational standards and inspection and termination rights commonly included in franchise agreements do not establish the close supervisory control or right of control over a franchisee necessary to support imposing vicarious liability against the franchisor for all purposes or as a general matter. We hold that *a franchisor may be subject to vicarious liability for the tortious conduct of its franchisee only if the franchisor had control or a right of control over the daily operation of the specific aspect of the franchisee's business that is alleged to have caused the harm.* Because Arby's did not have control or a right of control over DRI's supervision of its employees, there was no master/servant relationship between Arby's and DRI for purposes of the plaintiffs' *respondeat superior* claim against Arby's. Arby's cannot be held vicariously liable for DRI's negligent supervision of Pierce. [Emphasis added.]

DECISION AND REMEDY   The Wisconsin Supreme Court affirmed the lower court's decision, holding that Arby's was not vicariously liable for DRI's actions. The state supreme court concluded that Arby's had neither a right of control nor actual control over DRI's allegedly negligent actions.

WHY IS THIS CASE IMPORTANT?   *This case addresses an important issue for franchisors—vicarious (indirect) liability for franchisees' actions. Many franchisors understandably want to exercise enough control over the franchisee to protect the identity and reputation of the franchise. Yet the more control a franchisor exercises, the more likely it is that a court will hold the franchisor liable for any injuries sustained at the franchise or as a result of the franchisee's conduct.*

Pricing Arrangements   Depending on the nature of the business, the franchisor may require the franchisee to purchase certain supplies from the franchisor at an established price. A franchisor who sets the prices at which the franchisee will resell the goods may violate state or federal antitrust laws, or both, however.

Termination of the Franchise   The duration of the franchise is a matter to be determined between the parties. Generally, a franchise will start out for a short period, such as a year, so that the franchisee and the franchisor can determine whether they want to stay in business with one another. Usually, the franchise agreement will specify that termination must be "for cause," such as death or disability of the franchisee, insolvency of the franchisee, breach of the franchise agreement, or failure to meet specified sales quotas. Most franchise contracts provide that notice of termination must be given. If no set time for termination is specified, then a reasonable time, with notice, will be implied. A franchisee must be given reasonable time to wind up the business—that is, to do the accounting and return the copyright or trademark or any other property of the franchisor.

Because a franchisor's termination of a franchise often has adverse consequences for the franchisee, much franchise litigation involves claims of wrongful termination. Generally, the termination provisions of contracts are more favorable to the franchisor. This means that the franchisee, who normally invests a substantial amount of time and funds in the franchise operation to make it successful, may receive little or nothing for the business on termination. The franchisor owns the trademark and hence the business.

It is in this area that statutory and case law become important. The federal and state laws discussed earlier attempt, among other things, to protect franchisees from the arbitrary or unfair termination of their franchises by the franchisors. Generally, both statutory and case law emphasize the importance of good faith and fair dealing in terminating a franchise relationship. If a court perceives that a franchisor has arbitrarily or unfairly terminated a franchise, the franchisee will be provided with a remedy for wrongful termination.

THE NATURE OF THE CORPORATION

The corporation is a creature of statute. Its existence depends generally on state law. Each state has its own body of corporate law, and these laws are not entirely uniform. The Model Business Corporation Act (MBCA) is a codification of modern corporation law that has been influential in the drafting and revision of state corporation statutes. Today, the majority of state statutes are guided by the revised version of the MBCA, known as the Revised Model Business Corporation Act (RMBCA).

A *corporation* can consist of one or more *natural* persons (as opposed to the artificial "person" of the corporation) identified under a common name. The primary document needed to incorporate (that is, form the corporation according to state law) is the **articles of incorporation,** or *corporate charter,* which include such information about the corporation as its functions and the structure of its organization. As soon as a corporation is formed, an organizational meeting is held to adopt **bylaws** (rules for managing the firm) and to elect a board of directors.

The corporation substitutes itself for its shareholders in conducting corporate business and in incurring liability, yet its authority to act and the liability for its actions are separate and apart from the individuals who own it. (In certain limited situations, the "corporate veil" can be pierced; that is, liability for the corporation's obligations can be extended to shareholders—a topic to be discussed later in this chapter.)

Corporate Personnel

Responsibility for the overall management of the corporation is entrusted to a *board of directors,* which is elected by the shareholders. The board of directors hires *corporate officers* and other employees to run the daily business operations of the corporation.

> " A corporation is an artificial being, invisible, intangible, and existing only in contemplation of law. "
>
> —JOHN MARSHALL, 1755–1835
> (Chief justice of the United
> States Supreme Court, 1801–1835)

ARTICLES OF INCORPORATION
The document filed with the appropriate governmental agency, usually the secretary of state, when a business is incorporated; state statutes usually prescribe what kind of information must be contained in the articles of incorporation.

BYLAWS
A set of governing rules adopted by a corporation or other association.

When an individual purchases a share of stock in a corporation, that person becomes a *shareholder* and an owner of the corporation. Unlike the members in a partnership, the body of shareholders can change constantly without affecting the continued existence of the corporation. A shareholder can sue the corporation, and the corporation can sue a shareholder. Additionally, under certain circumstances, a shareholder can sue on behalf of a corporation.

Corporate Taxation

DIVIDEND

A distribution to corporate shareholders of corporate profits or income, disbursed in proportion to the number of shares held.

Corporate profits are taxed by state and federal governments. Corporations can do one of two things with corporate profits—retain them or pass them on to shareholders in the form of **dividends.** The corporation receives no tax deduction for dividends distributed to shareholders. Dividends are again taxable (except when they represent distributions of capital) to the shareholder receiving them. This double-taxation feature of the corporation is one of its major disadvantages.

RETAINED EARNINGS

The portion of a corporation's profits that has not been paid out as dividends to shareholders.

Profits not distributed are retained by the corporation. These **retained earnings,** if invested properly, will yield higher corporate profits in the future and thus normally cause the price of the company's stock to rise. Individual shareholders can then reap the benefits of these retained earnings in the capital gains they receive when they sell their shares.

The consequences of a failure to pay taxes can be severe. Indeed, the state may dissolve a corporation for this reason. Alternatively, corporate status may be suspended until the taxes are paid.

Another taxation issue of increasing importance to corporations today is whether corporations that sell goods or services to consumers via the Internet are required to collect state sales taxes. See this chapter's *Online Developments* feature for a discussion of this issue.

The U.S. Constitution. Does it grant corporations the same rights as individuals? (Library of Congress)

Constitutional Rights of Corporations

A corporation is recognized under state and federal law as a "person," and it enjoys many of the same rights and privileges that U.S. citizens enjoy. The Bill of Rights guarantees a person, as a citizen, certain protections, and corporations are considered persons in most instances. Accordingly, a corporation has the same right as a natural person to equal protection of the laws under the Fourteenth Amendment. It has the right of access to the courts as an entity that can sue or be sued. It also has the right of due process before denial of life, liberty, or property, as well as freedom from unreasonable searches and seizures and from double jeopardy.

Under the First Amendment, corporations are entitled to freedom of speech. As we pointed out in Chapter 4, however, commercial speech (such as advertising) and political speech (such as contributions to political causes or candidates) receive significantly less protection than noncommercial speech.

Generally, a corporation is not entitled to claim the Fifth Amendment privilege against self-incrimination. Agents or officers of the corporation therefore cannot refuse to produce corporate records on the ground that it might incriminate

The Internet Taxation Debate

Since the advent of the Internet, governments at the state and federal levels have debated the following question: Should state governments be able to collect sales taxes on goods sold via the Internet? Many state governments claim that sales taxes should be imposed on such transactions. They argue that their inability to tax online sales of goods to in-state customers by out-of-state corporations has caused them to suffer significant losses in sales tax revenues. Opponents of Internet taxation argue that taxing online sales will impede the growth of e-commerce. They also claim that because online sellers do not benefit from the state services that are typically paid for by tax revenues (such as fire departments and road construction), they should not be required to collect sales taxes.

The Supreme Court's Approach

According to a United States Supreme Court ruling in 1992, no individual state can compel an out-of-state business that lacks a substantial physical presence within that state to collect and remit state taxes.[a] If the corporation has a warehouse, office, or retail store within the state, though, the state can compel the collection of state taxes. Nevertheless, as the Court recognized in that ruling, Congress has the power to pass legislation requiring out-of-state corporations to collect and remit state sales taxes. Congress so far has chosen not to tax Internet transactions. In fact, in 1998 Congress passed the Internet Tax Freedom Act, which temporarily prohibited states from taxing sales of products conducted over the Internet. This ban expired in November 2003. Proposed legislation that would permanently prohibit state and local taxation of Internet sales has not been enacted.

A State Court's Decision

The issue of Internet taxation came before a Tennessee appellate court in *Prodigy Services Corp. v. Johnson.*[b] Prodigy, a Delaware corporation with its principal place of business in New York, is an Internet service provider (ISP) that offers two software programs for purchase online. A Tennessee statute imposes an obligation to collect sales taxes on anyone supplying "telecommunication services" to state residents. The Tennessee Department of Revenue determined that Prodigy's services constituted telecommunication services and assessed sales taxes. Prodigy appealed this tax assessment.

Ultimately, the state appellate court held that Prodigy did not have to charge its Tennessee customers the sales taxes. After looking closely at the wording of the statute and its legislative history, the court reasoned that the legislature had not intended the statute to apply to ISPs. The court also concluded that even if Prodigy had provided some telecommunication services, these services "were not the 'true object' of the Prodigy sale." The customer had to supply her or his own telephone services, and Prodigy had paid to use a telecommunications network to connect the customer to the main computer in New York. Thus, in the court's opinion, Prodigy was a consumer of telecommunication services rather than a provider.

For Critical Analysis *Although most states currently do not require corporations that sell goods and services online to collect state sales taxes, businesspersons should be aware that the law in this area is still developing. Thus, corporations may be required to collect state taxes on Internet sales in the future.*

a. See *Quill Corp. v. North Dakota,* 504 U.S. 298, 112 S.Ct. 1904, 119 L.Ed.2d 91 (1992).

b. 125 S.W.3d 413 (Tenn.Ct.App. 2003).

---

them. Additionally, the privileges and immunities clause of the Constitution (Article IV, Section 2) does not protect corporations. This clause requires each state to treat citizens of other states equally with respect to access to courts, travel rights, and so forth.

Classification of Corporations

The classification of a corporation depends on its purpose, ownership characteristics, and location. A corporation is referred to as a **domestic corporation** by its home state (the state in which it incorporates). A corporation formed in

DOMESTIC CORPORATION
In a given state, a corporation that does business in, and is organized under the law of, that state.

FOREIGN CORPORATION
In a given state, a corporation that does business in the state without being incorporated therein.

ALIEN CORPORATION
A designation in the United States for a corporation formed in another country but doing business in the United States.

"Did you expect a corporation to have a conscience, when it has no soul to be damned and no body to be kicked?"
—EDWARD THURLOW, 1731–1806
(English jurist)

one state but doing business in another is referred to in that other state as a **foreign corporation.** A corporation formed in another country—say, Mexico—but doing business in the United States is referred to in the United States as an **alien corporation.**

A corporation does not have an automatic right to do business in a state other than its state of incorporation. In certain circumstances, it must obtain a *certificate of authority* in any state in which it plans to do business. Once the certificate has been issued, the powers conferred on a corporation by its home state generally can be exercised in the other state.

Torts and Criminal Acts

A corporation is liable for the torts committed by its agents or officers within the course and scope of their employment. This principle applies to a corporation exactly as it applies to the ordinary agency relationships discussed in Chapter 13.

As you learned in Chapter 6, under modern criminal law, a corporation can sometimes be held liable for the criminal acts of its agents and employees, provided the punishment is one that can be applied to the corporation. Corporate criminal prosecutions were at one time relatively rare, but in the past decade they have increased significantly in number. Obviously, corporations cannot be imprisoned, but they can be fined. Of course, corporate directors and officers can be imprisoned, and in recent years, many have faced criminal penalties for their own actions or for the actions of employees under their supervision.

The question in the following case was whether a corporation could be convicted for its employee's criminal negligence.

CASE 11.2   Commonwealth v. Angelo Todesca Corp.

Supreme Judicial Court of Massachusetts, 2006.
446 Mass. 128,
842 N.E.2d 930.
www.findlaw.com/11stategov/ma/maca.html[a]

BACKGROUND AND FACTS Brian Gauthier worked as a truck driver for Angelo Todesca Corporation, a trucking and paving company. During 2000, Gauthier drove a ten-wheel tri-axle dump truck, which was designated AT-56. Angelo's safety manual required its trucks to be equipped with back-up alarms, which were to sound automatically whenever the

a. In the "Supreme Court Opinions" section, in the "2006" row, click on "March." When that page opens, scroll to the name of the case and click on its docket number to access the opinion.

vehicles were in reverse gear. In November, Gauthier discovered that AT-56's alarm was missing. Angelo ordered a new alarm. Meanwhile, Gauthier continued to drive AT-56. On December 1, Angelo assigned Gauthier to haul asphalt to a work site in Centerville, Massachusetts. At the site, as Gauthier backed up AT-56 to dump its load, he struck a police officer who was directing traffic through the site and facing away from the truck. The officer died of his injuries. The Commonwealth of Massachusetts charged Gautier and Angelo in a Massachusetts state court with, among other wrongful acts, motor vehicle homicide. Angelo was convicted and fined $2,500. Angelo appealed, and a state intermediate appellate court reversed the conviction. The state appealed to the Massachusetts Supreme Judicial Court, the state's highest court.

IN THE WORDS OF THE COURT . . . SPINA, J. [Justice]

* * * *

* * * To prove that a corporation is guilty of a criminal offense, the Commonwealth must prove the following three elements beyond a reasonable doubt: (1) that an individual committed a criminal offense; (2) that at the time of committing the offense, the indi-

vidual was engaged in some particular corporate business or project; and (3) that the individual had been vested by the corporation with the authority to act for it, and on its behalf, in carrying out that particular corporate business or project when the offense occurred.

* * * [On this appeal] the essence of the defendant's arguments deals with the first element of corporate criminal liability: namely, the requirement that an employee committed a criminal offense. The defendant maintains that a corporation never can be criminally liable for motor vehicle homicide * * * because * * * a "corporation" cannot "operate" a vehicle. The Commonwealth, however, argues that corporate liability is necessarily vicarious, and that a corporation can be held accountable for criminal acts committed by its agents, including negligent operation of a motor vehicle causing the death of another, if the elements of corporate criminal liability discussed above are satisfied.

We agree with the Commonwealth. Because a corporation is not a living person, it can act only through its agents. By the defendant's reasoning, a corporation never could be liable for any crime. A "corporation" can no more serve alcohol to minors, or bribe government officials, or falsify data on loan applications, than operate a vehicle negligently: only human agents, acting for the corporation, are capable of these actions. *Nevertheless, * * * a corporation may be criminally liable for such acts when performed by corporate employees, acting within the scope of their employment and on behalf of the corporation. * * ** [Emphasis added.]

The defendant further contends that it cannot be found vicariously [indirectly] liable for the victim's death because corporate criminal liability requires criminal conduct by the agent, which is lacking in this case. Operating a truck without a back-up alarm, the defendant notes, is not a criminal act: no State or Federal statute requires that a vehicle be equipped with such a device. Although the defendant is correct that criminal conduct of an agent is necessary before criminal liability may be imputed to the corporation, it mischaracterizes the agent's conduct in this case. Gauthier's criminal act, and the conduct imputed to the defendant, was not simply backing up without an alarm, as the defendant contends; rather, the criminal conduct was Gauthier's negligent operation of the defendant's truck, resulting in the victim's death * * * . Clearly, a corporation cannot be criminally liable for acts of employee negligence that are not criminal; however, [a Massachusetts state statute] criminalizes negligence in a very specific context (the operation of a motor vehicle on a public way) and with a specific outcome (resulting in death). Furthermore, nothing in that statute requires that the negligence be based on a statutory violation; the fact that a back-up alarm is not required by statute, then, is irrelevant to the issue whether vehicular homicide committed by an employee can be imputed to the corporation. If a corporate employee violates [this statute] while engaged in corporate business that the employee has been authorized to conduct, we can see no reason why the corporation cannot be vicariously liable for the crime.

DECISION AND REMEDY The Massachusetts Supreme Judicial Court affirmed Angelo's conviction. The court recognized that a corporation is not a "living person" and "can act only through its agents," which may include its employees. The court reasoned that if an employee commits a crime "while engaged in corporate business that the employee has been authorized to conduct," a corporation can be held liable for the crime.

WHY IS THIS CASE IMPORTANT? *Other states' courts that have considered the question at issue in this case have concluded that a corporation may be criminally liable for vehicular homicide under those states' statutes. This was the first case in which Massachusetts state courts determined the question under a Massachusetts statute.*

CORPORATE MANAGEMENT–SHAREHOLDERS

The acquisition of a share of stock makes a person an owner and shareholder in a corporation. Shareholders thus own the corporation. Although they have no legal title to corporate property, such as buildings and equipment, they do have an *equitable* (ownership) interest in the firm.

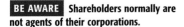
BE AWARE Shareholders normally are not agents of their corporations.

As a general rule, shareholders have no responsibility for the daily management of the corporation, although they are ultimately responsible for choosing the board of directors, which does have such control. Ordinarily, corporate officers and other employees owe no direct duty to individual shareholders. Their duty is to the corporation as a whole. A director, however, is in a fiduciary relationship to the corporation and therefore serves the interests of the shareholders. Generally, there is no legal relationship between shareholders and creditors of the corporation. Shareholders can, in fact, be creditors of the corporation and thus have the same rights of recovery against the corporation as any other creditor.

In this section, we look at the powers and voting rights of shareholders, which are generally established in the articles of incorporation and under the state's general incorporation law.

Shareholders' Powers

Shareholders must approve fundamental corporate changes before the changes can be effected. Hence, shareholders are empowered to amend the articles of incorporation (charter) and bylaws, approve a merger or the dissolution of the corporation, and approve the sale of all or substantially all of the corporation's assets. Some of these powers are subject to prior board approval.

Directors are elected to (and removed from) the board of directors by a vote of the shareholders. The first board of directors is either named in the articles of incorporation or chosen by the incorporators to serve until the first share-

BMW automobiles are inspected at a plant in the United States. BMW is classified as an alien corporation. What is the difference between an alien corporation and a foreign corporation? (McIntyre, Photo Researchers)

holders' meeting. From that time on, the selection and retention of directors are exclusively shareholder functions.

Directors usually serve their full terms; if the directors are unsatisfactory, they are simply not reelected. Shareholders have the inherent power, however, to remove a director from office *for cause* (breach of duty or misconduct) by a majority vote.[5] Some state statutes (and some corporate charters) even permit removal of directors *without cause* by the vote of a majority of the holders of outstanding shares entitled to vote.

Shareholders' Meetings

Shareholders' meetings must occur at least annually, and additional, special meetings can be called as needed to take care of urgent matters. Because it is usually not practical for owners of only a few shares of stock of publicly traded corporations to attend shareholders' meetings, such stockholders normally give third parties written authorization to vote their shares at the meeting. This authorization is called a **proxy** (from the Latin *procurare,* "to manage, take care of"). Proxies are often solicited by management, but any person can solicit proxies to concentrate voting power.

Shareholder Voting   For shareholders to act during a meeting, a quorum must be present. (A **quorum** is the minimum number of members of a body of officials or other group that must be present in order for business to be validly transacted.) Generally, a quorum exists when shareholders holding more than 50 percent of the outstanding shares are present. Corporate business matters are presented in the form of *resolutions,* which shareholders vote to approve or disapprove. Some state statutes have set forth specific voting requirements, and corporations' articles or bylaws must abide by these statutory requirements. Some states provide that the unanimous written consent of shareholders is a permissible alternative to holding a shareholders' meeting.

Once a quorum is present, voting can proceed. A majority vote of the shares represented at the meeting is usually required to pass resolutions. At times, more than a simple majority vote will be required either by a statute or by the corporate charter. Extraordinary corporate matters, such as a merger, consolidation, or dissolution of the corporation, require a higher percentage of the representatives of all corporate shares entitled to vote, not just a majority of those present at that particular meeting.

Cumulative Voting   Most states permit or even require shareholders to elect directors by *cumulative voting,* a method of voting designed to allow minority shareholders representation on the board of directors. When cumulative voting is allowed or required, the number of members of the board to be elected is multiplied by the total number of voting shares. The result equals the number of votes a shareholder has, and this total can be cast for one or more nominees for director. All nominees stand for election at the same time. When cumulative voting is not required either by statute or under the articles, the entire board can be elected by a simple majority of shares at a shareholders' meeting.

| **Example #2**   Suppose that a corporation has 10,000 shares issued and outstanding. One group of shareholders (the minority shareholders) holds only

PROXY
In corporation law, a written agreement between a stockholder and another under which the stockholder authorizes the other to vote the stockholder's shares in a certain manner.

QUORUM
The number of members of a decision-making body that must be present before business may be transacted.

BE CAREFUL   Once a quorum is present, a vote can be taken even if some shareholders leave without casting their votes.

---

5. A director can often demand court review of removal for cause.

3,000 shares, and the other group of shareholders (the majority shareholders) holds the other 7,000 shares. Three members of the board are to be elected. The majority shareholders' nominees are Acevedo, Barkley, and Craycik. The minority shareholders' nominee is Drake. Can Drake be elected by the minority shareholders?

If cumulative voting is allowed, the answer is yes. The minority shareholders have 9,000 votes among them (the number of directors to be elected times the number of shares held by the minority shareholders equals 3 times 3,000, which equals 9,000 votes). All of these votes can be cast to elect Drake. The majority shareholders have 21,000 votes (3 times 7,000 equals 21,000 votes), but these votes have to be distributed among their three nominees. The principle of cumulative voting is that no matter how the majority shareholders cast their 21,000 votes, they will not be able to elect all three directors if the minority shareholders cast all of their 9,000 votes for Drake, as illustrated in Exhibit 11–2.

CORPORATE MANAGEMENT–DIRECTORS

A corporation typically is governed by a board of directors. Subject to statutory limitations, the number of directors is set forth in the corporation's articles or bylaws.

Election of Directors

The first board of directors is normally appointed by the incorporators on the creation of the corporation, or directors are named by the corporation itself in the articles. The initial board serves until the first annual shareholders' meeting. Subsequent directors are elected by a majority vote of the shareholders.

The term of office for a director is usually one year—from annual meeting to annual meeting. Longer and staggered terms are permissible under most state statutes. A common practice is to elect one-third of the board members each year for a three-year term. In this way, there is greater management continuity.

More than 50 percent of the publicly traded companies in the United States are incorporated under Delaware law.[6] Consequently, decisions of the Delaware

---

6. *Publicly traded* means that the stock of a company can be bought and sold among members of the general public. In contrast, the shares of a *closely held*, or *close*, *corporation* are often owned by only a few individuals whose right to buy or sell those shares may be restricted, at least initially, to each other.

EXHIBIT 11–2   RESULTS OF CUMULATIVE VOTING

This exhibit illustrates how cumulative voting gives minority shareholders a greater chance of electing a director of their choice. By casting all of their 9,000 votes for one candidate (Drake), the minority shareholders will succeed in electing Drake to the board of directors.

BALLOT	MAJORITY SHAREHOLDERS' VOTES			MINORITY SHAREHOLDERS' VOTES	DIRECTORS ELECTED
	Acevedo	Barkley	Craycik	Drake	
1	10,000	10,000	1,000	9,000	Acevedo/Barkley/Drake
2	9,001	9,000	2,999	9,000	Acevedo/Barkley/Drake
3	6,000	7,000	8,000	9,000	Barkley/Craycik/Drake

courts on questions of corporate law have a wide impact. In the following case, a board increased the number of its members to diminish the effect that subsequently elected directors would have on the board's decisions. This may have been acceptable under the firm's bylaws, but was it valid under Delaware law?

CASE 11.3 **MM Companies, Inc. v. Liquid Audio, Inc.**

Delaware Supreme Court, 2003.
813 A.2d 1118.

COMPANY PROFILE *Liquid Audio, Inc. (***www.liquidaudio. com***), is a Delaware corporation, with its principal place of business in Redwood City, California. Liquid Audio provides software and services for the delivery of music over the Internet. Formed in 1996, Liquid Audio offered the first digital music-commerce system featuring copy protection and copyright management, as well as the first and largest digital music-distribution network. Liquid Audio's catalogue of secure music downloads is one of the world's largest.*

BACKGROUND AND FACTS MM Companies, Inc., a Delaware corporation with its principal place of business in New York City, owned 7 percent of Liquid Audio's stock. In

October 2001, MM sent a letter to Liquid Audio's board of directors offering to buy all of the company's stock for about $3 per share. The board rejected the offer. Liquid Audio's bylaws provide for a board of five directors divided into three classes; one class is elected each year. The next election, at which two directors would be chosen, was set for September 2002. By mid-August, it appeared that MM's nominees, Seymour Holtzman and James Mitarotonda, would win the election. The board amended the bylaws to increase the number of directors to seven and appointed Judith Frank and James Somes to fill the new positions. In September, MM's nominees were elected to the board, but their influence was diminished because there were now seven directors. MM filed a suit in a Delaware state court against Liquid Audio and others, challenging the board's actions. The court ruled in favor of the defendants. MM appealed to the Delaware Supreme Court.

IN THE WORDS OF THE COURT . . . HOLLAND, Justice.

* * * *

The most fundamental principles of corporate governance are a function of the allocation of power within a corporation between its stockholders and its board of directors. The stockholders' power is the right to vote on specific matters, in particular, in an election of directors. The power of managing the corporate enterprise is vested in the shareholders' duly elected board representatives. * * *

Maintaining a proper balance in the allocation of power between the stockholders' right to elect directors and the board of directors' right to manage the corporation is dependent upon the stockholders' unimpeded right to vote effectively in an election of directors. * * * [Emphasis added.]

* * * *

When the *primary purpose* of a board of directors' [action] is to interfere with or impede the effective exercise of the shareholder franchise in a contested election for directors, the board must first demonstrate a compelling justification for such action as a condition precedent to any judicial consideration of reasonableness and proportionality. * * * [S]uch * * * actions by a board need not actually prevent the shareholders from attaining any success in seating one or more nominees in a contested election for directors and the election contest need not involve a challenge for outright control of the board of directors. * * * [T]he * * * actions of the board only need to be taken for the primary purpose of interfering with or impeding the effectiveness of the stockholder vote in a contested election for directors.

* * * *

* * * [In this case, the directors] amended the bylaws to provide for a board of seven and appointed two additional members of the Board for the primary purpose of

CASE 11.3–CONTINUED ▶

diminishing the influence of MM's two nominees * * * . That * * * action * * * compromised the essential role of corporate democracy in maintaining the proper allocation of power between the shareholders and the Board, because that action was taken in the context of a contested election for successor directors. Since the * * * Defendants did not demonstrate a compelling justification for that * * * action, the bylaw amendment that expanded the size of the Liquid Audio board, and permitted the appointment of two new members on the eve of a contested election, should have been invalidated.

DECISION AND REMEDY   The Delaware Supreme Court reversed the judgment of the lower court and remanded the case for further proceedings. The state supreme court concluded that the board's amending the bylaws to increase the number of directors and filling the new positions with appointments was invalid, because the board acted primarily to impede the shareholders' right to vote in an impending election for successor directors.

FOR CRITICAL ANALYSIS–Political Consideration   *How could MM's newly elected nominees, or any two directors, affect the decisions of a five-member board?*

Directors' Qualifications and Compensation

Few legal requirements exist concerning directors' qualifications. Only a handful of states impose minimum age and residency requirements. A director is sometimes a shareholder, but this is not a necessary qualification—unless, of course, statutory provisions or corporate articles or bylaws require ownership.

Compensation for directors is ordinarily specified in the corporate articles or bylaws. Because directors have a fiduciary relationship to the shareholders and to the corporation, an express agreement or provision for compensation often is necessary for them to receive money from the funds that they control and for which they have responsibilities.

Board of Directors' Meetings

The board of directors conducts business by holding formal meetings with recorded minutes. The date on which regular meetings are held is usually established in the articles or bylaws or by board resolution, and no further notice is customarily required. Special meetings can be called, with notice sent to all directors.

Quorum requirements can vary among jurisdictions. Many states leave decisions regarding quorum requirements to the corporate articles or bylaws. In the absence of specific state statutes, most states provide that a quorum is a majority of the number of directors authorized in the articles or bylaws. Voting is done in person (unlike voting at shareholders' meetings, which can be done by proxy, as discussed earlier in this chapter).[7] The rule is one vote per director. Ordinary matters generally require a simple majority vote; certain extraordinary issues may require a greater-than-majority vote.

Directors' Management Responsibilities

Directors have responsibility for all policymaking decisions necessary to the management of corporate affairs. Just as shareholders cannot act individually to bind the corporation, the directors must act as a body in carrying out routine corpo-

---

7. Except in Louisiana, which allows a director to vote by proxy under certain circumstances.

rate business. One director has one vote, and generally the majority rules. The general areas of responsibility of the board of directors include the following:

1. Declaration and payment of corporate dividends to shareholders.
2. Authorization for major corporate policy decisions—for example, the initiation of proceedings for the sale or lease of corporate assets outside the regular course of business, the determination of new product lines, and the supervision of major contract negotiations and major management-labor negotiations.
3. Appointment, supervision, and removal of corporate officers and other managerial employees and the determination of their compensation.
4. Financial decisions, such as the issuance of authorized shares and bonds.

The board of directors can delegate some of its functions to an executive committee or to corporate officers. In doing so, the board is not relieved of its overall responsibility for directing the affairs of the corporation, but corporate officers and managerial personnel are empowered to make decisions relating to ordinary, daily corporate affairs within well-defined guidelines.

Role of Officers and Directors

A director occupies a position of responsibility unlike that of other corporate personnel. Directors are sometimes inappropriately characterized as *agents* (see Chapter 13) because they act on behalf of the corporation. No *individual* director, however, can act as an agent to bind the corporation; and as a group, directors collectively control the corporation in a way that no agent is able to control a principal.

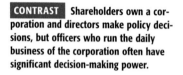

CONTRAST Shareholders own a corporation and directors make policy decisions, but officers who run the daily business of the corporation often have significant decision-making power.

Officers and Executive Employees The officers and other executive employees are hired by the board of directors or, in rare instances, by the shareholders. In addition to carrying out the duties articulated in the bylaws, corporate

Corporate executives discuss the business of their firm. How do the rights and duties of corporate officers differ from those of corporate directors? (PhotoDisc)

and managerial officers act as agents of the corporation, and the ordinary rules of agency (discussed in Chapter 13) normally apply to their employment. The qualifications required of officers and executive employees are determined at the discretion of the corporation and are included in the articles or bylaws. In most states, a person can hold more than one office and can be both an officer and a director of the corporation.

Fiduciary Duties   Directors and officers have *fiduciary duties* to the corporation, because their relationship with the corporation and its shareholders is one of trust and confidence. The term *fiduciary* is from a Latin root word meaning "faithful." The fiduciary duties of the directors and officers include the duty of care and the duty of loyalty. The duty of care requires directors and officers to be honest and use prudent business judgment in the conduct of corporate affairs. Directors and officers must carry out their responsibilities in an informed, businesslike manner. The duty of loyalty requires the subordination of the self-interest of the directors and officers to the interest of the corporation. In general, it prohibits directors and officers from using corporate funds or confidential corporate information for personal advantage. Directors and officers can be held liable to the corporation and to the shareholders for breach of either of these duties.

A breach of the duty of loyalty occurs when an officer or director, for his or her personal gain, takes advantage of a business opportunity that is financially within the corporation's reach, is in line with the firm's business, is to the firm's practical advantage, and is one in which the corporation has an interest.

Conflicts of Interest

The duty of loyalty also requires officers and directors to disclose fully to the board of directors any possible conflict of interest that might occur in conducting corporate transactions. The various state statutes contain different standards, but a contract will generally *not* be voidable if it was fair and reasonable to the corporation at the time it was made, if there was a full disclosure of the interest of the officers or directors involved in the transaction, and if the contract was approved by a majority of the disinterested directors or shareholders.

| **Example #3**   Southwood Corporation needs more office space. Lambert Alden, one of its five directors, owns the building adjoining the corporation's main office building. He negotiates a lease with Southwood for the space, making a full disclosure to Southwood and the other four board directors. The lease arrangement is fair and reasonable, and it is unanimously approved by the corporation's board of directors. In this situation, Alden has not breached his duty of loyalty to the corporation, and the contract is thus valid. The rule is one of reason. If it were otherwise, directors would be prevented from ever giving financial assistance to the corporations they serve. |

The Business Judgment Rule

Directors and officers are expected to exercise due care and to use their best judgment in guiding corporate management, but they are not insurers of business success. Honest mistakes of judgment and poor business decisions on their part do not make them liable to the corporation for resulting damages. This is the **business judgment rule.** The rule generally immunizes directors and officers from liability for the consequences of a decision that is within mana-

> " It is not the crook in modern business that we fear but the honest man who does not know what he is doing. "
> —OWEN D. YOUNG, 1874–1962
> (American corporate executive and public official)

BUSINESS JUDGMENT RULE
A rule that immunizes corporate management from liability for actions that result in corporate losses or damages if the actions are undertaken in good faith and are within both the power of the corporation and the authority of management to make.

gerial authority, as long as the decision complies with management's fiduciary duties and as long as acting on the decision is within the powers of the corporation. Consequently, if there is a reasonable basis for a business decision, it is unlikely that the court will interfere with that decision, even if the corporation suffers as a result.

To benefit from the rule, directors and officers must act in good faith, in what they consider to be the best interests of the corporation, and with the care that an ordinarily prudent person in a similar position would exercise in similar circumstances. This requires an informed decision, with a rational basis, and with no conflict between the decision maker's personal interest and the interest of the corporation. To be informed, the director or officer must do what is necessary to become informed: attend presentations, ask for information from those who have it, read reports, review other written materials such as contracts—in other words, carefully study a situation and its alternatives.

To be free of conflicting interests, the director must not engage in self-dealing. **| Example #4** A director should not oppose a *tender offer* (an offer to purchase shares in the company made by another company directly to the shareholders) that is in the corporation's best interest simply because its acceptance may cost the director her or his position. Similarly, a director should not accept a tender offer with only a moment's consideration based solely on the market price of the corporation's shares.**|**

> " All business proceeds on beliefs, or judgments of probabilities, and not on certainties. "
>
> —CHARLES ELIOT, 1834–1916
> (American educator and editor)

RIGHTS AND DUTIES OF OFFICERS AND MANAGERS

The rights of corporate officers and other high-level managers are defined by employment contracts, because these persons are employees of the company. Corporate officers normally can be removed by the board of directors at any time with or without cause and regardless of the terms of the employment contracts—although in so doing, the corporation may be liable for breach of contract. The duties of corporate officers are the same as those of directors, because both groups are involved in decision making and are in similar positions of control. Hence, officers are viewed as having the same fiduciary duties of care and loyalty in their conduct of corporate affairs as directors have.

RIGHTS OF SHAREHOLDERS

Shareholders possess numerous rights. A significant right—the right to vote their shares—has already been discussed. We now look at some additional rights of shareholders.

Stock Certificates

A **stock certificate** is a certificate issued by a corporation that evidences ownership of a specified number of shares in the corporation. Stock is intangible personal property, and the ownership right exists independently of the certificate itself. A stock certificate may be lost or destroyed, but ownership is not destroyed with it. A new certificate can be issued to replace one that has been lost or destroyed.[8] Notice of shareholders' meetings, dividends, and operational

STOCK CERTIFICATE
A certificate issued by a corporation evidencing the ownership of a specified number of shares in the corporation.

Stock certificates are displayed. To be a shareholder, is it necessary to have physical possession of a certificate? Why or why not? (Amy C. Etra/PhotoEdit)

---

8. For a lost or destroyed certificate to be reissued, a shareholder normally must furnish an indemnity bond to protect the corporation against potential loss should the original certificate reappear at some future time in the hands of a bona fide purchaser [UCC 8–302, 8–405(2)].

and financial reports are all distributed according to the recorded ownership listed in the corporation's books, not on the basis of possession of the certificate.

Preemptive Rights

A **preemptive right** is a common law concept under which a preference is given to shareholders over all other purchasers to subscribe to or purchase shares of a *new issue* of stock in proportion to the percentage of total shares they already hold. This allows each shareholder to maintain his or her portion of control, voting power, or financial interest in the corporation. Most statutes either (1) grant preemptive rights but allow them to be negated in the corporation's articles or (2) deny preemptive rights except to the extent that they are granted in the articles. The result is that the articles of incorporation determine the existence and scope of preemptive rights. Generally, preemptive rights apply only to additional, newly issued stock sold for cash, and the preemptive rights must be exercised within a specified time period (usually thirty days).

| **Example #5**   Tran Corporation authorizes and issues 1,000 shares of stock. Lebow purchases 100 shares, making her the owner of 10 percent of the company's stock. Subsequently, Tran, by vote of its shareholders, authorizes the issuance of another 1,000 shares (amending the articles of incorporation). This increases its capital stock to a total of 2,000 shares. If preemptive rights have been provided, Lebow can purchase one additional share of the new stock being issued for each share she already owns—or 100 additional shares. Thus, she can own 200 of the 2,000 shares outstanding, and she will maintain her relative position as a shareholder. If preemptive rights are not allowed, her proportionate control and voting power may be diluted from that of a 10 percent shareholder to that of a 5 percent shareholder because of the issuance of the additional 1,000 shares. |

Preemptive rights are most important in close corporations because each shareholder owns a relatively small number of shares but controls a substantial interest in the corporation. Without preemptive rights, it would be possible for a shareholder to lose his or her proportionate control over the firm.

Dividends

As mentioned earlier in this chapter, a *dividend* is a distribution of corporate profits or income ordered by the directors and paid to the shareholders in proportion to their respective shares in the corporation. Dividends can be paid in cash, property, stock of the corporation that is paying the dividends, or stock of other corporations.[9]

State laws vary, but each state determines the general circumstances and legal requirements under which dividends are paid. State laws also control the sources of revenue to be used; only certain funds are legally available for paying dividends.

Illegal Dividends   A dividend paid while the corporation is insolvent is automatically an illegal dividend, and shareholders may be liable for returning the

---

9. Technically, dividends paid in stock are not dividends. They maintain each shareholder's proportional interest in the corporation. On one occasion, a distillery declared and paid a "dividend" in bonded whiskey.

payment to the corporation or its creditors. Furthermore, as just discussed, dividends that are improperly paid from an unauthorized account may be illegal. Whenever dividends are illegal or improper, the board of directors can be held personally liable for the amount of the payment. When directors can show that a shareholder knew that a dividend was illegal when it was received, however, the directors are entitled to reimbursement from the shareholder.

Directors' Failure to Declare a Dividend   When directors fail to declare a dividend, shareholders can ask a court to compel the directors to meet and to declare a dividend. For the shareholders to succeed, they must show that the directors have acted so unreasonably in withholding the dividend that the directors' conduct is an abuse of their discretion.

Often, large cash reserves are accumulated for a bona fide purpose, such as expansion, research, or other legitimate corporate goals. The mere fact that sufficient corporate earnings or surplus is available to pay a dividend is not enough to compel directors to distribute funds that, in the board's opinion, should not be paid. The courts are reluctant to interfere with corporate operations and will not compel directors to declare dividends unless abuse of discretion is clearly shown.

Inspection Rights

Shareholders in a corporation enjoy both common law and statutory inspection rights. The shareholder's right of inspection is limited, however, to the inspection and copying of corporate books and records for a *proper purpose*, provided the request is made in advance. The shareholder can inspect in person, or an attorney, agent, accountant, or other type of assistant can do so.

Transfer of Shares

Stock certificates generally are negotiable and freely transferable by indorsement and delivery. Transfer of stock in closely held corporations, however, usually is restricted by the bylaws, by a restriction stamped on the stock certificate, or by a shareholder agreement. The existence of any restrictions on transferability must always be noted on the face of the stock certificate, and these restrictions must be reasonable.

Sometimes, corporations or their shareholders restrict transferability by reserving the option to purchase any shares offered for resale by a shareholder. This **right of first refusal** remains with the corporation or the shareholders for only a specified time or a reasonable time. Variations on the purchase option are possible. For example, a shareholder might be required to offer the shares to other shareholders first or to the corporation first.

RIGHT OF FIRST REFUSAL
The right to purchase personal or real property—such as corporate shares or real estate—before the property is offered for sale to others.

Shareholder's Derivative Suit

When those in control of a corporation—the corporate directors—fail to sue in the corporate name to redress a wrong suffered by the corporation, shareholders are permitted to do so "derivatively" in what is known as a **shareholder's derivative suit.** Some wrong must have been done to the corporation, and before a derivative suit can be brought, the shareholders must first state their complaint to the board of directors. Only if the directors fail to solve the problem or fail to take appropriate action can the derivative suit go forward.

SHAREHOLDER'S DERIVATIVE SUIT
A suit brought by a shareholder to enforce a corporate cause of action against a third person.

The right of shareholders to bring a derivative action is especially important when the wrong suffered by the corporation results from the actions of corporate directors or officers. This is because the directors and officers would probably want to prevent any action against themselves. (For a discussion of shareholder's suits in other nations, see this chapter's *Beyond Our Borders* feature.)

The shareholder's derivative suit is unusual in that those suing are not pursuing rights or benefits for themselves personally but are acting as guardians of the corporate entity. Therefore, any damages recovered by the suit normally go into the corporation's treasury, not to the shareholders personally. This is true even if the company is a small, closely held corporation. **| Example #6** Zeon Corporation is owned by two shareholders, each holding 50 percent of the corporate shares. Suppose that one of the shareholders wants to sue the other for misusing corporate assets or usurping corporate opportunities. The plaintiff-shareholder will have to bring a shareholder's derivative suit (not a suit in his or her own name) because the alleged harm was suffered by Zeon, not by the plaintiff personally. Any damages awarded will go to the corporation, not to the plaintiff-shareholder.**|**

LIABILITY OF SHAREHOLDERS

One of the hallmarks of the corporate organization is that shareholders are not personally liable for the debts of the corporation. If the corporation fails, shareholders can lose their investments, but that is generally the limit of their liability.

Disregarding the Corporate Entity

In some unusual situations, a corporate entity is used by its owners to perpetrate a fraud, circumvent the law, or in some other way accomplish an illegitimate objective. In these cases, the court will ignore the corporate structure and *pierce the corporate veil,* thus exposing the shareholders to personal liability [RMBCA 2.04]. In other words, when the facts show that great injustice would result from the use of a corporation to avoid individual responsibility, a court will look behind the corporate structure to the individual stockholder.

The following are some of the factors that may cause the courts to pierce the corporate veil:

1. A party is tricked or misled into dealing with the corporation rather than the individual.
2. The corporation is set up never to make a profit or always to be insolvent, or it is too "thinly" capitalized—that is, it has insufficient capital at the time it is formed to meet its prospective debts or potential liabilities.
3. Statutory corporate formalities, such as holding required corporation meetings, are not followed.
4. Personal and corporate interests are mixed together, or *commingled,* to the extent that the corporation has no separate identity.

Although they are rare, certain other instances arise where a shareholder can be personally liable. One relates to illegal dividends, which were discussed previously. Two others relate to *stock subscriptions* and *watered stock,* which we discuss here.

BEYOND OUR BORDERS
Derivative Actions in Other Nations

Today, most of the claims brought against directors and officers are those alleged in shareholders' derivative suits. Other nations, however, are more restrictive in regard to the use of such suits. In Germany, for example, there is no provision for derivative litigation, and a corporation's duty to its employees is just as significant as its duty to the shareholder-owners of the company. The United Kingdom has no statute authorizing derivative actions, which are permitted only to challenge directors' actions that the shareholders could not legally ratify. Japan authorizes derivative actions but also permits a company to bring a suit against the shareholder-plaintiff for damages if the action is unsuccessful.

For Critical Analysis *Do corporations benefit from shareholders' derivative suits? If so, how?*

Stock-Subscription Agreements

Sometimes stock-subscription agreements—written contracts by which one agrees to buy capital stock of a corporation—exist prior to incorporation. Normally, these agreements are treated as continuing offers and are irrevocable (for up to six months under RMBCA 6.20). Once the corporation has been formed, it can sell shares to shareholder investors. In either situation, once the subscription agreement or stock offer is accepted, a binding contract is formed. Any refusal to pay constitutes a breach resulting in the personal liability of the shareholder.

Shares of stock can be paid for by property or by services rendered instead of cash. They cannot be purchased with promissory notes, however. The general rule is that for **par-value shares** (shares that have a specific face value, or formal cash-in value, written on them, such as one penny or one dollar), the corporation must receive a value at least equal to the par-value amount. For **no-par shares** (shares that have no face value—no specific amount printed on their face), the corporation must receive the value of the shares as determined by the board or the shareholders when the stock was issued.

PAR-VALUE SHARES
Corporate shares that have a specific face value, or formal cash-in value, written on them, such as one dollar.

NO-PAR SHARES
Corporate shares that have no face value—that is, no specific dollar amount is printed on their face.

Watered Stock

When the corporation issues shares for less than the values stated above, the shares are referred to as **watered stock.**[10] Usually, the shareholder who receives watered stock must pay the difference to the corporation (the shareholder is personally liable). In some states, the shareholder who receives watered stock may be liable to creditors of the corporation for unpaid corporate debts.

WATERED STOCK
Shares of stock issued by a corporation for which the corporation receives, as payment, less than the stated value of the shares.

DUTIES OF MAJORITY SHAREHOLDERS

In some cases, a majority shareholder is regarded as having a fiduciary duty to the corporation and to the minority shareholders. This occurs when a single shareholder (or a few shareholders acting in concert) owns a sufficient number

---

10. The phrase *watered stock* was originally used to describe cattle that—kept thirsty during a long drive—were allowed to drink large quantities of water just prior to their sale. The increased weight of the "watered stock" allowed the seller to reap a higher profit.

of shares to exercise *de facto* control over the corporation. In these situations, majority shareholders owe a fiduciary duty to the minority shareholders when they sell their shares, because such a sale would be, in fact, a transfer of control of the corporation.

A breach of fiduciary duties by those who control a closely held corporation may constitute *oppressive conduct*. The court in the following case was asked to review a pattern of allegedly oppressive conduct by the person in control and determine whether that conduct fell within a two-year statute of limitations.

CASE 11.4   **Robbins v. Sanders**

Supreme Court of Alabama, 2004.
890 So.2d 998.

BACKGROUND AND FACTS   James and Mary Bailey owned fifty-three acres of land, subject to mortgages totaling $450,000, in Birmingham, Alabama. The Baileys rented buildings on the property and used part of the land as a landfill. In 1988, an underground fire broke out in the landfill. Pete Robbins offered to extinguish the fire and to pay the mortgages. The parties formed Corridor Enterprises, Inc., to which the Baileys contributed the land. Half of the stock—one thousand shares—was issued to Robbins. In 1991, the Baileys agreed to sell their thousand shares to Robbins at the rate of two shares per month. The Baileys both died in 1997. Terrill Sanders was appointed administrator of their estates. Over the next twelve months, Sanders had problems obtaining information from Robbins and uncovered discrepancies in Corridor's corporate records. On the estates' behalf, Sanders filed a suit in an Alabama state court, alleging, among other things, oppression of minority shareholders. The court assessed more than $4 million in damages against Robbins, who appealed to the Alabama Supreme Court, arguing in part that a two-year statute of limitations barred the suit.

IN THE WORDS OF THE COURT ... *PER CURIAM.* [By the whole court]

* * * *

Robbins argues that the claims asserted by the estates * * * are barred by the two-year statute of limitations found in [Alabama Code] Section 6-2-38. He argues that the "undisputed evidence" presented at trial established that, more than two years before this action was filed, the Baileys had "such knowledge * * * sufficient to provoke inquiry in reasonable minds which would have led to the facts on which the claims in this action are based." We reject this argument.

* * * James Bailey and Mary Bailey have not asserted personal claims against Robbins. The claims of breach * * * [and] oppression asserted in this action were asserted by the estate of James Bailey and the estate of Mary Bailey, not by James Bailey and Mary Bailey. Thus, the issue to be considered is when the minority shareholders had knowledge of, or had reason to know of, the activities that resulted in their alleged injuries.

The estates of James Bailey and Mary Bailey became minority shareholders in Corridor Enterprises in 1997, after James and Mary died. The evidence established that Robbins engaged in * * * oppression * * * and that he attempted to squeeze out the minority shareholders after the estates became the minority shareholders in Corridor Enterprises. For example, in 1998, Robbins used funds of Corridor Enterprises to purchase real estate in his own name, to invest in other businesses in his own name, and to purchase personal property for himself; he refused to provide an accounting of the corporate finances when he was requested to do so; he failed to pay the corporate property and income taxes, failed to have tax returns prepared and filed, and failed to maintain proper corporate records; he entered into a contract to sell property belonging to Corridor Enterprises without notice to or approval of the minority shareholders; and he

CASE 11.4–CONTINUED

failed to declare dividends during the entire time the estates were shareholders while he paid himself an exorbitant salary and drained the corporate funds.

The minority shareholders filed their complaint on August 4, 1998, within approximately a year of becoming shareholders and in the same year that many of the above-described activities occurred. *Therefore, the estates' claims of * * * squeeze-out/ oppression were not time-barred to the extent those claims sought to recover damages for injuries occurring to the estates * * *.* [Emphasis added.]

* * * *

* * * However, every award of damages made by the trial court was "in favor of Corridor Enterprises, Inc., and the plaintiffs." * * *

Because each award of damages was made jointly to the corporation and to the minority shareholders, the manner in which the trial court structured its damages award is improper. We are unable to determine whether the trial court intended all or some portion of the awards made "in favor of Corridor Enterprises, Inc., and the plaintiffs" to represent a recovery for the estates on their claims * * *. We point out that we find * * * no error in the trial court's determination that Robbins is liable for oppression and attempting to squeeze out the minority shareholders (the estates). We simply find that the trial court's order, as it pertains to damages, is improper.

DECISION AND REMEDY The Alabama Supreme Court held that Sanders's claims on behalf of the Baileys' estates were timely. The court remanded the case, though, so that the lower court could clearly state how the damages should be apportioned among the estates and Corridor.[a]

a. For a summary of the components of the damages ultimately awarded, see *Robbins v. Sanders,* 927 So.2d 777 (Ala. 2005).

FOR CRITICAL ANALYSIS–Economic Consideration
What should be the basis for determining the specific amount of damages to be awarded the minority shareholders in this case?

REVIEWING . . . BUSINESS ORGANIZATIONS

David Brock is on the board of directors of Firm Body Fitness, Inc., which owns a string of fitness clubs in New Mexico. Brock owns 15 percent of the Firm Body stock, and he is also employed as a tanning technician at one of the fitness clubs. After the January financial report showed that Firm Body's tanning division was operating at a substantial net loss, the board of directors, led by Marty Levinson, discussed the possibility of terminating the tanning operations. Brock successfully convinced a majority of the board that the tanning division was necessary to market the clubs' overall fitness package. By April, the tanning division's financial losses had risen. The board hired a business analyst, who conducted surveys and determined that the tanning operations did not significantly increase membership. A shareholder, Diego Peñada, discovered that Brock owned stock in Sunglow, Inc., the company from which Firm Body purchased its tanning equipment, and he had not informed the other directors of this interest. Peñada notified Levinson, who privately reprimanded Brock. Using the information presented in the chapter, answer the following questions.

1. What duties did Brock, as a director, owe to Firm Body?

2. Does the fact that Brock owned shares in Sunglow establish a conflict of interest? Why or why not?

3. Suppose that Firm Body brought an action against Brock claiming that he had breached the duty of loyalty by not disclosing his interest in Sunglow to the other directors. Can Brock use the business judgment rule as a defense? Explain.

4. Now suppose that Firm Body did not file an action against Brock. What type of a lawsuit might Peñada be able to bring based on these facts?

KEY TERMS

alien corporation 370	general partner 354	preemptive right 380
articles of incorporation 367	limited liability	proxy 373
articles of organization 355	company (LLC) 355	quorum 373
business judgment rule 378	limited liability	retained earnings 368
bylaws 367	partnership (LLP) 359	right of first refusal 381
corporation 354	limited partner 354	S corporation 354
dividend 368	limited partnership 354	shareholder's derivative suit 381
domestic corporation 369	member 355	sole proprietorship 353
foreign corporation 370	no-par share 383	stock certificate 379
franchise 360	operating agreement 357	watered stock 383
franchisee 360	par-value share 383	
franchisor 360	partnership 353	

CHAPTER SUMMARY • BUSINESS ORGANIZATIONS

Major Traditional Business Forms (See pages 352–355.)	1. *Sole proprietorships*—The simplest form of business; used by anyone who does business without creating an organization. The owner is the business. The owner pays personal income taxes on all profits and is personally liable for all business debts.
	2. *Partnerships*—
	a. General partnerships—Created by agreement of the parties; not treated as an entity except for limited purposes. Partners have unlimited liability for partnership debts, and each partner normally has an equal voice in management. Income is "passed through" the partnership to the individual partners, who pay personal taxes on the income.
	b. Limited partnerships—Must be formed in compliance with statutory requirements. A limited partnership consists of one or more general partners, who have unlimited liability for partnership losses, and one or more limited partners, who are liable only to the extent of their contributions. Only general partners can participate in management.
	3. *Corporations*—A corporation is formed in compliance with statutory requirements, is a legal entity separate and distinct from its owners, and can have perpetual existence. The shareholder-owners elect directors, who set policy and hire officers to run the day-to-day business of the corporation. Shareholders normally are not personally liable for the debts of the corporation. The corporation pays income tax on net profits; shareholders pay income tax on disbursed dividends.
Limited Liability Companies (LLCs) (See pages 355–359.)	1. *Formation*—Articles of organization must be filed with the appropriate state office—usually the office of the secretary of state—setting forth the name of the business, its principal address, the names of the owners (called *members*), and other relevant information.
	2. *Advantages of the LLC*—Advantages of the LLC include limited liability, the option to be taxed as a partnership or as a corporation, and flexibility in deciding how the business will be managed and operated.
	3. *Operating agreement*—When an LLC is formed, the members decide, in an operating agreement, how the business will be managed and what rules will apply to the organization.
Limited Liability Partnerships (LLPs) (See pages 359–360.)	1. *Formation*—Articles must be filed with the appropriate state agency, usually the secretary of state's office. Typically, an LLP is formed by professionals who work together as partners in a partnership. Under most state LLP statutes, it is relatively easy to convert a traditional partnership into an LLP.

CHAPTER SUMMARY • BUSINESS ORGANIZATIONS—CONTINUED

Limited Liability Partnerships (LLPs)— Continued	2. *Liability of partners*—LLP statutes vary, but generally they allow professionals to avoid personal liability for the malpractice of other partners. Partners in an LLP continue to be liable for their own wrongful acts and for the wrongful acts of those whom they supervise.

Private Franchises (See pages 360–367.)	1. *Types of franchises*—
	
	  a. Distributorship (for example, automobile dealerships).
	
	  b. Chain-style operation (for example, fast-food chains).
	
	  c. Manufacturing/processing-plant arrangement (for example, soft-drink bottling companies, such as Coca-Cola).
	
	2. *Laws governing franchising*—Franchises are governed by contract law, occasionally by agency law, and by federal and state statutory and regulatory laws.
	
	3. *The franchise contract*—
	
	  a. Ordinarily requires the franchisee (purchaser) to pay a price for the franchise license.
	
	  b. Specifies the territory to be served by the franchisee's firm.
	
	  c. May require the franchisee to purchase certain supplies from the franchisor at an established price.
	
	  d. May require the franchisee to abide by certain standards of quality relating to the product or service offered but cannot set retail resale prices.
	
	  e. Usually provides for the date and/or conditions of termination of the franchise arrangement. Both federal and state statutes attempt to protect certain franchisees from franchisors who unfairly or arbitrarily terminate franchises.

The Nature of the Corporation (See pages 367–371.)	The corporation is a legal entity distinct from its owners. Formal statutory requirements, which vary somewhat from state to state, must be followed in forming a corporation. The corporation can have perpetual existence or be chartered for a specific period of time. 1. *Corporate personnel*—The shareholders own the corporation. They elect a board of directors to govern the corporation. The board of directors hires corporate officers and other employees to run the daily business of the firm. 2. *Corporate taxation*—The corporation pays income tax on net profits; shareholders pay income tax on the disbursed dividends that they receive from the corporation (double-taxation feature). 3. *Classification of corporations*—A corporation is referred to as a *domestic corporation* within its home state (the state in which it incorporates). A corporation is referred to as a *foreign corporation* by any state that is not its home state. A corporation is referred to as an *alien corporation* if it originates in another country but does business in the United States. 4. *Torts and criminal acts*—The corporation is liable for the torts committed by its agents or officers within the course and scope of their employment. In some circumstances, a corporation can be held liable (and be fined) for the criminal acts of its agents and employees. In certain situations, corporate officers may be held personally liable for corporate crimes.
Directors and Officers (See pages 374–379.)	1. *Election of directors*—The first board of directors is usually appointed by the incorporators; thereafter, directors are elected by the shareholders. Directors usually serve a one-year term, although longer and staggered terms are permitted under most state statutes. 2. *Directors' qualifications and compensation*—Few qualifications are mandated; a director can be a shareholder but is not required to be. Compensation is usually specified in the corporate articles or bylaws.

(Continued)

CHAPTER SUMMARY • BUSINESS ORGANIZATIONS–CONTINUED

Directors and Officers–Continued	3. *Board of directors' meetings*—The board of directors conducts business by holding formal meetings with recorded minutes. The date of regular meetings is usually established in the corporate articles or bylaws; special meetings can be called, with notice sent to all directors. Quorum requirements vary from state to state; usually, a quorum is the majority of the corporate directors. Voting must usually be done in person, and in ordinary matters only a majority vote is required.
	4. *Directors' management responsibilities*—Directors are responsible for declaring and paying corporate dividends to shareholders; authorizing major corporate decisions; appointing, supervising, and removing corporate officers and other managerial employees; determining employees' compensation; making financial decisions necessary to the management of corporate affairs; and issuing authorized shares and bonds. Directors may delegate some of their responsibilities to executive committees and corporate officers and executives.
	5. *Duties*—Directors are obligated to act in good faith, to use prudent business judgment in the conduct of corporate affairs, and to act in the corporation's best interests. Directors have a fiduciary duty to subordinate their own interests to those of the corporation in matters relating to the corporation. If a director fails to exercise these duties, he or she can be answerable to the corporation and to the shareholders for breaching the duties.
	6. *Business judgment rule*—This rule immunizes a director from liability for a corporate decision as long as the decision was within the powers of the corporation and the authority of the director to make and was an informed, reasonable, and loyal decision.
Shareholders (See pages 372–374 and 379–385.)	1. *Shareholders' meetings*—Shareholders' meetings must occur at least annually; special meetings can be called when necessary. Notice of the date, time, and place of the meeting (and its purpose, if it is specially called) must be sent to shareholders. Shareholders may vote by proxy (authorizing someone else to vote their shares) and may submit proposals to be included in the company's proxy materials sent to shareholders before meetings.
	2. *Shareholder voting*—A minimum number of shareholders (a quorum—generally, more than 50 percent of shares held) must be present at a meeting for business to be conducted; resolutions are passed (usually) by simple majority vote. Cumulative voting may or may not be required or permitted. Cumulative voting gives minority shareholders a better chance to be represented on the board of directors.
	3. *Shareholders' rights*—Shareholders have numerous rights, which may include the following: a. The right to a stock certificate and preemptive rights. b. The right to obtain a dividend (at the discretion of the directors). c. Voting rights. d. The right to inspect the corporate records. e. The right to sue on behalf of the corporation (bring a shareholder's derivative suit) when the directors fail to do so.
	4. *Shareholders' liability*—Shareholders may be liable for the retention of illegal dividends, for breach of a stock-subscription agreement, and for the value of watered stock.
	5. *Duties of majority shareholders*—In certain situations, majority shareholders may be regarded as having a fiduciary duty to minority shareholders and will be liable if that duty is breached.

FOR REVIEW

Answers for the even-numbered questions in this For Review *section can be found in Appendix O at the end of this text.*

1. Which form of business organization is the simplest?

2. What are some advantages and disadvantages of doing business as a partnership or a corporation, respectively?

3. How do limited liability companies and limited liability partnerships differ from traditional corporations and partnerships?

4. What is a franchise? What are the most common types of franchises?

5. What are the rights and duties of the directors and officers of a corporation? What are the rights of shareholders in a corporate enterprise?

QUESTIONS AND CASE PROBLEMS

11–1. Forms of Business Organization. In each of the following situations, determine whether Georgio's Fashions is a sole proprietorship, a partnership, a limited partnership, or a corporation.

1. Georgio's defaults on a payment to supplier Dee Creations. Dee sues Georgio's and each of the owners of Georgio's personally for payment of the debt.

2. Georgio's raises $200,000 through the sale of shares of its stock.

3. At tax time, Georgio's files a tax return with the IRS and pays taxes on the firm's net profits.

4. Georgio's is owned by three persons, two of whom are not allowed to participate in the firm's management.

Question with Sample Answer

11–2. Jorge, Marta, and Jocelyn are college graduates, and Jorge has come up with an idea for a new product that he believes could make the three of them very rich. His idea is to manufacture soft-drink dispensers for home use and market them to consumers throughout the Midwest. Jorge's personal experience qualifies him to be both first-line supervisor and general manager of the new firm. Marta is a born salesperson. Jocelyn has little interest in sales or management but would like to invest a large sum of money that she has inherited from her aunt. What factors should Jorge, Marta, and Jocelyn consider in deciding which form of business organization to adopt?

For a sample answer to this question, go to Appendix P at the end of this text.

11–3. Rights of Shareholders. Dmitri has acquired one share of common stock of a multimillion-dollar corporation with over 500,000 shareholders. Dmitri's ownership is so small that he is questioning what his rights are as a shareholder. For example, he wants to know whether this one share entitles him to attend and vote at shareholders' meetings, inspect the corporate books, and receive periodic dividends. Discuss Dmitri's rights in these matters.

11–4. Duties of Directors. Overland Corp. is negotiating with Wharton Construction Co. for the renovation of Overland's corporate headquarters. Wharton, the owner of Wharton Construction, is also one of the five members of the board of directors of Overland. The contract terms are standard for this type of contract. Wharton has previously informed two of the other Overland directors of his interest in the construction company. Overland's board approves the contract on a three-to-two vote, with Wharton voting with the majority. Discuss whether this contract is binding on the corporation.

11–5. Business Judgment Rule. Charles Pace and Maria Fuentez were shareholders of Houston Industries, Inc. (HII), and employees of Houston Lighting & Power, a subsidiary of HII, when they lost their jobs because of a company-wide reduction in its workforce. Pace, as a shareholder, three times wrote to HII, demanding that the board of directors terminate certain HII directors and officers and file a suit to recover damages for breach of fiduciary duty. Three times, the directors referred the charges to board committees and an outside law firm, which found that the facts did not support the charges. The board also received input from federal regulatory authorities about the facts behind some of the charges. The board notified Pace that it would refuse his demands. In response, Pace and Fuentez filed a shareholder's derivative suit against Don Jordan and the other HII directors, contending that the board's investigation was inadequate. The defendants moved for summary judgment, arguing that the suit was barred by the business judgment rule. How should the court rule? Why? [*Pace v. Jordan*, 999 S.W.2d 615 (Tex.App.—Houston [1 Dist.] 1999)]

11–6. Good Faith. Walik Elkhatib, a Palestinian Arab, emigrated to the United States in 1971 and became an American citizen. Eight years later, Elkhatib bought a Dunkin' Donuts, Inc., franchise in Bellwood, Illinois. Dunkin' Donuts began offering breakfast sandwiches with bacon, ham, or sausage through its franchises in 1984, but Eklhatib refused to sell these items at his store on the ground that his religion forbade the handling of pork. In 1995, Elkhatib opened a second franchise in Berkeley, Illinois, at which he also refused to sell pork products. The next year, at both locations, Elkhatib began selling meatless sandwiches. In 1998, Elkhatib opened a third franchise in Westchester, Illinois. When he proposed to relocate this franchise, Dunkin' Donuts refused to approve the new location and added that it would not renew any of his franchise agreements because he did not carry the full sandwich line. Elkhatib filed a suit in a federal district court against Dunkin' Donuts and others. The defendants filed a motion for summary judgment. Did Dunkin' Donuts act in good faith in its relationship with Elkhatib? Explain. [*Elkhatib v. Dunkin' Donuts, Inc.,* __ F.Supp.2d __ (N.D.Ill. 2004)]

Case Problem with Sample Answer

11–7. Thomas Persson and Jon Nokes founded Smart Inventions, Inc., in 1991 to market household consumer products. The success of their first product, the Smart Mop, continued with later products, which were sold through infomercials and other means. Persson and Nokes were the firm's officers and equal shareholders, with Persson responsible for product development and Nokes in charge of day-to-day operations. By 1998, they had become dissatisfied with each other's efforts. Nokes represented the firm as financially "dying," "in a grim state, . . . worse than ever," and offered to buy all of Persson's shares for $1.6 million. Persson accepted. On the day that they signed the agreement to transfer the shares, Smart Inventions began marketing a new product—the Tap Light—which was an instant success, generating millions of dollars in revenues. In negotiating with Persson, Nokes had intentionally kept the Tap Light a secret. Persson filed a suit in a California state court against Smart Inventions and others, asserting fraud and other claims. Under what principle might Smart Inventions be liable for Nokes's fraud? Is Smart Inventions liable in this case? Explain. [*Persson v. Smart Inventions, Inc.,* 125 Cal.App.4th 1141, 23 Cal.Rptr.3d 335 (2 Dist. 2005)]

After you have answered this problem, compare your answer with the sample answer given on the Web site that accompanies this text. Go to www.thomsonedu.com/westbuslaw/let, select "Chapter 11," and click on "Case Problem with Sample Answer."

11–8. Duty of Loyalty. Digital Commerce, Ltd., designed software to enable its clients to sell their products or services over the Internet. Kevin Sullivan served as a Digital vice president until 2000, when he became president. Sullivan was dissatisfied that his compensation did not include stock in Digital, but he was unable to negotiate a deal that included equity (referring to shares of ownership in the company). In May, Sullivan solicited ASR Corp.'s business for Digital while he investigated employment opportunities with ASR for himself. When ASR would not include an "equity component" in a job offer, Sullivan refused to negotiate further on Digital's behalf. A few months later, Sullivan began to form his own firm to compete with Digital, conducting organizational and marketing activities on Digital's time, including soliciting ASR's business. In August, Sullivan resigned after first having

all e-mail pertaining to the new firm deleted from Digital's computers. ASR signed a contract with Sullivan's new firm and paid it $400,000 for work through October 2001. Digital filed a suit in a federal district court against Sullivan, claiming that he had usurped a corporate opportunity. Did Sullivan breach his fiduciary duty to Digital? Explain. [*In re Sullivan,* 305 Bankr. 809 (W.D.Mich. 2004)]

11–9. Duties of Majority Shareholders. Steve and Marie Venturini were involved in the operation of Steve's Sizzling Steakhouse in Carlstadt, New Jersey, from the day their parents opened it in the 1930s. By the 1980s, Steve, Marie, and Marie's husband, Joe, were running it. The business was incorporated, with Steve and Marie each owning half of the stock. Steve died in 2001, leaving his stock in equal shares to his sons, Steve and Gregg. Steve, Jr., had never worked there; Gregg performed occasional maintenance work until his father's death. Despite their lack of participation, the sons were each paid more than $750 a week. In 2002, Marie's son, Blaise, who had obtained a college degree in restaurant management while working part-time at the steakhouse, took over its management. When his cousins became threatening, he denied them access to the business and its books. Marie refused Gregg and Steve's offer of about $1.4 million for her stock in the restaurant, and they refused her offer of about $800,000 for theirs. They filed a suit in a New Jersey state court against her, claiming in part a breach of fiduciary duty. Should the court order the aunt to buy out the nephews or the nephews to buy out the aunt, or neither? Why? [*Venturini v. Steve's Steakhouse, Inc.,* __ N.J.Super. __, __ A.2d __ (Ch.Div. 2006)]

A Question of Ethics

11–10. In 1990, American Design Properties, Inc. (ADP), leased premises at 8604 Olive Blvd. in St. Louis County, Missouri. Under the lease agreement, ADP had the right to terminate the lease on 120 days' written notice, but it did not have the right to sublease the premises without the lessor's (landowner's) consent. ADP had no bank account, no employees, and no money. ADP had never filed an income tax return or held a directors' or shareholders' meeting. In fact, ADP's only business was to collect and pay the exact amount of rent due under the lease. American Design Group, Inc. (ADG), a wholesale distributor of jewelry and other merchandise, actually occupied 8604 Olive Blvd. J. H. Blum owned ADG and was an officer and director of both ADG and ADP. Blum's husband, Marvin, was an officer of ADG and signed the lease as an officer of ADP. Marvin's former son-in-law, Matthew Smith, was a salaried employee of ADG, an officer of ADG, and an officer and director of ADP. In 1995, Nusrala Four, Inc. (later known as Real Estate Investors Four, Inc.), purchased the property at 8604 Olive Blvd. and became the lessor. No one told Nusrala that ADG was the occupant of the premises leased by ADP. ADP continued to pay the rent until November 1998, when Smith paid with a check drawn on ADG's account. No more payments were made. On February 26, 1999, Marvin sent Nusrala a note that read, "We have vacated the property at 8604 Olive." Nusrala discovered the property had been damaged and filed a suit in a Missouri state court against ADG and ADP, seeking money for the damage. In view of these facts, consider the following questions. [*Real Estate Investors Four, Inc. v. American Design Group, Inc.*, 46 S.W.3d 51 (Mo.App. E.D. 2001)]

1. Given that ADG had not signed the lease and was not rightfully a sublessee, could ADG be held liable, at least in part, for the damage to the premises? Under what theory might the court ignore the separate corporate identities of ADG and ADP? If you were the judge, how would you rule in this case?
2. Assuming that ADP had few, if any, corporate assets, would it be fair to preclude Nusrala from recovering money for the damage from ADG?
3. Is it ever appropriate for a court to ignore the corporate structure? Why or why not?

Critical-Thinking Managerial Question

11-11. Tim Rodale, one of the directors of First National Bank, fails to attend any board of directors' meetings in five and a half years, never inspects any of the bank's books or records, and generally neglects to supervise the efforts of the bank president and the loan committee. Meanwhile, the bank president makes various improper loans and permits large overdrafts. Can Rodale be held liable to the bank for losses resulting from the unsupervised actions of the bank president and the loan committee? Explain.

Video Question

11-12. Go to this text's Web site at **www.thomsonedu.com/westbuslaw/let** and select "Chapter 11." Click on "Video Questions" and view the video titled *Corporation or LLC: Which Is Better?* Then answer the following questions.

1. Compare the liability that Anna and Caleb would be exposed to as shareholders/owners in a corporation versus being members in a limited liability company (LLC).
2. How are corporations taxed differently than LLCs?
3. Suppose that you were in the position of Anna and Caleb. Would you choose to create a corporation or an LLC? Why?

INTERACTING WITH THE INTERNET

For updated links to resources available on the Web, as well as a variety of other materials, visit this text's Web site at

www.thomsonedu.com/westbuslaw/let

To learn how the U.S. Small Business Administration assists in forming, financing, and operating businesses, go to

www.sbaonline.sba.gov

For information on the FTC regulations on franchising, as well as state laws regulating franchising, go to

www.ftc.gov/bcp/franchise/netfran.htm

One of the best sources on the Web for information on corporations, including their directors, is the EDGAR database of the Securities and Exchange Commission (SEC) at

www.sec.gov/edgar.shtml

Cornell University's Legal Information Institute has links to state corporation statutes at

www.law.cornell.edu/topics/state_statutes.html

INTERNET EXERCISES

Go to **www.thomsonedu.com/westbuslaw/let,** the Web site that accompanies this text. Select "Chapter 11" and click on "Internet Exercises." There you will find the following Internet research exercises that you can perform to learn more about topics covered in this chapter.

Internet Exercise 11–1: LEGAL PERSPECTIVE—Limited Liability Companies
Internet Exercise 11–2: ECONOMIC PERSPECTIVE—D&O Insurance
Internet Exercise 11–3: MANAGEMENT PERSPECTIVE—Franchises

BEFORE THE TEST

Go to **www.thomsonedu.com/westbuslaw/let,** the Web site that accompanies this text. Select "Chapter 11" and click on "Interactive Quizzes." You will find a number of interactive questions relating to this chapter.

CHAPTER 12

Creditors' Rights and Bankruptcy

CHAPTER OBJECTIVES

After reading this chapter, you should be able to answer the following questions:

1 What is a prejudgment attachment? What is a writ of execution? How does a creditor use these remedies?

2 What is garnishment? When might a creditor undertake a garnishment proceeding?

3 In a bankruptcy proceeding, what constitutes the debtor's estate in property? What property is exempt from the estate under federal bankruptcy law?

4 What is the difference between an exception to discharge and an objection to discharge?

5 In a Chapter 11 reorganization, what is the role of the debtor in possession?

CONTENTS

AMERICA'S FONT of practical wisdom, Benjamin Franklin, observed a truth known to all debtors—that creditors do observe "set days and times" and will expect to recover their loaned funds by the agreed-on dates. Historically, debtors and their families have been subjected to punishment, including involuntary servitude and imprisonment, for their inability to pay debts. The modern legal system, however, has moved away from a punishment philosophy in dealing with debtors.

Normally, creditors have no problem collecting the debts owed to them. When disputes arise over the amount owed, however, or when the debtor simply cannot or will not pay, what happens? What remedies are available to creditors when a debtor **defaults** (fails to pay as promised)? In this chapter, we first focus on some basic laws that assist the debtor and creditor in resolving their dispute. We then examine the process of bankruptcy as a last resort in resolving debtor-creditor problems. We specifically include changes resulting from the 2005 Bankruptcy Reform Act.

> "Creditors are . . . great observers of set days and times."
>
> —BENJAMIN FRANKLIN, 1706–1790
> (American diplomat, author, and scientist)

DEFAULT
The failure to observe a promise or to discharge an obligation. The term is commonly used to mean the failure to pay a debt when it is due.

LAWS ASSISTING CREDITORS

Both the common law and statutory laws other than Article 9 of the UCC create various rights and remedies for creditors. We discuss here some of these rights and remedies.

Painters finish the trim on a house. If the homeowner does not pay for the work, what can the painters do to collect what they are owed? (Myrleen Ferguson, PhotoEdit)

LIEN
An encumbrance on a property to satisfy a debt or protect a claim for payment of a debt.

MECHANIC'S LIEN
A statutory lien on the real property of another, created to ensure payment for work performed and materials furnished in the repair or improvement of real property, such as a building.

ARTISAN'S LIEN
A possessory lien given to a person who has made improvements and added value to another person's personal property as security for payment for services performed.

Liens

A **lien** is an encumbrance on (claim against) property to satisfy a debt or protect a claim for the payment of a debt. Creditors' liens may arise under the common law or under statutory law. Statutory liens include *mechanic's liens*. Liens created at common law include *artisan's liens*. *Judicial liens* include those that represent a creditor's efforts to collect on a debt before or after a judgment is entered by a court.

Mechanic's Lien   When a person contracts for labor, services, or materials to be furnished for the purpose of making improvements on real property (land and things attached to the land, such as buildings and trees—see Chapter 19) but does not immediately pay for the improvements, the creditor can file a **mechanic's lien** on the property. This creates a special type of debtor-creditor relationship in which the real estate itself becomes security for the debt.

| **Example #1**   A painter agrees to paint a house for a homeowner for an agreed-on price to cover labor and materials. If the homeowner refuses to pay for the work or pays only a portion of the charges, a mechanic's lien against the property can be created. The painter is the lienholder, and the real property is encumbered (burdened) with a mechanic's lien for the amount owed. If the homeowner does not pay the lien, the property can be sold to satisfy the debt. Notice of the foreclosure (the process by which the creditor deprives the debtor of his or her property) and sale must be given to the debtor in advance, however. |

Note that state law governs the procedures that must be followed to create a mechanic's lien. Generally, the lienholder must file a written notice of lien against the particular property involved. The notice of lien must be filed within a specific time period, normally measured from the last date on which materials or labor were provided (usually within 60 to 120 days). If the property owner fails to pay the debt, the lienholder is entitled to foreclose on the real estate on which the work or materials were provided and to sell it to satisfy the amount of the debt.

Artisan's Lien   An **artisan's lien** is a security device created at common law through which a creditor can recover payment from a debtor for labor and materials furnished for the repair or improvement of personal property. In contrast to a mechanic's lien, an artisan's lien is *possessory*. The lienholder ordinarily must have retained possession of the property and have expressly or impliedly agreed to provide the services on a cash, not a credit, basis. The lien remains in existence as long as the lienholder maintains possession, and the lien is terminated once possession is voluntarily surrendered—unless the surrender is only temporary.

| **Example #2**   Tenetia leaves her diamond ring at the jeweler's to be repaired and to have her initials engraved on the band. In the absence of an agreement, the jeweler can keep the ring until Tenetia pays for the services. Should Tenetia

fail to pay, the jeweler has a lien on Tenetia's ring for the amount of the bill and normally can sell the ring in satisfaction of the lien.

Modern statutes permit the holder of an artisan's lien to foreclose and sell the property subject to the lien to satisfy payment of the debt. As with the mechanic's lien, the holder of an artisan's lien is required to give notice to the owner of the property prior to foreclosure and sale. The sale proceeds are used to pay the debt and the costs of the legal proceedings, and the surplus, if any, is paid to the former owner.

Judicial Lien   When a debt is past due, a creditor can bring a legal action against the debtor to collect the debt. If the creditor is successful in the action, the court awards the creditor a judgment against the debtor (usually for the amount of the debt plus any interest and legal costs incurred in obtaining the judgment). Frequently, however, the creditor is unable to collect the awarded amount.

To ensure that a judgment in the creditor's favor will be collectible, creditors are permitted to request that certain nonexempt property of the debtor be seized to satisfy the debt. (As will be discussed later in this chapter, under state or federal statutes, certain property is exempt from attachment by creditors.) If the court orders the debtor's property to be seized prior to a judgment in the creditor's favor, the court's order is referred to as a *writ of attachment*. If the court orders the debtor's property to be seized following a judgment in the creditor's favor, the court's order is referred to as a *writ of execution*.

Attachment   In the context of judicial liens, **attachment** is a court-ordered seizure and taking into custody of property prior to the securing of a judgment for a past-due debt. Attachment rights are created by state statutes. Attachment is a *prejudgment* remedy because it occurs either at the time of or immediately after the commencement of a lawsuit and before the entry of a final judgment. By statute, to attach before judgment, a creditor must comply with specific restrictions and requirements.

ATTACHMENT
In the context of judicial liens, a court-ordered seizure and taking into custody of property prior to the securing of a judgment for a past-due debt.

To use attachment as a remedy, the creditor must have an enforceable right to payment of the debt under law and must follow certain procedures. Otherwise, the creditor can be liable for damages for wrongful attachment. She or he must file with the court an *affidavit* (a written or printed statement, made under oath or sworn to) stating that the debtor is in default and indicating the statutory grounds under which attachment is sought. The creditor must also post a bond to cover at least the court costs, the value of the loss of use of the good suffered by the debtor, and the value of the property attached. When the court is satisfied that all the requirements have been met, it issues a **writ of attachment**, which directs the sheriff or other public officer to seize nonexempt property. If the creditor prevails at trial, the seized property can be sold to satisfy the judgment.

WRIT OF ATTACHMENT
A court's order, issued prior to a trial to collect a debt, directing the sheriff or other officer to seize nonexempt property of the debtor. If the creditor prevails at trial, the seized property can be sold to satisfy the judgment.

Writ of Execution   If the debtor will not or cannot pay the judgment, the creditor is entitled to go back to the court and obtain a court order directing the sheriff to seize (levy) and sell any of the debtor's nonexempt real or personal property that is within the court's geographic jurisdiction (usually the county in which the courthouse is located). This order is called a **writ of execution.** The proceeds of the sale are used to pay off the judgment, accrued interest, and costs of the sale. Any excess is paid to the debtor. The debtor can pay the judgment

WRIT OF EXECUTION
A court's order, issued after a judgment has been entered against the debtor, directing the sheriff to seize (levy) and sell any of the debtor's nonexempt real or personal property. The proceeds of the sale are used to pay off the judgment, accrued interest, and costs of the sale; any surplus is paid to the debtor.

and redeem the nonexempt property any time before the sale takes place. (Because of exemption laws and bankruptcy laws, however, many judgments are virtually uncollectible.)

Garnishment

GARNISHMENT
A legal process used by a creditor to collect a debt by seizing property of the debtor (such as wages) that is being held by a third party (such as the debtor's employer).

Garnishment occurs when a creditor is permitted to collect a debt by seizing property of the debtor that is being held by a third party. Typically, a garnishment judgment is served on a debtor's employer so that part of the debtor's usual paycheck will be paid to the creditor. As a result of a garnishment proceeding, the court orders the debtor's employer to turn over a portion of the debtor's wages to pay the debt.

The legal proceeding for a garnishment action is governed by state law, and garnishment operates differently from state to state. According to the laws in some states, the creditor needs to obtain only one order of garnishment, which will then continuously apply to the debtor's weekly wages until the entire debt is paid. In other states, the creditor must go back to court for a separate order of garnishment for each pay period. Garnishment is usually a postjudgment remedy, but it can be a prejudgment remedy with a proper hearing by a court.

Both federal laws and state laws limit the amount of money that can be garnished from a debtor's weekly take-home pay.[1] Federal law provides a framework to protect debtors from suffering unduly when paying judgment debts.[2] State laws also provide dollar exemptions, and these amounts are often larger than those provided by federal law. Under federal law, garnishment of an employee's wages for any one indebtedness cannot be a ground for dismissal of an employee.

Creditors' Composition Agreements

CREDITORS' COMPOSITION AGREEMENT
An agreement formed between a debtor and his or her creditors in which the creditors agree to accept a lesser sum than that owed by the debtor in full satisfaction of the debt.

Creditors may contract with the debtor for discharge of the debtor's liquidated debts (debts that are definite, or fixed, in amount) on payment of a sum less than that owed. These agreements are called **creditors' composition agreements,** or simply *composition agreements,* and are usually held to be enforceable.

Mortgage Foreclosure

MORTGAGEE
Under a mortgage agreement, the creditor who takes a security interest in the debtor's property.

MORTGAGOR
Under a mortgage agreement, the debtor who gives the creditor a security interest in the debtor's property in return for a mortgage loan.

Mortgage holders have the right to foreclose on mortgaged property in the event of a debtor's default. The usual method of foreclosure is by judicial sale of the property, although the statutory methods of foreclosure vary from state to state. If the proceeds of the foreclosure sale are sufficient to cover both the costs of the foreclosure and the mortgaged debt, the debtor receives any surplus. If the sale proceeds are insufficient to cover the foreclosure costs and the mortgaged debt, however, the **mortgagee** (the creditor-lender) can seek to recover the difference from the **mortgagor** (the debtor) by obtaining a deficiency judgment representing the difference between the mortgaged debt and the amount actually received from the proceeds of the foreclosure sale.

---

1. Some states (for example, Texas) do not permit garnishment of wages by private parties except under a child-support order.
2. For example, the federal Consumer Credit Protection Act of 1968, 15 U.S.C. Sections 1601–1693r, provides that a debtor can retain either 75 percent of the disposable earnings per week or a sum equivalent to thirty hours of work paid at federal minimum-wage rates, whichever is greater.

The mortgagee obtains a deficiency judgment in a separate legal action pursued subsequent to the foreclosure action. The deficiency judgment entitles the mortgagee to recover the amount of the deficiency from other property owned by the debtor.

Suretyship and Guaranty

When a third person promises to pay a debt owed by another in the event the debtor does not pay, either a *suretyship* or a *guaranty* relationship is created. Suretyship and guaranty have a long history under the common law and provide creditors with the right to seek payment from the third party if the primary debtor defaults on her or his obligations. Exhibit 12–1 illustrates the relationship between a suretyship or guaranty party and the creditor.

Surety A contract of strict **suretyship** is a promise made by a third person to be responsible for the debtor's obligation. It is an express contract between the **surety** (the third party) and the creditor. The surety in the strictest sense is primarily liable for the debt of the principal. The creditor need not exhaust all legal remedies against the principal debtor before holding the surety responsible for payment. The creditor can demand payment from the surety from the moment the debt is due.

Example #3 Roberto Delmar wants to borrow from the bank to buy a used car. Because Roberto is still in college, the bank will not lend him the funds unless his father, José Delmar, who has dealt with the bank before, will cosign the note (add his signature to the note, thereby becoming a surety and thus jointly liable for payment of the debt). When José Delmar cosigns the note, he becomes primarily liable to the bank. On the note's due date, the bank has the option of seeking payment from either Roberto or José Delmar, or both jointly.

SURETYSHIP
An express contract in which a third party to a debtor-creditor relationship (the surety) promises to be primarily responsible for the debtor's obligation.

SURETY
A person, such as a cosigner on a note, who agrees to be primarily responsible for the debt of another.

EXHIBIT 12–1 SURETYSHIP AND GUARANTY PARTIES

In a suretyship or guaranty arrangement, a third party promises to be responsible for a debtor's obligations. A third party who agrees to be responsible for the debt even if the primary debtor does not default is known as a surety; a third party who agrees to be *secondarily* responsible for the debt—that is, responsible only if the primary debtor defaults—is known as a guarantor. Normally, a promise of guaranty (a collateral, or secondary, promise) must be in writing to be enforceable.

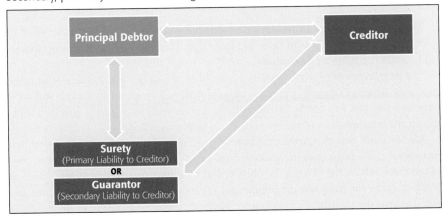

GUARANTOR
A person who agrees to satisfy the debt of another (the debtor) only after the principal debtor defaults. Thus, a guarantor's liability is secondary.

Guaranty With a suretyship arrangement, the surety is *primarily* liable for the debtor's obligation. With a guaranty arrangement, the **guarantor**—the third person making the guaranty—is *secondarily* liable. The guarantor can be required to pay the obligation *only after the principal debtor defaults*, and default usually takes place only after the creditor has made an attempt to collect from the debtor.

| Example #4 A small corporation, BX Enterprises, needs to borrow funds to meet its payroll. The bank is skeptical about the creditworthiness of BX and requires Dawson, its president, who is a wealthy businessperson and the owner of 70 percent of BX Enterprises, to sign an agreement making himself personally liable for payment if BX does not pay off the loan. As a guarantor of the loan, Dawson cannot be held liable until BX Enterprises is in default.**|**

The Statute of Frauds requires that a guaranty contract between the guarantor and the creditor must be in writing to be enforceable unless the *main purpose* exception applies. (A suretyship agreement, by contrast, need not be in writing to be enforceable.) Under this exception, if the main purpose of the guaranty agreement is to benefit the guarantor, then the contract need not be in writing to be enforceable.

In the following case, the issue was whether a guaranty of a lease signed by the officer of a corporation was enforceable against the officer personally even though he claimed to have signed the guaranty only as a representative of the corporation.

CASE 12.1 JSV, Inc. v. Hene Meat Co.

Court of Appeals of Indiana, 2003.
794 N.E.2d 555.

BACKGROUND AND FACTS On August 30, 1999, JSV, Inc., signed a lease to rent a portion of a building in Indianapolis, Indiana, from Hene Meat Company. Mark Kennedy signed the lease on behalf of JSV as one of its corporate officers. Kennedy also signed a document titled "GUARANTY," which stated that it was "an absolute and unconditional guaranty" of

the lease's performance by JSV. Kennedy's printed name and signature on the document were not followed by any corporate officer designation. JSV stopped paying rent to Hene in September 2000. Hene filed a suit in an Indiana state court against JSV and Kennedy, alleging, among other things, that Kennedy was personally liable on the guaranty. He responded in part that he signed the guaranty only as an officer of JSV. The court issued a summary judgment against Kennedy for $75,041.07 in favor of Hene. Kennedy appealed to a state intermediate appellate court.

IN THE WORDS OF THE COURT . . . *BARNES*, Judge.

* * * *

The * * * argument of Kennedy's that we address is whether the trial court erred in granting summary judgment in favor of Hene on its claim that Kennedy was personally liable under the guaranty he executed. * * *

The interpretation of a guaranty is governed by the same rules applicable to other contracts. Absent ambiguity, the terms of a contract will be given their plain and ordinary meaning and will not be considered ambiguous solely because the parties dispute the proper interpretation of the terms. * * * [Emphasis added.]

We conclude that the guaranty Kennedy executed was unambiguously a personal guaranty * * * . It is axiomatic under Indiana law that a guaranty agreement must consist of three parties: the obligor, the obligee, and the surety or guarantor. Here, Hene as landlord under the lease was the obligee and JSV as the tenant was the obligor; the disputed issue is the identity of the guarantor. Kennedy claims he signed both the lease *and* the guaranty as an officer of JSV.

CASE 12.1–CONTINUED

However, there would have been no point in Hene's obtaining Kennedy's guaranty of the lease if he was doing so only in his official capacity as an officer of JSV. Such an action would have been equivalent to JSV guaranteeing JSV's performance of the lease and to JSV being both the obligor under the lease and the guarantor under the guaranty. * * * [S]uch a result would be paradoxical and untenable. In [a different case] we concluded that where a corporate officer executed a guaranty with respect to credit extended to the corporation, the guaranty was a personal one and the officer personally was the guarantor despite the fact that the officer placed his corporate title after his signature on the guaranty. We further concluded that this was apparent as a matter of law and summary judgment on the issue was appropriate. In this case, the guaranty is even more clearly a personal one * * * because Kennedy's signature thereon is not followed by any corporate officer designation. The trial court did not err in concluding that the guaranty Kennedy executed was a personal one as a matter of law and in granting summary judgment against Kennedy personally.

DECISION AND REMEDY The state intermediate appellate court affirmed the judgment of the lower court, holding that the document Kennedy signed was "unambiguously a personal guaranty."

WHY IS THIS CASE IMPORTANT? *This case emphasizes the need to use explicit language in contracts with persons who are officers and directors of corporations. While this court ultimately concluded that the guaranty was personal even though it was not designated as such, other courts may reach different conclusions. To avoid potential problems and costly litigation, businesspersons would be wise to require those affiliated with corporations to clearly indicate whether they are signing each document in their individual or official capacities.*

Defenses of the Surety and the Guarantor The defenses of the surety and the guarantor are basically the same. Therefore, the following discussion applies to both, although it refers only to the surety.

Actions Releasing the Surety Certain actions will release the surety from the obligation. For example, any binding material modification in the terms of the original contract made between the principal debtor and the creditor—including a binding agreement to extend the time for making payment—without first obtaining the consent of the surety will discharge a gratuitous surety completely and discharge a compensated surety to the extent that the surety suffers a loss.
| Example #5 A father who agrees to assume responsibility for his daughter's obligation is a gratuitous surety; a venture capitalist who will profit from a loan made to the principal debtor is a compensated surety.**|**

Naturally, if the principal obligation is paid by the debtor or by another person on behalf of the debtor, the surety is discharged from the obligation. Similarly, if valid tender of payment is made, and the creditor rejects it with knowledge of the surety's existence, the surety is released from any obligation on the debt.

Defenses of the Principal Debtor Generally, the surety can use any defenses available to a principal debtor to avoid liability on the obligation to the creditor. Defenses available to the principal debtor that the surety *cannot* use include the principal debtor's incapacity or bankruptcy and the statute of limitations. The ability of the surety to assert any defenses the debtor may have against the creditor is the most important concept in suretyship; it means that most of the defenses available to the surety are also those of the debtor.

Surrender or Impairment of Collateral   In addition, if a creditor surrenders the collateral to the debtor or impairs the collateral while knowing of the surety and without the surety's consent, the surety is released to the extent of any loss suffered from the creditor's actions. The primary reason for this requirement is to protect a surety who agreed to become obligated only because the debtor's collateral was in the possession of the creditor.

Other Defenses   Obviously, a surety may also have his or her own defenses—for example, incapacity or bankruptcy. If the creditor fraudulently induced the surety to guarantee the debt of the debtor, the surety can assert fraud as a defense. In most states, the creditor has a legal duty to inform the surety, prior to the formation of the suretyship contract, of material facts known by the creditor that would substantially increase the surety's risk. Failure to so inform may constitute fraud and makes the suretyship obligation voidable.

Rights of the Surety and the Guarantor   Generally, when the surety or guarantor pays the debt owed to the creditor, the surety or guarantor is entitled to certain rights. Because the rights of the surety and guarantor are basically the same, the following discussion applies to both.

RIGHT OF SUBROGATION
The right of a person to stand in the place of (be substituted for) another, giving the substituted party the same legal rights that the original party had.

RIGHT OF REIMBURSEMENT
The legal right of a person to be restored, repaid, or indemnified for costs, expenses, or losses incurred or expended on behalf of another.

CO-SURETY
A joint surety; a person who assumes liability jointly with another surety for the payment of an obligation.

RIGHT OF CONTRIBUTION
The right of a co-surety who pays more than his or her proportionate share on a debtor's default to recover the excess paid from other co-sureties.

Subrogation and Reimbursement   The surety has the legal **right of subrogation.** Simply stated, this means that any right the creditor had against the debtor now becomes the right of the surety. Included are creditor rights in bankruptcy, rights to collateral possessed by the creditor, and rights to judgments secured by the creditor. In short, the surety now stands in the shoes of the creditor and may pursue any remedies that were available to the creditor against the debtor.

The surety also has a right to be reimbursed by the debtor. This **right of reimbursement** may stem either from the suretyship contract or from equity (fairness). Basically, the surety is entitled to receive from the debtor all outlays made on behalf of the suretyship arrangement. Such outlays can include expenses incurred as well as the actual amount of the debt paid to the creditor.

The Right of Contribution   In a situation involving **co-sureties** (two or more sureties on the same obligation owed by the debtor), a surety who pays more than her or his proportionate share on a debtor's default is entitled to recover from the co-sureties the amount paid above the surety's obligation. This is the **right of contribution.** Generally, a co-surety's liability either is determined by agreement between the co-sureties or, in the absence of an agreement, can be specified in the suretyship contract itself.

| **Example #6**   Assume that two co-sureties are obligated under a suretyship contract to guarantee the debt of a debtor. Together, the sureties' maximum liability is $25,000. As specified in the suretyship contract, surety A's maximum liability is $15,000, and surety B's is $10,000. The debtor owes $10,000 and is in default. Surety A pays the creditor the entire $10,000. In the absence of any agreement between the two co-sureties, surety A can recover $4,000 from surety B ($10,000/$25,000 × $10,000 = $4,000).|

LAWS ASSISTING DEBTORS

The law protects debtors as well as creditors. Certain property of the debtor, for example, is exempt from creditors' actions. In most states, certain types of property are exempt from execution or attachment. State exemption statutes usually include both real and personal property.

Exempted Real Property

Probably the most familiar exemption is the **homestead exemption.** Each state permits the debtor to retain the family home, either in its entirety or up to a specified dollar amount, free from the claims of unsecured creditors or trustees in bankruptcy (a bankruptcy trustee is appointed by the court to hold and protect estate property, as will be discussed later in this chapter). The purpose of the homestead exemption is to ensure that the debtor will retain some form of shelter.

HOMESTEAD EXEMPTION
A law permitting a debtor to retain the family home, either in its entirety or up to a specified dollar amount, free from the claims of unsecured creditors or trustees in bankruptcy.

| **Example #7** Suppose that Van Cleave owes Acosta $40,000. The debt is the subject of a lawsuit, and the court awards Acosta a judgment of $40,000 against Van Cleave. Van Cleave's home is valued at around $50,000, and the state exemption on homesteads is $25,000. There are no outstanding mortgages or other liens. To satisfy the judgment debt, Van Cleave's family home is sold at public auction for $45,000. The proceeds of the sale are distributed as follows:

1. Van Cleave is given $25,000 as his homestead exemption.
2. Acosta is paid $20,000 toward the judgment debt, leaving a $20,000 deficiency judgment that can be satisfied from any other nonexempt property (personal or real) that Van Cleave may have, if allowed by state law. |

Exempted Personal Property

Various types of personal property may also be exempt from satisfaction of judgment debts. Personal property that is most often exempt includes the following:

1. Household furniture up to a specified dollar amount.
2. Clothing and certain personal possessions, such as family pictures or a Bible or other religious text.
3. A vehicle (or vehicles) for transportation (at least up to a specified dollar amount).
4. Certain classified animals, usually livestock but including pets.
5. Equipment that the debtor uses in a business or trade, such as tools or professional instruments, up to a specified dollar amount.

Livestock, such as the cattle shown here, is usually considered exempt property under laws that assist debtors. Why is this? (PhotoDisc)

BANKRUPTCY PROCEEDINGS

Bankruptcy law in the United States has two goals—to protect a debtor by giving him or her a fresh start, free from creditors' claims, and to ensure equitable treatment to creditors who are competing for a debtor's assets. Federal bankruptcy legislation was first enacted in 1898 and has undergone several modifications since that time.

Bankruptcy law prior to 2005 was based on the Bankruptcy Reform Act of 1978, as amended. In 2005, Congress enacted a new Bankruptcy Reform Act.[3] As you will read in the following sections, the 2005 act significantly overhauled certain provisions of the Bankruptcy Code—for the first time in twenty-five years. Because of its significance for creditors and debtors alike, we present the Bankruptcy Reform Act as this chapter's *Landmark in the Legal Environment* feature on the following page.

---

3. The full title of the act is the Bankruptcy Abuse Prevention and Consumer Protection Act of 2005, Pub. L. No. 109-8, 119 Stat. 23 (April 20, 2005).

The Bankruptcy Reform Act of 2005

When Congress enacted the Bankruptcy Reform Act of 1978, many claimed that the new act made it too easy for debtors to file for bankruptcy protection. The Bankruptcy Reform Act of 2005 was passed, in part, in response to businesses' concerns about the rise in personal bankruptcy filings. Certainly, the facts cannot be denied: from 1978 to 2005, personal bankruptcy filings increased ninefold, reaching a peak of 1,613,097 in the year ending June 30, 2003. By the early 2000s, various business groups—including credit-card companies, banks, and firms providing loans for automobile purchases—were claiming that the bankruptcy process was being abused and that reform was necessary. As Mallory Duncan of the National Retail Federation put it, bankruptcy had gone from being a "stigma" to being a "financial planning tool" for many.[a]

The bulk of the act became effective 180 days after being signed by the president on April 20, 2005. Thus, the new provisions took effect in October 2005. Bankruptcy petitions that were filed before the act became effective continued to be administered and governed by the 1978 Reform Act, as amended.

More Repayment Plans, Fewer Liquidation Bankruptcies   One of the major goals of the Bankruptcy Reform Act of 2005 is to require consumers to pay as many of their debts as they possibly can instead of having those debts fully discharged in bankruptcy. Prior to the new law, only about 20 percent of personal bankruptcies were filed under Chapter 13 of the Bankruptcy Code. As you will read later in this chapter, this part of the Bankruptcy Code involves establishing a repayment plan under which a debtor pays off as many of his or her debts as possible over a maximum period of five years. The remaining bankruptcies were filed under Chapter 7 of the Code, which permits debtors, with some exceptions, to have all of their debts discharged in bankruptcy.

The distinction has been important for all creditors. Given that most individuals who declare personal bankruptcy have few durable assets, filing for bankruptcy protection under Chapter 7 essentially means that creditors lose out. Under the new law, in contrast, whenever a debtor has an annual income in excess of the mean income in that debtor's state of residence, the debtor may be forced into a Chapter 13 repayment plan.

Other Significant Provisions of the Act   One of the provisions of the Bankruptcy Reform Act of 2005 involves the homestead exemption. Prior to the passage of the bankruptcy reform legislation, some states allowed debtors petitioning for bankruptcy to exempt all of the equity (the market value minus the outstanding mortgage owed) in their homes during bankruptcy proceedings. The 2005 act leaves these exemptions in place but puts some limits on their use. The 2005 act also includes a number of other changes. For example, one provision requires credit-card companies to make fuller disclosures about their interest rates and payment schedules. Another provision gives child-support obligations priority over other debts and allows enforcement agencies to continue efforts to collect child-support payments. Additionally, the act expands protections for family farmers and provides more protection for personal information about customers that is owned by businesses undergoing bankruptcy.

Application to Today's Legal Environment

The Bankruptcy Reform Act of 2005 subjects a large class of individuals in the United States to increased financial risk. Supporters of the law hope that it will curb abuse by deterring financially troubled debtors from looking at bankruptcy as a mere "planning tool" instead of as a last resort. Certainly, fewer debtors will be allowed to have their debts discharged in Chapter 7 liquidation proceedings. At the same time, the 2005 act will make it more difficult for debtors to obtain a "fresh start" financially—one of the major goals of bankruptcy law in the United States. Under the 2005 act, more debtors will be forced to file under Chapter 13. Additionally, the act has made the bankruptcy process more time consuming and costly because of its more extensive documentation and certification requirements.

RELEVANT WEB SITES

To locate information on the Web concerning the 2005 bankruptcy reform legislation, go to this text's Web site at **www.thomsonedu.com/westbuslaw/let**, *select "Chapter 12," and click on "URLs for Landmarks."*

a. As cited in Nedra Pickler, "Bush Signs Big Rewrite of Bankruptcy Law," *The Los Angeles Times,* April 20, 2005.

Bankruptcy Courts

Bankruptcy proceedings are held in federal bankruptcy courts, which are under the authority of the U.S. district courts, and rulings from bankruptcy courts can be appealed to the district courts. Essentially, a bankruptcy court fulfills the role of an administrative court for the federal district court concerning matters in bankruptcy. The bankruptcy court holds proceedings dealing with the procedures required to administer the estate of the debtor in bankruptcy. A bankruptcy court can conduct a jury trial if the appropriate district court has authorized it and the parties to the bankruptcy consent. Bankruptcy court judges are federally appointed for fourteen-year terms. The 2005 Bankruptcy Reform Act included a section entitled the Bankruptcy Judgeship Act of 2005, which enlarged the number of bankruptcy judges by twenty-eight (including four for the Delaware District).

Types of Bankruptcy Relief

Title 11 of the *United States Code* encompasses the Bankruptcy Code, which has eight chapters. Chapters 1, 3, and 5 of the Code contain general definitional provisions, as well as provisions governing case administration, creditors, the debtor, and the estate. These three chapters apply generally to all kinds of bankruptcies. The next five chapters of the Code set forth the different types of relief that debtors may seek. Chapter 7 provides for **liquidation** proceedings (the selling of all nonexempt assets and the distribution of the proceeds to the debtor's creditors). Chapter 9 governs the adjustment of a municipality's debts. Chapter 11 governs reorganizations. Chapters 12 and 13 provide for the adjustment of debts by parties with regular incomes (family farmers and family fishermen under Chapter 12 and individuals under Chapter 13).[4] A debtor (except for a municipality) need not be insolvent[5] to file for bankruptcy relief under any chapter of the Bankruptcy Code. Anyone obligated to a creditor can declare bankruptcy.

LIQUIDATION
The sale of all the nonexempt assets of a debtor and the distribution of the proceeds to the debtor's creditors. Chapter 7 of the Bankruptcy Code provides for liquidation bankruptcy proceedings.

Special Treatment of Consumer-Debtors

To fully inform a consumer-debtor of the various types of relief available, the Code requires that the clerk of the court provide certain information to all consumer-debtors prior to the commencement of a bankruptcy filing. A **consumer-debtor** is a debtor whose debts result primarily from the purchase of goods for personal, family, or household use. First, the clerk must give consumer-debtors written notice of the general purpose, benefits, and costs of each chapter of the Bankruptcy Code under which they might proceed. Second, under the 2005 act, the clerk must provide consumer-debtors with informational materials on the types of services available from credit counseling agencies.

CONSUMER-DEBTOR
A debtor whose debts result primarily from the purchase of goods for personal, family, or household use.

---

4. There are no Chapters 2, 4, 6, 8, or 10 in Title 11. Such "gaps" are not uncommon in the *United States Code.* This is because chapter numbers (or other subdivisional unit numbers) are sometimes reserved for future use when a statute is enacted. (A gap may also appear if a law has been repealed.)

5. The inability to pay debts as they become due is known as *equitable* insolvency. A *balance sheet* insolvency, which exists when a debtor's liabilities exceed assets, is not the test. Thus, it is possible for debtors to voluntarily petition for bankruptcy or to be thrown into involuntary bankruptcy even though their assets far exceed their liabilities. This may occur when a debtor's cash flow problems become severe.

A mother and her daughter look over a collection of antiques and collectibles on display at a public auction. The auction is part of a company's liquidation bankruptcy proceeding. What other types of property might be included in the debtor's estate in property? (AP Photo/Christoper Record/ *The Charlotte Observer*)

within ninety days of the creditors' meeting.[14] The proof of claim lists the creditor's name and address, as well as the amount that the creditor asserts is owed to the creditor by the debtor. A creditor need not file a proof of claim if the debtor's schedules list the creditor's claim as liquidated (exactly determined) and the creditor does not dispute the amount of the claim. A proof of claim is necessary if there is any dispute concerning the claim. If a creditor fails to file a proof of claim, the bankruptcy court or trustee may file the proof of claim on the creditor's behalf but is not obligated to do so.

Generally, any legal obligation of the debtor is a claim (except claims for breach of employment contracts or real estate leases for terms longer than one year). When a claim is disputed, or unliquidated, the bankruptcy court will set the value of the claim. Any creditor holding a debtor's obligation can file a claim against the debtor's estate. These claims are automatically allowed unless contested by the trustee, the debtor, or another creditor. A creditor who files a false claim commits a crime.

Exemptions

The trustee takes control over the debtor's property, but an individual debtor is entitled to exempt certain property from the bankruptcy. The Bankruptcy Code exempts the following property:[15]

1. Up to $18,450 in equity in the debtor's residence and burial plot (the homestead exemption).
2. Interest in a motor vehicle up to $2,950.
3. Interest, up to $475 for a particular item, in household goods and furnishings, wearing apparel, appliances, books, animals, crops, and musical instruments (the aggregate total of all items is limited, however, to $9,850).
4. Interest in jewelry up to $1,225.
5. Interest in any other property up to $975, plus any unused part of the $18,450 homestead exemption up to $9,250.
6. Interest in any tools of the debtor's trade up to $1,850.
7. Any unmatured life insurance contract owned by the debtor.
8. Certain interests in accrued dividends and interest under life insurance contracts owned by the debtor, not to exceed $9,850.
9. Professionally prescribed health aids.
10. The right to receive Social Security and certain welfare benefits, alimony and support, certain retirement funds and pensions, and education savings accounts held for specific periods of time.
11. The right to receive certain personal-injury and other awards up to $18,450.

Individual states have the power to pass legislation precluding debtors from using the federal exemptions within the state; a majority of the states have done this. In those states, debtors may use only state, not federal, exemptions. In the rest of the states, an individual debtor (or a husband and wife filing

---

14. This ninety-day rule applies in Chapter 12 and Chapter 13 bankruptcies as well.
15. The dollar amounts stated in the Bankruptcy Code are adjusted automatically every three years on April 1 based on changes in the Consumer Price Index. The adjusted amounts are rounded to the nearest $25. The amounts stated in this chapter are in accordance with those computed on April 1, 2004.

jointly) may choose either the exemptions provided under state law or the federal exemptions.[16]

Note also that the 2005 Bankruptcy Reform Act clarified specifically what is included in "household goods and furnishings" (referred to in number 3 in the previous list). For example, the category includes one computer, one radio, one television, one videocassette recorder, educational materials or equipment primarily for use by minor dependent children, and furniture that is used exclusively by a minor dependent (or by an elderly or disabled dependent). Other items—such as works of art; electronic entertainment equipment with a fair market value of over $500; antiques and jewelry (except wedding rings) valued at more than $500; and motor vehicles, tractors, lawn mowers, watercraft, and aircraft—are not included in household goods.

The Homestead Exemption

The 2005 Bankruptcy Reform Act significantly changed the law for those debtors seeking to use state homestead exemption statutes. In six states, among them Florida and Texas, homestead exemptions allow debtors petitioning for bankruptcy to shield unlimited amounts of equity in their homes from creditors. In this context, the term *equity* refers to the difference between the market value of the property and any claims held against it (such as a mortgage debt or tax lien). The prior Bankruptcy Code required that the debtor must have been domiciled in the state for at least six months to apply any of the state exemptions. Under the 2005 act, however, the domicile period is now two years. In other words, the debtor must have lived in the state for two years prior to filing the petition to be able to use the state homestead exemption.

In addition, if the homestead is acquired within three and a half years preceding the date of filing, the maximum equity exempted is $125,000, even if the state law would permit a higher amount. (This does not apply to equity that has been rolled over during the specified period from the sale of a previous homestead in the same state.) Also, if the debtor owes a debt arising from a violation of securities law or if the debtor committed certain criminal or tortious acts in the previous five years that indicate the filing was substantial abuse, the debtor may not exempt any amount of equity.[17]

The Trustee

Promptly after the order for relief in the liquidation proceeding has been entered, an interim, or provisional, trustee is appointed by the U.S. Trustee. The interim, or provisional, trustee presides over the debtor's property until the first meeting of creditors. At this first meeting, either a permanent trustee is elected, or the interim trustee becomes the permanent trustee.

---

16. State exemptions may or may not be limited with regard to value. Under state exemption laws, a debtor may enjoy an unlimited value exemption on a motor vehicle, for example, even though the federal bankruptcy scheme exempts a vehicle only up to a value of $2,950. A state's law may also define the property coming within an exemption differently than the federal law or may exclude, or except, specific items from an exemption, making it unavailable to a debtor who fits within the exception.

17. Specifically, the debtor may not claim the homestead exemption if the debtor has committed any criminal act, intentional tort, or willful or reckless misconduct that caused serious physical injury or death to another individual in the preceding five years. Also, if the debtor has been convicted of a felony, he or she may not be able to claim the exemption.

The basic duty of the trustee is to collect the debtor's available estate and reduce it to cash for distribution, preserving the interests of both the debtor and unsecured creditors. This requires that the trustee be accountable for administering the debtor's estate. To enable the trustee to accomplish this duty, the Code gives the trustee certain powers, stated in both general and specific terms. These powers must be exercised within two years of the order for relief.

New Duties under the 2005 Act   The Bankruptcy Reform Act of 2005 imposes new duties on trustees (and bankruptcy administrators) with regard to means-testing all debtors who file Chapter 7 petitions. Under the new law, the U.S. Trustee or bankruptcy administrator is required to promptly review all materials filed by the debtor. Not later than ten days after the first meeting of the creditors, the trustee must file a statement as to whether the case is presumed to be an abuse under the means test. The trustee must then provide a copy of this statement concerning abuse to all creditors within five days. Not later than forty days after the first creditors' meeting, the trustee must either file a motion to dismiss the petition (or convert it to a Chapter 13 case) or file a statement setting forth the reasons why the motion would not be appropriate.

Under the 2005 act, the trustee also has new duties designed to protect domestic-support creditors (those to whom a domestic-support obligation is owed). The trustee is required to provide written notice of the bankruptcy to the claim holder (a former spouse who is owed child support, for example). The notice must also include certain information, such as the debtor's address, the name and address of the debtor's last known employer, and the address and phone number of the state child-support enforcement agency. (Note that these requirements are not limited to Chapter 7 bankruptcies, and the trustee may have additional duties in other types of bankruptcy to collect assets for distribution to the domestic-support creditor.)

The Trustee's Powers   The trustee occupies a position *equivalent* in rights to that of certain other parties. For example, the trustee has the same rights as a creditor and can obtain a judicial lien or levy execution on the debtor's property. This means that a trustee has priority over an unperfected secured party to the debtor's property. This right of a trustee, equivalent to that of a lien creditor, is known as the *strong-arm power*. A trustee also has power equivalent to that of a *bona fide purchaser* of real property from the debtor.

The Right to Possession of the Debtor's Property   The trustee has the power to require persons holding the debtor's property at the time the petition is filed to deliver the property to the trustee. Usually, a trustee does not take actual physical possession of a debtor's property, but instead takes constructive possession by exercising control over the property. **|Example #8** Suppose that a trustee needs to obtain possession of a debtor's trucks. The trustee could notify the debtor and take the keys to the trucks—without actually moving the trucks—to effectively take possession of them.**|**

Avoidance Powers   The trustee also has specific powers of *avoidance*—that is, the trustee can set aside a sale or other transfer of the debtor's property, taking it back as a part of the debtor's estate. These powers include any voidable rights available to the debtor, preferences, certain statutory liens, and fraudulent transfers by the debtor. Each of these powers is discussed in more detail below.

The debtor shares most of the trustee's avoidance powers. Thus, if the trustee does not take action to enforce one of the rights mentioned above, the debtor in a liquidation bankruptcy can nevertheless enforce that right.[18]

Note that under the 2005 act, the trustee no longer has the power to avoid any transfer that was a bona fide payment of a domestic-support debt.

Voidable Rights A trustee steps into the shoes of the debtor. Thus, any reason that a debtor can use to obtain the return of her or his property can be used by the trustee as well. These grounds include fraud, duress, incapacity, and mutual mistake.

| Example #9 Ben sells his boat to Tara. Tara gives Ben a check, knowing that she has insufficient funds in her bank account to cover the check. Tara has committed fraud. Ben has the right to avoid that transfer and recover the boat from Tara. Once an order for relief under Chapter 7 of the Code has been entered for Ben, the trustee can exercise the same right to recover the boat from Tara, and the boat becomes a part of the debtor's estate.|

Preferences A debtor is not permitted to transfer property or to make a payment that favors—or gives a **preference** to—one creditor over others. The trustee is allowed to recover payments made both voluntarily and involuntarily to one creditor in preference over another. If a **preferred creditor** (one who has received a preferential transfer from the debtor) has sold the property to an innocent third party, the trustee cannot recover the property from the innocent party. The preferred creditor, however, generally can be held accountable for the value of the property.

To have made a preferential payment that can be recovered, an *insolvent* debtor generally must have transferred property, for a *preexisting* debt, within *ninety days* prior to the filing of the petition in bankruptcy. The transfer must give the creditor more than the creditor would have received as a result of the bankruptcy proceedings. The trustee need not prove insolvency, as the Code provides that the debtor is presumed to be insolvent during this ninety-day period.

Preferences to Insiders Sometimes, the creditor receiving the preference is an *insider*—an individual, a partner, a partnership, a corporation, or an officer or a director of a corporation (or a relative of one of these) who has a close relationship with the debtor. In this situation, the avoidance power of the trustee is extended to transfers made within *one year* before filing; however, the *presumption* of insolvency is confined to the ninety-day period. Therefore, the trustee must prove that the debtor was insolvent at the time of a transfer that occurred prior to the ninety-day period.

Transfers That Do Not Constitute Preferences Not all transfers are preferences. To be a preference, the transfer must be made for something other than current consideration. Most courts generally assume that payment for services rendered within ten to fifteen days prior to the payment of the current consideration is not a preference. If a creditor receives payment in the ordinary

PREFERENCE
In bankruptcy proceedings, property transfers or payments made by the debtor that favor (give preference to) one creditor over others. The bankruptcy trustee is allowed to recover payments made both voluntarily and involuntarily to one creditor in preference over another.

PREFERRED CREDITOR
A creditor who has received a preferential transfer from a debtor.

---

18. Under a Chapter 11 bankruptcy (to be discussed later), for which no trustee other than the debtor generally exists, the debtor has the same avoidance powers as a trustee under Chapter 7. Under Chapters 12 and 13 (also to be discussed later), a trustee must be appointed.

course of business from an individual or business debtor, such as payment of last month's telephone bill, the payment cannot be recovered by the trustee in bankruptcy. To be recoverable, a preference must be a transfer for an antecedent (preexisting) debt, such as a year-old printing bill. In addition, the Code permits a consumer-debtor to transfer any property to a creditor up to a total value of $5,000, without the transfer's constituting a preference (this amount was increased from $600 to $5,000 by the 2005 act). Payment of domestic-support debts does not constitute a preference. Also, transfers that were made as part of an alternative repayment schedule negotiated by an approved credit counseling agency are not preferences.

Liens on Debtor's Property   The trustee has the power to avoid certain statutory liens against the debtor's property, such as a landlord's lien for unpaid rent. The trustee can avoid statutory liens that first became effective against the debtor when the bankruptcy petition was filed or when the debtor became insolvent. The trustee can also avoid any lien against a bona fide purchaser that was not perfected or enforceable on the date of the bankruptcy filing.

Fraudulent Transfers   The trustee may avoid fraudulent transfers or obligations if they were made within two years of the filing of the petition or if they were made with actual intent to hinder, delay, or defraud a creditor. Transfers made for less than a reasonably equivalent consideration are also vulnerable if by making them, the debtor became insolvent, was left engaged in business with an unreasonably small amount of capital, or intended to incur debts that he or she could not pay. When a fraudulent transfer is made outside the Code's two-year limit, creditors may seek alternative relief under state laws. Some state laws allow creditors to recover for transfers made up to three years prior to the filing of a petition.

Distribution of Property

The Code provides specific rules for the distribution of the debtor's property to secured and unsecured creditors. (We will examine these distributions shortly.) If any amount remains after the priority classes of creditors have been satisfied, it is turned over to the debtor. Exhibit 12–2 illustrates graphically the collection and distribution of property in most voluntary bankruptcies.

In a bankruptcy case in which the debtor has no assets,[19] creditors are notified of the debtor's petition for bankruptcy but are instructed not to file a claim. In such a case, the unsecured creditors will receive no payment, and most, if not all, of these debts will be discharged.

Distribution to Secured Creditors   The rights of perfected secured creditors were discussed earlier in this chapter. The Code provides that a consumer-debtor, either within thirty days of filing a liquidation petition or before the date of the first meeting of the creditors (whichever is first), must file with the clerk a statement of intention with respect to the secured collateral. The statement must indicate whether the debtor will redeem the collateral (make a single payment equal to the current value of the property), reaffirm the debt

---

19. This type of bankruptcy is called a "no-asset" case.

EXHIBIT 12-2 COLLECTION AND DISTRIBUTION OF
PROPERTY IN MOST VOLUNTARY BANKRUPTCIES

This exhibit illustrates the property that might be collected in a debtor's voluntary
bankruptcy and how it might be distributed to creditors. Involuntary bankruptcies and some
voluntary bankruptcies could include additional types of property and other creditors.

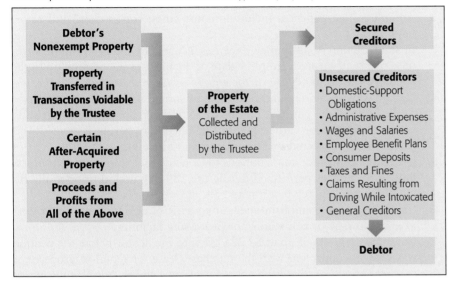

(continue making payments on the debt), or surrender the property to the
secured party.[20] The trustee is obligated to enforce the debtor's statement
within forty-five days after the meeting of the creditors. As noted previously,
failure of the debtor to redeem or reaffirm within forty-five days terminates
the automatic stay.

If the collateral is surrendered to the perfected secured party, the secured creditor can enforce the security interest either by accepting the property in full satisfaction of the debt or by foreclosing on the collateral and using the proceeds to
pay off the debt. Thus, the perfected secured party has priority over unsecured
parties as to the proceeds from the disposition of the collateral. Indeed, the Code
provides that if the value of the collateral exceeds the perfected secured party's
claim and if the security agreement so provides, the secured party also has priority as to the proceeds in an amount that will cover reasonable fees and costs
incurred because of the debtor's default. Fees include reasonable attorneys' fees.
Any excess over this amount is used by the trustee to satisfy the claims of unsecured creditors. Should the collateral be insufficient to cover the secured debt
owed, the secured creditor becomes an unsecured creditor for the difference.

Distribution to Unsecured Creditors   Bankruptcy law establishes an order of
priority for classes of debts owed to *unsecured* creditors, and they are paid in
the order of their priority. Each class must be fully paid before the next class is
entitled to any of the remaining proceeds. If there are insufficient proceeds to
pay fully all the creditors in a class, the proceeds are distributed *proportionately*
to the creditors in that class, and classes lower in priority receive nothing. The
new bankruptcy law elevated domestic-support obligations to the highest

---

20. Also, if applicable, the debtor must specify whether the collateral will be claimed as exempt
property.

priority of unsecured claims. The order of priority among classes of unsecured creditors is as follows:

1. Claims for domestic-support obligations, such as child support and alimony (subject to the priority of the administrative costs that the trustee incurred in administering assets to pay the obligations).
2. Administrative expenses including court costs, trustee fees, and attorneys' fees.
3. In an involuntary bankruptcy, expenses incurred by the debtor in the ordinary course of business from the date of the filing of the petition up to the appointment of the trustee or the court's issuance of an order for relief.
4. Unpaid wages, salaries, and commissions earned within ninety days prior to the filing of the petition, limited to $4,925 per claimant. Any claim in excess of $4,925 or earned before the ninety-day period is treated as a claim of a general creditor (listed as item 10 below).
5. Unsecured claims for contributions to be made to employee benefit plans, limited to services performed during the 180-day period prior to the filing of the bankruptcy petition and $4,925 per employee.
6. Claims by farmers and fishermen, up to $4,925, against debtor-operators of grain storage or fish storage or processing facilities.
7. Consumer deposits of up to $2,225 given to the debtor before the petition was filed in connection with the purchase, lease, or rental of property or purchase of services that were not received or provided. Any claim in excess of $2,225 is treated as a claim of a general creditor (listed as item 10 below).
8. Certain taxes and penalties due to government units, such as income and property taxes.
9. Claims for death or personal injury resulting from the operation of a motor vehicle or vessel if such operation was unlawful because the debtor was intoxicated as a result of using alcohol, a drug, or another substance. (This provision was added by the 2005 act.)
10. Claims of general creditors.

Discharge

From the debtor's point of view, the primary purpose of liquidation is to obtain a fresh start through a discharge of debts.[21] As mentioned earlier, once the debtor's assets have been distributed to creditors as permitted by the Code, the debtor's remaining debts are then discharged, meaning that the debtor is not obligated to pay them. Certain debts, however, are not dischargeable in bankruptcy. Also, certain debtors may not qualify to have all debts discharged in bankruptcy. These situations are discussed below.

Exceptions to Discharge   Discharge of a debt may be denied because of the nature of the claim or the conduct of the debtor. Claims that are not dischargeable in a liquidation bankruptcy include the following:

1. Claims for back taxes accruing within two years prior to bankruptcy.
2. Claims for amounts borrowed by the debtor to pay federal taxes or any nondischargeable taxes.

---

21. Discharges are granted under Chapter 7 only to individuals, not to corporations or partnerships. The latter may use Chapter 11, or they may terminate their existence under state law.

3. Claims against property or funds obtained by the debtor under false pretenses or by false representations.

4. Claims by creditors who were not notified and did not know of the bankruptcy; these claims did not appear on the schedules the debtor was required to file.

5. Claims based on fraud or misuse of funds by the debtor while he or she was acting in a fiduciary capacity or claims involving the debtor's embezzlement or larceny.

6. Domestic-support obligations and property settlements as provided for in a separation agreement or divorce decree.

7. Claims for amounts due on a retirement account loan.

8. Claims based on willful or malicious conduct by the debtor toward another or the property of another.

9. Certain government fines and penalties, which under the 2005 act also include penalties imposed under federal election laws.

10. Certain student loans or obligations to repay funds received as an educational benefit, scholarship, or stipend—unless payment of the loans imposes an undue hardship on the debtor and the debtor's dependents.

11. Consumer debts of more than $500 for luxury goods or services owed to a single creditor incurred within ninety days of the order for relief. (Prior to the passage of the 2005 act, the amount was $1,150 and the period was sixty days.) This denial of discharge is a rebuttable presumption (that is, the denial may be challenged by the debtor), however, and any debts reasonably incurred to support the debtor or dependents are not classified as luxuries.

12. Cash advances totaling more than $750 that are extensions of open-end consumer credit obtained by the debtor within seventy days of the order for relief. (The prior law allowed $1,150 in cash advances that were obtained within sixty days.) A denial of discharge of these debts is also a rebuttable presumption.

13. Judgments or consent decrees against a debtor as a result of the debtor's operation of a motor vehicle or any vessel or aircraft while intoxicated.

14. Fees or assessments arising from a lot in a homeowners' association, as long as the debtor retained an interest in the lot.

15. Failure of the debtor to provide required or requested tax documents. (This exception to discharge also applies to Chapter 11 and Chapter 13 bankruptcies.)

In the following case, the court considered whether to order the discharge of a debtor's student loan obligations. Is it "undue hardship" if, to repay the loans, a debtor has to forgo her son's private school tuition?

CASE 12.2   In re Savage

United States Bankruptcy Appellate Panel,
First Circuit, 2004.
311 Bankr. 835.

BACKGROUND AND FACTS Brenda Savage attended college in the mid-1980s—taking out five student loans—but she did not graduate. In 2003, at the age of forty-one, single, and in good health, she lived with her fifteen-year-old son in an apartment in Boston, Massachusetts. Her son attended Boston Trinity Academy, a private school. Savage worked 37.5 hours per week for Blue Cross/Blue Shield of Massachusetts. Her monthly gross wages were $3,079.79. Her employment provided health insurance, dental insurance, life insurance, a

CASE 12.2–CONTINUED ▶

retirement savings plan, and paid vacations and personal days. She also received monthly child-support income of $180.60. After deductions, her total net monthly income was $2,030.72. Her monthly expenses included, among other things, $607 for rent, $221 for utilities, $76 for phone, $23.99 for an Internet connection, $430 for food, $75 for clothing, $12.50 for laundry and dry cleaning, $23 for medical expenses, $95.50 for transportation, $193.50 for charitable

contributions, $43 for entertainment, $277.50 for her son's tuition, and $50 for his books. In February, Savage filed a petition in bankruptcy, seeking to discharge her student loan obligations to Educational Credit Management Corporation (ECMC). At the time, she owed $32,248.45. The court ordered a discharge of all but $3,120. ECMC appealed to the U.S. Bankruptcy Appellate Panel for the First Circuit.

IN THE WORDS OF THE COURT . . . *HAINES*, Bankruptcy Judge.

* * * *

Under 11 U.S.C. Section 523(a)(8), debtors are not permitted to discharge educational loans unless excepting the loans from discharge will impose an undue hardship on the debtor and the debtor's dependents. * * *

* * * *

Under "totality of the circumstances" analysis, a debtor seeking discharge of student loans must prove by a preponderance of evidence that (1) her past, present, and reasonably reliable future financial resources; (2) her and her dependents' reasonably necessary living expenses, and; (3) other relevant facts or circumstances unique to the case prevent her from paying the student loans in question while still maintaining a minimal standard of living, even when aided by a discharge of other prepetition debts.

* * * *

The debtor must show not only that her current income is insufficient to pay her student loans, but also that her prospects for increasing her income in the future are too limited to afford her sufficient resources to repay the student loans and provide herself and her dependents with a minimal (but fair) standard of living. [Emphasis added.]

Ms. Savage has not demonstrated that her current level of income and future prospects warrant discharge of her loans. Her present income may be insufficient to pay her student loans and still maintain precisely the standard of living she now has. But * * * it would enable her to repay the loans without undue hardship. Moreover, the record plainly establishes that her prospects for a steady increase in income over time are promising. She has been steadily employed at the same job and regularly receives annual raises. Nothing indicates change is in the wind. Moreover, Ms. Savage currently works 37½ hours a week, leaving time for some part-time work (or longer hours at her present job) * * * .

* * * *

To prove undue hardship for purposes of Section 523(a)(8), a debtor must show that her necessary and reasonable expenses leave her with too little to afford repayment. * * * [Emphasis added.]

* * * *

Private school tuition is not *generally* considered a reasonably necessary expense in bankruptcy cases * * * . Although compelling circumstances may distinguish a given case, the [courts] uniformly hold that a debtor's mere preference for private schooling is insufficient to qualify the attendant expense as necessary and reasonable.

Ms. Savage did not demonstrate a satisfactory reason why her son needs to attend private school at a monthly cost of $277.50 (plus $50 for books). When asked to explain why she did so, she testified:

There were a lot of fights, a lot of swearing, a lot of other things going on. I mean he would wake up every morning crying because he didn't want to go to school. * * * So I had to find

CASE 12.2–CONTINUED

a school to put him in * * * where he was going to—I mean, he didn't do well that whole year. I had to keep going down to the school several times. He was just a mess the whole school year. * * * So I had to find another school.

Although we understand why Ms. Savage prefers that her son attend private school, she has not demonstrated that the public school system cannot adequately meet her son's educational needs. Her preference appears sincere, but that alone is not sufficient to sustain the bankruptcy court's implicit conclusion that forgoing this expense would constitute undue hardship * * * .

* * * *

Given the fact that at least $327.50 (private school tuition and books) in expense can be eliminated from Ms. Savage's budget without creating undue hardship, her student loans cannot be discharged under Section 523(a)(8). It is worth noting, as well, that Ms. Savage's son will reach majority in just a few years, a consequence that will reduce her required expenses considerably.

DECISION AND REMEDY The U.S. Bankruptcy Appellate Panel for the First Circuit reversed the order of the bankruptcy court and remanded the case for the entry of a judgment in ECMC's favor. The appellate panel was "satisfied" that "Ms. Savage has now (and will increasingly have) the ability to repay her five student loans without undue hardship."

WHY IS THIS CASE IMPORTANT? *This case emphasizes the courts' reluctance to discharge student loan obligations in bankruptcy unless a debtor can show that repaying the loans would genuinely create an "undue hardship." Generally, a student loan will be discharged in bankruptcy only if the debtor's present and foreseeable financial circumstances indicate that it would be virtually impossible to pay the debt.*

Objections to Discharge In addition to the exceptions to discharge previously listed, a bankruptcy court may also deny the discharge of the *debtor* (as opposed to the debt). In the latter situation, the assets of the debtor are still distributed to the creditors, but the debtor remains liable for the unpaid portion of all claims. Grounds for the denial of discharge of the debtor include the following:

1. The debtor's concealment or destruction of property with the intent to hinder, delay, or defraud a creditor.
2. The debtor's fraudulent concealment or destruction of financial records.
3. The granting of a discharge to the debtor within eight years of the filing of the petition. (This period was increased from six to eight years by the 2005 act.)
4. Failure of the debtor to complete the required consumer education course (unless such a course is unavailable). (This ground for denial was added by the 2005 act and also applies to Chapter 13 petitions.)
5. Proceedings in which the debtor could be found guilty of a felony (basically, the 2005 act states that a court may not discharge any debt until the completion of felony proceedings against the debtor).

Effect of Discharge The primary effect of a discharge is to void any judgment on a discharged debt and enjoin any action to collect a discharged debt. A discharge does not affect the liability of a co-debtor.

Revocation of Discharge On petition by the trustee or a creditor, the bankruptcy court can, within one year, revoke the discharge decree. The discharge decree will be revoked if it is discovered that the debtor acted fraudulently or dishonestly during the bankruptcy proceedings. The revocation renders the discharge void, allowing creditors not satisfied by the distribution of the debtor's estate to proceed with their claims against the debtor.

Reaffirmation of Debt

REAFFIRMATION AGREEMENT
An agreement to pay a debt that is dischargeable in bankruptcy.

An agreement to pay a debt dischargeable in bankruptcy is called a **reaffirmation agreement**. A debtor may wish to pay a debt—such as, for example, a debt owed to a family member, physician, bank, or some other creditor—even though the debt could be discharged in bankruptcy. Also, as noted previously, under the new Code a debtor cannot retain secured property while continuing to pay without entering into a reaffirmation agreement.

To be enforceable, reaffirmation agreements must be made before the debtor is granted a discharge. The agreement must be signed and filed with the court (along with the original disclosure documents, as you will read shortly). Court approval is required unless the debtor is represented by an attorney during the negotiation of the reaffirmation and submits the proper documents and certifications. Nevertheless, court approval may be required even if the debtor is represented by an attorney when it appears that the reaffirmation will result in undue hardship on the debtor. When court approval is required, a separate hearing will take place. The court will approve the reaffirmation only if it finds that the agreement will not result in undue hardship to the debtor and that the reaffirmation is consistent with the debtor's best interests.

Presumption of Undue Hardship   Under the provisions of the 2005 act, if the debtor's monthly income minus the debtor's monthly expenses is less than the scheduled payments on the reaffirmed debt, undue hardship will be presumed. A presumption of undue hardship can be rebutted, however. The debtor can file a written statement with the court or appear in person to explain and identify additional sources of funds from which to make the agreed-on payments. If the court is not satisfied with the explanation, it may disapprove of the reaffirmation or hold a hearing.

If the debtor has an attorney, the attorney must certify in writing that he or she has fully advised the debtor of the legal effect and consequences of reaffirmation. In addition, to rebut the presumption of undue hardship, the attorney must certify that, in the attorney's opinion, the debtor is able to make the payments.

New Reaffirmation Disclosures   To discourage creditors from engaging in abusive reaffirmation practices, the 2005 act added new requirements for reaffirmation. The Code now provides the specific language for several pages of disclosures that must be given to debtors entering reaffirmation agreements.[22] These disclosures explain that the debtor is not required to reaffirm any debt, but that liens on secured property, such as mortgages and cars, will remain in effect even if the debt is not reaffirmed. The reaffirmation agreement must disclose the amount of the debt reaffirmed, the rates of interest, the date payments begin, and the right to rescind. The disclosures also caution the debtor, "Only agree to reaffirm a debt if it is in your best interest. Be sure you can afford the payments you agree to make." The original disclosure documents

---

22. Note that credit unions are exempted from these disclosure requirements.

must be signed by the debtor, certified by the debtor's attorney, and filed with the court at the same time as the reaffirmation agreement. A reaffirmation agreement that is not accompanied by the original signed disclosures will not be effective.

If the debtor is represented by an attorney and no presumption of undue hardship arises, then the reaffirmation becomes effective immediately on filing with the court. If the debtor is not represented, the reaffirmation is not effective until the court approves it. The debtor can rescind, or cancel, the agreement at any time before the court enters a discharge order, or within sixty days of the filing of the agreement, whichever is *later.*

CHAPTER 11—REORGANIZATION

The type of bankruptcy proceeding most commonly used by corporate debtors is the Chapter 11 *reorganization.* In a reorganization, the creditors and the debtor formulate a plan under which the debtor pays a portion of the debts and is discharged of the remainder. The debtor is allowed to continue in business. Although this type of bankruptcy is generally a corporate reorganization, any debtors (including individuals but excluding stockbrokers and commodities brokers)[23] who are eligible for Chapter 7 relief are eligible for relief under Chapter 11.[24] In 1994, Congress established a "fast-track" Chapter 11 procedure for small-business debtors whose liabilities do not exceed $2 million and who do not own or manage real estate. This allows for bankruptcy proceedings without the appointment of committees and can save time and costs.

WorldCom president and chief executive officer John Sidgmore discusses the company's filing for Chapter 11 bankruptcy protection in 2002. The company filed for bankruptcy after the disclosure that it had hidden almost $4 billion in expenses through deceptive accounting practices. What procedures are followed in a Chapter 11 reorganization? (AP Photo/Diane Bondareff)

The same principles that govern the filing of a liquidation (Chapter 7) petition apply to reorganization (Chapter 11) proceedings. The case may be brought either voluntarily or involuntarily. The same guidelines govern the entry of the order for relief. The automatic-stay and adequate protection provisions are applicable in reorganizations as well. The 2005 Bankruptcy Reform Act's exceptions to the automatic stay also apply to Chapter 11 proceedings, as do the new provisions regarding substantial abuse and additional grounds for dismissal (or conversion) of bankruptcy petitions. Also, the 2005 act contains specific rules and limitations for individual debtors who file a Chapter 11 petition. For example, an individual debtor's postpetition acquisitions and earnings become the property of the bankruptcy estate.

Must Be in the Best Interests of the Creditors

Under Section 305(a) of the Bankruptcy Code, a court, after notice and a hearing, may dismiss or suspend all proceedings in a case at any time if dismissal or suspension would better serve the interests of the creditors. Section 1112 also allows a court, after notice and a hearing, to dismiss a case under reorganization "for cause." Cause includes the absence of a reasonable likelihood of rehabilitation, the inability to effect a plan, and an unreasonable delay by the debtor that is prejudicial to (may harm the interests of) creditors.[25]

---

23. In *Toibb v. Radloff,* 501 U.S. 157, 111 S.Ct. 2197, 115 L.Ed.2d 145 (1991), the United States Supreme Court ruled that a nonbusiness debtor may petition for relief under Chapter 11.
24. In addition, railroads are eligible for Chapter 11 relief.
25. See 11 U.S.C. Section 1112(b). Debtors are not prohibited from filing successive petitions, however. A debtor whose petition is dismissed, for example, can file a new Chapter 11 petition (which may be granted unless it is filed in bad faith).

Workouts

WORKOUT
An out-of-court agreement between a debtor and his or her creditors in which the parties work out a payment plan or schedule under which the debtor's debts can be discharged.

In some instances, creditors may prefer private, negotiated adjustments of creditor-debtor relations, also known as **workouts,** to bankruptcy proceedings. Often, these out-of-court workouts are much more flexible and thus more conducive to a speedy settlement. Speed is critical because delay is one of the most costly elements in any bankruptcy proceeding. Another advantage of workouts is that they avoid the various administrative costs of bankruptcy proceedings.

Debtor in Possession

DEBTOR IN POSSESSION (DIP)
In Chapter 11 bankruptcy proceedings, a debtor who is allowed to continue in possession of the estate in property (the business) and to continue business operations.

On entry of the order for relief, the debtor generally continues to operate the business as a **debtor in possession (DIP).** The court, however, may appoint a trustee (often referred to as a *receiver*) to operate the debtor's business if gross mismanagement of the business is shown or if appointing a trustee is in the best interests of the estate.

The DIP's role is similar to that of a trustee in a liquidation. The DIP is entitled to avoid prepetition preferential payments made to creditors and prepetition fraudulent transfers of assets. The DIP has the power to decide whether to cancel or assume prepetition executory contracts (those that are not yet performed) or unexpired leases.

Under the strong-arm clause[26] of the Bankruptcy Code, a DIP can avoid any obligation or any transfer of property of the debtor that could be avoided by certain parties. These parties include (1) a creditor who extended credit to the debtor at the time of bankruptcy (petition) and who consequently obtained a lien on the debtor's property; (2) a creditor who extended credit to the debtor at the time of bankruptcy and who consequently obtained a writ of execution against the debtor that was returned unsatisfied; and (3) a bona fide purchaser of real property from the debtor if, at the time of the bankruptcy, the transfer was perfected.

ETHICAL ISSUE 12.1 *Should those who "bankrupt" a firm be allowed to continue to manage the firm as debtors in possession?*

Chapter 11 reorganizations have become the target of substantial criticism. One of the arguments against Chapter 11 is that it allows the very managers who "bankrupted" a firm to continue to manage it as debtors in possession while the firm is in Chapter 11 proceedings. According to some critics, the main beneficiaries of Chapter 11 corporate reorganizations are not the shareholder-owners of the corporations but rather attorneys and current management. Basically, these critics argue that reorganizations do not preserve companies' assets because large firms must pay millions of dollars for attorneys and accountants during the reorganization process, which can take years to complete.

Creditors' Committees

As soon as practicable after the entry of the order for relief, a creditors' committee of unsecured creditors is appointed. If the debtor has filed a plan accepted by the creditors, however, the trustee may decide not to call a meet-

---

26. 11 U.S.C. Section 544(a).

ing of the creditors. The committee may consult with the trustee or the DIP concerning the administration of the case or the formulation of the plan. Additional creditors' committees may be appointed to represent special interest creditors. Under the 2005 act, a court may order the trustee to change the membership of a committee or to increase the number of committee members to include a small-business concern if the court deems it necessary to ensure adequate representation of the creditors.

Orders affecting the estate generally will be entered only with the consent of the committee or after a hearing in which the judge is informed of the position of the committee. As mentioned earlier, businesses with debts of less than $2 million that do not own or manage real estate can avoid creditors' committees. In these cases, orders can be entered without a committee's consent.

The Reorganization Plan

A reorganization plan to rehabilitate the debtor is a plan to conserve and administer the debtor's assets in the hope of an eventual return to successful operation and solvency.

Filing the Plan   Only the debtor may file a plan within the first 120 days after the date of the order for relief. Under the 2005 act, the 120-day period may be extended, but not beyond 18 months from the date of the order for relief. If the debtor does not meet the 120-day deadline or obtain an extension, and if the debtor fails to procure the required creditor consent (discussed below) within 180 days, any party may propose a plan up to 20 months from the date of the order for relief. (In other words, the 180-day period cannot be extended beyond 20 months past the date of the order for relief.) For a small-business debtor, the time for the debtor's filing is 180 days.

The plan must be fair and equitable and must do the following:

1. Designate classes of claims and interests.
2. Specify the treatment to be afforded the classes. (The plan must provide the same treatment for all claims in a particular class.)
3. Provide an adequate means for execution. (The 2005 Bankruptcy Reform Act requires individual debtors to utilize postpetition assets as necessary to execute the plan.)
4. Provide for payment of tax claims over a five-year period.

Acceptance and Confirmation of the Plan   Once the plan has been developed, it is submitted to each class of creditors for acceptance. The plan need not provide for full repayment to unsecured creditors. Each class must accept the plan unless the class is not adversely affected by it. A class has accepted the plan when a majority of the creditors, representing two-thirds of the amount of the total claim, vote to approve it. Confirmation is conditioned on the debtor certifying that all postpetition domestic-support obligations have been paid in full. For small-business debtors, if the plan meets the listed requirements, the court must confirm the plan within forty-five days (unless this period is extended).

Even when all classes of creditors accept the plan, the court may refuse to confirm it if it is not "in the best interests of the creditors." A former spouse or child of the debtor can block the plan if it does not provide for payment of her or his claims in cash. Under the 2005 act, if an unsecured creditor objects to the plan, specific rules apply to the value of property to be distributed under the plan. The plan can also be modified on the request of the debtor, trustee, U.S. Trustee, or holder of the unsecured claim. Tax claims must be paid over a five-year period.

Even if only one class of creditors has accepted the plan, the court may still confirm the plan under the Code's so-called **cram-down provision.** In other words, the court may confirm the plan over the objections of a class of creditors. Before the court can exercise this right of cram-down confirmation, it must be demonstrated that the plan does not discriminate unfairly against any creditors and that the plan is fair and equitable.

CRAM-DOWN PROVISION
A provision of the Bankruptcy Code that allows a court to confirm a debtor's Chapter 11 reorganization plan even though only one class of creditors has accepted it.

Discharge   The plan is binding on confirmation; however, the Bankruptcy Reform Act of 2005 provides that confirmation of a plan does not discharge an individual debtor. For individual debtors, plan completion is required prior to discharge, unless the court orders otherwise. For all other debtors, the court may order discharge at any time after the plan is confirmed. The debtor is given a reorganization discharge from all claims not protected under the plan. This discharge does not apply to any claims that would be denied discharge under liquidation.

BANKRUPTCY RELIEF UNDER CHAPTER 13 AND CHAPTER 12

In addition to bankruptcy relief through liquidation and reorganization, the Code also provides for individuals' repayment plans (Chapter 13), and family-farmer and family-fishermen debt adjustments (Chapter 12).

Individuals' Repayment Plan

Chapter 13 of the Bankruptcy Code provides for "Adjustment of Debts of an Individual with Regular Income." Individuals (not partnerships or corporations) with regular income who owe fixed unsecured debts of less than $307,675 or fixed secured debts of less than $922,975 may take advantage of bankruptcy repayment plans. Among those eligible are salaried employees; sole proprietors; and individuals who live on welfare, Social Security, fixed pensions, or investment income. Many small-business debtors have a choice of filing a plan for reorganization or for repayment. Repayment plans offer several advantages, however. One benefit is that they are less expensive and less complicated than reorganization proceedings or, for that matter, even liquidation proceedings.

Filing the Petition   A repayment plan case can be initiated only by the filing of a voluntary petition by the debtor or by the conversion of a Chapter 7 petition (because of a finding of substantial abuse under the means test, for example). Certain liquidation and reorganization cases may be converted to repayment plan cases with the consent of the debtor.[27] A trustee, who will

---

27. A Chapter 13 case may be converted to a Chapter 7 case either at the request of the debtor or, under certain circumstances, "for cause" by a creditor. A Chapter 13 case may be converted to a Chapter 11 case after a hearing.

make payments under the plan, must be appointed. On the filing of a repayment plan petition, the automatic stay previously discussed takes effect. Although the stay applies to all or part of the debtor's consumer debt, it does not apply to any business debt incurred by the debtor. The automatic stay also does not apply to domestic-support obligations.

The Bankruptcy Code imposes the requirement of good faith on a debtor at both the time of the filing of the petition and at the time of the filing of the plan. The Code does not define good faith—it is determined in each case through a consideration of "the totality of the circumstances." Bad faith can be cause for the dismissal of a Chapter 13 petition, as the following case illustrates.

CASE 12.3 In re Buis

United States Bankruptcy Court,
Northern District of Florida,
Pensacola Division, 2006.
337 Bankr. 243.

BACKGROUND AND FACTS In 2000, Roger and Pauline Buis bought an air show business (including a helicopter, a trailer, and props) from Robert and Annette Hosking. The price was $275,000, which the Buises agreed to pay in installments. The Buises formed Otto Airshows and decorated the helicopter as "Otto the Clown." They performed in air shows and took passengers on flights for a fee. In 2003, the Buises began accusing a competitor, Army Aviation Heritage Foundation and Museum, Inc. (AAHF), of safety lapses. AAHF filed a suit in a federal district court against the Buises and their company, alleging defamation. The court issued a summary judgment in AAHF's favor. While a determination of the amount of the damages was pending, the Buises stopped doing business as Otto Airshows. They formed a new firm, Prop and Rotor Aviation, Inc., to which they leased the Otto equipment. Within a month, they filed a bankruptcy petition under Chapter 13. The plan and the schedules did not mention AAHF, the Prop and Rotor lease, a settlement that the Buises received in an unrelated suit, and other items. AAHF filed a motion to dismiss the case, asserting in part that the Buises filed their petition in bad faith.

IN THE WORDS OF THE COURT . . . *LEWIS M. KILLIAN, JR.,* Bankruptcy Judge.

* * * *

* * * In considering the totality of circumstances surrounding the debtors' filing of their petition, it is clear to me that *this case was filed in bad faith and therefore should be dismissed.* [Emphasis added.]

First, *the debtors did not accurately state their assets and liabilities on their initial bankruptcy petition.* The debtors failed to list AAHF as a creditor, which is especially hard for the court to comprehend when the debtor admitted that it was AAHF's judgment that pushed them into bankruptcy. The debtors listed income on their schedules from "[r]ent from personal property lease," but did not list any such lease on [the schedules] and did not report any income from leases in their statement of financial affairs or list any agreement with Prop and Rotor anywhere in their schedules * * * . The debtors also did not disclose the $55,000.00 personal-injury settlement they received prepetition. In addition to all of these omissions, the debtors also "forgot" about a Kubota lawn tractor worth $10,000 and their generator, worth $400. The debtors did not amend their schedules to reflect any of this until the day of the hearing on this motion. [Emphasis added.]

Next, the timing of the debtors' petition leads to the conclusion of bad faith, in two ways. First, the debtors filed their Chapter 13 petition after they were found liable in the District Court Action and after an unsuccessful mediation with AAHF, but before a final judgment could be entered. * * * It appears to me that *the timing of the bankruptcy*

CASE 12.3—CONTINUED ➡

filing was an ultimately futile attempt to keep the debtors eligible to file for relief under Chapter 13, because the debts owed to AAHF would be dischargeable [under Chapter 13]. The other reason the timing of the petition is suspect involves the grant of [certain] interests in [some of the Buises' assets to some of their creditors]. While the granting of these * * * interests may not have been fraudulent transfers as a matter of law, they certainly would have been preferences subject to avoidance * * * had they been made within 90 days of the filing of the petition. All of these transfers appear to have been made between 90 and 120 days prepetition. Thus, the debtors granted these * * * interests, * * * waited 90 days so they would "stick," then filed their petition. The debtor admitted that he began planning to avoid AAHF's judgment through a Chapter 13 bankruptcy shortly after the adverse ruling on summary judgment in the District Court. The timing of the bankruptcy petition further demonstrates both the debtors' attempt to continue in their prepetition pattern of egregious behavior towards AAHF and their bad faith in filing their petition. [Emphasis added.]

DECISION AND REMEDY The court dismissed the Buises' petition. The debtors had not included all of their assets and liabilities on their initial petition and had timed its filing to avoid payment on the judgment to AAHF. They had also attempted to transfer interests in some of their assets in preference to certain creditors. The court determined that "the debtors filed their petition in bad faith and it is in the creditors' and estate's best interests that this case be dismissed."

WHAT IF THE FACTS WERE DIFFERENT? *If AAHF had lost its defamation suit against the Buises, would the result in this case have been the same? Why or why not?*

The Repayment Plan   A plan of rehabilitation by repayment must provide for the following:

1. The turnover to the trustee of such future earnings or income of the debtor as is necessary for execution of the plan.
2. Full payment in deferred cash payments of all claims entitled to priority.[28]
3. Identical treatment of all claims within a particular class. (The Code permits the debtor to list co-debtors, such as guarantors or sureties, as a separate class.)

Filing the Plan   Only the debtor may file for a repayment plan. This plan may provide either for payment of all obligations in full or for payment of a lesser amount.[29] Prior to the 2005 act, the time for repayment was usually three years unless the court approved an extension for up to five years. Under the new Code, the length of the payment plan (three or five years) is determined by the debtor's median family income. If the debtor's family income is greater than the state median family income under the means test (previously discussed), the proposed plan must be for five years. The term may not exceed five years, however.

The Code requires the debtor to make "timely" payments from the debtor's disposable income, and the trustee must ensure that the debtor com-

---

28. As with a Chapter 11 reorganization plan, full repayment of all claims is not always required.

29. Under the 2005 act, a plan under Chapter 13 or Chapter 12 (to be discussed shortly) might propose to pay less than 100 percent of prepetition domestic-support obligations that had been assigned, but only if disposable income is dedicated to a five-year plan. Disposable income is also redefined to exclude the amounts reasonably necessary to pay current domestic-support obligations.

mences these payments. The plan cannot materially alter terms of repayment on a retirement loan account, however. These payment amounts must take into consideration the scheduled payments to lessors of personal property and must provide adequate protection to secured creditors of personal property. Proof of adequate insurance on personal property is required. The debtor must begin making payments under the proposed plan within thirty days after the plan has been *filed*. Failure of the debtor to make timely payments or to commence payments within the thirty-day period will allow the court to convert the case to a liquidation bankruptcy or to dismiss the petition.

Confirmation of the Plan   After the plan is filed, the court holds a confirmation hearing, at which interested parties (such as creditors) may object to the plan. Under the 2005 act, the hearing must be held at least twenty days, but no more than forty-five days, after the meeting of the creditors. Confirmation of the plan is dependent on the debtor's certification that postpetition domestic-support obligations have been paid in full and that all prepetition tax returns have been filed. The court will confirm a plan with respect to each claim of a secured creditor under any of the following circumstances:

1. If the secured creditors have accepted the plan.
2. If the plan provides that secured creditors retain their liens until there is payment in full or until the debtor receives a discharge.
3. If the debtor surrenders the property securing the claims to the creditors.

In addition, for confirmation, the plan must provide that a creditor with a purchase-money security interest (PMSI) retains its lien until payment of the entire debt for a motor vehicle purchased within 910 days before filing the petition. (A PMSI is created when a seller or lender agrees to extend credit for part or all of the price of goods being purchased. A PMSI in consumer goods is perfected automatically at the time of the sale.) For PMSIs on other personal property, the payment plan must cover debts incurred within a one-year period preceding the filing.

Objection to the Plan   Unsecured creditors do not have the power to confirm a repayment plan, but they can object to it. The court can approve a plan over the objection of the trustee or any unsecured creditor only in either of the following situations:

1. When the value of the property (replacement value as of the date of filing) to be distributed under the plan is at least equal to the amount of the claims.
2. When all of the debtor's projected disposable income to be received during the plan period will be applied to making payments. Disposable income is all income received less amounts needed to pay domestic-support obligations and/or amounts needed to meet ordinary expenses to continue the operation of a business. The 2005 act also excludes from disposable income charitable contributions up to 15 percent of the debtor's gross income and the reasonable and necessary costs for health insurance for the debtor and his or her dependents.

Modification of the Plan   Prior to completion of payments, the plan may be modified at the request of the debtor, the trustee, or an unsecured creditor. If any interested party objects to the modification, the court must hold a hearing to determine whether the modified plan will be approved.

Discharge　After completion of all payments, the court grants a discharge of all debts provided for by the repayment plan. Except for allowed claims not provided for by the plan, certain long-term debts provided for by the plan, certain tax claims, payments on retirement accounts, and claims for domestic-support obligations, all other debts are dischargeable. Under prior law, a discharge of debts under a Chapter 13 repayment plan was sometimes referred to as a "superdischarge" because it allowed the discharge of fraudulently incurred debt and claims resulting from malicious or willful injury.

The 2005 Bankruptcy Reform Act, however, deleted most of the "superdischarge" provisions, especially for debts based on fraud. Today, debts for trust fund taxes, taxes for which returns were never filed or filed late (within two years of filing), domestic-support payments, student loans, and injury or property damage from driving under the influence of alcohol or drugs are nondischargeable. The new law also excludes fraudulent tax obligations, criminal fines and restitution, fraud by a person acting in a fiduciary capacity, and restitution for willfully and maliciously causing personal injury or death.

Even if the debtor does not complete the plan, a hardship discharge may be granted if failure to complete the plan was due to circumstances beyond the debtor's control and if the value of the property distributed under the plan was greater than what would have been paid in a liquidation. A discharge can be revoked within one year if it was obtained by fraud.

Family Farmers and Fishermen

In 1986, to help relieve economic pressure on small farmers, Congress created Chapter 12 of the Bankruptcy Code. In 2005, Congress extended this protection to family fishermen,[30] modified its provisions somewhat, and made it a permanent chapter in the Bankruptcy Code (previously the statutes authorizing Chapter 12 had to be periodically renewed by Congress).

Definitions　For purposes of Chapter 12, a *family farmer* is one whose gross income is at least 50 percent farm dependent and whose debts are at least 50 percent farm related. The total debt for a family farmer must not exceed $3.237 million. (Prior law required a farmer's debts to be 80 percent farm related and not to exceed $1.5 million.) A partnership or closely held corporation (at least 50 percent owned by the farm family) can also qualify as a family farmer.

A *family fisherman* is defined by the 2005 act as one whose gross income is at least 50 percent dependent on commercial fishing operations[31] and whose debts are at least 80 percent related to commercial fishing. The total debt for a family fisherman must not exceed $1.5 million. As with family farmers, a partnership or closely held corporation can also qualify.

---

30. Although the Code uses the terms *fishermen* and *fisherman,* Chapter 12 provisions apply equally to men and women.

31. Commercial fishing operations include catching, harvesting, or aquaculture raising fish, shrimp, lobsters, urchins, seaweed, shellfish, or other aquatic species or products.

Filing the Petition The procedure for filing a family-farmer or family-fishermen bankruptcy plan is very similar to the procedure for filing a repayment plan under Chapter 13. The debtor must file a plan not later than ninety days after the order for relief. The filing of the petition acts as an automatic stay against creditors' and co-obligors' actions against the estate.

A farmer or fisherman who has already filed a reorganization or repayment plan may convert it to a Chapter 12 plan. The debtor may also convert a Chapter 12 plan to a liquidation plan.

Content and Confirmation of the Plan The content of a plan under Chapter 12 is basically the same as that of a Chapter 13 repayment plan. The plan can be modified by the debtor but, except for cause, must be confirmed or denied within forty-five days of filing.

Court confirmation of the plan is the same as for a repayment plan. In summary, the plan must provide for payment of secured debts at the value of the collateral. If the secured debt exceeds the value of the collateral, the remaining debt is unsecured. For unsecured debtors, the plan must be confirmed if either the value of the property to be distributed under the plan equals the amount of the claim or the plan provides that all of the debtor's disposable income to be received in a three-year period (or longer, by court approval) will be applied to making payments. Disposable income is all income received less amounts needed to support the farmer or fisherman and his or her family and to continue the farming or commercial fishing operation. Completion of payments under the plan discharges all debts provided for by the plan.

REVIEWING . . . CREDITORS' RIGHTS AND BANKRUPTCY

Three months ago, Janet Hart's husband of twenty years died of cancer. Although he had medical insurance, he left Janet with outstanding medical bills of more than $50,000. Janet has worked at the local library for the past ten years, earning $1,700 per month. Since her husband's death, Janet also receives $1,500 in Social Security benefits and $1,100 in life insurance proceeds every month, which leaves her with a monthly income of $4,300. After she pays the monthly mortgage payment of $1,500 and the monthly amounts due on other debts, Janet barely has enough left over to buy groceries for her family. (She has two teenaged daughters at home.) She decides to file for Chapter 7 bankruptcy, hoping for a fresh start. Using the information presented in the chapter, answer the following questions.

1. Under the Bankruptcy Code after the enactment of the 2005 revisions, what must Janet do prior to filing a petition for relief under Chapter 7?

2. How much time does Janet have after filing the bankruptcy petition to submit the required schedules? What happens if Janet does not meet the deadline?

3. Assume that Janet files a petition under Chapter 7. Further assume that the median family income in the state in which Janet lives is $49,300. What steps would a court take to determine whether Janet's petition is presumed to be "substantial abuse" using the means test?

4. Suppose that the court determines that no presumption of substantial abuse applies in Janet's case. Nevertheless, the court finds that Janet does have the ability to repay at least a portion of the amount due on the medical bills out of her disposable income. What would the court likely order in that situation?

KEY TERMS

artisan's lien 394
attachment 395
automatic stay 408
consumer-debtor 403
co-surety 400
cram-down provision 424
creditors' composition
   agreement 396
debtor in possession (DIP) 422
default 393
discharge 404
garnishment 396

guarantor 398
homestead exemption 401
lien 394
liquidation 403
mechanic's lien 394
mortgagee 396
mortgagor 396
order for relief 407
petition in bankruptcy 405
preference 413
preferred creditor 413
reaffirmation agreement 420

right of contribution 400
right of reimbursement 400
right of subrogation 400
surety 397
suretyship 397
trustee 404
U.S. Trustee 405
workout 422
writ of attachment 395
writ of execution 395

CHAPTER SUMMARY • CREDITORS' RIGHTS AND BANKRUPTCY

REMEDIES AVAILABLE TO CREDITORS

Liens
(See pages 394–396.)
	1. *Mechanic's lien*—A nonpossessory, filed lien on an owner's real estate for labor, services, or materials furnished to or made on the realty.
	
	2. *Artisan's lien*—A possessory lien on an owner's personal property for labor performed or value added.
	
	3. *Judicial liens*—
	
	  a. Attachment—A court-ordered seizure of property prior to a court's final determination of the creditor's rights to the property. Attachment is available only on the creditor's posting of a bond and strict compliance with the applicable state statutes.
	
	  b. Writ of execution—A court order directing the sheriff to seize (levy) and sell a debtor's nonexempt real or personal property to satisfy a court's judgment in the creditor's favor.

Garnishment (See page 396.)	A collection remedy that allows the creditor to attach a debtor's money (such as wages owed or bank accounts) and property that are held by a third person.
Creditors' Composition Agreement (See page 396.)	A contract between a debtor and his or her creditors by which the debtor's debts are discharged by payment of a sum less than the amount that is actually owed.
Mortgage Foreclosure (See pages 396–397.)	On the debtor's default, the entire mortgage debt is due and payable, allowing the creditor to foreclose on the realty by selling it to satisfy the debt.
Suretyship or Guaranty (See pages 397–400.)	Under contract, a third person agrees to be primarily or secondarily liable for the debt owed by the principal debtor. A creditor can turn to this third person for satisfaction of the debt.

LAWS ASSISTING DEBTORS

Exemptions (See pages 400–401.)	Numerous laws, including consumer protection statutes, assist debtors. Additionally, state laws exempt certain types of real and personal property from levy of execution or attachment. 1. *Real property*—Each state permits a debtor to retain the family home, either in its entirety or up to a specified dollar amount, free from the claims of unsecured creditors or trustees in bankruptcy (homestead exemption).

CHAPTER SUMMARY • CREDITORS' RIGHTS AND BANKRUPTCY—CONTINUED

Exemptions— Continued	2. *Personal property*—Personal property that is most often exempt from satisfaction of judgment debts includes the following:
	a. Household furniture up to a specified dollar amount.
	b. Clothing and certain personal possessions.
	c. Transportation vehicles up to a specified dollar amount.
	d. Certain classified animals, such as livestock and pets.
	e. Equipment used in a business or trade up to a specified dollar amount.

REMEDIES AVAILABLE TO CREDITORS

BANKRUPTCY—A COMPARISON OF CHAPTERS 7, 11, 12, AND 13

Issue	Chapter 7	Chapter 11	Chapters 12 and 13
Purpose	Liquidation.	Reorganization.	Adjustment.
Who Can Petition	Debtor (voluntary) or creditors (involuntary).	Debtor (voluntary) or creditors (involuntary).	Debtor (voluntary) only.
Who Can Be a Debtor	Any "person" (including partnerships, corporations, and municipalities) except railroads, insurance companies, banks, savings and loan institutions, investment companies licensed by the Small Business Administration, and credit unions. Farmers and charitable institutions also cannot be involuntarily petitioned. If the court finds the petition to be a substantial abuse of the use of Chapter 7, the debtor may be required to convert to a Chapter 13 repayment plan.	Any debtor eligible for Chapter 7 relief; railroads are also eligible. Individuals have specific rules and limitations.	*Chapter 12*—Any family farmer (one whose gross income is at least 50 percent farm dependent and whose debts are at least 50 percent farm related) or family fisherman (one whose gross income is at least 50 percent dependent on commercial fishing operations and whose debts are at least 80 percent related to commercial fishing) or any partnership or closely held corporation at least 50 percent owned by a family farmer or fisherman, when total debt does not exceed a specified amount ($3.237 million for farmers and $1.5 million for fishermen). *Chapter 13*—Any individual (not partnerships or corporations) with regular income who owes fixed unsecured debts of less than $307,675 or fixed secured debts of less than $922,975.
Procedure Leading to Discharge	Nonexempt property is sold with proceeds to be distributed (in order) to priority groups. Dischargeable debts are terminated.	Plan is submitted; if it is approved and followed, debts are discharged.	Plan is submitted and must be approved if the value of the property to be distributed equals the amount of the claims or if the debtor turns over disposable income for a

(Continued)

CHAPTER SUMMARY • CREDITORS' RIGHTS AND BANKRUPTCY—CONTINUED

Issue	Chapter 7	Chapter 11	Chapters 12 and 13
Procedure Leading to Discharge—Continued			three-year or five-year period; if the plan is followed, debts are discharged.
Advantages	On liquidation and distribution, most debts are discharged, and the debtor has an opportunity for a fresh start.	Debtor continues in business. Creditors can either accept the plan, or it can be "crammed down" on them. The plan allows for the reorganization and liquidation of debts over the plan period.	Debtor continues in business or possession of assets. If the plan is approved, most debts are discharged after the plan period.

FOR REVIEW

Answers for the even-numbered questions in this For Review *section can be found in Appendix O at the end of this text.*

1. What is a prejudgment attachment? What is a writ of execution? How does a creditor use these remedies?

2. What is garnishment? When might a creditor undertake a garnishment proceeding?

3. In a bankruptcy proceeding, what constitutes the debtor's estate in property? What property is exempt from the estate under federal bankruptcy law?

4. What is the difference between an exception to discharge and an objection to discharge?

5. In a Chapter 11 reorganization, what is the role of the debtor in possession?

QUESTIONS AND CASE PROBLEMS

12–1. Artisan's Lien. Air Ruidoso, Ltd., operated a commuter airline and air charter service between Ruidoso, New Mexico, and airports in Albuquerque and El Paso. Executive Aviation Center, Inc., provided services for airlines at the Albuquerque International Airport. When Air Ruidoso failed to pay more than $10,000 that it owed for fuel, oil, and oxygen, Executive Aviation took possession of Air Ruidoso's plane. Executive Aviation claimed that it had a lien on the plane and filed a suit in a New Mexico state court to foreclose. Do supplies such as fuel, oil, and oxygen qualify as "materials" for the purpose of creating an artisan's lien? Why or why not?

Question with Sample Answer

12–2. Meredith, a farmer, borrowed $5,000 from Farmer's Bank and gave the bank $4,000 in bearer bonds to hold as collateral for the loan. Meredith's neighbor, Peterson, who had known Meredith for years, signed as a surety on the note. Because of a drought, Meredith's harvest that year was only a fraction of the normal amount, and he was forced to default on his payments to Farmer's Bank. The bank did not immediately sell the bonds but instead requested $5,000 from Peterson. Peterson paid the $5,000 and then demanded that the bank give him the $4,000 in securities. Can Peterson enforce this demand? Explain.

For a sample answer to this question, go to Appendix P at the end of this text.

12–3. Liens. Sylvia takes her car to Caleb's Auto Repair Shop. A sign in the window states that all repairs must be paid for in cash unless credit is approved in advance. Sylvia and Caleb agree that Caleb will repair Sylvia's car engine and put in a new transmission. No mention is made of credit. Because Caleb is not sure how much engine repair will be necessary, he refuses to give Sylvia an estimate. He repairs the engine and puts in a new transmission. When Sylvia comes to pick up her car, she learns that the bill is $995. Sylvia is furious, refuses to pay Caleb that amount, and demands possession of her car. Caleb demands payment. Discuss the rights of the parties in this matter.

12–4. Voluntary versus Involuntary Bankruptcy. Burke has been a rancher all her life, raising cattle and crops. Her ranch is valued at $500,000, almost all of which is exempt under state law. Burke has eight creditors and a total indebtedness of $70,000. Two of her largest creditors are Oman ($30,000 owed) and Sneed ($25,000 owed). The other six creditors have claims of less than $5,000 each. A drought has ruined all of Burke's crops and forced her to sell many of her cattle at a loss. She cannot pay off her creditors.

1. Under the Bankruptcy Code, can Burke, with a $500,000 ranch, voluntarily petition herself into bankruptcy? Explain.
2. Could either Oman or Sneed force Burke into involuntary bankruptcy? Explain.

12–5. Automatic Stay. David Sisco had about $600 in an account in Tinker Federal Credit Union. Sisco owed DPW Employees Credit Union a little more than $1,100. To collect on the debt, DPW obtained a garnishment judgment and served it on Tinker. The next day, Sisco filed a bankruptcy petition. Tinker then told DPW that because of the bankruptcy filing, it could not pay the garnishment. DPW objected, and Tinker asked an Oklahoma state court to resolve the issue. What effect, if any, does Sisco's bankruptcy filing have on DPW's garnishment action? [*DPW Employees Credit Union v. Tinker Federal Credit Union*, 925 P.2d 93 (Okla.App.4th 1996)]

Case Problem with Sample Answer

12–6. Between 1980 and 1987, Craig Hanson borrowed funds from Great Lakes Higher Education Corp. to finance his education at the University of Wisconsin. Hanson defaulted on the debt in 1989, and Great Lakes obtained a judgment against him for $31,583.77. Three years later, Hanson filed a bankruptcy petition under Chapter 13. Great Lakes timely filed a proof of claim in the amount of $35,531.08. Hanson's repayment plan proposed to pay $135 monthly to Great Lakes over sixty months, which in total was only 19 percent of the claim, but said nothing about discharging the remaining balance. The plan was confirmed without objection. After Hanson completed the payments under the plan, without any additional proof or argument being offered, the court granted a discharge of his student loans. In 2003, Educational Credit Management Corp. (ECMC), which had taken over Great Lakes' interest in the loans, filed a motion for relief from the discharge. What is the requirement for the discharge of a student loan obligation in bankruptcy? Did Hanson meet this requirement? Should the court grant ECMC's motion? Discuss. [*In re Hanson*, 397 F.3d 482 (7th Cir. 2005)]

After you have answered this problem, compare your answer with the sample answer given on the Web site that accompanies this text. Go to www.thomsonedu.com/westbuslaw/let, select "Chapter 12," and click on "Case Problem with Sample Answer."

12–7. Discharge in Bankruptcy. Jon Goulet attended the University of Wisconsin in Eau Claire and Regis University in Denver, Colorado, from which he earned a bachelor's degree in history in 1972. Over the next ten years, he worked as a bartender and restaurant manager. In 1984, he became a life insurance agent, and his income ranged from $20,000 to

$30,000. In 1989, however, his agent's license was revoked for insurance fraud, and he was arrested for cocaine possession. From 1991 to 1995, Goulet was again at the University of Wisconsin, working toward, but failing to obtain, a master's degree in psychology. To pay for his studies, he took out student loans totaling $76,000. Goulet then returned to bartending and restaurant management and tried real estate sales. His income for the year 2000 was $1,490, and his expenses, excluding a child-support obligation, were $5,904. When the student loans came due, Goulet filed a petition for bankruptcy. On what ground might the loans be dischargeable? Should the court grant a discharge on this ground? Why or why not? [*Goulet v. Educational Credit Management Corp.*, 284 F.3d 773 (7th Cir. 2002)]

12–8. Automatic Stay. On January 22, 2001, Marlene Moffett bought a used 1998 Honda Accord from Hendrick Honda in Woodbridge, Virginia. Moffett agreed to pay $20,024.25, with interest, in sixty monthly installments, and Hendrick retained a security interest in the car. Hendrick assigned its rights under the sales agreement to Tidewater Finance Co., which perfected its security interest. The car was Moffett's only means of traveling the forty miles from her home to her workplace. In March and April 2002, Moffett missed two monthly payments. On April 25, Tidewater repossessed the car. On the same day, Moffett filed a Chapter 13 plan in a federal bankruptcy court. Moffett asked that the car be returned to her, in part under the Bankruptcy Code's automatic-stay provision. Tidewater asked the court to terminate the automatic stay so that it could sell the car. How can the interests of both the debtor and the creditor be fully protected in this case? What should the court rule? Explain. [*In re Moffett*, 356 F.3d 518 (4th Cir. 2004)]

12–9. Liquidation. James Stout, a professor of economics and business at Cornell College in Iowa City, Iowa, filed a petition in bankruptcy under Chapter 7, seeking to discharge about $95,000 in credit-card debts. At the time, Stout had been divorced for ten years and had custody of his children: Z.S., who attended college, and G.S., who was twelve years old. Stout's ex-wife did not contribute child support. According to Stout, G.S. was an "elite" ice-skater who practiced twenty hours a week and had placed between first and third at more than forty competitive events. He had decided to homeschool G.S., whose achievements were average for her grade level despite her frequent absences from public school. His petition showed monthly income of $4,227 and expenses of $4,806. The expenses included annual homeschool costs of $8,400 and annual skating expenses of $6,000. They did not include Z.S.'s college costs, such as airfare for his upcoming studies in Europe, and other items. The trustee allowed monthly expenses of $3,227—with nothing for skating—and asked the court to dismiss the petition. Can the court grant this request? Should it? If so, what might it encourage Stout to do? Explain. [*In re Stout*, 336 Bankr. 138 (N.D. Iowa 2006)]

A Question of Ethics

12–10. Herpel, Inc., agreed to make a stone fireplace mantel for a house owned by Straub Capital Corp. When the mantel was first delivered, Straub was not satisfied, so Herpel took the mantel back, refinished it, and redelivered it five weeks later. The mantel was installed, but Straub did not pay. Herpel filed a mechanic's lien 113 days after the first delivery but less than 90 days after the second delivery. Herpel then filed an action in a Florida district court to foreclose on the lien. The trial court ruled in favor of Straub because the lien had been filed more than 90 days from the time the mantel was first delivered. The appellate court reversed, noting that although the time for filing a lien is not extended by repair, corrective, or warranty work, "work done in fulfillment of the contract will extend the time for filing of the claim of lien." In view of these events, consider the following questions. [*Herpel, Inc. v. Straub Capital Corp.*, 682 So.2d 661 (S.D.Fla. 1996)]

1. The court's ruling hinges on the fact that Herpel took the fireplace mantel back, attempted to cure the alleged defects, and then offered it again for acceptance by Straub. Do you agree that this work was "in fulfillment of the contract," rather than to correct the defects?
2. Would the outcome of this case have been different if the fireplace mantel had been left with the buyer at the time of delivery and the seller had attempted to make repairs to it while it was in the buyer's possession? Why or why not?
3. Generally, do you think that it is fair for the court to consider who was in possession of the mantel at the time of repair when determining whether the lien was filed within the statutory time period?

Critical-Thinking Ethical Question

12–11. The Bankruptcy Reform Act of 2005 subjects a large class of individuals in the United States to increased financial risk. Supporters of the 2005 law contend that it

will curb abuse by deterring financially troubled debtors from looking at bankruptcy as a mere "planning tool" instead of as a last resort. Critics of the act argue that the reform legislation will make it difficult for debtors to obtain a "fresh start" financially—one of the goals of bankruptcy law in the United States. Do you believe that the 2005 act adequately balances the interests of creditors and debtors? Why or why not?

Video Question

12–12. Go to this text's Web site at **www.thomsonedu.com/westbuslaw/let** and select "Chapter 12." Click on "Video Questions" and view the video titled *The River*. Then answer the following questions.

1. In the video, a crowd (including Mel Gibson) is gathered at a farm auction in which a neighbor's (Jim Antonio's) farming goods are being sold. The people in the crowd, who are upset because they believe that the bank is selling out the farmer, begin chanting "no sale, no sale." In an effort to calm the group, the farmer tells the crowd that "they've already foreclosed" on his farm. What does he mean?
2. Assume that the auction is a result of Chapter 7 bankruptcy proceedings. Was the farmer's petition for bankruptcy voluntary or involuntary? Explain.
3. Suppose that the farmer purchased the homestead three years prior to filing a petition for bankruptcy and that the current market value of the farm is $215,000. What is the maximum amount of equity the farmer could claim as exempt under the 2005 Bankruptcy Reform Act?
4. Compare the results of a Chapter 12 bankruptcy as opposed to a Chapter 7 bankruptcy for the farmer in the video.

INTERACTING WITH THE INTERNET

For updated links to resources available on the Web, as well as a variety of other materials, visit this text's Web site at

www.thomsonedu.com/westbuslaw/let

The Legal Information Institute at Cornell University offers a collection of law materials concerning debtor-creditor relationships, including federal statutes and recent Supreme Court decisions on this topic, at

www.law.cornell.edu/topics/debtor_creditor.html

The U.S. Department of Labor's Web site contains a page on garnishment and employees' rights in relation to garnishment proceedings at

www.dol.gov/dol/topic/wages/garnishments.htm

The U.S. Bankruptcy Code is online at

www.law.cornell.edu:80/uscode/11

For information and news on bankruptcy reform legislation, go to the site maintained by Bankruptcy Media at

www.bankruptcyfinder.com/bankruptcyreformnews.html

INTERNET EXERCISES

Go to **www.thomsonedu.com/westbuslaw/let**, the Web site that accompanies this text. Select "Chapter 12" and click on "Internet Exercises." There you will find the following Internet research exercises that you can perform to learn more about topics covered in this chapter.

Internet Exercise 12–1: LEGAL PERSPECTIVE—Debtor-Creditor Relations
Internet Exercise 12–2: MANAGEMENT PERSPECTIVE—Bankruptcy Alternatives

BEFORE THE TEST

Go to **www.thomsonedu.com/westbuslaw/let**, the Web site that accompanies this text. Select "Chapter 12" and click on "Interactive Quizzes." You will find a number of interactive questions relating to this chapter.

UNIT THREE CUMULATIVE BUSINESS HYPOTHETICAL

Samuel Polson has an idea for a new software application. Polson hires an assistant and invests a considerable amount of his own time and funds developing the application. To develop other software, and to manufacture and market his applications, Polson needs financial capital.

1. Polson borrows $5,000 from his friend Michael Brant. Polson promises to repay Brant the $5,000 in three weeks. Brant, in urgent need of money, borrows $5,000 from his friend Mary Viva and assigns his rights to the $5,000 Polson owes him to Viva in return for the loan. Viva notifies Polson of the assignment. Polson pays Brant the $5,000 on the date stipulated in their contract. Brant refuses to give the money to Viva, and Viva sues Polson. Is Polson obligated to pay Viva $5,000 also? Discuss.

2. Polson learns that a competitor, Trivan, Inc., has already filed for a patent on a nearly identical program and has manufactured and sold the software to some customers. Polson learns from a reliable source that Trivan paid Polson's assistant a substantial sum of money to obtain a copy of the program. What legal recourse does Polson have against Trivan? Discuss fully.

3. While Polson is developing his idea and founding his business, he has no income. He continues to have living expenses, however, as well as payments due on his mortgage, various credit-card debts, and some loans that he took out to pay for his son's college tuition. As his business begins to make money, Polson files for Chapter 7 liquidation to be rid of his personal debts entirely, even though he believes he could probably pay them off over a four-year period if he scrimped and used every cent available to pay his creditors. Are all of Polson's personal debts dischargeable under Chapter 7, including the debts incurred for his son's education? Given the fact that Polson could foreseeably pay off his debts over a four-year period, will the court allow Polson to obtain relief under Chapter 7? Why or why not?

4. Polson is the sole owner of the business and pays no business income taxes. What is the form of Polson's business organization? What other options, in terms of business organizational forms, does Polson have? What are the advantages and disadvantages of each option? If Polson decides to incorporate the business under the name Polson Software, Inc., what steps will he need to take to do so?

UNIT 4 The Employment Environment

13 Employment Relationships

CONTENTS

> " [It] is a universal principle in the law of agency, that the powers of the agent are to be exercised for the benefit of the principal only, and not of the agent or of third parties. "

—JOSEPH STORY, 1779–1845
(Associate justice of the
United States Supreme Court, 1811–1844)

AGENCY
A relationship between two parties in which one party (the agent) agrees to represent or act for the other (the principal).

CHAPTER OBJECTIVES

After reading this chapter, you should be able to answer the following questions:

1 What is an agency relationship, and how do agency relationships arise?

2 What is the difference between an employee and an independent contractor?

3 What are the rights and duties of parties to an agency relationship?

4 What federal statutes govern wages and worker health and safety in the workplace? What is the purpose of workers' compensation laws?

5 How does the government provide for income security? What are some issues relating to employee privacy rights?

EMPLOYMENT RELATIONSHIPS are agency relationships. Indeed, one of the most common, important, and pervasive legal relationships is that of **agency.** In an agency relationship between two parties, one of the parties, called the *agent,* agrees to represent or act for the other, called the *principal.* The principal has the right to control the agent's conduct in matters entrusted to the agent, and the agent must exercise his or her powers "for the benefit of the principal only," as Justice Joseph Story indicated in the chapter-opening quotation. By using agents, a principal can conduct multiple business operations simultaneously in various locations. Thus, for example, contracts that bind the principal, such as a corporation or other business firm, can be made at different places with different persons at the same time. Because agency relationships permeate the business world, an understanding of the law of agency is crucial to understanding the legal environment of business.

Also important to the framework of the legal environment of business are employment statutes. For most of this century, the relationship of employer and employee has been the subject of federal and state legislation. Many of these statutes are discussed in the last part of this chapter.

AGENCY RELATIONSHIPS

Section 1(1) of the *Restatement (Second) of Agency*[1] defines agency as "the fiduciary relation which results from the manifestation of consent by one person to another that the other shall act in his [or her] behalf and subject to his

---

1. The *Restatement (Second) of Agency* is an authoritative summary of the law of agency and is often referred to by jurists in their decisions and opinions.

[or her] control, and consent by the other so to act." In other words, in a principal-agent relationship, the parties have agreed that the agent will act *on behalf and instead of* the principal in negotiating and transacting business with third parties.

The term **fiduciary** is at the heart of agency law. The term can be used both as a noun and as an adjective. When used as a noun, it refers to a person having a duty created by her or his undertaking to act primarily for another's benefit in matters connected with the undertaking. When used as an adjective, as in "fiduciary relationship," it means that the relationship involves trust and confidence.

Agency relationships commonly exist between employers and employees. Agency relationships may sometimes also exist between employers and independent contractors who are hired to perform special tasks or services.

FIDUCIARY

As a noun, a person having a duty created by his or her undertaking to act primarily for another's benefit in matters connected with the undertaking. As an adjective, a relationship founded on trust and confidence.

Employer-Employee Relationships

Normally, all employees who deal with third parties are deemed to be agents.
| **Example #1**   A salesperson in a department store is an agent of the store's owner (the principal) and acts on the owner's behalf. Any sale of goods made by the salesperson to a customer is binding on the principal. Similarly, most representations of fact made by the salesperson with respect to the goods sold are binding on the principal.|

Because employees who deal with third parties are normally deemed to be agents of their employers, agency law and employment law overlap considerably. Agency relationships, though, as will become apparent, can exist outside an employer-employee relationship and thus have a broader reach than employment laws do. Additionally, bear in mind that agency law is based on the common law. In the employment realm, many common law doctrines have been displaced by statutory law and government regulations governing employment relationships.

Employment laws (state and federal) apply only to the employer-employee relationship. Statutes governing Social Security, withholding taxes, workers' compensation, unemployment compensation, workplace safety, employment discrimination, and the like are applicable only if employer-employee status exists. *These laws do not apply to an independent contractor.*

Employer–Independent Contractor Relationships

Independent contractors are not employees because, by definition, those who hire them have no control over the details of their physical performance. Section 2 of the *Restatement (Second) of Agency* defines an **independent contractor** as follows:

INDEPENDENT CONTRACTOR

One who works for, and receives payment from, an employer but whose working conditions and methods are not controlled by the employer. An independent contractor is not an employee but may be an agent.

> [An independent contractor is] a person who contracts with another to do something for him [or her] but who is not controlled by the other nor subject to the other's right to control with respect to his [or her] physical conduct in the performance of the undertaking. *He [or she] may or may not be an agent.* [Emphasis added.]

Building contractors and subcontractors are independent contractors; a property owner does not control the acts of either of these professionals. Truck drivers who own their equipment and hire themselves out on a per-job basis are independent contractors, but truck drivers who drive company trucks on a regular basis are usually employees.

A businessperson (an independent contractor) sits on the floor working on his laptop computer in a computer server facility. What are some significant differences between employees and independent contractors? (Thinkstock Photo)

The relationship between a person or firm and an independent contractor may or may not involve an agency relationship. **Example #2** An owner of real estate who hires a real estate broker to negotiate a sale of the property not only has contracted with an independent contractor (the real estate broker) but also has established an agency relationship for the specific purpose of assisting in the sale of the property.

Determining Employee Status

The courts are frequently asked to determine whether a particular worker is an employee or an independent contractor. How a court decides this issue can have a significant effect on the rights and liabilities of the parties.

Criteria Used by the Courts   In determining whether a worker has the status of an employee or an independent contractor, the courts often consider the following questions:

1. How much control can the employer exercise over the details of the work? (If an employer can exercise considerable control over the details of the work, this would indicate employee status. This is perhaps the most important factor weighed by the courts in determining employee status.)
2. Is the worker engaged in an occupation or business distinct from that of the employer? (If so, this points to independent-contractor status, not employee status.)
3. Is the work usually done under the employer's direction or by a specialist without supervision? (If the work is usually done under the employer's direction, this would indicate employee status.)
4. Does the employer supply the tools at the place of work? (If so, this would indicate employee status.)
5. For how long is the person employed? (If the person is employed for a long period of time, this would indicate employee status.)
6. What is the method of payment—by time period or at the completion of the job? (Payment by time period, such as once every two weeks or once a month, would indicate employee status.)
7. What degree of skill is required of the worker? (If little skill is required, this may indicate employee status.)

Sometimes, it is beneficial for workers to have employee status—to take advantage of laws protecting employees, for example. In contrast, independent-contractor status can sometimes be an advantage—to maintain ownership rights in copyrighted works, for example.

Criteria Used by the IRS   Often, the criteria for determining employee status are established by a statute or an administrative agency regulation. Businesspersons should be aware that the Internal Revenue Service (IRS) has established its own criteria for determining whether a worker is an independent contractor or an employee. Although the IRS once considered twenty factors in determining a worker's status, guidelines effective in 1997 encourage IRS examiners to focus on just one of those factors—the degree of control the business exercises over the worker.

The IRS tends to closely scrutinize a firm's classification of its workers because employers can avoid certain tax liabilities by hiring independent con-

tractors instead of employees. Even when a firm classifies a worker as an independent contractor, if the IRS decides that the worker is actually an employee, then the employer will be responsible for paying any applicable Social Security, withholding, and unemployment taxes.

In contrast, when a worker is a corporate officer, the exercise of control may be the opposite of the usual situation involving an employer and an employee. In that circumstance, the question may concern the degree of control that the officer (the employee) exercises over the corporation (the employer). In the following case, the issue was whether a corporate officer was an employee of the corporation.

CASE 13.1   Nu-Look Design, Inc. v. Commissioner of Internal Revenue

United States Court of Appeals,
Third Circuit, 2004.
356 F.3d 290.

BACKGROUND AND FACTS Nu-Look Design, Inc., is a home-improvement company that provides carpentry, siding installation, and general residential construction services. During 1996, 1997, and 1998, Ronald Stark was Nu-Look's president, manager, and sole shareholder. He solicited business for the company, performed the bookkeeping, handled the firm's finances, and hired and supervised its workers. Instead of paying Stark a salary or wages, Nu-Look

distributed its income to him "as Mr. Stark's needs arose." Nu-Look reported on its tax returns for those years net income of $10,866.14, $14,216.37, and $7,103.60, respectively. Stark reported the same amounts as income on his tax returns. In 2001, the Internal Revenue Service (IRS) classified Stark as Nu-Look's employee and assessed federal employment taxes for 1996, 1997, and 1998. Nu-Look filed a suit in the U.S. Tax Court against the commissioner of the IRS, seeking relief from this liability. Nu-Look contended in part that Stark was not an employee because Nu-Look did not control Stark—Stark controlled Nu-Look. The court ruled against the firm, which appealed to the U.S. Court of Appeals for the Third Circuit.

IN THE WORDS OF THE COURT . . . SMITH, Circuit Judge.

This appeal challenges the determination by the United States Tax Court that the Internal Revenue Service ("IRS") appropriately classified Ronald A. Stark, who was an officer and the sole shareholder of Nu-Look Design, Inc. ("Nu-Look"), as an employee of Nu-Look. That determination resulted in Nu-Look's liability for certain employment taxes under the Federal Insurance Contributions Act ("FICA") and the Federal Unemployment Tax Act ("FUTA"). * * *

    * * * *

Nu-Look contends that the Tax Court erred in determining that Stark was an employee under the FICA and the FUTA. We begin by looking to the statutory language. Where the statutory language is plain and unambiguous, further inquiry is not required * * * .

*Both the FICA and the FUTA impose taxes on employers based on the wages paid to individuals in their employ. "Wages," as defined by both Acts, includes, with certain exceptions not applicable here, "all remuneration for employment * * * ." Employment is "any service of whatever nature, performed * * * by an employee for the person employing him * * * ." Employee is defined by the FICA [to include] * * * any officer of a corporation * * * .* Under the FUTA, the term *employee*, with certain exceptions not relevant here, has the same meaning * * * . [Under the IRS regulations] there is an exception for an "officer of a corporation who as such does not perform any services or performs only minor services and who neither receives nor is entitled to receive, directly or indirectly, any remuneration." [Emphasis added.]

CASE 13.1—CONTINUED ▶

* * * *

Mindful of these statutory provisions and Stark's status as a corporate officer, the Tax Court appropriately focused on the nature of the services Stark rendered and whether the distributions Nu-Look paid were remuneration for those services. It found that Stark performed more than minor services and that the distributions Stark received were, in fact, remuneration for his services. Those findings led the Tax Court to conclude that Stark was an employee for purposes of the FICA and the FUTA.

We agree. The record establishes that Stark was a corporate officer and that he single-handedly managed Nu-Look's entire operation. The services that Stark rendered for Nu-Look were, therefore, substantial and the Tax Court appropriately concluded that Stark was an employee * * * .

* * * *

In sum, we conclude that Stark was properly classified by the IRS as an employee of Nu-Look and that Nu-Look lacked a reasonable basis for failing to treat Stark as an employee. We will affirm the decision of the Tax Court that Nu-Look is liable for certain employment taxes under the FICA and the FUTA for calendar years 1996, 1997 and 1998.

DECISION AND REMEDY   The U.S. Court of Appeals for the Third Circuit affirmed the ruling of the lower court. For federal tax purposes, Stark was to be considered an employee of Nu-Look, in light of the nature of the services that he rendered to the company and the income that the firm distributed to him as payment for those services.

WHY IS THIS CASE IMPORTANT?   *Businesspersons should be aware that the mere designation of a person as either an independent contractor or a corporate officer does not mean the employer can avoid tax liability. The courts and the IRS look behind the label to ascertain the true relationship between the worker and the business entity.*

AGENCY FORMATION

Agency relationships normally are consensual; that is, they come about by voluntary consent and agreement between the parties. Generally, the agreement need not be in writing,[2] and consideration is not required. A principal must have contractual capacity. A person who cannot legally enter into contracts directly should not be allowed to do so indirectly through an agent.

An agency relationship can be created for any legal purpose. An agency relationship that is created for an illegal purpose or that is contrary to public policy is unenforceable. **| Example #3**   Suppose that Sharp (as principal) contracts with Blesh (as agent) to sell illegal narcotics. This agency relationship is unenforceable because selling illegal narcotics is a felony and is contrary to public policy.| It is also illegal for physicians and other licensed professionals to employ unlicensed agents to perform professional actions.

Generally, an agency relationship can arise in four ways: by agreement of the parties, by ratification, by estoppel, and by operation of law. We look here at each of these possibilities.

---

2. There are two main exceptions to the statement that agency agreements need not be in writing: (1) Whenever agency authority empowers the agent to enter into a contract that the Statute of Frauds requires to be in writing, the agent's authority from the principal must likewise be in writing. (2) A power of attorney, which confers authority to an agent, must be in writing.

Agency by Agreement

Most agency relationships are based on an express or implied agreement that the agent will act for the principal and that the principal agrees to have the agent so act. An agency agreement can take the form of an express written or oral contract. An agency agreement can also be implied by conduct. **Example #4** A hotel expressly allows only Boris Koontz to park cars, but Boris has no employment contract there. The hotel's manager tells Boris when to work, as well as where and how to park the cars. The hotel's conduct amounts to a manifestation of its willingness to have Boris park its customers' cars, and Boris can infer from the hotel's conduct that he has authority to act as a parking valet. It can be inferred that Boris is an agent-employee for the hotel, his purpose being to provide valet parking services for hotel guests.

Agency by Ratification

On occasion, a person who is in fact not an agent (or who is an agent acting outside the scope of her or his authority) may make a contract on behalf of another (a principal). If the principal approves or affirms that contract by word or by action, an agency relationship is created by **ratification.** Ratification is a question of intent, and intent can be expressed by either words or conduct.

Agency by Estoppel

When a principal causes a third person to believe that another person is his or her agent, and the third person deals with the supposed agent, the principal is "estopped to deny" the agency relationship. In such a situation, the principal's actions create the *appearance* of an agency that does not in fact exist. The third person must prove that she or he *reasonably* believed that an agency relationship existed, however.[3] Facts and circumstances must show that an ordinary, prudent person familiar with business practice and custom would have been justified in concluding that the agent had authority.

Example #5 Suppose that Andrew accompanies Grant, a seed sales representative, to call on a customer, Steve, the proprietor of the General Seed Store. Andrew has done independent sales work but has never signed an employment agreement with Grant. Grant boasts to Steve that he wishes he had three more assistants "just like Andrew." By making this representation, Grant creates the impression that Andrew is his agent and has authority to solicit orders. Steve has reason to believe from Grant's statements that Andrew is an agent for Grant. Steve then places seed orders with Andrew. If Grant does not correct the impression that Andrew is an agent, Grant will be bound to fill the orders just as if Andrew were really his agent. Grant's representation to Steve created the impression that Andrew was Grant's agent and had authority to solicit orders.

The acts or declarations of a purported *agent* in and of themselves do not create an agency by estoppel. Rather, it is the deeds or statements of the *principal* that create an agency by estoppel. **Example #6** If Andrew walks into Steve's store and claims to be Grant's agent, when in fact he is not, and Grant has no

A restaurant offers valet parking services. Can it be inferred that the parking attendant shown here is an agent of the restaurant? Why or why not? (Michael Newman/PhotoEdit)

RATIFICATION
The act of accepting and giving legal force to an obligation that previously was not enforceable.

---

3. These concepts also apply when a person who is in fact an agent undertakes an action that is beyond the scope of her or his authority, as will be discussed later in this chapter.

A buyer from New York examines the inventory of a clothing supplier in China. If the buyer tells the clothing supplier that she is working for a particular retail outlet in the United States, would this be sufficient to create an agency by estoppel? Why or why not? (Comstock Images)

knowledge of Andrew's representations, Grant will not be bound to any deal struck by Andrew and Steve. Andrew's acts and declarations alone do not create an agency by estoppel.|

Agency by Operation of Law

The courts may find an agency relationship in the absence of a formal agreement in other situations as well. This can occur in family relationships. For instance, suppose that one spouse purchases certain basic necessaries and charges them to the other spouse's charge account. The courts will often rule that the latter is liable for payment for the necessaries, either because of a social policy of promoting the general welfare of the spouse or because of a legal duty to supply necessaries to family members.

Agency by operation of law may also occur in emergency situations, when the agent's failure to act outside the scope of his or her authority would cause the principal substantial loss. If the agent is unable to contact the principal, the courts will often grant this emergency power. For instance, a railroad engineer may contract on behalf of her or his employer for medical care for an injured motorist hit by the train.

DUTIES OF AGENTS AND PRINCIPALS

Once the principal-agent relationship has been created, both parties have duties that govern their conduct. As discussed previously, an agency relationship is *fiduciary*—one of trust. In a fiduciary relationship, each party owes the other the duty to act with the utmost good faith.

We now examine the various duties of agents and principals. In general, for every duty of the principal, the agent has a corresponding right, and vice versa. When one party to the agency relationship violates his or her duty to the other party, the remedies available to the nonbreaching party arise out of contract and tort law. These remedies include monetary damages, termination of the agency relationship, injunction, and required accountings.

Agent's Duties to the Principal

Generally, the agent owes the principal five duties—performance, notification, loyalty, obedience, and accounting.

Performance   An implied condition in every agency contract is the agent's agreement to use reasonable diligence and skill in performing the work. When an agent fails to perform her or his duties entirely, liability for breach of contract normally will result. The degree of skill or care required of an agent is usually that expected of a reasonable person under similar circumstances. Generally, this is interpreted to mean ordinary care. If an agent has represented himself or herself as possessing special skills, however, the agent is expected to exercise the degree of skill or skills claimed. Failure to do so constitutes a breach of the agent's duty.

Notification   According to a maxim in agency law, notice to the agent is notice to the principal. An agent is thus required to notify the principal of all

A real estate agent sets up a sign to attract potential home buyers to new properties for sale. If this agent knows a buyer who is willing to pay more than the asking price for a property, what duty would the agent breach if she bought the property from the seller and sold it at a profit to that buyer? (AP Photo/Don Ryan)

matters that come to her or his attention concerning the subject matter of the agency. This is the duty of notification, or the duty to inform.

The law assumes that the principal knows of any information acquired by the agent that is relevant to the agency—regardless of whether the agent actually passes on this information to the principal.

Loyalty Loyalty is one of the most fundamental duties in a fiduciary relationship. Basically, the agent has the duty to act *solely for the benefit of his or her principal* and not in the interest of the agent or a third party. For example, an agent cannot represent two principals in the same transaction unless both know of the dual capacity and consent to it. The duty of loyalty also means that any information or knowledge acquired through the agency relationship is considered confidential. It would be a breach of loyalty to disclose such information either during the agency relationship or after its termination. Typical examples of confidential information are trade secrets and customer lists compiled by the principal.

BE AWARE An agent's disclosure of confidential information could constitute the business tort of misappropriation of trade secrets.

In short, the agent's loyalty must be undivided. The agent's actions must be strictly for the benefit of the principal and must not result in any secret profit for the agent. **| Example #7** Suppose that Ryder contracts with Alton, a real estate agent, to sell Ryder's property. Alton knows that she can find a buyer who will pay substantially more for the property than Ryder is asking. If Alton were to secretly purchase Ryder's property, however, and then resell it at a profit to another buyer, Alton would breach her duty of loyalty as Ryder's agent. Alton has a duty to act in Ryder's best interests and can only become the purchaser in this situation with Ryder's knowledge and approval.**|**

Obedience When acting on behalf of a principal, an agent has a duty to follow all lawful and clearly stated instructions of the principal. Any deviation from such instructions is a violation of this duty. During emergency situations, however, when the principal cannot be consulted, the agent may deviate from the instructions without violating this duty. Whenever instructions are not clearly stated, the agent can fulfill the duty of obedience by acting in good faith and in a manner reasonable under the circumstances.

Accounting Unless an agent and a principal agree otherwise, the agent has the duty to keep and make available to the principal an account of all property and funds received and paid out on behalf of the principal. This includes gifts from third parties in connection with the agency. For example, a gift from a customer to a salesperson for prompt deliveries made by the salesperson's firm, in the absence of a company policy to the contrary, belongs to the firm. The agent has a duty to maintain separate accounts for the principal's funds and for the agent's personal funds, and no intermingling of these accounts is allowed.

Principal's Duties to the Agent

The principal also owes certain duties to the agent. These duties relate to compensation, reimbursement and indemnification, cooperation, and safe working conditions.

Compensation In general, when a principal requests certain services from an agent, the agent reasonably expects payment. The principal therefore has a duty to pay the agent for services rendered. For example, when an accountant or an attorney is asked to act as an agent, an agreement to compensate the agent for such service is implied. The principal also has a duty to pay that compensation in a timely manner. Except in a gratuitous agency relationship, in which an agent does not act for payment in return, the principal must pay the agreed-on value for an agent's services. If no amount has been expressly agreed on, the principal owes the agent the customary compensation for such services.

Reimbursement and Indemnification Whenever an agent disburses funds to fulfill the request of the principal or to pay for necessary expenses in the course of a reasonable performance of his or her agency duties, the principal has the duty to reimburse the agent for these payments. Agents cannot recover for expenses incurred through their own misconduct or negligence, though.

Subject to the terms of the agency agreement, the principal has the duty to compensate, or *indemnify,* an agent for liabilities incurred because of authorized and lawful acts and transactions. For instance, if the principal fails to perform a contract formed by the agent with a third party and the third party then sues the agent, the principal is obligated to compensate the agent for any costs incurred in defending against the lawsuit.

Additionally, the principal must indemnify (pay) the agent for the value of benefits that the agent confers on the principal. The amount of indemnification is usually specified in the agency contract. If it is not, the courts will look to the nature of the business and the type of loss to determine the amount.

Cooperation A principal has a duty to cooperate with the agent and to assist the agent in performing her or his duties. The principal must do nothing to prevent such performance. **|Example #8** Suppose that Akers (the principal) grants Johnson (the agent) an exclusive territory within which Johnson may sell Akers's products, thus creating an exclusive agency. In this situation, Akers cannot compete with Johnson within that territory—or appoint or allow another agent to so compete—because this would violate the exclusive agency. If Akers did so, he would be exposed to liability for Johnson's lost sales or profits.|

Safe Working Conditions The common law requires the principal to provide safe working premises, equipment, and conditions for all agents and employees. The principal has a duty to inspect the working conditions and to warn agents and employees about any unsafe areas. When the agent is an employee, the employer's liability is frequently covered by state workers' compensation insurance, and federal and state statutes often require the employer to meet certain safety standards (discussed further later in this chapter).

AGENT'S AUTHORITY

An agent's authority to act can be either *actual* (express or implied) or *apparent*. *Express authority* is authority declared in clear, direct, and definite terms. Express authority can be given orally or in writing. *Implied authority* is conferred by custom, can be inferred from the position the agent occupies, or is implied by virtue of being reasonably necessary to carry out express authority. |**Example #9** Mueller is employed by Al's Supermarket to manage one of its stores. Al's has not expressly stated that Mueller has authority to contract with third persons. In this situation, though, authority to manage a business implies authority to do what is reasonably required (as is customary or can be inferred from a manager's position) to operate the business. This includes forming contracts to hire employees, to buy merchandise and equipment, and to advertise the products sold in the store.|

Actual authority (express or implied) arises from what the principal manifests *to the agent*. *Apparent authority* exists when the principal, by either words or actions, causes a *third party* reasonably to believe that an agent has authority to act, even though the agent has no express or implied authority. If the third party changes her or his position in reliance on the principal's representations, the principal may be *estopped* (prevented) from denying that the agent had authority. Note that here, in contrast to agency formation by estoppel, the issue has to do with the apparent authority of an *agent*, not the apparent authority of a person who is in fact not an agent.

> "The law is not a series of calculating machines where definitions and answers come tumbling out when the right levers are pushed."
> —WILLIAM O. DOUGLAS, 1898–1980
> (Associate Justice of the
> United States Supreme Court, 1939–1975)

ETHICAL ISSUE 13.1

Does an agent's breach of loyalty terminate the agent's authority?

Suppose that an employee-agent who is authorized to access company trade secrets contained in computer files e-mails those secrets to a competitor for whom the employee is about to begin working. Clearly, in this situation the employee has violated the ethical—and legal—duty of loyalty to the employer. Does this breach of loyalty mean that the employee's act of accessing the trade secrets was unauthorized? The question has significant implications because if the act was unauthorized, the employee would be subject to state and federal laws prohibiting unauthorized access to computer information and data. If the act was authorized, the employee would not be subject to such laws. When this unusual question came before a federal district court, the court held that the moment the employee accessed trade secrets for the purpose of divulging them to a competitor, the employee's

A truck lies on its side following an accident. If the driver had stopped at a bar during working hours and become inebriated, and this accident was caused by the driver's inebriated state, who would be held responsible for the damage? (Michael Newman/PhotoEdit)

DISCLOSED PRINCIPAL
A principal whose identity is known to a third party at the time the agent makes a contract with the third party.

PARTIALLY DISCLOSED PRINCIPAL
A principal whose identity is unknown by a third party, but the third party knows that the agent is or may be acting for a principal at the time the agent and the third party form a contract.

UNDISCLOSED PRINCIPAL
A principal whose identity is unknown by a third person, and the third person has no knowledge that the agent is acting for a principal at the time the agent and the third person form a contract.

authority as an agent terminated. Thus, the employee could be subject to both criminal and civil sanctions under a federal law prohibiting unauthorized access to protected computer information. In reaching its decision, the court cited Section 112 of the *Restatement (Second) of Agency.* That section reads, in part, "Unless otherwise agreed, the authority of an agent terminates if, without knowledge of the principal, he acquires adverse interests or if he is otherwise guilty of a serious breach of loyalty to the principal."[4]

LIABILITY IN AGENCY RELATIONSHIPS

Frequently, a question arises as to which party, the principal or the agent, should be held liable for contracts formed by the agent or for torts or crimes committed by the agent. We look here at these aspects of agency law.

Liability for Contracts

Liability for contracts formed by an agent depends on how the principal is classified and on whether the actions of the agent were authorized or unauthorized. Principals are classified as disclosed, partially disclosed, or undisclosed.[5]

A **disclosed principal** is a principal whose identity is known by the third party at the time the contract is made by the agent. A **partially disclosed principal** is a principal whose identity is not known by the third party, but the third party knows that the agent is or may be acting for a principal at the time the contract is made. | **Example #10** Sarah has contracted with a real estate agent to sell certain property. She wishes to keep her identity a secret, but the agent can make it perfectly clear to a purchaser of the real estate that the agent is acting in an agency capacity. In this situation, Sarah is a partially disclosed principal. | An **undisclosed principal** is a principal whose identity is totally unknown by the third party, and the third party has no knowledge that the agent is acting in an agency capacity at the time the contract is made.

Authorized Acts   If an agent acts within the scope of her or his authority, normally the principal is obligated to perform the contract regardless of whether the principal was disclosed, partially disclosed, or undisclosed. Whether the agent may also be held liable under the contract, however, depends on the disclosed, partially disclosed, or undisclosed status of the principal. A disclosed or partially disclosed principal is liable to a third party for a contract made by an agent who is acting within the scope of her or his authority. If the principal is disclosed, an agent has no contractual liability for the nonperformance of the principal or the third party. If the principal is partially disclosed, in most states the agent is also treated as a party to the contract, and the third party can hold the agent liable for contractual nonperformance.[6] When neither the fact of agency nor the identity of the principal is disclosed, the undisclosed principal is fully bound to perform just as if the principal had been fully disclosed at the time the contract was made. The agent is also liable as a party to the contract.

4. *Shurgard Storage Centers, Inc. v. Safeguard Self Storage, Inc.,* 119 F.Supp.2d 1121 (W.D.Wash. 2000).
5. *Restatement (Second) of Agency,* Section 4.
6. *Restatement (Second) of Agency,* Section 321.

Unauthorized Acts   If an agent has no authority but nevertheless contracts with a third party, the principal cannot be held liable on the contract. It does not matter whether the principal was disclosed, partially disclosed, or undisclosed. The *agent* is liable, however. |**Example #11** Scranton signs a contract for the purchase of a truck, purportedly acting as an agent under authority granted by Johnson. In fact, Johnson has not given Scranton any such authority. Johnson refuses to pay for the truck, claiming that Scranton had no authority to purchase it. The seller of the truck is entitled to hold Scranton liable for payment.|

If the principal is disclosed or partially disclosed, the agent is liable to the third party as long as the third party relied on the agency status. The agent's liability here is based on the breach of an implied warranty that the agent had authority to enter the contract, not on breach of the contract itself.[7] If the third party knows at the time the contract is made that the agent is mistaken about the extent of her or his authority, though, the agent is not liable. Similarly, if the agent indicates to the third party *uncertainty* about the extent of the authority, the agent is not personally liable.

Liability for Torts and Crimes

Obviously, any person, including an agent, is liable for her or his own torts and crimes. Whether a principal can also be held liable for an agent's torts and crimes depends on several factors. A principal may be liable for harm an agent caused to a third party under the doctrine of ***respondeat superior***,[8] a Latin term meaning "let the master respond." This doctrine, which is discussed in this chapter's *Landmark in the Legal Environment* feature on the following page, is similar to the theory of strict liability discussed in Chapter 5. The doctrine imposes **vicarious liability,** or indirect liability, on the employer—that is, liability without regard to the personal fault of the employer for torts committed by an employee in the course or scope of employment.

Liability for Agent's Torts   The key to determining whether a principal may be liable for the torts of an agent under the doctrine of *respondeat superior* is whether the torts are committed within the scope of the agency or employment. The *Restatement (Second) of Agency,* Section 229, indicates the factors that today's courts will consider in determining whether a particular act occurred within the course and scope of employment. These factors are as follows:

1. Whether the employee's act was authorized by the employer.
2. The time, place, and purpose of the act.
3. Whether the act was one commonly performed by employees on behalf of their employers.
4. The extent to which the employer's interest was advanced by the act.
5. The extent to which the private interests of the employee were involved.
6. Whether the employer furnished the means or instrumentality (for example, a truck or a machine) by which the injury was inflicted.
7. Whether the employer had reason to know that the employee would do the act in question and whether the employee had ever done it before.
8. Whether the act involved the commission of a serious crime.

RESPONDEAT SUPERIOR
Latin for "let the master respond." A doctrine under which a principal or an employer is held liable for the wrongful acts committed by agents or employees while acting within the course and scope of their agency or employment.

VICARIOUS LIABILITY
Legal responsibility placed on one person for the acts of another; indirect liability imposed on a supervisory party (such as an employer) for the actions of a subordinate (such as an employee) because of the relationship between the two parties.

NOTE An agent-employee going to or from work or meals usually is not considered to be within the scope of employment. An agent-employee whose job requires travel, however, is considered to be within the scope of employment for the entire trip, including the return.

---

7. The agent is not liable on the contract because the agent was never intended personally to be a party to the contract.
8. Pronounced ree-*spahn*-dee-uht soo-*peer*-ee-your.

LANDMARK IN THE LEGAL ENVIRONMENT
The Doctrine of *Respondeat Superior*

The idea that a master (employer) must respond to third persons for losses negligently caused by the master's servant (employee) first appeared in Lord Holt's opinion in *Jones v. Hart* (1698).[a] By the early nineteenth century, this maxim had been adopted by most courts and was referred to as the doctrine of *respondeat superior.*

Theories of Liability   The vicarious (indirect) liability of the master for the acts of the servant has been supported primarily by two theories. The first theory rests on the issue of *control,* or *fault:* the master has control over the acts of the servant and is thus responsible for injuries arising out of such service. The second theory is economic in nature: because the master takes the benefits or profits of the servant's service, he or she should also suffer the losses; moreover, the master is better able than the servant to absorb such losses.

The *control* theory is clearly recognized in the *Restatement (Second) of Agency,* which defines a master as "a principal who employs an agent to perform service in his [or her] affairs and who controls, or has the right to control, the physical conduct of the other in the performance of the service." Accordingly, a servant is defined as "an agent employed by a master to perform service in his [or her] affairs whose physical conduct in his [or her] performance of the service is controlled, or is subject to control, by the master."

a. K.B. 642, 90 Eng. Reprint 1255 (1698).

Limitations on the Employer's Liability   There are limitations on the master's liability for the acts of the servant, however. An employer (master) is only responsible for the wrongful conduct of an employee (servant) that occurs in "the scope of employment." The criteria used by the courts in determining whether an employee is acting within the scope of employment are set forth in the *Restatement (Second) of Agency* as discussed on page 449. Generally, the act must be of a kind the servant was employed to do; must have occurred within "authorized time and space limits"; and must have been "activated, at least in part, by a purpose to serve the master."

Application to Today's Legal Environment
The courts have accepted the doctrine of respondeat superior *for nearly two centuries. This theory of vicarious liability is laden with practical implications in all situations in which a principal-agent (master-servant, employer-employee) relationship exists. Today, the small-town grocer with one clerk and the multinational corporation with thousands of employees are equally subject to the doctrinal demand of "let the master respond."*

RELEVANT WEB SITES
To locate information on the Web concerning the doctrine of respondeat superior, *go to this text's Web site at* **www.thomsonedu.com/westbuslaw/let**, *select "Chapter 13," and click on "URLs for Landmarks."*

The doctrine of *respondeat superior* applies to intentional torts as well as to negligence. Thus, an employer can be held indirectly liable for the intentional torts of an employee that are committed within the course and scope of employment. For instance, an employer is liable when an employee (such as a "bouncer" at a nightclub or a security guard at a department store) commits the tort of assault and battery or false imprisonment while acting within the scope of employment. A principal is exposed to tort liability whenever a third person sustains a loss due to an agent's misrepresentation. The principal's liability depends on whether the agent was actually or apparently authorized to make representations and whether such representations were made within the scope of the agency. The principal is always directly responsible for an agent's misrepresentation made within the scope of the agent's authority.

Liability for Independent Contractor's Torts   Generally, an employer is not liable for physical harm caused to a third person by the negligent act of an independent contractor in the performance of the contract. This is because the

employer does not have *the right to control* the details of an independent contractor's performance. Exceptions to this rule are made in certain situations,
though, such as when unusually hazardous activities are involved. Typical
examples of such activities include blasting operations, the transportation of
highly volatile chemicals, or the use of poisonous gases. In these situations, an
employer cannot be shielded from liability merely by using an independent
contractor. Strict liability is imposed on the employer-principal as a matter of
law. Also, in some states, strict liability may be imposed by statute.

Liability for Agent's Crimes   An agent is liable for his or her own crimes. A
principal or employer is not liable for an agent's crime even if the crime was
committed within the scope of authority or employment—unless the principal
participated by conspiracy or other action. In some jurisdictions, under specific statutes, a principal may be liable for an agent's violation, in the course
and scope of employment, of regulations, such as those governing sanitation,
prices, weights, and the sale of liquor.

WAGE-HOUR LAWS

In the 1930s, Congress enacted several laws regulating the wages and working
hours of employees. In 1931, Congress passed the Davis-Bacon Act,[9] which
requires contractors and subcontractors working on government construction
projects to pay "prevailing wages" to their employees. In 1936, the Walsh-
Healey Act[10] was passed. This act requires that a minimum wage, as well as
overtime pay of time and a half, be paid to employees of manufacturers or suppliers entering into contracts with agencies of the federal government.

   In 1938, Congress passed the Fair Labor Standards Act (FLSA).[11] This act
extended wage-hour requirements to cover all employers engaged in interstate
commerce or in the production of goods for interstate commerce, plus selected
types of other businesses. We examine here the FLSA's provisions in regard to
child labor, maximum hours, and minimum wages.

Child Labor

The FLSA prohibits oppressive child labor. Children under fourteen years of
age are allowed to do certain types of work, such as deliver newspapers, work
for their parents, and work in the entertainment and (with some exceptions)
agricultural areas. Children who are fourteen or fifteen years of age are allowed
to work, but not in hazardous occupations. There are also numerous restric-
tions on how many hours per day and per week they can work. **| Example #12**
Children under the age of sixteen cannot work during school hours, for more
than three hours on a school day (or eight hours on a nonschool day), for
more than eighteen hours during a school week (or forty hours during a non-
school week), or before 7 A.M. or after 7 P.M. (9 P.M. during the summer).| Many
states require persons under sixteen years of age to obtain work permits.

   Working times and hours are not restricted for persons between the ages of
sixteen and eighteen, but they cannot be employed in hazardous jobs or in jobs

---

9. 40 U.S.C. Sections 276a–276a-5.
10. 41 U.S.C. Sections 35–45.
11. 29 U.S.C. Sections 201–260.

OSHA. Whenever an employee is killed in a work-related accident or when five or more employees are hospitalized as a result of one accident, the employer must notify the Department of Labor within forty-eight hours. If the company fails to do so, it will be fined. Following the accident, a complete inspection of the premises is mandatory.

Criminal penalties for willful violation of the Occupational Safety and Health Act are limited. Employers may also be prosecuted under state laws, however. In other words, the act does not preempt state and local criminal laws.[16]

Workers' Compensation

WORKERS' COMPENSATION LAWS
State statutes establishing an administrative procedure for compensating workers' injuries that arise out of—or in the course of—their employment, regardless of fault.

State **workers' compensation laws** establish an administrative procedure for compensating workers injured on the job. Instead of suing, an injured worker files a claim with the administrative agency or board that administers local workers' compensation claims.

Covered Employees   Most workers' compensation statutes are similar. No state covers all employees. Typically excluded are domestic workers, agricultural workers, temporary employees, and employees of common carriers (companies that provide transportation services to the public). Typically, the statutes cover minors. Usually, the statutes allow employers to purchase insurance from a private insurer or a state fund to pay workers' compensation benefits in the event of a claim. Most states also allow employers to be self-insured—that is, employers who show an ability to pay claims do not need to buy insurance.

Requirements for Receiving Workers' Compensation   In general, the right to recover benefits is predicated wholly on the existence of an employment relationship and the fact that the injury was *accidental* and *occurred on the job or in the course of employment,* regardless of fault. Intentionally inflicted self-injury, for example, would not be considered accidental and hence would not be covered. If an injury occurred while an employee was commuting to or from work, it usually would not be considered to have occurred on the job or in the course of employment and hence would not be covered.

An employee must notify her or his employer promptly (usually within thirty days) of an injury. Generally, an employee must also file a workers' compensation claim with the appropriate state agency or board within a certain period (sixty days to two years) from the time the injury is first noticed, rather than from the time of the accident.

Workers' Compensation versus Litigation   An employee's acceptance of workers' compensation benefits bars the employee from suing for injuries caused by the employer's negligence. By barring lawsuits for negligence, workers' compensation laws also bar employers from raising common law defenses to negligence, such as contributory negligence, assumption of risk, or injury caused by a "fellow servant" (another employee). A worker may sue an employer who *intentionally* injures the worker, however.

---

16. *Pedraza v. Shell Oil Co.*, 942 F.2d 48 (1st Cir. 1991); *cert.* denied, *Shell Oil Co. v. Pedraza*, 502 U.S. 1082, 112 S.Ct. 993, 117 L.Ed.2d 154 (1992).

INCOME SECURITY

Federal and state governments participate in insurance programs designed to protect employees and their families by covering the financial impact of retirement, disability, death, hospitalization, and unemployment. The key federal law on this subject is the Social Security Act of 1935.[17]

Social Security

The Social Security Act provides for old-age (retirement), survivors, and disability insurance. The act is therefore often referred to as OASDI. Both employers and employees must "contribute" under the Federal Insurance Contributions Act (FICA)[18] to help pay for benefits that will partially make up for the employees' loss of income on retirement.

The basis for the employee's and the employer's contribution is the employee's annual wage base—the maximum amount of the employee's wages that are subject to the tax. The employer withholds the employee's FICA contribution from the employee's wages and then matches this contribution. (In 2006, employers were required to withhold 6.2 percent of each employee's wages, up to a maximum wage base of $94,200, and to match this contribution.)

Retired workers are then eligible to receive monthly payments from the Social Security Administration, which administers the Social Security Act. Social Security benefits are fixed by statute but increase automatically with increases in the cost of living.

NOTE Social Security covers almost all jobs in the United States. More than nine out of ten workers "contribute" to this protection for themselves and their families.

Medicare

Medicare, a federal government health-insurance program, is administered by the Social Security Administration for people sixty-five years of age and older and for some under the age of sixty-five who are disabled. It has two parts, one pertaining to hospital costs and the other to nonhospital medical costs, such as visits to physicians' offices. People who have Medicare hospital insurance can also obtain additional federal medical insurance if they pay small monthly premiums, which increase as the cost of medical care increases.

As with Social Security contributions, both the employer and the employee contribute to Medicare. As of this writing, both the employer and the employee pay 1.45 percent of the amount of *all* wages and salaries to finance Medicare. Unlike Social Security contributions, there is no cap on the amount of wages subject to the Medicare tax.

Private Pension Plans

Significant legislation has been enacted to regulate employee retirement plans set up by employers to supplement Social Security benefits. The major federal act covering these retirement plans is the Employee Retirement Income Security Act (ERISA) of 1974.[19] This act empowers the Labor Management Services Administration of the Department of Labor to enforce its provisions

---

17. 42 U.S.C. Sections 301–1397e.
18. 26 U.S.C. Sections 3101–3125.
19. 29 U.S.C. Sections 1001 *et seq.*

VESTING

The creation of an absolute or unconditional right or power.

governing employers who have private pension funds for their employees. ERISA does not require an employer to establish a pension plan. When a plan exists, however, ERISA establishes standards for its management.

A key provision of ERISA concerns vesting. **Vesting** gives an employee a legal right to receive pension benefits at some future date when he or she stops working. Before ERISA was enacted, some employees who had worked for companies for as long as thirty years received no pension benefits when their employment terminated, because those benefits had not vested. ERISA establishes complex vesting rules. Generally, however, all employee contributions to pension plans vest immediately, and employee rights to employer contributions to a plan vest after five years of employment.

In an attempt to prevent mismanagement of pension funds, ERISA has established rules on how they must be invested. Pension managers must be cautious in their investments and refrain from investing more than 10 percent of the funds in securities of the employer. ERISA also contains detailed record-keeping and reporting requirements.

Unemployment Insurance

To ease the financial impact of unemployment, the United States has a system of unemployment insurance. The Federal Unemployment Tax Act (FUTA) of 1935[20] created a state-administered system that provides unemployment compensation to eligible individuals. Under this system, employers pay into a fund, and the proceeds are paid out to qualified unemployed workers. The FUTA and state laws require employers that fall under the provisions of the act to pay unemployment taxes at regular intervals.

WATCH OUT If an employer does not pay unemployment taxes, a state government can place a lien (claim) on the employer's property to secure the debt.

To be eligible for unemployment compensation, a worker must be willing and able to work and be actively seeking employment. Workers who have been fired for misconduct or who have voluntarily left their jobs are not eligible for benefits. To leave a job voluntarily is to leave it without good cause. In the following case, an unemployed worker left his job. The question was whether he left the job for good cause and was therefore eligible for unemployment benefits.

---

20. 26 U.S.C. Sections 3301–3310.

CASE 13.2   Lewis v. Director, Employment Security Department

Court of Appeals of Arkansas,
Division I, 2004.
141 S.W.3d 896.
courts.state.ar.us/opinions/ca2004a.htm[a]

BACKGROUND AND FACTS   The jobs in the warehouse unit of Ace Hardware Corporation in Arkansas are divided between two departments: break order and full case. Break-order positions involve lifting no more than fifty pounds. The full-case department fills heavier orders (up to five thousand pounds). Employees who complete orders in less time than

Ace allows earn incentive pay. Employees believe that incentive pay is lower in the full-case department. Jobs are awarded on a seniority basis: new hires start in the full-case department but bid for other positions as soon as possible. Jimmy Lewis had worked for Ace since 1984, primarily in the break-order department. Ace had a high turnover in the full-case department, however, and whenever additional workers were needed, Ace reassigned Lewis. In 1998, Lewis began to complain regularly to his superiors about the reassignments. He offered to train others to fill the position, but his managers declined. In 2003, Lewis quit and applied for unemployment benefits. Ace questioned Lewis's entitlement. An Arkansas state employment tribunal ruled in Lewis's favor, a state review board reversed the ruling, and Lewis appealed to a state intermediate appellate court.

---

a. Click on "January 21, 2004." On the next page, scroll to the name of the case and click on the appropriate link to access the opinion. The Arkansas Judiciary maintains this Web site.

CASE 13.2–CONTINUED

IN THE WORDS OF THE COURT . . . *WENDELL L. GRIFFEN*, Judge.

* * * *

An individual shall be disqualified for unemployment benefits if he or she left his or her last work voluntarily and without good cause connected with the work. Good cause is a cause that would reasonably impel an average, able-bodied, qualified worker to give up his or her employment. *Good cause is dependent not only on the reaction of the average employee, but also on the good faith of the employee involved, which includes the presence of a genuine desire to work and to be self-supporting.* In addition, in order to receive unemployment benefits, an employee must make reasonable efforts to preserve his or her job rights. [Emphasis added.]

We hold that the [Arkansas Board of Review] erred in finding that appellant [Lewis] did not leave his work for good cause. The Board concluded that Ace had a legitimate, business-related reason for not training women to work in the full-case department, in that if women were required to call for assistance to lift the heavier objects, that would compound Ace's staffing problems. However, Ace made no such assertion. By Ace's own admission, the only reason that it failed to train other workers was because appellant was already trained and it was easier to reassign him. Appellant testified that some orders in the full-case department weighed as much as 5,000 pounds. Thus, presumably even men who are reassigned to the full-case department will be required to call for the assistance of a forklift to handle such heavy material.

While an employer has managerial discretion, it may not use that discretion in a discriminatory manner. Even if we agree that Ace had a legitimate, business-related reason for not training women to work in the full-case department, it advanced no such reason for not training other men to work in that department. We cannot ignore that Ace's staffing problems were self-created and that its reassignment policy seems to violate its own rules regarding seniority upon which its employees rely. [Emphasis added.]

Appellant left his job when he realized that Ace was never going to permanently address the underlying situation that caused his reassignment to the full-case department: in spite of the fact that employees regularly bid out of the full-case department, causing staffing shortages in that department, Ace refused to train other existing workers to fill those shortages. *An element in determining good cause is whether the employee took appropriate steps to prevent mistreatment from continuing.* Appellant had worked for Ace for nearly twenty years. After five years of complaining to all levels of management about being reassigned to a position that, in his experience, caused him to lose pay, after offering to assist with training other employees, and after having management violate its own seniority rules and take virtually no action to provide a permanent remedy, appellant quit. We agree with appellant that his circumstances would reasonably impel an average, able-bodied, qualified worker to give up his or her employment. [Emphasis added.]

DECISION AND REMEDY   The state intermediate appellate court reversed the review board's decision and remanded the case for an order to award benefits. The court held that Lewis left his job for good cause and was therefore entitled to unemployment benefits.

FOR CRITICAL ANALYSIS–Social Consideration   *The court in the* Lewis *case based its decision, in part, on the employee's reaction to the situation on the job. What other factors should be considered in deciding whether a worker had "good cause" to quit?*

COBRA

Federal legislation also addresses the issue of health insurance for workers whose jobs have been terminated—and who are thus no longer eligible for group health-insurance plans. The Consolidated Omnibus Budget Reconciliation Act

(COBRA) of 1985[21] prohibits the elimination of a worker's medical, optical, or dental insurance on the voluntary or involuntary termination of the worker's employment. The act applies to most workers who have either lost their jobs or had their hours decreased so that they are no longer eligible for coverage under the employer's health plan. Only workers fired for gross misconduct are excluded from protection.

The worker has sixty days (beginning with the date that the group coverage would stop) to decide whether to continue with the employer's group insurance plan. If the worker chooses to discontinue the coverage, the employer has no further obligation. If the worker chooses to continue coverage, though, the employer is obligated to keep the policy active for up to eighteen months. If the worker is disabled, the employer must extend coverage for up to twenty-nine months. The coverage provided must be the same as that enjoyed by the worker prior to the termination or reduction of work. If family members were originally included, for example, COBRA prohibits their exclusion. To receive continued benefits, however, the worker may be required to pay all of the premiums, as well as a 2 percent administrative charge.

Employers, with some exceptions, must comply with COBRA if they employ twenty or more workers and provide a benefit plan to those workers. An employer must inform an employee of COBRA's provisions when that worker faces termination or a reduction of hours that would affect his or her eligibility for coverage under the plan. The employer need not provide benefit coverage if the employer eliminates its group benefit plan or if the worker becomes eligible for Medicare, becomes covered under a spouse's health plan, becomes insured under a different plan (with a new employer, for example), or fails to pay the premium. An employer that does not comply with COBRA risks substantial penalties, such as a tax of up to 10 percent of the annual cost of the group plan or $500,000, whichever is less.

FAMILY AND MEDICAL LEAVE

In 1993, Congress passed the Family and Medical Leave Act (FMLA)[22] to allow employees to take time off from work for family or medical reasons. A majority of the states also have legislation allowing for a leave from employment for family or medical reasons, and many employers maintain private family-leave plans for their workers.

Coverage and Applicability of the FMLA

The FMLA requires employers who have fifty or more employees to provide employees with up to twelve weeks of unpaid family or medical leave during any twelve-month period. Generally, an employee may take family leave to care for a newborn baby, an adopted child, or a foster child and take medical leave when the employee or the employee's spouse, child, or parent has a "serious health condition" requiring care.[23] The employer must continue the worker's health-care coverage and guarantee employment in the same position or a com-

> " It is the job of the legislature to follow the spirit of the nation, provided it is not contrary to the principles of government. "
> —CHARLES-LOUIS DE SECONDAT, BARON DE MONTESQUIEU, 1689–1755
> (French philosopher and jurist)

---

21. 29 U.S.C. Sections 1161–1169.
22. 29 U.S.C. Sections 2601, 2611–2619, 2651–2654.
23. The foster care must be state sanctioned before such an arrangement falls within the coverage of the FMLA.

parable position when the employee returns to work. An important exception to the FMLA, however, allows the employer to avoid reinstating a *key employee*—defined as an employee whose pay falls within the top 10 percent of the firm's workforce. Also, the act does not apply to part-time or newly hired employees (those who have worked for less than one year).

Employees suffering from certain chronic health conditions, such as asthma, diabetes, and pregnancy, may take FMLA leave for their own incapacities that require absences of less than three days. | **Example #13** Estel, an employee who has asthma, suffers from periodic episodes of illness. According to regulations issued by the Department of Labor, employees with such conditions are covered by the FMLA. Thus, Estel may take a medical leave.|

The FMLA expressly covers private and public (government) employees. Nevertheless, some states argued that public employees could not sue their state employers in federal courts to enforce their FMLA rights unless the states consented to be sued.[24] This argument came before the United States Supreme Court in the following case.

---

24. Under the Eleventh Amendment to the U.S. Constitution, a state is immune from suit in a federal court unless the state agrees to be sued.

CASE 13.3 **Nevada Department of Human Resources v. Hibbs**

Supreme Court of the United States, 2003.
538 U.S. 721,
123 S.Ct. 1972,
155 L.Ed.2d 953.

BACKGROUND AND FACTS William Hibbs worked for the Nevada Department of Human Resources. In April 1997, Hibbs asked for time off under the FMLA to care for his sick wife, who was recovering from a car accident and neck surgery. The department granted Hibbs's request, allowing him to use the leave intermittently, as needed, beginning in May.

Hibbs did this until August 5, after which he did not return to work. In October, the department told Hibbs that he had exhausted his FMLA leave, that no further leave would be granted, and that he must return to work by November 12. When he did not return, he was discharged. Hibbs filed a suit in a federal district court against the department. The court held that the Eleventh Amendment to the U.S. Constitution barred the suit. On Hibbs's appeal, the U.S. Court of Appeals for the Ninth Circuit reversed this holding. The department appealed to the United States Supreme Court.

IN THE WORDS OF THE COURT . . . Chief Justice *REHNQUIST* delivered the opinion of the Court.

* * * *

[After the enactment of Title VII of the Civil Rights Act of 1964] state gender discrimination did not cease. * * * According to evidence that was before Congress when it enacted the FMLA, States continue[d] to rely on invalid gender stereotypes in the employment context, specifically in the administration of leave benefits. * * *

* * * *

Congress * * * heard testimony that "[p]arental leave for fathers * * * is rare. Even * * * [w]here child-care leave policies do exist, men, *both in the public and private sectors*, receive notoriously discriminatory treatment in their requests for such leave." Many States offered women extended "maternity" leave that far exceeded the typical 4- to 8-week period of physical disability due to pregnancy and childbirth, but very few States granted men a parallel benefit: Fifteen States provided women up to one year of extended maternity leave, while only four provided men with the same. This and

CASE 13.3–CONTINUED ▶

other differential leave policies were not attributable to any differential physical needs of men and women, but rather to the pervasive sex-role stereotype that caring for family members is women's work. [Emphasis added.]

* * * *

* * * Because employers continued to regard the family as the woman's domain, they often denied men similar accommodations or discouraged them from taking leave. These mutually reinforcing stereotypes created a self-fulfilling cycle of discrimination that forced women to continue to assume the role of primary family caregiver, and fostered employers' stereotypical views about women's commitment to work and their value as employees. * * *

We believe that Congress's chosen remedy, the family-care leave provision of the FMLA, is congruent [corresponds to] and [is] proportional to the targeted violation. * * *

By creating an across-the-board, routine employment benefit for all eligible employees, Congress sought to ensure that family-care leave would no longer be stigmatized as an inordinate drain on the workplace caused by female employees, and that employers could not evade leave obligations simply by hiring men. By setting a minimum standard of family leave for *all* eligible employees, irrespective of gender, the FMLA attacks the formerly state-sanctioned stereotype that only women are responsible for family caregiving, thereby reducing employers' incentives to engage in discrimination by basing hiring and promotion decisions on stereotypes.

DECISION AND REMEDY The United States Supreme Court affirmed the lower court's decision, concluding that the FMLA corresponds to and is proportional to the discrimination that Congress intended the FMLA to address. Thus, the FMLA, which expressly covers public employees, can serve as the basis for a suit against a state employer regardless of whether the state consents to the suit.

FOR CRITICAL ANALYSIS–Social Consideration *The Court emphasized how men frequently have received discriminatory treatment in family-leave policies. If the plaintiff had been a woman, would that have changed the outcome in this case? Why or why not?*

Violations of the FMLA

An employer who violates the FMLA may be held liable for damages to compensate an employee for unpaid wages (or salary), lost benefits, denied compensation, and actual monetary losses (such as the cost of providing for care of the family member) up to an amount equivalent to the employee's wages for twelve weeks. Supervisors may also be subject to personal liability, as employers, for violations of the act. A court may require the employer to reinstate the employee in her or his job or to grant a promotion that had been denied. A successful plaintiff is entitled to court costs; attorneys' fees; and, in cases involving bad faith on the part of the employer, two times the amount of damages awarded by a judge or jury.

Regulations issued by the Department of Labor (DOL) impose additional sanctions on employers who fail to notify employees when an absence will be counted against leave authorized under the act. Under one such rule, if an employer failed to provide notice, then the employee's absence would not count as a portion of the leave time available under the FMLA. | **Example #14** An employee had been absent from work for thirty weeks while undergoing treatment for cancer. The employer had not designated any of the employee's time off as FMLA leave. Thus, under the DOL's regulation, the employee was entitled to an additional leave of twelve weeks. In 2002, however, the United States Supreme Court invalidated this rule. The Court reasoned that it would be unjust for an employee to obtain additional protected leave as a windfall.[25]

EMPLOYEE PRIVACY RIGHTS

In the last several decades, concerns about the privacy rights of employees have arisen in response to the sometimes invasive tactics used by employers to monitor and screen workers. Perhaps the greatest privacy concern in today's employment arena has to do with electronic performance monitoring. Clearly, employers need to protect themselves from liability for their employees' online activities. They also have a legitimate interest in monitoring the productivity of their workers. At the same time, employees expect to have a certain zone of privacy in the workplace. Indeed, many lawsuits have involved allegations that employers' intrusive monitoring practices violate employees' privacy rights.

A number of laws protect privacy rights. We look here at laws that apply in the employment context. Recall from Chapter 4 that the U.S. Constitution does not contain a provision that explicitly guarantees a right to privacy. A personal right to privacy, however, has been inferred from other constitutional guarantees provided by the First, Third, Fourth, Fifth, and Ninth Amendments to the Constitution. Tort law (see Chapter 5), state constitutions, and a number of state and federal statutes also provide for privacy rights.

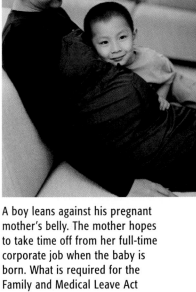

A boy leans against his pregnant mother's belly. The mother hopes to take time off from her full-time corporate job when the baby is born. What is required for the Family and Medical Leave Act (FMLA) to apply to her employer? If the employer is covered by the FMLA, how much family leave does the act authorize? (PhotoDisc)

Electronic Monitoring in the Workplace

A variety of specially designed software products have made it easier for an employer to track employees' Internet use. Software now allows an employer to track virtually every move made by an employee using the Internet, including the specific Web sites visited and the time spent surfing the Web. Filtering software can also be used to prevent employees from accessing certain Web sites, such as sites containing pornographic or sexually explicit images. Other filtering software may be used to screen incoming e-mail for viruses and block junk mail (spam).

Although the use of filtering software by public employers (government agencies) has led to charges that blocking access to Web sites violates employees' rights to free speech, this issue does not arise in private businesses. This is because the First Amendment's protection of free speech applies only to *government* restraints on speech, and not normally to restraints imposed in the private sector.

> "We are rapidly entering the age of no privacy, where everyone is open to surveillance at all times; where there are no secrets."
>
> —WILLIAM O. DOUGLAS, 1898–1980
> (Associate justice of the
> United States Supreme Court, 1939–1975)

The Electronic Communications Privacy Act The major statute with which employers must comply is the Electronic Communications Privacy Act (ECPA) of 1986.[26] This act amended existing federal wiretapping law to cover electronic forms of communications, such as communications via cellular telephones or e-mail. The ECPA prohibits the intentional interception of any wire or electronic communication and the intentional disclosure or use of the information obtained by the interception. Excluded from coverage, however, are

25. *Ragsdale v. Wolverine World Wide, Inc.*, 535 U.S. 81, 122 S.Ct. 1155, 152 L.Ed.2d 167 (2002).
26. 18 U.S.C. Sections 2510–2521.

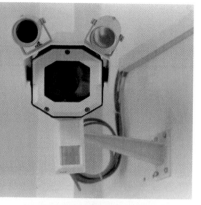

Employers are increasingly using surveillance cameras, such as this one, to monitor their employees' conduct in the workplace. What legitimate interests might employers have for using surveillance cameras? (Bill Stryker)

any electronic communications through devices that are "furnished to the subscriber or user by a provider of wire or electronic communication service" and that are being used by the subscriber or user, or by the provider of the service, "in the ordinary course of its business."

This "business-extension exception" to the ECPA permits employers to monitor employees' electronic communications made in the ordinary course of business. It does not, however, permit employers to monitor employees' personal communications. Under another exception to the ECPA, however, an employer may avoid liability under the act if the employees consent to having their electronic communications intercepted by the employer. Thus, an employer may be able to avoid liability under the ECPA by simply requiring employees to sign forms indicating that they consent to such monitoring.

Factors Considered by the Courts in Employee Privacy Cases   When determining whether an employer should be held liable for violating an employee's privacy rights, the courts generally weigh the employer's interests against the employee's reasonable expectation of privacy. Generally, if employees are informed that their communications are being monitored, they cannot reasonably expect those communications to be private. If employees are not informed that certain communications are being monitored, however, the employer may be held liable for invading their privacy.

For the most part, cases in which the courts have held that an employer's monitoring of electronic communications in the workplace violated employees' privacy rights are relatively rare. (For a further discussion of this issue, see this chapter's *Management Perspective* feature.)

Other Types of Monitoring

In addition to monitoring their employees' online activities, employers also engage in other types of employee screening and monitoring practices. These practices, which have included lie-detector tests, drug tests, AIDS tests, and genetic testing, have often been subject to challenge as violations of employee privacy rights.

Lie-Detector Tests   At one time, many employers required employees or job applicants to take polygraph examinations (lie-detector tests) in connection with their employment. To protect the privacy interests of employees and job applicants, in 1988 Congress passed the Employee Polygraph Protection Act.[27] The act prohibits employers from (1) requiring or causing employees or job applicants to take lie-detector tests or suggesting or requesting that they do so; (2) using, accepting, referring to, or asking about the results of lie-detector tests taken by employees or applicants; and (3) taking or threatening negative employment-related action against employees or applicants based on results of lie-detector tests or on their refusal to take the tests.

Employers excepted from these prohibitions include federal, state, and local government employers; certain security service firms; and companies manufacturing and distributing controlled substances. Other employers may use polygraph tests when investigating losses attributable to theft, including embezzlement and the theft of trade secrets.

---

27. 29 U.S.C. Sections 2001 *et seq.*

E-Mail and Employee Privacy Rights

Management Faces a Legal Issue Business owners and managers today routinely provide their employees with e-mail access to facilitate the performance of job duties. Sometimes, however, an employee may use e-mail to spread rumors or make sexually explicit and unprofessional comments about other employees. Clearly, an employer has both a legal and an ethical obligation to prevent harassment and discrimination in the workplace, as well as a practical interest in avoiding liability for such actions. Other uses of e-mail by employees—such as to send important trade secrets to unauthorized persons—have also caused employers to be concerned about their employees' use of company e-mail systems. An important question for many business owners and managers involves the extent to which they have a legal right to monitor or intercept their employees' e-mail.

What the Courts Say Generally, in disputes concerning e-mail monitoring and privacy rights, the courts have tended to side with the employers, reasoning that employees have no reasonable expectation of privacy in e-mail. This is true even when employees are not informed that their e-mail will be monitored. Indeed, in one case, a company's stated policy was that it would not monitor its employees' e-mail. When the company later fired an employee based on e-mail messages that the employee had sent, the employee sued the company, alleging that his privacy rights had been violated. The court held that the employee had no reasonable

expectation of privacy in the e-mail communications that he voluntarily made over the company's e-mail system.[a] The courts have also held that employees have no reasonable expectation of privacy even when their e-mail messages are stored in a password-protected location on their computers at work.[b] In 2004, a federal appellate court held that even an independent contractor's e-mail can be monitored by the employer. That case involved a company that had made e-mail services available to an independent contractor who was working at a separate location. The worker's status as an independent contractor was irrelevant, in the court's view, because the employer had provided the e-mail service to the worker.[c]

Implications for Managers Business owners and managers who provide Internet access to their employees can usually monitor or access their employees' e-mail messages without liability for invasion of privacy. Although courts have been reluctant to hold that employees have a reasonable expectation of privacy in their e-mail, it is likely that this issue will continue to come before the courts. Business owners should therefore be fair and judicious in their monitoring policies and inform employees not to expect e-mail on their office computers to be private.

a. *Smyth v. Pillsbury Co.*, 914 F.Supp. 97 (E.D.Pa. 1996).
b. *McLaren v. Microsoft Corp.*, 1999 WL 339015 (Tex.App.—Dallas 1999).
c. *Fraser v. Nationwide Mutual Insurance Co.*, 352 F.3d 107 (3d Cir. 2004).

Drug Testing In the interests of public safety, many employers, including the government, require their employees to submit to drug testing. State laws relating to the privacy rights of private-sector employees vary from state to state. Some state constitutions may prohibit private employers from testing for drugs, and state statutes may restrict drug testing by private employers in any number of ways. A collective bargaining agreement may also provide protection against drug testing. In some instances, employees have brought an action against the employer for the tort of invasion of privacy (discussed in Chapter 5).

Constitutional limitations apply to the testing of certain employees. The Fourth Amendment provides that individuals have the right to be "secure in their persons" against "unreasonable searches and seizures" conducted by government agents. Nonetheless, drug tests have been held constitutional when there was a reasonable basis for suspecting government employees of using drugs. Additionally, when drug use in a particular job could threaten public safety, testing has been upheld. For example, a Department of Transportation rule that requires employees engaged in oil and gas pipeline

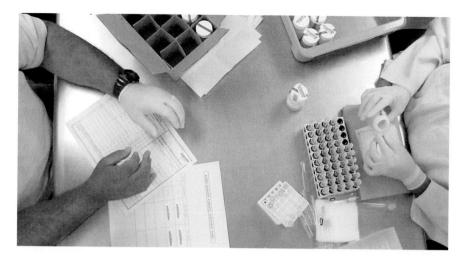

Workers at a toxicology lab place employees' urine samples in bar-coded test tubes before screening the samples for drugs. Many private employers today routinely require their employees to submit to drug testing. What recourse, if any, does an employee who does not consent to a drug test have against the employer? (U.S. Navy/ Jim Watson)

operations to submit to random drug testing was upheld, even though the rule did not require that before being tested the individual must have been suspected of drug use.[28] The court held that the government's interest in promoting public safety in the pipeline industry outweighed the employees' privacy interests.

AIDS Testing A number of employers test their workers for acquired immune deficiency syndrome (AIDS). Some state laws restrict AIDS testing, and federal statutes offer some protection to employees or job applicants who have AIDS or have tested positive for HIV, the virus that causes AIDS. The federal Americans with Disabilities Act of 1990[29] (which will be discussed in Chapter 14), for example, prohibits discrimination against persons with disabilities, and the term *disability* has been broadly defined to include those individuals with diseases such as AIDS. The law also requires employers to reasonably accommodate the needs of persons with disabilities. As a rule, although the law may not prohibit AIDS testing, it may prohibit the discharge of employees based on the results of those tests.

Genetic Testing A serious privacy issue arose when some employers began conducting genetic testing of employees or prospective employees in an effort to identify individuals who might develop significant health problems in the future. To date, however, only a few cases involving this issue have come before the courts. In one case, the Lawrence Berkeley Laboratory screened prospective employees for the gene that causes sickle-cell anemia, although the applicants were not informed of this. In a lawsuit subsequently brought by the prospective employees, a federal appellate court held that they had a cause of action for violation of their privacy rights.[30] The case was later settled for $2.2 million.

In another case, the Equal Employment Opportunity Commission (EEOC), the federal agency in charge of administering laws prohibiting employment discrimination, brought an action against a railroad company that had genet-

---

28. *Electrical Workers Local 1245 v. Skinner,* 913 F.2d 1454 (9th Cir. 1990).
29. 42 U.S.C. Sections 12102–12118.
30. *Norman-Bloodsaw v. Lawrence Berkeley Laboratory,* 135 F.3d 1260 (9th Cir. 1998).

ically tested its employees. The EEOC contended that the genetic testing violated the Americans with Disabilities Act (see Chapter 14). In 2002, this case was settled out of court, also for $2.2 million.

KEEP IN MIND An employer may act on the basis of any professionally developed test, provided the test relates to the employment and does not violate the law.

REVIEWING . . . EMPLOYMENT RELATIONSHIPS

Rick Saldona began working as a traveling salesperson for Aimer Winery in 1977. Sales constituted 90 percent of Saldona's work time. Saldona worked an average of fifty hours per week but received no overtime pay. In June 2006, Saldona's new supervisor, Caesar Braxton, claimed that Saldona had been inflating his reported sales calls and required Saldona to submit to a polygraph test. Saldona reported Braxton to the U.S. Department of Labor, which prohibited Aimer from requiring Saldona to take a polygraph test for this purpose. In August 2006, Saldona's wife, Venita, fell from a ladder and sustained a head injury while employed as a full-time agricultural harvester. Saldona delivered to Aimer's Human Resources Department a letter from his wife's physician indicating that she would need daily care for several months, and Saldona took leave until December 2006. Aimer had sixty-three employees at that time. When Saldona returned to Aimer, he was informed that his position had been eliminated because his sales territory had been combined with an adjacent territory. Using the information presented in the chapter, answer the following questions.

1. Saldona, as a salesperson for Aimer, clearly is an agent for the company. As an agent, what duties does Saldona owe to Aimer, the principal?

2. Would Saldona have been legally entitled to receive overtime pay at a higher rate? Why or why not?

3. What is the maximum length of time Saldona would have been allowed to take leave to care for his injured spouse?

4. Under what circumstances would Aimer have been allowed to require a polygraph test of an employee?

KEY TERMS

agency   438
disclosed principal   448
fiduciary   439
independent contractor   439

minimum wage   452
partially disclosed principal   448
ratification   443
respondeat superior   449

undisclosed principal   448
vesting   456
vicarious liability   449
workers' compensation laws   454

CHAPTER SUMMARY • EMPLOYMENT RELATIONSHIPS

Agency Relationships (See pages 438–442.)	In a *principal-agent* relationship, an agent acts on behalf of and instead of the principal in dealing with third parties. An employee who deals with third parties is normally an agent. An independent contractor is not an employee, and the employer has no control over the details of physical performance. The independent contractor may or may not be an agent.
Agency Formation (See pages 442–444.)	1. *By agreement*—Through express consent (oral or written) or implied by conduct. 2. *By ratification*—The principal, either by act or agreement, ratifies the conduct of an agent who acted outside the scope of authority or the conduct of a person who is in fact not an agent.

(Continued)

CHAPTER SUMMARY • EMPLOYMENT RELATIONSHIPS—CONTINUED

Agency Formation—Continued	3. *By estoppel*—When the principal causes a third person to believe that another person is his or her agent, and the third person deals with the supposed agent in reasonable reliance on the agency's existence, the principal is "estopped to deny" the agency relationship.
	4. *By operation of law*—Based on a social duty (such as the need to support family members) or created in emergency situations when the agent is unable to contact the principal.
Duties of Agents and Principals (See pages 444–447.)	1. *Duties of the agent*—
	a. *Performance*—The agent must use reasonable diligence and skill in performing his or her duties or use the special skills that the agent has represented to the principal that the agent possesses.
	b. *Notification*—The agent is required to notify the principal of all matters that come to his or her attention concerning the subject matter of the agency.
	c. *Loyalty*—The agent has a duty to act solely for the benefit of his or her principal and not in the interest of the agent or a third party.
	d. *Obedience*—The agent must follow all lawful and clearly stated instructions of the principal.
	e. *Accounting*—The agent has a duty to make available to the principal records of all property and money received and paid out on behalf of the principal.
	2. *Duties of the principal*—
	a. *Compensation*—Except in a gratuitous agency relationship, the principal must pay the agreed-on value (or reasonable value) for an agent's services.
	b. *Reimbursement and indemnification*—The principal must reimburse the agent for all sums of money disbursed at the request of the principal and for all sums of money the agent disburses for necessary expenses in the course of reasonable performance of his or her agency duties.
	c. *Cooperation*—A principal must cooperate with and assist an agent in performing his or her duties.
	d. *Safe working conditions*—A principal must provide safe working conditions for the agent-employee.
Agent's Authority (See pages 447–448.)	1. *Actual authority*—Can be either express or implied. *Express authority* can be oral or in writing. Authorization must be in writing if the agent is to execute a contract that must be in writing. *Implied authority* is authority that is customarily associated with the position of the agent or authority that is deemed necessary for the agent to carry out expressly authorized tasks.
	2. *Apparent authority*—Exists when the principal, by word or action, causes a third party reasonably to believe that an agent has authority to act, even though the agent has no express or implied authority.
Liability in Agency Relationships (See pages 448–451.)	1. *Liability for contracts*—If the principal's identity is disclosed or partially disclosed at the time the agent forms a contract with a third party, the principal is liable to the third party under the contract if the agent acted within the scope of his or her authority. If the principal's identity is undisclosed at the time of contract formation, the agent is personally liable to the third party, but if the agent acted within the scope of authority, the principal is also bound by the contract.
	2. *Liability for agent's torts*—Under the doctrine of *respondeat superior,* the principal is liable for any harm caused to another through the agent's torts if the agent was acting within the scope of his or her employment at the time the harmful act occurred. The principal is also liable for an agent's misrepresentation, whether made knowingly or by mistake.
	3. *Liability for independent contractor's torts*—A principal is not liable for harm caused by an independent contractor's negligence, unless hazardous activities are involved (in which situation the principal is strictly liable for any resulting harm) or other exceptions apply.

CHAPTER SUMMARY • EMPLOYMENT RELATIONSHIPS—CONTINUED

Liability in Agency Relationships—Continued	4. *Liability for agent's crimes*—An agent is responsible for his or her own crimes, even if the crimes were committed while the agent was acting within the scope of authority or employment. A principal will be liable for an agent's crime only if the principal participated by conspiracy or other action or (in some jurisdictions) if the agent violated certain government regulations in the course of employment.
Wage-Hour Laws (See pages 451–452.)	1. *Davis-Bacon Act (1931)*—Requires the payment of "prevailing wages" to employees of contractors and subcontractors working on federal government construction projects. 2. *Walsh-Healey Act (1936)*—Requires that a minimum wage and overtime pay be paid to employees of firms that contract with federal agencies. 3. *Fair Labor Standards Act (1938)*—Extended wage-hour requirements to cover all employers whose activities affect interstate commerce plus certain businesses. The act has specific requirements in regard to child labor, maximum hours, and minimum wages.
Worker Health and Safety (See pages 453–454.)	1. The Occupational Safety and Health Act of 1970 requires employers to meet specific safety and health standards that are established and enforced by the Occupational Safety and Health Administration (OSHA). 2. State workers' compensation laws establish an administrative procedure for compensating workers who are injured in accidents that occur on the job, regardless of fault.
Income Security (See pages 455–458.)	1. *Social Security and Medicare*—The Social Security Act of 1935 provides for old-age (retirement), survivors, and disability insurance. Both employers and employees must make contributions under the Federal Insurance Contributions Act (FICA) to help pay for the employees' loss of income on retirement. The Social Security Administration administers Medicare, a health-insurance program for older or disabled persons. 2. *Private pension plans*—The federal Employee Retirement Income Security Act (ERISA) of 1974 establishes standards for the management of employer-provided pension plans. 3. *Unemployment insurance*—The Federal Unemployment Tax Act of 1935 created a system that provides unemployment compensation to eligible individuals. Covered employers are taxed to help cover the costs of unemployment compensation. 4. *COBRA*—The Consolidated Omnibus Budget Reconciliation Act (COBRA) of 1985 requires employers to give employees, on termination of employment, the option of continuing their medical, optical, or dental insurance coverage for a certain period.
Family and Medical Leave (See pages 458–461.)	The Family and Medical Leave Act (FMLA) of 1993 requires employers with fifty or more employees to provide their employees (except for key employees) with up to twelve weeks of unpaid family or medical leave during any twelve-month period for the following reasons: 1. *Family leave*—May be taken to care for a newborn baby, an adopted child, or a foster child. 2. *Medical leave*—May be taken when the employee or the employee's spouse, child, or parent has a serious health condition requiring care.
Employee Privacy Rights (See pages 461–465.)	A right to privacy has been inferred from guarantees provided by the First, Third, Fourth, Fifth, and Ninth Amendments to the U.S. Constitution. State laws may also provide for privacy rights. Employer practices that have been challenged by employees as invasive of their privacy rights include electronic performance monitoring, drug testing, AIDS testing, and genetic testing and screening procedures.

FOR REVIEW

Answers for the even-numbered questions in this For Review *section can be found in Appendix O at the end of this text.*

1. What is an agency relationship, and how do agency relationships arise?

2. What is the difference between an employee and an independent contractor?

Video Question

13-11. Go to this text's Web site at <u>www. thomsonedu.com/westbuslaw/let</u> and select "Chapter 13." Click on "Video Questions" and view the video titled *Fast Times*. Then answer the following questions.

1. Recall from the video that Brad (Judge Reinhold) is told to deliver an order of Captain Hook Fish and Chips to IBM. Is Brad an employee or an independent contractor? Why?

2. Assume that Brad is an employee and agent of Captain Hook Fish and Chips. What duties does he owe Captain Hook Fish and Chips? What duties does Captain Hook Fish and Chips, as principal, owe to Brad?

3. In the video, Brad throws part of his uniform and several bags of the food that he is supposed to deliver out of his car window while driving. If Brad is an agent-employee and his actions cause injury to a person or property, can Captain Hook Fish and Chips be held liable? Why or why not? What should Captain Hook argue to avoid liability for Brad's actions?

INTERACTING WITH THE INTERNET

For updated links to resources available on the Web, as well as a variety of other materials, visit this text's Web site at

www.thomsonedu.com/westbuslaw/let

A good Web site for information on employee benefits—including the full text of the FMLA, COBRA, other relevant statutes and case law, and current articles—is BenefitsLink. Go to

benefitslink.com/index.html

The Occupational Safety and Health Administration (OSHA) offers information related to workplace health and safety at

www.osha.gov

The Bureau of Labor Statistics provides a wide variety of data on employment, including data on employment compensation, working conditions, and productivity. Go to

www.bls.gov

INTERNET EXERCISES

Go to **www.thomsonedu.com/westbuslaw/let**, the Web site that accompanies this text. Select "Chapter 13" and click on "Internet Exercises." There you will find the following Internet research exercises that you can perform to learn more about topics covered in this chapter.

Internet Exercise 13–1: LEGAL PERSPECTIVE—Employees or Independent Contractors?
Internet Exercise 13–2: LEGAL PERSPECTIVE—Workers' Compensation
Internet Exercise 13–3: MANAGEMENT PERSPECTIVE—Workplace Monitoring

BEFORE THE TEST

Go to **www.thomsonedu.com/westbuslaw/let**, the Web site that accompanies this text. Select "Chapter 13" and click on "Interactive Quizzes." You will find a number of interactive questions relating to this chapter.

Equal Employment Opportunities

CHAPTER OBJECTIVES

After reading this chapter, you should be able to answer the following questions:

1. Generally, what kind of conduct is prohibited by Title VII of the Civil Rights Act of 1964, as amended?

2. What is the difference between disparate-treatment discrimination and disparate-impact discrimination?

3. What remedies are available under Title VII of the 1964 Civil Rights Act, as amended?

4. What federal acts prohibit discrimination based on age and discrimination based on disability?

5. What are three defenses to claims of employment discrimination?

CONTENTS

O UT OF THE 1960s civil rights movement to end racial and other forms of discrimination grew a body of law protecting employees against discrimination in the workplace. This protective legislation eroded the common law doctrine of employment at will—still recognized in most states—under which employers may hire and terminate employees "at will," at any time and for any reason. In the past several decades, judicial decisions, administrative agency actions, and legislation have restricted the ability of employers, as well as unions, to discriminate against workers on the basis of race, color, religion, national origin, gender, age, or disability. A class of persons defined by one or more of these criteria is known as a **protected class.**

Several federal statutes prohibit **employment discrimination** against members of protected classes. The most important statute is Title VII of the Civil Rights Act of 1964.[1] Title VII prohibits discrimination on the basis of race, color, religion, national origin, or gender at any stage of employment. The Age Discrimination in Employment Act of 1967[2] and the Americans with Disabilities Act of 1990[3] prohibit discrimination on the basis of age and disability, respectively.

This chapter focuses on the kinds of discrimination prohibited by these federal statutes. Note, though, that discrimination against employees on the basis of any of these criteria may also violate state human rights statutes or other state laws or public policies prohibiting discrimination.

> **"**Nor shall any State . . . deny to any person within its jurisdiction the equal protection of the laws.**"**
>
> —THE FOURTEENTH AMENDMENT TO THE U.S. CONSTITUTION

PROTECTED CLASS
A group of persons protected by specific laws because of the group's defining characteristics. Under the laws prohibiting employment discrimination, these characteristics include race, color, religion, national origin, gender, age, and disability.

EMPLOYMENT DISCRIMINATION
Treating employees or job applicants unequally on the basis of race, color, national origin, religion, gender, age, or disability; prohibited by federal statutes.

---

1. 42 U.S.C. Sections 2000e–2000e-17.
2. 29 U.S.C. Sections 621–634.
3. 42 U.S.C. Sections 12102–12118.

TITLE VII OF THE CIVIL RIGHTS ACT OF 1964

Title VII of the Civil Rights Act of 1964 and its amendments prohibit job discrimination against employees, applicants, and union members on the basis of race, color, national origin, religion, or gender at any stage of employment. Title VII applies to employers with fifteen or more employees, labor unions with fifteen or more members, labor unions that operate hiring halls (to which members go regularly to be rationed jobs as they become available), employment agencies, and state and local governing units or agencies. A special section of the act prohibits discrimination in most federal government employment.

An employer with fewer than fifteen employees is not automatically shielded from a lawsuit filed under Title VII, however, as the following case illustrates.

CASE 14.1　**Arbaugh v. Y & H Corp.**

Supreme Court of the United States, 2006.
__ U.S. __,
126 S.Ct. 1235,
163 L.Ed.2d 1097.
www.findlaw.com/casecode/supreme.html[a]

BACKGROUND AND FACTS　For nine months, Jenifer Arbaugh worked as a bartender and waitress at the Moonlight Café, a restaurant in New Orleans, Louisiana, owned and operated by Y & H Corporation (Y & H). Yalcin Hatipoglu was one of Y & H's owners. Arbaugh quit working for the Moonlight and filed a suit in a federal district court against Y & H under Title VII. She alleged that Hatipoglu's improper conduct had

forced her to resign. (This is known as *constructive discharge*, a topic discussed in more detail later in this chapter.) The court entered a judgment in her favor, awarding damages of $40,000. Two weeks later, Y & H filed a motion to dismiss, arguing that the court did not have "federal subject-matter jurisdiction." Y & H asserted—for the first time in the case—that it had fewer than fifteen employees and therefore was not subject to a suit under Title VII. The dispute turned on the status of eight drivers who made deliveries for the restaurant and the company's owners, including two managers and their spouses. The court concluded that none of these individuals qualified as "employees" for Title VII purposes and dismissed the case. Arbaugh appealed to the U.S. Court of Appeals for the Fifth Circuit, which affirmed the lower court's decision. Arbaugh appealed to the United States Supreme Court.

a. In the "Browsing" section, click on "2006 Decisions." When that page opens, scroll to the name of the case and click on it to read the opinion.

IN THE WORDS OF THE COURT . . . Justice *GINSBURG* delivered the opinion of the Court.

* * * The question here presented is whether the numerical qualification contained in Title VII's definition of "employer" affects federal-court subject-matter jurisdiction or, instead, delineates a substantive ingredient of a Title VII claim for relief.

* * * *

* * * To spare very small businesses from Title VII liability, Congress provided that:

"[t]he term 'employer' means a person engaged in an industry affecting commerce who has fifteen or more employees for each working day in each of twenty or more calendar weeks in the current or preceding calendar year, and any agent of such a person * * * ."

Congress has broadly authorized the federal courts to exercise subject-matter jurisdiction over all civil actions arising under the Constitution, laws, or treaties of the United States. * * * In 1964, however, when Title VII was enacted, * * * [federal] jurisdiction contained an amount-in-controversy limitation: Claims could not be brought * * * unless the amount in controversy exceeded $10,000. Title VII, framed in that light, assured that the amount-in-controversy limitation would not impede an employment-discrimination complainant's access to a federal forum. The Act thus contains its own jurisdiction-conferring provision, which reads:

"Each United States district court and each United States court of a place subject to the jurisdiction of the United States shall have jurisdiction of actions brought under this subchapter." [Emphasis added.]

CASE 14.1–CONTINUED

* * * *

The objection that a federal court lacks subject-matter jurisdiction may be raised by a party * * * at any stage in the litigation, even after trial and the entry of judgment. * * * By contrast, the objection that a complaint fails to state a claim upon which relief can be granted may not be asserted [after a] trial. * * *

* * * *

* * * *[S]ubject-matter jurisdiction, because it involves the court's power to hear a case, can never be forfeited or waived.* Moreover, courts, including this Court, have an independent obligation to determine whether subject-matter jurisdiction exists, even in the absence of a challenge from any party. Nothing in the text of Title VII indicates that Congress intended courts, on their own motion, to assure that the employee-numerosity [number] requirement is met. [Emphasis added.]

* * * *

Of course, Congress could make the employee-numerosity requirement "jurisdictional" * * * . Instead, the 15-employee threshold appears in a separate provision that does not speak in jurisdictional terms * * * . Given the unfairness and waste of judicial resources entailed in tying the employee-numerosity requirement to subject-matter jurisdiction, we think it the sounder course to refrain from constricting * * * Title VII's jurisdictional provision and to leave the ball in Congress'[s] court. If the Legislature clearly states that a threshold limitation on a statute's scope shall count as jurisdictional, then courts and litigants will be duly instructed and will not be left to wrestle with the issue. But *when Congress does not rank a statutory limitation on coverage as jurisdictional, courts should treat the restriction as nonjurisdictional in character.* Applying that readily administrable bright line to this case, we hold that the threshold number of employees for application of Title VII is an element of a plaintiff's claim for relief, not a jurisdictional issue. [Emphasis added.]

DECISION AND REMEDY   The United States Supreme Court reversed the lower court's decision and remanded the case for further proceedings. The Court held that "the numerical threshold does not circumscribe federal-court subject-matter jurisdiction. Instead, the employee-numerosity requirement relates to the substantive adequacy of Arbaugh's Title VII claim, and therefore could not be raised defensively late in the lawsuit." Y & H waited too long to argue that it had too few employees to be subject to Title VII.

WHAT IF THE FACTS WERE DIFFERENT?   *Suppose that the lower court had determined that the Moonlight's drivers and owners qualified as employees for Title VII purposes. How might the course of this case have been changed?*

The Equal Employment Opportunity Commission

Compliance with Title VII is monitored by the Equal Employment Opportunity Commission (EEOC). A victim of alleged discrimination, before bringing a suit against the employer, must first file a claim with the EEOC. The EEOC may investigate the dispute and attempt to obtain the parties' voluntary consent to an out-of-court settlement. If voluntary agreement cannot be reached, the EEOC may then file a suit against the employer on the employee's behalf. If the EEOC decides not to investigate the claim, the victim may bring her or his own lawsuit against the employer.

The EEOC does not investigate every claim of employment discrimination, regardless of the merits of the claim. Generally, it investigates only "priority cases," such as cases involving retaliatory discharge (firing an employee in retaliation for submitting a claim to the EEOC) and cases involving types of discrimination that are of particular concern to the EEOC.

Intentional and Unintentional Discrimination

Title VII prohibits both intentional and unintentional discrimination.

DISPARATE-TREATMENT DISCRIMINATION
A form of employment discrimination that results when an employer intentionally discriminates against employees who are members of protected classes.

Intentional Discrimination   Intentional discrimination by an employer against an employee is known as **disparate-treatment discrimination.** Because intent may sometimes be difficult to prove, courts have established certain procedures for resolving disparate-treatment cases. Suppose that a woman applies for employment with a construction firm and is rejected. If she sues on the basis of disparate-treatment discrimination in hiring, she must show that (1) she is a member of a protected class, (2) she applied and was qualified for the job in question, (3) she was rejected by the employer, and (4) the employer continued to seek applicants for the position or filled the position with a person not in a protected class.

PRIMA FACIE CASE
A case in which the plaintiff has produced sufficient evidence of his or her conclusion that the case can go to a jury; a case in which the evidence compels the plaintiff's conclusion if the defendant produces no affirmative defense or evidence to disprove it.

If the woman can meet these relatively easy requirements, she has made out a *prima facie* **case** of illegal discrimination. Making out a *prima facie* case of discrimination means that the plaintiff has met her initial burden of proof and will win in the absence of a legally acceptable employer defense (defenses to claims of employment discrimination will be discussed later in this chapter). The burden then shifts to the employer-defendant, who must articulate a legal reason for not hiring the plaintiff. To prevail, the plaintiff must then show that the employer's reason is a *pretext* (not the true reason) and that discriminatory intent actually motivated the employer's decision.

DISPARATE-IMPACT DISCRIMINATION
A form of employment discrimination that results from certain employer practices or procedures that, although not discriminatory on their face, have a discriminatory effect.

Unintentional Discrimination   Employers often use interviews and testing procedures to choose from among a large number of applicants for job openings. Minimum educational requirements are also common. These practices and procedures may have an unintended discriminatory impact on a protected class. **Disparate-impact discrimination** occurs when, as a result of educational or other job requirements or hiring procedures, an employer's workforce does not reflect the percentage of nonwhites, women, or members of other protected classes that characterizes qualified individuals in the local labor market. If a person challenging an employment practice having a discriminatory effect can show a connection between the practice and the disparity, he or she has made out a *prima facie* case, and no evidence of discriminatory intent needs to be shown.

Disparate-impact discrimination can also occur when an educational or other job requirement or hiring procedure excludes members of a protected class from an employer's workforce at a substantially higher rate than nonmembers, regardless of the racial balance in the employer's workforce. The EEOC has devised a test, called the "four-fifths rule," to determine whether an employment examination is discriminatory on its face. Under this rule, a selection rate for protected classes that is less than four-fifths, or 80 percent, of the rate for the group with the highest rate will generally be regarded as evidence of disparate impact.

| **Example #1**   One hundred white applicants take an employment test, and fifty pass the test and are hired. One hundred minority applicants take the test, and twenty pass the test and are hired. Because twenty is less than four-fifths (80 percent) of fifty, the test would be considered discriminatory under the EEOC guidelines.|

Discrimination Based on Race, Color, and National Origin

If a company's standards or policies for selecting or promoting employees have the effect of discriminating against employees or job applicants on the basis of race, color, or national origin, they are illegal—unless (except for race) they have a substantial, demonstrable relationship to realistic qualifications for the job in question. Discrimination against these protected classes in regard to employment conditions and benefits is also illegal.

| **Example #2** In one case, Cynthia McCullough, an African American woman with a college degree, worked at a deli in a grocery store. More than a year later, the owner of the store promoted a white woman to the position of "deli manager." The white woman had worked in the deli for only three months, had only a sixth-grade education, and could not calculate prices or read recipes. Although the owner gave various reasons for promoting the white woman instead of McCullough, a federal appellate court held that these reasons were likely just excuses and that the real reason was discriminatory intent.[4]|

ETHICAL ISSUE 14.1 ***Are English-only policies in the workplace a form of national-origin discrimination?***

As the U.S. population becomes more multilingual, so does the workforce. In response to this development, many employers have instituted English-only policies in their workplaces, particularly in states with large immigrant populations, such as Texas and California. Are English-only policies fair to workers who do not speak English? Do they violate Title VII's prohibition against discrimination on the basis of race or national origin, as workers in a number of lawsuits have alleged? Generally, the courts have shown a fair degree of tolerance with respect to English-only rules, especially when an employer can show that there is a legitimate business reason for the rules, such as improved communication among employees or worker safety. Some courts, however, tend to regard with suspicion policies that require that English be spoken not only during work time but also on breaks, lunch hours, and the like. For example, one federal district court held that a Texas firm had engaged in disparate-treatment discrimination based on national origin by requiring that English be spoken exclusively in the workplace, including during breaks, except when employees were communicating with customers who could not speak English.[5]

Discrimination Based on Religion

Title VII of the Civil Rights Act of 1964 also prohibits government employers, private employers, and unions from discriminating against persons because of their religion. An employer must "reasonably accommodate" the religious practices of its employees, unless to do so would cause undue hardship to the employer's business. For example, if an employee's religion prohibits him or her from working on a certain day of the week or at a certain type of job, the

---

4. *McCullough v. Real Foods, Inc.*, 140 F.3d 1123 (8th Cir. 1998). The federal district court had granted summary judgment for the employer in this case. The Eighth Circuit Court of Appeals reversed the district court's decision and remanded the case for trial.
5. *EEOC v. Premier Operator Services, Inc.*, 113 F.Supp.2d 1066 (N.D.Tex. 2000).

employer must make a reasonable attempt to accommodate these religious requirements. Employers must reasonably accommodate an employee's religious belief even if the belief is not based on the tenets or dogma of a particular church, sect, or denomination. The only requirement is that the belief be sincerely held by the employee.[6]

Discrimination Based on Gender

Under Title VII, as well as other federal acts, employers are forbidden to discriminate against employees on the basis of gender. Employers are prohibited from classifying jobs as male or female and from advertising in help-wanted columns that are designated male or female unless the employer can prove that the gender of the applicant is essential to the job. Furthermore, employers cannot have separate male and female seniority lists. Generally, to succeed in a suit for gender discrimination, a plaintiff must demonstrate that gender was a determining factor in the employer's decision to hire, fire, or promote her or him. Typically, this involves looking at all of the surrounding circumstances.

The Pregnancy Discrimination Act of 1978,[7] which amended Title VII, expanded the definition of gender discrimination to include discrimination based on pregnancy. Women affected by pregnancy, childbirth, or related medical conditions must be treated—for all employment-related purposes, including the receipt of benefits under employee benefit programs—the same as other persons not so affected but similar in ability to work.

Sometimes employees claim that they were "constructively discharged" from their jobs. **Constructive discharge** occurs when the employer causes the employee's working conditions to be so intolerable that a reasonable person in the employee's position would feel compelled to quit. Title VII encompasses employer liability for constructive discharge.[8] In the case that follows, the question was whether the employer should have been aware of the employee's mistreatment and unbearable working conditions and done something about them.

> **"** A sign that says 'men only' looks very different on a bathroom door than a courthouse door. **"**
>
> —THURGOOD MARSHALL, 1908–1993
> (Associate justice of the United States Supreme Court, 1967–1991)

CONSTRUCTIVE DISCHARGE
A termination of employment brought about by making the employee's working conditions so intolerable that the employee reasonably feels compelled to leave.

---

6. *Frazee v. Illinois Department of Employment Security,* 489 U.S. 829, 109 S.Ct. 1514, 103 L.Ed.2d 914 (1989).
7. 42 U.S.C. Section 2000e(k).
8. *Pennsylvania State Police v. Suders,* 542 U.S. 129, 124 S.Ct. 2342, 159 L.Ed.2d 204 (2004).

CASE 14.2   **Conway-Jepsen v. Small Business Administration**

United States District Court, District of Montana, 2004.
303 F.Supp.2d 1155.

BACKGROUND AND FACTS   In August 1992, Jo Alice Mospan took charge of the Helena, Montana, office of the U.S. Small Business Administration (SBA) as the district director. At the time, there were no other females above a certain pay level in the Helena office, and most of the senior employees and supervisors were male. Mospan was an "in-your-face" micromanager, frequently disciplining employees. In Helena, her purportedly express purpose was to harass and ultimately

rid the office of certain male employees so that they could be replaced by females. In 1993, Mospan recruited Mary Conway-Jepsen from the SBA office in Santa Ana, California. Conway-Jepsen soon learned what Mospan was doing, told her that it was wrong, and refused to cooperate. Mospan retaliated. Among other things, she overloaded Conway-Jepsen with irrelevant assignments, took counterproductive actions to her projects, and set her up to make mistakes. Conway-Jepsen's physician recommended that she quit her job. She applied for a transfer, but when none was forthcoming, she resigned in August 1997. By 2000, all of the targeted males were also gone. Conway-Jepsen filed a suit in a federal district court against the SBA, claiming a violation of Title VII.

IN THE WORDS OF THE COURT . . . *LOVELL,* Senior District Judge.

* * * *

Title VII prohibits an employer from discriminating against any employee because he or she has opposed * * * *an unlawful employment practice* * * * . In order to prove retaliation, Plaintiff must show that (1) she opposed an unlawful employment practice, (2) she suffered an adverse employment action, and (3) a causal connection existed between the adverse employment action and the protected activity or opposition. * * * [Emphasis added.]

Among the unlawful employment practices forbidden by Title VII is the rule that employers must not * * * *discharge any individual, or otherwise* * * * *discriminate against any individual with respect to his compensation, terms, conditions, or privileges of employment, because of such individual's race, color, religion, sex, or national origin.* * * * [Emphasis added.]

* * * *

In order to meet her burden of proving that she was constructively discharged, Plaintiff must show that a reasonable person in her position would have felt compelled to resign because of intolerable working conditions. * * *

In addition, Plaintiff must show that the intolerable working conditions were created by the very conduct that constituted a violation of Title VII (in this case, e.g., the retaliation) and that her resignation resulted from the intolerable working conditions.

* * * *

At all pertinent times herein, Mospan was the duly appointed and acting agent and [district director] of Helena SBA, acting within the scope and course of her authority and employment so to act, and Defendant is answerable for actionable wrongs committed by [its] agent Mospan against Plaintiff in violation of Title VII. Defendant knew or should have known of the hostile working conditions at Helena SBA, yet failed to prevent or remedy these conditions.

* * * [T]he Court concludes that Plaintiff reasonably found her hostile working conditions intolerable, that the intolerable working conditions were created by conduct that constituted a violation of Title VII, and that Plaintiff's resignation resulted from the hostile and intolerable working conditions. The Court concludes that Plaintiff was a diligent and competent SBA employee who was constructively discharged from her position by Mospan's lengthy, continuous, and pervasive pattern of retaliatory treatment for the reason that she had objected to employment practices which were unlawful under Title VII.

* * * *

* * * Plaintiff believes that Mospan ruined her career, and the Court views this belief as justifiable under all the circumstances. * * * The Court finds that Mospan continued to retaliate against Plaintiff after Plaintiff's resignation by interfering with Plaintiff's ability to obtain [further] work in Montana. * * *

DECISION AND REMEDY The court concluded that Conway-Jepsen was constructively discharged in violation of Title VII. The hostile working conditions at the Helena SBA office were created by conduct in violation of Title VII, Conway-Jepsen reasonably found the conditions intolerable, and her resignation resulted from these conditions. On her behalf, the court awarded back pay, job reinstatement, compensatory damages, and attorneys' fees.

WHY IS THIS CASE IMPORTANT? *Employers should be aware that if a manager or supervisor creates intolerable working conditions because of his or her own personal bias, the employer could be held liable under Title VII.*

Sexual Harassment

Title VII also protects employees against **sexual harassment** in the workplace. Sexual harassment has often been classified as either *quid pro quo* harassment or hostile-environment harassment. *Quid pro quo* harassment[9] occurs when sexual favors are demanded in return for job opportunities, promotions, salary increases, and the like. According to the United States Supreme Court, hostile-environment harassment occurs when "the workplace is permeated with discriminatory intimidation, ridicule, and insult, that is sufficiently severe or pervasive to alter the conditions of the victim's employment and create an abusive working environment."[10]

Generally, the courts apply this Supreme Court guideline on a case-by-case basis. Some courts have held that just one incident of sexually offensive conduct—such as a sexist remark by a co-worker or a photo on an employer's desk of his bikini-clad wife—can create a hostile environment.[11] According to some employment specialists, employers should assume that hostile-environment harassment has occurred if an employee claims that it has. (For a discussion of sexual harassment in other nations, see this chapter's *Beyond Our Borders* feature.)

> "Justice is better than chivalry if we cannot have both."
>
> —ALICE STONE BLACKWELL,
> 1857–1950
> (American suffragist and editor)

Harassment by Supervisors What if an employee is harassed by a manager or supervisor of a large firm, and the firm itself (the "employer") is not aware of the harassment? Should the employer be held liable for the harassment nonetheless? For some time, the courts were in disagreement on this issue. Typically, employers were held liable for Title VII violations by the firm's managerial or supervisory personnel in *quid pro quo* harassment cases regardless of whether the employer knew about the harassment. In hostile-environment cases, the majority of courts tended to hold employers liable only if the employer knew or should have known of the harassment and failed to take prompt remedial action.

Tangible Employment Action For an employer to be held liable for a supervisor's sexual harassment, the supervisor must have taken a tangible employment action against the employee. A *tangible employment action* is a significant change in employment status, such as firing or failing to promote an employee, reassigning the employee to a position with significantly different responsibilities, or effecting a significant change in employment benefits.

Only a supervisor, or another person acting with the authority of the employer, can cause this sort of injury. A co-worker can sexually harass another employee, and anyone who has regular contact with an employee can inflict psychological injuries by offensive conduct. A co-worker cannot dock another's pay, demote her or him, or set conditions for continued employment, though.

| **Example #3** Jin was a sales agent at Metropolitan Life Insurance Company (MetLife). Morabito was Jin's supervisor. Morabito made sexual remarks to Jin, offensively touched her, and forced her to engage in sexual acts by threat-

---

9. *Quid pro quo* is a Latin phrase that is often translated to mean "something in exchange for something else."
10. *Harris v. Forklift Systems*, 510 U.S. 17, 114 S.Ct. 367, 126 L.Ed.2d 295 (1993).
11. For other examples, see *Radtke v. Everett*, 442 Mich. 368, 501 N.W.2d 155 (1993); and *Nadeau v. Rainbow Rugs, Inc.*, 675 A.2d 973 (Me. 1996).

Sexual Harassment in Other Nations

The problem of sexual harassment in the workplace is not confined to the United States. Indeed, it is a worldwide problem for female workers. In Argentina, Brazil, Egypt, Turkey, and many other countries, there is no legal protection against any form of employment discrimination. Even in those countries that do have laws prohibiting discriminatory employment practices, including gender-based discrimination, those laws often do not specifically include sexual harassment as a discriminatory practice. Several countries have attempted to remedy this omission by passing new laws or amending others to specifically prohibit sexual harassment in the workplace. Japan, for example, has amended its Equal Employment Opportunity Law to include a provision making sexual harassment illegal.

Thailand has also passed its first sexual-harassment law. In 2002, the European Union, which some years ago outlawed gender-based discrimination, adopted a directive that specifically identifies sexual harassment as a form of discrimination. Nevertheless, women's groups throughout Europe contend that corporations in European countries tend to view sexual harassment with "quiet tolerance." They contrast this attitude with that of most U.S. corporations, which have implemented specific procedures to deal with harassment claims.

For Critical Analysis *Why do you think U.S. corporations are more aggressive than European companies in taking steps to prevent sexual harassment in the workplace?*

ening to fire her and physically harm her if she did not submit to his demands. When Jin sued MetLife for sexual harassment, the jury found that she was not subjected to a tangible employment action. A federal appellate court reversed, however. The court reasoned that Morabito had used his authority as a supervisor to impose on Jin the added job requirement that she submit to sexual abuse to keep her job.[12]

Supreme Court Guidelines   In 1998, in two separate cases, the United States Supreme Court issued some significant guidelines relating to the liability of employers for their supervisors' harassment of employees in the workplace. In *Faragher v. City of Boca Raton,*[13] the Court held that an employer (a city) could be held liable for a supervisor's harassment of employees even though the employer was unaware of the behavior. The Court reached this conclusion primarily because, although the city had a written policy against sexual harassment, the policy had not been distributed to city employees. Additionally, the city had not established any procedures that could be followed by employees who felt that they were victims of sexual harassment. In *Burlington Industries, Inc. v. Ellerth,*[14] the Court ruled that a company could be held liable for the harassment of an employee by one of its vice presidents even though the employee suffered no adverse job consequences.

In these two cases, the Court set forth some guidelines on workplace harassment that are helpful to employers and employees alike. On the one hand, employees benefit by the ruling that employers may be held liable for their supervisors' harassment even though the employers were unaware of the

12. *Jin v. Metropolitan Life Insurance Co.,* 295 F.3d 335 (2d Cir. 2002), republished at 310 F.3d 84 (2d Cir. 2002).
13. 524 U.S. 775, 118 S.Ct. 2275, 141 L.Ed.2d 662 (1998).
14. 524 U.S. 742, 118 S.Ct. 2257, 141 L.Ed.2d 633 (1998).

actions and even though the employees suffered no adverse job consequences. On the other hand, the Court made it clear in both decisions that employers have an affirmative defense against liability for their supervisors' harassment of employees if the employers can show the following:

1. That they have taken "reasonable care to prevent and correct promptly any sexually harassing behavior" (by establishing effective harassment policies and complaint procedures, for example).
2. That the employees suing for harassment failed to follow these policies and procedures.

In 2004, the Supreme Court further clarified the tangible employment action requirement in the following case. The Court had to decide how the guidelines apply to a state police employee's constructive discharge caused by her supervisors' sexual harassment. Does a constructive discharge count as a tangible employment action and preclude the employer's assertion of the affirmative defense? That was the issue before the Court.

CASE 14.3   **Pennsylvania State Police v. Suders**

Supreme Court of the United States, 2004.
542 U.S. 129,
124 S.Ct. 2342,
159 L.Ed.2d 204.
www.findlaw.com/casecode/supreme.html[a]

BACKGROUND AND FACTS   In March 1998, the Pennsylvania State Police (PSP) hired Nancy Suders to work as a communications operator. Suders's supervisors—Sergeant Eric Easton, Corporal William Baker, and Corporal Eric Prendergast—subjected her to a continuous barrage of sexual harassment. In June, Suders told Officer Virginia Smith-Elliott, whom PSP had designated as its equal employment

opportunity officer, that Suders might need help. Two months later, again to Smith-Elliott, Suders reported that she was being harassed and was afraid. Smith-Elliott told Suders to file a complaint, but did not tell her how to obtain the necessary form. Two days later, Suders's supervisors arrested her for the theft of her own computer-skills exam paper, which she had removed after they reported falsely that she had failed the exam. Suders resigned and filed a suit in a federal district court against PSP, alleging, in part, sexual harassment. The court issued a summary judgment in PSP's favor. Suders appealed to the U.S. Court of Appeals for the Third Circuit, which reversed the judgment and remanded the case for trial, holding that the *Ellerth/Faragher* affirmative defense is never available in constructive discharge cases. PSP appealed to the United States Supreme Court.

a. In the "Browsing" section, click on "2004 Decisions." When that page opens, click on the name of the case to access the opinion.

IN THE WORDS OF THE COURT . . . Justice *GINSBURG* delivered the opinion of the Court.

*   *   *   *

This case concerns an employer's liability for * * * constructive discharge resulting from sexual harassment, or hostile work environment, attributable to a supervisor. Our starting point is the framework [the] *Ellerth* and *Faragher* [decisions, discussed previously in this chapter] established to govern employer liability for sexual harassment by supervisors. * * * [T]hose decisions delineate two categories of hostile work environment claims: (1) harassment that culminates in a tangible employment action, for which employers are strictly liable, and (2) harassment that takes place in the absence of a tangible employment action, to which employers may assert an affirmative defense * * * .

*   *   *   *

Suders'[s] claim is of the same genre as the hostile work environment claims the Court analyzed in [the] *Ellerth* and *Faragher* [decisions]. Essentially, Suders presents a "worse case" harassment scenario, harassment ratcheted up to the breaking point. Like the harassment considered in our pathmarking decisions, harassment so intolerable as

CASE 14.3–CONTINUED

to cause a resignation may be effected through co-worker conduct, unofficial supervisory conduct, or official company acts. Unlike an actual termination, which is *always* effected through an official act of the company, a constructive discharge need not be. *A constructive discharge involves both an employee's decision to leave and precipitating conduct: The former involves no official action; the latter, like a harassment claim without any constructive discharge assertion, may or may not involve official action.* [Emphasis added.]

To be sure, a constructive discharge is functionally the same as an actual termination in [some] respects. * * * [B]oth end the employer-employee relationship, and both inflict * * * direct economic harm. But when an official act does not underlie the constructive discharge, the *Ellerth* and *Faragher* analysis, we here hold, calls for extension of the affirmative defense to the employer. As those leading decisions indicate, official directions and declarations are the acts most likely to be brought home to the employer, the measures over which the employer can exercise greatest control. Absent an official act of the enterprise as the last straw, the employer ordinarily would have no particular reason to suspect that a resignation is not the typical kind daily occurring in the work force. And as [the] *Ellerth* and *Faragher* [decisions] further point out, an official act reflected in company records—a demotion or a reduction in compensation, for example—shows beyond question that the supervisor has used his managerial or controlling position to the employee's disadvantage. *Absent such an official act, the extent to which the supervisor's misconduct has been aided by the [employment] relation is less certain. That uncertainty * * * justifies affording the employer the chance to establish, through the Ellerth/Faragher affirmative defense, that it should not be held vicariously liable.* [Emphasis added.]

* * * *

We agree with the Third Circuit that the case, in its current posture, presents genuine issues of material fact concerning Suders'[s] hostile work environment and constructive discharge claims. We hold, however, that the Court of Appeals erred in declaring the affirmative defense described in [the] *Ellerth* and *Faragher* [decisions] never available in constructive discharge cases. Accordingly, we vacate the Third Circuit's judgment and remand the case for further proceedings consistent with this opinion.

DECISION AND REMEDY The United States Supreme Court vacated the lower court's judgment and remanded the case for further proceedings. To establish constructive discharge, a plaintiff alleging sexual harassment must show that the work environment became so intolerable that resignation was a fitting response. An employer may then assert the *Ellerth/Faragher* affirmative defense unless the plaintiff quit in reasonable response to a tangible employment action.

WHAT IF THE FACTS WERE DIFFERENT? *If the plaintiff had filed a complaint with the employer's equal employment opportunity officer, how might the result have been different?*

Harassment by Co-Workers and Nonemployees Often, employees alleging harassment complain that the actions of co-workers, not supervisors, are responsible for creating a hostile working environment. In such cases, the employee may still have a cause of action against the employer. Normally, though, the employer will be held liable only if the employer knew, or should have known, about the harassment and failed to take immediate remedial action. (For a further discussion of the importance of taking immediate and *effective* remedial action in response to complaints of sexual harassment, see this chapter's *Management Perspective* feature on the next page.)

Responding to Sexual Harassment in the Workplace

Management Faces a Legal Issue   As discussed elsewhere in this chapter, in two cases decided in 1998, the United States Supreme Court issued guidelines concerning the liability of employers for their supervisors' harassment of employees in the workplace. Generally, these guidelines allow employers to avoid liability if they take reasonable steps to prevent sexual harassment in the workplace and take prompt remedial action to correct sexually harassing behavior. Although these cases involved harassment of workers by supervisors, the principles expressed in the rulings have also been applied to harassment by co-workers. One question remains, though: When an employee complains of an incident of sexual harassment, what steps must the employer take to satisfy the requirement of "prompt remedial action"? The answer to this question has important implications for today's business owners and managers.

What the Courts Say   Generally, when it can be shown that a worker was sexually harassed (by either a supervisor *or* a co-worker), management must make sure that whatever action it takes will effectively prevent similar incidents of harassment in the future. Consider the outcome of two cases dealing with just this issue. One case, decided by the Supreme Court of Hawaii, involved a plaintiff—a female worker in a restaurant—who had experienced a short, isolated instance of unwanted contact from a male co-worker (the co-worker had squeezed her buttock for approximately one second). She asked him to stop and then asked a manager, who had witnessed the incident, to ask the co-worker to not do it again. The manager did so immediately. A few weeks later, the co-worker again squeezed the plaintiff's buttock for a second or so. Management immediately suspended the co-worker and terminated him shortly thereafter. The trial court granted the employer's motion for summary judgment, concluding that the manager's response was sufficient to avoid liability. The Hawaii Supreme Court,

however, reversed the trial court's decision and remanded the case for trial. The state supreme court held that reasonable minds could differ as to whether the manager's response was reasonably calculated to end the harassment. The court noted that the co-worker was given only an oral warning, which, the manager later admitted to the plaintiff, the co-worker did not take seriously. Second, the co-worker was not threatened with a future written reprimand, nor was he informed that he could be suspended or terminated if his behavior continued (even though he was, in fact, later terminated, when the harassment continued).[a]

In the other case, the plaintiff, Jamie McCurdy, worked as a radio dispatcher for the Arkansas State Police. After a police sergeant allegedly groped her breast, touched her hair, and made suggestive sexual comments to her, she immediately reported the incident to her supervisor. Shortly thereafter, supervisory officers investigated the incident and ultimately demoted the sergeant and transferred him to a different location. In this case, a federal appellate court concluded that these actions were sufficient to justify the lower court's grant of summary judgment for the employer.[b]

Implications for Managers   These cases both illustrate that a key factor in a court's determination of employer liability for harassment in the workplace is the *effectiveness* of the response. Is the employer's response effective in the sense that it will help to prevent incidents of harassment? To avoid liability, managers would be wise to give more than just oral warnings to offending employees and to take definite preventive steps. These steps range from removing the offending supervisor or co-worker from a complainant's work area to terminating the offender.

a. *Arquero v. Hilton Hawaiian Village, L.L.C.,* 104 Hawaii 423, 91 P.3d 505 (2004).
b. *McCurdy v. Arkansas State Police,* 375 F.3d 762 (8th Cir. 2004).

Employers may also be liable for harassment by *nonemployees* in certain circumstances. **Example #4**   A restaurant owner or manager knows that a certain customer repeatedly harasses a waitress and permits the harassment to continue. The restaurant owner may be liable under Title VII even though the customer is not an employee of the restaurant. The issue turns on the control that the employer exerts over a nonemployee. In one case, an owner of a Pizza Hut franchise was held liable for the harassment of a waitress by two male customers because no steps were taken to prevent the harassment.[15]

15. *Lockard v. Pizza Hut, Inc.,* 162 F.3d 1062 (10th Cir. 1998).

Same-Gender Harassment   The courts have also had to address the issue of whether men who are harassed by other men, or women who are harassed by other women, are protected by laws that prohibit gender-based discrimination in the workplace. For example, what if the male president of a firm demands sexual favors from a male employee? Does this action qualify as sexual harassment? For some time, the courts were widely split on this issue. In 1998, in *Oncale v. Sundowner Offshore Services, Inc.,*[16] the Supreme Court resolved the issue by holding that Title VII protection extends to situations in which individuals are harassed by members of the same gender.

Nevertheless, it can be difficult to prove that the harassment in same-gender harassment cases is "based on sex." **| Example #5** Suppose that a gay man is harassed by another man at the workplace. The harasser is not a homosexual and does not treat all men with hostility—just this one man. Does the victim in this situation have a cause of action under Title VII? A court may find that this does not qualify as sexual harassment under Title VII because the harasser's conduct was because of the employee's sexual orientation, not "because of sex."[17]**|**

Online Harassment

Employees' online activities can create a hostile working environment in many ways. Racial jokes, ethnic slurs, or other comments contained in e-mail may become the basis for a claim of hostile-environment harassment or other forms of discrimination. A worker who sees sexually explicit images on a co-worker's computer screen may find the images offensive and claim that they create a hostile working environment.

Avoiding Liability through Prompt Remedial Action   Generally, employers may be able to avoid liability for online harassment if they take prompt remedial action. **| Example #6** In *Daniels v. WorldCom, Inc.,*[18] Angela Daniels, an employee of Robert Half International under contract to WorldCom, Inc., received racially harassing e-mailed jokes from another employee. After receiving the jokes, Daniels complained to WorldCom managers. Shortly afterward, the company issued a warning to the offending employee about the proper use of the e-mail system and held two meetings to discuss company policy on the use of the system. In Daniels's suit against WorldCom for racial discrimination, a federal district court concluded that the employer was not liable for its employee's racially harassing e-mails because the employer took prompt remedial action.**|**

An Ongoing Challenge   Employers who have taken steps to avoid online harassment in the workplace continue to face challenging problems. Clearly, if they do not take effective steps to curb such harassment, they may face liability for violating Title VII. At the same time, if they monitor their employees' communications, they may face liability under other laws—for invading their employees' privacy, for instance.

---

16. 523 U.S. 75, 118 S.Ct. 998, 140 L.Ed.2d 207 (1998).
17. See, for example, *McCown v. St. John's Health System*, 349 F.3d 540 (8th Cir. 2003); and *Rene v. MGM Grand Hotel, Inc.*, 305 F.3d 1061 (9th Cir. 2002).
18. 1998 WL 91261 (N.D.Tex. 1998).

Additionally, an employee who is fired for misusing the employer's computer system to, say, e-mail pornographic images to co-workers or others may claim that he or she was wrongfully discharged. Finally, there are constitutional rights to be considered. In one case, a court held that religious speech that unintentionally creates a hostile environment is constitutionally protected.[19]

Remedies under Title VII

Employer liability under Title VII may be extensive. If the plaintiff successfully proves that unlawful discrimination occurred, he or she may be awarded reinstatement, back pay, retroactive promotions, and damages. Compensatory damages are available only in cases of intentional discrimination. Punitive damages may be recovered against a private employer only if the employer acted with malice or reckless indifference to an individual's rights. The statute limits the total amount of compensatory and punitive damages that the plaintiff can recover from specific employers—ranging from $50,000 against employers with one hundred or fewer employees to $300,000 against employers with more than five hundred employees.

EQUAL PAY ACT OF 1963

The Equal Pay Act of 1963 was enacted as an amendment to the Fair Labor Standards Act of 1938. Basically, the act prohibits gender-based discrimination in the wages paid for similar work on jobs that require the same amount of skill, effort, and responsibility. For the act's equal pay requirements to apply, the male and female employees must work at the same establishment.

A person alleging wage discrimination in violation of the Equal Pay Act may sue her or his employer. To determine whether the Equal Pay Act has been violated, a court will look to the primary duties of the two jobs. It is job content rather than job description that controls in all cases. The jobs of a barber and a beautician, for example, are considered essentially "equal." So, too, are those of a tailor and a seamstress. Nevertheless, an employer will *not* be found liable for violating the act if it can show that the wage differential for equal work was based on (1) a seniority system, (2) a merit system, (3) a system that pays according to quality or quantity of production, or (4) any factor other than gender. Small differences in job content, however, do not justify higher pay for one gender. The Equal Pay Act is administered by the EEOC.

DISCRIMINATION BASED ON AGE

Age discrimination is potentially the most widespread form of discrimination, because anyone—regardless of race, color, national origin, or gender—could be a victim at some point in life. The Age Discrimination in Employment Act (ADEA) of 1967, as amended, prohibits employment discrimination on the basis of age against individuals forty years of age or older. The act also prohibits mandatory retirement for nonmanagerial workers. For the act to apply, an employer must have twenty or more employees, and the employer's business activities must affect interstate commerce. The EEOC administers the

---

19. *Meltebeke v. B.O.L.I.*, 903 P.2d 351 (Or. 1995).

ADEA, but the act also permits private causes of action against employers for age discrimination.

Procedures under the ADEA

The burden-shifting procedure under the ADEA is similar to that under Title VII. If a plaintiff can establish that she or he (1) was a member of the protected age group, (2) was qualified for the position from which she or he was discharged, and (3) was discharged under circumstances that give rise to an inference of discrimination, the plaintiff has established a *prima facie* case of unlawful age discrimination. The burden then shifts to the employer, who must articulate a legitimate reason for the discrimination. If the plaintiff can prove that the employer's reason is only a pretext (excuse) and that the plaintiff's age was a determining factor in the employer's decision, the employer will be held liable under the ADEA.

Numerous age discrimination cases have been brought against employers who, to cut costs, replaced older, higher-salaried employees with younger, lower-salaried workers. Whether a firing is discriminatory or simply part of a rational business decision to prune the company's ranks is not always clear. Companies often defend a decision to discharge a worker by asserting that the worker could no longer perform his or her duties or that the worker's skills were no longer needed. The employee must prove that the discharge was motivated, at least in part, by age bias. Proof that qualified older employees are generally discharged before younger employees or that co-workers continually made unflattering age-related comments about the discharged worker may be enough.

The plaintiff need not prove that he or she was replaced by a person outside the protected class—that is, by a person under the age of forty years.[20] Rather, the issue in all ADEA cases is whether age discrimination has, in fact, occurred, regardless of the age of the replacement worker.

State Employees Not Covered by the ADEA

The United States Supreme Court has generally held that the states are immune from lawsuits brought by private individuals in federal court—unless a state consents to the suit. This immunity stems from the Supreme Court's interpretation of the Eleventh Amendment (the text of this amendment is included in Appendix B). In *Kimel v. Florida Board of Regents*,[21] decided in 2000, the United States Supreme Court held that the Eleventh Amendment bars private parties (in this case, employees of two Florida state universities) from suing state employers for violations of the ADEA. According to the Court, Congress had exceeded its constitutional authority when it included in the ADEA a provision stating that "all employers," including state employers, were subject to the act.

State immunity under the Eleventh Amendment is not absolute, however, as the Supreme Court explained in 2004. A case was brought under the Americans with Disabilities Act (a statute that will be discussed shortly), alleging that disabled individuals were denied access to the courts. The Court held that in

> **REMEMBER !** The Fourteenth Amendment prohibits any state from denying to any person "the equal protection of the laws." This prohibition applies to the *federal* government through the due process clause of the Fifth Amendment.

20. *O'Connor v. Consolidated Coin Caterers Corp.*, 517 U.S. 308, 116 S.Ct. 1307, 134 L.Ed.2d 433 (1996).
21. 528 U.S. 62, 120 S.Ct. 631, 145 L.Ed.2d 522 (2000).

some situations, such as when fundamental rights are at stake, Congress has the power to abrogate (abolish) state immunity to private suits through legislation that unequivocally shows Congress's intent to subject states to private suits.[22]

DISCRIMINATION BASED ON DISABILITY

The Americans with Disabilities Act (ADA) of 1990 is designed to eliminate discriminatory employment practices that prevent otherwise qualified workers with disabilities from fully participating in the national labor force. Prior to 1990, the major federal law providing protection to those with disabilities was the Rehabilitation Act of 1973. That act covered only federal government employees and those employed under federally funded programs. The ADA extends federal protection against disability-based discrimination to all workplaces with fifteen or more workers. Basically, the ADA requires that employers "reasonably accommodate" the needs of persons with disabilities unless to do so would cause the employer to suffer an "undue hardship." Note, though, that with the exception of the one 2004 case mentioned above, the Supreme Court has normally held that lawsuits under the ADA cannot be brought against state government employers.[23]

Procedures under the ADA

To prevail on a claim under the ADA, a plaintiff must show that he or she (1) has a disability, (2) is otherwise qualified for the employment in question, and (3) was excluded from the employment solely because of the disability. As in Title VII cases, a claim alleging a violation of the ADA may be commenced only after the plaintiff has pursued the claim through the EEOC. Plaintiffs may sue for many of the same remedies available under Title VII. The EEOC may decide to investigate and perhaps even sue the employer on behalf of the employee. If the EEOC decides not to sue, then the employee is entitled to sue.

Significantly, the United States Supreme Court held in 2002 that the EEOC could bring a suit against an employer for disability-based discrimination even though the employee had agreed to submit any job-related disputes to arbitration (see Chapter 3). The Court reasoned that because the EEOC was not a party to the arbitration agreement, the agreement was not binding on the EEOC.[24]

Plaintiffs in lawsuits brought under the ADA may seek many of the same remedies available under Title VII. These include reinstatement, back pay, a limited amount of compensatory and punitive damages (for intentional discrimination), and certain other forms of relief. Repeat violators may be ordered to pay fines of up to $100,000.

What Is a Disability?

The ADA is broadly drafted to cover persons with a wide range of disabilities. Specifically, the ADA defines *disability* as "(1) a physical or mental impairment that substantially limits one or more of the major life activities of such

22. *Tennessee v. Lane,* 541 U.S. 509, 124 S.Ct. 1978, 158 L.Ed.2d 820 (2004).

23. *Board of Trustees of the University of Alabama v. Garrett,* 531 U.S. 356, 121 S.Ct. 955, 148 L.Ed.2d 866 (2001).

24. *EEOC v. Waffle House, Inc.,* 534 U.S. 279, 122 S.Ct. 754, 151 L.Ed.2d 75 (2002).

individuals; (2) a record of such impairment; or (3) being regarded as having such an impairment."

Health conditions that have been considered disabilities under the federal law include blindness, alcoholism, heart disease, cancer, muscular dystrophy, cerebral palsy, paraplegia, diabetes, acquired immune deficiency syndrome (AIDS), testing positive for the human immunodeficiency virus (HIV, the virus that causes AIDS), and morbid obesity (defined as existing when an individual's weight is two times that of a normal person).[25] The ADA excludes from coverage certain conditions, such as kleptomania (the obsessive desire to steal).

Although the ADA's definition of disability is broad, starting in 1999 the United States Supreme Court has issued a series of decisions narrowing the definition of what constitutes a disability under the act.

Correctable Conditions   The Supreme Court held in 1999 that the determination of whether a person is substantially limited in a major life activity is based on how the person functions when taking medication or using corrective devices, not on how the person functions without these measures.[26] In a 2002 case, a federal appellate court held that a pharmacist suffering from diabetes, which could be corrected by insulin, had no cause of action against his employer under the ADA.[27] In other cases decided in the early 2000s, the courts have held that plaintiffs with bipolar disorder, epilepsy, and other such conditions do not fall under the ADA's protections if the conditions can be corrected.

Repetitive-Stress Injuries   For some time, the courts were divided on the issue of whether carpal tunnel syndrome (or other repetitive-stress injury) constituted a disability under the ADA. Carpal tunnel syndrome is a condition of pain and weakness in the hand caused by repetitive compression of a nerve in the wrist. In 2002, in a case involving this issue, the Supreme Court unanimously held that it did not constitute a disability. The Court stated that although the employee could not perform the manual tasks associated with her job, the condition did not amount to a disability under the ADA because it did not "substantially limit" the major life activity of performing manual tasks.[28]

Co-workers discuss business matters. What is a disability under the Americans with Disabilities Act? (Johnny Stockshooter/International Stock)

Reasonable Accommodation

The ADA does not require that employers accommodate the needs of job applicants or employees with disabilities who are not otherwise qualified for the work. If a job applicant or an employee with a disability, with reasonable accommodation, can perform essential job functions, however, the employer must make the accommodation. Required modifications may include installing ramps for a wheelchair, establishing flexible working hours, creating or modifying job assignments, and creating or improving training materials and procedures.

Considering Employees' Preferences   Generally, employers should give primary consideration to employees' preferences in deciding what accommodations

---

25. *Cook v. Rhode Island Department of Mental Health*, 10 F.3d 17 (1st Cir. 1993).

26. *Sutton v. United Airlines, Inc.*, 527 U.S. 471, 119 S.Ct. 2139, 144 L.Ed.2d 450 (1999).

27. *Orr v. Walmart Stores, Inc.*, 297 F.3d 720 (8th Cir. 2002).

28. *Toyota Motor Manufacturing, Kentucky, Inc. v. Williams*, 534 U.S. 184, 122 S.Ct. 681, 151 L.Ed.2d 615 (2002).

should be made. What happens if a job applicant or employee does not indicate to the employer how her or his disability can be accommodated so that the employee can perform essential job functions? In this situation, the employer may avoid liability for failing to hire or retain the individual on the ground that the applicant or employee has failed to meet the "otherwise qualified" requirement.[29]

Undue Hardship   Employers who do not accommodate the needs of persons with disabilities must demonstrate that the accommodations will cause "undue hardship." Generally, the law offers no uniform standards for identifying what is an undue hardship other than the imposition of a "significant difficulty or expense" on the employer.

Usually, the courts decide whether an accommodation constitutes an undue hardship on a case-by-case basis. In one case, the court decided that paying for a parking space near the office for an employee with a disability was not an undue hardship.[30] In another case, the court held that accommodating the request of an employee with diabetes for indefinite leave until his disease was under control would create an undue hardship for the employer because the employer would not know when the employee was returning to work. The court stated that reasonable accommodation under the ADA means accommodation so that the employee can perform the job now or "in the immediate future" rather than at some unspecified distant time.[31]

Job Applications and Preemployment Physical Exams   Employers must modify their job-application process so that those with disabilities can compete for jobs with those who do not have disabilities. | **Example #7** A job announcement that includes only a phone number would discriminate against potential job applicants with hearing impairments. Thus, the job announcement must also provide an address.|

DON'T FORGET Preemployment screening procedures must be applied equally with regard to all job applicants.

Employers are restricted in the kinds of questions they may ask on job-application forms and during preemployment interviews. Furthermore, they cannot require persons with disabilities to submit to preemployment physicals unless such exams are required of all other applicants. Employers can condition an offer of employment on the applicant's successfully passing a medical examination, but can disqualify the applicant only if the medical problems they discover would render the applicant unable to perform the job.

Dangerous Workers   Employers are not required to hire or retain workers who, because of their disabilities, pose a "direct threat to the health or safety" of their co-workers or the public.[32] This danger must be substantial and immediate; it cannot be speculative. In the wake of the AIDS epidemic, many employers have been concerned about hiring or continuing to employ a worker who has AIDS under the assumption that the worker might pose a direct threat to the health or safety of others in the workplace. Courts have generally held, however, that

---

29. See, for example, *Beck v. University of Wisconsin Board of Regents*, 75 F.3d 1130 (7th Cir. 1996); and *White v. York International Corp.*, 45 F.3d 357 (10th Cir. 1995).
30. *Lyons v. Legal Aid Society*, 68 F.3d 1512 (2d Cir. 1995).
31. *Myers v. Hose*, 50 F.3d 278 (4th Cir. 1995).
32. Note that the United States Supreme Court has also upheld regulations that permit an employer to refuse to hire a worker when the job would pose a threat to that person's own health. *Chevron USA, Inc. v. Echazabal*, 536 U.S. 73, 122 S.Ct. 2045, 153 L.Ed.2d 82 (2002).

AIDS is not so contagious as to disqualify employees in most jobs. Therefore, employers must reasonably accommodate job applicants or employees who have AIDS or who test positive for HIV, the virus that causes AIDS.

Substance Abusers   Drug addiction is a disability under the ADA because drug addiction is a substantially limiting impairment. Those who are currently using illegal drugs are not protected by the act, however. The ADA protects only persons with *former* drug addictions—those who have completed a supervised drug rehabilitation program or are currently in a supervised rehabilitation program. Individuals who have used drugs casually in the past are not protected under the act. They are not considered addicts and therefore do not have a disability (addiction).

People suffering from alcoholism are protected by the ADA. Employers cannot legally discriminate against employees simply because they are suffering from alcoholism and must treat them in the same way they treat other employees. In other words, an employee with alcoholism who comes to work late because she or he was drinking excessively the night before cannot be disciplined any differently than someone else who is late for another reason. Of course, employers have the right to prohibit the use of alcohol in the workplace and can require that employees not be under the influence of alcohol while working. Employers can also fire or refuse to hire a person with alcoholism if he or she poses a substantial risk of harm to either himself or herself or to others and the risk cannot be reduced by reasonable accommodation.

Health-Insurance Plans   Workers with disabilities must be given equal access to any health insurance provided to other employees. Employers can exclude from coverage preexisting health conditions and certain types of diagnostic or surgical procedures, though. An employer can also put a limit, or cap, on health-care payments under its particular group health policy—as long as such caps are "applied equally to all insured employees" and do not "discriminate

A discussion occurs at a meeting of Alcoholics Anonymous. Should employers be allowed to discriminate against persons suffering from alcoholism? Why or why not? (John Boykin/PhotoEdit)

on the basis of disability." Whenever a group health-care plan makes a disability-based distinction in its benefits, the plan violates the ADA. The employer must then be able to justify the distinction by proving one of the following:

1. That limiting coverage of certain ailments is required to keep the plan financially sound.
2. That coverage of certain ailments would cause such a significant increase in premium payments or their equivalent that the plan would be unappealing to a significant number of workers.
3. That the disparate treatment is justified by the risks and costs associated with a particular disability.

Hostile-Environment Claims under the ADA

As discussed earlier in this chapter, under Title VII of the Civil Rights Act of 1964, an employee may base certain types of employment-discrimination causes of action on a hostile-environment theory. Using this theory, a worker may successfully sue her or his employer, even if the worker was not fired or otherwise discriminated against.

Can a worker file a suit founded on a hostile-environment claim under the ADA? The ADA does not expressly provide for such suits, but some courts have allowed them.[33] Others have assumed that the claim was possible without deciding whether the ADA allowed it. To succeed, such a claim would likely have to be based on conduct that a reasonable person would find so offensive that it would change the conditions of the person's employment.

DEFENSES TO EMPLOYMENT DISCRIMINATION

The first line of defense for an employer charged with employment discrimination is, of course, to assert that the plaintiff has failed to meet his or her initial burden of proving that discrimination occurred. As noted, plaintiffs bringing cases under the ADA sometimes find it difficult to meet this initial burden because they must prove that their alleged disabilities are disabilities covered by the ADA. Furthermore, plaintiffs in ADA cases must prove that they were otherwise qualified for the job and that their disabilities were the sole reason they were not hired or were fired.

Once a plaintiff succeeds in proving that discrimination occurred, the burden shifts to the employer to justify the discriminatory practice. Often, employers attempt to justify the discrimination by claiming that it was the result of a business necessity, a bona fide occupational qualification, or a seniority system. In some cases, as noted earlier, an effective antiharassment policy and prompt remedial action when harassment occurs may shield employers from liability under Title VII for sexual harassment.

Business Necessity

BUSINESS NECESSITY
A defense to allegations of employment discrimination in which the employer demonstrates that an employment practice that discriminates against members of a protected class is related to job performance.

An employer may defend against a claim of disparate-impact (unintentional) discrimination by asserting that a practice that has a discriminatory effect is a **business necessity.** | **Example #8** If requiring a high school diploma is shown

---

33. See, for example, *Flowers v. Southern Regional Physician Services, Inc.,* 247 F.3d 229 (5th Cir. 2001).

to have a discriminatory effect, an employer might argue that a high school education is necessary for workers to perform the job at a required level of competence. If the employer can demonstrate to the court's satisfaction that a definite connection exists between a high school education and job performance, the employer will normally succeed in this business necessity defense.

Bona Fide Occupational Qualification

Another defense applies when discrimination against a protected class is essential to a job—that is, when a particular trait is a **bona fide occupational qualification (BFOQ).** | **Example #9** A women's clothing store might legitimately hire only female sales attendants if part of an attendant's job involves assisting clients in the store's dressing rooms. Similarly, the Federal Aviation Administration can legitimately impose age limits for airline pilots.|

Race, however, can never be a BFOQ. Generally, courts have restricted the BFOQ defense to instances in which the employee's gender is essential to the job. The United States Supreme Court has even held that a policy that was adopted to protect the unborn children of female employees from the harmful effects of exposure to lead was an unacceptable BFOQ.[34]

BONA FIDE OCCUPATIONAL QUALIFICATION (BFOQ)
Identifiable characteristics reasonably necessary to the normal operation of a particular business. These characteristics can include gender, national origin, and religion, but not race.

Seniority Systems

An employer with a history of discrimination may have no members of protected classes in upper-level positions. Even if the employer now seeks to be unbiased, it may face a lawsuit in which the plaintiff asks a court to order that minorities be promoted ahead of schedule to compensate for past discrimination. If no present intent to discriminate is shown, however, and if promotions or other job benefits are distributed according to a fair **seniority system** (in which workers with more years of service are promoted first or laid off last), the employer has a good defense against the suit. According to the Supreme Court in 2002, this defense may also apply to alleged discrimination under the ADA. If an employee with a disability requests an accommodation (such as an assignment to a particular position) that conflicts with an employer's seniority system, the accommodation will generally not be considered "reasonable" under the act.[35]

SENIORITY SYSTEM
In regard to employment relationships, a system in which those who have worked longest for the company are first in line for promotions, salary increases, and other benefits; they are also the last to be laid off if the workforce must be reduced.

After-Acquired Evidence of Employee Misconduct

In some situations, employers have attempted to avoid liability for employment discrimination on the basis of "after-acquired evidence"—that is, evidence that the employer discovers after a lawsuit is filed—of an employee's misconduct. | **Example #10** Suppose that an employer fires a worker, who then sues the employer for employment discrimination. During pretrial investigation, the employer learns that the employee made material misrepresentations on his or her employment application—misrepresentations that, had the employer known about them, would have served as a ground to fire the individual.|

---

34. *United Auto Workers v. Johnson Controls, Inc.,* 499 U.S. 187, 111 S.Ct. 1196, 113 L.Ed.2d 158 (1991).
35. *U.S. Airways, Inc. v. Barnett,* 535 U.S. 391, 122 S.Ct. 1516, 152 L.Ed.2d 589 (2002).

According to the United States Supreme Court, after-acquired evidence of wrongdoing cannot be used to shield an employer entirely from liability for employment discrimination. It may, however, be used to limit the amount of damages for which the employer is liable.[36]

AFFIRMATIVE ACTION

Federal statutes and regulations providing for equal opportunity in the workplace were designed to reduce or eliminate discriminatory practices with respect to hiring, retaining, and promoting employees. **Affirmative action** programs go a step further and attempt to "make up" for past patterns of discrimination by giving members of protected classes preferential treatment in hiring or promotion. During the 1960s, all federal and state government agencies, private companies that contract to do business with the federal government, and institutions that receive federal funding were required to implement affirmative action policies.

Title VII of the Civil Rights Act of 1964 neither requires nor prohibits affirmative action. Thus, most private firms have not been required to implement affirmative action policies, though many have chosen to do so.

Affirmative action programs have aroused much controversy since the 1960s, particularly when they have resulted in what is frequently called "reverse discrimination"—discrimination against "majority" individuals, such as white males. At issue is whether affirmative action programs, because of their inherently discriminatory nature, violate the equal protection clause of the Fourteenth Amendment to the Constitution.

The *Bakke* Case

An early case addressing this issue, *Regents of the University of California v. Bakke,*[37] involved an affirmative action program implemented by the University of California at Davis. Allan Bakke, who had been turned down for medical school at the Davis campus, sued the university for reverse discrimination after he discovered that his academic record was better than those of some of the minority applicants who had been admitted to the program.

The United States Supreme Court held that affirmative action programs were subject to "intermediate scrutiny." Recall from the discussion of the equal protection clause in Chapter 4 that any law or action evaluated under a standard of intermediate scrutiny, to be constitutionally valid, must be substantially related to important government objectives. Applying this standard, the Court held that the university could give favorable weight to minority applicants as part of a plan to increase minority enrollment so as to achieve a more culturally diverse student body. The Court stated, however, that the use of a quota system, which explicitly reserved a certain number of places for minority applicants, violated the equal protection clause of the Fourteenth Amendment.

---

36. *McKennon v. Nashville Banner Publishing Co.,* 513 U.S. 352, 115 S.Ct. 879, 130 L.Ed.2d 852 (1995).
37. 438 U.S. 265, 98 S.Ct. 2733, 57 L.Ed.2d 750 (1978).

The *Adarand* Case

Although the *Bakke* case and later court decisions alleviated the harshness of the quota system, today's courts are going even further in questioning the constitutional validity of affirmative action programs. In 1995, in its landmark decision in *Adarand Constructors, Inc. v. Peña,*[38] the United States Supreme Court held that any federal, state, or local affirmative action program that uses racial or ethnic classifications as the basis for making decisions is subject to strict scrutiny by the courts.

In effect, the Court's opinion in *Adarand* means that an affirmative action program is constitutional only if it attempts to remedy past discrimination and does not make use of quotas or preferences. Furthermore, once such a program has succeeded in the goal of remedying past discrimination, it must be changed or dropped. Since then, other federal courts have followed the Supreme Court's lead by declaring affirmative action programs invalid unless they attempt to remedy specific practices of past or current discrimination.[39]

The *Hopwood* Case

In 1996, the U.S. Court of Appeals for the Fifth Circuit, in *Hopwood v. State of Texas,*[40] held that an affirmative action program at the University of Texas School of Law in Austin violated the equal protection clause. In that case, two white law school applicants sued the university when they were denied admission. The court decided that the affirmative action policy unlawfully discriminated in favor of minority applicants. In its opinion, the court directly challenged the *Bakke* decision by stating that the use of race even as a means of achieving diversity on college campuses "undercuts the Fourteenth Amendment." The United States Supreme Court declined to hear the case, thus letting the lower court's decision stand. Over the next years, federal courts were divided over the constitutionality of such programs.[41]

Subsequent Court Decisions

In 2003, the United States Supreme Court reviewed two cases involving issues similar to that in the *Hopwood* case. Both cases involved admissions programs at the University of Michigan. In *Gratz v. Bollinger,*[42] two white applicants who were denied undergraduate admission to the university alleged reverse discrimination. The school's policy gave each applicant a score based on a number of factors, including grade point average, standardized test scores, and personal achievements. The system *automatically* awarded every "underrepresented" minority (African American, Hispanic, and Native American) applicant twenty points—one-fifth of the points needed to guarantee admission. The Court held that this policy violated the equal protection clause.

Students at the University of Michigan show their support for the Supreme Court's ruling in 2003 that allowed race to be considered as a "plus factor" in university admissions. Why did the Court find that the undergraduate admissions policy at the University of Michigan violated the equal protection clause, but the law school's admissions policy did not? (Reuters/Gregory Shamus/Landov)

38. 515 U.S. 200, 115 S.Ct. 2097, 132 L.Ed.2d 158 (1995).
39. See, for example, *Taxman v. Board of Education of the Township of Piscataway,* 91 F.3d 1547 (3d Cir. 1996); and *Schurr v. Resorts International Hotel, Inc.,* 196 F.3d 486 (3d Cir. 1999).
40. 84 F.3d 720 (5th Cir. 1996).
41. See, for example, *Johnson v. Board of Regents of the University of Georgia,* 106 F.Supp.2d 1362 (S.D.Ga. 2000); and *Smith v. University of Washington School of Law,* 233 F.3d 1188 (9th Cir. 2000).
42. 539 U.S. 244, 123 S.Ct. 2411, 156 L.Ed.2d 257 (2003).

In contrast, in *Grutter v. Bollinger*,[43] the Court held that the University of Michigan Law School's admissions policy was constitutional. In that case, the Court concluded that "[u]niversities can, however, consider race or ethnicity more flexibly as a 'plus' factor in the context of individualized consideration of each and every applicant." The significant difference between the two admissions policies, in the Court's view, was that the law school's approach did not apply a mechanical formula giving "diversity bonuses" based on race or ethnicity.

STATE STATUTES

Although the focus of this chapter has been on federal legislation, most states also have statutes that prohibit employment discrimination. Generally, the same kinds of discrimination are prohibited under federal and state legislation. In addition, state statutes often provide protection for certain individuals who are not protected under federal laws. For example, a New Jersey appellate court has held that anyone over the age of eighteen is entitled to sue for age discrimination under the state law, which specifies no threshold age limit.[44]

Furthermore, state laws prohibiting discrimination may apply to firms with fewer employees than the threshold number required under federal statutes, thus offering protection to more workers. State laws may also allow for additional damages, such as damages for emotional distress, that are not available under federal statutes. Finally, some states, including California and Washington, have passed laws that end affirmative action programs in that state or modify admissions policies at state-sponsored universities.

---

43. 539 U.S. 306, 123 S.Ct. 2325, 156 L.Ed.2d 304 (2003).
44. *Bergen Commercial Bank v. Sisler*, 307 N.J.Super. 333, 704 A.2d 1017 (1998).

REVIEWING . . . EQUAL EMPLOYMENT OPPORTUNITIES

Amaani Lyle, an African American woman, took a job as a scriptwriters' assistant at Warner Brothers Television Productions, working for the writers of *Friends,* a popular, adult-oriented television series. One of her essential job duties was to type detailed notes for the scriptwriters during brainstorming sessions in which they discussed jokes, dialogue, and story lines. The writers then combed through Lyle's notes after the meetings for script material. During these meetings, the three male scriptwriters told lewd and vulgar jokes and made sexually explicit comments and gestures. They often talked about their personal sexual experiences and fantasies, and some of these conversations were then used in episodes of *Friends.*

Lyle never complained that she found the writers' conduct during the meetings offensive. After four months, Lyle was fired because she could not type fast enough to keep up with the writers' conversations during the meetings. She filed a suit against Warner Brothers, alleging sexual harassment and claiming that her termination was based on racial discrimination. Using the information presented in the chapter, answer the following questions.

1. Would Lyle's claim of racial discrimination be for intentional (disparate-treatment) or unintentional (disparate-impact) discrimination? Explain.

2. Can Lyle establish a *prima facie* case of racial discrimination? Why or why not?

3. Lyle was told when she was hired that typing speed was extremely important to her position. At the time, she maintained that she could type eighty words per minute, so she was not given a typing test. It later turned out that Lyle could type only fifty words per minute. What impact might typing speed have on Lyle's lawsuit?

4. Lyle's sexual-harassment claim is based on the hostile work environment created by the writers' sexually offensive conduct at meetings that she was required to attend. The writers, however, argue that their behavior was essential to the "creative process" of writing for *Friends*, a show that routinely contained sexual innuendos and adult humor. Which defense discussed in the chapter might Warner Brothers assert using this argument?

KEY TERMS

affirmative action 492
bona fide occupational qualification (BFOQ) 491
business necessity 490
constructive discharge 476

disparate-impact discrimination 474
disparate-treatment discrimination 474
employment discrimination 471

prima facie case 474
protected class 471
seniority system 491
sexual harassment 478

CHAPTER SUMMARY • EQUAL EMPLOYMENT OPPORTUNITIES

Title VII of the Civil Rights Act of 1964 (See pages 472–484.)	Title VII prohibits employment discrimination based on race, color, national origin, religion, or gender.
	1. *Procedures*—Employees must file a claim with the Equal Employment Opportunity Commission (EEOC). The EEOC may sue the employer on the employee's behalf; if not, the employee may sue the employer directly.
	2. *Types of discrimination*—Title VII prohibits both intentional (disparate-treatment) and unintentional (disparate-impact) discrimination. Disparate-impact discrimination occurs when an employer's practice, such as hiring only persons with a certain level of education, has the effect of discriminating against a class of persons protected by Title VII. Title VII also extends to discriminatory practices, such as various forms of harassment, in the online environment.
	3. *Remedies for discrimination under Title VII*—If a plaintiff proves that unlawful discrimination occurred, he or she may be awarded reinstatement, back pay, and retroactive promotions. Damages (both compensatory and punitive) may be awarded for intentional discrimination.
Equal Pay Act of 1963 (See page 484.)	The Equal Pay Act of 1963 prohibits gender-based discrimination in the wages paid for equal work on jobs when their performance requires equal skill, effort, and responsibility under similar conditions.
Discrimination Based on Age (See pages 484–486.)	The Age Discrimination in Employment Act (ADEA) of 1967 prohibits employment discrimination on the basis of age against individuals forty years of age or older. Procedures for bringing a case under the ADEA are similar to those for bringing a case under Title VII.
Discrimination Based on Disability (See pages 486–490.)	The Americans with Disabilities Act (ADA) of 1990 prohibits employment discrimination against persons with disabilities who are otherwise qualified to perform the essential functions of the jobs for which they apply.
	1. *Procedures and remedies*—To prevail on a claim under the ADA, the plaintiff must show that she or he has a disability, is otherwise qualified for the employment in question, and was excluded from the employment solely because of the disability. Procedures under the ADA are similar to those required in Title VII cases; remedies are also similar to those under Title VII.
	2. *Definition of disability*—The ADA defines the term *disability* as a physical or mental impairment that substantially limits one or more major life activities, a record of such impairment, or being regarded as having such an impairment.

(Continued)

CHAPTER SUMMARY • EQUAL EMPLOYMENT OPPORTUNITIES–CONTINUED

Discrimination Based on Disability– Continued	3. *Reasonable accommodation*—Employers are required to reasonably accommodate the needs of persons with disabilities. Reasonable accommodations may include altering job-application procedures, modifying the physical work environment, and permitting more flexible work schedules. Employers are not required to accommodate the needs of all workers with disabilities. For example, employers need not accommodate workers who pose a definite threat to health and safety in the workplace or those who are not otherwise qualified for their jobs.
Defenses to Employment Discrimination (See pages 490–492.)	If a plaintiff proves that employment discrimination occurred, employers may avoid liability by successfully asserting certain defenses. Employers may assert that the discrimination was required for reasons of business necessity, to meet a bona fide occupational qualification, or to maintain a legitimate seniority system. Evidence of prior employee misconduct acquired after the employee has been fired is not a defense to discrimination.
Affirmative Action (See pages 492–494.)	Affirmative action programs attempt to "make up" for past patterns of discrimination by giving members of protected classes preferential treatment in hiring or promotion. Increasingly, such programs are being strictly scrutinized by the courts and struck down as violating the Fourteenth Amendment.
State Statutes (See page 494.)	Generally, state laws also prohibit the kinds of discrimination prohibited by federal statutes. State laws may provide for more extensive protection and remedies than federal laws. Also, some states, such as California and Washington, have banned state-sponsored affirmative action programs.

FOR REVIEW

Answers for the even-numbered questions in this For Review *section can be found in Appendix O at the end of this text.*

1. Generally, what kind of conduct is prohibited by Title VII of the Civil Rights Act of 1964, as amended?

2. What is the difference between disparate-treatment discrimination and disparate-impact discrimination?

3. What remedies are available under Title VII of the 1964 Civil Rights Act, as amended?

4. What federal acts prohibit discrimination based on age and discrimination based on disability?

5. What are three defenses to claims of employment discrimination?

QUESTIONS AND CASE PROBLEMS

14–1. Title VII Violations. Discuss fully whether any of the following actions would constitute a violation of Title VII of the 1964 Civil Rights Act, as amended.

1. Tennington, Inc., is a consulting firm and has ten employees. These employees travel on consulting jobs in seven states. Tennington has an employment record of hiring only white males.
2. Novo Films, Inc., is making a film about Africa and needs to employ approximately one hundred extras for this picture. Novo advertises in all major newspapers in Southern California for the hiring of these extras. The ad states that only African Americans need apply.

Question with Sample Answer

14–2. Tavo Jones had worked since 1974 for Westshore Resort, where he maintained golf carts. During the first decade, he received positive job evaluations and numerous merit pay

raises. He was promoted to the position of supervisor of golf-cart maintenance at three courses. Then a new employee, Ben Olery, was placed in charge of the golf courses. He demoted Jones, who was over the age of forty, to running one of the three cart facilities, and he froze Jones's salary indefinitely. Olery also demoted five other men over the age of forty. Another cart facility was placed under the supervision of Blake Blair. Later, the cart facilities for the three courses were again consolidated, but Blair—not Jones—was put in charge. At the time, Blair was in his twenties. Jones overheard Blair say that "we are going to have to do away with these . . . old and senile" men. Jones quit and sued Westshore for employment discrimination. Should he prevail? Explain.

For a sample answer to this question, go to Appendix P at the end of this text.

14–3. Discrimination Based on Disability. Vaughn Murphy was first diagnosed with hypertension (high blood pressure) when he was ten years old. Unmedicated, his blood pressure is approximately 250/160. With medication, however, he can function normally and engage in the same activities as anyone else. In 1994, United Parcel Service, Inc. (UPS), hired Murphy to be a mechanic, a position that required him to drive commercial motor vehicles. To get the job, Murphy had to meet a U.S. Department of Transportation (DOT) regulation that a driver have "no current clinical diagnosis of high blood pressure likely to interfere with his/her ability to operate a commercial vehicle safely." At the time, Murphy's blood pressure was measured at 186/124, but he was erroneously certified and started work. Within a month, the error was discovered and he was fired. Murphy obtained another mechanic's job—one that did not require DOT certification—and filed a suit in a federal district court against UPS, claiming discrimination under the Americans with Disabilities Act. UPS filed a motion for summary judgment. Should the court grant UPS's motion? Explain. [*Murphy v. United Parcel Service, Inc.*, 527 U.S. 516, 119 S.Ct. 2133, 144 L.Ed.2d 484 (1999)]

Case Problem with Sample Answer

 14–4. PGA Tour, Inc., sponsors professional golf tournaments. A player may enter in several ways, but the most common method is to successfully compete in a three-stage qualifying tournament known as the "Q-School." Anyone may enter the Q-School by submitting two letters of recommendation and paying $3,000 to cover greens fees and the cost of a golf cart, which is permitted during the first two stages, but is prohibited during the third stage. The rules governing the events include the "Rules of Golf," which apply at all levels of amateur and professional golf and do not prohibit the use of golf carts, and the "hard card," which applies specifically to the PGA tour and requires the players to walk the course during most of a tournament. Casey Martin is a talented golfer with a degenerative circulatory disorder that prevents him from walking golf courses. Martin entered the Q-School and asked for permission to use a cart during the third stage. PGA refused. Martin filed a suit in a federal district court against PGA, alleging a violation of the Americans with Disabilities Act. Is a golf cart in these circumstances a "reasonable accommodation" under the ADA? Why or why not? [*PGA Tour, Inc. v. Martin*, 532 U.S. 661, 121 S.Ct. 1879, 149 L.Ed.2d 904 (2001)]

After you have answered this problem, compare your answer with the sample answer given on the Web site that accompanies this text. Go to www.thomsonedu.com/westbuslaw/let, select "Chapter 14," and click on "Case Problem with Sample Answer."

14–5. Discrimination Based on Race. The hiring policy of Phillips Community College of the University of Arkansas (PCCUA) is to conduct an internal search for qualified applicants before advertising outside the college. Steven Jones, the university's chancellor, can determine the application and appointment process for vacant positions, however, and is the ultimate authority in hiring decisions. Howard Lockridge, an

African American, was the chair of PCCUA's Technical and Industrial Department. Between 1988 and 1998, Lockridge applied for several different positions, some of which were unadvertised, some of which were unfilled for years, and some of which were filled with less qualified persons from outside the college. In 1998, when Jones advertised an opening for the position of dean of industrial technology and workforce development, Lockridge did not apply for the job. Jones hired Tracy McGraw, a white male. Lockridge filed a suit in a federal district court against the university under Title VII. The university filed a motion for summary judgment in its favor. What are the elements of a *prima facie* case of disparate-treatment discrimination? Can Lockridge pass this test, or should the court issue a judgment in the university's favor? Explain. [*Lockridge v. Board of Trustees of the University of Arkansas*, 315 F.3d 1005 (8th Cir. 2003)]

14–6. Discrimination Based on Age. The United Auto Workers (UAW) is the union that represents the employees of General Dynamics Land Systems, Inc. In 1997, a collective bargaining agreement between UAW and General Dynamics eliminated the company's obligation to provide health insurance to employees who retired after the date of the agreement, except for current workers at least fifty years old. Dennis Cline and 194 other employees, who were over forty years old but under fifty, objected to this term. They complained to the Equal Employment Opportunity Commission, claiming that the agreement violated the Age Discrimination in Employment Act (ADEA) of 1967. The ADEA forbids discriminatory preference for the "young" over the "old." Does the ADEA also prohibit favoring the old over the young? How should the court rule? Explain. [*General Dynamics Land Systems, Inc. v. Cline*, 540 U.S. 581, 124 S.Ct. 1236, 157 L.Ed.2d 1094 (2004)]

14–7. Discrimination Based on Gender. For twenty years, Darlene Jespersen worked as a bartender at Harrah's Casino in Reno, Nevada. In 2000, Harrah's implemented a "Personal Best" program that included new grooming standards. Among other requirements, women were told to wear make-up "applied neatly in complimentary colors." Jespersen, who never wore make-up off the job, felt so uncomfortable wearing it at work that it interfered with her ability to perform. Unwilling to wear make-up and not qualifying for another position at Harrah's that paid similar compensation, Jespersen quit the casino. She filed a suit in a federal district court against Harrah's Operating Co., the casino's owner, alleging that the make-up policy discriminated against women in violation of Title VII of the Civil Rights Act of 1964. Harrah's argued that any burdens under the new program fell equally on both sexes, citing the "Personal Best" short-hair standard that applied only to men. Jespersen responded by describing her personal reaction to the make-up policy and emphasizing her exemplary record during her tenure at Harrah's. In whose favor should the court rule? Why? [*Jespersen v. Harrah's Operating Co.*, 444 F.3d 1104 (9th Cir. 2006)]

A Question of Ethics

14–8. Luz Long and three other Hispanic employees (the plaintiffs) worked as bank tellers for the Culmore branch of the First Union Corp. of Virginia. The plaintiffs often conversed with one another in Spanish, their native language. In 1992, the Culmore branch manager adopted an "English-only" policy, which required all employees to speak English during working hours unless they had to speak another language to assist customers. The plaintiffs refused to cooperate with the new policy and were eventually fired. In a suit against the bank, the plaintiffs alleged that the English-only policy discriminated against them on the basis of their national origin. The court granted the bank's motion for summary judgment, concluding that "[t]here is nothing in Title VII which . . . provides that an employee has a right to speak his or her native tongue while on the job." [*Long v. First Union Corp. of Virginia*, 894 F.Supp. 933 (E.D.Va. 1995)]

1. The bank argued that the policy was implemented in response to complaints made by fellow employees that the Spanish-speaking employees were creating a hostile environment by speaking Spanish among themselves in the presence of other employees. From an ethical perspective, is this a sufficient reason to institute an English-only policy?
2. Is it ever ethically justifiable for employers to deny bilingual employees the opportunity to speak their native language while on the job?
3. Might there be situations in which English-only policies are necessary to promote worker health and safety?
4. Generally, what are the pros and cons of English-only policies in the workplace?

Case Briefing Assignment

14–9. Go to www.thomsonedu.com/westbuslaw/let, the Web site that accompanies this text. Select "Chapter 14" and click on "Case Briefing Assignments." Examine Case A.4 [*Sutton v. United Airlines, Inc.*, 527 U.S. 471, 119 S.Ct. 2139, 144 L.Ed.2d 450 (1999)]. This case has been excerpted there in great detail. Review and then brief the case, making sure that your brief answers the following questions.

1. For what jobs were the plaintiffs applying, and what disability did the plaintiffs claim that they had?
2. Did United Airlines refuse to interview the plaintiffs? Did United reject all applicants with less than perfect vision?
3. What did the lower court hold regarding the plaintiffs' claims of disability-based discrimination?
4. Did the Supreme Court conclude that the plaintiffs were not disabled under the terms of the ADA? Why or why not?

Critical-Thinking Legal Qustion

14–10. Why has the federal government limited the application of the statutes discussed in this chapter to firms with a specified number of employees, such as fifteen or twenty? Should these laws apply to all employers, regardless of size? Why or why not?

Video Question

14–11. Go to this text's Web site at www.thomsonedu.com/westbuslaw/let and select "Chapter 14." Click on "Video Questions" and view the video titled *Parenthood*. Then answer the following questions.

1. In the video, Gil (Steve Martin) threatens to leave his job when he discovers that his boss is promoting another person to partner instead of him. His boss (Dennis Dugan) laughs and tells him that the threat is not realistic because if Gil leaves, he will be competing for positions with workers who are younger than he is and willing to accept lower salaries. If Gil takes his employer's advice and stays in his current position, can he sue his boss for age discrimination based on the boss's statements? Why or why not?
2. Suppose that Gil leaves his current position and applies for a job at another firm. The prospective employer refuses to hire him based on his age. What would Gil have to prove to establish a *prima facie* case of age discrimination? Explain your answer.
3. What defenses might Gil's current employer raise if Gil sues for age discrimination?

INTERACTING WITH THE INTERNET

For updated links to resources available on the Web, as well as a variety of other materials, visit this text's Web site at

www.thomsonedu.com/westbuslaw/let

An abundance of helpful information on disability-based discrimination, including the text of the Americans with Disabilities Act of 1990, can be found at the following Web site:

www.jan.wvu.edu/links/adalinks.htm

An excellent source for information on various forms of employment discrimination is the Equal Employment Opportunity Commission's Web site at

www.eeoc.gov

INTERNET EXERCISES

Go to **www.thomsonedu.com/westbuslaw/let**, the Web site that accompanies this text. Select "Chapter 14" and click on "Internet Exercises." There you will find the following Internet research exercises that you can perform to learn more about topics covered in this chapter.

Internet Exercise 14–1: LEGAL PERSPECTIVE—Americans with Disabilities
Internet Exercise 14–2: MANAGEMENT PERSPECTIVE—Equal Employment Opportunity
Internet Exercise 14–3: MANAGEMENT PERSPECTIVE—Religious and National-Origin Discrimination

BEFORE THE TEST

Go to **www.thomsonedu.com/westbuslaw/let**, the Web site that accompanies this text. Select "Chapter 14" and click on "Interactive Quizzes." You will find a number of interactive questions relating to this chapter.

CONTENTS

CHAPTER OBJECTIVES

After reading this chapter, you should be able to answer the following questions:

1. What federal statutes govern labor unions and collective bargaining?

2. How does the way in which a union election is conducted protect the rights of employees and employers?

3. What types of strikes are illegal?

4. What activities are prohibited as unfair employer practices?

5. What are the rights of nonunion employees?

> "Experience has proved that protection by law of the right of employees to organize and bargain collectively . . . promotes the flow of commerce."
>
> NATIONAL LABOR RELATIONS ACT
> OF 1935, SECTION 1

THROUGH THE FIRST HALF of the nineteenth century, most Americans were self-employed, often in agriculture. For those who were employed by others, the employers generally set the terms of employment. The nature of employment changed with the growth of the Industrial Revolution, which had begun about 1760. Fewer Americans were self-employed. Terms of employment were sometimes set through bargaining between employees and employers. Most industrial enterprises were in their infancies, however, and to encourage their development, the government gave employers considerable freedom to hire, fire, and determine other employment standards in response to changing conditions in the marketplace.

With increasing industrialization, the size of workplaces and the number of workplace hazards increased. Workers came to believe that to counter the power and freedom of their employers and to protect themselves, they needed to organize into unions. Employers discouraged—sometimes forcibly—collective activities such as unions. In support of unionization, Congress enacted such legislation as the Railway Labor Act of 1926.[1] These laws were often restricted to particular industries. Beginning in 1932, Congress enacted a number of statutes that increased employees' rights in general. As the chapter-opening quotation indicates, at the heart of these rights is the right to join unions and engage in collective bargaining with management to negotiate working conditions, salaries, and benefits for a group of workers.

---

1. 45 U.S.C. Sections 151–188.

This chapter describes the development of labor law and legal recognition of the right to form unions. The laws that govern the management-union relationship are set forth in historical perspective. Then we discuss the process of unionizing a company, the collective bargaining required of a unionized employer, the "industrial war" of strikes and lockouts that may result if bargaining fails, and the labor practices that are considered unfair under federal law.

FEDERAL LABOR LAW

Federal labor laws governing union-employer relations have developed considerably since the first law was enacted in 1932. Initially, the laws were concerned with protecting the rights and interests of workers. Subsequent legislation placed some restraints on unions and granted rights to employers. This section summarizes the four major federal labor law statutes.

An employer's rules. How do federal labor laws influence the adoption of such rules?

Norris-LaGuardia Act

Congress protected peaceful strikes, picketing, and boycotts in 1932 in the Norris-LaGuardia Act.[2] The statute restricted federal courts in their power to issue injunctions against unions engaged in peaceful strikes. The act also provided that contracts limiting an employee's right to join a union are unlawful. Such contracts are known as **yellow dog contracts.** (In the early part of the twentieth century, "yellow dog" meant "coward.") In effect, this act declared a national policy permitting employees to organize.

YELLOW DOG CONTRACT
An agreement under which an employee promises his or her employer, as a condition of employment, not to join a union.

National Labor Relations Act

The National Labor Relations Act of 1935 (NLRA),[3] also called the Wagner Act, established the right of employees to form unions, the right of those unions to engage in collective bargaining (negotiate contracts for their members), and the right to strike. The act also created the National Labor Relations Board (NLRB) to oversee union elections and to prevent employers from engaging in unfair labor union activities and unfair labor practices. Details of the NLRA are provided in this chapter's *Landmark in the Legal Environment* feature on the following page.

To be protected under the NLRA, an individual must be an "employee," as that term is defined in the statute.[4] Courts have long held that job applicants fall within the definition (otherwise, the NLRA's ban on discrimination in regard to hiring would mean nothing). The United States Supreme Court has held that an individual can be a company's "employee" even if, at the same time, a union pays the individual to organize the company.[5]

---

2. 29 U.S.C. Sections 101–115.
3. 29 U.S.C. Sections 151–169.
4. 29 U.S.C. Section 152(3).
5. *NLRB v. Town & Country Electric, Inc.,* 516 U.S. 85, 116 S.Ct. 450, 133 L.Ed.2d 371 (1995).

The National Labor Relations Act (1935)

The National Labor Relations Act of 1935 is often referred to as the Wagner Act because it was sponsored by Senator Robert Wagner. (Appendix E presents excerpts from the National Labor Relations Act.) During the 1930s, Wagner sponsored several pieces of legislation, particularly in the field of labor law. Until the early 1930s, employers had been free to establish the terms and conditions of employment. Collective activities by employees, such as participation in unions, were discouraged by employers. In 1934, when Wagner introduced the bill subsequently enacted as the National Labor Relations Act (NLRA), he saw it as a vehicle through which the disparate balance of power between employers and employees could be corrected.

Section 1 of the NLRA justifies the act under the commerce clause of the Constitution. Section 1 states that unequal bargaining power between employees and employers leads to economic instability, and refusals of employers to bargain collectively lead to strikes. These disturbances impede the flow of interstate commerce. It is declared to be the policy of the United States, under the authority given to the federal government under the commerce clause, to ensure the free flow of commerce by encouraging collective bargaining and unionization.

Purposes of the NLRA   The pervading purpose of the NLRA was to protect interstate commerce by securing for employees the rights established by Section 7 of the act: to organize, to bargain collectively through representatives of their own choosing, and to engage in concerted activities for that and other purposes. In Section 8, the act specifically defined a number of employer practices as unfair to labor:

1. Interference with the efforts of employees to form, join, or assist labor organizations or to engage in concerted activities for their mutual aid or protection [Section 8(a)(1)].
2. Domination of a labor organization or contribution of financial or other support to it [Section 8(a)(2)].

3. Discrimination in the hiring or awarding of tenure to employees because of union affiliation [Section 8(a)(3)].
4. Discrimination against employees for filing charges under the act or giving testimony under the act [Section 8(a)(4)].
5. Refusal to bargain collectively with the duly designated representative of the employees [Section 8(a)(5)].

The Creation of the NLRB   Another purpose of the act was to promote fair and just settlements of disputes by peaceful processes and to avoid industrial warfare. The act created the National Labor Relations Board (NLRB) to oversee elections and to prevent employers from engaging in unfair and illegal union activities and unfair labor practices. The board was granted investigatory powers and was authorized to issue and serve complaints against employers in response to employee charges of unfair labor practices. The board was further empowered to issue cease-and-desist orders—which could be enforced by a federal court of appeals if necessary—when violations were found.

Application to Today's Legal Environment

The NLRA was initially viewed by employers as a drastic piece of legislation, and the act elicited a great deal of opposition. Some even claimed that, by passing the act, Congress had exceeded its authority under the commerce clause. In 1937, however, in National Labor Relations Board v. Jones & Laughlin Steel Corp.,[a] *the United States Supreme Court held that the act and its application were constitutionally valid. Today, the NLRB continues to investigate employees' charges of unfair labor practices and to serve complaints against employers in response to these charges.*

RELEVANT WEB SITES

To locate information on the Web concerning the National Labor Relations Act of 1935, go to this text's Web site at **www.thomsonedu.com/westbuslaw/let**, *select "Chapter 15," and click on "URLs for Landmarks."*

a. 301 U.S. 1, 57 S.Ct. 615, 81 L.Ed. 893 (1937).

Labor-Management Relations Act

The Labor-Management Relations Act of 1947 (LMRA, or Taft-Hartley Act)[6] was passed to proscribe certain union practices. The Taft-Hartley Act contained provisions protecting employers as well as employees. The act was bit-

6. 29 U.S.C. Sections 141, 504.

terly opposed by organized labor groups. It provided a detailed list of unfair labor activities that unions as well as management were now forbidden to practice. In addition, the law gave the president the authority to intervene in labor disputes and delay strikes that would "imperil the national health or safety."

An important provision of the LMRA concerned the **closed shop**—a firm that requires union membership of its workers as a condition of obtaining employment. Closed shops were made illegal under the Taft-Hartley Act. The act preserved the legality of the **union shop,** which does not require membership as a prerequisite for employment but can, and usually does, require that workers join the recognized union after a specified amount of time on the job. The act also allowed individual states to pass their own **right-to-work laws**— laws making it illegal for union membership to be required for *continued* employment in any establishment. Thus, union shops are technically illegal in states with right-to-work laws.

Labor-Management Reporting and Disclosure Act

The Labor-Management Reporting and Disclosure Act of 1959 (Landrum-Griffin Act)[7] established an employee bill of rights, as well as reporting requirements for union activities to prevent corruption. The Landrum-Griffin Act strictly regulated internal union business procedures.

Union elections, for example, are regulated by the Landrum-Griffin Act, which requires that regularly scheduled elections of officers occur and that secret ballots be used. Ex-convicts are prohibited from holding union office. Moreover, union officials are made accountable for union property and funds. Members have the right to attend and to participate in union meetings, to nominate officers, and to vote in most union proceedings.

Coverage and Procedures

Coverage of the federal labor laws is broad and extends to all employers whose business activity either involves or affects interstate commerce. Some workers are specifically excluded from these laws. Railroads and airlines are not covered by the NLRA but are covered by a separate act, the Railway Labor Act, which closely parallels the NLRA. Other types of employees, such as agricultural workers and domestic servants, are excluded from the NLRA and have no coverage under separate legislation.

When a union or employee believes that an employer has violated federal labor law (or vice versa), the union or employee files a charge with a regional office of the NLRB. The form for an employee to use to file an unfair labor practice charge against an employer is shown in Exhibit 15–1 on the next page. The charge is investigated, and if it is found worthy, the regional director files a complaint. An administrative law judge (ALJ) initially hears the complaint and rules on it (as will be discussed in Chapter 16). The NLRB reviews the ALJ's findings and decision. If the board finds a violation, it may issue remedial orders (including requiring rehiring of discharged workers). The NLRB decision may be appealed to a U.S. court of appeals.

CLOSED SHOP
A firm that requires union membership by its workers as a condition of employment. The closed shop was made illegal by the Labor-Management Relations Act of 1947.

UNION SHOP
A place of employment in which all workers, once employed, must become union members within a specified period of time as a condition of their continued employment.

RIGHT-TO-WORK LAW
A state law providing that employees are not to be required to join a union as a condition of obtaining or retaining employment.

---

7. 29 U.S.C. Sections 153, 1111.

EXHIBIT 15-1　UNFAIR LABOR PRACTICE COMPLAINT FORM

FORM EXEMPT UNDER 44 U.S.C. 3512

FORM NLRB-501 (11-94)	UNITED STATES OF AMERICA NATIONAL LABOR RELATIONS BOARD **CHARGE AGAINST EMPLOYER**	**DO NOT WRITE IN THIS SPACE**	
		Case	Date Filed

INSTRUCTIONS: File an original and 4 copies of this charge with NLRB Regional Director for the region in which the alleged unfair labor practice occurred or is occurring.

1. EMPLOYER AGAINST WHOM CHARGE IS BROUGHT

a. Name of Employer	b. Number of workers employed

c. Address *(street, city, state, ZIP code)*	d. Employer Representative	e. Telephone No.
		Fax No.

f. Type of Establishment *(factory, mine, wholesaler, etc.)*	g. Identify Principal Product or Service

h. The above-named employer has engaged in and is engaging in unfair labor practices within the meaning of Section 8(a), subsections (1) and *(list subsections)* _____ of the National Labor Relations Act, and these unfair labor practices are unfair practices affecting commerce within the meaning of the Act.

2. Basis of the Charge *(set forth a clear and concise statement of the facts constituting the alleged unfair labor practices)*

By the above and other acts, the above-named employer has interfered with, restrained, and coerced employees in the exercise of the rights guaranteed in Section 7 of the Act

3. Full name of party filing charge *(if labor organization, give full name, including local name and number)*

4a. Address *(street and number, city, state, and ZIP code)*	4b. Telephone No.
	Fax No.

5. Full name of national or international labor organization of which it is an affiliate or constituent unit *(to be filled in when charge is filed by a labor organization)*

6. DECLARATION

I declare that I have read the above charge and that the statements are true to the best of my knowledge and belief.

By _____   _____
　　(signature of representative or person making charge)　　　　*(Title, if any)*

Address _____   _____   _____
　　　　　　　　　　　　　　　　　(Telephone No.)　　　*(Date)*

WILLFUL FALSE STATEMENTS ON THIS CHARGE CAN BE PUNISHED BY FINE AND IMPRISONMENT (U.S. CODE, TITLE 18, SECTION 1001)

THE DECISION TO FORM OR SELECT A UNION

The key starting point for labor relations law is the decision by a company's employees to form a union, which is usually referred to in the law as their bargaining representative. Most workplaces have no union, and workers bargain individually with the employer. If the workers decide that they want the added power of collective union representation, they must follow certain steps to have a union certified. Usually, the employer will fight these efforts to unionize.

Preliminary Organizing

Suppose that a national union, such as the Communications Workers of America (CWA), wants to organize workers who produce semiconductor chips. The union would visit the manufacturing plant of a company—SemiCo in this example. If some SemiCo workers are interested in joining the union, they must begin organizing. An essential part of the process is to decide exactly which workers will be covered in the planned union. Will all manufacturing workers be covered or just those engaged in a single step in the manufacturing process?

The first step in forming a union is to get the relevant workers to sign **authorization cards.** These cards usually state that the worker desires to have a certain union, such as the CWA, represent the workforce. If those in favor of the union can obtain authorization cards from over 50 percent of the workers, they may present the cards to the employer and ask the employer, SemiCo, to recognize the union formally. SemiCo is not required to do so, however.

If the employer (SemiCo) refuses to recognize the union based on authorization cards, an election is necessary to determine whether unionization has majority support among the workers. If at least 30 percent of the workers to be represented sign authorization cards, the unionizers present these cards to the NLRB regional office with a petition for an election.

This 30 percent support is generally considered a sufficient showing of interest to justify an election on union representation. Union backers are not required to obtain authorization cards but generally must have some evidence that at least 30 percent of the relevant workforce supports a union or an election on unionization.

AUTHORIZATION CARD
A card signed by an employee that gives a union permission to act on his or her behalf in negotiations with management.

Appropriate Bargaining Unit

The NLRB considers the employees' petition as a basis for calling an election. In addition to a sufficient showing of interest in unionization, the proposed union must represent an **appropriate bargaining unit.**

Not every group of workers can form together into a single union. One key requirement of an appropriate bargaining unit is a *mutuality of interest* among all the workers to be represented. Groups of workers with significantly conflicting interests may not be represented in a single union.

APPROPRIATE BARGAINING UNIT
A designation based on job duties, skill levels, and so on, of the proper entity that should be covered by a collective bargaining agreement.

Job Similarity One factor in determining the mutuality of interest is the *similarity of the jobs* of all the workers to be unionized. The NLRB considers factors such as similar levels of skill and qualifications, similar levels of wages and benefits, and similar working conditions. If represented workers have vastly different working conditions, they are unlikely to have the mutuality of interest necessary to bargain as a single unit with their employer.

One issue of job similarity has involved companies that employ both general industrial workers and craft workers (those with specialized skills, such as electricians). On many occasions, the NLRB has found that industrial and craft workers should be represented by different unions, although this is not an absolute rule.

Work Site Proximity   A second important factor in determining the appropriate bargaining unit is *geographical*. If workers at only a single manufacturing plant are to be unionized, the geographical factor is not a problem. Even if the workers desire to join a national union, such as the CWA, they can join together in a single "local" division of that union. Geographical disparity may become a problem if a union is attempting to join workers at many different manufacturing sites together into a single union.

Nonmanagement Employees   A third factor to be considered is the rule against unionization of *management* employees. The labor laws differentiate between labor and management and preclude members of management from being part of a union. There is no clear-cut definition of management, but supervisors are considered management and may not be included in worker unions. A supervisor is an individual who has the discretionary authority, as a representative of the employer, to make decisions such as hiring, suspending, promoting, firing, or disciplining other workers.[8] Professional employees, including legal and medical personnel, may be considered labor rather than management.

Moving toward Certification

A union, then, becomes certified through a procedure that begins with petitioning the NLRB. The proposed union must present authorization cards or other evidence showing an employee interest level of at least 30 percent. The organization must also show that the proposed union represents an appropriate bargaining unit. If the workers are under the NLRA's jurisdiction and if no other union has been certified within the past twelve months for these workers, the NLRB will schedule an election.

UNION ELECTION

Labor law provides for an election to determine whether employees choose to be represented by a union and, if so, which union. The NLRB supervises this election, ensuring secret voting and voter eligibility. The election is usually held about a month after the NLRB orders the vote (although it may be much longer, if management disputes the composition of an appropriate bargaining unit). If the election is a fair one, and if the proposed union receives majority support, the board certifies the union as the bargaining representative. Otherwise, the board will not certify the union.

Sometimes, a plant with an existing union may attempt to *decertify* the union (de-unionize). Although this action may be encouraged by management, it must be conducted by the employees. This action also requires a petition to the NLRB, with a showing of 30 percent employee support and no certifica-

---

8. *Waldau v. Merit Systems Protection Board*, 19 F.3d 1395 (Fed.Cir. 1994).

tion within the past year. The NLRB may grant this petition and call for a decertification election.

Union Election Campaign

Union organizers may campaign among workers to solicit votes for unionization. Considerable litigation has arisen over the rights of workers and outside union supporters to conduct such campaigns.

The Employer's Right to Limit Campaign Activities   The employer retains great control over any activities, including unionization campaigns, that take place on company property and on company time. Employers may lawfully use this authority to limit the campaign activities of union supporters.
| Example #1 Management may prohibit all solicitations and distribution of pamphlets on company property as long as it has a legitimate business reason for doing so (such as to ensure safety or to prevent interference with business). The employer may also reasonably limit the places where solicitation occurs (for example, limit it to the lunchroom), limit the times during which solicitation can take place, and prohibit all outsiders from access to the workplace. All these actions are lawful.**|**

Suppose that a union seeks to organize clerks at a department store. Courts have reasoned that an employer can prohibit all solicitation in areas of the store open to the public. Union campaign activities in these circumstances could seriously interfere with the store's business.

Restrictions on Management   There are some legal restrictions on management regulation of union solicitation. The key restriction is the *nondiscrimination* rule. An employer may prohibit all solicitation during work time or in certain places but may not selectively prohibit union solicitation during work hours. If the employer permits political candidates to campaign on the employer's premises, for example, it also must permit union solicitation.[9] Additionally, companies cannot prevent union-related solicitation in work areas as long as the activity is conducted outside working hours—during lunch hours or coffee breaks, for example.

ETHICAL ISSUE 15.1 *Is an employer's e-mail system a "work area"?*

An emerging issue has to do with whether employers, if they allow employees to use company-owned e-mail systems for nonbusiness purposes, must permit employees to use e-mail to exchange messages related to unionization or union activities. In the few cases involving this issue, the NLRB has ruled that, in these circumstances, employees can use e-mail for communicating union-related messages. Suppose, however, that a company's policy prohibits employees from using e-mail for nonbusiness purposes. Given that employees are permitted to engage in union-related solicitation in work areas as long as they are on a break from work, should they also be able to use their employer's e-mail system while on

---

9. *Nonemployee* union organizers do not have the right to trespass on an employer's property to organize employees, however. See *Lechmere, Inc. v. NLRB*, 502 U.S. 527, 112 S.Ct. 841, 117 L.Ed.2d 79 (1992).

a break? Is an e-mail system a "work area"? To date, the NLRB has not ruled on this question, which clearly involves issues of fairness—for both employers and employees. Even if the NLRB were to decide that an employer's e-mail system is a work area, questions would remain. For example, what if an employee sends a union-related e-mail message while on a break but the employee receiving it, without knowing its contents, opens it during working hours? Can anything be done to prevent this kind of situation from occurring?

Workers' Rights and Obligations   Workers have a right to some reasonable opportunity to campaign. | **Example #2**   The United States Supreme Court held that employees have a right to distribute a pro-union newsletter in nonworking areas on the employer's property during nonworking time. In this case, management had the burden of showing some material harm from this action and could not do so.[10]|

Like an employer, a union and its supporters may not engage in unfair labor practices during a union election campaign. In the following case, the court considered the impact of a union proponent's allegedly unfair labor practice on the outcome of an election.

---

10. *Eastex, Inc. v. NLRB*, 437 U.S. 556, 98 S.Ct. 2505, 57 L.Ed.2d 428 (1978).

CASE 15.1   **Associated Rubber Co. v. National Labor Relations Board**

United States Court of Appeals,
Eleventh Circuit, 2002.
296 F.3d 1055.
www.law.emory.edu/11circuit [a]

BACKGROUND AND FACTS   Associated Rubber Company owns three rubber-production plants in Tallapoosa, Georgia. In June 1999, the United Steelworkers of America, AFL-CIO-CLC, filed a petition with the National Labor Relations Board (NLRB), seeking an election to obtain certification as the collective bargaining representative of maintenance workers, truck drivers, and mechanics employed at Associated Rubber's

plants. During the election campaign, Leroy Brown, an Associated Rubber employee and a union supporter, threatened Tim Spears, an employee and a union opponent. Three days before the election, Brown speeded up the rate at which heavy, scalding batches of rubber compound were mixed and sent to Spears. Barely able to handle the speed, Spears told his foreman that if the union won the election, he would quit his job out of fear the incident would be repeated. Other employees were aware of Brown's threat and the "Banbury incident" (Banbury was the brand name of the compound mixer). The union won the election by a vote of 53 to 50. Associated Rubber filed an objection on the basis of Brown's conduct. The NLRB concluded that the election was not tainted, certified the union, and ordered Associated Rubber to bargain. Associated Rubber appealed the order to the U.S. Court of Appeals for the Eleventh Circuit.

a. In the "Listing by Month of Decision" section, in the "2002" row, click on "July." In the result, click on the name of the case to access the opinion. Emory University School of Law in Atlanta, Georgia, maintains this Web site.

IN THE WORDS OF THE COURT . . . *CARNES,* **Circuit Judge.**

* * * *

When the union itself engages in objectionable misconduct, the Board will overturn the election if the conduct interfered with the employees' exercise of free choice to such an extent that it materially affected the results of the election. If, however, a third party engages in misconduct, the party objecting to the election has the burden of showing that the misconduct was so aggravated as to create a general atmosphere of fear and reprisal rendering a free election impossible. * * * [Emphasis added.]

* * * *

CASE 15.1–CONTINUED

Applying these legal standards to the record in this case convinces us that the Board's conclusion that the Banbury mixer incident did not warrant overturning the election should itself be overturned. To begin with, the record shows that Brown accelerated the mixer in retaliation for Spears'[s] refusal to accept union literature. Brown threatened to make Spears "pay" for refusing to accept union literature, and he did so. Seven or eight days after the threat, and as the election drew near, Brown accelerated the Banbury mixer during Spears'[s] shift as mill operator, causing the hot 450-pound batches of rubber compound to drop at a faster rate, a rate that made things more difficult and more dangerous than would have been the case but for Brown's malicious behavior. * * *

* * * *

* * * No employee ought to be subjected to any increased danger because of his position in a union certification election, and an increased risk of injury can itself be enough to have a chilling effect on the employees' right to freely decide whether they wish to be represented by a union.

* * * *

Importantly, the incident occurred only three days before the election took place. That fact makes the incident worse and increases the impact it had on the election. * * *

* * * *

In sum, the fact that Spears was threatened and then retaliated against in a way that placed him in personal danger would reasonably create fear in the minds of employees who were voting in the certification election. Although there apparently is no evidence that Spears'[s] own vote was affected, at least seven people, including Spears, knew of the incident and connected it to Brown's earlier threat, and the election results turned on two votes.

DECISION AND REMEDY The U.S. Court of Appeals for the Eleventh Circuit set aside the NLRB's order. The court held that given the seriousness of the incident, the degree to which news of it was disseminated before the election, its proximity to the election, and the closeness of the vote, the NLRB should have ordered a new election.

FOR CRITICAL ANALYSIS–Social Consideration *If Brown's conduct in the "Banbury incident" had been motivated by something other than his support for the union and Spears's refusal to accept union literature, would the result in this case have been different?*

Management Election Campaign

Management may also campaign among its workers against the union (or for decertification of an existing union). Campaign tactics, however, are carefully monitored and regulated by the NLRB. Otherwise, the economic power of management might allow coercion of the workers.

Management still has many advantages in the campaign. For example, management is allowed to call all workers together during work time and make a speech against unionization. Management need not give the union supporters an equal opportunity for rebuttal. The NLRB does restrict what management may say in such a speech, however.

No Threats In campaigning against the union, the employer may not make threats of reprisals if employees vote to unionize. **| Example #3** A supervisor may not state, "If the union wins, you'll all be fired." This would be a threat. Even if an employer says, "Our competitor's plant in town became unionized, and half the workers lost their jobs," the NLRB might consider this to be a veiled threat and therefore unfair.|

"Laboratory Conditions" Obviously, union election campaigns are not like national political campaigns, in which a political party can make almost any claim. The NLRB tries to maintain "laboratory conditions" for a fair election that is unaffected by pressure. In establishing such conditions, the board considers the totality of circumstances in the campaign. The NLRB is especially strict about promises (or threats) made by the employer at the last minute, immediately before the election, because the union lacks an opportunity to respond effectively to these last-minute statements.

There is even a specific rule that prohibits an employer from making any election speech on company time, to massed assemblies of workers, within twenty-four hours of the time for voting. Such last-minute speeches are permitted only if employees attend voluntarily and on their own time.[11]

The employer is also prohibited from taking actions that might intimidate its workers. Employers may not undertake certain types of surveillance of workers or even create the impression of observing workers to identify union sympathizers. Management also is limited in its ability to question individual workers about their positions on unionization. These actions are deemed to contain implicit threats.

NLRB Options If the employer issues threats or engages in other unfair labor practices and then wins the election, the NLRB may invalidate the results. The NLRB may certify the union, even though it lost the election, and direct the employer to recognize the union as the employees' exclusive bargaining representative. Alternatively, the NLRB may ask a court to order a new election.

COLLECTIVE BARGAINING

If a fair election is held and the union wins, the NLRB will certify the union as the *exclusive bargaining representative* of the workers polled. Unions may provide a variety of services to their members, but the central legal right of a union is to serve as the sole representative of the group of workers in bargaining with the employer over the workers' rights.

The concept of bargaining is at the heart of the federal labor laws. When a union is officially recognized, it may make a demand to bargain with the employer. The union then sits at the table opposite the representatives of management to negotiate contracts for its workers. The terms of employment that result from the negotiations apply to all workers in the bargaining unit, even those who do not choose to belong to the union. This process is known as **collective bargaining.** Such bargaining is like most other business negotiations, and each side uses its economic power to pressure or persuade the other side to grant concessions.

Bargaining is a somewhat vague term. Bargaining does not mean that either side must give in to demands or even that the sides must always compromise.

COLLECTIVE BARGAINING
The process by which labor and management negotiate the terms and conditions of employment, including working hours and workplace conditions.

---

11. Political party–like electioneering on behalf of a union, on the day of a union election, however, has been held acceptable and does not invalidate the election. See *Overnite Transportation Co. v. NLRB*, 104 F.3d 109 (7th Cir. 1997).

Union Rights in Great Britain

A British union that has been recognized by an employer for collective bargaining purposes has certain rights. These rights include the right to receive information related to collective bargaining issues, the right to time off, the right to appoint a representative to handle safety matters, and the right to be consulted before an employer relocates its place of business.

For Critical Analysis *Do you think employees have rights that should apply in all countries around the world under all circumstances?*

It does mean that a demand must be taken seriously and considered as part of a package to be negotiated. Most important, both sides must bargain in "good faith."

Subjects of Bargaining

A common issue in collective bargaining concerns the subjects over which the parties can bargain. The law makes certain subjects mandatory for collective bargaining. These topics cannot be "taken off the table" unilaterally but must be discussed and bargained over. (To learn about union rights in Great Britain, see this chapter's *Beyond Our Borders* feature.)

Terms and Conditions of Employment The NLRA provides that employers may bargain with workers over wages, hours of work, and other terms and conditions of employment. These are broad terms that cover many employment issues. Suppose that a union wants a contract provision granting all

Union workers cast their votes in a special election held to determine whether they would accept or reject a third contract offer from their employer during collective bargaining negotiations. Suppose that the employer had threatened to fire any worker who did not vote to accept the contract offer. In that situation, which act would the employer be violating? (Larry W. Smith/Getty Images)

workers four weeks of paid vacation. The company need not give in to this demand but must at least consider it and bargain over it.

Many other employment issues are also considered appropriate subjects for collective bargaining. These include safety rules, insurance coverage, pension and other employee benefit plans, procedures for employee discipline, procedures for employee grievances against the company, and even the price of food sold in the company cafeteria.

A few subjects are illegal in collective bargaining. Management need not bargain over a provision that would be illegal if included in a contract. Thus, if a union presents a demand for **featherbedding** (the hiring of unnecessary excess workers) or for an unlawful closed shop, management need not respond to these demands.

FEATHERBEDDING
A requirement that more workers be employed to do a particular job than are actually needed.

SEVERANCE PAY
Funds in excess of normal wages or salaries paid to an employee on termination of his or her employment with a company.

Closing or Relocating a Plant   Management need not bargain with a union over the decision to close a particular facility. Similarly, management need not bargain over a decision to relocate a plant if the move involves a basic change in the nature of the employer's operation.[12] Management may, however, choose to bargain over such decisions to obtain concessions on other bargaining subjects.

Management must bargain over the economic consequences of such decisions, though. Thus, issues such as **severance pay** (compensation for the termination of employment) in the event of a plant shutdown are appropriate for collective bargaining. Also, if a relocation does *not* involve a basic change in the nature of an operation, management must bargain over the decision unless it can show (1) that the work performed at the new location varies significantly from the work performed at the former plant; (2) that the work performed at the former plant is to be discontinued entirely and not moved to the new location; (3) that the move involves a change in the scope and direction of the enterprise; (4) that labor costs were not a factor in the decision; or (5) that even if labor costs were a factor, the union could not have offered concessions that would have changed the decision to relocate.

Privacy Issues   Employee privacy rights were discussed in Chapter 13. Are these rights, and their potential or real violations, appropriate subjects for collective bargaining? The NLRB has determined that physical examinations, requirements for drug or alcohol testing, and polygraph (lie-detector) testing are mandatory subjects of bargaining. The question in the following case was whether the use of hidden surveillance cameras could also be bargained over.

---

12. *Dubuque Packing Co.*, 303 N.L.R.B. No. 386 (1991).

CASE 15.2   National Steel Corp. v. NLRB

United States Court of Appeals,
Seventh Circuit, 2003.
324 F.3d 928.
findlaw.com/casecode/courts/7th.html[a]

BACKGROUND AND FACTS   National Steel Corporation operates a plant in Granite City, Illinois, where it employs

a. In the "By Date" section, select "2003" and "April." In the list of results, click on "Nat'l Steel Corp. v. NLRB." This is a page within the Web site maintained by FindLaw (now a part of West Group).

approximately three thousand employees, who are represented by ten different unions and covered by seven different collective bargaining agreements. National Steel uses over one hundred video cameras in plain view to monitor areas of the plant and periodically employs hidden cameras to investigate suspected misconduct. In February 1999, National Steel installed a hidden camera to discover who was using a manager's office when the manager was not at work. The camera revealed a union member using the office to make long-distance phone calls. When National Steel discharged the

CASE 15.2–CONTINUED

employee, the union asked the company about other hidden cameras and indicated that it wanted to bargain over their use. National Steel refused to supply the information. The union filed a charge with the NLRB, which ordered National Steel to provide the information and bargain over the use of the cameras. National Steel appealed to the U.S. Court of Appeals for the Seventh Circuit.

IN THE WORDS OF THE COURT . . . *WILLIAMS,* Circuit Judge.

* * * *

The [National Labor Relations] Board determined * * * that the use of hidden surveillance cameras is a mandatory subject of collective bargaining because it found the installation and use of such cameras "analogous to physical examinations, drug/alcohol testing requirements, and polygraph testing, all of which the Board has found to be mandatory subjects of bargaining." It found that hidden cameras are focused primarily on the "working environment" that employees experience on a daily basis and are used to expose misconduct or violations of the law by employees or others. The Board held that such changes in an employer's methods have "serious implications for its employees' job security." The Board found that the use of such devices "is not entrepreneurial in character [and] is not fundamental to the basic direction of the enterprise." We find the Board's legal conclusion * * * objectively reasonable and wholly supported. * * *

* * * According to National Steel, requiring it to bargain over hidden surveillance cameras, especially as to their locations precludes an employer from meaningfully using such devices because bargaining itself will compromise the secrecy that is required for them to be effective. * * *

* * * [T]he Board acknowledged an employer's need for secrecy if hidden surveillance cameras are to serve a purpose. The Board's order to National Steel preserves those managerial interests while also honoring the union's collective bargaining rights. It only requires National Steel to negotiate with the unions over the company's installation and use of hidden surveillance cameras and * * * does not dictate how the legitimate interests of the parties are to be accommodated in the process. The Board's order does not mandate an outcome of negotiations, nor does it make any suggestion that National Steel must yield any prerogatives, other than yielding the right to proceed exclusive of consultation with the union. * * * *Here, the Board's order is consistent with the [National Labor Relations] Act's requirement that parties resolve their differences through good-faith bargaining;* it simply directs National Steel to initiate an accommodation process, and to provide assertedly confidential information in accord with whatever accommodation the parties agree upon (such as a confidentiality agreement * * *). The Board's order does not eliminate National Steel's management right to use hidden cameras and it seeks to preserve the level of confidentiality necessary to allow for the continued effective use of such devices. [Emphasis added.]

DECISION AND REMEDY The U.S. Court of Appeals for the Seventh Circuit upheld the NLRB's order to National Steel to bargain over the use of hidden surveillance cameras in the workplace. The court emphasized that this order did not prohibit their use, but only made that use a subject of collective bargaining.

FOR CRITICAL ANALYSIS–Social Consideration *Can an employer's interests ever justify the use of hidden video cameras in the workplace?*

Good Faith Bargaining

Parties engaged in collective bargaining often claim that the other side is not bargaining in good faith, as required by labor law. Although good faith is a matter of subjective intent, a party's actions are used to evaluate the finding of good or bad faith in bargaining. Obviously, the employer must be willing to meet with union representatives. Excessive delaying tactics may be proof of bad faith, as is insistence on obviously unreasonable contract terms. Suppose that a company makes a single overall contract offer on a "take-it-or-leave-it" basis and refuses to consider modifications of individual terms. This also is considered bad faith in bargaining.

While bargaining is going on, management may not make unilateral changes in important working conditions, such as wages or hours of employment. These changes must be bargained over. Once bargaining reaches an impasse, management may make such unilateral changes. The law also includes an exception permitting unilateral changes in cases of business necessity. A series of decisions have found other actions to constitute bad faith in bargaining, including the following:

- Engaging in a campaign among workers to undermine the union.
- Constantly shifting positions on disputed contract terms.
- Sending bargainers who lack authority to commit the company to a contract.

If an employer (or a union) refuses to bargain in good faith without justification, it has committed an unfair labor practice, and the other party may petition the NLRB for an order requiring good faith bargaining. Except in extreme cases, the NLRB does not have authority to require a party to accede to any specific contract terms. The NLRB may require a party to reimburse the other side for its litigation expenses.

STRIKES

The law does not require parties to reach a contract agreement in collective bargaining. Even when parties have bargained in good faith, they may be unable to reach a final agreement. When extensive collective bargaining has been conducted and the parties still cannot agree, an impasse has been reached. The union may call a strike against the employer to pressure it into making concessions. A *strike* occurs when the unionized workers leave their jobs and refuse to work. The workers also typically picket the plant, standing outside the facility with signs that complain of management's unfairness.

A strike is an extreme action. Striking workers lose their right to be paid. Management loses production and may lose customers, whose orders cannot be filled. Labor law regulates the circumstances and conduct of strikes. Most strikes are "economic strikes," which are initiated because the union wants a better contract. A union may also strike when the employer has engaged in unfair labor practices.

The right to strike is guaranteed by the NLRA, within limits, and strike activities, such as picketing, are protected by the free speech guarantee of the First Amendment to the Constitution. Nonworkers have a right to participate in picketing an employer. The NLRA also gives workers the right to refuse to cross a picket line of fellow workers who are engaged in a lawful strike. Not all strikes are lawful, however.

> "I see an America where the workers are really free and through their great unions . . . can take their proper place in the council tables with the owners and managers of business."
>
> —FRANKLIN D. ROOSEVELT,
> 1882–1945
> (Thirty-second president of the United States, 1932–1945)

Illegal Strikes

An otherwise lawful strike may become illegal because of the conduct of the strikers. Violent strikes (including the threat of violence) are illegal. The use of violence against management employees or substitute workers is illegal. Certain forms of "massed picketing" are also illegal. If the strikers form a barrier and deny management or other nonunion workers access to the plant, the strike is illegal. Similarly, "sit-down" strikes, in which employees simply stay in the plant without working, are illegal.

Secondary Boycotts   A strike directed against someone other than the strikers' employer, such as the companies that sell materials to the employer, is a **secondary boycott.** Suppose that the unionized workers of SemiCo (our hypothetical semiconductor company) go out on strike. To increase their economic leverage, the workers picket the leading suppliers and customers of SemiCo in an attempt to hurt the company's business. SemiCo is considered the primary employer, and its suppliers and customers are considered secondary employers. Picketing of the suppliers or customers is a secondary boycott, which was made illegal by the Taft-Hartley Act.

Common Situs Picketing   A controversy may arise in a strike when both the primary employer and a secondary employer occupy the same job site. In this case, it may be difficult to distinguish between lawful picketing of the primary employer and an unlawful strike against a secondary employer. The law permits a union to picket a site occupied by both primary and secondary employers, an act called **common situs picketing.** If evidence indicates that the strike is directed against the secondary employer, however, it may become illegal. **| Example #4** A union sends a threatening letter to the secondary employer about the strike. That fact may show that the picketing includes an illegal secondary boycott. |

Hot-Cargo Agreements   In what is called a **hot-cargo agreement,** employers voluntarily agree with unions not to handle, use, or deal in goods produced by nonunion employees of other firms. This particular type of secondary boycott was *not* made illegal by the Taft-Hartley Act, because that act only prevented unions from inducing *employees* to strike or otherwise act to force employers not to handle these goods. The Landrum-Griffin Act addressed this problem:

> It shall be [an] unfair labor practice for any labor organization and any employer to enter into any contract or any agreement . . . whereby such employer . . . agrees to refrain from handling, using, selling, transporting or otherwise dealing in any of the products of any other employer, or to cease doing business with any other person.

Hot-cargo agreements are therefore illegal. Parties injured by an illegal hot-cargo agreement or other secondary boycott may sue the union for damages.

A union may legally urge consumer boycotts of the primary employer, even at the site of a secondary employer.

SECONDARY BOYCOTT
A union's refusal to work for, purchase from, or handle the products of a secondary employer, with whom the union has no dispute, for the purpose of forcing that employer to stop doing business with the primary employer, with whom the union has a labor dispute.

COMMON SITUS PICKETING
The illegal picketing of a primary employer's site by workers who are involved in a labor dispute with a secondary employer.

HOT-CARGO AGREEMENT
An agreement in which employers voluntarily agree with unions not to handle, use, or deal in goods produced by nonunion employees of other firms; a type of secondary boycott explicitly prohibited by the Labor-Management Reporting and Disclosure Act of 1959.

Striking workers picket to publicize their labor dispute. Why is the right to strike important to unions? (AP Photo/Ric Francis)

| **Example #5** A union is on strike against SemiCo, which manufactures semiconductors that are bought by Intellect, Inc., a distributor of electronic components. Intellect sells SemiCo's semiconductors to computer manufacturers. The striking workers can urge the manufacturers not to buy SemiCo's products. The workers cannot urge a total boycott of Intellect, as that would constitute a secondary boycott. |

WILDCAT STRIKE
A strike that is not authorized by the union that ordinarily represents the striking employees.

Wildcat Strikes   A **wildcat strike** occurs when a group of workers, perhaps dissatisfied with a union's representation, calls its own strike. The union is the exclusive bargaining representative of a group of workers, and only the union can call a strike. A wildcat strike, unauthorized by the certified union, is illegal.

| **Example #6** In one case, several concrete workers left their jobs because it was raining and went on "strike." The court found the strike illegal because it was not preceded by a demand on the employer for action and because the employer had made shelter available for the workers and paid them for waiting time. |

Strikes That Threaten National Health or Safety   The law also places some restrictions on strikes that threaten national health or safety. The law does not prohibit such strikes, nor does it require the settlement of labor disputes that threaten the national welfare. The Taft-Hartley Act simply provides time to encourage the settlement of these disputes, called the "cooling-off period."

EIGHTY-DAY COOLING-OFF PERIOD
A provision of the Taft-Hartley Act that allows federal courts to issue injunctions against strikes that might create a national emergency.

One of the most controversial aspects of the Taft-Hartley Act was the establishment of this **eighty-day cooling-off period**—a provision allowing federal courts to issue injunctions against strikes that would create a national emergency. The president of the United States can obtain a court injunction that will last for eighty days, and presidents have occasionally used this provision. During these eighty days, the president and other government officials can work with the employer and the union to produce a settlement and avoid a strike that may cause a national emergency.

NO-STRIKE CLAUSE
A provision in a collective bargaining agreement that states that the employees will not strike for any reason and labor disputes will be resolved by arbitration.

Strikes That Contravene No-Strike Clauses   A strike may also be illegal if it contravenes a **no-strike clause.** The previous collective bargaining agreement between a union and an employer may have contained a clause in which the union agreed not to strike (a no-strike clause). The law permits the employer to enforce this no-strike clause and obtain an injunction against the strike in some circumstances.

The Supreme Court held that a no-strike clause could be enforced with an injunction if the contract contained a clause providing for arbitration of unresolved disputes.[13] The Court held that the arbitration clause was an effective substitute for the right to strike. In the absence of an applicable arbitration provision, however, an employer cannot enjoin (forbid) a strike, even if the contract contains a no-strike clause.

Replacement Workers

Suppose that SemiCo's workers go out on strike. SemiCo is not required to shut down its operations but may find substitute workers to replace the strikers, if possible. These substitute workers are often called "scabs" by union

---

13. *Boys Markets, Inc. v. Retail Clerks Local 770, 398 U.S. 235, 90 S.Ct. 1583, 26 L.Ed.2d 199 (1970).*

supporters. An employer may even give the replacement workers permanent positions with the company.

In the 1930s and 1940s, strikes were powerful in part because employers often had difficulty finding trained replacements to keep their businesses running during strikes. Since the illegal air traffic controller strike in 1981, when President Ronald Reagan successfully hired replacement workers, employers have increasingly used this strategy, with considerable success. | **Example #7** The National Football League (NFL), when struck by the players in 1987, found replacements to play for the NFL teams. Although some scoffed at the ability of the replacement players, the tactic was largely successful for management, as the strike was called off after only three weeks.| An employer can even use an employment agency to recruit replacement workers.[14]

Rights of Strikers after the Strike

An important issue concerns the rights of strikers after the strike ends. In a typical economic strike over working conditions, the employer has a right to hire permanent replacements during the strike, and need not terminate the replacement workers when the economic strikers seek to return to work. In other words, striking workers are not guaranteed the right to return to their jobs after the strike if satisfactory replacement workers have been found. If the employer has not hired replacement workers to fill the strikers' positions, however, then the employer must rehire the economic strikers to fill any vacancies. Employers may not discriminate against former economic strikers, and those who are rehired retain their seniority rights.

Different rules apply when a union strikes because the employer has engaged in unfair labor practices. If an employer is discriminating against a union's workers, they may go out on an unfair labor practice strike. Furthermore, an economic strike may become an unfair labor practice strike if the employer refuses to bargain in good faith. In the case of an unfair labor practice strike, the employer may still hire replacements but must give the strikers back their jobs once the strike is over. An employer may, however, refuse to rehire unfair labor practice strikers if the strike was deemed unlawful or if there is simply no longer any work for them to do.

LOCKOUTS

Lockouts are the employer's counterpart to the worker's right to strike. A **lockout** occurs when the employer shuts down to prevent employees from working. Lockouts are usually used when the employer believes that a strike is imminent.

Lockouts may be a legal employer response. | **Example #8** In the leading Supreme Court case on this issue, a union and an employer had reached a stalemate in collective bargaining. The employer feared that the union would delay a strike until the busy season and thereby cause the employer to suffer more greatly from the strike. The employer called a lockout before the busy season to deny the union this leverage, and the Supreme Court held that this action was legal.[15]|

LOCKOUT

The closing of a plant to employees by an employer to gain leverage in collective bargaining negotiations.

---

14. *Professional Staff Nurses Association v. Dimensions Health Corp.*, 110 Md.App. 270, 677 A.2d 87 (1996).
15. *American Ship Building Co. v. NLRB*, 380 U.S. 300, 85 S.Ct. 955, 13 L.Ed.2d 855 (1965).

Some lockouts are illegal, however. An employer may not use its lockout weapon as a tool to break the union and pressure employees into decertification. Consequently, an employer must show some economic justification for instituting a lockout.

UNFAIR LABOR PRACTICES

The preceding sections have discussed unfair labor practices involved in the significant acts of union elections, collective bargaining, and strikes. Many unfair labor practices may occur within the normal working relationship as well. The most important of these practices are discussed in the following sections. Exhibit 15–2 lists the basic unfair labor practices.

Employer's Refusal to Recognize the Union and to Negotiate

As noted above, once a union has been certified as the exclusive representative of a bargaining unit, an employer must recognize and bargain in good faith with the union over issues affecting all employees who are within the bargaining unit. Failure to do so is an unfair labor practice. Because the National Labor Relations Act embraces a policy of majority rule, certification of the union as the bargaining unit's representative binds *all* of the employees in that bargaining unit. Thus, the union must fairly represent all the members of the bargaining unit.

Certification does not mean that a union will continue indefinitely as the exclusive representative of the bargaining unit. If the union loses the majority support of those it represents, an employer is not obligated to continue recognition of, or negotiation with, the union. As a practical matter, a newly elected representative needs time to establish itself among the workers and to begin to formulate and implement its programs. Therefore, as a matter of labor policy, a union is immune from attack by employers and from repudiation by the employees for a period of one year after certification. During this period, it is *presumed* that the union enjoys majority support among the employees; the employer cannot refuse to deal with the union as the employees' exclusive representative, even if the employees prefer not to be represented by that union.

Beyond the one-year period, the presumption of majority support continues, but it is *rebuttable*. An employer may rebut (attempt to refute) the presumption

EXHIBIT 15–2 BASIC UNFAIR LABOR PRACTICES

Employers *It is unfair to . . .*	**Unions** *It is unfair to . . .*
1. Refuse to recognize a union and refuse to bargain in good faith.	1. Refuse to bargain in good faith.
2. Interfere with, restrain, or coerce employees in their efforts to form a union and bargain collectively.	2. Picket to coerce unionization without the support of a majority of the employees.
3. Dominate a union.	3. Demand the hiring of unnecessary excess workers.
4. Discriminate against union workers.	4. Discriminate against nonunion workers.
5. Agree to participate in a secondary boycott.	5. Agree to participate in a secondary boycott.
6. Punish employees for engaging in concerted activity.	6. Engage in an illegal strike.
	7. Charge excessive membership fees.

with objective evidence that a majority of employees do not wish to be represented by the union. If the evidence is sufficient to support a *good faith belief* that the union no longer enjoys majority support among the employees, the employer may refuse to continue to recognize and negotiate with the union.[16]

Employer's Interference in Union Activities

The NLRA declares it to be an unfair labor practice for an employer to interfere with, restrain, or coerce employees in the exercise of their rights to form a union and bargain collectively. Unlawful employer interference may take a variety of forms.

Courts have found it an unfair labor practice for an employer to make threats that may interfere with an employee's decision to join a union. Even asking employees about their views on the union may be considered coercive. Employees responding to such questioning must be able to remain anonymous and must receive assurances against employer reprisals. Employers also may not prohibit certain forms of union activity in the workplace. If an employee has a grievance with the company, the employer cannot prevent the union's participation in support of the employee, for example.

If an employer has unlawfully interfered with the operation of a union, the NLRB or a reviewing court may issue a cease-and-desist order halting the practice. The company typically is required to post the order on a bulletin board and renounce its past unlawful conduct.

Employer's Domination of a Union

In the early days of unionization, employers fought back by forming employer-sponsored unions to represent employees. These "company unions" were seldom more than the puppets of management. The NLRA outlawed company unions and any other form of employer domination of workers' unions.

Under the law against employer domination, an employer can have no say in which employees belong to the union or which employees serve as union officers. Nor may supervisors or other management personnel participate in union meetings.

Company actions that support a union may be considered improper potential domination. For this reason, a company cannot give union workers pay for time spent on union activities, because this is considered undue support for the union. The company may not provide financial aid to a union and may not solicit workers to join a union.

Employer's Discrimination against Union Employees

The NLRA prohibits employers from discriminating against workers because they are union officers or are otherwise associated with a union. When workers must be laid off, the company cannot consider union participation as a criterion for deciding whom to fire.

---

16. An employer cannot agree to a collective bargaining agreement and later refuse to abide by it, however, on the ground of a good faith belief that the union did not have majority support when the agreement was negotiated. See *Auciello Iron Works, Inc. v. NLRB*, 517 U.S. 781, 116 S.Ct. 1754, 135 L.Ed.2d 64 (1996).

The provisions prohibiting discrimination also apply to hiring decisions.
| **Example #9** Certain employees of SemiCo are represented by a union, but the company is attempting to weaken the union's strength. The company is prohibited from requiring potential new hires to guarantee that they will not join the union. |

Discriminatory punishment of union members or officers can be difficult to prove. The company will claim to have good reasons for its action. The NLRB has specified a series of factors to be considered in determining whether an action had an unlawful, discriminatory motivation. These include giving inconsistent reasons for the action, applying rules inconsistently and more strictly against union members, failing to give an expected warning prior to discharge or other discipline, and acting contrary to worker seniority.

The decision to close a facility cannot be made with a discriminatory motive. If a company has several facilities and only one is unionized, the company cannot shut down the union plant simply because of the union. The company could shut down the union plant if it were demonstrably less efficient than the other facilities, however.

Union's Unfair Labor Practices

Certain union activities are declared to be unfair labor practices by the Taft-Hartley Act. Secondary boycotts, discussed above, are one such union unfair labor practice.

Coercion   Another significant union unfair labor practice is coercion or restraint on an employee's decision to participate in or refrain from participating in union activities. Obviously, it is unlawful for a union to threaten an employee or a family with violence for failure to join the union. The law's prohibition includes economic coercion as well. Suppose that a union official declares, "We have a lot of power here; you had better join the union, or you may lose your job." This threat is an unfair labor practice.

The NLRA provides unions with the authority to regulate their own internal affairs, which includes disciplining union members. This discipline cannot be used in an improperly coercive fashion, however. | **Example #10** Stan Kowalski is a union member who feels that the union is no longer providing proper representation for employees at his workplace. He starts a campaign to decertify the union. The union may expel Kowalski from membership, but it may not fine or otherwise discipline the worker. |

Discrimination   Another significant union unfair labor practice is discrimination. A union may not discriminate against workers because they refuse to join. This provision also prohibits a union from using its influence to cause an employer to discriminate against workers who refuse to join the union. A union cannot force an employer to deny promotions to workers who fail to join the union.

Other Unfair Practices   Other union unfair labor practices include featherbedding (discussed earlier in this chapter), participation in picketing to coerce unionization without majority employee support, and refusal to engage in good faith bargaining with employer representatives.

Unions are allowed to bargain for certain "union security clauses" in contracts. Although closed shops are illegal, a union can bargain for a provision that requires workers to contribute to the union within thirty days after they are hired. This is typically called an *agency shop*, or *union shop*, *clause*.

The union shop clause can compel workers to begin paying dues to the certified union but cannot require the worker to "join" the union. Dues payment can be required to prevent workers from taking the benefits of union bargaining without contributing to the union's efforts. The clause cannot require workers to contribute their efforts to the union, however, or to go out on strike.

Even a requirement of dues payment has its limits. Excessive initiation fees or dues may be illegal. Unions often use their revenues to contribute to causes or to lobby politicians. A nonunion employee subject to a union shop clause who must pay dues cannot be required to contribute to this sort of union expenditure.

RIGHTS OF NONUNION EMPLOYEES

Most labor law involves the formation of unions and associated rights. Even nonunion employees have some similar rights, however. Most workers do not belong to unions, so this issue is significant. The NLRA protects concerted employee action, for example, and does not limit its protection to certified unions.

Concerted Activity

Data from the NLRB indicate that growing numbers of nonunion employees are challenging employer barriers to their **concerted action.** Protected concerted action is that taken by employees for their mutual benefit regarding wages, hours, or terms and conditions of employment.

Even an action by a *single* employee may be protected concerted activity, if that action is taken for the benefit of other employees and if the employee has at least discussed the action with other approving workers. If only a single worker engages in a protest or walkout, the employer will not be liable for an unfair labor practice if it fires the worker unless the employer is aware that this protest or walkout is concerted activity taken with the assent of other workers.

In the following case, an employer discharged an employee for "complaining." The employee claimed that this "complaining" constituted concerted activity on behalf of herself and other employees.

CONCERTED ACTION
Action by employees, such as a strike or picketing, with the purpose of furthering their bargaining demands or other mutual interests.

CASE 15.3   NLRB v. Hotel Employees and Restaurant Employees International Union Local 26, AFL-CIO

United States Court of Appeals, First Circuit, 2006.
446 F.3d 200.
www.ca1.uscourts.gov[a]

BACKGROUND AND FACTS   The Hotel Employees and Restaurant Employees International Union, Local 26, AFL-CIO

(the Union), represents 5,800 hotel workers in Boston, Massachusetts. In 1997, the Union hired Janice Loux as its president. In September 1998, Loux hired Emma Johnson as a researcher. In June 1999, the Logan Airport Ramada Inn near Boston announced that it would be closing and all employees would be discharged. Hilton Hotels Corporation would reopen the hotel, but the discharged employees would not be given a right of reemployment. Loux scheduled a leafleting campaign against Hilton. Each Union employee was to leaflet in a two-hour shift at times varying from day to day, in addition to other job duties. During the campaign, Johnson repeatedly asked Loux to allow employees to switch shifts.

a. In the right-hand column, click on "Opinions." When that page opens, in the "Opinion Number begins with" box, type "05-1924" and click on "Submit Search." From the result, in the "Click for Opinion" column, click on the link to read the case. The U.S. Court of Appeals for the First Circuit maintains this Web site.

CASE 15.3–CONTINUED ▶

Loux refused. On August 6, the Union reached an agreement with Hilton and the leafleting stopped. Less than two weeks later, Loux fired Johnson for "complaining about the Hilton campaign." Johnson filed an unfair labor practice charge with the National Labor Relations Board (NLRB) against the Union.

The NLRB concluded that the Union discharged Johnson "because of her protected concerted activity." The Union petitioned the U.S. Court of Appeals for the First Circuit for review.

IN THE WORDS OF THE COURT . . . *BOWMAN,* Senior Circuit Judge.

* * * *

* * * The Union argues that Johnson did not engage in concerted activity, but rather engaged in self-motivated complaining about her schedule.

To qualify as concerted activity, conduct need not take place in a union setting and it is not necessary that a collective bargaining agreement be in effect. It is sufficient that the complaining employee intends or contemplates, as an end result, group activity which will also benefit some other employees. We recognize that even a conversation can constitute concerted activity, but to qualify as such, it must appear at the very least that it was engaged in with the object of initiating or inducing or preparing for group action or that it had some relation to group action in the interest of the employees. [Emphasis added.]

We conclude * * * that Johnson engaged in concerted activity. * * * Johnson polled co-employees about their desire to switch shifts and/or work only one day per weekend, she informed co-employees that she would present her ideas to Loux at a staff meeting, and she later presented her ideas that would benefit all employees to Loux. Johnson also gave Loux alternative weekend schedules that either would have granted employees one weekend day off per week or at least ensured that the employees did not work in the middle of both weekend days. Some employees supported Johnson's ideas. * * * *Johnson's conduct related to group action that would have benefited the Union's employees such that it constituted concerted activity.* [Emphasis added.]

* * * *

[Next] we ask whether * * * Loux discharged Johnson because she engaged in protected concerted activity. * * * After Loux announced that the leafletting campaign could last up to four months, that employees could not take any vacations until it was concluded, and that employees would work seven days per week during the campaign, Johnson began to discuss schedule changes openly with co-employees. Johnson then advocated to Loux on behalf of the employees for the ability to switch shifts or be allowed to work four-hour shifts on one weekend day so that they could enjoy one day off per week.

* * * Loux knew about this activity [and] * * * Loux's motivation for discharging Johnson was rooted in Johnson's protesting the leafletting schedule. For instance, * * * Johnson's [job performance was rated in May 1999] as very good * * * . Soon after, in July 1999, Loux initiated the leafletting campaign against the Hilton and Johnson began voicing complaints about the leafletting schedule. That is when Loux became extremely critical of Johnson's performance and attitude. * * * Johnson was discharged because she complained about the Hilton campaign. * * * Thus, we conclude * * * that *a motivating factor in the Union's discharge of Johnson was her protected concerted activity.* [Emphasis added.]

* * * *

The Union admits that Johnson's poor attitude during the leafletting activities was a reason for her discharge. * * * [T]his criticism is inextricably related to the fact that Johnson made herself a pest in Loux's eyes by continually complaining about the * * *

CASE 15.3–CONTINUED leafletting schedule. * * * Johnson may have been an irritant to Loux because she was challenging the schedule; but that irritating activity by Johnson is protected by * * * the NLRA.

DECISION AND REMEDY The U.S. Court of Appeals for the First Circuit denied the Union's petition for review. The court affirmed the NLRB's conclusion that the Union was liable for discharging Johnson. "A consistent theme runs through the * * * testimony and supports the * * * finding that Johnson's protected concerted activity motivated Loux to discharge her."

WHY IS THIS CASE IMPORTANT? *The unique circumstances in this case—a union's discharge of its own employee for concerted activity on behalf of other union employees—make the case notable. When a union acts as an employer, it is subject to the legal principles that apply to employers generally.*

Safety

A common circumstance for nonunion activity is concern over workplace safety. The Labor-Management Relations Act authorizes an employee to walk off the job if he or she has a good faith belief that the working conditions are abnormally dangerous. The employer cannot lawfully discharge the employee under these conditions.

| **Example #11** Knight Company operates a plant building mobile homes. A large ventilation fan at the plant blows dust and abrasive materials into the faces of workers. The workers have complained, but Knight Company has done nothing. The workers finally refuse to work until the fan is modified, and Knight fires them. The NLRB will find that the walkout is a protected activity and can command Knight to rehire the workers with back pay.|

To be protected under federal labor law, a safety walkout must be *concerted* activity. If a single worker walks out over a safety complaint, other workers must be affected by the safety issue for the walkout to be protected under the LMRA.

Employee Committees

Personnel specialists note that worker problems are often attributable to a lack of communication between labor and management. In a nonunion workforce, a company may wish to create some institution to communicate with workers and act together with them to improve workplace conditions. This institution, generally called an **employee committee,** is composed of representatives from both management and labor. The committee meets periodically and has some authority to create rules. The committee gives employees a forum to voice their dissatisfaction with certain conditions and gives management a conduit to inform workers fully of policy decisions.

The creation of an employee committee may be entirely motivated by good intentions on the company's part and may serve the interests of workers as well as management. Nevertheless, employee committees are fraught with potential problems under federal labor laws, and management must be aware of these difficulties. The central problem with employee committees is that they may become the functional equivalent of unions dominated by management, in violation of the NLRA. Thus, these committees cannot perform union functions. | **Example #12** The employee representatives on an employee committee should not present a package of proposals on wages and terms of employment, because this is the role of a union negotiating committee.|

EMPLOYEE COMMITTEE
A committee created by an employer and composed of representatives of management and nonunion employees to act together to improve workplace conditions.

REVIEWING . . . LABOR-MANAGEMENT RELATIONS

In April 2005, several employees of Javatech, Inc., a computer hardware developer with 250 employees, formed the Javatech Employees Union (JEU). In June, the National Labor Relations Board (NLRB) conducted an election that showed that a majority of Javatech employees supported the union. JEU began bargaining with management over wages and benefits. In January 2006, Javatech management offered JEU a 1 percent annual wage increase to all employees with no other changes in employment benefits. JEU countered by requesting a 3 percent wage increase and an employee health-insurance package. Javatech management responded that the 1 percent wage increase was the company's only offer. JEU petitioned the NLRB for an order requesting good faith bargaining. After meeting with an NLRB representative, Javatech management still refused to consider modifying its position. JEU leaders then became embroiled in a dispute about whether JEU should accept this offer or go on strike. New union leaders were elected in July 2006, and the employer refused to meet with the new JEU representatives, claiming that the union no longer had majority support from employees. In August 2006, a group of seven Javatech engineers began feeling ill while working with a new adhesive used in creating motherboards. The seven engineers discussed going on strike without union support. Before reaching agreement, one of the engineers, Rosa Molina, became dizzy while working with the adhesive and walked out of the workplace. Using the information presented in the chapter, answer the following questions.

1. How many of Javatech's 250 employees must have signed authorization cards to allow JEU to petition the NLRB for an election?

2. What must Javatech change in its collective bargaining negotiations to demonstrate that it is bargaining in good faith with JEU, as required by labor law?

3. Could the seven engineers legally call a strike? What would this be called?

4. Would Molina's safety walkout be protected under the Labor-Management Relations Act?

KEY TERMS

CHAPTER SUMMARY • LABOR-MANAGEMENT RELATIONS

Federal Labor Law (See pages 501–504.)	1. *Norris-LaGuardia Act of 1932*—Extended legal protection to peaceful strikes, picketing, and boycotts. Restricted the power of the courts to issue injunctions against unions engaged in peaceful strikes.
	2. *National Labor Relations Act of 1935 (Wagner Act)*—Established the rights of employees to engage in collective bargaining and to strike. Created the National Labor Relations Board (NLRB) to oversee union elections and prevent employers from engaging in unfair labor practices (such as refusing to recognize and negotiate with a certified union or interfering in union activities).

CHAPTER SUMMARY • LABOR-MANAGEMENT RELATIONS—CONTINUED

Federal Labor Law— Continued	3. *Labor-Management Relations Act of 1947 (Taft-Hartley Act)*—Extended to employers protections already enjoyed by employees. Provided a list of activities prohibited to unions (secondary boycotts, use of coercion or discrimination to influence employees' decisions to participate or refrain from union activities) and allowed employers to propagandize against unions before any NLRB election. Prohibited closed shops (which require that all workers belong to a union as a condition of employment), allowed states to pass right-to-work laws, and provided for an eighty-day cooling-off period.
	4. *Labor-Management Reporting and Disclosure Act of 1959 (Landrum-Griffin Act)*—Regulated internal union business procedures and union elections. Imposed restrictions on the types of persons who may serve as union officers and outlawed hot-cargo agreements.
Union Organizing (See pages 505–510.)	1. *Authorization cards*—Before beginning an organizing effort, a union will attempt to assess worker support for unionization by obtaining signed authorization cards from the employees. It can then ask the employer to recognize the union, or it can submit the cards with a petition to the National Labor Relations Board.
	2. *Appropriate bargaining unit*—In determining whether workers constitute an appropriate bargaining unit, the NLRB will consider whether the skills, tasks, and jobs of the workers are sufficiently similar so that they can all be adequately served by a single negotiating position.
	3. *Union election campaign*—The NLRB is charged with monitoring union elections. During an election campaign, an employer may legally limit union activities as long as it can offer legitimate business justifications for those limitations. In regulating the union's presence on the business premises, the employer must treat the union in the same way it would treat any other entity having on-site contact with its workers. The NLRB is particularly sensitive to any threats in an employer's communications to workers, such as declarations that a union victory will result in the closing of the plant. The NLRB will also closely monitor sudden policy changes regarding compensation, hours, or working conditions that the employer makes before the election.
	4. *Union certification*—Certification by the NLRB means that the union is the exclusive representative of a bargaining unit and that the employer must recognize the union and bargain in good faith with it over issues affecting all employees who are within the bargaining unit.
Collective Bargaining (See pages 510–514.)	Once a union is elected, its representatives will engage in collective bargaining with the employer. Topics such as wages, hours of work, and other conditions of employment are discussed during collective bargaining sessions. Some demands, such as a demand for featherbedding or for a closed shop, are illegal. If the parties reach an impasse, the union may call a strike against the employer to bring additional economic pressure to bear. This is one way in which the union can offset management's superior bargaining power.
Strikes and Lockouts (See pages 514–518.)	1. *Right to strike*—The right to strike is guaranteed by the National Labor Relations Act, and strike activities are protected by the U.S. Constitution. During a strike, an employer is no longer obligated to pay union members, and union members are no longer required to show up for work.
	2. *Secondary boycott*—Strikers are not permitted to engage in a secondary boycott by picketing the suppliers of an employer. Similarly, striking employees are not permitted to coerce the employer's customers into agreeing not to do business with it.
	3. *Wildcat strike*—A wildcat strike occurs when a small group of union members engages in a strike against the employer without the permission of the union.
	4. *Replacement workers*—An employer may hire permanent replacement employees in the event of an economic strike. If the strike is called by the union to protest the employer's unwillingness to engage in good faith negotiations, then the employer must rehire the striking workers after the strike is settled, even if it has since replaced them with other workers.

(Continued)

CHAPTER SUMMARY • LABOR-MANAGEMENT RELATIONS—CONTINUED

Strikes and Lockouts—Continued	5. *Lockouts*—Employers may respond to threatened employee strikes by shutting down the plant altogether to prevent employees from working. Lockouts are used when the employer believes a strike is imminent.
Unfair Labor Practices (See pages 518–521.)	1. An employer's refusal to recognize or negotiate with the union, interference in union activities, domination of the union, and discrimination against union employees. 2. A union's coercive actions against employees, discrimination against nonunion members, featherbedding, and other practices.
Rights of Nonunion Employees (See pages 521–523.)	The National Labor Relations Act protects concerted action on the part of nonunion employees. Protected concerted action includes walkouts and other activities regarding wages, hours, workplace safety, or other terms or conditions of employment.

FOR REVIEW

Answers for the even-numbered questions in this For Review *section can be found in Appendix O at the end of this text.*

1. What federal statutes govern labor unions and collective bargaining?

2. How does the way in which a union election is conducted protect the rights of employees and employers?

3. What types of strikes are illegal?

4. What activities are prohibited as unfair employer practices?

5. What are the rights of nonunion employees?

QUESTIONS AND CASE PROBLEMS

15–1. Preliminary Organizing. A group of employees at the Briarwood Furniture Co.'s manufacturing plant were interested in joining a union. A representative of the American Federation of Labor and Congress of Industrial Organizations (AFL-CIO) told the group that her union was prepared to represent the workers and suggested that the group members begin organizing by obtaining authorization cards from their fellow employees. After obtaining 252 authorization cards from among Briarwood's 500 nonmanagement employees, the organizers requested that the company recognize the AFL-CIO as the official representative of the employees. The company refused. Has the company violated federal labor laws? What should the organizers do?

15–2. Appropriate Bargaining Unit. The Briarwood Furniture Co., discussed in the preceding problem, employs 400 unskilled workers and 100 skilled workers in its plant. The unskilled workers operate the industrial machinery used in processing Briarwood's line of standardized plastic office furniture. The skilled workers, who work in an entirely separate part of the plant, are experienced artisans who craft Briarwood's line of expensive wood furniture products. Do you see any problems with a single union's representing all the workers at the Briarwood plant? Explain. Would your answers to Problem 15–1 change if you knew that 51 of the authorization cards had been signed by the skilled workers, with the remainder signed by the unskilled workers?

Question with Sample Answer

15–3. Suppose that Consolidated Stores is undergoing a unionization campaign. Prior to the election, management says that the union is unnecessary to protect workers. Management also provides bonuses and wage increases to the workers during this period. The employees reject the union. Union organizers protest that the wage increases during the election campaign unfairly prejudiced the vote. Should these wage increases be regarded as an unfair labor practice? Discuss.

For a sample answer to this question, go to Appendix P at the end of this text.

15–4. Unfair Labor Practices. SimpCo was engaged in ongoing negotiations over a new labor contract with the union representing the company's employees. As the deadline for expiration of the old labor contract drew near, several employees who were active in union activities were disciplined for being late to work. The union claimed that other employees had not been dealt with as harshly and that the company was discriminating on the basis of union activity. When the negotiations failed to prove fruitful and the old contract expired, the union called a strike. The company claimed the action was an economic strike to press the union's demands for higher wages. The union contended the action was an unfair labor practice strike because of the alleged discrimination. What importance does the distinction have for the striking workers and the company?

15-5. Secondary Boycotts. For many years, grapefruit was shipped to Japan from Fort Pierce and Port Canaveral, Florida. In 1990, Coastal Stevedoring Co. in Fort Pierce and Port Canaveral Stevedoring, Ltd., in Port Canaveral—nonunion firms—were engaged in a labor dispute with the International Longshoremen's Association (ILA). The ILA asked the National Council of Dockworkers' Unions of Japan to prevent Japanese shippers from using nonunion stevedores in Florida, and the council warned Japanese firms that their workers would not unload fruit loaded in the United States by nonunion labor. The threat caused all citrus shipments from Florida to Japan to go through Tampa, where they were loaded by stevedores represented by the ILA. Coastal, Canaveral, and others complained to the National Labor Relations Board (NLRB), alleging that the ILA's request of the Japanese unions was an illegal secondary boycott. How should the NLRB rule? [*International Longshoremen's Association, AFL-CIO,* 313 N.L.R.B. No. 53 (1993)]

Case Problem with Sample Answer

15-6. The Teamsters Union represented twenty-seven employees of Curtin Matheson Scientific, Inc. When a collective bargaining agreement between the union and the company expired, the company made an offer for a new agreement, which the union rejected. The company locked out the twenty-seven employees, and the union began an economic strike. The company hired replacement workers. When the union ended its strike and offered to accept the company's earlier offer, the company refused. The company also refused to bargain further, asserting doubt that the union was supported by a majority of the employees. The union sought help from the National Labor Relations Board (NLRB), which refused to presume that the replacement workers did not support the union. On the company's appeal, a court overturned the NLRB's ruling. The union appealed to the United States Supreme Court. How should the Court rule? [*NLRB v. Curtin Matheson Scientific, Inc.,* 494 U.S. 775, 110 S.Ct. 1542, 108 L.Ed.2d 801 (1990)]

After you have answered this problem, compare your answer with the sample answer given on the Web site that accompanies this text. Go to www.thomsonedu.com/westbuslaw/let, select "Chapter 15," and click on "Case Problem with Sample Answer."

15-7. Unfair Labor Practice. The New York Department of Education's e-mail policy prohibits the use of the e-mail system for unofficial purposes, except that officials of the New York Public Employees Federation (PEF), the union representing state employees, can use the system for some limited communications, including the scheduling of union meetings and activities. In 1998, Michael Darcy, an elected PEF official, began sending mass, union-related e-mails to employees,

including a summary of a union delegates' convention, a union newsletter, a criticism of proposed state legislation, and a criticism of the state governor and the Governor's Office of Employee Relations. Richard Cate, the department's chief operating officer, met with Darcy and reiterated the department's e-mail policy. When Darcy refused to stop his use of the e-mail system, Cate terminated his access to it. Darcy filed a complaint with the New York Public Employment Relations Board, alleging an unfair labor practice. Do the circumstances support Cate's action? Why or why not? [*Benson v. Cuevas,* 293 A.D.2d 927, 741 N.Y.S.2d 310 (3 Dept. 2002)]

15-8. Collective Bargaining. Verizon New York, Inc. (VNY), provides telecommunications services. VNY and the Communications Workers of America (CWA) are parties to collective bargaining agreements covering installation and maintenance employees. At one time, VNY supported annual blood drives. VNY, CWA, and charitable organizations jointly set dates, arranged appointments, and adjusted work schedules for the drives. For each drive, about a thousand employees, including managers, spent up to four hours traveling to a donor site, giving blood, recovering, and returning to their jobs. Employees received full pay for the time. In 2001, VNY told CWA that it would no longer allow employees to participate "on Company time," claiming that it experienced problems meeting customer requests for service during the drives. CWA filed a complaint with the National Labor Relations Board (NLRB), asking that VNY be ordered to bargain over the decision. Did VNY commit an unfair labor practice? Should the NLRB grant CWA's request? Why or why not? [*Verizon New York, Inc. v. National Labor Relations Board,* 360 F.3d 206 (D.C.Cir. 2004)]

15-9. Collective Bargaining. Ceridian Corp. provides employment services to other companies. One of its divisions offers counseling to its customers' employees through a call-in center in Eagan, Minnesota. Under Ceridian's "Personal Days Off" (PDO) policy, employees can use a certain amount of paid time off each year for whatever purpose they wish, but unpaid leave is not available. Employees who take time off in excess of their PDO are subject to discipline, including discharge. In June 2003, the National Labor Relations Board (NLRB) certified Service Employees International Union 113 as the exclusive collective bargaining representative for 130 employees at the call-in center. The union assembled a six-employee team to negotiate a collective bargaining agreement. Ceridian refused to meet with the team during nonworking hours or to grant the members unpaid leave to attend bargaining sessions during working hours, but required them to use their PDO instead. The union filed an unfair-labor-practice charge with the NLRB against Ceridian, alleging that the employer impermissibly interfered with its employees' choice of bargaining representatives. Did Ceridian commit an unfair labor practice? Explain. [*Ceridian Corp. v. National Labor Relations Board,* 435 F.3d 352 (D.C.Cir. 2006)]

A Question of Ethics

15–10. Salvatore Monte was president of Kenrich Petrochemicals, Inc. Helen Chizmar had been Kenrich's office manager since 1963. Among the staff that Chizmar supervised were her sister, daughter, and daughter-in-law. In 1987, Chizmar's relatives and four other staff members designated the Oil, Chemical, and Atomic Workers International Union as their bargaining representative. Chizmar was not involved, but when Monte was notified that his office was unionizing, he told Chizmar that someone else could do her job for "$20,000 less" and fired her. He told another employee that one of his reasons for firing Chizmar was that he "was not going to put up with any union bullsh—." During negotiations with the union, Monte said that he planned to "get rid of the whole family." Chizmar's family complained to the National Labor Relations Board (NLRB) that the firing was an unfair labor practice. The NLRB agreed and ordered that Chizmar be reinstated with back pay. Kenrich appealed. In view of these facts, consider the following questions. [*Kenrich Petrochemicals, Inc. v. NLRB*, 907 F.2d 400 (3d Cir. 1990)]

1. The National Labor Relations Act does not protect supervisors who engage in union activities. Should the appellate court affirm the NLRB's order nonetheless?
2. If the appellate court does not affirm the NLRB's order, what message will be sent to the supervisors and employees of Kenrich?
3. Is there anything Kenrich could (legally) do to avoid the unionization of its employees? Would it be ethical to counter the wishes of the employees to unionize?

Critical-Thinking Legal Question

15–11. Suppose that a disaffected union member feels that the union is no longer providing proper representation for employees and starts a campaign to decertify the union. In these circumstances, what can the union do?

INTERACTING WITH THE INTERNET

For updated links to resources available on the Web, as well as a variety of other materials, visit this text's Web site at

www.thomsonedu.com/westbuslaw/let

The American Federation of Labor–Congress of Industrial Organizations (AFL-CIO) provides links to a broad variety of labor-related resources at

www.aflcio.org

The National Labor Relations Board is online at the following URL:

www.nlrb.gov

INTERNET EXERCISES

Go to **www.thomsonedu.com/westbuslaw/let**, the Web site that accompanies this text. Select "Chapter 15" and click on "Internet Exercises." There you will find the following Internet research exercises that you can perform to learn more about topics covered in this chapter.

Internet Exercise 15–1: LEGAL PERSPECTIVE—The National Labor Relations Board
Internet Exercise 15–2: MANAGEMENT PERSPECTIVE—Mail Policies and Union Activity
Internet Exercise 15–3: MANAGEMENT PERSPECTIVE—Unions and Labor Laws

BEFORE THE TEST

Go to **www.thomsonedu.com/westbuslaw/let**, the Web site that accompanies this text. Select "Chapter 15" and click on "Interactive Quizzes." You will find a number of interactive questions relating to this chapter.

UNIT FOUR CUMULATIVE BUSINESS HYPOTHETICAL

Falwell Motors, Inc., is a large corporation that manufactures automobile batteries.

1. One of Falwell's salespersons, Loren, puts in long hours every week. He spends most of his time away from the office generating sales. Less than 10 percent of his work time is devoted to other duties. Usually, he receives a substantial bonus at the end of each year from his employer, and Loren now relies on this supplement to his annual salary and commission. One year, the employer does not give any of its employees year-end bonuses. Loren calculates the number of hours he had worked during the year beyond the required forty hours a week. Then he tells Falwell's president that if he is not paid for these overtime hours, he will sue the company for the overtime pay he has "earned." Falwell's president tells Loren that Falwell is not obligated to pay Loren overtime because Loren is a salesperson. What federal statute governs this dispute? Under this statute, is Falwell required to pay Loren for the "overtime hours"? Why or why not?

2. One day Barry, one of the salespersons, anxious to make a sale, intentionally quotes a price to a customer that is $500 lower than Falwell has authorized for that particular product. The customer purchases the product at the quoted price. When Falwell learns of the deal, it claims that it is not legally bound to the sales contract because it did not authorize Barry to sell the product at that price. Is Falwell bound by the contract? Discuss fully.

3. One day Gina, a Falwell employee, suffered a serious burn when she accidentally spilled some acid on her hand. The accident occurred because another employee, who was suspected of using illegal drugs, carelessly bumped into her. The hand required a series of skin grafting operations before it healed sufficiently to allow Gina to return to work. Gina wants to obtain compensation for her lost wages and medical expenses. Can she do so? If so, how?

4. After Gina's injury, Falwell decides to conduct random drug tests on all of its employees. Several employees claim that the testing violates their privacy rights. If the dispute is litigated, what factors will the court consider in deciding whether the random drug testing is legally permissible?

5. Aretha, a Falwell employee, is disgusted by the sexually offensive behavior of several male employees. She has complained to her supervisor on several occasions about the offensive behavior, but the supervisor merely laughs at her concerns. Aretha decides to bring a legal action against the company for sexual harassment. Does Aretha's complaint concern *quid pro quo* harassment or hostile-environment harassment? What federal statute protects employees from sexual harassment? What remedies are available under that statute? What procedures must Aretha follow in pursuing her legal action?

UNIT 5 The Regulatory Environment

CONTENTS

CHAPTER 16 Powers and Functions of Administrative Agencies

CHAPTER OBJECTIVES

After reading this chapter, you should be able to answer the following questions:

1. **How are federal administrative agencies created?**

2. **What are the three operations that make up the basic functions of most administrative agencies?**

3. **What sequence of events must normally occur before an agency rule becomes law?**

4. **How do administrative agencies enforce their rules?**

5. **How do the three branches of government limit the power of administrative agencies?**

"[P]erhaps more values today are affected by [administrative] decisions than by those of all the courts."

—ROBERT H. JACKSON, 1892–1954
(Associate justice of the United States Supreme Court, 1941–1954)

AS THE CHAPTER-OPENING quotation suggests, government agencies established to administer the law have a tremendous impact on the day-to-day operation of the government and the economy. In the early years of our nation, the United States had a relatively simple, nonindustrial economy that required little regulation. Because administrative agencies often create and enforce such regulations, there were relatively few such agencies. Today, however, there are rules covering virtually every aspect of a business's operation. Consequently, agencies have multiplied. At the federal level, the Securities and Exchange Commission regulates a firm's capital structure and financing, as well as its financial reporting. The National Labor Relations Board oversees relations between a firm and any unions with which it may deal. The Equal Employment Opportunity Commission also regulates employment relationships. The Environmental Protection Agency and the Occupational Safety and Health Administration affect the way a firm manufactures its products. The Federal Trade Commission affects the way the firm markets these products.

Added to this layer of federal regulation is a second layer of state regulation that, when not preempted by federal legislation, may cover many of the same activities or regulate independently those activities not covered by federal regulation. Finally, agency regulations at the county and municipal levels also affect certain types of business activities.

Administrative agencies issue rules, orders, and decisions. These regulations make up the body of *administrative law*. You were introduced briefly to some of the main principles of administrative law in Chapter 1. In the following pages, these principles are presented in much greater detail.

AGENCY CREATION AND POWERS

Congress creates federal administrative agencies. By delegating some of its authority to make and implement laws, Congress can monitor indirectly a particular area in which it has passed legislation without becoming bogged down in the details relating to enforcement—details that are often best left to specialists.

To create an administrative agency, Congress passes **enabling legislation,** which specifies the name, purposes, functions, and powers of the agency being created. Federal administrative agencies can exercise only those powers that Congress has delegated to them in enabling legislation. Through similar enabling acts, state legislatures create state administrative agencies.

ENABLING LEGISLATION
Statutes enacted by Congress that authorize the creation of an administrative agency and specify the name, composition, and powers of the agency being created.

Enabling Legislation—An Example

Congress created the Federal Trade Commission (FTC) in the Federal Trade Commission Act of 1914.[1] The act prohibits unfair and deceptive trade practices. It also describes the procedures that the agency must follow to charge persons or organizations with violations of the act, and it provides for judicial review of agency orders. The act grants the FTC the power to

1. Create "rules and regulations for the purpose of carrying out the Act."
2. Conduct investigations of business practices.
3. Obtain reports from interstate corporations concerning their business practices.
4. Investigate possible violations of federal antitrust statutes. (The FTC shares this task with the Antitrust Division of the U.S. Department of Justice.)
5. Publish findings of its investigations.
6. Recommend new legislation.
7. Hold trial-like hearings to resolve certain kinds of trade disputes that involve FTC regulations or federal antitrust laws.

The commission that heads the FTC is composed of five members, each of whom the president appoints, with the advice and consent of the Senate, for a term of seven years. The president designates one of the commissioners to be chairperson. Various offices and bureaus of the FTC undertake different administrative activities for the agency. The organization of the FTC is illustrated in Exhibit 16–1 on the next page.

Types of Agencies

There are two basic types of administrative agencies: executive agencies and independent regulatory agencies. Federal *executive agencies* include the cabinet departments of the executive branch, which were formed to assist the president in carrying out executive functions, and the subagencies within the cabinet departments. The Occupational Safety and Health Administration, for example, is a subagency within the Department of Labor. Exhibit 16–2 on page 535 lists the cabinet departments and their most important subagencies.

All administrative agencies are part of the executive branch of government, but *independent regulatory agencies* are outside the major executive departments. The Federal Trade Commission and the Securities and Exchange

---

1. 15 U.S.C. Sections 41–58.

EXHIBIT 16-1   ORGANIZATION OF THE FEDERAL TRADE COMMISSION

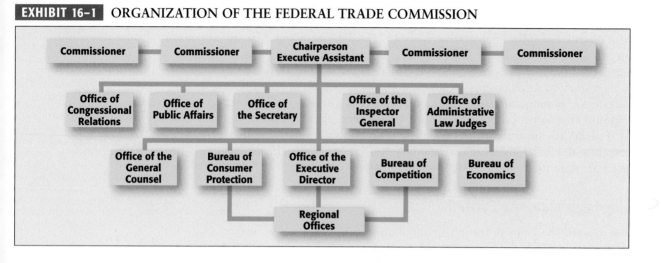

Commission are examples of independent regulatory agencies. These and other selected independent regulatory agencies, as well as their principal functions, are listed in Exhibit 16–3 on page 536.

The significant difference between the two types of agencies lies in the accountability of the regulators. Agencies that are considered part of the executive branch are subject to the authority of the president, who has the power to appoint and remove federal officers. In theory, this power is less pronounced in regard to independent agencies, whose officers serve for fixed terms and cannot be removed without just cause. In practice, however, the president's power to exert influence over independent agencies is often considerable.

Agency Powers and the Constitution

Administrative agencies occupy an unusual niche in the American legal scheme, because they exercise powers that are normally divided among the three branches of government. | **Example #1** In the FTC's enabling legislation discussed above, the FTC's grant of power incorporates functions associated with the legislature (rulemaking), the executive branch (enforcement of the rules), and the courts (adjudication, or the formal resolution of disputes). |

The constitutional principle of *checks and balances* allows each branch of government to act as a check on the actions of the other two branches. Furthermore, the Constitution authorizes only the legislative branch to create laws. Yet administrative agencies, to which the Constitution does not specifically refer, make **legislative rules,** or *substantive rules,* that are as legally binding as laws that Congress passes.

LEGISLATIVE RULE
An administrative agency rule that carries the same weight as a congressionally enacted statute.

Courts generally hold that Article I of the U.S. Constitution authorizes delegating such powers to administrative agencies. In fact, courts generally hold that Article I is the basis for all administrative law. Section 1 of that article grants all legislative powers to Congress and requires Congress to oversee the implementation of all laws. Article I, Section 8, gives Congress the power to make all laws necessary for executing its specified powers. The courts interpret these passages, under what is known as the **delegation doctrine,** as granting Congress the power to establish administrative agencies that can create rules for implementing those laws.

DELEGATION DOCTRINE
A doctrine based on Article I, Section 8, of the U.S. Constitution, which has been construed to allow Congress to delegate some of its power to make and implement laws to administrative agencies.

EXHIBIT 16–2 EXECUTIVE DEPARTMENTS AND IMPORTANT SUBAGENCIES

DEPARTMENT AND DATE FORMED	SELECTED SUBAGENCIES
State (1789)	Passport Office; Bureau of Diplomatic Security; Foreign Service; Bureau of Human Rights and Humanitarian Affairs; Bureau of Consular Affairs; Bureau of Intelligence and Research
Treasury (1789)	Internal Revenue Service; U.S. Mint
Interior (1849)	U.S. Fish and Wildlife Service; National Park Service; Bureau of Indian Affairs; Bureau of Land Management
Justice (1870)[a]	Federal Bureau of Investigation; Drug Enforcement Administration; Bureau of Prisons; U.S. Marshals Service
Agriculture (1889)	Soil Conservation Service; Agricultural Research Service; Food Safety and Inspection Service; Forest Service
Commerce (1913)[b]	Bureau of the Census; Bureau of Economic Analysis; Minority Business Development Agency; U.S. Patent and Trademark Office; National Oceanic and Atmospheric Administration
Labor (1913)[b]	Occupational Safety and Health Administration; Bureau of Labor Statistics; Employment Standards Administration; Office of Labor-Management Standards; Employment and Training Administration
Defense (1949)[c]	National Security Agency; Joint Chiefs of Staff; Departments of the Air Force, Navy, Army; service academies
Housing and Urban Development (1965)	Office of Community Planning and Development; Government National Mortgage Association; Office of Fair Housing and Equal Opportunity
Transportation (1967)	Federal Aviation Administration; Federal Highway Administration; National Highway Traffic Safety Administration; Federal Transit Administration
Energy (1977)	Office of Civilian Radioactive Waste Management; Office of Nuclear Energy; Energy Information Administration
Health and Human Services (1980)[d]	Food and Drug Administration; Centers for Medicare and Medicaid Services; Centers for Disease Control; National Institutes of Health
Education (1980)[d]	Office of Special Education and Rehabilitation Services; Office of Elementary and Secondary Education; Office of Postsecondary Education; Office of Vocational and Adult Education
Veterans' Affairs (1989)	Veterans Health Administration; Veterans Benefits Administration; National Cemetery System
Homeland Security (2002)	U.S. Citizenship and Immigration Services; Directorate of Border and Transportation Services; U.S. Coast Guard; Federal Emergency Management Agency

a. Formed from the Office of the Attorney General (created in 1789).
b. Formed from the Department of Commerce and Labor (created in 1903).
c. Formed from the Department of War (created in 1789) and the Department of the Navy (created in 1798).
d. Formed from the Department of Health, Education, and Welfare (created in 1953).

The three branches of government exercise certain controls over agency powers and functions, as is discussed later in this chapter, but in many ways administrative agencies function independently. For this reason, administrative agencies, which constitute the **bureaucracy,** are sometimes referred to as the "fourth branch" of the American government.

BUREAUCRACY
The organizational structure, consisting of government bureaus and agencies, through which the government implements and enforces the laws.

ADMINISTRATIVE PROCESS

The three functions mentioned previously—rulemaking, enforcement, and adjudication—make up what is called the administrative process. **Administrative process** involves the administration of law by administrative agencies, in

ADMINISTRATIVE PROCESS
The procedure used by administrative agencies in the administration of law.

EXHIBIT 16–3   SELECTED INDEPENDENT REGULATORY AGENCIES

NAME AND DATE FORMED	PRINCIPAL DUTIES
Federal Reserve System Board of Governors (Fed) (1913)	Determines policy with respect to interest rates, credit availability, and the money supply.
Federal Trade Commission (FTC) (1914)	Prevents businesses from engaging in unfair trade practices; stops the formation of monopolies in the business sector; protects consumer rights.
Securities and Exchange Commission (SEC) (1934)	Regulates the nation's stock exchanges, in which shares of stock are bought and sold; enforces the securities laws, which require full disclosure of the financial profiles of companies that wish to sell stock and bonds to the public.
Federal Communications Commission (FCC) (1934)	Regulates all communications by telegraph, cable, telephone, radio, satellite, and television.
National Labor Relations Board (NLRB) (1935)	Protects employees' rights to join unions and bargain collectively with employers; attempts to prevent unfair labor practices by both employers and unions.
Equal Employment Opportunity Commission (EEOC) (1964)	Works to eliminate discrimination in employment based on religion, gender, race, color, disability, national origin, or age; investigates claims of discrimination.
Environmental Protection Agency (EPA) (1970)	Undertakes programs aimed at reducing air and water pollution; works with state and local agencies to help fight environmental hazards. (It has been suggested recently that its status be elevated to that of a department.)
Nuclear Regulatory Commission (NRC) (1975)	Ensures that electricity-generating nuclear reactors in the United States are built and operated safely; regularly inspects operations of such reactors.

JUDICIAL PROCESS
The procedures relating to, or connected with, the administration of justice through the judicial system.

contrast to **judicial process,** which involves the administration of law by the courts.

The Administrative Procedure Act (APA) of 1946[2] imposes procedural requirements that all federal agencies must follow in their rulemaking, adjudication, and other functions. The APA is such an integral part of the administrative process that we examine its application as we go through the basic functions carried out by administrative agencies.

Rulemaking

RULEMAKING
The actions undertaken by administrative agencies when formally adopting new regulations or amending old ones. Under the Administrative Procedure Act, rulemaking includes notifying the public of proposed rules or changes and receiving and considering the public's comments.

A major function of an administrative agency is **rulemaking**—the formulation of new regulations. In an agency's enabling legislation, Congress confers the agency's power to make rules. **▍Example #2** The Occupational Safety and Health Act of 1970 authorized the Occupational Health and Safety Administration (OSHA) to develop and issue rules governing safety in the workplace. In 1991, OSHA deemed it in the public interest to issue a new rule regulating the health-care industry to prevent the spread of such diseases as acquired immune deficiency syndrome (AIDS). OSHA created a rule specifying various standards—on how contaminated instruments should be handled, for example—with which employers in that industry must comply.▍

In addition to making legislative rules, administrative agencies also make *interpretive rules.* These rules are not legally binding on the public but simply

---

2. 5 U.S.C. Sections 551–706.

indicate how an agency plans to interpret and enforce its statutory authority. For example, the Equal Employment Opportunity Commission periodically issues interpretive rules, usually referred to as enforcement guidelines, indicating how it plans to interpret and apply a provision of a certain statute, such as the Americans with Disabilities Act. When making interpretive rules, an agency need not follow the requirements of the APA.

In formulating rules, administrative agencies follow specific rulemaking procedures required under the APA. The most commonly used rulemaking procedure is called **notice-and-comment rulemaking.** This procedure involves three basic steps: notice of the proposed rulemaking, a comment period, and the final rule.

NOTICE-AND-COMMENT RULEMAKING
A procedure in agency rulemaking that requires (1) notice, (2) opportunity for comment, and (3) a published draft of the final rule.

Notice of the Proposed Rulemaking   When a federal agency decides to create a new rule, the agency publishes a notice of the proposed rulemaking proceedings in the *Federal Register,* a daily publication of the executive branch that prints government orders, rules, and regulations. The notice states where and when the proceedings will be held, the agency's legal authority for making the rule (usually its enabling legislation), and the terms or subject matter of the proposed rule.

Comment Period   Following the publication of the notice of the proposed rulemaking proceedings, the agency must allow ample time for persons to comment on the proposed rule. The purpose of this comment period is to give interested parties the opportunity to express their views on the proposed rule in an effort to influence agency policy. The comments may be in writing or, if a hearing is held, may be given orally. The agency need not respond to all comments, but it must respond to any significant comments that bear directly on the proposed rule. The agency responds by either modifying its final rule or explaining, in a statement accompanying the final rule, why it did not make any changes. In some circumstances, particularly when the procedure being used in a specific instance is less formal, an agency may accept comments after the comment period is closed. The agency should summarize these *ex parte* (private, off-the-record) comments for possible review.

> "In some respects matters of procedure constitute the very essence of ordered liberty under the Constitution."
> —WILEY B. RUTLEDGE, 1894–1949
> (Associate justice of the
> United States Supreme Court, 1943–1949)

The Final Rule   After the agency reviews the comments, it drafts the final rule and publishes it in the *Federal Register.* The final rule is later compiled with the rules and regulations of other federal administrative agencies in the *Code of Federal Regulations (C.F.R.).* Final rules have binding legal effect unless the courts later overturn them.

The court in the following case considered whether to enforce rules that were issued outside of the rulemaking procedure.

CASE 16.1 **Hemp Industries Association v. Drug Enforcement Administration**

United States Court of Appeals,
Ninth Circuit, 2004.
357 F.3d 1012.

BACKGROUND AND FACTS   The members of the Hemp Industries Association (HIA) import and distribute sterilized hemp seed and oil and cake derived from hemp seed, and make and sell food and cosmetic products made from hemp seed and oil. These products contain only nonpsychoactive trace amounts of tetrahydrocannabinols (THC).[a] On October

a. A *nonpsychoactive substance* is one that does not affect a person's mind or behavior. Nonpsychoactive hemp is derived from industrial hemp plants grown in Canada and Europe, the flowers of which contain only a trace amount of the THC contained in marijuana varieties grown for psychoactive use.

CASE 16.1—CONTINUED ➡

9, 2001, the U.S. Drug Enforcement Administration (DEA) published an interpretive rule declaring that "any product that contains any amount of THC is a Schedule I controlled substance."[b] On the same day, the DEA proposed two legislative rules. One rule—DEA-205F—amended the listing of THC in "Schedule I" to include natural, as well as synthetic,

THC. The second rule—DEA-206F—exempted from control nonpsychoactive hemp products that contain trace amounts of THC not intended to enter the human body. On March 21, 2003, without following formal rulemaking procedures, the DEA declared that these rules were final. This effectively banned the possession and sale of the food products of the HIA's members. The HIA petitioned the U.S. Court of Appeals for the Ninth Circuit to review the rules, asserting that they could not be enforced.

b. A *controlled substance* is a drug whose availability is restricted by law.

IN THE WORDS OF THE COURT . . . *BETTY B. FLETCHER*, Circuit Judge.

* * * *

* * * Appellants * * * argue that DEA-205F is a scheduling action—placing nonpsychoactive hemp in Schedule I for the first time—that fails to follow the procedures for such actions required by the Controlled Substances Act ("CSA"). * * *

* * * *

Under 21 U.S.C. [Section] 811(a) [of the CSA]:

the Attorney General may by rule—
(1) add to * * * a schedule * * * any drug or other substance if he—
* * *

(B) makes with respect to such drug or other substance the findings prescribed by subsection (b) of [S]ection 812 of this title * * * .

Rules of the Attorney General under this subsection shall be made on the record after opportunity for a hearing pursuant to the rulemaking procedures prescribed by [the Administrative Procedure Act (APA).]

* * * *Formal rulemaking requires hearings on the record, and [the APA] invites parties to submit proposed findings and oppose the stated bases of tentative agency decisions, and requires the agency to issue formal rulings on each finding, conclusion, or exception on the record.* We will not reproduce the entirety of the [APA] here; it suffices to say that the DEA did not and does not claim to have followed formal rulemaking procedures. [Emphasis added.]

In addition, the DEA did not comply with [Section] 811(a)(1)(B), because the findings required by [Section] 812(b) were not made. Section 812(b) states:

(b) Placement on schedules; findings required. * * * [A] drug or other substance may not be placed in any schedule unless the findings required for such schedule are made with respect to such drug or other substance.

* * * *

The DEA does not purport to have met the requirements for placement of nonpsychoactive hemp on Schedule I * * * . Instead, the DEA argues that naturally occurring THC in those parts of the hemp plant excluded from the definition of "marijuana" have always been included under the listing for "THC" * * * .

* * * *

Two CSA provisions are relevant to determining whether Appellants' hemp products were banned before [DEA-205F and DEA-206F]: the definition of THC and the definition of marijuana. Both are unambiguous * * * : Appellants' products do not contain the "synthetic" "substances or derivatives" that are covered by the definition of THC, and nonpsychoactive hemp is explicitly excluded from the definition of marijuana.

* * * *

CASE 16.1–CONTINUED Under 21 U.S.C. [Section] 802(16) [of the CSA]:

> The term "marihuana" means all parts of the plant *Cannabis sativa L.* * * * . Such term does not include the mature stalks of such plant, fiber produced from such stalks, oil or cake made from the seeds of such plant, any other compound, manufacture, salt, derivative, mixture, or preparation of such mature stalks (except the resin extracted therefrom), fiber, oil, or cake, or the sterilized seed of such plant which is incapable of germination.

The nonpsychoactive hemp in Appellants' products is derived from the "mature stalks" or is "oil and cake made from the seeds" of the Cannabis plant, and therefore fits within the plainly stated exception to the CSA definition of marijuana.

* * * Congress knew what it was doing, and its intent to exclude nonpsychoactive hemp from regulation is entirely clear.

DECISION AND REMEDY The U.S. Court of Appeals for the Ninth Circuit held that DEA-205F and DEA-206F "are inconsistent with the unambiguous meaning of the CSA definitions of marijuana and THC," and that the DEA did not follow the proper administrative procedures required to schedule a substance. The court issued an injunction against the enforcement of the rules with respect to nonpsychoactive hemp or products containing it.

FOR CRITICAL ANALYSIS–Social Consideration *Suppose that the statutory definitions of THC and marijuana covered naturally occurring THC and nonpsychoactive hemp. Would the result in this case have been different?*

Investigation

Administrative agencies conduct investigations of the entities that they regulate. Agencies investigate a wide range of activities, including coal mining, automobile manufacturing, and the industrial discharge of pollutants into the environment. A typical agency investigation occurs during the rulemaking process to obtain information about a certain individual, firm, or industry. The purpose of such an investigation is to avoid issuing a rule that is arbitrary and capricious and instead to issue a rule based on a consideration of relevant factors. After final rules are issued, agencies conduct investigations to monitor compliance with those rules. A typical agency investigation of this kind might begin when a citizen reports a possible violation.

Inspections and Tests Many agencies gather information through on-site inspections. Sometimes, inspecting an office, a factory, or some other business facility is the only way to obtain the evidence needed to prove a regulatory violation. At other times, an inspection or test is used in place of a formal hearing to show the need to correct or prevent an undesirable condition. Administrative inspections and tests cover a wide range of activities, including safety inspections of underground coal mines, safety tests of commercial equipment and automobiles, and environmental monitoring of factory emissions. An agency may also ask a firm or individual to submit certain documents or records to the agency for examination.

Normally, business firms comply with agency requests to inspect facilities or business records because it is in any firm's interest to maintain a good relationship with regulatory bodies. In some instances, however, such as when a firm thinks an agency's request is unreasonable and may be detrimental to the firm's interest, the firm may refuse to comply with the request. In such situations, an agency may resort to the use of a subpoena or a search warrant.

Subpoenas   There are two basic types of subpoenas. The subpoena *ad testificandum* ("to testify") is an ordinary subpoena. It is a writ, or order, compelling a witness to appear at an agency hearing. The subpoena *duces tecum* ("bring it with you") compels an individual or organization to hand over books, papers, records, or documents to the agency. An administrative agency may use either type of subpoena to obtain testimony or documents.

There are limits on what an agency can demand. To determine whether an agency is abusing its discretion in its pursuit of information as part of an investigation, a court may consider such factors as the following:

1. The purpose of the investigation. An investigation must have a legitimate purpose. An improper purpose is, for example, harassment. An agency may not issue an administrative subpoena to inspect business records if the agency's motive is to harass or pressure the business into settling an unrelated matter.
2. The relevancy of the information being sought. Information is relevant if it reveals that the law is being violated or if it assures the agency that the law is not being violated.
3. The specificity of the demand for testimony or documents. A subpoena must, for example, adequately describe the material being sought.
4. The burden of the demand on the party from whom the information is sought. In responding to a request for information, a party must bear the costs of, for example, copying the documents that must be handed over, but a business is generally protected from revealing information such as trade secrets.

In addition, a subpoena might not be enforced when the subject matter of an investigation is not within the authority of an agency to investigate. The issue in the following case was whether the subject matter of a certain subpoena issued by the National Labor Relations Board exceeded the agency's statutory authority.

CASE 16.2   National Labor Relations Board v. American Medical Response, Inc.

United States Court of Appeals,
Second Circuit, 2006.
438 F.3d 188.

BACKGROUND AND FACTS   American Medical Response, Inc. (AMR), provides ambulance service to cities and counties in fifteen states. AMR employs paramedics and emergency medical technicians (EMTs) at nearly fifty-five nonunionized facilities, including a facility in Bridgeport, Connecticut. The International Association of EMTs and Paramedics, SEIU/NAGE, AFL-CIO (the Union), began an organizing campaign in January 2003 at the Bridgeport location. In April, AMR's management announced a plan to set up "action teams" at all

of its nonunionized facilities. The teams would be "composed of supervisory and rank-and-file employees, whose purpose would be to discuss and develop improvements on a range of issues, such as employee safety and cash incentive awards." Employees would receive extra pay for serving on the teams. The Union filed a charge with the National Labor Relations Board (the Board), alleging that the offer of extra pay at the Bridgeport facility violated the National Labor Relations Act (NLRA). The Board issued a subpoena *duces tecum* that sought certain documents related to the action teams at all of AMR's nonunionized facilities and asked a federal district court to enforce the subpoena. The court ordered AMR to comply. AMR appealed to the U.S. Court of Appeals for the Second Circuit.

IN THE WORDS OF THE COURT . . . FEINBERG, Circuit Judge.

* * * *

AMR argues primarily that only AMR's offer to pay employees for participation in employee "action teams" * * * is under investigation, not the action teams themselves,

CASE 16.2–CONTINUED

and thus, the operation of action teams at other facilities is irrelevant to the investigation of that conduct. * * *

* * * *

* * * [T]he documents sought are relevant for two reasons. First, the Board's investigation of the * * * charge clearly requires its investigation of AMR's Bridgeport action teams, and the documents sought are relevant to that purpose. Second, the Board may extend its investigation of the * * * charge to AMR's action teams, regardless of location, as a closely related matter, and the documents sought are also relevant to that purpose.

As to the first reason why the documents sought by the * * * subpoena are relevant, it is clear that AMR's Bridgeport action teams, and not just the offer of compensation * * * , are properly a matter under investigation. The Union's * * * charge alleges that AMR violated the NLRA at its Bridgeport facility by "offering to pay employees for participation in employee *'action teams'* to improve the company." *Under * * * the NLRA it is unlawful for an employer to "dominate or interfere with the formation or administration of any labor organization or to contribute financial or other support to it."* * * * Thus, an investigation of whether an alleged offer to pay employees for their participation in the Bridgeport action teams violates [the NLRA] necessarily encompasses investigation of the Bridgeport action teams themselves to resolve the prior issue of whether they are "labor organizations" at all. [Emphasis added.]

The documents sought by the * * * subpoena are clearly relevant to that investigation. Determination of whether an entity is a "labor organization" within the meaning of * * * the NLRA requires examination of whether employees participate; whether the entity in question addresses grievances, labor disputes, wages, rates of pay, hours of employment, or conditions of work; and whether it has a purpose, in whole or in part, of dealing with the employer about the foregoing subject matters. While this is, as AMR contends, a fact-specific inquiry, AMR has implemented its action teams pursuant to a uniform, nationwide scheme. It is reasonable to expect that the operation of action teams at other AMR facilities pursuant to that scheme may shed light on the operation of the Bridgeport action teams and, in turn, aid the Board's investigation of whether they are "labor organizations."

The second reason why the documents sought by the * * * subpoena are relevant is that a charge serves merely to set in motion the investigatory machinery of the Board. In carrying out its investigation, the Board is not left *carte blanche* to expand the charge as it might please or to ignore the charge altogether. But because the Board was created not to adjudicate private controversies but to advance the public interest neither is the Board confined in its inquiry and in framing the complaint to the specific matters alleged in the charge. In issuing a complaint, the Board may properly include certain allegations closely related to the original charge. It follows that the Board's investigation may permissibly extend to certain closely related matters that may become the subject of its complaint.

We have little difficulty concluding that AMR's conduct generally with regard to its Bridgeport action teams may be a matter closely related to its offer of compensation. This conduct may similarly raise the possibility of unlawful "dominat[ion] or interfere[nce] with the formation or administration of any labor organization" in violation of * * * the NLRA. And because AMR's action teams are operated pursuant to a national scheme, AMR's conduct generally with regard to its action teams at other facilities may also be closely related. The documents sought by the * * * subpoena are therefore relevant for the further reason that they may shed light on the legality of AMR's action teams, a subject within the scope of the investigation * * * .

CASE 16.2–CONTINUED ▶

DECISION AND REMEDY   The U.S. Court of Appeals for the Second Circuit affirmed the lower court's order to enforce the Board's subpoena, which asked for certain documents related to AMR's action teams at its nonunionized facilities nationwide. The appellate court reasoned that the documents were relevant in more than one respect to the agency's investigation of unfair labor practices at the employer's facility in Bridgeport.

WHAT IF THE FACTS WERE DIFFERENT?   *Suppose that compliance with the agency's subpoena would have been unnecessarily burdensome for the employer. What might the court have ruled?*

Search Warrants   The Fourth Amendment protects against unreasonable searches and seizures by requiring that in most instances a physical search for evidence must be conducted under the authority of a search warrant. An agency's search warrant is an order directing law enforcement officials to search a specific place for a specific item and present it to the agency. Although it was once thought that administrative inspections were exempt from the warrant requirement, the United States Supreme Court held in *Marshall v. Barlow's, Inc.,*[3] that the requirement does apply to the administrative process.

Agencies can conduct warrantless searches in several situations. Warrants are not required to conduct searches in highly regulated industries. Firms that sell firearms or liquor, for example, are automatically subject to inspections without warrants. Sometimes, a statute permits warrantless searches of certain types of hazardous operations, such as coal mines. Also, a warrantless inspection in an emergency situation is normally considered reasonable.

Adjudication

After conducting an investigation of a suspected rule violation, an agency may begin to take administrative action against an individual or organization. Most administrative actions are resolved through negotiated settlements at their initial stages, without the need for formal **adjudication** (the resolution of the dispute through a hearing conducted by the agency).

ADJUDICATION
The act of rendering a judicial decision. In an administrative process, the proceeding in which an administrative law judge hears and decides on issues that arise when an administrative agency charges a person or a firm with violating a law or regulation enforced by the agency.

Formal Complaints and Hearings   If a settlement cannot be reached, the agency may issue a formal complaint against the suspected violator. **| Example #3** The Environmental Protection Agency (EPA) finds that Acme Manufacturing, Inc., is polluting groundwater in violation of federal pollution laws. The EPA issues a complaint against the violator in an effort to bring the plant into compliance with federal regulations.**|** This complaint is a public document, and a press release may accompany it. The party charged in the complaint responds by filing an answer to the allegations. If the charged party and the agency cannot agree on a settlement, the case will be adjudicated. Agency adjudication may involve a trial-like setting before an *administrative law judge (ALJ).*

The ALJ presides over the hearing and has the power to administer oaths, take testimony, rule on questions of evidence, and make determinations of fact. Although formally the ALJ works for the agency prosecuting the case, the law requires an ALJ to be an unbiased adjudicator (judge). Certain safeguards

---

3. 436 U.S. 307, 98 S.Ct. 1816, 56 L.Ed.2d 305 (1978).

prevent bias on the part of the ALJ and promote fairness in the proceedings. For example, the Administrative Procedure Act requires that the ALJ be separate from the agency's investigative and prosecutorial staff. The APA also prohibits *ex parte* (private, one-sided) communications between the ALJ and any party to an agency proceeding, including a party charged with a complaint and the agency itself. Finally, provisions of the APA protect the ALJ from agency disciplinary actions unless the agency can show good cause for such an action.

Hearing procedures vary widely from agency to agency. Administrative agencies generally can exercise substantial discretion over the type of hearing procedures that will be used. Frequently, disputes are resolved through informal adjudication proceedings. **│ Example #4** The Federal Trade Commission (FTC) charges Good Foods, Inc., with deceptive advertising. Representatives of Good Foods and of the FTC, their counsel, and the ALJ meet at a table in a conference room to resolve the dispute informally.│ A formal adjudicatory hearing, in contrast, resembles a trial in many respects. Prior to the hearing, the parties are permitted to undertake extensive discovery proceedings (involving depositions, interrogatories, and requests for documents or other information, as described in Chapter 3). During the hearing, the parties may give testimony, present other evidence, and cross-examine adverse witnesses. A significant difference between a trial and an administrative agency hearing, though, is that normally, much more information, including hearsay (secondhand information), can be introduced as evidence during an administrative hearing.

Agency Orders　Following a hearing, the ALJ renders an **initial order,** or decision, on the case. Either party can appeal the ALJ's decision, first to the board or commission that governs the agency and then, if still dissatisfied, to a federal appeals court. If no party appeals the case, the ALJ's decision becomes the **final order** of the agency. If a party does appeal the case, the final order comes from the commission's decision or that of the reviewing court. If a party appeals and the commission and the court decline to review the case, the ALJ's decision also becomes final.

LIMITATIONS ON AGENCY POWERS

Combining the functions normally divided among the three branches of government into an administrative agency concentrates considerable power in a single organization. Because of this concentration of authority, one of the major policy objectives of the government is to control the risks of arbitrariness and overreaching by administrative agencies without hindering the effective use of agency power to deal with particular problem areas, as Congress intends.

The judicial branch of the government exercises control over agency powers through the courts' review of agency actions. The executive and legislative branches also exercise control over agency authority.

Judicial Controls

The APA provides for judicial review of most agency decisions. As discussed above, if a charged party is dissatisfied with an agency's order, it can appeal the decision to a federal appeals court. Agency actions are not automatically

INITIAL ORDER
In the context of administrative law, an agency's disposition in a matter other than a rulemaking. An administrative law judge's initial order becomes final unless it is appealed.

FINAL ORDER
The final decision of an administrative agency on an issue. If no appeal is taken, or if the case is not reviewed or considered anew by the agency commission, the administrative law judge's initial order becomes the final order of the agency.

subject to judicial review, however. Parties seeking review must demonstrate that they meet certain requirements, including those listed here:

1. The action must be *reviewable* by the court. The APA creates a presumption that agency actions are reviewable, making this requirement easy to satisfy.
2. The party must have *standing to sue* the agency (the party must have a direct stake in the outcome of the judicial proceeding).
3. The party must have *exhausted all possible administrative remedies*. Each agency has its chain of review, and the party must follow agency appeal procedures before a court will deem that administrative remedies have been exhausted.
4. There must be an *actual controversy* at issue. Courts will not review cases before it is necessary to decide them.

Recall from Chapter 3 that appellate courts normally defer to the decisions of trial courts on questions of fact. In reviewing administrative actions, the courts are similarly reluctant to review the factual findings of agencies. In most cases, the courts accept the facts as found in the agency proceedings. Normally, when a court reviews an administrative agency decision, the court considers the following types of issues:

1. Whether the agency has exceeded its authority under its enabling legislation.
2. Whether the agency has properly interpreted laws applicable to the agency action under review.
3. Whether the agency has violated any constitutional provisions.
4. Whether the agency has acted in accordance with procedural requirements of the law.
5. Whether the agency's actions were arbitrary, capricious, or an abuse of discretion.
6. Whether any conclusions drawn by the agency are not supported by substantial evidence.

In the following case, the Cellular Telecommunications & Internet Association and others asked a court to review an order of the Federal Communications Commission (FCC) relating to the enforcement of an FCC rule. The court considered how the FCC interpreted and applied a phrase in the Telecommunications Act of 1996 when the agency issued its order.

CASE 16.3   **Cellular Telecommunications & Internet Association v. Federal Communications Commission**

United States Court of Appeals,
District of Columbia Circuit, 2003.
330 F.3d 502.
www.findlaw.com/casecode/courts/dc.html[a]

HISTORICAL AND TECHNOLOGICAL SETTING Congress enacted the Telecommunications Act of 1996 to "promote competition and reduce regulation in order to secure lower prices and higher quality services for American

telecommunications consumers and encourage the rapid deployment of new telecommunications technologies." The act directs the Federal Communications Commission (FCC) to "forbear from applying any regulation * * * if the [FCC] determines that * * * enforcement * * * is not necessary for the protection of consumers."[b] At the time, a wireless telephone customer who wished to switch from one wireless service provider to another also had to change phone numbers.

a. In the "By Date" section, select "2003" and "June." Click on "search." In the list of results, click on "Cell Telecom v. FCC" to access the opinion.

b. 47 U.S.C. Section 160(a).

CASE 16.3–CONTINUED

BACKGROUND AND FACTS In 1996, the FCC issued rules that required wireless service providers to offer number portability[c] by June 30, 1999. In 1999, the FCC granted a request from the Cellular Telecommunications & Internet Association (CTIA) and others that the FCC temporarily refrain from enforcing these rules and extended the deadline to November 24, 2002 (later extended again to November 24, 2003), partly because the industry needed more time to develop its technology. The FCC issued an order refusing to permanently refrain from enforcing the rules, however, on finding that consumers would otherwise be "forced to stay with carriers with whom they may be dissatisfied," due to price, service, or coverage, "because the cost of giving up their wireless phone number in order to move to another carrier is too high." The CTIA and others filed a suit against the FCC in the U.S. Court of Appeals for the District of Columbia Circuit for a review of this order. The plaintiffs argued, in part, that the FCC misinterpreted and misapplied the statutory phrase requiring the agency to forbear (refrain) from enforcing its regulations if "enforcement * * * is not necessary for the protection of consumers."

c. *Number portability* is the ability of consumers to retain their phone numbers when they switch carriers.

IN THE WORDS OF THE COURT . . . *HARRY T. EDWARDS*, Circuit Judge.

* * * *

Petitioners' challenge to the Commission's [order] centers on the meaning of the statutory term "necessary." Petitioners contend that * * * the Commission erred in failing to construe "necessary" to mean "absolutely required," "indispensable," or "essential." Petitioners' position is that the Commission must forbear from enforcement of its wireless number portability rules if enforcement is not *absolutely required* to protect consumers. Petitioners argue that enforcement of the wireless number portability rules is not absolutely required to protect consumers * * * .

* * * *

[In the context of this case], *application of petitioners' definition of "necessary" would lead to an absurd result, because it is difficult to imagine a regulation whose enforcement is absolutely required or indispensable to protect consumers.* Indeed, when counsel for petitioners was questioned about this, he could not give a viable example of a "necessary" regulation. None. In the forbearance context, we think that it would defy common sense to adopt a construction of "necessary" that results in a criterion that can never be met. What would follow is that every regulation would, strictly speaking, be "not necessary for the protection of consumers." * * * The Commission always would be required to forbear from enforcement * * * . [Emphasis added.]

Adopting petitioners' rigid construction of "necessary" in the forbearance context would result in a further absurdity. Under petitioners' view, the FCC, which is permitted to promulgate regulations * * * , could be required, the very next day, to forbear from enforcement of the same regulations, because the unattainable criterion of "necessary" cannot be met. * * *

* * * *

* * * [W]e find the Commission's interpretation of "necessary" eminently reasonable. In the forbearance context, for the reasons already stated, it is reasonable to construe "necessary" as referring to the existence of a strong connection between what the agency has done by way of regulation and what the agency permissibly sought to achieve with the disputed regulation. In other words, the number portability rules are required to achieve the desired goal of consumer protection. That is essentially the definition of "necessary" that the Commission embraced and applied in its Order. We therefore find that deference to the agency's reasonable interpretation * * * is appropriate.

CASE 16.3–CONTINUED ▶

DECISION AND REMEDY The U.S. Court of Appeals for the District of Columbia Circuit dismissed the plaintiffs' challenge to the FCC's decision not to forbear from enforcing its number portability rules. The court concluded that the FCC's interpretation of the term *necessary* was reasonable. The FCC applied this interpretation to find that the number portability rules were required to achieve the goal of consumer protection.

FOR CRITICAL ANALYSIS–Social Consideration *On what basis might an agency decide that a temporary forbearance from the enforcement of a rule is justified while a permanent forbearance is not?*

Executive Controls

The executive branch of government exercises control over agencies both through the president's powers to appoint federal officers and through the president's veto powers. The president can veto enabling legislation presented by Congress or congressional attempts to modify an existing agency's authority.

Legislative Controls

Congress also exercises authority over agency powers. Through enabling legislation, Congress gives power to an agency. Of course, an agency cannot exceed the power that Congress delegates to it. Through subsequent legislation, Congress can take away that power or even abolish an agency altogether. Legislative authority is required to fund an agency, and enabling legislation usually sets certain time and monetary limits relating to the funding of particular programs. Congress can always revise these limits.

In addition to its power to create and fund agencies, Congress has the authority to investigate the implementation of its laws and the agencies that it has created. Individual legislators may also affect agency policy through their casework activities, which involve attempts to help their constituents deal with agencies.

Congress also has the power to "freeze" the enforcement of most federal regulations before the regulations take effect. Under the Small Business Regulatory Enforcement Fairness Act of 1996,[4] all federal agencies must submit final rules to Congress before the rules become effective. If, within sixty days, Congress passes a joint resolution of disapproval concerning a rule, enforcement of the regulation is frozen while the rule is reviewed by congressional committees.

Other legislative checks on agency actions include the Administrative Procedure Act, discussed earlier in this chapter, and the laws discussed in the next section.

PUBLIC ACCOUNTABILITY

As a result of growing public concern over the powers exercised by administrative agencies, Congress passed several laws to make agencies more accountable through public scrutiny. We discuss here the most significant of these laws.

---

4. 5 U.S.C. Sections 801–808.

Freedom of Information Act

Enacted in 1966, the Freedom of Information Act (FOIA)[5] requires the federal government to disclose certain records to any person on request, even without any reason being given for the request. The FOIA exempts certain types of records. For other records, though, a request that complies with the FOIA procedures need only contain a reasonable description of the information sought. An agency's failure to comply with such a request can be challenged in a federal district court. The media, industry trade associations, public-interest groups, and even companies seeking information about competitors rely on these FOIA provisions to obtain information from government agencies.

> "Law . . . is a human institution, created by human agents to serve human ends."
>
> —HARLAN F. STONE, 1872–1946
> (Chief justice of the United States Supreme Court, 1941–1946)

Government in the Sunshine Act

Congress passed the Government in the Sunshine Act,[6] or open meeting law, in 1976. It requires that "every portion of every meeting of an agency" be open to "public observation." The act also requires procedures to ensure that the public is provided with adequate advance notice of the agency's scheduled meeting and agenda. Like the FOIA, the Sunshine Act contains certain exceptions. Closed meetings are permitted when (1) the subject of the meeting concerns accusing any person of a crime, (2) open meetings would frustrate implementation of future agency actions, or (3) the subject of the meeting involves matters relating to future litigation or rulemaking. Courts interpret these exceptions to allow open access whenever possible.

Regulatory Flexibility Act

Concern over the effects of regulation on the efficiency of businesses, particularly smaller ones, led Congress to pass the Regulatory Flexibility Act in 1980.[7] Under this act, whenever a new regulation will have a "significant impact upon a substantial number of small entities," the agency must conduct a regulatory flexibility analysis. The analysis must measure the cost that the rule would impose on small businesses and must consider less burdensome alternatives. The act also contains provisions to alert small businesses about forthcoming regulations. The act relieved small businesses of some record-keeping burdens, especially with regard to hazardous waste management.

Small Business Regulatory Enforcement Fairness Act

As mentioned above, the Small Business Regulatory Enforcement Fairness Act (SBREFA) of 1996 allows Congress to review new federal regulations for at least sixty days before they take effect. This period gives opponents of the rules time to present their arguments to Congress.

The SBREFA also authorizes the courts to enforce the Regulatory Flexibility Act. This helps to ensure that federal agencies, such as the Internal Revenue Service, consider ways to reduce the economic impact of new regulations on small businesses. Federal agencies are required to prepare guides that explain in plain English how small businesses can comply with federal regulations.

---

5. 5 U.S.C. Section 552.
6. 5 U.S.C. Section 552b.
7. 5 U.S.C. Sections 601–612.

At the Small Business Administration, the SBREFA set up the National Enforcement Ombudsman to receive comments from small businesses about their dealings with federal agencies. Based on these comments, Regional Small Business Fairness Boards rate the agencies and publicize their findings.

Finally, the SBREFA allows small businesses to recover their expenses and legal fees from the government when an agency makes demands for fines or penalties that a court considers excessive.

STATE ADMINISTRATIVE AGENCIES

Although much of this chapter deals with federal administrative agencies, state agencies also play a significant role in regulating activities within the states. Many of the factors that encouraged the proliferation of federal agencies also fostered the growing presence of state agencies. For example, reasons for the growth of administrative agencies at all levels of government include the inability of Congress and state legislatures to oversee the actual implementation of their laws and the greater technical competence of the agencies.

Commonly, a state creates an agency as a parallel to a federal agency to provide similar services on a more localized basis. For example, a state department of public welfare shoulders some of the same responsibilities at the state level as the Social Security Administration does at the federal level. A state pollution-control agency parallels the federal Environmental Protection Agency. Not all federal agencies have parallel state agencies, however. For example, the Central Intelligence Agency has no parallel agency at the state level.

If the actions of parallel state and federal agencies conflict, the actions of the federal agency will prevail. **| Example #5** The Federal Aviation Administration (FAA) specifies the hours during which airplanes may land at and depart from airports. A California state agency issues inconsistent regulations governing the same activities. In a proceeding initiated by Interstate Distribution Corporation, an air transport company, to challenge the state rules, the FAA regulations would be held to prevail.**|** The priority of federal law over conflicting state laws is based on the supremacy clause of the U.S. Constitution. This clause, which is found in Article VI of the Constitution, states that the Constitution and "the Laws of the United States which shall be made in Pursuance thereof . . . shall be the supreme Law of the Land."

REVIEWING . . . POWERS AND FUNCTIONS OF ADMINISTRATIVE AGENCIES

Assume that the Securities and Exchange Commission (SEC) has a rule that it will enforce statutory provisions prohibiting insider trading only when the insiders make monetary profits for themselves. Then the SEC makes a new rule, declaring that it has the statutory authority to bring an enforcement action against an individual even if she or he does not personally profit from the insider trading.

In making the new rule, the SEC does not conduct a rulemaking proceeding but simply announces its new decision. A stockbrokerage firm objects and says that the new rule was unlawfully developed without opportunity for public comment. The brokerage firm challenges the rule in an action that ultimately is reviewed by a federal appellate court. Using the information presented in the chapter, answer the following questions.

1. Is the SEC an executive agency or an independent regulatory agency? Explain.

2. Is the SEC's new rule a legislative rule or an interpretive rule? Why?

3. Under the Administrative Procedure Act, was the SEC required to follow notice-and-comment rule-making procedures when making the new rule? Why or why not?

4. Assuming that the SEC has not exceeded its authority, will the reviewing court be likely to conclude that the SEC's conduct in enacting the new rule was arbitrary and capricious? Why or why not?

KEY TERMS

adjudication   542
administrative process   535
bureaucracy   535
delegation doctrine   534

enabling legislation   533
final order   543
initial order   543
judicial process   536

legislative rule   534
notice-and-comment
  rulemaking   537
rulemaking   536

CHAPTER SUMMARY • POWERS AND FUNCTIONS OF ADMINISTRATIVE AGENCIES

Agency Creation and Powers (See pages 533–535.)	1. Under the U.S. Constitution, Congress can delegate the task of implementing its laws to government agencies. By delegating the task, Congress can indirectly monitor an area in which it has passed legislation without becoming bogged down in details relating to enforcement of the legislation.
	2. Administrative agencies are created by enabling legislation, which usually specifies the name, composition, and powers of the agency.
	3. Administrative agencies exercise enforcement, rulemaking, and adjudicatory powers.
Administrative Process—Rulemaking (See pages 536–539.)	1. Agencies are authorized to create new regulations—their rulemaking function. This power is conferred on an agency in the enabling legislation.
	2. Agencies can create legislative rules, which are as important as formal acts of Congress.
	3. Notice-and-comment rulemaking is the most common rulemaking procedure. It begins with the publication of the proposed regulation in the *Federal Register*. Publication of the notice is followed by a comment period to allow private parties to comment on the proposed rule.
Administrative Process—Investigation (See pages 539–542.)	1. Administrative agencies investigate the entities that they regulate. Investigations are conducted during the rulemaking process to obtain information and after rules are issued to monitor compliance.
	2. The most important investigative tools available to an agency are the following:
	a. Inspections and tests—Used to gather information and to correct or prevent undesirable conditions.
	b. Subpoenas—Orders that direct individuals to appear at a hearing or to hand over specified documents.
	3. Limits on administrative investigations include the following:
	a. The investigation must be for a legitimate purpose.
	b. The information sought must be relevant, and the investigative demands must be specific and not unreasonably burdensome.
	c. The Fourth Amendment protects companies and individuals from unreasonable searches and seizures by requiring search warrants in most instances.

(Continued)

CHAPTER SUMMARY • POWERS AND FUNCTIONS OF ADMINISTRATIVE AGENCIES—CONTINUED

Administrative Process—Adjudication (See pages 542–543.)	1. After a preliminary investigation, an agency may initiate an administrative action against an individual or organization by filing a complaint. Most such actions are resolved at this stage before they go through the formal adjudicatory process.
	2. If there is no settlement, the case is presented to an administrative law judge (ALJ) in a proceeding similar to a trial.
	3. After a case is concluded, the ALJ renders an initial order, which can be appealed by either party to the board or commission that governs the agency and ultimately to a federal appeals court. If no appeal is taken or the case is not reviewed, then the order becomes the final order of the agency. The charged party may be ordered to pay damages or to stop carrying on some specified activity.
Limitations on Agency Powers (See pages 543–546.)	1. *Judicial controls*—Administrative agencies are subject to the judicial review of the courts. For example, a court may review whether an agency has exceeded the scope of its enabling legislation or has properly interpreted the laws.
	2. *Executive controls*—The president can control administrative agencies through appointments of federal officers and through vetoes of legislation creating or affecting agency powers.
	3. *Legislative controls*—Congress can give power to an agency, take it away, increase or decrease the agency's funding, or abolish the agency. The Administrative Procedure Act of 1946 also limits agencies.
Public Accountability (See pages 546–548.)	Congress has passed several laws to make agencies more accountable through public scrutiny. These laws include the Freedom of Information Act of 1966, the Government in the Sunshine Act of 1976, the Regulatory Flexibility Act of 1980, and the Small Business Regulatory Enforcement Fairness Act of 1996.
State Administrative Agencies (See page 548.)	States create agencies that parallel federal agencies to provide similar services on a more localized basis. If the actions of parallel state and federal agencies conflict, the actions of the federal agency will prevail.

FOR REVIEW

Answers for the even-numbered questions in this For Review *section can be found in Appendix O at the end of this text.*

1. How are federal administrative agencies created?

2. What are the three operations that make up the basic functions of most administrative agencies?

3. What sequence of events must normally occur before an agency rule becomes law?

4. How do administrative agencies enforce their rules?

5. How do the three branches of government limit the power of administrative agencies?

QUESTIONS AND CASE PROBLEMS

16–1. Rulemaking and Adjudication Powers. For decades, the Federal Trade Commission (FTC) resolved fair trade and advertising disputes through individual adjudications. In the 1960s, the FTC began promulgating rules that defined fair and unfair trade practices. In cases involving violations of these rules, the due process rights of participants were more limited and did not include cross-examination. This was because, although anyone found violating a rule would receive a full adjudication, the legitimacy of the rule itself could not be challenged in the adjudication. Any party charged with violating a rule was almost certain to lose the adjudication. Affected parties complained to a court, arguing

that their rights before the FTC were unduly limited by the new rules. What will the court examine to determine whether to uphold the new rules?

Question with Sample Answer

16–2. Assume that the Food and Drug Administration (FDA), using proper procedures, adopts a rule describing its future investigations. This new rule covers all future circumstances in which the FDA wants to regulate food additives. Under the new rule, the FDA is not to regulate food additives without giving food companies an opportunity to cross-examine witnesses. At a subsequent time, the FDA wants to regulate methylisocyanate, a food additive. The FDA undertakes an informal rulemaking procedure, without cross-examination, and regulates methylisocyanate. Producers protest, saying that the FDA promised them the opportunity for cross-examination. The FDA responds that the Administrative Procedure Act does not require such cross-examination and that it is free to withdraw the promise made in its new rule. If the producers challenge the FDA in court, on what basis would the court rule in their favor?

For a sample answer to this question, go to Appendix P at the end of this text.

16–3. Executive Controls. In 1982, the president of the United States appointed Matthew Chabal, Jr., to the position of U.S. marshal. U.S. marshals are assigned to the federal courts. In the fall of 1985, Chabal received an unsatisfactory annual performance rating, and he was fired shortly thereafter by the president. Given that U.S. marshals are assigned to the federal courts, are these appointees members of the executive branch? Did the president have the right to fire Chabal without consulting Congress about the decision? [*Chabal v. Reagan,* 841 F.2d 1216 (3d Cir. 1988)]

16–4. Investigation. In 1990, Maureen Droge began working for United Air Lines, Inc. (UAL), as a flight attendant. In 1995, she was assigned to Paris, France, where she became pregnant. Because UAL does not allow its flight attendants to fly during their third trimester of pregnancy, Droge was placed on involuntary leave. She applied for temporary disability benefits through the French social security system, but her request was denied because UAL does not contribute to the French system on behalf of its U.S.-based flight attendants. Droge filed a charge of discrimination with the U.S. Equal Employment Opportunity Commission (EEOC), alleging that UAL had discriminated against her and other Americans. The EEOC issued a subpoena, asking UAL to detail all benefits received by all UAL employees living outside the United States. UAL refused to provide the information, in part on the grounds that it was irrelevant and compliance would be unduly burdensome. The EEOC filed a suit in a federal district court against UAL. Should the court enforce the subpoena? Why or why not? [*Equal Employment Opportunity Commission v. United Air Lines, Inc.,* 287 F.3d 643 (7th Cir. 2002)]

16–5. *Ex Parte* Comments. In 1976, the Environmental Protection Agency (EPA) proposed a rule establishing new standards for coal-fired steam generators. The agency gave notice and received comments in the manner prescribed by the Administrative Procedure Act. After the public comments had been received, the EPA received informal comments from members of Congress and other federal officials. In 1979, the EPA published its final standards. Several environmental groups protested these standards, arguing that they were too lax. As part of this protest, the groups complained that political influence from Congress and other federal officials had

encouraged the EPA to relax the proposed standards. The groups went on to argue that the *ex parte* comments of the government officials were themselves illegal or that the comments should at least have been summarized in the record. What will the court decide? Discuss fully. [*Sierra Club v. Costle,* 657 F.2d 298 (D.C.Cir. 1981)]

16–6. Judicial Review. American Message Centers (AMC) provides answering services to retailers. Calls to a retailer are automatically forwarded to AMC, which pays for the calls. AMC obtains telephone service at a discount from major carriers, including Sprint. Sprint's tariff (a public document setting out rates and rules relating to Sprint's services) states that the "subscriber shall be responsible for the payment of all charges for service." When AMC learned that computer hackers had obtained the access code for AMC's lines and had made long-distance calls costing nearly $160,000, it asked Sprint to absorb the charges. Sprint refused. AMC filed a complaint with the Federal Communications Commission (FCC), claiming in part that Sprint's tariff was vague and ambiguous, in violation of the Communications Act of 1934 and FCC rules. These laws require that a carrier's tariff "clearly and definitely" specify any "exceptions or conditions which in any way affect the rates named in the tariff." The FCC rejected AMC's complaint. AMC appealed the FCC's decision to a federal appellate court, claiming that the FCC's decision to reject AMC's complaint was arbitrary and capricious. What should the court decide? Discuss fully. [*American Message Centers v. Federal Communications Commission,* 50 F.3d 35 (D.C.Cir. 1995)]

16–7. Arbitrary and Capricious Test. Lion Raisins, Inc., is a family-owned, family-operated business that grows and markets raisins to private enterprises. In the 1990s, Lion also successfully bid on more than fifteen contracts awarded by the U.S. Department of Agriculture (USDA). In May 1999, a USDA investigation reported that Lion appeared to have falsified inspectors' signatures, given false moisture content, and changed the grade of raisins on three USDA raisin certificates issued between 1996 and 1998. Lion was subsequently awarded five more USDA contracts. Then, in November 2000, the company was the low bidder on two new USDA contracts for school lunch programs. In January 2001, however, the USDA awarded these contracts to other bidders and, on the basis of the May 1999 report, suspended Lion from participating in government contracts for one year. Lion filed a suit in the U.S. Court of Federal Claims against the USDA, seeking, in part, lost profits on the school lunch contracts on the ground that the USDA's suspension was arbitrary and capricious. On what reasoning might the court grant a summary judgment in Lion's favor? [*Lion Raisins, Inc. v. United States,* 51 Fed.Cl. 238 (2001)]

Case Problem with Sample Answer

16–8. Riverdale Mills Corp. makes plastic-coated steel wire products in Northbridge, Massachusetts. Riverdale uses a water-based cleaning process that generates acidic and alkaline wastewater. To meet federal clean-water requirements, Riverdale has a system within its plant to treat the water. It then flows through a pipe that opens into a manhole-covered test pit outside the plant in full view of Riverdale's employees. Three hundred feet away, the pipe merges into the public sewer system. In October 1997, the U.S. Environmental Protection Agency (EPA) sent Justin Pimpare and Daniel Granz to inspect the plant. Without a search warrant and without Riverdale's express consent, the agents took samples from the test pit. Based on the samples, Riverdale and James Knott, the company's owner, were charged with criminal violations of the federal Clean Water Act. The defendants filed a suit in a federal district court against the EPA agents and others, alleging violations of the Fourth Amendment. What right does the Fourth Amendment provide in this context? This right is based on a "reasonable expectation of privacy." Should the agents be held liable? Why or why not? [*Riverdale Mills Corp. v. Pimpare*, 392 F.3d 55 (1st Cir. 2004)]

After you have answered this problem, compare your answer with the sample answer given on the Web site that accompanies this text. Go to www.thomsonedu.com/westbuslaw/let, select "Chapter 16," and click on "Case Problem with Sample Answer."

16–9. Rulemaking. The Investment Company Act of 1940 prohibits a mutual fund from engaging in certain transactions in which there may be a conflict of interest between the manager of the fund and its shareholders. Under rules issued by the Securities and Exchange Commission (SEC), however, a fund that meets certain conditions may engage in an otherwise prohibited transaction. In June 2004, the SEC added two new conditions. A year later, the SEC reconsidered the new conditions in terms of the costs that they would impose on the funds. Within eight days, and without asking for public input, the SEC readopted the conditions. The Chamber of Commerce of the United States—which is both a mutual fund shareholder and an association with mutual fund managers among its members—asked the U.S. Court of Appeals for the Second Circuit to review the new rules. The Chamber charged, in part, that in readopting the rules, the SEC relied on materials not in the "rulemaking record" without providing an opportunity for public comment. The SEC countered that the information was otherwise "publicly available." In adopting a rule, should an agency consider information that is not part of the rulemaking record? Why or why not? [*Chamber of Commerce of the United States v. Securities and Exchange Commission*, 443 F.3d 890 (D.C.Cir. 2006)]

A Question of Ethics

16–10. The Marine Mammal Protection Act was enacted in 1972 to reduce incidental killing and injury of marine mammals during commercial fishing operations. Under the act,

commercial fishing vessels are required to allow an employee of the National Oceanic and Atmospheric Administration (NOAA) to accompany the vessels to conduct research and observe operations. In December 1986, after NOAA had adopted a new policy of recruiting female as well as male observers, NOAA notified Caribbean Marine Services Co. that female observers would be assigned to accompany two of the company's fishing vessels on their next voyages. The owners and crew members of the ships (the plaintiffs) moved for an injunction against the implementation of the NOAA directive. The plaintiffs contended that the presence of a female onboard a fishing vessel would be very awkward, because the female would have to share the crew's quarters, and crew members enjoyed little or no privacy with respect to bodily functions. Further, they alleged that the presence of a female would be disruptive to fishing operations, because some of the crew members were "crude" men with little formal education who might harass or sexually assault a female observer, and the officers would therefore have to devote time to protecting the female from the crew. Finally, the plaintiffs argued that the presence of a female observer could destroy morale and distract the crew, thus affecting the crew's efficiency and decreasing the vessel's profits. [*Caribbean Marine Services Co. v. Baldrige*, 844 F.2d 668 (9th Cir. 1988)]

1. In general, do you think that the public policy of promoting equal employment opportunity should override the concerns of the vessel owners and crew? If you were the judge, would you grant the injunction? Why or why not?

2. The plaintiffs pointed out that fishing voyages could last three months or longer. Would the length of a particular voyage affect your answer to the preceding question?

3. The plaintiffs contended that even if the indignity of sharing bunk rooms and toilet facilities with a female observer could be overcome, the observer's very presence in the common areas of the vessel, such as the dining area, would unconstitutionally infringe on the crew members' right to privacy in these areas. Evaluate this claim.

Critical-Thinking Legal Question

16–11. Does Congress delegate too much power to federal administrative agencies? Do the courts defer too much to Congress in its grant of power to those agencies? What are the alternatives to the agencies that we encounter in every facet of our lives?

INTERACTING WITH THE INTERNET

For updated links to resources available on the Web, as well as a variety of other materials, visit this text's Web site at

www.thomsonedu.com/westbuslaw/let

To view the text of the Administrative Procedure Act of 1946, go to

www.archives.gov/federal-register/laws/administrative-procedure

The Internet Law Library contains links to federal and state regulatory materials, including the *Code of Federal Regulations*. This page can be found at

www.lawguru.com/ilawlib

INTERNET EXERCISES

Go to **www.thomsonedu.com/westbuslaw/let**, the Web site that accompanies this text. Select "Chapter 16" and click on "Internet Exercises." There you will find the following Internet research exercises that you can perform to learn more about topics covered in this chapter.

Internet Exercise 16–1: LEGAL PERSPECTIVE—The Freedom of Information Act
Internet Exercise 16–2: MANAGEMENT PERSPECTIVE—Agency Inspections

BEFORE THE TEST

Go to **www.thomsonedu.com/westbuslaw/let**, the Web site that accompanies this text. Select "Chapter 16" and click on "Interactive Quizzes." You will find a number of interactive questions relating to this chapter.

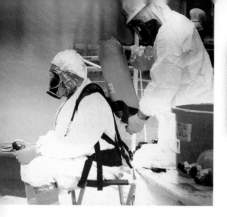

CHAPTER
17 Consumer Protection

CHAPTER OBJECTIVES

After reading this chapter, you should be able to answer the following questions:

1   **When will advertising be deemed deceptive?**

2   **What special rules apply to telephone solicitation?**

3   **What is Regulation Z, and to what type of transactions does it apply?**

4   **How does the Federal Food, Drug and Cosmetic Act protect consumers?**

5   **What are the major federal statutes providing for consumer protection in credit transactions?**

> "Subject to specific constitutional limitations, when the legislature has spoken, the public interest has been declared in terms well nigh conclusive."
>
> —WILLIAM O. DOUGLAS, 1898–1980
> (Associate justice of the United States Supreme Court, 1939–1975)

THE "PUBLIC INTEREST" referred to by Justice William O. Douglas in the chapter-opening quotation was evident during the 1960s and 1970s in what has come to be known as the consumer movement. Some have labeled the 1960s and 1970s "the age of the consumer" because so much legislation was passed to protect consumers against purportedly unsafe products and unfair practices of sellers. Since the 1980s, the impetus driving the consumer movement has lessened, to a great extent because so many of its goals have been achieved. *Consumer law* consists of all of the statutes, administrative agency rules, and judicial decisions that serve to protect the interests of consumers.

In the first part of this chapter, we examine some of the sources and some of the major issues of consumer protection. Sources of consumer protection exist at all levels of government. At the federal level, a number of laws have been passed to define the duties of sellers and the rights of consumers. Federal administrative agencies, such as the Federal Trade Commission (FTC), also provide an important source of consumer protection. Nearly every agency and department of the federal government has an office of consumer affairs, and most states have one or more such offices, including the offices of state attorneys general, to assist consumers.

Because of the wide variation among state consumer protection laws, our primary focus here will be on federal legislation—specifically, on legislation governing deceptive advertising, telemarketing and electronic advertising, labeling and packaging, sales, health protection, product safety, and credit protection. Realize, though, that state laws often provide more sweeping and significant protections for the consumer than do federal laws. State consumer protection laws will be discussed at the end of this chapter.

ADVERTISING

One of the earliest—and still one of the most important—federal consumer protection laws is the Federal Trade Commission Act of 1914 (mentioned in Chapter 16). The act created the FTC to carry out the broadly stated goal of preventing unfair and deceptive trade practices, including deceptive advertising, within the meaning of Section 5 of the act. We look here at deceptive advertising and at laws regulating telemarketing and electronic advertising.

Deceptive Advertising

Generally, **deceptive advertising** occurs if a reasonable consumer would be misled by the advertising claim. Vague generalities and obvious exaggerations are permissible. These claims are known as *puffery*. Recall from Chapter 10 that puffery consists of statements about a product that a reasonable person would not believe to be true. When a claim takes on the appearance of literal authenticity, however, it may create problems. Advertising that *appears* to be based on factual evidence but in fact is scientifically untrue will be deemed deceptive. A classic example occurred in a 1944 case in which the claim that a skin cream would restore youthful qualities to aged skin was deemed deceptive.[1]

Some advertisements contain "half-truths," meaning that the presented information is true but incomplete and, therefore, leads consumers to a false conclusion. **| Example #1** The makers of Campbell's soups advertised that "most" Campbell's soups were low in fat and cholesterol and thus were helpful in fighting heart disease. What the ad did not say was that Campbell's soups were high in sodium, and high-sodium diets may increase the risk of heart disease. The FTC ruled that Campbell's claims were thus deceptive.**|** Advertising that contains an endorsement by a celebrity may be deemed deceptive if the celebrity does not actually use the product.

Bait-and-Switch Advertising The FTC has issued rules that govern specific advertising techniques. One of the most important rules is contained in the FTC's "Guides on Bait Advertising."[2] The rule is designed to prevent **bait-and-switch advertising**—that is, advertising a very low price for a particular item that will likely be unavailable to the consumer and then encouraging him or her to purchase a more expensive item. The low price is the "bait" to lure the consumer into the store. The salesperson is instructed to "switch" the consumer to a different, more expensive item. According to the FTC guidelines, bait-and-switch advertising occurs if the seller refuses to show the advertised item, fails to have reasonable quantities of it available, fails to promise to deliver the advertised item within a reasonable time, or discourages employees from selling the item.

Online Deceptive Advertising Deceptive advertising may occur in the online environment as well. For several years, the FTC has actively monitored online advertising and has identified hundreds of Web sites that have made false or deceptive advertising claims for products ranging from medical treatments for various diseases to exercise equipment and weight-loss aids.

DECEPTIVE ADVERTISING
Advertising that misleads consumers, either by unjustified claims concerning a product's performance or by the omission of a material fact concerning the product's composition or performance.

BAIT-AND-SWITCH ADVERTISING
Advertising a product at a very attractive price (the "bait") and then, once the consumer is in the store, saying that the advertised product is either not available or is of poor quality; the customer is then urged to purchase ("switched" to) a more expensive item.

---

1. *Charles of the Ritz Distributing Corp. v. Federal Trade Commission*, 143 F.2d 676 (2d Cir. 1944).
2. 16 C.F.R. Section 288.

In 2000, the FTC issued new guidelines to help online businesses comply with existing laws prohibiting deceptive advertising.[3] The guidelines did not set forth new rules but rather described how existing laws apply to online advertising. Generally, the rules emphasize that any ads—online or offline—must be truthful and not misleading and that any claims made in any ads must be substantiated. Additionally, ads cannot be unfair, defined in the guidelines as "caus[ing] or . . . likely to cause substantial consumer injury that consumers could not reasonably avoid and that is not outweighed by the benefit to consumers or competition."

The guidelines also call for "clear and conspicuous" disclosure of any qualifying or limiting information. The FTC suggests that advertisers should assume that consumers will not read an entire Web page. Therefore, to satisfy the "clear and conspicuous" requirement, advertisers should place the disclosure as close as possible to the claim being qualified or include the disclosure within the claim itself. If such placement is not feasible, the next-best placement is on a section of the page to which a consumer can easily scroll. Generally, hyperlinks to a disclosure are recommended only for lengthy disclosures or for disclosures that must be repeated in a variety of locations on the Web page.

REMEMBER ! Changes in technology often require changes in the law.

FTC Actions against Deceptive Advertising　The FTC receives complaints from many sources, including competitors of alleged violators, consumers, consumer organizations, trade associations, Better Business Bureaus, government organizations, and state and local officials. If enough consumers complain and the complaints are widespread, the FTC will investigate the problem. If the FTC concludes that a given advertisement is unfair or deceptive, it sends a formal complaint to the alleged offender. The company may agree to settle the complaint without further proceedings; if not, the FTC can conduct a hearing before an administrative law judge (discussed in Chapter 16) in which the company can present its defense.

If the FTC succeeds in proving that an advertisement is unfair or deceptive, it usually issues a **cease-and-desist order** requiring that the challenged advertising be stopped. It might also require **counteradvertising** in which the company advertises anew—in print, on radio, and on television—to inform the public about the earlier misinformation.

In some cases, the FTC may seek other remedies. In the following case, for example, after receiving over five hundred consumer complaints, the FTC sought restitution of the amounts that the consumers had paid. Each payment had been based on a false representation that a charge for Web site content accessed over a consumer's phone line could not be avoided, even if the consumer did not access the content or authorize another party to do so.

CEASE-AND-DESIST ORDER
An administrative or judicial order prohibiting a person or business firm from conducting activities that an agency or court has deemed illegal.

COUNTERADVERTISING
New advertising that is undertaken pursuant to a Federal Trade Commission order for the purpose of correcting earlier false claims that were made about a product.

---

3. *Advertising and Marketing on the Internet: Rules of the Road*, September 2000.

CASE 17.1　Federal Trade Commission v. Verity International, Ltd.

United States Court of Appeals,
Second Circuit, 2006.
443 F.3d 48.

BACKGROUND AND FACTS　Robert Green and Marilyn Shein founded and, between May 1997 and September 2000, controlled Verity International, Ltd., and Automatic

Communications, Ltd. (ACL). Through these firms, Green and Shein designed and implemented a billing system that ensured consumers paid charges for accessing pornography and other adult-entertainment Web sites. The system identified the user of an online adult-entertainment service by the phone line used to access the service and billed the phone-line subscriber for the cost the same as for an international phone call to Madagascar. Revenue was divided among Verity, the phone companies, and others. Under this system, a party could access an adult-entertainment service over a phone line without authorization from the phone-line subscriber, who was led to believe that he or she was legally bound to pay the charge, which was untrue. For example, Verity maintained a call center that told complaining consumers that the charges were valid, they must be paid,

and nonpayment would result in further collection activity. The FTC filed a suit in a federal district court against Verity, ACL, Green, and Shein, alleging violations of the FTC Act. The court issued an injunction freezing the defendants' assets and ordered them to pay nearly $18 million in restitution. The defendants appealed to the U.S. Court of Appeals for the Second Circuit.

IN THE WORDS OF THE COURT . . . *John M. WALKER, Jr.,* Chief Judge.

* * * *

* * * *To prove a deceptive act or practice under [Section] 5(a)(1) [of the FTC Act], the FTC must show three elements: (1) a representation, omission, or practice, that (2) is likely to mislead consumers acting reasonably under the circumstances, and [that] (3)* * * * *is material. The deception need not be made with intent to deceive; it is enough that the representations or practices were likely to mislead consumers acting reasonably.* [Emphasis added.]

The FTC contends that the first element is satisfied by proof that the defendants-appellants caused telephone-line subscribers to receive explicit and implicit representations that they could not successfully avoid paying charges for adult entertainment that had been accessed over their phone lines—what we call a "representation of uncontestability [impossible to dispute]." * * * [T]he defendants-appellants caused charges for adult entertainment to appear on * * * phone bills as telephone calls, thereby capitalizing on the common and well-founded perception held by consumers that they must pay their telephone bills, irrespective of whether they made or authorized the calls. * * * [T]his representation was also made * * * by * * * the call-center messages delivered to bill recipients. Upon reviewing the bills and call-center practices, we find that * * * they conveyed a representation of uncontestability.

The second requirement for [Section] 5(a)(1) liability is that the defendants-appellants' representation be likely to mislead consumers acting reasonably. The FTC contends that the representation of uncontestability was false and therefore likely to mislead consumers who did not use or authorize others to use the adult entertainment in question; the defendants-appellants contend that the representation was rendered true by * * * common law agency principles. * * *

Under common law agency principles, a person is liable to pay for services that she does not herself contract for if another person has actual, apparent, or implied authority to consent on her behalf to pay for the services. The defendants-appellants rely on apparent authority, contending that all calls made over a subscriber's telephone line were necessarily made with the subscriber's apparent authority because any user of a computer connected to that telephone line must have been given authority by the line subscriber to use the computer. [Emphasis added.]

Apparent authority * * * would derive here either from manifestations of the principal (the line subscriber) to a third party (an entity involved in the billing system) or from the putative agent's (the computer user's) position, when justified by ordinary expectations and habits. The defendants-appellants analogize the present case to * * * purchases by a company's employee * * * with a properly issued company credit card * * * made with the apparent authority of the company. * * * Here, in contrast, the computer is a multipurpose tool that is not primarily understood as a payment mechanism, and in the ordinary habits of human behavior, one does not reasonably infer that because a person is authorized to use a computer, the subscriber to the telephone line

CASE 17.1–CONTINUED ▶

connected to that computer has authorized the computer user to purchase online content on the subscriber's account. Apparent authority does not exist on these facts.

The representation of uncontestability is therefore false, unsupported by * * * common law agency principles. Because the defendants-appellants offer no reason why this misrepresentation would not be likely to mislead consumers acting reasonably, we find that * * * the FTC proved the second element of its * * * claim.

Finally, to establish a deceptive act or practice under [Section] 5(a)(1), the FTC must prove that the misrepresentation was material to consumers. * * * The FTC submitted evidence * * * that telephone-line subscribers found the representation material to their decision whether to pay the billed charges because of the worry of telephone-line disconnection, the perception of the futility of challenging the charges, the desire to avoid credit-score injury, or some combination of these factors.

DECISION AND REMEDY   The U.S. Court of Appeals for the Second Circuit affirmed the lower court's holding that the defendants had violated the FTC Act. "[T]he FTC proved all three elements of its [Section] 5(a)(1) claim premised on the deceptive representation of uncontestability." The court upheld the injunction and the order of restitution but changed the measure of damages to the amount of the defendants' "unjust gain"—not to include amounts paid to the phone companies and other innocent third parties—and remanded the case for a determination of the size of this award.

WHY IS THIS CASE IMPORTANT?   *One significant aspect of this case is the order for restitution. The FTC Act does not expressly provide for this remedy, but the court reasoned that because the statute allows for the issuance of injunctions, other equitable relief—such as restitution—is also possible. Equitable restitution allows a plaintiff to recover money or property in a defendant's possession that can clearly be traced to money or property identified as the plaintiff's.*

Telemarketing and Electronic Advertising

The pervasive use of the telephone to market goods and services to homes and businesses led to the passage in 1991 of the Telephone Consumer Protection Act (TCPA).[4] The act prohibits telephone solicitation using an automatic telephone dialing system or a prerecorded voice. Most states also have laws regulating telephone solicitation. The TCPA also makes it illegal to transmit ads via fax without first obtaining the recipient's permission. (Similar issues have arisen with respect to junk e-mail, called "spam"—see Chapter 5.)

The act is enforced by the Federal Communications Commission and also provides for a private right of action. Consumers can recover any actual monetary loss resulting from a violation of the act or receive $500 in damages for each violation, whichever is greater. If a court finds that a defendant willfully or knowingly violated the act, the court has the discretion to treble (triple) the damages awarded.

The Telemarketing and Consumer Fraud and Abuse Prevention Act[5] of 1994 directed the FTC to establish rules governing telemarketing and to bring actions against fraudulent telemarketers. The FTC's Telemarketing Sales Rule[6] of 1995 requires a telemarketer, before making a sales pitch, to inform the recipient that the call is a sales call and to identify the seller's name and the product being sold. The rule makes it illegal for telemarketers to misrepresent information (including facts about their goods or services and earnings potential, for example). Additionally, telemarketers must inform the people they call

---

4. 47 U.S.C. Sections 227 *et seq.*
5. 15 U.S.C. Sections 6101–6108.
6. 16 C.F.R. Sections 310.1–310.8.

of the total cost of the goods being sold, any restrictions on obtaining or using the goods, and whether a sale will be considered final and nonrefundable. A telemarketer must also remove a consumer's name from its list of potential contacts if the consumer so requests. A 2002 amendment to the Telemarketing Sales Rule established a national "Do Not Call" registry, which became effective in October 2003. Telemarketers must refrain from calling those consumers who have placed their names on the list.

LABELING AND PACKAGING

A number of federal and state laws deal specifically with the information given on labels and packages. The rules are designed to ensure that labels provide accurate information

What federal act prohibits telemarketers from using an automatic telephone dialing system, and what agency enforces that act? (Corbis. All rights reserved.)

about the product and to warn about possible dangers from its use or misuse. In general, labels must be accurate and must use words that are understood by the ordinary consumer. For example, a box of cereal cannot be labeled "giant" if that would exaggerate the amount of cereal contained in the box. In some instances, labels must specify the raw materials used in the product, such as the percentage of cotton, nylon, or other fibers used in a garment. In other instances, the products must carry a warning. Cigarette packages and advertising, for example, must include one of several warnings about the health hazards associated with smoking.[7] Some cigar manufacturers have also agreed to voluntarily put similar warnings on cigar packages and labels.

Food Labeling

The Fair Packaging and Labeling Act requires that product labels identify (1) the product; (2) the net quantity of the contents and, if the number of servings is stated, the size of a serving; (3) the manufacturer; and (4) the packager or distributor.[8] The act also provides for additional requirements concerning descriptions on packages, savings claims, components of nonfood products, and standards for the partial filling of packages.

Food products must bear labels detailing the food's nutrition content, including how much fat the food contains and what kind of fat it is. The Department of Health and Human Services, as well as the FTC, enforces these rules. The Nutrition Labeling and Education Act of 1990 requires standard nutrition facts (including fat content) on food labels; regulates the use of such terms as *fresh* and *low fat;* and, subject to the federal Food and Drug Administration's approval, authorizes certain health claims.

Other Federal Statutes

Federal laws regulating the labeling and packaging of products include the Wool Products Labeling Act of 1939,[9] the Fur Products Labeling Act of 1951,[10] the Flammable Fabrics Act of 1953,[11] the Fair Packaging and

---

7. 15 U.S.C. Sections 1331 *et seq.*
8. 15 U.S.C. Section 1453.
9. 15 U.S.C. Section 68.
10. 15 U.S.C. Section 69.
11. 15 U.S.C. Section 1191.

Today's consumers are increasingly concerned about eating genetically modified crops and the potential presence of pesticides, hormones, and mad cow disease in foods. Many consumers have thus switched to buying organic foods. How might an organic label be deceptive to consumers? Do ordinary consumers understand what is required for a food to be labeled "organic"? Why or why not? (PhotoDisc)

REGULATION Z
A set of rules promulgated by the Federal Reserve Board of Governors to implement the provisions of the Truth-in-Lending Act.

"COOLING-OFF" LAWS
Laws that allow buyers a period of time, such as three days, in which to cancel door-to-door sales contracts.

Labeling Act of 1966,[12] the Comprehensive Smokeless Tobacco Health Education Act of 1986,[13] and the Nutrition Labeling and Education Act of 1990.[14] The Comprehensive Smokeless Tobacco Health Education Act, for example, requires that producers, packagers, and importers of smokeless tobacco label their product with one of several warnings about the health hazards associated with the use of smokeless tobacco; the warnings are similar to those required on cigarette packages.

SALES

A number of statutes protect consumers by requiring the disclosure of certain terms in sales transactions and providing rules governing home or door-to-door sales, mail-order transactions, referral sales, and unsolicited merchandise. The Federal Reserve Board of Governors, for example, has issued **Regulation Z**, which governs credit provisions associated with sales contracts. Many states have also passed laws providing remedies to consumers in home sales. Furthermore, states have provided a number of consumer protection measures, such as implied warranties, through the adoption of the Uniform Commercial Code. In some states, the Uniform Consumer Credit Code's requirements, including disclosure requirements, also protect consumers in credit transactions.

Door-to-Door Sales

The laws of most states single out door-to-door sales for special treatment in part because of the nature of the sales transaction. Repeat purchases are less likely than in stores, so the seller has less incentive to cultivate the goodwill of the purchaser. Furthermore, the seller is unlikely to present alternative products and their prices. Thus, a number of states have passed **"cooling-off" laws** that permit the buyers of goods sold door to door to cancel their contracts within a specified period of time, usually two to three days after the sale.

An FTC regulation also requires sellers to give consumers three days to cancel any door-to-door sale. Because this rule applies in addition to the relevant state statutes, consumers are given the benefits of both the FTC rule and their own state statutes. In addition, the FTC rule requires that consumers be notified in Spanish of this right if the oral negotiations for the sale were in that language.

Telephone and Mail-Order Sales

The nation's Better Business Bureaus receive more complaints about sales made by telephone or mail order than about any other transactions. Many mail-order houses are far removed from the buyers who order from them, making it difficult for a consumer to bring a complaint against a seller. To a certain extent, consumers are protected under federal laws prohibiting mail fraud, which were discussed in Chapter 6, and under state consumer protection laws that parallel and supplement the federal laws.

---

12. 15 U.S.C. Sections 1451 *et seq.*
13. 15 U.S.C. Sections 4401–4408.
14. 21 U.S.C. Section 343-1.

The FTC's Mail or Telephone Order Merchandise Rule of 1993, which amended the FTC's Mail Order Rule of 1975,[15] provides specific protections for consumers who purchase goods via phone lines or through the mails. The 1993 rule extended the 1975 rule to include sales in which orders are transmitted using computers, fax machines, or any similar means involving telephone lines. Among other things, the rule requires mail-order merchants to ship orders within the time promised in their catalogues or advertisements, to notify consumers when orders cannot be shipped on time, and to issue a refund within a specified period of time when a consumer cancels an order.

In addition, the Postal Reorganization Act of 1970[16] provides that unsolicited merchandise sent by U.S. mail may be retained, used, discarded, or disposed of in any manner the recipient deems appropriate, without the recipient's incurring any obligation to the sender.

Online Sales

In recent years, the Internet has become a vehicle for a wide variety of business-to-consumer (B2C) sales transactions. Most mail-order houses now have a Web presence, and other Web sites offer consumers an increasing array of goods, ranging from airline tickets to books to xylophones. Protecting consumers from fraudulent and deceptive sales practices conducted via the Internet has proved to be a challenging task. Nonetheless, the FTC and other federal agencies have brought a number of enforcement actions against those who perpetrate online fraud. Additionally, the laws mentioned earlier, such as the federal statute prohibiting wire fraud, apply to online transactions.

Some states have amended their consumer protection statutes to cover Internet transactions as well. For example, the California legislature revised its Business and Professional Code to include transactions conducted over the Internet or by "any other electronic means of communication." Previously, that code covered only telephone, mail-order catalogue, radio, and television sales. Now any entity selling over the Internet in California must explicitly create an on-screen notice indicating its refund and return policies, where its business is physically located, its legal name, and a number of other details. Various states are also setting up information sites to help consumers protect themselves.

HEALTH AND SAFETY PROTECTION

The laws discussed earlier regarding the labeling and packaging of products go a long way toward promoting consumer health and safety. There is a significant distinction, however, between regulating the information dispensed about a product and regulating the actual content of the product. The classic example is tobacco products. Producers of tobacco products are required to warn consumers about the hazards associated with the use of their products. Yet the sale of tobacco products has not yet been subject to significant restrictions or banned outright despite their obvious hazards. We now examine various laws that regulate the actual products made available to consumers.

---

15. 16 C.F.R. Sections 435.1–435.2.
16. 39 U.S.C. Section 3009.

Food and Drugs

The first federal legislation regulating food and drugs was enacted in 1906 as the Pure Food and Drugs Act.[17] That law, as amended in 1938, exists now as the Federal Food, Drug and Cosmetic Act (FFDCA).[18] The act protects consumers against adulterated and misbranded foods and drugs. More recent amendments to the act added other substantive and procedural requirements. In its present form, the act establishes food standards, specifies safe levels of potentially hazardous food additives, and sets classifications of food and food advertising.

Most of these statutory requirements are monitored and enforced by the Food and Drug Administration (FDA). Under an extensive set of procedures established by the FDA, drugs must be shown to be effective as well as safe before they may be marketed to the public, and the use of some food additives suspected of being carcinogenic is prohibited. A 1976 amendment to the FFDCA[19] authorizes the FDA to regulate medical devices, such as pacemakers and other health devices or equipment, and to withdraw from the market any such device that is mislabeled.

Consumer Product Safety

Legislation regulating the safety of consumer products began in 1953 with the enactment of the Flammable Fabrics Act, which prohibits the sale of highly flammable clothing or materials. Over the next two decades, Congress enacted legislation regarding the design or composition of specific classes of products. Then, in 1972, Congress enacted the Consumer Product Safety Act,[20] which created a comprehensive scheme of regulation over matters concerning consumer safety. The act also established the Consumer Product Safety Commission (CPSC) and gave it far-reaching authority over consumer safety.

The CPSC conducts research on the safety of individual products and maintains a clearinghouse on the risks associated with various products. The Consumer Product Safety Act authorizes the CPSC to set standards for con-

---

17. 21 U.S.C. Sections 1–5, 7–15.
18. 21 U.S.C. Section 301.
19. 21 U.S.C. Sections 352(o), 360(j), 360(k), and 360c–360k.
20. 15 U.S.C. Section 2051.

These stuffed teddy bears were recalled because the plastic beads inside the toy could come out and create a choking hazard for young children. Which area of consumer protection law governs such a recall? (Photo by the Consumer Product Safety Commission/Getty Images)

sumer products and to ban the manufacture and sale of any product that the commission deems to be potentially hazardous to consumers. The CPSC also has authority to remove from the market any products it believes to be imminently hazardous and to require manufacturers to report on any products already sold or intended for sale if the products have proved to be hazardous. Additionally, the CPSC administers other product-safety legislation, such as the Child Protection and Toy Safety Act of 1969[21] and the Federal Hazardous Substances Act of 1960.[22] The CPSC's authority is sufficiently broad to allow it to ban any product that the commission believes poses merely an "unreasonable risk" to the consumer.

The Consumer Product Safety Act imposes notification requirements on distributors of consumer products. Distributors must immediately notify the CPSC when they receive information that a product "contains a defect which . . . creates a substantial risk to the public" or "an unreasonable risk of serious injury or death." The following case illustrates the consequences of failing to fulfill this requirement.

---

21. 15 U.S.C. Section 1262(e).
22. 15 U.S.C. Sections 1261–1273.

CASE 17.2 **United States v. Mirama Enterprises, Inc.**

United States District Court,
Southern District of California, 2002.
185 F.Supp.2d 1148.

BACKGROUND AND FACTS Mirama Enterprises, Inc., began operations in 1996 and today does business as Aroma Housewares Company. From 1996 until 1998, Aroma distributed a juice extractor, or juicer, made by a company in Taiwan, to retail stores throughout the United States. In early January 1998, Aroma received a complaint from a consumer whose juicer had broken. In February, consumer Richard Norton wrote Aroma to report that his juicer had shattered. In capital letters, Norton stated that the juicer

SUDDENLY EXPLODED, THROWING WITH GREAT VIOLENCE PIECES OF THE CLEAR PLASTIC COVER AND SHREDS OF THE

RAZOR-SHARP SEPARATOR SCREEN AS FAR AS EIGHT FEET IN MY KITCHEN. * * *

Over the next months, Aroma received twenty-three complaints about exploding juicers, some of which had caused injuries. One consumer, Jan Griffin, concluded her complaint by saying, "I feel that this juicer should be recalled, as it is very unsafe. The injuries that I suffered could have been a lot worse." In August, consumer Sylvia Mendoza filed a suit against Aroma, alleging injuries caused by a shattering juicer. On November 16, Aroma filed a report with the CPSC, which recalled the juicer on June 30, 1999. The federal government filed a suit against Mirama, seeking damages for its alleged failure to notify the CPSC of the danger earlier. The federal government then filed a motion for summary judgment.

IN THE WORDS OF THE COURT . . . *KEEP*, District Judge.

* * * *

[The] reporting requirement was imposed upon consumer product manufacturers to protect the public health and safety—the sooner the [Consumer Product Safety] Commission knows of a potential problem, the sooner it can investigate and take necessary action. This notification requirement was statutorily imposed upon manufacturers * * * because they are often the first to receive information about hazardous consumer products. * * *

CASE 17.2–CONTINUED ▶

CASE 17.2–CONTINUED

The thrust of the Act is clearly for firms to quickly inform the Commission as soon as they might "reasonably believe" that their product, through defect or otherwise, poses a significant threat to consumers. Upon receipt of "first information," a company is required to report within 24 hours to the Commission. Companies are advised that they should not await complete or accurate risk estimates before reporting * * * . While a firm may investigate to determine whether the information is reportable, a firm should not take more than 10 days unless it can demonstrate that such additional time is reasonable. * * * [Emphasis added.]

* * * The issue is whether, prior to [its reporting] date, Aroma received information which "reasonably supported" the conclusion that the juicer either * * * contained a "defect" which created a "substantial product hazard," such that it "created a substantial risk to the public," or created an "unreasonable risk of serious injury or death."

* * * *

The Court finds that Aroma was in receipt of overwhelming evidence such that a reasonable person could conclude that the juicer contained a defect which created a substantial risk to the public. The Court will not set forth again the litany of phone calls and letters with which scared, angry, and often injured consumers bombarded the company. The Court finds particularly noteworthy, however, several items in particular. * * * [I]n a period of approximately only one month, Aroma received three telephone calls and two letters recounting exploding juicers, flying pieces of razor-sharp metal, and one emergency room visit. Hence, by at least early March, Aroma had enough information for a reasonable person to conclude that the juicer contained a defect, whether in the actual unit or in the instructions and warnings, that created a substantial risk to the public.

DECISION AND REMEDY   The court granted the plaintiff's motion for summary judgment. The defendant had sufficient knowledge from consumer complaints that the juicer contained "a defect which . . . creates a substantial risk to the public" to report to the CPSC as early as March 1998.

WHY IS THIS CASE IMPORTANT?   *This case emphasizes that the law imposes a strict requirement on all businesses that sell goods to notify the CPSC immediately of any reports indicating that a product poses a substantial risk to the public.*

CREDIT PROTECTION

Considering the extensive use of credit by U.S. consumers, credit protection is one of the most important aspects of consumer protection legislation. A key statute regulating the credit and credit-card industries is the Truth-in-Lending Act (TILA), the name commonly given to Title 1 of the Consumer Credit Protection Act (CCPA),[23] which was passed by Congress in 1968.

Truth in Lending

NOTE   The Federal Reserve Board is part of the Federal Reserve System, which influences the lending and investing activities of commercial banks and the cost and availability of credit.

The TILA is basically a *disclosure law.* It is administered by the Federal Reserve Board and requires sellers and lenders to disclose credit terms or loan terms so that individuals can shop around for the best financing arrangements. TILA requirements apply only to persons who, in the ordinary course of business, lend funds, sell on credit, or arrange for the extension of credit. Thus, sales or loans made between two consumers do not come under the protection

---

23. 15 U.S.C. Sections 1601–1693r. The act was amended in 1980 by the Truth-in-Lending Simplification and Reform Act.

of the act. Additionally, this law protects only debtors who are *natural* persons (as opposed to the artificial "person" of a corporation); it does not extend to other legal entities.

The disclosure requirements are found in Regulation Z, which, as mentioned earlier in this chapter, was promulgated by the Federal Reserve Board. If the contracting parties are subject to the TILA, the requirements of Regulation Z apply to any transaction involving an installment sales contract that calls for payment to be made in more than four installments. Transactions subject to Regulation Z typically include installment loans, retail and installment sales, car loans, home-improvement loans, and certain real estate loans if the amount of financing is less than $25,000.

Under the provisions of the TILA, all of the terms of a credit instrument must be clearly and conspicuously disclosed. The TILA provides for contract rescission (cancellation) if a creditor fails to follow the exact procedures required by the act.[24]

Equal Credit Opportunity In 1974, Congress enacted, as an amendment to the TILA, the Equal Credit Opportunity Act (ECOA).[25] The ECOA prohibits the denial of credit solely on the basis of race, religion, national origin, color, gender, marital status, or age. The act also prohibits credit discrimination on the basis of whether an individual receives certain forms of income, such as public-assistance benefits.

Under the ECOA, a creditor may not require the signature of an applicant's spouse, or a cosigner, on a credit instrument if the applicant qualifies under the creditor's standards of creditworthiness for the amount requested. **Example #2** Tonja, an African American, applied for financing with a used-car dealer. The dealer looked at Tonja's credit report and, without submitting the application to the lender, decided that she would not qualify. Instead of informing Tonja that she did not qualify, the dealer told her that she needed a cosigner on the loan to purchase the car. According to a federal appellate court in 2004, the dealer qualified as a creditor in this situation because the dealer unilaterally denied the credit and thus could be held liable under the ECOA.[26]

Credit-Card Rules The TILA also contains provisions regarding credit cards. One provision limits the liability of a cardholder to $50 per card for unauthorized charges made before the creditor is notified that the card has been lost. Another provision prohibits a credit-card company from billing a consumer for any unauthorized charges if the credit card was improperly issued by the company. **Example #3** A consumer receives an unsolicited credit card in the mail, and the card is later stolen and used by the thief to make purchases. In this situation, the consumer to whom the card was sent will not be liable for the unauthorized charges.

Further provisions of the act concern billing disputes related to credit-card purchases. If a debtor thinks that an error has occurred in billing or wishes to withhold payment for a faulty product purchased by credit card, the act outlines

---

24. Note, though, that amendments to the TILA enacted in 1995 prevent borrowers from rescinding loans for minor clerical errors in closing documents [15 U.S.C. Sections 1605, 1631, 1635, 1640, and 1641].
25. 15 U.S.C. Section 1643.
26. *Treadway v. Gateway Chevrolet Oldsmobile, Inc.*, 362 F.3d 971 (7th Cir. 2004).

specific procedures for both the consumer and the credit-card company in settling the dispute.

Consumer Leases   The Consumer Leasing Act (CLA) of 1988[27] amended the TILA to provide protection for consumers who lease automobiles and other goods. The CLA applies to those who lease or arrange to lease consumer goods in the ordinary course of their business. The act applies only if the goods are priced at $25,000 or less and if the lease term exceeds four months. The CLA and its implementing regulation, Regulation M,[28] require lessors to disclose in writing all of the material terms of the lease.

Fair Credit Reporting

In 1970, to protect consumers against inaccurate credit reporting, Congress enacted the Fair Credit Reporting Act (FCRA).[29] The act provides that consumer credit reporting agencies may issue credit reports to users only for specified purposes, including the extension of credit, the issuance of insurance policies, compliance with a court order, and compliance with a consumer's request for a copy of her or his own credit report. The act further provides that any time a consumer is denied credit or insurance on the basis of the consumer's credit report, or is charged more than others ordinarily would be for credit or insurance, the consumer must be notified of that fact and of the name and address of the credit reporting agency that issued the credit report.

Consumers Must Be Given Access to Information   Under the FCRA, consumers may request the source of any information being given out by a credit agency, as well as the identity of anyone who has received an agency's report. Consumers are also permitted to have access to the information contained about them in a credit reporting agency's files. If a consumer discovers that the agency's files contain inaccurate information about the consumer's credit standing, the agency, on the consumer's written request, must investigate the matter and delete any unverifiable or erroneous information within a reasonable period of time.

ETHICAL ISSUE 17.1

Are agencies that report whether a consumer has a history of litigation subject to the Fair Credit Reporting Act?

Today, some consumer credit reporting agencies will also investigate and report a person's litigation history online. Physicians and landlords frequently use such services to find out whether prospective patients or tenants have a prior history of suing their physicians or landlords. One service, for example, allows physicians, for a membership fee of $4.95, to perform over two hundred name searches online to find out if a prospective patient was a plaintiff in a previous malpractice suit. Users say that these services are an ideal way to screen out undesirable applicants and reduce the risk of being sued, but

---

27. 15 U.S.C. Sections 1667–1667e.
28. 12 C.F.R. Part 213.
29. 15 U.S.C. Sections 1681 *et seq.*

consumer rights advocates argue that it is akin to "blacklisting." Is it fair to allow physicians and landlords to obtain information about consumers' involvement in prior court proceedings without allowing the consumers to challenge the information?

Not according to one California court. In that case, five tenants sued U. D. Registry, Inc. (UDR), a credit reporting agency, for disseminating false, misleading, and incomplete information about them. UDR had compiled the data from court records of eviction proceedings. Although in each case the court had dismissed the proceedings against the tenant, UDR's report stated that no judgment had been entered in the proceedings. Under the FCRA, companies that sell consumer information must report the information accurately and must provide a remedy for consumers who seek to dispute the information. UDR did not have any procedures in place to enable consumers to obtain copies of the reports so that they could challenge the information provided. Thus, the court ruled that UDR had violated the FCRA.[30]

Reporting Agencies Must Investigate Disputed Information   An agency's investigation should include contacting the creditor whose information a consumer disputes. The creditor, after receiving notice of the dispute, should conduct a reasonable investigation of its records to determine whether the disputed information can be verified.

Fair and Accurate Credit Transactions Act

In an effort to combat rampant identity theft (discussed in Chapter 6), Congress passed the Fair and Accurate Credit Transactions (FACT) Act of 2003.[31] The act established a national fraud alert system so that consumers who suspect that they have been or may be victimized by identity theft can place an alert in their credit files. The FACT Act also requires the major credit reporting agencies to provide consumers with a free copy of their credit reports every twelve months. Another provision requires account numbers on credit-card receipts to be shortened ("truncated") so that merchants, employees, and others who have access to the receipts cannot obtain a consumer's name and full credit-card numbers. The act also mandates that financial institutions work with the Federal Trade Commission to identify "red flag" indicators of identity theft and to develop rules on how to dispose of sensitive credit information.

The FACT Act also gives consumers who have been victimized by identity theft some assistance in rebuilding their credit reputations. For example, credit reporting agencies must stop reporting allegedly fraudulent account information once the consumer establishes that identify theft has occurred. Business owners and creditors are required to provide a consumer with copies of any records that can help the consumer prove that a particular account or transaction is fraudulent (such as when an account was created by a fraudulent signature, for example). In addition, to help prevent the spread of erroneous credit information, the act allows consumers to report the accounts affected by identity theft directly to the creditors.

---

30. *Decker v. U. D. Registry, Inc.*, 105 Cal.App.4th 1382, 129 Cal.Rptr.2d 892 (2003).
31. Pub. L. No. 108-159, 117 Stat. 1952 (December 4, 2003).

Fair Debt-Collection Practices

In 1977, Congress enacted the Fair Debt Collection Practices Act (FDCPA)[32] in an attempt to curb what were perceived to be abuses by collection agencies. The act applies only to specialized debt-collection agencies that regularly attempt to collect debts on behalf of someone else, usually for a percentage of the amount owed. Creditors attempting to collect debts are not covered by the act unless, by misrepresenting themselves, they cause the debtors to believe that they are collection agencies.

Requirements under the Act   The act explicitly prohibits a collection agency from using any of the following tactics:

1. Contacting the debtor at the debtor's place of employment if the debtor's employer objects.
2. Contacting the debtor during inconvenient or unusual times (for example, calling the debtor at three o'clock in the morning) or at any time if the debtor is being represented by an attorney. (If a collection agency is not aware that the debtor is represented by an attorney, will contacting the debtor about a debt subject the collection agency to liability? For the answer to this question, see this chapter's *Management Perspective* feature.)
3. Contacting third parties other than the debtor's parents, spouse, or financial adviser about payment of a debt unless a court authorizes such action.
4. Using harassment or intimidation (for example, using abusive language or threatening violence) or employing false and misleading information (for example, posing as a police officer).
5. Communicating with the debtor at any time after receiving notice that the debtor is refusing to pay the debt, except to advise the debtor of further action to be taken by the collection agency.

The FDCPA also requires collection agencies to include a "validation notice" whenever they initially contact a debtor for payment of a debt or within five days of that initial contact. The notice must state that the debtor has thirty days within which to dispute the debt and to request a written verification of the debt from the collection agency. The debtor's request for debt validation must be in writing.

Enforcement of the Act   The enforcement of the FDCPA is primarily the responsibility of the Federal Trade Commission. The FDCPA provides that a debt collector who fails to comply with the act is liable for actual damages, plus additional damages not to exceed $1,000[33] and attorneys' fees.

Cases brought under the FDCPA often raise questions as to who qualifies as a debt collector or debt-collecting agency subject to the act. For example, for several years it was not clear whether attorneys who attempted to collect debts owed to their clients were subject to the FDCPA's provisions. In 1995, the United States Supreme Court addressed this issue to resolve conflicting opinions in the lower courts. The Court held that an attorney who regularly

---

32. 15 U.S.C. Section 1692.
33. According to the U.S. Court of Appeals for the Sixth Circuit, the $1,000 limit on damages applies to each lawsuit, not to each violation. See *Wright v. Finance Service of Norwalk, Inc.,* 22 F.3d 647 (6th Cir. 1994).

MANAGEMENT PERSPECTIVE
Dealing with the FDCPA's Requirements

Management Faces a Legal Issue Collection agencies are, as the term indicates, in the business of collecting debts. Yet as you read elsewhere in this chapter, owners and managers of such agencies are constrained in the tactics they can use when collecting debts by the requirements of the Fair Debt Collection Practices Act (FDCPA). One of these requirements is that a collection agency is prohibited from contacting a debtor about an overdue debt "if the debt collector knows the consumer is represented by an attorney." What happens, though, if a collection agency, not knowing that the debtor has hired an attorney to represent him or her, contacts the debtor directly? Has the agency violated the FDCPA?

What the Courts Say This question has come before the courts on a number of occasions. Consider a case involving a debt owed by Paul Schmitt to First Bank U.S.A. Schmitt retained an attorney and was considering the possibility of filing for bankruptcy. The attorney advised the bank that Schmitt was unable to pay the debt and that the bank, if the account was turned over to a collection agency, should let the agency know of the attorney's representation. The bank later transferred Schmitt's account to FMA Alliance, a collection agency, but it did not inform the agency of the legal representation. When FMA sent a letter directly to Schmitt seeking immediate payment of the debt, Schmitt brought an action against FMA, alleging that the agency had violated the FDCPA. FMA responded that it could

not be liable under the act because FMA did not *know* of the legal representation. Schmitt countered that even if FMA did not have *actual* knowledge of Schmitt's legal representation, FMA had *implied* knowledge of the representation—because, as the bank's agent, such knowledge could be imputed to FMA.

When Schmitt's case ultimately reached the U.S. Court of Appeals for the Eighth Circuit, that court stated that Schmitt's argument contradicted established agency law (see Chapter 13). The court noted that although under agency law, knowledge of the agent is imputed to the principal, the reverse is not true—a principal's knowledge cannot be imputed to an agent. The court thus held that FMA had not violated the FDCPA because FMA did not have knowledge of the debtor's legal representation.[a]

Implications for Managers Although some courts have agreed with the federal appellate court's reasoning in this case, others have not.[b] Therefore, managers of collection agencies would be wise to (1) always check with their creditor-clients to find out if any debtors involved are represented by attorneys and (2) learn how courts in their jurisdictions have ruled on this issue.

a. *Schmitt v. FMA Alliance,* 398 F.3d 995 (8th Cir. 2005). For another case in which the court held that a creditor's knowledge cannot be imputed to debt collectors, see *Randolph v. I.M.B.S., Inc.,* 368 F.3d 726 (7th Cir. 2004).
b. See, for example, *Powers v. Professional Credit Services,* 107 F.Supp.2d 166 (N.D.N.Y. 2000); and *Micare v. Foster & Garbus,* 132 F.Supp.2d 77 (N.D.N.Y. 2001).

tries to obtain payment of consumer debts through legal proceedings meets the FDCPA's definition of "debt collector."[34]

STATE CONSUMER PROTECTION LAWS

Thus far, our primary focus has been on federal legislation. State laws, however, often provide more extensive protections for consumers than do federal laws. The warranty and unconscionability provisions of the Uniform Commercial Code (discussed in Chapter 10) offer important protections for consumers against unfair practices on the part of sellers. Virtually all states have specific consumer protection acts, often titled "deceptive trade practices acts." Although the provisions of state consumer protection statutes vary widely, a common thread runs through most of them. Typically, these laws are directed at sellers' deceptive practices, such as providing false or misleading

34. *Heintz v. Jenkins,* 514 U.S. 291, 115 S.Ct. 1489, 131 L.Ed.2d 395 (1995).

information to consumers. An example of the broad protection such legislation may provide is the Texas Deceptive Trade Practices Act of 1973, which forbids a seller from selling to a buyer anything that the buyer does not need or cannot afford.

In California, in the 1950s, unscrupulous promoters were misrepresenting their services to exact unjustified payments from property owners for real estate transactions. Therefore, in 1959 the state restricted the collection of "advance fees" to those with state-issued licenses, except for "newspapers of general circulation," which were found not to have engaged in any fraud. In the following case, the court considered whether this interpretation could be applied to an out-of-state, Internet-based service.

CASE 17.3 ForSaleByOwner.com v. Zinnemann

United States District Court,
Eastern District of California, 2004.
347 F.Supp.2d 868.

BACKGROUND AND FACTS ForSaleByOwner.com (FSBO) advertises residential real property for sale. FSBO charges a flat fee to owners to advertise their homes. The Web site lists the properties in a nationwide database that prospective buyers can view at no charge. FSBO also provides information about home sales, crime, schools, costs of living in specific locales, mortgage payments, and interest rates. To providers of related services (home-improvement contractors and others), FSBO sells listings in an online directory. FSBO is not a real estate agent and proclaims on its site that it is "legally prohibited from taking part in the actual sales transaction of any of the properties." Under California Business and Professions Code Section 10130, it is unlawful for any person or company to act as a real estate broker without first obtaining a state license. Sections 10026, 10131, and 10131.2 define *real estate broker* to include anyone—except newspapers—who, for an "advance fee," lists residential real property for sale. FSBO filed a suit in a federal district court against Paula Zinnemann, commissioner of the California Department of Real Estate, and others, claiming that this statute violated FSBO's rights under the First Amendment to the U.S. Constitution. FSBO filed a motion for summary judgment.

IN THE WORDS OF THE COURT . . . *ENGLAND*, District Judge.

* * * *

FSBO argues that California's real estate licensing laws * * * "single out" publishers of real estate advertising and information, like FSBO, for a burden the state places on no other speech and is directed only at works with a specified content. FSBO contends that publishers of other sales magazines or websites for different products (like automobiles, jewelry or boats, for instance) are not required to be licensed, and even more significantly argues that newspapers * * * are exempt from real estate licensing requirements despite the fact that they offer services virtually identical to those provided by FSBO. According to FSBO, this *differential treatment is unconstitutional unless the State's regulation is necessary to serve a compelling state interest and is narrowly drawn to achieve that end.* [Emphasis added.]

FSBO's argument that [the statute] unconstitutionally discriminates based on media type is persuasive. The Court agrees that California's real estate licensing scheme impermissibly differentiates between certain types of publications carrying the same basic content. * * * Given the uncontroverted fact that FSBO's activities are virtually identical to those pursued online by California newspapers, the distinction drawn between the two publishing mediums appears wholly arbitrary.

* * * *

* * * Indeed, given the fact that the online newspaper services and the FSBO website are virtually identical, there appears to be no justification whatsoever for any dis-

CASE 17.3–CONTINUED

tinction between the two mediums. Even if a distinction was warranted in 1959, when the statute was amended to include the newspaper exemption, that does not mean that the same rationale for exempting newspapers remains viable in 2004, given the vast advances in technology that have occurred in the meantime.

As FSBO points out, if use of the Internet itself justifies state regulation, that would logically suggest that both online newspaper services and websites like FSBO's should be equally restricted. Instead, however, online newspaper advertising for real property is not subject to licensing, whereas the very same information disseminated by FSBO requires a real estate broker's license. That license entails substantial coursework requirements as well as passage of a rigorous broker's exam. Defendants have simply shown no compelling need why such requirements must be satisfied in the case of FSBO but need not be adhered to by newspapers.

* * * Defendants suggest that FSBO accepts fees from mortgage brokers for business generated through a website referral process, despite the fact that no such referral service is even available on the FSBO website for users in California. The only other specific activity targeted by Defendants concerns referral fees paid by FSBO for customers directed through other websites.

Defendants have not demonstrated that these arrangements are improper, or that licensing will do anything to prevent or regulate any resulting improprieties. Defendants make no effort to show how regulating such activities constitutes a compelling state interest, not to mention whether requiring FSBO to obtain a broker's license is a remedy narrowly tailored to address such an interest. Otherwise, while Defendants vaguely attempt to paint newspapers as geographically situated and relatively more stable than Internet companies, they have not established why this should require websites like FSBO's to obtain a California broker's license as a prerequisite to listing properties for sale, when online services doing exactly the same thing are not subject to any licensing requirement so long as they are operated by a "newspaper." Defendants provide no reasonable explanation whatsoever for this differential treatment, let alone a compelling interest to justify it.

DECISION AND REMEDY The court granted FSBO's motion for summary judgment. The court reasoned that the California statute, as applied to FSBO, was unconstitutional, based on the "disparity of treatment" between newspapers and Web sites such as that of FSBO. The defendants failed to show "any compelling state interest" for requiring FSBO to obtain a broker's license, while identical online services were exempt if newspapers operated them.

FOR CRITICAL ANALYSIS–Technological Consideration
If newspapers published real estate listings only in print and did not provide the same services as FSBO online, would the result have been different?

REVIEWING . . . CONSUMER PROTECTION

Leota Sage saw a local motorcycle dealer's newspaper advertisement for a MetroRider EZ electric scooter for $1,699. When she met the salesperson at the dealership, however, she learned that the EZ model had been sold out. The salesperson told Sage that he still had the higher-end MetroRider FX model in stock for $2,199 and would offer her one for $1,999. Sage was disappointed but decided to purchase the FX model. Sage told the sales representative that she wished to purchase the scooter on credit and was directed to the dealer's credit department. As she filled out the credit forms, the clerk told Sage, an African American female, that she would need a cosigner to obtain a loan. Sage could not understand why she would need a cosigner and asked to speak to the store manager. The manager apologized, told her that the clerk was mistaken, and said that he would "speak to" the clerk about that. The manager completed Sage's credit application, and Sage then rode the scooter home. Seven months later, Sage received a letter from the manufacturer informing her that a flaw had been discovered in the scooter's braking system and that the model had been recalled. Using the information presented in the chapter, answer the following questions.

1. Did the dealer engage in deceptive advertising? Why or why not?

2. Suppose that Sage had ordered the scooter through the dealer's Web site but the dealer had been unable to deliver it by the date promised. What would the FTC require the merchant to do in that situation?

3. Assuming that the clerk had required a cosigner based on Sage's race or gender, what act prohibits such credit discrimination?

4. What organization has the authority to ban the sale of scooters based on safety concerns?

KEY TERMS

bait-and-switch advertising 555	"cooling-off" laws 560	deceptive advertising 555
cease-and-desist order 556	counteradvertising 556	Regulation Z 560

CHAPTER SUMMARY • CONSUMER PROTECTION

Deceptive Advertising (See pages 555–558.)	1. *Definition of deceptive advertising*—Generally, an advertising claim will be deemed deceptive if it would mislead a reasonable consumer.
	2. *Bait-and-switch advertising*—Advertising a lower-priced product (the "bait") when the intention is not to sell the advertised product but to lure consumers into the store and convince them to buy a higher-priced product (the "switch") is prohibited by the FTC.
	3. *Online deceptive advertising*—The FTC has issued guidelines to help online businesses comply with existing laws prohibiting deceptive advertising. The guidelines do not set forth new rules but rather describe how existing laws apply to online advertising.
	4. *FTC actions against deceptive advertising*—
	a. Cease-and-desist orders—Requiring the advertiser to stop the challenged advertising.
	b. Counteradvertising—Requiring the advertiser to advertise to correct the earlier misinformation.
Telemarketing and Electronic Advertising (See pages 558–559.)	The Telephone Consumer Protection Act of 1991 prohibits telephone solicitation using an automatic telephone dialing system or a prerecorded voice, as well as the transmission of advertising materials via fax without first obtaining the recipient's permission to do so.
Labeling and Packaging (See pages 559–560.)	Manufacturers must comply with labeling or packaging requirements for their specific products. In general, all labels must be accurate and not misleading.
Sales (See pages 560–561.)	1. *Door-to-door sales*—The FTC requires all door-to-door sellers to give consumers three days (a "cooling-off" period) to cancel any sale. States also provide for similar protection.
	2. *Telephone and mail-order sales*—Federal and state statutes and regulations govern certain practices of sellers who solicit over the telephone or through the mails and prohibit the use of the mails to defraud individuals.
	3. *Online sales*—Increasingly, the Internet is being used to conduct business-to-consumer (B2C) transactions. Both state and federal laws protect consumers to some extent against fraudulent and deceptive online sales practices.

CHAPTER SUMMARY • CONSUMER PROTECTION—CONTINUED

Health and Safety Protection (See pages 561–564.)	1. *Food and drugs*—The Federal Food, Drug and Cosmetic Act of 1938, as amended, protects consumers against adulterated and misbranded foods and drugs. The act establishes food standards, specifies safe levels of potentially hazardous food additives, and sets classifications of food and food advertising.
	2. *Consumer product safety*—The Consumer Product Safety Act of 1972 seeks to protect consumers from risk of injury from hazardous products. The Consumer Product Safety Commission has the power to remove products that are deemed imminently hazardous from the market and to ban the manufacture and sale of hazardous products.
Credit Protection (See pages 564–569.)	1. *Consumer Credit Protection Act, Title I (Truth-in-Lending Act, or TILA)*—A disclosure law that requires sellers and lenders to disclose credit terms or loan terms in certain transactions, including retail and installment sales and loans, car loans, home-improvement loans, and certain real estate loans. Additionally, the TILA provides rules governing equal credit opportunity, credit-card protection, and consumer leases.
	2. *Fair Credit Reporting Act*—Entitles consumers to request verification of the accuracy of a credit report and to have unverified or false information removed from their files.
	3. *Fair Debt Collection Practices Act*—Prohibits debt collectors from using unfair debt-collection practices, such as contacting the debtor at his or her place of employment if the employer objects or at unreasonable times, contacting third parties about the debt, and harassing the debtor, for example.
State Consumer Protection Laws (See pages 569–571.)	State laws often provide for greater consumer protection against deceptive trade practices than do federal laws. In addition, the warranty and unconscionability provisions of the Uniform Commercial Code protect consumers against sellers' deceptive practices.

FOR REVIEW

Answers for the even-numbered questions in this For Review *section can be found in Appendix O at the end of this text.*

1. When will advertising be deemed deceptive?
2. What special rules apply to telephone solicitation?
3. What is Regulation Z, and to what type of transactions does it apply?

4. How does the Federal Food, Drug and Cosmetic Act protect consumers?
5. What are the major federal statutes providing for consumer protection in credit transactions?

QUESTIONS AND CASE PROBLEMS

17–1. Unsolicited Merchandise. Andrew, a California resident, received a flyer in the U.S. mail announcing a new line of regional cookbooks distributed by the Every-Kind Cookbook Co. Andrew was not interested and threw the flyer away. Two days later, Andrew received in the mail an introductory cookbook entitled *Lower Mongolian Regional Cookbook*, as announced in the flyer, on a "trial basis" from Every-Kind. Andrew was not interested but did not go to the trouble to return the cookbook. Every-Kind demanded payment of $20.95 for the *Lower Mongolian Regional Cookbook*. Discuss whether Andrew can be required to pay for the cookbook.

Question with Sample Answer

17–2. On June 28, a salesperson for Renowned Books called on the Gonchars at their home. After a very persuasive sales pitch by the agent, the Gonchars agreed in writing

to purchase a twenty-volume set of historical encyclopedias from Renowned Books for a total of $299. A down payment of $35 was required, with the remainder of the cost to be paid in monthly payments over a one-year period. Two days later the Gonchars, having second thoughts, contacted the book company and stated that they had decided to rescind the contract. Renowned Books said this would be impossible. Has Renowned Books violated any consumer law by not allowing the Gonchars to rescind their contract? Explain.

For a sample answer to this question, go to Appendix P at the end of this text.

17–3. Credit Protection. Maria Ochoa receives two new credit cards on May 1. She has solicited one of them from Midtown Department Store, and the other arrives unsolicited from High-Flying Airlines. During the month of May, Ochoa makes numerous credit-card purchases from Midtown

Department Store, but she does not use the High-Flying Airlines card. On May 31, a burglar breaks into Ochoa's home and steals both credit cards, along with other items. Ochoa notifies the Midtown Department Store of the theft on June 2, but she fails to notify High-Flying Airlines. Using the Midtown credit card, the burglar makes a $500 purchase on June 1 and a $200 purchase on June 3. The burglar then charges a vacation flight on the High-Flying Airlines card for $1,000 on June 5. Ochoa receives the bills for these charges and refuses to pay them. Discuss Ochoa's liability in these situations.

17–4. Deceptive Advertising. Kraft, Inc., produces individually wrapped cheese slices, called "Singles Slices," which are made from real cheese and which cost more than the imitation cheese slices on the market. In the early 1980s, Kraft began losing its market share to an increasing number of producers of imitation cheese slices. Kraft responded with a series of advertisements collectively known as the "Five Ounces of Milk" campaign. The ads claimed that Kraft Singles cost more than imitation slices because they were made from five ounces of milk rather than less expensive ingredients. The ads also implied that because each slice contained five ounces of milk, Kraft Singles contained a higher calcium content than imitation cheese slices. The Federal Trade Commission (FTC) filed a complaint against Kraft, charging that Kraft had materially misrepresented the calcium content and relative calcium benefit of Kraft Singles. Was Kraft's advertising campaign deceptive and likely to mislead consumers? [*Kraft, Inc. v. FTC*, 970 F.2d 311 (7th Cir. 1992)]

Case Problem with Sample Answer

17–5. CrossCheck, Inc., provides check-authorization services to retail merchants. When a customer presents a check, the merchant contacts CrossCheck, which estimates the probability that the check will clear the bank. If the check is within an acceptable statistical range, CrossCheck notifies the merchant. If the check is dishonored, the merchant sends it to CrossCheck, which pays it. CrossCheck then attempts to redeposit the check. If this fails, CrossCheck takes further steps to collect the amount. CrossCheck attempts to collect on more than two thousand checks per year and spends $2 million on these efforts, which involve about 7 percent of its employees and 6 percent of its total expenses. William Winterstein took his truck to C&P Auto Service Center, Inc., for a tune-up and paid for the service with a check. C&P contacted CrossCheck and, on its recommendation, accepted the check. When the check was dishonored, C&P mailed it to CrossCheck, which reimbursed C&P and sent a letter to Winterstein, requesting payment. Winterstein filed a suit in a federal district court against CrossCheck, asserting that the letter violated the Fair Debt Collection Practices Act. CrossCheck filed a motion for summary judgment. On what ground might the court grant the motion? Explain.

[*Winterstein v. CrossCheck, Inc.*, 149 F.Supp.2d 466 (N.D.Ill. 2001)]

After you have answered this problem, compare your answer with the sample answer given on the Web site that accompanies this text. Go to www.thomsonedu.com/westbuslaw/let, select "Chapter 17," and click on "Case Problem with Sample Answer."

17–6. Fair Credit Reporting Act. Source One Associates, Inc., is based in Poughquag, New York. Peter Easton, Source One's president, is responsible for its daily operations. Between 1995 and 1997, Source One received requests from persons in Massachusetts seeking financial information about individuals and businesses. To obtain this information, Easton first obtained the targeted individuals' credit reports through Equifax Consumer Information Services by claiming the reports would be used only in connection with credit transactions involving the consumers. From the reports, Easton identified financial institutions at which the targeted individuals held accounts and then called the institutions to learn the account balances by impersonating either officers of the institutions or the account holders. The information was then provided to Source One's customers for a fee. Easton did not know why the customers wanted the information. The state ("Commonwealth") of Massachusetts filed a suit in a Massachusetts state court against Source One and Easton, alleging, among other things, violations of the Fair Credit Reporting Act (FCRA). Did the defendants violate the FCRA? Explain. [*Commonwealth v. Source One Associates, Inc.*, 436 Mass. 118, 763 N.E.2d 42 (2002)]

17–7. Deceptive Advertising. "Set up & Ready to Make Money in Minutes Guaranteed!" the ads claimed. "The Internet Treasure Chest (ITC) will give you everything you need to start your own exciting Internet business including your own worldwide website all for the unbelievable price of only $59.95." The ITC "contains virtually everything you need to quickly and easily get your very own worldwide Internet business up, running, stocked with products, able to accept credit cards and ready to take orders almost immediately." What ITC's marketers—Damien Zamora and end70 Corp.—did not disclose were the significant additional costs required to operate the business: domain name registration fees, monthly Internet access and hosting charges, monthly fees to access the ITC product warehouse, and other "upgrades." The Federal Trade Commission filed a suit in a federal district court against end70 and Zamora, seeking an injunction and other relief. Are the defendants' claims "deceptive advertising"? If so, what might the court order the defendants to do to correct any misrepresentations? [*Federal Trade Commission v. end70 Corp.*, __F.Supp.2d__ (N.D.Tex. 2003)]

17–8. Debt Collection. 55th Management Corp. in New York City owns residential property that it leases to various tenants. In June 2000, claiming that one of the tenants, Leslie Goldman, owed more than $13,000 in back rent, 55th retained Jeffrey Cohen, an attorney, to initiate nonpayment proceedings. Cohen filed a petition in a New York state court against Goldman, seeking recovery of the unpaid rent and at least $3,000 in attorneys' fees. After receiving notice of the petition, Goldman filed a suit in a federal district court against Cohen. Goldman alleged that the notice of the petition constituted the initial contact under the Fair Debt Collection Practices Act (FDCPA) that required a validation notice. Because Cohen did not give Goldman a validation notice at the time, or within five days, of the notice of the petition, Goldman argued that Cohen was in violation of the FDCPA. Should the filing of a suit in a state court be considered "communication," requiring a debt collector to provide a validation notice under the FDCPA? Why or why not? [*Goldman v. Cohen*, 445 F.3d 152 (2d Cir. 2006)]

A Question of Ethics

17–9. Renee Purtle bought a 1986 Chevrolet Blazer from Eldridge Auto Sales, Inc. To finance the purchase through Eldridge, Purtle filled out a credit application on which she misrepresented her employment status. Based on the misrepresentation, Eldridge extended credit. In the credit contract, Eldridge did not disclose the finance charge, the annual percentage rate, or the total sales price or use the term *amount financed*, as the Truth-in-Lending Act (TILA) and its regulations require. Purtle defaulted on the loan, and Eldridge repossessed the vehicle. Purtle filed a suit in a federal district court against Eldridge, alleging violations of the TILA. The court awarded Purtle $1,000 in damages, plus attorneys' fees and costs. Eldridge appealed, arguing in part that Purtle was not entitled to damages because she had committed fraud on her credit application. Considering these facts, answer the following questions. [*Purtle v. Eldridge Auto Sales, Inc.*, 91 F.3d 797 (6th Cir. 1996)]

1. How will the appellate court rule in this case? Why?
2. The trial court awarded Purtle money damages for the car dealer's violation of the TILA even though Purtle

had lied about her job on the credit application. Do you think it is fair for the court to reward a plaintiff who has committed fraud? What should the court do?
3. The plaintiff in this case also defaulted on the loan. Generally, should a person who defaults on a loan be prohibited from suing the creditor for violating the TILA? Why or why not?

Critical-Thinking Legal Question

17–10. As discussed in the text, many states have enacted laws that go even further than federal law to protect the interests of consumers. These laws vary tremendously from state to state. Generally, do you think it is fair that citizens of one state receive more protection than citizens of another state? What about fairness to sellers, who may be prohibited from engaging in a practice in one state that is perfectly legal in another? Should all consumer protection statutes be federally legislated? Why or why not?

Video Question

17–11. Go to this text's Web site at **www.thomsonedu.com/westbuslaw/let** and select "Chapter 17." Click on "Video Questions" and view the video titled *Advertising Communication Law: Bait and Switch.* Then answer the following questions.

1. Is the auto dealership's advertisement for the truck in the video deceptive? Why or why not?
2. Is the advertisement for the truck an offer to which the dealership is bound? Does it matter if Betty detrimentally relied on the advertisement?
3. Is Tony committed to buying Betty's trade-in truck for $3,000 because that is what he told her over the phone?

INTERACTING WITH THE INTERNET

For updated links to resources available on the Web, as well as a variety of other materials, visit this text's Web site at

www.thomsonedu.com/westbuslaw/let

For a government-sponsored Web site containing reports on consumer issues, go to

www.consumer.com

The Web site of the Federal Trade Commission (FTC) offers extensive information on consumer protection laws, consumer problems, enforcement issues, and other topics relevant to consumer law. Go to the consumer protection home page at

www.ftc.gov/ftc/consumer/home.html

To learn more about the FTC's "cooling-off" rule, you can access it directly by going to the following URL:

www.ftc.gov/bcp/conline/pubs/buying/cooling.htm

INTERNET EXERCISES

Go to **www.thomsonedu.com/westbuslaw/let**, the Web site that accompanies this text. Select "Chapter 17" and click on "Internet Exercises." There you will find the following Internet research exercises that you can perform to learn more about topics covered in this chapter.

Internet Exercise 17–1: LEGAL PERSPECTIVE—The Food and Drug Administration
Internet Exercise 17–2: MANAGEMENT PERSPECTIVE—Internet Advertising and Marketing

BEFORE THE TEST

Go to **www.thomsonedu.com/westbuslaw/let**, the Web site that accompanies this text. Select "Chapter 17" and click on "Interactive Quizzes." You will find a number of interactive questions relating to this chapter.

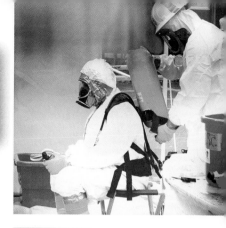

CHAPTER 18 — Protecting the Environment

CHAPTER OBJECTIVES

After reading this chapter, you should be able to answer the following questions:

1. Under what common law theories can polluters be held liable?

2. What is an environmental impact statement, and who must file one?

3. What does the Environmental Protection Agency do?

4. What major federal statutes regulate air and water pollution?

5. What is Superfund? To what categories of persons does liability under Superfund extend?

CONTENTS

CONCERN OVER the degradation of the environment has increased over time in response to the environmental effects of population growth, urbanization, and industrialization. Environmental protection is not without a price, however. For many businesses, the costs of complying with environmental regulations are high, and for some they are too high. A constant tension exists between the desirability of increasing profits and productivity and the need to protect the environment.

To a great extent, environmental law consists of statutes passed by federal, state, or local governments and regulations issued by administrative agencies. Before examining statutory and regulatory environmental laws, however, we look at the remedies available under the common law against environmental pollution.

> "Man, however much he may like to pretend the contrary, is part of nature."
> —RACHEL CARSON, 1907–1964
> (American writer and conservationist)

COMMON LAW ACTIONS

Common law remedies against environmental pollution originated centuries ago in England. Those responsible for operations that created dirt, smoke, noxious odors, noise, or toxic substances were sometimes held liable under common law theories of nuisance or negligence. Today, injured individuals continue to rely on the common law to obtain damages and injunctions against business polluters.

Nuisance

Under the common law doctrine of **nuisance**, persons may be held liable if they use their property in a manner that unreasonably interferes with others' rights to use or enjoy their own property. In these situations, the courts commonly

NUISANCE
A common law doctrine under which persons may be held liable for using their property in a manner that unreasonably interferes with others' rights to use or enjoy their own property.

577

balance the equities between the harm caused by the pollution and the costs of stopping it.

Courts have often denied injunctive relief on the ground that the hardships that would be imposed on the polluter and on the community are relatively greater than the hardships suffered by the plaintiff. **| Example #1** A factory that causes neighboring landowners to suffer from smoke, dirt, and vibrations may be left in operation if it is the core of a local economy. The injured parties may be awarded only money damages. These damages may include compensation for the decrease in the value of the neighbors' property that results from the factory's operation.**|**

A property owner may be given relief from pollution if he or she can identify a distinct harm separate from that affecting the general public. This harm is referred to as a "private" nuisance. Under the common law, citizens were denied standing (access to the courts—see Chapter 3) unless they suffered a harm distinct from the harm suffered by the public at large. Some states still require this. **| Example #2** A group of individuals who made their living by commercial fishing in a major river in New York sued for damages and to obtain an injunction against a company that was polluting the river. The court found that the plaintiffs had standing because they were particularly harmed by the pollution in the river.[1]**|** A public authority (such as a state's attorney general), though, can sue to abate a "public" nuisance.

Negligence and Strict Liability

An injured party may sue a business polluter in tort under the negligence and strict liability theories discussed in Chapter 5. The basis for a negligence action is the business's alleged failure to use reasonable care toward the party whose injury was foreseeable and, of course, caused by the lack of reasonable care. For example, employees might sue an employer whose failure to use proper pollution controls contaminated the air and caused the employees to suffer respiratory illnesses. A developing area of tort law involves **toxic torts**—civil wrongs arising from exposure to a toxic substance, such as asbestos, radiation, or hazardous waste.

TOXIC TORT
A civil wrong arising from exposure to a toxic substance, such as asbestos, radiation, or hazardous waste.

Businesses that engage in ultrahazardous activities—such as the transportation of radioactive materials—are strictly liable for whatever injuries the activities cause. In a strict liability action, the injured party does not need to prove that the business failed to exercise reasonable care.

FEDERAL, STATE, AND LOCAL REGULATION

All levels of government in the United States regulate some aspect of the environment. In this section, we look at some of the ways in which the federal, state, and local governments control business activities and land use in the interests of environmental preservation and protection.

Federal Regulation

Congress has enacted a number of statutes to control the impact of human activities on the environment. Some of these laws have been passed to improve the quality of air and water. Some of them specifically regulate toxic chemicals, including pesticides, herbicides, and hazardous wastes.

---

1. *Lee v. General Electric Co.,* 538 N.Y.S.2d 844, 145 A.D.2d 291 (1989).

Environmental Regulatory Agencies   Much of the body of federal law governing business activities consists of the regulations issued and enforced by administrative agencies. The most well known of the agencies regulating environmental law is, of course, the Environmental Protection Agency (EPA), which was created in 1970 to coordinate federal environmental responsibilities. Other federal agencies with authority to regulate specific environmental matters include the Department of the Interior, the Department of Defense, the Department of Labor, the Food and Drug Administration, and the Nuclear Regulatory Commission. These regulatory agencies—and all other agencies of the federal government—must take environmental factors into consideration when making significant decisions.

Most federal environmental laws provide that citizens can sue to enforce environmental regulations if government agencies fail to do so—or if agencies go too far in their enforcement actions. Typically, a threshold hurdle in such suits is meeting the requirements for standing to sue.

State and local regulatory agencies also play a significant role in implementing federal environmental legislation. Typically, the federal government relies on state and local governments to enforce federal environmental statutes and regulations such as those regulating air quality.

Environmental Impact Statements   The National Environmental Policy Act (NEPA) of 1969[2] requires that an **environmental impact statement (EIS)** be prepared for every major federal action that significantly affects the quality of the environment. An EIS must analyze (1) the impact on the environment that the action will have, (2) any adverse effects on the environment and alternative actions that might be taken, and (3) irreversible effects the action might generate.

An action qualifies as "major" if it involves a substantial commitment of resources (monetary or otherwise). An action is "federal" if a federal agency has the power to control it. Construction by a private developer of a ski resort on federal land, for example, may require an EIS.[3] Building or operating a nuclear plant, which requires a federal permit,[4] would require an EIS, as would constructing a dam as part of a federal project.[5] If an agency decides that an EIS is unnecessary, it must issue a statement supporting this conclusion. EISs have become instruments for private citizens, consumer interest groups, businesses, and others to challenge federal agency actions on the basis that the actions improperly threaten the environment.

State and Local Regulation

Many states regulate the degree to which the environment may be polluted. Thus, for example, even when state zoning laws permit a business's proposed development, the proposal may have to be altered to lessen the development's impact on the environment. State laws may restrict a business's discharge of chemicals into the air or water or regulate its disposal of toxic wastes. States

ENVIRONMENTAL IMPACT STATEMENT (EIS)
A statement required by the National Environmental Policy Act for any major federal action that will significantly affect the quality of the environment. The statement must analyze the action's impact on the environment and explore alternative actions that might be taken.

---

2. 42 U.S.C. Sections 4321–4370d.
3. *Robertson v. Methow Valley Citizens' Council,* 490 U.S. 332, 109 S.Ct. 1835, 104 L.Ed.2d 351 (1989).
4. *Calvert Cliffs Coordinating Committee v. Atomic Energy Commission,* 449 F.2d 1109 (D.C. Cir. 1971).
5. *Marsh v. Oregon Natural Resources Council,* 490 U.S. 360, 109 S.Ct. 1851, 104 L.Ed.2d 377 (1989).

CASE 18.1   Clean Air Markets Group v. Pataki

United States District Court,
Northern District of New York, 2002.
194 F.Supp.2d 147.

HISTORICAL AND ENVIRONMENTAL SETTING   *Acid rain allegedly has negative effects on water, forests, human health, and buildings and other structures. Acid rain consists of atmospheric sulfates and nitrates, which are formed from sulfur dioxide (SO_2) and nitrogen oxides (NO_x). These substances are emitted as by-products of the combustion of fossil fuels, most notably during the generation of electricity. Emissions originating in fourteen midwestern, eastern, and southern states, referred to as "upwind states," contribute significantly to acid rain in New York.*

BACKGROUND AND FACTS   By 1999, it was clear to some scientists that SO_2 emissions at the rates allowed by the Clean Air Act would not permit the environmental restoration of parts of the state of New York. Additional reductions in SO_2 emissions would be required. George Pataki, the governor of

New York, ordered New York utilities to cut SO_2 emissions to half of the amount permitted by the Clean Air Act by January 2, 2007. By doing this, the New York utilities would have additional SO_2 credits to sell. In May 2000, the New York state legislature enacted the Air Pollution Mitigation Law (APML), which stipulated that most sums received for the sale or trade of SO_2 allowances to a polluter in an upwind state would be forfeited to the New York Public Service Commission (PSC), which regulates New York utilities. This effectively lowered the market value of credits originating with New York utilities. Clean Air Markets Group (CAMG) filed a suit in a federal district court against Pataki and others, claiming in part that the APML was preempted under the U.S. Constitution's supremacy clause.[a] All parties filed motions for summary judgment.

a. As explained in Chapter 4, if federal law has not supplanted a whole field of state law, state law is preempted to the extent that it actually conflicts with federal law. A conflict between state and federal law occurs when compliance with both is physically impossible or when the state law is an obstacle to accomplishing the objective of federal law.

IN THE WORDS OF THE COURT . . . HURD, District Judge.

* * * *

* * * [The APML] creates an obstacle to the accomplishment and execution of the full purposes and objectives of Congress. [The Clean Air Act] provides that SO_2 allowances "may be transferred among designated representatives of the owners or operators of [covered units (utilities)] and *any* other person who holds such allowances." [The APML's] restrictions on transferring allowances to units in the Upwind States [are] contrary to the federal provision that allowances be tradeable to *any* other person. Additionally, Congress considered geographically restricted allowance transfers and rejected it. The EPA, in setting regulations to implement [the Clean Air Act], also considered geographically restricted allowance trading and rejected it * * * . *The rejection of a regionally restricted allowance trading system illustrates the Congressional objective of having a nationwide trading market for SO_2 allowances. New York's regional restrictions on SO_2 allowance trading by New York units are an obstacle to the execution of that objective.* [Emphasis added.]

Pataki argues that the Air Pollution Mitigation Law * * * imposes a more stringent requirement for air pollution control or abatement, as expressly permitted. However, * * * the Air Pollution Mitigation Law sets no emissions requirements. It sets no requirements for air pollution control or abatement at all. Rather, the New York law is a state regulation of federally allocated SO_2 allowances. Further, it is a restriction on the nationwide trading system for which the Clean Air Act provides. It is insufficient to merely say that it imposes requirements for air pollution control, or that the goal is air pollution control or abatement. New York's Air Pollution Mitigation Law is preempted because it interferes with the Clean Air Act's method for achieving the goal of air pollution control: a cap and nationwide SO_2 allowance trading system.

In addition to interfering with the nationwide trading of SO_2 allowances, the Air Pollution Mitigation Law would result in decreased availability of SO_2 allowances in the

CASE 18.1–CONTINUED Upwind States. Restricted availability of SO$_2$ allowances could indirectly reduce emissions in the Upwind States. No doubt that the New York legislators had this in mind when the Air Pollution Mitigation Law was enacted. However, the Clean Air Act permits restrictions on emissions by a state in that state, but it does not permit one state to control emissions in another state. Thus, the inevitable result of laws such as New York's Air Pollution Mitigation Law would be the indirect regulation of allowance trading and emissions in other states, which could not be done directly.

DECISION AND REMEDY The court granted the CAMG's motion for summary judgment, holding that New York's Air Pollution Mitigation Law is preempted, under the supremacy clause, by the Clean Air Act because it interferes with that law's methods for achieving air-pollution control. The court enjoined the enforcement of the state law.

FOR CRITICAL ANALYSIS–Environmental Consideration
Suppose that the APML also provided for a subsidy to those who claimed that the value of their pollution credits had been reduced. Would this have affected the outcome of the case? Why or why not?

Hazardous Air Pollutants

Hazardous air pollutants are those likely to cause death or serious irreversible or incapacitating illness. In all, there are 189 of these pollutants, including asbestos, benzene, beryllium, cadmium, mercury, and vinyl chloride. These pollutants may cause cancer as well as neurological and reproductive damage. They are emitted from stationary sources by a variety of business activities, including smelting (melting ore to produce metal), dry cleaning, house painting, and commercial baking. Instead of establishing specific emissions standards for each hazardous air pollutant, the 1990 amendments to the Clean Air Act require industry to use pollution-control equipment that represents the maximum achievable control technology to limit emissions. The EPA issues

This worker is cleaning asbestos, a hazardous air pollutant, from the interior of an old building. Does the Clean Air Act establish specific emission standards for hazardous air pollutants? Why or why not? What is the EPA's role in controlling hazardous air pollutants? (Corbis)

guidelines as to what equipment meets this standard. In 1996, the EPA issued a rule to regulate hazardous air pollutants emitted by landfills.[8]

Violations of the Clean Air Act

For violations of emission limits under the Clean Air Act, the EPA can assess civil penalties of up to $25,000 per day. Additional fines of up to $5,000 per day can be assessed for other violations, such as failing to maintain the required records. To penalize those who find it more cost-effective to violate the act than to comply with it, the EPA is authorized to obtain a penalty equal to the violator's economic benefits from noncompliance. Persons who provide information about violators may be paid up to $10,000. Private citizens can also sue violators.

Those who knowingly violate the act may be subject to criminal penalties, including fines of up to $1 million and imprisonment for up to two years (for false statements or failures to report violations). Corporate officers are among those who may be subject to these penalties.

WATER POLLUTION

Water pollution stems mostly from industrial, municipal, and agricultural sources. Pollutants entering streams, lakes, and oceans include organic wastes, heated water, sediments from soil runoff, nutrients (including fertilizers and human and animal wastes), and toxic chemicals and other hazardous substances. We look here at laws and regulations governing water pollution.

Navigable Waters

Federal regulations governing the pollution of water can be traced back to the Rivers and Harbors Appropriations Act of 1899.[9] These regulations prohibited ships and manufacturers from discharging or depositing refuse in navigable waterways without a permit. In 1948, Congress passed the Federal Water Pollution Control Act (FWPCA),[10] but its regulatory system and enforcement powers proved to be inadequate.

In 1972, amendments to the FWPCA—known as the Clean Water Act—established the following goals: (1) make waters safe for swimming, (2) protect fish and wildlife, and (3) eliminate the discharge of pollutants into the water. The amendments set specific time schedules, which were extended by amendment in 1977 and by the Water Quality Act of 1987.[11] Under these schedules, the EPA limits the discharge of various types of pollutants based on the technology available for controlling them. The 1972 act also requires municipal and industrial polluters to apply for permits before discharging wastes into navigable waters.

Under the act, violators are subject to a variety of civil and criminal penalties. Depending on the violation, civil penalties range from $10,000 per day to as much as $25,000 per day, but not more than $25,000 per violation.

8. 40 C.F.R. Sections 60.750–759.
9. 33 U.S.C. Sections 401–418.
10. 33 U.S.C. Sections 1251–1387.
11. This act amended 33 U.S.C. Section 1251.

Criminal penalties, which apply only if a violation was intentional, range from a fine of $2,500 per day and imprisonment for up to one year to a fine of $1 million and fifteen years' imprisonment. Injunctive relief and damages can also be imposed. The polluting party can be required to clean up the pollution or pay for the cost of doing so.

To obtain a federal license to "discharge" into navigable waters requires a state's certification that water-protection laws will not be violated. Can a river routed through a hydropower dam "discharge" into itself for purposes of the Clean Water Act, thus requiring the dam's owner to obtain state approval? That was the question in the following case.

CASE 18.2 S.D. Warren Co. v. Maine Board of Environmental Protection

Supreme Court of the United States, 2006.
__ U.S. __,
126 S.Ct. 1843,
164 L.Ed.2d 625.
www.findlaw.com/casecode/supreme.html [a]

BACKGROUND AND FACTS S.D. Warren Company operates hydropower dams to generate electricity for a paper mill in the Presumpscot River, which runs for twenty-five miles through southern Maine. Each dam creates a pond, from which water funnels into a canal, through turbines, and back to the riverbed. Operating the dams requires a license from the Federal Energy Regulatory Commission (FERC). Under the Clean Water Act, a license for an activity that causes a

a. In the "Browsing" section, click on "2006 Decisions." When that page opens, scroll to the name of the case and click on it to read the opinion.

"discharge" into navigable waters requires the certification of the state in which the discharge occurs that it will not violate water-quality standards. To renew the licenses for the dams in 1999, Warren applied for certification from the Maine Department of Environmental Protection. The agency told Warren to maintain a minimum stream flow in the river and to allow passage for migratory fish and eels. Warren appealed to the state Board of Environmental Protection, which upheld the requirements. FERC licensed the dams subject to the conditions. Warren filed a suit in a Maine state court against the state agency, arguing that the dams do not result in discharges. The court ruled in the agency's favor. Warren appealed to the Supreme Judicial Court of Maine, the state's highest court, which affirmed the lower court's ruling. Warren appealed to the United States Supreme Court.

IN THE WORDS OF THE COURT . . . Justice *SOUTER* delivered the opinion of the Court.

* * * *

The dispute turns on the meaning of the word "discharge," the key to the state certification requirement under [the Clean Water Act]. * * * [S]ince it is neither defined in the statute nor a term of art, we are left to construe it in accordance with its ordinary or natural meaning. [Emphasis added.]

When it applies to water, "discharge" commonly means a "flowing or issuing out," [according to] *Webster's New International Dictionary * * * , and this ordinary sense has consistently been the meaning intended when this Court has used the term in prior water cases.* [Emphasis added.]

* * * *

* * * [T]his Court has not been alone, for the Environmental Protection Agency (EPA) and FERC have each regularly read "discharge" as having its plain meaning and thus covering releases from hydroelectric dams. Warren is, of course, entirely correct in cautioning us that because neither the EPA nor FERC has formally settled the definition, or even set out agency reasoning, these expressions of agency understanding do not command deference from this Court. But even so, the administrative usage of "discharge" in this way confirms our understanding of the everyday sense of the term.

* * * *

CASE 18.2–CONTINUED ▶

CASE 18.2–CONTINUED

Congress passed the Clean Water Act to "restore and maintain the chemical, physical, and biological integrity of the Nation's waters," the "national goal" being to achieve "water quality which provides for the protection and propagation of fish, shellfish, and wildlife and provides for recreation in and on the water." To do this, the Act does not stop at controlling the "addition of pollutants," but deals with "pollution" generally, which Congress defined to mean "the man-made or man-induced alteration of the chemical, physical, biological, and radiological integrity of water."

The alteration of water quality as thus defined is a risk inherent in limiting river flow and releasing water through turbines. Warren itself admits that its dams "can cause changes in the movement, flow, and circulation of a river * * * caus[ing] a river to absorb less oxygen and to be less passable by boaters and fish." And several [other parties who submitted briefs in this case] alert us to the chemical modification caused by the dams, with "immediate impact on aquatic organisms, which of course rely on dissolved oxygen in water to breathe." Then there are the findings of the Maine Department of Environmental Protection that led to this appeal:

> "The record in this case demonstrates that Warren's dams have caused long stretches of the natural riverbed to be essentially dry and thus unavailable as habitat for indigenous [native, or original] populations of fish and other aquatic organisms; that the dams have blocked the passage of eels and sea-run fish to their natural spawning and nursery waters; that the dams have eliminated the opportunity for fishing in long stretches of river, and that the dams have prevented recreational access to and use of the river."

Changes in the river like these fall within a State's legitimate legislative business, and the Clean Water Act provides for a system that respects the States' concerns. [Emphasis added.]

State certifications under [the Clean Water Act] are essential in the scheme to preserve state authority to address the broad range of pollution * * * .

Reading [the Clean Water Act] to give "discharge" its common and ordinary meaning preserves the state authority apparently intended.

DECISION AND REMEDY The United States Supreme Court affirmed the decision of the Maine Supreme Judicial Court. Under the Clean Water Act, an activity that may result in a "discharge" into navigable waters under a federal license requires state approval. Water flowing through a hydropower dam operated under a federal license constitutes such a "discharge."

WHAT IF THE FACTS WERE DIFFERENT? *Would the result in this case have been different if the quality of the water flowing through the turbines of Warren's dams improved before returning to the river? Why or why not?*

- -

Wetlands

WETLANDS
Water-saturated areas of land that are designated by government agencies (such as the Army Corps of Engineers or the Environmental Protection Agency) as protected areas that support wildlife and therefore cannot be filled in or dredged by private contractors or parties without a permit.

The Clean Water Act prohibits the filling or dredging of **wetlands** unless a permit is obtained from the Army Corps of Engineers. The EPA defines *wetlands* as "those areas that are inundated or saturated by surface or ground water at a frequency and duration sufficient to support, and that under normal circumstances do support, a prevalence of vegetation typically adapted for life in saturated soil conditions." In recent years, the broad interpretation of what constitutes a wetland subject to the regulatory authority of the federal government has generated substantial controversy.

Example #3 Perhaps one of the most controversial regulations was the "migratory-bird rule" issued by the Army Corps of Engineers. Under this rule, any bodies of water that could affect interstate commerce, including seasonal ponds or waters "used or suitable for use by migratory birds" that fly over state borders, were "navigable waters" subject to federal regulation as wetlands under the Clean Water Act. The rule was challenged in a case brought by a group of communities in the Chicago suburbs that wanted to build a landfill in a tract of land northwest of Chicago that had once been used as a strip mine. Over time, areas that were once pits in the mine became ponds used by a variety of migratory birds. The Army Corps of Engineers, claiming that the shallow ponds formed a habitat for migratory birds, refused to grant a permit for the landfill.

Ultimately, the United States Supreme Court held that the Army Corps of Engineers had exceeded its authority under the Clean Water Act. The Court stated that it was not prepared to hold that isolated and seasonable ponds, puddles, and "prairie potholes" become "navigable waters of the United States" simply because they serve as a habitat for migratory birds.[12]

Drinking Water

Another statute governing water pollution is the Safe Drinking Water Act of 1974.[13] This act requires the EPA to set maximum levels for pollutants in public water systems. Public water system operators must come as close as possible to meeting the EPA's standards by using the best available technology that is economically and technologically feasible. The EPA is particularly concerned about contamination from underground sources. Pesticides and wastes leaked from landfills or disposed of in underground injection wells are among the more than two hundred pollutants known to exist in groundwater used for drinking in at least thirty-four states. Many of these substances may be associated with cancer and may cause damage to the central nervous system, liver, and kidneys. The act was amended in 1996 to give the EPA more flexibility in setting regulatory standards.

> "Among the treasures of our land is water—fast becoming our most valuable, most prized, most critical resource."
> —DWIGHT D. EISENHOWER,
> 1890–1969
> (Thirty-fourth president of the United States, 1953–1961)

Ocean Dumping

The Marine Protection, Research, and Sanctuaries Act of 1972[14] (popularly known as the Ocean Dumping Act), as amended in 1983, regulates the transportation and dumping of material into ocean waters. It prohibits entirely the ocean dumping of radiological, chemical, and biological warfare agents and high-level radioactive waste. Each violation of any provision may result in a civil penalty of up to $50,000, and a knowing violation is a criminal offense that may result in a $50,000 fine, imprisonment for not more than a year, or both. The court may also grant an injunction to prevent an imminent or continuing violation of the Ocean Dumping Act.

Oil Spills

In 1989, the supertanker *Exxon Valdez* caused the worst oil spill in North American history in the waters of Alaska's Prince William Sound. A quarter of a million barrels of crude oil—more than ten million gallons—leaked out of

---

12. *Solid Waste Agency of Northern Cook County v. U.S. Army Corps of Engineers*, 531 U.S. 159, 121 S.Ct. 675, 148 L.Ed.2d 576 (2001).
13. 42 U.S.C. Sections 300f to 300j-25.
14. 16 U.S.C. Sections 1401–1445.

Clean-up efforts in Alaska's Prince William Sound following the *Exxon Valdez* oil spill. How did this disaster change the law regarding oil spills? Who can be held responsible for clean-up costs? (*Exxon Valdez* Oil Spill Trustee Council/National Oceanic & Atmospheric Administration)

> **"** All property in this country is held under the implied obligation that the owner's use of it shall not be injurious to the community. **"**
>
> —JOHN HARLAN, 1899–1971
> (Associate justice of the United States Supreme Court, 1955–1971)

the ship's broken hull. In response to the *Exxon Valdez* disaster, Congress passed the Oil Pollution Act of 1990.[15] Any onshore or offshore oil facility, oil shipper, vessel owner, or vessel operator that discharges oil into navigable waters or onto an adjoining shore may be liable for clean-up costs, as well as damages.

Under the act, damage to natural resources, private property, and the local economy, including the increased cost of providing public services, is compensable. The act provides for civil penalties of $1,000 per barrel spilled or $25,000 for each day of the violation. The party held responsible for the clean-up costs can bring a civil suit for contribution from other potentially liable parties. The act also decreed that by the year 2011, oil tankers using U.S. ports must be double hulled to limit the severity of accidental spills.

TOXIC CHEMICALS

Originally, most environmental clean-up efforts were directed toward reducing smog and making water safe for fishing and swimming. Over time, however, control of toxic chemicals has become an important part of environmental law.

Pesticides and Herbicides

The Federal Insecticide, Fungicide, and Rodenticide Act (FIFRA) of 1947 regulates pesticides and herbicides.[16] Under FIFRA, pesticides and herbicides must be (1) registered before they can be sold, (2) certified and used only for approved applications, and (3) used in limited quantities when applied to food crops. The EPA can cancel or suspend registration of substances that are identified as harmful and may also inspect factories where the chemicals are made. Under 1996 amendments to FIFRA, there must be no more than a one-in-a-million risk to people of developing cancer from any kind of exposure to the substance, including eating food that contains pesticide residues.[17] Also, the EPA must distribute brochures to grocery stores on the high-risk pesticides that are in or on food, and the stores must display these brochures for consumers.

It is a violation of FIFRA to sell a pesticide or herbicide that is unregistered or has had its registration canceled or suspended. It is also a violation to sell a pesticide or herbicide with a false or misleading label or to destroy or deface any labeling required under the act. Penalties for commercial dealers include imprisonment for up to one year and a fine of no more than $25,000. Farmers

15. 33 U.S.C. Sections 2701–2761.
16. 7 U.S.C. Sections 135–136y.
17. 21 U.S.C. Section 346a.

and other private users of pesticides or herbicides who violate the act are subject to a $1,000 fine and incarceration for up to thirty days.

Can a state regulate the sale and use of federally registered pesticides? Tort suits against pesticide manufacturers were common long before the enactment of the FIFRA in 1947 and continued to be a feature of the legal landscape at the time the FIFRA was amended. Until it heard the following case, however, the United States Supreme Court had never considered whether that statute preempts claims arising under state law.

CASE 18.3 Bates v. Dow Agrosciences, LLC

Supreme Court of the United States, 2005.
544 U.S. 431,
125 S.Ct. 1788,
161 L.Ed.2d 687.
www.findlaw.com/casecode/supreme.html[a]

BACKGROUND AND FACTS The Environmental Protection Agency (EPA) conditionally registered Strongarm, a new weed-killing pesticide, on March 8, 2000.[b] Dow Agrosciences, LLC, immediately sold Strongarm to Texas peanut farmers, who

a. In the "Browsing" section, click on "2005 Decisions." In the result, click on the name of the case to access the opinion.
b. Strongarm might more commonly be called a herbicide, but the FIFRA classifies it as a pesticide.

normally plant their crops around May 1. The label stated, "Use of Strongarm is recommended in all areas where peanuts are grown." When the farmers applied Strongarm to their fields, the pesticide damaged their crops while failing to control the growth of weeds. After unsuccessfully attempting to negotiate with Dow, the farmers announced their intent to sue Strongarm's maker for violations of Texas state law. Dow filed a suit in a federal district court against the peanut farmers, asserting that FIFRA preempted their claims. The court issued a summary judgment in Dow's favor. The farmers appealed to the U.S. Court of Appeals for the Fifth Circuit, which affirmed the lower court's judgment. The farmers appealed to the United States Supreme Court.

IN THE WORDS OF THE COURT . . . Justice STEVENS delivered the opinion of the Court.

* * * *

Under FIFRA * * * , [a] pesticide is misbranded if its label contains a statement that is false or misleading in any particular, including a false or misleading statement concerning the efficacy of the pesticide. *A pesticide is also misbranded if its label does not contain adequate instructions for use, or if its label omits necessary warnings or cautionary statements.* [Emphasis added.]

* * * *

* * * [Section] 136v provides:

"(a) * * * A State may regulate the sale or use of any federally registered pesticide or device in the State, but only if and to the extent the regulation does not permit any sale or use prohibited by [FIFRA].

"(b) * * * Such State shall not impose or continue in effect any requirements for labeling or packaging in addition to or different from those required under [FIFRA]. * * * "

* * * *

* * * *Nothing in the text of FIFRA would prevent a State from making the violation of a federal labeling or packaging requirement a state offense,* thereby imposing its own sanctions on pesticide manufacturers who violate federal law. The imposition of state sanctions for violating state rules that merely duplicate federal requirements is equally consistent with the text of [Section] 136v. [Emphasis added.]

* * * *

* * * For a particular state rule to be preempted, it must satisfy two conditions. First, it must be a requirement "for labeling or packaging"; rules governing the design

CASE 18.3—CONTINUED ▶

CASE 18.3–CONTINUED

of a product, for example, are not preempted. Second, it must impose a labeling or packaging requirement that is "in addition to or different from those required under [FIFRA]." A state regulation requiring the word "poison" to appear in red letters, for instance, would not be preempted if an EPA regulation imposed the same requirement.

* * * Rules that require manufacturers to design reasonably safe products, to use due care in conducting appropriate testing of their products, to market products free of manufacturing defects, and to honor their express warranties or other contractual commitments plainly do not qualify as requirements for "labeling or packaging." None of these common-law rules requires that manufacturers label or package their products in any particular way. Thus, petitioners' claims for defective design, defective manufacture, negligent testing, and breach of express warranty are not preempted.

* * * *

Dow * * * argues that [this] "parallel requirements" reading of [Section] 136v(b) would "give juries in 50 States the authority to give content to FIFRA's misbranding prohibition, establishing a crazy-quilt of anti-misbranding requirements * * * ." Conspicuously absent from the submissions by Dow * * * is any plausible alternative interpretation of "in addition to or different from" that would give that phrase meaning. Instead, they appear to favor reading those words out of the statute * * * . This amputated version of [Section] 136v(b) would no doubt have clearly and succinctly commanded the preemption of all state requirements concerning labeling. *That Congress added the remainder of the provision is evidence of its intent to draw a distinction between state labeling requirements that are preempted and those that are not.* [Emphasis added.]

* * * *

In sum, under our interpretation, [Section] 136v(b) * * * preempts competing state labeling standards—imagine 50 different labeling regimes prescribing the color, font size, and wording of warnings—that would create significant inefficiencies for manufacturers. The provision also preempts any statutory or common-law rule that would impose a labeling requirement that diverges from those set out in FIFRA * * * . It does not, however, preempt any state rules that are fully consistent with federal requirements.

- -

DECISION AND REMEDY   The United States Supreme Court vacated the lower court's judgment. A state can regulate the sale and use of federally registered pesticides to the extent that it does not permit anything that FIFRA prohibits, but a state cannot impose any requirements for labeling or packaging in addition to or different from those that FIFRA requires. The Court remanded the case, however, for further proceedings subject to this standard, concerning certain state law claims "on which we have not received sufficient briefing."

WHAT IF THE FACTS WERE DIFFERENT?   *Suppose that FIFRA required Strongarm's label to include the word* caution, *and the Texas peanut farmers filed their claims under a state regulation that required the label to use the word* danger. *Would the result have been different?*

Toxic Substances

The first comprehensive law covering toxic substances was the Toxic Substances Control Act of 1976.[18] The act was passed to regulate chemicals and chemical compounds that are known to be toxic—such as asbestos and polychlorinated biphenyls, popularly known as PCBs—and to institute investi-

---

18. 15 U.S.C. Sections 2601–2692.

gation of any possible harmful effects from new chemical compounds. The regulations authorize the EPA to require that manufacturers, processors, and other organizations planning to use chemicals first determine their effects on human health and the environment. The EPA can regulate substances that potentially pose an imminent hazard or an unreasonable risk of injury to health or the environment. The EPA may require special labeling, limit the use of a substance, set production quotas, or prohibit the use of a substance altogether.

HAZARDOUS WASTE DISPOSAL

Some industrial, agricultural, and household wastes pose more serious threats than others. If not properly disposed of, these toxic chemicals may present a substantial danger to human health and the environment. If released into the environment, they may contaminate public drinking water resources.

A hazardous waste–disposal team cleans up toxic chemicals that spilled from a semitrailer onto a public highway. If the substance was not properly labeled in violation of the RCRA, what civil penalty might a court impose on the company that operated the vehicle? (Photo Courtesy of Minnesota Pollution Control Agency)

Resource Conservation and Recovery Act

In 1976, Congress passed the Resource Conservation and Recovery Act (RCRA)[19] in reaction to the growing concern over the effects of hazardous waste materials on the environment. The RCRA required the EPA to determine which forms of solid waste should be considered hazardous and to establish regulations to monitor and control hazardous waste disposal. The act also requires all producers of hazardous waste materials to label and package properly any hazardous waste to be transported. The RCRA was amended in 1984 and 1986 to decrease the use of land containment in the disposal of hazardous waste and to require smaller generators of hazardous waste to comply with the act.

Under the RCRA, a company may be assessed a civil penalty of up to $25,000 for each violation.[20] Penalties are based on the seriousness of the violation, the probability of harm, and the extent to which the violation deviates from RCRA requirements. Criminal penalties include fines of up to $50,000 for each day of violation, imprisonment for up to two years (in most instances), or both.[21] Criminal fines and the period of imprisonment can be doubled for certain repeat offenders.

Superfund

In 1980, the U.S. Congress passed the Comprehensive Environmental Response, Compensation, and Liability Act (CERCLA),[22] commonly known as Superfund. The basic purpose of CERCLA, which was amended in 1986, is to regulate the clean-up of leaking hazardous waste–disposal sites. A special federal fund was created for that purpose. Because of its impact on the business community, the act is presented at this chapter's *Landmark in the Legal Environment* feature on the next page.

19. 42 U.S.C. Sections 6901 *et seq.*
20. 42 U.S.C. Section 6928(a).
21. 42 U.S.C. Section 6928(d).
22. 42 U.S.C. Sections 9601–9675.

LANDMARK IN THE LEGAL ENVIRONMENT
Superfund

The origins of the Comprehensive Environmental Response, Compensation, and Liability Act (CERCLA) of 1980, commonly referred to as Superfund, can be traced to drafts that the Environmental Protection Agency (EPA) started to circulate in 1978.

Dump Sites Characterized as "Ticking Time Bombs"
EPA officials emphasized the necessity of new legislation by pointing to what they characterized as "ticking time bombs"—dump sites around the country that were ready to explode and injure the public with toxic fumes.

The popular press was also running prominent stories about hazardous waste–dump sites at the time. The New York Love Canal disaster first made headlines in 1978 when residents in the area complained about health problems, contaminated sludge oozing into their basements, and chemical "volcanoes" erupting in their yards. These problems were the result of approximately 21,000 tons of chemicals that Hooker Chemical had dumped into the canal from 1942 to 1953. By the middle of May 1980, the Love Canal situation was making the national news virtually every day, and it remained in the headlines for a month.

CERCLA—Its Purpose and Primary Elements
The basic purpose of CERCLA, which was amended in 1986, is to regulate the clean-up of leaking hazardous waste–disposal sites. The act has four primary elements:

- It established an information-gathering and analysis system that enables the government to identify chemical dump sites and determine the appropriate action.
- It authorized the EPA to respond to hazardous substance emergencies and to arrange for the clean-up of a leaking site directly if the persons responsible for the problem fail to clean up the site.
- It created a Hazardous Substance Response Trust Fund (Superfund) to pay for the clean-up of hazardous sites using funds obtained through taxes on certain businesses.
- It allowed the government to recover the cost of clean-up from the persons who were (even remotely) responsible for hazardous substance releases.

Application to Today's Legal Environment
The provisions of CERCLA profoundly affect today's businesses. Virtually any business decision relating to the purchase and sale of property, for example, requires an analysis of previous activities on the property to determine whether they resulted in contamination. Additionally, to avoid violating CERCLA, owners and managers of manufacturing plants must be extremely careful in arranging for the removal and disposal of any hazardous waste materials. Unless Congress significantly changes CERCLA and the way that it is implemented, businesses will continue to face potentially extensive liability for violations under this act.

RELEVANT WEB SITES
To locate information on the Web concerning Superfund, go to this text's Web site at **www.thomsonedu.com/ westbuslaw/let**, *select "Chapter 18," and click on "URLs for Landmarks."*

POTENTIALLY RESPONSIBLE PARTY (PRP)

A party liable for the costs of cleaning up a hazardous waste–disposal site under the Comprehensive Environmental Response, Compensation, and Liability Act (CERCLA). Any person who generated the hazardous waste, transported it, owned or operated the waste site at the time of disposal, or currently owns or operates the site may be responsible for some or all of the clean-up costs.

Potentially Responsible Parties under Superfund   Superfund provides that when a release or a threatened release of hazardous chemicals from a site occurs, the EPA can clean up the site and recover the cost of the clean-up from the following persons: (1) the person who generated the wastes disposed of at the site, (2) the person who transported the wastes to the site, (3) the person who owned or operated the site at the time of the disposal, or (4) the current owner or operator. A person falling within one of these categories is referred to as a **potentially responsible party (PRP)**.

Joint and Several Liability under Superfund   Liability under Superfund is usually joint and several—that is, a person who generated *only a fraction of the hazardous waste* disposed of at the site may nevertheless be liable for *all* of the clean-up costs. CERCLA authorizes a party who has incurred clean-up costs to bring a "contribution action" against any other person who is liable or potentially liable for a percentage of the costs, however.

REVIEWING . . . PROTECTING THE ENVIRONMENT

In the late 1980s, various residents of Lake Caliopa, Minnesota, began noticing an unusually high number of lung ailments among their population. A group of concerned local citizens pooled their resources and commissioned a study of the frequency of these health conditions per capita as compared with national averages. The study concluded that Lake Caliopa had four to seven times the usual frequency of asthma, bronchitis, and emphysema when compared with national data. During the study period, citizens began expressing concerns about the large volumes of smog emitted by the Cotton Design apparel manufacturing plant on the outskirts of town. The plant had opened its production facility two miles east of town beside the Tawakoni River in 1977 and employed seventy full-time workers by 1991. Just downstream on the Tawakoni River, the city of Lake Caliopa operated a public waterworks facility, which supplied all city residents with water. In August 1991, the Minnesota Pollution Control Agency required Cotton Design to install new equipment to control air and water pollution. In May 1992, thirty citizens brought a class-action lawsuit in a Minnesota state court against Cotton Design for various respiratory ailments allegedly caused or compounded by smog from Cotton Design's factory. Using the information presented in the chapter, answer the following questions.

1. Under the common law, what would each plaintiff be required to identify in order to be given relief by the court?

2. Are air-quality regulations typically overseen by federal, state, or local governments?

3. The equipment to control air pollution has to meet what standard for limiting emissions from Cotton Design?

4. What information must the city send to every household that the city supplies with water?

KEY TERMS

environmental impact statement (EIS)   579

nuisance   577

potentially responsible party (PRP)   592

toxic tort   578

wetlands   586

CHAPTER SUMMARY • PROTECTING THE ENVIRONMENT

Common Law Actions (See pages 577–578.)	1. *Nuisance*—A common law doctrine under which actions against pollution-causing activities may be brought. An action is permissible only if an individual suffers a harm separate and distinct from that of the general public.
	2. *Negligence and strict liability*—Parties may recover damages for injuries sustained as a result of a firm's pollution-causing activities if it can be demonstrated that the harm was a foreseeable result of the firm's failure to exercise reasonable care (negligence); businesses engaging in ultrahazardous activities are liable for whatever injuries the activities cause, regardless of whether the firms exercise reasonable care.
Federal, State, and Local Regulation (See pages 578–592.)	Activities affecting the environment are controlled at the local and state levels through regulations relating to land use, the disposal and recycling of garbage and waste, and pollution-causing activities in general. Federal regulation involves the following:
	1. *Environmental protection agencies*—The most well known of the agencies regulating environmental law is the federal Environmental Protection Agency (EPA), which was created in 1970 to coordinate federal environmental programs. The EPA administers most federal environmental policies and statutes.

(Continued)

CHAPTER SUMMARY • PROTECTING THE ENVIRONMENT—CONTINUED

Federal, State, and Local Regulation—Continued

2. *Assessing environmental impact*—The National Environmental Policy Act of 1969 imposes environmental responsibilities on all federal agencies and requires the preparation of an environmental impact statement (EIS) for every major federal action. An EIS must analyze the action's impact on the environment, its adverse effects and possible alternatives, and its irreversible effects on environmental quality.

3. *Important areas regulated by the federal government*—Important areas regulated by the federal government include the following:

   a. Air pollution—Regulated under the authority of the Clean Air Act of 1963 and its amendments, particularly those of 1970, 1977, and 1990.

   b. Water pollution—Regulated under the authority of the Rivers and Harbors Appropriation Act of 1899, as amended, and the Federal Water Pollution Control Act of 1948, as amended by the Clean Water Act of 1972.

   c. Toxic chemicals and hazardous waste—Pesticides and herbicides, toxic substances, and hazardous waste are regulated under the authority of the Federal Insecticide, Fungicide, and Rodenticide Act of 1947; the Toxic Substances Control Act of 1976; and the Resource Conservation and Recovery Act of 1976, respectively. The Comprehensive Environmental Response, Compensation, and Liability Act (CERCLA) of 1980, as amended, regulates the clean-up of hazardous waste–disposal sites.

FOR REVIEW

Answers for the even-numbered questions in this For Review *section can be found in Appendix O at the end of this text.*

1. Under what common law theories can polluters be held liable?

2. What is an environmental impact statement, and who must file one?

3. What does the Environmental Protection Agency do?

4. What major federal statutes regulate air and water pollution?

5. What is Superfund? To what categories of persons does liability under Superfund extend?

QUESTIONS AND CASE PROBLEMS

18–1. Clean Air Act. Current scientific knowledge indicates that there is no safe level of exposure to a cancer-causing agent. In theory, even one molecule of such a substance has the potential for causing cancer. Section 112 of the Clean Air Act requires that all cancer-causing substances be regulated to ensure a margin of safety. Some environmental groups have argued that all emissions of such substances must be eliminated if a margin of safety is to be reached. Such a total elimination would likely shut down many major U.S. industries. Should the Environmental Protection Agency totally eliminate all emissions of cancer-causing chemicals? Discuss.

Question with Sample Answer

18–2. Fruitade, Inc., is a processor of a soft drink called Freshen Up. Fruitade uses returnable bottles, which it cleans with a special acid to allow for further beverage processing. The acid is diluted with water and then allowed to pass into a navigable stream. Fruitade crushes its broken bottles and throws the crushed glass into the stream. Discuss fully any environmental laws that Fruitade has violated.

For a sample answer to this question, go to Appendix P at the end of this text.

18–3. Common Law Actions. Moonbay is a home-building corporation that primarily develops retirement communities. Farmtex owns a number of feedlots in Sunny Valley. Moonbay purchased 20,000 acres of farmland in the same area and began building and selling homes on this acreage. In the meantime, Farmtex continued to expand its feedlot business, and eventually only 500 feet separated the two operations. Because of the odor and flies from the feedlots, Moonbay found it difficult to sell the homes in its development. Moonbay wants to enjoin Farmtex from operating its feedlots in the vicinity of the retirement home development. Under what common law theory would Moonbay file this action? Has Farmtex violated any federal environmental laws? Discuss.

18-4. Strict Liability. Cities Service Co. operated a phosphate rock mine that included large settling ponds for the extraction of phosphate. A dam outside of one of these ponds broke, sending a billion gallons of phosphate slime into the nearby Peace River. This killed fish and caused other damage. The state of Florida sued Cities Service under a theory of strict liability for damages. Given these facts, should Cities Service be liable? [*Cities Service Co. v. State*, 312 So.2d 799 (Fla.App. 1975)]

18-5. Clean Water Act. Attique Ahmad owned the Spin-N-Market, a convenience store and gas station. The gas pumps were fed by underground tanks, one of which had a leak at its top that allowed water to enter. Ahmad emptied the tank by pumping its contents into a storm drain and a sewer system. Through the storm drain, gasoline flowed into a creek, forcing the city to clean the water. Through the sewer system, gasoline flowed into a sewage treatment plant, forcing the city to evacuate the plant and two nearby schools. Ahmad was charged with discharging a pollutant without a permit, which is a criminal violation of the Clean Water Act. The act provides that a person who "knowingly violates" the act commits a felony. Ahmad claimed that he had believed he was discharging only water. Did Ahmad commit a felony? Why or why not? Discuss fully. [*United States v. Ahmad*, 101 F.3d 386 (5th Cir. 1996)]

18-6. Environmental Impact Statement. Greers Ferry Lake is in Arkansas, and its shoreline is under the management of the U.S. Army Corps of Engineers, which is part of the U.S. Department of Defense (DOD). The Corps's 2000 Shoreline Management Plan (SMP) rezoned numerous areas along the lake, authorized the Corps to issue permits for the construction of new boat docks in the rezoned areas, increased by 300 percent the area around habitable structures that could be cleared of vegetation, and instituted a Wildlife Enhancement Permit to allow limited modifications of the shoreline. In relation to the SMP's adoption, the Corps issued a Finding of No Significant Impact, which declared that no environmental impact statement (EIS) was necessary. The Corps issued thirty-two boat dock construction permits under the SMP before Save Greers Ferry Lake, Inc., filed a suit in a federal district court against the DOD, asking the court to, among other things, stop the Corps from acting under the SMP and order it to prepare an EIS. What are the requirements for an EIS? Is an EIS needed in this case? Explain. [*Save Greers Ferry Lake, Inc. v. Department of Defense*, 255 F.3d 498 (8th Cir. 2001)]

18-7. CERCLA. Beginning in 1926, Marietta Dyestuffs Co. operated an industrial facility in Marietta, Ohio, to make dyes and other chemicals. In 1944, Dyestuffs became part of American Home Products Corp. (AHP), which sold the Marietta facility to American Cyanamid Co. in 1946. In 1950, AHP sold the rest of the Dyestuffs assets and all of its stock to Goodrich Co., which immediately liquidated the acquired corporation. Goodrich continued to operate the dis-

solved corporation's business, however. Cyanamid continued to make chemicals at the Marietta facility, and in 1993, it created Cytec Industries, Inc., which expressly assumed all environmental liabilities associated with Cyanamid's ownership and operation of the facility. Cytec spent nearly $25 million on clean-up costs and filed a suit in a federal district court against Goodrich to recover, under CERCLA, a portion of the costs attributable to the clean-up of hazardous wastes that may have been discarded at the site between 1926 and 1946. Cytec filed a motion for summary judgment in its favor. Should the court grant Cytec's motion? Explain. [*Cytec Industries, Inc. v. B. F. Goodrich Co.*, 196 F.Supp.2d 644 (S.D. Ohio 2002)]

Case Problem with Sample Answer

 18-8. William Gurley was the president and majority stockholder in Gurley Refining Co. (GRC). GRC bought used oil, treated it, and sold it. The refining process created a by-product residue of oily waste. GRC disposed of this waste by dumping it at, among other locations, a landfill in West Memphis, Arkansas. In February 1992, after detecting hazardous chemicals at the site, the Environmental Protection Agency (EPA) asked Gurley about his assets, the generators of the material disposed of at the landfill, site operations, and the structure of GRC. Gurley refused to respond, except to suggest that the EPA ask GRC. In October, the EPA placed the site on its clean-up list and again asked Gurley for information. When he still refused to respond, the EPA filed a suit in a federal district court against him, asking the court to impose a civil penalty. In February 1999, Gurley finally answered the EPA's questions. Under CERCLA, a court may impose a civil penalty "not to exceed $25,000 for each day of noncompliance against any person who unreasonably fails to comply" with an information request. Should the court assess a penalty in this case? Why or why not? [*United States v. Gurley*, 384 F.3d 316 (6th Cir. 2004)]

After you have answered this problem, compare your answer with the sample answer given on the Web site that accompanies this text. Go to www.thomsonedu.com/westbuslaw/let, select "Chapter 18," and click on "Case Problem with Sample Answer."

18-9. Clean Water Act. The Anacostia River, which flows through Washington, D.C., is one of the ten most polluted rivers in the country. For bodies of water such as the Anacostia, the Clean Water Act (CWA) requires states (which, under the CWA, includes the District of Columbia) to set a "total maximum daily load" (TMDL) for pollutants. A TMDL is to be set "at a level necessary to implement the applicable water-quality standards with seasonal variations." The Anacostia contains biochemical pollutants that consume oxygen, putting the river's aquatic life at risk for suffocation. In addition, the river is murky, stunting the growth of plants that rely on sunlight and impairing recreational use. The

Environmental Protection Agency (EPA) approved one TMDL limiting the *annual* discharge of oxygen-depleting pollutants, and a second limiting the *seasonal* discharge of pollutants contributing to turbidity. Neither TMDL limited daily discharges. Friends of the Earth, Inc. (FoE), asked a federal district court to review the TMDLs. What is FoE's best argument in this dispute? What is the EPA's likely response? What should the court rule, and why? [*Friends of Earth, Inc. v. Environmental Protection Agency*, 446 F.3d 140 (D.C.Cir. 2006)]

A Question of Ethics

18–10. The Endangered Species Act of 1973 makes it unlawful for any person to "take" endangered or threatened species. The act defines *take* to mean "harass, harm, pursue," "wound," or "kill." The secretary of the interior (Bruce Babbitt) issued a regulation that further defined *harm* to include "significant habitat modification or degradation where it actually kills or injures wildlife." A group of businesses and individuals involved in the timber industry brought an action against the secretary of the interior and others. The group complained that the application of the "harm" regulation to the red-cockaded woodpecker and the northern spotted owl had injured the group economically by preventing logging operations (habitat modification) in Pacific Northwest forests containing these species. The group challenged the regulation's validity, contending that Congress had not intended the word *take* to include habitat modification. The case ultimately reached the United States Supreme Court, which held that the secretary had reasonably construed Congress's intent when he defined *harm* to include habitat modification. [*Babbitt v. Sweet Home Chapter of Communities for a Great Oregon*, 515 U.S. 687, 115 S.Ct. 2407, 132 L.Ed.2d 597 (1995)]

1. Traditionally, the term *take* has been used to refer to the capture or killing of wildlife, usually for private gain. Is the secretary's regulation prohibiting habitat modification consistent with this definition?
2. One of the issues in this case was whether Congress intended to protect existing generations of species or future generations. How do the terms *take* and *habitat modification* relate to this issue?
3. Three dissenting Supreme Court justices contended that construing the act as prohibiting habitat modification "imposes unfairness to the point of financial ruin—not just upon the rich, but upon the simplest farmer who finds his land conscripted to national zoological use." Should private parties be required to bear the burden of preserving habitats for wildlife?
4. Generally, should the economic welfare of private parties be taken into consideration in the creation and application of environmental statutes and regulations?

Critical-Thinking Economic Question

18–11. It has been estimated that for every dollar spent cleaning up hazardous waste sites, administrative agencies spend seven dollars in overhead. Can you think of any way to trim the administrative costs associated with the clean-up of contaminated sites?

INTERACTING WITH THE INTERNET

For updated links to resources available on the Web, as well as a variety of other materials, visit this text's Web site at

www.thomsonedu.com/westbuslaw/let

For information on the EPA's standards, guidelines, and regulations, go to the EPA's Web site at

www.epa.gov

To learn about the RCRA's "buy-recycled" requirements and other steps that the federal government has taken toward "greening the environment," go to

www.epa.gov/cpg

The Law Library of the Indiana University School of Law provides numerous links to online environmental law sources. Go to

www.law.indiana.edu/library/services/onl_env.shtml

INTERNET EXERCISES

Go to **www.thomsonedu.com/westbuslaw/let**, the Web site that accompanies this text. Select "Chapter 18" and click on "Internet Exercises." There you will find the following Internet research exercises that you can perform to learn more about topics covered in this chapter.

Internet Exercise 18–1: LEGAL PERSPECTIVE—Nuisance Law
Internet Exercise 18–2: MANAGEMENT PERSPECTIVE—Complying with Environmental Regulation
Internet Exercise 18–3: ETHICAL PERSPECTIVE—Environmental Justice

BEFORE THE TEST

Go to **www.thomsonedu.com/westbuslaw/let**, the Web site that accompanies this text. Select "Chapter 18" and click on "Interactive Quizzes." You will find a number of interactive questions relating to this chapter.

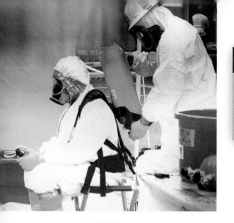

CHAPTER 19

Land-Use Control and Real Property

CHAPTER OBJECTIVES

After reading this chapter, you should be able to answer the following questions:

1 What are the different types of ownership interests in real property?

2 How can ownership interests in real property be transferred?

3 What is a leasehold estate, and how does it arise?

4 What are the respective duties of the landlord and tenant concerning the use and maintenance of leased property?

5 What limitations may be imposed on the rights of property owners?

> " The right of property is the most sacred of all the rights of citizenship. "
> —JEAN-JACQUES ROUSSEAU,
> 1712–1778
> (French writer and philosopher)

REAL PROPERTY
Land and everything attached to it, such as vegetation and buildings.

PERSONAL PROPERTY
Property that is movable; any property that is not real property.

F ROM EARLIEST TIMES, property has provided a means for survival. Primitive peoples lived off the fruits of the land, eating the vegetation and wildlife. Later, as the wildlife was domesticated and the vegetation cultivated, property provided pasturage and farmland. In the twelfth and thirteenth centuries, the power of feudal lords was determined by the amount of land that they held; the more land they held, the more powerful they were. After the age of feudalism passed, property continued to be an indicator of family wealth and social position. In the Western world, the protection of an individual's right to his or her property has become, in the words of Jean-Jacques Rousseau in the chapter-opening quotation, one of the "most sacred of all the rights of citizenship."

Real property (sometimes called *realty* or *real estate*) means the land and everything permanently attached to the land. Everything else is **personal property** (or *personalty*). In this chapter, we first examine the nature of real property. We then look at the various ways in which real property can be owned and at how ownership rights in real property are transferred from one person to another. We also include a discussion of leased property and landlord-tenant relationships. Although real property includes more than land, it is generally referred to simply as "land." Hence, the dominion over land ownership and use that we discuss in the concluding pages of this chapter is commonly referred to as *land-use control*.

THE NATURE OF REAL PROPERTY

Real property consists of land and the buildings, plants, and trees that it contains. Real property also includes subsurface and air rights, as well as personal property that has become permanently attached to real property. Whereas personal property is movable, real property—also called *real estate* or *realty*—is immovable.

Land

Land includes the soil on the surface of the earth and the natural products or artificial structures that are attached to it. It further includes all the waters contained on or under the earth's surface and the airspace above it. In other words, absent a contrary statute or case law, a landowner has the right to everything existing permanently below the surface of his or her property to the center of the earth and above it to the sky (subject to certain qualifications).

Airspace and Subsurface Rights

The owner of real property has relatively exclusive rights to the airspace above the land, as well as to the soil and minerals underneath it. When no limitations on airspace rights or subsurface rights are indicated on the document transferring title at the time of purchase, a purchaser can generally expect to have an unrestricted right to possession of the property (subject to the limits on ownership rights, which will be examined in detail later in this chapter).

Cases involving air rights present questions such as the right of commercial and private planes to fly over property and the right of individuals and governments to seed clouds and produce artificial rain. Flights over private land do not normally violate the property owners' rights unless the flights are low and frequent, causing a direct interference with the enjoyment and use of the land.[1]

Ownership of the surface of land can be separated from ownership of its subsurface. Subsurface rights can be extremely valuable when minerals, oil, or natural gas is located beneath the surface. A subsurface owner's rights would be of little value if he or she could not use the surface to exercise those rights. Hence, a subsurface owner will have a right (called a *profit*—discussed later in this chapter) to use the surface of the land to, for example, find and remove minerals. If the owners of the subsurface rights excavate and their excavation causes the surface to subside, however, they may be liable to the owner of the surface rights.

Plant Life and Vegetation

Plant life, both natural and cultivated, is also considered to be real property. In many instances, the natural vegetation, such as trees, adds greatly to the value of the realty. When a parcel of land is sold and the land has growing crops on it, the sale includes the crops, unless otherwise specified in the sales contract. When crops are sold by themselves, however, they are considered to be personal property or goods. Consequently, the sale of crops is a sale of goods, and therefore it is governed by the Uniform Commercial Code (see Chapter 10) rather than by real property law.

Fixtures

Certain personal property can become so closely associated with the real property to which it is attached that the law views it as real property. Such property is known as a **fixture**—a thing *affixed* to realty, meaning it is attached to it by roots; embedded in it; permanently situated on it; or permanently attached by means of cement, plaster, bolts, nails, or screws. The fixture can be physically attached to real property, be attached to another fixture, or even be

FIXTURE

A thing that was once personal property but that has become attached to real property in such a way that it takes on the characteristics of real property and becomes part of that real property.

---

1. *United States v. Causby*, 328 U.S. 256, 66 S.Ct. 1062, 90 L.Ed. 1206 (1946).

without any actual physical attachment to the land (such as a statue). As long as the owner intends the property to be a fixture, normally it will be a fixture.

Fixtures are included in the sale of land if the sales contract does not provide otherwise. The sale of a house includes the land and the house and the garage on the land, as well as the cabinets, plumbing, and windows. Because these are permanently affixed to the property, they are considered to be a part of it. Unless otherwise agreed, however, the curtains and throw rugs are not included. Items such as drapes and window-unit air conditioners are difficult to classify. Thus, a contract for the sale of a house or commercial realty should indicate which items of this sort are included in the sale to avoid disputes.

OWNERSHIP OF REAL PROPERTY

Ownership of property is an abstract concept that cannot exist independently of the legal system. No one can actually possess or *hold* a piece of land, the air above it, the earth below it, and all the water contained on it. The legal system therefore recognizes certain rights and duties that constitute ownership interests in real property.

Property ownership is often viewed as a bundle of rights. One who possesses the entire bundle of rights is said to hold the property in *fee simple,* which is the most complete form of ownership. When only some of the rights in the bundle are transferred to another person, the effect is to limit the ownership rights of both the one transferring the rights and the one receiving them.

Ownership in Fee Simple

The most common type of property ownership today is the fee simple. Generally, the term *fee simple* is used to designate a **fee simple absolute,** in which the owner has the greatest possible aggregation of rights, privileges, and power. The fee simple is limited absolutely to a person and his or her heirs and is assigned forever without limitation or condition. The rights that accompany a fee simple include the right to use the land for whatever purpose the owner sees fit, subject to laws that prevent the owner from unreasonably interfering with another person's land and subject to applicable zoning laws. Furthermore, the owner has the rights of *exclusive* possession and use of the property. A fee simple is potentially infinite in duration and can be disposed of by deed or by will (by selling or giving away). When there is no will, the fee simple passes to the owner's legal heirs.

Life Estates

A **life estate** is an estate that lasts for the life of some specified individual. A conveyance "to A for his life" creates a life estate.[2] In a life estate, the life tenant has fewer rights of ownership than the holder of a fee simple, because the rights necessarily cease to exist on the life tenant's death.

The life tenant has the right to use the land, provided that he or she commits no waste (injury to the land). In other words, the life tenant cannot injure the land in a manner that would adversely affect its value. The life tenant can use the land to harvest crops or, if mines and oil wells are already on the land, can extract minerals and oil from it, but the life tenant cannot exploit the land

---

> "Few . . . men own their property. The property owns them."
> —ROBERT G. INGERSOLL, 1833–1899
> (American politician and lecturer)

FEE SIMPLE ABSOLUTE
An ownership interest in land in which the owner has the greatest possible aggregation of rights, privileges, and power. Ownership in fee simple absolute is limited absolutely to a person and his or her heirs.

LIFE ESTATE
An interest in land that exists only for the duration of the life of some person, usually the holder of the estate.

---

2. A less common type of life estate is created by the conveyance "to A for the life of B." This is known as an estate *pur autre vie,* or an estate for the duration of the life of another.

by creating new wells or mines. The life tenant is entitled to any rents or royalties generated by the realty and has other rights, such as the right to mortgage or lease the life estate. These cannot extend beyond the life of the tenant, however. In addition, with few exceptions, the owner of a life estate has an exclusive right to possession during his or her life.

Along with these rights, the life tenant also has some duties—to keep the property in repair and to pay property taxes. In short, the owner of the life estate has the same rights as a fee simple owner except that he or she must maintain the value of the property during his or her tenancy, less the decrease in value resulting from the normal use of the property allowed by the life tenancy.

Nonpossessory Interests

In contrast to the types of property interests just described, some interests in land do not include any rights to possess the property. These interests are thus known as **nonpossessory interests**. Three forms of nonpossessory interests are easements, profits, and licenses.

An **easement** is the right of a person to make limited use of another person's real property without taking anything from the property. An easement, for example, can be the right to travel over another's property. In contrast, a **profit**[3] is the right to go onto land owned by another and take away some part of the land itself or some product of the land. If Akmed, the owner of Sandy View, gives Carmen the right to go there and remove all the sand and gravel that she needs for her cement business, Carmen has a profit.

A **license** is the revocable right of a person to come onto another person's land. It is a personal privilege that arises from the consent of the owner of the land and that can be revoked by the owner. A ticket to attend a movie at a theater is an example of a license. **Example #1** Assume that a Broadway theater owner issues to Carla a ticket to see a play. If Carla is refused entry into the theater because she is improperly dressed, she has no right to force her way into the theater. The ticket is only a revocable license, not a conveyance of an interest in property.

TRANSFER OF OWNERSHIP

Ownership of real property can pass from one person to another in a number of ways. Commonly, ownership interests in land are transferred by sale—the terms of the transfer are specified in a real estate sales contract. Often, real estate brokers or agents who are licensed by the state assist the buyers and sellers during sales transactions. (For a discussion of some issues involving online advertising by real estate professionals, see this chapter's *Online Developments* feature on page 602.) When real property is sold or transferred as a gift, title to the property is conveyed by means of a **deed**—the instrument of **conveyance** (transfer) of real property. We look here at transfers of real property by deed, as well as some other ways in which ownership rights in real property can be transferred.

Deeds

A valid deed must contain the following elements:

1. The names of the buyer (grantee) and seller (grantor).

NONPOSSESSORY INTEREST
In the context of real property, an interest in land that does not include any right to possess the property.

EASEMENT
A nonpossessory right to use another's property in a manner established by either express or implied agreement.

PROFIT
In real property law, the right to enter on and remove things from the property of another (for example, the right to enter onto a person's land and remove sand and gravel from it).

LICENSE
A revocable right or privilege of a person to come on another person's land.

DEED
A document by which title to property (usually real property) is passed.

CONVEYANCE
The transfer of a title to land from one person to another by deed; a document (such as a deed) by which an interest in land is transferred from one person to another.

---

3. The term *profit*, as used here, does not refer to the "profits" made by a business firm. Rather, it means a gain or an advantage.

ONLINE DEVELOPMENTS
Potential Problems When Real Estate Is Advertised Online

The Internet has transformed the real estate business, just as it has transformed other industries. Today's real estate professionals market properties—and themselves—online. Given that the Internet knows no physical borders, what happens when an online advertisement reaches people outside the state in which the real estate professional is licensed? Is this illegal? Can the agent be sued for fraud if the ad contains misrepresentations? Such questions are likely to arise in the future as more and more people use the Internet to search for properties.

State Licensing Statutes and Advertising

Every state requires anyone who sells or offers to sell real property in that state to obtain a license. To be licensed, a person normally must pass a state examination and pay a fee and then must take a minimum number of continuing education courses periodically (every year or two) to maintain the license. The purpose of requiring real estate licenses is to protect the public and to maintain quality standards for real property transactions in that state. Usually, a person must also be licensed to list real property for sale or to negotiate the purchase, sale, lease, or exchange of real property or a business opportunity involving real property.[a] Often, a state agency, such as a real estate commission, is in charge of granting licenses and enforcing the laws and regulations governing real estate professionals.

Although some states have rules regarding the advertising of real property, these regulations usually do not specifically address Internet advertising, which necessarily reaches consumers beyond the state's borders. At least one state, California, flatly prohibits Internet advertising of real estate by individuals not licensed in the state.[b] But how can a state enforce such a law or check the credentials of Web advertisers? California's Department of Real Estate *suggests* that anyone who advertises real property online and is not licensed in California should include a disclaimer on the ad—but this is not required.

Actions for Misrepresentations (Fraud)

Suppose that a real estate agent, either inadvertently or intentionally, makes a misstatement online about some important aspect of real property that is for sale. Someone, relying on the statements, responds to the ad and eventually contracts to buy the property, only to discover later that the ad misrepresented it. What remedies does the buyer have? In this situation, the buyer can complain to the state authority that granted the agent's license, and the state may even revoke the license for such conduct. If the buyer wants to obtain damages or cancel the contract, however, he or she will have to sue the agent for fraud (see Chapters 5 and 9). At this point, jurisdiction problems may arise.

If the real estate agent and the buyer are located in different states and the Internet ad was the agent's only contact with the buyer's state, the buyer may have to travel to the agent's state to file the suit. Courts have reached different conclusions on the type of Internet advertising that permits a court to have jurisdiction over an out-of-state advertiser. In many states, a court will not have jurisdiction unless the Web site advertisement is *interactive*. In other states, the courts have held that a passive Web site that solicited business in the state,[c] or a passive Web site coupled with a toll-free phone number or downloadable forms,[d] provided the minimum contacts necessary for jurisdiction. Thus, people who are deceived when buying real property from an online ad and wish to sue the perpetrator of the fraud may be in a precarious position, depending on the state where they live.

For Critical Analysis *Do you think that the federal government should regulate the advertising of real property on the Internet to protect consumers from potential fraud? If so, what kind of regulations would be appropriate, and how might they be enforced?*

c. *Telco Communications v. An Apple A Day*, 977 F.Supp. 404 (E.D.Va. 1997); and *Inset Systems, Inc. v. Instruction Set, Inc.*, 937 F.Supp. 161 (D.Conn. 1996).
d. *State by Humphrey v. Granite Gate Resorts, Inc.*, 1996 WL 767431 (Minn.Dist.Ct. 1996); aff'd, 568 N.W.2d 715 (Minn.App. 1997); aff'd again, 576 N.W.2d 747 (Minn. 1998); and *Hasbro, Inc. v. Clue Computing, Inc.*, 994 F.Supp. 34 (D.Mass. 1997).

a. See, for example, Section 10131 of the Cal. Bus. & Prof. Code and Vermont's 26 V.S.A. Sections 2211–2212.
b. 9 Cal. Code of Regs. Section 2770.

---

   2. Words evidencing an intent to convey the property (for example, "I hereby bargain, sell, grant, or give").
   3. A legally sufficient description of the land.
   4. The grantor's (and, sometimes, the spouse's) signature.

Additionally, to be valid, a deed must be delivered to the person to whom the property is being conveyed or to his or her agent.

Warranty Deeds Different types of deeds provide different degrees of protection against defects of title. A **warranty deed** warrants the greatest number of things and thus provides the greatest protection for the buyer, or grantee. In most states, special language is required to make a deed a general warranty deed; normally, the deed must include a written promise to protect the buyer against all claims of ownership of the property. A sample warranty deed is shown in Exhibit 19–1 on page 604. Warranty deeds commonly include a number of *covenants,* or promises, that the grantor makes to the grantee.

A *covenant of seisin*[4] and a *covenant of the right to convey* warrant that the seller has title to the estate that the deed describes and the power to convey the estate, respectively. The covenant of seisin specifically assures the buyer that the seller has the property in the purported quantity and quality. A *covenant against encumbrances* is a covenant that the property being sold or conveyed is not subject to any outstanding rights or interests that will diminish the value of the land, except as explicitly stated. Examples of common encumbrances include mortgages, liens, profits, easements, and private deed restrictions on the use of the land.

A *covenant of quiet enjoyment* guarantees that the buyer will not be disturbed in his or her possession of the land by the seller or any third persons.

| **Example #2** Assume that Julio sells a two-acre lot and office building by warranty deed. Subsequently, a third person shows better title than Julio had and proceeds to evict the buyer. Here, the covenant of quiet enjoyment has been breached, and the buyer can sue to recover the purchase price of the land plus any other damages incurred as a result of the eviction. |

Quitclaim Deeds A **quitclaim deed** offers the least amount of protection against defects in the title. Basically, a quitclaim deed conveys to the buyer whatever interest the seller had; so, if the seller had no interest, then the buyer receives no interest. Quitclaim deeds are often used when the seller is uncertain as to the extent of his or her rights in the property.

Recording Statutes Every jurisdiction has **recording statutes,** which allow deeds to be recorded. Recording a deed gives notice to the public that a certain person is now the owner of a particular parcel of real estate. Thus, prospective buyers can check the public records to see whether there have been earlier transactions creating interests or rights in specific parcels of real property. Placing everyone on notice as to the identity of the true owner is intended to prevent the previous owners from fraudulently conveying the land to other purchasers. Deeds are recorded in the county in which the property is located. Many state statutes require that the grantor sign the deed in the presence of two witnesses before it can be recorded.

Will or Inheritance

Property that is transferred on an owner's death is passed either by will or by state inheritance laws. If the owner of land dies with a will, the land passes in accordance with the terms of the will. If the owner dies without a will, state inheritance statutes prescribe how and to whom the property will pass.

WARRANTY DEED
A deed in which the seller assures (warrants to) the buyer that the grantor has title to the property conveyed in the deed, that there are no encumbrances on the property other than what the seller has represented, and that the buyer will enjoy quiet possession of the property; a deed that provides the greatest amount of protection for the grantee.

QUITCLAIM DEED
A deed intended to pass any title, interest, or claim that the seller may have in the property but not warranting that such title is valid. A quitclaim deed offers the least amount of protection against defects in the title.

RECORDING STATUTE
A statute that allows deeds, mortgages, and other real property transactions to be recorded so as to provide notice to future purchasers or creditors of an existing claim on the property.

---

4. Pronounced *see*-zuhn.

EXHIBIT 19–1   A SAMPLE WARRANTY DEED

Date: May 31, 2007

Grantor: GAYLORD A. JENTZ AND WIFE, JOANN H. JENTZ

Grantor's Mailing Address (including county):
> 4106 North Loop Drive
> Austin, Travis County, Texas

Grantee: DAVID F. FRIEND AND WIFE, JOAN E. FRIEND AS JOINT TENANTS
WITH RIGHT OF SURVIVORSHIP

Grantee's Mailing Address (including county):
> 5929 Fuller Drive
> Austin, Travis County, Texas

Consideration:
For and in consideration of the sum of Ten and No/100 Dollars ($10.00) and other valuable consideration to the undersigned paid by the grantees herein named, the receipt of which is hereby acknowledged, and for which no lien is retained, either express or implied.

Property (including any improvements):
Lot 23, Block "A", Northwest Hills, Green Acres Addition, Phase 4, Travis County, Texas, according to the map or plat of record in volume 22, pages 331-336 of the Plat Records of Travis County, Texas.

Reservations from and Exceptions to Conveyance and Warranty:

This conveyance with its warranty is expressly made subject to the following:

Easements and restrictions of record in Volume 7863, Page 53, Volume 8430, Page 35, Volume 8133, Page 152 of the Real Property Record of Travis County, Texas; Volume 22, Pages 335-339, of the Plat Records of Travis County, Texas; and to any other restrictions and easements affecting said property which are of record in Travis County, Texas.

    Grantor, for the consideration and subject to the reservations from and exceptions to conveyance and warranty, grants, sells, and conveys to Grantee the property, together with all and singular the rights and appurtenances thereto in any wise belonging, to have and hold it to Grantee, Grantee's heirs, executors, administrators, successors, or assigns forever. Grantor binds Grantor and Grantor's heirs, executors, administrators, and successors to warrant and forever defend all and singular the property to Grantee and Grantee's heirs, executors, administrators, successors, and assigns against every person whomsoever lawfully claiming or to claim the same or any part thereof, except as to the reservations from and exceptions to conveyance and warranty.

    When the context requires, singular nouns and pronouns include the plural.

BY: _Gaylord A. Jentz_
Gaylord A. Jentz

BY: _JoAnn H. Jentz_
JoAnn H. Jentz

(Acknowledgment)

STATE OF TEXAS
COUNTY OF TRAVIS

    This instrument was acknowledged before me on the 31st day of May, 2007
by Gaylord A. and JoAnn H. Jentz

Rosemary Potter
Notary Public.State of Texas
Notary's name (printed): Rosemary Potter

     Notary Seal

Notary's commission expires: 1/31/2011

Adverse Possession

Adverse possession is a means of obtaining title to land without delivery of a deed. Essentially, when one person possesses the property of another for a certain statutory period of time (three to thirty years, with ten years being most common), that person, called the *adverse possessor*, acquires title to the land and cannot be removed from it by the original owner. The adverse possessor is vested with a perfect title just as if there had been a conveyance by deed.

For property to be held adversely, four elements must be satisfied:

1. Possession must be actual and exclusive; that is, the possessor must take sole physical occupancy of the property.
2. The possession must be open, visible, and notorious, not secret or clandestine. The possessor must occupy the land for all the world to see.
3. Possession must be continuous and peaceable for the required period of time. This requirement means that the possessor must not be interrupted in the occupancy by the true owner or by the courts.
4. Possession must be hostile and adverse. In other words, the possessor must claim the property as against the whole world. He or she cannot be living on the property with the permission of the owner.

ADVERSE POSSESSION
The acquisition of title to real property by occupying it openly, without the consent of the owner, for a period of time specified by a state statute. The occupation must be actual, open, notorious, exclusive, and in opposition to all others, including the owner.

Intestate

ETHICAL ISSUE 19.1 ***What public policies underlie the doctrine of adverse possession?***

There are a number of public-policy reasons for the adverse possession doctrine. One reason is that it furthers society's interest in resolving boundary disputes in as fair a manner as possible. For example, suppose that a couple mistakenly assumes that they own a certain strip of land by their driveway. They plant grass and shrubs in the area, and maintain the property over the years. The shrubs contribute to the beauty of their lot and to the value of the property. Some thirty years later, their neighbors have a survey taken, and the results show that the strip of property actually belongs to them. In this situation, the couple could claim that they owned the property by adverse possession, and a court would likely agree.

The doctrine of adverse possession thus helps to determine ownership rights when title to property is in question. The doctrine also furthers the policies of rewarding possessors for putting land to productive use, keeping land in the stream of commerce, and not rewarding owners who sit on their rights too long.

LEASEHOLD ESTATES

Often, real property is used by those who do not own it. A **lease** is a contract by which the owner of real property (the landlord, or lessor) grants to a person (the tenant, or lessee) an exclusive right to use and possess the property, usually for a specified period of time, in return for rent or some other form of payment. Property in the possession of a tenant is referred to as a **leasehold estate.**

The respective rights and duties of the landlord and tenant that arise under a lease agreement will be discussed shortly. Here we look at the types of leasehold estates, or tenancies, that can be created when real property is leased.

LEASE
In real property law, a contract by which the owner of real property (the landlord, or lessor) grants to a person (the tenant, or lessee) an exclusive right to use and possess the property, usually for a specified period of time, in return for rent or some other form of payment.

LEASEHOLD ESTATE
An estate in realty held by a tenant under a lease. In every leasehold estate, the tenant has a qualified right to possess and/or use the land.

Tenancy for Years

A **tenancy for years** is created by an express contract by which property is leased for a specified period of time, such as a day, a month, a year, or a period of years. For example, signing a one-year lease to occupy an apartment creates a tenancy for years. At the end of the period specified in the lease, the lease ends (without notice), and possession of the apartment returns to the lessor. If the tenant dies during the period of the lease, the lease interest passes to the tenant's heirs as personal property. Often, leases include renewal or extension provisions.

Periodic Tenancy

A **periodic tenancy** is created by a lease that does not specify how long it is to last but does specify that rent is to be paid at certain intervals. This type of tenancy is automatically renewed for another rental period unless properly terminated. For example, a periodic tenancy is created by a lease that states, "Rent is due on the tenth day of every month." This provision creates a tenancy from month to month. This type of tenancy can also extend from week to week or from year to year.

Under the common law, to terminate a periodic tenancy, the landlord or tenant must give at least one period's notice to the other party. If the tenancy extends from month to month, for example, one month's notice must be given prior to the last month's rent payment. State statutes may require a different period for notice of termination in a periodic tenancy, however.

Tenancy at Will

Suppose that a landlord rents an apartment to a tenant "for as long as both agree." In such a situation, the tenant receives a leasehold estate known as a **tenancy at will.** Under the common law, either party can terminate the tenancy without notice (that is, "at will"). This type of estate usually arises when a tenant who has been under a tenancy for years retains possession after the termination date of that tenancy with the landlord's consent. Before the tenancy has been converted into a periodic tenancy (by the periodic payment of rent), it is a tenancy at will, terminable by either party without notice. Once the tenancy is treated as a periodic tenancy, termination notice must conform to the one already discussed for that type of tenancy. The death of either party or the voluntary commission of waste (harm to the premises) by the tenant will terminate a tenancy at will.

Tenancy at Sufferance

The mere possession of land without right is called a **tenancy at sufferance.** It is not a true tenancy. A tenancy at sufferance is not an estate, because it is created when a tenant *wrongfully* retains possession of property. Whenever a tenancy for years, periodic tenancy, or tenancy at will ends and the tenant continues to retain possession of the premises without the owner's permission, a tenancy at sufferance is created. When a tenancy at sufferance arises, the owner can immediately evict the tenant.

LANDLORD-TENANT RELATIONSHIPS

In the past several decades, landlord-tenant relationships have become much more complex, as has the law governing them. Generally, the law has come to apply contract doctrines, such as those relating to implied warranties and unconscionability, to the landlord-tenant relationship. Increasingly, landlord-tenant relationships have become subject to specific state and local statutes and ordinances as well. In 1972, in an effort to create more uniformity in the law governing landlord-tenant relationships, the National Conference of Commissioners on Uniform State Laws issued the Uniform Residential Landlord and Tenant Act (URLTA). More than one-third of the states have adopted variations of the URLTA.

A landlord-tenant relationship is established by a lease contract. A lease contract may be oral or written. In most states, statutes mandate that leases be in writing for some tenancies (such as those exceeding one year). Generally, to ensure the validity of a lease agreement, it should be in writing and do the following:

1. Express an intent to establish the relationship.
2. Provide for the transfer of the property's possession to the tenant at the beginning of the term.
3. Provide that the property owner is entitled to retake possession at the end of the term.
4. Describe the property—for example, give its street address.
5. Indicate the length of the term, the amount of the rent, and how and when it is to be paid.

Illegality

State or local law often dictates permissible lease terms. For example, a state law might prohibit gambling houses. Thus, if a landlord and tenant intend that the leased premises be used only to house an illegal betting operation, their lease is unenforceable.

A property owner cannot legally discriminate against prospective tenants on the basis of race, color, national origin, religion, gender, or disability. In addition, a tenant cannot legally promise to do something counter to laws prohibiting discrimination. A commercial tenant, for example, cannot legally promise to do business only with members of a particular race.

Rights and Duties

The rights and duties of landlords and tenants generally pertain to four broad areas of concern—the possession, use, maintenance, and, of course, rent of leased property.

Possession   A landlord is obligated to give a tenant possession of the property that the tenant has agreed to lease. Many states follow the "English" rule, which requires the landlord to provide actual *physical possession* to the tenant (making sure that the previous tenant has vacated). Other states follow the "American" rule, which requires the landlord to transfer only the *legal right to possession* (thus, the new tenant is responsible for removing a previous tenant).

After obtaining possession, the tenant retains the property exclusively until the lease expires, unless the lease states otherwise.

The covenant of quiet enjoyment mentioned previously also applies to leased premises. Under this covenant, the landlord promises that during the lease term, neither the landlord nor anyone having a superior title to the property will disturb the tenant's use and enjoyment of the property. This covenant forms the essence of the landlord-tenant relationship, and if it is breached, the tenant can terminate the lease and sue for damages.

If the landlord deprives the tenant of possession of the leased property or interferes with the tenant's use or enjoyment of it, an **eviction** occurs. An eviction occurs, for instance, when the landlord changes the lock and refuses to give the tenant a new key. A **constructive eviction** occurs when the landlord wrongfully performs or fails to perform any of the duties the lease requires, thereby making the tenant's further use and enjoyment of the property exceedingly difficult or impossible. Examples of constructive eviction include a landlord's failure to provide heat in the winter, light, or other essential utilities.

EVICTION
A landlord's act of depriving a tenant of possession of the leased premises.

CONSTRUCTIVE EVICTION
A form of eviction that occurs when a landlord fails to perform adequately any of the undertakings (such as providing heat in the winter) required by the lease, thereby making the tenant's further use and enjoyment of the property exceedingly difficult or impossible.

Use and Maintenance of the Premises   If the parties do not limit by agreement the uses to which the property may be put, the tenant may make any use of it, as long as the use is legal and reasonably relates to the purpose for which the property is adapted or ordinarily used and does not injure the landlord's interest.

The tenant is responsible for any damage to the premises that he or she causes, intentionally or negligently, and may be held liable for the cost of returning the property to the physical condition it was in at the lease's inception. Also, the tenant is not entitled to create a *nuisance* by substantially interfering with others' quiet enjoyment of their property rights (the tort of nuisance was discussed in Chapter 18). Unless the parties have agreed otherwise, the tenant is not responsible for ordinary wear and tear and the property's consequent depreciation in value.

In some jurisdictions, landlords of residential property are required by statute to maintain the premises in good repair. Landlords must also comply with any applicable state statutes and city ordinances regarding maintenance and repair of buildings.

IMPLIED WARRANTY OF HABITABILITY
An implied promise by a landlord that rented residential premises are fit for human habitation—that is, in a condition that is safe and suitable for people to live in.

Implied Warranty of Habitability   The **implied warranty of habitability** requires a landlord who leases residential property to furnish premises that are in a habitable condition—that is, in a condition that is safe and suitable for people to live in. Also, the landlord must make repairs to maintain the premises in that condition for the lease's duration. Some state legislatures have enacted this warranty into law. In other jurisdictions, courts have based the warranty on the existence of a landlord's statutory duty to keep leased premises in good repair, or they have simply applied it as a matter of public policy. Generally, this warranty applies to major, or *substantial,* physical defects that the landlord knows or should know about and has had a reasonable time to repair—for example, a large hole in the roof.

NOTE Options that may be available to a tenant on a landlord's breach of the implied warranty of habitability include repairing the defect and deducting the amount from the rent, canceling the lease, and suing for damages.

Rent   *Rent* is the tenant's payment to the landlord for the tenant's occupancy or use of the landlord's real property. Usually, the tenant must pay the rent even if she or he refuses to occupy the property or moves out, as long as the refusal or the move is unjustified and the lease is in force. Under the common law, if the leased premises were destroyed by fire or flood, the tenant still had to pay rent. Today, however, most state's statutes provide that if an apartment building burns down, tenants are not required to continue to pay rent.

In some situations, such as when a landlord breaches the implied warranty of habitability, a tenant may be allowed to withhold rent as a remedy. When rent withholding is authorized under a statute, the tenant must usually put the amount withheld into an *escrow account*. This account is held in the name of the depositor (the tenant) and an *escrow agent* (usually the court or a government agency), and the funds are returnable to the depositor if the third person (the landlord) fails to make the premises habitable. Generally, the tenant may withhold an amount equal to the amount by which the defect rendering the premises unlivable reduces the property's rental value. How much that is may be determined in different ways, and a tenant who withholds more than is legally permissible is liable to the landlord for the excessive amount withheld.

Transferring Rights to Leased Property

Either the landlord or the tenant may wish to transfer her or his rights to the leased property during the term of the lease. If complete title to the leased property is transferred, the tenant becomes the tenant of the new owner. The new owner may collect subsequent rent but must abide by the terms of the existing lease agreement.

The tenant's transfer of his or her entire interest in the leased property to a third person is an *assignment of the lease*. Many leases require that the assignment have the landlord's written consent. An assignment that lacks consent can be avoided (nullified) by the landlord. State statutes may specify that the landlord may not unreasonably withhold such consent, though. Also, a landlord who knowingly accepts rent from the assignee may be held to have waived the consent requirement. When an assignment is valid, the assignee acquires all of the tenant's rights under the lease. But an assignment does not release the assigning tenant from the obligation to pay rent should the assignee default.

The tenant's transfer of all or part of the premises for a period shorter than the lease term is a **sublease**. The same restrictions that apply to an assignment of the tenant's interest in leased property apply to a sublease. If the landlord's consent is required, a sublease without such permission is ineffective. Also, a sublease does not release the tenant from her or his obligations under the lease any more than an assignment does.

SUBLEASE
A lease executed by the lessee of real estate to a third person, conveying the same interest that the lessee enjoys but for a shorter term than that held by the lessee.

LAND-USE CONTROL

Property owners—even those who possess the entire bundle of rights set out earlier in this chapter—cannot do whatever they wish with their property. The rights of every property owner are subject to certain conditions and limitations.

There are three sources of land-use control. First, the law of torts (see Chapter 5) places on the owners of land obligations to protect the interests of individuals who come on the land and the interests of the owners of nearby land. Second, landowners may agree with others to restrict or limit the use of their property. Such agreements may "run with the land" when ownership is transferred to others. Thus, one who acquires real property with actual or *constructive* (imputed by law) notice of a restriction may be bound by an earlier, voluntary agreement to which he or she was not a party.

Third, controls are imposed by the government. Land use is subject to regulation by the state within whose political boundaries the land is located. Most states authorize control over land use through various planning boards and zoning authorities at a city or county level. The federal government does not engage in land-use control under normal circumstances, except with respect to federally owned land.[5] The federal government does influence state and local regulation, however, through the allocation of federal funds. Stipulations on land use may be a condition to the states' receiving such funds.

Sources of Public Control

The states' power to control the use of land through legislation is derived from their *police power* and the doctrine of *eminent domain*. Under their police power, state governments enact legislation that promotes the health, safety, and welfare of their citizens. This legislation includes land-use controls. The power of **eminent domain** is the government's authority to take private property for public use or purpose without the owner's consent. Typically, this is accomplished through a judicial proceeding to obtain title to the land.

EMINENT DOMAIN
The power of a government to take land for public use from private citizens for just compensation.

Police Power

As an exercise of its police power,[6] a state can regulate the use of land within its jurisdiction. A few states control land use at the state level. Hawaii, for instance, employs a statewide land-use classification scheme. Some states have a land-permit process that operates in conjunction with local control. Florida, for example, uses such a scheme in certain areas of "critical environmental concern" to permit or prohibit development on the basis of available roads, sewers, and so on. Vermont also utilizes a statewide land-permit program.

Usually, however, a state authorizes its city or county governments to regulate the use of land within their local jurisdictions. A state confers this power through *enabling legislation*. Enabling legislation normally requires local governments to devise *general plans* before imposing other land-use controls. Enabling acts also typically authorize local bodies to enact *zoning laws* to regulate the use of land and the types of, and specifications for, structures. Local planning boards may regulate the development of subdivisions, in which private developers subdivide tracts of land and construct commercial or residential units for resale to others. Local governments may also enact growth-management ordinances to control development in their jurisdictions.

Government Plans   Most states require that land-use laws follow a local government's general plan. A **general plan** is a comprehensive, long-term scheme dealing with the physical development, and in some cases redevelopment, of a city or community. It addresses such concerns as types of housing, protection

GENERAL PLAN
A comprehensive document that local jurisdictions are often required by state law to devise and implement as a precursor to specific land-use regulations.

---

5. Federal (and state) laws concerning environmental matters such as air and water quality, the protection of endangered species, and the preservation of natural wetlands are also a source of land-use control. Some of these laws were discussed in Chapter 18.

6. As pointed out in Chapter 4, the police power of a state encompasses the right to regulate private activities to protect or promote the public order, health, safety, morals, and general welfare.

of natural resources, provision of public facilities and transportation, and other issues related to land use. A plan indicates the direction of growth in a community and the contributions that private developers must make toward providing public facilities, such as roads. If a proposed use is not authorized by the general plan, the plan may be amended to permit the use. (A plan may also be amended to preclude a proposed use.)

Even when a proposed use complies with a general plan, it may not be allowed. Most jurisdictions have requirements in addition to those in the general plan. These requirements are then included in *specific plans*—also called special, area, or community plans. Specific plans typically pertain to only a portion of a jurisdiction's area. For example, a specific plan may concern a downtown area subject to redevelopment efforts, an area with special environmental concerns, or an area with increased public transportation needs arising from population growth.

Zoning Laws   In addition to complying with a general plan and any specific plans, a particular land use must comply with zoning laws. The term **zoning** refers to the dividing of an area into districts to which specific land-use regulations apply. A typical zoning law consists of a zoning map and a zoning ordinance. The zoning map indicates the characteristics of each parcel of land within an area and divides that area into districts. The zoning ordinance specifies the restrictions on land use within those districts.

Zoning ordinances generally include two types of restrictions. One type pertains to the kind of land use—such as commercial versus residential—to which property within a particular district may be put. The second type dictates the engineering features and architectural design of structures built within that district.

Use Restrictions   Districts are typically zoned for residential, commercial, industrial, or agricultural use. Each district may be further subdivided for degree or intensity of use. **| Example #3**   A residential district may be subdivided to permit a certain number of apartment buildings and a specific number of units in each building. Commercial and industrial districts are often zoned to permit *heavy* or *light* activity. Heavy activity might include the operation of large factories. Light activity might encompass the operation of professional office buildings or small retail shops.**|** Zoning that specifies the use to which property may be put is referred to as **use zoning**.

Structural Restrictions   Restrictions known as *bulk regulations* cover such details as minimum floor-space requirements and minimum lot-size restrictions. **| Example #4**   A particular district's minimum floor-space requirements might specify that a one-story building contain a minimum of 1,240 square feet of floor space. Minimum lot-size restrictions might mandate that each single-family dwelling be built on a lot that is at least one acre in size.**|** Referred to collectively as **bulk zoning**, these regulations also dictate *setback* (the distance between a building and a street, sidewalk, or other boundary) and the height of buildings, with different requirements for buildings in different areas.

Restrictions related to structure may also be concerned with such matters as architectural control, the overall appearance of a community, and the preservation of historic buildings. An ordinance may require that all proposed construction be approved by a design review board composed of local architects. A

ZONING

The division of a city by legislative regulation into districts and the application in each district of regulations having to do with structural and architectural designs of buildings and prescribing the use to which buildings within designated districts may be put.

USE ZONING

Zoning classifications within a particular municipality that may be distinguished based on the uses to which the land is to be put.

BULK ZONING

Zoning regulations that restrict the amount of structural coverage on a particular parcel of land.

community may restrict the size and placement of outdoor advertising, such as billboards and business signs. A property owner may be prohibited from tearing down or remodeling a historic landmark or building. In challenges against these types of restrictions, the courts have generally upheld the regulations.

ZONING VARIANCE

The granting of permission by a municipality or other public board to a landowner to use his or her property in a way that does not strictly conform with the zoning regulations so as to avoid causing the landowner undue hardship.

Variances   A **zoning variance** allows property to be used or structures to be built in some way that varies from the restrictions of a zoning ordinance. **| Example #5** A variance may exempt property from a use restriction to allow, for example, a bakery shop in a residential area. Or a variance may exempt a building from a height restriction so that, for example, a two-story house can be built in a district in which houses are otherwise limited to one floor.| Some jurisdictions do not permit variances from use restrictions.

Variances are normally granted by local adjustment boards. In general, a property owner must meet three criteria to obtain a variance:

1. The owner must find it impossible to realize a reasonable return on the land as currently zoned.
2. The adverse effect of the zoning ordinance must be particular to the party seeking the variance and not have a similar effect on other owners in the same zone.
3. Granting the variance must not substantially alter the essential character of the zoned area.

Perhaps the most important of these criteria is whether the variance would substantially alter the character of the area. Courts are more lenient about the other requirements when reviewing decisions of adjustment boards.

In contrast to a "use" provision, an "area" restriction regulates the area, height, density, setback, or sideline attributes of a building or other development on a piece of property. For example, an area provision may dictate the distance between buildings. In the following case, a builder sought a variance from an area provision.

CASE 19.1   Richard Roeser Professional Builder, Inc. v. Anne Arundel County

Maryland Court of Appeals, 2002.
386 Md. 294,
793 A.2d 545.
www.courts.state.md.us/opinions.html[a]

HISTORICAL AND ECONOMIC SETTING   *For decades, it has been a common practice in most states for a buyer to contract to buy property subject to the condition that the contract will be consummated (will become binding) only if a local zoning board grants a variance to permit development of the property. Although it has been argued that this practice constitutes a "self-created" hardship for the buyer, the courts have generally approved requests for variances in such circumstances.*[b]

a. At the bottom of the screen, click on the "Search" link. In the result, choose "Both Appellate Courts" from the drop-down menu, enter "Roeser," and click on "Google Search." Click on the case name in the resulting list to access the opinion. The Maryland Judiciary maintains this Web site.
b. See, for example, *Myron v. City of Plymouth,* 562 N.W.2d 21 (Minn.App. 1997).

BACKGROUND AND FACTS   In 1999, with a certain project in mind, Richard Roeser Professional Builder, Inc. (RRPB), contracted to buy two lots near Annapolis, Maryland, in Anne Arundel County, for $62,000. Part of one of the lots was adjacent to wetlands. County "Critical Area" zoning provisions required a setback "buffer zone" between wetlands and any development on the property. At the time, RRPB knew that variances from the provisions would be required to build the firm's project on the lot. RRPB applied for those variances, but the county zoning board denied the request on the ground that "[t]he conditions surrounding the Petitioners' request for a variance have been self-created." RRPB filed a suit in a Maryland state court against the county. The court rejected the board's decision. The board appealed to a state intermediate appellate court, which reversed the judgment of the lower court and directed it to reinstate the decision of the board. RRPB appealed to the Maryland Court of Appeals, the state's highest court.

IN THE WORDS OF THE COURT . . . CATHELL, Judge.

*   *   *   *

*   *   *   [Z]oning constitutes restrictions on land, not on title. Both the Maryland Declaration of Rights and the Fifth Amendment of the United States Constitution guarantee rights to property owners. Property owners start out with the unrestricted right to use their land as they see fit. Under the common law, those rights are limited only by a restriction as to uses that create traditional nuisances. *   *   *   [H]owever, *   *   * reasonable regulation is constitutional. That said, it must, nonetheless, be recognized that *regulation of land, including zoning regulations, are limitations on the full exercise of a property owner's constitutional rights as well as his or her rights under the common law.* [Emphasis added.]

*   *   *   [W]e must not forget the underlying principle that *   *   * zoning ordinances are in derogation of [deviate from] the common law right to so use private property as to realize its highest utility, and while they should be liberally construed to accomplish their plain purpose and intent, they should not be extended by implication to cases not clearly within the scope of the purpose and intent manifest in their language. In that respect, reasonable zoning limitations are always directed to the property, itself, and its uses and structures, not to the completely separate matter of title to property, which is another whole field of law. In zoning, it is the property that is regulated, not the title.

In Maryland, when title is transferred, it takes with it all the encumbrances and burdens that attach to title; but it also takes with it all the benefits and rights inherent in ownership. If a predecessor in title was subject to a claim that he had created his own hardship, that burden, for variance purposes, passes with the title. But, at the same time, if the prior owner has not self-created a hardship, a self-created hardship is not immaculately conceived merely because the new owner obtains title.

DECISION AND REMEDY The Maryland Court of Appeals reversed the judgment of the lower court and remanded the case for further proceedings. The Maryland Court of Appeals held that RRPB's purchase of the property, with notice that it was subject to restrictions, including a "Critical Area" buffer zone for wetlands under county zoning provisions, was not a self-created hardship that precluded RRPB from receiving a variance.

FOR CRITICAL ANALYSIS–Social Consideration *Why should it matter whether a hardship was "self-created" when determining whether a variance should be granted?*

Subdivision Regulations When subdividing a parcel of land into smaller plots, a private developer must comply not only with local zoning ordinances but also with local subdivision regulations. Subdivision regulations are different from zoning ordinances, although they may be administered by the same local agencies that oversee the zoning process. In the design of a subdivision, the local authorities may demand, for example, the allocation of space for a public park or school or may require a developer to construct streets to accommodate a specific level of traffic.

Growth-Management Ordinances To prevent population growth from racing ahead of the community's ability to provide necessary public services, local authorities may enact a growth-management ordinance to limit, for example, the number of residential building permits. A property owner may thus be precluded from constructing a residential building on his or her property even if the area is zoned for the use and the proposed structure complies with all other requirements. A growth-management ordinance may prohibit the issuance of residential building permits for a specific period of time, until the occurrence of a specific event (such as a decline in the total number of residents in the community), or on the basis of the availability of necessary public services (such as the capacity for drainage in the area or the proximity of hospitals and police stations).

Limitations on the Exercise of Police Power   The government's exercise of its police power to regulate the use of land is limited in at least three ways. Two of these limitations arise under the Fourteenth Amendment to the Constitution. The third limitation arises under the Fifth Amendment and requires that, under certain circumstances, the government must compensate an owner who is deprived of the use of his or her property.

Due Process and Equal Protection   A government cannot regulate the use of land in a way that violates either the due process clause or the equal protection clause of the Fourteenth Amendment. A government may be deemed to violate the due process clause if it acts arbitrarily or unreasonably. Thus, there must be a *rational basis* for classifications that are imposed on property. Any classification that is reasonably related to the health or general welfare of the public is deemed to have a rational basis.

Under the equal protection clause, land-use controls cannot be discriminatory. A zoning ordinance is discriminatory if it affects one parcel of land in a way in which it does not affect surrounding parcels and if there is no rational basis for the difference. For example, classifying a single parcel in a way that does not accord with a general plan is discriminatory. Similarly, a zoning ordinance cannot be racially discriminatory. |**Example #6**   A community may not zone itself to exclude all low-income housing if the intention is to exclude minorities.|

As explained in Chapter 4, *procedural* due process concerns the fairness of the procedures that a government uses to take an action, while *substantive* due process focuses on the substance of that action. A challenge to a state law based on both aspects of due process was at issue in the following case.

CASE 19.2   MacPherson v. Department of Administrative Services

Supreme Court of Oregon, 2006.
340 Or. 117,
130 P.3d 308.
159.121.112.45/supreme.htm [a]

BACKGROUND AND FACTS   In 1973, Oregon began to impose regulations to protect farmland, forestland, and other nonurban uses and limit most new construction to areas within urban boundaries. In 2004, voters in the state approved an initiative known as Ballot Measure 37—later codified as Oregon Revised Statute (ORS) Section 197.352. The measure required a state or local government entity, on a property

owner's claim, to pay the owner for any reduction in the fair market value of his or her real property due to certain "land-use regulation" or to modify, remove, or avoid applying the regulation. If the government entity chose not to apply the regulation, the owner could put the property to a use permitted at the time the property was acquired, even if the regulation would have otherwise prohibited that use. Hector MacPherson and others filed a suit in an Oregon state court against the Oregon Department of Administrative Services and other state agencies. Believing that their property could be adversely affected by their neighbors' conflicting use of property, the plaintiffs argued in part that Measure 37 violated the due process clause of the Fourteenth Amendment. The court declared the measure unconstitutional. The defendants appealed to the Oregon Supreme Court.

a. Click on "February" under "Cases decided in 2006." When that page opens, click on the name of the case to read the opinion. The Oregon Judicial Department maintains this Web site.

IN THE WORDS OF THE COURT . . . _De MUNIZ_, C.J. [Chief Justice]

* * * *

* * * [T]he trial court held that Measure 37 violated the procedural due process rights of [the plaintiffs] because the measure failed to provide * * * procedures for those property owners to challenge governmental actions that adversely would affect their property interests. The trial court held that, because nearby property owners may suffer "irreparable harm" as a result of a governmental decision to modify, remove, or not apply a land-use regulation, property owners so affected "must be given notice and an opportunity to be heard _before_ a public entity decides the Measure 37 claim."

In so ruling, the trial court asked more of Measure 37 than the measure was required to deliver. While it is true that Measure 37 does not expressly provide the * * * procedures that the trial court outlined, it does not follow that that omission renders Measure 37 unconstitutional under the Fourteenth Amendment. * * *

Nothing in Measure 37 denies * * * procedures to individuals such as plaintiffs who may wish to challenge particular governmental actions that may harm individual property interests. Neither does Measure 37 preclude responsible governmental entities from implementing such * * * procedures. To the contrary, Measure 37 contemplates that a "metropolitan service district, city, or county, or state agency may adopt or apply procedures for the processing of claims under this act." And, as the trial court noted, for claims that a state entity must decide, the state has adopted rules that provide for notice and an opportunity to be heard to affected third parties. * * * We therefore conclude that Measure 37 * * * does not violate plaintiffs' procedural due process rights.

The trial court also concluded that Measure 37 violated the substantive component of the Fourteenth Amendment's due process clause. The trial court explained that * * * "the government, through the initiative process, could not have had a legitimate reason for enacting Measure 37, because * * * the compensation provision of Measure 37 impedes the [government's power to regulate land use]." On appeal, plaintiffs argue that the trial court correctly held that Measure 37 was unable to withstand rational basis review, [that is,] that the measure was not reasonably related to a legitimate state interest.

* * * Plaintiffs assert that compensating persons who suffer economic loss due to governmental regulation furthers "private interests," which is not a legitimate state interest. * * *

* * * [Plaintiffs also] assert * * * that, before the enactment of Measure 37, no law required governments to offer such compensation. Plaintiffs reason from that fact that it would be "manifestly destructive" to society to burden the public with compensating individuals when the government has enacted land-use regulations for the public good. * * *

We find none of those arguments persuasive. * * * _Although it is true that_ * * * _the [Constitution does not require] compensation to individuals who suffer any loss in property value as a consequence of land-use regulation, it is equally true that [the Constitution does not forbid] requiring such compensation in the manner provided for in Measure 37._ The people, in exercising their initiative power, were free to enact Measure 37 in furtherance of policy objectives such as compensating landowners for a diminution in property value resulting from certain land-use regulations or otherwise relieving landowners from some of the financial burden of certain land-use regulations. Neither policy is irrational; no one seriously can assert that Measure 37 is not reasonably related to those policy objectives. [Emphasis added.]

CASE 19.2–CONTINUED ▶

DECISION AND REMEDY   The Oregon Supreme Court reversed the judgment of the lower court and remanded the case for the entry of a judgment in favor of the defendants. The state supreme court concluded that Measure 37 did not violate either the procedural or the substantive component of the due process clause of the Fourteenth Amendment.

WHAT IF THE FACTS WERE DIFFERENT?   *If Measure 37 had authorized the payment of compensation but not a waiver of land-use regulations for certain property owners, is it likely that their neighbors would have challenged the statute? If so, would the result have been the same? Discuss.*

* * *

Just Compensation   Under the Fifth Amendment, private property may not be taken for a public purpose without the payment of just compensation.[7] If government restrictions on a landowner's property rights are overly burdensome, the regulation may be deemed a taking. A *taking* occurs when a regulation denies an owner the ability to use his or her property for any reasonable income-producing or private purpose for which it is suited. This requires the government to pay the owner.

| **Example #7**   Suppose that Perez purchases a large tract of land with the intent to subdivide and develop it into residential properties. At the time of the purchase, there are no zoning laws restricting use of the land. After Perez has taken significant steps to develop the property, the county attempts to zone the tract for use as "public parkland only." If this prohibits Perez from developing any of the land, normally it will be deemed a taking. If the county does not fairly compensate Perez, the regulation will be held unconstitutional and void. |

The distinction between an ordinance that merely restricts land use and an outright taking is crucial. A restriction is simply an exercise of the state's police

---

7. Although the Fifth Amendment pertains to actions taken by the federal government, the Fourteenth Amendment has been interpreted as extending this limitation to state actions.

A view of the ocean from a public park. If this had once been private property, why would the government have been prohibited from taking it for public use without paying the owner? (PhotoDisc)

power; even though it limits a property owner's land use, the owner generally need not be compensated for the limitation. If an ordinance or other government action completely deprives an owner of use or benefit of property or constitutes an outright governmental taking of property, however, the owner normally must be compensated.

The United States Supreme Court has held that restrictions do not constitute a taking of an owner's property if they "substantially advance legitimate state interests" and do not "den[y] an owner economically viable use of his land."[8] It is not clear, however, exactly what constitutes a "legitimate state interest" or when particular restrictions "substantially advance" that interest. Furthermore, the term "economically viable use" has not yet been clearly defined.

> "[A] strong public desire to improve the public condition is not enough to warrant achieving the desire by a shorter cut than . . . paying for the change."
>
> —OLIVER WENDELL HOLMES, JR., 1841–1935
> (Associate justice of the United States Supreme Court, 1902–1932)

Eminent Domain

As already noted, governments have an inherent power to take property for public use or purpose without the consent of the owner. This is the power of eminent domain, and it is very important in the public control of land use.

Every property owner holds his or her interest in land subject to a superior interest. Just as in medieval England the king was the ultimate landowner, so in the United States the government retains an ultimate ownership right in all land. This right, known as eminent domain, is sometimes referred to as the *condemnation power* of the government to take land for public use. It gives to the government a right to acquire possession of real property in the manner directed by the Constitution and the laws of the state whenever the public interest requires it. Property may not be taken for private benefit, but only for public use.

| **Example #8** When a new public highway is to be built, the government must decide where to build it and how much land to condemn. After the government determines that a particular parcel of land is necessary for public use, it brings a judicial proceeding to obtain title to the land. |

Under the Fifth Amendment, although the government may take land for public use, it must pay fair and just compensation for it. Thus, in the previous highway example, after the proceeding to obtain title to the land, there is a second proceeding in which the court determines the *fair value* of the land. Fair value is usually approximately equal to market value.

Can the power of eminent domain be used to further economic development? That was the question in the following case.

---

8. *Agins v. Tiburon*, 447 U.S. 255, 100 S.Ct. 2138, 65 L.Ed.2d 106 (1980).

CASE 19.3 **Kelo v. City of New London, Connecticut**

Supreme Court of the United States, 2005.
__ U.S. __,
125 S.Ct. 2655,
162 L.Ed.2d 439.
www.findlaw.com/casecode/supreme.html[a]

BACKGROUND AND FACTS Decades of economic decline led a Connecticut state agency in 1990 to designate the city

a. In the "Browsing" section, click on "2005 Decisions." In the result, click on "Kelo v. New London" to access the opinion.

of New London as a "distressed municipality." In 1996, the federal government closed the Naval Undersea Warfare Center, which had been located in the Fort Trumbull area of the city and had employed over 1,500 people. Within two years, the city's unemployment rate was nearly double that of the state. In 1998, Pfizer, Inc., announced that it would build a $300 million research facility on a site next to Fort Trumbull. Hoping that this would draw new business to the city, the city council approved a plan to redevelop the area that once

CASE 19.3–CONTINUED ▶

housed the federal facility. The city bought most of the land for the project, but negotiations with some of the property owners fell through, and the city began condemnation proceedings. Susette Kelo and other affected owners filed a suit in a Connecticut state court against the city and others. The plaintiffs claimed, among other things, that the taking of

their property would violate the "public-use" restriction in the U.S. Constitution's Fifth Amendment. The court issued a ruling partly in favor of both sides. On appeal, the Connecticut Supreme Court held that all of the city's proposed takings were valid. The owners appealed to the United States Supreme Court.

IN THE WORDS OF THE COURT . . . Justice *STEVENS* delivered the opinion of the Court.

* * * *

We granted *certiorari* to determine whether a city's decision to take property for the purpose of economic development satisfies the "public-use" requirement of the Fifth Amendment.

* * * *

* * * [T]he City would no doubt be forbidden from taking petitioners' land for the purpose of conferring a private benefit on a particular private party. Nor would the City be allowed to take property under the mere pretext of a public purpose, when its actual purpose was to bestow a private benefit. The takings before us, however, would be executed pursuant to a carefully considered development plan. * * * The City's development plan was not adopted to benefit a particular class of identifiable individuals.

On the other hand, this is not a case in which the City is planning to open the condemned land—at least not in its entirety—to use by the general public. Nor will the private lessees of the land in any sense be required to operate like common carriers, making their services available to all comers. But although such a projected use would be sufficient to satisfy the public-use requirement, this Court long ago rejected any literal requirement that condemned property be put into use for the general public. Indeed, while many state courts in the mid-19th century endorsed "use by the public" as the proper definition of public use, that narrow view steadily eroded over time. Not only was the "use by the public" test difficult to administer (*e.g.*, what proportion of the public need have access to the property? at what price?), but it proved to be impractical given the diverse and always evolving needs of society. Accordingly, * * * *this Court* * * * *embraced the broader and more natural interpretation of public use as "public purpose."* * * * [Emphasis added.]

The disposition of this case therefore turns on the question whether the City's development plan serves a "public purpose." Without exception, our cases have defined that concept broadly, reflecting our longstanding policy of deference to legislative judgments in this field.

* * * *

Viewed as a whole, our jurisprudence has recognized that the needs of society have varied between different parts of the Nation, just as they have evolved over time in response to changed circumstances. Our earliest cases in particular embodied a strong theme of federalism, emphasizing the great respect that we owe to state legislatures and state courts in discerning local public needs. For more than a century, our public use jurisprudence has wisely eschewed [avoided] rigid formulas and intrusive scrutiny in favor of affording legislatures broad latitude in determining what public needs justify the use of the takings power.

* * * *

Those who govern the City were not confronted with the need to remove blight in the Fort Trumbull area, but their determination that the area was sufficiently distressed to justify a program of economic rejuvenation is entitled to our deference. The City has

CASE 19.3–CONTINUED

carefully formulated an economic development plan that it believes will provide appreciable benefits to the community, including—but by no means limited to—new jobs and increased tax revenue. As with other exercises in urban planning and development, the City is endeavoring to coordinate a variety of commercial, residential, and recreational uses of land, with the hope that they will form a whole greater than the sum of its parts. To effectuate this plan, the City has invoked a state statute that specifically authorizes the use of eminent domain to promote economic development. Given the comprehensive character of the plan, the thorough deliberation that preceded its adoption, and the limited scope of our review, it is appropriate for us * * * to resolve the challenges of the individual owners, not on a piecemeal basis, but rather in light of the entire plan. *Because that plan unquestionably serves a public purpose, the takings challenged here satisfy the public use requirement of the Fifth Amendment.* [Emphasis added.]

DECISION AND REMEDY   The United States Supreme Court affirmed the lower court's judgment. The Court held that economic development can constitute "public use" within the meaning of the Fifth Amendment's takings clause to justify a local government's exercise of its power of eminent domain to take private property. The Court reasoned that the development "unquestionably serves a public purpose," even though it would also benefit private parties.

WHY IS THIS CASE IMPORTANT?   *The Kelo decision was widely criticized. It reawakened a national debate over the government's ability to seize property, particularly for urban redevelopment projects that benefit private developers. In the wake of the case, numerous states enacted laws to limit the government's power of eminent domain. Most of the other states—and Congress—also took a new look at the law on the subject.*

REVIEWING . . . LAND-USE CONTROL AND REAL PROPERTY

Vern Shoepke purchased a two-story home on a one-acre lot in the town of Roche, Maine, from Walter and Eliza Bruster. The warranty deed that effected the transfer did not specify what covenants would be included in the conveyance. The property was adjacent to a public park that included a popular Frisbee golf course. (Frisbee golf is a sport similar to golf but using Frisbees.) Wayakichi Creek ran along the north end of the park and along Shoepke's property as part of a two-mile public trail system. The deed allowed Roche citizens the right to walk across a five-foot-wide section of the lot beside Wayakichi Creek. Teenagers regularly threw Frisbee golf discs from the walking path behind Shoepke's property over his yard to the adjacent park. Shoepke habitually shouted and cursed at the teenagers, demanding that they not throw objects over his yard. Two months after moving into his Roche home, Shoepke signed a lease agreement with Lauren Slater under which Slater agreed to rent the second floor for $645 per month for nine months. (The lease did not specify that Shoepke's consent would be required to sublease the second floor.) After three months of tenancy, Slater sublet the second floor to a local artist, Javier Indalecio. Over the remaining six months, Indalecio's use of oil paints damaged the carpeting in Shoepke's home. Using the information presented in the chapter, answer the following questions.

1. What is the term for the right of Roche citizens to walk across Shoepke's land on the trail?

2. In the warranty deed effecting the transfer of the property from the Brusters to Shoepke, what covenants would be inferred by most courts?

3. Suppose that Shoepke wants to file a trespass lawsuit against some teenagers who continually throw Frisbees over his land. Shoepke discovers, however, that when the city put in the Frisbee golf course, the neighborhood homeowners signed an agreement that limited their right to complain about errant Frisbees. What is this type of promise or agreement called in real property law?

4. Can Shoepke hold Slater financially responsible for the carpeting damaged by Indalecio?

KEY TERMS

adverse possession   605
bulk zoning   611
constructive eviction   608
conveyance   601
deed   601
easement   601
eminent domain   610
eviction   608
fee simple absolute   600
fixture   599
general plan   610

implied warranty of
    habitability   608
lease   605
leasehold estate   605
license   601
life estate   600
nonpossessory interest   601
periodic tenancy   606
personal property   598
profit   601
quitclaim deed   603

real property   598
recording statute   603
sublease   609
tenancy at sufferance   606
tenancy at will   606
tenancy for years   606
use zoning   611
warranty deed   603
zoning   611
zoning variance   612

CHAPTER SUMMARY • LAND-USE CONTROL AND REAL PROPERTY

The Nature of Real Property (See pages 598–600.)	Real property (also called real estate or realty) is immovable. It includes land, subsurface and air rights, plant life and vegetation, and fixtures.
Ownership of Real Property (See pages 600–601.)	1. *Fee simple absolute*—The most complete form of ownership. 2. *Life estate*—An estate that lasts for the life of a specified individual; ownership rights in a life estate necessarily cease to exist on the life tenant's death. 3. *Nonpossessory interest*—An interest that involves the right to use real property but not to possess it. Easements, profits, and licenses are nonpossessory interests.
Transfer of Ownership (See pages 601–605.)	1. *By deed*—When real property is sold or transferred as a gift, title to the property is conveyed by means of a deed. A deed must meet specific legal requirements. A *warranty deed* warrants the most extensive protection against defects of title. A *quitclaim deed* conveys to the grantee whatever interest the grantor had; it warrants less than any other deed. A deed may be recorded in the manner prescribed by *recording statutes* in the appropriate jurisdiction to give third parties notice of the owner's interest. 2. *By will or inheritance*—If the owner dies after having made a valid will, the land passes as specified in the will. If the owner dies without having made a will, the heirs inherit according to state inheritance statutes. 3. *By adverse possession*—When a person possesses the property of another for a statutory period of time (three to thirty years, with ten years being the most common), that person acquires title to the property, provided the possession is actual and exclusive, open and visible, continuous and peaceable, and hostile and adverse (without the permission of the owner).
Leasehold Estates (See pages 605–606.)	A leasehold estate is an interest in real property that is held only for a limited period of time, as specified in the lease agreement. Types of tenancies relating to leased property include the following: 1. *Tenancy for years*—Tenancy for a period of time stated by express contract. 2. *Periodic tenancy*—Tenancy for a period determined by the frequency of rent payments; automatically renewed unless proper notice is given. 3. *Tenancy at will*—Tenancy for as long as both parties agree; no notice of termination is required. 4. *Tenancy at sufferance*—Possession of land without legal right.

CHAPTER SUMMARY • LAND-USE CONTROL AND REAL PROPERTY—CONTINUED

Landlord-Tenant Relationships (See pages 607–609.)	1. *Lease agreement*—The landlord-tenant relationship is created by a lease agreement. State or local laws may dictate whether the lease must be in writing and what lease terms are permissible.
	2. *Rights and duties*—The rights and duties that arise under a lease agreement generally pertain to the following areas:
	a. Possession—The tenant has an exclusive right to possess the leased premises, which must be available to the tenant at the agreed-on time. Under the covenant of quiet enjoyment, the landlord promises that during the lease term neither the landlord nor anyone having superior title to the property will disturb the tenant's use and enjoyment of the property.
	b. Use and maintenance of the premises—Unless the parties agree otherwise, the tenant may make any legal use of the property. The tenant is responsible for any damage that he or she causes. The landlord must comply with laws that set specific standards for the maintenance of real property. The implied warranty of habitability requires that a landlord furnish and maintain residential premises in a habitable condition (that is, in a condition safe and suitable for human life).
	c. Rent—The tenant must pay the rent as long as the lease is in force, unless the tenant justifiably refuses to occupy the property or withholds the rent because of the landlord's failure to maintain the premises properly.
	3. *Transferring rights to leased property*—
	a. If the landlord transfers complete title to the leased property, the tenant becomes the tenant of the new owner. The new owner may then collect the rent but must abide by the existing lease.
	b. Generally, tenants may assign their rights (but not their duties) under a lease contract to a third person. Tenants may also sublease leased property to a third person, but the original tenant is not relieved of any obligations to the landlord under the lease. In either case, the landlord's consent may be required.
Land-Use Control— Private Control (See pages 609–610.)	1. *The law of torts*—Owners are obligated to protect the interests of those who come on the land and those who own nearby land.
	2. *Private agreements*—Owners may agree with others to limit the use of their property.
Land-Use Control— Government Police Power (See pages 610–617.)	1. *Government plans*—Most states require that local land-use laws follow a general plan.
	2. *Zoning laws*—Laws that divide an area into districts to which specific land-use regulations apply. Districts may be zoned for residential, commercial, industrial, or agricultural use. Within all districts there may be minimum lot-size requirements, structural restrictions, and other bulk zoning regulations. A variance allows for the use of property in ways that vary from the restrictions.
	3. *Subdivision regulations*—Laws directing the dedication of specific plots of land to specific uses within a subdivision.
	4. *Growth-management ordinances*—Limits on, for example, the number of residential building permits.
	5. *Limits on the police power:*
	a. Due process and equal protection—Land-use controls cannot be arbitrary, unreasonable, or discriminatory.
	b. Just compensation—Private property taken for a public purpose requires payment of just compensation. "Taking" for a public purpose includes enacting overly burdensome regulations.

(Continued)

CHAPTER SUMMARY • LAND-USE CONTROL AND REAL PROPERTY—CONTINUED

| Land-Use Control— Eminent Domain (See pages 617–619.) | 1. *Condemnation power*—Governments have the inherent power to take property for public use without the consent of the owner. |
| | 2. *Limits on the power of eminent domain*—Private property taken for a public purpose requires payment of just compensation. |

FOR REVIEW

Answers for the even-numbered questions in this For Review *section can be found in Appendix O at the end of this text.*

1. What are the different types of ownership interests in real property?

2. How can ownership interests in real property be transferred?

3. What is a leasehold estate, and how does it arise?

4. What are the respective duties of the landlord and tenant concerning the use and maintenance of leased property?

5. What limitations may be imposed on the rights of property owners?

QUESTIONS AND CASE PROBLEMS

19–1. Tenant's Rights and Responsibilities. You are a student in college and plan to attend classes for nine months. You sign a twelve-month lease for an apartment. Discuss fully each of the following situations.

1. You have a summer job in another town and wish to assign the balance of your lease (three months) to a fellow student who will be attending summer school. Can you do so?

2. You are graduating in May. The lease will have three months remaining. Can you terminate the lease without liability by giving a thirty-day notice to the landlord?

Question with Sample Answer

19–2. The county intends to rezone an area from industrial use to residential use. Land within the affected area is largely undeveloped, but nonetheless it is expected that the proposed action will reduce the market value of the affected land by as much as 50 percent. Will the landowners be successful in suing to have the action declared a taking of their property, entitling them to just compensation?

For a sample answer to this question, go to Appendix P at the end of this text.

19–3. Property Ownership. Lorenz was a wanderer twenty-two years ago. At that time, he decided to settle down on an unoccupied, three-acre parcel of land that he did not own. People in the area indicated to him that they had no idea who owned the property. Lorenz built a house on the land, got married, and raised three children while living there. He fenced in the land, placed a gate with a sign above it that read "Lorenz's Homestead," and had trespassers removed. Lorenz is now confronted by Joe Reese, who has a deed in his name as owner of the property. Reese, claiming ownership of the land, orders Lorenz and his family off the property. Discuss who has the better "title" to the property.

19–4. Deeds. Wiley and Gemma are neighbors. Wiley's lot is extremely large, and his present and future use of it will not involve the entire area. Gemma wants to build a single-car garage and driveway along the present lot boundary. Because of ordinances requiring buildings to be set back fifteen feet from an adjoining property line, and because of the placement of her existing structures, Gemma cannot build the garage. Gemma contracts to purchase ten feet of Wiley's property along their boundary line for $3,000. Wiley is willing to sell but will give Gemma only a quitclaim deed, whereas Gemma wants a warranty deed. Discuss the differences between these deeds as they would affect the rights of the parties if the title to this ten feet of land later proved to be defective.

19–5. Subdivision Regulations. Suppose that as a condition of a developer's receiving approval for constructing a new residential community, the local authorities insist that the developer dedicate, or set aside, land for a new hospital. The hospital would serve not only the proposed residential community but also the rest of the city. If the developer challenges the condition in court, under what standard might the court invalidate the condition?

Case Problem with Sample Answer

19–6. Jennifer Tribble leased an apartment from Spring Isle II, a limited partnership. The written lease agreement provided that if Tribble was forced to move because of a job transfer or because she accepted a new job, she could vacate on sixty days' notice and owe only an extra two months' rent plus no more than a $650 rerenting fee. The initial term was for one year, and the parties renewed the lease for a second one-year term. The security deposit was $900. State law allowed a landlord to withhold a security deposit for the non-payment of rent but required timely notice stating valid reasons for the withholding or the tenant would be entitled to twice the amount of the deposit as damages. One month into the second term, Tribble notified Spring Isle in writing that she had accepted a new job and would move out within a week. She paid the extra rent required by the lease, but not the rerental fee, and vacated the apartment. Spring Isle wrote her a letter, stating that it was keeping the entire security deposit until the apartment was rerented or the lease term ended, whichever came first. Spring Isle later filed a suit in a Wisconsin state court against Tribble, claiming that she owed, among other things, the rest of the rent until the apartment had been rented again and the costs of rerenting. Tribble responded that withholding the security deposit was improper and that she was entitled to "any penalties." Does Tribble owe Spring Isle anything? Does Spring Isle owe Tribble anything? Explain. [*Spring Isle II v. Tribble,* 610 N.W.2d 229 (Wis.App. 2000)]

After you have answered this problem, compare your answer with the sample answer given on the Web site that accompanies this text. Go to www.thomson.edu.com/westbuslaw/let, select "Chapter 19," and click on "Case Problem with Sample Answer."

19–7. Easements. In 1988, Gary Dubin began leasing property from Robert Chesebrough at 26011 Bouquet Canyon Road in Los Angeles County, California, to operate Alert Auto, a vehicle repair shop. There was a narrow driveway on one side of the premises, but blocking the widest means of access were crash posts on the adjacent unoccupied property, which Chesebrough also owned. The lease did not mention a means of access, but Dubin's primary customers were to be large trucks and motor homes, which could reach Alert Auto only over the wide driveway. Chesebrough had the posts removed. After his death, the Robert Newhall Chesebrough Trust became the owner of both properties, which Wespac Management Group, Inc., managed. In 2000, Wespac reinstalled the posts. Dubin filed a suit in a California state court against the Trust and others, alleging that he had an easement, which the posts were obstructing, and sought damages and an injunction. The defendants denied the existence of any easement. Does Dubin have an easement? If so, how was it created? Explain. [*Dubin v. Robert Newhall Chesebrough Trust,* 96 Cal.App.4th 465, 116 Cal.Rptr.2d 872 (2 Dist. 2002)]

19–8. Commercial Lease Terms. Metropolitan Life Insurance Co. leased space in its Trail Plaza Shopping Center in Florida to Winn-Dixie Stores, Inc., to operate a supermarket. Under the lease, the landlord agreed not to permit "any [other] property located within the shopping center to be used for or occupied by any business dealing in or which shall keep in stock or sell for off-premises consumption any staple or fancy groceries" in more than "500 square feet of sales area." In 1999, Metropolitan leased 22,000 square feet of space in Trail Plaza to 99 Cent Stuff-Trail Plaza, LLC, under a lease that prohibited it from selling "groceries" in more than 500 square feet of "sales area." Shortly after 99 Cent Stuff opened, it began selling food and other products, including soap, matches, and paper napkins. Alleging that these sales violated the parties'

leases, Winn-Dixie filed a suit in a Florida state court against 99 Cent Stuff and others. The defendants argued in part that the groceries provision covered only food and the 500-square-foot restriction included only shelf space, not store aisles. How should these lease terms be interpreted? Should the court grant an injunction in Winn-Dixie's favor? Explain. [*Winn-Dixie Stores, Inc. v. 99 Cent Stuff-Trail Plaza, LLC,* 811 So.2d 719 (Fla.App. 3 Dist. 2002)]

19–9. Eminent Domain. The Hope Partnership for Education, a religious organization, proposed to build a private independent middle school in a blighted neighborhood in Philadelphia, Pennsylvania. In 2002, the Hope Partnership asked the Redevelopment Authority of the City of Philadelphia to acquire specific land for the project and sell it to the Hope Partnership for a nominal price. The land included a house at 1839 North Eighth Street owned by Mary Smith, whose daughter Veronica lived there with her family. The Authority offered Smith $12,000 for the house and initiated a taking of the property. Smith filed a suit in a Pennsylvania state court against the Authority, admitting that the house was a "substandard structure in a blighted area," but arguing that the taking was unconstitutional because its beneficiary was private. The Authority asserted that only the public purpose of the taking should be considered, not the status of the property's developer. On what basis can a government entity use the power of eminent domain to take property? What are the limits to this power? How should the court rule? Why? [*In re Redevelopment Authority of City of Philadelphia,* 891 A.2d 820 (Pa.Cmwlth. 2006)]

A Question of Ethics

19–10. John and Terry Hoffius own property in Jackson, Michigan, which they rent. Kristal McCready and Keith Kerr responded to the Hoffiuses' ad about the property. The Hoffiuses refused to rent to McCready and Kerr, however, when they learned that the two were single and intended to live together. John Hoffius told all prospective tenants that unmarried cohabitation violated his religious beliefs. McCready and others filed a suit in a Michigan state court against the Hoffiuses. They alleged in part that the Hoffiuses' actions violated the plaintiffs' civil rights under a state law that prohibits discrimination on the basis of "marital status." The Hoffiuses responded in part that forcing them to rent to unmarried couples in violation of the Hoffiuses' religious beliefs would be unconstitutional. [*McCready v. Hoffius,* 459 Mich. 131, 586 N.W.2d 723 (Mich. 1998)]

1. Was it the plaintiffs' "marital status" or their conduct to which the defendants objected? Did the defendants violate the plaintiffs' civil rights? Explain.
2. Should a court, in the interest of preventing discrimination in housing, compel a landlord to violate his or her conscience? In other words, whose rights should prevail in this case? Why?
3. Is there an objective rule that determines when civil rights or religious freedom, or any two similarly

important principles, should prevail? If so, what is it? If not, should there be?

Case Briefing Assignment

19–11. Go to www.thomsonedu.com/westbuslaw/let, the Web site that accompanies this text. Select "Chapter 19" and click on "Case Briefing Assignments." Examine Case A.5 [*City of Monterey v. Del Monte Dunes at Monterey*, 526 U.S. 687, 119 S.Ct. 1624, 143 L.Ed.2d 882 (1999)]. The case has been excerpted there in great detail. Review and then brief the case, making sure that your brief answers the following questions.

1. What actions taken by the city of Monterey led to this lawsuit?
2. Why did Del Monte Dunes claim that the city of Monterey had taken its property?
3. What did the trial court decide in this case?
4. What primary issue is in dispute before the Supreme Court?
5. What was the question that the jury was asked to determine and that the Court considered to be "essentially fact-bound"?

Critical-Thinking Legal Question

19–12. Garza Construction Co. erects a silo (a grain storage facility) on Reeve's ranch. Garza also lends Reeve the money to pay for the silo under an agreement providing that the silo is not to become part of the land until Reeve completes the loan payments. Before the silo is paid for, Metropolitan State Bank, the mortgage holder on Reeve's land, forecloses on the property. Metropolitan contends that the silo is a fixture to the realty and that the bank is therefore entitled to the proceeds from its sale. Garza argues that the silo is personal property and that the proceeds should therefore go to Garza. Is the silo a fixture? Why or why not?

INTERACTING WITH THE INTERNET

For updated links to resources available on the Web, as well as a variety of other materials, visit this text's Web site at

www.thomsonedu.com/westbuslaw/let

Information on the buying and financing of homes, as well as the full text of the Real Estate Settlement Procedures Act, is online at

www.hud.gov/buying

For links to numerous sources relating to real property, go to

www.findlaw.com/01topics/33property/index.html

For information on condemnation procedures and rules under one state's (California's) law, go to

www.eminentdomainlaw.net/propertyguide.html

INTERNET EXERCISES

Go to **www.thomsonedu.com/westbuslaw/let**, the Web site that accompanies this text. Select "Chapter 19" and click on "Internet Exercises." There you will find the following Internet research exercises that you can perform to learn more about topics covered in this chapter.

Internet Exercise 19–1: LEGAL PERSPECTIVE—Eminent Domain
Internet Exercise 19–2: MANAGEMENT PERSPECTIVE—How to Challenge a
                        Condemnation of Property

BEFORE THE TEST

Go to **www.thomsonedu.com/westbuslaw/let**, the Web site that accompanies this text. Select "Chapter 19" and click on "Interactive Quizzes." You will find a number of interactive questions relating to this chapter.

CHAPTER 20 Promoting Competition

CHAPTER OBJECTIVES

After reading this chapter, you should be able to answer the following questions:

1 What is a monopoly? What is market power? How do these concepts relate to each other?

2 What type of activity is prohibited by Section 1 of the Sherman Act? What type of activity is prohibited by Section 2 of the Sherman Act?

3 What are the four major provisions of the Clayton Act, and what types of activities do these provisions prohibit?

4 What agencies of the federal government enforce the federal antitrust laws?

5 What are four activities that are exempt from the antitrust laws?

CONTENTS

TODAY'S ANTITRUST LAWS are the direct descendants of common law actions intended to limit *restraints on trade* (agreements between firms that have the effect of reducing competition in the marketplace). Such actions date to the fifteenth century in England. In the United States, concern over monopolistic practices arose following the Civil War with the growth of large corporate enterprises and their attempts to reduce or eliminate competition. In an attempt to thwart competition, they legally tied themselves together in business trusts. A *business trust* is a form of business organization in which trustees hold title to property for the benefit of others. The most powerful of these trusts, the Standard Oil trust, is discussed in this chapter's *Landmark in the Legal Environment* feature on the following page.

Many states attempted to curb such monopolistic behavior by enacting statutes outlawing the use of trusts. That is why all the laws regulating economic competition today are referred to as **antitrust laws.** At the national level, Congress passed the Sherman Antitrust Act in 1890. In 1914, Congress passed the Clayton Act and the Federal Trade Commission Act in an attempt to further curb anticompetitive or unfair business practices. Congress later amended the 1914 acts to broaden and strengthen their coverage.

This chapter examines these major antitrust statutes, focusing particularly on the Sherman Act and the Clayton Act, as amended, and the types of activities they prohibit. Remember in reading this chapter that the basis of antitrust legislation is the desire to foster competition. Antitrust legislation was initially created—and continues to be enforced—because of our belief that competition leads to lower prices, generates more product information, and results in a more equitable distribution of wealth between consumers and producers. As

> **"** Free competition is worth more to society than it costs. **"**
>
> —OLIVER WENDELL HOLMES, JR.,
> 1841–1935
> (Associate justice of the United States Supreme Court, 1902–1932)

ANTITRUST LAW
A law protecting commerce from unlawful restraints.

625

LANDMARK IN THE LEGAL ENVIRONMENT
The Sherman Antitrust Act of 1890

The author of the Sherman Antitrust Act of 1890, Senator John Sherman, was the brother of the famed Civil War general William Tecumseh Sherman and a recognized financial authority. Sherman had been concerned for years with the diminishing competition within U.S. industry and the emergence of monopolies, such as the Standard Oil trust.

The Standard Oil Trust   By 1890, the Standard Oil trust had become the foremost petroleum refining and marketing combination in the United States. Streamlined, integrated, and centrally and efficiently controlled, its monopoly over the industry could not be disputed. Standard Oil controlled 90 percent of the U.S. market for refined petroleum products, and small manufacturers were incapable of competing with such an industrial leviathan.

The increasing consolidation occurring in U.S. industry, and particularly the Standard Oil trust, came to the attention of the public for the first time in March 1881. Henry Demarest Lloyd, a young journalist from Chicago, published an article in the *Atlantic Monthly* entitled "The Story of a Great Monopoly." The article discussed the success of the Standard Oil Company and clearly demonstrated that the petroleum industry in the United States was dominated by one firm—Standard Oil. Lloyd's article, which was so popular that the issue was reprinted six times, marked the beginning of the U.S. public's growing awareness of, and concern over, the growth of monopolies.

The Passage of the Sherman Antitrust Act   The common law regarding trade regulation was not always consistent. Certainly, it was not very familiar to the members of Congress. The public concern over large business integrations and trusts was familiar, however. In 1888, 1889, and again in 1890, Senator Sherman introduced in Congress bills designed to destroy the large combinations of capital that he felt were creating a lack of balance within the nation's economy. Sherman told Congress that the Sherman Act "does not announce a new principle of law, but applies old and well-recognized principles of the common law." [a] In 1890, the Fifty-first Congress enacted the bill into law.

In the pages that follow, we look closely at the major provisions of this act. Generally, the act prohibits business combinations and conspiracies that restrain trade and commerce, as well as certain monopolistic practices.

Application to Today's Legal Environment

The Sherman Antitrust Act remains very relevant to today's world. The widely publicized monopolization case brought in 2001 by the U.S. Department of Justice and a number of state attorneys general against Microsoft Corporation is just one example of the relevance of the Sherman Act to modern business developments and practices.

RELEVANT WEB SITES

To locate information on the Web concerning the Sherman Antitrust Act, go to this text's Web site at **www.thomsonedu.com/westbuslaw/let**, *select "Chapter 20," and click on "URLs for Landmarks."*

a. 21 *Congressional Record* 2456 (1890).

Oliver Wendell Holmes, Jr., indicated in the chapter-opening quotation, free competition is worth more to our society than the cost we pay for it. The cost is, of course, government regulation of business behavior.

THE SHERMAN ANTITRUST ACT

In 1890, Congress passed "An Act to Protect Trade and Commerce against Unlawful Restraints and Monopolies"—commonly known as the Sherman Antitrust Act or, more simply, the Sherman Act. The Sherman Act was and remains one of the government's most powerful weapons in the effort to maintain a competitive economy. Because of the act's significance, we examined its passage more closely in this chapter's *Landmark in the Legal Environment* feature.

Major Provisions of the Sherman Act

Sections 1 and 2 contain the main provisions of the Sherman Act:

1: Every contract, combination in the form of trust or otherwise, or conspiracy, in restraint of trade or commerce among the several States, or with foreign nations, is hereby declared to be illegal [and is a felony punishable by fine and/or imprisonment].

2: Every person who shall monopolize, or attempt to monopolize, or combine or conspire with any other person or persons, to monopolize any part of the trade or commerce among the several States, or with foreign nations, shall be deemed guilty of a felony [and is similarly punishable].

Differences between Section 1 and Section 2

These two sections of the Sherman Act are quite different. Violation of Section 1 requires two or more persons, as a person cannot contract or combine or conspire alone. Thus, the essence of the illegal activity is *the act of joining together.* Section 2, though, can apply either to one person or to two or more persons because it refers to "[e]very person." Thus, unilateral conduct can result in a violation of Section 2.

The cases brought to court under Section 1 of the Sherman Act differ from those brought under Section 2. Section 1 cases are often concerned with finding an agreement (written or oral) that leads to a restraint of trade. Section 2 cases deal with the structure of a monopoly that already exists in the marketplace. The term **monopoly** is generally used to describe a market in which there is a single seller or a very limited number of sellers. Whereas Section 1 focuses on agreements that are restrictive—that is, agreements that have a wrongful purpose—Section 2 looks at the so-called misuse of **monopoly power** in the marketplace.

Monopoly power exists when a firm has an extremely great amount of **market power**—the power to affect the market price of its product. Both Section 1 and Section 2 seek to curtail market practices that result in undesired monopoly pricing and output behavior. For a case to be brought under Section 2, however, the "threshold" or "necessary" amount of monopoly power must already exist. We will return to a discussion of these two sections of the Sherman Act after we look at the act's jurisdictional requirements.

MONOPOLY
A term generally used to describe a market in which there is a single seller or a very limited number of sellers.

MONOPOLY POWER
The ability of a monopoly to dictate what takes place in a given market.

MARKET POWER
The power of a firm to control the market price of its product. A monopoly has the greatest degree of market power.

Jurisdictional Requirements

The Sherman Act applies only to restraints that have a significant impact on interstate commerce. The Sherman Act also extends to U.S. nationals abroad when they are engaged in activities that have an effect on U.S. foreign commerce. (The extraterritorial application of U.S. antitrust laws will be discussed in Chapter 22.) State laws regulate local restraints on competition.

Courts have generally held that any activity that substantially affects interstate commerce falls within the scope of the Sherman Act. As discussed in Chapter 4, courts have construed the meaning of *interstate commerce* broadly, bringing even local activities within the regulatory power of the national government.

SECTION 1 OF THE SHERMAN ACT

The underlying assumption of Section 1 of the Sherman Act is that society's welfare is harmed if rival firms are permitted to join in an agreement that consolidates their market power or otherwise restrains competition. The types of trade restraints that Section 1 of the Sherman Act prohibits generally fall into two broad categories: *horizontal restraints* and *vertical restraints*, both of which will be discussed shortly. First, though, we look at the rules that the courts may apply when assessing the anticompetitive impact of alleged restraints on trade.

Per Se Violations versus the Rule of Reason

Some restraints are so blatantly and substantially anticompetitive that they are deemed *per se* violations—illegal *per se* (on their face, or inherently)—under Section 1. Other agreements, however, even though they result in enhanced market power, do not *unreasonably* restrain trade. Using what is called the **rule of reason,** the courts analyze anticompetitive agreements that allegedly violate Section 1 of the Sherman Act to determine whether they may, in fact, constitute reasonable restraints on trade.

The need for a rule-of-reason analysis of some agreements in restraint of trade is obvious—if the rule of reason had not been developed, virtually any business agreement could conceivably be held to violate the Sherman Act. Justice Louis Brandeis effectively phrased this sentiment in *Chicago Board of Trade v. United States,* a case decided in 1918:

> Every agreement concerning trade, every regulation of trade, restrains. To bind, to restrain, is of their very essence. The true test of legality is whether the restraint imposed is such as merely regulates and perhaps thereby promotes competition or whether it is such as may suppress or even destroy competition.[1]

When analyzing an alleged Section 1 violation under the rule of reason, a court will consider several factors. These factors include the purpose of the agreement, the parties' power to implement the agreement to achieve that purpose, and the effect or potential effect of the agreement on competition. Yet another factor that a court might consider is whether the parties could have relied on less restrictive means to achieve their purpose. (See this chapter's *Management Perspective* feature for a discussion of a case decided under the rule of reason.)

Horizontal Restraints

The term **horizontal restraint** is encountered frequently in antitrust law. A horizontal restraint is any agreement that in some way restrains competition between rival firms competing in the same market. In the following subsections, we look at several types of horizontal restraints.

Price Fixing   Any **price-fixing agreement**—an agreement among competitors to fix prices—constitutes a *per se* violation of Section 1. Perhaps the definitive case regarding price-fixing agreements is still the 1940 case of *United States v.*

PER SE VIOLATION
A type of anticompetitive agreement that is considered to be so injurious to the public that there is no need to determine whether it actually injures market competition; rather, it is in itself *(per se)* a violation of the Sherman Act.

RULE OF REASON
A test by which a court balances the positive effects (such as economic efficiency) of an agreement against its potentially anticompetitive effects. In antitrust litigation, many practices are analyzed under the rule of reason.

HORIZONTAL RESTRAINT
Any agreement that in some way restrains competition between rival firms competing in the same market.

PRICE-FIXING AGREEMENT
An agreement between competitors to fix the prices of products or services at a certain level.

---

1. 246 U.S. 231, 38 S.Ct. 242, 62 L.Ed. 683 (1918).

MANAGEMENT PERSPECTIVE
Antitrust Laws and the Credit-Card Industry

Management Faces a Legal Issue Business owners and managers of banks and other entities doing business with the credit-card industry have long realized that MasterCard and Visa largely control the credit-card market. Although American Express and Discover are also major players in this industry, these networks, as well as other credit-card entities, find it extremely difficult to compete with MasterCard and Visa. Why isn't there greater competition in the credit-card industry? Are MasterCard and Visa violating the antitrust laws in any way?

What the Courts Say In a case brought against MasterCard and Visa by the U.S. Department of Justice, one of the agencies that enforces antitrust laws, the U.S. Court of Appeals for the Second Circuit issued a significant ruling. The court held that the defendants, Visa and MasterCard, had conspired to restrain trade in violation of Section 1 of the Sherman Act. The court noted that the defendants had significant market power (combined, their market power exceeded 70 percent) and had made it very difficult for others to enter the credit-card market through their "exclusionary rules." Under these rules, any bank that chose to issue the credit cards of competitors, including American Express and Discover, forfeited its right to issue Visa and MasterCard products. The court cited evidence that three major U.S. issuer banks—Banco Popular, Advanta, and Bank One—would have contracted with American Express (Amex) to issue Amex cards in the United States if it had not been for the exclusionary rules.

The court applied the rule of reason when analyzing the case. As mentioned elsewhere, under the rule of reason the test of whether a violation of Section 1 of the Sherman Act has occurred is whether the procompetitive

effects of a restraint on trade outweigh its anticompetitive effects. The defendants argued that even if the exclusivity rules did harm competition, those harms were outweighed by the procompetitive effects of the rules. The exclusionary rules promoted "cohesion" within the MasterCard and Visa networks, therefore making it possible for the networks to compete effectively in the marketplace. Thus, the defendants argued, the exclusivity rules were merely part of a legitimate, procompetitive business strategy. The court did not agree. The court observed that "MasterCard members have long been permitted to issue Visa cards, and vice versa, without such consequences. Moreover, . . . there is no evidence that the defendants' network cohesion has been harmed overseas, where, in the absence of exclusionary rules, Amex has contracted with Visa and MasterCard member banks to issue Amex-branded payment cards." "In sum," concluded the court, "the defendants have failed to show that the anticompetitive effects of their exclusionary rules are outweighed by the procompetitive benefits." The court ordered that the exclusionary rules be revoked and permanently enjoined the defendants from promulgating similar rules in the future.[a]

Implications for Managers The court's decision in this case opened the door to greater competition within the credit-card industry. Clearly, the immediate beneficiaries of the decision were American Express and Discover, because banking institutions could now enter into agreements with these networks without having to forgo the issuance of MasterCard and Visa products. But the decision also opened the door for the entry of other firms into the credit-card industry.

a. *United States v. Visa U.S.A., Inc.,* 344 F.3d 229 (2d Cir. 2003).

Socony-Vacuum Oil Co.[2] In that case, a group of independent oil producers in Texas and Louisiana were caught between falling demand due to the Great Depression of the 1930s and increasing supply from newly discovered oil fields in the region. In response to these conditions, a group of major refining companies agreed to buy "distress" gasoline (excess supplies) from the independents so as to dispose of it in an "orderly manner." Although there was no explicit agreement as to price, it was clear that the purpose of the agreement was to limit the supply of gasoline on the market and thereby raise prices.

There may have been good reasons for the agreement. Nonetheless, the United States Supreme Court recognized the dangerous effects that such an

2. 310 U.S. 150, 60 S.Ct. 811, 84 L.Ed. 1129 (1940).

agreement could have on open and free competition. The Court held that the reasonableness of a price-fixing agreement is never a defense; any agreement that restricts output or artificially fixes price is a *per se* violation of Section 1. The rationale of the *per se* rule was best stated in what is now the most famous portion of the Court's opinion—footnote 59. In that footnote, Justice William O. Douglas compared a freely functioning price system to a body's central nervous system, condemning price-fixing agreements as threats to "the central nervous system of the economy."

At issue in the following case was whether an agreement between two pharmaceutical manufacturers violated the Sherman Act.

CASE 20.1   In re Cardizem CD Antitrust Litigation

United States Court of Appeals,
Sixth Circuit, 2003.
332 F.3d 896.

BACKGROUND AND FACTS Hoescht Marion Roussel, Inc. (HMR), is the manufacturer of the prescription drug Cardizem CD, which is used to treat angina and hypertension and to prevent heart attacks and strokes. HMR's patent for the drug expired in November 1992. Andrx Pharmaceuticals, Inc., developed a generic version. On receiving the approval of the Food and Drug Administration (FDA), Andrx would have 180

days within which to sell the generic without competition from other drugmakers. HMR and Andrx became involved in litigation over the patent, however, which delayed FDA approval. In 1997, after the FDA tentatively approved the generic, Andrx agreed not to market it in exchange for $40 million per year from HMR until their dispute was resolved in an "unappealable determination." Louisiana Wholesale Drug Company and other buyers of Cardizem CD filed a suit in a federal district court against the two firms, challenging their agreement as a violation of antitrust law. The court issued a summary judgment in the plaintiffs' favor. The defendants appealed to the U.S. Court of Appeals for the Sixth Circuit.

IN THE WORDS OF THE COURT . . . *OBERDORFER*, District Judge.

* * * *

* * * By delaying Andrx's entry into the market, the Agreement also delayed the entry of other generic competitors, who could not enter until the expiration of Andrx's 180-day period of marketing exclusivity * * * . There is simply no escaping the conclusion that the Agreement, all of its other conditions and provisions notwithstanding, was, at its core, a horizontal agreement to eliminate competition in the market for Cardizem CD throughout the entire United States, a classic example of a *per se* illegal restraint of trade.

None of the defendants' attempts to avoid *per se* treatment is persuasive. * * * [T]he Agreement cannot be fairly characterized as merely an attempt to enforce patent rights or an interim settlement of the patent litigation. As the plaintiffs point out, it is one thing to take advantage of a monopoly that naturally arises from a patent, but another thing altogether to bolster the patent's effectiveness in inhibiting competitors by paying the only potential competitor $40 million per year to stay out of the market. Nor does the fact that this is a "novel" area of law preclude *per se* treatment. To the contrary, whatever may be its peculiar problems and characteristics, *the Sherman Act, so far as price-fixing agreements are concerned, establishes one uniform rule applicable to all industries alike.* We see no reason not to apply that rule here, especially when the record does not support the defendants' claim that the district court made "errors" in its analysis. Finally, the defendants' claims that the Agreement lacked anticompetitive effects and had procompetitive benefits are simply irrelevant. * * * *[T]he virtue/vice of the* per se *rule is that it allows courts to presume that certain behaviors as a class are anticompetitive without expending judicial resources to evaluate the actual anticompetitive effects or procompetitive justifications in a particular case.* * * * [Emphasis added.]

CASE 20.1–CONTINUED

The respondents' principal argument is that the *per se* rule is inapplicable because their agreements are alleged to have procompetitive justifications. The argument indicates a misunderstanding of the *per se* concept. *The anticompetitive potential inherent in all price-fixing agreements justifies their facial invalidation even if procompetitive justifications are offered for some.* Those claims of enhanced competition are so unlikely to prove significant in any particular case that we adhere to the rule of law that is justified in its general application. [Emphasis added.]

Thus, the law is clear that once it is decided that a restraint is subject to *per se* analysis, the claimed lack of any actual anticompetitive effects or presence of procompetitive effects is irrelevant.

DECISION AND REMEDY The U.S. Court of Appeals for the Sixth Circuit held that the agreement between HMR and Andrx was illegal *per se* under Section 1 of the Sherman Act. The appellate court affirmed the lower court's summary judgment on this issue.

FOR CRITICAL ANALYSIS–Social Consideration *The defendants claimed that their agreement had procompetitive benefits. Why did the court hold that this claim was "simply irrelevant"?*

Group Boycotts A **group boycott** is an agreement by two or more sellers to refuse to deal with (boycott) a particular person or firm. Such group boycotts have been held to constitute *per se* violations of Section 1 of the Sherman Act. Section 1 has been violated if it can be demonstrated that the boycott or joint refusal to deal was undertaken with the intention of eliminating competition or preventing entry into a given market. Some boycotts, such as group boycotts against a supplier for political reasons, may be protected under the First Amendment right to freedom of expression, however. The rule of *per se* illegality does not apply to college and professional league sports. In that context, the validity of an allegedly illegal agreement is analyzed under the rule of reason.

GROUP BOYCOTT
The refusal by a group of competitors to deal with a particular person or firm; prohibited by the Sherman Act.

A quarterback for the Miami Dolphins prepares to throw the football to a teammate. If the teams in the National Football League (NFL) agree that players are not eligible for the NFL until three years after their high school graduation, is this a group boycott? How would a court evaluate the legality of this agreement? (Reuters/Pierre DuCharme/Landov)

Horizontal Market Division It is a *per se* violation of Section 1 of the Sherman Act for competitors to divide up territories or customers. | **Example #1** | Manufacturers A, B, and C compete against one another in the states of Kansas, Nebraska, and Iowa. By agreement, A sells products only in Kansas; B sells only in Nebraska; and C sells only in Iowa. This concerted action not only reduces marketing costs but also allows all three (assuming there is no other competition) to raise the price of the goods sold in their respective states. The same violation would take place if A, B, and C simply agreed that A would sell only to institutional purchasers (such as school districts, universities, state agencies and departments, and cities) in all three states, B only to wholesalers, and C only to retailers. |

Trade Associations Businesses in the same general industry or profession frequently organize trade associations to pursue common interests. The joint activities of the trade association may include exchanges of information, representation of the members' business interests before governmental bodies, advertising campaigns, and the setting of regulatory standards to govern the industry or profession.

Generally, the rule of reason is applied to many of these horizontal actions. If a court finds that a trade association practice or agreement that restrains

trade is sufficiently beneficial both to the association and to the public, it may deem the restraint reasonable.

Other trade association agreements may have such substantially anticompetitive effects that the court will consider them to be in violation of Section 1 of the Sherman Act. **| Example #2** A professional engineering society's code of ethics prohibited members from discussing prices with a potential customer until after the customer had chosen an engineer. When this ban on competitive bidding was challenged as a violation of Section 1, the United States Supreme Court held that it was "nothing less than a frontal assault on the basic policy of the Sherman Act."[3] **|**

Vertical Restraints

A **vertical restraint** of trade results from an agreement between firms at different levels in the manufacturing and distribution process. In contrast to horizontal relationships, which occur at the same level of operation, vertical relationships encompass the entire chain of production. The chain of production normally includes the purchase of inventory, basic manufacturing, distribution to wholesalers, and eventual sale of a product at the retail level. For some products, these distinct phases may be carried out by different firms. In other instances, a single firm carries out two or more of the separate functional phases. Such enterprises are considered to be **vertically integrated firms.**

Even though firms operating at different functional levels are not in direct competition with one another, they are in competition with other firms. Thus, agreements between firms standing in a vertical relationship may affect competition. Some vertical restraints are *per se* violations of Section 1; others are judged under the rule of reason.

Territorial or Customer Restrictions   In arranging for the distribution of its products, a manufacturing firm often wishes to insulate dealers from direct competition with other dealers selling the product. To this end, it may institute territorial restrictions or attempt to prohibit wholesalers or retailers from reselling the product to certain classes of buyers, such as competing retailers.

A firm may have legitimate reasons for imposing such territorial or customer restrictions. **| Example #3** A computer manufacturer may wish to prevent a dealer from cutting costs and undercutting rivals by selling computers without promotion or customer service, while relying on nearby dealers to provide these services. In this situation, the cost-cutting dealer reaps the benefits (sales of the product) paid for by other dealers who undertake promotion and arrange for customer service. By not providing customer service, the cost-cutting dealer may also harm the manufacturer's reputation. **|**

Territorial and customer restrictions are judged under the rule of reason. In *United States v. Arnold, Schwinn & Co.,*[4] a case decided in 1967, the Supreme Court had held that vertical territorial and customer restrictions were *per se* violations of Section 1 of the Sherman Act. Ten years later, however, in *Continental T.V., Inc. v. GTE Sylvania, Inc.,*[5] the Court overturned the *Schwinn* decision and held that such vertical restrictions should be judged

---

3. *National Society of Professional Engineers v. United States*, 435 U.S. 679, 98 S.Ct. 1355, 55 L.Ed.2d 637 (1978).
4. 388 U.S. 365, 87 S.Ct. 1856, 18 L.Ed.2d 1249 (1967).
5. 433 U.S. 36, 97 S.Ct. 2549, 53 L.Ed.2d 568 (1977).

under the rule of reason. The *Continental* case marked a definite shift from rigid characterization of these kinds of vertical restraints to a more flexible, economic analysis of the restraints under the rule of reason.

Resale Price Maintenance Agreements   An agreement between a manufacturer and a distributor or retailer in which the manufacturer specifies what the retail prices of its products must be is referred to as a **resale price maintenance agreement.** This type of agreement may violate Section 1 of the Sherman Act. As with territorial restrictions, the Supreme Court originally held that resale price maintenance agreements were *per se* violations.[6] Subsequently, however, in 1997 the Court reversed this decision.[7] Today, such price-fixing arrangements are evaluated under the rule of reason.

Refusals to Deal   As discussed previously, joint refusals to deal (group boycotts) are subject to close scrutiny under Section 1 of the Sherman Act. A single manufacturer acting unilaterally, though, is generally free to deal, or not to deal, with whomever it wishes. In vertical arrangements, even though a manufacturer cannot set retail prices for its products, it can refuse to deal with retailers or dealers that cut prices to levels substantially below the manufacturer's suggested retail prices. In *United States v. Colgate & Co.,*[8] for example, the United States Supreme Court held that a manufacturer's advance announcement that it would not sell to price cutters was not a violation of the Sherman Act.

Nevertheless, in some instances, a unilateral refusal to deal will violate antitrust laws. These instances involve offenses proscribed under Section 2 of the Sherman Act and occur only if (1) the firm refusing to deal has—or is likely to acquire—monopoly power and (2) the refusal is likely to have an anticompetitive effect on a particular market.

SECTION 2 OF THE SHERMAN ACT

Section 1 of the Sherman Act proscribes certain concerted, or joint, activities that restrain trade. In contrast, Section 2 condemns "every person who shall monopolize, or attempt to monopolize." Thus, two distinct types of behavior are subject to sanction under Section 2: *monopolization* and *attempts to monopolize.* One tactic that may be involved in either offense is **predatory pricing.** Predatory pricing involves an attempt by one firm to drive its competitors from the market by selling its product at prices substantially *below* the normal costs of production. Once the competitors are eliminated, the firm will attempt to recapture its losses and go on to earn higher profits by driving prices up far above their competitive levels.

Monopolization

In *United States v. Grinnell Corp.,*[9] the United States Supreme Court defined the offense of **monopolization** as involving the following two elements: "(1) the possession of monopoly power in the relevant market and (2) the willful acquisition or maintenance of [that] power as distinguished from growth

RESALE PRICE MAINTENANCE AGREEMENT
An agreement between a manufacturer and a retailer in which the manufacturer specifies what the retail prices of its products must be.

PREDATORY PRICING
The pricing of a product below cost with the intent to drive competitors out of the market.

MONOPOLIZATION
The possession of monopoly power in the relevant market and the willful acquisition or maintenance of that power, as distinguished from growth or development as a consequence of a superior product, business acumen, or historic accident.

---

6. *Albrecht v. Herald Co.,* 390 U.S. 145, 88 S.Ct. 869, 19 L.Ed.2d 998 (1968).
7. *State Oil Co. v. Khan,* 522 U.S. 3, 118 S.Ct. 275, 139 L.Ed.2d 199 (1997).
8. 250 U.S. 300, 39 S.Ct. 465, 63 L.Ed. 992 (1919).
9. 384 U.S. 563, 86 S.Ct. 1698, 16 L.Ed.2d 778 (1966).

A retail store displays a well-known designer's clothing. Is an agreement between the manufacturer and an independent retailer to sell the clothing at a certain price considered a violation of the Sherman Act? Why or why not? (AP Photo/Kathy Willens)

or development as a consequence of a superior product, business acumen, or historic accident." A violation of Section 2 requires that both these elements—monopoly power and an intent to monopolize—be established.

Monopoly Power   The Sherman Act does not define *monopoly*. In economic parlance, monopoly refers to control of a specific market by a single entity. It is well established in antitrust law, however, that a firm may be deemed a monopolist even though it is not the sole seller in a market. Additionally, size alone does not determine whether a firm is a monopoly. For example, a "mom and pop" grocery located in an isolated desert town is a monopolist if it is the only grocery serving that particular market. Size in relation to the market is what matters, because monopoly involves the power to affect prices.

Market Power   Monopoly power, as mentioned earlier in this chapter, exists when a firm has an extremely large amount of market power. If a firm has sufficient market power to control prices and exclude competition, that firm has monopoly power. As difficult as it is to define market power precisely, it is even more difficult to measure it. In determining the extent of a firm's market power, courts often use the so-called **market-share test,**[10] which measures the firm's percentage share of the "relevant market." A firm may be considered to have monopoly power if its share of the relevant market is 70 percent or more. This is merely a rule of thumb, though; it is not a binding principle of law. In some cases, a smaller share may be held to constitute monopoly power.[11]

MARKET-SHARE TEST

The primary measure of monopoly power. A firm's market share is the percentage of a market that the firm controls.

---

10. Other measures of market power have been devised, but the market-share test is the most widely used.

11. This standard was first articulated by Judge Learned Hand in *United States v. Aluminum Co. of America,* 148 F.2d 416 (2d Cir. 1945). A 90 percent share was held to be clear evidence of monopoly power. Anything less than 64 percent, said Judge Hand, made monopoly power doubtful, and anything less than 30 percent was clearly not monopoly power.

Relevant Market   The relevant market consists of two elements: (1) a relevant product market and (2) a relevant geographic market. What should the relevant product market include? No doubt, it must include all products that, although produced by different firms, have identical attributes, such as sugar. Products that are not identical, however, may be substituted for one another. Coffee may be substituted for tea, for example. In defining the relevant product market, the issue is the degree of interchangeability between products. If one product is a sufficient substitute for another, the two products are considered to be part of the same product market. (For a case discussing the "relevant market" for domain names, see this chapter's *Online Developments* feature on page 636.)

The second component of the relevant market is the geographic boundaries of the market. For products that are sold nationwide, the geographic boundaries of the market encompass the entire United States. If a producer and its competitors sell in only a limited area (one in which customers have no access to other sources of the product), the geographic market is limited to that area. A national firm may thus compete in several distinct areas and have monopoly power in one area but not in another.

The Intent Requirement   Monopoly power, in and of itself, does not constitute the offense of monopolization under Section 2 of the Sherman Act. The offense also requires an *intent* to monopolize. A dominant market share may be the result of business acumen or the development of a superior product. It may simply be the result of historic accident. In these situations, the acquisition of monopoly power is not an antitrust violation. Indeed, it would be contrary to society's interest to condemn every firm that acquired a position of power because it was well managed and efficient and marketed a product desired by consumers.

If a firm possesses market power as a result of carrying out some purposeful act to acquire or maintain that power through anticompetitive means, then it is in violation of Section 2. In most monopolization cases, intent may be inferred from evidence that the firm had monopoly power and engaged in anticompetitive behavior.

> **KEEP IN MIND** Section 2 of the Sherman Act essentially condemns the act of monopolizing, not the possession of monopoly power.

Attempts to Monopolize

Section 2 also prohibits **attempted monopolization** of a market. Any action challenged as an attempt to monopolize must have been specifically intended to exclude competitors and garner monopoly power. In addition, the attempt must have had a "dangerous" probability of success—only *serious* threats of monopolization are condemned as violations. The probability cannot be dangerous unless the alleged offender possesses some degree of market power.

> **ATTEMPTED MONOPOLIZATION** Any actions by a firm to eliminate competition and gain monopoly power.

ETHICAL ISSUE 20.1   *Are we destined for more monopolies in the future?*

Knowledge and information form the building blocks of the so-called new economy. Some observers believe that the nature of this new economy means that we will see an increasing number of monopolies. Consider that the justification for all antitrust law is that monopoly leads to restricted output and hence higher prices for consumers. That is how a monopolist maximizes profits relative to a competitive firm. In the knowledge-based sector, however, firms face *economies of scale* (defined as decreases in long-run average costs resulting from increases in output), so

What Is the Relevant Product Market for Domain Names?

Most attempts to measure monopoly power involve quantifying the degree of concentration in a relevant market and/or the extent of a particular firm's ability to control that market. Accordingly, defining the relevant market is a necessary step in any monopolization case brought under Section 2 of the Sherman Act. Thus, when Stan Smith brought a monopolization case against Network Solutions, Inc. (NSI), a domain name registrar (see Chapter 7), for not allowing Smith and others to register for expired domain names, a threshold question before the court was the following: What is the relevant product market for domain names?

The Registry
At one time, NSI was the only registrar for domain names in this country. In 1998, however, the federal government opened domain name registration to competition and set up a nonprofit corporation, the Internet Corporation for Assigned Names and Numbers (ICANN), to oversee the distribution of domain names. At that time, NSI's domain name registration service was divided into two separate units: a registrar and a registry (the Registry).[a]

The registrar unit continues to register domain names, although it is now only one of eighty or so accredited registrars in operation. The Registry, in contrast, is the only entity of its kind. It maintains a centralized "WHOIS" database of all domain names using the ".com," ".org," and ".net" top level domains, regardless of whether the names have been registered by NSI or one of the other accredited registrars. The Registry's WHOIS database allows all registrars to determine almost

instantaneously which domain names are already registered and therefore unavailable. The public can also access the Registry's WHOIS database.

At the time Smith brought his suit, the WHOIS database included approximately 163,000 expired domain names—names that had been registered but belonged to registrants who had failed to pay the required registration renewal fees. NSI's policy was to give registrants a "grace period" of two to three months in which they could renew their expired registrations. In the meantime, the names remained on the WHOIS database and were unavailable for others.

What Is the Relevant Product Market?
Smith claimed that by failing to make expired domain names available to himself and others, NSI had intentionally maintained an unlawful monopoly over expired domain names in violation of Section 2 of the Sherman Act. The court, however, concluded that the relevant product market was not expired domain names but all domain names—and NSI did not have monopoly power over all domain names. The court reasoned that "the relevant market includes those commodities or services that are reasonably interchangeable." Because of the "virtually limitless" supply of domain names, said the court, "there will always be reasonable substitute names available for any given name kept out of circulation."[b]

For Critical Analysis *Do you agree that the relevant market for domain names should include all domain names and not just those that have expired? Why or why not?*

---

a. In 2000, NSI became a wholly owned subsidiary of VeriSign, Inc., and the Registry was subsequently renamed VeriSign Global Registry Services. Both NSI and VeriSign were defendants in this case.

b. *Smith v. Network Solutions, Inc.*, 135 F.Supp.2d 1159 (N.D.Ala. 2001).

---

they will do the exact opposite of a traditional monopolist—they will increase output and reduce prices. That is precisely what Microsoft Corporation has done over the years—developed and maintained monopoly power in the market for Intel-compatible personal computer (PC) operating systems.[12] Despite this monopoly power, the prices of Microsoft's operating systems have fallen, particularly when corrected for inflation.

This characteristic of knowledge-based monopolies may mean that antitrust authorities will have to have greater tolerance for these monopolies to allow them to benefit from full economies of scale. After all, consumers are the ultimate beneficiaries of such economies of scale. In the early 1900s, economist

---

12. See *United States v. Microsoft Corp.*, 253 F.3d 34 (C.A.D.C. 2001), in which a federal appellate court held that Microsoft did willfully acquire monopoly power in Intel-compatible operating systems in violation of Section 2 of the Sherman Act.

Joseph Schumpeter argued in favor of allowing monopolies. According to his theory of "creative destruction," monopolies stimulate innovation and economic growth because firms that capture monopoly profits have a greater incentive to innovate. Those that do not survive—the firms that are "destroyed"—leave room for the more efficient firms that will survive.

THE CLAYTON ACT

In 1914, Congress attempted to strengthen federal antitrust laws by enacting the Clayton Act. The Clayton Act was aimed at specific anticompetitive or monopolistic practices that the Sherman Act did not cover. The substantive provisions of the act deal with four distinct forms of business behavior, which are declared illegal but not criminal. With regard to each of the four provisions, the act's prohibitions are qualified by the general condition that the behavior is illegal only if it substantially tends to lessen competition or create monopoly power. The major offenses under the Clayton Act are set out in Sections 2, 3, 7, and 8 of the act.

Section 2—Price Discrimination

Section 2 of the Clayton Act prohibits **price discrimination**, which occurs when a seller charges different prices to competitive buyers for identical goods. Because businesses frequently circumvented Section 2 of the act, Congress strengthened this section by amending it with the passage of the Robinson-Patman Act in 1936.

As amended, Section 2 prohibits price discrimination that cannot be justified by differences in production costs or transportation costs, or cost differences due to other reasons. To violate Section 2, the seller must be engaged in interstate commerce, and the effect of the price discrimination must be to substantially lessen competition or create a competitive injury. Under Section 2, as amended, a seller is prohibited from reducing a price to one buyer below the price charged to that buyer's competitor. Even offering goods to different customers at the same price but with different delivery arrangements may violate Section 2 in some circumstances.[13]

An exception is made if the seller can justify the price reduction by demonstrating that the lower price was charged temporarily and in good faith to meet another seller's equally low price to the buyer's competitor. To be predatory, a seller's pricing policies must also include a reasonable prospect that the seller will recoup its losses.[14]

PRICE DISCRIMINATION
Setting prices in such a way that two competing buyers pay two different prices for an identical product or service.

Microsoft's founder, Bill Gates, demonstrates the future of Windows computing at an industry conference. Suppose that Microsoft stops requiring companies that make computers to install Windows to also install Microsoft's browser (Explorer) and exclude competing browsers. Also suppose that despite this change, Microsoft continues to maintain monopoly power in the relevant operating-system market. Can Microsoft still be guilty of the offense of monopolization? Why or why not? How might a rival firm prove the required intent? (AP Photo/Damian Dovarganes)

---

13. *Bell v. Fur Breeders Agricultural Cooperative,* 3 F.Supp.2d 1241 (D. Utah 1998).
14. See, for example, *Brooke Group, Ltd. v. Brown & Williamson Tobacco Corp.,* 509 U.S. 209, 113 S.Ct. 2578, 125 L.Ed.2d 168 (1993), in which the United States Supreme Court held that a seller's price-cutting policies could not be predatory "[g]iven the market's realities"— the size of the seller's market share and the expanding output by other sellers, as well as additional factors.

Section 3—Exclusionary Practices

Under Section 3 of the Clayton Act, sellers or lessors cannot sell or lease goods "on the condition, agreement or understanding that the . . . purchaser or lessee thereof shall not use or deal in the goods . . . of a competitor or competitors of the seller." In effect, this section prohibits two types of vertical agreements involving exclusionary practices—*exclusive-dealing contracts* and *tying arrangements*.

EXCLUSIVE-DEALING CONTRACT

An agreement under which a seller forbids a buyer to purchase products from the seller's competitors.

Exclusive-Dealing Contracts   A contract under which a seller forbids a buyer to purchase products from the seller's competitors is called an **exclusive-dealing contract.** A seller is prohibited from making an exclusive-dealing contract under Section 3 if the effect of the contract is "to substantially lessen competition or tend to create a monopoly."

| **Example #4**   In *Standard Oil Co. of California v. United States,*[15] a leading case decided by the United States Supreme Court in 1949, the then-largest gasoline seller in the nation made exclusive-dealing contracts with independent stations in seven western states. The contracts involved 16 percent of all retail outlets, with sales amounting to approximately 7 percent of all retail sales in that market. The Court noted that the market was substantially concentrated because the seven largest gasoline suppliers all used exclusive-dealing contracts with their independent retailers and together controlled 65 percent of the market. Looking at market conditions after the arrangements were instituted, the Court found that market shares were extremely stable and that entry into the market was apparently restricted. Thus, the Court held that Section 3 of the Clayton Act had been violated because competition was "foreclosed in a substantial share" of the relevant market. |

TYING ARRANGEMENT

An agreement between a buyer and a seller in which the buyer of a specific product or service becomes obligated to purchase additional products or services from the seller.

Tying Arrangements   When a seller conditions the sale of a product (the tying product) on the buyer's agreement to purchase another product (the tied product) produced or distributed by the same seller, a **tying arrangement,** or *tie-in sales agreement,* results. The legality of a tie-in agreement depends on many factors, particularly the purpose of the agreement and its likely effect on competition in the relevant markets (the market for the tying product and the market for the tied product).

Section 3 of the Clayton Act has been held to apply only to commodities, not to services. Tying arrangements, however, can also be considered agreements that restrain trade in violation of Section 1 of the Sherman Act. Thus, cases involving tying arrangements of services have been brought under Section 1 of the Sherman Act. Traditionally, the courts have held tying arrangements challenged under the Sherman Act to be illegal *per se.* In recent years, however, courts have shown a willingness to look at factors that are important in a rule-of-reason analysis.

Does a party claiming a violation of antitrust law in a deal tying patented and unpatented products have to offer proof of the relevant market and the patent holder's power in that market? Or, because of the existence of the patent, can these factors be presumed without proof? That was the question in the following case.

---

15. 337 U.S. 293, 69 S.Ct. 1051, 93 L.Ed. 1371 (1949).

CASE 20.2   Illinois Tool Works Inc. v. Independent Ink, Inc.

Supreme Court of the United States, 2006.
__ U.S. __,
126 S.Ct. 1281,
164 L.Ed.2d 26.
www.findlaw.com/casecode/supreme.html [a]

BACKGROUND AND FACTS   Illinois Tool Works Inc., in Glenview, Illinois, owns Trident, Inc. The firms make printing systems that include three components: a patented inkjet printhead, a patented ink container that attaches to the printhead, and specially designed, but unpatented, ink. They sell the systems to original equipment manufacturers (OEMs) who incorporate the systems into printers that are sold to other companies to use in printing bar codes on packaging

a. In the "Browsing" section, click on "2006 Decisions." When that page opens, scroll to the name of the case and click on it to read the opinion.

materials. As part of each deal, the OEMs agree to buy ink exclusively from Illinois and Trident and not to refill the patented containers with ink of any other kind. Independent Ink, Inc., in Gardena, California, sells ink with the same chemical composition as Illinois and Trident's product at lower prices. Independent filed a suit in a federal district court against Illinois and Trident, alleging in part that they were engaged in illegal tying in violation of the Sherman Act. Independent filed a motion for summary judgment, arguing that because the defendants owned patents in their products, market power could be presumed. The court issued a summary judgment in the defendants' favor, holding that market power could not be presumed. The U.S. Court of Appeals for the Federal Circuit reversed this judgment. Illinois and Trident appealed to the United States Supreme Court.

IN THE WORDS OF THE COURT . . . Justice *STEVENS* delivered the opinion of the Court.

* * * *

American courts first encountered tying arrangements in the course of patent infringement litigation [in 1912]. * * *

In the years since [1912], four different rules of law have supported challenges to tying arrangements. They have been condemned as improper extensions of the patent monopoly under the patent misuse doctrine, as unfair methods of competition under [Section] 5 of the Federal Trade Commission Act, as contracts tending to create a monopoly under [Section] 3 of the Clayton Act, and as contracts in restraint of trade under [Section] 1 of the Sherman Act. In all of those instances, the justification for the challenge rested on either an assumption or a showing that the defendant's position of power in the market for the tying product was being used to restrain competition in the market for the tied product. * * * [T]he essential characteristic of an invalid tying arrangement lies in the seller's exploitation of its control over the tying product to force the buyer into the purchase of a tied product that the buyer either [does] not want at all, or might [prefer] to purchase elsewhere on different terms.

Over the years, however, this Court's strong disapproval of tying arrangements has substantially diminished. Rather than relying on assumptions, in its more recent opinions the Court has required a showing of market power in the tying product. * * *

* * * *

* * * [T]he presumption that a patent confers market power arose outside the antitrust context as part of the patent misuse doctrine. * * *

Without any analysis of actual market conditions, [the] patent misuse [doctrine] assumed that, by tying the purchase of unpatented goods to the sale of [a] patented good, the patentee was restraining competition or securing a limited monopoly of an unpatented material. In other words, [the doctrine] presumed the requisite economic power over the tying product such that the patentee could extend its economic control to unpatented products.

* * * *

Although the patent misuse doctrine and our antitrust jurisprudence became intertwined in [a case decided in 1947], subsequent events initiated their untwining. * * *

CASE 20.2–CONTINUED ▶

* * * *

Shortly thereafter, *Congress* * * * *excluded some conduct, such as a tying arrangement involving the sale of a patented product tied to an "essential" or "nonstaple" product that has no use except as part of the patented product or method, from the scope of the patent misuse doctrine. Thus,* * * * *Congress began chipping away at the assumption in the patent misuse context from whence it came.* [Emphasis added.]

It is Congress'[s] most recent narrowing of the patent misuse defense * * * that is directly relevant to this case. * * * [In 1988] Congress amended the [patent laws] to eliminate [the patent-equals-market-power] presumption in the patent misuse context. * * *

While the 1988 amendment does not expressly refer to the antitrust laws, it certainly invites a reappraisal of the *per se* rule * * * . [G]iven the fact that the patent misuse doctrine provided the basis for the market power presumption, it would be anomalous to preserve the presumption in antitrust after Congress has eliminated its foundation.

After considering the congressional judgment reflected in the 1988 amendment, we conclude that tying arrangements involving patented products should be evaluated under [such factors as those that apply in a rule-of-reason analysis] rather than under the *per se* rule * * * . While some such arrangements are still unlawful, such as those that are the product of a true monopoly or a marketwide conspiracy, that conclusion must be supported by proof of power in the relevant market rather than by a mere presumption thereof.

DECISION AND REMEDY   The United States Supreme Court vacated the judgment of the lower court and remanded the case to the trial court to give Independent "a fair opportunity" to offer evidence of the relevant market and the defendants' power within it. The Supreme Court ruled that a plaintiff who alleges an illegal tying arrangement involving a patented product must prove that the defendant has market power in the tying product. A company does not automatically possess market power in a product for antitrust purposes just because the firm holds a patent in the product.

WHY IS THIS CASE IMPORTANT?   *In this decision, the United States Supreme Court overruled nearly sixty years of case law in which it had been presumed that a patent always confers significant market power on the holder of the patent. A conclusion of an unlawful tying arrangement involving a patented product must now be supported by proof rather than by presumption.*

Section 7–Mergers

Under Section 7 of the Clayton Act, a person or business organization cannot hold stock and/or assets in another entity "where the effect . . . may be to substantially lessen competition." Section 7 is the statutory authority for preventing mergers or acquisitions that could result in monopoly power or a substantial lessening of competition in the marketplace. Section 7 applies to horizontal mergers and vertical mergers, both of which we discuss in the following subsections.

A crucial consideration in most merger cases is the **market concentration** of a product or business. Determining market concentration involves allocating percentage market shares among the various companies in the relevant market. When a small number of companies control a large share of the market, the market is concentrated. For example, if the four largest grocery stores in Chicago accounted for 80 percent of all retail food sales, the market clearly would be concentrated in those four firms. Competition, however, is not necessarily diminished solely as a result of market concentration, and other fac-

MARKET CONCENTRATION
The degree to which a small number of firms control a large percentage share of a relevant market; determined by calculating the percentages held by the largest firms in that market.

tors will be considered in determining whether a merger will violate Section 7. One factor of particular importance in evaluating the effects of a merger is whether the merger will make it more difficult for potential competitors to enter the relevant market.

Horizontal Mergers   Mergers between firms that compete with each other in the same market are called **horizontal mergers.** If a horizontal merger creates an entity with anything other than a small percentage market share, the merger will be presumed illegal. This is because the United States Supreme Court has held that Congress, in amending Section 7 of the Clayton Act in 1950, intended to prevent mergers that increase market concentration.[16] When analyzing the legality of a horizontal merger, the courts also consider three other factors: overall concentration of the relevant product market, the relevant market's history of tending toward concentration, and whether the apparent design of the merger is to establish market power or to restrict competition.

HORIZONTAL MERGER
A merger between two firms that are competing in the same marketplace.

The Federal Trade Commission and the U.S. Department of Justice have established guidelines indicating which mergers will be challenged. Under the guidelines, the first factor to be considered is the degree of concentration in the relevant market. Other factors to be considered include the ease of entry into the relevant market, economic efficiency, the financial condition of the merging firms, the nature and price of the product or products involved, and so on. If a firm is a leading one—having at least a 35 percent share and twice that of the next leading firm—any merger with a firm having as little as a 1 percent share will probably be challenged.

Vertical Mergers   A **vertical merger** occurs when a company at one stage of production acquires a company at a higher or lower stage of production. An example of a vertical merger is a company merging with one of its suppliers or retailers. In the past, courts focused almost exclusively on "foreclosure" in assessing vertical mergers. Foreclosure occurs because competitors of the merging firms lose opportunities to sell or buy products from the merging firms.

VERTICAL MERGER
The acquisition by a company at one level in a marketing chain of a company at a higher or lower level in the chain (such as a company merging with one of its suppliers or retailers).

| **Example #5**   In *United States v. E. I. du Pont de Nemours & Co.,*[17] du Pont was challenged for acquiring a considerable amount of General Motors (GM) stock. In holding that the transaction was illegal, the United States Supreme Court noted that the stock acquisition would enable du Pont to prevent other sellers of fabrics and finishes from selling to GM, which then accounted for 50 percent of all auto fabric and finishes purchases. |

Today, whether a vertical merger will be deemed illegal generally depends on several factors, including market concentration, barriers to entry into the market, and the apparent intent of the merging parties. Mergers that do not prevent competitors of either merging firm from competing in a segment of the market will not be condemned as "foreclosing" competition and are legal.

Section 8–Interlocking Directorates

Section 8 of the Clayton Act deals with *interlocking directorates*—that is, the practice of having individuals serve as directors on the boards of two or more competing companies simultaneously. Specifically, no person may be a director

---

16. *Brown Shoe v. United States,* 370 U.S. 294, 82 S.Ct. 1502, 8 L.Ed.2d 510 (1962).
17. 353 U.S. 586, 77 S.Ct. 872, 1 L.Ed.2d 1057 (1957).

in two or more competing corporations at the same time if either of the corporations has capital, surplus, or undivided profits aggregating more than $22,761,000 or competitive sales of $2,276,100 or more. The Federal Trade Commission (FTC) adjusts the threshold amounts each year. (The amounts given here are those announced by the FTC in 2006.)

ENFORCEMENT OF ANTITRUST LAWS

The federal agencies that enforce the federal antitrust laws are the U.S. Department of Justice (DOJ) and the Federal Trade Commission (FTC). The FTC was established by the Federal Trade Commission Act of 1914. Section 5 of that act condemns all forms of anticompetitive behavior that are not covered under other federal antitrust laws. Only the DOJ can prosecute violations of the Sherman Act, which can be either criminal or civil offenses. Either the DOJ or the FTC can enforce the Clayton Act, but violations of that statute are not crimes and can be pursued only through civil proceedings. The DOJ or the FTC may ask the courts to impose various remedies, including **divestiture** (making a company give up one or more of its operating functions) and dissolution. The FTC has the sole authority to enforce violations of Section 5 of the Federal Trade Commission Act. FTC actions are effected through administrative orders, but if a firm violates an FTC order, the FTC can seek court sanctions for the violation. For a discussion of the enforcement of antitrust laws in the global context, see this chapter's *Beyond Our Borders* feature.

A private party who has been injured as a result of a violation of the Sherman Act or the Clayton Act can sue for damages and attorneys' fees. In some instances, private parties may also seek injunctive relief to prevent antitrust violations. The courts have determined that the ability to sue depends on the directness of the injury suffered by the would-be plaintiff. Thus, a person wishing to sue under the Sherman Act must prove (1) that the antitrust violation either caused or was a substantial factor in causing the injury that was suffered and (2) that the unlawful actions of the accused party affected business activities of the plaintiff that were protected by the antitrust laws.

In recent years, more than 90 percent of all antitrust actions have been brought by private plaintiffs. One reason for this is that successful plaintiffs may recover **treble damages**—three times the damages that they have suffered as a result of the violation. Such recoveries by private plaintiffs for antitrust violations have been rationalized as encouraging people to act as "private attorneys general" who will vigorously pursue antitrust violators on their own initiative.

EXEMPTIONS FROM ANTITRUST LAWS

There are many legislative and constitutional limitations on antitrust enforcement. Most statutory and judicially created exemptions to the antitrust laws apply to the following areas or activities:

1. *Labor.* Section 6 of the Clayton Act generally permits labor unions to organize and bargain without violating antitrust laws. Section 20 of the Clayton Act specifies that strikes and other labor activities are not violations of any law of the United States. A union can lose its exemption, however, if it combines with a nonlabor group rather than acting simply in its own self-interest.

CONTRAST Section 5 of the Federal Trade Commission Act is broader than the other antitrust laws. It covers virtually all anticompetitive behavior, including conduct that does not violate either the Sherman Act or the Clayton Act.

DIVESTITURE
The act of selling one or more of a company's divisions or parts, such as a subsidiary or plant; often mandated by the courts in merger or monopolization cases.

TREBLE DAMAGES
Damages that, by statute, are three times the amount that the fact finder determines is owed.

BEYOND OUR BORDERS

Antitrust Laws in the Global Context

As mentioned earlier in this chapter, the reach of U.S. antitrust laws extends beyond the territorial borders of the United States. The U.S. government (the Department of Justice or the Federal Trade Commission) and private parties may bring an action against a foreign party that has violated Section 1 of the Sherman Act. The Federal Trade Commission Act may also be applied to foreign trade. Foreign mergers, if Section 7 of the Clayton Act applies, may also be brought within the jurisdiction of U.S. courts. Before U.S. courts will exercise jurisdiction and apply antitrust laws to actions occurring in other countries, however, normally it must be shown that the alleged violation had a substantial effect on U.S. commerce. (See Chapter 22 for a further discussion of the extraterritorial application of U.S. antitrust laws.)

In the past, companies usually had to be concerned only with U.S. antitrust laws. Today, however, many countries have adopted antitrust laws. The European Union has antitrust provisions that are broadly analogous to Sections 1 and 2 of the Sherman Act, as well as laws governing mergers. Japanese antitrust laws prohibit unfair trade practices, monopolization, and restrictions that unreasonably restrain trade. Several nations in Southeast Asia, including Indonesia, Malaysia, and Vietnam, have enacted statutes protecting competition. Argentina, Brazil, Chile, Peru, and several other Latin American countries have adopted modern antitrust laws as well. Most of the antitrust laws apply extraterritorially, as U.S. antitrust laws do. This means that a U.S. company may be subject to another nation's antitrust laws if the company's conduct has a substantial effect on that nation's commerce.

For Critical Analysis *In what ways might antitrust laws place too great a burden on commerce in the global marketplace?*

2. *Agricultural associations and fisheries.* Section 6 of the Clayton Act (along with the Capper-Volstead Act of 1922) exempts agricultural cooperatives from the antitrust laws. The Fisheries Cooperative Marketing Act of 1976 exempts from antitrust legislation individuals in the fishing industry who collectively catch, produce, and prepare for market their products. Both exemptions allow members of such co-ops to combine and set prices for a particular product, but do not allow them to engage in exclusionary practices or restraints of trade directed at competitors.

3. *Insurance.* The McCarran-Ferguson Act of 1945 exempts the insurance business from the antitrust laws whenever state regulation exists. This exemption does not cover boycotts, coercion, or intimidation on the part of insurance companies.

4. *Foreign trade.* Under the provisions of the Webb-Pomerene Act of 1918, U.S. exporters may engage in cooperative activity to compete with similar foreign associations. This type of cooperative activity may not, however, restrain trade within the United States or injure other U.S. exporters. The Export Trading Company Act of 1982 broadened the Webb-Pomerene Act by permitting the Department of Justice to certify properly qualified export trading companies. Any activity within the scope described by the certificate is exempt from public prosecution under the antitrust laws.

5. *Professional baseball.* In 1922, the United States Supreme Court held that professional baseball was not within the reach of federal antitrust laws because it did not involve "interstate commerce."[18] Some of the effects of

---

18. *Federal Baseball Club of Baltimore, Inc. v. National League of Professional Baseball Clubs,* 259 U.S. 200, 42 S.Ct. 465, 66 L.Ed. 898 (1922).

this decision, however, were modified by the Curt Flood Act of 1998. Essentially, the act allows players the option of suing team owners for anticompetitive practices if, for example, the owners collude to "blacklist" players, hold down players' salaries, or force players to play for specific teams.[19]

6. *Oil marketing.* The Interstate Oil Compact of 1935 allows states to determine quotas on oil that will be marketed in interstate commerce.

7. *Cooperative research and production.* Cooperative research among small-business firms is exempt under the Small Business Act of 1958, as amended. Research or production of a product, process, or service by joint ventures consisting of competitors is exempt under special federal legislation, including the National Cooperative Research Act of 1984 and the National Cooperative Production Amendments of 1993.

8. *Joint efforts by businesspersons to obtain legislative or executive action.* This is often referred to as the *Noerr-Pennington* doctrine.[20] For example, DVD producers may jointly lobby Congress to change the copyright laws without being held liable for attempting to restrain trade. Though selfish rather than purely public-minded conduct is permitted, there is an exception: an action will not be protected if it is clear that the action is "objectively baseless in the sense that no reasonable [person] could reasonably expect success on the merits" and it is an attempt to make anticompetitive use of government processes.[21]

9. *Other exemptions.* Other activities exempt from antitrust laws include activities approved by the president in furtherance of the defense of our nation (under the Defense Production Act of 1950, as amended); state actions, when the state policy is clearly articulated and the policy is actively supervised by the state;[22] and activities of regulated industries (such as the communication and banking industries) when federal commissions, boards, or agencies (such as the Federal Communications Commission and the Federal Maritime Commission) have primary regulatory authority.

> **NOTE** State actions include the regulation of public utilities, whose rates may be set by the states in which they do business.

The following case concerns the first exemption (labor) in the above list.

---

19. In 2003, a federal appellate court held that because baseball was exempt from federal antitrust laws, it was also exempt from the reach of state antitrust laws due to the supremacy clause. *Major League Baseball v. Crist,* 331 F.3d 1177 (11th Cir. 2003).
20. See *Eastern Railroad Presidents Conference v. Noerr Motor Freight, Inc.,* 365 U.S. 127, 81 S.Ct. 523, 5 L.Ed.2d 464 (1961); and *United Mine Workers of America v. Pennington,* 381 U.S. 657, 85 S.Ct. 1585, 14 L.Ed.2d 626 (1965).
21. *Professional Real Estate Investors, Inc. v. Columbia Pictures Industries, Inc.,* 508 U.S. 49, 113 S.Ct. 1920, 123 L.Ed.2d 611 (1993).
22. See *Parker v. Brown,* 317 U.S. 341, 63 S.Ct. 307, 87 L.Ed. 315 (1943).

CASE 20.3   Clarett v. National Football League

United States Court of Appeals, Second Circuit, 2004.
369 F.3d 124.

BACKGROUND AND FACTS Maurice Clarett was a star football player attending Ohio State University (OSU). In his freshman year, Clarett led his team to an undefeated season. The season was capped by a double-overtime victory over the University of Miami in the Fiesta Bowl, OSU's first national championship in thirty-four years. Clarett's goal was to play in the National Football League (NFL) in the fall of 2004. The NFL, an unincorporated association of thirty-two member clubs, consistently outperforms all other professional sports leagues, in both revenues and television ratings, representing an unparalleled opportunity for an aspiring football player in terms of salary and level of competition. The only thing preventing Clarett from achieving his goal was an NFL rule that limited eligibility to players three seasons removed from their high school graduation. Clarett filed a suit in a federal district court against the NFL, claiming that the rule was an illegal restraint of trade. Clarett argued that by adopting the rule, the NFL teams had agreed to exclude a broad class of players from the NFL labor market. The court issued a summary judgment in Clarett's favor. The NFL appealed to the U.S. Court of Appeals for the Second Circuit.

IN THE WORDS OF THE COURT . . . *SOTOMAYOR*, Circuit Judge.

* * * *

* * * [T]o accommodate the collective bargaining process, certain concerted activity among and between labor and employers [is] held to be beyond the reach of the antitrust laws. * * * [Emphasis added.]

* * * *

Although the NFL has maintained draft eligibility rules in one form or another for much of its history, the inception of a collective bargaining relationship between the NFL and its players union some thirty years ago irrevocably altered the governing legal regime. * * * [P]rospective players no longer have the right to negotiate directly with the NFL teams over the terms and conditions of their employment. That responsibility is instead committed to the NFL and the players union to accomplish through the collective bargaining process, and throughout that process the NFL and the players union are to have the freedom to craft creative solutions to their differences in light of the economic imperatives of their industry. Furthermore, the NFL teams are permitted to engage in joint conduct with respect to the terms and conditions of players' employment as a multiemployer bargaining unit without risking antitrust liability. * * *

* * * *

Clarett's argument that antitrust law should permit him to circumvent this scheme established by federal labor law starts with the contention that the eligibility rules do not constitute a mandatory subject of collective bargaining and thus cannot fall within the protection of the * * * exemption. * * * [H]owever, we find that the eligibility rules are mandatory bargaining subjects. Though tailored to the unique circumstances of a professional sports league, the eligibility rules for the draft represent a quite literal condition for initial employment and for that reason alone might constitute a mandatory bargaining subject. But moreover, the eligibility rules constitute a mandatory bargaining subject because they have tangible effects on the wages and working conditions of current NFL players. *Because the unusual economic imperatives of professional sports raise numerous problems with little or no precedent in standard industrial relations, * * * many of the arrangements in professional sports that, at first glance, might not appear to deal with wages or working conditions are indeed mandatory bargaining subjects. * * ** [Emphasis added.]

Furthermore, by reducing competition in the market for entering players, the eligibility rules also affect the job security of veteran players. Because the size of NFL teams is capped, the eligibility rules diminish a veteran player's risk of being replaced by either a drafted rookie or a player who enters the draft and, though not drafted, is then hired as a rookie free agent. Consequently, * * * we find that to regard the NFL's eligibility rules as merely permissive bargaining subjects would ignore the reality of collective bargaining in sports.

DECISION AND REMEDY The U.S. Court of Appeals for the Second Circuit reversed the judgment of the lower court and remanded the case for the entry of a judgment in favor of the NFL. The appellate court vacated the order designating Clarett eligible to participate in the year's NFL draft.

FOR CRITICAL ANALYSIS–Social Consideration *Why are the NFL's member clubs permitted to agree that a player will not be hired until three full football seasons after the player's high school graduation?*

REVIEWING . . . PROMOTING COMPETITION

The Internet Corporation for Assigned Names and Numbers (ICANN) is a nonprofit entity organizing Internet domain names. It is governed by a board of directors elected by various groups with commercial interests in the Internet. One of ICANN's functions is to authorize an entity as a registry for certain "top level domains" (TLDs). ICANN entered into an agreement with VeriSign to serve as registry for the ".com" TLD and to provide registry services in accordance with ICANN's specifications. VeriSign complained that ICANN was restricting the services that it could make available as a registrar and blocking new services, imposing unnecessary conditions on those services, and setting prices at which the services were offered. VeriSign claimed that ICANN's control of the registry services for domain names violated Section 1 of the Sherman Act.

1. Should ICANN's actions be judged under the rule of reason or deemed a *per se* violation of Section 1 of the Sherman Act?

2. Should ICANN's actions be viewed as a horizontal or a vertical restraint of trade?

3. Does it matter that ICANN's leadership is chosen by those with a commercial interest in the Internet?

4. If judged under the rule of reason, what might be ICANN's defense for having a standardized set of registry services that must be used?

KEY TERMS

antitrust law   625
attempted monopolization   635
divestiture   642
exclusive-dealing contract   638
group boycott   631
horizontal merger   641
horizontal restraint   628
market concentration   640
market power   627

market-share test   634
monopolization   633
monopoly   627
monopoly power   627
per se violation   628
predatory pricing   633
price discrimination   637
price-fixing agreement   628

resale price maintenance
   agreement   633
rule of reason   628
treble damages   642
tying arrangement   638
vertical merger   641
vertical restraint   632
vertically integrated firm   632

CHAPTER SUMMARY • PROMOTING COMPETITION

The Sherman Antitrust Act (1890) (See pages 626–637.)	1. *Major provisions*—
	a. Section 1—Prohibits contracts, combinations, and conspiracies in restraint of trade.
	(1) Horizontal restraints subject to Section 1 include price-fixing agreements, group boycotts (joint refusals to deal), horizontal market divisions, and trade association agreements.
	(2) Vertical restraints subject to Section 1 include territorial or customer restrictions, resale price maintenance agreements, and refusals to deal.
	b. Section 2—Prohibits monopolies and attempts to monopolize.
	2. *Jurisdictional requirements*—The Sherman Act applies only to activities that have a significant impact on interstate commerce.
	3. *Interpretive rules*—
	a. *Per se* rule—Applied to restraints on trade that are so inherently anticompetitive that they cannot be justified and are deemed illegal as a matter of law.

The Sherman Antitrust Act (1890)—Continued	b. Rule of reason—Applied when an anticompetitive agreement may be justified by legitimate benefits. Under the rule of reason, the lawfulness of a trade restraint will be determined by the purpose and effects of the restraint.

The Clayton Act (1914) (See pages 637–642.)	The major provisions are as follows:
	
	 1. *Section 2*—As amended in 1936 by the Robinson-Patman Act, prohibits price discrimination that substantially lessens competition and prohibits a seller engaged in interstate commerce from selling to two or more buyers goods of similar grade and quality at different prices when the result is a substantial lessening of competition or the creation of a competitive injury.
	
	 2. *Section 3*—Prohibits exclusionary practices, such as exclusive-dealing contracts and tying arrangements, when the effect may be to substantially lessen competition.
	
	 3. *Section 7*—Prohibits mergers when the effect may be to substantially lessen competition or to tend to create a monopoly.
	
	    a. Horizontal mergers—The acquisition by merger or consolidation of a competing firm engaged in the same relevant market. Will be unlawful only if the merger results in the merging firms' holding a disproportionate share of the market, resulting in a substantial lessening of competition, and if the merger does not enhance consumer welfare by increasing efficiency of production or marketing.
	
	    b. Vertical mergers—The acquisition by a seller of one of its buyers or vice versa. Will be unlawful if the merger prevents competitors of either merging firm from competing in a segment of the market that otherwise would be open to them, resulting in a substantial lessening of competition.
	
	 4. *Section 8*—Prohibits interlocking directorates.

Enforcement of Antitrust Laws (See page 642.)	Federal agencies that enforce antitrust laws are the Department of Justice and the Federal Trade Commission, which was established by the Federal Trade Commission Act of 1914. Private parties who have been injured as a result of violations of the Sherman Act or Clayton Act may also bring civil suits. In recent years, many private parties have filed such suits largely because, if successful, they may be awarded treble damages and attorneys' fees.
Exemptions from Antitrust Laws (See pages 642–645.)	1. Labor unions (under Section 6 of the Clayton Act of 1914). 2. Agricultural associations and fisheries (under Section 6 of the Clayton Act of 1914, the Capper-Volstead Act of 1922, and the Fisheries Cooperative Marketing Act of 1976). 3. Insurance when state regulation exists (under the McCarran-Ferguson Act of 1945). 4. Export trading companies (under the Webb-Pomerene Act of 1918 and the Export Trading Company Act of 1982). 5. Professional baseball (by a 1922 judicial decision, although modified by a 1998 federal statute). 6. Oil marketing (under the Interstate Oil Compact of 1935). 7. Cooperative research and production (under various acts, including the Small Business Act of 1958, as amended, the National Cooperative Research Act of 1984, and the National Cooperative Production Amendments of 1993). 8. Joint efforts by businesspersons to obtain legislative or executive action (under the *Noerr-Pennington* doctrine). 9. Other activities, including certain national defense activities, state actions, and activities of certain regulated industries.

FOR REVIEW

Answers for the even-numbered questions in this For Review *section can be found in Appendix O at the end of this text.*

1. What is a monopoly? What is market power? How do these concepts relate to each other?
2. What type of activity is prohibited by Section 1 of the Sherman Act? What type of activity is prohibited by Section 2 of the Sherman Act?
3. What are the four major provisions of the Clayton Act, and what types of activities do these provisions prohibit?
4. What agencies of the federal government enforce the federal antitrust laws?
5. What are four activities that are exempt from the antitrust laws?

QUESTIONS AND CASE PROBLEMS

20–1. Sherman Act. An agreement that is blatantly and substantially anticompetitive is deemed a *per se* violation of Section 1 of the Sherman Act. Under what rule is an agreement analyzed if it appears to be anticompetitive but is not a *per se* violation? In making this analysis, what factors will a court consider?

Question with Sample Answer

20–2. Allitron, Inc., and Donovan, Ltd., are interstate competitors selling similar appliances, principally in the states of Illinois, Indiana, Kentucky, and Ohio. Allitron and Donovan agree that Allitron will no longer sell in Ohio and Indiana and that Donovan will no longer sell in Kentucky and Illinois. Have Allitron and Donovan violated any antitrust laws? If so, which law or laws? Explain.

For a sample answer to this question, go to Appendix P at the end of this text.

20–3. Horizontal Restraints. Jorge's Appliance Corp. was a new retail seller of appliances in Sunrise City. Because of its innovative sales techniques and financing, Jorge's caused the appliance department of No-Glow Department Store, a large chain store with a great deal of buying power, to lose a substantial amount of sales. No-Glow told a number of appliance manufacturers that if they continued to sell to Jorge's, No-Glow would discontinue its large volume of purchases from them. The manufacturers immediately stopped selling appliances to Jorge's. Jorge's filed suit against No-Glow and the manufacturers, claiming that their actions constituted an antitrust violation. No-Glow and the manufacturers were able to prove that Jorge's was a small retailer with a small portion of the market. They claimed that because the relevant market was not substantially affected, they were not guilty of restraint of trade. Discuss fully whether there was an antitrust violation.

20–4. Exclusionary Practices. Instant Foto Corp. is a manufacturer of photography film. At the present time, Instant Foto has approximately 50 percent of the market. Instant Foto advertises that the purchase price for its film includes

photo processing by Instant Foto Corp. Instant Foto claims that its film processing is specially designed to improve the quality of photos taken with Instant Foto film. Is Instant Foto's combination of film and film processing an antitrust violation? Explain.

20–5. Tying Arrangement. Public Interest Corp. (PIC) owned and operated the television station WTMV-TV in Lakeland, Florida. MCA Television, Ltd., owns and licenses syndicated television programs. The parties entered into a licensing contract with respect to several television shows. MCA conditioned the license on PIC's agreeing to take another show, *Harry and the Hendersons.* PIC agreed to this arrangement, although it would not have chosen to license *Harry* if it had not had to do so to secure the licenses for the other shows. More than two years into the contract, a dispute arose over PIC's payments, and negotiations failed to resolve the dispute. In a letter, MCA suspended PIC's broadcast rights for all of its shows and stated that "[a]ny telecasts of MCA programming by WTMV-TV . . . will be deemed unauthorized and shall constitute an infringement of MCA's copyrights." PIC nonetheless continued broadcasting MCA's programs, with the exception of *Harry.* MCA filed a suit in a federal district court against PIC, alleging breach of contract and copyright infringement. PIC filed a counterclaim, contending in part that MCA's deal was an illegal tying arrangement. Is PIC correct? Explain. [*MCA Television, Ltd. v. Public Interest Corp.,* 171 F.3d 1265 (11th Cir. 1999)]

Case Problem with Sample Answer

20–6. In 1995, to make personal computers (PCs) easier to use, Intel Corp. and other companies developed a standard, called the Universal Serial Bus (USB) specification, to enable peripherals (printers and other hardware) to be easily attached to PCs. Intel and others formed the Universal Serial Bus Implementers Forum (USB-IF) to promote USB technology and products. Intel, however, makes relatively few USB products and does not make any USB interconnect devices. Multivideo Labs, Inc. (MVL), designed and distributed Active Extension Cables (AECs) to connect peripheral devices to each other or to a PC. The AECs were not USB compliant, a fact that Intel employees told other USB-IF members. Asserting that this caused a "general cooling of the market" for AECs, MVL filed a suit in a federal district court against Intel, claiming in part attempted monopolization in violation of the Sherman Act. Intel filed a motion for summary judgment. How should the court rule, and why? [*Multivideo Labs, Inc. v. Intel Corp.,* __ F.Supp.2d __ (S.D.N.Y. 2000)]

After you have answered this problem, compare your answer with the sample answer given on the Web site that accompanies this text. Go to www.thomsonedu.com/westbuslaw/let, select "Chapter 20," and click on "Case Problem with Sample Answer."

20–7. Monopolization. Moist snuff is a smokeless tobacco product sold in small round cans from racks, which include point-of-sale (POS) ads. POS ads are critical because tobacco advertising is restricted and the number of people who use smokeless tobacco products is relatively small. In the moist snuff market in the United States, there are only four competitors, including U.S. Tobacco Co. and its affiliates (USTC) and Conwood Co. In 1990, USTC, which held 87 percent of the market, began to convince major retailers, including Wal-Mart Stores, Inc., to use USTC's "exclusive racks" to display its products and those of all other snuff makers. USTC agents would then destroy competitors' racks. USTC also began to provide retailers with false sales data to convince them to maintain its poor-selling items and drop competitors' less expensive products. Conwood's Wal-Mart market share fell from 12 percent to 6.5 percent. In stores in which USTC did not have rack exclusivity, however, Conwood's market share increased to 25 percent. Conwood filed a suit in a federal district court against USTC, alleging in part that USTC used its monopoly power to exclude competitors from the moist snuff market. Should the court rule in Conwood's favor? What is USTC's best defense? Discuss. [*Conwood Co., L.P. v. U.S. Tobacco Co.,* 290 F.3d 768 (6th Cir. 2002)]

20–8. Sherman Act. Dentsply International, Inc., is one of a dozen manufacturers of artificial teeth for dentures and other restorative devices. Dentsply sells its teeth to twenty-three dealers of dental products. The dealers supply the teeth to dental laboratories, which fabricate dentures for sale to dentists. There are hundreds of other dealers who compete with one another on the basis of price and service. Some manufacturers sell directly to the laboratories. There are also thousands of laboratories that compete with one another on the basis of price and service. Because of advances in dental medicine, however, artificial tooth manufacturing is marked by low growth potential, and Dentsply dominates the industry. Dentsply's market share is greater than 75 percent and is about fifteen times larger than that of its next-closest competitor. Dentsply prohibits its dealers from marketing competitors' teeth unless they were selling the teeth before 1993. The federal government filed a suit in a federal district court against Dentsply, alleging in part a violation of Section 2 of

the Sherman Act. What must the government show to succeed in its suit? Are those elements present in this case? What should the court rule? Explain. [*United States v. Dentsply International, Inc.,* 399 F.3d 181 (3d Cir. 2005)]

20–9. Price Fixing. Texaco Inc. and Shell Oil Co. are competitors in the national and international oil and gasoline markets. They refine crude oil into gasoline and sell it to service station owners and others. Between 1998 and 2002, Texaco and Shell engaged in a joint venture, Equilon Enterprises, to consolidate their operations in the western United States, and in a separate venture, Motiva Enterprises, for the same purpose in the eastern United States. This ended their competition in the domestic refining and marketing of gasoline. As part of the ventures, Texaco and Shell agreed to pool their resources and share the risks and profits of their joint activities. The Federal Trade Commission and several states approved the formation of these entities without restricting the pricing of their gasoline, which the ventures began to sell at a single price under the original Texaco and Shell brand names. Fouad Dagher and other service station owners filed a suit in a federal district court against Texaco and Shell, alleging that the defendants were engaged in illegal price fixing. Do the circumstances in this case fit the definition of a price-fixing agreement? Explain. [*Texaco Inc. v. Dagher,* __ U.S. __, 126 S.Ct. 1276, 164 L.Ed.2d 1 (2006)]

A Question of Ethics

20–10. A group of lawyers in the District of Columbia regularly acted as court-appointed attorneys for indigent defendants in District of Columbia criminal cases. At a meeting of the Superior Court Trial Lawyers Association (SCTLA), the attorneys agreed to stop providing this representation until the district increased their compensation. Their subsequent boycott had a severe impact on the district's criminal justice system, and the District of Columbia gave in to the lawyers' demands for higher pay. After the lawyers had returned to work, the Federal Trade Commission filed a complaint against the SCTLA and four of its officers and, after an investigation, ruled that the SCTLA's activities constituted an illegal group boycott in violation of antitrust laws. [*Federal Trade Commission v. Superior Court Trial Lawyers Association,* 493 U.S. 411, 110 S.Ct. 768, 107 L.Ed.2d 851 (1990)]

1. The SCTLA obviously was aware of the negative impact its decision would have on the district's criminal justice system. Given this fact, do you think the lawyers behaved ethically?

2. On appeal, the SCTLA claimed that its boycott was undertaken to publicize that the attorneys were underpaid and that the boycott thus constituted an expression protected by the First Amendment. Do you agree with this argument?

3. Labor unions have the right to strike when negotiations between labor and management fail to result in

agreement. Is it fair to prohibit members of the SCTLA from "striking" against their employer, the District of Columbia, simply because the SCTLA is a professional organization and not a labor union?

Critical-Thinking Legal Question

20–11. Critics of antitrust law claim that in the long run, competitive market forces will eliminate private monopolies unless they are fostered by government regulation. Do you agree? Why or why not?

INTERACTING WITH THE INTERNET

For updated links to resources available on the Web, as well as a variety of other materials, visit this text's Web site at

www.thomsonedu.com/westbuslaw/let

The Federal Trade Commission offers an abundance of information on antitrust law, including a handbook titled *Promoting Competition, Protecting Consumers: A Plain English Guide to Antitrust Laws,* which is available at

www.ftc.gov/bc/compguide/index.htm

The *Tech Law Journal* presents "news, records, and analysis of legislation, litigation, and regulation affecting the computer and Internet industry" in the area of antitrust law at

www.techlawjournal.com/atr/default.htm

To see the American Bar Association's Web page on antitrust law, go to

www.abanet.org/antitrust

INTERNET EXERCISES

Go to **www.thomsonedu.com/westbuslaw/let**, the Web site that accompanies this text. Select "Chapter 20" and click on "Internet Exercises." There you will find the following Internet research exercises that you can perform to learn more about topics covered in this chapter.

Internet Exercise 20–1: LEGAL PERSPECTIVE—The Standard Oil Trust
Internet Exercise 20–2: MANAGEMENT PERSPECTIVE—Avoiding Antitrust Problems

BEFORE THE TEST

Go to **www.thomsonedu.com/westbuslaw/let**, the Web site that accompanies this text. Select "Chapter 20" and click on "Interactive Quizzes." You will find a number of interactive questions relating to this chapter.

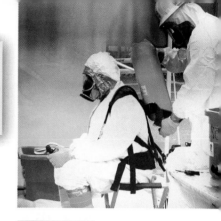

CHAPTER OBJECTIVES

After reading this chapter, you should be able to answer the following questions:

1. What is meant by the term *securities*?

2. What are the two major statutes regulating the securities industry? When was the Securities and Exchange Commission created, and what are its major purposes and functions?

3. What is insider trading? Why is it prohibited?

4. What are some of the features of state securities laws?

5. How are securities laws being applied in the online environment?

AFTER THE STOCK market crash of 1929, many members of Congress argued in favor of regulating securities markets. Basically, legislation for such regulation was enacted to provide investors with more information to help them make buying and selling decisions about **securities**—generally defined as any documents evidencing corporate ownership (stock) or debts (bonds)—and to prohibit deceptive, unfair, and manipulative practices. Today, the sale and transfer of securities are heavily regulated by federal and state statutes and by government agencies.

This chapter discusses the nature of federal securities regulation and its effect on the business world. We first examine the major traditional laws governing securities offerings and trading. We then discuss the Sarbanes-Oxley Act of 2002,[1] which significantly affects certain types of securities transactions. In the concluding pages of this chapter, we look at how securities laws are being adapted to the online environment. Before we begin, though, the important role played by the Securities and Exchange Commission (SEC) in the regulation of federal securities laws requires some attention. We examine the origin and functions of the SEC in this chapter's *Landmark in the Legal Environment* feature on the following page.

SECURITIES ACT OF 1933

The Securities Act of 1933[2] governs initial sales of stock by businesses. The act was designed to prohibit various forms of fraud and to stabilize the securities industry by requiring that all essential information concerning the issuance of

> " It shall be unlawful for any person in the offer or sale of any security . . . to engage in any transaction, practice, or course of business which operates or would operate as a fraud or deceit upon the purchaser. "
>
> —SECURITIES ACT OF 1933, SECTION 17

SECURITY
Generally, a stock certificate, bond, note, debenture, warrant, or other document given as evidence of an ownership interest in a corporation or as a promise of repayment by a corporation.

---

1. 15 U.S.C. Sections 7201 *et seq.*
2. 15 U.S.C. Sections 77–77aa.

LANDMARK IN THE LEGAL ENVIRONMENT
The Securities and Exchange Commission

In 1931, the Senate passed a resolution calling for an extensive investigation of securities trading. The investigation led, ultimately, to the passage by Congress of the Securities Act of 1933, which is also known as the *truth-in-securities* bill. In the following year, Congress passed the Securities Exchange Act. This 1934 act created the Securities and Exchange Commission (SEC).

Major Responsibilities of the SEC   The SEC was created as an independent regulatory agency with the function of administering the 1933 and 1934 acts. Its major responsibilities in this respect are as follows:

1. Requiring disclosure of facts concerning offerings of securities listed on national securities exchanges and of certain securities traded over the counter (OTC).
2. Regulating the trade in securities on national and regional securities exchanges and in the OTC markets.
3. Investigating securities fraud.
4. Regulating the activities of securities brokers, dealers, and investment advisers and requiring their registration.
5. Supervising the activities of mutual funds.
6. Recommending administrative sanctions, injunctive remedies, and criminal prosecution against those who violate securities laws. (The SEC can bring enforcement actions for civil violations of federal securities laws. The Fraud Section of the Criminal Division of the Department of Justice prosecutes criminal violations.)

The SEC's Expanding Regulatory Powers   Since its creation, the SEC's regulatory functions have gradually been increased by legislation granting it authority in different areas. For example, to further curb securities fraud, the Securities Enforcement Remedies and Penny Stock Reform Act of 1990[a] amended existing securities laws to

allow SEC administrative law judges to hear many more types of securities violation cases; the SEC's enforcement options were also greatly expanded. The act also provides that courts can prevent persons who have engaged in securities fraud from serving as officers and directors of publicly held corporations. The Securities Acts Amendments of 1990 authorized the SEC to seek sanctions against those who violate foreign securities laws.[b]

The National Securities Markets Improvement Act of 1996 expanded the power of the SEC to exempt persons, securities, and transactions from the requirements of the securities laws.[c] (This part of the act is also known as the Capital Markets Efficiency Act.) The act also limited the authority of the states to regulate certain securities transactions and particular investment advisory firms.[d] The Sarbanes-Oxley Act of 2002, which you will read about later in this chapter, further expanded the authority of the SEC by directing the agency to issue new rules relating to corporate disclosure requirements and by creating an SEC oversight board.

Application to Today's Legal Environment
Congress and the SEC have been attempting to streamline the regulatory process generally. The goal is to make it more efficient and more relevant to today's securities trading practices, including those occurring in the online environment. Another goal is to establish more oversight over securities transactions and accounting practices. Additionally, as the number and types of online securities frauds increase, the SEC is trying to keep pace by expanding its online fraud division.

RELEVANT WEB SITES
To locate information on the Web concerning the SEC, go to this text's Web site at **www.thomsonedu.com/ westbuslaw/let**, *select "Chapter 21," and click on "URLs for Landmarks."*

b. 15 U.S.C. Section 78a.
c. 15 U.S.C. Sections 77z-3, 78mm.
d. 15 U.S.C. Section 80b-3a.

a. 15 U.S.C. Section 77g.

securities be made available to the investing public. Basically, the purpose of this act is to require disclosure.

What Is a Security?

Section 2(1) of the Securities Act states that securities include the following:

> [A]ny note, stock, treasury stock, bond, debenture, evidence of indebtedness, certificate of interest or participation in any profit-sharing agreement, collateral-trust certificate, preorganization certificate or subscription, transferable share, investment

contract, voting-trust certificate, certificate of deposit for a security, fractional undivided interest in oil, gas, or other mineral rights, or, in general, any interest or instrument commonly known as a "security," or any certificate of interest or participation in, temporary or interim certificate for, receipt for, guarantee of, or warrant or right to subscribe to or purchase, any of the foregoing.[3]

The courts have interpreted the act's definition of what constitutes a security[4] to include investment contracts. An *investment contract* is any transaction in which a person (1) invests (2) in a common enterprise (3) reasonably expecting profits (4) derived *primarily* or *substantially* from others' managerial or entrepreneurial efforts.[5]

For our purposes, it is probably convenient to think of securities in their most common forms—stocks and bonds issued by corporations. Bear in mind, though, that securities can take many forms and have been held to include whiskey, cosmetics, worms, beavers, boats, vacuum cleaners, muskrats, and cemetery lots, as well as investment contracts in condominiums, franchises, limited partnerships, oil or gas or other mineral rights, and farm animals accompanied by care agreements.

Registration Statement

Section 5 of the Securities Act of 1933 broadly provides that unless a security qualifies for an exemption, that security must be *registered* before it is offered to the public either through the mails or through any facility of interstate commerce, including securities exchanges. Issuing corporations must file a *registration statement* with the SEC. Investors must be provided with a prospectus that describes the security being sold, the issuing corporation, and the investment or risk attaching to the security. In principle, the registration statement and the prospectus supply sufficient information to enable unsophisticated investors to evaluate the financial risk involved.

DON'T FORGET The purpose of the Securities Act of 1933 is disclosure—the SEC does not consider whether a security is worth the investment price.

Contents of the Registration Statement   The registration statement must be written in plain English and include the following:

1. A description of the significant provisions of the security offered for sale, including the relationship between that security and the other securities of the registrant. Also, the corporation must disclose how it intends to use the proceeds of the sale.
2. A description of the corporation's properties and business.
3. A description of the management of the corporation and its security holdings; remuneration; and other benefits, including pensions and stock options. Any interests of directors or officers in any material transactions with the corporation must be disclosed.
4. A financial statement certified by an independent public accounting firm.
5. A description of pending lawsuits.

A registration statement discusses a security that is being offered to the public. What are the major contents of a registration statement? (David Young-Wolff/PhotoEdit)

Other Requirements   Before filing the registration statement and the prospectus with the SEC, the corporation is allowed to obtain an *underwriter*—a company that agrees to purchase the new issue of securities for resale to the public.

---

3. 15 U.S.C. Section 77b(1). Amendments in 1982 added stock options.
4. See 15 U.S.C. Section 77b(a)(1).
5. *SEC v. W. J. Howey Co.,* 328 U.S. 293, 66 S.Ct. 1100, 90 L.Ed. 1244 (1946).

RED HERRING
A preliminary prospectus that can be distributed to potential investors after the registration statement (for a securities offering) has been filed with the Securities and Exchange Commission. The name derives from the red legend printed across the prospectus stating that the registration has been filed but has not become effective.

TOMBSTONE AD
An advertisement, historically in a format resembling a tombstone, of a securities offering. The ad tells potential investors where and how they may obtain a prospectus.

There is a twenty-day waiting period (which can be accelerated by the SEC) after registration before the securities can be sold. During this period, oral offers between interested investors and the issuing corporation concerning the purchase and sale of the proposed securities may take place, and very limited written advertising is allowed. At this time, the so-called **red herring** prospectus may be distributed. The name comes from the red legend printed across the prospectus stating that the registration has been filed but has not become effective.

After the waiting period, the registered securities can be legally bought and sold. Written advertising is allowed in the form of a **tombstone ad,** so named because historically the format resembled a tombstone. Such ads simply tell the investor where and how to obtain a prospectus. Normally, any other type of advertising is prohibited until the registration becomes effective.

Exempt Securities

A number of specific securities are exempt from the registration requirements of the Securities Act of 1933. These securities—which can also generally be resold without being registered—are listed in Exhibit 21–1.[6] Note that issues of up to $5 million in securities in any twelve-month period are exempt from registration requirements under Regulation A.[7] The issuer must file with the SEC a notice of the issue and an offering circular, which must also be provided to investors before the sale. This is a much simpler and less expensive process than the procedures associated with full registration. Companies are allowed to "test the waters" for potential interest before preparing the offering circular. To *test the waters* means to determine potential interest without actually selling any securities or requiring any commitment on the part of those who express interest. Small-business issuers (companies with annual revenues of less than $25 million) can also use an integrated registration and reporting system that uses simpler forms than the full registration system.

BE AWARE   The issuer of an exempt security does not have to disclose the same information that other issuers do.

Exempt Transactions

An issuer of securities that are not exempt under one of the ten categories listed in Exhibit 21–1 can avoid the high cost and complicated procedures associated with registration by taking advantage of certain transaction exemptions. These exemptions are very broad, and thus many sales occur without registration. Because the coverage of the exemptions overlaps somewhat, an offering may qualify for more than one.

Small Offerings—Regulation D   The SEC's Regulation D contains four separate exemptions from registration requirements for limited offers (offers that either involve a small amount or are made in a limited manner). Regulation D provides that any of these offerings made during any twelve-month period are exempt from the registration requirements.

Rule 504   Noninvestment company offerings up to $1 million in any twelve-month period are exempt.[8] In contrast to investment companies (discussed

6. See 15 U.S.C. Section 77c.
7. 17 C.F.R. Sections 230.251–230.263.
8. 17 C.F.R. Section 230.504. Rule 504 is the exemption used by most small businesses, but that could change under new SEC Rule 1001. This rule permits, under certain circumstances, "testing the waters" for offerings of up to $5 million *per transaction.* These offerings can be made only to "qualified purchasers" (knowledgeable, sophisticated investors), though.

EXHIBIT 21–1 EXEMPTIONS UNDER THE 1933 SECURITIES ACT

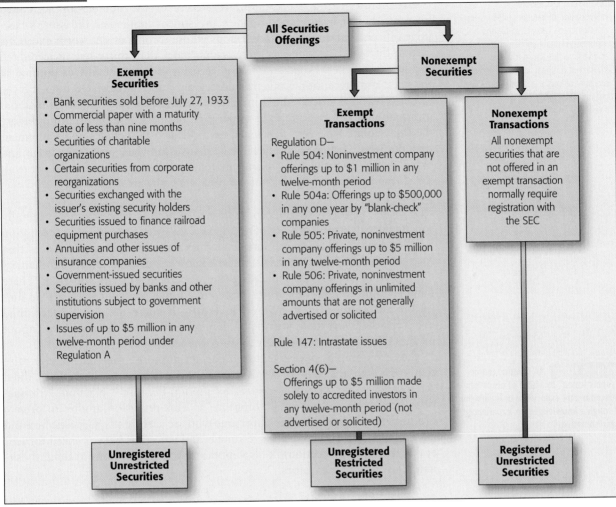

later in this chapter), noninvestment companies are firms that are not engaged primarily in the business of investing or trading in securities.

Rule 504a   Offerings up to $500,000 in any one year by so-called blank-check companies—companies with no specific business plans except to locate and acquire currently unknown businesses or opportunities—are exempt if no general solicitation or advertising is used; the SEC is notified of the sales; and precaution is taken against nonexempt, unregistered resales.[9] The limits on advertising and unregistered resales do not apply if the offering is made solely in states that provide for registration and disclosure and the securities are sold in compliance with those provisions.[10]

---

9. Precautions to be taken against nonexempt, unregistered resales include asking the investor whether he or she is buying the securities for others; before the sale, disclosing to each purchaser in writing that the securities are unregistered and thus cannot be resold, except in an exempt transaction, without first being registered; and indicating on the certificates that the securities are unregistered and restricted.

10. 17 C.F.R. Section 230.504a.

ACCREDITED INVESTOR
In the context of securities offerings, an investor who is knowledgeable and sophisticated about financial matters such as a bank, an insurance company, an investment company, any of the issuer's executive officers and directors, and any person whose income or net worth exceeds a certain threshold.

Rule 505   Private, noninvestment company offerings up to $5 million in any twelve-month period are exempt, regardless of the number of **accredited investors** (banks, insurance companies, investment companies, the issuer's executive officers and directors, and persons whose income or net worth exceeds a certain threshold), so long as there are no more than thirty-five unaccredited investors; no general solicitation or advertising is used; the SEC is notified of the sales; and precaution is taken against nonexempt, unregistered resales. If the sale involves *any* unaccredited investors, *all* investors must be given material information about the offering company, its business, and the securities before the sale. Unlike Rule 506 (discussed next), Rule 505 includes no requirement that the issuer believe each unaccredited investor "has such knowledge and experience in financial and business matters that he [or she] is capable of evaluating the merits and the risks of the prospective investment."[11]

Rule 506   Private offerings in unlimited amounts that are not generally solicited or advertised are exempt if the SEC is notified of the sales; precaution is taken against nonexempt, unregistered resales; and the issuer believes that each unaccredited investor has sufficient knowledge or experience in financial matters to be capable of evaluating the investment's merits and risks. There may be no more than thirty-five unaccredited investors, but there are no limits on the number of accredited investors. If there are *any* unaccredited investors, the issuer must provide to *all* purchasers material information about itself, its business, and the securities before the sale.[12]

This exemption is perhaps most important to those firms that want to raise funds through the sale of securities without registering them. It is often referred to as the *private placement* exemption because it exempts "transactions not involving any public offering."[13] This provision applies to private offerings to a limited number of persons who are sufficiently sophisticated and able to assume the risk of the investment (and who thus have no need for federal registration protection). It also applies to private offerings to similarly situated institutional investors.

Small Offerings—Section 4(6)   Under Section 4(6) of the Securities Act of 1933, an offer made *solely* to accredited investors is exempt if its amount is not more than $5 million. Any number of accredited investors may participate, but no unaccredited investors may do so. No general solicitation or advertising may be used; the SEC must be notified of all sales; and precaution must be taken against nonexempt, unregistered resales. Precaution is necessary because these are *restricted* securities and may be resold only by registration or in an exempt transaction.[14] (The securities purchased and sold by most people who deal in stock are called, in contrast, *unrestricted* securities.)

Intrastate Issues—Rule 147   Also exempt are intrastate transactions involving purely local offerings.[15] This exemption applies to most offerings that are restricted to residents of the state in which the issuing company is organized

11. 17 C.F.R. Section 230.505.
12. 17 C.F.R. Section 230.506.
13. 15 U.S.C. Section 77d(2).
14. 15 U.S.C. Section 77d(6).
15. 15 U.S.C. Section 77c(a)(11); 17 C.F.R. Section 230.147.

and doing business. For nine months after the last sale, virtually no resales may be made to nonresidents, and precautions must be taken against this possibility. These offerings remain subject to applicable laws in the state of issue.

Resales Most securities can be resold without registration (although some resales may be subject to restrictions, as discussed above in connection with specific exemptions). The Securities Act of 1933 provides exemptions for resales by most persons other than issuers or underwriters. The average investor who sells shares of stock need not file a registration statement with the SEC. Resales of restricted securities acquired under Rule 504a, Rule 505, Rule 506, or Section 4(6), however, trigger the registration requirements unless the party selling them complies with Rule 144 or Rule 144A. These rules are sometimes referred to as "safe harbors."

Rule 144 Rule 144 exempts restricted securities from registration on resale if there is adequate current public information about the issuer, the person selling the securities has owned them for at least one year, they are sold in certain limited amounts in unsolicited brokers' transactions, and the SEC is given notice of the resale.[16] "Adequate current public information" consists of the reports that certain companies are required to file under the Securities Exchange Act of 1934. A person who has owned the securities for at least three years is subject to none of these requirements, unless the person is an affiliate. An *affiliate* is one who controls, is controlled by, or is in common control with the issuer.

Rule 144A Securities that at the time of issue are not of the same class as securities listed on a national securities exchange or quoted in a U.S. automated interdealer quotation system may be resold under Rule 144A.[17] They may be sold only to a qualified institutional buyer (an institution, such as an insurance company or a bank, that owns and invests at least $100 million in securities). The seller must take reasonable steps to ensure that the buyer knows that the seller is relying on the exemption under Rule 144A. A sample restricted stock certificate is shown in Exhibit 21–2 on page 658.

Violations of the 1933 Act

As mentioned, the SEC has the power to investigate and bring civil enforcement actions against companies that violate federal securities laws. It is a violation of the Securities Act of 1933 to intentionally defraud investors by misrepresenting or omitting facts in a registration statement or prospectus. Liability is also imposed on those who are negligent for not discovering the fraud. Selling securities before the effective date of the registration statement or under an exemption for which the securities do not qualify results in liability.

Criminal violations are prosecuted by the Department of Justice. Violators may be fined up to $10,000, imprisoned for up to five years, or both. The SEC is authorized to seek civil sanctions against those who willfully violate the 1933 act. It can request an injunction to prevent further sales of the securities involved or ask the court to grant other relief, such as an order to a violator

---

16. 17 C.F.R. Section 230.144.
17. 17 C.F.R. Section 230.144A.

EXHIBIT 21-2 A SAMPLE RESTRICTED STOCK CERTIFICATE

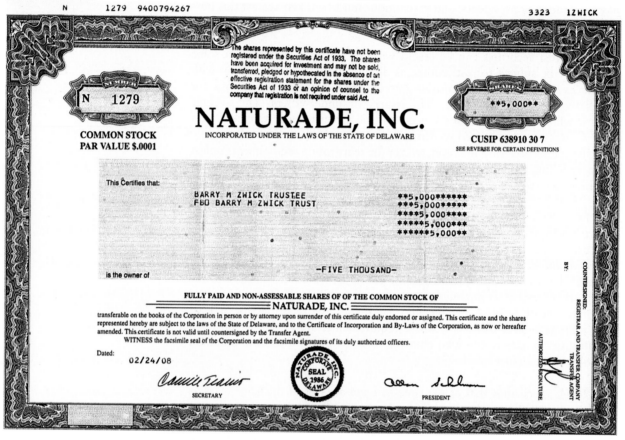

to refund profits. Those parties who purchase securities and suffer harm as a result of false or omitted statements may also bring suits in a federal court to recover their losses and other damages.

SECURITIES EXCHANGE ACT OF 1934

The Securities Exchange Act of 1934 provides for the regulation and registration of securities exchanges, brokers, dealers, and national securities associations such as the National Association of Securities Dealers (NASD). The SEC regulates the markets in which securities are traded by maintaining a continuous disclosure system for all corporations with securities on the securities exchanges and for those companies that have assets in excess of $10 million and five hundred or more shareholders. These corporations are referred to as Section 12 companies because they are required to register their securities under Section 12 of the 1934 act.

The act also authorizes the SEC to regulate proxy solicitations for voting (discussed in Chapter 11) and to engage in market surveillance to deter undesirable market practices such as fraud, market manipulation, and misrepresentation.

Section 10(b), SEC Rule 10b-5, and Insider Trading

Section 10(b) is one of the most important sections of the Securities Exchange Act of 1934. This section proscribes the use of any manipulative or deceptive device in violation of SEC rules and regulations. Among the rules that the SEC has promulgated pursuant to the 1934 act is **SEC Rule 10b-5,** which prohibits the commission of fraud in connection with the purchase or sale of any security.

One of the major goals of Section 10(b) and SEC Rule 10b-5 is to prevent so-called **insider trading.** Because of their positions, corporate directors and officers often obtain advance inside information that can affect the future market value of the corporate stock. Obviously, their positions give them a trading advantage over the general public and shareholders. The 1934 Securities Exchange Act defines inside information and extends liability to officers and directors for taking advantage of such information in their personal transactions when they know that it is unavailable to the persons with whom they are dealing.

Section 10(b) of the 1934 act and SEC Rule 10b-5 cover not only corporate officers, directors, and majority shareholders but also any persons having access to or receiving information of a nonpublic nature on which trading is based.

Disclosure under SEC Rule 10b-5 Any material omission or misrepresentation of material facts in connection with the purchase or sale of a security may violate not only the Securities Act of 1933 but also the antifraud provisions of Section 10(b) and SEC Rule 10b-5 of the 1934 act. The key to liability (which can be civil or criminal) under Section 10(b) and SEC Rule 10b-5 is whether the insider's information is *material.*

Examples of Material Facts Calling for Disclosure The following are some examples of material facts calling for disclosure under the rule:

1. Fraudulent trading in the company stock by a broker-dealer.
2. A dividend change (whether up or down).
3. A contract for the sale of corporate assets.
4. A new discovery, a new process, or a new product.
5. A significant change in the firm's financial condition.
6. Potential litigation against the company.

Note that any one of these facts, by itself, will not automatically be considered a material fact. Rather, it will be regarded as a material fact if it is significant enough that it will likely affect an investor's decision as to whether to purchase or sell certain securities.

The following case is one of the landmark decisions interpreting SEC Rule 10b-5. The SEC sued Texas Gulf Sulphur Company for issuing a misleading press release. The release underestimated the magnitude and value of a mineral discovery. The SEC also sued several of Texas Gulf Sulphur's directors, officers, and employees under SEC Rule 10b-5 for purchasing large amounts of the corporate stock prior to the announcement of the corporation's rich ore discovery.

A former executive of Enron Corporation leaves the federal courthouse in Houston in May 2004 after pleading guilty to an insider-trading charge. What is the reasoning behind laws that make insider trading illegal? (AP Photo/Pat Sullivan)

SEC RULE 10b-5
A rule of the Securities and Exchange Commission that makes it unlawful, in connection with the purchase or sale of any security, to make any untrue statement of a material fact or to omit a material fact if such omission causes the statement to be misleading.

INSIDER TRADING
The purchase or sale of securities on the basis of information that has not been made available to the public.

LANDMARK & CLASSIC CASES

CASE 21.1   SEC v. Texas Gulf Sulphur Co.

United States Court of Appeals,
Second Circuit, 1968.
401 F.2d 833.

BACKGROUND AND FACTS   Texas Gulf Sulphur Company (TGS) conducted aerial geophysical surveys over more than 15,000 square miles of eastern Canada. The operations indicated concentrations of commercially exploitable minerals. At one site near Timmins, Ontario, TGS drilled a hole that appeared to yield a core with an exceedingly high mineral content. TGS kept secret the results of the core sample. Officers and employees of the company made substantial purchases of

TGSs stock or accepted stock options after learning of the ore discovery, even though further drilling was necessary to establish whether there was enough ore to be mined commercially. Several months later, TGS announced that the strike was expected to yield at least 25 million tons of ore. Subsequently, the price of TGS stock rose substantially. The Securities and Exchange Commission (SEC) brought a suit against the officers and employees of TGS for violating SEC Rule 10b-5. The officers and employees argued that the information on which they had traded had not been material at the time of their trades because the mine had not then been commercially proved. The trial court held that most of the defendants had not violated SEC Rule 10b-5, and the SEC appealed.

IN THE WORDS OF THE COURT . . . *WATERMAN*, Circuit Judge.

* * * *

* * * [W]hether facts are material within Rule 10b-5 when the facts relate to a particular event and are undisclosed by those persons who are knowledgeable thereof *will depend at any given time upon a balancing of both the indicated probability that the event will occur and the anticipated magnitude of the event in light of the totality of the company activity.* Here, * * * knowledge of the possibility, which surely was more than marginal, of the existence of a mine of the vast magnitude indicated by the remarkably rich drill core located rather close to the surface (suggesting mineability by the less expensive openpit method) within the confines of a large anomaly (suggesting an extensive region of mineralization) might well have affected the price of TGS stock and would certainly have been an important fact to a reasonable, if speculative, investor in deciding whether he should buy, sell, or hold. [Emphasis added.]

* * * *

* * * [A] major factor in determining whether the * * * discovery was a material fact is the importance attached to the drilling results by those who knew about it. * * * [T]he timing by those who knew of it of their stock purchases * * *—purchases in some cases by individuals who had never before purchased * * * TGS stock—virtually compels the inference that the insiders were influenced by the drilling results.

DECISION AND REMEDY   The appellate court ruled in favor of the SEC. All of the trading by insiders who knew of the mineral find before its true extent had been publicly announced violated SEC Rule 10b-5.

IMPACT OF THIS CASE ON TODAY'S LEGAL ENVIRONMENT
This landmark case affirmed the principle that the test of whether information is "material," for SEC Rule 10b-5 purposes, is whether it would affect the judgment of reasonable investors. The corporate insiders' purchases of

stock and stock options (rights to purchase stock) indicated that they were influenced by the drilling results and that the information about the drilling results was material. The courts continue to cite this case when applying SEC Rule 10b-5 to cases of alleged insider trading.

RELEVANT WEB SITES   *To locate information on the Web concerning the* Texas Gulf Sulphur *case, go to this text's Web site at* **www.thomsonedu.com/westbuslaw/let***, select "Chapter 21," and click on "URLs for Landmarks."*

■ ▪ ■

The Private Securities Litigation Reform Act of 1995   One of the unintended effects of SEC Rule 10b-5 was to deter the disclosure of some material information, such as financial forecasts. To understand why, consider an example.

| **Example #1** A company announces that its projected earnings in a certain time period will be X amount. It turns out that the forecast is wrong. The earnings are in fact much lower, and the price of the company's stock is affected—negatively. The shareholders then bring a class-action suit against the company, alleging that the directors violated SEC Rule 10b-5 by disclosing misleading financial information. |

In an attempt to rectify this problem and promote disclosure, Congress passed the Private Securities Litigation Reform Act of 1995. Among other things, the act provides a "safe harbor" for publicly held companies that make forward-looking statements, such as financial forecasts. Companies that make such statements are protected against liability for securities fraud as long as the statements are accompanied by "meaningful cautionary statements identifying important factors that could cause actual results to differ materially from those in the forward-looking statement."[18]

Wall Street in New York has become nearly synonymous with securities trading. What federal laws regulate the purchase and sale of securities? What are the costs and benefits of such regulation? (Brand X Pictures)

After the 1995 act was passed, a number of securities class-action suits were filed in state courts to skirt the requirements of the 1995 federal act. In response to this problem, Congress passed the Securities Litigation Uniform Standards Act (SLUSA) of 1998. The act placed stringent limits on the ability of plaintiffs to bring class-action suits in state courts against firms whose securities are traded on national stock exchanges.

Does the SLUSA deny state law securities fraud class-action claims only for the purchasers and sellers of securities? Or does it also cover those investors who are fraudulently induced to hold on to their securities? That was the question in the following case.

---

18. 15 U.S.C. Sections 77z-2, 78u-5.

CASE 21.2 Merrill Lynch, Pierce, Fenner & Smith, Inc. v. Dabit

Supreme Court of the United States, 2006.
__ U.S. __,
126 S.Ct. 1503,
164 L.Ed.2d 179.
www.findlaw.com/casecode/supreme.html[a]

BACKGROUND AND FACTS Merrill Lynch, Pierce, Fenner & Smith, Inc., is an investment banking firm that offers research and brokerage services to investors. In 2002, the state of New York began to investigate charges that Merrill Lynch had given bad investment advice to its clients. The firm settled this dispute. Meanwhile, Shadi Dabit, a former Merrill Lynch broker, filed a class-action suit in an Oklahoma state court against the

a. In the "Browsing" section, click on "2006 Decisions." When that page opens, scroll to the name of the case and click on it to read the opinion.

firm on behalf of all its brokers who bought for themselves or their clients certain stock between December 1, 1999, and December 31, 2000. Basing his claims on state law, Dabit alleged in part that the firm had issued overly optimistic appraisals of stocks' values on which its brokers relied to buy and sell their shares and to advise their clients whether to sell their holdings. When New York began its investigation, "the truth was actually revealed" and the stocks' prices plummeted. The suit was moved to a federal district court, where it was consolidated with others' claims. Merrill Lynch filed a motion to dismiss Dabit's complaint, arguing in part that the SLUSA blocked it. The court agreed and dismissed the complaint. Dabit appealed to the U.S. Court of Appeals for the Second Circuit, which vacated the lower court's decision. Merrill Lynch appealed to the United States Supreme Court.

IN THE WORDS OF THE COURT . . . Justice STEVENS delivered the opinion of the Court.

* * * *

The magnitude of the federal interest in protecting the integrity and efficient operation of the market for nationally traded securities cannot be overstated. In response to

CASE 21.2–CONTINUED ▶

the sudden and disastrous collapse in prices of listed stocks in 1929, and the Great Depression that followed, Congress enacted the Securities Act of 1933, and the Securities Exchange Act of 1934. Since their enactment, these two statutes have anchored federal regulation of vital elements of our economy.

* * * *

Policy considerations * * * prompted Congress, in 1995, to adopt [the Private Securities Litigation Reform Act] targeted at perceived abuses of the class-action vehicle in litigation involving nationally traded securities. * * *

* * * *

* * * Rather than face the obstacles set in their path by the Reform Act, plaintiffs and their representatives began bringing class actions under state law, often in state court. * * * To stem this shift from Federal to State courts * * * , Congress enacted SLUSA.

* * * *

The core provision of SLUSA reads as follows:

* * * No covered class action based upon the statutory or common law of any State or subdivision thereof may be maintained in any State or Federal court by any private party alleging—
* * * a misrepresentation or omission of a material fact in connection with the purchase or sale of a covered security * * * .

* * * The only disputed issue [in this case] is whether the alleged wrongdoing was "in connection with the purchase or sale" of securities.

Respondent [Dabit] urges that the operative language must be read narrowly to encompass (and therefore preempt) only those actions in which the [actual purchasers or sellers of the securities are involved]. * * *

* * * Under our precedents, it is enough that the fraud alleged "coincide" with a securities transaction—whether by the plaintiff or by someone else. The requisite showing, in other words, is deception "in connection with the purchase or sale of any security," not deception of an identifiable purchaser or seller. Notably, this broader interpretation of the statutory language comports [is consistent] with the longstanding views of the SEC.

Congress can hardly have been unaware of the broad construction adopted by both this Court and the SEC when it imported the key phrase—"in connection with the purchase or sale"—into SLUSA's core provision. And *when judicial interpretations have settled the meaning of an existing statutory provision, repetition of the same language in a new statute indicates* * * * *the intent to incorporate its* * * * *judicial interpretations as well.* * * * [Emphasis added.]

The presumption that Congress envisioned a broad construction follows * * * from the particular concerns that culminated in SLUSA's enactment. A narrow reading of the statute would undercut the effectiveness of the 1995 Reform Act and thus run contrary to SLUSA's stated purpose, [which is] "to prevent certain State private securities class-action lawsuits alleging fraud from being used to frustrate the objectives" of the 1995 Act. * * *

Respondent's preferred construction also would give rise to wasteful, duplicative litigation. Facts supporting an action by purchasers under Rule 10b-5 (which must proceed in federal court if at all) typically support an action by holders [of stock or stock options and other contractual rights or duties to purchase or sell securities] as well, at least in those States that recognize holder claims. The prospect is raised, then, of parallel class actions proceeding in state and federal court, with different standards governing claims asserted on identical facts. That prospect * * * squarely conflicts with the congressional preference for national standards for securities class-action lawsuits involving nationally traded securities.

DECISION AND REMEDY The United States Supreme Court vacated the judgment of the lower court and remanded the case for further proceedings. The SLUSA prevents state law class-action claims by certain shareholders who traded their securities based on a "misrepresentation or omission of a material fact in connection with the purchase or sale of a covered security." That is to say, those who buy or hold rights to buy specific stocks based on "incorrect" advice cannot file a class-action lawsuit in state court. The act also bars such claims by shareholders who refrained from trading their securities.

WHAT IF THE FACTS WERE DIFFERENT? *If Dabit had filed his suit only on his own behalf, rather than on the behalf of other brokers and investors, how might the result in this case have been different?*

Applicability of SEC Rule 10b-5   SEC Rule 10b-5 applies in virtually all cases concerning the trading of securities, whether on organized exchanges, in over-the-counter markets, or in private transactions. The rule covers, among other things, notes, bonds, agreements to form a corporation, and joint-venture agreements. Generally, it covers just about any form of security. It is immaterial whether a firm has securities registered under the 1933 act for the 1934 act to apply.

Although SEC Rule 10b-5 is applicable only when the requisites of federal jurisdiction—such as the use of the mails, of stock exchange facilities, or of any instrumentality of interstate commerce—are present, virtually no commercial transaction can be completed without such contact. In addition, the states have corporate securities laws, many of which include provisions similar to SEC Rule 10b-5.

Outsiders and SEC Rule 10b-5   The traditional insider-trading case involves true insiders—corporate officers, directors, and majority shareholders who have access to (and trade on) inside information. Increasingly, liability under Section 10(b) of the 1934 act and SEC Rule 10b-5 is being extended to include certain "outsiders"—those persons who trade on inside information acquired indirectly. Two theories have been developed under which outsiders may be held liable for insider trading: the *tipper/tippee theory* and the *misappropriation theory*.

Tipper/Tippee Theory   Anyone who acquires inside information as a result of a corporate insider's breach of his or her fiduciary duty can be liable under SEC Rule 10b-5. This liability extends to **tippees** (those who receive "tips" from insiders) and even remote tippees (tippees of tippees).

TIPPEE
A person who receives inside information.

The key to liability under this theory is that the inside information must be obtained as a result of someone's breach of a fiduciary duty to the corporation whose shares are involved in the trading. The tippee is liable under this theory only if there is a breach of a duty not to disclose inside information, the disclosure is in exchange for personal benefit, and the tippee knows (or should know) of this breach and benefits from it.[19]

Misappropriation Theory   Liability for insider trading may also be established under the misappropriation theory. This theory holds that if an individual wrongfully obtains (misappropriates) inside information and trades on it

---

19. See, for example, *Chiarella v. United States*, 445 U.S. 222, 100 S.Ct. 1108, 63 L.Ed.2d 348 (1980); and *Dirks v. SEC*, 463 U.S. 646, 103 S.Ct. 3255, 77 L.Ed.2d 911 (1983).

for her or his personal gain, then the individual should be held liable because, in essence, the individual stole information rightfully belonging to another.

The misappropriation theory has been controversial because it significantly extends the reach of SEC Rule 10b-5 to outsiders who ordinarily would not be deemed fiduciaries of the corporations in whose stock they trade. The United States Supreme Court, however, has held that liability under SEC Rule 10b-5 can be based on the misappropriation theory.[20]

Insider Reporting and Trading—Section 16(b)

Officers, directors, and certain large stockholders[21] of Section 12 corporations (corporations that are required to register their securities under Section 12 of the 1934 act) must file reports with the SEC concerning their ownership and trading of the corporations' securities.[22] To discourage such insiders from using nonpublic information about their companies for their personal benefit in the stock market, Section 16(b) of the 1934 act provides for the recapture by the corporation of all profits realized by an insider on any purchase and sale or sale and purchase of the corporation's stock within any six-month period.[23] It is irrelevant whether the insider actually uses inside information; *all such short-swing profits must be returned to the corporation.*

Section 16(b) applies not only to stock but also to warrants, options, and securities convertible into stock. In addition, the courts have fashioned complex rules for determining profits. Note that the SEC exempts a number of transactions under Rule 16b-3.[24] For all of these reasons, corporate insiders are wise to seek specialized counsel prior to trading in the corporation's stock. Exhibit 21–3 compares the effects of SEC Rule 10b-5 and Section 16(b).

Proxy Statements

Section 14(a) of the Securities Exchange Act of 1934 regulates the solicitation of proxies (documents granting a person authority to vote another's stock shares— see Chapter 11) from shareholders of Section 12 companies. The SEC regulates the content of proxy statements. A *proxy statement* is sent to shareholders when corporate officials are requesting authority to vote on behalf of the shareholders in a particular election on specified issues. Whoever solicits a proxy must fully and accurately disclose in the proxy statement all of the facts that are pertinent to the matter on which the shareholders are to vote. SEC Rule 14a-9 is similar to the antifraud provisions of SEC Rule 10b-5. Remedies for violations are extensive; they range from injunctions that prevent a vote from being taken to monetary damages.

A proxy statement. Who regulates the content of proxy statements, and how? (Courtesy of Prudential Financial)

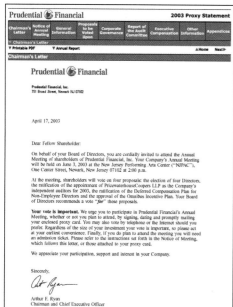

20. *United States v. O'Hagan*, 521 U.S. 642, 117 S.Ct. 2199, 138 L.Ed.2d 724 (1997).
21. Those stockholders owning 10 percent of the class of equity securities registered under Section 12 of the 1934 act.
22. 15 U.S.C. Section 78l.
23. A person who expects the price of a particular stock to decline can realize profits by "selling short"—selling at a high price and repurchasing later at a lower price to cover the "short sale."
24. 17 C.F.R. Section 240.16b-3.

Violations of the 1934 Act

Violations of Section 10(b) of the Securities Exchange Act of 1934 and SEC Rule 10b-5 include insider trading. This is a criminal offense, with criminal penalties. Violators of these laws may also be subject to civil liability. For any sanctions to be imposed, however, there must be *scienter*—the violator must have had an intent to defraud or knowledge of her or his misconduct. *Scienter* can be proved by showing that a defendant made false statements or wrongfully failed to disclose material facts.

Violations of Section 16(b) include the sale by insiders of stock acquired less than six months before the sale. These violations are subject to civil sanctions. Liability under Section 16(b) is strict liability. Thus, liability is imposed regardless of whether *scienter* or negligence existed.

Criminal Penalties   For violations of Section 10(b) and Rule 10b-5, an individual may be fined up to $5 million, imprisoned for up to twenty years, or both.[25] A partnership or a corporation may be fined up to $25 million. Under Section 807 of the Sarbanes-Oxley Act of 2002, for a willful violation of the 1934 act the violator may, in addition to being subject to a fine, be imprisoned for up to twenty-five years.

To be found guilty of a crime under the securities laws, the jury must conclude beyond a reasonable doubt that the defendant knew he or she was acting wrongfully. The issue in the following case was whether, in light of this principle, there was enough evidence that Martha Stewart, founder of a well-known media and homemaking empire, intended to deceive investors to present the matter to a jury.

25. These numbers reflect the increased penalties imposed by the Sarbanes-Oxley Act of 2002, discussed later in this chapter.

EXHIBIT 21–3 COMPARISON OF COVERAGE, APPLICATION, AND LIABILITIES UNDER SEC RULE 10b–5 AND SECTION 16(b)

AREA OF COMPARISON	SEC RULE 10b-5	SECTION 16(b)
What is the subject matter of the transaction?	Any security (does not have to be registered).	Any security (does not have to be registered).
What transactions are covered?	Purchase or sale.	Short-swing purchase and sale or short-swing sale and purchase.
Who is subject to liability?	Virtually anyone with inside information under a duty to disclose—including officers, directors, controlling stockholders, and tippees.	Officers, directors, and certain 10 percent stockholders.
Is omission or misrepresentation necessary for liability?	Yes.	No.
Are there any exempt transactions?	No.	Yes, there are a variety of exemptions.
Is direct dealing with the party necessary?	No.	No.
Who may bring an action?	A person transacting with an insider, the SEC, or a purchaser or seller damaged by a wrongful act.	A corporation or a shareholder by derivative action.

CASE 21.3   United States v. Stewart

United States District Court,
Southern District of New York, 2004.
305 F.Supp.2d 368.

BACKGROUND AND FACTS   Samuel Waksal, the chief executive officer of ImClone Systems, Inc., a biotechnology company, was a client of stockbroker Peter Bacanovic. Bacanovic's other clients included Martha Stewart, then the chief executive officer of Martha Stewart Living Omnimedia (MSLO). On December 27, 2001, Waksal began selling his ImClone stock. Bacanovic allegedly had Stewart informed of Waksal's sales, and she also sold her ImClone shares. The next day, ImClone announced that the Food and Drug Administration had rejected the company's application for approval of its leading product, a medication called Erbitux. The government began to investigate Stewart's ImClone trades, the media began to report on the investigation, and the value of MSLO stock began to drop. In June 2002, at a "Mid-Year Media Review" conference attended by investment professionals and investors, Stewart said that she had previously agreed with Bacanovic to sell her ImClone stock if the price fell to $60 per share. "I have nothing to add on this matter today. And I'm here to talk about our terrific company." Her statements were followed by a forty-minute presentation on MSLO. Subsequently, Stewart was charged with, among other things, fraud in connection with the purchase and sale of MSLO securities in violation of the Securities Exchange Act of 1934. She filed a motion for a judgment of acquittal on this charge.

IN THE WORDS OF THE COURT . . . *CEDARBAUM,* District Judge.

*   *   *   *

*   *   *   "[S]cienter," or intent, in the civil securities fraud context, indicates a mental state embracing intent to deceive, manipulate, or defraud, and is a required element of any claim of securities fraud. *In a criminal prosecution, the Government must also prove that the defendant acted willfully, that is, with a realization that she was acting wrongfully.* *   *   * The issue at hand is *   *   * whether, taking into account the heightened standard of proof in criminal cases, there is sufficient evidence of Stewart's intent to deceive investors to present the matter to the jury. [Emphasis added.]

*   *   *   *

The Government contends that a reasonable jury could draw inferences from the evidence *   *   * that would permit it to find beyond a reasonable doubt that Stewart intended to deceive investors with her statements. Specifically, the Government argues that the evidence supports the inferences that Stewart was aware of the impact of the negative publicity about her ImClone trade on the market value of MSLO securities *   *   * and that Stewart deliberately directed her statements to investors in MSLO securities.

*   *   * I hold that a reasonable juror could not, without resorting to speculation and surmise [guesswork], find beyond a reasonable doubt that Stewart's purpose was to influence the market in MSLO securities.

*   *   *   *

With respect to the June *   *   * statement, the Government contends that Stewart's awareness that she was speaking to analysts and investors, her prefatory statement that she was embarking upon a topic about which her audience was "probably interested," and the timing of the statement, which occurred as the stock continued to fall, are sufficient *   *   * to permit the jury to infer that she intended to deceive investors in MSLO securities when she made the statement.

*   *   * [T]he fact that the *   *   * statement was read to an audience of analysts and investors *   *   * cannot be viewed in isolation—the entire context of the statement must be considered. Thus, any inference to be drawn from the makeup of the audience must also take into account the fact that Stewart was only one of several representatives of MSLO, and that MSLO was only one of several corporations making presentations at the conference. The evidence does not show that the conference was organized by Stewart or her company. There is no evidence that the negative publicity about ImClone influenced Stewart's decision to attend and take advantage of a platform from which to reach investors directly. To the contrary, her statement—a very brief portion of a much longer presentation—indicates otherwise. The Government argues that her statement indicating an awareness that the audience was "probably interested" in what she had to say about the ImClone trade is meaningful. Yet her remarks at the close of the statement—"I have nothing to add on this matter today. And I'm here to talk about our terrific company * * * ."—support an inference that she wanted to dispose of the issue and begin to address the subjects of the conference.

* * * *

In sum, when the nature of the audience is viewed within the overall context of the statement, this is too slight an addition to the total mix of evidence of intent to carry the burden of proving criminal intent beyond a reasonable doubt.

DECISION AND REMEDY The court granted Stewart's motion for a judgment of acquittal on the charge at issue in this case. The court reasoned that "to find the essential element of criminal intent beyond a reasonable doubt" and conclude that Stewart lied to influence the market for the securities of her company "a rational juror would have to speculate."**a**

a. Stewart was later convicted on other charges related to her sale of ImClone stock, including obstruction of justice and lying to federal officials, and was sentenced to, and served, five months in prison and five months and three weeks of house arrest. In May 2005, the SEC filed a lawsuit against Stewart seeking civil sanctions for violations of the 1934 Act and the SEC's rules prohibiting insider trading. The civil action had been stayed pending the resolution of the criminal case against Stewart.

FOR CRITICAL ANALYSIS–Social Consideration *How does the scienter, or intent, requirement in the context of criminal securities fraud differ from its counterpart in the context of civil securities fraud?*

Civil Sanctions The SEC can bring a suit in a federal district court against anyone violating or aiding in a violation of the 1934 act or SEC rules by purchasing or selling a security while in the possession of material nonpublic information.[26] The violation must occur on or through the facilities of a national securities exchange or from or through a broker or dealer. Transactions pursuant to a public offering by an issuer of securities are excepted. The court may assess as a penalty as much as triple the profits gained or the loss avoided by the guilty party. Profit or loss is defined as "the difference between the purchase or sale price of the security and the value of that security as measured by the trading price of the security at a reasonable period of time after public dissemination of the nonpublic information."[27]

The Insider Trading and Securities Fraud Enforcement Act of 1988 enlarged the class of persons who may be subject to civil liability for insider-trading violations. This act also gave the SEC authority to award **bounty payments** (rewards given by government officials for acts beneficial to the state) to persons providing information leading to the prosecution of insider-trading violations.[28]

Private parties may also sue violators of Section 10(b) and Rule 10b-5. A private party may obtain rescission (cancellation) of a contract to buy securities or

BOUNTY PAYMENT
A reward (payment) given to a person or persons who perform a certain service, such as informing legal authorities of illegal actions.

---

26. The Insider Trading Sanctions Act of 1984. 15 U.S.C. Section 78u(d)(2)(A).
27. 15 U.S.C. Section 78u(d)(2)(C).
28. 15 U.S.C. Section 78u-1.

damages to the extent of the violator's illegal profits. Those found liable have a right to seek contribution from those who share responsibility for the violations, including accountants, attorneys, and corporations.[29] For violations of Section 16(b), a corporation can bring an action to recover the short-swing profits.

CORPORATE GOVERNANCE

Corporate governance can be narrowly defined as the relationship between a corporation and its shareholders. The Organization of Economic Cooperation and Development (OECD) provides a broader definition:

> Corporate governance is the system by which business corporations are directed and controlled. The corporate governance structure specifies the distribution of rights and responsibilities among different participants in the corporation, such as the board of directors, managers, shareholders, and other stakeholders, and spells out the rules and procedures for making decisions on corporate affairs.[30]

While this definition has no true legal value, it does set the tone for the ways in which modern corporations should be governed. In other words, effective corporate governance requires more than compliance with laws and regulations.

The Need for Good Corporate Governance

The need for effective corporate governance arises in large corporations because corporate ownership (by shareholders) is separated from corporate control (by officers and managers). In the real world, officers and managers are tempted to advance their own interests, even when such interests conflict with those of the shareholders. The reason for concern about managerial opportunism can be illustrated by the well-publicized scandals in the corporate world during the last ten years.

Attempts at Aligning the Interests of Shareholders with Those of Officers

Some corporations have sought to align the financial interests of their officers with those of the company's shareholders. Thus, many officers have been provided with *stock options* for the corporation, which could be exercised at a set price and sold for a profit above that per-share price. When a corporation's share value grows, these options become more valuable for the officers, thereby giving them a financial stake in the share price.

Options have turned out to be an imperfect device for controlling governance, however. Executives in some companies have been tempted to "cook" the company's books in order to keep share prices higher so that they could exercise their

---

29. The United States Supreme Court has ruled that no private cause of action can be brought against those who "aid and abet" under Section 10(b) and SEC Rule 10b-5. *Central Bank of Denver, N.A. v. First Interstate Bank of Denver, N.A.*, 511 U.S. 164, 114 S.Ct. 1439, 128 L.Ed.2d 119 (1994). Only the SEC can bring actions against so-called aiders and abettors. Nevertheless, some courts have held accountants and attorneys liable as primary violators under Section 10(b), and a conflict exists in the federal circuit courts on precisely what course of conduct subjects a secondary actor to primary liability.

30. *Governance in the 21st Century: Future Studies*, OECD, 2001.

options for a profit. Executives in other corporations experienced no losses when share prices dropped; instead, some had their options "repriced" so that they did not suffer from the share price decline and could still profit from future increases above the lowered share price. Although stock options theoretically can motivate officers to protect shareholder interests, stock option plans became a way for officers to take advantage of shareholders.

Because of numerous headline-making scandals within major corporations, there has been an outcry for more "outside" directors—the theory is that independent directors will more closely monitor the actions of corporate officers. Today, we see more boards with outside directors (those with no formal employment affiliation with the company). Note, though, that outside directors may not be truly independent of corporate officers; they may be friends or business associates of the leading officers. A study of board appointments found that the best way to increase one's probability of appointment was to "suck up" to the chief executive officer.[31]

Corporate Governance and Corporate Law

Good corporate governance standards are designed to address problems (such as those briefly discussed above) and to motivate officers to make decisions to promote the financial interests of the company's shareholders. Generally, corporate governance entails corporate decision-making structures that monitor employees (particularly officers) to ensure that they are acting for the benefit of the shareholders. Thus, corporate governance involves, at a minimum:

1. The audited reporting of financial conditions at the corporation, so that managers can be evaluated.
2. Legal protections for shareholders, so that violators of the law, who attempt to take advantage of shareholders, can be punished for misbehavior and victims may recover damages for any associated losses.

The Practical Significance of Good Corporate Governance   Effective corporate governance may have considerable practical significance. A study by researchers at Harvard University and the Wharton School of Business found that firms providing greater shareholder rights had higher profits, higher sales growth, higher firm value, and other economic advantages.[32] Better corporate governance in the form of greater accountability to investors may therefore offer the opportunity to considerably enhance institutional wealth.

Governance and Corporation Law   Corporate governance is the essential purpose of corporation law in the United States. These statutes set up the legal framework for corporate governance. Under the corporate law of Delaware, where most major companies incorporate, all corporations must have in place certain structures of corporate governance. The key structure of corporate law is, of course, the board of directors. Directors make the most important decisions about the future of the corporation and monitor the actions of corporate officers. Directors are elected by shareholders to look out for their best interests.

---

31. Jennifer Reingold, "Suck Up and Move Fast," *Fast Company,* January 2005, p. 34.
32. Paul A. Gompers, Joy L. Ishii, and Andrew Metrick, "Corporate Governance and Equity Prices," *Quarterly Journal of Economics,* Vol. 118 (2003), p. 107.

The Board of Directors   Some argue that shareholder democracy is key to improving corporate governance. If shareholders could vote on major corporate decisions, shareholders could presumably have more control over the corporation. Essential to shareholder democracy is the concept of electing the board of directors, usually at the corporation's annual meeting. Under corporate law, a corporation must have a board of directors elected by shareholders. Virtually anyone can become a director, though some organizations, such as the New York Stock Exchange, require certain standards of service for directors of their listed corporations.

Directors have the responsibility of ensuring that officers are operating wisely and in the exclusive interest of shareholders. Directors receive reports from the officers and give them managerial directions. The board in theory controls the compensation of officers (presumably tied to performance). The reality, though, is that corporate directors devote a relatively small amount of time to monitoring officers.

Ideally, shareholders would monitor the directors' supervision of officers. As one leading board monitor stated, "Boards of directors are like subatomic particles—they behave differently when they are observed." Consequently, monitoring directors, and holding them responsible for corporate failings, can induce the directors to do a better job of monitoring officers and ensuring that the company is being managed in the interest of shareholders. While the directors can be sued for failing to effectively do their jobs, directors are rarely held personally liable.

Importance of the Audit Committee   One crucial board committee is known as the *audit committee*. Members of the audit committee oversee the corporation's accounting and financial reporting processes, including both internal and outside auditors. These audit committee members must, however, have sufficient expertise and be willing to spend the time necessary to carefully examine the corporation's bookkeeping methods. Otherwise, the audit committee may be ineffective.

The audit committee also oversees the corporation's "internal controls." These are the measures taken to ensure that reported results are accurate; they are carried out largely by the company's internal auditing staff. As an example, these controls help to determine whether a corporation's debts are collectible. If the debts are not collectible, it is up to the audit committee to make sure that the corporation's financial officers cannot simply pretend that payment will eventually be made.

The Compensation Committee   Another important committee of the board of directors is the *compensation committee*. This committee monitors and determines the compensation to be paid to a company's officers. In the process, it has the responsibility for assessing the officers' performance, and its members may try to design compensation systems that encourage better performance by the officers on behalf of shareholders.

The Sarbanes-Oxley Act of 2002

As discussed in Chapter 2, in 2002, following a series of corporate scandals, Congress passed the Sarbanes-Oxley Act (see Appendix N for excerpts and explanatory comments). The act separately addresses certain issues relating to corporate governance. Generally, the act attempts to increase corporate accountability by imposing strict disclosure requirements and harsh penalties for violations of securities laws. Among other things, the act requires chief corporate executives to take responsibility for the accuracy of financial statements and reports that are filed with the SEC. Chief executive officers and chief financial officers must personally certify that the statements and reports are accurate and complete.

Additionally, the new rules require that certain financial and stock-transaction reports be filed with the SEC earlier than was required under the previous rules. The act also mandates SEC oversight over a new entity, called the Public Company Accounting Oversight Board, that regulates and oversees public accounting firms. Other provisions of the act created new private civil actions and expanded the SEC's remedies in administrative and civil actions.

Because of the importance of this act for those dealing with securities transactions, we present some of the act's key provisions relating to corporate accountability in Exhibit 21–4 on the following page. We also discuss the act and its effect on corporate governance procedures in this section.

The New York Stock Exchange (NYSE). The Sarbanes-Oxley Act has imposed millions of dollars of additional annual costs on publicly listed corporations. Consequently, New York is no longer the preferred market for raising capital by large multinational companies. Where can such companies go instead? (Photo Courtesy of NYSE)

More Internal Controls and Accountability   The Sarbanes-Oxley Act includes some traditional securities law provisions but also introduces direct *federal* corporate governance requirements for public companies (companies whose shares are traded in the public securities markets). The law addresses many of the corporate governance procedures just discussed and creates new requirements in an attempt to make the system work more effectively. The requirements deal with independent monitoring of company officers by both the board of directors and auditors.

Sections 302 and 404 of Sarbanes-Oxley require high-level managers (the most senior officers) to establish and maintain an effective system of internal controls. Moreover, senior management must reassess the system's effectiveness on an annual basis. Some companies already had strong and effective internal control systems in place before the passage of the act, but others had to take expensive steps to bring their internal controls up to the new federal standard. These include "disclosure controls and procedures" to ensure that company financial reports are accurate and timely. Assessment must involve the documenting of financial results and accounting policies before reporting them. By the beginning of 2007, hundreds of companies had reported that they had identified and corrected shortcomings in their internal control systems.

Certification and Monitoring Requirements   Section 906 requires that chief executive officers (CEOs) and chief financial officers (CFOs) certify that the corporate financial statements "fairly present, in all material respects, the financial condition and results of operation of the issuer." These corporate officers are subject to both civil and criminal penalties for violation of this section. This requirement makes officers directly accountable for the accuracy of their financial reporting and avoids any "ignorance defense" if shortcomings are later discovered.

EXHIBIT 21–4   SOME KEY PROVISIONS OF THE SARBANES-OXLEY ACT
OF 2002 RELATING TO CORPORATE ACCOUNTABILITY

Certification Requirements—Under Section 906 of the Sarbanes-Oxley Act, the chief executive officers (CEOs) and chief financial officers (CFOs) of most major companies listed on public stock exchanges must now certify financial statements that are filed with the SEC. For virtually all filed financial reports, CEOs and CFOs have to certify that such reports "fully comply" with SEC requirements and that all of the information reported "fairly represents in all material respects, the financial conditions and results of operations of the issuer."

Under Section 302 of the act, for each quarterly and annual filing with the SEC, CEOs and CFOs of reporting companies are required to certify that a signing officer reviewed the report and that it contains no untrue statements of material fact. Also, the signing officer or officers must certify that they have established an internal control system to identify all material information, and that any deficiencies in the system were disclosed to the auditors.

Loans to Directors and Officers—Section 402 prohibits any reporting company, as well as any private company that is filing an initial public offering, from making personal loans to directors and executive officers (with a few limited exceptions, such as for certain consumer and housing loans).

Protection for Whistleblowers—Section 806 protects "whistleblowers"—those employees who report ("blow the whistle" on) securities violations by their employers—from being fired or in any way discriminated against by their employers.

Blackout Periods—Section 306 prohibits certain types of securities transactions during "blackout periods"—periods during which the issuer's ability to purchase, sell, or otherwise transfer funds in individual account plans (such as pension funds) is suspended.

Enhanced Penalties for—

- *Violations of Section 906 Certification Requirements*—A CEO or CFO who certifies a financial report or statement filed with the SEC knowing that the report or statement does not fulfill all of the requirements of Section 906 will be subject to criminal penalties of up to $1 million in fines, ten years in prison, or both. *Willful* violators of the certification requirements may be subject to $5 million in fines, twenty years in prison, or both.

- *Violations of the Securities Exchange Act of 1934*—Penalties for securities fraud under the 1934 act were also increased (as discussed earlier in this chapter). Individual violators may be fined up to $5 million, imprisoned for up to twenty years, or both. *Willful* violators may be imprisoned for up to twenty-five years in addition to being fined.

- *Destruction or Alteration of Documents*—Anyone who alters, destroys, or conceals documents or otherwise obstructs any official proceeding will be subject to fines, imprisonment for up to twenty years, or both.

- *Other Forms of White-Collar Crime*—The act stiffened the penalties for certain criminal violations, such as federal mail and wire fraud, and ordered the U.S. Sentencing Commission to revise the sentencing guidelines for white-collar crimes (see Chapter 6).

Statute of Limitations for Securities Fraud—Section 804 provides that a private right of action for securities fraud may be brought no later than two years after the discovery of the violation or five years after the violation, whichever is earlier.

Sarbanes-Oxley also adopts requirements to improve directors' monitoring of officers' activities. All members of the corporate audit committee for public companies must be outside directors. The New York Stock Exchange (NYSE) has a similar rule that also extends to the board's compensation committee. The audit committee must have a written charter that sets out its duties and provides for performance appraisal. At least one "financial expert" must serve on the audit committee, which must hold executive meetings without company officers being present. The audit committee must establish procedures for "whistleblowers." In addition to reviewing the internal controls, the committee also monitors the actions of the outside auditor.

The Separation of Audit and Nonaudit Services   The law includes other provisions to improve accounting accuracy. Auditors are prohibited from providing a company with substantial nonaudit services of any kind that might compromise the auditors' independence. The lead audit partner and reviewing partner must rotate off each assignment every five years. This rotation is aimed at preventing them from establishing unduly close relationships with the management officers they are auditing. Other rules apply to lawyers representing public companies and require them to blow the whistle on their clients when they determine a client is engaged in illegal behavior.

Corporate Ethical Codes   Sarbanes-Oxley also contains provisions for corporate ethical codes. A company regulated by the SEC must report whether it has established an ethical code governing high-level officers. The contents of that code must be publicly available. The NYSE similarly requires that each listed company adopt a code of conduct and ethics for its officers and post it on the company's Web site. This code of conduct and ethics must specifically prohibit self-dealing at the expense of shareholders. Of course, the code must also prohibit violations of the law.

ETHICAL ISSUE 21.1   ***Should lawyers be required to withdraw as counsel and notify the SEC if a corporate client is violating securities laws?***

The attorney-client privilege generally prevents lawyers from disclosing confidential client information—even when the client has committed an unlawful act. The idea is to encourage clients to be open and honest with their attorneys to ensure competent representation. The Sarbanes-Oxley Act of 2002 requires an attorney to report any material violations of securities laws to the corporation's highest authority.[33] The act does not require that the lawyer reveal client confidences, though, because the lawyer is still reporting to officials within the corporation.

The SEC now wants to go one step further than the Sarbanes-Oxley Act and mandate a "noisy withdrawal." Under the SEC's proposal, attorneys whose corporate clients are violating securities laws would have to withdraw publicly from representing the corporation and notify the SEC. This proposal is controversial and has been the subject of much debate. Should the SEC be able to force lawyers to disclose privileged client information? Would this be fair to the corporation? In 2003, the American Bar Association (ABA) modified its ethics rules to allow attorneys to break confidence with a client to report possible corporate fraud. The ABA rules do not *require* attorneys to do so, however. Nonetheless, the SEC wants to make the disclosure mandatory. In the SEC's view, lawyers owe a duty to the corporation and its investors, not to the individual officers and directors.

THE REGULATION OF INVESTMENT COMPANIES

Investment companies, and mutual funds in particular, grew rapidly after World War II. **Investment companies** act on behalf of many smaller shareholders by buying a large portfolio of securities and professionally managing that portfolio. A **mutual fund** is a specific type of investment company that continually buys or sells to investors shares of ownership in a portfolio. Such companies are

INVESTMENT COMPANY
A company that acts on behalf of many smaller shareholders/owners by buying a large portfolio of securities and professionally managing that portfolio.

MUTUAL FUND
A specific type of investment company that continually buys or sells to investors shares of ownership in a portfolio.

---

33. See Section 307 of the Sarbanes-Oxley Act.

regulated by the Investment Company Act of 1940,[34] which provides for SEC regulation of their activities. The act was expanded by the 1970 amendments to the Investment Company Act. Further minor changes were made in the Securities Act Amendments of 1975 and in later years.

Definition of an Investment Company

For the purposes of the act, an *investment company* is any entity that (1) is engaged primarily "in the business of investing, reinvesting, or trading in securities" or (2) is engaged in such business and has more than 40 percent of its assets in investment securities. Excluded from coverage by the act are banks, insurance companies, savings and loan associations, finance companies, oil and gas drilling firms, charitable foundations, tax-exempt pension funds, and other special types of institutions, such as closely held corporations.

Registration and Reporting Requirements

The 1940 act requires that every investment company register with the SEC by filing a notification of registration. Each year, registered investment companies must file reports with the SEC. To safeguard company assets, all securities must be held in the custody of a bank or stock exchange member, which must follow strict procedures established by the SEC.

Restrictions on Investment Companies

The 1940 act also imposes restrictions on the activities of investment companies and persons connected with them. For example, investment companies are not allowed to purchase securities on the margin (pay only part of the total price, borrowing the rest), sell short (sell shares not yet owned), or participate in joint trading accounts. In addition, no dividends may be paid from any source other than accumulated, undistributed net income.

STATE SECURITIES LAWS

BE AWARE Federal securities laws do not take priority over state securities laws.

Today, all states have their own corporate securities laws, or "blue sky laws," that regulate the offer and sale of securities within individual state borders. (The phrase *blue sky laws* dates to a 1917 decision by the United States Supreme Court in which the Court declared that the purpose of such laws was to prevent "speculative schemes which have no more basis than so many feet of 'blue sky.'")[35] Article 8 of the Uniform Commercial Code, which has been adopted by all of the states, also imposes various requirements relating to the purchase and sale of securities.

Requirements under State Securities Laws

Despite some differences in philosophy, all state blue sky laws have certain features. Typically, state laws have disclosure requirements and antifraud provisions, many of which are patterned after Section 10(b) of the Securities

---

34. 15 U.S.C. Sections 80a-1 to 64.
35. *Hall v. Geiger-Jones Co.*, 242 U.S. 539, 37 S.Ct. 217, 61 L.Ed. 480 (1917).

Exchange Act of 1934 and SEC Rule 10b-5. State laws also provide for the registration or qualification of securities offered or issued for sale within the state and impose disclosure requirements. Unless an exemption from registration is applicable, issuers must register or qualify their stock with the appropriate state official, often called a *corporations commissioner*. Additionally, most state securities laws regulate securities brokers and dealers.

Concurrent Regulation

State securities laws apply mainly to intrastate transactions. Since the adoption of the 1933 and 1934 federal securities acts, the state and federal governments have regulated securities concurrently. Issuers must comply with both federal and state securities laws, and exemptions from federal law are not exemptions from state laws.

The dual federal and state system has not always worked well, particularly during the early 1990s, when the securities markets underwent considerable expansion. In response, Congress passed the National Securities Markets Improvement Act of 1996, which eliminated some of the duplicate regulations and gave the SEC exclusive power to regulate most national securities activities. The National Conference of Commissioners on Uniform State Laws then substantially revised the Uniform Securities Act and recommended it to the states for adoption in 2002. Unlike the previous version of this law, the new act is designed to coordinate state and federal securities regulation and enforcement efforts. Since 2002, ten states have adopted the Uniform Securities Act, and a number of other states are considering adoption.[36]

ONLINE SECURITIES OFFERINGS AND DISCLOSURES

The Spring Street Brewing Company, headquartered in New York, made history when it became the first company to attempt to sell securities via the Internet. Through its online initial public offering (IPO), which ended in early 1996, Spring Street raised about $1.6 million—without having to pay any commissions to brokers or underwriters. The offering was made pursuant to Regulation A, which, as mentioned earlier in this chapter, allows small-business issuers to use a simplified registration procedure.

Such online IPOs are particularly attractive to small companies and start-up ventures that may find it difficult to raise capital from institutional investors or through underwriters. By making the offering online under Regulation A, the company can avoid both commissions and the costly and time-consuming filings required for a traditional IPO under federal and state law.

Regulations Governing Online Securities Offerings

One of the early questions posed by online offerings was whether the delivery of securities information via the Internet met the requirements of the 1933 Securities Act, which traditionally were applied to the delivery of paper documents. In an

---

36. At the time this book went to press, the 2002 Uniform Securities Act had been adopted in Idaho, Iowa, Kansas, Maine, Minnesota, Missouri, Oklahoma, South Carolina, South Dakota, and Vermont, as well as in the U.S. Virgin Islands. Adoption legislation was pending in Alabama, Alaska, Hawaii, and Washington. You can find current information on state adoptions at www.nccusl.org.

The home page of E*Trade. Online trading through a firm such as E*Trade does not involve personal contact with a broker. Does this mean that online trading is unregulated? (Courtesy of E-Trade Financial Group)

interpretive release issued in 1995, the SEC stated that "[t]he use of electronic media should be at least an equal alternative to the use of paper-based media" and that anything that can be delivered in paper form under the current securities laws might also be delivered in electronic form.[37]

Basically, there has been no change in the substantive law of disclosure; only the delivery vehicle has changed. When the Internet is used for delivery of a prospectus, the same rules apply as for the delivery of a paper prospectus. Once the three requirements listed below have been satisfied, the prospectus has been successfully delivered.

1. *Timely and adequate notice of the delivery of information is required.* Hosting a prospectus on a Web site does not constitute adequate notice, but separate e-mails or even postcards stating the URL where the prospectus can be viewed will satisfy the SEC's notice requirements.

2. *The online communication system must be easily accessible.* This is very simple to do today because virtually anyone interested in purchasing securities has access to the Web.

3. *Some evidence of delivery must be created.* This requirement is relatively easy to satisfy. Those making online offerings can require an e-mail return receipt verification of any materials sent electronically.

Potential Liability Created by Online Offering Materials

Every printed prospectus indicates that only the information given in the prospectus can be used in conjunction with making an investment decision in the securities offered. The same wording, of course, appears on Web-based offerings. What happens if an electronic prospectus contains information that conflicts with the information provided in a printed prospectus? Will such an error render the registration statement ineffective? See this chapter's *Online Developments* feature for a discussion of a case involving this issue.

Hyperlinks to Other Web Pages   Those who create such Web-based offerings may be tempted to insert hyperlinks to other Web pages. They may include links to other sites that have analyzed the future prospects of the company, the products and services sold by the company, or the offering itself. To avoid potential liability, however, online offerors (the entities making the offerings) need to exercise caution when including such hyperlinks.

| **Example #2**   Suppose that a hyperlink goes to an analyst's Web page that makes optimistic statements concerning the financial outlook of the offering company. Further suppose that after the IPO, the stock price falls. By including the hyperlink on its Web site, the offering company is impliedly supporting the information presented on the linked page. If it turns out that the company knew the statements made on the analyst's Web page were false or misleading, the company may be liable for violating sections of the Securities Exchange Act of 1934.[38]|

---

37. "Use of Electronic Media for Delivery Purposes," Securities Act Release No. 33-7233 (October 6, 1995). The rules governing the use of electronic transmissions for delivery purposes were subsequently confirmed in Securities Act Release No. 33-7289 (May 9, 1996) and expanded in Securities Act Release No. 33-7856 (April 28, 2000).

38. See, for example, *In re Syntex Corp. Securities Litigation*, 95 F.3d. 922 (9th Cir. 1996), involving alleged violations of Sections 10(b) and 20(a) of the 1934 act.

ONLINE DEVELOPMENTS
Will Inaccurate Information in an Electronic Prospectus Invalidate the Registration?

Many companies now submit registration statements, prospectuses, and other information to the Securities and Exchange Commission (SEC) via the Internet. The SEC's Electronic Data Gathering, Analysis, and Retrieval (EDGAR) system then posts much of this information online to inform investors about the corporation, the security being sold, and the risk of investing in that security. Some corporations also send investors a printed prospectus. Theoretically, a corporation should provide the same information in electronic form as it does in a printed prospectus, but practical difficulties can arise in transmitting digital information.

The Problem with Graphics
As anyone who is familiar with the Internet knows, the graphics, images, and audio files created by one computer are not always readable by another computer when they are exchanged online. The SEC has created Rule 304 to deal with this situation.[a] The first part of the rule states that if graphic, image, or audio material in a prospectus cannot be reproduced in an electronic form on EDGAR, the electronic prospectus must include a fair and accurate narrative description of the omitted data. The second part of Rule 304 provides that the graphic, image, and audio material contained in the version of a document delivered to investors is *deemed to be part of the electronic document* filed with the SEC.

As a result, a corporation can have two versions of a prospectus—a print version that contains graphics and an electronic version that describes the information shown in the graphics. What if the summary describing the graphics in an electronic prospectus is inaccurate but the investors received an accurate print version? That was the issue before a federal appellate court in *DeMaria v. Andersen.*[b]

The Electronic Prospectus Contained Inaccuracies
In anticipation of an initial public offering (IPO), ILife.com, Inc., filed a registration statement and a prospectus with the SEC via the EDGAR database. ILife.com also distributed a printed version of the prospectus to the public. The printed prospectus contained a bar graph that provided historical financial information about the company, while the EDGAR prospectus contained a table that summarized the bar graph inaccurately (without mentioning losses). Brian DeMaria and other investors filed a suit against officers of ILife.com. The investors claimed that because of the inaccurate summary, the securities in the IPO were "unregistered" and thus were sold in violation of the Securities Act of 1933. The lower court dismissed the case, and DeMaria appealed.

The Registration Held Valid
Despite the inaccurate summary of the bar graph in the electronic prospectus, the appellate court had no trouble deciding that the securities sold were still registered as required by the Securities Act of 1933. Federal courts are bound to follow the SEC's interpretation of its own regulations unless the interpretations are plainly erroneous. Here, the SEC had filed a brief explaining that because the graphics in the printed prospectus are deemed to be part of the electronic registration statement, it did not matter that the narrative description was inaccurate.

For Critical Analysis *Does the part of Rule 304 that deems a printed prospectus to be part of a registration statement completely eliminate liability for any inaccuracies in the electronic materials filed? Why or why not?*

a. 17 C.F.R. Section 232.304.
b. 318 F.3d 170 (2d Cir. 2003).

Regulation D Offerings Potential problems may also occur with some Regulation D offerings, if the offeror places the offering circular on its Web site for general consumption by anybody on the Internet. Because Regulation D offerings are private placements, general solicitation is restricted. If anyone can have access to the offering circular on the Web, the Regulation D exemption may be disqualified.

Case Problem with Sample Answer

21–5. 2TheMart.com, Inc., was conceived in January 1999 to launch a Web auction site to compete with eBay, Inc. On January 19, 2TheMart announced that its Web site was in its "final development" stages and was expected to be active by the end of July as a "preeminent" auction site. The company also said that it had "retained the services of leading Web site design and architecture consultants to design and construct" the site. Based on the announcement, investors rushed to buy 2TheMart's stock, causing a rapid increase in the price. On February 3, 2TheMart entered into an agreement with IBM to take preliminary steps to plan the site. Three weeks later, 2TheMart announced that the site was "currently in final development." On June 1, 2TheMart signed a contract with IBM to design, build, and test the site, with a target delivery date of October 8. When 2TheMart's site did not debut as announced, Mary Harrington and others who had bought the stock filed a suit in a federal district court against the firm's officers, alleging violations of the Securities Exchange Act of 1934. The defendants responded, in part, that any alleged misrepresentations were not material and asked the court to dismiss the suit. How should the court rule, and why? [*In re 2TheMart.com, Inc. Securities Litigation,* 114 F.Supp.2d 955 (C.D.Cal. 2000)]

After you have answered this problem, compare your answer with the sample answer given on the Web site that accompanies this text. Go to www.thomsonedu.com/westbuslaw/let, select "Chapter 21," and click on "Case Problem with Sample Answer."

21–6. Insider Reporting and Trading. Ronald Bleakney, an officer at Natural Microsystems Corp. (NMC), a Section 12 corporation, directed NMC sales in North America, South America, and Europe. In November 1998, Bleakney sold more than 7,500 shares of NMC stock. The following March, Bleakney resigned from the firm, and the next month, he bought more than 20,000 shares of its stock. NMC provided some guidance to employees concerning the rules of insider trading, but with regard to Bleakney's transactions, the corporation said nothing about potential liability. Richard Morales, an NMC shareholder, filed a suit against NMC and Bleakney to compel recovery, under Section 16(b) of the Securities Exchange Act of 1934, of Bleakney's profits from the sale and purchase of his shares. (When Morales died, his executor Deborah Donoghue became the plaintiff.) Bleakney argued that he should not be liable because he relied on NMC's advice. Should the court order Bleakney to disgorge his profits? Explain. [*Donoghue v. Natural Microsystems Corp.,* 198 F.Supp.2d 487 (S.D.N.Y. 2002)]

21–7. SEC Rule 10b–5. Scott Ginsburg was chief executive officer (CEO) of Evergreen Media Corp. In 1996, Evergreen became interested in acquiring EZ Communications, Inc. Ginsburg met with EZ's CEO, Alan Box, on July 12. Evergreen and EZ executives began negotiating confidentially for the purchase of EZ at the specific price of $50 a share. Ginsburg called his brother, Mark, who spoke to their father, Jordan, about the deal. Mark and Jordan bought almost 75,000 shares of EZ stock. Evergreen's bid for EZ fell through, but in August, EZ announced its merger with another company. The price of EZ stock rose 30 percent, increasing the value of Mark and Jordan's shares by more than $1.76 million. The Securities and Exchange Commission (SEC) filed a suit in a federal district court against Ginsburg, alleging, among other things, violations of SEC Rule 10b–5 for communicating material nonpublic information to Mark and Jordan, who traded on the basis of that information. Ginsburg contended in part that the information was not material and filed a motion for a judgment as a matter of law. What is the test for materiality in this context? Does the information in this case meet the test, or should the court grant the motion? Explain. [*SEC v. Ginsburg,* 362 F.3d 1292 (11th Cir. 2004)]

21–8. Securities Laws. In 1997, WTS Transnational, Inc., required financing to develop a prototype of an unpatented fingerprint-verification system. At the time, WTS had no revenue, $655,000 in liabilities, and only $10,000 in assets. Thomas Cavanagh and Frank Nicolois, who operated an investment banking company called U.S. Milestone (USM), arranged the financing using Curbstone Acquisition Corp. Curbstone had no assets but had registered approximately 3.5 million shares of stock with the Securities and Exchange Commission (SEC). Under the terms of the deal, Curbstone acquired WTS, and the resulting entity was named Electro-Optical Systems Corp. (EOSC). New EOSC shares were issued to all of the WTS shareholders. Only Cavanagh and others affiliated with USM could sell EOSC stock to the public, however. Over the next few months, these individuals issued false press releases, made small deceptive purchases of EOSC shares at high prices, distributed hundreds of thousands of shares to friends and relatives, and sold their own shares at inflated prices through third party companies they owned. When the SEC began to investigate, the share price fell to its actual value, and innocent investors lost over $15 million. Were any securities laws violated in this case? If so, what might be an appropriate remedy? [*SEC v. Cavanagh,* 445 F.3d 105 (2d Cir. 2006)]

A Question of Ethics

21–9. Susan Waldbaum was a niece of the president and controlling shareholder of Waldbaum, Inc. Susan's mother (the president's sister) told Susan that the company was going to be sold at a favorable price and that a tender offer was soon to be made. She told Susan not to tell anyone except her husband, Keith Loeb, about the sale. (Loeb did not work for the company and was never brought into the family's inner circle, in which family members discussed confidential business information.) The next day, Susan told her husband of the sale and cautioned him not to tell anyone because "it could possibly ruin the sale." The day after he learned of the sale, Loeb told Robert Chestman, his broker, about the sale, and Chestman purchased shares of the company for both Loeb and himself. Chestman was later convicted by a jury of, among other things, trading on misappropriated inside information in violation of SEC Rule 10b-5. [*United States v. Chestman*, 947 F.2d 551 (2d Cir. 1991)]

1. On appeal, the central question was whether Chestman had acquired the inside information about the tender offer as a result of an insider's breach of a fiduciary duty. Could Loeb—the "tipper" in this case—be considered an insider?

2. If Loeb was not an insider, did he owe any fiduciary (legal) duty to his wife or his wife's family to keep the information confidential? Would it be fair of the court to impose such a legal duty on Loeb?

Critical-Thinking Ethical Question

21-10. Do you think that the tipper/tippee and misappropriation theories extend liability under SEC Rule 10b-5 too far? Why or why not?

Video Question

21-11. Go to this text's Web site at **www.thomsonedu.com/westbuslaw/let** and select "Chapter 21." Click on "Video Questions" and view the video titled *Mergers and Acquisitions*. Then answer the following questions.

1. Analyze whether the purchase of Onyx Advertising is a material fact that the Quigley Co. had a duty to disclose under SEC Rule 10b-5.

2. Does it matter whether Quigley personally knew about or authorized the company spokesperson's statements? Why or why not?

3. Which case discussed in the chapter presented issues that are very similar to those raised in the video? Under the holding of that case, would Onyx Advertising be able to maintain a suit against the Quigley Co. for violation of SEC Rule 10b-5?

4. Who else might be able to bring a suit against the Quigley Co. for insider trading under SEC Rule 10b-5?

INTERACTING WITH THE INTERNET

For updated links to resources available on the Web, as well as a variety of other materials, visit this text's Web site at

www.thomsonedu.com/westbuslaw/let

To access the SEC's EDGAR database, go to

www.sec.gov/edgar.shtml

The Center for Corporate Law at the University of Cincinnati College of Law examines many of the laws discussed in this chapter, including the Securities Act of 1933 and the Securities Exchange Act of 1934. Go to

www.law.uc.edu/CCL

INTERNET EXERCISES

Go to **www.thomsonedu.com/westbuslaw/let**, the Web site that accompanies this text. Select "Chapter 21" and click on "Internet Exercises." There you will find the following Internet research exercises that you can perform to learn more about topics covered in this chapter.

Internet Exercise 21-1: LEGAL PERSPECTIVE—Electronic Delivery
Internet Exercise 21-2: MANAGEMENT PERSPECTIVE—The SEC's Role

BEFORE THE TEST

Go to **www.thomsonedu.com/westbuslaw/let**, the Web site that accompanies this text. Select "Chapter 21" and click on "Interactive Quizzes." You will find a number of interactive questions relating to this chapter.

UNIT FIVE CUMULATIVE BUSINESS HYPOTHETICAL

Falwell Motors, Inc., is a large corporation that manufactures automobile batteries.

1. The Federal Trade Commission (FTC) learns that one of the retail stores that sells Falwell's batteries engages in deceptive advertising practices. What actions can the FTC take against the retailer?

2. For years, Falwell has shipped the toxic waste created by its manufacturing process to a waste-disposal site in the next county. The waste site has become contaminated by leakage from toxic waste containers delivered to the site by other manufacturers. Can Falwell be held liable for clean-up costs, even though its containers were not the ones that leaked? If so, what is the extent of its liability?

3. Falwell faces stiff competition from Alchem, Inc., another battery manufacturer. To acquire control over Alchem, Falwell makes a tender offer to Alchem's shareholders. If Falwell succeeds in its attempt and Alchem is merged into Falwell, will the merger violate any antitrust laws? Suppose the merger falls through. The vice president of Falwell's battery division and the president of Alchem agree to divide up the market between them, so they will not have to compete for customers. Is this agreement legal? Explain.

4. One of Falwell's employees learns that Falwell is contemplating a takeover of a rival. The employee tells her husband about the possibility. The husband calls their broker, who purchases shares in the target corporation for the employee and her husband, as well as for himself. Has the employee violated any securities law? Has her husband? Has the broker? Explain.

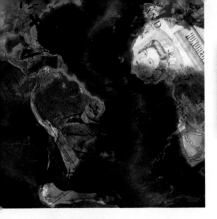

The Regulation of International Transactions

CHAPTER OBJECTIVES

After reading this chapter, you should be able to answer the following questions:

1 What is the principle of comity, and why do courts deciding disputes involving a foreign law or judicial decree apply this principle?

2 What is the act of state doctrine? In what circumstances is this doctrine applied?

3 Under the Foreign Sovereign Immunities Act of 1976, on what bases might a foreign state be considered subject to the jurisdiction of U.S. courts?

4 In what circumstances will U.S. antitrust laws be applied extraterritorially?

5 Do U.S. laws prohibiting employment discrimination apply in all circumstances to U.S. employees working for U.S. employers abroad?

" Our interests are those of the open door—a door of friendship and mutual advantage. This is the only door we care to enter. **"**

—WOODROW WILSON, 1856–1924
(Twenty-eighth president of the United States, 1913–1921)

INTERNATIONAL LAW
The law that governs relations among nations. International customs and treaties are important sources of international law.

NATIONAL LAW
Laws that pertain to a particular nation (as opposed to international law).

INTERNATIONAL BUSINESS TRANSACTIONS are not unique to the modern world. Indeed, as suggested by President Woodrow Wilson's statement in the chapter-opening quotation, people have always found that they can benefit from exchanging goods with others. What is new in our day is the dramatic growth in world trade and the emergence of a global business community. Because the exchange of goods, services, and ideas on a global level is now routine, students of business law should be familiar with the laws pertaining to international business transactions. In this chapter, we first examine the legal context of international business transactions. We then look at some selected areas relating to business activities in a global context, including international sales contracts, civil dispute resolution, letters of credit, and investment protection. We conclude the chapter with a discussion of the application of certain U.S. laws in a transnational setting.

INTERNATIONAL PRINCIPLES AND DOCTRINES

Recall from our discussion in Chapter 1 that **international law** can be defined as a body of law—formed as a result of international customs, treaties, and organizations—that governs relations among or between nations. **National law,** in contrast, is the law of a particular nation, such as Brazil, Germany, Japan, or the United States. Here, we look at some legal principles and doctrines of international law that have evolved over time and that the courts of various nations have employed—to a greater or lesser extent—to resolve or reduce conflicts that involve a foreign element. The three important legal principles and doctrines discussed in the following subsections are based primarily on courtesy and respect and are applied in the interests of maintaining harmonious relations among nations.

The Principle of Comity

Under what is known as the principle of **comity,** one nation will defer and give effect to the laws and judicial decrees of another country, as long as those laws and judicial decrees are consistent with the law and public policy of the accommodating nation.

| **Example #1** Assume that a Swedish seller and a U.S. buyer have formed a contract, which the buyer breaches. The seller sues the buyer in a Swedish court, which awards damages. The buyer's assets, however, are in the United States and cannot be reached unless the judgment is enforced by a U.S. court of law. In this situation, if a U.S. court determines that the procedures and laws applied in the Swedish court were consistent with U.S. national law and policy, that court will likely defer to (and enforce) the foreign court's judgment. |

COMITY
The principle by which one nation defers and gives effect to the laws and judicial decrees of another nation. This recognition is based primarily on respect.

The Act of State Doctrine

The **act of state doctrine** is a judicially created doctrine that provides that the judicial branch of one country will not examine the validity of public acts committed by a recognized foreign government within its own territory. This doctrine is premised on the theory that the judicial branch should not "pass upon the validity of foreign acts when to do so would vex the harmony of our international relations with that foreign nation."[1]

The act of state doctrine can have important consequences for individuals and firms doing business with, and investing in, other countries. For example, this doctrine is frequently employed in situations involving expropriation or confiscation. **Expropriation** occurs when a government seizes a privately owned business or privately owned goods for a proper public purpose and awards just compensation. When a government seizes private property for an illegal purpose or without just compensation, the taking is referred to as a **confiscation.** The line between these two forms of taking is sometimes blurred because of differing interpretations of what is illegal and what constitutes just compensation.

When applicable, both the act of state doctrine and the doctrine of *sovereign immunity* (to be discussed next) tend to immunize (protect) foreign governments from the jurisdiction of U.S. courts. This means that firms or individuals who own property overseas often have diminished legal protection against government actions in the countries in which they operate.

ACT OF STATE DOCTRINE
A doctrine providing that the judicial branch of one country will not examine the validity of public acts committed by a recognized foreign government within its own territory.

EXPROPRIATION
The seizure by a government of a privately owned business or personal property for a proper public purpose and with just compensation.

CONFISCATION
A government's taking of a privately owned business or personal property without a proper public purpose or an award of just compensation.

The Doctrine of Sovereign Immunity

When certain conditions are satisfied, the doctrine of **sovereign immunity** immunizes foreign nations from the jurisdiction of U.S. courts. In 1976, Congress codified this rule in the Foreign Sovereign Immunities Act (FSIA).[2] The FSIA exclusively governs the circumstances in which an action may be

SOVEREIGN IMMUNITY
A doctrine that immunizes foreign nations from the jurisdiction of U.S. courts when certain conditions are satisfied.

---

1. *Libra Bank, Ltd. v. Banco Nacional de Costa Rica, S.A.,* 570 F.Supp. 870 (S.D.N.Y. 1983).
2. 28 U.S.C. Sections 1602–1611.

brought in the United States against a foreign nation, including attempts to attach a foreign nation's property.

Section 1605 of the FSIA sets forth the major exceptions to the jurisdictional immunity of a foreign state or country. A foreign state is not immune from the jurisdiction of U.S. courts when the state has "waived its immunity either explicitly or by implication" or when the action is taken "in connection with a commercial activity carried on in the United States by the foreign state" or having "a direct effect in the United States."[3]

The question frequently arises as to whether an entity falls within the category of a foreign state. The question of what is a commercial activity has also been the subject of dispute. Under Section 1603 of the FSIA, a *foreign state* includes both a political subdivision of a foreign state and an instrumentality (department or agency of any branch of a government) of a foreign state. Section 1603 broadly defines a *commercial activity* as a commercial activity that is carried out by a foreign state within the United States, but it does not describe the particulars of what constitutes a commercial activity. Thus, the courts are left to decide whether a particular activity is governmental or commercial in nature. In the following case, the United States Supreme Court considered whether the principles of the FSIA should apply to a dispute dating back to World War II, before the FSIA had been enacted.

---

3. See, for example, *Keller v. Central Bank of Nigeria*, 277 F.3d 811 (6th Cir. 2002), in which the court held that failure to pay promised funds to a Cleveland account was an action having a direct effect in the United States.

CASE 22.1   Republic of Austria v. Altmann

Supreme Court of the United States, 2004.
541 U.S. 677,
124 S.Ct. 2240,
159 L.Ed.2d 1.
www.findlaw.com/casecode/supreme.html[a]

BACKGROUND AND FACTS   Maria Altmann escaped Austria after it was annexed by Nazi Germany in 1938 and moved to California. She was an heir of Ferdinand Bloch-Bauer, who had owned valuable artworks that had been seized by the Nazis. Six paintings by the artist Gustav Klimt were eventually displayed in the Austrian Gallery, an "instrumentality" of the Republic of Austria, along with other art that had been seized by the Nazis

or expropriated by Austria after World War II. Altmann filed a suit in a U.S. federal district court against Austria and the gallery to recover the Klimt paintings. Altmann asserted jurisdiction under the Foreign Sovereign Immunities Act (FSIA), despite the fact that the defendants' alleged wrongdoing (the seizure and expropriation of the art) had occurred before the FSIA was enacted in 1976. The defendants filed a motion to dismiss, arguing that Austria possessed absolute sovereign immunity from suit because the conduct took place prior to the FSIA's enactment. The court ruled in Altmann's favor, holding that the FSIA applied retroactively and the defendants were not entitled to immunity. The defendants appealed to the U.S. Court of Appeals for the Ninth Circuit, which affirmed the lower court's ruling. The defendants appealed to the United States Supreme Court.

a. In the "Browsing" section, click on "2004 Decisions." When that page opens, scroll to the name of the case and click on it to read the opinion.

IN THE WORDS OF THE COURT . . . Justice *STEVENS* delivered the opinion of the Court.

* * * *

To begin with, the preamble of the FSIA expresses Congress'[s] understanding that the Act would apply to all postenactment claims of sovereign immunity. That section provides:

"Claims of foreign states to immunity should henceforth be decided by courts of the United States and of the States in conformity with the principles set forth in this [Act]."

CASE 22.1–CONTINUED

* * * [T]his language is unambiguous: Immunity "claims"—not actions protected by immunity, but assertions of immunity to suits arising from those actions—are the relevant conduct regulated by the Act; those claims are "henceforth" to be decided by the courts. * * * *[T]his language suggests Congress intended courts to resolve all such claims "in conformity with the principles set forth" in the Act, regardless of when the underlying conduct occurred.* [Emphasis added.]

The FSIA's overall structure strongly supports this conclusion. Many of the Act's provisions unquestionably apply to cases arising out of conduct that occurred before 1976. * * * [F]or example, * * * whether an entity qualifies as an "instrumentality" of a "foreign state" for purposes of the FSIA's grant of immunity depends on the relationship between the entity and the state at the time suit is brought rather than when the conduct occurred. * * * [T]here has never been any doubt that the Act's procedural provisions relating to venue, removal, execution, and attachment apply to all pending cases. Thus, the FSIA's preamble indicates that it applies "henceforth," and its body includes numerous provisions that unquestionably apply to claims based on pre-1976 conduct.

Finally, applying the FSIA to all pending cases regardless of when the underlying conduct occurred is most consistent with two of the Act's principal purposes: clarifying the rules that judges should apply in resolving sovereign immunity claims and eliminating political participation in the resolution of such claims. * * * [T]o accomplish these purposes, Congress established a comprehensive framework for resolving any claim of sovereign immunity: * * * *the text and structure of the FSIA demonstrate Congress'[s] intention that the FSIA be the sole basis for obtaining jurisdiction over a foreign state in our courts.* * * * Section 1604 bars federal and state courts from exercising jurisdiction when a foreign state is entitled to immunity, and Section 1330(a) confers jurisdiction on district courts to hear suits brought by United States citizens and by aliens when a foreign state is not entitled to immunity. * * * [Emphasis added.]

* * * Quite obviously, Congress'[s] purposes in enacting such a comprehensive jurisdictional scheme would be frustrated if, in postenactment cases concerning preenactment conduct, courts were to continue to follow the same ambiguous and politically charged standards that the FSIA replaced.

DECISION AND REMEDY The United States Supreme Court affirmed the lower court's decision "because the Act * * * clearly applies to conduct, like petitioners' alleged wrongdoing, that occurred prior to 1976." The complaint was not dismissed, and the case was remanded for trial.

WHAT IF THE FACTS WERE DIFFERENT? *If the court had held that the FSIA did not apply to Altmann's claim, could Altmann still have established that the U.S. courts had jurisdiction over Austria? Why or why not?*

DOING BUSINESS INTERNATIONALLY

A U.S. domestic firm can engage in international business transactions in a number of ways. The simplest way is to seek out foreign markets for domestically produced products or services. In other words, U.S. firms can look abroad for **export** markets for their goods and services. Alternatively, a U.S. firm can establish foreign production facilities so as to be closer to the foreign market or markets in which its products are sold. A domestic firm can also obtain revenues by licensing its technology to an existing foreign company or by selling franchises to overseas entities.

EXPORT
The goods and services that domestic firms sell to buyers located in other countries.

Exporting

Exporting can take two forms: direct exporting and indirect exporting. In *direct exporting,* a U.S. company signs a sales contract with a foreign purchaser that provides for the conditions of shipment and payment for the goods. (How payments are made in international transactions is discussed later in this chapter.) If sufficient business develops in a foreign country, a U.S. corporation may set up a specialized marketing organization in that foreign market by appointing a foreign agent or a foreign distributor. This is called *indirect exporting.*

When a U.S. firm desires to limit its involvement in an international market, it will typically establish an *agency relationship* with a foreign firm. In an agency relationship (discussed in Chapter 13), one person (the agent) agrees to act on behalf of another (the principal). The foreign agent is thereby empowered to enter into contracts in the agent's country on behalf of the U.S. principal.

When a substantial market exists in a foreign country, a U.S. firm may wish to appoint a distributor located in that country. The U.S. firm and the distributor enter into a **distribution agreement,** which is a contract between the seller and the distributor setting out the terms and conditions of the distributorship—for example, price, currency of payment, availability of supplies, and method of payment. The terms and conditions primarily involve contract law. Disputes concerning distribution agreements may involve jurisdictional or other issues (discussed in detail later in this chapter). In addition, some **exclusive distributorships**—in which distributors agree to distribute only the sellers' goods—have raised antitrust problems.

DISTRIBUTION AGREEMENT
A contract between a seller and a distributor of the seller's products setting out the terms and conditions of the distributorship.

EXCLUSIVE DISTRIBUTORSHIP
A distributorship in which the seller and the distributor of the seller's products agree that the distributor has the exclusive right to distribute the seller's products in a certain geographic area.

Manufacturing Abroad

An alternative to direct or indirect exporting is the establishment of foreign manufacturing facilities. Typically, U.S. firms establish manufacturing plants abroad if they believe that doing so will reduce their costs—particularly for labor, shipping, and raw materials—and enable them to compete more effectively in foreign markets. A U.S. firm can manufacture goods in other countries in several ways. They include licensing and franchising, as well as investing in a wholly owned subsidiary or a joint venture.

Licensing   A U.S. firm can obtain business from abroad by licensing a foreign manufacturing company to use its copyrighted, patented, or trademarked intellectual property or trade secrets. Like any other licensing agreement (see Chapter 7), a licensing agreement with a foreign-based firm calls for a payment of royalties on some basis—such as so many cents per unit produced or a certain percentage of profits from units sold in a particular geographic territory.

Franchising   Franchising is a well-known form of licensing. Recall from Chapter 11 that in a franchise arrangement the owner of a trademark, trade name,

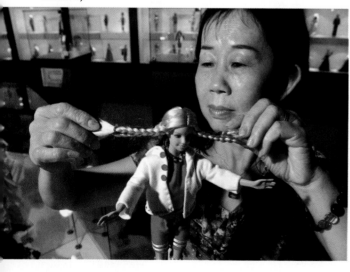

A woman in Taiwan holds a Barbie doll that was manufactured in Taiwan. Why would a U.S. corporation, such as Mattel, Inc., outsource its manufacturing jobs to a foreign firm? (AP Photo/Wally Santana)

or copyright (the franchisor) licenses another (the franchisee) to use the trademark, trade name, or copyright under certain conditions or limitations in the selling of goods or services. In return, the franchisee pays a fee, which is usually based on a percentage of gross or net sales. Examples of international franchises include Holiday Inn and Hertz.

Investing in a Wholly Owned Subsidiary or a Joint Venture Another way to expand into a foreign market is to establish a wholly owned subsidiary firm in a foreign country. When a wholly owned subsidiary is established, the parent company, which remains in the United States, retains complete ownership of all the facilities in the foreign country, as well as complete authority and control over all phases of the operation. A U.S. firm can also expand into international markets through a joint venture. In a joint venture, the U.S. company owns only part of the operation; the rest is owned either by local owners in the foreign country or by another foreign entity. All of the firms involved in a joint venture share responsibilities, as well as profits and liabilities.

COMMERCIAL CONTRACTS IN AN INTERNATIONAL SETTING

Like all commercial contracts, an international contract should be in writing. For an example of an actual international sales contract, refer back to the fold-out contract in Chapter 10.

Contract Clauses

Language and legal differences among nations can create special problems for parties to international contracts when disputes arise. It is possible to avoid these problems by including in a contract special provisions designating the official language of the contract, the legal forum (court or place) in which disputes under the contract will be settled, and the substantive law that will be applied in settling any disputes. Parties to international contracts should also indicate in their contracts what acts or events will excuse the parties from performance under the contract and whether disputes under the contract will be arbitrated or litigated.

Choice of Language A deal struck between a U.S. company and a company in another country normally involves two languages. Typically, many phrases in one language are not readily translatable into another. Consequently, the complex contractual terms involved may not be understood by one party in the other party's language. To make sure that no disputes arise out of this language problem, an international sales contract should have a **choice-of-language clause** designating the official language by which the contract will be interpreted in the event of disagreement.

CHOICE-OF-LANGUAGE CLAUSE
A clause in a contract designating the official language by which the contract will be interpreted in the event of a future disagreement over the contract's terms.

Choice of Forum When parties from several countries are involved, litigation may be pursued in courts in different nations. There are no universally accepted rules as to which court has jurisdiction over particular subject matter or parties to a dispute. Consequently, parties to an international transaction should always include in the contract a **forum-selection clause** indicating what court, jurisdiction, or tribunal will decide any disputes arising under the contract. It is especially important to indicate the specific court that will have

FORUM-SELECTION CLAUSE
A provision in a contract designating the court, jurisdiction, or tribunal that will decide any disputes arising under the contract.

BEYOND OUR BORDERS

Arbitration versus Litigation

One of the reasons many businesspersons find it advantageous to include arbitration clauses in their international contracts is that arbitration awards are usually easier to enforce than court judgments. As mentioned, the New York Convention provides for the enforcement of arbitration awards in those countries that have signed the convention. In contrast, the enforcement of court judgments normally depends on the principle of comity and bilateral agreements providing for such enforcement. How the principle of comity is applied varies from one nation to another, and many countries have not signed bilateral agreements agreeing to enforce judgments rendered in U.S. courts. Furthermore, even a

U.S. court may not enforce a foreign court's judgment if it conflicts with U.S. laws or policies. For example, a U.S. federal appellate court refused to enforce the judgment of a British court in a libel case. The court pointed out that the judgment was contrary to the public policy of the United States, which generally favors a much broader and more protective freedom of the press than has ever been provided for under English law.[a]

For Critical Analysis *What might be some other advantages of arbitrating disputes involving international transactions? Are there any disadvantages?*

a. *Telnikoff v. Matusevitch,* 159 F.3d 636 (D.C. Cir. 1998).

country will enforce the judgment. (For a further discussion of this issue, see this chapter's *Beyond Our Borders* feature.)

MAKING PAYMENT ON INTERNATIONAL TRANSACTIONS

Currency differences between nations and the geographic distance between parties to international sales contracts add a degree of complexity to international sales that does not exist in the domestic market. Because international contracts involve greater financial risks, special care should be taken in drafting these contracts to specify both the currency in which payment is to be made and the method of payment.

Monetary Systems

Although our national currency, the U.S. dollar, is one of the primary forms of international currency, any U.S. firm undertaking business transactions abroad must be prepared to deal with one or more other currencies. Currencies are convertible when they can be freely exchanged one for the other at some specified market rate in a **foreign exchange market.** Foreign exchange markets make up a worldwide system for the buying and selling of foreign currencies. At any point in time, the foreign exchange rate is set by the forces of supply and demand in unrestricted foreign exchange markets. The foreign exchange rate is simply the price of a unit of one country's currency in terms of another country's currency. For example, if today's exchange rate is one hundred Japanese yen for one dollar, that means that anybody with one hundred yen can obtain one dollar, and vice versa.

Frequently, a U.S. company can rely on its domestic bank to take care of all international transfers of funds. Commercial banks often transfer funds internationally through their **correspondent banks** in other countries. **| Example #2** Suppose that a customer of Citibank wishes to pay a bill in euros to a company in Paris. Citibank can draw a bank check payable in euros on its account in

FOREIGN EXCHANGE MARKET
A worldwide system in which foreign currencies are bought and sold.

CORRESPONDENT BANK
A bank in which another bank has an account (and vice versa) for the purpose of facilitating fund transfers.

Crédit Agricole, a Paris correspondent bank, and then send the check to the French company to which its customer owes the funds. Alternatively, Citibank's customer can request a wire transfer of the funds to the French company. Citibank instructs Crédit Agricole by wire to pay the necessary amount in euros.

The Clearinghouse Interbank Payment System (CHIPS) handles about 90 percent of both national and international interbank transfers of U.S. funds. In addition, the Society for Worldwide International Financial Telecommunications (SWIFT) is a communication system that provides banks with messages concerning international transactions.

Letters of Credit

Because buyers and sellers engaged in international business transactions are frequently separated by thousands of miles, special precautions are often taken to ensure performance under the contract. Sellers want to avoid delivering goods for which they might not be paid. Buyers desire the assurance that sellers will not be paid until there is evidence that the goods have been shipped. Thus, **letters of credit** are frequently used to facilitate international business transactions.

LETTER OF CREDIT
A written instrument, usually issued by a bank on behalf of a customer or other person, in which the issuer promises to honor drafts or other demands for payment by third persons in accordance with the terms of the instrument.

In a simple letter-of-credit transaction, the *issuer* (a bank) agrees to issue a letter of credit and to ascertain whether the *beneficiary* (seller) performs certain acts. In return, the *account party* (buyer) promises to reimburse the issuer for the amount paid to the beneficiary. The transaction may also involve an *advising bank* that transmits information and a *paying bank* that expedites payment under the letter of credit. See Exhibit 22–1 on the following page for an illustration of a letter-of-credit transaction.

Under a letter of credit, the issuer is bound to pay the beneficiary (seller) when the beneficiary has complied with the terms and conditions of the letter of credit. The beneficiary looks to the issuer, not to the account party (buyer), when it presents the documents required by the letter of credit. Typically, the letter of credit will require that the beneficiary deliver a *bill of lading* to the issuing bank to prove that shipment has been made. A letter of credit assures the beneficiary (seller) of payment and at the same time assures the account party (buyer) that payment will not be made until the beneficiary has complied with the terms and conditions of the letter of credit.

The Value of a Letter of Credit The basic principle behind letters of credit is that payment is made against the documents presented by the beneficiary and not against the facts that the documents purport to reflect. Thus, in a letter-of-credit transaction, the issuer does not police the underlying contract; a letter of credit is independent of the underlying contract between the buyer and the seller. Eliminating the need for banks (issuers) to inquire into whether actual contractual conditions have been satisfied greatly reduces the costs of letters of credit. Moreover, the use of a letter of credit protects both buyers and sellers.

DON'T FORGET A letter of credit is independent of the underlying contract between the buyer and the seller.

Compliance with a Letter of Credit A letter-of-credit transaction generally involves at least three separate and distinct contracts: the contract between the account party (buyer) and the beneficiary (seller); the contract between the issuer (bank) and the account party (buyer); and, finally, the letter of credit itself, which involves the issuer (bank) and the beneficiary (seller). These

EXHIBIT 22-1 A LETTER-OF-CREDIT TRANSACTION

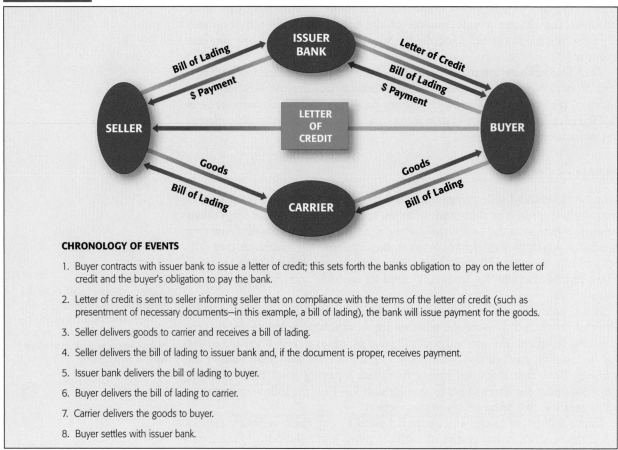

CHRONOLOGY OF EVENTS

1. Buyer contracts with issuer bank to issue a letter of credit; this sets forth the banks obligation to pay on the letter of credit and the buyer's obligation to pay the bank.

2. Letter of credit is sent to seller informing seller that on compliance with the terms of the letter of credit (such as presentment of necessary documents—in this example, a bill of lading), the bank will issue payment for the goods.

3. Seller delivers goods to carrier and receives a bill of lading.

4. Seller delivers the bill of lading to issuer bank and, if the document is proper, receives payment.

5. Issuer bank delivers the bill of lading to buyer.

6. Buyer delivers the bill of lading to carrier.

7. Carrier delivers the goods to buyer.

8. Buyer settles with issuer bank.

contracts are separate and distinct, and the issuer's obligations under the letter of credit do not concern the underlying contract between the buyer and the seller. Rather, it is the issuer's duty to ascertain whether the documents presented by the beneficiary (seller) comply with the terms of the letter of credit.

If the documents presented by the beneficiary comply with the terms of the letter of credit, the issuer (bank) must honor the letter of credit. If the issuing bank refuses to pay the beneficiary (seller) even though the beneficiary has complied with all the requirements, the beneficiary can bring an action to enforce payment. Sometimes, however, it can be difficult to determine exactly what a letter of credit requires. Traditionally, courts required strict compliance with the terms of a letter of credit, but in recent years, some courts have moved to a standard of *reasonable* compliance.

REGULATION OF SPECIFIC BUSINESS ACTIVITIES

Doing business abroad can affect the economies, foreign policies, domestic policies, and other national interests of the countries involved. For this reason, nations impose laws to restrict or facilitate international business. Controls may also be imposed by international agreements. We discuss here how different types of international activities are regulated.

Investing

Firms that invest in foreign nations face the risk that the foreign government may take possession of the investment property. Expropriation, as already mentioned, occurs when property is taken and the owner is paid just compensation for what is taken. Expropriation does not violate generally observed principles of international law. Such principles are normally violated, however, when a government confiscates property without compensation (or without adequate compensation). Few remedies are available for confiscation of property by a foreign government. Claims are often resolved by lump-sum settlements after negotiations between the United States and the taking nation.

To counter the deterrent effect that the possibility of confiscation may have on potential investors, many countries guarantee that foreign investors will be compensated if their property is taken. A guaranty can take the form of national constitutional or statutory laws or provisions in international treaties. As further protection for foreign investments, some countries provide insurance for their citizens' investments abroad.

Export Controls

The U.S. Constitution provides in Article I, Section 9, that "No Tax or Duty shall be laid on Articles exported from any State." Thus, Congress cannot impose any export taxes. Congress can, however, use a variety of other devices to control exports. Congress may set export quotas on various items, such as grain being sold abroad. Under the Export Administration Act of 1979,[4] the flow of technologically advanced products and technical data can be restricted. In recent years, the U.S. Department of Commerce has made a controversial attempt to restrict the export of encryption software.

NOTE Most countries restrict exports for the same reasons: to protect national security, to further foreign policy objectives, to prevent the spread of nuclear weapons, and to preserve commodities deemed by the government to be "essential."

While restricting certain exports, the United States (and other nations) also use devices such as export incentives and subsidies to stimulate other exports and thereby aid domestic businesses. The Revenue Act of 1971,[5] for instance, gave tax benefits to firms marketing their products overseas through certain foreign sales corporations by exempting income produced by the exports. Under the Export Trading Company Act of 1982,[6] U.S. banks are encouraged to invest in export trading companies, which are formed when exporting firms join together to export a line of goods. The Export-Import Bank of the United States provides financial assistance, consisting primarily of credit guaranties given to commercial banks that in turn lend funds to U.S. exporting companies.

Import Controls

All nations have restrictions on imports, and the United States is no exception. Restrictions include strict prohibitions, quotas, and tariffs. Under the Trading with the Enemy Act of 1917,[7] for instance, no goods may be imported from nations that have been designated enemies of the United States. Other laws prohibit the importation of illegal drugs, books that urge insurrection against the United States, and agricultural products that pose dangers to domestic crops or animals.

> "The notion dies hard that in some sort of way exports are patriotic but imports are immoral."
> —LORD HARLECH (DAVID ORMSLEY GORE), 1918–1985
> (English writer)

---

4. 50 U.S.C. Sections 2401–2420.
5. 26 U.S.C. Sections 991–994.
6. 15 U.S.C. Sections 4001, 4003.
7. 12 U.S.C. Section 95a.

Quotas and Tariffs   Limits on the amounts of goods that can be imported are known as **quotas.** At one time, the United States had legal quotas on the number of automobiles that could be imported from Japan. Today, Japan "voluntarily" restricts the number of automobiles exported to the United States. **Tariffs** are taxes on imports. A tariff is usually a percentage of the value of the import, but it can be a flat rate per unit (for example, per barrel of oil). Tariffs raise the prices of goods, causing some consumers to purchase less expensive, domestically manufactured goods.

Dumping   The United States has specific laws directed at what it sees as unfair international trade practices. **Dumping,** for example, is the sale of imported goods at "less than fair value." "Fair value" is usually determined by the price of those goods in the exporting country. Foreign firms that engage in dumping in the United States hope to undersell U.S. businesses to obtain a larger share of the U.S. market. To prevent this, an extra tariff—known as an *antidumping duty*—may be assessed on the imports.

Minimizing Trade Barriers   Restrictions on imports are also known as *trade barriers.* The elimination of trade barriers is sometimes seen as essential to the world's economic well-being. Most of the world's leading trading nations are members of the World Trade Organization (WTO), which was established in 1995. To minimize trade barriers among nations, each member country of the WTO is required to grant **normal trade relations (NTR) status** (formerly known as *most-favored-nation status*) to other member countries. This means each member is obligated to treat other members at least as well as it treats the country that receives its most favorable treatment with regard to imports or exports.

Various regional trade agreements and associations also help to minimize trade barriers between nations. The European Union (EU), for example, is working to minimize or remove barriers to trade among its member countries. The EU is a single integrated trading unit made up of twenty-five European nations. Another important regional trade agreement is the North American Free Trade Agreement (NAFTA). NAFTA, which became effective on January 1, 1994, created a regional trading unit consisting of Mexico, the United States, and Canada. The primary goal of NAFTA is to eliminate tariffs among these three countries on substantially all goods over a period of fifteen to twenty years.

A more recent trade agreement is the Central America–Dominican Republic–United States Free Trade Agreement (CAFTA-DR), which was signed into law by President George W. Bush in 2005. This agreement was formed by Costa Rica, the Dominican Republic, El Salvador, Guatemala, Honduras, Nicaragua, and the United States. Once the parties agree on an effective date, CAFTA-DR will reduce trade tariffs and improve market access among all of the signatory nations, including the United States.

Bribing Foreign Officials

Giving cash or in-kind benefits to foreign government officials to obtain business contracts and other favors is often considered normal practice. To reduce such bribery by representatives of U.S. corporations, Congress enacted the Foreign Corrupt Practices Act in 1977.[8] This act and its implications for American businesspersons engaged in international business transactions were discussed in Chapter 2.

---

8. 15 U.S.C. Sections 78m–78ff.

U.S. LAWS IN A GLOBAL CONTEXT

The internationalization of business raises questions about the extraterritorial application of a nation's laws—that is, the effect of the country's laws outside its boundaries. To what extent do U.S. domestic laws apply to other nations' businesses? To what extent do U.S. domestic laws apply to U.S. firms doing business abroad? Here, we discuss these questions in the context of the Sarbanes-Oxley Act, U.S. antitrust law, and U.S. laws prohibiting employment discrimination.

The Sarbanes-Oxley Act

The Sarbanes-Oxley Act of 2002 (discussed in Chapters 2 and 21) is designed to improve the quality and clarity of financial reporting and auditing of public companies. The act prescribes the issuance of codes of ethics, increases the criminal penalties for securities fraud, and utilizes other means to hold public companies to higher reporting standards.

Three provisions protect whistleblowers. One section requires public companies to adopt procedures that encourage employees to expose "questionable" accounting practices. Another section imposes criminal sanctions for retaliation against anyone who reports the commission of any federal offense to law enforcement officers.

A third section—18 U.S.C. Section 1514A—creates an administrative complaint procedure and a federal civil cause of action for employees who report violations of the federal laws relating to fraud committed against the shareholders of public companies. The extraterritorial application of this section was at issue in the following case.

CASE 22.3 **Carnero v. Boston Scientific Corp.**

United States Court of Appeals,
First Circuit, 2006.
433 F.3d 1.
www.ca1.uscourts.gov [a]

BACKGROUND AND FACTS Boston Scientific Corporation (BSC) is a Delaware corporation with headquarters in Natick, Massachusetts. BSC, which makes medical equipment, operates in many countries throughout the world. BSC's subsidiaries include Boston Scientific Argentina S.A. (BSA) in

Argentina and Boston Scientific Do Brasil Ltda. (BSB) in Brazil. In 1997, Ruben Carnero, a citizen of Argentina, began working for BSA in Buenos Aires. Four years later, Carnero accepted a simultaneous assignment with BSB. Soon afterward, he reported to BSC that its Latin American subsidiaries were improperly inflating sales figures and engaging in other accounting misconduct. His employment with BSA and BSB was terminated. Carnero filed a complaint with the U.S. Department of Labor (DOL) against BSC under the Sarbanes-Oxley Act, seeking reinstatement. The DOL rejected the claim. Carnero filed a suit in a federal district court against BSC on the same basis. The court dismissed the complaint. Carnero appealed to the U.S. Court of Appeals for the First Circuit.

a. In the right-hand column, click on "Opinions." When that page opens, in the "Short Title *contains*" box, type "Carnero" and click on "Submit Search." Then click on one of the numbers in the "Click for Opinion" column to access the opinion.

IN THE WORDS OF THE COURT . . . LEVIN H. CAMPBELL, Senior Circuit Judge.

* * * *

Carnero argues that [18 U.S.C. Section 1514A] should be given extraterritorial effect, so as to allow him to pursue in federal court his whistleblower claim brought under its provisions. He says his claim not only fits within the literal language of the statute but that to limit the operation of the statute to purely domestic conduct in the United States would improperly insulate the foreign operations of covered companies. This, he says, would frustrate the basic purpose of the Sarbanes-Oxley Act of which the whistleblower

CASE 22.3–CONTINUED ▶

protection statute at issue is a part, to protect both the investors in U.S. securities markets and the integrity of those markets.

While Carnero's argument has some force, it faces a high and we think insurmountable hurdle in the well-established presumption against the extraterritorial application of Congressional statutes. Where, as here, a statute is silent as to its territorial reach, and no contrary congressional intent clearly appears, there is generally a presumption against its extraterritorial application. * * *

    *   *   *   *

The presumption serves at least two purposes. It protects against unintended clashes between our laws and those of other nations which could result in international discord, and it reflects the notion that when Congress legislates, it is primarily concerned with domestic conditions. * * * [Emphasis added.]

    *   *   *   *

* * * [P]ertinent factors run strongly counter to finding an extraterritorial legislative intent. These contrary *indicia* [signs or indications] prevent our determining that Congress has evidenced its "clear intent" for extraterritorial application. Not only is the text of 18 U.S.C. Section 1514A silent as to any intent to apply it abroad, the statute's legislative history indicates that Congress gave no consideration to either the possibility or the problems of overseas application. In sharp contrast with this silence, Congress has provided expressly elsewhere in the Sarbanes-Oxley Act for extraterritorial enforcement of a different, criminal, whistleblower statute. By so providing, Congress demonstrated that it was well able to call for extraterritorial application when it so desired. Also in the Act, Congress has provided expressly for the exterritorial application of certain other unrelated statutes, tailoring these so as to cope with problems of sovereignty and the like—again demonstrating Congress's ability to provide for foreign application when it wished. Here, however, while placing the whistleblower provision's enforcement in the hands of the DOL, a domestic agency, Congress has made no provision for possible problems arising when that agency seeks to regulate employment relationships in foreign nations, nor has Congress provided the DOL with special powers and resources to conduct investigations abroad. Furthermore, judicial venue provisions written into the whistleblower protection statute were made expressly applicable only to whistleblower violations within the United States and to complainants residing here on the date of violation, with no corresponding basis being provided for venue as to foreign complainants claiming violations in foreign countries.

These factors * * * not only fail to imply a clear congressional intent for extraterritorial application, but indicate that Congress never expected such application.

DECISION AND REMEDY   The U.S. Court of Appeals for the First Circuit affirmed the lower court's dismissal of Carnero's complaint under 18 U.S.C. Section 1514A. Congress "made no reference to [the statute's] application abroad and tailored the * * * statute to purely domestic application." This section of the Sarbanes-Oxley Act "does not reflect the necessary clear expression of congressional intent to extend its reach beyond our nation's borders."

WHY IS THIS CASE IMPORTANT?   *This is the first federal appellate court decision on the application of this section of the Sarbanes-Oxley Act's whistleblower protection to a foreign citizen working outside the United States for a foreign subsidiary of a U.S. company. Under this decision, employee whistleblowers working abroad may not be protected from their employers' retaliation.*

U.S. Antitrust Laws

U.S. antitrust laws (discussed in Chapter 20) have a wide application. They may *subject* persons in foreign nations to their provisions, as well as *protect* foreign consumers and competitors from violations committed by U.S. citizens. Consequently, *foreign persons,* a term that by definition includes foreign governments, may sue under U.S. antitrust laws in U.S. courts.

Section 1 of the Sherman Act provides for the extraterritorial effect of the U.S. antitrust laws. The United States is a major proponent of free competition in the global economy. Thus, any conspiracy that has a *substantial effect* on U.S. commerce is within the reach of the Sherman Act. The law applies even if the violation occurs outside the United States, and foreign governments as well as persons can be sued for violations.

Before U.S. courts will exercise jurisdiction and apply antitrust laws, however, it must be shown that the alleged violation had a substantial effect on U.S. commerce. U.S. jurisdiction is automatically invoked when a *per se* violation occurs.[9] An example of a *per se* violation is a price-fixing contract.

Antidiscrimination Laws

As explained in Chapter 14, federal laws in the United States prohibit discrimination on the basis of race, color, national origin, religion, gender, age, and disability. These laws, as they affect employment relationships, generally apply extraterritorially. Since 1984, for example, the Age Discrimination in Employment Act of 1967 has covered U.S. employees working abroad for U.S. employers. The Americans with Disabilities Act of 1990, which requires employers to accommodate the needs of workers with disabilities, also applies to U.S. nationals working abroad for U.S. firms. Title VII of the Civil Rights Act of 1964 also applies to all U.S. employees working for U.S. employers abroad. Generally, U.S. employers must abide by U.S. antidiscrimination laws unless to do so would violate the laws of the country where their workplaces are located. This "foreign laws exception" allows employers to avoid being subjected to conflicting laws.

---

9. Certain types of restrictive contracts, such as price-fixing agreements, are deemed inherently anticompetitive and thus in restraint of trade as a matter of law. Such a restrictive contract constitutes a *per se* violation of the antitrust laws. See Chapter 20.

REVIEWING . . . THE REGULATION OF INTERNATIONAL TRANSACTIONS

Robco, Inc., was a Florida arms dealer. The armed forces of Honduras contracted to purchase weapons from Robco over a six-year period. After the government was replaced and a democracy installed, the Honduran government sought to reduce the size of its military, and its relationship with Robco deteriorated. Honduras refused to go through with the contract and purchase the inventory of arms, which Robco could sell elsewhere only at a much lower price. Robco filed a suit in a federal district court in the United States to recover damages for this breach of contract by the government of Honduras. Using the information presented in the chapter, answer the following questions.

1. Should the Foreign Sovereign Immunities Act (FSIA) preclude this lawsuit? Why or why not?

2. Does the act of state doctrine bar Robco from seeking to enforce the contract? Explain.

3. Suppose that prior to this lawsuit, the new government of Honduras had enacted a law making it illegal to purchase weapons from foreign arms dealers. What doctrine of deference might lead a U.S. court to dismiss Robco's case in that situation?

4. Now suppose that the U.S. court hears the case and awards damages to Robco, but the government of Honduras has no assets in the United States that can be used to satisfy the judgment. Under which doctrine might Robco be able to collect the damages by asking another nation's court to enforce the U.S. judgment?

KEY TERMS

act of state doctrine   687
choice-of-language clause   691
choice-of-law clause   693
comity   687
confiscation   687
correspondent bank   694
distribution agreement   690
dumping   698

exclusive distributorship   690
export   689
expropriation   687
force majeure clause   693
foreign exchange market   694
forum-selection clause   691
international law   686
letter of credit   695

national law   686
normal trade relations (NTR)
   status   698
quota   698
sovereign immunity   687
tariff   698

CHAPTER SUMMARY • THE REGULATION OF INTERNATIONAL TRANSACTIONS

International Principles and Doctrines (See pages 686–689.)	1. *The principle of comity*—Under this principle, nations give effect to the laws and judicial decrees of other nations for reasons of courtesy and international harmony. 2. *The act of state doctrine*—A doctrine under which U.S. courts avoid passing judgment on the validity of public acts committed by a recognized foreign government within its own territory. 3. *The doctrine of sovereign immunity*—When certain conditions are satisfied, foreign nations are immune from U.S. jurisdiction under the Foreign Sovereign Immunities Act of 1976. Exceptions are made (a) when a foreign state has "waived its immunity either explicitly or by implication" or (b) when the action is based on a "commercial activity carried on in the United States by the foreign state."
Doing Business Internationally (See pages 689–691.)	Ways in which U.S. domestic firms engage in international business transactions include (a) exporting, which may involve foreign agents or distributors, and (b) manufacturing abroad through licensing arrangements, franchising operations, wholly owned subsidiaries, or joint ventures.
Commercial Contracts in an International Setting (See pages 691–694.)	International business contracts often include choice-of-language, forum-selection, and choice-of-law clauses to reduce the uncertainties associated with interpreting the language of the agreement and dealing with legal differences. Most domestic and international contracts include *force majeure* clauses. They commonly stipulate that certain events, such as floods, fires, accidents, labor strikes, and government orders, may excuse a party from liability for nonperformance of the contract. Arbitration clauses are also frequently found in international contracts.
Making Payment on International Transactions (See pages 694–696.)	1. *Currency conversion*—Because nations have different monetary systems, payment on international contracts requires currency conversion at a rate specified in a foreign exchange market. 2. *Correspondent banking*—Correspondent banks facilitate the transfer of funds from a buyer in one country to a seller in another. 3. *Letters of credit*—Letters of credit facilitate international transactions by ensuring payment to sellers and assuring buyers that payment will not be made until the sellers have complied with the terms of the letters of credit. Typically, compliance occurs when a bill of lading is delivered to the issuing bank.
Regulation of Specific Business Activities (See pages 696–699.)	National laws regulate foreign investments, exporting, and importing. The World Trade Organization attempts to minimize trade barriers among nations, as do regional trade agreements and associations, including the European Union and the North American Free Trade Agreement.
U.S. Laws in a Global Context (See pages 699–701.)	1. *Antitrust laws*—U.S. antitrust laws may be applied beyond the borders of the United States. Any conspiracy that has a substantial effect on commerce within the United States may be subject to the Sherman Act, even if the violation occurs outside the United States. 2. *Antidiscrimination laws*—The major U.S. laws prohibiting employment discrimination, including Title VII of the Civil Rights Act of 1964, the Age Discrimination in Employment Act of 1967, and the Americans with Disabilities Act of 1990, cover U.S. employees working abroad for U.S. firms—*unless* to apply the U.S. laws would violate the laws of the host country.

Answers for the even-numbered questions in this For Review *section can be found in Appendix O at the end of this text.*

1. What is the principle of comity, and why do courts deciding disputes involving a foreign law or judicial decree apply this principle?

2. What is the act of state doctrine? In what circumstances is this doctrine applied?

3. Under the Foreign Sovereign Immunities Act of 1976, on what bases might a foreign state be considered subject to the jurisdiction of U.S. courts?

4. In what circumstances will U.S. antitrust laws be applied extraterritorially?

5. Do U.S. laws prohibiting employment discrimination apply in all circumstances to U.S. employees working for U.S. employers abroad?

QUESTIONS AND CASE PROBLEMS

Question with Sample Answer

22–1. In 1995, France implemented a law making the use of the French language mandatory in certain legal documents. Documents relating to securities offerings, such as prospectuses, for example, must be written in French. So must instruction manuals and warranties for goods and services offered for sale in France. Additionally, all agreements entered into with French state or local authorities, with entities controlled by state or local authorities, and with private entities carrying out a public service (such as providing utilities) must be written in French. What kinds of problems might this law pose for U.S. businesspersons who wish to form contracts with French individuals or business firms?

For a sample answer to this question, go to Appendix P at the end of this text.

22–2. Discrimination Claims. Radio Free Europe and Radio Liberty (RFE/RL), a U.S. corporation doing business in Germany, employs more than three hundred U.S. citizens at its principal place of business in Munich, Germany. The concept of mandatory retirement is deeply embedded in German labor policy, and a contract formed in 1982 between RFE/RL and a German labor union contained a clause that required workers to be retired when they reach the age of sixty-five. When William Mahoney and other U.S. employees (the plaintiffs) reached the age of sixty-five, RFE/RL terminated their employment as required under its contract with the labor union. The plaintiffs sued RFE/RL for discriminating against them on the basis of age, in violation of the Age Discrimination in Employment Act of 1967. Will the plaintiffs succeed in their suit? Discuss fully. [*Mahoney v. RFE/RL, Inc.,* 47 F.3d 447 (D.C. Cir. 1995)]

22–3. Sovereign Immunity. Nuovo Pignone, Inc., is an Italian company that designs and manufactures turbine systems. Nuovo sold a turbine system to Cabinda Gulf Oil Co. (CABGOC). The system was manufactured, tested, and inspected in Italy; then it was sent to Louisiana for mounting on a platform by CABGOC's contractor. Nuovo sent a representative to consult on the mounting. The platform went to a CABGOC site off the coast of West Africa. Marcus Pere, an instrument technician at the site, was killed when a turbine within the system exploded. Pere's widow filed a suit in a U.S. district court against Nuovo and others. Nuovo claimed sovereign immunity on the ground that its majority shareholder at the time of the explosion was Ente Nazionale Idrocaburi, which was created by the government of Italy to lead its oil and gas exploration and development. Is Nuovo exempt from suit under the doctrine of sovereign immunity? Is it subject to suit under the "commercial activity" exception? Why or why not? [*Pere v. Nuovo Pignone, Inc.,* 150 F.3d 477 (5th Cir. 1998)]

22–4. Dumping. In response to a petition filed on behalf of the U.S. pineapple industry, the U.S. Commerce Department initiated an investigation of canned pineapple imported from Thailand. The investigation concerned Thai producers of the canned fruit, including the Thai Pineapple Public Co. The Thai producers also turned out products, such as pineapple juice and juice concentrate, outside the scope of the investigation. These products use separate parts of the same fresh pineapple, so they share raw material costs. To determine fair value and antidumping duties, the Commerce Department had to calculate the Thai producers' cost of production and, in so doing, had to allocate a portion of the shared fruit costs to the canned fruit. These allocations were based on the producers' own financial records, which were consistent with Thai generally accepted accounting principles. The result was a determination that more than 90 percent of the canned fruit sales were below the cost of production. The producers filed a suit in the U.S. Court of International Trade against the federal government, challenging this allocation. The producers argued that their records did not reflect actual production costs, which instead should be based on the weight of fresh fruit used to make the products. Did the Commerce Department act reasonably in determining the cost of production? Why or why not? [*Thai Pineapple Public Co. v. United States,* 187 F.3d 1362 (Fed.Cir. 1999)]

Case Problem with Sample Answer

22–5. Tonoga, Ltd., doing business as Taconic Plastics, Ltd., is a manufacturer incorporated in Ireland with its principal place of business in New York. In 1997, Taconic entered into a contract with a German construction company to supply special material for a tent project designed to shelter religious pilgrims visiting holy sites in Saudi Arabia. Most of the material was made in, and shipped from, New York. The company did not pay Taconic and eventually filed for bankruptcy. Another German firm, Werner Voss Architects and Engineers, acting as an agent for the government of Saudi Arabia, guaranteed the payments due Taconic to induce it to complete the project. When it did not receive the final payment, Taconic filed a suit in a U.S. district court against the government of Saudi Arabia, claiming a breach of the guaranty and seeking to collect, in part, about $3 million. The defendant filed a motion to dismiss based, in part, on the doctrine of sovereign immunity. Under what circumstances does this doctrine apply? What are its exceptions? Should this suit be dismissed under the "commercial activity" exception? Explain. [*Tonoga, Ltd. v. Ministry of Public Works and Housing of Kingdom of Saudi Arabia*, 135 F.Supp.2d 350 (N.D.N.Y. 2001)]

After you have answered this problem, compare your answer with the sample answer given on the Web site that accompanies this text. Go to **www.thomsonedu.com/westbuslaw/let**, select "Chapter 22," and click on "Case Problem with Sample Answer."

22–6. Imports. DaimlerChrysler Corp. makes and markets motor vehicles. DaimlerChrysler assembled the 1993 and 1994 model years of its trucks at plants in Mexico. Assembly involved sheet metal components sent from the United States. DaimlerChrysler subjected some of the parts to a complicated treatment process, which included applying coats of paint to prevent corrosion, impart color, and protect the finish. Under U.S. law, goods that are assembled abroad using U.S.-made parts can be imported tariff free. A U.S. *statute* provides that painting is "incidental" to assembly and does not affect the status of the goods. A U.S. *regulation,* however, states that "painting primarily intended to enhance the appearance of an article or to impart distinctive features or characteristics" is not incidental. The U.S. Customs Service levied a tariff on the trucks. DaimlerChrysler filed a suit in the U.S. Court of International Trade, challenging the levy. Should the court rule in DaimlerChrysler's favor? Why or why not? [*DaimlerChrysler Corp. v. United States*, 361 F.3d 1378 (Fed.Cir. 2004)]

22–7. Dumping. A newspaper printing press system is over a hundred feet long, stands four or five stories tall, and weighs two million pounds. Only about ten sales of these systems occur each year in the United States. Because of the size and cost, rather than replace its system, a newspaper may update by buying "additions." By the 1990s, Goss International Corp. was the only domestic maker of this equipment in the United States and represented the entire U.S. market. Tokyo Kikai

Seisakusho (TKSC), a Japanese corporation, makes the systems in Japan. In the 1990s, TKSC began to compete in the U.S. market, requiring Goss to cut its prices below cost. TKSC's tactics included offering its customers "secret" rebates on prices that were ultimately substantially less than the products' actual market value in Japan. The goal was, according to TKSC office memos, to "win completely this survival game" against Goss, the "enemy." Goss filed a suit in a federal district court against TKSC and others (including a German manufacturer whose name is reflected in the case title), alleging illegal dumping. At what point does a foreign firm's attempt to compete with a domestic manufacturer in the United States become illegal dumping? Was that point reached in this case? Discuss. [*Goss International Corp. v. Man Roland Druckmaschinen Aktiengesellschaft*, 434 F.3d 1081 (8th Cir. 2006)]

A Question of Ethics

22–8. Ronald Riley, a U.S. citizen, and Council of Lloyd's, a British insurance corporation with its principal place of business in London, entered into an agreement in 1980 that allowed Riley to underwrite insurance through Lloyd's. The agreement provided that if any dispute arose between Lloyd's and Riley, the courts of England would have exclusive jurisdiction, and the laws of England would apply. Over the next decade, some of the parties insured under policies that Riley underwrote experienced large losses, for which they filed claims. Instead of paying his share of the claims, Riley filed a lawsuit in a U.S. district court against Lloyd's and its managers and directors (all British citizens or entities), seeking, among other things, rescission of the 1980 agreement. Riley alleged that the defendants had violated the Securities Act of 1933, the Securities Exchange Act of 1934, and Rule 10b-5. The defendants asked the court to enforce the forum-selection clause in the agreement. Riley argued that if the clause was enforced, he would be deprived of his rights under the U.S. securities laws. The court held that the parties were to resolve their dispute in England. [*Riley v. Kingsley Underwriting Agencies, Ltd.*, 969 F.2d 953 (10th Cir. 1992)]

1. Did the court's decision fairly balance the rights of the parties? How would you argue in support of the court's decision in this case? How would you argue against it?
2. Should the fact that an international transaction may be subject to laws and remedies different from or less favorable than those of the United States be a valid basis for denying enforcement of forum-selection and choice-of-law clauses?
3. All parties to this litigation other than Riley were British. Should the court consider this fact in deciding this case?

Case Briefing Assignment

22–9. Go to **www.thomsonedu.com/ westbuslaw/let**, the Web site that accompanies this text. Select "Chapter 22" and click on "Case Briefing Assignments." Examine

Case A.6 [*Trans-Orient Marine Corp. v. Star Trading & Marine, Inc.,* 731 F.Supp. 619 (S.D.N.Y. 1990)]. This case has been excerpted there in great detail. Review and then brief the case, making sure that your brief answers the following questions.

1. What specific circumstances led to this lawsuit?
2. What was the central international legal issue addressed by the court?
3. How did the court distinguish a "succession of state" from a "succession of government," and what was the effect of the distinction on executory contracts of the state?

Critical-Thinking International Question

22–10. Business cartels and monopolies that are legal in some countries may engage in practices that violate U.S. antitrust laws. In view of this fact, what are some of the implications of applying U.S. antitrust laws extraterritorially?

Video Question

22–11. Go to this text's Web site at **www.thomsonedu.com/westbuslaw/let** and select "Chapter 22." Click on "Video Questions" and view the video titled *International Letter of Credit.* Then answer the following questions.

1. Do banks always require the same documents to be presented in letter-of-credit transactions? If not, who dictates what documents will be required in the letter of credit?
2. At what point does the seller receive payment in a letter-of-credit transaction?
3. What assurances does a letter of credit provide to the buyer and the seller involved in the transaction?

INTERACTING WITH THE INTERNET

For updated links to resources available on the Web, as well as a variety of other materials, visit this text's Web site at

www.thomsonedu.com/westbuslaw/let

FindLaw, which is now a part of West Group, includes an extensive array of links to international doctrines and treaties, as well as to the laws of other nations, on its Web site. Go to

www.findlaw.com/12international

For information on the legal requirements of doing business internationally, a good source is the Internet Law Library's collection of laws of other countries. You can access this source at

www.lawguru.com/ilawlib/index.html

INTERNET EXERCISES

Go to **www.thomsonedu.com/westbuslaw/let**, the Web site that accompanies this text. Select "Chapter 22" and click on "Internet Exercises." There you will find the following Internet research exercises that you can perform to learn more about topics covered in this chapter.

Internet Exercise 22–1: LEGAL PERSPECTIVE—The World Trade Organization
Internet Exercise 22–2: MANAGEMENT PERSPECTIVE—Overseas Business Opportunities

BEFORE THE TEST

Go to **www.thomsonedu.com/westbuslaw/let**, the Web site that accompanies this text. Select "Chapter 22" and click on "Interactive Quizzes." You will find a number of interactive questions relating to this chapter.

UNIT SIX CUMULATIVE BUSINESS HYPOTHETICAL

Macrotech, Inc., has obtained a patent on an innovative computer chip that it makes and markets under the trademarked brand name "Flash."

1. Macrotech wants to sell the Flash chip to Nitron, Ltd., in Pacifica, a foreign country. Macrotech is concerned, however, that after an initial purchase, Nitron will duplicate the chip, pirate it, and sell the pirated version to computer manufacturers in Pacifica. To avoid this situation, Macrotech could establish its own manufacturing facility in Pacifica, but it does not want to do this. How can Macrotech, without establishing a manufacturing facility in Pacifica, protect Flash from being pirated by Nitron?

2. A representative of Pixel, S.A., in Raretania, a foreign country, contacts Macrotech, says that Pixel may be interested in buying a quantity of the Flash chips, and asks for a demonstration and a list of prices. Before Pixel makes a buy, Macrotech learns that there is a proposal in Congress to tax certain exports, including products such as Flash. Macrotech also learns of a proposal to impose restrictions on the export of Flash and similar products. Which of these proposals is most likely to be implemented, and why? If Congress wanted to stimulate, rather than restrict, the export of Flash, what steps might it take to do so?

3. Quaro Corp. and Selecta Corp., which are manufacturers in Techuan, a foreign country, make products that compete with the Flash chip. When Quaro and Selecta products seem to flood the U.S. market at low prices, Macrotech believes that its competitors have conspired to fix their prices. Can Macrotech file a suit against Quaro and Selecta in a U.S. court? If Quaro thought Macrotech was conspiring with other firms against it, could Quaro file a suit against Macrotech in a U.S. court? What could the U.S. government do if it found that Quaro and Selecta were selling their products in U.S. markets at "less than fair value"?

How to Brief Cases and Analyze Case Problems

HOW TO BRIEF CASES

To fully understand the law with respect to business, you need to be able to read and understand court decisions. To make this task easier, you can use a method of case analysis that is called *briefing*. There is a fairly standard procedure that you can follow when you "brief" any court case. You must first read the case opinion carefully. When you feel you understand the case, you can prepare a brief of it.

Although the format of the brief may vary, typically it will present the essentials of the case under headings such as those listed below.

1. **Citation.** Give the full citation for the case, including the name of the case, the date it was decided, and the court that decided it.
2. **Facts.** Briefly indicate (a) the reasons for the lawsuit; (b) the identity and arguments of the plaintiff(s) and defendant(s), respectively; and (c) the lower court's decision—if appropriate.
3. **Issue.** Concisely phrase, in the form of a question, the essential issue before the court. (If more than one issue is involved, you may have two—or even more—questions here.)
4. **Decision.** Indicate here—with a "yes" or "no," if possible—the court's answer to the question (or questions) in the Issue section above.
5. **Reason.** Summarize as briefly as possible the reasons given by the court for its decision (or decisions) and the case or statutory law relied on by the court in arriving at its decision.

AN EXAMPLE OF A BRIEFED SAMPLE COURT CASE

As an example of the format used in briefing cases, we present here a briefed version of the sample court case that was presented in the appendix to Chapter 1 in Exhibit 1A–3.

IN RE DIXON
Bankruptcy Appellate Panel,
United States Court of Appeals,
Eighth Circuit, 2006.
338 Bankr. 383.

FACTS   Before October 22, 2005, Keith Dixon was notified that his home was scheduled for foreclosure—at 12:00 P.M. on November 10, his creditors were going to sell the house to pay his debts. The night before the sale, at 6:30 P.M., Dixon contacted an attorney, who said that the proceeding could be stopped if, before it occurred, Dixon filed a petition in bankruptcy. To be eligible to file such a petition, a party must undergo credit counseling within 180 days *before* the filing. Unable to arrange counseling in the limited time before the foreclosure, Dixon asked a federal bankruptcy court to waive the requirement "based on exigent circumstances," claiming that the situation demanded immediate action. The court ruled that Dixon's request "did not describe exigent circumstances which merited a waiver." The court concluded that Dixon was therefore not "eligible to be a debtor" and dismissed the case. Dixon appealed to the Bankruptcy Appellate Panel of the U.S. Court of Appeals for the Eighth Circuit.

ISSUE   Did Dixon's situation constitute such exigent circumstances as to merit a waiver of the counseling requirement?

DECISION   No. The Bankruptcy Appellate Panel of the U.S. Court of Appeals for the Eighth Circuit affirmed the lower court's judgment. The appellate court concluded that "the bankruptcy court did not abuse its discretion in determining that the debtor had not demonstrated exigent circumstances." Dixon "was therefore not eligible to be a debtor" and "dismissal of his case was appropriate."

REASON   The court explained that for an individual to obtain a waiver of the credit-counseling requirement, "first, there must be exigent circumstances and, second, those circumstances must merit a waiver of the briefing requirements." Exigent refers to "adverse events" that will occur before the party can receive the counseling. Because in all cases in which parties request such waivers, "they feel that they are unable to wait," the "real question" is "whether or not those exigent circumstances merit the * * * waiver." In this case, Dixon had at least twenty days' notice of the foreclosure. "In the face of that much notice," Dixon's exigent circumstances did not merit the waiver." Because Dixon did not meet the counseling requirement and did not qualify for the waiver, he was not eligible to be a debtor under the Bankruptcy Code. "[V]irtually every court that has visited this issue has [concluded] that once that determination is made, dismissal of the case is appropriate."

REVIEW OF SAMPLE COURT CASE

Here we provide a review of the briefed version to indicate the kind of information that is contained in each section.

CITATION   The name of the case is *In re Dixon*. Dixon is the appellant. The Bankruptcy Appellate Panel of the U.S. Court of Appeals for the Eighth Circuit decided this case in 2006.

FACTS   The *Facts* section identifies the parties and describes the events leading up to this appeal, the request of the appellant in the initial petition to the lower court, and (because this case is an appellate court decision) the lower court's determinations and the identification of the party appealing those rulings. The appellant's contention on appeal is also sometimes included here.

ISSUE   The *Issue* section presents the central issue (or issues) decided by the court. In this case, the Bankruptcy Appellate Panel of the U.S. Court of Appeals for the Eighth Circuit reviews the lower court's conclusion that an individual was not entitled to a waiver of a certain requirement to file a bankruptcy petition. The relevant law includes the applicable statutes.

DECISION   The *Decision* section includes the court's decision on the issues before it. The decision reflects the opinion of the majority of the judges or justices hearing the case. Decisions by appellate courts are frequently phrased in reference to the lower court's decision. That is, the appellate court may "affirm" the lower court's ruling or "reverse" it. Here, the appellate court concluded that the lower court was correct in determining the debtor had not shown "exigent circumstances" and "was therefore not eligible to be a debtor." The appellate court affirmed the lower court's dismissal of the case.

REASON   The *Reason* section includes references to the relevant laws and legal principles that were applied in coming to

a conclusion in the case before the court. The relevant law here consisted of the provisions of the Bankruptcy Code that set out the counseling requirement and define its exception, as well as other courts' interpretations and applications of these provisions. This section also explains this court's application of the law to the facts in the case.

ANALYZING CASE PROBLEMS

In addition to learning how to brief cases, students of business law and the legal environment also find it helpful to know how to analyze case problems. Part of the study of business law and the legal environment usually involves analyzing case problems, such as those included in this text at the end of each chapter.

For each case problem in this book, we provide the relevant background and facts of the lawsuit and the issue before the court. When you are assigned one of these problems, your job will be to determine how the court should decide the issue, and why. In other words, you will need to engage in legal analysis and reasoning. Here we offer some suggestions on how to make this task less daunting. We begin by presenting a sample problem:

> While Janet Lawson, a famous pianist, was shopping in Quality Market, she slipped and fell on a wet floor in one of the aisles. The floor had recently been mopped by one of the store's employees, but there were no signs warning customers that the floor in that area was wet. As a result of the fall, Lawson injured her right arm and was unable to perform piano concerts for the next six months. Had she been able to perform the scheduled concerts, she would have earned approximately $60,000 over that period of time. Lawson sued Quality Market for this amount, plus another $10,000 in medical expenses. She claimed that the store's failure to warn customers of the wet floor constituted negligence and therefore the market was liable for her injuries. Will the court agree with Lawson? Discuss.

UNDERSTAND THE FACTS

This may sound obvious, but before you can analyze or apply the relevant law to a specific set of facts, you must clearly understand those facts. In other words, you should read through the case problem carefully—more than once, if necessary—to make sure you understand the identity of the plaintiff(s) and defendant(s) in the case and the progression of events that led to the lawsuit.

In the sample case just given, the identity of the parties is fairly obvious. Janet Lawson is the one bringing the suit; therefore, she is the plaintiff. Quality Market, against whom she is bringing the suit, is the defendant. Some of the case problems you may work on have multiple plaintiffs or defendants. Often, it is helpful to use abbreviations for the parties. To indicate a reference to a plaintiff, for example, the *pi* symbol—π—is often used, and a defendant is denoted by a *delta*—Δ—a triangle.

The events leading to the lawsuit are also fairly straight-forward. Lawson slipped and fell on a wet floor, and she contends that Quality Market should be liable for her injuries because it was negligent in not posting a sign warning customers of the wet floor.

When you are working on case problems, realize that the facts should be accepted as they are given. For example, in our sample problem, it should be accepted that the floor was wet and that there was no sign. In other words, avoid making conjectures, such as "Maybe the floor wasn't too wet," or "Maybe an employee was getting a sign to put up," or "Maybe someone stole the sign." Questioning the facts as they are presented only adds confusion to your analysis.

LEGAL ANALYSIS AND REASONING

Once you understand the facts given in the case problem, you can begin to analyze the case. The *IRAC method* is a helpful tool to use in the legal analysis and reasoning process. IRAC is an acronym for Issue, Rule, Application, Conclusion. Applying this method to our sample problem would involve the following steps:

1. First, you need to decide what legal **issue** is involved in the case. In our sample case, the basic issue is whether Quality Market's failure to warn customers of the wet floor constituted negligence. As discussed in Chapter 5, negligence is a *tort*—a civil wrong. In a tort lawsuit, the plaintiff seeks to be compensated for another's wrongful act. A defendant will be deemed negligent if he or she breached a duty of care owed to the plaintiff and the breach of that duty caused the plaintiff to suffer harm.

2. Once you have identified the issue, the next step is to determine what *rule of law* applies to the issue. To make this determination, you will want to review carefully the text of the chapter in which the problem appears to find the relevant rule of law. Our sample case involves the tort of negligence, covered in Chapter 5. The applicable rule of law is the tort law principle that business owners owe a duty to exercise reasonable care to protect their customers ("business invitees"). Reasonable care, in this context, includes either removing or warning customers

of *foreseeable* risks about which the owner *knew* or *should have known*. Business owners need not warn customers of "open and obvious" risks, however. If a business owner breaches this duty of care (fails to exercise the appropriate degree of care toward customers), and the breach of duty causes a customer to be injured, the business owner will be liable to the customer for the customer's injuries.

3. The next—and usually the most difficult—step in analyzing case problems is the *application* of the relevant rule of law to the specific facts of the case you are studying. In our sample problem, applying the tort law principle just discussed presents few difficulties. An employee of the store had mopped the floor in the aisle where Lawson slipped and fell, but no sign was present indicating that the floor was wet. That a customer might fall on a wet floor is clearly a foreseeable risk. Therefore, the failure to warn customers about the wet floor was a breach of the duty of care owed by the business owner to the store's customers.

4. Once you have completed step 3 in the IRAC method, you should be ready to draw your *conclusion*. In our sample case, Quality Market is liable to Lawson for her injuries, because the market's breach of its duty of care caused Lawson's injuries.

The fact patterns in the case problems presented in this text are not always as simple as those presented in our sample problem. Often, for example, there may be more than one plaintiff or defendant. There also may be more than one issue involved in a case and more than one applicable rule of law. Furthermore, in some case problems the facts may indicate that the general rule of law should not apply. For example, suppose a store employee advised Lawson not to walk on the floor in the aisle because it was wet, but Lawson decided to walk on it anyway. This fact could alter the outcome of the case because the store could then raise the defense of assumption of risk (see Chapter 5). Nonetheless, a careful review of the chapter should always provide you with the knowledge you need to analyze the problem thoroughly and arrive at accurate conclusions.

The Constitution of the United States

Note: You can access the full text of the Constitution online by going to **memory.loc.gov/const/const.html**. This is a page within the THOMAS Web site, which the U.S. Library of Congress maintains. To read the Bill of Rights or other amendments to the U.S. Constitution, click on the link at the top of the page.

PREAMBLE

We the People of the United States, in Order to form a more perfect Union, establish Justice, insure domestic Tranquility, provide for the common defence, promote the general Welfare, and secure the Blessings of Liberty to ourselves and our Posterity, do ordain and establish this Constitution for the United States of America.

ARTICLE I

Section 1. All legislative Powers herein granted shall be vested in a Congress of the United States, which shall consist of a Senate and House of Representatives.

Section 2. The House of Representatives shall be composed of Members chosen every second Year by the People of the several States, and the Electors in each State shall have the Qualifications requisite for Electors of the most numerous Branch of the State Legislature.

No Person shall be a Representative who shall not have attained to the Age of twenty five Years, and been seven Years a Citizen of the United States, and who shall not, when elected, be an Inhabitant of that State in which he shall be chosen.

Representatives and direct Taxes shall be apportioned among the several States which may be included within this Union, according to their respective Numbers, which shall be determined by adding to the whole Number of free Persons, including those bound to Service for a Term of Years, and excluding Indians not taxed, three fifths of all other Persons. The actual Enumeration shall be made within three Years after the first Meeting of the Congress of the United States, and within every subsequent Term of ten Years, in such Manner as they shall by Law direct. The Number of Representatives shall not exceed one for every thirty Thousand, but each State shall have at Least one Representative; and until such enumeration shall be made, the State of New Hampshire shall be entitled to chuse three, Massachusetts eight, Rhode Island and Providence Plantations one, Connecticut five, New York six, New Jersey four, Pennsylvania eight, Delaware one, Maryland six, Virginia ten, North Carolina five, South Carolina five, and Georgia three.

When vacancies happen in the Representation from any State, the Executive Authority thereof shall issue Writs of Election to fill such Vacancies.

The House of Representatives shall chuse their Speaker and other Officers; and shall have the sole Power of Impeachment.

Section 3. The Senate of the United States shall be composed of two Senators from each State, chosen by the Legislature thereof, for six Years; and each Senator shall have one Vote.

Immediately after they shall be assembled in Consequence of the first Election, they shall be divided as equally as may be into three Classes. The Seats of the Senators of the first Class shall be vacated at the Expiration of the second Year, of the second Class at the Expiration of the fourth Year, and of the third Class at the Expiration of the sixth Year, so that one third may be chosen every second Year; and if Vacancies happen by Resignation, or otherwise, during the Recess of the Legislature of any State, the Executive thereof may make temporary Appointments until the next Meeting of the Legislature, which shall then fill such Vacancies.

No Person shall be a Senator who shall not have attained to the Age of thirty Years, and been nine Years a Citizen of the United States, and who shall not, when elected, be an Inhabitant of that State for which he shall be chosen.

The Vice President of the United States shall be President of the Senate, but shall have no Vote, unless they be equally divided.

The Senate shall chuse their other Officers, and also a President pro tempore, in the Absence of the Vice President, or when he shall exercise the Office of President of the United States.

The Senate shall have the sole Power to try all Impeachments. When sitting for that Purpose, they shall be on Oath or Affirmation. When the President of the United States is tried, the Chief Justice shall preside: And no Person shall be convicted without the Concurrence of two thirds of the Members present.

Judgment in Cases of Impeachment shall not extend further than to removal from Office, and disqualification to hold and enjoy any Office of honor, Trust, or Profit under the United States: but the Party convicted shall nevertheless be liable and subject to Indictment, Trial, Judgment, and Punishment, according to Law.

Section 4. The Times, Places and Manner of holding Elections for Senators and Representatives, shall be prescribed in each State by the Legislature thereof; but the Congress may at any time by Law make or alter such Regulations, except as to the Places of chusing Senators.

The Congress shall assemble at least once in every Year, and such Meeting shall be on the first Monday in December, unless they shall by Law appoint a different Day.

Section 5. Each House shall be the Judge of the Elections, Returns, and Qualifications of its own Members, and a Majority of each shall constitute a Quorum to do Business; but a smaller Number may adjourn from day to day, and may be authorized to compel the Attendance of absent Members, in such Manner, and under such Penalties as each House may provide.

Each House may determine the Rules of its Proceedings, punish its Members for disorderly Behavior, and, with the Concurrence of two thirds, expel a Member.

Each House shall keep a Journal of its Proceedings, and from time to time publish the same, excepting such Parts as may in their Judgment require Secrecy; and the Yeas and Nays of the Members of either House on any question shall, at the Desire of one fifth of those Present, be entered on the Journal.

Neither House, during the Session of Congress, shall, without the Consent of the other, adjourn for more than three days, nor to any other Place than that in which the two Houses shall be sitting.

Section 6. The Senators and Representatives shall receive a Compensation for their Services, to be ascertained by Law, and paid out of the Treasury of the United States. They shall in all Cases, except Treason, Felony and Breach of the Peace, be privileged from Arrest during their Attendance at the Session of their respective Houses, and in going to and returning from the same; and for any Speech or Debate in either House, they shall not be questioned in any other Place.

No Senator or Representative shall, during the Time for which he was elected, be appointed to any civil Office under the Authority of the United States, which shall have been created, or the Emoluments whereof shall have been increased during such time; and no Person holding any Office under the United States, shall be a Member of either House during his Continuance in Office.

Section 7. All Bills for raising Revenue shall originate in the House of Representatives; but the Senate may propose or concur with Amendments as on other Bills.

Every Bill which shall have passed the House of Representatives and the Senate, shall, before it become a Law, be presented to the President of the United States; If he approve he shall sign it, but if not he shall return it, with his Objections to the House in which it shall have originated, who shall enter the Objections at large on their Journal, and proceed to reconsider it. If after such Reconsideration two thirds of that House shall agree to pass the Bill, it shall be sent together with the Objections, to the other House, by which it shall likewise be reconsidered, and if approved by two thirds of that House, it shall become a Law. But in all such Cases the Votes of both Houses shall be determined by Yeas and Nays, and the Names of the Persons voting for and against the Bill shall be entered on the Journal of each House respectively. If any Bill shall not be returned by the President within ten Days (Sundays excepted) after it shall have been presented to him, the Same shall be a Law, in like Manner as if he had signed it, unless the Congress by their Adjournment prevent its Return in which Case it shall not be a Law.

Every Order, Resolution, or Vote, to which the Concurrence of the Senate and House of Representatives may be necessary (except on a question of Adjournment) shall be presented to the President of the United States; and before the Same shall take Effect, shall be approved by him, or being disapproved by him, shall be repassed by two thirds of the Senate and House of Representatives, according to the Rules and Limitations prescribed in the Case of a Bill.

Section 8. The Congress shall have Power To lay and collect Taxes, Duties, Imposts and Excises, to pay the Debts and provide for the common Defence and general Welfare of the United States; but all Duties, Imposts and Excises shall be uniform throughout the United States;

To borrow Money on the credit of the United States;

To regulate Commerce with foreign Nations, and among the several States, and with the Indian Tribes;

To establish an uniform Rule of Naturalization, and uniform Laws on the subject of Bankruptcies throughout the United States;

To coin Money, regulate the Value thereof, and of foreign Coin, and fix the Standard of Weights and Measures;

To provide for the Punishment of counterfeiting the Securities and current Coin of the United States;

To establish Post Offices and post Roads;

To promote the Progress of Science and useful Arts, by securing for limited Times to Authors and Inventors the exclusive Right to their respective Writings and Discoveries;

To constitute Tribunals inferior to the supreme Court;

To define and punish Piracies and Felonies committed on the high Seas, and Offenses against the Law of Nations;

To declare War, grant Letters of Marque and Reprisal, and make Rules concerning Captures on Land and Water;

To raise and support Armies, but no Appropriation of Money to that Use shall be for a longer Term than two Years;

To provide and maintain a Navy;

To make Rules for the Government and Regulation of the land and naval Forces;

To provide for calling forth the Militia to execute the Laws of the Union, suppress Insurrections and repel Invasions;

To provide for organizing, arming, and disciplining, the Militia, and for governing such Part of them as may be employed in the Service of the United States, reserving to the States respectively, the Appointment of the Officers, and the Authority of training the Militia according to the discipline prescribed by Congress;

To exercise exclusive Legislation in all Cases whatsoever, over such District (not exceeding ten Miles square) as may, by Cession of particular States, and the Acceptance of Congress, become the Seat of the Government of the United States, and to exercise like Authority over all Places purchased by the Consent of the Legislature of the State in which the Same shall be, for the Erection of Forts, Magazines, Arsenals, dock-Yards, and other needful Buildings;—And

To make all Laws which shall be necessary and proper for carrying into Execution the foregoing Powers, and all other Powers vested by this Constitution in the Government of the United States, or in any Department or Officer thereof.

Section 9.   The Migration or Importation of such Persons as any of the States now existing shall think proper to admit, shall not be prohibited by the Congress prior to the Year one thousand eight hundred and eight, but a Tax or duty may be imposed on such Importation, not exceeding ten dollars for each Person.

The privilege of the Writ of Habeas Corpus shall not be suspended, unless when in Cases of Rebellion or Invasion the public Safety may require it.

No Bill of Attainder or ex post facto Law shall be passed.

No Capitation, or other direct, Tax shall be laid, unless in Proportion to the Census or Enumeration herein before directed to be taken.

No Tax or Duty shall be laid on Articles exported from any State.

No Preference shall be given by any Regulation of Commerce or Revenue to the Ports of one State over those of another: nor shall Vessels bound to, or from, one State be obliged to enter, clear, or pay Duties in another.

No Money shall be drawn from the Treasury, but in Consequence of Appropriations made by Law; and a regular Statement and Account of the Receipts and Expenditures of all public Money shall be published from time to time.

No Title of Nobility shall be granted by the United States: And no Person holding any Office of Profit or Trust under them, shall, without the Consent of the Congress, accept of any present, Emolument, Office, or Title, of any kind whatever, from any King, Prince, or foreign State.

Section 10.   No State shall enter into any Treaty, Alliance, or Confederation; grant Letters of Marque and Reprisal; coin Money; emit Bills of Credit; make any Thing but gold and silver Coin a Tender in Payment of Debts; pass any Bill of Attainder, ex post facto Law, or Law impairing the Obligation of Contracts, or grant any Title of Nobility.

No State shall, without the Consent of the Congress, lay any Imposts or Duties on Imports or Exports, except what may be absolutely necessary for executing its inspection Laws: and the net Produce of all Duties and Imposts, laid by any State on Imports or Exports, shall be for the Use of the Treasury of the United States; and all such Laws shall be subject to the Revision and Controul of the Congress.

No State shall, without the Consent of Congress, lay any Duty of Tonnage, keep Troops, or Ships of War in time of Peace, enter into any Agreement or Compact with another State, or with a foreign Power, or engage in War, unless actually invaded, or in such imminent Danger as will not admit of delay.

ARTICLE II

Section 1.   The executive Power shall be vested in a President of the United States of America. He shall hold his Office during the Term of four Years, and, together with the Vice President, chosen for the same Term, be elected, as follows:

Each State shall appoint, in such Manner as the Legislature thereof may direct, a Number of Electors, equal to the whole Number of Senators and Representatives to which the State may be entitled in the Congress; but no Senator or Representative, or Person holding an Office of Trust or Profit under the United States, shall be appointed an Elector.

The Electors shall meet in their respective States, and vote by Ballot for two Persons, of whom one at least shall not be an Inhabitant of the same State with themselves. And they shall make a List of all the Persons voted for, and of the Number of Votes for each; which List they shall sign and certify, and transmit sealed to the Seat of the Government of the United States, directed to the President of the Senate. The President of the Senate shall, in the Presence of the Senate and House of Representatives, open all the Certificates, and the Votes shall then be counted. The Person having the greatest Number of Votes shall be the President, if such Number be a Majority of the whole Number of Electors appointed; and if there be more than one who have such Majority, and have an equal Number of Votes, then the House of Representatives shall immediately chuse by Ballot one of them for President; and if no Person have a Majority, then from the five highest on the List the said House shall in like Manner chuse the President. But in chusing the President, the Votes shall be taken by States, the Representation from each State having one Vote; A quorum for this Purpose shall consist of a Member or Members from two thirds of the States, and a Majority of all the States shall be necessary to a Choice. In every Case, after the Choice of the President, the Person having the greater Number of Votes of the Electors shall be the Vice President. But if there should remain two or more who have equal Votes, the Senate shall chuse from them by Ballot the Vice President.

The Congress may determine the Time of chusing the Electors, and the Day on which they shall give their Votes; which Day shall be the same throughout the United States.

No person except a natural born Citizen, or a Citizen of the United States, at the time of the Adoption of this Constitution, shall be eligible to the Office of President; neither shall any Person be eligible to that Office who shall not have attained to the Age of thirty five Years, and been fourteen Years a Resident within the United States.

In Case of the Removal of the President from Office, or of his Death, Resignation or Inability to discharge the Powers and Duties of the said Office, the same shall devolve on the Vice President, and the Congress may by Law provide for the Case of Removal, Death, Resignation or Inability, both of the President and Vice President, declaring what Officer shall then act as President, and such Officer shall act accordingly, until the Disability be removed, or a President shall be elected.

The President shall, at stated Times, receive for his Services, a Compensation, which shall neither be increased nor diminished during the Period for which he shall have been elected, and he shall not receive within that Period any other Emolument from the United States, or any of them.

Before he enter on the Execution of his Office, he shall take the following Oath or Affirmation: "I do solemnly swear (or affirm) that I will faithfully execute the Office of President of the United States, and will to the best of my Ability, preserve, protect and defend the Constitution of the United States."

Section 2. The President shall be Commander in Chief of the Army and Navy of the United States, and of the Militia of the several States, when called into the actual Service of the United States; he may require the Opinion, in writing, of the principal Officer in each of the executive Departments, upon any Subject relating to the Duties of their respective Offices, and he shall have Power to grant Reprieves and Pardons for Offenses against the United States, except in Cases of Impeachment.

He shall have Power, by and with the Advice and Consent of the Senate to make Treaties, provided two thirds of the Senators present concur; and he shall nominate, and by and with the Advice and Consent of the Senate, shall appoint Ambassadors, other public Ministers and Consuls, Judges of the supreme Court, and all other Officers of the United States, whose Appointments are not herein otherwise provided for, and which shall be established by Law; but the Congress may by Law vest the Appointment of such inferior Officers, as they think proper, in the President alone, in the Courts of Law, or in the Heads of Departments.

The President shall have Power to fill up all Vacancies that may happen during the Recess of the Senate, by granting Commissions which shall expire at the End of their next Session.

Section 3. He shall from time to time give to the Congress Information of the State of the Union, and recommend to their Consideration such Measures as he shall judge necessary and expedient; he may, on extraordinary Occasions, convene both Houses, or either of them, and in Case of Disagreement between them, with Respect to the Time of Adjournment, he may adjourn them to such Time as he shall think proper; he shall receive Ambassadors and other public Ministers; he shall take Care that the Laws be faithfully executed, and shall Commission all the Officers of the United States.

Section 4. The President, Vice President and all civil Officers of the United States, shall be removed from Office on Impeachment for, and Conviction of, Treason, Bribery, or other high Crimes and Misdemeanors.

ARTICLE III

Section 1. The judicial Power of the United States, shall be vested in one supreme Court, and in such inferior Courts as the Congress may from time to time ordain and establish. The Judges, both of the supreme and inferior Courts, shall hold their Offices during good Behaviour, and shall, at stated Times, receive for their Services a Compensation, which shall not be diminished during their Continuance in Office.

Section 2. The judicial Power shall extend to all Cases, in Law and Equity, arising under this Constitution, the Laws of the United States, and Treaties made, or which shall be made, under their Authority;—to all Cases affecting Ambassadors, other public Ministers and Consuls;—to all Cases of admiralty and maritime Jurisdiction;—to Controversies to which the United States shall be a Party;—to Controversies between two or more States;—between a State and Citizens of another State;—between Citizens of different States;—between Citizens of the same State claiming Lands under Grants of different States, and between a State, or the Citizens thereof, and foreign States, Citizens or Subjects.

In all Cases affecting Ambassadors, other public Ministers and Consuls, and those in which a State shall be a Party, the supreme Court shall have original Jurisdiction. In all the other Cases before mentioned, the supreme Court shall have appellate Jurisdiction, both as to Law and Fact, with such Exceptions, and under such Regulations as the Congress shall make.

The Trial of all Crimes, except in Cases of Impeachment, shall be by Jury; and such Trial shall be held in the State where the said Crimes shall have been committed; but when not committed within any State, the Trial shall be at such Place or Places as the Congress may by Law have directed.

Section 3. Treason against the United States, shall consist only in levying War against them, or, in adhering to their Enemies, giving them Aid and Comfort. No Person shall be convicted of Treason unless on the Testimony of two Witnesses to the same overt Act, or on Confession in open Court.

The Congress shall have Power to declare the Punishment of Treason, but no Attainder of Treason shall work Corruption of Blood, or Forfeiture except during the Life of the Person attainted.

ARTICLE IV

Section 1.   Full Faith and Credit shall be given in each State to the public Acts, Records, and judicial Proceedings of every other State. And the Congress may by general Laws prescribe the Manner in which such Acts, Records and Proceedings shall be proved, and the Effect thereof.

Section 2.   The Citizens of each State shall be entitled to all Privileges and Immunities of Citizens in the several States.

A Person charged in any State with Treason, Felony, or other Crime, who shall flee from Justice, and be found in another State, shall on Demand of the executive Authority of the State from which he fled, be delivered up, to be removed to the State having Jurisdiction of the Crime.

No Person held to Service or Labour in one State, under the Laws thereof, escaping into another, shall, in Consequence of any Law or Regulation therein, be discharged from such Service or Labour, but shall be delivered up on Claim of the Party to whom such Service or Labour may be due.

Section 3.   New States may be admitted by the Congress into this Union; but no new State shall be formed or erected within the Jurisdiction of any other State; nor any State be formed by the Junction of two or more States, or Parts of States, without the Consent of the Legislatures of the States concerned as well as of the Congress.

The Congress shall have Power to dispose of and make all needful Rules and Regulations respecting the Territory or other Property belonging to the United States; and nothing in this Constitution shall be so construed as to Prejudice any Claims of the United States, or of any particular State.

Section 4.   The United States shall guarantee to every State in this Union a Republican Form of Government, and shall protect each of them against Invasion; and on Application of the Legislature, or of the Executive (when the Legislature cannot be convened) against domestic Violence.

ARTICLE V

The Congress, whenever two thirds of both Houses shall deem it necessary, shall propose Amendments to this Constitution, or, on the Application of the Legislatures of two thirds of the several States, shall call a Convention for proposing Amendments, which, in either Case, shall be valid to all Intents and Purposes, as part of this Constitution, when ratified by the Legislatures of three fourths of the several States, or by Conventions in three fourths thereof, as the one or the other Mode of Ratification may be proposed by the Congress; Provided that no Amendment which may be made prior to the Year One thousand eight hundred and eight shall in any Manner affect the first and fourth Clauses in the Ninth Section of the first Article; and that no State, without its Consent, shall be deprived of its equal Suffrage in the Senate.

ARTICLE VI

All Debts contracted and Engagements entered into, before the Adoption of this Constitution shall be as valid against the United States under this Constitution, as under the Confederation.

This Constitution, and the Laws of the United States which shall be made in Pursuance thereof; and all Treaties made, or which shall be made, under the Authority of the United States, shall be the supreme Law of the Land; and the Judges in every State shall be bound thereby, any Thing in the Constitution or Laws of any State to the Contrary notwithstanding.

The Senators and Representatives before mentioned, and the Members of the several State Legislatures, and all executive and judicial Officers, both of the United States and of the several States, shall be bound by Oath or Affirmation, to support this Constitution; but no religious Test shall ever be required as a Qualification to any Office or public Trust under the United States.

ARTICLE VII

The Ratification of the Conventions of nine States shall be sufficient for the Establishment of this Constitution between the States so ratifying the Same.

AMENDMENT I [1791]

Congress shall make no law respecting an establishment of religion, or prohibiting the free exercise thereof; or abridging the freedom of speech, or of the press; or the right of the people peaceably to assembly, and to petition the Government for a redress of grievances.

AMENDMENT II [1791]

A well regulated Militia, being necessary to the security of a free State, the right of the people to keep and bear Arms, shall not be infringed.

AMENDMENT III [1791]

No Soldier shall, in time of peace be quartered in any house, without the consent of the Owner, nor in time of war, but in a manner to be prescribed by law.

AMENDMENT IV [1791]

The right of the people to be secure in their persons, houses, papers, and effects, against unreasonable searches and seizures, shall not be violated, and no Warrants shall issue, but upon probable cause, supported by Oath or affirmation, and particularly describing the place to be searched, and the persons or things to be seized.

AMENDMENT V [1791]

No person shall be held to answer for a capital, or otherwise infamous crime, unless on a presentment or indictment of a Grand Jury, except in cases arising in the land or naval forces, or in the Militia, when in actual service in time of War or public danger; nor shall any person be subject for the same offence to be twice put in jeopardy of life or limb; nor shall be compelled in any criminal case to be a witness against himself, nor be deprived of life, liberty, or property, without due process of law; nor shall private property be taken for public use, without just compensation.

AMENDMENT VI [1791]

In all criminal prosecutions, the accused shall enjoy the right to a speedy and public trial, by an impartial jury of the State and district wherein the crime shall have been committed, which district shall have been previously ascertained by law, and to be informed of the nature and cause of the accusation; to be confronted with the witnesses against him; to have compulsory process for obtaining witnesses in his favor, and to have the Assistance of Counsel for his defence.

AMENDMENT VII [1791]

In Suits at common law, where the value in controversy shall exceed twenty dollars, the right of trial by jury shall be preserved, and no fact tried by jury, shall be otherwise re-examined in any Court of the United States, than according to the rules of the common law.

AMENDMENT VIII [1791]

Excessive bail shall not be required, nor excessive fines imposed, nor cruel and unusual punishments inflicted.

AMENDMENT IX [1791]

The enumeration in the Constitution, of certain rights, shall not be construed to deny or disparage others retained by the people.

AMENDMENT X [1791]

The powers not delegated to the United States by the Constitution, nor prohibited by it to the States, are reserved to the States respectively, or to the people.

AMENDMENT XI [1798]

The Judicial power of the United States shall not be construed to extend to any suit in law or equity, commenced or prosecuted against one of the United States by Citizens of another State, or by Citizens or Subjects of any Foreign State.

AMENDMENT XII [1804]

The Electors shall meet in their respective states, and vote by ballot for President and Vice-President, one of whom, at least, shall not be an inhabitant of the same state with themselves; they shall name in their ballots the person voted for as President, and in distinct ballots the person voted for as Vice-President, and they shall make distinct lists of all persons voted for as President, and of all persons voted for as Vice-President, and of the number of votes for each, which lists they shall sign and certify, and transmit sealed to the seat of the government of the United States, directed to the President of the Senate;—The President of the Senate shall, in the presence of the Senate and House of Representatives, open all the certificates and the votes shall then be counted;—The person having the greatest number of votes for President, shall be the President, if such number be a majority of the whole number of Electors appointed; and if no person have such majority, then from the persons having the highest numbers not exceeding three on the list of those voted for as President, the House of Representatives shall choose immediately, by ballot, the

President. But in choosing the President, the votes shall be taken by states, the representation from each state having one vote; a quorum for this purpose shall consist of a member or members from two-thirds of the states, and a majority of all states shall be necessary to a choice. And if the House of Representatives shall not choose a President whenever the right of choice shall devolve upon them, before the fourth day of March next following, then the Vice-President shall act as President, as in the case of the death or other constitutional disability of the President.—The person having the greatest number of votes as Vice-President, shall be the Vice-President, if such number be a majority of the whole number of Electors appointed, and if no person have a majority, then from the two highest numbers on the list, the Senate shall choose the Vice-President; a quorum for the purpose shall consist of two-thirds of the whole number of Senators, and a majority of the whole number shall be necessary to a choice. But no person constitutionally ineligible to the office of President shall be eligible to that of Vice-President of the United States.

AMENDMENT XIII [1865]

Section 1. Neither slavery nor involuntary servitude, except as a punishment for crime whereof the party shall have been duly convicted, shall exist within the United States, or any place subject to their jurisdiction.

Section 2. Congress shall have power to enforce this article by appropriate legislation.

AMENDMENT XIV [1868]

Section 1. All persons born or naturalized in the United States, and subject to the jurisdiction thereof, are citizens of the United States and of the State wherein they reside. No State shall make or enforce any law which shall abridge the privileges or immunities of citizens of the United States; nor shall any State deprive any person of life, liberty, or property, without due process of law; nor deny to any person within its jurisdiction the equal protection of the laws.

Section 2. Representatives shall be apportioned among the several States according to their respective numbers, counting the whole number of persons in each State, excluding Indians not taxed. But when the right to vote at any election for the choice of electors for President and Vice President of the United States, Representatives in Congress, the Executive and Judicial officers of a State, or the members of the Legislature thereof, is denied to any of the male inhabitants of such State, being twenty-one years of age, and citizens of the United States, or in any way abridged, except for participation in rebellion, or other crime, the basis of representation therein shall be reduced in the proportion which the number of such male citizens shall bear to the whole number of male citizens twenty-one years of age in such State.

Section 3. No person shall be a Senator or Representative in Congress, or elector of President and Vice President, or hold any office, civil or military, under the United States, or under any State, who having previously taken an oath, as a member of Congress, or as an officer of the United States, or as a member of any State legislature, or as an executive or judicial officer of any State, to support the Constitution of the United States, shall have engaged in insurrection or rebellion against the same, or given aid or comfort to the enemies thereof. But Congress may by a vote of two-thirds of each House, remove such disability.

Section 4.   The validity of the public debt of the United States, authorized by law, including debts incurred for payment of pensions and bounties for services in suppressing insurrection or rebellion, shall not be questioned. But neither the United States nor any State shall assume or pay any debt or obligation incurred in aid of insurrection or rebellion against the United States, or any claim for the loss or emancipation of any slave; but all such debts, obligations and claims shall be held illegal and void.

Section 5.   The Congress shall have power to enforce, by appropriate legislation, the provisions of this article.

AMENDMENT XV [1870]

Section 1.   The right of citizens of the United States to vote shall not be denied or abridged by the United States or by any State on account of race, color, or previous condition of servitude.

Section 2.   The Congress shall have power to enforce this article by appropriate legislation.

AMENDMENT XVI [1913]

The Congress shall have power to lay and collect taxes on incomes, from whatever source derived, without apportionment among the several States, and without regard to any census or enumeration.

AMENDMENT XVII [1913]

Section 1.   The Senate of the United States shall be composed of two Senators from each State, elected by the people thereof, for six years; and each Senator shall have one vote. The electors in each State shall have the qualifications requisite for electors of the most numerous branch of the State legislatures.

Section 2.   When vacancies happen in the representation of any State in the Senate, the executive authority of such State shall issue writs of election to fill such vacancies: Provided, That the legislature of any State may empower the executive thereof to make temporary appointments until the people fill the vacancies by election as the legislature may direct.

Section 3.   This amendment shall not be so construed as to affect the election or term of any Senator chosen before it becomes valid as part of the Constitution.

AMENDMENT XVIII [1919]

Section 1.   After one year from the ratification of this article the manufacture, sale, or transportation of intoxicating liquors within, the importation thereof into, or the exportation thereof from the United States and all territory subject to the jurisdiction thereof for beverage purposes is hereby prohibited.

Section 2.   The Congress and the several States shall have concurrent power to enforce this article by appropriate legislation.

Section 3.   This article shall be inoperative unless it shall have been ratified as an amendment to the Constitution by the legislatures of the several States, as provided in the Constitution, within seven years from the date of the submission hereof to the States by the Congress.

AMENDMENT XIX [1920]

Section 1.   The right of citizens of the United States to vote shall not be denied or abridged by the United States or by any State on account of sex.

Section 2.   Congress shall have power to enforce this article by appropriate legislation.

AMENDMENT XX [1933]

Section 1.   The terms of the President and Vice President shall end at noon on the 20th day of January, and the terms of Senators and Representatives at noon on the 3d day of January, of the years in which such terms would have ended if this article had not been ratified; and the terms of their successors shall then begin.

Section 2.   The Congress shall assemble at least once in every year, and such meeting shall begin at noon on the 3d day of January, unless they shall by law appoint a different day.

Section 3.   If, at the time fixed for the beginning of the term of the President, the President elect shall have died, the Vice President elect shall become President. If the President shall not have been chosen before the time fixed for the beginning of his term, or if the President elect shall have failed to qualify, then the Vice President elect shall act as President until a President shall have qualified; and the Congress may by law provide for the case wherein neither a President elect nor a Vice President elect shall have qualified, declaring who shall then act as President, or the manner in which one who is to act shall be selected, and such person shall act accordingly until a President or Vice President shall have qualified.

Section 4.   The Congress may by law provide for the case of the death of any of the persons from whom the House of Representatives may choose a President whenever the right of choice shall have devolved upon them, and for the case of the death of any of the persons from whom the Senate may choose a Vice President whenever the right of choice shall have devolved upon them.

Section 5.   Sections 1 and 2 shall take effect on the 15th day of October following the ratification of this article.

Section 6.   This article shall be inoperative unless it shall have been ratified as an amendment to the Constitution by the legislatures of three-fourths of the several States within seven years from the date of its submission.

AMENDMENT XXI [1933]

Section 1.   The eighteenth article of amendment to the Constitution of the United States is hereby repealed.

Section 2.   The transportation or importation into any State, Territory, or possession of the United States for delivery or use therein of intoxicating liquors, in violation of the laws thereof, is hereby prohibited.

Section 3. This article shall be inoperative unless it shall have been ratified as an amendment to the Constitution by conventions in the several States, as provided in the Constitution, within seven years from the date of the submission hereof to the States by the Congress.

AMENDMENT XXII [1951]

Section 1. No person shall be elected to the office of the President more than twice, and no person who has held the office of President, or acted as President, for more than two years of a term to which some other person was elected President shall be elected to the office of President more than once. But this Article shall not apply to any person holding the office of President when this Article was proposed by the Congress, and shall not prevent any person who may be holding the office of President, or acting as President, during the term within which this Article becomes operative from holding the office of President or acting as President during the remainder of such term.

Section 2. This article shall be inoperative unless it shall have been ratified as an amendment to the Constitution by the legislatures of three-fourths of the several States within seven years from the date of its submission to the States by the Congress.

AMENDMENT XXIII [1961]

Section 1. The District constituting the seat of Government of the United States shall appoint in such manner as the Congress may direct:

A number of electors of President and Vice President equal to the whole number of Senators and Representatives in Congress to which the District would be entitled if it were a State, but in no event more than the least populous state; they shall be in addition to those appointed by the states, but they shall be considered, for the purposes of the election of President and Vice President, to be electors appointed by a state; and they shall meet in the District and perform such duties as provided by the twelfth article of amendment.

Section 2. The Congress shall have power to enforce this article by appropriate legislation.

AMENDMENT XXIV [1964]

Section 1. The right of citizens of the United States to vote in any primary or other election for President or Vice President, for electors for President or Vice President, or for Senator or Representative in Congress, shall not be denied or abridged by the United States, or any State by reason of failure to pay any poll tax or other tax.

Section 2. The Congress shall have power to enforce this article by appropriate legislation.

AMENDMENT XXV [1967]

Section 1. In case of the removal of the President from office or of his death or resignation, the Vice President shall become President.

Section 2. Whenever there is a vacancy in the office of the Vice President, the President shall nominate a Vice President who shall take office upon confirmation by a majority vote of both Houses of Congress.

Section 3. Whenever the President transmits to the President pro tempore of the Senate and the Speaker of the House of Representatives his written declaration that he is unable to discharge the powers and duties of his office, and until he transmits to them a written declaration to the contrary, such powers and duties shall be discharged by the Vice President as Acting President.

Section 4. Whenever the Vice President and a majority of either the principal officers of the executive departments or of such other body as Congress may by law provide, transmit to the President pro tempore of the Senate and the Speaker of the House of Representatives their written declaration that the President is unable to discharge the powers and duties of his office, the Vice President shall immediately assume the powers and duties of the office as Acting President.

Thereafter, when the President transmits to the President pro tempore of the Senate and the Speaker of the House of Representatives his written declaration that no inability exists, he shall resume the powers and duties of his office unless the Vice President and a majority of either the principal officers of the executive department or of such other body as Congress may by law provide, transmit within four days to the President pro tempore of the Senate and the Speaker of the House of Representatives their written declaration that the President is unable to discharge the powers and duties of his office. Thereupon Congress shall decide the issue, assembling within forty-eight hours for that purpose if not in session. If the Congress, within twenty-one days after receipt of the latter written declaration, or, if Congress is not in session, within twenty-one days after Congress is required to assemble, determines by two-thirds vote of both Houses that the President is unable to discharge the powers and duties of his office, the Vice President shall continue to discharge the same as Acting President; otherwise, the President shall resume the powers and duties of his office.

AMENDMENT XXVI [1971]

Section 1. The right of citizens of the United States, who are eighteen years of age or older, to vote shall not be denied or abridged by the United States or by any State on account of age.

Section 2. The Congress shall have power to enforce this article by appropriate legislation.

AMENDMENT XXVII [1992]

No law, varying the compensation for the services of the Senators and Representatives, shall take effect, until an election of Representatives shall have intervened.

The Administrative Procedure Act of 1946 (Excerpts)

Note: You can access the full text of the Administrative Procedure Act online by going to **uscode.house.gov/search/ criteria.shtml**. In the "Title" box, type "5," and in the "Section" box, type a relevant section number (such as "551"). Click on "Search," and in the list of "documents found," click on the citation to access the text of the statute. The Office of the Law Revision Council of the U.S. House of Representatives maintains this Web site.

Section 551. Definitions

For the purpose of this subchapter—

* * * *

(4) "rule" means the whole or a part of an agency statement of general or particular applicability and future effect designed to implement, interpret, or prescribe law or policy or describing the organization, procedure, or practice requirements of an agency and includes the approval or prescription for the future of rates, wages, corporate or financial structures or reorganizations thereof, prices, facilities, appliances, services or allowances therefor or of valuations, costs, or accounting, or practices bearing on any of the foregoing[.]

* * * *

Section 552. Public Information; Agency Rules, Opinions, Orders, Records, and Proceedings

(a) Each agency shall make available to the public information as follows:

(1) Each agency shall separately state and currently publish in the Federal Register for the guidance of the public—

(A) descriptions of its central and field organization and the established places at which, the employees * * * from whom, and the methods whereby, the public may obtain information, make submittals or requests, or obtain decisions;

* * * *

(C) rules of procedure, descriptions of forms available or the places at which forms may be obtained, and instructions as to the scope and contents of all papers, reports, or examinations;

(D) substantive rules of general applicability adopted as authorized by law, and statements of general policy or interpretations of general applicability formulated and adopted by the agency[.]
* * *

* * * *

Section 552b. Open Meetings

* * * *

(j) Each agency subject to the requirements of this section shall annually report to Congress regarding its compliance with such requirements, including a tabulation of the total number of agency meetings open to the public, the total number of meetings closed to the public, the reasons for closing such meetings, and a description of any litigation brought against the agency under this section, including any costs assessed against the agency in such litigation * * *.

* * * *

Section 553. Rule Making

* * * *

(b) General notice of proposed rule making shall be published in the Federal Register, unless persons subject thereto are named and either personally served or otherwise have actual notice thereof in accordance with law. * * *

(c) After notice required by this section, the agency shall give interested persons an opportunity to participate in the rule making through submission of written data, views, or arguments with or without opportunity for oral presentation. * * *

* * * *

Section 554. Adjudications

* * * *

(b) Persons entitled to notice of an agency hearing shall be timely informed of—

(1) the time, place, and nature of the hearing;

(2) the legal authority and jurisdiction under which the hearing is to be held; and

(3) the matters of fact and law asserted.

* * * *

(c) The agency shall give all interested parties opportunity for—

(1) the submission and consideration of facts, arguments, offers of settlement, or proposals of adjustment when time, the nature of the proceeding, and the public interest permit; and

(2) to the extent that the parties are unable so to determine a controversy by consent, hearing and decision on notice * * *.

* * * *

Section 555. Ancillary Matters

* * * *

(c) Process, requirement of a report, inspection, or other investigative act or demand may not be issued, made, or enforced except as authorized by law. A person compelled to submit data or evidence is entitled to retain or, on payment of lawfully prescribed costs, procure a copy or transcript thereof, except that in a nonpublic investigatory proceeding the witness may for good cause be limited to inspection of the official transcript of his testimony.

* * * *

(e) Prompt notice shall be given of the denial in whole or in part of a written application, petition, or other request of an interested person made in connection with any agency proceeding. * * *

Section 556. Hearings; Presiding Employees; Powers and Duties; Burden of Proof; Evidence; Record as Basis of Decision

* * * *

(b) There shall preside at the taking of evidence—

(1) the agency;

(2) one or more members of the body which comprises the agency; or

(3) one or more administrative law judges * * *.

* * * *

(c) Subject to published rules of the agency and within its powers, employees presiding at hearings may—

(1) administer oaths and affirmations;

(2) issue subpoenas authorized by law;

(3) rule on offers of proof and receive relevant evidence;

(4) take depositions or have depositions taken when the ends of justice would be served;

(5) regulate the course of the hearing;

(6) hold conferences for the settlement or simplification of the issues by consent of the parties or by the use of alternative means of dispute resolution as provided in subchapter IV of this chapter;

(7) inform the parties as to the availability of one or more alternative means of dispute resolution, and encourage use of such methods;

* * * *

(9) dispose of procedural requests or similar matters;

(10) make or recommend decisions in accordance with * * * this title; and

(11) take other action authorized by agency rule consistent with this subchapter.

* * * *

Section 702. Right of Review

A person suffering legal wrong because of agency action * * * is entitled to judicial review thereof. An action in a court of the United States seeking relief other than money damages and stating a claim that an agency or an officer or employee thereof acted or failed to act in an official capacity or under color of legal authority shall not be dismissed nor relief therein be denied on the ground that it is against the United States or that the United States is an indispensable party. The United States may be named as a defendant in any such action, and a judgment or decree may be entered against the United States: Provided, [t]hat any mandatory or injunctive decree shall specify the [f]ederal officer or officers (by name or by title), and their successors in office, personally responsible for compliance. * * *

* * * *

Section 704. Actions Reviewable

Agency action made reviewable by statute and final agency action for which there is no other adequate remedy in a court are subject to judicial review. A preliminary, procedural, or intermediate agency action or ruling not directly reviewable is subject to review on the review of the final agency action.

Article 2 of the Uniform Commercial Code

Note: You can access the full text of Article 2 of the Uniform Commercial Code (UCC) online at **www.law.cornell.edu/ucc/2**. The Legal Information Institute of the Cornell Law School maintains this Web site. This online version of the UCC does not include the official comments or the 2003 amendments to UCC Article 2.

Article 2
SALES

Part 1 Short Title, General Construction and Subject Matter

§ 2–101. Short Title.

This Article shall be known and may be cited as Uniform Commercial Code—Sales.

§ 2–102. Scope; Certain Security and Other Transactions Excluded From This Article.

Unless the context otherwise requires, this Article applies to transactions in goods; it does not apply to any transaction which although in the form of an unconditional contract to sell or present sale is intended to operate only as a security transaction nor does this Article impair or repeal any statute regulating sales to consumers, farmers or other specified classes of buyers.

§ 2–103. Definitions and Index of Definitions.

(1) In this Article unless the context otherwise requires

(a) "Buyer" means a person who buys or contracts to buy goods.

(b) "Good faith" in the case of a merchant means honesty in fact and the observance of reasonable commercial standards of fair dealing in the trade.

(c) "Receipt" of goods means taking physical possession of them.

(d) "Seller" means a person who sells or contracts to sell goods.

(2) Other definitions applying to this Article or to specified Parts thereof, and the sections in which they appear are:

"Acceptance". Section 2–606.
"Banker's credit". Section 2–325.
"Between merchants". Section 2–104.
"Cancellation". Section 2–106(4).
"Commercial unit". Section 2–105.
"Confirmed credit". Section 2–325.
"Conforming to contract". Section 2–106.
"Contract for sale". Section 2–106.
"Cover". Section 2–712.
"Entrusting". Section 2–403.
"Financing agency". Section 2–104.
"Future goods". Section 2–105.
"Goods". Section 2–105.
"Identification". Section 2–501.
"Installment contract". Section 2–612.
"Letter of Credit". Section 2–325.
"Lot". Section 2–105.
"Merchant". Section 2–104.
"Overseas". Section 2–323.
"Person in position of seller". Section 2–707.
"Present sale". Section 2–106.
"Sale". Section 2–106.
"Sale on approval". Section 2–326.
"Sale or return". Section 2–326.
"Termination". Section 2–106.

(3) The following definitions in other Articles apply to this Article:

"Check". Section 3–104.
"Consignee". Section 7–102.
"Consignor". Section 7–102.
"Consumer goods". Section 9–109.
"Dishonor". Section 3–507.
"Draft". Section 3–104.

(4) In addition Article 1 contains general definitions and principles of construction and interpretation applicable throughout this Article.

As amended in 1994 and 1999.

§ 2–104. Definitions: "Merchant"; "Between Merchants"; "Financing Agency".

(1) "Merchant" means a person who deals in goods of the kind or otherwise by his occupation holds himself out as having knowledge or skill peculiar to the practices or goods involved in the transaction or to whom such knowledge or skill may be attributed by his employment of an agent or broker or other intermediary who by his occupation holds himself out as having such knowledge or skill.

(2) "Financing agency" means a bank, finance company or other person who in the ordinary course of business makes advances against goods or documents of title or who by arrangement with either the seller or the buyer intervenes in ordinary course to make or collect payment due or claimed under the contract for sale, as by purchasing or paying the seller's draft or making advances against it or by merely taking it for collection whether or not documents of title accompany the draft. "Financing agency" includes also a bank or other person who similarly intervenes between persons who are in the position of seller and buyer in respect to the goods (Section 2–707).

(3) "Between merchants" means in any transaction with respect to which both parties are chargeable with the knowledge or skill of merchants.

§ 2–105. Definitions: Transferability; "Goods"; "Future" Goods; "Lot"; "Commercial Unit".

(1) "Goods" means all things (including specially manufactured goods) which are movable at the time of identification to the contract for sale other than the money in which the price is to be paid, investment securities (Article 8) and things in action. "Goods" also includes the unborn young of animals and growing crops and other identified things attached to realty as described in the section on goods to be severed from realty (Section 2–107).

(2) Goods must be both existing and identified before any interest in them can pass. Goods which are not both existing and identified are "future" goods. A purported present sale of future goods or of any interest therein operates as a contract to sell.

(3) There may be a sale of a part interest in existing identified goods.

(4) An undivided share in an identified bulk of fungible goods is sufficiently identified to be sold although the quantity of the bulk is not determined. Any agreed proportion of such a bulk or any quantity thereof agreed upon by number, weight or other measure may to the extent of the seller's interest in the bulk be sold to the buyer who then becomes an owner in common.

(5) "Lot" means a parcel or a single article which is the subject matter of a separate sale or delivery, whether or not it is sufficient to perform the contract.

(6) "Commercial unit" means such a unit of goods as by commercial usage is a single whole for purposes of sale and division of which materially impairs its character or value on the market or in use. A commercial unit may be a single article (as a machine) or a set of articles (as a suite of furniture or an assortment of sizes) or a quantity (as a bale, gross, or carload) or any other unit treated in use or in the relevant market as a single whole.

§ 2–106. Definitions: "Contract"; "Agreement"; "Contract for Sale"; "Sale"; "Present Sale"; "Conforming" to Contract; "Termination"; "Cancellation".

(1) In this Article unless the context otherwise requires "contract" and "agreement" are limited to those relating to the present or future sale of goods. "Contract for sale" includes both a present sale of goods and a contract to sell goods at a future time. A "sale" consists in the passing of title from the seller to the buyer for a price (Section 2–401). A "present sale" means a sale which is accomplished by the making of the contract.

(2) Goods or conduct including any part of a performance are "conforming" or conform to the contract when they are in accordance with the obligations under the contract.

(3) "Termination" occurs when either party pursuant to a power created by agreement or law puts an end to the contract otherwise than for its breach. On "termination" all obligations which are still executory on both sides are discharged but any right based on prior breach or performance survives.

(4) "Cancellation" occurs when either party puts an end to the contract for breach by the other and its effect is the same as that of "termination" except that the cancelling party also retains any remedy for breach of the whole contract or any unperformed balance.

§ 2–107. Goods to Be Severed From Realty: Recording.

(1) A contract for the sale of minerals or the like (including oil and gas) or a structure or its materials to be removed from realty is a contract for the sale of goods within this Article if they are to be severed by the seller but until severance a purported present sale thereof which is not effective as a transfer of an interest in land is effective only as a contract to sell.

(2) A contract for the sale apart from the land of growing crops or other things attached to realty and capable of severance without material harm thereto but not described in subsection (1) or of timber to be cut is a contract for the sale of goods within this Article whether the subject matter is to be severed by the buyer or by the seller even though it forms part of the realty at the time of contracting, and the parties can by identification effect a present sale before severance.

(3) The provisions of this section are subject to any third party rights provided by the law relating to realty records, and the contract for sale may be executed and recorded as a document transferring an interest in land and shall then constitute notice to third parties of the buyer's rights under the contract for sale.

As amended in 1972.

Part 2 Form, Formation and Readjustment of Contract

§ 2–201. Formal Requirements; Statute of Frauds.

(1) Except as otherwise provided in this section a contract for the sale of goods for the price of $500 or more is not enforceable by way of action or defense unless there is some writing sufficient to indicate that a contract for sale has been made between the parties and signed by the party against whom enforcement is sought or by his authorized agent or broker. A writing is not insufficient because it omits or incorrectly states a term agreed upon but the contract is not enforceable under this paragraph beyond the quantity of goods shown in such writing.

(2) Between merchants if within a reasonable time a writing in confirmation of the contract and sufficient against the sender is received and the party receiving it has reason to know its contents, its satisfies the requirements of subsection (1) against such party unless written notice of objection to its contents is given within ten days after it is received.

(3) A contract which does not satisfy the requirements of subsection (1) but which is valid in other respects is enforceable

(a) if the goods are to be specially manufactured for the buyer and are not suitable for sale to others in the ordinary course of the seller's business and the seller, before notice of repudiation is received and under circumstances which reasonably indicate that the goods are for the buyer, has made either a substantial beginning of their manufacture or commitments for their procurement; or

(b) if the party against whom enforcement is sought admits in his pleading, testimony or otherwise in court that a contract for sale was made, but the contract is not enforceable under this provision beyond the quantity of goods admitted; or

(c) with respect to goods for which payment has been made and accepted or which have been received and accepted (Sec. 2–606).

§ 2–202. Final Written Expression: Parol or Extrinsic Evidence.

Terms with respect to which the confirmatory memoranda of the parties agree or which are otherwise set forth in a writing intended by the parties as a final expression of their agreement with respect to such terms as are included therein may not be contradicted by evidence of any prior agreement or of a contemporaneous oral agreement but may be explained or supplemented

(a) by course of dealing or usage of trade (Section 1–205) or by course of performance (Section 2–208); and

(b) by evidence of consistent additional terms unless the court finds the writing to have been intended also as a complete and exclusive statement of the terms of the agreement.

§ 2–203. Seals Inoperative.

The affixing of a seal to a writing evidencing a contract for sale or an offer to buy or sell goods does not constitute the writing of a sealed instrument and the law with respect to sealed instruments does not apply to such a contract or offer.

§ 2–204. Formation in General.

(1) A contract for sale of goods may be made in any manner sufficient to show agreement, including conduct by both parties which recognizes the existence of such a contract.

(2) An agreement sufficient to constitute a contract for sale may be found even though the moment of its making is undetermined.

(3) Even though one or more terms are left open a contract for sale does not fail for indefiniteness if the parties have intended to make a contract and there is a reasonably certain basis for giving an appropriate remedy.

§ 2–205. Firm Offers.

An offer by a merchant to buy or sell goods in a signed writing which by its terms gives assurance that it will be held open is not revocable, for lack of consideration, during the time stated or if no time is stated for a reasonable time, but in no event may such period of irrevocability exceed three months; but any such term of assurance on a form supplied by the offeree must be separately signed by the offeror.

§ 2–206. Offer and Acceptance in Formation of Contract.

(1) Unless other unambiguously indicated by the language or circumstances

(a) an offer to make a contract shall be construed as inviting acceptance in any manner and by any medium reasonable in the circumstances;

(b) an order or other offer to buy goods for prompt or current shipment shall be construed as inviting acceptance either by a prompt promise to ship or by the prompt or current shipment of conforming or nonconforming goods, but such a shipment of non-conforming goods does not constitute an acceptance if the seller seasonably notifies the buyer that the shipment is offered only as an accommodation to the buyer.

(2) Where the beginning of a requested performance is a reasonable mode of acceptance an offeror who is not notified of acceptance within a reasonable time may treat the offer as having lapsed before acceptance.

§ 2–207. Additional Terms in Acceptance or Confirmation.

(1) A definite and seasonable expression of acceptance or a written confirmation which is sent within a reasonable time operates as an acceptance even though it states terms additional to or different from those offered or agreed upon, unless acceptance is expressly made conditional on assent to the additional or different terms.

(2) The additional terms are to be construed as proposals for addition to the contract. Between merchants such terms become part of the contract unless:

(a) the offer expressly limits acceptance to the terms of the offer;

(b) they materially alter it; or

(c) notification of objection to them has already been given or is given within a reasonable time after notice of them is received.

(3) Conduct by both parties which recognizes the existence of a contract is sufficient to establish a contract for sale although the writings of the parties do not otherwise establish a contract. In such case the terms of the particular contract consist of those terms on which the writings of the parties agree, together with any supplementary terms incorporated under any other provisions of this Act.

§ 2–208.   Course of Performance or Practical Construction.

(1) Where the contract for sale involves repeated occasions for performance by either party with knowledge of the nature of the performance and opportunity for objection to it by the other, any course of performance accepted or acquiesced in without objection shall be relevant to determine the meaning of the agreement.

(2) The express terms of the agreement and any such course of performance, as well as any course of dealing and usage of trade, shall be construed whenever reasonable as consistent with each other; but when such construction is unreasonable, express terms shall control course of performance and course of performance shall control both course of dealing and usage of trade (Section 1–205).

(3) Subject to the provisions of the next section on modification and waiver, such course of performance shall be relevant to show a waiver or modification of any term inconsistent with such course of performance.

§ 2–209.   Modification, Rescission and Waiver.

(1) An agreement modifying a contract within this Article needs no consideration to be binding.

(2) A signed agreement which excludes modification or rescission except by a signed writing cannot be otherwise modified or rescinded, but except as between merchants such a requirement on a form supplied by the merchant must be separately signed by the other party.

(3) The requirements of the statute of frauds section of this Article (Section 2–201) must be satisfied if the contract as modified is within its provisions.

(4) Although an attempt at modification or rescission does not satisfy the requirements of subsection (2) or (3) it can operate as a waiver.

(5) A party who has made a waiver affecting an executory portion of the contract may retract the waiver by reasonable notification received by the other party that strict performance will be required of any term waived, unless the retraction would be unjust in view of a material change of position in reliance on the waiver.

§ 2–210.   Delegation of Performance; Assignment of Rights.

(1) A party may perform his duty through a delegate unless otherwise agreed or unless the other party has a substantial interest in having his original promisor perform or control the acts required by the contract. No delegation of performance relieves the party delegating of any duty to perform or any liability for breach.

(2) Except as otherwise provided in Section 9–406, unless otherwise agreed, all rights of either seller or buyer can be assigned except where the assignment would materially change the duty of the other party, or increase materially the burden or risk imposed on him by his contract, or impair materially his chance of obtaining return performance. A right to damages for breach of the whole contract or a right arising out of the assignor's due performance of his entire obligation can be assigned despite agreement otherwise.

(3) The creation, attachment, perfection, or enforcement of a security interest in the seller's interest under a contract is not a transfer that materially changes the duty of or increases materially the burden or risk imposed on the buyer or impairs materially the buyer's chance of obtaining return performance within the purview of subsection (2) unless, and then only to the extent that, enforcement actually results in a delegation of material performance of the seller. Even in that event, the creation, attachment, perfection, and enforcement of the security interest remain effective, but (i) the seller is liable to the buyer for damages caused by the delegation to the extent that the damages could not reasonably be prevented by the buyer, and (ii) a court having jurisdiction may grant other appropriate relief, including cancellation of the contract for sale or an injunction against enforcement of the security interest or consummation of the enforcement.

(4) Unless the circumstances indicate the contrary a prohibition of assignment of "the contract" is to be construed as barring only the delegation to the assignees of the assignor's performance.

(5) An assignment of "the contract" or of "all my rights under the contract" or an assignment in similar general terms is an assignment of rights and unless the language or the circumstances (as in an assignment for security) indicate the contrary, it is a delegation of performance of the duties of the assignor and its acceptance by the assignee constitutes a promise by him to perform those duties. This promise is enforceable by either the assignor or the other party to the original contract.

(6) The other party may treat any assignment which delegates performance as creating reasonable grounds for insecurity and may without prejudice to his rights against the assignor demand assurances from the assignee (Section 2–609).

As amended in 1999.

Part 3 General Obligation and Construction of Contract

§ 2–301. General Obligations of Parties.

The obligation of the seller is to transfer and deliver and that of the buyer is to accept and pay in accordance with the contract.

§ 2–302. Unconscionable Contract or Clause.

(1) If the court as a matter of law finds the contract or any clause of the contract to have been unconscionable at the time it was made the court may refuse to enforce the contract, or it may enforce the remainder of the contract without the unconscionable clause, or it may so limit the application of any unconscionable clause as to avoid any unconscionable result.

(2) When it is claimed or appears to the court that the contract or any clause thereof may be unconscionable the parties shall be afforded a reasonable opportunity to present evidence as to its commercial setting, purpose and effect to aid the court in making the determination.

§ 2–303. Allocations or Division of Risks.

Where this Article allocates a risk or a burden as between the parties "unless otherwise agreed", the agreement may not only shift the allocation but may also divide the risk or burden.

§ 2–304. Price Payable in Money, Goods, Realty, or Otherwise.

(1) The price can be made payable in money or otherwise. If it is payable in whole or in part in goods each party is a seller of the goods which he is to transfer.

(2) Even though all or part of the price is payable in an interest in realty the transfer of the goods and the seller's obligations with reference to them are subject to this Article, but not the transfer of the interest in realty or the transferor's obligations in connection therewith.

§ 2–305. Open Price Term.

(1) The parties if they so intend can conclude a contract for sale even though the price is not settled. In such a case the price is a reasonable price at the time for delivery if

(a) nothing is said as to price; or

(b) the price is left to be agreed by the parties and they fail to agree; or

(c) the price is to be fixed in terms of some agreed market or other standard as set or recorded by a third person or agency and it is not so set or recorded.

(2) A price to be fixed by the seller or by the buyer means a price for him to fix in good faith.

(3) When a price left to be fixed otherwise than by agreement of the parties fails to be fixed through fault of one party the other may at his option treat the contract as cancelled or himself fix a reasonable price.

(4) Where, however, the parties intend not to be bound unless the price be fixed or agreed and it is not fixed or agreed there is no contract. In such a case the buyer must return any goods already received or if unable so to do must pay their reasonable value at the time of delivery and the seller must return any portion of the price paid on account.

§ 2–306. Output, Requirements and Exclusive Dealings.

(1) A term which measures the quantity by the output of the seller or the requirements of the buyer means such actual output or requirements as may occur in good faith, except that no quantity unreasonably disproportionate to any stated estimate or in the absence of a stated estimate to any normal or otherwise comparable prior output or requirements may be tendered or demanded.

(2) A lawful agreement by either the seller or the buyer for exclusive dealing in the kind of goods concerned imposes unless otherwise agreed an obligation by the seller to use best efforts to supply the goods and by the buyer to use best efforts to promote their sale.

§ 2–307. Delivery in Single Lot or Several Lots.

Unless otherwise agreed all goods called for by a contract for sale must be tendered in a single delivery and payment is due only on such tender but where the circumstances give either party the right to make or demand delivery in lots the price if it can be apportioned may be demanded for each lot.

§ 2–308. Absence of Specified Place for Delivery.

Unless otherwise agreed

(a) the place for delivery of goods is the seller's place of business or if he has none his residence; but

(b) in a contract for sale of identified goods which to the knowledge of the parties at the time of contracting are in some other place, that place is the place for their delivery; and

(c) documents of title may be delivered through customary banking channels.

§ 2–309. Absence of Specific Time Provisions; Notice of Termination.

(1) The time for shipment or delivery or any other action under a contract if not provided in this Article or agreed upon shall be a reasonable time.

(2) Where the contract provides for successive performances but is indefinite in duration it is valid for a reasonable time but unless otherwise agreed may be terminated at any time by either party.

(3) Termination of a contract by one party except on the happening of an agreed event requires that reasonable notification be received by the other party and an agreement dispensing with notification is invalid if its operation would be unconscionable.

§ 2–310. Open Time for Payment or Running of Credit; Authority to Ship Under Reservation.

Unless otherwise agreed

(a) payment is due at the time and place at which the buyer is to receive the goods even though the place of shipment is the place of delivery; and

(b) if the seller is authorized to send the goods he may ship them under reservation, and may tender the documents of title, but the buyer may inspect the goods after their arrival before payment is due unless such inspection is inconsistent with the terms of the contract (Section 2–513); and

(c) if delivery is authorized and made by way of documents of title otherwise than by subsection (b) then payment is due at the time and place at which the buyer is to receive the documents regardless of where the goods are to be received; and

(d) where the seller is required or authorized to ship the goods on credit the credit period runs from the time of shipment but post-dating the invoice or delaying its dispatch will correspondingly delay the starting of the credit period.

§ 2–311. Options and Cooperation Respecting Performance.

(1) An agreement for sale which is otherwise sufficiently definite (subsection (3) of Section 2–204) to be a contract is not made invalid by the fact that it leaves particulars of performance to be specified by one of the parties. Any such specification must be made in good faith and within limits set by commercial reasonableness.

(2) Unless otherwise agreed specifications relating to assortment of the goods are at the buyer's option and except as otherwise provided in subsections (1)(c) and (3) of Section 2–319 specifications or arrangements relating to shipment are at the seller's option.

(3) Where such specification would materially affect the other party's performance but is not seasonably made or where one party's cooperation is necessary to the agreed performance of the other but is not seasonably forthcoming, the other party in addition to all other remedies

(a) is excused for any resulting delay in his own performance; and

(b) may also either proceed to perform in any reasonable manner or after the time for a material part of his own performance treat the failure to specify or to cooperate as a breach by failure to deliver or accept the goods.

§ 2–312. Warranty of Title and Against Infringement; Buyer's Obligation Against Infringement.

(1) Subject to subsection (2) there is in a contract for sale a warranty by the seller that

(a) the title conveyed shall be good, and its transfer rightful; and

(b) the goods shall be delivered free from any security interest or other lien or encumbrance of which the buyer at the time of contracting has no knowledge.

(2) A warranty under subsection (1) will be excluded or modified only by specific language or by circumstances which give the buyer reason to know that the person selling does not claim title in himself or that he is purporting to sell only such right or title as he or a third person may have.

(3) Unless otherwise agreed a seller who is a merchant regularly dealing in goods of the kind warrants that the goods shall be delivered free of the rightful claim of any third person by way of infringement or the like but a buyer who furnishes specifications to the seller must hold the seller harmless against any such claim which arises out of compliance with the specifications.

§ 2–313. Express Warranties by Affirmation, Promise, Description, Sample.

(1) Express warranties by the seller are created as follows:

(a) Any affirmation of fact or promise made by the seller to the buyer which relates to the goods and becomes part of the basis of the bargain creates an express warranty that the goods shall conform to the affirmation or promise.

(b) Any description of the goods which is made part of the basis of the bargain creates an express warranty that the goods shall conform to the description.

(c) Any sample or model which is made part of the basis of the bargain creates an express warranty that the whole of the goods shall conform to the sample or model.

(2) It is not necessary to the creation of an express warranty that the seller use formal words such as "warrant" or "guarantee" or that he have a specific intention to make a warranty, but an affirmation merely of the value of the goods or a statement purporting to be merely the seller's opinion or commendation of the goods does not create a warranty.

§ 2–314. Implied Warranty: Merchantability; Usage of Trade.

(1) Unless excluded or modified (Section 2–316), a warranty that the goods shall be merchantable is implied in a contract for their sale if the seller is a merchant with respect to goods of that kind. Under this section the serving for value of food or drink to be consumed either on the premises or elsewhere is a sale.

(2) Goods to be merchantable must be at least such as

(a) pass without objection in the trade under the contract description; and

(b) in the case of fungible goods, are of fair average quality within the description; and

(c) are fit for the ordinary purposes for which such goods are used; and

(d) run, within the variations permitted by the agreement, of even kind, quality and quantity within each unit and among all units involved; and

(e) are adequately contained, packaged, and labeled as the agreement may require; and

(f) conform to the promises or affirmations of fact made on the container or label if any.

(3) Unless excluded or modified (Section 2–316) other implied warranties may arise from course of dealing or usage of trade.

§ 2–315. Implied Warranty: Fitness for Particular Purpose.

Where the seller at the time of contracting has reason to know any particular purpose for which the goods are required and that the buyer is relying on the seller's skill or judgment to select or furnish suitable goods, there is unless excluded or modified under the next section an implied warranty that the goods shall be fit for such purpose.

§ 2–316. Exclusion or Modification of Warranties.

(1) Words or conduct relevant to the creation of an express warranty and words or conduct tending to negate or limit warranty shall be construed wherever reasonable as consistent with each other; but subject to the provisions of this Article on parol or extrinsic evidence (Section 2–202) negation or limitation is inoperative to the extent that such construction is unreasonable.

(2) Subject to subsection (3), to exclude or modify the implied warranty of merchantability or any part of it the language must mention merchantability and in case of a writing must be conspicuous, and to exclude or modify any implied warranty of fitness the exclusion must be by a writing and conspicuous. Language to exclude all implied warranties of fitness is sufficient if it states, for example, that "There are no warranties which extend beyond the description on the face hereof."

(3) Notwithstanding subsection (2)

(a) unless the circumstances indicate otherwise, all implied warranties are excluded by expressions like "as is", "with all faults" or other language which in common understanding calls the buyer's attention to the exclusion of warranties and makes plain that there is no implied warranty; and

(b) when the buyer before entering into the contract has examined the goods or the sample or model as fully as he desired or has refused to examine the goods there is no implied warranty with regard to defects which an examination ought in the circumstances to have revealed to him; and

(c) an implied warranty can also be excluded or modified by course of dealing or course of performance or usage of trade.

(4) Remedies for breach of warranty can be limited in accordance with the provisions of this Article on liquidation or limitation of damages and on contractual modification of remedy (Sections 2–718 and 2–719).

§ 2–317. Cumulation and Conflict of Warranties Express or Implied.

Warranties whether express or implied shall be construed as consistent with each other and as cumulative, but if such construction is unreasonable the intention of the parties shall determine which warranty is dominant. In ascertaining that intention the following rules apply:

(a) Exact or technical specifications displace an inconsistent sample or model or general language of description.

(b) A sample from an existing bulk displaces inconsistent general language of description.

(c) Express warranties displace inconsistent implied warranties other than an implied warranty of fitness for a particular purpose.

§ 2–318. Third Party Beneficiaries of Warranties Express or Implied.

Note: If this Act is introduced in the Congress of the United States this section should be omitted. (States to select one alternative.)

Alternative A

A seller's warranty whether express or implied extends to any natural person who is in the family or household of his buyer or who is a guest in his home if it is reasonable to expect that such person may use, consume or be affected by the goods and who is injured in person by breach of the warranty. A seller may not exclude or limit the operation of this section.

Alternative B

A seller's warranty whether express or implied extends to any natural person who may reasonably be expected to use, consume or be affected by the goods and who is injured in person by breach of the warranty. A seller may not exclude or limit the operation of this section.

Alternative C

A seller's warranty whether express or implied extends to any person who may reasonably be expected to use, consume or be affected by the goods and who is injured by breach of the warranty. A seller may not exclude or limit the operation of this section with respect to injury to the person of an individual to whom the warranty extends.

As amended 1966.

§ 2–319. F.O.B. and F.A.S. Terms.

(1) Unless otherwise agreed the term F.O.B. (which means "free on board") at a named place, even though used only in connection with the stated price, is a delivery term under which

(a) when the term is F.O.B. the place of shipment, the seller must at that place ship the goods in the manner provided in this Article (Section 2–504) and bear the expense and risk of putting them into the possession of the carrier; or

(b) when the term is F.O.B. the place of destination, the seller must at his own expense and risk transport the goods to that place and there tender delivery of them in the manner provided in this Article (Section 2–503);

(c) when under either (a) or (b) the term is also F.O.B. vessel, car or other vehicle, the seller must in addition at his own expense and risk load the goods on board. If the term is F.O.B. vessel the buyer must name the vessel and in an appropriate case the seller must comply with the provisions of this Article on the form of bill of lading (Section 2–323).

(2) Unless otherwise agreed the term F.A.S. vessel (which means "free alongside") at a named port, even though used only in connection with the stated price, is a delivery term under which the seller must

(a) at his own expense and risk deliver the goods alongside the vessel in the manner usual in that port or on a dock designated and provided by the buyer; and

(b) obtain and tender a receipt for the goods in exchange for which the carrier is under a duty to issue a bill of lading.

(3) Unless otherwise agreed in any case falling within subsection (1)(a) or (c) or subsection (2) the buyer must seasonably give any needed instructions for making delivery, including when the term is F.A.S. or F.O.B. the loading berth of the vessel and in an appropriate case its name and sailing date. The seller may treat the failure of needed instructions as a failure of cooperation under this Article (Section 2–311). He may also at his option move the goods in any reasonable manner preparatory to delivery or shipment.

(4) Under the term F.O.B. vessel or F.A.S. unless otherwise agreed the buyer must make payment against tender of the required documents and the seller may not tender nor the buyer demand delivery of the goods in substitution for the documents.

§ 2–320. C.I.F. and C. & F. Terms.

(1) The term C.I.F. means that the price includes in a lump sum the cost of the goods and the insurance and freight to the named destination. The term C. & F. or C.F. means that the price so includes cost and freight to the named destination.

(2) Unless otherwise agreed and even though used only in connection with the stated price and destination, the term C.I.F. destination or its equivalent requires the seller at his own expense and risk to

(a) put the goods into the possession of a carrier at the port for shipment and obtain a negotiable bill or bills of lading covering the entire transportation to the named destination; and

(b) load the goods and obtain a receipt from the carrier (which may be contained in the bill of lading) showing that the freight has been paid or provided for; and

(c) obtain a policy or certificate of insurance, including any war risk insurance, of a kind and on terms then current at the port of shipment in the usual amount, in the currency of the contract, shown to cover the same goods covered by the bill of lading and providing for payment of loss to the order of the buyer or for the account of whom it may concern; but the seller may add to the price the amount of the premium for any such war risk insurance; and

(d) prepare an invoice of the goods and procure any other documents required to effect shipment or to comply with the contract; and

(e) forward and tender with commercial promptness all the documents in due form and with any indorsement necessary to perfect the buyer's rights.

(3) Unless otherwise agreed the term C. & F. or its equivalent has the same effect and imposes upon the seller the same obligations and risks as a C.I.F. term except the obligation as to insurance.

(4) Under the term C.I.F. or C. & F. unless otherwise agreed the buyer must make payment against tender of the required documents and the seller may not tender nor the buyer demand delivery of the goods in substitution for the documents.

§ 2–321. C.I.F. or C. & F.: "Net Landed Weights"; "Payment on Arrival"; Warranty of Condition on Arrival.

Under a contract containing a term C.I.F. or C. & F.

(1) Where the price is based on or is to be adjusted according to "net landed weights", "delivered weights", "out turn" quantity or quality or the like, unless otherwise agreed the seller must reasonably estimate the price. The payment due on tender of the documents called for by the contract is the amount so estimated, but after final adjustment of the price a settlement must be made with commercial promptness.

(2) An agreement described in subsection (1) or any warranty of quality or condition of the goods on arrival places upon the seller the risk of ordinary deterioration, shrinkage and the like in transportation but has no effect on the place or time of identification to the contract for sale or delivery or on the passing of the risk of loss.

(3) Unless otherwise agreed where the contract provides for payment on or after arrival of the goods the seller must before payment allow such preliminary inspection as is feasible; but if the goods are lost delivery of the documents and payment are due when the goods should have arrived.

§ 2–322. Delivery "Ex-Ship".

(1) Unless otherwise agreed a term for delivery of goods "exship" (which means from the carrying vessel) or in equivalent

language is not restricted to a particular ship and requires delivery from a ship which has reached a place at the named port of destination where goods of the kind are usually discharged.

(2) Under such a term unless otherwise agreed

(a) the seller must discharge all liens arising out of the carriage and furnish the buyer with a direction which puts the carrier under a duty to deliver the goods; and

(b) the risk of loss does not pass to the buyer until the goods leave the ship's tackle or are otherwise properly unloaded.

§ 2–323. Form of Bill of Lading Required in Overseas Shipment; "Overseas".

(1) Where the contract contemplates overseas shipment and contains a term C.I.F. or C. & F. or F.O.B. vessel, the seller unless otherwise agreed must obtain a negotiable bill of lading stating that the goods have been loaded on board or, in the case of a term C.I.F. or C. & F., received for shipment.

(2) Where in a case within subsection (1) a bill of lading has been issued in a set of parts, unless otherwise agreed if the documents are not to be sent from abroad the buyer may demand tender of the full set; otherwise only one part of the bill of lading need be tendered. Even if the agreement expressly requires a full set

(a) due tender of a single part is acceptable within the provisions of this Article on cure of improper delivery (subsection (1) of Section 2–508); and

(b) even though the full set is demanded, if the documents are sent from abroad the person tendering an incomplete set may nevertheless require payment upon furnishing an indemnity which the buyer in good faith deems adequate.

(3) A shipment by water or by air or a contract contemplating such shipment is "overseas" insofar as by usage of trade or agreement it is subject to the commercial, financing or shipping practices characteristic of international deep water commerce.

§ 2–324. "No Arrival, No Sale" Term.

Under a term "no arrival, no sale" or terms of like meaning, unless otherwise agreed,

(a) the seller must properly ship conforming goods and if they arrive by any means he must tender them on arrival but he assumes no obligation that the goods will arrive unless he has caused the non-arrival; and

(b) where without fault of the seller the goods are in part lost or have so deteriorated as no longer to conform to the contract or arrive after the contract time, the buyer may proceed as if there had been casualty to identified goods (Section 2–613).

§ 2–325. "Letter of Credit" Term; "Confirmed Credit".

(1) Failure of the buyer seasonably to furnish an agreed letter of credit is a breach of the contract for sale.

(2) The delivery to seller of a proper letter of credit suspends the buyer's obligation to pay. If the letter of credit is dishonored, the seller may on seasonable notification to the buyer require payment directly from him.

(3) Unless otherwise agreed the term "letter of credit" or "banker's credit" in a contract for sale means an irrevocable credit issued by a financing agency of good repute and, where the shipment is overseas, of good international repute. The term "confirmed credit" means that the credit must also carry the direct obligation of such an agency which does business in the seller's financial market.

§ 2–326. Sale on Approval and Sale or Return; Rights of Creditors.

(1) Unless otherwise agreed, if delivered goods may be returned by the buyer even though they conform to the contract, the transaction is

(a) a "sale on approval" if the goods are delivered primarily for use, and

(b) a "sale or return" if the goods are delivered primarily for resale.

(2) Goods held on approval are not subject to the claims of the buyer's creditors until acceptance; goods held on sale or return are subject to such claims while in the buyer's possession.

(3) Any "or return" term of a contract for sale is to be treated as a separate contract for sale within the statute of frauds section of this Article (Section 2–201) and as contradicting the sale aspect of the contract within the provisions of this Article or on parol or extrinsic evidence (Section 2–202).

As amended in 1999.

§ 2–327. Special Incidents of Sale on Approval and Sale or Return.

(1) Under a sale on approval unless otherwise agreed

(a) although the goods are identified to the contract the risk of loss and the title do not pass to the buyer until acceptance; and

(b) use of the goods consistent with the purpose of trial is not acceptance but failure seasonably to notify the seller of election to return the goods is acceptance, and if the goods conform to the contract acceptance of any part is acceptance of the whole; and

(c) after due notification of election to return, the return is at the seller's risk and expense but a merchant buyer must follow any reasonable instructions.

(2) Under a sale or return unless otherwise agreed

(a) the option to return extends to the whole or any commercial unit of the goods while in substantially their original condition, but must be exercised seasonably; and

(b) the return is at the buyer's risk and expense.

§ 2–328. Sale by Auction.

(1) In a sale by auction if goods are put up in lots each lot is the subject of a separate sale.

(2) A sale by auction is complete when the auctioneer so announces by the fall of the hammer or in other customary manner. Where a bid is made while the hammer is falling in acceptance of a prior bid the auctioneer may in his discretion reopen the bidding or declare the goods sold under the bid on which the hammer was falling.

(3) Such a sale is with reserve unless the goods are in explicit terms put up without reserve. In an auction with reserve the auctioneer may withdraw the goods at any time until he announces completion of the sale. In an auction without reserve, after the auctioneer calls for bids on an article or lot, that article or lot cannot be withdrawn unless no bid is made within a reasonable time. In either case a bidder may retract his bid until the auctioneer's announcement of completion of the sale, but a bidder's retraction does not revive any previous bid.

(4) If the auctioneer knowingly receives a bid on the seller's behalf or the seller makes or procures such as bid, and notice has not been given that liberty for such bidding is reserved, the buyer may at his option avoid the sale or take the goods at the price of the last good faith bid prior to the completion of the sale. This subsection shall not apply to any bid at a forced sale.

Part 4 Title, Creditors and Good Faith Purchasers

§ 2–401. Passing of Title; Reservation for Security; Limited Application of This Section.

Each provision of this Article with regard to the rights, obligations and remedies of the seller, the buyer, purchasers or other third parties applies irrespective of title to the goods except where the provision refers to such title. Insofar as situations are not covered by the other provisions of this Article and matters concerning title became material the following rules apply:

(1) Title to goods cannot pass under a contract for sale prior to their identification to the contract (Section 2–501), and unless otherwise explicitly agreed the buyer acquires by their identification a special property as limited by this Act. Any retention or reservation by the seller of the title (property) in goods shipped or delivered to the buyer is limited in effect to a reservation of a security interest. Subject to these provisions and to the provisions of the Article on Secured Transactions (Article 9), title to goods passes from the seller to the buyer in any manner and on any conditions explicitly agreed on by the parties.

(2) Unless otherwise explicitly agreed title passes to the buyer at the time and place at which the seller completes his performance with reference to the physical delivery of the goods, despite any reservation of a security interest and even though a document of title is to be delivered at a different time or place; and in particular and despite any reservation of a security interest by the bill of lading

(a) if the contract requires or authorizes the seller to send the goods to the buyer but does not require him to deliver them at destination, title passes to the buyer at the time and place of shipment; but

(b) if the contract requires delivery at destination, title passes on tender there.

(3) Unless otherwise explicitly agreed where delivery is to be made without moving the goods,

(a) if the seller is to deliver a document of title, title passes at the time when and the place where he delivers such documents; or

(b) if the goods are at the time of contracting already identified and no documents are to be delivered, title passes at the time and place of contracting.

(4) A rejection or other refusal by the buyer to receive or retain the goods, whether or not justified, or a justified revocation of acceptance revests title to the goods in the seller. Such revesting occurs by operation of law and is not a "sale".

§ 2–402. Rights of Seller's Creditors Against Sold Goods.

(1) Except as provided in subsections (2) and (3), rights of unsecured creditors of the seller with respect to goods which have been identified to a contract for sale are subject to the buyer's rights to recover the goods under this Article (Sections 2–502 and 2–716).

(2) A creditor of the seller may treat a sale or an identification of goods to a contract for sale as void if as against him a retention of possession by the seller is fraudulent under any rule of law of the state where the goods are situated, except that retention of possession in good faith and current course of trade by a merchant-seller for a commercially reasonable time after a sale or identification is not fraudulent.

(3) Nothing in this Article shall be deemed to impair the rights of creditors of the seller

(a) under the provisions of the Article on Secured Transactions (Article 9); or

(b) where identification to the contract or delivery is made not in current course of trade but in satisfaction of or as security for a pre-existing claim for money, security or the like and is made under circumstances which under any rule of law of the state where the goods are situated would apart from this Article constitute the transaction a fraudulent transfer or voidable preference.

§ 2–403. Power to Transfer; Good Faith Purchase of Goods; "Entrusting".

(1) A purchaser of goods acquires all title which his transferor had or had power to transfer except that a purchaser of a limited interest acquires rights only to the extent of the interest purchased. A person with voidable title has power to transfer a good title to a good faith purchaser for value. When goods have been delivered under a transaction of purchase the purchaser has such power even though

(a) the transferor was deceived as to the identity of the purchaser, or

(b) the delivery was in exchange for a check which is later dishonored, or

(c) it was agreed that the transaction was to be a "cash sale", or

(d) the delivery was procured through fraud punishable as larcenous under the criminal law.

(2) Any entrusting of possession of goods to a merchant who deals in goods of that kind gives him power to transfer all rights of the entruster to a buyer in ordinary course of business.

(3) "Entrusting" includes any delivery and any acquiescence in retention of possession regardless of any condition expressed between the parties to the delivery or acquiescence and regardless of whether the procurement of the entrusting or the possessor's disposition of the goods have been such as to be larcenous under the criminal law.

(4) The rights of other purchasers of goods and of lien creditors are governed by the Articles on Secured Transactions (Article 9), Bulk Transfers (Article 6) and Documents of Title (Article 7).
As amended in 1988.

Part 5 Performance

§ 2–501. Insurable Interest in Goods; Manner of Identification of Goods.

(1) The buyer obtains a special property and an insurable interest in goods by identification of existing goods as goods to which the contract refers even though the goods so identified are non-conforming and he has an option to return or reject them. Such identification can be made at any time and in any manner explicitly agreed to by the parties. In the absence of explicit agreement identification occurs

(a) when the contract is made if it is for the sale of goods already existing and identified;

(b) if the contract is for the sale of future goods other than those described in paragraph (c), when goods are shipped, marked or otherwise designated by the seller as goods to which the contract refers;

(c) when the crops are planted or otherwise become growing crops or the young are conceived if the contract is for the sale of unborn young to be born within twelve months after contracting or for the sale of crops to be harvested within twelve months or the next normal harvest season after contracting whichever is longer.

(2) The seller retains an insurable interest in goods so long as title to or any security interest in the goods remains in him and where the identification is by the seller alone he may until default or insolvency or notification to the buyer that the identification is final substitute other goods for those identified.

(3) Nothing in this section impairs any insurable interest recognized under any other statute or rule of law.

§ 2–502. Buyer's Right to Goods on Seller's Insolvency.

(1) Subject to subsections (2) and (3) and even though the goods have not been shipped a buyer who has paid a part or all of the price of goods in which he has a special property under the provisions of the immediately preceding section may on making and keeping good a tender of any unpaid portion of their price recover them from the seller if:

(a) in the case of goods bought for personal, family, or household purposes, the seller repudiates or fails to deliver as required by the contract; or

(b) in all cases, the seller becomes insolvent within ten days after receipt of the first installment on their price.

(2) The buyer's right to recover the goods under subsection (1)(a) vests upon acquisition of a special property, even if the seller had not then repudiated or failed to deliver.

(3) If the identification creating his special property has been made by the buyer he acquires the right to recover the goods only if they conform to the contract for sale.
As amended in 1999.

§ 2–503. Manner of Seller's Tender of Delivery.

(1) Tender of delivery requires that the seller put and hold conforming goods at the buyer's disposition and give the buyer any notification reasonably necessary to enable him to take delivery. The manner, time and place for tender are determined by the agreement and this Article, and in particular

(a) tender must be at a reasonable hour, and if it is of goods they must be kept available for the period reasonably necessary to enable the buyer to take possession; but

(b) unless otherwise agreed the buyer must furnish facilities reasonably suited to the receipt of the goods.

(2) Where the case is within the next section respecting shipment tender requires that the seller comply with its provisions.

(3) Where the seller is required to deliver at a particular destination tender requires that he comply with subsection (1) and also in any appropriate case tender documents as described in subsections (4) and (5) of this section.

(4) Where goods are in the possession of a bailee and are to be delivered without being moved

(a) tender requires that the seller either tender a negotiable document of title covering such goods or procure acknowledgment by the bailee of the buyer's right to possession of the goods; but

(b) tender to the buyer of a non-negotiable document of title or of a written direction to the bailee to deliver is sufficient tender unless the buyer seasonably objects, and receipt by the bailee of notification of the buyer's rights fixes those rights as against the bailee and all third persons; but risk of loss of the goods and of any failure by the bailee to honor the non-negotiable document of title or to obey the direction remains on the seller until the buyer has had a reasonable time to present the document or direction, and a refusal by the bailee to honor the document or to obey the direction defeats the tender.

(5) Where the contract requires the seller to deliver documents

(a) he must tender all such documents in correct form, except as provided in this Article with respect to bills of lading in a set (subsection (2) of Section 2–323); and

(b) tender through customary banking channels is sufficient and dishonor of a draft accompanying the documents constitutes non-acceptance or rejection.

§ 2–504. Shipment by Seller.

Where the seller is required or authorized to send the goods to the buyer and the contract does not require him to deliver them at a particular destination, then unless otherwise agreed he must

(a) put the goods in the possession of such a carrier and make such a contract for their transportation as may be reasonable having regard to the nature of the goods and other circumstances of the case; and

(b) obtain and promptly deliver or tender in due form any document necessary to enable the buyer to obtain possession of the goods or otherwise required by the agreement or by usage of trade; and

(c) promptly notify the buyer of the shipment.

Failure to notify the buyer under paragraph (c) or to make a proper contract under paragraph (a) is a ground for rejection only if material delay or loss ensues.

§ 2–505. Seller's Shipment under Reservation.

(1) Where the seller has identified goods to the contract by or before shipment:

(a) his procurement of a negotiable bill of lading to his own order or otherwise reserves in him a security interest in the goods. His procurement of the bill to the order of a financing agency or of the buyer indicates in addition only the seller's expectation of transferring that interest to the person named.

(b) a non-negotiable bill of lading to himself or his nominee reserves possession of the goods as security but except in a case of conditional delivery (subsection (2) of Section 2–507) a non-negotiable bill of lading naming the buyer as consignee reserves no security interest even though the seller retains possession of the bill of lading.

(2) When shipment by the seller with reservation of a security interest is in violation of the contract for sale it constitutes an improper contract for transportation within the preceding section but impairs neither the rights given to the buyer by shipment and identification of the goods to the contract nor the seller's powers as a holder of a negotiable document.

§ 2–506. Rights of Financing Agency.

(1) A financing agency by paying or purchasing for value a draft which relates to a shipment of goods acquires to the extent of the payment or purchase and in addition to its own rights under the draft and any document of title securing it any rights of the shipper in the goods including the right to stop delivery and the shipper's right to have the draft honored by the buyer.

(2) The right to reimbursement of a financing agency which has in good faith honored or purchased the draft under commitment to or authority from the buyer is not impaired by subsequent discovery of defects with reference to any relevant document which was apparently regular on its face.

§ 2–507. Effect of Seller's Tender; Delivery on Condition.

(1) Tender of delivery is a condition to the buyer's duty to accept the goods and, unless otherwise agreed, to his duty to pay for them. Tender entitles the seller to acceptance of the goods and to payment according to the contract.

(2) Where payment is due and demanded on the delivery to the buyer of goods or documents of title, his right as against the seller to retain or dispose of them is conditional upon his making the payment due.

§ 2–508. Cure by Seller of Improper Tender or Delivery; Replacement.

(1) Where any tender or delivery by the seller is rejected because non-conforming and the time for performance has not yet expired, the seller may seasonably notify the buyer of his intention to cure and may then within the contract time make a conforming delivery.

(2) Where the buyer rejects a non-conforming tender which the seller had reasonable grounds to believe would be acceptable with or without money allowance the seller may if he seasonably notifies the buyer have a further reasonable time to substitute a conforming tender.

§ 2–509. Risk of Loss in the Absence of Breach.

(1) Where the contract requires or authorizes the seller to ship the goods by carrier

(a) if it does not require him to deliver them at a particular destination, the risk of loss passes to the buyer when the goods are duly delivered to the carrier even though the shipment is under reservation (Section 2–505); but

(b) if it does require him to deliver them at a particular destination and the goods are there duly tendered while in the possession of the carrier, the risk of loss passes to the buyer when the goods are there duly so tendered as to enable the buyer to take delivery.

(2) Where the goods are held by a bailee to be delivered without being moved, the risk of loss passes to the buyer

(a) on his receipt of a negotiable document of title covering the goods; or

(b) on acknowledgment by the bailee of the buyer's right to possession of the goods; or

(c) after his receipt of a non-negotiable document of title or other written direction to deliver, as provided in subsection (4)(b) of Section 2–503.

(3) In any case not within subsection (1) or (2), the risk of loss passes to the buyer on his receipt of the goods if the seller is a merchant; otherwise the risk passes to the buyer on tender of delivery.

(4) The provisions of this section are subject to contrary agreement of the parties and to the provisions of this Article on sale on approval (Section 2–327) and on effect of breach on risk of loss (Section 2–510).

§ 2–510. Effect of Breach on Risk of Loss.

(1) Where a tender or delivery of goods so fails to conform to the contract as to give a right of rejection the risk of their loss remains on the seller until cure or acceptance.

(2) Where the buyer rightfully revokes acceptance he may to the extent of any deficiency in his effective insurance coverage treat the risk of loss as having rested on the seller from the beginning.

(3) Where the buyer as to conforming goods already identified to the contract for sale repudiates or is otherwise in breach before risk of their loss has passed to him, the seller may to the extent of any deficiency in his effective insurance coverage treat the risk of loss as resting on the buyer for a commercially reasonable time.

§ 2–511. Tender of Payment by Buyer; Payment by Check.

(1) Unless otherwise agreed tender of payment is a condition to the seller's duty to tender and complete any delivery.

(2) Tender of payment is sufficient when made by any means or in any manner current in the ordinary course of business unless the seller demands payment in legal tender and gives any extension of time reasonably necessary to procure it.

(3) Subject to the provisions of this Act on the effect of an instrument on an obligation (Section 3–310), payment by check is conditional and is defeated as between the parties by dishonor of the check on due presentment.

As amended in 1994.

§ 2–512. Payment by Buyer Before Inspection.

(1) Where the contract requires payment before inspection non-conformity of the goods does not excuse the buyer from so making payment unless

    (a) the non-conformity appears without inspection; or

    (b) despite tender of the required documents the circumstances would justify injunction against honor under this Act (Section 5–109(b)).

(2) Payment pursuant to subsection (1) does not constitute an acceptance of goods or impair the buyer's right to inspect or any of his remedies.

As amended in 1995.

§ 2–513. Buyer's Right to Inspection of Goods.

(1) Unless otherwise agreed and subject to subsection (3), where goods are tendered or delivered or identified to the contract for sale, the buyer has a right before payment or acceptance to inspect them at any reasonable place and time and in any reasonable manner. When the seller is required or authorized to send the goods to the buyer, the inspection may be after their arrival.

(2) Expenses of inspection must be borne by the buyer but may be recovered from the seller if the goods do not conform and are rejected.

(3) Unless otherwise agreed and subject to the provisions of this Article on C.I.F. contracts (subsection (3) of Section 2–321), the buyer is not entitled to inspect the goods before payment of the price when the contract provides

    (a) for delivery "C.O.D." or on other like terms; or

    (b) for payment against documents of title, except where such payment is due only after the goods are to become available for inspection.

(4) A place or method of inspection fixed by the parties is presumed to be exclusive but unless otherwise expressly agreed it does not postpone identification or shift the place for delivery or for passing the risk of loss. If compliance becomes impossible, inspection shall be as provided in this section unless the place or method fixed was clearly intended as an indispensable condition failure of which avoids the contract.

§ 2–514. When Documents Deliverable on Acceptance; When on Payment.

Unless otherwise agreed documents against which a draft is drawn are to be delivered to the drawee on acceptance of the draft if it is payable more than three days after presentment; otherwise, only on payment.

§ 2–515. Preserving Evidence of Goods in Dispute.

In furtherance of the adjustment of any claim or dispute

    (a) either party on reasonable notification to the other and for the purpose of ascertaining the facts and preserving evidence has the right to inspect, test and sample the goods including such of them as may be in the possession or control of the other; and

    (b) the parties may agree to a third party inspection or survey to determine the conformity or condition of the goods and may agree that the findings shall be binding upon them in any subsequent litigation or adjustment.

Part 6 Breach, Repudiation and Excuse

§ 2–601. Buyer's Rights on Improper Delivery.

Subject to the provisions of this Article on breach in installment contracts (Section 2–612) and unless otherwise agreed under the sections on contractual limitations of remedy (Sections 2–718 and 2–719), if the goods or the tender of delivery fail in any respect to conform to the contract, the buyer may

    (a) reject the whole; or

    (b) accept the whole; or

(c) accept any commercial unit or units and reject the rest.

§ 2–602. Manner and Effect of Rightful Rejection.

(1) Rejection of goods must be within a reasonable time after their delivery or tender. It is ineffective unless the buyer seasonably notifies the seller.

(2) Subject to the provisions of the two following sections on rejected goods (Sections 2–603 and 2–604),

(a) after rejection any exercise of ownership by the buyer with respect to any commercial unit is wrongful as against the seller; and

(b) if the buyer has before rejection taken physical possession of goods in which he does not have a security interest under the provisions of this Article (subsection (3) of Section 2–711), he is under a duty after rejection to hold them with reasonable care at the seller's disposition for a time sufficient to permit the seller to remove them; but

(c) the buyer has no further obligations with regard to goods rightfully rejected.

(3) The seller's rights with respect to goods wrongfully rejected are governed by the provisions of this Article on Seller's remedies in general (Section 2–703).

§ 2–603. Merchant Buyer's Duties as to Rightfully Rejected Goods.

(1) Subject to any security interest in the buyer (subsection (3) of Section 2–711), when the seller has no agent or place of business at the market of rejection a merchant buyer is under a duty after rejection of goods in his possession or control to follow any reasonable instructions received from the seller with respect to the goods and in the absence of such instructions to make reasonable efforts to sell them for the seller's account if they are perishable or threaten to decline in value speedily. Instructions are not reasonable if on demand indemnity for expenses is not forthcoming.

(2) When the buyer sells goods under subsection (1), he is entitled to reimbursement from the seller or out of the proceeds for reasonable expenses of caring for and selling them, and if the expenses include no selling commission then to such commission as is usual in the trade or if there is none to a reasonable sum not exceeding ten per cent on the gross proceeds.

(3) In complying with this section the buyer is held only to good faith and good faith conduct hereunder is neither acceptance nor conversion nor the basis of an action for damages.

§ 2–604. Buyer's Options as to Salvage of Rightfully Rejected Goods.

Subject to the provisions of the immediately preceding section on perishables if the seller gives no instructions within a reasonable time after notification of rejection the buyer may store the rejected goods for the seller's account or reship them to him or resell them for the seller's account with reimbursement as provided in the preceding section. Such action is not acceptance or conversion.

§ 2–605. Waiver of Buyer's Objections by Failure to Particularize.

(1) The buyer's failure to state in connection with rejection a particular defect which is ascertainable by reasonable inspection precludes him from relying on the unstated defect to justify rejection or to establish breach

(a) where the seller could have cured it if stated seasonably; or

(b) between merchants when the seller has after rejection made a request in writing for a full and final written statement of all defects on which the buyer proposes to rely.

(2) Payment against documents made without reservation of rights precludes recovery of the payment for defects apparent on the face of the documents.

§ 2–606. What Constitutes Acceptance of Goods.

(1) Acceptance of goods occurs when the buyer

(a) after a reasonable opportunity to inspect the goods signifies to the seller that the goods are conforming or that he will take or retain them in spite of their nonconformity; or

(b) fails to make an effective rejection (subsection (1) of Section 2–602), but such acceptance does not occur until the buyer has had a reasonable opportunity to inspect them; or

(c) does any act inconsistent with the seller's ownership; but if such act is wrongful as against the seller it is an acceptance only if ratified by him.

(2) Acceptance of a part of any commercial unit is acceptance of that entire unit.

§ 2–607. Effect of Acceptance; Notice of Breach; Burden of Establishing Breach After Acceptance; Notice of Claim or Litigation to Person Answerable Over.

(1) The buyer must pay at the contract rate for any goods accepted.

(2) Acceptance of goods by the buyer precludes rejection of the goods accepted and if made with knowledge of a nonconformity cannot be revoked because of it unless the acceptance was on the reasonable assumption that the nonconformity would be seasonably cured but acceptance does not of itself impair any other remedy provided by this Article for non-conformity.

(3) Where a tender has been accepted

(a) the buyer must within a reasonable time after he discovers or should have discovered any breach notify the seller of breach or be barred from any remedy; and

(b) if the claim is one for infringement or the like (subsection (3) of Section 2–312) and the buyer is sued as a result of such a breach he must so notify the seller within a reasonable time after he receives notice of the litigation or be barred from any remedy over for liability established by the litigation.

(4) The burden is on the buyer to establish any breach with respect to the goods accepted.

(5) Where the buyer is sued for breach of a warranty or other obligation for which his seller is answerable over

(a) he may give his seller written notice of the litigation. If the notice states that the seller may come in and defend and that if the seller does not do so he will be bound in any action against him by his buyer by any determination of fact common to the two litigations, then unless the seller after seasonable receipt of the notice does come in and defend he is so bound.

(b) if the claim is one for infringement or the like (subsection (3) of Section 2–312) the original seller may demand in writing that his buyer turn over to him control of the litigation including settlement or else be barred from any remedy over and if he also agrees to bear all expense and to satisfy any adverse judgment, then unless the buyer after seasonable receipt of the demand does turn over control the buyer is so barred.

(6) The provisions of subsections (3), (4) and (5) apply to any obligation of a buyer to hold the seller harmless against infringement or the like (subsection (3) of Section 2–312).

§ 2–608. Revocation of Acceptance in Whole or in Part.

(1) The buyer may revoke his acceptance of a lot or commercial unit whose non-conformity substantially impairs its value to him if he has accepted it

(a) on the reasonable assumption that its nonconformity would be cured and it has not been seasonably cured; or

(b) without discovery of such non-conformity if his acceptance was reasonably induced either by the difficulty of discovery before acceptance or by the seller's assurances.

(2) Revocation of acceptance must occur within a reasonable time after the buyer discovers or should have discovered the ground for it and before any substantial change in condition of the goods which is not caused by their own defects. It is not effective until the buyer notifies the seller of it.

(3) A buyer who so revokes has the same rights and duties with regard to the goods involved as if he had rejected them.

§ 2–609. Right to Adequate Assurance of Performance.

(1) A contract for sale imposes an obligation on each party that the other's expectation of receiving due performance will not be impaired. When reasonable grounds for insecurity arise with respect to the performance of either party the other may in writing demand adequate assurance of due performance and until he receives such assurance may if commercially reasonable suspend any performance for which he has not already received the agreed return.

(2) Between merchants the reasonableness of grounds for insecurity and the adequacy of any assurance offered shall be determined according to commercial standards.

(3) Acceptance of any improper delivery or payment does not prejudice the party's right to demand adequate assurance of future performance.

(4) After receipt of a justified demand failure to provide within a reasonable time not exceeding thirty days such assurance of due performance as is adequate under the circumstances of the particular case is a repudiation of the contract.

§ 2–610. Anticipatory Repudiation.

When either party repudiates the contract with respect to a performance not yet due the loss of which will substantially impair the value of the contract to the other, the aggrieved party may

(a) for a commercially reasonable time await performance by the repudiating party; or

(b) resort to any remedy for breach (Section 2–703 or Section 2–711), even though he has notified the repudiating party that he would await the latter's performance and has urged retraction; and

(c) in either case suspend his own performance or proceed in accordance with the provisions of this Article on the seller's right to identify goods to the contract notwithstanding breach or to salvage unfinished goods (Section 2–704).

§ 2–611. Retraction of Anticipatory Repudiation.

(1) Until the repudiating party's next performance is due he can retract his repudiation unless the aggrieved party has since the repudiation cancelled or materially changed his position or otherwise indicated that he considers the repudiation final.

(2) Retraction may be by any method which clearly indicates to the aggrieved party that the repudiating party intends to perform, but must include any assurance justifiably demanded under the provisions of this Article (Section 2–609).

(3) Retraction reinstates the repudiating party's rights under the contract with due excuse and allowance to the aggrieved party for any delay occasioned by the repudiation.

§ 2–612. "Installment Contract"; Breach.

(1) An "installment contract" is one which requires or authorizes the delivery of goods in separate lots to be separately accepted, even though the contract contains a clause "each delivery is a separate contract" or its equivalent.

(2) The buyer may reject any installment which is nonconforming if the non-conformity substantially impairs the value of that installment and cannot be cured or if the non-conformity is a defect in the required documents; but if the non-conformity does not fall within subsection (3) and the seller gives adequate assurance of its cure the buyer must accept that installment.

(3) Whenever non-conformity or default with respect to one or more installments substantially impairs the value of the whole contract there is a breach of the whole. But the aggrieved party reinstates the contract if he accepts a non-conforming installment without seasonably notifying of cancellation or if he brings an action with respect only to past installments or demands performance as to future installments.

§ 2–613. Casualty to Identified Goods.

Where the contract requires for its performance goods identified when the contract is made, and the goods suffer casualty without fault of either party before the risk of loss passes to the buyer, or in a proper case under a "no arrival, no sale" term (Section 2–324) then

(a) if the loss is total the contract is avoided; and

(b) if the loss is partial or the goods have so deteriorated as no longer to conform to the contract the buyer may nevertheless demand inspection and at his option either treat the contract as voided or accept the goods with due allowance from the contract price for the deterioration or the deficiency in quantity but without further right against the seller.

§ 2–614. Substituted Performance.

(1) Where without fault of either party the agreed berthing, loading, or unloading facilities fail or an agreed type of carrier becomes unavailable or the agreed manner of delivery otherwise becomes commercially impracticable but a commercially reasonable substitute is available, such substitute performance must be tendered and accepted.

(2) If the agreed means or manner of payment fails because of domestic or foreign governmental regulation, the seller may withhold or stop delivery unless the buyer provides a means or manner of payment which is commercially a substantial equivalent. If delivery has already been taken, payment by the means or in the manner provided by the regulation discharges the buyer's obligation unless the regulation is discriminatory, oppressive or predatory.

§ 2–615. Excuse by Failure of Presupposed Conditions.

Except so far as a seller may have assumed a greater obligation and subject to the preceding section on substituted performance:

(a) Delay in delivery or non-delivery in whole or in part by a seller who complies with paragraphs (b) and (c) is not a breach of his duty under a contract for sale if performance as agreed has been made impracticable by the occurrence of a contingency the nonoccurrence of which was a basic assumption on which the contract was made or by compliance in good faith with any applicable foreign or domestic governmental regulation or order whether or not it later proves to be invalid.

(b) Where the causes mentioned in paragraph (a) affect only a part of the seller's capacity to perform, he must allo-

cate production and deliveries among his customers but may at his option include regular customers not then under contract as well as his own requirements for further manufacture. He may so allocate in any manner which is fair and reasonable.

(c) The seller must notify the buyer seasonably that there will be delay or non-delivery and, when allocation is required under paragraph (b), of the estimated quota thus made available for the buyer.

§ 2–616. Procedure on Notice Claiming Excuse.

(1) Where the buyer receives notification of a material or indefinite delay or an allocation justified under the preceding section he may by written notification to the seller as to any delivery concerned, and where the prospective deficiency substantially impairs the value of the whole contract under the provisions of this Article relating to breach of installment contracts (Section 2–612), then also as to the whole,

(a) terminate and thereby discharge any unexecuted portion of the contract; or

(b) modify the contract by agreeing to take his available quota in substitution.

(2) If after receipt of such notification from the seller the buyer fails so to modify the contract within a reasonable time not exceeding thirty days the contract lapses with respect to any deliveries affected.

(3) The provisions of this section may not be negated by agreement except in so far as the seller has assumed a greater obligation under the preceding section.

Part 7 Remedies

§ 2–701. Remedies for Breach of Collateral Contracts Not Impaired.

Remedies for breach of any obligation or promise collateral or ancillary to a contract for sale are not impaired by the provisions of this Article.

§ 2–702. Seller's Remedies on Discovery of Buyer's Insolvency.

(1) Where the seller discovers the buyer to be insolvent he may refuse delivery except for cash including payment for all goods theretofore delivered under the contract, and stop delivery under this Article (Section 2–705).

(2) Where the seller discovers that the buyer has received goods on credit while insolvent he may reclaim the goods upon demand made within ten days after the receipt, but if misrepresentation of solvency has been made to the particular seller in writing within three months before delivery the ten day limitation does not apply. Except as provided in this subsection the seller may not base a right to reclaim goods on the buyer's fraudulent or innocent misrepresentation of solvency or of intent to pay.

(3) The seller's right to reclaim under subsection (2) is subject to the rights of a buyer in ordinary course or other good faith purchaser under this Article (Section 2–403). Successful reclamation of goods excludes all other remedies with respect to them.

§ 2–703. Seller's Remedies in General.

Where the buyer wrongfully rejects or revokes acceptance of goods or fails to make a payment due on or before delivery or repudiates with respect to a part or the whole, then with respect to any goods directly affected and, if the breach is of the whole contract (Section 2–612), then also with respect to the whole undelivered balance, the aggrieved seller may

> (a) withhold delivery of such goods;
>
> (b) stop delivery by any bailee as hereafter provided (Section 2–705);
>
> (c) proceed under the next section respecting goods still unidentified to the contract;
>
> (d) resell and recover damages as hereafter provided (Section 2–706);
>
> (e) recover damages for non-acceptance (Section 2–708) or in a proper case the price (Section 2–709);
>
> (f) cancel.

§ 2–704. Seller's Right to Identify Goods to the Contract Notwithstanding Breach or to Salvage Unfinished Goods.

(1) An aggrieved seller under the preceding section may

> (a) identify to the contract conforming goods not already identified if at the time he learned of the breach they are in his possession or control;
>
> (b) treat as the subject of resale goods which have demonstrably been intended for the particular contract even though those goods are unfinished.

(2) Where the goods are unfinished an aggrieved seller may in the exercise of reasonable commercial judgment for the purposes of avoiding loss and of effective realization either complete the manufacture and wholly identify the goods to the contract or cease manufacture and resell for scrap or salvage value or proceed in any other reasonable manner.

§ 2–705. Seller's Stoppage of Delivery in Transit or Otherwise.

(1) The seller may stop delivery of goods in the possession of a carrier or other bailee when he discovers the buyer to be insolvent (Section 2–702) and may stop delivery of carload, truckload, planeload or larger shipments of express or freight when the buyer repudiates or fails to make a payment due before delivery or if for any other reason the seller has a right to withhold or reclaim the goods.

(2) As against such buyer the seller may stop delivery until

> (a) receipt of the goods by the buyer; or
>
> (b) acknowledgment to the buyer by any bailee of the goods except a carrier that the bailee holds the goods for the buyer; or

> (c) such acknowledgment to the buyer by a carrier by reshipment or as warehouseman; or
>
> (d) negotiation to the buyer of any negotiable document of title covering the goods.

(3) (a) To stop delivery the seller must so notify as to enable the bailee by reasonable diligence to prevent delivery of the goods.

> (b) After such notification the bailee must hold and deliver the goods according to the directions of the seller but the seller is liable to the bailee for any ensuing charges or damages.
>
> (c) If a negotiable document of title has been issued for goods the bailee is not obliged to obey a notification to stop until surrender of the document.
>
> (d) A carrier who has issued a non-negotiable bill of lading is not obliged to obey a notification to stop received from a person other than the consignor.

§ 2–706. Seller's Resale Including Contract for Resale.

(1) Under the conditions stated in Section 2–703 on seller's remedies, the seller may resell the goods concerned or the undelivered balance thereof. Where the resale is made in good faith and in a commercially reasonable manner the seller may recover the difference between the resale price and the contract price together with any incidental damages allowed under the provisions of this Article (Section 2–710), but less expenses saved in consequence of the buyer's breach.

(2) Except as otherwise provided in subsection (3) or unless otherwise agreed resale may be at public or private sale including sale by way of one or more contracts to sell or of identification to an existing contract of the seller. Sale may be as a unit or in parcels and at any time and place and on any terms but every aspect of the sale including the method, manner, time, place and terms must be commercially reasonable. The resale must be reasonably identified as referring to the broken contract, but it is not necessary that the goods be in existence or that any or all of them have been identified to the contract before the breach.

(3) Where the resale is at private sale the seller must give the buyer reasonable notification of his intention to resell.

(4) Where the resale is at public sale

> (a) only identified goods can be sold except where there is a recognized market for a public sale of futures in goods of the kind; and
>
> (b) it must be made at a usual place or market for public sale if one is reasonably available and except in the case of goods which are perishable or threaten to decline in value speedily the seller must give the buyer reasonable notice of the time and place of the resale; and
>
> (c) if the goods are not to be within the view of those attending the sale the notification of sale must state the place where the goods are located and provide for their reasonable inspection by prospective bidders; and

(d) the seller may buy.

(5) A purchaser who buys in good faith at a resale takes the goods free of any rights of the original buyer even though the seller fails to comply with one or more of the requirements of this section.

(6) The seller is not accountable to the buyer for any profit made on any resale. A person in the position of a seller (Section 2–707) or a buyer who has rightfully rejected or justifiably revoked acceptance must account for any excess over the amount of his security interest, as hereinafter defined (subsection (3) of Section 2–711).

§ 2–707. "Person in the Position of a Seller".

(1) A "person in the position of a seller" includes as against a principal an agent who has paid or become responsible for the price of goods on behalf of his principal or anyone who otherwise holds a security interest or other right in goods similar to that of a seller.

(2) A person in the position of a seller may as provided in this Article withhold or stop delivery (Section 2–705) and resell (Section 2–706) and recover incidental damages (Section 2–710).

§ 2–708. Seller's Damages for Non-Acceptance or Repudiation.

(1) Subject to subsection (2) and to the provisions of this Article with respect to proof of market price (Section 2–723), the measure of damages for non-acceptance or repudiation by the buyer is the difference between the market price at the time and place for tender and the unpaid contract price together with any incidental damages provided in this Article (Section 2–710), but less expenses saved in consequence of the buyer's breach.

(2) If the measure of damages provided in subsection (1) is inadequate to put the seller in as good a position as performance would have done then the measure of damages is the profit (including reasonable overhead) which the seller would have made from full performance by the buyer, together with any incidental damages provided in this Article (Section 2–710), due allowance for costs reasonably incurred and due credit for payments or proceeds of resale.

§ 2–709. Action for the Price.

(1) When the buyer fails to pay the price as it becomes due the seller may recover, together with any incidental damages under the next section, the price

(a) of goods accepted or of conforming goods lost or damaged within a commercially reasonable time after risk of their loss has passed to the buyer; and

(b) of goods identified to the contract if the seller is unable after reasonable effort to resell them at a reasonable price or the circumstances reasonably indicate that such effort will be unavailing.

(2) Where the seller sues for the price he must hold for the buyer any goods which have been identified to the contract and are still in his control except that if resale becomes possible he may resell them at any time prior to the collection of the judgment. The net proceeds of any such resale must be credited to the buyer and payment of the judgment entitles him to any goods not resold.

(3) After the buyer has wrongfully rejected or revoked acceptance of the goods or has failed to make a payment due or has repudiated (Section 2–610), a seller who is held not entitled to the price under this section shall nevertheless be awarded damages for non-acceptance under the preceding section.

§ 2–710. Seller's Incidental Damages.

Incidental damages to an aggrieved seller include any commercially reasonable charges, expenses or commissions incurred in stopping delivery, in the transportation, care and custody of goods after the buyer's breach, in connection with return or resale of the goods or otherwise resulting from the breach.

§ 2–711. Buyer's Remedies in General; Buyer's Security Interest in Rejected Goods.

(1) Where the seller fails to make delivery or repudiates or the buyer rightfully rejects or justifiably revokes acceptance then with respect to any goods involved, and with respect to the whole if the breach goes to the whole contract (Section 2–612), the buyer may cancel and whether or not he has done so may in addition to recovering so much of the price as has been paid

(a) "cover" and have damages under the next section as to all the goods affected whether or not they have been identified to the contract; or

(b) recover damages for non-delivery as provided in this Article (Section 2–713).

(2) Where the seller fails to deliver or repudiates the buyer may also

(a) if the goods have been identified recover them as provided in this Article (Section 2–502); or

(b) in a proper case obtain specific performance or replevy the goods as provided in this Article (Section 2–716).

(3) On rightful rejection or justifiable revocation of acceptance a buyer has a security interest in goods in his possession or control for any payments made on their price and any expenses reasonably incurred in their inspection, receipt, transportation, care and custody and may hold such goods and resell them in like manner as an aggrieved seller (Section 2–706).

§ 2–712. "Cover"; Buyer's Procurement of Substitute Goods.

(1) After a breach within the preceding section the buyer may "cover" by making in good faith and without unreasonable delay any reasonable purchase of or contract to purchase goods in substitution for those due from the seller.

(2) The buyer may recover from the seller as damages the difference between the cost of cover and the contract price together with any incidental or consequential damages as hereinafter defined (Section 2–715), but less expenses saved in consequence of the seller's breach.

(3) Failure of the buyer to effect cover within this section does not bar him from any other remedy.

§ 2–713. Buyer's Damages for Non-Delivery or Repudiation.

(1) Subject to the provisions of this Article with respect to proof of market price (Section 2–723), the measure of damages for non-delivery or repudiation by the seller is the difference between the market price at the time when the buyer learned of the breach and the contract price together with any incidental and consequential damages provided in this Article (Section 2–715), but less expenses saved in consequence of the seller's breach.

(2) Market price is to be determined as of the place for tender or, in cases of rejection after arrival or revocation of acceptance, as of the place of arrival.

§ 2–714. Buyer's Damages for Breach in Regard to Accepted Goods.

(1) Where the buyer has accepted goods and given notification (subsection (3) of Section 2–607) he may recover as damages for any non-conformity of tender the loss resulting in the ordinary course of events from the seller's breach as determined in any manner which is reasonable.

(2) The measure of damages for breach of warranty is the difference at the time and place of acceptance between the value of the goods accepted and the value they would have had if they had been as warranted, unless special circumstances show proximate damages of a different amount.

(3) In a proper case any incidental and consequential damages under the next section may also be recovered.

§ 2–715. Buyer's Incidental and Consequential Damages.

(1) Incidental damages resulting from the seller's breach include expenses reasonably incurred in inspection, receipt, transportation and care and custody of goods rightfully rejected, any commercially reasonable charges, expenses or commissions in connection with effecting cover and any other reasonable expense incident to the delay or other breach.

(2) Consequential damages resulting from the seller's breach include

(a) any loss resulting from general or particular requirements and needs of which the seller at the time of contracting had reason to know and which could not reasonably be prevented by cover or otherwise; and

(b) injury to person or property proximately resulting from any breach of warranty.

§ 2–716. Buyer's Right to Specific Performance or Replevin.

(1) Specific performance may be decreed where the goods are unique or in other proper circumstances.

(2) The decree for specific performance may include such terms and conditions as to payment of the price, damages, or other relief as the court may deem just.

(3) The buyer has a right of replevin for goods identified to the contract if after reasonable effort he is unable to effect cover for such goods or the circumstances reasonably indicate that such effort will be unavailing or if the goods have been shipped under reservation and satisfaction of the security interest in them has been made or tendered. In the case of goods bought for personal, family, or household purposes, the buyer's right of replevin vests upon acquisition of a special property, even if the seller had not then repudiated or failed to deliver.

As amended in 1999.

§ 2–717. Deduction of Damages From the Price.

The buyer on notifying the seller of his intention to do so may deduct all or any part of the damages resulting from any breach of the contract from any part of the price still due under the same contract.

§ 2–718. Liquidation or Limitation of Damages; Deposits.

(1) Damages for breach by either party may be liquidated in the agreement but only at an amount which is reasonable in the light of the anticipated or actual harm caused by the breach, the difficulties of proof of loss, and the inconvenience or nonfeasibility of otherwise obtaining an adequate remedy. A term fixing unreasonably large liquidated damages is void as a penalty.

(2) Where the seller justifiably withholds delivery of goods because of the buyer's breach, the buyer is entitled to restitution of any amount by which the sum of his payments exceeds

(a) the amount to which the seller is entitled by virtue of terms liquidating the seller's damages in accordance with subsection (1), or

(b) in the absence of such terms, twenty per cent of the value of the total performance for which the buyer is obligated under the contract or $500, whichever is smaller.

(3) The buyer's right to restitution under subsection (2) is subject to offset to the extent that the seller establishes

(a) a right to recover damages under the provisions of this Article other than subsection (1), and

(b) the amount or value of any benefits received by the buyer directly or indirectly by reason of the contract.

(4) Where a seller has received payment in goods their reasonable value or the proceeds of their resale shall be treated as payments for the purposes of subsection (2); but if the seller has notice of the buyer's breach before reselling goods received in part performance, his resale is subject to the conditions laid down in this Article on resale by an aggrieved seller (Section 2–706).

§ 2–719. **Contractual Modification or Limitation of Remedy.**

(1) Subject to the provisions of subsections (2) and (3) of this section and of the preceding section on liquidation and limitation of damages,

(a) the agreement may provide for remedies in addition to or in substitution for those provided in this Article and may limit or alter the measure of damages recoverable under this Article, as by limiting the buyer's remedies to return of the goods and repayment of the price or to repair and replacement of nonconforming goods or parts; and

(b) resort to a remedy as provided is optional unless the remedy is expressly agreed to be exclusive, in which case it is the sole remedy.

(2) Where circumstances cause an exclusive or limited remedy to fail of its essential purpose, remedy may be had as provided in this Act.

(3) Consequential damages may be limited or excluded unless the limitation or exclusion is unconscionable. Limitation of consequential damages for injury to the person in the case of consumer goods is prima facie unconscionable but limitation of damages where the loss is commercial is not.

§ 2–720. **Effect of "Cancellation" or "Rescission" on Claims for Antecedent Breach.**

Unless the contrary intention clearly appears, expressions of "cancellation" or "rescission" of the contract or the like shall not be construed as a renunciation or discharge of any claim in damages for an antecedent breach.

§ 2–721. **Remedies for Fraud.**

Remedies for material misrepresentation or fraud include all remedies available under this Article for non-fraudulent breach. Neither rescission or a claim for rescission of the contract for sale nor rejection or return of the goods shall bar or be deemed inconsistent with a claim for damages or other remedy.

§ 2–722. **Who Can Sue Third Parties for Injury to Goods.**

Where a third party so deals with goods which have been identified to a contract for sale as to cause actionable injury to a party to that contract

(a) a right of action against the third party is in either party to the contract for sale who has title to or a security interest or a special property or an insurable interest in the goods; and if the goods have been destroyed or converted a right of action is also in the party who either bore the risk of loss under the contract for sale or has since the injury assumed that risk as against the other;

(b) if at the time of the injury the party plaintiff did not bear the risk of loss as against the other party to the contract for sale and there is no arrangement between them for disposition of the recovery, his suit or settlement is, subject to his own interest, as a fiduciary for the other party to the contract;

(c) either party may with the consent of the other sue for the benefit of whom it may concern.

§ 2–723. **Proof of Market Price: Time and Place.**

(1) If an action based on anticipatory repudiation comes to trial before the time for performance with respect to some or all of the goods, any damages based on market price (Section 2–708 or Section 2–713) shall be determined according to the price of such goods prevailing at the time when the aggrieved party learned of the repudiation.

(2) If evidence of a price prevailing at the times or places described in this Article is not readily available the price prevailing within any reasonable time before or after the time described or at any other place which in commercial judgment or under usage of trade would serve as a reasonable substitute for the one described may be used, making any proper allowance for the cost of transporting the goods to or from such other place.

(3) Evidence of a relevant price prevailing at a time or place other than the one described in this Article offered by one party is not admissible unless and until he has given the other party such notice as the court finds sufficient to prevent unfair surprise.

§ 2–724. **Admissibility of Market Quotations.**

Whenever the prevailing price or value of any goods regularly bought and sold in any established commodity market is in issue, reports in official publications or trade journals or in newspapers or periodicals of general circulation published as the reports of such market shall be admissible in evidence. The circumstances of the preparation of such a report may be shown to affect its weight but not its admissibility.

§ 2–725. **Statute of Limitations in Contracts for Sale.**

(1) An action for breach of any contract for sale must be commenced within four years after the cause of action has accrued. By the original agreement the parties may reduce the period of limitation to not less than one year but may not extend it.

(2) A cause of action accrues when the breach occurs, regardless of the aggrieved party's lack of knowledge of the breach. A breach of warranty occurs when tender of delivery is made, except that where a warranty explicitly extends to future performance of the goods and discovery of the breach must await the time of such performance the cause of action accrues when the breach is or should have been discovered.

(3) Where an action commenced within the time limited by subsection (1) is so terminated as to leave available a remedy by another action for the same breach such other action may be commenced after the expiration of the time limited and within six months after the termination of the first action unless the termination resulted from voluntary discontinuance or from dismissal for failure or neglect to prosecute.

(4) This section does not alter the law on tolling of the statute of limitations nor does it apply to causes of action which have accrued before this Act becomes effective.

Article 2 Amendments (Excerpts)[1]

Part 1 Short Title, General Construction and Subject Matter

*   *   *   *

§ 2–103. Definitions and Index of Definitions.

(1) In this article unless the context otherwise requires

*   *   *   *

(b) "Conspicuous", with reference to a term, means so written, displayed, or presented that a reasonable person against which it is to operate ought to have noticed it. A term in an electronic record intended to evoke a response by an electronic agent is conspicuous if it is presented in a form that would enable a reasonably configured electronic agent to take it into account or react to it without review of the record by an individual. Whether a term is "conspicuous" or not is a decision for the court. Conspicuous terms include the following:

    (i) for a person:

        (A) a heading in capitals equal to or greater in size than the surrounding text, or in contrasting type, font, or color to the surrounding text of the same or lesser size and;

        (B) language in the body of a record or display in larger type than the surrounding text, or in contrasting type, font, or color to the surrounding text of the same size, or set off from surrounding text of the same size by symbols or other marks that call attention to the language; and

    (ii) for a person or an electronic agent, a term that is so placed in a record or display that the person or electronic agent cannot proceed without taking action with respect to the particular term.

(c) "Consumer" means an individual who buys or contracts to buy goods that, at the time of contracting, are intended by the individual to be used primarily for personal, family, or household purposes.

(d) "Consumer contract" means a contract between a merchant seller and a consumer.

*   *   *   *

(j) "Good faith" means honesty in fact and the observance of reasonable commercial standards of fair dealing.

(k) "Goods" means all things that are movable at the time of identification to a contract for sale. The term includes future goods, specially manufactured goods, the unborn young of animals, growing crops, and other identified things attached to realty as described in Section 2–107. The term does not include information, the money in which the price is to be paid, investment securities under Article 8, the subject matter of foreign exchange transactions, and choses in action.

*   *   *   *

(m) "Record" means information that is inscribed on a tangible medium or that is stored in an electronic or other medium and is retrievable in perceivable form.

(n) "Remedial promise" means a promise by the seller to repair or replace the goods or to refund all or part of the price upon the happening of a specified event.

*   *   *   *

(p) "Sign" means, with present intent to authenticate or adopt a record,

    (i) to execute or adopt a tangible symbol; or

    (ii) to attach to or logically associate with the record an electronic sound, symbol, or process.

*   *   *   *

Part 2 Form, Formation, Terms and Readjustment of Contract; Electronic Contracting

§ 2–201. Formal Requirements; Statute of Frauds.

(1) A contract for the sale of goods for the price of $5,000 or more is not enforceable by way of action or defense unless there is some record sufficient to indicate that a contract for sale has been made between the parties and signed by the party against which enforcement is sought or by the party's authorized agent or broker. A record is not insufficient because it omits or incorrectly states a term agreed upon but the contract is not enforceable under this subsection beyond the quantity of goods shown in the record.

(2) Between merchants if within a reasonable time a record in confirmation of the contract and sufficient against the sender is received and the party receiving it has reason to know its contents, it satisfies the requirements of subsection (1) against the recipient unless notice of objection to its contents is given in a record within 10 days after it is received.

(3) A contract which does not satisfy the requirements of subsection (1) but which is valid in other respects is enforceable

    (a) if the goods are to be specially manufactured for the buyer and are not suitable for sale to others in the ordinary course of the seller's business and the seller, before notice of repudiation is received and under circumstances which reasonably indicate that the goods are for the buyer, has made either a substantial beginning of their manufacture or commitments for their procurement; or

    (b) if the party against which enforcement is sought admits in the party's pleading, or in the party's testimony

---

[1]. Additions and new wording are underlined. What follows represents only selected changes made by the 2003 amendments. Although the National Conference of Commissioners on Uniform State Laws and the American Law Institute approved the amendments in May of 2003, as of this writing, they have not as yet been adopted by any state.

or otherwise under oath that a contract for sale was made, but the contract is not enforceable under this paragraph beyond the quantity of goods admitted; or

(c) with respect to goods for which payment has been made and accepted or which have been received and accepted (Sec. 2–606).

(4) A contract that is enforceable under this section is not rendered unenforceable merely because it is not capable of being performed within one year or any other applicable period after its making.

*　*　*　*

§ 2–207. Terms of Contract; Effect of Confirmation.

Subject to Section 2–202, if (i) conduct by both parties recognizes the existence of a contract although their records do not otherwise establish a contract, (ii) a contract is formed by an offer and acceptance, or (iii) a contract formed in any manner is confirmed by a record that contains terms additional to or different from those in the contract being confirmed, the terms of the contract, are:

(a) terms that appear in the records of both parties;

(b) terms, whether in a record or not, to which both parties agree; and

(c) terms supplied or incorporated under any provision of this Act.

*　*　*　*

Part 3 General Obligation and Construction of Contract

*　*　*　*

§ 2–312. Warranty of Title and Against Infringement; Buyer's Obligation Against Infringement.

(1) Subject to subsection (3) there is in a contract for sale a warranty by the seller that

(a) the title conveyed shall be, good and its transfer rightful and shall not, unreasonably expose the buyer to litigation because of any colorable claim to or interest in the goods; and

(b) the goods shall be delivered free from any security interest or other lien or encumbrance of which the buyer at the time of contracting has no knowledge.

(2) Unless otherwise agreed a seller that is a merchant regularly dealing in goods of the kind warrants that the goods shall be delivered free of the rightful claim of any third person by way of infringement or the like but a buyer that furnishes specifications to the seller must hold the seller harmless against any such claim that arises out of compliance with the specifications.

(3) A warranty under this section may be disclaimed or modified only by specific language or by circumstances that give the buyer reason to know that the seller does not claim title, that the seller is purporting to sell only the right or title as

the seller or a third person may have, or that the seller is selling subject to any claims of infringement or the like.

§ 2–313. Express Warranties by Affirmation, Promise, Description, Sample; Remedial Promise.

(1) In this section, "immediate buyer" means a buyer that enters into a contract with the seller.

*　*　*　*

(4) Any remedial promise made by the seller to the immediate buyer creates an obligation that the promise will be performed upon the happening of the specified event.

§ 2–313A. Obligation to Remote Purchaser Created by Record Packaged with or Accompanying Goods.

(1) In this section:

(a) "Immediate buyer" means a buyer that enters into a contract with the seller.

(b) "Remote purchaser" means a person that buys or leases goods from an immediate buyer or other person in the normal chain of distribution.

(2) This section applies only to new goods and goods sold or leased as new goods in a transaction of purchase in the normal chain of distribution.

(3) If in a record packaged with or accompanying the goods the seller makes an affirmation of fact or promise that relates to the goods, provides a description that relates to the goods, or makes a remedial promise, and the seller reasonably expects the record to be, and the record is, furnished to the remote purchaser, the seller has an obligation to the remote purchaser that:

(a) the goods will conform to the affirmation of fact, promise or description unless a reasonable person in the position of the remote purchaser would not believe that the affirmation of fact, promise or description created an obligation; and

(b) the seller will perform the remedial promise.

(4) It is not necessary to the creation of an obligation under this section that the seller use formal words such as "warrant" or "guarantee" or that the seller have a specific intention to undertake an obligation, but an affirmation merely of the value of the goods or a statement purporting to be merely the seller's opinion or commendation of the goods does not create an obligation.

(5) The following rules apply to the remedies for breach of an obligation created under this section:

(a) The seller may modify or limit the remedies available to the remote purchaser if the modification or limitation is furnished to the remote purchaser no later than the time of purchase or if the modification or limitation is contained in the record that contains the affirmation of fact, promise or description.

(b) Subject to a modification or limitation of remedy, a seller in breach is liable for incidental or consequential damages under Section 2–715, but not for lost profits.

(c) The remote purchaser may recover as damages for breach of a seller's obligation arising under subsection (2) the loss resulting in the ordinary course of events as determined in any reasonable manner.

(5) An obligation that is not a remedial promise is breached if the goods did not conform to the affirmation of fact, promise or description creating the obligation when the goods left the seller's control.

§ 2–313B. Obligation to Remote Purchaser Created by Communication to the Public.

(1) In this section:

(a) "Immediate buyer" means a buyer that enters into a contract with the seller.

(b) "Remote purchaser" means a person that buys or leases goods from an immediate buyer or other person in the normal chain of distribution.

(2) This section applies only to new goods and goods sold or leased as new goods in a transaction of purchase in the normal chain of distribution.

(3) If in an advertisement or a similar communication to the public a seller makes an affirmation of fact or promise that relates to the goods, provides a description that relates to the goods, or makes a remedial promise, and the remote purchaser enters into a transaction of purchase with knowledge of and with the expectation that the goods will conform to the affirmation of fact, promise, or description, or that the seller will perform the remedial promise, the seller has an obligation to the remote purchaser that:

(a) the goods will conform to the affirmation of fact, promise or description unless a reasonable person in the position of the remote purchaser would not believe that the affirmation of fact, promise or description created an obligation; and

(b) the seller will perform the remedial promise.

(4) It is not necessary to the creation of an obligation under this section that the seller use formal words such as "warrant" or "guarantee" or that the seller have a specific intention to undertake an obligation, but an affirmation merely of the value of the goods or a statement purporting to be merely the seller's opinion or commendation of the goods does not create an obligation.

(5) The following rules apply to the remedies for breach of an obligation created under this section:

(a) The seller may modify or limit the remedies available to the remote purchaser if the modification or limitation is furnished to the remote purchaser no later than the time of purchase. The modification or limitation may be

furnished as part of the communication that contains the affirmation of fact, promise or description.

(b) Subject to a modification or limitation of remedy, a seller in breach is liable for incidental or consequential damages under Section 2–715, but not for lost profits.

(c) The remote purchaser may recover as damages for breach of a seller's obligation arising under subsection (2) the loss resulting in the ordinary course of events as determined in any reasonable manner.

(6) An obligation that is not a remedial promise is breached if the goods did not conform to the affirmation of fact, promise or description creating the obligation when the goods left the seller's control.

*   *   *   *

§ 2–316. Exclusion or Modification of Warranties.
*   *   *   *

(2) Subject to subsection (3), to exclude or modify the implied warranty of merchantability or any part of it in a consumer contract the language must be in a record, be conspicuous, and state "The seller undertakes no responsibility for the quality of the goods except as otherwise provided in this contract," and in any other contract the language must mention merchantability and in case of a record must be conspicuous. Subject to subsection (3), to exclude or modify the implied warranty of fitness the exclusion must be in a record and be conspicuous. Language to exclude all implied warranties of fitness in a consumer contract must state "The seller assumes no responsibility that the goods will be fit for any particular purpose for which you may be buying these goods, except as otherwise provided in the contract," and in any other contract the language is sufficient if it states, for example, that "There are no warranties that extend beyond the description on the face hereof." Language that satisfies the requirements of this subsection for the exclusion and modification of a warranty in a consumer contract also satisfies the requirements for any other contract.

(3) Notwithstanding subsection (2):

(a) unless the circumstances indicate otherwise, all implied warranties are excluded by expressions like "as is", "with all faults" or other language which in common understanding calls the buyer's attention to the exclusion of warranties, makes plain that there is no implied warranty, and in a consumer contract evidenced by a record is set forth conspicuously in the record; and

(b) when the buyer before entering into the contract has examined the goods or the sample or model as fully as desired or has refused to examine the goods after a demand by the seller there is no implied warranty with regard to defects which an examination ought in the circumstances to have revealed to the buyer; and

(c) an implied warranty can also be excluded or modified by course of dealing or course of performance or usage of trade.

* * * *

§ 2–318. Third Party Beneficiaries of Warranties and Obligations.

(1) In this section:

(a) "Immediate buyer" means a buyer that enters into a contract with the seller.

(b) "Remote purchaser" means a person that buys or leases goods from an immediate buyer or other person in the normal chain of distribution.

Alternative A to subsection (2)

(2) A seller's warranty to an immediate buyer, whether express or implied, a seller's remedial promise to an immediate buyer, or a seller's obligation to a remote purchaser under Section 2–313A or 2–313B extends to any natural person who is in the family or household of the immediate buyer or the remote purchaser or who is a guest in the home of either if it is reasonable to expect that the person may use, consume or be affected by the goods and who is injured in person by breach of the warranty, remedial promise or obligation. A seller may not exclude or limit the operation of this section.

Alternative B to subsection (2)

(2) A seller's warranty to an immediate buyer, whether express or implied, a seller's remedial promise to an immediate buyer, or a seller's obligation to a remote purchaser under Section 2–313A or 2–313B extends to any natural person who may reasonably be expected to use, consume or be affected by the goods and who is injured in person by breach of the warranty, remedial promise or obligation. A seller may not exclude or limit the operation of this section.

Alternative C to subsection (2)

(2) A seller's warranty to an immediate buyer, whether express or implied, a seller's remedial promise to an immediate buyer, or a seller's obligation to a remote purchaser under Section 2–313A or 2–313B extends to any person that may reasonably be expected to use, consume or be affected by the goods and that is injured by breach of the warranty, remedial promise or obligation. A seller may not exclude or limit the operation of this section with respect to injury to the person of an individual to whom the warranty, remedial promise or obligation extends.

* * * *

Part 5 Performance

* * * *

§ 2–502. Buyer's Right to Goods on Seller's Insolvency.

(1) Subject to subsections (2) and (3) and even though the goods have not been shipped a buyer that has paid a part or all of the price of goods in which the buyer has a special property under the provisions of the immediately preceding section may on making and keeping good a tender of any unpaid portion of their price recover them from the seller if:

(a) in the case of goods bought by a consumer, the seller repudiates or fails to deliver as required by the contract; or

(b) in all cases, the seller becomes insolvent within ten days after receipt of the first installment on their price.

(2) The buyer's right to recover the goods under subsection (1) vests upon acquisition of a special property, even if the seller had not then repudiated or failed to deliver.

(3) If the identification creating the special property has been made by the buyer, the buyer acquires the right to recover the goods only if they conform to the contract for sale.

* * * *

§ 2–508. Cure by Seller of Improper Tender or Delivery; Replacement.

(1) Where the buyer rejects goods or a tender of delivery under Section 2–601 or 2–612 or, except in a consumer contract, justifiably revokes acceptance under Section 2–608(1)(b) and the agreed time for performance has not expired, a seller that has performed in good faith, upon seasonable notice to the buyer and at the seller's own expense, may cure the breach of contract by making a conforming tender of delivery within the agreed time. The seller shall compensate the buyer for all of the buyer's reasonable expenses caused by the seller's breach of contract and subsequent cure.

(2) Where the buyer rejects goods or a tender of delivery under Section 2–601 or 2–612 or except in a consumer contract justifiably revokes acceptance under Section 2–608(1)(b) and the agreed time for performance has expired, a seller that has performed in good faith, upon seasonable notice to the buyer and at the seller's own expense, may cure the breach of contract, if the cure is appropriate and timely under the circumstances, by making a tender of conforming goods. The seller shall compensate the buyer for all of the buyer's reasonable expenses caused by the seller's breach of contract and subsequent cure.

§ 2–509. Risk of Loss in the Absence of Breach.

(1) Where the contract requires or authorizes the seller to ship the goods by carrier

(a) if it does not require the seller to deliver them at a particular destination, the risk of loss passes to the buyer when the goods are delivered to the carrier even though the shipment is under reservation (Section 2–505); but

(b) if it does require <u>the seller</u> to deliver them at a particular destination and the goods are there tendered while in the possession of the carrier, the risk of loss passes to the buyer when the goods are there so tendered as to enable the buyer to take delivery.

(2) Where the goods are held by a bailee to be delivered without being moved, the risk of loss passes to the buyer

(a) on <u>the buyer's</u> receipt of a negotiable document of title covering the goods; or

(b) on acknowledgment by the bailee <u>to the buyer</u> of the buyer's right to possession of the goods; or

(c) after <u>the buyer's</u> receipt of a non-negotiable document of title or other direction to deliver <u>in a record,</u> as provided in subsection (4)(b) of Section 2–503.

(3) In any case not within subsection (1) or (2), the risk of loss passes to the buyer on <u>the buyer's</u> receipt of the goods.

(4) The provisions of this section are subject to contrary agreement of the parties and to the provisions of this Article on sale on approval (Section 2–327) and on effect of breach on risk of loss (Section 2–510).

*   *   *   *

§ 2–513. Buyer's Right to Inspection of Goods.

*   *   *   *

(3) Unless otherwise agreed, the buyer is not entitled to inspect the goods before payment of the price when the contract provides

(a) for delivery <u>on terms that under applicable course of performance, course of dealing, or usage of trade are interpreted to preclude inspection before payment;</u> or

(b) for payment against documents of title, except where such payment is due only after the goods are to become available for inspection.

*   *   *   *

Part 6 Breach, Repudiation and Excuse

*   *   *   *

§ 2–605. Waiver of Buyer's Objections by Failure to Particularize.

(1) The buyer's failure to state in connection with rejection a particular defect <u>or in connection with revocation of acceptance a defect that justifies revocation</u> precludes <u>the buyer</u> from relying on the unstated defect to justify rejection or <u>revocation of acceptance if the defect is ascertainable by reasonable inspection</u>

(a) where the seller <u>had a right to cure the defect and</u> could have cured it if stated seasonably; or

(b) between merchants when the seller has after rejection made a request in <u>a record for a full and</u> final statement <u>in record form</u> of all defects on which the buyer proposes to rely.

(2) <u>A buyer's payment</u> against documents <u>tendered to the buyer</u> made without reservation of rights precludes recovery of the payment for defects apparent on the face of the documents.

*   *   *   *

§ 2–607. Effect of Acceptance; Notice of Breach; Burden of Establishing Breach After Acceptance; Notice of Claim or Litigation to Person Answerable Over.

*   *   *   *

(3) Where a tender has been accepted

(a) the buyer must within a reasonable time after <u>the buyer</u> discovers or should have discovered any breach notify the seller. <u>However, failure to give timely notice bars the buyer from a remedy only to the extent that the seller is prejudiced by the failure</u> and

(b) if the claim is one for infringement or the like (subsection (3) of Section 2–312) and the buyer is sued as a result of such a breach <u>the buyer</u> must so notify the seller within a reasonable time after <u>the buyer</u> receives notice of the litigation or be barred from any remedy over for liability established by the litigation.

*   *   *   *

§ 2–608. Revocation of Acceptance in Whole or in Part.

*   *   *   *

<u>(4) If a buyer uses the goods after a rightful rejection or justifiable revocation of acceptance, the following rules apply:</u>

<u>(a) Any use by the buyer which is unreasonable under the circumstances is wrongful as against the seller and is an acceptance only if ratified by the seller.</u>

<u>(b) Any use of the goods which is reasonable under the circumstances is not wrongful as against the seller and is not an acceptance, but in an appropriate case the buyer shall be obligated to the seller for the value of the use to the buyer.</u>

*   *   *   *

§ 2–612. "Installment Contract"; Breach.

*   *   *   *

(2) The buyer may reject any installment which is non-conforming if the non-conformity substantially impairs the value of that installment <u>to the buyer</u> or if the non-conformity is a defect in the required documents; but if the non-conformity does not fall within subsection (3) and the seller gives adequate assurance of its cure the buyer must accept that installment.

(3) Whenever non-conformity or default with respect to one or more installments substantially impairs the value of the whole contract there is a breach of the whole. But the aggrieved party reinstates the contract if <u>the party</u> accepts a non-conforming installment without seasonably notifying of cancellation or if <u>the party</u> brings an action with respect only to past installments or demands performance as to future installments.

* * * *

Part 7 Remedies

§ 2–702. Seller's Remedies on Discovery of Buyer's Insolvency.

* * * *

(2) Where the seller discovers that the buyer has received goods on credit while insolvent <u>the seller</u> may reclaim the goods upon demand made within <u>a reasonable time</u> after the <u>buyer's</u> receipt <u>of the goods</u>. Except as provided in this subsection the seller may not base a right to reclaim goods on the buyer's fraudulent or innocent misrepresentation of solvency or of intent to pay.

* * * *

§ 2–703. Seller's Remedies in General.

<u>(1) A breach of contract by the buyer includes the buyer's wrongful rejection or wrongful attempt to revoke acceptance of goods, wrongful failure to perform a contractual obligation, failure to make a payment when due, and repudiation.</u>

<u>(2) If the buyer is in breach of contract the seller, to the extent provided for by this Act or other law, may:</u>

<u>(a) withhold delivery of the goods:</u>

<u>(b) stop delivery of the goods under Section 2–705;</u>

<u>(c) proceed under Section 2–704 with respect to goods unidentified to the contract or unfinished;</u>

<u>(d) reclaim the goods under Section 2–507(2) or 2–702(2);</u>

<u>(e) require payment directly from the buyer under Section 2–325(c);</u>

<u>(f) cancel;</u>

<u>(g) resell and recover damages under Section 2–706;</u>

<u>(h) recover damages for nonacceptance or repudiation under Section 2–708(1);</u>

<u>(i) recover lost profits under Section 2–708(2);</u>

<u>(j) recover the price under Section 2–709;</u>

<u>(k) obtain specific performance under Section 2–716;</u>

<u>(l) recover liquidated damages under Section 2–718;</u>

<u>(m) in other cases, recover damages in any manner that is reasonable under the circumstances.</u>

<u>(3) If a buyer becomes insolvent, the seller may:</u>

<u>(a) withhold delivery under Section 2–702(1);</u>

<u>(b) stop delivery of the goods under Section 2–705;</u>

<u>(c) reclaim the goods under Section 2–702(2).</u>

* * * *

§ 2–705. Seller's Stoppage of Delivery in Transit or Otherwise.

(1) The seller may stop delivery of goods in the possession of a carrier or other bailee when <u>the seller</u> discovers the buyer to be insolvent (Section 2–702) <u>or</u> when the buyer repudiates or fails to make a payment due before delivery or if for any other reason the seller has a right to withhold or reclaim the goods.

* * * *

§ 2–706. Seller's Resale Including Contract for Resale.

(1) <u>In an appropriate case involving breach by the buyer,</u> the seller may resell the goods concerned or the undelivered balance thereof. Where the resale is made in good faith and in a commercially reasonable manner the seller may recover the difference between the <u>contract price and the</u> resale price together with any incidental <u>or consequential</u> damages allowed under the provisions of this Article (Section 2–710), but less expenses saved in consequence of the buyer's breach.

* * * *

§ 2–708. Seller's Damages for Non-Acceptance or Repudiation.

(1) Subject to subsection (2) and to the provisions of this Article with respect to proof of market price (Section 2–723)

<u>(a)</u> the measure of damages for non-acceptance by the buyer is the difference between the <u>contract price and the</u> market price at the time and place for tender together with any incidental <u>or consequential</u> damages provided in this Article (Section 2–710), but less expenses saved in consequence of the buyer's breach; <u>and</u>

<u>(b) the measure of damages for repudiation by the buyer is the difference between the contract price and the market price at the place for tender at the expiration of a commercially reasonable time after the seller learned of the repudiation, but no later than the time stated in paragraph (a), together with any incidental or consequential damages provided in this Article (Section 2–710), but less expenses saved in consequence of the buyer's breach.</u>

(2) If the measure of damages provided in subsection (1) <u>or in Section 2–706</u> is inadequate to put the seller in as good a position as performance would have done then the measure of damages is the profit (including reasonable overhead) which the seller would have made from full performance by the buyer, together with any incidental <u>or consequential</u> damages provided in this Article (Section 2–710).

§ 2–709. Action for the Price.

(1) When the buyer fails to pay the price as it becomes due the seller may recover, together with any incidental <u>or consequential</u> damages under the next section, the price

(a) of goods accepted or of conforming goods lost or damaged within a commercially reasonable time after risk of their loss has passed to the buyer; and

(b) of goods identified to the contract if the seller is unable after reasonable effort to resell them at a reasonable price or the circumstances reasonably indicate that such effort will be unavailing.

* * * *

§ 2–710. Seller's Incidental <u>and Consequential Damages.</u>

<u>(1)</u> Incidental damages to an aggrieved seller include any commercially reasonable charges, expenses or commissions incurred in stopping delivery, in the transportation, care and custody of goods after the buyer's breach, in connection with return or resale of the goods or otherwise resulting from the breach.

<u>(2) Consequential damages resulting from the buyer's breach include any loss resulting from general or particular requirements and needs of which the buyer at the time of contracting had reason to know and which could not reasonably be prevented by resale or otherwise.</u>

<u>(3) In a consumer contract, a seller may not recover consequential damages from a consumer.</u>

* * * *

§ 2–711. Buyer's Remedies in General; Buyer's Security Interest in Rejected Goods.

<u>(1) A breach of contract by the seller includes the seller's wrongful failure to deliver or to perform a contractual obligation, making of a nonconforming tender of delivery or performance, and repudiation.</u>

<u>(2) If a seller is in breach of contract under subsection (1) the buyer, to the extent provided for by this Act or other law, may:</u>

<u>(a) in the case of rightful cancellation, rightful rejection or justifiable revocation of acceptance recover so much of the price as has been paid;</u>

<u>(b) deduct damages from any part of the price still due under Section 2–717;</u>

<u>(c) cancel;</u>

<u>(d) cover and have damages under Section 2–712 as to all goods affected whether or not they have been identified to the contract;</u>

<u>(e) recover damages for non-delivery or repudiation under Section 2–713;</u>

<u>(f) recover damages for breach with regard to accepted goods or breach with regard to a remedial promise under Section 2–714;</u>

<u>(g) recover identified goods under Section 2–502;</u>

<u>(h) obtain specific performance or obtain the goods by replevin or similar remedy under Section 7–716;</u>

<u>(i) recover liquidated damages under Section 2–718;</u>

<u>(j) in other cases, recover damages in any manner that is reasonable under the circumstances.</u>

(3) On rightful rejection or justifiable revocation of acceptance a buyer has a security interest in goods in <u>the buyer's</u> possession or control for any payments made on their price and any expenses reasonably incurred in their inspection, receipt, transportation, care and custody and may hold such goods and resell them in like manner as an aggrieved seller (Section 2–706).

* * * *

§ 2–713. Buyer's Damages for Non-Delivery or Repudiation.

(1) Subject to the provisions of this Article with respect to proof of market price (Section 2–723), <u>if the seller wrongfully fails to deliver or repudiates or the buyer rightfully rejects or justifiably revokes acceptance</u>

(a) the measure of damages <u>in the case of wrongful failure to deliver</u> by the seller <u>or rightful rejection or justifiable revocation of acceptance by the buyer</u> is the difference between the market price at the time <u>for tender under the contract</u> and the contract price together with any incidental or consequential damages provided in this Article (Section 2–715), but less expenses saved in consequence of the seller's <u>breach; and</u>

<u>(b) the measure of damages for repudiation by the seller is the difference between the market price at the expiration of a commercially reasonable time after the buyer learned of the repudiation, but no later than the time stated in paragraph (a), and the contract price together with any incidental or consequential damages provided in this Article (Section 2–715), less expenses saved in consequence of the seller's breach.</u>

* * * *

§ 2–725. Statute of Limitations in Contracts for Sale.

<u>(1) Except as otherwise provided in this section, an action for breach of any contract for sale must be commenced within the later of four years after the right of action has accrued under subsection (2) or (3) or one year after the breach was or should have been discovered, but no longer than five years after the right of action accrued. By the original agreement the parties may reduce the period of limitation to not less than one year but may not extend it.</u>

However, in a consumer contract, the period of limitation may not be reduced.

(2) Except as otherwise provided in subsection (3), the following rules apply:

(a) Except as otherwise provided in this subsection, a right of action for breach of a contract accrues when the breach occurs, even if the aggrieved party did not have knowledge of the breach.

(b) For breach of a contract by repudiation, a right of action accrues at the earlier of when the aggrieved party elects to treat the repudiation as a breach or when a commercially reasonable time for awaiting performance has expired.

(c) For breach of a remedial promise, a right of action accrues when the remedial promise is not performed when performance is due.

(d) In an action by a buyer against a person that is answerable over to the buyer for a claim asserted against the buyer, the buyer's right of action against the person answerable over accrues at the time the claim was originally asserted against the buyer.

(3) If a breach of a warranty arising under Section 2–312, 2–313(2), 2–314, or 2–315, or a breach of an obligation, other than a remedial promise, arising under Section 2–313A or 2–313B, is claimed the following rules apply:

(a) Except as otherwise provided in paragraph (c), a right of action for breach of a warranty arising under Section 2–313(2), 2–314 or 2–315 accrues when the seller has tendered delivery to the immediate buyer, as defined in Section 2–313, and has completed performance of any agreed installation or assembly of the goods.

(b) Except as otherwise provided in paragraph (c), a right of action for breach of an obligation other than a remedial promise arising under Section 2–313A or 2–313B accrues when the remote purchaser, as defined in sections 2–313A and 2–313B, receives the goods.

(c) Where a warranty arising under Section 2–313(2) or an obligation, other than a remedial promise, arising under 2–313A or 2–313B explicitly extends to future performance of the goods and discovery of the breach must await the time for performance the right of action accrues when the immediate buyer as defined in Section 2–313 or the remote purchaser as defined in Sections 2–313A and 2–313B discovers or should have discovered the breach.

(d) A right of action for breach of warranty arising under Section 2–312 accrues when the aggrieved party discovers or should have discovered the breach. However, an action for breach of the warranty of non-infringement may not be commenced more than six years after tender of delivery of the goods to the aggrieved party.

*   *   *   *

APPENDIX E

The National Labor Relations Act of 1935 (Excerpts)

Note: You can access the full text of the National Labor Relations Act of 1935 online at **uscode.house.gov/search/criteria.shtml**. The official citation to this act includes 29 U.S.C. Sections 151–169. In the "Title" box, type "29," and in the "Section" box, type a relevant section number (such as, for example, "151"). Click on "Search." In the list of "documents found," click on the citation to access the text of the statute.

§ 157. Right of Employees as to Organization, Collective Bargaining, etc.

Employees shall have the right to self-organization, to form, join, or assist labor organizations, to bargain collectively through representatives of their own choosing, and to engage in other concerted activities for the purpose of collective bargaining or other mutual aid or protection, and shall also have the right to refrain from any or all of such activities except to the extent that such right may be affected by an agreement requiring membership in a labor organization as a condition of employment as authorized in section 158(a)(3) of this title.

§ 158. Unfair Labor Practices

(a) Unfair labor practices for an employer

It shall be an unfair labor practice for an employer—

(1) to interfere with, restrain, or coerce employees in the exercise of the rights guaranteed in section 157 of this title;

(2) to dominate or interfere with the formation or administration of any labor organization or contribute financial or other support to it: Provided, [t]hat subject to rules and regulations made and published by the Board pursuant to section 156 of this title, an employer shall not be prohibited from permitting employees to confer with him during working hours without loss of time or pay;

(3) by discrimination in regard to hire or tenure of employment or any term or condition of employment to encourage or discourage membership in any labor organization: Provided, [t]hat nothing in this subchapter, or in any other statute of the United States, shall preclude an employer from making an agreement with a labor organization (not established, maintained, or assisted by any action defined in this subsection as an unfair labor practice) to require as a condition of employment membership therein on or after the thirtieth day following the beginning of such employment or the effective date of such agreement, whichever is the later, (i) if such labor organization is the representative of the employees as provided in section 159(a) of this title, in the appropriate collective-bargaining unit covered by such agreement when made, and (ii) unless following an election held as provided in section 159(e) of this title within one year preceding the effective date of such agreement, the Board shall have certified that at least a majority of the employees eligible to vote in such election have voted to rescind the authority of such labor organization to make such an agreement: Provided further, [t]hat no employer shall justify any discrimination against an employee for nonmembership in a labor organization (A) if he has reasonable grounds for believing that such membership was not available to the employee on the same terms and conditions generally applicable to other members, or (B) if he has reasonable grounds for believing that membership was denied or terminated for reasons other than the failure of the employee to tender the periodic dues and the initiation fees uniformly required as a condition of acquiring or retaining membership;

(4) to discharge or otherwise discriminate against an employee because he has filed charges or given testimony under this subchapter;

(5) to refuse to bargain collectively with the representatives of his employees, subject to the provisions of section 159(a) of this title.

(b) Unfair labor practices by labor organization

It shall be an unfair labor practice for a labor organization or its agents—

(1) to restrain or coerce (A) employees in the exercise of the rights guaranteed in section 157 of this title: Provided, [t]hat this paragraph shall not impair the right of a labor organization to prescribe its own rules with respect to the acquisition or retention of membership therein; or (B) an employer in the selection of his representatives for the purposes of collective bargaining or the adjustment of grievances;

(2) to cause or attempt to cause an employer to discriminate against an employee in violation of subsection (a)(3) of this section or to discriminate against an employee with respect to whom membership in such organization has been denied or terminated on some ground other than his failure to tender the periodic dues and the initiation fees uniformly required as a condition of acquiring or retaining membership;

(3) to refuse to bargain collectively with an employer, provided it is the representative of his employees subject to the provisions of section 159(a) of this title;

(4) (i) to engage in, or to induce or encourage any individual employed by any person engaged in commerce or in an industry affecting commerce to engage in, a strike or a refusal in the course of his employment to use, manufacture, process, transport, or otherwise handle or work on any goods, articles, materials, or commodities or to perform any services; or (ii) to threaten, coerce, or restrain any person engaged in commerce or in an industry affecting commerce[.] * * *

(5) to require of employees covered by an agreement authorized under subsection (a)(3) of this section the payment, as a condition precedent to becoming a member of such organization, of a fee in an amount which the Board finds excessive or discriminatory under all the circumstances. In making such a finding, the Board shall consider, among other relevant factors, the practices and customs of labor organizations in the particular industry, and the wages currently paid to the employees affected;

(6) to cause or attempt to cause an employer to pay or deliver or agree to pay or deliver any money or other thing of value, in the nature of an exaction, for services which are not performed or not to be performed; and

(7) to picket or cause to be picketed, or threaten to picket or cause to be picketed, any employer where an object thereof is forcing or requiring an employer to recognize or bargain with a labor organization as the representative of his employees, or forcing or requiring the employees of an employer to accept or select such labor organization as their collective bargaining representative[.] * * *

(c) Expression of views without threat of reprisal or force or promise of benefit

The expressing of any views, argument, or opinion, or the dissemination thereof, whether in written, printed, graphic, or visual form, shall not constitute or be evidence of an unfair labor practice under any of the provisions of this subchapter, if such expression contains no threat of reprisal or force or promise of benefit.

(d) Obligation to bargain collectively

For the purposes of this section, to bargain collectively is the performance of the mutual obligation of the employer and the representative of the employees to meet at reasonable times and confer in good faith with respect to wages, hours, and other terms and conditions of employment, or the negotiation of an agreement, or any question arising thereunder, and the execution of a written contract incorporating any agreement reached if requested by either party, but such obligation does not compel either party to agree to a proposal or require the making of a concession: Provided, [t]hat where there is in effect a collective-bargaining contract covering employees in an industry affecting commerce, the duty to bargain collectively shall also mean that no party to such contract shall terminate or modify such contract, unless the party desiring such termination or modification—

(1) serves a written notice upon the other party to the contract of the proposed termination or modification sixty days prior to the expiration date thereof, or in the event such contract contains no expiration date, sixty days prior to the time it is proposed to make such termination or modification;

(2) offers to meet and confer with the other party for the purpose of negotiating a new contract or a contract containing the proposed modifications;

(3) notifies the Federal Mediation and Conciliation Service within thirty days after such notice of the existence of a dispute, and simultaneously therewith notifies any State or Territorial agency established to mediate and conciliate disputes within the State or Territory where the dispute occurred, provided no agreement has been reached by that time; and

(4) continues in full force and effect, without resorting to strike or lock-out, all the terms and conditions of the existing contract for a period of sixty days after such notice is given or until the expiration date of such contract, whichever occurs later[.] * * *

The Sherman Act of 1890 (Excerpts)

Note: You can access the full text of the Sherman Act of 1890 online at **uscode.house.gov/search/criteria.shtml**. In the "Title" box, type "15," and in the "Section" box, type a relevant section number (such as, for example, "1"). Click on "Search." In the list of "documents found," scroll to the citation with the appropriate title (such as, in this example, "Sec. 1. Trusts, etc., in restraint of trade illegal; penalty"). Click on the citation to access the text of the statute.

Section 1. Every contract, combination in the form of trust or otherwise, or conspiracy, in restraint of trade or commerce among the several States, or with foreign nations, is declared to be illegal. Every person who shall make any contract or engage in any combination or conspiracy hereby declared to be illegal shall be deemed guilty of a felony, and, on conviction thereof, shall be punished by fine not exceeding $10,000,000 if a corporation, or, if any other person, $350,000, or by imprisonment not exceeding three years, or by both said punishments, in the discretion of the court.

Section 2. Every person who shall monopolize, or attempt to monopolize, or combine or conspire with any other person or persons, to monopolize any part of the trade or commerce among the several States, or with foreign nations, shall be deemed guilty of a felony, and, on conviction thereof, shall be punished by fine not exceeding $10,000,000 if a corporation, or, if any other person, $350,000, or by imprisonment not exceeding three years, or by both said punishments, in the discretion of the court.

Section 3. Every contract, combination in form of trust or otherwise, or conspiracy, in restraint of trade or commerce in any Territory of the United States or of the District of Columbia, or in restraint of trade or commerce between any such Territory and another, or between any such Territory or Territories and any State or States or the District of Columbia, or with foreign nations, or between the District of Columbia and any State or States or foreign nations, is declared illegal. Every person who shall make any such contract or engage in any such combination or conspiracy, shall be deemed guilty of a felony, and, on conviction thereof, shall be punished by fine not exceeding $10,000,000 if a corporation, or, if any other person, $350,000, or by imprisonment not exceeding three years, or by both said punishments, in the discretion of the court.

*   *   *   *

Section 7. Every combination, conspiracy, trust, agreement, or contract is declared to be contrary to public policy, illegal, and void when the same is made by or between two or more persons or corporations, either of whom, as agent or principal, is engaged in importing any article from any foreign country into the United States, and when such combination, conspiracy, trust, agreement, or contract is intended to operate in restraint of lawful trade, or free competition in lawful trade or commerce, or to increase the market price in any part of the United States of any article or articles imported or intended to be imported into the United States, or of any manufacture into which such imported article enters or is intended to enter. Every person who shall be engaged in the importation of goods or any commodity from any foreign country in violation of this section, or who shall combine or conspire with another to violate the same, is guilty of a misdemeanor, and on conviction thereof in any court of the United States such person shall be fined in a sum not less than $100 and not exceeding $5,000, and shall be further punished by imprisonment, in the discretion of the court, for a term not less than three months nor exceeding twelve months.

Section 8. The word "person", or "persons", wherever used in sections 1 to 7 of this title shall be deemed to include corporations and associations existing under or authorized by the laws of either the United States, the laws of any of the Territories, the laws of any State, or the laws of any foreign country.

The Clayton Act of 1914 (Excerpts)

Note: You can access the full text of the Clayton Act of 1914 online at **uscode.house.gov/search/criteria.shtml**. In the "Title" box, type "15," and in the "Section" box, type a relevant section number (such as, for example, "12"). Click on "Search." In the list of "documents found," click on the citation with the appropriate title (such as, in this example, "Sec. 12. Definitions; short title") to access the text of the statute.

Section 3. That it shall be unlawful for any person engaged in commerce, in the course of such commerce, to lease or make a sale or contract for sale of goods, wares, merchandise, machinery, supplies, or other commodities, whether patented or unpatented, for use, consumption, or resale within the United States or *   *   * other place under the jurisdiction of the United States, or fix a price charged therefor, or discount from, or rebate upon, such price, on the condition, agreement, or understanding that the lessee or purchaser thereof shall not use or deal in the goods, wares, merchandise, machinery, supplies, or other commodities of a competitor or competitors of the lessor or seller, where the effect of such lease, sale, or contract for sale or such condition, agreement, or understanding may be to substantially lessen competition to tend to create a monopoly in any line of commerce.

Section 4. That any person who shall be injured in his business or property by reason of anything forbidden in the antitrust laws may sue therefor in any district court of the United States in the district in which the defendant resides or is found, or has an agent, without respect to the amount in controversy, and shall recover threefold the damages by him sustained, and the cost of suit, including a reasonable attorney's fee.

Section 4A. Whenever the United States is hereafter injured in its business or property by reason of anything forbidden in the antitrust laws it may sue therefor in the United States district court for the district in which the defendant resides or is found or has an agent, without respect to the amount in controversy, and shall recover actual damages by it sustained and the cost of suit.

Section 4B. Any action to enforce any cause of action under sections 4 or 4A shall be forever barred unless commenced within four years after the cause of action accrued. No cause of action barred under existing law on the effective date of this act shall be revived by this Act.

*   *   *   *   *

Section 6. That the labor of a human being is not a commodity or article of commerce. Nothing contained in the antitrust laws shall be construed to forbid the existence and operation of labor, agricultural or horticultural organizations, instituted for the purposes of mutual help, and not having capital stock or conducted for profit, or to forbid or restrain individual members of such organizations from lawfully carrying out the legitimate objects thereof; nor shall such organizations or the members thereof, be held or construed to be illegal combinations or conspiracies in restraint of trade, under the antitrust laws.

Section 7. That no person engaged in commerce shall acquire, directly or indirectly, the whole or any part of the stock or other share capital and no corporation subject to the jurisdiction of the Federal Trade Commission shall acquire the whole or any part of the assets of another corporation engaged also in commerce, where in any line of commerce in any section of the country, the effect of such acquisition may be substantially to lessen competition, or to tend to create a monopoly.

No person shall acquire, directly or indirectly, the whole or any part of the stock or other share capital and no corporation subject to the jurisdiction of the Federal Trade Commission shall acquire the whole or any part of the assets of one or more corporations engaged in commerce, where in any line of commerce in any section of the country, the effect of such acquisition, of such stocks or assets, or of the use of such stock by the voting or granting of proxies or otherwise, may be substantially to lessen competition, or to tend to create a monopoly.

This section shall not apply to persons purchasing such stock solely for investment and not using the same by voting or otherwise to bring about, or in attempting to bring about, the substantial lessening of competition *   *   *   .

Section 8. *   *   * No person at the same time shall be a director in any two or more corporations any one of which has capital, surplus, and undivided profits aggregating more than $1,000,000 engaged in whole or in part in commerce, *   *   * if such corporations are or shall have been theretofore, by virtue of their business and location of operation, competitors, so that the elimination of competition by agreement between them would constitute a violation of any of the provisions of the antitrust laws. *   *   *

751

The Federal Trade Commission Act of 1914 (Excerpts)

Note: You can access the full text of the Federal Trade Commission Act of 1914 online at **uscode.house.gov/search/criteria.shtml**. In the "Title" box, type "15," and in the "Section" box, type a relevant section number (such as, for example, "45"). Click on "Search." In the list of "documents found," click on the citation with the appropriate title (such as, in this example, "Sec. 45. Unfair methods of competition unlawful; prevention by Commission") to access the text of the statute.

Section 5.

(a)(1) Unfair methods of competition in or affecting commerce, and unfair or deceptive acts or practices in or affecting commerce, are hereby declared unlawful.

(2) The Commission is hereby empowered and directed to prevent persons, partnerships, or corporations from using unfair methods of competition in or affecting commerce and unfair or deceptive acts or practices in or affecting commerce.

(1) Any person, partnership, or corporation who violates an order of the Commission after it has become final, and while such order is in effect, shall forfeit and pay to the United States a civil penalty of not more than $10,000 for each violation, which shall accrue to the United States and may be recovered in a civil action brought by the Attorney General of the United States. Each separate violation of such an order shall be a separate offense, except that in the case of a violation through continuing failure to obey or neglect to obey a final order of the Commission, each day of continuance of such failure or neglect shall be deemed a separate offense. In such actions, the United States district courts are empowered to grant mandatory injunctions and such other and further equitable relief as they deem appropriate in the enforcement of such final orders of the Commission.

The Securities Act of 1933 (Excerpts)

Note: You can access the full text of the Securities Act of 1933 online at **uscode.house.gov/search/criteria.shtml**. In the "Title" box, type "15," and in the "Section" box, type a relevant section number (such as, for example, "77b"). Click on "Search." In the list of "documents found," click on the citation with the appropriate title (such as, in this example, "Sec. 77b. Definitions; promotion of efficiency, competition, and capital formation") to access the text of the statute.

Definitions

Section 2. When used in this title, unless the context requires—

(1) The term "security" means any note, stock, treasury stock, bond, debenture, evidence of indebtedness, certificate of interest or participation in any profit-sharing agreement, collateral-trust certificate, preorganization certificate or subscription, transferable share, investment contract, voting-trust certificate, certificate of deposit for a security, fractional undivided interest in oil, gas, or other mineral rights, any put, call, straddle, option, or privilege on any security, certificate of deposit, or group or index of securities (including any interest therein or based on the value thereof), or any put, call, straddle, option, or privilege entered into on a national securities exchange relating to foreign currency, or, in general, any interest or participation in, temporary or interim certificate for, receipt for, guarantee of, or warrant or right to subscribe to or purchase, any of the foregoing.

Exempted Securities

Section 3. (a) Except as hereinafter expressly provided the provisions of this title shall not apply to any of the following classes of securities:

* * * *

(2) Any security issued or guaranteed by the United States or any territory thereof, or by the District of Columbia, or by any State of the United States, or by any political subdivision of a State or Territory, or by any public instrumentality of one or more States or Territories, or by any person controlled or supervised by and acting as an instrumentality of the Government of the United States pursuant to authority granted by the Congress of the United States; or any certificate of deposit for any of the foregoing; or any security issued or guaranteed by any bank; or any security issued by or representing an interest in or a direct obligation of a Federal Reserve Bank. * * * *

(3) Any note, draft, bill of exchange, or banker's acceptance which arises out of a current transaction or the proceeds of which have been or are to be used for current transactions, and which has a maturity at the time of issuance of not exceeding nine months, exclusive of days of grace, or any renewal thereof the maturity of which is likewise limited;

(4) Any security issued by a person organized and operated exclusively for religious, educational, benevolent, fraternal, charitable, or reformatory purposes and not for pecuniary profit, and no part of the net earnings of which inures to the benefit of any person, private stockholder, or individual;

* * * *

(11) Any security which is a part of an issue offered and sold only to persons resident within a single State or Territory, where the issuer of such security is a person resident and doing business within, or, if a corporation, incorporated by and doing business within, such State or Territory.

(b) The Commission may from time to time by its rules and regulations and subject to such terms and conditions as may be described therein, add any class of securities to the securities exempted as provided in this section, if it finds that the enforcement of this title with respect to such securities is not necessary in the public interest and for the protection of investors by reason of the small amount involved or the limited character of the public offering; but no issue of securities shall be exempted under this subsection where the aggregate amount at which such issue is offered to the public exceeds $5,000,000.

Exempted Transactions

Section 4. The provisions of section 5 shall not apply to—

(1) transactions by any person other than an issuer, underwriter, or dealer.

(2) transactions by an issuer not involving any public offering.

(3) transactions by a dealer (including an underwriter no longer acting as an underwriter in respect of the security involved in such transactions), except—

(A) transactions taking place prior to the expiration of forty days after the first date upon which the security was bona fide offered to the public by the issuer or by or through an underwriter.

(B) transactions in a security as to which a registration statement has been filed taking place prior to the expiration of forty days after the effective date of such registration statement or prior to the expiration of forty days after the first date upon which the security was bona fide offered to the public by the issuer or by or through an underwriter after such effective date, whichever is later (excluding in the computation of such forty days any time during which a stop order issued under section 8 is in effect as to the security), or such shorter period as the Commission may specify by rules and regulations or order, and

(C) transactions as to the securities constituting the whole or a part of an unsold allotment to or subscription by such dealer as a participant in the distribution of such securities by the issuer or by or through an underwriter.

With respect to transactions referred to in clause (B), if securities of the issuer have not previously been sold pursuant to an earlier effective registration statement the applicable period, instead of forty days, shall be ninety days, or such shorter period as the Commission may specify by rules and regulations or order.

(4) brokers' transactions, executed upon customers' orders on any exchange or in the over-the-counter market but not the solicitation of such orders.

*   *   *   *

(6) transactions involving offers or sales by an issuer solely to one or more accredited investors, if the aggregate offering price of an issue of securities offered in reliance on this paragraph does not exceed the amount allowed under Section 3(b) of this title, if there is no advertising or public solicitation in connection with the transaction by the issuer or anyone acting on the issuer's behalf, and if the issuer files such notice with the Commission as the Commission shall prescribe.

Prohibitions Relating to Interstate Commerce and the Mails

Section 5. (a) Unless a registration statement is in effect as to a security, it shall be unlawful for any person, directly or indirectly—

(1) to make use of any means or instruments of transportation or communication in interstate commerce or of the mails to sell such security through the use or medium of any prospectus or otherwise; or

(2) to carry or cause to be carried through the mails or in interstate commerce, by any means or instruments of transportation, any such security for the purpose of sale or for delivery after sale.

(b) It shall be unlawful for any person, directly or indirectly—

(1) to make use of any means or instruments of transportation or communication in interstate commerce or of the mails to carry or transmit any prospectus relating to any security with respect to which a registration statement has been filed under this title, unless such prospectus meets the requirements of section 10, or

(2) to carry or to cause to be carried through the mails or in interstate commerce any such security for the purpose of sale or for delivery after sale, unless accompanied or preceded by a prospectus that meets the requirements of subsection (a) of section 10.

(c) It shall be unlawful for any person, directly, or indirectly, to make use of any means or instruments of transportation or communication in interstate commerce or of the mails to offer to sell or offer to buy through the use or medium of any prospectus or otherwise any security, unless a registration statement has been filed as to such security, or while the registration statement is the subject of a refusal order or stop order or (prior to the effective date of the registration statement) any public proceeding of examination under section 8.

The Securities Exchange Act of 1934 (Excerpts)

Note: You can access the full text of the Securities Exchange Act of 1934 online at **uscode.house.gov/search/criteria.shtml**. In the "Title" box, type "15," and in the "Section" box, type a relevant section number (such as, for example, "78b"). Click on "Search." In the list of "documents found," click on the citation to access the text of the statute.

Definitions and Application of Title

Section 3. (a) When used in this title, unless the context otherwise requires—

* * * *

(4) The term "broker" means any person engaged in the business of effecting transactions in securities for the account of others, but does not include a bank.

(5) The term "dealer" means any person engaged in the business of buying and selling securities for his own account, through a broker or otherwise, but does not include a bank, or any person insofar as he buys or sells securities for his own account, either individually or in some fiduciary capacity, but not as part of a regular business.

* * * *

(7) The term "director" means any director of a corporation or any person performing similar functions with respect to any organization, whether incorporated or unincorporated.

(8) The term "issuer" means any person who issues or proposes to issue any security; except that with respect to certificates of deposit for securities, voting-trust certificates, or collateral-trust certificates, or with respect to certificates of interest or shares in an unincorporated investment trust not having a board of directors or the fixed, restricted management, or unit type, the term "issuer" means the person or persons performing the acts and assuming the duties of depositor or manager pursuant to the provisions of the trust or other agreement or instrument under which such securities are issued; and except that with respect to equipment-trust certificates or like securities, the term "issuer" means the person by whom the equipment or property is, or is to be, used.

(9) The term "person" means a natural person, company, government, or political subdivision, agency, or instrumentality of a government.

Regulation of the Use of Manipulative and Deceptive Devices

Section 10. It shall be unlawful for any person, directly or indirectly, by the use of any means or instrumentality of interstate commerce or of the mails, or of any facility of any national securities exchange—

(a) To effect a short sale, or to use or employ any stop-loss order in connection with the purchase or sale, of any security registered on a national securities exchange, in contravention of such rules and regulations as the Commission may prescribe as necessary or appropriate in the public interest or for the protection of investors.

(b) To use or employ, in connection with the purchase or sale of any security registered on a national securities exchange or any security not so registered, any manipulative or deceptive device or contrivance in contravention of such rules and regulations as the Commission may prescribe as necessary or appropriate in the public interest or for the protection of investors.

Electronic Signatures in Global and National Commerce Act of 2000 (Excerpts)

Note: You can access the full text of the Electronic Signatures in Global and National Commerce Act of 2000 online at **uscode.house.gov/search/criteria.shtml**. In the "Title" box, type "15," and in the "Section" box, type a relevant section number (such as "7001"). Click on "Search." In the list of "documents found," click on the citation to access the text of the statute.

SEC. 101. GENERAL RULE OF VALIDITY.

(a) IN GENERAL—Notwithstanding any statute, regulation, or other rule of law (other than this title and title II), with respect to any transaction in or affecting interstate or foreign commerce—

(1) a signature, contract, or other record relating to such transaction may not be denied legal effect, validity, or enforceability solely because it is in electronic form; and

(2) a contract relating to such transaction may not be denied legal effect, validity, or enforceability solely because an electronic signature or electronic record was used in its formation.

*　　*　　*　　*

(d) RETENTION OF CONTRACTS AND RECORDS—

(1) ACCURACY AND ACCESSIBILITY—If a statute, regulation, or other rule of law requires that a contract or other record relating to a transaction in or affecting interstate or foreign commerce be retained, that requirement is met by retaining an electronic record of the information in the contract or other record that—

   (A) accurately reflects the information set forth in the contract or other record; and

   (B) remains accessible to all persons who are entitled to access by statute, regulation, or rule of law, for the period required by such statute, regulation, or rule of law, in a form that is capable of being accurately reproduced for later reference, whether by transmission, printing, or otherwise.

(2) EXCEPTION—A requirement to retain a contract or other record in accordance with paragraph (1) does not apply to any information whose sole purpose is to enable the contract or other record to be sent, communicated, or received.

(3) ORIGINALS—If a statute, regulation, or other rule of law requires a contract or other record relating to a transaction in or affecting interstate or foreign commerce to be provided, available, or retained in its original form, or provides consequences if the contract or other record is not provided, available, or retained in its original form, that statute, regulation, or rule of law is satisfied by an electronic record that complies with paragraph (1).

(4) CHECKS—If a statute, regulation, or other rule of law requires the retention of a check, that requirement is satisfied by retention of an electronic record of the information on the front and back of the check in accordance with paragraph (1).

*　　*　　*　　*

(g) NOTARIZATION AND ACKNOWLEDGMENT—If a statute, regulation, or other rule of law requires a signature or record relating to a transaction in or affecting interstate or foreign commerce to be notarized, acknowledged, verified, or made under oath, that requirement is satisfied if the electronic signature of the person authorized to perform those acts, together with all other information required to be included by other applicable statute, regulation, or rule of law, is attached to or logically associated with the signature or record.

(h) ELECTRONIC AGENTS—A contract or other record relating to a transaction in or affecting interstate or foreign commerce may not be denied legal effect, validity, or enforceability solely because its formation, creation, or delivery involved the action of one or more electronic agents so long as the action of any such electronic agent is legally attributable to the person to be bound.

(i) INSURANCE—It is the specific intent of the Congress that this title and title II apply to the business of insurance.

(j) INSURANCE AGENTS AND BROKERS—An insurance agent or broker acting under the direction of a party that enters into a contract by means of an electronic record or electronic signature may not be held liable for any deficiency in the electronic procedures agreed to by the parties under that contract if—

(1) the agent or broker has not engaged in negligent, reckless, or intentional tortious conduct;

(2) the agent or broker was not involved in the development or establishment of such electronic procedures; and

(3) the agent or broker did not deviate from such procedures.

* * * *

SEC. 103. SPECIFIC EXCEPTIONS.

(a) EXCEPTED REQUIREMENTS—The provisions of section 101 shall not apply to a contract or other record to the extent it is governed by—

(1) a statute, regulation, or other rule of law governing the creation and execution of wills, codicils, or testamentary trusts;

(2) a State statute, regulation, or other rule of law governing adoption, divorce, or other matters of family law; or

(3) the Uniform Commercial Code, as in effect in any State, other than sections 1–107 and 1–206 and Articles 2 and 2A.

(b) ADDITIONAL EXCEPTIONS—The provisions of section 101 shall not apply to—

(1) court orders or notices, or official court documents (including briefs, pleadings, and other writings) required to be executed in connection with court proceedings;

(2) any notice of—

(A) the cancellation or termination of utility services (including water, heat, and power);

(B) default, acceleration, repossession, foreclosure, or eviction, or the right to cure, under a credit agreement secured by, or a rental agreement for, a primary residence of an individual;

(C) the cancellation or termination of health insurance or benefits or life insurance benefits (excluding annuities); or

(D) recall of a product, or material failure of a product, that risks endangering health or safety; or

(3) any document required to accompany any transportation or handling of hazardous materials, pesticides, or other toxic or dangerous materials.

The Uniform Electronic Transactions Act (Excerpts)

Note: You can access the full text of the Uniform Electronic Transactions Act online at **www.law.upenn.edu/bll/ulc/fnact99/1990s/ueta99.htm**. This is a page within the Web site of the University of Pennsylvania Law School, which provides drafts of uniform and model acts in association with the National Conference of Commissioners on Uniform State Laws.

*　　*　　*　　*

Section 5. USE OF ELECTRONIC RECORDS AND ELECTRONIC SIGNATURES; VARIATION BY AGREEMENT.

(a) This [Act] does not require a record or signature to be created, generated, sent, communicated, received, stored, or otherwise processed or used by electronic means or in electronic form.

(b) This [Act] applies only to transactions between parties each of which has agreed to conduct transactions by electronic means. Whether the parties agree to conduct a transaction by electronic means is determined from the context and surrounding circumstances, including the parties' conduct.

(c) A party that agrees to conduct a transaction by electronic means may refuse to conduct other transactions by electronic means. The right granted by this subsection may not be waived by agreement.

(d) Except as otherwise provided in this [Act], the effect of any of its provisions may be varied by agreement. The presence in certain provisions of this [Act] of the words "unless otherwise agreed," or words of similar import, does not imply that the effect of other provisions may not be varied by agreement.

(e) Whether an electronic record or electronic signature has legal consequences is determined by this [Act] and other applicable law.

Section 6. CONSTRUCTION AND APPLICATION. This [Act] must be construed and applied:

(1) to facilitate electronic transactions consistent with other applicable law; (2) to be consistent with reasonable practices concerning electronic transactions and with the continued expansion of those practices; and

(3) to effectuate its general purpose to make uniform the law with respect to the subject of this [Act] among States enacting it.

Section 7. LEGAL RECOGNITION OF ELECTRONIC RECORDS, ELECTRONIC SIGNATURES, AND ELECTRONIC CONTRACTS.

(a) A record or signature may not be denied legal effect or enforceability solely because it is in electronic form.

(b) A contract may not be denied legal effect or enforceability solely because an electronic record was used in its formation.

(c) If a law requires a record to be in writing, an electronic record satisfies the law.

(d) If a law requires a signature, an electronic signature satisfies the law.

*　　*　　*　　*

Section 10. EFFECT OF CHANGE OR ERROR. If a change or error in an electronic record occurs in a transmission between parties to a transaction, the following rules apply:

(1) If the parties have agreed to use a security procedure to detect changes or errors and one party has conformed to the procedure, but the other party has not, and the nonconforming party would have detected the change or error had that party also conformed, the conforming party may avoid the effect of the changed or erroneous electronic record.

(2) In an automated transaction involving an individual, the individual may avoid the effect of an electronic record that resulted from an error made by the individual in dealing with the electronic agent of another person if the electronic agent did not provide an opportunity for the prevention or correction of the error and, at the time the individual learns of the error, the individual:

(A) promptly notifies the other person of the error and that the individual did not intend to be bound by the electronic record received by the other person;

(B) takes reasonable steps, including steps that conform to the other person's reasonable instructions, to return to the other person or, if instructed by the other person, to destroy the consideration received, if any, as a result of the erroneous electronic record; and

(C) has not used or received any benefit or value from the consideration, if any, received from the other person.

(3) If neither paragraph (1) nor paragraph (2) applies, the change or error has the effect provided by other law, including the law of mistake, and the parties' contract, if any.

(4) Paragraphs (2) and (3) may not be varied by agreement.

The Sarbanes-Oxley Act of 2002 (Excerpts and Explanatory Comments)

Note: The author's explanatory comments appear in italics following the excerpt from each section.

SECTION 302

Corporate responsibility for financial reports[1]

(a) Regulations required

The Commission shall, by rule, require, for each company filing periodic reports under section 13(a) or 15(d) of the Securities Exchange Act of 1934 (15 U.S.C. 78m, 78o(d)), that the principal executive officer or officers and the principal financial officer or officers, or persons performing similar functions, certify in each annual or quarterly report filed or submitted under either such section of such Act that—

(1) the signing officer has reviewed the report;

(2) based on the officer's knowledge, the report does not contain any untrue statement of a material fact or omit to state a material fact necessary in order to make the statements made, in light of the circumstances under which such statements were made, not misleading;

(3) based on such officer's knowledge, the financial statements, and other financial information included in the report, fairly present in all material respects the financial condition and results of operations of the issuer as of, and for, the periods presented in the report;

(4) the signing officers—

(A) are responsible for establishing and maintaining internal controls;

(B) have designed such internal controls to ensure that material information relating to the issuer and its consolidated subsidiaries is made known to such officers by others within those entities, particularly during the period in which the periodic reports are being prepared;

(C) have evaluated the effectiveness of the issuer's internal controls as of a date within 90 days prior to the report; and

(D) have presented in the report their conclusions about the effectiveness of their internal controls based on their evaluation as of that date;

(5) the signing officers have disclosed to the issuer's auditors and the audit committee of the board of directors (or persons fulfilling the equivalent function)—

(A) all significant deficiencies in the design or operation of internal controls which could adversely affect the issuer's ability to record, process, summarize, and report financial data and have identified for the issuer's auditors any material weaknesses in internal controls; and

(B) any fraud, whether or not material, that involves management or other employees who have a significant role in the issuer's internal controls; and

(6) the signing officers have indicated in the report whether or not there were significant changes in internal controls or in other factors that could significantly affect internal controls subsequent to the date of their evaluation, including any corrective actions with regard to significant deficiencies and material weaknesses.

(b) Foreign reincorporations have no effect

Nothing in this section shall be interpreted or applied in any way to allow any issuer to lessen the legal force of the statement required under this section, by an issuer having reincorporated or having engaged in any other transaction that resulted in the transfer of the corporate domicile or offices of the issuer from inside the United States to outside of the United States.

(c) Deadline

The rules required by subsection (a) of this section shall be effective not later than 30 days after July 30, 2002.

EXPLANATORY COMMENTS: *Section 302 requires the chief executive officer (CEO) and chief financial officer (CFO) of each public company to certify that they have reviewed the company's quarterly and annual reports to be filed with the Securities and Exchange Commission (SEC). The CEO and CFO must certify that, based on their knowledge, the reports do not contain any untrue statement of a*

---

1. This section of the Sarbanes-Oxley Act is codified at 15 U.S.C. Section 7241.

material fact or any half-truth that would make the report misleading, and that the information contained in the reports fairly presents the company's financial condition.

In addition, this section also requires the CEO and CFO to certify that they have created and designed an internal control system for their company and have recently evaluated that system to ensure that it is effectively providing them with relevant and accurate financial information. If the signing officers have found any significant deficiencies or weaknesses in the company's system or have discovered any evidence of fraud, they must have reported the situation, and any corrective actions they have taken, to the auditors and the audit committee.

SECTION 306

Insider trades during pension fund blackout periods[2]

(a) Prohibition of insider trading during pension fund blackout periods

(1) In general

Except to the extent otherwise provided by rule of the Commission pursuant to paragraph (3), it shall be unlawful for any director or executive officer of an issuer of any equity security (other than an exempted security), directly or indirectly, to purchase, sell, or otherwise acquire or transfer any equity security of the issuer (other than an exempted security) during any blackout period with respect to such equity security if such director or officer acquires such equity security in connection with his or her service or employment as a director or executive officer.

(2) Remedy

(A) In general

Any profit realized by a director or executive officer referred to in paragraph (1) from any purchase, sale, or other acquisition or transfer in violation of this subsection shall inure to and be recoverable by the issuer, irrespective of any intention on the part of such director or executive officer in entering into the transaction.

(B) Actions to recover profits

An action to recover profits in accordance with this subsection may be instituted at law or in equity in any court of competent jurisdiction by the issuer, or by the owner of any security of the issuer in the name and in behalf of the issuer if the issuer fails or refuses to bring such action within 60 days after the date of request, or fails diligently to prosecute the action thereafter, except that no such suit shall be brought more than 2 years after the date on which such profit was realized.

(3) Rulemaking authorized

The Commission shall, in consultation with the Secretary of Labor, issue rules to clarify the application of this subsection and to prevent evasion thereof. Such rules shall provide for the application of the requirements of para-

graph (1) with respect to entities treated as a single employer with respect to an issuer under section 414(b), (c), (m), or (o) of Title 26 to the extent necessary to clarify the application of such requirements and to prevent evasion thereof. Such rules may also provide for appropriate exceptions from the requirements of this subsection, including exceptions for purchases pursuant to an automatic dividend reinvestment program or purchases or sales made pursuant to an advance election.

(4) Blackout period

For purposes of this subsection, the term "blackout period", with respect to the equity securities of any issuer—

(A) means any period of more than 3 consecutive business days during which the ability of not fewer than 50 percent of the participants or beneficiaries under all individual account plans maintained by the issuer to purchase, sell, or otherwise acquire or transfer an interest in any equity of such issuer held in such an individual account plan is temporarily suspended by the issuer or by a fiduciary of the plan; and

(B) does not include, under regulations which shall be prescribed by the Commission—

(i) a regularly scheduled period in which the participants and beneficiaries may not purchase, sell, or otherwise acquire or transfer an interest in any equity of such issuer, if such period is—

(I) incorporated into the individual account plan; and

(II) timely disclosed to employees before becoming participants under the individual account plan or as a subsequent amendment to the plan; or

(ii) any suspension described in subparagraph (A) that is imposed solely in connection with persons becoming participants or beneficiaries, or ceasing to be participants or beneficiaries, in an individual account plan by reason of a corporate merger, acquisition, divestiture, or similar transaction involving the plan or plan sponsor.

(5) Individual account plan

For purposes of this subsection, the term "individual account plan" has the meaning provided in section 1002(34) of Title 29, except that such term shall not include a one-participant retirement plan (within the meaning of section 1021(i)(8)(B) of Title 29).

(6) Notice to directors, executive officers, and the Commission

In any case in which a director or executive officer is subject to the requirements of this subsection in connection with a blackout period (as defined in paragraph (4)) with respect to any equity securities, the issuer of such equity securities shall timely notify such director or officer and the Securities and Exchange Commission of such blackout period.

---

2. Codified at 15 U.S.C. Section 7244.

* * * *

EXPLANATORY COMMENTS: *Corporate pension funds typically prohibit employees from trading shares of the corporation during periods when the pension fund is undergoing significant change. Prior to 2002, however, these blackout periods did not affect the corporation's executives, who frequently received shares of the corporate stock as part of their compensation. During the collapse of Enron, for example, its pension plan was scheduled to change administrators at a time when Enron's stock price was falling. Enron's employees therefore could not sell their shares while the price was dropping, but its executives could and did sell their stock, consequently avoiding some of the losses. Section 306 was Congress's solution to the basic unfairness of this situation. This section of the act required the SEC to issue rules that prohibit any director or executive officer from trading during pension fund blackout periods. (The SEC later issued these rules, entitled Regulation Blackout Trading Restriction, or Reg BTR.) Section 306 also provided shareholders with a right to file a shareholder's derivative suit against officers and directors who have profited from trading during these blackout periods (provided that the corporation has failed to bring a suit). The officer or director can be forced to return to the corporation any profits received, regardless of whether the director or officer acted with bad intent.*

SECTION 402

Periodical and other reports[3]

* * * *

(i) Accuracy of financial reports

Each financial report that contains financial statements, and that is required to be prepared in accordance with (or reconciled to) generally accepted accounting principles under this chapter and filed with the Commission shall reflect all material correcting adjustments that have been identified by a registered public accounting firm in accordance with generally accepted accounting principles and the rules and regulations of the Commission.

(j) Off-balance sheet transactions

Not later than 180 days after July 30, 2002, the Commission shall issue final rules providing that each annual and quarterly financial report required to be filed with the Commission shall disclose all material off-balance sheet transactions, arrangements, obligations (including contingent obligations), and other relationships of the issuer with unconsolidated entities or other persons, that may have a material current or future effect on financial condition, changes in financial condition, results of operations, liquidity, capital expenditures, capital resources, or significant components of revenues or expenses.

(k) Prohibition on personal loans to executives

(1) In general

It shall be unlawful for any issuer (as defined in section 7201 of this title), directly or indirectly, including through any subsidiary, to extend or maintain credit, to arrange for the extension of credit, or to renew an extension of credit, in the form of a personal loan to or for any director or executive officer (or equivalent thereof) of that issuer. An extension of credit maintained by the issuer on July 30, 2002, shall not be subject to the provisions of this subsection, provided that there is no material modification to any term of any such extension of credit or any renewal of any such extension of credit on or after July 30, 2002.

(2) Limitation

Paragraph (1) does not preclude any home improvement and manufactured home loans (as that term is defined in section 1464 of Title 12), consumer credit (as defined in section 1602 of this title), or any extension of credit under an open end credit plan (as defined in section 1602 of this title), or a charge card (as defined in section 1637(c)(4)(e) of this title), or any extension of credit by a broker or dealer registered under section 78o of this title to an employee of that broker or dealer to buy, trade, or carry securities, that is permitted under rules or regulations of the Board of Governors of the Federal Reserve System pursuant to section 78g of this title (other than an extension of credit that would be used to purchase the stock of that issuer), that is—

(A) made or provided in the ordinary course of the consumer credit business of such issuer;

(B) of a type that is generally made available by such issuer to the public; and

(C) made by such issuer on market terms, or terms that are no more favorable than those offered by the issuer to the general public for such extensions of credit.

(3) Rule of construction for certain loans

Paragraph (1) does not apply to any loan made or maintained by an insured depository institution (as defined in section 1813 of Title 12), if the loan is subject to the insider lending restrictions of section 375b of Title 12.

(l) Real time issuer disclosures

Each issuer reporting under subsection (a) of this section or section 78o(d) of this title shall disclose to the public on a rapid and current basis such additional information concerning material changes in the financial condition or operations of the issuer, in plain English, which may include trend and qualitative information and graphic presentations, as the Commission determines, by rule, is necessary or useful for the protection of investors and in the public interest.

EXPLANATORY COMMENTS: *Corporate executives during the Enron era typically received extremely large salaries, significant bonuses, and abundant stock options, even when*

---

3. This section of the Sarbanes-Oxley Act amended some of the provisions of the 1934 Securities Exchange Act and added the paragraphs reproduced here at 15 U.S.C. Section 78m.

the companies for which they worked were suffering. Executives were also routinely given personal loans from corporate funds, many of which were never paid back. The average large company during that period loaned almost $1 million a year to top executives, and some companies, including Tyco International and Adelphia Communications Corporation, loaned hundreds of millions of dollars to their executives every year. Section 402 amended the 1934 Securities Exchange Act to prohibit public companies from making personal loans to executive officers and directors. There are a few exceptions to this prohibition, such as home-improvement loans made in the ordinary course of business. Note also that while loans are forbidden, outright gifts are not. A corporation is free to give gifts to its executives, including cash, provided that these gifts are disclosed on its financial reports. The idea is that corporate directors will be deterred from making substantial gifts to their executives by the disclosure requirement—particularly if the corporation's financial condition is questionable—because making such gifts could be perceived as abusing their authority.

SECTION 403

Directors, officers, and principal stockholders[4]

(a) Disclosures required

(1) Directors, officers, and principal stockholders required to file

Every person who is directly or indirectly the beneficial owner of more than 10 percent of any class of any equity security (other than an exempted security) which is registered pursuant to section 78l of this title, or who is a director or an officer of the issuer of such security, shall file the statements required by this subsection with the Commission (and, if such security is registered on a national securities exchange, also with the exchange).

(2) Time of filing

The statements required by this subsection shall be filed—

(A) at the time of the registration of such security on a national securities exchange or by the effective date of a registration statement filed pursuant to section 78l(g) of this title;

(B) within 10 days after he or she becomes such beneficial owner, director, or officer;

(C) if there has been a change in such ownership, or if such person shall have purchased or sold a security-based swap agreement (as defined in section 206(b) of the Gramm-Leach-Bliley Act (15 U.S.C. 78c note)) involving such equity security, before the end of the second business day following the day on which the subject transaction has been executed, or at such other

time as the Commission shall establish, by rule, in any case in which the Commission determines that such 2-day period is not feasible.

(3) Contents of statements

A statement filed—

(A) under subparagraph (A) or (B) of paragraph (2) shall contain a statement of the amount of all equity securities of such issuer of which the filing person is the beneficial owner; and

(B) under subparagraph (C) of such paragraph shall indicate ownership by the filing person at the date of filing, any such changes in such ownership, and such purchases and sales of the security-based swap agreements as have occurred since the most recent such filing under such subparagraph.

(4) Electronic filing and availability

Beginning not later than 1 year after July 30, 2002—

(A) a statement filed under subparagraph (C) of paragraph (2) shall be filed electronically;

(B) the Commission shall provide each such statement on a publicly accessible Internet site not later than the end of the business day following that filing; and

(C) the issuer (if the issuer maintains a corporate website) shall provide that statement on that corporate website, not later than the end of the business day following that filing.

* * * *

EXPLANATORY COMMENTS: *This section dramatically shortens the time period provided in the Securities Exchange Act of 1934 for disclosing transactions by insiders. The prior law stated that most transactions had to be reported within ten days of the beginning of the following month, although certain transactions did not have to be reported until the following fiscal year (within the first forty-five days). Because some of the insider trading that occurred during the Enron fiasco did not have to be disclosed (and was therefore not discovered) until long after the transactions, Congress added this section to reduce the time period for making disclosures. Under Section 403, most transactions by insiders must be electronically filed with the SEC within two business days. Also, any company that maintains a Web site must post these SEC filings on its site by the end of the next business day. Congress enacted this section in the belief that if insiders are required to file reports of their transactions promptly with the SEC, companies will do more to police themselves and prevent insider trading.*

SECTION 404

Management assessment of internal controls[5]

(a) Rules required

---

4. This section of the Sarbanes-Oxley Act amended the disclosure provisions of the 1934 Securities Exchange Act, at 15 U.S.C. Section 78p.

5. Codified at 15 U.S.C. Section 7262.

The Commission shall prescribe rules requiring each annual report required by section 78m(a) or 78o(d) of this title to contain an internal control report, which shall—

(1) state the responsibility of management for establishing and maintaining an adequate internal control structure and procedures for financial reporting; and

(2) contain an assessment, as of the end of the most recent fiscal year of the issuer, of the effectiveness of the internal control structure and procedures of the issuer for financial reporting.

(b) Internal control evaluation and reporting

With respect to the internal control assessment required by subsection (a) of this section, each registered public accounting firm that prepares or issues the audit report for the issuer shall attest to, and report on, the assessment made by the management of the issuer. An attestation made under this subsection shall be made in accordance with standards for attestation engagements issued or adopted by the Board. Any such attestation shall not be the subject of a separate engagement.

EXPLANATORY COMMENTS: *This section was enacted to prevent corporate executives from claiming they were ignorant of significant errors in their companies' financial reports. For instance, several CEOs testified before Congress that they simply had no idea that the corporations' financial statements were off by billions of dollars. Congress therefore passed Section 404, which requires each annual report to contain a description and assessment of the company's internal control structure and financial reporting procedures. The section also requires that an audit be conducted of the internal control assessment, as well as the financial statements contained in the report. This section goes hand in hand with Section 302 (which, as discussed previously, requires various certifications attesting to the accuracy of the information in financial reports).*

Section 404 has been one of the more controversial and expensive provisions in the Sarbanes-Oxley Act because it requires companies to assess their own internal financial controls to make sure that their financial statements are reliable and accurate. A corporation might need to set up a disclosure committee and a coordinator, establish codes of conduct for accounting and financial personnel, create documentation procedures, provide training, and outline the individuals who are responsible for performing each of the procedures. Companies that were already well managed have not experienced substantial difficulty complying with this section. Other companies, however, have spent millions of dollars setting up, documenting, and evaluating their internal financial control systems. Although initially creating the internal financial control system is a onetime-only expense, the costs of maintaining and evaluating it are ongoing. Some corporations that spent considerable sums complying with Section 404 have been able to offset these costs by discovering and correcting inefficiencies or frauds within their systems. Nevertheless, it is unlikely that

any corporation will find compliance with this section to be inexpensive.

SECTION 802 (A)

Destruction, alteration, or falsification of records in Federal investigations and bankruptcy[6]

Whoever knowingly alters, destroys, mutilates, conceals, covers up, falsifies, or makes a false entry in any record, document, or tangible object with the intent to impede, obstruct, or influence the investigation or proper administration of any matter within the jurisdiction of any department or agency of the United States or any case filed under title 11, or in relation to or contemplation of any such matter or case, shall be fined under this title, imprisoned not more than 20 years, or both.

Destruction of corporate audit records[7]

(a) (1) Any accountant who conducts an audit of an issuer of securities to which section 10A(a) of the Securities Exchange Act of 1934 (15 U.S.C. 78j-1(a)) applies, shall maintain all audit or review workpapers for a period of 5 years from the end of the fiscal period in which the audit or review was concluded.

(2) The Securities and Exchange Commission shall promulgate, within 180 days, after adequate notice and an opportunity for comment, such rules and regulations, as are reasonably necessary, relating to the retention of relevant records such as workpapers, documents that form the basis of an audit or review, memoranda, correspondence, communications, other documents, and records (including electronic records) which are created, sent, or received in connection with an audit or review and contain conclusions, opinions, analyses, or financial data relating to such an audit or review, which is conducted by any accountant who conducts an audit of an issuer of securities to which section 10A(a) of the Securities Exchange Act of 1934 (15 U.S.C. 78j-1(a)) applies. The Commission may, from time to time, amend or supplement the rules and regulations that it is required to promulgate under this section, after adequate notice and an opportunity for comment, in order to ensure that such rules and regulations adequately comport with the purposes of this section.

(b) Whoever knowingly and willfully violates subsection (a)(1), or any rule or regulation promulgated by the Securities and Exchange Commission under subsection (a)(2), shall be fined under this title, imprisoned not more than 10 years, or both.

(c) Nothing in this section shall be deemed to diminish or relieve any person of any other duty or obligation imposed by Federal or State law or regulation to maintain, or refrain from destroying, any document.

EXPLANATORY COMMENTS: *Section 802(a) enacted two new statutes that punish those who alter or destroy documents.*

---

6. Codified at 15 U.S.C. Section 1519.
7. Codified at 15 U.S.C. Section 1520.

The first statute is not specifically limited to securities fraud cases. It provides that anyone who alters, destroys, or falsifies records in federal investigations or bankruptcy may be criminally prosecuted and sentenced to a fine or to up to twenty years in prison, or both. The second statute requires auditors of public companies to keep all audit or review working papers for five years but expressly allows the SEC to amend or supplement these requirements as it sees fit. The SEC has, in fact, amended this section by issuing a rule that requires auditors who audit reporting companies to retain working papers for seven years from the conclusion of the review. Section 802(a) further provides that anyone who knowingly and willfully violates this statute is subject to criminal prosecution and can be sentenced to a fine, imprisoned for up to ten years, or both if convicted.

This portion of the Sarbanes-Oxley Act implicitly recognizes that persons who are under investigation often are tempted to respond by destroying or falsifying documents that might prove their complicity in wrongdoing. The severity of the punishment should provide a strong incentive for these individuals to resist the temptation.

SECTION 804

Time limitations on the commencement of civil actions arising under Acts of Congress[8]

(a) Except as otherwise provided by law, a civil action arising under an Act of Congress enacted after the date of the enactment of this section may not be commenced later than 4 years after the cause of action accrues.

(b) Notwithstanding subsection (a), a private right of action that involves a claim of fraud, deceit, manipulation, or contrivance in contravention of a regulatory requirement concerning the securities laws, as defined in section 3(a)(47) of the Securities Exchange Act of 1934 (15 U.S.C. 78c(a)(47)), may be brought not later than the earlier of—

(1) 2 years after the discovery of the facts constituting the violation; or

(2) 5 years after such violation.

EXPLANATORY COMMENTS: *Prior to the enactment of this section, Section 10(b) of the Securities Exchange Act of 1934 had no express statute of limitations. The courts generally required plaintiffs to have filed suit within one year from the date that they should (using due diligence) have discovered that a fraud had been committed but no later than three years after the fraud occurred. Section 804 extends this period by specifying that plaintiffs must file a lawsuit within two years after they discover (or should have discovered) a fraud but no later than five years after the fraud's occurrence. This provision has prevented the courts from dismissing numerous securities fraud lawsuits.*

SECTION 806

Civil action to protect against retaliation in fraud cases[9]

(a) Whistleblower protection for employees of publicly traded companies.—

No company with a class of securities registered under section 12 of the Securities Exchange Act of 1934 (15 U.S.C. 78l), or that is required to file reports under section 15(d) of the Securities Exchange Act of 1934 (15 U.S.C. 78o(d)), or any officer, employee, contractor, subcontractor, or agent of such company, may discharge, demote, suspend, threaten, harass, or in any other manner discriminate against an employee in the terms and conditions of employment because of any lawful act done by the employee—

(1) to provide information, cause information to be provided, or otherwise assist in an investigation regarding any conduct which the employee reasonably believes constitutes a violation of section 1341, 1343, 1344, or 1348, any rule or regulation of the Securities and Exchange Commission, or any provision of Federal law relating to fraud against shareholders, when the information or assistance is provided to or the investigation is conducted by—

(A) a Federal regulatory or law enforcement agency;

(B) any Member of Congress or any committee of Congress; or

(C) a person with supervisory authority over the employee (or such other person working for the employer who has the authority to investigate, discover, or terminate misconduct); or

(2) to file, cause to be filed, testify, participate in, or otherwise assist in a proceeding filed or about to be filed (with any knowledge of the employer) relating to an alleged violation of section 1341, 1343, 1344, or 1348, any rule or regulation of the Securities and Exchange Commission, or any provision of Federal law relating to fraud against shareholders.

(b) Enforcement action.—

(1) In general.—A person who alleges discharge or other discrimination by any person in violation of subsection (a) may seek relief under subsection (c), by—

(A) filing a complaint with the Secretary of Labor; or

(B) if the Secretary has not issued a final decision within 180 days of the filing of the complaint and there is no showing that such delay is due to the bad faith of the claimant, bringing an action at law or equity for de novo review in the appropriate district court of the United States, which shall have jurisdiction over such an action without regard to the amount in controversy.

(2) Procedure.—

(A) In general.—An action under paragraph (1)(A) shall be governed under the rules and procedures set forth in section 42121(b) of title 49, United States Code.

---

8. Codified at 28 U.S.C. Section 1658.

9. Codified at 18 U.S.C. Section 1514A.

(B) Exception.—Notification made under section 42121(b)(1) of title 49, United States Code, shall be made to the person named in the complaint and to the employer.

(C) Burdens of proof.—An action brought under paragraph (1)(B) shall be governed by the legal burdens of proof set forth in section 42121(b) of title 49, United States Code.

(D) Statute of limitations.—An action under paragraph (1) shall be commenced not later than 90 days after the date on which the violation occurs.

(c) Remedies.—

(1) In general.—An employee prevailing in any action under subsection (b)(1) shall be entitled to all relief necessary to make the employee whole.

(2) Compensatory damages.—Relief for any action under paragraph (1) shall include—

(A) reinstatement with the same seniority status that the employee would have had, but for the discrimination;

(B) the amount of back pay, with interest; and

(C) compensation for any special damages sustained as a result of the discrimination, including litigation costs, expert witness fees, and reasonable attorney fees.

(d) Rights retained by employee.—Nothing in this section shall be deemed to diminish the rights, privileges, or remedies of any employee under any Federal or State law, or under any collective bargaining agreement.

EXPLANATORY COMMENTS: *Section 806 is one of several provisions that were included in the Sarbanes-Oxley Act to encourage and protect whistleblowers—that is, employees who report their employer's alleged violations of securities law to the authorities. This section applies to employees, agents, and independent contractors who work for publicly traded companies or testify about such a company during an investigation. It sets up an administrative procedure at the Department of Labor for individuals who claim that their employer retaliated against them (fired or demoted them, for example) for blowing the whistle on the employer's wrongful conduct. It also allows the award of civil damages—including back pay, reinstatement, special damages, attorneys' fees, and court costs—to employees who prove that they suffered retaliation. Since this provision was enacted, whistleblowers have filed numerous complaints with the Department of Labor under this section.*

SECTION 807

Securities fraud[10]

Whoever knowingly executes, or attempts to execute, a scheme or artifice—

(1) to defraud any person in connection with any security of an issuer with a class of securities registered under section 12 of the Securities Exchange Act of 1934 (15 U.S.C. 78l) or that is required to file reports under section 15(d) of the Securities Exchange Act of 1934 (15 U.S.C. 78o(d)); or

(2) to obtain, by means of false or fraudulent pretenses, representations, or promises, any money or property in connection with the purchase or sale of any security of an issuer with a class of securities registered under section 12 of the Securities Exchange Act of 1934 (15 U.S.C. 78l) or that is required to file reports under section 15(d) of the Securities Exchange Act of 1934 (15 U.S.C. 78o(d)); shall be fined under this title, or imprisoned not more than 25 years, or both.

EXPLANATORY COMMENTS: *Section 807 adds a new provision to the federal criminal code that addresses securities fraud. Prior to 2002, federal securities law had already made it a crime—under Section 10(b) of the Securities Exchange Act of 1934 and SEC Rule 10b-5, both of which are discussed in Chapter 21—to intentionally defraud someone in connection with a purchase or sale of securities, but the offense was not listed in the federal criminal code. Also, paragraph 2 of Section 807 goes beyond what is prohibited under securities law by making it a crime to obtain by means of false or fraudulent pretenses any money or property from the purchase or sale of securities. This new provision allows violators to be punished by up to twenty-five years in prison, a fine, or both.*

SECTION 906

Failure of corporate officers to certify financial reports[11]

(a) Certification of periodic financial reports.—Each periodic report containing financial statements filed by an issuer with the Securities Exchange Commission pursuant to section 13(a) or 15(d) of the Securities Exchange Act of 1934 (15 U.S.C. 78m(a) or 78o(d)) shall be accompanied by a written statement by the chief executive officer and chief financial officer (or equivalent thereof) of the issuer.

(b) Content.—The statement required under subsection (a) shall certify that the periodic report containing the financial statements fully complies with the requirements of section 13(a) or 15(d) of the Securities Exchange Act of 1934 (15 U.S.C. 78m or 78o(d)) and that information contained in the periodic report fairly presents, in all material respects, the financial condition and results of operations of the issuer.

(c) Criminal penalties.—Whoever—

(1) certifies any statement as set forth in subsections (a) and (b) of this section knowing that the periodic report accompanying the statement does not comport with all the

---

10. Codified at 18 U.S.C. Section 1348.

11. Codified at 18 U.S.C. Section 1350.

requirements set forth in this section shall be fined not more than $1,000,000 or imprisoned not more than 10 years, or both; or

(2) willfully certifies any statement as set forth in subsections (a) and (b) of this section knowing that the periodic report accompanying the statement does not comport with all the requirements set forth in this section shall be fined not more than $5,000,000, or imprisoned not more than 20 years, or both.

EXPLANATORY COMMENTS: *As previously discussed, under Section 302 a corporation's CEO and CFO are required to certify that they believe the quarterly and annual reports their company files with the SEC are accurate and fairly present the company's financial condition. Section 906 adds "teeth" to these requirements by authorizing criminal penalties for those officers who intentionally certify inaccurate SEC filings. Knowing violations of the requirements are punishable by a fine of up to $1 million, ten years in prison, or both. Willful violators may be fined up to $5 million, sentenced to up to twenty years in prison, or both. Although the difference between a knowing and a willful violation is not entirely clear, the section is obviously intended to remind corporate officers of the serious consequences of certifying inaccurate reports to the SEC.*

Chapter 1

2A. *What is common law tradition?*

Because of our colonial heritage, much of American law is based on the English legal system. In that system, after the Norman Conquest, the king's courts sought to establish a uniform set of rules for the entire country. What evolved in these courts was the common law—a body of general legal principles that applied throughout the entire English realm. Courts developed the common law rules from the principles underlying judges' decisions in actual legal controversies.

4A. *What is the difference between remedies at law and remedies in equity?*

An award of compensation in either money or property, including land, is a remedy at law. Remedies in equity include a decree for *specific performance* (an order to perform what was promised), an *injunction* (an order directing a party to do or refrain from doing a particular act), and *rescission* (cancellation) of a contract (and a return of the parties to the positions that they held before the contract's formation). As a rule, courts will grant an equitable remedy only when the remedy at law (money damages) is inadequate. Remedies in equity on the whole are more flexible than remedies at law.

Chapter 2

2A. *How can business leaders encourage their companies to act ethically?*

Ethical leadership is important to create and maintain an ethical workplace. Management can set standards and apply those standards to themselves and their firm's employees.

4A. *What duties do professionals owe to those who rely on their services?*

Generally, professionals are subject to standards of conduct established by codes of professional ethics, as well as the law. To those who rely on their services, professionals owe duties that include compliance with the standards of care, knowledge, and judgment set by these sources.

Chapter 3

2A. *Before a court can hear a case, it must have jurisdiction. Over what must it have jurisdiction? How are the courts applying traditional jurisdictional concepts to cases involving Internet transactions?*

To hear a case, a court must have jurisdiction over the person against whom the suit is brought or over the property involved in the suit. The court must also have jurisdiction over the subject matter. Generally, courts apply a "sliding-scale" standard to determine when it is proper to exercise jurisdiction over a defendant whose only connection with the jurisdiction is the Internet.

4A. *In a lawsuit, what are pleadings? What is discovery, and how does electronic discovery differ? What is electronic filing?*

The pleadings include a plaintiff's complaint and a defendant's answer (and the counterclaim and reply). The pleadings inform each party of the other's claims and specify the issues involved in a case. Discovery is the process of obtaining information and evidence about a case from the other party or third parties. Discovery entails gaining access to witnesses, documents, records, and other types of evidence. Electronic discovery differs in its subject (e-media rather than traditional sources of information). Electronic filing involves the filing of court documents in electronic media, typically over the Internet.

Chapter 4

2A. *What constitutional clause gives the federal government the power to regulate commercial activities among the various states?*

To prevent states from establishing laws and regulations that would interfere with trade and commerce among the states, the Constitution expressly delegated to the national government the power to regulate interstate commerce. The commerce clause (Article I, Section 8, of the U.S. Constitution) expressly permits Congress "[t]o regulate Commerce with foreign Nations, and among the several States, and with the Indian Tribes."

4A. *What is the Bill of Rights? What freedoms are guaranteed by the First Amendment?*

The Bill of Rights consists of the first ten amendments to the U.S. Constitution. Adopted in 1791, the Bill of Rights embodies protections for individuals against interference by the federal government. Some of the protections also apply to business entities. The First Amendment guarantees the freedoms of religion, speech, and the press, and the rights to assemble peaceably and to petition the government.

Chapter 5

2A. *What is the purpose of tort law? What are two basic categories of torts?*

Generally, the purpose of tort law is to provide remedies for the invasion of legally recognized and protected interests (personal safety, freedom of movement, property, and some intangibles, including privacy and reputation). The two broad categories of torts are intentional and unintentional.

4A. *What are the elements of a cause of action in strict product liability?*

Under Section 402A of the *Restatement (Second) of Torts,* the elements of an action for strict product liability are (1) the product must be in a defective condition when the defendant sells it, (2) the defendant must normally be engaged in the business of selling (or distributing) that product, (3) the product must be unreasonably dangerous to the user or consumer because of its defective condition (in most states), (4) the plaintiff must incur physical harm to self or property by use or consumption of the product, (5) the defective condition must be the proximate cause of the injury or damage, and (6) the goods must not have been substantially changed from the time the product was sold to the time the injury was sustained.

Chapter 6

2A. *What are five broad categories of crimes? What is white-collar crime?*

Traditionally, crimes have been grouped into the following categories: violent crime (crimes against persons), property crime, public order crime, white-collar crime, and organized crime. White-collar crime is an illegal act or series of acts committed by an individual or business entity using some nonviolent means usually in the course of a legitimate occupation.

4A. *What constitutional safeguards exist to protect persons accused of crimes? What are the basic steps in the criminal process?*

Under the Fourth Amendment, before searching or seizing private property, law enforcement officers must obtain a search warrant, which requires probable cause. Under the Fifth Amendment, no one can be deprived of "life, liberty, or property without due process of law." The Fifth Amendment also protects persons against double jeopardy and self-incrimination. The Sixth Amendment guarantees the right to a speedy trial, the right to a jury trial, the right to a public trial, the right to confront witnesses, and the right to counsel. All evidence obtained in violation of the Fourth, Fifth, and Sixth Amendments must be excluded from the trial, as well as all evidence derived from the illegally obtained evidence. Individuals who are arrested must be informed of certain constitutional rights, including their Fifth Amendment right to remain silent and their Sixth Amendment right to counsel. The Eighth Amendment prohibits excessive bail and fines, and cruel and unusual punishment.

The basic steps in the criminal process include an arrest, the booking, the initial appearance, a preliminary hearing, a grand jury or magistrate's review, the arraignment, a plea bargain (if any), and the trial or guilty plea.

Chapter 7

2A. *Why are trademarks and patents protected by the law?*

As stated in Article I, Section 8, of the Constitution, Congress is authorized "[t]o promote the Progress of Science and useful Arts, by securing for limited Times to Authors and Inventors the exclusive Right to their respective Writings and Discoveries." Laws protecting patents and trademarks, as well as copyrights, are designed to protect and reward inventive and artistic creativity.

4A. *What are trade secrets, and what laws offer protection for this form of intellectual property?*

Trade secrets are business processes and information that are not or cannot be patented, copyrighted, or trademarked. Trade secrets consist of generally anything that makes an individual company unique and that would have value to a competitor. The Uniform Trade Secrets Act, the Economic Espionage Act, and the common law offer trade secrets protection.

Chapter 8

2A. *What elements are necessary for an effective offer?*

Three elements are necessary for an offer to be effective: (1) a serious, objective intent by the offeror; (2) reasonably certain, or definite terms; and (3) communication of the offer to the offeree. Nonoffers include expressions of opinion, statements of intent, preliminary negotiations, advertisements, catalogues, and circulars. In an auction, the bidder, not the seller, is the offeror.

4A. *Does an intoxicated person have the capacity to enter into an enforceable contract?*

If a person who is sufficiently intoxicated to lack mental capacity enters into a contract, the contract is voidable at the option of that person. It must be proved that the person's reason and judgment were impaired to the extent that he or she did not comprehend the legal consequences of entering into the contract.

Chapter 9

2A. *How are most contracts discharged?*
The most common way to discharge, or terminate, a contract is by the performance of contractual duties.

4A. *What is the standard measure of compensatory damages when a contract is breached?*
In a contract for the sale of goods, the usual measure of compensatory damages is an amount equal to the difference between the contract price and the market price. When the buyer breaches and the seller has not yet produced the goods, compensatory damages normally equal the lost profits on the sale rather than the difference between the contract price and the market price.

Chapter 10

2A. *In a sales contract, if an offeree includes additional or different terms in an acceptance, will a contract result? If so, what happens to these terms?*
Under the UCC, a contract can be formed even if the acceptance includes an offeree's additional or different terms. If one of the parties is a nonmerchant, the contract does not include the additional terms. If both parties are merchants, the additional terms automatically become part of the contract unless (1) the original offer expressly limits acceptance to the terms of the offer, (2) the new or changed terms *materially* alter the contract, or (3) the offeror objects to the new or changed terms within a reasonable period of time. (If the additional terms expressly require the offeror's assent, the offeree's expression is not an acceptance, but a counteroffer.) Under some circumstances, a court might strike the additional terms.

4A. *What implied warranties arise under the UCC?*
Implied warranties that arise under the UCC include the implied warranty of merchantability; the implied warranty of fitness for a particular purpose; and implied warranties that may arise from, or be excluded or modified by, course of dealing, course of performance, or usage of trade.

Chapter 11

2A. *What are some advantages and disadvantages of doing business as a partnership or a corporation, respectively?*
The advantages and disadvantages of doing business in any form generally relate to the right of control, and the assessment of tax liability and of liability generally. A partner may have a right to manage a partnership, but also has unlimited liability for the firm's debts. A partnership has no tax liability on its profits, which are passed through directly to the partners. An owner of a corporation may have only limited liability with respect to the firm's debts, but may have no say in the business's management. A corporation's profits may also be subject to a double tax—once before they are distributed to shareholders and once as income to those shareholders.

4A. *What is a franchise? What are the most common types of franchises?*
A *franchise* is any arrangement in which the owner of a trademark, a trade name, or a copyright licenses others to use the trademark, trade name, or copyright in the selling of goods or services. The majority of franchises are distributorships, chain-style business operations, or manufacturing or processing-plant arrangements.

Chapter 12

2A. *What is garnishment? When might a creditor undertake a garnishment proceeding?*
Garnishment occurs when a creditor is permitted to collect a debt by seizing property of the debtor that is being held by a third party (such as a paycheck held by an employer or a checking account held by a bank).

Closely regulated, garnishment is used in some cases in which debts are not paid.

4A. *What is the difference between an exception to discharge and an objection to discharge?*
An *exception* to discharge is a claim that is not dischargeable in bankruptcy (such as a government claim for unpaid taxes). An *objection* to discharge is a circumstance that causes a discharge to be denied (such as concealing assets).

Chapter 13

2A. *What is the difference between an employee and an independent contractor?*
The difference between independent contractors and employees is that those who hire the former have no control over the details of their physical performance. Agency relationships normally are consensual: they arise by voluntary consent and agreement between the parties.

4A. *What federal statutes govern wages and worker health and safety in the workplace? What is the purpose of workers' compensation laws?*
The Fair Labor Standards Act is the most significant federal statute governing working hours and wages. To protect the health and safety of workers, Congress passed the Occupational Safety and Health Act. Workers' compensation laws are state statutes that establish administrative procedures for compensating workers injured on the job.

Chapter 14

2A. *What is the difference between disparate-treatment discrimination and disparate-impact discrimination?*
Intentional discrimination by an employer against an employee is known as *disparate-treatment discrimination.*

Disparate-impact discrimination occurs when, as a result of educational or other job requirements or hiring procedures, an employer's workforce does not reflect the percentage of nonwhites, women, or members of other protected classes that characterizes qualified individuals in the local labor market. Disparate-impact discrimination does not require evidence of intent.

4A. *What federal acts prohibit discrimination based on age and discrimination based on disability?*
The Age Discrimination in Employment Act of 1967 and the Americans with Disabilities Act of 1990 prohibit discrimination on the basis of age and disability, respectively.

Chapter 15

2A. *How does the way in which a union election is conducted protect the rights of employees and employers?*
During a union election campaign, management may prohibit all solicitations on company property for a legitimate business reason, or may reasonably limit the places where solicitation occurs, limit the times in which it takes place, or prohibit all outsiders from access to the workplace. Management cannot permit all solicitation by unions, however. Management also may not make threats of reprisals; offer special benefits for a nonunion vote; undertake certain types of surveillance of workers, or even create the impression of surveilling workers, to identify union sympathizers; or question individual workers about their position on unionization. If the election is unfair, the National Labor Relations Board may invalidate the results.

4A. *What activities are prohibited as unfair employer practices?*
Unfair employer practices include the refusal to recognize a union and negotiate with it, interference in union activities, the domination of unions, and discrimination against union employees. Each of these unfair practices may occur in different ways.

Chapter 16

2A. *What are the three operations that make up the basic functions of most administrative agencies?*
The three operations that make up the functions of most agencies are rulemaking (making rules), enforcement (including investigating possible violations and enforcing the rules), and adjudication (including administrative action against rule violators).

4A. *How do administrative agencies enforce their rules?*
Agencies enforce their rules by investigating the entities that they regulate to monitor compliance with the agency's rules. The agency uses a variety of investigative tools, including subpoenas and search warrants.

Chapter 17

2A. *What special rules apply to telephone solicitation?*
Federal statutes that protect consumers in credit transactions include the various titles of the Consumer Credit Protection Act—the Truth-in-Lending Act, of which the Equal Credit Opportunity Act and the Consumer Leasing Act are a part— as well as the Fair Credit Reporting Act and the Fair Debt Collection Practices Act.

4A. *How does the Federal Food, Drug and Cosmetic Act protect consumers?*
The Federal Food, Drug and Cosmetic Act protects consumers against adulterated and misbranded foods and drugs by establishing food standards, specifying safe levels of potentially hazardous food additives, setting classifications of food and food advertising, requiring that drugs be shown to be effective as well as safe before they are marketed to the public, and prohibiting the use of some food additives suspected of being carcinogenic.

Chapter 18

2A. *What is an environmental impact statement, and who must file one?*
An environmental impact statement (EIS) analyzes (1) the impact on the environment that an action will have, (2) any adverse effects on the environment and alternative actions that might be taken, and (3) irreversible effects the action might generate. For every major federal action that significantly affects the quality of the environment, an EIS must be prepared. An action is "major" if it involves a substantial commitment of resources (monetary or otherwise). An action is "federal" if a federal agency has the power to control it.

4A. *What major statutes regulate air and water pollution?*
Air pollution is regulated at the federal statutory level by the Clean Air Act and its many amendments. Water pollution is covered at the same level by the Federal Water Pollution Control Act (the Clean Water Act) and its amendments, including the Water Quality Act, as well as the Safe Drinking Water Act; the Marine Protection, Research, and Sanctuaries Act (the Ocean Dumping Act); and the Oil Pollution Act.

Chapter 19

2A. *How can ownership interests in real property be transferred?*
Ownership interests in real property may be transferred by deed, by will or inheritance, or by adverse possession. A deed can pass possession and title without consideration. A deed requires (1) the names of the grantor and grantee, (2) words evidencing an intent to convey, (3) a legally sufficient description of the land, (4) the grantor's (and some-

times his or her spouse's) signature, and (5) delivery. An adverse possessor's possession must be (1) actual and exclusive; (2) open, visible, and notorious, not secret or clandestine; (3) continuous and peaceable for the statutory period of time; and (4) hostile and adverse.

4A. *What are the respective duties of the landlord and tenant concerning the use and maintenance of leased property?*

If the parties do not limit by agreement the uses of the property, a tenant may make any use of it, as long as the use is legal, reasonably relates to the purpose for which the property is adapted or ordinarily used, and does not injure the landlord's interest. A tenant is responsible for damage that he or she causes, which may include the cost of returning the property to the condition it was in at a lease's inception. A landlord must comply with state statutes and city ordinances that delineate specific standards for the maintenance of buildings. This generally includes delivering possession of residential premises in habitable condition.

Chapter 20

2A. *What type of activity is prohibited by Section 1 of the Sherman Act? What type of activity is prohibited by Section 2 of the Sherman Act?*

Section 1 prohibits agreements that are anticompetitively restrictive—that is, agreements that have the wrongful purpose of restraining competition. Section 2 prohibits the misuse, and attempted misuse, of monopoly power in the marketplace.

4A. *What agencies of the federal government enforce the federal antitrust laws?*

The federal agencies that enforce the federal antitrust laws are the U.S. Department of Justice and the Federal Trade Commission.

Chapter 21

2A. *What are the two major statutes regulating the securities industry? When was the Securities and Exchange Commission created, and what are its major purposes and functions?*

The major statutes regulating the securities industry are the Securities Act of 1933 and the Securities Exchange Act of 1934, which created the Securities and Exchange Commission (SEC).

The SEC's major functions are to (1) require the disclosure of facts concerning offerings of securities listed on national securities exchanges and of certain securities traded over the counter; (2) regulate the trade in securities on the national and regional securities exchanges and in the over-the-counter markets; (3) investigate securities fraud; (4) regulate the activities of securities brokers, dealers, and investment advisers and require their registration; (5) supervise the activities of mutual funds; and (6) recommend administrative sanctions, injunctive remedies, and criminal prosecution against those who violate securities laws.

4A. *What are some of the features of state securities laws?*

Typically, state laws have disclosure requirements and antifraud provisions patterned after Section 10(b) of the Securities Exchange Act of 1934 and SEC Rule 10b-5. State laws provide for the registration or qualification of securities offered or issued for sale within the state with the appropriate state official. Also, most state securities laws regulate securities brokers and dealers.

Chapter 22

2A. *What is the act of state doctrine? In what circumstances is this doctrine applied?*

The *act of state doctrine* is a judicially created doctrine that provides that the judicial branch of one country will not examine the validity of public acts committed by a recognized foreign government within its own territory. This doctrine is often employed in cases involving expropriation or confiscation.

4A. *In what circumstances will U.S. antitrust laws be applied extraterritorially?*

U.S. courts will apply U.S. antitrust laws extraterritorially when it is shown that an alleged violation has a substantial effect on U.S. commerce.

1–2A. Question with Sample Answer

1. The U.S. Constitution—The U.S. Constitution is the supreme law of the land. A law in violation of the Constitution, no matter what its source, will be declared unconstitutional and will not be enforced.
2. The federal statute—Under the U.S. Constitution, when there is a conflict between federal law and state law, federal law prevails.
3. The state statute—State statutes are enacted by state legislatures. Areas not covered by state statutory law are governed by state case law.
4. The U.S. Constitution—State constitutions are supreme within their respective borders unless they conflict with the U.S. Constitution, which is the supreme law of the land.
5. The federal administrative regulation—Under the U.S. Constitution, when there is a conflict between federal law and state law, federal law prevails.

2–2A. Question with Sample Answer

It could be argued that businesses should not allow themselves to be dictated to by small groups of activists, just as it could be said that a government should not yield to activists who do not represent the governed. Small groups may not represent the best interests of those to whom a business owes its principal duties—consumers, employees, shareholders, and so on. It might also be asserted that businesses should yield to activist groups, however, when those groups do represent the best interests of all, or some, of those to whom a business owes a duty or the best interests of society at large. Small groups may be "cutting edge"—seeing and encouraging others to see the future, as in the case of global warming. Regardless of whether a business ultimately yields to the pressure of activists, however, the business should consider other factors before choosing which course to follow. Besides the interests of the business's stakeholders, there are the interests and the actions of those who may not have a direct stake in the business but whose interests may be parallel (competitors, for example). There are also the interests of the business itself to consider—its profitability and its continued viability should it do or not do what certain activists urge.

3–2A. Question with Sample Answer

Marya can bring suit in all three courts. The trucking firm did business in Florida, and the accident occurred there. Thus, the state of Florida would have jurisdiction over the defendant. Because the firm was headquartered in Georgia and had its principal place of business in that state, Marya could also sue in a Georgia court. Finally, because the amount in controversy exceeds $75,000, the suit could be brought in federal court on the basis of diversity of citizenship.

4–3A. Question with Sample Answer

As the text points out, Thomas has a constitutionally protected right to his religion and the free exercise of it. In denying his unemployment benefits, the state violated these rights. Employers are obligated to make reasonable accommodations for their employees' beliefs, right or wrong, that are openly and sincerely held. Thomas's beliefs were openly and sincerely held. By placing him in a department that made military goods, his employer effectively put him in a position of having to choose between his job and his religious principles. This unilateral decision on the part of the employer was the reason Thomas left his job and why the company was required to compensate Thomas for his resulting unemployment.

5–3A. Question with Sample Answer

The correct answer is (b). The *Restatement (Second) of Torts* defines negligence as "conduct that falls below the standard established by law for the protection of others against unreasonable risk of harm." The standard established by law is that of a reasonable person acting with due care in the circumstances. Mary was well aware that the medication she took would make her drowsy, and her failure to observe due care (that is, refrain from driving) under the circumstances was negligent. Answer (a) is incorrect because Mary had no reason to believe the golf club was defective, and she could not have prevented the injury by the exercise of due care.

6–2A. Question with Sample Answer

1. Sarah has wrongfully taken and carried away the personal property of another with the intent to perma-

nently deprive the owner of such property. She has committed the crime of larceny.
2. Sarah has unlawfully and forcibly taken the personal property of another. She has committed the crime of robbery.
3. Sarah has broken and entered a dwelling with the intent to commit a felony. She has committed the crime of burglary. (Most states have dispensed with the requirement that the act take place at night.)

Note the basic differences: Burglary requires breaking and entering into a building without the use of force against a person. Robbery does not involve any breaking and entering, but force is required. Larceny is the taking of personal property without force and without breaking and entering into a building. Generally, because force is used, robbery is considered the most serious of these crimes and carries the most severe penalties. Larceny involves no force or threat to human life; therefore, it carries the least severe penalty of the three. Burglary, because it involves breaking and entering, frequently where people live, carries a lesser penalty than robbery but a greater penalty than larceny.

7–2A. Question with Sample Answer

1. Making a photocopy of an article in a scholarly journal "for purposes such as . . . scholarship, or research, is not an infringement of copyright" under Section 107 of the Copyright Act.
2. This is an example of trademark infringement. Whenever a trademark is copied to a substantial degree or used in its entirety by one who is not entitled to its use, the trademark has been infringed.
3. This is the most likely example of copyright infringement. Generally, determining whether the reproduction of copyrighted material constitutes copyright infringement is made on a case-by-case basis under the "fair use" doctrine, as expressed in Section 107 of the Copyright Act. Courts look at such factors as the "purpose and character" of a use, such as whether it is "of a commercial nature"; "the amount and substantiality of the portion used in relation to the copyrighted work as a whole"; and "the effect of the use on the potential market" for the copied work. In this question, the video store owner is taping copyright-protected works in their entirety for commercial purposes, thereby affecting the market for the works.
4. Taping a television program "for purposes such as . . . teaching . . . is not an infringement of copyright" under Section 107 of the Copyright Act.

8–2A. Question with Sample Answer

According to the question, Janine was apparently unconscious or otherwise unable to agree to a contract for the nursing services she received while she was in the hospital. As you read in the chapter, however, sometimes the law will create a fictional contract in order to prevent one party from unjustly receiving a benefit at the expense of another. This is known as a *quasi contract* and provides a basis for Nursing Services to recover the value of the services it provided while Janine was in the hospital. As for the at-home services that were provided to Janine, because Janine was aware that those services were being provided for her, Nursing Services can recover for those services under an implied-in-fact contract. Under this type of contract, the conduct of the parties creates and defines the terms. Janine's acceptance of the services constitutes her agreement to form a contract, and she will probably be required to pay Nursing Services in full.

9–2A. Question with Sample Answer

A novation exists when a new, valid contract expressly or impliedly discharges a prior contract by the substitution of a party. Accord and satisfaction exists when the parties agree that the original obligation can be discharged by a substituted performance. In this case, Fred's agreement with Iba to pay off Junior's debt for $1,100 (as compared with the $1,000 owed) is definitely a valid contract. The terms of the contract substitute Fred as the debtor for Junior, and Junior is definitely discharged from further liability. This agreement is a *novation*.

10–2A. Question with Sample Answer

The entire answer falls under UCC 2–206(1)(b), because the situation deals with a buyer's order to buy goods for prompt shipment. The law is that such an order or offer invites acceptance by a prompt promise to ship conforming goods. If the promise (acceptance) is sent by a medium reasonable under the circumstances, the acceptance is effective when sent. Therefore, a contract was formed on October 8, and it required Martin to ship 100 Model Color-X television sets. Martin's shipment is nonconforming, and Flint is correct in claiming that Martin is in breach. Martin's claim would be valid if Martin had not sent its promise of shipment. The UCC provides that shipment of nonconforming goods constitutes an acceptance *unless* the seller seasonably notifies the buyer that such shipment is sent only as an accommodation. Thus, had a contract not been formed on October 8, the nonconforming shipment on the 28th would not be treated as an acceptance, and no contract would be in existence to breach.

11–2A. Question with Sample Answer

The three most important factors to consider are taxes, costs of organizing, and limited liability. Tax considerations are very important when deciding which form of business organization to adopt. A wealthy person, for example, might wish to incorporate, since incorporating often works to shelter an investor's home. In contrast, a person in a lower tax bracket might wish to engage in business as a partner or a sole proprietor, since income passes directly through the business to him or her. The decision will hinge, to a great extent, on whether the corporate tax rate is higher than the personal income tax rate for a particular individual. Another factor to consider in forming a business organization is the relative cost of establishing each type of organization. For example, incorporating involves the cost of filing with appropriate government agencies. No such filing is involved in a partnership arrangement. Finally, limited liability may be an important factor to consider in choosing a form of business organization under which to operate. Individual participants in a partnership are exposed to unlimited liability for partnership obligations. By law, the personal liability of investors in a corporation is limited to the amount of money or capital that they have invested. The personal liability of limited partners in a limited partnership is also limited to the amount of their investment—unless they participate in management.

12–2A. Question with Sample Answer

Yes. Peterson can enforce his demand. When a surety pays a debt owed to a creditor, the surety is entitled to certain rights, one of which is the legal right of subrogation. This means that the surety acquires any right against the debtor formerly held by the creditor. In other words, the surety now stands in the shoes of the creditor. Because of this right of subrogation, Peterson can enforce his demand that the bank give him the $4,000 in securities because Peterson now has acquired rights in the collateral given for the loan.

13–3A. Question with Sample Answer

The Occupational Health and Safety Act (OSHA) requires employers to provide safe working conditions for employees. The act prohibits employers from discharging or discriminating against any employee who refuses to work when the employee believes in good faith that he or she will risk death or great bodily harm by undertaking the employment activity. Denton and Carlo had sufficient reason to believe that the maintenance job required of them by their employer involved great risk, and therefore, under OSHA, their discharge was wrongful. Denton and Carlo can turn to the occupational Safety and Health Administration, which is part of the Department of Labor, for assistance.

14–2A. Question with Sample Answer

The Age Discrimination in Employment Act (ADEA) prohibits discrimination in employment on the basis of age against individuals forty years of age or older. For the ADEA to apply, an employer must have twenty or more employees, and interstate commerce must be affected by the employer's business activities. Because Jones worked at a resort (presumably employing more than twenty persons), the court would probably find that its activities affected interstate commerce because it was frequented by out-of-state travelers. Because Jones was not demoted due to any apparent job-

performance problems, the fact that he was replaced by a person half his age, coupled with Blair's statement about getting rid of all the "senile" men, would be enough to shift the burden to the employer to show that it was not discriminating on the basis of age.

15–3A. Question with Sample Answer

The National Labor Relations Board (NLRB) has consistently been suspicious of companies that grant added benefits during union election campaigns. These benefits will be considered as an unfair labor practice that biases elections, unless the employer can demonstrate that the benefits were unrelated to the unionization and would have been granted anyway.

16–2A. Question with Sample Answer

The court will consider first whether the agency followed the procedures prescribed in the Administrative Procedure Act (APA). Ordinarily, courts will not require agencies to use procedures beyond those of the APA. Courts will, however, compel agencies to follow their own rules. If an agency has adopted a rule granting extra procedures, the agency must provide those extra procedures, at least until the rule is formally rescinded. Ultimately, in this case, the court will most likely rule for the food producers.

17–2A. Question with Sample Answer

Yes. A regulation of the Federal Trade Commission (FTC) under Section 5 of the Federal Trade Commission Act makes it a violation for door-to-door sellers to fail to give consumers three days to cancel any sale. In addition, a number of state statutes require this three-day "cooling off" period to protect consumers from unscrupulous door-to-door sellers. Because the Gonchars sought to rescind the contract within the three-day period, Renowned Books was obligated to agree to cancel the contract. Its failure to allow rescission was in violation of the FTC regulation and of most state statutes.

18–2A. Question with Sample Answer

Fruitade has violated a number of federal environmental laws if such actions are being taken without a permit. First, because the dumping is in a navigable waterway, the River and Harbor Act of 1886, as amended, has been violated. Second, the Clean Water Act of 1972, as amended, has been violated. This act is designed to make the waters safe for swimming, to protect fish and wildlife, and to eliminate discharge of pollutants into the water. Both the crushed glass and the acid violate this act. Third, the Toxic Substances Control Act of 1976 was passed to regulate chemicals that are known to be toxic and that could have an effect on human health and the environment. The acid in the cleaning fluid or compound could come under this act.

19–2A. Question with Sample Answer

Because all land use regulations necessarily limit the ways in which property may be used, a regulation by itself will not generally be considered a compensable taking. Compensation will be required only if the regulation itself is found to be overly burdensome and thus subject to the requirement that just compensation be paid. Rezoning the land from industrial use to commercial use—despite the expected reduction in its market value—would probably not be considered a compensable taking because it would not prevent the owner from using the land for any reasonable income-producing or private purpose.

20–2A. Question with Sample Answer

Yes. The major antitrust law being violated is the Sherman Act, Section 1. Allitron and Donovan are engaged in interstate commerce, and the agreement to divide marketing territories between them is a contract in restraint of trade. The U.S. Department of Justice could seek fines for up to $1 million for each corporation, and the officers or directors responsible could be imprisoned for up to three years. In addition, the Department of Justice could institute civil proceedings to restrain this conduct.

21–2A. Question with Sample Answer

No. Under federal securities law, a stock split is exempt from registration requirements. This is because no *sale* of stock is involved. The existing shares are merely being split, and no consideration is received by the corporation for the additional shares created.

22–1A. Question with Sample Answer

The law could pose problems for some businesspersons because certain legal terms or phrases in documents governed by U.S. law have no equivalent terms or phrases in the French legal system. Thus, businesspersons who wish their contracts to be subject to, or at least incorporate, certain U.S. legal principles that are not part of French law may have difficulty drafting those principles into the contracts. Even without differences between U.S. and French law, however, the parties may have different understandings of the contractual terms involved. Typically, many phrases in one language are not readily translatable into another.

GLOSSARY

A

Acceptance • A voluntary act by the offeree that shows assent, or agreement, to the terms of an offer; may consist of words or conduct.

Accredited Investors • In the context of securities offerings, an investor who is knowledgeable and sophisticated about financial matters such as a bank, an insurance company, an investment company, any of the issuer's executive officers and directors, and any person whose income or net worth exceeds a certain threshold.

Act of State Doctrine • A doctrine providing that the judicial branch of one country will not examine the validity of public acts committed by a recognized foreign government within its own territory.

Actionable • Capable of serving as the basis of a lawsuit. An actionable claim can be pursued in a lawsuit or other court action.

Actual Malice • Knowledge (by the person who makes a defamatory statement) that a statement is false, or reckless disregard about whether it is true. In a defamation suit, a statement made about a public figure normally must be made with actual malice for liability to be incurred.

Adjudication • The act of rendering a judicial decision. In an administrative process, the proceeding in which an administrative law judge hears and decides on issues that arise when an administrative agency charges a person or a firm with violating a law or regulation enforced by the agency.

Administrative Agency • A federal or state government agency established to perform a specific function. Administrative agencies are authorized by legislative acts to make and enforce rules to administer and enforce the acts.

Administrative Law • The body of law created by administrative agencies (in the form of rules, regulations, orders, and decisions) in order to carry out their duties and responsibilities.

Administrative Process • The procedure used by administrative agencies in the administration of law.

Adverse Possession • The acquisition of title to real property by occupying it openly, without the consent of the owner, for a period of time specified by a state statute. The occupation must be actual, open, notorious, exclusive, and in opposition to all others, including the owner.

Affirmative Action • Job-hiring policies that give special consideration to members of protected classes in an effort to overcome present effects of past discrimination.

Agency • A relationship between two parties in which one party (the agent) agrees to represent or act for the other (the principal).

Agreement • A meeting of two or more minds in regard to the terms of a contract, usually broken down into two events—an offer and an acceptance.

Alien Corporation • A designation in the United States for a corporation formed in another country but doing business in the United States.

Alternative Dispute Resolution (ADR) • The resolution of disputes in ways other than those involved in the traditional judicial process. Negotiation, mediation, and arbitration are forms of ADR.

Answer • Procedurally, a defendant's response to the plaintiff's complaint.

Anticipatory Repudiation • An assertion or action by a party indicating that he or she will not perform an obligation that the party is contractually obligated to perform at a future time.

Antitrust Law • A law protecting commerce from unlawful restraints.

Appropriate Bargaining Unit • A designation based on job duties, skill levels, and so on, of the proper entity that should be covered by a collective bargaining agreement.

Appropriation • In tort law, the use by one person of another person's name, likeness, or other identifying characteristic without permission and for the benefit of the user.

Arbitration • The settling of a dispute by submitting it to a disinterested third party (other than a court), who renders a decision that is (most often) legally binding.

Arbitration Clause • A clause in a contract that provides that, in the event of a dispute, the parties will submit the dispute to arbitration rather than litigate the dispute in court.

Arson • The intentional burning of another's dwelling. Some statutes have expanded this to include any real property regardless of ownership and the destruction of property by other means—for example, by explosion.

Articles of Incorporation • The document filed with the appropriate governmental agency, usually the secretary of state, when a business is incorporated; state statutes usually prescribe what kind of information must be contained in the articles of incorporation.

Articles of Organization • The document filed with a designated state official by which a limited liability company is formed.

Artisan's Lien • A possessory lien given to a person who has made improvements and added value to another person's personal property as security for payment for services performed.

Assault • Any word or action intended to make another person fearful of immediate physical harm; a reasonably believable threat.

Assignment • The act of transferring to another all or part of one's rights arising under a contract.

Assumption of Risk • A doctrine under which a plaintiff may not recover for injuries or damages suffered from risks he or she knows of and has voluntarily assumed.

Attachment • In the context of judicial liens, a court-ordered seizure and taking into custody of property prior to the securing of a judgment for a past-due debt.

Attempted Monopolization • Any actions by a firm to eliminate competition and gain monopoly power.

Authorization Card • A card signed by an employee that gives a union permission to act on his or her behalf in negotiations with management.

Automatic Stay • In bankruptcy proceedings, the suspension of virtually all litigation and other action by creditors against the debtor or the debtor's property. The stay is effective the moment the debtor files a petition in bankruptcy.

Award • In litigation, the amount awarded to a plaintiff in a civil lawsuit as damages. In the context of alternative dispute resolution, the decision rendered by an arbitrator.

B

Bait-and-Switch Advertising • Advertising a product at a very attractive price (the "bait") and then, once the consumer is in the store, saying that the advertised product is either not available or is of poor quality; the customer is then urged to purchase ("switched" to) a more expensive item.

Bankruptcy Court • A federal court of limited jurisdiction that handles only bankruptcy proceedings. Bankruptcy proceedings are governed by federal bankruptcy law.

Battery • The unprivileged, intentional touching of another.

Beyond a Reasonable Doubt • The burden of proof used in criminal cases. If there is any reasonable doubt that a criminal defendant committed the crime with which she or he has been charged, then the verdict must be "not guilty."

Bill of Rights • The first ten amendments to the U.S. Constitution.

Binding Authority • Any source of law that a court must follow when deciding a case. Binding authorities include constitutions, statutes, and regulations that govern the issue being decided, as well as court decisions that are controlling precedents within the jurisdiction.

Bona Fide Occupational Qualification (BFOQ) • Identifiable characteristics reasonably necessary to the normal operation of a particular business. These characteristics can include gender, national origin, and religion, but not race.

Bounty Payment • A reward (payment) given to a person or persons who perform a certain service, such as informing legal authorities of illegal actions.

Breach • The failure to perform a legal obligation.

Breach of Contract • The failure, without legal excuse, of a promisor to perform the obligations of a contract.

Brief • A formal legal document submitted by the attorney for the appellant or the appellee (in answer to the appellant's brief) to an appellate court when a case is appealed. The appellant's brief outlines the facts and issues of the case, the judge's rulings or jury's findings that should be reversed or modified, the applicable law, and the arguments on the client's behalf.

Browse-Wrap Terms • Terms and conditions of use that are presented to an Internet user at the time certain products, such as software, are being downloaded but to which the user need not agree (by clicking "I agree," for example) before being able to install or use the product.

Bulk Zoning • Zoning regulations that restrict the amount of structural coverage on a particular parcel of land.

Bureaucracy • The organizational structure, consisting of government bureaus and agencies, through which the government implements and enforces the laws.

Burglary • The unlawful entry or breaking into a building with the intent to commit a felony. (Some state statutes expand this to include the intent to commit any crime.)

Business Ethics • Ethics in a business context; a consensus of what constitutes right or wrong behavior in the world of business and the application of moral principles to situations that arise in a business setting.

Business Invitee • A person, such as a customer or a client, who is invited onto business premises by the owner of those premises for business purposes.

Business Judgment Rule • A rule that immunizes corporate management from liability for actions that result in corporate losses or damages if the actions are undertaken in good faith and are within both the power of the corporation and the authority of management to make.

Business Necessity • A defense to allegations of employment discrimination in which the employer demonstrates that an employment practice that discriminates against members of a protected class is related to job performance.

Business Tort • Wrongful interference with another's business rights.

Bylaws • A set of governing rules adopted by a corporation or other association.

C

Case Law • Case law includes the aggregate of reported cases that interpret judicial precedents, statutes, regulations, and constitutional provisions.

Categorical Imperative • A concept developed by the philosopher Immanuel Kant as an ethical guideline for behavior. In deciding whether an action is right or wrong, or desirable or undesirable, a person should evaluate the action in terms of what would happen if everybody else in the same situation, or category, acted the same way.

Causation in Fact • An act or omission without which an event would not have occurred.

Cease-and-Desist Order • An administrative or judicial order prohibiting a person or business firm from conducting activities that an agency or court has deemed illegal.

Checks and Balances • The principle under which the powers of the national government are divided among three separate branches—the executive, legislative, and judicial branches—each of which exercises a check on the actions of the others.

Choice-of-Language Clause • A clause in a contract designating the official language by which the contract will be interpreted in the event of a future disagreement over the contract's terms.

Choice-of-Law Clause • A clause in a contract designating the law (such as the law of a particular state or nation) that will govern the contract.

Citation • A reference to a publication in which a legal authority—such as a statute or a court decision—or other source can be found.

Civil Law • The branch of law dealing with the definition and enforcement of all private or public rights, as opposed to criminal matters.

Click-On Agreement • An agreement that arises when a buyer, engaging in a transaction on a computer, indicates his or her assent to be bound by the terms of an offer by clicking on a button that says, for example, "I agree"; sometimes referred to as a *click-on license* or a *click-wrap agreement.*

Closed Shop • A firm that requires union membership by its workers as a condition of employment. The closed shop was made illegal by the Labor-Management Relations Act of 1947.

Collective Bargaining • The process by which labor and management negotiate the terms and conditions of employment, including working hours and workplace conditions.

Comity • The principle by which one nation defers and gives effect to the laws and judicial decrees of another nation. This recognition is based primarily on respect.

Commerce Clause • The provision in Article I, Section 8, of the U.S. Constitution that gives Congress the power to regulate interstate commerce.

Commercial Impracticability • A doctrine under which a court might excuse the parties from performing a contract when the performance becomes much more difficult or costly due to an event that the parties did not foresee or anticipate at the time the contract was made.

Common Law • That body of law derived from judicial decisions or custom in English and U.S. courts, not attributable to a legislature.

Common Situs Picketing • The illegal picketing of a primary employer's site by workers who are involved in a labor dispute with a secondary employer.

Comparative Negligence • A rule in tort law that reduces the plaintiff's recovery in proportion to the plaintiff's degree of fault, rather than barring recovery completely; used in the majority of states.

Compensatory Damages • A money award equivalent to the actual value of injuries or damages sustained by the aggrieved party.

Complaint • The pleading made by a plaintiff alleging wrongdoing on the part of the defendant; the document that, when filed with a court, initiates a lawsuit.

Computer Crime • Any act that is directed against computers and computer parts, that uses computers as instruments of crime, or that involves computers and constitutes abuse.

Concerted Action • Action by employees, such as a strike or picketing, with the purpose of furthering their bargaining demands or other mutual interests.

Concurrent Conditions • Conditions that must occur or be performed at the same time; they are mutually dependent. No obligations arise until these conditions are simultaneously performed.

Concurrent Jurisdiction • Jurisdiction that exists when two different courts have the power to hear a case. For example, some cases can be heard in either a federal or a state court.

Condition • A qualification, provision, or clause in a contractual agreement, the occurrence or nonoccurrence of which creates, suspends, or terminates the obligations of the contracting parties.

Condition Precedent • In a contractual agreement, a condition that must be met before a party's promise becomes absolute.

Condition Subsequent • A condition in a contract that, if not fulfilled, operates to terminate a party's absolute promise to perform.

Confiscation • A government's taking of a privately owned business or personal property without a proper public purpose or an award of just compensation.

Conforming Goods • Goods that conform to contract specifications.

Consent • The voluntary agreement to a proposition or an act of another; a concurrence of wills.

Consequential Damages • Special damages that compensate for a loss that does not directly or immediately result from the breach (for example, lost profits). For the plaintiff to collect consequential damages, they must have been reasonably foreseeable at the time the breach or injury occurred.

Consideration • Generally, the value given in return for a promise. The consideration must be something of legally sufficient value, and there must be a bargained-for exchange.

Constitutional Law • The body of law derived from the U.S. Constitution and the constitutions of the various states.

Constructive Discharge • A termination of employment brought about by making the employee's working conditions so intolerable that the employee reasonably feels compelled to leave.

Constructive Eviction • A form of eviction that occurs when a landlord fails to perform adequately any of the undertakings (such as providing heat in the winter) required by the lease, thereby making the tenant's further use and enjoyment of the property exceedingly difficult or impossible.

Consumer-Debtor • A debtor whose debts result primarily from the purchase of goods for personal, family, or household use.

Contract • An agreement that can be enforced in court; formed by two or more competent parties who agree, for consideration, to perform or to refrain from performing some legal act now or in the future.

Contributory Negligence • A rule in tort law that completely bars the plaintiff from recovering any damages if the damage suffered is partly the plaintiff's own fault; used in a minority of states.

Conversion • Wrongfully taking or retaining possession of an individual's personal property and placing it in the service of another.

Conveyance • The transfer of a title to land from one person to another by deed; a document (such as a deed) by which an interest in land is transferred from one person to another.

Copyright • The exclusive right of "authors" to publish, print, or sell an intellectual production for a statutory period of time. A copyright has the same monopolistic nature as a patent or trademark, but it differs in that it applies exclusively to works of art, literature, and other works of authorship (including computer programs).

Corporate Governance • The system by which business corporations are governed, including policies and procedures for making decisions on corporate affairs.

Corporation • A legal entity formed in compliance with statutory requirements. The entity is distinct from its shareholder-owners.

Correspondent Bank • A bank in which another bank has an account (and vice versa) for the purpose of facilitating fund transfers.

Cost-Benefit Analysis • A decision-making technique that involves weighing the costs of a given action against the benefits of that action.

Co-Surety • A joint surety; a person who assumes liability jointly with another surety for the payment of an obligation.

Counteradvertising • New advertising that is undertaken pursuant to a Federal Trade Commission order for the purpose of correcting earlier false claims that were made about a product.

"Cooling-Off" Laws • Laws that allow buyers a period of time, such as three days, in which to cancel door-to-door sales contracts.

Counterclaim • A claim made by a defendant in a civil lawsuit against the plaintiff. In effect, the defendant is suing the plaintiff.

Counteroffer • An offeree's response to an offer in which the offeree rejects the original offer and at the same time makes a new offer.

Cover • A buyer or lessee's purchase on the open market of goods to substitute for those promised but never delivered by the seller. Under the UCC, if the cost of cover exceeds the cost of the contract goods, the buyer or lessee can recover the difference, plus incidental and consequential damages.

Cram-Down Provision • A provision of the Bankruptcy Code that allows a court to confirm a debtor's Chapter 11 reorganization plan even though only one class of creditors has accepted it.

Creditors' Composition Agreement • An agreement formed between a debtor and his or her creditors in which the creditors agree to accept a lesser sum than that owed by the debtor in full satisfaction of the debt.

Crime • A wrong against society proclaimed in a statute and punishable by society through fines and/or imprisonment—and, in some cases, death.

Criminal Law • Law that defines and governs actions that constitute crimes. Generally, criminal law has to do with wrongful actions committed against society for which society demands redress.

Cure • The right of a party who tenders nonconforming performance to correct that performance within the contract period [UCC 2-508(1)].

Cyber Crime • A crime that occurs online, in the virtual community of the Internet, as opposed to the physical world.

Cyber Mark • A trademark in cyberspace.

Cyber Tort • A tort committed in cyberspace.

Cyberlaw • An informal term used to refer to all laws governing electronic communications and transactions, particularly those conducted via the Internet.

Cybersquatting • The act of registering a domain name that is the same as, or confusingly similar to, the trademark of another and then offering to sell that domain name back to the trademark owner.

Cyberstalker • A person who commits the crime of stalking in cyberspace. Generally, stalking consists of harassing a person and putting that person in reasonable fear for his or her safety or the safety of the person's immediate family.

Cyberterrorist • A hacker whose purpose is to exploit a target computer for a serious impact, such as corrupting a program to sabotage a business.

D

Damages • Money sought as a remedy for a breach of contract or a tortious action.

Debtor In Possession (DIP) • In Chapter 11 bankruptcy proceedings, a debtor who is allowed to continue in possession of the estate in property (the business) and to continue business operations.

Deceptive Advertising • Advertising that misleads consumers, either by unjustified claims concerning a product's performance or by the omission of a material fact concerning the product's composition or performance.

Deed • A document by which title to property (usually real property) is passed.

Defamation • Anything published or publicly spoken that causes injury to another's good name, reputation, or character.

Default • The failure to observe a promise or to discharge an obligation. The term is commonly used to mean the failure to pay a debt when it is due.

Default Judgment • A judgment entered by a court against a defendant who has failed to appear in court to answer or defend against the plaintiff's claim.

Defendant • One against whom a lawsuit is brought; the accused person in a criminal proceeding.

Defense • A reason offered and alleged by a defendant in an action or suit as to why the plaintiff should not recover or establish what she or he seeks.

Delegation • The transfer of a contractual duty to a third party. The party delegating the duty (the delegator) to the third party (the delegatee) is still obliged to perform on the contract should the delegatee fail to perform.

Delegation Doctrine • A doctrine based on Article I, Section 8, of the U.S. Constitution, which has been construed to allow Congress to delegate some of its power to make and implement laws to administrative agencies.

Deposition • The testimony of a party to a lawsuit or a witness taken under oath before a trial.

Disaffirmance • The legal avoidance, or setting aside, of a contractual obligation.

Discharge • The termination of an obligation. In contract law, discharge occurs when the parties have fully performed their contractual obligations or when events, conduct of the parties, or operation of law releases the parties from performance. In bankruptcy proceedings, the release of a debtor from the obligation to pay debts.

Disclosed Principal • A principal whose identity is known to a third party at the time the agent makes a contract with the third party.

Discovery • A phase in the litigation process during which the opposing parties may obtain information from each other and from third parties prior to trial.

Disparagement of Property • An economically injurious falsehood made about another's product or property. A general term for torts that are more specifically referred to as *slander of quality* or *slander of title*.

Disparate-Impact Discrimination • A form of employment discrimination that results from certain employer practices or procedures that, although not discriminatory on their face, have a discriminatory effect.

Disparate-Treatment Discrimination • A form of employment discrimination that results when an employer intentionally discriminates against employees who are members of protected classes.

Distributed Network • A network that can be used by persons located (distributed) around the country or the globe to share computer files.

Distribution Agreement • A contract between a seller and a distributor of the seller's products setting out the terms and conditions of the distributorship.

Diversity of Citizenship • Under Article III, Section 2, of the Constitution, a basis for federal district court jurisdiction over a lawsuit between (1) citizens of different states, (2) a foreign country and citizens of a state or of different states, or (3) citizens of a state and citizens or subjects of a foreign country. The amount in controversy must be more than $75,000 before a federal district court can take jurisdiction in such cases.

Divestiture • The act of selling one or more of a company's divisions or parts, such as a subsidiary or plant; often mandated by the courts in merger or monopolization cases.

Dividend • A distribution to corporate shareholders of corporate profits or income, disbursed in proportion to the number of shares held.

Docket • The list of cases entered on a court's calendar and thus scheduled to be heard by the court.

Domain Name • The last part of an Internet address, such as "westlaw.com." The top level (the part of the name to the right of the period) indicates the type of entity that operates the site ("com" is an abbreviation for "commercial"). The second level (the part of the name to the left of the period) is chosen by the entity.

Domestic Corporation • In a given state, a corporation that does business in, and is organized under the law of, that state.

Double Jeopardy • A situation occurring when a person is tried twice for the same criminal offense; prohibited by the Fifth Amendment to the Constitution.

Dram Shop Act • A state statute that imposes liability on the owners of bars and taverns, as well as those who serve alcoholic drinks to the public, for injuries resulting from accidents caused by intoxicated persons when the sellers or servers of alcoholic drinks contributed to the intoxication.

Due Process Clause • The provisions in the Fifth and Fourteenth Amendments to the Constitution that guarantee that no person shall be deprived of life, liberty, or property without due process of law. Similar clauses are found in most state constitutions.

Dumping • The selling of goods in a foreign country at a price below the price charged for the same goods in the domestic market.

Duress • Unlawful pressure brought to bear on a person, causing the person to perform an act that she or he would not otherwise perform.

Duty of Care • The duty of all persons, as established by tort law, to exercise a reasonable amount of care in their dealings with others. Failure to exercise due care, which is normally determined by the "reasonable person standard," constitutes the tort of negligence.

E

Early Neutral Case Evaluation • A form of alternative dispute resolution in which a neutral third party evaluates the strengths and weaknesses of the disputing parties' positions. The evaluator's opinion then forms the basis for negotiating a settlement.

Easement • A nonpossessory right to use another's property in a manner established by either express or implied agreement.

E-Contract • A contract that is formed electronically.

E-Evidence • A type of evidence that consists of computer-generated or electronically recorded information, including e-mail, voice mail, spreadsheets, word-processing documents, and other data.

Eighty-Day Cooling-Off Period • A provision of the Taft-Hartley Act that allows federal courts to issue injunctions against strikes that might create a national emergency.

Embezzlement • The fraudulent appropriation of funds or other property by a person to whom the funds or property has been entrusted.

Eminent Domain • The power of a government to take land for public use from private citizens for just compensation.

Employee Committee • A committee created by an employer and composed of representatives of management and nonunion employees to act together to improve workplace conditions.

Employment Discrimination • Treating employees or job applicants unequally on the basis of race, color, national origin, religion, gender, age, or disability; prohibited by federal statutes.

Enabling Legislation • Statutes enacted by Congress that authorize the creation of an administrative agency and specify the name, composition, and powers of the agency being created.

Entrapment • In criminal law, a defense in which the defendant claims that he or she was induced by a public official—usually an undercover agent or police officer—to commit a crime that he or she would otherwise not have committed.

Environmental Impact Statement (EIS) • A statement required by the National Environmental Policy Act for any major federal action that will significantly affect the quality of the environment. The statement must analyze the action's impact on the environment and explore alternative actions that might be taken.

Equal Protection Clause • The provision in the Fourteenth Amendment to the Constitution that guarantees that no state will "deny to any person within its jurisdiction the equal protection of the laws." This clause mandates that the state governments treat similarly situated individuals in a similar manner.

Equitable Principles and Maxims • General propositions or principles of law that have to do with fairness (equity).

E-Signature • Under the Uniform Electronic Transactions Act, a signature can be any electronic sound, symbol, or process attached to electronically stored information. This definition is intentionally broad in order to give legal effect to acts that people intend to be the equivalent of their written signatures.

Establishment Clause • The provision in the First Amendment to the Constitution that prohibits the government from establishing any state-sponsored religion or enacting any law that promotes religion or favors one religion over another.

Ethical Reasoning • A reasoning process in which an individual links his or her moral convictions or ethical standards to the particular situation at hand.

Ethics • Moral principles and values applied to social behavior.

Eviction • A landlord's act of depriving a tenant of possession of the leased premises.

Exclusionary Rule • In criminal procedure, a rule under which any evidence that is obtained in violation of the accused's constitutional rights guaranteed by the Fourth, Fifth, and Sixth Amendments, as well as any evidence derived from illegally obtained evidence, will not be admissible in court.

Exclusive Distributorship • A distributorship in which the seller and the distributor of the seller's products agree that the distributor has the exclusive right to distribute the seller's products in a certain geographic area.

Exclusive Jurisdiction • Jurisdiction that exists when a case can be heard only in a particular court or type of court.

Exclusive-Dealing Contract • An agreement under which a seller forbids a buyer to purchase products from the seller's competitors.

Executive Agency • An administrative agency within the executive branch of government. At the federal level, executive agencies are those within the cabinet departments.

Export • The goods and services that domestic firms sell to buyers located in other countries.

Express Warranty • A seller's or lessor's oral or written promise or affirmation of fact, ancillary to an underlying sales or lease agreement, as to the quality, description, or performance of the goods being sold or leased.

Expropriation • The seizure by a government of a privately owned business or personal property for a proper public purpose and with just compensation.

F

Featherbedding • A requirement that more workers be employed to do a particular job than are actually needed.

Federal Form of Government • A system of government in which the states form a union and the sovereign power is divided between the central government and the member states.

Federal Question • A question that pertains to the U.S. Constitution, acts of Congress, or treaties. A federal question provides a basis for federal jurisdiction.

Fee Simple Absolute • An ownership interest in land in which the owner has the greatest possible aggregation of rights, privileges, and power. Ownership in fee simple absolute is limited absolutely to a person and his or her heirs.

Felony • A crime—such as arson, murder, rape, or robbery—that carries the most severe sanctions, which range from more than one year in a state or federal prison to the death penalty.

Fiduciary • As a noun, a person having a duty created by his or her undertaking to act primarily for another's benefit in matters connected with the undertaking. As an adjective, a relationship founded on trust and confidence.

Filtering Software • A computer program that includes a pattern through which data are passed. When designed to block access to certain Web sites, the pattern blocks the retrieval of a site whose URL or key words are on a list within the program.

Final Order • The final decision of an administrative agency on an issue. If no appeal is taken, or if the case is not reviewed or considered anew by the agency commission, the administrative law judge's initial order becomes the final order of the agency.

Firm Offer • An offer (by a merchant) that is irrevocable without consideration for a stated period of time or, if no definite period is stated, for a reasonable time (neither period to exceed three months). A firm offer by a merchant must be in writing and must be signed by the offeror.

Fixture • A thing that was once personal property but that has become attached to real property in such a way that it takes on the characteristics of real property and becomes part of that real property.

Force Majeure **Clause** • A provision in a contract stipulating that certain unforeseen events—such as war, political upheavals, or acts of God—will excuse a party from liability for nonperformance of contractual obligations.

Foreign Corporation • In a given state, a corporation that does business in the state without being incorporated therein.

Foreign Exchange Market • A worldwide system in which foreign currencies are bought and sold.

Forgery • The fraudulent making or altering of any writing in a way that changes the legal rights and liabilities of another.

Forum-Selection Clause • A provision in a contract designating the court, jurisdiction, or tribunal that will decide any disputes arising under the contract.

Franchise • Any arrangement in which the owner of a trademark, trade name, or copyright licenses another to use that trade-mark, trade name, or copyright, under specified conditions or limitations, in the selling of goods and services.

Franchisee • One receiving a license to use another's (the franchisor's) trademark, trade name, or copyright in the sale of goods and services.

Franchisor • One licensing another (the franchisee) to use his or her trademark, trade name, or copyright in the sale of goods or services.

Fraudulent Misrepresentation • Any misrepresentation, either by misstatement or omission of a material fact, knowingly made with the intention of deceiving another and on which a reasonable person would and does rely to his or her detriment.

Free Exercise Clause • The provision in the First Amendment to the Constitution that prohibits the government from interfering with people's religious practices or forms of worship.

Frustration of Purpose • A court-created doctrine under which a party to a contract will be relieved of his or her duty to perform when the objective purpose for performance no longer exists (due to reasons beyond that party's control).

G

Garnishment • A legal process used by a creditor to collect a debt by seizing property of the debtor (such as wages) that is being held by a third party (such as the debtor's employer).

General Partner • In a limited partnership, a partner who assumes responsibility for the management of the partnership and liability for all partnership debts.

General Plan • A comprehensive document that local jurisdictions are often required by state law to devise and implement as a precursor to specific land-use regulations.

Generally Accepted Accounting Principles (GAAP) • The conventions, rules, and procedures necessary to define accepted accounting practices at a particular time. The source of the principles is the Financial Accounting Standards Board (FASB).

Generally Accepted Auditing Standards (GAAS) • Standards concerning an auditor's professional qualities and the judgment exercised by him or her in the performance of an examination and report. The source of the standards is the American Institute of Certified Public Accountants.

Genuineness of Assent • Knowledge of, and voluntary assent to, the terms of a contract. If a contract is formed as a result of a mistake, misrepresentation, undue influence, or duress, genuineness of assent is lacking, and the contract will be voidable.

Good Samaritan Statute • A state statute stipulating that persons who provide emergency services to, or rescue, someone in peril cannot be sued for negligence, unless they act recklessly, thereby causing further harm.

Grand Jury • A group of citizens called to decide, after hearing the state's evidence, whether a reasonable basis (probable cause) exists for believing that a crime has been committed and whether a trial ought to be held.

Group Boycott • The refusal by a group of competitors to deal with a particular person or firm; prohibited by the Sherman Act.

Guarantor • A person who agrees to satisfy the debt of another (the debtor) only after the principal debtor defaults. Thus, a guarantor's liability is secondary.

H

Hacker • A person who uses one computer to break into another. Professional computer programmers refer to such persons as "crackers."

Historical School • A school of legal thought that emphasizes the evolutionary process of law and that looks to the past to discover what the principles of contemporary law should be.

Homestead Exemption • A law permitting a debtor to retain the family home, either in its entirety or up to a specified dollar amount, free from the claims of unsecured creditors or trustees in bankruptcy.

Horizontal Merger • A merger between two firms that are competing in the same marketplace.

Horizontal Restraint • Any agreement that in some way restrains competition between rival firms competing in the same market.

Hot-Cargo Agreement • An agreement in which employers voluntarily agree with unions not to handle, use, or deal in goods produced by nonunion employees of other firms; a type of secondary boycott explicitly prohibited by the Labor-Management Reporting and Disclosure Act of 1959.

I

Identity Theft • The act of stealing another's identifying information—such as a name, date of birth, or Social Security number—and using that information to access the victim's financial resources.

Implied Warranty of Fitness for a Particular Purpose • A warranty that goods sold or leased are fit for a particular purpose. The warranty arises when any seller or lessor knows the particular purpose for which a buyer or lessee will use the goods and knows that the buyer or lessee is relying on the skill and judgment of the seller or lessor to select suitable goods.

Implied Warranty of Habitability • An implied promise by a landlord that rented residential premises are fit for human habitation—that is, in a condition that is safe and suitable for people to live in.

Implied Warranty of Merchantability • A warranty that goods being sold or leased are reasonably fit for the ordinary purpose for which they are sold or leased, are properly packaged and labeled, and are of fair quality. The

warranty automatically arises in every sale or lease of goods made by a merchant who deals in goods of the kind sold or leased.

Implied Warranty • A warranty that arises by law by implication or inference from the nature of the transaction or the relative situations or circumstances of the parties.

Impossibility of Performance • A doctrine under which a party to a contract is relieved of his or her duty to perform when performance becomes objectively impossible or totally impracticable (through no fault of either party).

Incidental Beneficiary • A third party who incidentally benefits from a contract but whose benefit was not the reason the contract was formed; an incidental beneficiary has no rights in a contract and cannot sue to have the contract enforced.

Independent Contractor • One who works for, and receives payment from, an employer but whose working conditions and methods are not controlled by the employer. An independent contractor is not an employee but may be an agent.

Independent Regulatory Agency • An administrative agency that is not considered part of the government's executive branch and is not subject to the authority of the president. Independent agency officials cannot be removed without cause.

Indictment • A charge by a grand jury that a named person has committed a crime.

Information • A formal accusation or complaint (without an indictment) issued in certain types of actions (usually criminal actions involving lesser crimes) by a law officer, such as a magistrate.

Initial Order • In the context of administrative law, an agency's disposition in a matter other than a rulemaking. An administrative law judge's initial order becomes final unless it is appealed.

Insider Trading • The purchase or sale of securities on the basis of information that has not been made available to the public.

Intellectual Property • Property resulting from intellectual, creative processes.

Intended Beneficiary • A third party for whose benefit a contract is formed; an intended beneficiary can sue the promisor if such a contract is breached.

Intentional Tort • A wrongful act knowingly committed.

International Law • The law that governs relations among nations. International customs and treaties are important sources of international law.

Interrogatories • A series of written questions for which written answers are prepared, usually with the assistance of

jury and to direct a verdict for the party who filed the motion on the ground that the other party has not produced sufficient evidence to support her or his claim.

Motion for a New Trial • A motion asserting that the trial was so fundamentally flawed (because of error, newly discovered evidence, prejudice, or other reason) that a new trial is necessary to prevent a miscarriage of justice.

Motion for Judgment N.O.V. • A motion requesting the court to grant judgment in favor of the party making the motion on the ground that the jury's verdict against him or her was unreasonable and erroneous.

Motion for Judgment on the Pleadings • A motion by either party to a lawsuit at the close of the pleadings requesting the court to decide the issue solely on the pleadings without proceeding to trial. The motion will be granted only if no facts are in dispute.

Motion for Summary Judgment • A motion requesting the court to enter a judgment without proceeding to trial. The motion can be based on evidence outside the pleadings and will be granted only if no facts are in dispute.

Motion to Dismiss • A pleading in which a defendant asserts that the plaintiff's claim fails to state a cause of action (that is, has no basis in law) or that there are other grounds on which a suit should be dismissed.

Mutual Assent • The element of agreement in the formation of a contract. The manifestation of contract parties' mutual assent to the same bargain is required to establish a contract.

Mutual Fund • A specific type of investment company that continually buys or sells to investors shares of ownership in a portfolio.

Mutual Rescission • An agreement between the parties to cancel their contract, releasing the parties from further obligations under the contract. The object of the agreement is to restore the parties to the positions they would have occupied had no contract ever been formed.

N

National Law • Laws that pertain to a particular nation (as opposed to international law).

Natural Law • The belief that government and the legal system should reflect universal moral and ethical principles that are inherent in human nature. The natural law school is the oldest and one of the most significant schools of legal thought.

Negligence • The failure to exercise the standard of care that a reasonable person would exercise in similar circumstances.

Negligence *Per Se* • An action or failure to act in violation of a statutory requirement.

Negotiation • A process in which parties attempt to settle their dispute informally, with or without attorneys to represent them.

Nonpossessory Interest • In the context of real property, an interest in land that does not include any right to possess the property.

No-Par Shares • Corporate shares that have no face value—that is, no specific dollar amount is printed on their face.

Normal Trade Relations (NTR) Status • A status granted in an international treaty by a provision stating that the citizens of the contracting nations may enjoy the privileges accorded by either party to citizens of its NTR nations. Generally, this status is designed to establish equality of international treatment.

No-Strike Clause • A provision in a collective bargaining agreement that states that the employees will not strike for any reason and labor disputes will be resolved by arbitration.

Notice-and-Comment Rulemaking • A procedure in agency rulemaking that requires (1) notice, (2) opportunity for comment, and (3) a published draft of the final rule.

Novation • The substitution, by agreement, of a new contract for an old one, with the rights under the old one being terminated. Typically, novation involves the substitution of a new party for one of the original parties to the contract.

Nuisance • A common law doctrine under which persons may be held liable for using their property in a manner that unreasonably interferes with others' rights to use or enjoy their own property.

O

Offer • A promise or commitment to perform or refrain from performing some specified act in the future.

Online Dispute Resolution (ODR) • The resolution of disputes with the assistance of organizations that offer dispute-resolution services via the Internet.

Operating Agreement • In a limited liability company, an agreement in which the members set forth the details of how the business will be managed and operated. State statutes typically give the members wide latitude in deciding for themselves the rules that will govern their organization.

Order for Relief • In bankruptcy proceedings, a court's grant of assistance to a debtor. The order relieves the debtor of the immediate obligation to pay the debts listed in the bankruptcy petition.

Ordinance • A regulation enacted by a city or county legislative body that becomes part of that state's statutory law.

P

Partially Disclosed Principal • A principal whose identity is unknown by a third party, but the third party knows that the agent is or may be acting for a principal at the time the agent and the third party form a contract.

Partnership • An agreement by two or more persons to carry on, as co-owners, a business for profit.

Par-Value Shares • Corporate shares that have a specific face value, or formal cash-in value, written on them, such as one dollar.

Past Consideration • An act done before the contract is made, which ordinarily, by itself, cannot be consideration for a later promise to pay for the act.

Patent • A government grant that gives an inventor the exclusive right or privilege to make, use, or sell his or her invention for a limited time period.

Peer-to-Peer (P2P) Networking • The sharing of resources (such as files, hard drives, and processing styles) among multiple computers without necessarily requiring a central network server.

Penalty • An amount, stipulated in the contract, to be paid in the event of a default or breach of contract. When the amount is not a reasonable measure of damages, the court will not enforce it but will limit recovery to actual damages.

***Per Se* Violation** • A type of anticompetitive agreement that is considered to be so injurious to the public that there is no need to determine whether it actually injures market competition; rather, it is in itself *(per se)* a violation of the Sherman Act.

Perfect Tender Rule • A rule under which a seller or lessor is required to deliver goods that conform perfectly to the requirements of the contract. A tender of nonconforming goods automatically constitutes a breach of contract.

Performance • In contract law, the fulfillment of one's duties arising under a contract with another; the normal way of discharging one's contractual obligations.

Periodic Tenancy • A lease interest in land for an indefinite period involving payment of rent at fixed intervals, such as week to week, month to month, or year to year.

Personal Property • Property that is movable; any property that is not real property.

Persuasive Authority • Any legal authority or source of law that a court may look to for guidance but on which it need not rely in making its decision. Persuasive authorities include cases from other jurisdictions and secondary sources of law.

Petition in Bankruptcy • A document filed with a bankruptcy court to initiate bankruptcy proceedings. The official forms required for a petition in bankruptcy must be completed accurately, sworn to under oath, and signed by the debtor.

Petty Offense • In criminal law, the least serious kind of criminal offense, such as a minor traffic or building-code violation.

Plaintiff • One who initiates a lawsuit.

Plea Bargaining • The process by which a defendant and the prosecutor in a criminal case work out a mutually satisfactory disposition of the case, subject to court approval; usually involves the defendant's pleading guilty to a lesser offense in return for a lighter sentence.

Pleadings • Statements made by the plaintiff and the defendant in a lawsuit that detail the facts, charges, and defenses involved in the litigation. The complaint and answer are part of the pleadings.

Police Powers • Powers possessed by the states as part of their inherent sovereignty. These powers may be exercised to protect or promote the public order, health, safety, morals, and general welfare.

Positive Law • The body of conventional, or written, law of a particular society at a particular point in time.

Potentially Responsible Party (PRP) • A party liable for the costs of cleaning up a hazardous waste-disposal site under the Comprehensive Environmental Response, Compensation, and Liability Act (CERCLA). Any person who generated the hazardous waste, transported it, owned or operated the waste site at the time of disposal, or currently owns or operates the site may be responsible for some or all of the clean-up costs.

Precedent • A court decision that furnishes an example or authority for deciding subsequent cases involving identical or similar facts.

Predatory Behavior • Business behavior that is undertaken with the intention of unlawfully driving competitors out of the market.

Predatory Pricing • The pricing of a product below cost with the intent to drive competitors out of the market.

Preemption • A doctrine under which certain federal laws preempt, or take precedence over, conflicting state or local laws.

Preemptive Rights • Rights held by shareholders that entitle them to purchase newly issued shares of a corporation's stock, equal in percentage to shares already held, before the stock is offered to any outside buyers. Preemptive rights enable shareholders to maintain their proportionate ownership and voice in the corporation.

Preference • In bankruptcy proceedings, property transfers or payments made by the debtor that favor (give preference to) one creditor over others. The bankruptcy trustee is allowed to recover payments made both voluntarily and involuntarily to one creditor in preference over another.

Preferred Creditor • A creditor who has received a preferential transfer from a debtor.

Price Discrimination • Setting prices in such a way that two competing buyers pay two different prices for an identical product or service.

Price-Fixing Agreement • An agreement between competitors to fix the prices of products or services at a certain level.

Prima Facie Case • A case in which the plaintiff has produced sufficient evidence of his or her conclusion that the case can go to a jury; a case in which the evidence compels the plaintiff's conclusion if the defendant produces no affirmative defense or evidence to disprove it.

Primary Source of Law • Any authority, such as a constitution, a statute, an administrative rule, or a court decision, that establishes the law governing a particular area.

Principle of Rights • The principle that human beings have certain fundamental rights (to life, freedom, and the pursuit of happiness, for example). Those who adhere to this "rights theory" believe that a key factor in determining whether a business decision is ethical is how that decision affects the rights of various groups. These groups include the firm's owners, its employees, the consumers of its products or services, its suppliers, the community in which it does business, and society as a whole.

Privilege • A legal right, exemption, or immunity granted to a person or a class of persons. In the context of defamation, an absolute privilege immunizes the person making the statements from suit, regardless of whether the person's statements were malicious. A qualified privilege immunizes a person from suit only when the statements were made in good faith by a person having an interest in the subject, or a moral or societal duty to speak.

Probable Cause • Reasonable grounds for believing that a person should be arrested or searched.

Probate Court • A state court of limited jurisdiction that conducts proceedings relating to the settlement of a deceased person's estate.

Procedural Law • Law that establishes the methods of enforcing the rights established by substantive law.

Product Liability • The legal liability of manufacturers, sellers, and lessors of goods to consumers, users, and bystanders for injuries or damages that are caused by the goods.

Profit • In real property law, the right to enter on and remove things from the property of another (for example, the right to enter onto a person's land and remove sand and gravel from it).

Promise • A person's assurance that the person will or will not do something.

Promissory Estoppel • A doctrine that applies when a promisor makes a clear and definite promise on which the promisee justifiably relies; such a promise is binding if justice will be better served by the enforcement of the promise.

Protected Class • A group of persons protected by specific laws because of the group's defining characteristics. Under the laws prohibiting employment discrimination, these characteristics include race, color, religion, national origin, gender, age, and disability.

Proximate Cause • Legal cause; exists when the connection between an act and an injury is strong enough to justify imposing liability.

Proxy • In corporation law, a written agreement between a stockholder and another under which the stockholder authorizes the other to vote the stockholder's shares in a certain manner.

Puffery • A salesperson's exaggerated claims concerning the quality of property offered for sale. Such claims involve opinions rather than facts and are not considered to be legally binding promises or warranties.

Punitive Damages • Money damages that may be awarded to a plaintiff to punish the defendant and deter future similar conduct.

Q

Quasi Contract • A fictional contract imposed on parties by a court in the interests of fairness and justice; usually imposed to avoid the unjust enrichment of one party at the expense of another.

Quitclaim Deed • A deed intended to pass any title, interest, or claim that the seller may have in the property but not warranting that such title is valid. A quitclaim deed offers the least amount of protection against defects in the title.

Quorum • The number of members of a decision-making body that must be present before business may be transacted.

Quota • A set limit on the amount of goods that can be imported.

R

Ratification • The act of accepting and giving legal force to an obligation that previously was not enforceable.

Reaffirmation Agreement • An agreement to pay a debt that is dischargeable in bankruptcy.

Real Property • Land and everything attached to it, such as vegetation and buildings.

Reasonable Person Standard • The standard of behavior expected of a hypothetical "reasonable person"; the standard against which negligence is measured and that must be observed to avoid liability for negligence.

Recording Statute • A statute that allows deeds, mortgages, and other real property transactions to be recorded so as to provide notice to future purchasers or creditors of an existing claim on the property.

Red Herring • A preliminary prospectus that can be distributed to potential investors after the registration statement (for a securities offering) has been filed with the Securities and Exchange Commission. The name derives from the red legend printed across the prospectus stating that the registration has been filed but has not become effective.

Reformation • A court-ordered correction of a written contract so that it reflects the true intentions of the parties.

Regulation Z • A set of rules promulgated by the Federal Reserve Board of Governors to implement the provisions of the Truth-in-Lending Act.

Remedy • The relief given to an innocent party to enforce a right or compensate for the violation of a right.

Reply • Procedurally, a plaintiff's response to a defendant's answer.

Res Ipsa Loquitur • A doctrine under which negligence may be inferred simply because an event occurred, if it is the type of event that would never occur in the absence of negligence. Literally, the term means "the facts speak for themselves."

Resale Price Maintenance Agreement • An agreement between a manufacturer and a retailer in which the manufacturer specifies what the retail prices of its products must be.

Respondeat superior • Latin for "let the master respond." A doctrine under which a principal or an employer is held liable for the wrongful acts committed by agents or employees while acting within the course and scope of their agency or employment.

Restitution • An equitable remedy under which a person is restored to his or her original position prior to loss or injury, or placed in the position he or she would have been in had the breach not occurred.

Retained Earnings • The portion of a corporation's profits that has not been paid out as dividends to shareholders.

Revocation • In contract law, the withdrawal of an offer by an offeror; unless the offer is irrevocable, it can be revoked at any time prior to acceptance without liability.

Right of Contribution • The right of a co-surety who pays more than his or her proportionate share on a debtor's default to recover the excess paid from other co-sureties.

Right of First Refusal • The right to purchase personal or real property—such as corporate shares or real estate—before the property is offered for sale to others.

Right of Reimbursement • The legal right of a person to be restored, repaid, or indemnified for costs, expenses, or losses incurred or expended on behalf of another.

Right of Subrogation • The right of a person to stand in the place of (be substituted for) another, giving the substituted party the same legal rights that the original party had.

Right-to-Work Law • A state law providing that employees are not to be required to join a union as a condition of obtaining or retaining employment.

Robbery • The act of forcefully and unlawfully taking personal property of any value from another. Force or intimidation is usually necessary for an act of theft to be considered a robbery.

Rule of Four • A rule of the United States Supreme Court under which the Court will not issue a writ of *certiorari* unless at least four justices approve of the decision to issue the writ.

Rule of Reason • A test by which a court balances the positive effects (such as economic efficiency) of an agreement against its potentially anticompetitive effects. In antitrust litigation, many practices are analyzed under the rule of reason.

Rulemaking • The actions undertaken by administrative agencies when formally adopting new regulations or amending old ones. Under the Administrative Procedure Act, rulemaking includes notifying the public of proposed rules or changes and receiving and considering the public's comments.

S

S Corporation • A close business corporation that has met certain requirements as set out by the Internal Revenue Code and thus qualifies for special income tax treatment.

Essentially, an S corporation is taxed the same as a partnership, but its owners enjoy the privilege of limited liability.

Sale • The passing of title to property from the seller to the buyer for a price.

Sales Contract • A contract for the sale of goods under which the ownership of goods is transferred from a seller to a buyer for a price.

Search Warrant • An order granted by a public authority, such as a judge, that authorizes law enforcement personnel to search particular premises or property.

SEC Rule 10b-5 • A rule of the Securities and Exchange Commission that makes it unlawful, in connection with the purchase or sale of any security, to make any untrue statement of a material fact or to omit a material fact if such omission causes the statement to be misleading.

Secondary Boycott • A union's refusal to work for, purchase from, or handle the products of a secondary employer, with whom the union has no dispute, for the purpose of forcing that employer to stop doing business with the primary employer, with whom the union has a labor dispute.

Secondary Source of Law • A publication that summarizes or interprets the law, such as a legal encyclopedia, a legal treatise, or an article in a law review.

Security • Generally, a stock certificate, bond, note, debenture, warrant, or other document given as evidence of an ownership interest in a corporation or as a promise of repayment by a corporation.

Self-Defense • The legally recognized privilege to protect oneself or one's property against injury by another. The privilege of self-defense protects only acts that are reasonably necessary to protect oneself, one's property, or another person.

Self-Incrimination • The giving of testimony that may subject the testifier to criminal prosecution. The Fifth Amendment to the Constitution protects against self-incrimination by providing that no person "shall be compelled in any criminal case to be a witness against himself."

Seniority System • In regard to employment relationships, a system in which those who have worked longest for the company are first in line for promotions, salary increases, and other benefits; they are also the last to be laid off if the workforce must be reduced.

Service Mark • A mark used in the sale or advertising of services to distinguish the services of one person from those of others. Titles, character names, and other distinctive features of radio and television programs may be registered as service marks.

Severance Pay • Funds in excess of normal wages or salaries paid to an employee on termination of his or her employment with a company.

Sexual Harassment • In the employment context, the demanding of sexual favors in return for job promotions or other benefits, or language or conduct that is so sexually offensive that it creates a hostile working environment.

Shareholder's Derivative Suit • A suit brought by a shareholder to enforce a corporate cause of action against a third person.

Slander • Defamation in oral form.

Slander of Quality (Trade Libel) • The publication of false information about another's product, alleging that it is not what its seller claims.

Slander of Title • The publication of a statement that denies or casts doubt on another's legal ownership of any property, causing financial loss to that property's owner.

Small Claims Court • A special court in which parties may litigate small claims (such as those involving $5,000 or less). Attorneys are not required in small claims courts and, in some states, are not allowed to represent the parties.

Sociological School • A school of legal thought that views the law as a tool for promoting justice in society.

Sole Proprietorship • The simplest form of business, in which the owner is the business; the owner reports business income on his or her personal income tax return and is legally responsible for all debts and obligations incurred by the business.

Sovereign Immunity • A doctrine that immunizes foreign nations from the jurisdiction of U.S. courts when certain conditions are satisfied.

Spam • Bulk, unsolicited ("junk") e-mail.

Specific Performance • An equitable remedy requiring exactly the performance that was specified in a contract; usually granted only when money damages would be an inadequate remedy and the subject matter of the contract is unique (for example, real property).

Standing to Sue • The requirement that an individual must have a sufficient stake in a controversy before he or she can bring a lawsuit. The plaintiff must demonstrate that he or she has been either injured or threatened with injury.

Stare Decisis • A common law doctrine under which judges are obligated to follow the precedents established in prior decisions.

Statute of Frauds • A state statute under which certain types of contracts must be in writing to be enforceable.

Statute of Limitations • A federal or state statute setting the maximum time period during which a certain action can be brought or certain rights enforced.

Statute of Repose • Basically, a statute of limitations that is not dependent on the happening of a cause of action.

Statutes of repose generally begin to run at an earlier date and run for a longer period of time than statutes of limitations.

Statutory Law • The body of law enacted by legislative bodies (as opposed to constitutional law, administrative law, or case law).

Stock Certificate • A certificate issued by a corporation evidencing the ownership of a specified number of shares in the corporation.

Strict Liability • Liability regardless of fault. In tort law, strict liability is imposed on a manufacturer or seller that introduces into commerce a good that is unreasonably dangerous when in a defective condition.

Sublease • A lease executed by the lessee of real estate to a third person, conveying the same interest that the lessee enjoys but for a shorter term than that held by the lessee.

Substantive Law • Law that defines, describes, regulates, and creates legal rights and obligations.

Summary Jury Trial (SJT) • A method of settling disputes, used in many federal courts, in which a trial is held, but the jury's verdict is not binding. The verdict acts only as a guide to both sides in reaching an agreement during the mandatory negotiations that immediately follow the summary jury trial.

Summons • A document informing a defendant that a legal action has been commenced against him or her and that the defendant must appear in court on a certain date to answer the plaintiff's complaint. The document is delivered by a sheriff or any other person so authorized.

Supremacy Clause • The provision in Article VI of the Constitution that provides that the Constitution, laws, and treaties of the United States are "the supreme Law of the Land." Under this clause, state and local laws that directly conflict with federal law will be rendered invalid.

Surety • A person, such as a cosigner on a note, who agrees to be primarily responsible for the debt of another.

Suretyship • An express contract in which a third party to a debtor-creditor relationship (the surety) promises to be primarily responsible for the debtor's obligation.

Symbolic Speech • Nonverbal expressions of beliefs. Symbolic speech, which includes gestures, movements, and articles of clothing, is given substantial protection by the courts.

T

Tangible Property • Property that has physical existence and can be distinguished by the senses of touch, sight, and so on. A car is tangible property; a patent right is intangible property.

Tariff • A tax on imported goods.

Tenancy at Sufferance • A type of tenancy under which one who, after rightfully being in possession of leased premises, continues (wrongfully) to occupy the property after the lease has been terminated. The tenant has no rights to possess the property and occupies it only because the person entitled to evict the tenant has not done so.

Tenancy at Will • A type of tenancy under which either party can terminate the tenancy without notice; usually arises when a tenant who has been under a tenancy for years retains possession, with the landlord's consent, after the tenancy for years has terminated.

Tenancy for Years • A type of tenancy under which property is leased for a specified period of time, such as a month, a year, or a period of years.

Tender • An unconditional offer to perform an obligation by a person who is ready, willing, and able to do so.

Tender of Delivery • Under the Uniform Commercial Code, a seller's or lessor's act of placing conforming goods at the disposal of the buyer or lessee and giving the buyer or lessee whatever notification is reasonably necessary to enable the buyer or lessee to take delivery.

Third Party Beneficiary • One for whose benefit a promise is made in a contract but who is not a party to the contract.

Tippee • A person who receives inside information.

Tombstone Ad • An advertisement, historically in a format resembling a tombstone, of a securities offering. The ad tells potential investors where and how they may obtain a prospectus.

Tort • A civil wrong not arising from a breach of contract. A breach of a legal duty that proximately causes harm or injury to another.

Tortfeasor • One who commits a tort.

Toxic Tort • A civil wrong arising from exposure to a toxic substance, such as asbestos, radiation, or hazardous waste.

Trade Dress • The image and overall appearance of a product—for example, the distinctive decor, menu, layout, and style of service of a particular restaurant. Basically, trade dress is subject to the same protection as trademarks.

Trade Name • A term that is used to indicate part or all of a business's name and that is directly related to the business's reputation and goodwill. Trade names are protected under the common law (and under trademark law, if the name is the same as that of the firm's trademarked property).

Trade Secrets • Business information that is kept confidential to maintain an advantage over competitors.

Trademark • A distinctive mark, motto, device, or emblem that a manufacturer stamps, prints, or otherwise affixes to the goods it produces so that they may be identified on the market and their origins made known. Once a trademark is established (under the common law or through registration), the owner is entitled to its exclusive use.

Treble Damages • Damages that, by statute, are three times the amount that the fact finder determines is owed.

Trespass to Land • The entry onto, above, or below the surface of land owned by another without the owner's permission or legal authorization.

Trespass to Personal Property • The unlawful taking or harming of another's personal property; interference with another's right to the exclusive possession of his or her personal property.

Trustee • One who holds title to property for the use or benefit of another.

Tying Arrangement • An agreement between a buyer and a seller in which the buyer of a specific product or service becomes obligated to purchase additional products or services from the seller.

U

U.S. Trustee • A government official who performs certain administrative tasks that a bankruptcy judge would otherwise have to perform.

Undisclosed Principal • A principal whose identity is unknown by a third person, and the third person has no knowledge that the agent is acting for a principal at the time the agent and the third person form a contract.

Union Shop • A place of employment in which all workers, once employed, must become union members within a specified period of time as a condition of their continued employment.

Unreasonably Dangerous Product • In product liability, a product that is defective to the point of threatening a consumer's health and safety. A product will be considered unreasonably dangerous if (1) it is dangerous beyond the expectation of the ordinary consumer or if (2) a less dangerous alternative was economically feasible for the manufacturer, but the manufacturer failed to produce it.

Use Zoning • Zoning classifications within a particular municipality that may be distinguished based on the uses to which the land is to be put.

Utilitarianism • An approach to ethical reasoning that evaluates behavior not on the basis of any absolute ethical or moral values but on the consequences of that behavior for those who will be affected by it. In utilitarian reasoning, a "good" decision is one that results in the greatest good for the greatest number of people affected by the decision.

V

Venue • The geographic district in which an action is tried and from which the jury is selected.

Vertical Merger • The acquisition by a company at one level in a marketing chain of a company at a higher or lower level in the chain (such as a company merging with one of its suppliers or retailers).

Vertical Restraint • Any restraint on trade created by agreements between firms at different levels in the manufacturing and distribution process.

Vertically Integrated Firm • A firm that carries out two or more functional phases (manufacture, distribution, and retailing, for example) of the chain of production.

Vesting • The creation of an absolute or unconditional right or power.

Vicarious Liability • Legal responsibility placed on one person for the acts of another; indirect liability imposed on a supervisory party (such as an employer) for the actions of a subordinate (such as an employee) because of the relationship between the two parties.

Voir Dire • An old French phrase meaning "to speak the truth." In legal language, the phrase refers to the process in which the attorneys question prospective jurors to learn about their backgrounds, attitudes, biases, and other characteristics that may affect their ability to serve as impartial jurors.

W

Waiver • An intentional, knowing relinquishment of a legal right.

Warranty Deed • A deed in which the seller assures (warrants to) the buyer that the grantor has title to the property conveyed in the deed, that there are no encumbrances on the property other than what the seller has represented, and that the buyer will enjoy quiet possession of the property; a deed that provides the greatest amount of protection for the grantee.

Watered Stock • Shares of stock issued by a corporation for which the corporation receives, as payment, less than the stated value of the shares.

Wetlands • Water-saturated areas of land that are designated by government agencies (such as the Army Corps of

Engineers or the Environmental Protection Agency) as protected areas that support wildlife and therefore cannot be filled in or dredged by private contractors or parties without a permit.

White-Collar Crime • Nonviolent crime committed by individuals or corporations to obtain a personal or business advantage.

Wildcat Strike • A strike that is not authorized by the union that ordinarily represents the striking employees.

Workers' Compensation Laws • State statutes establishing an administrative procedure for compensating workers' injuries that arise out of—or in the course of—their employment, regardless of fault.

Workout • An out-of-court agreement between a debtor and his or her creditors in which the parties work out a payment plan or schedule under which the debtor's debts can be discharged.

Writ of Attachment • A court's order, issued prior to a trial to collect a debt, directing the sheriff or other officer to seize nonexempt property of the debtor. If the creditor prevails at trial, the seized property can be sold to satisfy the judgment.

Writ of *Certiorari* • A written order from a higher court asking the lower court for the record of a case.

Writ of Execution • A court's order, issued after a judgment has been entered against the debtor, directing the sheriff to seize (levy) and sell any of the debtor's nonexempt real or personal property. The proceeds of the sale are used to pay off the judgment, accrued interest, and costs of the sale; any surplus is paid to the debtor.

Yellow Dog Contract • An agreement under which an employee promises his or her employer, as a condition of employment, not to join a union.

Z

Zoning Variance • The granting of permission by a municipality or other public board to a landowner to use his or her property in a way that does not strictly conform with the zoning regulations so as to avoid causing the landowner undue hardship.

Zoning • The division of a city by legislative regulation into districts and the application in each district of regulations having to do with structural and architectural designs of buildings and prescribing the use to which buildings within designated districts may be put.

TABLE OF CASES

INDEX

Ethical Issues